Studies in Social and Demographic History

General editors Peter Laslett, R. S. Schofield, E. A. Wrigley

The Population History of England 1541–1871

A reconstruction

E. A. Wrigley and R. S. Schofield

with contributions by Ronald Lee and Jim Oeppen

Harvard University Press
Cambridge, Massachusetts
1981

Library of Congress Cataloging in Publication Data

Wrigley, E. A. (Edward Anthony), 1931-
  The population history of England, 1541–1871.

  (Studies in social and demographic history)
  Includes index.
  1. England – Population – History. I. Schofield, R. S.
II. Title. III. Series.
HB 3585.W74   304.6′0942   81-5010

ISBN 0-674-69007-9   AACR2

Printed in the United States of America

To the local population historians of England

Contents

Preface

All research, even that of the most isolated and independent scholar, is collaborative in the sense that it must rest upon and be related to the work of those who came earlier in the field. Some is collaborative also in the more obvious sense that it is the work of many hands. The research upon which this book is based was collaborative in both these senses. Its contents reflect the preoccupations of earlier scholars, and the issues that concern population historians today, though the debate about the nature and significance of long-term demographic change is of such fundamental importance to the understanding both of the past and of the pressing problems of the contemporary world that the context of the discussion extends well beyond the confines of population history. But the research was also collaborative in the second sense; it has been pursued over several years at the SSRC Cambridge Group for the History of Population and Social Structure, and all those who have been members of the Group in that period can justly claim to have played a part in bringing it to fruition. This is true not only of those who have been engaged full-time in the affairs of the Group, but also of those who have been present from time to time as visiting scholars, or have been research students attached to the Group. Their help, both direct and indirect, has been so great and so pervasive that at times the author's position might be likened to the literary tip of a research iceberg, the visible part of a much larger whole.

When so many have contributed to an enterprise, it is invidious to make distinctions, but some of our obligations are so signal that it would be wrong not to acknowledge, indeed to stress them.

First and foremost it is both proper and a pleasure to pay tribute to the local historians without whose help the research upon which this book draws could not have taken place, for it was they who carried out the aggregative tabulations of monthly frequencies of baptisms, burials, and marriages in Anglican parish registers that form the ultimate source of all the demographic data used. The nature and scale of their work is more fully described in the introductory chapter, but it may be appropriate to remark here that at the time when work on the aggregative tabulations was at its height most parish registers were still kept in parish chests. Carrying out a tabulation often involved many hours of cramped work in a chilly vestry. Yet several hundred men, women, and schoolchildren gave their time generously to the work, which would have been far beyond the capacity of the small number of people working at the Cambridge Group itself. Their help did not stop with the counting of entries. The letters sent with the tabulations, and in many cases substantial later correspondence, were immensely valuable in revealing the individual peculiarities of particular parishes or registers, which in turn often threw light not simply on local circumstances but also on much wider questions of population history. The names of those local historians whose work contributed directly to the data used in the book are listed in appendix 1. We have felt it fitting as a mark of our appreciation to dedicate this book to the local population historians of England.

There were in all almost four million monthly totals of events to be key-punched for computer input when the aggregative tabulations had been returned to Cambridge. This work devolved chiefly on Selma Berksoy, Lynn Bilsborough, Christine Cooke, Marina Hamilton, Marianne Leach, Christine Roberts, Alan Simon, Valerie Smith, and Margaret Thompson. Olivia Skulsky supervized the handling of the data and was in charge of the checking operations by which clean data files were produced from the initial computer input. Her punctilious regard for detail and her stamina in carrying out what must be times have seemed an endless task had much to do with the success of this phase of the work. Since the volume of the data was very large, their input and subsequent manipulation within the computer put a heavy premium on efficiency. We have been exceptionally fortunate in this regard in having available the skill and foresight of Ros Davies who has designed and implemented a flexible computer file-handling system which allows easy and efficient access to the data.

Our most important technical innovation, designed to help to make the most of very long runs of aggregative data, has been the development of a technique that we have called back projection. Its implementation, and many of its most valuable features, stand to the credit of Jim Oeppen, who developed the original conception into a sophisticated and efficient program, patiently exploring the theoretical and operational characteristics of many alternative strategies until a stable and satisfactory solution was found. The description of the program contained in appendix 15 is from his pen.

In one instance the collaboration on which this book is based extended overseas. Professor Ronald Lee of the University of California at Berkeley has been studying a wide range of the substantive and technical problems of population history, and from a fairly early stage in the construction of our data files he has made use of them to pursue questions in which he has a special interest. It became apparent as work progressed that it might prove a happy example of the division of labour if he were willing to undertake the analysis of some aspects of short-term change in demographic, economic, and climatic variables. Chapter 9 is the outcome of his acceptance of our invitation and contains, in our view, some important and challenging findings.

The great bulk of the typing of the manuscript was done by Les Pepper. It forms a long book which has evolved slowly and painfully through many drafts. Its text is at times made difficult by technical terms, and it is liberally endowed with large and complex tables. She has borne with these trials, and with the waywardness of the authors, with remarkable patience and understanding, for which we are most grateful.

We are also grateful to the Computing Service of the University of Cambridge for their helpfulness and consideration in making available the substantial computing resources which were required to carry out the work described in this book; and to the Computing Laboratory of the University of Newcastle upon Tyne where the early input and processing of data were carried out.

Work on the book itself began in earnest at much the same time as the Cambridge Group became a unit of the Social Science Research Council. The change of status gave a most welcome additional impetus to the work since additional resources became available, and because it gave a longer term of assured life to the Group, a matter of great moment to the planning and execution of a project on this scale. One of the authors (Wrigley) is also indebted to Erasmus University in Rotterdam. The opportunity to spend some months there as the Tinbergen visiting professor during the later stages of the writing of the book was of great help in bringing draft chapters to their final form.

Introduction

It is a commonplace of the history of all pre-industrial societies that the changing fortunes of a community from year to year tended to be affected by the harvest more than by any other single influence. The land was the source of all food and of most of the raw materials needed by industry. A harvest failure therefore meant distress and depression; an abundant harvest an interlude of comparative plenty. Those who lived in town or who worked outside agriculture were as vulnerable as the husbandmen. And fluctuations in the size of the harvest were unavoidable, though their effects might be mitigated by trade and by the storage of grain from one year to another. They caused an abrupt change in the balance between a population and its economic resources which, if severe, could entail disaster rather than merely distress.

But the balance between a population and its productive resources was also subject to secular change. Underlying the frequent and sometimes violent fluctuations imposed on every society by the harvest cycle, there were slow sea changes at work which continued for many decades, sometimes for more than a century. Thus, almost throughout the sixteenth century the balance between the English population and the resources to which it could gain access with the material technology of the day steadily deteriorated because the growth in numbers outstripped the rise in production. Conversely, between the mid seventeenth and mid eighteenth centuries it improved with the sharp reduction in the rate of population increase. In both periods the underlying trends were temporarily alleviated or aggravated by the short-term effects of good or bad harvests, but in both they displayed a remarkable persistence.

The consequences of short-term alterations in the balance of people and resources brought about by the vagaries of the harvest were plainly apparent to contemporaries and have proved comparatively easy for historians to study both in quantitative terms and for their social and political significance. Secular trends have been harder to grasp. They were little remarked by contemporaries, if noticed at all, and there are few sources which give consistently reliable information about demographic or economic trends over periods of time measured in centuries. Moreover, where they exist they may demand novel analytic techniques for their effective exploitation. Yet long-term changes in the balance between a people and the means of sustenance and economic activity available to them had profound effects both upon individual welfare and on the course of institutional and attitudinal change. And since pre-industrial societies normally experienced great difficulty in achieving a rapid expansion in their capacity to produce goods and services, population was the more dynamic element in the striking of a balance with production. Accordingly, any source that offers the possibility of tracing out demographic change over a period of three centuries deserves close attention.

English parish registers are such a source. In this book we have tried to ensure that they are used to best advantage to provide detailed and continuous information about trends in population size and in fertility and mortality from their institution in 1538 until the state assumed responsibility for vital registration 300 years later. This makes it possible for the first time to establish with some precision what changes took place in a pre-industrial population over a period of time long enough to encompass a secular cycle of population development, and to investigate the relationship between demographic and economic change during its course. Since the economic series available for long periods of time are both less representative than the demographic and subject to wider margins of error, some parts of the argument based on the examination of the relationship between population and the economy are necessarily tentative. But much of the dynamic seems clear.

England is exceptionally fortunate in having several thousand parish registers that begin before 1600. A substantial proportion of these early registers are unusable for a variety of reasons, but collectively they form a source which may be unrivalled for its combination of an early start and wide coverage.[1] Indeed, the lack of comparable national information for any other country until the mid eighteenth century proved one of our chief handicaps in attempting to assess the significance of English demographic characteristics in the sixteenth and seventeenth centuries.

Very long runs of data are, paradoxically, just as valuable for the study of short-term variation as for the studies of secular trends. They make it possible to pick out more confidently not only the relationships that are visible in the more spectacular episodes of short-term change, but also the subtler links that obtained both between the demographic variables themselves, and between them and external factors, whether economic, such as price change, or environmental, such as extremes of temperature. Moreover, many of the relationships changed over time, and a data series stretching over three centuries permits the nature and timing of such changes to be investigated.

The realization that English parish registers afforded an exceptional opportunity for the study of the country's population history over a very long period of time is not new. John Rickman was well aware of their value in this regard when planning the first census in 1801. As part of the census he sought to obtain from every Anglican parish minister totals of the number of events recorded in his registers for one year in each decade throughout the first 80 years of the eighteenth century and for every year in its last two decades.[2] Having the advantage of the authority and resources of the state to back his inquiry, he succeeded in obtaining returns from the vast majority of

---

1. French registers, for example, often suffer from defective burial registration until the late seventeenth century and even beyond. Swedish registers survive in numbers only from the 1680s. In general it appears to be the case that while occasional individual registers may survive from a very early date, it is very difficult to find the combination of characteristics needed for the systematic study of population history covering large regions in continental Europe before the eighteenth century. The same is also true, of course, of Scotland and Ireland. Fleury and Henry, *Nouveau manuel*, pp. 25–6 and Henry and Blayo, 'La population de la France de 1740 à 1860', pp. 87–9; Gaunt, 'Early Swedish parish records'.

Rickman drew attention to this point after having made the exhaustive inventory of English parish registers published in summary in the 1831 census. 'The preservation of parish registers retrospectively is a matter of degree; no person will be surprised that one half of the registers anterior to A.D. 1600 should have disappeared. If any other nation possesses similar registers of that date (a valuable proof of uninterrupted civilisation), a comparison might be instituted, and the preservation of such records through three hundred years would not prove to have been of frequent occurrence.' *1831 Census*, I, Enumeration abstract, p. xxix.

2. Rickman noted in 1801 that 'The second object of the Population Act was to ascertain the increase or diminution of the population of Great Britain, throughout the last century'. *1801 Census*, Observations, p. 4. The 1801 returns covered every tenth year from 1700 to 1770 and every year from 1780 to 1800 for baptisms and burials; for marriages, however, returns were sought for every year from 1754 to 1800.

parishes. He added to the store of data acquired in 1801 by prosecuting a further inquiry in 1836 and securing additional information from all those parishes whose registers began before 1600. This second inquiry covered a few widely spaced groups of years reaching back into the sixteenth century.[3] Rickman's labours laid the foundation for most subsequent discussions of English population history in early modern times. Indeed, all scholars have remained primarily dependent on him for their empirical information, but have attempted in various ways to overcome the shortcomings of his data, and to improve upon his techniques of analysis and interpretation.

The data used: the parish registers and their shortcomings

Rickman's work has been of great value to us as to others, for no other study based on parish registers can hope to rival the scope of his surveys. They afford invaluable checks upon the accuracy of totals obtained from other studies covering only a relatively small percentage of the 10,000 ancient parishes of England. Nor is there any alternative to the parish registers as a source of information about fertility, mortality, and nuptiality before the nineteenth century. But Rickman's data refer only to a few widely scattered points in time before 1700 and to only one year in ten for most of the eighteenth century. In order to address the range of issues outlined above, we have found it necessary, in the manner foreshadowed by Glass, to construct a more comprehensive national series of vital events providing monthly totals from the inception of parochial registration in 1538 through to its supersession by civil registration in 1837 and on to 1871, the closing date for the present study.[4] For the period down to 1837 we have sought to achieve this by using monthly totals of events taken from the registers of a total of 404 parishes; for the later period by making corrections to the material collected by the Registrar General and published in his *Annual Reports*.[5] The construction of such a series was a necessary preliminary to

3. The 1836 returns, which were made the basis of the estimates of population totals by county from the sixteenth century onwards published in the 1841 census, covered the following years: 1569–71, 1599–1601, 1629–31, 1669–71, 1699–1701, 1749–51, and 1800.

4. Glass made the following comment on Rickman's work. 'There are already several sets of estimates of the population of England and Wales in the eighteenth century, and most of them have been derived in one way or another from Rickman's compilation of parish register data. But the returns supplied to Rickman no longer exist and we do not know how accurately those returns were transcribed from the registers, to what extent dissenters were included, or whether the interpolations used by Rickman to fill gaps in the returns were acceptable approximations. Hence any further serious attempt to investigate population growth during the eighteenth century on the basis of parish register material must break away from Rickman's series and begin with a new compilation (no doubt on a sample basis) of accurate year-by-year transcriptions and an equivalent analysis of the records of dissenting groups. But this would represent only the initial step. To work backwards from the first periodic censuses of England and Wales requires a much closer assessment than has so far been undertaken of the changing completeness of ecclesiastical registration; a study of the reliability – in respect both of completeness and of the accuracy of the age data recorded in 1821, 1841 and 1851 – of the early nineteenth century censuses; and new attempts to estimate the volume of net migration from England and Wales in the eighteenth and first half of the nineteenth centuries'. What Glass wrote of work on the eighteenth century is equally applicable to the parish register period as a whole. In the course of assembling and correcting the data on which this book is based we have had occasion to tackle all the issues listed by Glass, and indeed to consider others (such as the problem of detecting periods in individual registers when registration was defective without failing entirely). Glass, 'Introduction', pp. 8–9.

5. The Registrar General's returns did not extend to monthly totals. In his *Annual Reports* he published no national data for units of time shorter than the quarter. For this reason our monthly series of vital events are not continued beyond the end of the parish register period (table A2.4). It may be noted that it was

bypassing the increasingly sterile debates about the ways in which Rickman's data should be corrected and manipulated in order to derive measures of fertility and mortality in the past.

Our starting date was forced upon us because no suitable source exists to enable the series to be pushed back beyond 1538. The closing date was chosen with three chief considerations in mind. First, in the early years of civil registration coverage of births was seriously incomplete and the shortfall did not shrink to negligible proportions until about 1870. The fertility data derived from the Registrar General's *Annual Reports* cannot therefore be used with any confidence until the last quarter of the nineteenth century. Second, it became increasingly clear in the course of research connected with this book that there was a major discontinuity in the history of both fertility and mortality at about this date. Third, the technique of back projection, which was developed to make the best use of the aggregative data assembled, requires a census with tolerably accurate age information as a starting point. The censuses of 1851 or 1861 would have been equally suitable for this purpose, but the first two considerations both pointed to a date about 1870: so preference was given to 1871.

The totals of events collected by Rickman suffer not only from the fact that few years were covered, but also from another crippling weakness. They are totals of Anglican baptisms, burials, and marriages, and not totals of births, deaths, and marriages. In the sixteenth century the former do not differ very greatly from the latter, but in the course of time the growth of nonconformity, the developing custom of delaying baptisms for weeks or months after the birth of a child (whose early death might then mean that his or her name was never recorded in a register), and the increasing importance of other causes of non-registration, all conspired to make the Anglican registers a less and less satisfactory source for the study of English population history. It was essential to find some way of establishing the scale of these several causes of under-registration in Anglican registers, and to estimate their changing levels over time.

Furthermore, there are other inescapable problems in using Anglican registers as a basic source for the study of population history. It is very rare to find a register in which the recording of events was continuously complete from its beginning until 1837. Breaks in registration, or periods when registration was seriously defective, occur in almost all registers. In cases where a break is prolonged the simplest course is to exclude the parish from the sample used, but a satisfactory method of identifying and dealing with short breaks, and with periods when registration does not break down entirely but is incomplete, had to be devised and implemented systematically. The extent of the necessary correction varies greatly over time, being very large in periods such as the reign of Queen Mary or during the Civil War, when the influence of political or religious crises superimposed upon the continuing background level of under-registration a large special element arising from the disturbances of the day. Again, although all parishes began registration in 1538, the earliest surviving register books may start in any year from 1538 onwards. Few survive from 1538 itself. Since it was desirable to be able to make use of information from those registers that began early rather than to wait until all the registers in the sample had begun registration, it was necessary to devise a method of using data from a growing number of parishes

---

occasionally necessary to use data for years beyond 1871 in order to complete series ending in that year. For example, the calculation of fertility and mortality rates for the 5-year period centring on 1871 meant using birth and death totals down to 1873.

which eliminated that element in the rising totals of events which occurred simply because more and more parishes were coming into observation.

Aggregative tabulations and local historians

The problems touched upon so far would have arisen in any project aimed at producing a national series of vital events from the baptisms, burials, and marriages recorded in the Anglican parish registers. But in addition there were certain problems peculiar to the data set assembled by the Cambridge Group to which solutions had to be found. When the first aggregative tabulations were made there was no intention of using them as the prime data source for a major independent project. The tabulations were made as a subsidiary element in another research undertaking. In the middle 1960s it became apparent that the technique of family reconstitution could be applied successfully to certain English parish registers but that the number of suitable registers was very limited.[6] It was important to try to discover how many such registers existed and to identify them. Available lists of registers usually gave only the starting and finishing dates of each register without indicating whether there were breaks in registration, or whether the individual entries in the register contained simply the date of the event and the name of the person concerned or included additional information about relationship to the head of the family, occupation, age, residence, or other types of information necessary or helpful to family reconstitution. Accordingly, lists of registers that appeared *prima facie* suitable were drawn up county by county. Only parishes whose earliest registers began before *c*.1620 were considered, so that a long sweep of time could be covered, and parishes with a small population were excluded because of a fear that a reconstitution based on the register of a small parish would yield too small a total of events to permit changes in demographic behaviour to be distinguished with confidence from random fluctuations.

The resulting county lists identified registers that might prove suitable for reconstitution but many of them, of course, were sure to fall by the wayside because of breaks in registration or entries too uninformative to allow nominal record linkage to be undertaken with confidence. Both possible reasons for rejection could be checked by having an aggregative tabulation made and a check-list filled in. The former, by revealing the monthly totals of events, would immediately make clear whether there were breaks in registration or periods of defective registration, while the latter, which consisted of questions about the presence or absence of information concerning relationship to head of family, occupation, and so on, covered other aspects of register quality germane to a decision about proceeding to carry out family reconstitution.

An appeal was then made to local historians known to have an interest in parish registers for help in carrying out aggregative tabulations of any register on the county lists. Each volunteer was sent the list for his or her county and invited to choose whatever register or registers were most accessible. At the time it seemed prudent to hope for no more than about 50 completed tabulations. In the event there was an overwhelming response which continues to this day. By the late 1960s it was

---

6. This is especially true if a starting date earlier than, say, 1650 is sought. But even with a later starting date the choice is restricted. The most widespread problem is the paucity of information given at each entry. Wrigley, 'Some problems of family reconstitution'.

becoming clear that it was reasonable to expect to receive several hundred tabulations, and that they constituted a store of information of such high value in their own right that careful consideration would have to be given to making the fullest use of this vast mass of information.

The tabulations returned were not a *random* sample. Some counties were over-represented, though in the main the sample was not seriously unrepresentative geographically. But it was badly defective in two respects: large parishes were over-represented, and no London parishes were included in the set. Both defects were the result of the initial object of the survey as an adjunct to reconstitution work. The reason for the exclusion of small parishes has already been noted. London parishes were ruled out because it was thought at the time that the high turnover of population in London parishes precluded successful reconstitution.[7] The under-representation of small parishes could be partially corrected by removing the earlier size restriction when answering new requests for guidance about aggregative tabulations to be carried out. But a bias remained, and establishing its nature and extent in the sample of parishes for which returns were available, and then devising ways of correcting it, entailed much thought and effort. The problem of the omission of London parishes had also to be tackled. Once these issues had been dealt with, moreover, the conversion of the resulting corrected totals of events occurring within the aggregative sample into totals of events intended to represent the national whole, also meant a careful testing of alternative possible strategies.

By 1974 the number of tabulations returned was approaching 550, and the rate of inflow of new tabulations was declining. It seemed an appropriate time to take stock and make up the tally of registers that could be incorporated in the aggregative study. Tabulations arriving later could not be incorporated in the main sample, though they may well prove of great value in later work, for example in the study of regional population trends. Many of the tabulations available in 1974 proved unsuitable for inclusion in the aggregative sample either because they started too late, ended too early, contained serious gaps, or gave evidence of inaccurate compilation, but a total of 404 registers passed the various tests. They provided a total of approximately 3.7 million monthly totals of baptisms, burials, and marriages, which form the basis of almost all the demographic description and analysis presented in this book. It is perhaps unnecessary to add that the formidable size of the data set and the complexity of the operations that were required to be carried out upon it would have represented an insuperable obstacle to its full exploitation at any time before the availability of electronic computers. Their advent is one important reason why it is now possible to progress beyond the point reached by Rickman and his census clerks.

The first half of this book is devoted to a more detailed examination of the problems just adumbrated and to a description of the strategies adopted in an attempt to overcome them. Each step in the conversion of Anglican baptism, burial, and marriage totals drawn from the aggregative sample of 404 parishes into national series of vital events is fully set out. But although the complexity of the problems has meant that much space has had to be allotted to a discussion of their solution, the entire sequence of operations was only a preliminary to the main object of the enterprise, namely the construction of new national demographic series extending over several centuries, and the examination of the relationship between economic and demo-

---

7. Subsequently Finlay has shown that valuable results can be obtained from London parish registers using a modified form of family reconstitution. Finlay, *Population of London*.

graphic change. These issues are discussed in the second half of the book, to which those who are prepared to take on trust the accuracy of our estimates of the national totals of births, deaths, and marriages may move directly.

The problem of demographic inference from aggregative data

Aggregative data can be used directly for many purposes. For example, they require no further modifications to be used in the study of seasonality of birth, death, and marriage. And they are also immediately useful for the study of some aspects of short-term variations. If, say, the number of deaths doubles between one year and the next it is safe to assume that a mortality crisis of some sort has occurred. It is unlikely in the extreme that the population has doubled and the mortality rate has remained unchanged. But for other purposes, and especially for the study of secular trends, such data are of limited value when used on their own. If the number of deaths doubles over a century, there can be no initial presumption that mortality has worsened. The numbers at risk may have risen even more than the numbers of deaths. Demographic measurement for all but the simplest purposes depends upon knowing both the number of events of a particular type and the size of the population at risk. Until recently historical population studies of periods earlier than the nineteenth century were greatly handicapped by the fact that although parish registers might provide a fair guide to the numbers of vital events, it was rare to find a satisfactory source of information about the numbers at risk such as national censuses were later to provide. It therefore appeared to be extremely difficult to discover whether, for example, mortality in Elizabethan England was higher or lower than mortality in Georgian England.

In the second half of this book we have tried both to use the best of the old methods of measuring demographic characteristics and change and to develop new techniques of analysis. The most important of the latter we have called back projection. It represents an attempt to provide for aggregative studies the type of solution to the problem of demographic measurement that has already been provided for nominative studies by family reconstitution. In both cases a way has to be found to discover the size of the population producing the events recorded in the registers. Where no censuses exist to provide the necessary data they have to be derived from the flows of vital events themselves. In reconstitution this is achieved by defining the period during which a particular individual may be regarded as being in observation for a particular class of event. Once this has been done the number of years at risk can be set against the number of events occurring (as, for example, live births to a woman in observation during her child-bearing period).

Aggregative back projection takes a different approach, deriving ultimately from a well-known method of population forecasting. If the size and age structure, and the fertility and mortality characteristics, of a population are known, and the population is closed in the sense that there is nil net migration in all age groups, it is possible to forecast future totals of births and deaths as a function of the assumptions made about fertility and mortality trends in the future. However, given the same initial information about the size and age structure of the population the logic of the model can be inverted and changes in the underlying levels of fertility and mortality can be calculated from a knowledge of the flows of births and deaths. Furthermore, information about changes in the size and age structure of the population can also be obtained. This method, which its author Ronald Lee has called inverse projection, appeared to be a promising way of extracting demographic information from the birth and death totals that we had estimated for England from the mid sixteenth century.[8]

For inverse projection to be applicable to our English data, however, it seemed essential to overcome two of its limitations. First, the technique assumes population closure, whereas some net migration is likely to have occurred throughout early modern English history and at times migration is known to have been on a large scale. Second, inverse projection runs forward in time and therefore involves creating a fictitious population at the starting point of the data and endowing it with an assumed age structure. Back projection was designed to avoid having to make the assumption of a closed population by enabling the volume of net migration to be estimated throughout the period studied; and, as the name suggests, it moves backwards in time from a date when the size and age structure of the population is known. Like inverse projection it furnishes estimates of the size and age structure of the population, and of summary measures of fertility and mortality. It provides this information every five years from the mid sixteenth century onwards, thus producing substantially longer runs of basic demographic data than are available as yet for any other country.[9] Once such data have been derived, of course, it is then a comparatively simple matter to settle some long-standing points of controversy: to establish, for example, the relative importance of changes in fertility and mortality in causing the rapid acceleration in population growth that occurred during the eighteenth century.

Both in treating secular changes and in analysing short-term fluctuations we have begun by using simple methods of inference and analysis and then moved on to more complex techniques. Where the findings of both the simple and the complex are in agreement, there must be enhanced confidence that the findings themselves are not an artefact of the particular method employed. Comparison with other countries can also be illuminating where the data exist to permit it. For example, for both France and Sweden there is comparable information covering most demographic characteristics after 1750, and scattered data exist from these and other countries for earlier periods. We have made use of such information where it appeared to be valuable in giving a wider setting to the English experience or served to emphasize the diversity to be found in the demographic history of early modern western Europe.

Demographic structure and environment

To give a new precision and depth to knowledge of English demographic history is a worthwhile objective in its own right, but it is also a necessary first step towards attaining a better understanding of the interplay between population characteristics and the economic, social, and physical environment in which they developed. Throughout the second half of the book, and particularly in the last four chapters, we have sought both to examine certain particular issues (such as the extent to which years of high food prices provoked an increase in the number of deaths) and to look at wider issues related to the functioning of the pre-industrial economy and the changes that occurred in the course of the industrial revolution.

8. Lee, 'Estimating vital rates'.
9. The estimates of expectation of life at birth and of the gross reproduction rate begin in 1541. There is comparable French data from 1740 onwards, and Swedish data from 1750 onwards (see figure 7.13 and its accompanying note on sources). Other Scandinavian countries also possess national demographic series beginning from various dates in the eighteenth century. See, for example, Turpeinen, 'Fertility and mortality in Finland'; Drake, *Population and society in Norway*, pp. 169–84.

What can be attempted is limited, of course, both by the range of the questions to be addressed and by the paucity of reliable data series stretching back to the sixteenth century. One of the few such series, the index of the price of a basket of consumables compiled by Phelps Brown and Hopkins, proved to be particularly valuable. Used in conjunction with their wage data, it made possible the construction of an annual real wage index covering the whole period.[10] And the consumables index itself could be used to examine the influence of population changes on price movements and vice-versa, both in the short and long term. Some of the relationships revealed were striking. For example, when secular changes in population and price levels were compared, a remarkably strong, almost rigid, relationship between rates of change in the two variables became apparent. Significantly this relationship, after having subsisted unchanged from the mid sixteenth to the end of the eighteenth century, then abruptly disappeared during the early decades of the industrial revolution.

Although the price and real-wage series proved especially useful, as might have been expected, other series also showed their worth. For example, monthly temperature data exist from 1659, and rainfall data from 1697. It was therefore possible to investigate the nature and extent of fluctuations in the weather and their impact on birth, death, and marriage rates. Inter-relationships between movements in the demographic series themselves were, of course, also examined, both for their intrinsic interest and for what they implied about the physical, social, and economic circumstances of the population. Here, as in other contexts, one of the most important advantages of the availability of long runs of data lay in the opportunity they afforded to go beyond the discovery of general relationships between two or more variables to a study of how the relationships changed over time.

There proved to be evidence about the relationship between a sufficient number of economic, social, and demographic variables to justify an attempt to construct a general model of their joint functioning in early modern England, which would also take account of the changes that occurred between Elizabethan and Victorian times. The construction of the model is no more than a *ballon d' essai* and the model itself has no pretensions towards comprehensiveness or rigour. Its purpose is more modest, namely to identify some of the basic features of population and the economy in early modern England, and to draw out the implications of the mutual influences upon each other of economic and demographic change. For example, a simple model of this kind facilitates a juster assessment of the circumstances leading up to the industrial revolution and of the changes occurring once it was in train. It can also help to bring out more fully the significance of some of the substantive findings first reported elsewhere in the book. The virtual absence of the Malthusian positive check from early modern England, for example, and the complementary dominance of the preventive check, carry general implications for the nature of English economy and society that can conveniently be examined in terms of a model of this kind.

The unit of analysis

It is a major limitation of this volume that it is devoted almost exclusively to England considered as an undivided whole. No examination of the population history of a country can be complete or satisfactory which is restricted to a national level of

10. The price and wage data and the method used to construct a real wage series from them are described in appendix 9.

aggregation. Lack of change in the national picture may conceal substantial changes of opposite sign in its constituent parts. Equally, a national index may change because of shifts in the relative size of the populations of different constituent groups, whether geographical or socio-economic, even though each group experiences no change. Such dangers are not simply hypothetical. It is probable that the virtual absence of improvement in national mortality between 1820 and 1870 conceals a widespread tendency for mortality rates to fall, which was offset by compositional change in the English population due to the rapid increase in the numbers living in the very unhealthy large manufacturing towns.

To have attempted regional analyses, however, appeared impracticable, both because it would have made an already large book over long and because it would have entailed much additional research. It would have been necessary, for example, not only to have increased the number of registers input and analysed to ensure satisfactory totals of events and parishes in each region, but also to have carried out additional work on matters such as regional nonconformity and registration coverage because the inflation factors used to correct national data would not necessarily have been appropriate for each region.

In the future it may prove possible to calculate regional demographic indices to parallel those published in this book for England as a whole, but in any case we hope to take a first step towards the provision of sub-national data by publishing a volume devoted to the description and analysis of the results obtained from some 20 family reconstitution studies which have been carried out in recent years under the aegis of the Cambridge Group. Indeed, some summary data from a first batch of 12 reconstitutions are reported in this book, because they throw light on demographic characteristics, such as age at marriage and marital fertility, that cannot be directly measured by aggregative techniques.

It should be emphasized that all data and estimates given in this book refer to England only. Scotland did not, of course, share the Anglican system of parochial registration, and its population history has to be approached differently, as in the recent major study by Flinn and his associates.[11] Welsh parish registers are in principle comparable to the English, but in practice they appear to have been more defectively kept, and proportionately far fewer begin at an early date. Monmouth was very Welsh in this respect and was therefore also excluded: unless otherwise stated, any reference to England in this book relates to England less Monmouth.[12]

The presentation of results

One of the many debts owed to Louis Henry by historical demography lies in his establishment of new standards of scrupulousness in the presentation of evidence, no less than in the devising of new techniques and the refinement of old. Reconstitution monographs in the style of *Crulai*[13] present the original data on which the subsequent tabulations and analysis are based in sufficient detail to make it possible for the reader

---

11. Flinn, *Scottish population history*.
12. Rickman drew attention to the poorer coverage of Welsh registers, singling out Wentlloog Hundred in Monmouthshire where in the early nineteenth century 'baptisms and burials respectively do not always outnumber marriages, although four births to a marriage is a very moderate calculation, and the mortality cannot be very different from that of adjoining English counties'. *1831 Census*, I, Enumeration abstract, p. xxxi.
13. Gautier and Henry, *Crulai*.

to retrace each step taken, or to use the data for a different purpose. This is an excellent convention to have established and we have tried to conform to it in this volume. Excessive predigestion of raw material reduces the value of many studies and inhibits the assessment of results while doing nothing to allay any anxiety that may be felt about the way in which they have been obtained. On the other hand, we have tried to avoid encumbering the main text unnecessarily and have therefore made extensive use of appendices, of which there are 16 in all, devoted both to the presentation of data and to the description of analytical techniques.

The raw material upon which many of the findings of this book were based consists of about 3.7 million monthly totals of baptisms, burials, and marriages, each drawn from one of the 404 registers in the aggregative sample. To have printed them in full would have occupied several thousand pages. They lie compactly enough on magnetic tape but their bulk precludes their reproduction even in an appendix.[14] Although parish-level data could not be reproduced in full, however, we have printed the national totals of events for each month after correction for the several causes of under-registration or bias, and we have tried to ensure that each step taken in modifying the original Anglican totals of events should be identifiable in detail. For example, the methods designed to detect periods of under-registration in parish registers and to generate replacement values for such periods produce major changes in the original values in periods like the Civil War. It is important that the reader should be able both to examine their operation in detail and to test the effect of alternative assumptions by referring to the original values. The data necessary for this to be done are given in table A4.1, where the annual totals of events counted in the registers of the 404 parishes in the aggregative sample are set out in the first column and the effect of each intermediate modification, which together produce national totals of births, deaths, and marriages, may be examined.

The national series have been extended from 1837 to 1873 by making use of the totals of vital events returned by the Registrar General corrected to take account of the under-registration of births and deaths which was still a problem in the early years of the civil registration system. The extent of the corrections we have made can be gauged from the original and corrected totals given in tables 5.20 to 5.22 and in table A8.5. The final national totals of births, deaths, and marriages from 1539 to 1873 are set out in appendix 2 in tabulations of successively greater detail, beginning with decadal totals and ending with the monthly totals for the period up to 1836. The figures are printed unrounded and so have the appearance of perfect accuracy as if each birth, death, and marriage occurring in the whole country had been recorded and incorporated into the totals. The appearance is spurious, of course, and the reason for presenting totals in such fine detail is not a wish to conceal the existence of a margin of uncertainty surrounding each final figure. Rather we hope that by printing a precise outcome to the sequence of corrections we have made to the raw data we shall enable the end product to be more effectively judged through comparison with alternative totals that others may wish to derive as a result of making different assumptions about the extent and nature of the flaws in the original data.

Since it is just as desirable that the techniques used to amend or analyse the data should be set out in detail as that the data themselves should be fully described, a number of technical appendices have been included. Other appendices are devoted to presenting the demographic tabulations resulting from back projection in greater

14. However, they are to be published in microform on a regional basis by *Local Population Studies*, Tawney House, The Green, Matlock, Derbyshire.

detail than is convenient elsewhere. And there are a few topics of importance to the book that have been placed in appendices to avoid unbalancing the flow of argument in the main text: for example, earlier estimates of English population totals are compared with those obtained by back projection in appendix 5; the strengths and weaknesses of Rickman's work in attempting to collect parish register data on a nationwide basis are discussed in appendix 7; and local mortality crises are examined in appendix 10.

I From parish register data to national vital series

1

The basic data

The Anglican parish registers form a peculiarly tantalizing body of information, holding out the promise of studying in great detail a fundamental aspect of social history over a very long period of time, but presenting many difficulties. Parish registers were first required to be kept in 1538, and thereafter they record the baptisms, burials, and marriages taking place in the ten thousand or so ancient English parishes.[1] It is probable that no other country possesses such a considerable number of registers of fair quality from such an early date.[2] Furthermore the period covered by the registers includes both the bulk of a pre-industrial growth cycle and the decades of the industrial revolution out of which the modern world was born. Since in principle the registers record the vital events of almost everyone born in England from the mid sixteenth century onwards it would seem that no other aspect of economic and social life can be quantified so thoroughly throughout the early modern period. Yet the promise has very often appeared illusory, because the use of parish registers has proved to involve a number of intractable problems of interpretation so severe that uncertainty about the accuracy of the data has largely vitiated any conclusions that might be drawn from them.[3]

One set of difficulties springs from the very nature of parochial registration itself, for while demographic analysis requires information on the vital events of birth, marriage, and death, the registers normally only record the Anglican ceremonies of baptism, burial, and marriage. The discrepancy between what happened in the past and what was recorded in parish registers varied according to time and place. For example, during the eighteenth century more and more nonconformist chapels began to maintain their own registers both of baptisms and burials, while at times clandestine marriages were common. And even within the Anglican communion there could be a gap between register and reality, especially as a result of the steadily lengthening interval between the birth of a child and its baptism. An infant who died young might fail to appear in the baptism register, and after the end of the seventeenth century its burial was also often omitted.

Moreover on their own terms as a record of ecclesiastical events the parish registers

1. The classic work on parish registers is Cox, *The parish registers of England*. For a useful discussion of many aspects of registers and registration see Steel, *National index of parish registers*, I. The text of the 1538 royal injunctions which required registers to be kept of 'every wedding, christening, and burying' in every parish can be found in Frere and Kennedy, *Visitation articles*, II, pp. 39–40. For a convenient digest of the provisions of canon law relating to baptism, burial, and marriage see Gibson, *Codex iuris*, tit. xviii, xxii, and xxiii.
2. For a description of the quality of registration in several countries see Hollingsworth, *Historical demography*, pp. 160–81.
3. Flinn, in appraising a number of attempts to use national totals of baptisms and burials collected for sample years in the eighteenth century (the Parish Register Abstracts), characterizes the results as 'unacceptable for the purposes of modern scholarship'. Flinn, *British population growth*, p. 20.

may be less than perfect. The temporary absence or negligence of an incumbent, archival misfortune or neglect, and deliberate mutilation have all taken their toll. Since our purpose is to reconstruct the course of population change over a period of 300 years we shall need to spend some time examining each of the possible sources of error that lurk to trap those who try to use parish registers as a guide to long-term demographic development.

We have already described how we acquired our basic data, the tabulations of the monthly frequencies of baptisms, burials, and marriages, from a large number of parishes. In this chapter the steps taken to control the quality of the tabulations and to check the adequacy of each register as a record of ecclesiastical events will be outlined. In particular we shall explain how we have tried to identify periods of defective registration and make good the deficiencies. In subsequent chapters we consider how far the set of registers that pass our tests for completeness constitute a representative sample of the ancient parishes in the country, and what biases need to be eliminated before they can be used as a basis on which to estimate national totals of ecclesiastical events. We go on to make these national estimates, taking account of the absence of London from our figures, and compare them to the national totals of baptisms, burials, and marriages collected by Rickman in the early nineteenth century. Next the national series of ecclesiastical events is converted to one of vital events by correcting for the events missed from the Anglican registers through nonconformity and the lengthening interval between birth and baptism. Finally we compare the numbers of births and deaths in our vital series with those implied by the age structures recorded in the early-nineteenth-century censuses. The comparison reveals the full extent of under-registration at the time and allows a correction factor to be calculated to compensate for escapes from registration for reasons other than nonconformity and the gap between birth and baptism.

By this long and circuitous route we have tried to circumvent the pitfalls inherent in our documentary sources and so arrive at a series of estimated monthly national frequencies of births, deaths, and marriages from which the story of English population over the 300 years between the reigns of Henry VIII and Victoria can begin to be told. To help bring out the scale of the successive corrections that we have thought it advisable to make to the original parish register data, a full set of annual totals for each of the three vital series after each major stage in the process of revision is listed in appendix 4.

The parish tabulations

The first aggregative tabulations of parish registers carried out at our request were made in 1964. Thereafter there has been a steady flow of new tabulations which still continues. In order to prepare and process the data used in this book, however, it was necessary to take an arbitrary point in the flow as a limit, excluding from consideration all tabulations which were to arrive after the decision had been made.

At that date, in mid 1974, a total of 530 register tabulations had been returned, and of these 404 survived to form the basis of the subsequent demographic analysis. These parishes are listed in appendix 1, together with the names of the researchers who so generously provided us with their tabulations of the monthly frequencies. Some of the 530 tabulations were rejected because there was evidence that the counting of monthly totals in the register had not been accurately done, some because the tabulations covered too short a period of time, and some because in one or more periods registration failed to reach a minimum standard of completeness.

The first test we applied was an exercise in quality control. A set of instructions was sent out with each set of blank aggregative tabulation forms in an attempt to secure uniformity of practice and to cover the problems most commonly experienced in work on parish registers. Not everyone, however, has the gift of accuracy in the counting of events. To check this, specimen worksheets from each return were tested wherever possible. The test consisted of selecting a period of 20 years from one of the three series (baptisms, burials, and marriages) covered by the tabulation and making an independent count of the events recorded in the register for that period with great care. If the tabulation under test produced an overall total number of events for the 20 year period within 1 per cent of the control figure yielded by the independent count, the tabulation for the parish as a whole was accepted.[4] If it failed this test, it was then subjected to a further check to discover what proportion of the individual monthly totals had been wrongly recorded. If more than 3 per cent of the months were in error the tabulation was rejected, otherwise it was accepted. These critical error rates are admittedly arbitrary; but since perfection was unattainable it was essential to draw the line somewhere, and 3 per cent seemed about the greatest amount of error that could be tolerated.[5] The error rate was estimated by taking successive samples of 20 year periods until sufficient confidence could be had in the precision of the estimate to enable a decision about acceptance or rejection to be made. The statistical basis of this sequential sampling procedure, and the rules adopted in carrying out the test, are set out in appendix 11.[6]

In principle it is clearly desirable to check each return. In practice it was normally feasible to do so only when the register was available in print or in transcript so that the check could be carried out in a library.[7] Where a tabulation had been made from an original register still in the parish chest, it was only occasionally possible to make a check because of the cost in both time and money that was involved. In all, decisions about the accuracy of tabulations were made on 276 returns. Wherever possible registers were checked individually, but if a volunteer had done several tabulations and only one or two could be checked the other returns were judged by performance on those which had been checked. If any tabulation failed, all other tabulations by the same volunteer were rejected unless they could be checked individually and passed.

Table 1.1 shows that of the 213 registers that could be checked individually 15, or 7 per cent, were rejected. When tabulations judged by the person were amalgamated with those tested individually, the comparable total failing was 22 out of 276, or 8 per cent. A number of registers which passed this test failed other tests for completeness of registration, so that 203 out of the final total of 404 registers had been checked for accuracy of tabulation, leaving 201 that were not checked. It is reasonable to suppose that about 7 per cent of these might have failed if they had been tested since this was the percentage failing in the group of tabulations that were checked. This would have meant withdrawing a further 13 tabulations from the final pool or 3 per cent of the total of 404 which were retained. Since many of the tabulations rejected were only slightly inaccurate the gain in accuracy that would have accrued from excluding them would have been very small.

4. Errors of double-counting were as common as errors of omission and the 1 per cent rule tolerates a higher error rate providing that the mistakes offset each other numerically.
5. Following Henry in *Manuel*, p. 5.
6. As a working rule a tabulation was accepted if less than 3.5 per cent of the monthly totals were erroneous.
7. A large collection of typescript and manuscript transcripts of registers is held in the library of the Society of Genealogists in London.

Table 1.1: Results of checking registers for accuracy of tabulation

	Passed No.	Failed No.	Failed Percentage	Total No.
Decision taken				
By sample tabulation from register	213	15	7	228
By performance of volunteer on other registers	41	7	15	48
Total	254	22	8	276

Table 1.2 shows the number of tabulations that were made from the original registers, from printed or other transcripts, or from various combinations of sources among the 404 tabulations forming the final set. The largest single category, covering

Table 1.2: Sources used for parish register tabulations

		No.	Per cent
1	Original register	157	39
2	Printed or duplicated transcripts	92	23
3	Other transcripts	43	11
4	Bishops' transcripts	1	0
5	Combination of 1 and 2	44	11
6	Combination of 1 and 3	40	10
7	Other combinations	17	4
8	Unknown	10	2
	Total	404	100

39 per cent of the whole set, consists in tabulations made from original registers, followed by printed or duplicated transcripts with 23 per cent. Other transcripts were used in 11 per cent of cases while 25 per cent of the tabulations were based on various combinations of sources. Original registers are not necessarily the most complete source. Some transcripts are based on a comparison and conflation of the original registers with the Bishop's transcripts, which may result in a fuller coverage since some events missing from the original registers appear in the Bishop's transcripts, presumptively because both were made up from notebooks used from day to day by the incumbent or parish clerk. The fact that the volunteers did not indicate the sources used in 10 instances does not imply that the result is likely to be inaccurate. In 7 out of the 10 cases individual checks were possible and showed the work to have been done accurately.

Registration coverage over time

The second test was simpler, and concerned the length of the period covered by the tabulation. Those who volunteered to undertake a tabulation were normally asked to select a register which began in 1620 or earlier and contained no major breaks thereafter. To help narrow the field of choice they were sent lists of registers suitable for aggregative tabulation that appeared to meet this requirement among others.

Inevitably, however, some returns came in that began at a later date. Similarly, although it was intended that each tabulation should be carried down to 1837 when civil registration began, this proved impossible in some cases. Sometimes tabulations began too late or finished too early because of the loss or destruction of the original registers, but often the problem lay elsewhere. For example, where a tabulation was based on a printed transcript, the transcript might begin too late or end too early, and where access to the original register was not possible the tabulation would fail under this test even though the original registers might span a sufficiently long period of time.

As the number of returns mounted it seemed clear that the most suitable minimum requirement to adopt under this head was that all three series in all the registers in the sample should be in observation throughout a period beginning in January 1662 and ending in December 1811. The Civil War and the Commonwealth period in the 1640s and 1650s greatly disrupted the normal registration of baptisms, burials, and marriages, and for a time during the Commonwealth a civil registration system replaced the traditional ecclesiastical recording of events.[8] Although very few registers in the early returns began registration as late as the 1640s and 1650s, it was feared that many registers would prove to have such substantial gaps in these two decades that they would fail the third requirement of reasonably continuous registration if the latest date by which this should have begun were to be set at a date before the outbreak of civil war. In the event this fear proved groundless, but since a small number of registers began only in the 1640s and 1650s the minimum requirement was not altered.[9]

Setting 1811 as the end of the core period was determined by the fact that a very high percentage of all printed registers end with the coming into force of Rose's Act in January 1813 and therefore contain no entries later than a date towards the end of 1812.[10] In these registers therefore 1811 is often the last year in which registration was unambiguously complete. A total of 60 tabulations failed to cover the period 1662 to 1811 and were rejected on this ground.

Completeness of registration

The third test concerning a minimum standard of completeness of registration was designed to pick out registers that survived the first two tests but that contained so many years of deficient registration that to have included them would have heightened considerably the problems of data correction. The rule of thumb we adopted was to reject a tabulation if in any consecutive run of 40 years there were 20 years without a recorded baptism. The same test was applied to burials, while for marriages the

8. 'An act touching Marriages and the Registring thereof: and also touching Births and Burials' of 1653 replaced marriage before a priest by marriage before a Justice of the Peace, and put the registration of births, marriages, and burials in the hands of an elected secular official, 'the Register', who also had custody of the earlier registers. The text of the act is printed in Firth and Rait, *Acts and ordinances*, II, pp. 715–8. An earlier ordinance of 1645 required dates of birth and death to be recorded in addition to dates of baptism and burial, but this was little observed. For the text see *ibid.*, I, pp. 582–3. Although the 1653 act required births to be registered, only a minority of parishes complied and in general baptisms continued to be registered. See Berry and Schofield, 'Age at baptism', p. 455.
9. Some registers began in 1661 so 1662 was the first year in which registration was unambiguously complete.
10. 52 George III c.146. Section 1 of the act required registration in special books to be supplied by the king's printer, thereby causing the register current in 1812 to be terminated.

tabulation failed if there were 20 blank years in any period of 30 consecutive years. A failure in any one series caused the exclusion of the parish tabulation as a whole. If, however, there was a defective period or periods before January 1662 in any series but no defective period after that date, the series was deemed to enter into observation at the end of the latest period of incomplete registration and the tabulation of the frequencies of events in that series was accepted from that point on.

The test for marriages was less rigorous than for the other two series because the marriage registers usually recorded only between a quarter and a third as many events, and in a parish with a small population there might be a substantial proportion of years without marriages even if registration were complete. A parish of 100 souls, for example, would be likely to celebrate only one marriage each year on average. As an additional safeguard against the danger of excluding a very small parish with complete registration, years in which no events were recorded were ignored if on either side they were adjacent to a year in which only one event was recorded (the recording of only one event was used as an indication that the parish was small). Thus in the annual sequence of events (0, 1, 0, *0*, 0, 1, 0) only the (italicized) fourth year would count as a year of incomplete registration for the purpose of this test even though no events occurred in five of the seven years in the sequence. While clear cut instances of failure under this test can easily be picked out by eye, a computer program was found to be much more capable of dealing consistently with marginal cases in a large body of data. In the event 44 parishes were rejected on these grounds.

Any test of incomplete registration is inevitably somewhat arbitrary. In this case a tougher test, say 10 blank years in any 20, would have led to the rejection of a much higher proportion of the registers in the original sample because of the special problem presented by the 1640s and 1650s when many parishes suffered from incomplete registration. Basing the test on 20 blank years ensured that a parish would not be excluded if its only major defect under this head was confined to the period of Civil War and the Interregnum.

Table 1.3 summarizes the results of the steps taken to winnow out the poorer registers. The 404 parish tabulations remaining out of the initial set of 530 were not without internal defects, indeed it was rare to find a register that showed no sign of

Table 1.3: Stages in the selection of a final set of registers

Number of parishes in original set		530
Rejected because period covered by tabulation begins after 1661 or ends before 1812	60	
Rejected because of incompleteness in period 1662–1811	44	
Rejected because of inaccurate tabulation	22	
	126	
Number of parishes in final set		404

under-registration throughout a period of 250 years or more.[11] Where there is a complete break in registration lasting for many months there is normally little difficulty in establishing the existence of under-registration, though in small parishes with very low annual frequencies of events even a long run of months without entries is not necessarily evidence of neglect. But where the completeness of registration declines without ceasing altogether, there will be far more ambiguity about judging whether there was under-registration and if so where it began and ended. Small parishes once again present a particularly intractable problem. In a very big parish where, say, 15 baptisms are normally recorded each month, there is little room for doubt that registration has become defective if the number of baptisms falls to 3 a month for a period of half a year or so. In a small parish, on the other hand, where 9 months in 10 may pass without an entry being made in the marriage register even in a period of full registration, it is scarcely possible to identify short periods of under-registration at all and even periods of three or four years without an entry may not be adequate grounds for suspicion. In such circumstances identification by eye would have been wayward and inconsistent, and with 3.689 million monthly frequencies to survey it would also have been a very time-consuming operation. Accordingly a computer algorithm was devised to detect periods of under-registration. A full description of the algorithm is given in appendix 12 but it may be helpful to outline here the general approach adopted in tackling this issue.

The individual monthly totals in each series in each register are considered successively. The program may be pictured as a point moving forward in time through the body of the data with a search period ahead of it while behind it trails a reference set of monthly values that have already been accepted as reasonably well registered. The purpose of the reference set is to provide an estimate of the current average monthly number of events against which the total of events actually registered in the search period can be compared. The reference period therefore naturally excludes both under-registered months and months with untypically high totals, such as might occur during an epidemic, a baptismal 'round up', or during the operation of a 'marriage-shop'.[12] The length of the reference period for each series is determined before the process of testing begins so that it will contain on average a total of 100 events, with a minimum of 10 years and a maximum of 40 years.

The length of the search period is successively revised during the testing process to equal the number of months in which 20 events could be expected to be registered on the basis of the average monthly frequency calculated from the trailing reference set of months. In a very large parish the search period might be as short as one month, while in a small parish it might be as long as 200 months or more, though in practice an upper limit of 10 years was imposed Tests carried out on a number of registers showed that the totals of successive samples of events, taken in blocks of months of a size to yield on average approximately 20 events, were distributed in a manner that

11. Amongst the already select group of 404 parishes only 35, 50, and 37 parishes had no periods of defective registration in the baptism, burial, and marriage registers, respectively.
12. Baptisms of large numbers of people on the same day are rare at all times, and are generally confined to the years immediately after the Restoration and to the early nineteenth century. For a dramatic example of a steady decline in the numbers of baptisms recorded in the 1830s in Hinckley, Leics., followed by a mass baptism of 239 persons in two days just before the introduction of civil registration in July 1837, see Schofield, 'Comment on correspondence on age at baptism'. Before Hardwicke's Act of 1753 some vicars attracted marriages from a wide area. Among the 404 parishes the tiny village of Fledborough, Notts., was a conspicuous example of a 'marriage shop', registering large numbers of marriages between July 1729 and March 1754, when Hardwicke's Act put it out of business.

approached the normal distribution with a mean of 20 and a standard deviation of 6.0 (6.5 for burials).[13] If a large number of independent random samples of 20 events were to be drawn it might be expected that only 1 per cent of the samples would yield a total number of events more than 2.32 standard deviations below 20, and only 0.5 per cent of the samples would return a score more than 2.58 standard deviations below the mean.[14] Although we were not drawing independent random samples, these figures were used as a rough guide to setting threshold levels below which the frequencies were so low that it was highly unlikely that they would have arisen by chance, and so could be taken as an indication of defective registration.

The threshold numbers of events occurring in a test period that we considered low enough to warrant outright rejection were 4.5 for baptisms and marriages and 3.5 for burials. The lower figure for burials was to take account of the greater instability of this series. These figures are about 2.58 standard deviations from the mean of 20 events and so correspond to fluctuations that under conditions of independent random sampling would occur by chance with a probability of less than 1 in 200.

We were also prepared to accept less violent falls in the number of events in the test period as indicating under-registration provided that we did not find any countervailing evidence in the behaviour of the other series. For example, a period in which rather low totals of baptisms or marriages are registered is quite likely to be valid if at the same time the total of burials is higher than usual, since crisis mortality was often accompanied by a considerable fall in fertility and nuptiality. Similarly, in the months after a period of crisis mortality the number of burials recorded is often low, while the totals of baptisms and marriages tend to run at, or above, normal levels.

We therefore set further threshold numbers of events at 6.5 for baptisms and marriages and 5.5 for burials, below which the search period was provisionally regarded as a period of under-registration.[15] If the number of events in a test period was low enough to be rejected provisionally, but not so extreme as to warrant outright rejection, the burial series was consulted in the case of baptisms and marriages, and the baptism series in the case of burials, over the same test period. If this second series also recorded totals below the provisional threshold, the judgement that the first series was under-registered was confirmed, otherwise it was withdrawn.

Once a period of under-registration had been detected it was regarded as continuing until the search period, advancing a month at a time, came to contain a total of events greater than 11, representing 1.5 standard deviations below the expected figure of 20 events. A higher total of events was demanded from the search period as a sign of the end of a period of under-registration than was required as evidence that a period of defective registration was begining, because in each case what was being sought was some indication that the current state of registration had changed. The standards for

13. Our choice of 20 events was confirmed by a study of the variation of frequencies of vital events in a number of Belgian parishes which found that for baptisms and marriages samples of around 20 events constituted a 'critical number' below which the coefficient of variation increased markedly and above which 'there was relatively little change in the coefficient of variation, so that a researcher could be safe in the knowledge that increased size would not give an improved estimate'. Spencer, 'Variability of demographic data', pp. 27–30, 37–9; quotation from p. 28. Instabilities due to frequent crisis mortality prevented any equivalent results being reported for deaths, *ibid.*, p. 29.

14. The properties of the normal distribution are described in most statistical textbooks. The sampling distribution of a mean is discussed formally in Cochran, *Sampling techniques*, pp. 9–12 and chs. 2.3, 2.13, and informally in Schofield, 'Sampling in historical research', pp. 155–6.

15. These levels correspond to 2.25 standard deviations below the mean, a fluctuation that under conditions of independent random sampling would occur with a probability of less than 1 in 80.

determining the beginning and end of periods of defective registration were arrived at after much experimentation on a test file consisting of registers that appeared to present special difficulties for the accurate determination of the bounds of such periods.[16]

After the beginning or end of a period of defective registration has been detected the program then deals with fine adjustments to the edges of the period. This problem arises because the search period may be so long that it straddles the point at which the change in the quality of registration occurs. For example, a search period 10 months long may be identified as showing under-registration because it yields only 3 events, but if the first 2 months of the search period record 2 events and 1 event respectively, and the remaining 7 months are without events, it is desirable that the beginning of under-registration should be advanced three months from the point at which it was first detected. In more indeterminate cases the algorithm must be able to cope with more complex sequences of monthly totals, and these are discussed in appendix 12.

As the program advances along the monthly series the total of events in the trailing reference period is successively revised in the manner of a moving average. Normally as each new month is accepted the earliest month in the trailing set is deleted, but when under-registration has been detected the latest month is not accepted and so the trailing period is frozen. After a period of defective registration, or an unusual 'peak' of events, the trailing reference period 'snakes round' the months affected to preserve the representativeness of the moving average monthly frequency of events. In a period where the secular trend of totals of events is rising, therefore, the moving average monthly frequency will also rise and the search period within which 20 events are expected will shrink proportionately.

The early years of each series clearly present a special problem since there will be no trailing set of validated monthly frequencies by which to judge the totals of events in the search period. This difficulty was overcome by starting the process of testing well after the start of the monthly series, at a point six times the length of the reference period from the first year of the series. The program then tracks backwards towards the start of the series, identifying periods with under-registration or untypically high peaks of events. By the time the program has reached the start of the series the reference period has had plenty of time to lose any contamination from under- or over-registration it may have acquired at the point where the program began, and is by now composed of months in which registration has been tested and found to be normal. The program then turns round and runs forward along the series in chronological order, as described briefly above and in greater technical detail in appendix 12.

Patterns of defective registration

The set of 404 parishes contains 3,688,884 monthly frequencies of baptisms, marriages, and burials and the program identified 211,964 of them, or 5.5 per cent, as defective. This judgement was based on statistical grounds alone and reflects a wide variety of circumstances: missing registers, torn out pages, illegible entries, absent or apathetic incumbents, or parishioners who were indifferent or hostile to the religious

16. For example, standards had to be sensitive enough to detect a slow descent into, or recovery from, defective registration in some parishes and yet not be misled into identifying spurious periods of defective registration in other parishes that experienced a greater variation from month to month in the numbers of events being recorded.

celebration of vital events. Some of these underlying causes may have been present to a greater or lesser degree at all times, but others were subject to short-term changes, for the proportion of monthly frequencies judged to be defective was by no means constant over time, and variations in this statistic illustrate the degree to which some of the major religious and political events of the day made their mark in the parishes.

Table 1.4 provides a summary view of the proportions of monthly totals of baptisms, burials, and marriages identified as defective at different points in time. To bring out the variations as clearly as possible the 300 years from 1539 to 1839 have been divided into blocks at the points of greatest change. In the mid sixteenth century it was a change of monarch that had the greatest impact on the adequacy of parochial registration. After the reign of Elizabeth this was no longer the case, though the political and religious upheavals of the period of the Civil War and the Interregnum leave a clear mark. After the Restoration registration was most influenced by legal enactments, whether directly as in the cases of the Marriage Act of 1753 and the Registration Act of 1812, or indirectly as with the Marriage Duty Act of 1695.

From table 1.4 it is apparent that normally in the period before the Civil War about 5 to 7 per cent of the monthly totals of baptisms, burials, and marriages were defective in the sense described above. The detailed figures from which table 1.4 has been compiled show that this was a general background level, displaying no tendency to increase or decrease in the century between 1540 and 1640. It thus provides a convenient reference point from which to assess the relative impact of the more exceptional periods of the reigns of Edward VI and Mary in the mid sixteenth century, and of the Civil War and Interregnum in the mid seventeenth century.

Although the relatively small number of registers in observation makes it difficult to obtain a stable estimate of the proportion of defective months in Henry VIII's reign, it seems likely that the first decade of registration was similar to other 'normal' decades in the period before the Civil War.[17] With the accession of the young protestant king Edward VI, however, matters deteriorated rapidly. From 1548 the percentage of defective months rose to around three times its previous level (15 per cent) in the case of baptisms and marriages, and to 1.5 times the previous level (11 per cent) in the case of burials. Figure 1.1 charts this rise and shows how the accession of the catholic queen Mary in 1553 heralded a further dramatic increase in the proportion of registration that was defective. Baptisms and burials recorded maximum figures of 35.6 per cent and 31.5 per cent at the height of the government's anti-protestant activities in 1555, while defectiveness of marriage registration peaked a year later in 1556. This year is generally held to mark the beginning of the waning of Mary's power, and from this point the proportion of defective months in the parish registers begins to ebb.[18]

The accession of Elizabeth, although occasioning renewed uncertainty in matters of religion, brought a massive reduction in the proportion of defective registers. Within three years the figures for both baptisms and marriages fell almost to the level at which they had stood under Henry VIII. Defectiveness in burial registration, on the other hand, which had increased less under both Edward and Mary, fell less dramatically in the first few years of Elizabeth's reign, and even rose to a new lower peak in 1567, from which it declined once more by 1571. Both baptisms and

17. For the dates at which registers entered into observation see table 2.19 below.
18. Pollard, *History of England*, pp. 127–62. The avoidance of parochial registration, particularly in 1554, was probably even greater than figure 1.1 would suggest since the totals of events, and especially of marriages, was very low in that year even after correction. See table A4.1.

Table 1.4: Percentages of months with defective registration

Period	Dates	Baptisms Months observed	Baptisms Percentage defective	Burials Months observed	Burials Percentage defective	Marriages Months observed	Marriages Percentage defective
Henry VIII	Jan. 1539–Jan. 1547	4 950	5.3	4 695	7.0	4 320	6.1
Edward VI	Feb. 1547–Jul. 1553	5 425	15.2	5 205	11.3	4 871	15.1
Mary	Aug. 1553–Nov. 1558	5 052	33.5	5 056	25.3	4 600	28.0
Elizabeth–Charles I	Dec. 1558–Mar. 1640	303 150	5.6	303 119	6.3	293 175	5.8
Civil War	Apr. 1640–Sept. 1653	62 283	20.5	62 352	26.6	61 254	42.8
Civil registration	Oct. 1653–May 1660	31 849	16.5	31 858	17.5	31 315	31.0
Restoration	June 1660–Apr. 1695	169 219	4.8	169 219	7.0	169 129	15.5
Marriage Duty Act	May 1695–Mar. 1754	285 628	1.4	285 628	1.9	285 628	4.6
Hardwicke's Act	Apr. 1754–Dec. 1812	283 356	0.6	285 356	0.8	283 416	0.6
Rose's Act	Jan. 1813–Dec. 1839	82 080	0.1	82 776	0.1	82 920	0.4

Note: The dates are taken to the nearest whole month.

Source: See text.

Per cent

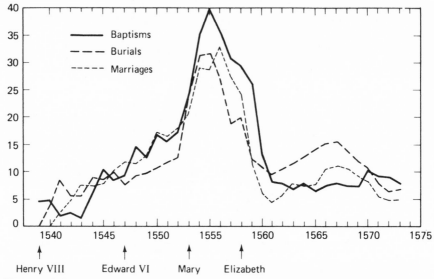

Figure 1.1: Proportions of months with defective registration 1539–73

marriages also experienced an increase in defective registration in the mid 1560s, though to a lesser extent. This period saw an intensification of the struggle between the ecclesiastical hierarchy and some of the more 'puritan' members of both church and laity, who objected to what they considered to be superstitious popish practices and customs still attaching to church ceremonies: the making of the sign of the cross at baptisms, the symbolic use of the ring at weddings, the ringing of bells, processions, and the wearing of mourning clothes at burials.[19]

The reformist clergy, who counted several bishops amongst their ranks, had narrowly failed to secure sweeping changes in the forms of service in the Prayer Book in the convocation of 1563, and the period in which the proportion of defectively registered months rises is precisely that in which the reformers switched their attack to parliament, while the official hierarchy counter-attacked by suspending incumbents who would not subscribe to the thirty-nine articles.[20] If there were indeed a connexion between these ecclesiastical controversies and the quality of parochial registration, then it would seem that the puritans' objections to the baptism and marriage ceremonies made less difference to the numbers of events being recorded than did their objections to the ritual connected with burial services. In the case of burials a general protestant dislike of superstition may have been reinforced by a specifically predestinarian antipathy to a burial service which implied the efficacy of human intercession in securing the salvation of a departed soul.[21]

19. See, for example, 'A view of popishe abuses yet remaining in the Englishe church, for which godly ministers have refused to subscribe', part of 'An admonition to the parliament' of 1571 in Frere and Douglas, *Puritan manifestoes*, pp. 26–8. Similar objections were expressed in the parliamentary ordinance of 1645 that replaced the Book of Common Prayer by a Directory for Publique Worship. Firth and Rait, *Acts and ordinances*, I, pp. 600–1, 604.
20. Knappen, *Tudor puritanism*, pp. 184–216, 225–9.
21. 'To pray over the grave and the burial of the dead carrieth some odour of prayer for all and calling everyone that is buried dear brother in what manner soever he lived or died argueth the opinion to be true

Per cent

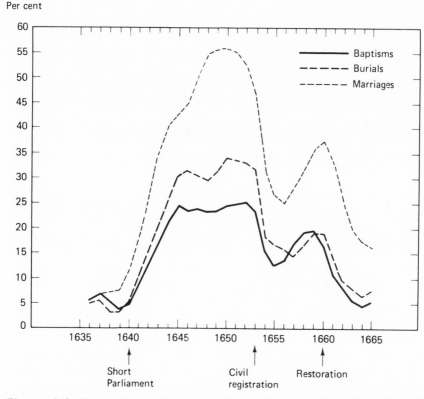

Figure 1.2: Proportions of months with defective registration 1636–65

After 1571 the proportion of defective months in each series remained remarkably constant at about 5 to 6 per cent despite a continuing religious debate. The next major increase in the proportion of defective months occurred in the years of uncertainty and civil strife following the calling of the Short Parliament in 1640. As is clear from figure 1.2, the marriage series was the most affected: the percentage of defective months rose earlier than with the other series and reached the staggering maximum of 55.9 per cent in 1650. Burials reached a lower maximum of 34.1 per cent defective in the same year, while baptisms attained a maximum of only 25.1 per cent defective two years later in 1651. Taking the period from 1640 to the establishment of civil registration in 1653 as a whole, baptism registration was less affected by the Civil War than by the difficulties of Mary's reign. On the other hand burial registration deteriorated to almost the same extent as it had in Mary's reign, while the registration of marriages was far more severely interrupted in the era of civil strife than during the catholic revival of the previous century.[22]

that all shall be saved'. From an undated manuscript headed 'Subscription (as it hath been required) is to be judged unlawfull', which probably relates to the 1583–4 subscription crisis. Lambeth Palace Library MSS 2550, ff. 130–1. We owe this reference and its dating to Dr P. Lake of Clare College, Cambridge. The Directory for Publique Worship of 1645 considered 'praying by, or towards the dead corps' to be superstitious and in 'no way beneficial to the dead'. Firth and Rait, *Acts and ordinances*, 1, p. 604.
22. The parliamentary ordinance establishing The Directory for Publique Worship in 1645 repeated the

Although the proportion of defective months was already beginning to decline in the early 1650s, the introduction of civil registration at the end of September 1653 brought about a considerable improvement.[23] Yet despite the clear intentions of parliament, the baptism and burial registers were still about three times more defective than they had been before the Civil War, while marriages were five times more defective. A return to the levels that had prevailed between 1570 and 1640 had to wait upon the Restoration, and even then it was not achieved in baptisms and burials until 1663, while the proportion of defective months in marriage registers stayed obstinately high around 15 per cent, some 2.5 times the level before the Civil War. During the reign of Charles II the position with all three series continued to improve gradually, though in 1688–9 the 'Glorious Revolution' was accompanied by a sharp, though modest and temporary, reversal of this trend.

The next event to have had a major impact on the quality of registration was the passing of the Marriage Duty Act in 1695, levying taxes on births, marriages, and deaths, and charging a poll tax on unmarried bachelors. Although the collectors were required to make their own inventories of the population and compile their own lists of vital events, they were empowered to search the parish registers to this end.[24] From 1696 every birth had to be notified to the incumbent who was required to record it and to produce his registers, including a register of births, to the tax commissioners twice a year.[25] As is apparent from figure 1.3 these enactments were followed by a substantial fall in the proportion of months that were defective. By 1705, the last year in which the Marriage Duty Act taxes were levied, the proportion of defective months had declined from 4 to just under 1 per cent in the case of baptisms, from 5 to 1 per cent in the case of burials, and from 12 to 4 per cent in the case of marriages. Although in 1705 the clergy were accorded statutory exemption from any penalties for negligent registration to which they may have become liable under Marriage Duty Acts, these Acts appear to have been conspicuously successful in driving down defective registration to unprecedentedly low levels.[26]

Immediately after the Marriage Duty Acts ceased to have any force the percentages of defectively registered months rose a little in each of the three series before settling down at about 1.5 per cent for baptisms, 2.0 per cent for burials, and 4.5 per cent for marriages until the mid eighteenth century. The century after the start of the Civil War was thus marked by a persistent relative deficiency in marriage registration. Why marriages should have first begun to be so much worse registered than baptisms and burials in the 1640s is not clear. Their continued defectiveness was accompanied by the existence of cut-rate 'marriage shops' where the ceremony was performed at a lower cost in fees, either by itinerant priests or in 'extra-parochial' locations in the countryside, as well as in the towns.[27]

---

requirement laid down by earlier canons and royal injunctions that every parish should register baptisms, marriages, and burials, but does not appear to have had any effect on the proportion of defective registers. Firth and Rait, *Acts and ordinances*, i, p. 583.

23. See note 8, above. The introduction of civil registration of marriages seems to have occasioned some apprehension, for the number of marriages recorded in September 1653 was over three times the number registered in the previous September. See table A2.4.

24. 6 and 7 William and Mary c. 6, s. 20.

25. 7 and 8 William and Mary c. 35, ss 4–5. The incumbent was liable to penalties of £2 for failure to register a birth and £5 for failure to produce his registers to the tax commissioners.

26. The exemption was contingent upon the taxes due in respect of the vital events having been paid. 4 and 5 Anne c. 23, s. 10.

27. For some examples of 'marriage shops' see Tate, *Parish chest*, pp. 81–2. For clandestine marriages

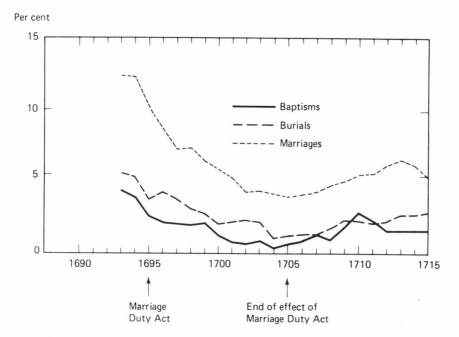

Per cent

Figure 1.3: Proportions of months with defective registration 1693–1715

Marriage registration was particularly vulnerable because in canon law a church wedding was not the only means by which a legally valid marriage could be contracted. Traditionally the medieval church had held that the essential elements of marriage were the exchange of vows before witnesses and a subsequent full sexual relationship (*cum copula*). After the Council of Trent in the mid sixteenth century the Roman Catholic church had required as a matter of discipline that the vows should be exchanged before a priest at a mass, but the Church of England retained the medieval Church's indifference as to where the exchange of promises took place.[28] By the mid eighteenth century the legal difficulties in determining whether the circumstances in particular cases were such as to constitute a valid marriage had become so irksome that the Lord Chancellor, Lord Hardwicke, persuaded parliament to pass an act declaring that only those marriages celebrated in a parish church according to the Prayer Book and registered in the Anglican registers in a specified manner were to have legal validity. Thus from 1754 to 1837, when the civil registration of marriages began, the parishes of the Church of England had a monopoly of legally valid marriages and a legal duty to register them, with the exception of the marriages of Jews, Quakers, and members of the royal family, who were exempted from the provisions of Hardwicke's Act.[29]

---

generally see the case law cited in Burn, *Ecclesiastical law*, II, pp. 465–78b. The most celebrated purveyor of extra-parochial marriages was the liberty of the Fleet in London in the early eighteenth century. See Brown, *Clandestine marriages in London*.

28. However, a bishop had the power to compel a church celebration of an existing marriage. The law of marriage is summarized in Burn, *Ecclesiastical law*, II, pp. 433–512. See especially p. 457.

29. 26 George II c. 33.

Per cent

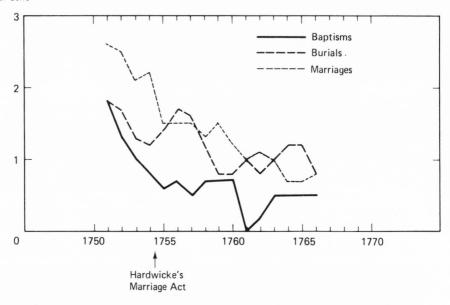

Figure 1.4: Proportions of months with defective registration 1751–66

From figure 1.4 it is clear that although marriage registration was already beginning to improve in the 1740s, Hardwicke's Act had an immediate impact in reducing the proportion of months with defective marriage registration. The full effects of the act were not felt until the 1770s, but taking the period between 1754 and 1812 as a whole, marriage registration at last came back on a par with the registration of baptisms and burials, with only 0.6 per cent of the monthly marriage frequencies judged to be defective. The next breakpoint falls in January 1813 when the first attempt to legislate comprehensively for the whole system of parish registration came into effect. Amongst other things, the act in question, usually known as Rose's Act, laid down a *pro forma* for baptism and burial registration, and marginally amended the layout of the *pro forma* for marriage registration established by Hardwicke's Act of 1753.[30] From 1813 the baptism and burial registers were made up of uniform, printed pages with separate columns for different items, such as dates and names. With the passing of the old, idiosyncratic manuscript registers, the proportion of defective months amongst baptisms and burials plunged to an insignificant figure of 0.1 per cent. Curiously, marriage registration, although equally subject to the act, improved only a little so that 0.4 per cent of the monthly figures were still defective in the way that we have described.

Correcting defective registration

While the temporal distribution of the proportion of defective months provided some interesting side-lights on the impact of national affairs at the parish level, our

30. 52 George III c. 146.

immediate practical concern was to make good these deficiencies and restore to the registers the missing events. Failure to do so would evidently lead to a very considerable under-enumeration of baptisms, burials, and marriages in periods such as the reigns of Edward VI and Mary, the Civil War, and the Interregnum.

The program that had detected the periods of defective registration in each series provided a list of the months in each parish judged to contain unacceptably low numbers of events. With 211,964 defective original monthly frequencies to be corrected, it seemed advisable to approach the problem in a straightforward manner. Since the periods of defective registration in a parish might occur when the numbers of events in a series were rising, stationary, or falling, it was important to preserve the underlying trend. Rather than embark upon elaborate curve-fitting exercises we calculated the trend line of events during a defective period by interpolating geometrically between the average monthly frequencies in the periods of sound registration immediately before and after the defective period.

The resulting estimates of monthly frequencies, however, were far too smooth to be realistic. In reality there was a marked seasonal periodicity of events in each of the three series, and in a period such as the Civil War, when a high proportion of monthly frequencies needed correcting, there would be a danger that relying exclusively on a simple interpolation would so dampen short-term variation as to jeopardize the investigation of oscillation in the combined 'national' series of events. We therefore generated a template of monthly frequencies from all the parishes that were fully registered to use as a guide to periodical variation occurring during defective periods.[31]

For each defective month in each parish we found the proportional deviation from trend of the corresponding value in the template series and applied it to the smooth geometric trend value calculated for that month in the defective register. This figure was then rounded to the nearest whole number, and assigned to the month in question, unless the original frequency happened to be greater than the replacement value in which case the original frequency was allowed to stand. Finally, if the sum of the whole numbers of events assigned to each month in the defective period did not equal the sum of the unrounded monthly frequencies assigned to the period, the difference to be added or subtracted was randomly distributed amongst the months comprising the defective period with a probability of selection proportionate to the number of events recorded for that month in the template series. Further details of these procedures for calculating the monthly replacement values can be found in appendix 13.

The effect of replacing the 211,964 defective monthly frequencies can be seen in table A4.1 where the annual totals of baptisms, burials, and marriages after replacement (column 2) can be compared with the original totals from the 404 parish registers (column 1). Column 7 of the table brings out the changing impact of defective registration from year to year in terms of the ratio between the annual totals before and after the replacement of the missing events. In table 1.5 we have grouped the years according to the same major periods of high and low defective registration identified in table 1.4. For each period we have calculated the percentage of the total number of events that were identified as missing and 'added back' by the replacement procedure. Providing both the months and the parishes that had defective registration

31. Since only 35, 50, and 37 parishes had no periods of defective registration in the baptism, burial, and marriage registers respectively, the replacement procedure was taken in two stages so as to increase the number of parishes on which the monthly template series could be based. For details see appendix 13.

were reasonably typical, then a comparison between the percentage of missing events and the percentage of defective months gives an indication of the severity of the deficiencies in registration detected and corrected at this stage. If the months identified as defective witnessed a total collapse in registration we would expect the two percentage figures to be approximately the same, while partial failures in registration would result in lower proportions of missing events compared to the proportion of months judged to be defective.

In the event table 1.5 shows that the two percentage figures were generally close together in periods of both high and low incidence of defective registration.

Table 1.5: Percentages of events missing and proportions of months defective

Period	Baptisms		Percentages defective Burials		Marriages	
	Events	Months	Events	Months	Events	Months
Henry VIII	5.4	5.3	5.1	7.0	5.2	6.1
Edward VI	12.4	15.2	11.7	11.3	17.2	15.1
Mary	35.1	33.5	24.8	25.3	30.6	28.0
Elizabeth–Charles I	4.8	5.6	5.4	6.3	5.2	5.8
Civil War	16.7	20.5	24.3	26.6	36.1	42.8
Civil registration	13.6	16.5	15.2	17.5	25.8	31.0
Restoration	3.5	4.8	5.3	7.0	10.9	15.5
Marriage Duty Act	1.4	1.4	1.6	1.9	3.3	4.6
Hardwicke's Act	0.5	0.6	0.6	0.8	0.6	0.6
Rose's Act	0.6	0.1	0.0	0.1	0.7	0.4

Note: For the months included in each period, see table 1.4.

Source: 'Events', see text; 'Months', see table 1.4.

Occasionally, the percentage of missing events was slightly higher than the percentage of defective months, implying that either the months, or the parishes that experienced defective registration, were not entirely typical. This feature was confined to the extremes of the date range covered, when not all of the 404 parishes were contributing events. Between 1558 and 1812, however, when the bulk of the parishes were in observation, the percentages of missing events were only a little below the percentages of defective months. This result implies that the months identified as defective witnessed a nearly complete collapse of registration. It is interesting, nonetheless, that there should have been a wider than usual gap between the two percentages in the case of marriages in the period 1640–1754, indicating that the exceptionally high proportions of defective months in the marriage registers at this time also covered cases where marriage registration declined suspiciously without ceasing altogether. But this gloss should not detract from the main message of table 1.5 which is that the registration deficiencies so far detected and corrected were gross ones and would probably have been picked up by any reasonable set of criteria. Thus the present results are likely to be robust and not dependent on the particular critical levels adopted in the procedures used to identify months of defective registration as outlined in appendix 12. On the other hand it is clear that the corrections made so far are only a first step and that other, more insidious, defects in the set of 404 registers need to be tackled before they can be used as a basis for demographic analysis.

2

The representativeness of the data

The correction of each series in each of the 404 parish registers to make good obvious defects has now been described, but two more issues need to be tackled before the figures can be aggregated together and used as a basis for national estimates of population change. First, the set of 404 parishes must be shown to be a representative selection from all 10,000 parishes in the country. If this is not the case then the data need to be modified to secure representativeness before the totals of events recorded in the 404 parishes can be inflated to yield estimates of national totals of baptisms, burials, and marriages. Second, the national series of ecclesiastical events need to be converted into series of vital events by estimating how many births, marriages, and deaths failed to be recorded in the parish registers because of nonconformity and for other reasons.

It has already been stressed that the set of 404 parishes was not drawn as strict random sample. Indeed, even if such a sample had been drawn, many registers would have been rejected on account of gross gaps in registration, and it would still have been necessary to check that the final sample of parishes had not been biased as a result. In the present case the set of 404 parishes is a selection from tabulations contributed by a large number of people scattered all over the country, so it is even more essential to check for bias.

A demographic check

Our main concern is with the demographic representativeness of the 404 parishes, but it is difficult to test this directly short of replicating the entire study with a random selection of parishes. However, a summary check can be made by comparing the rate of growth of the population of the aggregative parishes to that of a random sample of parishes using data on parish population totals at two different dates. The aggregative and random sample sets of parishes can also be compared to discover whether the aggregative parishes are typical with respect to a number of geographical, social, and economic characteristics.

The summary check consisted in finding the amount by which each of the 404 parishes grew during a given period and comparing the range of resulting growth ratios with similar figures for a representative set of parishes. Ideally the parish population figures should be spaced well apart in time. For the end of the period we took the census of 1811 to lessen the complications in identifying the areas covered by individual registers consequent upon rapid urbanization. Finding parish population figures for an earlier date is more problematical; very few sources provide anything like a national coverage and all pose severe difficulties of interpretation.[1] We decided

1. For a general survey of the sources see Thirsk, 'Sources of information on population'

to ignore all surveys of a fiscal nature, not only because they were notoriously prone to evasion, but also because it is impossible to specify at all accurately the proportion of the population that was legally exempt. The other major source for estimating parish population figures consists of ecclesiastical surveys, usually of households or parishioners of communicable age, but few have survived that provide information for the whole country, and none from the sixteenth century. We decided therefore to base our earlier population estimates on the comparatively late 'Compton Census' of 1676. This had the advantages of being available for a substantial proportion of parishes, of being currently the subject of a critical edition, and of being close in date to a national population estimate based on workings by Gregory King.

In principle the Compton Census gives for each parish in the province of Canterbury the number of persons, whether communicant, nonconforming, or recusant, over the age of 16 years. Dr Whiteman has shown that the incumbents sometimes misunderstood their instructions and returned either the number of adult males, or the number of householders, or the total number of parishioners, including children. Often whole areas are plagued by suspect returns, which suggests that the local version of the general instructions issued to incumbents departed radically from the standard form. Sometimes it is apparent that the return relates only to a part of the parish.[2]

We have tried to detect and eliminate those parish population figures that were obviously wrong in two ways. First, wherever possible we took advantage of comparative information, for example from the Protestation returns of 1642 and from the 1603 communicants returns.[3] Second, for the 404 aggregative parishes, we also checked the Compton Census population figures, where these were available, against estimates derived from the numbers of baptisms, burials, and marriages recorded in the parish registers. For each series we chose a very high and a very low vital rate based on what is known from family reconstitution studies so as to yield the widest plausible range of population sizes that could have produced that number of registered events. The range of rates for baptisms, burials, and marriages was 20–35, 20–40, and 5–10 per thousand respectively. Selecting the highest and lowest totals produced in this fashion gives a range of population sizes in which the largest is necessarily at least twice the smallest and is often three or more times greater. The Compton Census figure was therefore given considerable latitude before it was judged to be inconsistent with the evidence of the parish registers.

Because of these restrictions plausible Compton Census figures could be found for only just over one half (56 per cent) of the aggregative parishes. Taking advantage of a random sample of 289 parishes drawn for another purpose, we found acceptable Compton Census population figures for a similar proportion of the parishes (53 per cent).[4] For each parish we calculated the ratio between the total population figure in 1811 census and the number of over-16s enumerated in the Compton Census of 1676. Naturally there was considerable variation from parish to parish, so to bring out the underlying pattern more clearly the parishes in each set were grouped into four

2. We acknowledge gratefully the information and assistance that Dr Whiteman of Lady Margaret Hall, Oxford, has generously given us prior to the publication of her study of the Compton Census.

3. Information made available to us through the kindness of Dr Whiteman.

4. The random sample of parishes was drawn for a survey of illiteracy, reported in Schofield, 'Dimensions of illiteracy'. The original sample contained 291 parishes, two of which came from London and so are excluded from the present comparision with the aggregative set of parishes. In the literacy study 17 parishes were found to be incapable of registering marriages under Hardwicke's Act (1753), so the literacy results were based on 274 parishes.

categories according to their total population size in 1811. The results are shown in table 2.1 below.

For each population size-group the ratios between the 1811 and 1676 figures in the two sets of parishes are remarkably close. The only exception is the category of 1,500 inhabitants and above for which the random sample ratio is rather higher than the equivalent figure for the aggregative set. In fact the random sample contains two very large parishes with exceptionally high ratios (Sedgeley, Staffs. 11.61; and Rotherham, Yorks.W.R. 11.16). If the final category is limited to parishes with populations in the range 1,500–4,999 the ratios for the aggregative set and random sample come closer together at 2.94 and 3.18 respectively. Indeed the overall agreement between the ratios for the two sets of parishes is so close that it seems reasonable to conclude that within each size-group the aggregative parishes are behaving as if they were a random sample so that, at least so far as population growth between the late seventeenth and early nineteenth centuries is concerned, they can be considered a representative guide to the national experience.

However, it is also clear from table 2.1 that the size of the growth ratios increases with the size of the population of the parishes, which is not surprising in view of the fact that the parishes were assigned to size-groups according to their population at the end of the period in 1811. It is therefore very important to ensure that a set of parishes on which national estimates are to be based should have a representative distribution of population sizes. A glance at columns 2 and 7 of table 2.1 shows that the aggregative set contains proportionately more large parishes and fewer small parishes than the random sample. Thus a simple overall ratio summed over the aggregative parishes would be a misleading guide to national patterns, since it would exaggerate the rate of growth in the number of events. This discrepancy in the size distribution of the aggregative set is not confined to the 226 parishes for which Compton Census figures can be found, and several important consequences follow. We shall return to this point later.

Meanwhile it is instructive to consider how far these ratios between the 1811 and 1676 parish population figures are consistent with estimates of the national rate of population growth over the same period. To ensure the correct mix of parishes of different sizes we shall use the figures for the random sample. First, the total of the over-16s enumerated in the Compton Census must be converted into figures for the whole population. To do this stable population theory was used. A population subject to constant demographic rates ultimately acquires a fixed age-structure, and sets of model populations with different combinations of vital rates and hence with different age-structures have been conveniently tabulated and published. Family reconstitution studies and other sources suggest that fertility was relatively low and mortality rather high in the mid seventeenth century.[5] We therefore chose a model population with an expectation of life at birth of 35 years and a gross reproduction rate of about 2.0. Under these conditions about 30 per cent of the population is under 16 years of age.[6] This is admittedly a rough and ready procedure, and our assumptions about both the

5. Fertility and mortality estimates based on family reconstitutions will be discussed in a forthcoming volume. Some results have already been reported in Wrigley, 'Family limitation', and Schofield and Wrigley, 'Infant and child mortality'.

6. Coale and Demeny, *Regional model life tables*, p. 256. The age-structure selected is that of a population with the 'North' pattern of female mortality. With e_0 at 35 years and the GRR at 1.991 (mean age of maternity at 33) the population is stationary. The percentage under age 15 is 28.94 to which has been added one fifth of the proportion aged 15–19 (1.69), to yield 30.63 per cent under age 16.

Table 2.1: Enumerated population growth ratios 1811:1676

| Population size group in 1811 | Aggregative set | | | | | | Random sample | | | | |
| | Parishes | | Population 1811 (3) | Over-16s 1676 (4) | Ratio 1811/1676 (5) ((3)/(4)) | Parishes | | Population 1811 (8) | Over-16s 1676 (9) | Ratio 1811/1676 (10) ((8)/(9)) |
	No. (1)	Percentage (2)				No. (6)	Percentage (7)			
0–399	36	16	10 044	4 483	2.24	100	65	19 926	9 046	2.20
400–749	41	18	22 079	8 348	2.64	21	14	11 330	4 194	2.70
750–1499	74	33	77 606	27 674	2.80	21	14	21 629	7 796	2.77
1500+	75	33	224 002	64 931	3.45	12	8	45 803	9 322	4.91
Total	226	100				154	101			

Sources: 1676 Compton Census, figures supplied by Dr A. Whiteman, Lady Margaret Hall, Oxford
1811 Census, Enumeration.

level and stability of fertility and mortality may be contested. But for our present purpose a crude calculation is sufficient.

If the Compton Census only covered the 70 per cent of the population over age 16 the ratios between the 1811 and 1676 population figures given in table 1 need to be reduced by 70/100, as is shown below in table 2.2. Overall the random-sample parish populations grew by a factor of 2.28 between 1676 and 1811.

Table 2.2: Total population growth ratios, random sample, 1811:1676

Population size group in 1811	Ratio
0–399	1.54
400–749	1.89
750–1499	1.94
1500+	3.44
All	2.28

Source: Table 2.1

Unfortunately the Compton Census has too many missing or defective returns to yield a national population estimate for 1676, but a reduction of Gregory King's estimate for 1695 as revised by Glass so as to apply to England alone, omitting Wales, suggests a population figure of about 4.632 million. If we compare this to the 9.477 million recorded in the 1811 census we obtain a growth ratio of 2.05, slightly lower than the overall random sample ratio of 2.28.[7] Considering the risks of random variation attending the small size of the sample and the approximate nature of the estimates both of the parish population totals in 1676 and of the national population in 1695, the similarity in the two estimates of the national population growth ratio between 1695 and 1811 is satisfactory. The outcome increases confidence both in the usefulness of the Compton Census figures for testing purposes and in the representativeness of the random sample. Since within each population size-group the growth ratios of the aggregative set of parishes were in close agreement with those of the random sample, if those size-groups can be combined so as to reflect the national distribution of parish sizes, the aggregative parishes should be able to provide a representative basis on which to estimate national population trends.

Some indirect checks

Population growth over a period of a century and a quarter is a very summary measure of demographic experience: the same overall growth ratio can be the product of quite different combinations of fertility and mortality, or of varying phases of growth and

7. For the reworking of the 1695 estimates to refer to England rather than England and Wales see below pp. 571–2. For the population figure for the 1811 census see table A6.7. If King's original 1695 estimate is reduced so as to apply to England alone, the resulting figure (5.183 million) implies a growth ratio of 1.82 between 1695 and 1811, rather further from the 2.28 estimated on the basis of the random sample.

decline. It is therefore prudent to investigate the representativeness of the aggregative parishes more fully by testing how typical they were with regard to a number of geographical, social, and economic characteristics thought to be related to the different components of population change.

For example fertility, mortality, and nuptiality have been shown to vary according to region, farming type (arable, wood pasture), modes of production (agriculture, domestic industry, retail, and services), social organization (estate villages, open villages), and size and density of settlement.[8] Any set of parishes on which national figures are to be based should therefore be reasonably representative of the national distribution of each of these associated parish characteristics. The registers of a set of small, nuclear, landlord-dominated, midland villages, engaged exclusively in arable farming, would be unlikely to provide a reliable guide to national population trends.

To investigate fully the social, economic, and physiographic background of every parish would be a major research enterprise in its own right. Since our concern was only to discover whether the set of 404 parishes appeared to be biased in any significant respect, we were satisfied with summary indications which could be obtained for all parishes from standard sources. The range of information collected is displayed below in table 2.3. It will be clear that much of the social and economic data refers to specific dates, often in the early nineteenth century when standard information on many topics first becomes available on a nationwide basis.

Information was also collected on a number of other topics, including the important question of the strength of nonconformity in the early nineteenth century. The most comprehensive source on a parish basis appeared to be the standard returns on the adequacy of registration and the number of dissenters, which incumbents made to the government in 1831.[9] Unfortunately this promising material turned out to be seriously defective, for in the larger towns, where nonconformity is known to have been rife, incumbents often made no attempt to estimate the numbers involved and filed a blank return.

For many of the parish characteristics for which full information could be found, there were no summary tabulations available describing their national distribution with which the set of 404 parishes could be compared. The labour of compiling such tables for all 10,000 parishes in the country would have been immense, so the national distributions were estimated from information collected for the simple random sample of 289 parishes referred to above. These estimates are subject to sampling error, so minor discrepancies between them and the results for the aggregative parishes do not necessarily indicate that the latter are biased.

If we first consider the geographical location of the 404 aggregative parishes, whose names are listed in appendix 1, we find from figure 2.1 that they are reasonably well spread over the whole country, defined as England excluding Monmouth and London. The reason for the omission of London has already been explained. The special steps taken to correct for this when deriving national estimates will be described later. Despite the generally good spread of parishes, certain concentrations and lacunae leap to the eye. The aggregative set is clearly deficient in parishes for the whole of the south-west from the Thames Valley to Cornwall, despite some well

8. See, for example, Deane and Cole, *British economic growth*, ch. 3 for regions; Thirsk, 'Industries in the countryside' for farming type; Levine, *Family formation* for modes of production; Holderness ' "Open" and "close" parishes' for social organization; and Deprez 'Demographic development of Flanders', for size and density of population.
9. P.R.O. H.O.71/1–130.

Table 2.3: Parish Characteristics

	Heading	Content	Date applicable
Physiographic			
	Location	National grid co-ordinates	—
	Altitude	Feet above sea level	—
	Area	Hectares	—
	Soil-type	e.g. 'Calcareous', 'Lowland gley'	—
Economic			
	Farming-type	e.g. Arable, dairy, stockrearing	*c. 1600*
	Exchange	Market town status	*c. 1640, 1700*
	Employment	Per cent of adult males in manufacturing etc.	*1831*
	Landownership	Per cent of land owned by richest 1–3 landlords	*c. 1798*
Social			
	Elite presence	Number of resident gentry	*1700*
Demographic			
	Population size	Number of inhabitants	*1811*
	Dispersion	e.g. 'Nuclear village'. 'Scattered farms'.	*1817–35*

Sources: Location and Altitude: Ordnance Survey 1 inch to 1 mile (1946–7 edition)

Area:	*1851 Census,* Numbers of inhabitants.
Soil-type:	Bickmore and Shaw, *Atlas of Britain,* p. 40.
Farming type:	Thirsk, 'Farming Regions'. p. 4.
Exchange:	1640: Everitt, 'Marketing', pp. 468–75.
	1700: Adams, *Index villaris.*
Employment:	*1831 Census,* Enumeration abstract.
Landownership:	1798 Land Tax Returns, or nearest available assessment, in county record offices.
Elite presence:	Adams, *Index villaris.*
Population size:	1811 figures as revised in *1851 Census,* Numbers of inhabitants.
Dispersion:	Data taken from county maps published by Bryant (Bucks., Herefs., Norfolk, Oxon: 1824–35); Dury and Andrews (Herts.: 1782); Baker (Cambs.: 1830); and Greenwood (all other counties: 1818–31)

represented areas such as south Devon. Another conspicuously under-represented area runs from Northamptonshire up round the Wash, through Lincolnshire to East Yorkshire. On the other hand there is a notable concentration of rural parishes in Bedfordshire, and clusters of small urban parishes in Ipswich and Norwich. Other areas over-represented, though to a less dramatic extent, are the Weald and parts of the West Riding and Leicestershire.

However, the map is in some ways misleading as to the representativeness of the spread of the aggregative parishes, because in some parts of the country there are genuinely very few parishes, usually because the settlement is rather sparse. We have therefore calculated the proportion of the total number of parishes in each county included in the aggregative set.[10] The results are shown in table 2.4 and figure 2.2 and

10. The county totals of parishes refer to those that were registering baptisms, burials, and marriages by 1801, as described in appendix 7, fn. 2. This is a less rigorous condition than was applied to the selection of

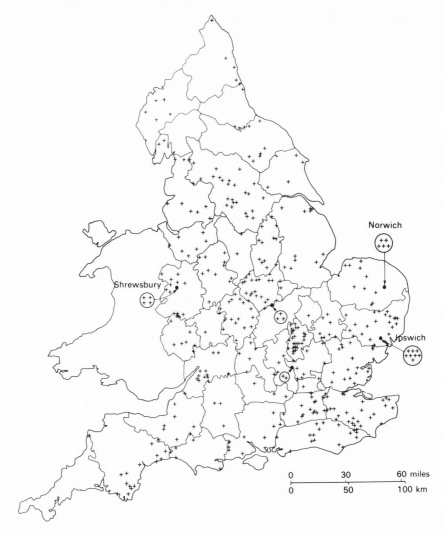

Figure 2.1: Geographical distribution of the set of aggregative parishes

reflect the geographical distribution of a number of factors: the excellence of registration, the survival of the documents, the accessibility of the registers today, and the place of residence of those who made the tabulations of the events recorded in the registers.

As is clear from table 2.4 the 404 parishes comprise 4.0 per cent of a national total of 10,141 parishes, as defined above. A glance down the final column of the table confirms and amplifies the geographical distortions we have noticed already. There are no parishes from Cornwall and Westmorland. Areas with less than half the

the aggregative set when a parish was included only if all three series were being registered without serious gaps by 1661.

Table 2.4: Aggregative parishes by county

County	Total no. of parishes (1)	Aggregative parishes (2)	Aggregative percentage (3) (2)/(1) × 100
Beds.	124	28	22.6
Berks.	158	3	1.9
Bucks.	205	3	1.5
Cambs.	172	8	4.7
Chesh.	122	7	5.7
Cornw.	201	–	–
Cumb.	135	5	3.7
Derbs.	181	2	1.1
Devon	468	15	3.2
Dors.	258	3	1.2
Durham	99	3	3.0
Essex	403	17	4.2
Glos.	332	14	4.2
Hants	307	10	3.3
Herefs.	222	6	2.7
Herts.	131	9	6.9
Hunts.	97	1	1.0
Kent	395	29	7.3
Lancs.	190	10	5.3
Leics.	251	26	10.4
Lincs.	607	13	2.1

County	Total no. of parishes (1)	Aggregative parishes (2)	Aggregative percentage (3) (2)/(1) × 100
Mddx.	190	2	1.1
Norf.	687	15	2.2
N'hants.	292	1	0.3
N'humb.	92	5	5.4
Notts.	214	9	4.2
Oxon	223	5	2.2
Rutl.	50	1	2.0
Salop	230	17	7.4
Soms.	476	10	2.1
Staffs.	177	11	6.2
Suff.	500	29	5.8
Surrey	143	13	9.1
Sussex	297	15	5.1
Warwicks.	208	16	7.7
Westm.	61	–	–
Wilts.	309	3	1.0
Worcs.	197	2	1.0
Yorks. E.R.	234	4	1.7
Yorks. N.R.	225	8	3.6
Yorks. W.R.	278	26	9.4
	10 141	404	4.0

Sources: Totals of parishes: table A7.10, col. 2.
Aggregative parishes: appendix 1.

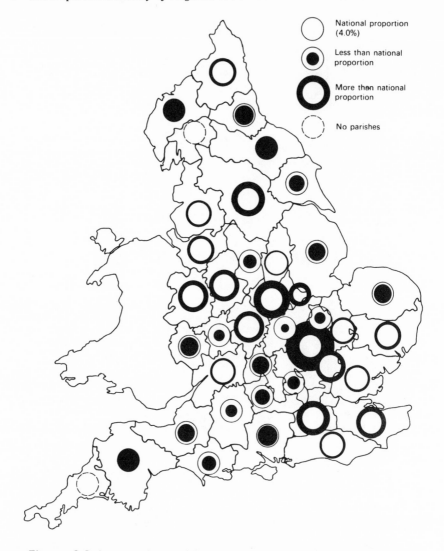

Figure 2.2 Aggregative parishes as a proportion of all parishes,
by county. Area of circle proportionate to
percentage of parishes in aggregative set.

national proportion (under 2 per cent) are to be found in the near south-west
(Wiltshire, Somerset, and Dorset), an arc of counties running from Middlesex
through Berkshire, Buckinghamshire, and Northamptonshire to Huntingdonshire,
and two isolated counties, Derbyshire and Worcestershire. Counties with more than
double the national proportion (above 8 per cent) are more scattered, and each of
them, namely Yorkshire, Leicestershire, Bedfordshire, and Surrey, is adjacent to one
or more of the under-represented counties. Figure 2.2 brings out a more general
pattern: the part of the country with less than average representation in the aggregative
set can be seen like a giant boomerang, starting in the south-west, running across the

Thames valley through Berkshire, Oxfordshire, and Buckinghamshire, then passing narrowly through Northamptonshire to the Wash, before curving north up the east coast to Durham, with a spur off into Norfolk. The over-represented part of the country comprises everything north of the central midlands, apart from the east coast counties and Derbyshire, and most of the south-east.

This general geographical pattern of over- and under-represented counties, although clearly visible, should not be over-emphasized, for many of the county deviations from the overall national proportion of 4.0 per cent are not very marked. Furthermore even major discrepancies often balance up over quite small distances, as when over-represented counties adjoin under-represented ones. Bedfordshire, for example, which is massively over-represented, with 23 per cent of its parishes in the aggregative set, is surrounded to the north and to the west by three heavily under-represented counties (Huntingdonshire, Northamptonshire, and Buckinghamshire). Table 2.5 shows how far these short-range differences even out when the 41 counties are combined into 8 regions. For example, the entry in the table for the south-east midlands shows that the surplus of parishes in Bedfordshire is almost exactly offset by the relative lack of parishes in neighbouring counties.

At a regional level the spread of the aggregative parishes is reasonably even across the country. There is one major exception, and that is the under-representation of the south-west, with only 1.8 per cent, instead of national figure of 4.0 per cent, of parishes in the aggregative set. The 'Pennine' group of counties also seems somewhat over-represented, but if it and the 'North' group are taken together as representing the whole of the 'north' of England, the percentage of parishes in the aggregative set comes to 4.7 per cent, not so far from the national figure.

We can explore the geographical representativeness of the aggregative parishes further by comparing their distributions for other parish characteristics linked to geographical location with those of the random sample of parishes. For example, table 2.6 compares the percentage distributions of the two sets of parishes according to their height above sea-level. In general while the aggregative parishes are reasonably well spread over the range, there are too few parishes at less than 100 feet above sea-level compared with the random sample.

With soil type, too, the overall distribution of the aggregative parishes is similar to that of the random sample. There are a few too many parishes on brown forest soils, especially where drainage is poor, but this is offset by there being too few on lowland gleys where the drainage is even worse (table 2.7).[11]

Location also greatly influences the kind of farming practised. When the parishes are classified into the 'farming regions' suggested by Thirsk for the period 1540–1640, the aggregative set is found to agree well with the random sample not only in the way the parishes divide into the three main types of agricultural activity (mixed arable and pasture, wood pasture, and open pasture), but also in the percentages of parishes engaged in more specific activities such as dairying, pig-keeping, and cereal culture (table 2.8).

Although not so closely tied to location, as is the case with farming type, another economic characteristic of the aggregative parishes showed an even closer fit with national patterns. Table 2.9 gives the proportions of adult males returned in the 1831 census as working in various occupational categories (agriculture, manufacture, retail and handicrafts, etc.) both in the aggregative parishes and nationally. In most

11. For the influence of drainage on mortality see ch. 6, fn. 12.

Table 2.5: Aggregative parishes as a percentage of all parishes by region

Region	Total no. of parishes (1)	Aggregative parishes (2)	Aggregative percentage (3) (2)/(1) ×100	Constituent Counties
North	612	21	3.4	N'humb., Durham, Cumb., Westm., Yorks. N. R.
Pennine	824	47	5.7	Lancs., Chesh., Yorks. W. R., Yorks. E. R.
N. E. Midland	1 303	51	3.9	Derbs., Notts., Lincs., Leics., Rutl.
W. Midland	1 366	66	4.8	Salop, Staffs., Warwicks., Worcs., Herefs., Glos.
S. E. Midland	1 262	49	3.9	N'hants., Hunts., Beds., Herts., Mddx., Bucks., Oxon
East Anglia	1 762	69	3.9	Norf., Suff., Cambs., Essex
South-east	1 300	70	5.4	Kent, Sussex, Surrey, Hants, Berks.
South-west	1 712	31	1.8	Cornwall, Devon, Dorset, Somerset, Wilts.
All	10 141	404	4.0	

Source: Table 2.4.

occupational groups the aggregative parishes reflect the national percentages exactly. They have slightly too many employed in manufacturing and as non-agricultural labourers, and slightly too few as labourers in agriculture, but these differences are only two or three percentage points.

Table 2.6: Altitude: percentage distributions of aggregative and random sample parishes

Feet above sea-level	Percentages	
	Aggregative Set	Random Sample
0–99	23	33
100–99	27	23
200–99	21	17
300–99	16	12
400+	13	15
No. of parishes	404	289

Source: See table 2.3.

Table 2.7: Soil-type: percentage distributions of aggregative and random sample parishes

Soil type	Percentages	
	Aggregative set	Random sample
Calcareous	13	16
Brown forest	29	24
Brown forest with gleying[1]	18	11
Podzolic[2]	15	15
Lowland gleys	21	26
Miscellaneous[3]	5	7
No. of parishes	404	289

Notes: [1] Including acid brown soils
[2] Grey-brown podzolic soils and podzolized soils of the lowlands
[3] Warp soils, warp gley soils, regosols, podzolised and gley soils of the uplands, lithosols and shallow podsols, hill and basin peat

Source: See table 2.3.

A bias discovered and corrected

So far the aggregative set has appeared to be a reasonable cross-section of the country on a number of counts. But the bias towards parishes with larger population sizes in 1811, which has already been mentioned in connexion with the calculation of population growth rates based on the Compton Census, proved on closer inspection to be a serious one. As a result not only were the aggregative parishes too large in area, but the set was also found to contain too many parishes that were market towns, too many with satellite hamlets, too many with resident gentry, and too few in which the ownership of land was concentrated in the hands of two or three people.

Table 2.8: Farming regions: percentage distributions of aggregative and random sample parishes

Type	Percentages Aggregative set	Random sample	Constituent elements
Mixed arable and pasture	53	57	1, 2, 3
Wood pasture	25	21	4, 5, 6, 7
Open pasture	22	21	8, 9, 10, 11, 12
of which cereal growing	56	60	1, 2, 3, 5
pig keeping	22	19	4, 6, 7
dairying	12	12	4, 12
No. of parishes	387	289	

Notes:
1 Key to constituent elements
   1   Sheep and corn on downland, wolds, and breckland
   2   Corn and stock variously combined in clay vales
   3   Corn and stock-fattening in marshland
   4   Dairying and pig-keeping, sometimes with horse-breeding
   5   Stock-keeping with corn-growing, sometimes with dairying
   6   Stock-fattening and pig-keeping
   7   Stock-rearing and pig-keeping, sometimes with horse-breeding
   8   Cattle and sheep-rearing on fells and moorland
   9   Rearing and fattening
  10   Fattening of sheep with some cattle
  11   Stock-fattening with horse-breeding, dairying, fishing, fowling in fenland
  12   Dairying
2 Wholly urban parishes were excluded.

Source: Thirsk, 'Farming regions', p. 4.

The bias towards larger parishes was not unexpected, in that it arose from the way in which the data were collected, but the potential consequences proved to be more serious than had been anticipated. Before describing the nature of the bias and the steps taken to eliminate it, it will be useful to show how far the aggregative parishes diverged from the random sample in their distribution over a number of parish characteristics strongly associated with population size.

First of all, the aggregative parishes were generally too large in area as well as in population size. Table 2.10 shows how great the discrepancy was at each extreme of the size range: while 26 per cent of the random sample parishes were under 500 hectares only 6 per cent of the aggregative parishes were as small as this. On the other hand 41 per cent of the aggregative parishes were above 2,000 hectares in area, while only 14 per cent of the random sample parishes reached this size.

The aggregative parishes were also more dispersed in their settlement patterns: single settlement parishes comprised 12 per cent of the aggregative set compared to 27 per cent of the random sample. They also had more resident gentry: only 13 per cent lacked a gentleman's seat in 1700, as against 20 per cent of the random sample. On average an aggregative parish contained 2.3 gentlemen's seats and a random sample

Table 2.9: Occupational categories of males over age 20 (1831 census): percentage distributions of aggregative parishes and national total

Occupational category[1]	Percentages Aggregative parishes	England[2]
Farmers	8	8
Agricultural labourers	23	26
Manufacturing	13	11
Non-agricultural labourers	16	14
Retail trade and handicrafts	28	28
Professions	4	4
Servants	2	2
Others	6	6
No. of parishes	404	

[1] The categories correspond to the following descriptions in the census.
Farmers: occupiers employing labourers, and occupiers not employing labourers.
Agricultural labourers: labourers employed in agriculture.
Manufacturing: employed in manufacture or in making manufacturing machinery.
Non-agricultural labourers: labourers employed in labour not agricultural.
Retail trade and handicrafts: employed in retail trade or in handicrafts as masters or workmen.
Professions: capitalists, bankers, professional and other educated men.
Servants: male servants 20 years of age.
Others: other males 20 years of age (except servants).

[2] Less Monmouth and London.

Source: 1831 Census, Enumeration abstract.

Table 2.10: Parish areas: percentage distributions of aggregative and random sample parishes

Hectares	Percentages Aggregative set	Random sample
0–499	6	26
500–999	16	36
1000–1999	36	23
2000+	41	14
No. of parishes	396	286
No information	8	3
	404	289

Source: 1851 Census, Numbers of inhabitants.

parish 1.2 seats.[12] Despite this greater presence of the social élite the aggregative parishes were considerably less dominated by small groups of landowners than were the random sample parishes, probably because the typical 'close' parish was also a small one. On the evidence of the 1798 land-tax returns, in only 16 per cent of the

12. Information was lacking for 28 aggregative parishes and 26 parishes in the random sample.

aggregative parishes was over half of the assessed value of the parish possessed by three landowners or fewer, while in the random sample the proportion of parishes dominated in this way was as high as 40 per cent.[13] A particularly marked consequence of the larger size of the aggregative parishes was that they contained far too many settlements with markets. According to two different sources, a modern list of markets for the period 1540–1640 and a classification of communities published in 1700, markets were held in 30 per cent of the aggregative parishes but in only 8 or 9 per cent of the parishes in the random sample.[14] This bias towards the larger 'market town' in the aggregative set is an unfortunate one from a demographic point of view. These communities were more densely settled than the smaller rural villages and seem to have experienced significantly higher mortality. Yet they continued to grow in size as an increasing proportion of economic activity involved commercial and specialist services. This combination of high mortality and strong immigration made them very unlike the country at large.[15]

The population size bias in the aggregative set therefore not only distorts the representativeness of the aggregative parishes for a number of related parish characteristics, but does so in a way likely to lead to biased demographic results. Indeed we have already seen how the population growth ratios calculated for the period between 1676 and 1811 increased with the size of the parish. The same pattern is visible amongst the aggregative parishes themselves. If a growth ratio is calculated for each parish by dividing the number of baptisms registered in the decade 1800–9 by the number registered in 1670–9, the median parish growth ratio amongst the 404 parishes works out at 1.74. In contrast, the median growth ratio of the 5 aggregative parishes with a population of over 10,000 in 1811 was 4.87 and their lowest growth ratio was 3.42. Again, amongst the 21 aggregative parishes with a population of over 5,000 in 1811 the median growth ratio was 3.21, almost double the median for the whole aggregative set of 1.74.

Thus there was a strong possibility that the presence of too many large parishes in the aggregative set would yield overall totals of baptisms, marriages, and burials that grew too much during the eighteenth century. Consequently it was important that any national series of events should be based on data furnished by a set of parishes with the correct distribution of population sizes. Lacking any summary national tabulation of the population sizes of fully registering ecclesiastical parishes in 1811, we have taken the random sample as an estimate of the national distribution.[16] However, the random sample has relatively few large parishes in it, and there is a danger that the random variation associated with small numbers may make it an imprecise guide to the national distribution just at the point where precision is most needed.

Accordingly we decided to check the representativeness of the random sample in

13. Information was lacking for 52 aggregative parishes and 26 parishes in the random sample. Where possible a land tax assessment for 1798 was used, and failing a return for that date the nearest available assessment was taken. In the event, 79 per cent of the assessments came from 1798, and 91 per cent from the 4 years 1797–1800. The earliest assessment used dated from 1790 and the latest from 1824.

14. Everitt, 'Marketing', pp. 468–75; Adams, *Index villaris*.

15. The numbers of events recorded in 'market towns' continued to grow despite continuing deficits of deaths over births, implying immigration. For the higher mortality of market towns see pp. 165–6 below and ch. 6. fn. 12.

16. In most cases the smallest area for which population totals are printed in the census is the ecclesiastical parish, but sometimes the figures refer to tithings, chapelries, townships, hamlets, precincts, and extra-parochial places. Some care needs to be taken to match the area covered by a parish register with the areas enumerated in the census, especially in the north. *1811 census*, Enumeration.

this sensitive area by a full enumeration of parishes with a population of 5,000 and above in 1811. The cut-off point was taken as 5,000 because below this figure the association between parish growth ratios and population sizes was very much less marked, both in the aggregative set, and in the random sample parishes for which information was available from the Compton Census. Nationally, we found that of the 9,884 fully registering parishes, 244 or 2.5 per cent had a population of 5,000 or above in 1811, compared with 2.8 per cent (8 out of 286) of the random sample parishes.[17] This is a fairly close agreement and the random sample was therefore accepted as a reasonable guide to the national distribution of parish population sizes in 1811.

The extent of the size bias in the aggregative parishes may be seen in table 2.11, which compares the distribution of the 1811 population sizes of the aggregative

Table 2.11: Population size in 1811: percentage distribution of aggregative and random sample parishes

| No. of inhabitants | Percentages | |
	Aggregative set	Random sample
0–399	13	58
400–749	14	16
750–1499	34	16
1500–2499	19	3
2500–4999	15	5
5000+	6	3
Mean size	1916	871
No. of parishes	404	286

Note: In three cases in the random sample set the population size of the parish
could not be determined.

Source: Revised figures for 1811 in *1851 census*, Numbers of inhabitants, with
boundary adjustments as necessary from *1811 Census*, Enumeration.

parishes with those of the random sample parishes. The size range has been divided into six categories to obtain a reasonable number of parishes in each category, while avoiding gross groupings of the larger parishes, where differences in growth ratios are most pronounced.

The aggregative set is clearly deficient in small parishes: only 13 per cent of the parishes have fewer than 400 inhabitants as against 58 per cent of the random sample parishes. At the other end of the range, in each of the larger population size groups the aggregative set has proportionately considerably more parishes than the random sample. A bias of this kind, if uncorrected, is likely to lead to faulty demographic conclusions; at the very least to a mis-estimation of the magnitude and timing of population growth after 1700. It therefore seemed essential to eliminate the bias by bringing the aggregative set of parishes back into line with the national distribution of parish population sizes as estimated by the random sample.

A simple method of achieving this result is to calculate for each parish size-group in table 2.11 the ratio between the proportions of parishes in that size-group in the

17. The set of fully registering parishes was calculated from the details of the status of, and dates covered by, individual register volumes in *1831 census*, Parish register abstract. See fn. 10 and table 2.4 above.

aggregative and random sets of parishes. These ratios are then used as factors, or weights, by which to multiply the numbers of baptisms, burials, and marriages contributed by parishes in each size-group. In this way the numbers of events contributed by the under-represented smaller parishes will be inflated, and those contributed by the over-represented larger parishes will be deflated, so that when aggregated they combine in the appropriate proportions, as if the aggregative set had possessed the same distribution of parish population sizes as the random sample.[18] For example, if a particular population size-group comprises 20 per cent of the aggregative parishes but only 10 per cent of the random sample, the parishes of this size are over-represented in the aggregative set by twice their true frequency, and thus the number of events they contribute towards the overall total needs to be halved.

The numbers of parishes in each of the six size-groups in the aggregative and random sets of parishes are given in table 2.12, together with the weighting factors necessary to bring the aggregative size distribution into line with that of the random sample. Thus, at the extremes, the relatively few small parishes in the aggregative set, with populations under 400 in 1811, have their baptism, burial, and marriage frequencies multiplied by 4.509, while the most over-represented group of parishes with 1,500 to 2,499 inhabitants have the number of events recorded in their registers

Table 2.12: Weighting factors to correct population size bias in the aggregative set

Population in 1811	Aggregative set Parishes	Random sample Parishes	Weighting factor (to 3 decimal places)
0–399	52	166	4.509
400–749	58	45	1.096
750–1499	137	45	0.464
1500–2499	75	9	0.170
2500–4999	59	13	0.311
5000+	23	8	0.491
No. of parishes	404	286	

Source: As for table 2.11.

reduced to almost one sixth (0.17) of the original frequencies. It is noteworthy that the largest size-group, that of 5,000 inhabitants and above, is less heavily over-represented in the aggregative set than the size-group immediately beneath it. Consequently the baptism, burial, and marriage frequencies recorded by these fast-growing parishes are only reduced to about one half (0.491) of their original numbers.

Strictly speaking, the weighting procedure we have just described only brings the size distribution of the aggregative parishes into balance with the national distribution as it was in 1811. However, the percentage size distributions of the aggregative and

18. More formally the corrected overall frequency (F*) contributed by the six population size-groups is calculated as $F^* = \sum_{s=1}^{6} f_{[s]}(p_{[ran,s]}/p_{[agg,s]})$, where in each size-group $[s]$, f is the original total frequency of events, $p_{[ran,]}$ is the proportion of parishes in that size-group in the random sample, and $p_{[agg,]}$ the corresponding proportion in the aggregative set.

random sample parishes shown in table 2.1 probably give an accurate indication of the extent of the size bias in 1676, for it is unlikely that the availability of reliable Compton Census totals of communicants was itself differentially biased as between the two sets of parishes. Since the weighting factors implied by the discrepancy between the size distributions in 1676 are close to those calculated for 1811 (table 2.12), it seems probable that the population size bias in the aggregative set was a stable and enduring one, and that corrective action based on the fuller information available for 1811 is both necessary and appropriate for earlier periods too.

We shall describe later the effect that this correction by weighting factors has on the total number of baptisms, burials, and marriages recorded by the 404 aggregative parishes. Meanwhile, it is instructive to consider how far the inflation of small parishes and deflation of large parishes inherent in the weighting scheme improves, or worsens, the representativeness of the aggregative set so far as the other parish characteristics we have been considering are concerned.

As before, we shall compare the frequency distribution of the aggregative parishes for each characteristic with that of the random sample parishes. In an unweighted frequency distribution each parish counts for one, while in a weighted distribution each parish scores its weight (for example 4.509 or 0.311). By definition, the sum of the weights is equal to the number of parishes (404 in the case of the aggregative set), so the effect of weighting is simply to change the individual contributions of large and small parishes from one of equality to a scheme whereby each of the few small parishes counts for much more than each of the more numerous larger parishes. As might be expected, correction for population size generally brings the distributions of those discrepant parish characteristics associated with population size back into line with those of the random sample. The most dramatic improvement occurs in the reduction of the percentage of parishes that are market towns. Applying the appropriate weighting factors (table 2.12) reduces the percentage of aggregative parishes that are market towns from an unweighted figure of 30 per cent to 10 per cent in 1700, a figure very close to the random sample figure of 9 per cent at that date. Weighting also brings the percentage of aggregative parishes with no resident gentleman up to 25, considerably nearer to the 29 per cent of the random sample parishes than the original, unweighted figure of 13 per cent. In addition the average number of gentlemen's seats per parish is reduced from 2.3 to 1.3, much closer to the random sample figure of 1.2. The distribution of settlement patterns in the aggregative set is also greatly improved by applying the population size weights, as is clear from table 2.13.

Table 2.13: Settlement patterns after weighting by population size

Settlement type	Aggregative Original	Aggregative Weighted	Random Sample
	Percentages		
Single settlement	12	20	27
Main village + hamlets only	64	49	39
Main village + hamlets + farms	24	30	30
Farms only	0	1	4
No. of parishes	404	404	289

Source: Early-nineteenth-century county maps, see table 2.3, above.

Correcting for population size has a less pronounced effect on the prevalence of landlord-dominated parishes in the aggregative set, increasing the proportion of parishes in which three or fewer landlords owned over half the land from 16 per cent to 28 per cent. Although this is a step in the right direction it still leaves the aggregative set well short of the 41 per cent of parishes dominated by landlords in the random sample.

Finally, correcting for population size produces rather uneven results so far as improving the distribution of the areas of the aggregative parishes is concerned. As can be seen in table 2.14 the discrepancy between the aggregative and random samples is just as bad as before in the smallest and next-to-largest area size-groups, but weighting markedly improves the correspondence in the other size-groups, leading to a better agreement overall.

Table 2.14: Parish areas after weighting by population size

| Hectares | Percentages | | Random Sample |
| | Aggregative | | |
	Original	Weighted	
0–499	6	6	25
500–999	17	41	37
1000–1999	36	37	24
2000+	41	16	15
No. of parishes	396	396	289

Source: See table 2.10.

Thus, weighting by population size reduces, and sometimes virtually eliminates, the most serious divergences between the aggregative parishes and the random sample. We must now discover whether these substantial improvements have been purchased at the price of destroying the reasonably representative distributions that the unweighted aggregative parishes achieved for a number of other parish characteristics.

Table 2.15 shows the effect of correcting for population size on the geographical location of the aggregative parishes. On the county level, it generally exacerbates the unevenness already present in the unweighted figures (table 2.4). However, as before, combining the counties into regions evens out most of the variation between the counties. Table 2.16 reveals that the south-east midlands is now over-represented, largely due to a massive increase in the contribution from Bedfordshire, whose already over-numerous parishes were smaller than average and thus inflated by the weighting procedure. The same is true of the north-east midlands, where weighting both increases the already over-large contribution from Leicestershire and removes the deficit in Lincolnshire which formerly offset it. On the other hand the 'Pennine' region, which contains many larger-than-average parishes, moves from its earlier position as the most over-represented area to a position close to the national average. Disappointingly, the under-representation of the south-west remains uncorrected: indeed it becomes a little worse. On the whole, despite some extreme results for individual counties, correcting for population size only marginally disturbs the unweighted regional distribution of the aggregative parishes. As before, each region, apart from the south-west, contributes something reasonably near to the national average of 4 per cent of its parishes to the aggregative set.

Table 2.15: Aggregative parishes by county, after weighting by population size

County	Total no. of parishes (1)	Weighted aggregative parishes (2)	Weighted percentage (3) (2)/(1) × 100	County	Total no. of parishes (1)	Weighted aggregative parishes (2)	Weighted percentage (3) (2)/(1) × 100
Beds.	124	50.12	40.4	Mddx.	190	5.00	2.9
Berks.	158	1.73	1.1	Norf.	687	7.33	1.1
Bucks.	205	0.94	0.5	N'hants.	292	1.10	0.4
Cambs.	172	6.24	3.6	N'humb.	92	2.22	2.4
Chesh.	122	2.19	1.8	Notts.	214	15.91	7.4
Cornw.	201	–	–	Oxon	223	2.50	1.1
Cumb.	135	1.13	0.8	Rutl.	50	0.17	0.3
Derbs.	181	0.80	0.4	Salop	230	6.98	3.0
Devon	461	10.94	2.4	Soms.	476	3.30	0.6
Dors.	258	1.39	0.5	Staffs.	177	5.36	3.0
Durham	99	5.46	5.5	Suff.	500	20.29	4.1
Essex	403	33.02	8.2	Surrey	143	15.61	10.9
Glos.	332	4.73	1.4	Sussex	297	16.84	5.7
Hants	307	12.17	4.0	Warwicks.	208	10.48	5.0
Herefs.	222	15.25	6.9	Westm.	61	–	–
Herts.	131	4.53	3.5	Wilts.	309	5.44	1.8
Hunts.	97	4.51	4.6	Worcs.	197	0.78	0.4
Kent	395	19.86	5.0	Yorks. E. R.	234	5.75	2.5
Lancs.	190	8.68	4.6	Yorks. N. R.	225	15.55	6.9
Leics.	251	33.73	13.4	Yorks. W. R.	278	14.96	5.4
Lincs.	607	31.00	5.1		10141	403.99	4.0

Source: See table 2.4.

Table 2.16: Aggregative parishes by region, after weighting by population size

Region	Total no. of parishes (1)	Aggregative parishes Weighted frequency (2)	Weighted percentage (3) (2)/(1) × 100	Unweighted percentage (4)	Constituent counties
North	612	24.4	4.0	3.4	N'humb., Durham, Cumb., Westm., Yorks. N. R.
Pennine	824	31.6	3.8	5.7	Lancs., Chesh., Yorks. W. R., Yorks. E. R.
N. E. Midland	1303	81.6	6.3	3.9	Derbs., Notts., Lincs., Leics., Rutl.
W. Midland	1366	43.6	3.2	4.8	Salop, Staffs., Warwicks., Worcs., Herefs., Glos.
S. E. Midland	1262	68.7	5.4	3.9	N'hants., Hunts., Beds., Herts., Mddx., Bucks., Oxon
East Anglia	1762	66.9	3.8	3.9	Norf., Suff., Cambs., Essex
South-east	1300	66.2	5.1	5.4	Kent, Sussex, Surrey, Hants, Berks.
South-west	1712	21.1	1.2	1.8	Cornwall, Devon, Dorset, Somerset, Wilts.
All	10141	404.1	4.0	4.0	

Sources: See tables 2.5 and 2.15

Table 2.17: Farming regions, after weighting by population size

Type	Percentages Aggregative set Original	Weighted	Random Sample	Constituent elements
Mixed arable and pasture	53	63	57	1, 2, 3
Wood pasture	25	23	21	4, 5, 6, 7
Open pasture	22	14	21	8, 9, 10, 11, 12
in which cereal growing	56	65	60	1, 2, 3, 5
pig keeping	22	21	19	4, 6, 7
dairying	12	9	12	4, 12
No. of parishes	387	387	289	

Note: See table 2.8 for key constituent elements. Wholly urban parishes were excluded.

Source: See table 2.8.

The effect of correcting for population size on the other parish characteristics is very much the same: sometimes the agreement between the aggregative and random sets of parishes is improved, sometimes it is made worse. But overall the earlier reasonable fit between the two sets of distributions remains. So far as farming regions are concerned, table 2.17 shows that weighting increases the proportion of aggregative parishes with mixed farming at the expense of those with open pasture, thereby raising the proportion of cereal-growing parishes. But overall the changes are relatively minor.

When the distributions of parishes by soil-type and by height are recalculated weighted by population size, the greatest change lies in a reduction by 7 per cent of the proportion of parishes on brown forest soils with gleying, which brings the aggregative percentage exactly into line with the figure for the random sample (see table 2.7). Otherwise the small percentage differences that weighting makes to the individual cells in tables 2.6 and 2.7 are relatively insignificant. Overall, the fit between the aggregative and random sets is slightly worse for height, but for soil-type it is somewhat improved.

Weighting by population size also marginally affected the previously excellent fit of the unweighted aggregative parishes to the national distribution of occupational categories in 1831. As table 2.18 shows, the general effect of weighting is to reduce the contribution of parishes with many people engaged in manufacturing, retail trade and handicrafts, and non-agricultural labouring and to boost that of parishes engaged primarily in agriculture. On the credit side, the weighted aggregative figures show a better fit with the national percentages engaged in manufacturing and non-agricultural labouring. On the other hand the proportion of agricultural labourers is driven as far above the national figure as it was below it before the weighting procedure was applied, while the occupational category comprising retail trade and handicrafts moves from a position of perfect representation to one of slight deficiency as against the national percentage. Overall, however, the aggregative set remains quite close to the national distribution of occupational groups.

Taking all the parish characteristics together, therefore, the strategy of weighting by population size must be regarded as a success. As well as achieving its prime objective of removing a serious bias towards larger parishes in the aggregative set, the

Table 2.18: Occupational categories of males over age 20 (1831 Census), after weighting by population size

Occupational category	Percentages Aggregative set		England[1]
	Original	Weighted	
Farmers	8	9	8
Agricultural labourers	23	29	26
Manufacturing	13	12	11
Non-agricultural labourers	16	14	14
Retail trade and handicrafts	28	26	28
Professions	4	4	4
Servants	2	2	2
Others	6	5	6
No. of parishes	404	404	

[1] Less Monmouth and London.

Source: 1831 Census, Enumeration abstract.

weighting procedure either eliminated or substantially reduced a number of other major biases. Furthermore, it achieved those results without inflicting any systematic or substantial distortions in fields where the aggregative parishes had already shown themselves reasonably representative of the country as a whole.

Although far from exhaustive, the tests described above have covered many geographical, social, and economic characteristics of parishes, some of which are closely connected with population trends. That the aggregative parishes, once their population size bias has been removed, should follow as closely as they do the national distribution of parishes for each characteristic augurs well for their general representativeness and inspires confidence in them as a basis from which a national series of baptisms, burials, and marriages can be estimated over a long period of time.

Compensating for differences in length of registration

In constructing such a series, however, we are immediately faced with the difficulty that not all parishes began registration at the same time. There is also a parallel difficulty in the nineteenth century because, while most tabulations ran on to the beginning of civil registration in 1837, in about a third of the parishes inaccessible or missing registers caused the tabulations to be halted at an earlier date, usually coinciding with the introduction of new register books in 1813, following Rose's Act. Table 2.19 shows the changing number of baptism registers in observation throughout the period of study. The comparable tables for burials and marriages are not reproduced as they differ only slightly from the pattern shown by the baptism registers. It may be noted that 25 per cent of the final total of 404 registers were in observation by 1558, 50 per cent by 1562, 75 per cent by 1596 and 90 per cent by 1613.[19]

19. A constitution of the province of Canterbury, which received royal approval in 1598 and was enforced generally by a Canon of 1603, required all names to be copied from older registers into new parchment books, 'but especially since the first year of her Majesty's reign'. This clause seems to have induced many copyists to exclude events registered before Elizabeth's reign, as the large number of surviving registers beginning in the period 1558–64 attests. For a discussion of starting dates of registration and regional differences see Cox, *The parish registers of England*, pp. 237–9; Steel, *National index of parish registers*, 1, pp. 23–7.

Table 2.19: Number of baptism registers in observation

	No. of parishes			No. of parishes			No. of parishes	
Year	Registration starts	Cumulative no. fully in observation	Year	Registration starts	Cumulative no. fully in observation	Year	Registration starts/stops	Cumulative no. fully in observation
1538	27	0	1590	0	296	1640	0	383
1539	13	27	1591	1	296	1641	0	383
			1592	1	297	1642	1	383
1540	5	40	1593	0	298	1643	0	384
1541	11	45	1594	3	298	1644	0	384
1542	1	56	1595	1	301	1645	0	384
1543	1	57	1596	5	302	1646	0	384
1544	3	58	1597	4	307	1647	0	384
1545	2	61	1598	6	311	1648	0	384
1546	3	63	1599	5	317	1649	1	384
1547	2	66						
1548	1	68	1600	4	322	1650	1	385
1549	0	69	1601	9	326	1651	1	386
			1602	11	335	1652	1	387
1550	1	69	1603	2	346	1653	6	388
1551	3	70	1604	1	348	1654	4	394
1552	0	73	1605	2	349	1655	1	398
1553	0	73	1606	1	351	1656	0	399
1554	2	73	1607	2	352	1657	0	399
1555	3	75	1608	1	354	1658	2	399
1556	5	78	1609	1	355	1659	0	401
1557	6	83						
1558	39	89	1610	1	356	1660	0	401
1559	27	128	1611	1	357	1661	3	401
			1612	4	358	1662	0	404
1560	7	155	1613	3	362			
1561	33	162	1614	1	365			
1562	10	195	1615	1	366			
1563	11	205	1616	3	367			
1564	10	216	1617	1	370	1811	0	404
1565	4	226	1618	0	371	1812	122	282
1566	4	230	1619	0	371	1813	2	280
1567	3	234				1814	0	280
1568	4	237	1620	1	371	1815	0	280
1569	4	241	1621	0	372	1816	0	280
			1622	0	372	1817	1	279
1570	7	245	1623	1	372	1818	0	279
1571	5	252	1624	0	373	1819	0	279
1572	0	257	1625	1	373			
1573	4	257	1626	1	374	1820	3	276
1574	3	261	1627	2	374	1821	0	276
1575	2	264	1628	1	376	1822	0	276
1576	2	266	1629	0	377	1823	0	276
1577	2	268				1824	0	276
1578	0	270	1630	0	377	1825	0	276
1579	1	270	1631	2	377	1826	0	276
			1632	0	379	1827	0	276
			1633	0	379	1828	0	276
1580	1	271	1634	0	379	1829	0	276
1581	7	272	1635	1	379			
1582	2	279	1636	1	380	1830	0	276
1583	4	281	1637	0	381	1831	0	276
1584	5	285	1638	1	381	1832	1	275
1585	3	290	1639	1	382	1833	0	275
1586	1	293				1834	1	274
1587	0	294				1835	1	273
1588	2	294				1836	15	258
1589	0	296				1837	173	85

Source: Parish register tabulations.

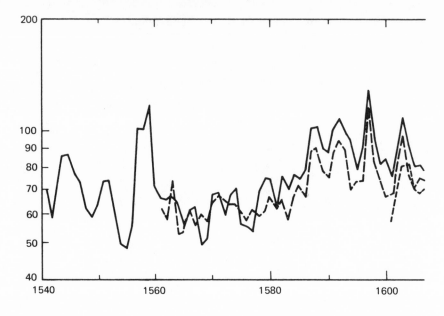

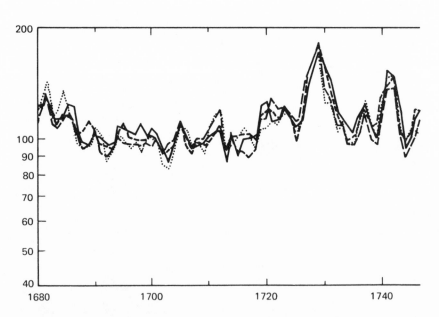

Figure 2.3: Annual burial totals in four groups: parishes in full
observation by 1541, after 1541 and before 1561,
after 1561 and before 1601, and after 1601 and
before 1662

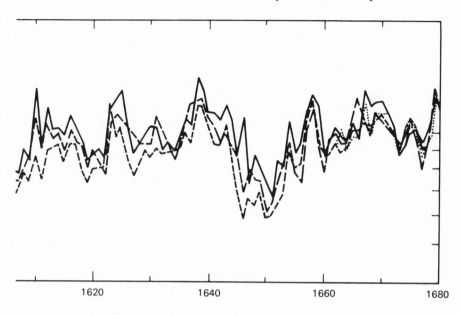

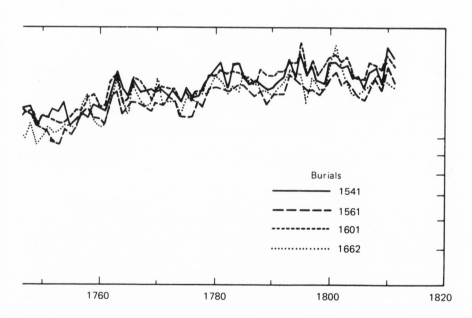

Burials

——————— 1541

— — — — 1561

------------- 1601

················ 1662

Note: The number of parishes in the four groups
was 43, 118, 192, 51 respectively, beginning
with the earliest group.

The period 1662–1811 presents no problem in this context. Throughout this period monthly totals of baptisms, burials, and marriages are available for all 404 parishes. Before and after the central period, however, some action is necessary if totals of events for particular months or years are to be compared with each other or with totals from the central period. Providing the parishes still in observation at any point in time are representative of the whole group of parishes, a simple solution is possible, for in this case the number of events they yield can be proportionately inflated to compensate for the absence of those parishes whose registers are lacking.

Although, of course, we cannot check the representativeness of the movements of the numbers of baptisms, burials, and marriages recorded by a group of parishes during a period when they alone remain in observation, we can compare the events they record at other periods with totals of events contributed by other parishes at the same time. In this way, for example, it can be seen whether those parishes which began registration especially early are typical or untypical in their later behaviour. If they behave typically during the period for which they can be compared with other parishes, this inspires confidence in their typicality during the period when they alone are in observation, and it will seem reasonable to take their experience as a proxy for the parishes that have passed out of observation. If, on the other hand, parishes that began registration early have an unusual population history later on, there is a strong probability that they are also untypical at an early period, and it would be foolhardy to assume that they represent the demographic experience of the missing parishes and take them as a guide to the general course of population change.

To test whether there was any systematic relationship between the date of entry into observation and subsequent demographic experience, the 404 parishes were split into four groups according to the date by which they had entered into observation, as in table 2.20. The total number of events recorded by the parishes in each group were then compared for the periods when they overlapped. Figure 2.3 shows the results of this test for burials; the graphs for baptisms and marriages are similar and have not been reproduced. The four series have been made visually comparable by indexing each on the average annual number of events recorded during the period 1700–19, which was set to equal 100.[20] In the event the four lines keep closely together as they move across the graph, indicating that the groups of parishes behave similarly regardless of the date of entry into observation.

We can therefore be confident that the date at which registration begins is not

Table 2.20: Burial registers: date of entry into full observation

Period	Number of parishes
1539–42	52
1543–62	148
1563–1602	131
1603–62	73
	404

Source: Parish register tabulations.

20. The annual totals are as recorded in the registers without any corrections for under-registration, and have not been weighted by population size.

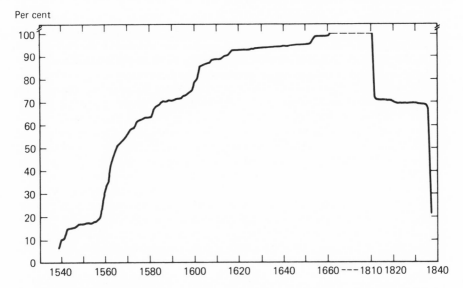

Figure 2.4: Proportion of 'all' baptisms recorded by registers still in observation

Note: For details of derivation see text.

systematically related to subsequent demographic experience and that those parishes remaining in observation can be taken as representative of those whose registers are unavailable. The problem now becomes one of discovering what proportion of all events would have been contributed by the missing parishes and then inflating the numbers of events recorded by the parishes still in observation to make good the deficiency. A convenient way of doing this is to start in the central period 1662–1811 when all parishes are in observation and work outwards, back to 1539 in one direction and forward to 1837 in the other, a year at a time. In most years a number of parishes move out of observation, because registration information either begins or ceases to be available in that year. The consequential loss is estimated by calculating what proportion of the weighted total number of baptisms, burials, or marriages the parishes in question contribute in the 10 years immediately before passing out of observation. This contribution is then added in to a cumulative total of the proportions contributed by parishes that have already passed out of observation in previous years. The complement of the cumulative proportion gives the proportion of all events still being recorded by the parishes remaining in observation at that time. Thus the number of events still being registered can be divided by this proportion to obtain the total number of weighted events that would have been recorded if information had been available from all 404 parishes.

Evidently, as the process continues to work back from 1662 and forward from 1811 the cumulative proportions associated with the parishes no longer in observation increase, and the total numbers of events recorded by the remaining parishes are successively inflated by progressively higher ratios. Figure 2.4 shows the estimated proportion of 'all' baptisms comprised by the events occurring in the parishes remaining in observation at different points in time. The graphs for burials and marriages are similar and are not reproduced here. For example, in 1560 the parishes remaining in observation are estimated as contributing one third of the total number of baptisms that would have been produced by the 404 parishes if all 404 baptism registers had survived, so the total number of events for the set of 404 parishes in 1560 is calculated by multiplying the number of recorded events by three.

Naturally there is a close correspondence between the numbers of parishes entering or leaving observation in each year as shown in table 2.19 and the proportions of baptisms still being recorded in figure 2.4. All parishes are in observation between 1662 and 1811 so no inflation needs to be made. In the seventeenth century almost all parishes had already begun registration so the estimated total numbers of events are based on a coverage of more than 90 per cent back to 1614 and of more than 75 per cent in 1600. The proportion of events contributed by parishes still in observation drifts down to 50 per cent by 1565. The great burst of parishes entering observation in the seven years between 1558 and 1564 reduces the proportion of events attributable to parishes still in observation to 20 per cent of the total by 1558. The figure falls a little lower to 14 per cent in 1542 and then rapidly declines to zero in 1538.

Before 1558, therefore, the events in our series are based on parishes contributing less than a fifth of the total numbers of events, and our estimates of these total numbers involve multiplying the recorded frequencies by factors greater than five. In these circumstances the random variation attendant on small numbers is likely to increase.

At the other end of the period, parishes contributing 29 per cent of the number of events between 1801 and 1811 pass out of observation in 1812. Thereafter very few leave until the advent of civil registration, so our figures for the period 1812–36 are based on approximately 70 per cent of the estimated true total number of events. The introduction of civil registration badly disturbed the quality of parish registration, but provided an alternative source of information, and the Registrar General's figures are used from 1837 onwards (1838 in the case of marriages), with corrections for under-registration where appropriate.

The consequences of weighting by parish population size

We have now constructed series of baptisms, burials, and marriages representing the aggregate frequencies of events in the 404 parishes over the whole period 1539–1837, corrected for population size. The next steps are to inflate them into national series, and then to convert them into series of vital events representing births, marriages, and deaths. But first it will be convenient to describe the effect of weighting the events registered in each parish using the factors designed to correct population size bias (table 2.12).

The total annual frequencies of baptisms, burials, and marriages recorded by the 404 parishes, weighted by population size, are given in table A4.1, column 4. Column 12 of the table contains an alternative series of annual totals corrected for date of entry into observation, but unweighted by parish size. Table 2.21 brings out the main relationships between the two series more clearly by grouping the data into 50-year periods. The table begins in 1550 so as to exclude the years based on small numbers of parishes, and ends in 1829 to avoid the problems caused by the onset of civil registration. The left hand panel of the table shows for each of the three series of baptisms, burials, and marriages, in each time period, the proportion of the unweighted frequencies of events comprised by the weighted total frequencies. It is clear from the panel that weighting approximately halves the numbers of events

Table 2.21: Ratios between weighted and unweighted aggregative frequencies by period

Period	Weighted events per 1000 unweighted events			Relative growth since previous period Unweighted growth ratio = 1000		
	Baptisms	Burials	Marriages	Baptisms	Burials	Marriages
1550-99	550	531	585	—	—	—
1600-49	537	518	583	975	977	997
1650-99	524	521	581	977	1000	997
1700-49	510	507	562	974	974	967
1750-99	499	492	501	979	971	892
1800-29	482	476	493	965	966	983
1550-1829	513	506	542	876	896	843

Source: Table A4.1, columns 4 and 12.

recorded by the 404 aggregative parishes, a reduction in line with the fact that in 1811 the mean size of the aggregative parishes was just over twice the mean size of the parishes in the random sample (table 2.11).

However, the proportion of weighted to unweighted events is not constant over time. For example, in the case of baptisms the proportion falls from 550 per 1,000 in the second half of the sixteenth century to 482 per 1,000 in the first 30 years of the nineteenth, showing that the weighted baptisms grow more slowly than the unweighted baptisms. Again this is not an unexpected result, since it is the larger parishes with the higher rates of growth whose contribution to the overall aggregative total is reduced by the weighting procedure. Thus the correction for parish population size has evidently succeeded in its primary task, which was to prevent the over-numerous, fast-growing, large parishes from dominating the aggregative set and giving it an untypically high rate of growth in the number of events recorded.

The right-hand panel of the table shows the extent to which weighting by population size reduced the growth shown by the unweighted time-series. In other words, it shows by how much the population size bias in the unweighted aggregative set would have overstated the growth in the numbers of baptisms, burials, and marriages from one period to the next. For each time period, the growth ratios of the unweighted and weighted frequencies of a series are calculated between the current and the previous period. The growth ratios of the unweighted frequencies are then indexed as 1,000, and the figures in the right-hand panel of the table give the relative movement of the growth ratios of the weighted frequencies. For example, the first figure in the panel indicates that between the two half centuries 1550–99 and 1600–49 the growth ratio of the weighted baptisms was 975 per 1,000, or 97.5 per cent, of the growth ratio registered by the unweighted baptisms over the same period.

Casting an eye down this column it is clear that the weighting procedure has reduced the growth ratios to something close to 97.5 per cent of those for unweighted baptisms over most of the parish register period. The reduction was only slightly greater (to 96.5 per cent) in the relative growth between the late eighteenth and early nineteenth century, the period that was the original cause for concern. Taking the parish register period as a whole, the weighting process reduced the increase in baptisms between the late sixteenth and the early nineteenth centuries to 87.6 per cent of the growth recorded by the unweighted frequencies.

Weighting affected burials to almost exactly the same degree, with two exceptions: it made no difference at all to the burial growth ratio for 1650–99, but reduced burials more than baptisms in the later eighteenth century. Since weighting by population size alters the relative contributions of large and small parishes to the overall frequencies of events, the greater the reduction in the growth ratios the more discrepant the demographic experiences of large and small parishes are likely to have been. Conversely, if weighting has no effect on the growth ratios, the demographic experiences of large and small parishes are more likely to have been the same. Thus the lack of any impact of weighting on the 1650–99 burial growth rates indicates that something was happening to mortality in the course of the seventeenth century affecting all parishes sufficiently strongly to overlay the normal differences in the growth of the number of burials between large and small parishes.

From the first half of the eighteenth century weighting by population size has a progressively greater effect. The relative growth figure is 974 for both baptisms and burials in the early eighteenth century falling to 965 and 966 respectively in the early nineteenth century. In this context the figure of 971 for burials in the period 1750–99 seems to be consistent with the falling trend, but the figure of 979 for baptisms in the same period is anomalous in that it is higher than the preceding figure, as if something were happening to nuptiality or fertility in the late eighteenth century that temporarily overlaid the tendency towards widening differences in the rates of growth of baptisms between large and small parishes. Although we cannot explore these possibilities here, the results of weighting by population size at least identify two periods where some change may have occurred in the differences between the fertility and mortality patterns of large and small communities.

Table 2.22: Ratios between weighted and unweighted baptism/burial ratios by period

| Period | Baptism/burial ratios | | Ratio of ratios |
	Unweighted	Weighted	Weighted/Unweighted
1550–99	1.263	1.309	1.036
1600–49	1.214	1.257	1.035
1650–99	1.026	1.033	1.007
1700–49	1.117	1.125	1.007
1750–99	1.293	1.312	1.015
1800–29	1.596	1.618	1.014

Source: Table A4.1, columns 4 and 12.

The differences we have noted between the impact of the weighting procedure on baptisms and burials, although small, alter the ratio between them at certain dates and thereby change a key element in the demographic story. In fact weighting generally reduces baptisms less than burials and so increases the baptism-to-burial ratios. The weighted and unweighted baptism-to-burial ratios and the ratios between them are given in table 2.22. The greatest proportional increases occur in the late sixteenth and early seventeenth centuries when the weighted baptism-to-burial ratios are 3.6 per cent and 3.5 per cent higher than the unweighted ratios. For the period 1650 to 1750 there is practically no difference between the weighted and unweighted series, but after 1750 the weighted baptism-to-burial ratios are 1.5 per cent higher than the unweighted. Thus the unweighted frequencies not only show a greater growth in the number of events recorded over the whole period, but also manage to achieve this with lower rates of natural increase, implying either more in-migration or less out-migration. A full investigation of the internal demographic consistency of each of the two sets of frequencies and rates would detain us too long here, but this last difference between them is consistent with the domination of the original set of parishes by large communities, which was removed by the weighting process. For many of those larger parishes were market towns and 'manufacturing' centres, which had modest rates of natural increase yet grew considerably in size largely as the result of in-migration.[21]

Weighting by population size affects marriages rather differently. Before 1700 weighting has little impact on the rates of growth, suggesting that in small parishes marriages, unlike baptisms, were growing as fast as in the larger parishes. This may reflect a tendency for smaller parishes to be more favoured as locations for cut-rate marriages, thus securing more than their fair share of marriage registrations. The relative growth ratio for 1700–49, indicating change since the late seventeenth century, is much more in line with the figures for baptisms and burials. This provides further evidence that the Marriage Duty Act, levied between 1696 and 1705, improved the quality of marriage registration, even though it failed to eliminate the cut-rate 'marriage shops'. These were finally killed by Hardwicke's Marriage Act of 1753, and the relative growth ratio in the later eighteenth century plunges to 892, indicating a major transfer of marriage registration from the smaller to the larger parishes.[22] In 1800–29 the relative growth ratio picks up again and attains a level a little higher than the ratios for baptisms and burials.

Thus weighting by population size appears to change the frequencies of all three series of ecclesiastical events recorded during the parish register period in a manner that is both coherent and consistent with what is known of the historical context within which registration took place. Weighting also appears to have been successful in correcting those untypical attributes of the demography of the larger parishes which otherwise would have led to a greater growth over time in the number of events furnished by the 404 parishes. Yet the differences that weighting makes are not very great: the baptism–burial ratios of the weighted and unweighted series are usually within 1.5 per cent of each other and never more than 4 per cent apart. Over the whole period from the sixteenth to the nineteenth century the growth in baptisms, which was more affected by weighting than burials, was reduced by only 12.4 per cent.

Even though the two series tell the same basic story, however, the apparently small differences between them are quite sufficient to produce a significant difference in the outline of the long-term course of population change. Since the unweighted series incorporates a serious bias towards larger parishes with untypical demographic régimes, and since weighting the individual parish figures reduces other associated biases in the social and economic characteristics of the aggregative set of parishes, we shall base all our subsequent evaluation and analysis on the series of aggregative frequencies weighted by parish population size.

21. See pp. 165–6.
22. The adequacy of marriage registration is also discussed on pp. 28–30 above. For the effect of Hardwicke's Act see also fn. 4, above.

3

Inflation to national frequencies

As a result of the operations so far described the original monthly frequencies of baptisms, burials, and marriages found in the 404 parishes have been corrected for under-registration and for differing starting and finishing dates, and the contribution of each size-group of parishes to the total of events has been reweighted to offset the biases arising because the parishes were not randomly chosen. We have thereby produced totals of baptisms, burials, and marriages that should reflect national trends and fluctuations in miniature, and we therefore turn now to the question of selecting an appropriate multiplier to be used in converting the reweighted totals for the 404 parishes into national totals. This will involve a comparison of the population of the 404 parishes in 1811 with the national total in that year, an examination of the parish register data collected by Rickman which can be used to test the aggregative sample totals, and an attempt to estimate London's contribution to national totals independently since there are no London parishes in the aggregative sample.

One of the standard elements of information collected for every parish both in the aggregative and random samples of parishes was its population in 1811. It is therefore a simple matter to calculate the total population of the 404 parishes at that date both as enumerated and after reweighting using the same weights as were used to produce representative totals of baptisms, burials, and marriages. The enumerated population of the 404 parishes in 1811 was 773,961 (mean 1,916), while the total after reweighting was 371,093 (mean 919). The total population of England (excluding Monmouth) was 9,476,700 in 1811. The population of London was 1,009,546, so that the population of England excluding London was 8,467,154. Since the 404 parishes did not include any from London, the behaviour of the reweighted totals of events from the aggregative sample of parishes should mirror that of England without London rather than England as a whole. The 1811 population data suggest that multiplying the reweighted series by 22.82 (8,467,154/371,093) should result in totals of events that mirror the behaviour of national totals excluding London. What evidence exists to enable this supposition to be tested?

The aggregative sample and Rickman's 1836 survey

The most important sources of information about national totals of events recorded in the Anglican parish registers are to be found in the two major enquiries instituted by Rickman during the long period when he directed census activities. In 1801 he asked the minister of every parish to make a return of the annual totals of baptisms and burials occurring in his parish for every tenth year from 1700 to 1780 and each subsequent year down to 1800. He also asked for marriage totals for each year from 1754 to 1800. Thirty-five years later he made a further inquiry. By 1836 he knew, from the answers to questions sent to every incumbent in 1831, the date at which the earliest registers began in every parish. He therefore circularized only those parishes whose registers began by 1600 at the latest, asking for the totals in the three series in three-year periods centring on 1570, 1600, 1630, 1670, 1700, and 1750, and in addition for the totals for 1800, expressing the hope that especial care would be taken in counting the 1800 totals since they were to serve as the reference point in making estimates of the size of the population at the earlier dates.[1]

Both enquiries produced, of course, an immense volume of data, though unhappily in neither case have the original parochial returns survived. The published results in both cases present problems. In 1801 there were many omissions and a plethora of clerical errors. The 1836 returns, which were published only in a very summary analysis in the 1841 census after Rickman's death, may also suffer either from sampling bias or other defects in some counties.[2] Nevertheless Rickman's initiatives have given us material of the greatest value, with a coverage beyond the scope of any enquiry not backed by the resources of the central government.

We may begin by considering how far the reweighted totals of events drawn from the aggregative sample of 404 parishes compare with the results of the later of the two inquiries made by Rickman. This covered almost the entire parish register period, though including only seven widely scattered points in time. It permits an examination of the degree of similarity in the long-term trends in the two sources. The material collected in 1801 can then be used to determine how close to the 'target' ratio of 22.82 were the totals in the national and aggregative sample series in the eighteenth century.

It is convenient to begin by converting the data published in 1841 into totals of events at each date for which returns were made. It is ironical that such a roundabout procedure is necessary, since the raw material of Rickman's enquiry was, of course, annual totals of baptisms, burials, and marriages. But Rickman converted the parish register returns into estimates of population totals and these must therefore be reconverted to allow comparison with the aggregative sample totals.

The totals shown in table 3.1 were produced by determining the baptism, burial, and marriage rates in 1800 for the English parishes approached by Rickman in 1836 from the unpublished manuscript calculations associated with the table published in 1841. Monmouth has as usual been excluded, and also Middlesex. London was not separately tabulated and Middlesex has therefore been substituted for London, and excluded to preserve comparability with the aggregative sample. The unpublished material enables baptism, burial, and marriage rates to be calculated for the parishes included in the survey.[3] The returns cover 47 per cent of all English parishes and the rates based on so large a sample, determined only by register survival, may therefore stand for the country as a whole. In 1800 there were 102,158 baptisms in these parishes, 77,166 burials, and 26,358 marriages. The population at risk was 3,596,299 and the rates were therefore 28.41, 21.46, and 7.33 per 1,000 respectively.[4] Applying these rates to the 1801 population of England without Monmouth or Middlesex (7,467,723) produces the totals of events in 1800 shown in table 3.1. The data published in the 1841 census then suffice to allow the calculation

1. The form of words which Rickman used may be found in appendix 7, p. 597. Fuller details both of the 1836 survey and the returns of 1801 are given in appendix 7.
2. See appendix 7, pp. 622–9.
3. Details of the manuscript source may be found in appendix 7, p. 624, fn. 30.
4. For further discussion of the population at risk and the level of the burial and marriage rates see appendix 7, pp. 624–6.

of totals of events at other dates since the size of the estimated populations at each date relative to that of 1801 reflects the ratio between the number of events registered at the two dates. There are separate estimates of population size at each date based on baptism, burial, and marriage frequencies, so that once the totals of events for 1800 have been calculated, the subsequent operations are straightforward. As an example, the estimated population of England without Monmouth and Middlesex in 1630 is given as 4,629,302 when based on marriage frequencies.[5] The average number of marriages in the years 1629–31 may therefore be taken to be 54,738 × 4,629,302/ 7,467,723 = 33,932.

The aggregative sample data would not have been directly comparable with the Rickman series totals if the reweighted totals arrived at by the operations described in chapter 2 had been used, because they include corrections made for under-registration. Since Rickman's totals were not corrected in any way so far as is known, it is necessary to remove the effect of correcting for under-registration from the aggregative sample data before comparing the two series. It will be remembered that the effect of correcting for under-registration was substantial in the earlier years of the aggregative series. For example, the number of burials in 1569–71 was increased by 8.6 per cent for this reason, whereas in 1800 the figure was only 0.6 per cent. The aggregative sample totals in the top half of table 3.1, therefore, have had an appropriate degree of under-registration restored to them, so to speak. The lower half of the table shows the number of events at each date relative to the number occurring in 1800. The agreement between comparable indexed figures based on the national and sample totals is impressively close in the main. There are six points in each indexed series at which comparison can be made (1569–71, 1599–1601, 1629–31, 1669–71, 1699–1701, and 1749–51). In the baptism series the sum of the differences between the paired index figures at the six points is 78 ignoring sign, and +34 if sign is taken into account. For burials and marriages the comparable figures are 90 and − 64, and 69 and + 69. The mean difference at the 18 comparison points in the three series is therefore 13 ignoring sign, and +2 if sign is taken into account. We take this as evidence of a satisfactory agreement overall between the trends revealed in data drawn from the two sources.

The relationship between Rickman's 1836 data and the aggregative sample can also be expressed in a form that bears more directly on the question of the most appropriate inflation factor to be used in converting the total of events in the aggregative series into national totals. Table 3.2 sets out the ratios between the national and aggregative sample totals of events shown in table 3.1. For example, the national total of baptisms for 1569–71 in the table is 96,820 and the aggregative sample total for the same period is 4,195 giving the ratio figure of 23.08 shown in table 3.2.

The ratios shown in table 3.2 are tolerably close to the 'target' ratio of 22.82 based upon 1811 population totals. The burial series contains rather higher figures in the two earliest periods as well as the anomalous figure for 1699–1701, and the marriage series figures show a consistent tendency to be a little above the 'target' ratio except in the first two periods. Too much should not be made of minor discrepancies between the expected and the observed. The margin of error necessarily involved when so much processing of raw data is involved is too great to allow firm conclusions to be drawn from slight variations in the ratios. The sensitivity of the ratios to alternative methods of using the same basic information is easily demonstrated. The national

---

5. See *1841 Census*, Enumeration abstract, Preface, p. 36.

Table 3.1: National and sample totals of baptisms, burials, and marriages

Year(s)	England			Aggregative sample		
	Baptisms	Burials	Marriages	Baptisms	Burials	Marriages
1569–71	96 820	76 270	27 532	4 195	3 129	1 250
1599–1601	118 627	80 353	32 773	5 288	3 420	1 441
1629–31	129 624	104 839	33 932	5 632	4 592	1 449
1669–71	121 954	127 628	29 856	5 107	5 588	1 290
1699–1701	130 472	115 228	34 651	5 807	4 783	1 483
1749–51	148 691	119 347	41 404	6 700	5 263	1 775
1800	212 158	160 257	54 738	9 215	6 994	2 333

Year(s)	Baptisms		Burials		Marriages	
	England	Sample	England	Sample	England	Sample
1569–71	456	455	476	447	503	536
1599–1601	559	574	501	489	599	618
1629–31	611	611	654	657	620	621
1669–71	575	554	796	799	545	553
1699–1701	615	630	719	684	633	636
1749–51	701	727	745	753	756	761
1800	1000	1000	1000	1000	1000	1000

Notes:
1 England is England without Monmouth and Middlesex.
2 All totals except those for 1800 are averages of the three years indicated.
3 The aggregative sample totals, other than those for 1800, are all based on the Old Style year (though running 1 April to 31 March rather than 25 March to 24 March: see appendix 7).

Source: The totals for England were derived from data published in the 1841 census (*1841 Census, Enumeration abstract*, Preface, pp. 36–7). For a description of the derivation see text.

Table 3.2: Ratios between national totals of events based on the returns made to Rickman in 1836 and the aggregative sample totals (national totals derived from published data in 1841 census)

Year(s)	Baptisms	Burials	Marriages
1569–71	23.08	24.38	22.03
1599–1601	22.43	23.50	22.74
1629–31	23.02	22.83	23.42
1669–71	23.88	22.84	23.14
1699–1701	22.46	24.09	23.37
1749–51	22.19	22.68	23.33
1800	23.02	22.91	23.46
Mean	22.87	23.32	23.07

Source: Table 3.1.

population estimates published in the 1841 census were the result of summing separate estimates made for each county. Rickman's method was to make three estimates of the population of each county at each date based on the number of baptisms, burials, and marriages at that date relative to the county total in 1800.[6] The proportion of registers beginning before 1600 and therefore included in his survey varied considerably from county to county and the absolute number of registers involved was sometimes very small.[7]

In the manuscript notebooks used in preparing the 1841 census table an alternative method of calculating national populations was also tried. England was treated as a single unit rather than as the sum of its constituent counties, and changes in the numbers of baptisms, burials, and marriages in the country as a whole were used to calculate national population totals. If this approach is used a rather different set of ratio figures results. They are set out in table 3.3. Once again Monmouth and

Table 3.3: Ratios between national totals of events based on the returns made to Rickman in 1836 and the aggregative sample totals (national totals derived from unpublished data)

Year(s)	Baptisms	Burials	Marriages
1569–71	22.83	23.79	21.39
1599–1601	22.46	22.95	21.93
1629–31	22.86	22.62	22.82
1669–71	23.46	22.41	22.72
1699–1701	22.04	23.68	22.70
1749–51	21.82	22.45	22.53
1800	23.02	22.91	23.46
Mean	22.64	22.97	22.51

Source: For derivation of national totals see text.
Aggregative sample totals from table 3.1.

6. See *1841 Census*, Enumeration abstract, Preface, p. 35; and appendix 7.
7. For example, although 30.2 per cent of the population of Northumberland in 1801 lived in parishes

Middlesex have been taken out of the national totals. Treating the 1841 data in this way leaves some of the anomalies noted in reference to table 3.2, such as the high burial ratio in 1699–1701, but produces a general tendency to undershoot rather than to overshoot the 'target' ratio. In general the ratios in the two tables provide encouraging evidence both that the aggregative series capture national trends well and that the 'target' ratio holds approximately true over the whole period. We may therefore turn now to consider the implications of Rickman's earlier exercise of 1801.

The aggregative sample and the parish register returns of 1801

Rickman had hoped to receive information from every English and Welsh parish in 1801. He was disappointed in this, and was also badly let down by the arithmetic of his census clerks which was prone to frequent and often serious error. It is therefore unsafe to use the 1801 returns in the form in which Rickman left them. We have made an attempt to remove the most serious arithmetical errors and have adopted a less arbitrary method of correcting for parishes which made no return. The details of this work, together with a critique of the accuracy of the work of individual incumbents may be found in appendix 7. The appendix contains a table showing both the original and the new national totals derived from the parochial returns.

Table 3.4 is based on the new totals given in the appendix.[8] They were adjusted to exclude London from the totals for England without Monmouth. Thus, for example, the revision of Rickman's data gives a baptism total for 1700 of 143,535. In the original returns the comparable total was 138,291 and the total for London (the area of the bills of mortality plus Chelsea, Kensington, Marylebone, Paddington, and St Pancras) was 16,585. Therefore the baptism total shown in table 3.4 for England less London is 126,321 (143,535 × (138,291 − 16,585)/138,291). The reweighted totals of events in the 404 parishes are also shown, and the ratios between comparable totals in the two series. The sample totals for each year up to 1750 are for years beginning in April and ending in March. In appendix 7 we show reason to think that the great majority of those making returns to Rickman used the Old Style year until the change to the New Style in 1752. The aggregative data consist of monthly totals and cannot therefore be remarshalled to match the O.S. year exactly but there is a better 'fit' between the sample and national data using a year beginning 1 April than if the N.S. year beginning 1 January had been used throughout.

The ratios shown in table 3.4 lend further weight to the view that the 'target' inflation factor of 22.82 is appropriate to use when converting the sample totals into a national series. In the case of baptisms and burials the ratios in the two final decades 1780–9 and 1790–9 lie very close to this value. If the two final years of the 20-year period are excluded, the ratios for the rest of the period (1780–97) for baptisms and burials are 22.73 and 22.70 respectively. In the years 1798–9 the ratios were higher at 23.25 and 23.41, while in 1800, the final year covered in the 1801 returns, the comparable figures are 23.25 and 23.12. It is probable that the returns made to

---

included in the 1836 survey, only 8 of the 92 parishes in the county were involved but all the 4 Newcastle parishes were included. There is clearly a serious risk of obtaining unrepresentative estimates in such circumstances. Northumberland was the most extreme case but there were other cases where either a small number or a small proportion of parishes were made the basis of the 1841 exercise. For example, only 15 Westmorland parishes out of 61 were included, with 25.6 per cent of the population. The figures for Cumberland were 18, 135, and 25.5 per cent. See table A7.11, and pp. 627–8.

8. See table A7.1.

Table 3.4: National and sample totals of baptisms, burials and marriages (national totals derived from 1801 returns to Rickman)

Year(s)	Baptisms (1)	(2)	(3)	Burials (1)	(2)	(3)
1700	126 321	5 931	21.30	103 865	4 883	21.27
1710	114 471	5 048	22.68	108 871	5 102	21.34
1720	126 320	5 545	22.78	128 732	5 997	21.47
1730	132 556	6 003	22.08	140 873	6 454	21.83
1740	140 577	6 470	21.73	128 229	5 761	22.26
1750	152 458	7 123	21.40	122 151	5 495	22.23
1760	159 379	7 034	22.66	126 152	5 528	22.82
1770	176 974	7 983	22.17	140 435	6 235	22.52
1780–9	1 969 800	86 603	22.75	1 522 793	67 474	22.57
1790–9	2 189 278	95 910	22.83	1 551 215	67 519	22.97
1800	215 146	9 252	23.25	162 653	7 036	23.12

Year(s)	Marriages (1)	(2)	(3)
1755–9	209 005	9 538	21.91
1760–9	473 313	21 807	21.70
1770–9	497 827	22 251	22.37
1780–9	542 400	23 740	22.85
1790–9	594 749	25 633	23.20
1800	55 770	2 325	23.71

(1)   Totals for England without Monmouth and London.
(2)   Totals for aggregative sample after reweighting.
(3)   Ratio of 1 to 2.

Note: The aggregative sample totals of baptisms and burials for 1700 to 1750 are for the year beginning 1 April (see text).

Source: National totals may be found in table A7.1. See text for a description of their adjustment for this table.

Rickman for the last few years before the census were slightly swollen by the inclusion of baptisms and burials of which the minister had knowledge though they were not recorded in the Anglican registers. Evidence of this tendency will be presented when reviewing the position after 1800. The fact that the 1800 totals derived from the 1841 returns, for which the incumbents probably confined their attention solely to their registers, are slightly lower than the comparable figures based on the 1801 returns (compare tables 3.1 and 3.4) may also be explained in part on these grounds.

In the earlier years of the eighteenth century the ratios are normally lower than in the 1780s and 1790s. For baptisms the average of the years 1700 to 1770 is 22.10; for burials 21.97. The tendency for the ratio to rise over time is more clearcut in the case of burials than with baptisms. The lower figures early in the century are not due simply to the corrections carried out on the aggregative series to offset periodic under-registration. Using uncorrected totals in the aggregative series would raise the average ratios for 1700–70 to 22.35 and 22.21 respectively, but, in contrast to the effect of this operation on the 1841 returns, this still leaves a slight rising trend during the century. Nor is it clear that it is proper to remove from the aggregative series the effect of correction for under-registration since Rickman was conscious of the existence of periods of defective registration and appends an observation to the page of the 1801 census on which the census questions are listed. 'In cases where the returns are stated to be in some years "defective", such defects have been supplied, in every instance, by an average number of baptisms, burials, and marriages (or of either) taken from the returns of the same parish, in such of the years specified in the respective tables as are immediately preceding and subsequent to such defect'.[9] But many such years probably escaped the notice and remark of incumbents, and where they were noticed, Rickman's clerks do not always appear to have followed his instruction.[10] Moreover, in a small proportion of cases the loss of early register volumes meant that registers began only part of the way through the eighteenth century. This problem is absent both from the aggregative sample and the registers on which the 1841 exercise was based since in both cases only registers beginning at an earlier date were admitted to the sample. A moderately lower ratio in the earlier years of the century is therefore to be expected, and its existence does not upset the general plausibility of the 'target' ratio.

The ratios between national and sample marriage totals rise to a slightly higher level than those in the other two series, and also appear to rise more strongly over the second half of the century. They suggest a less stable relationship between the two series than is the case with either baptisms or burials (though this effect does not appear at all in the comparison with Rickman's 1836 material). In this connexion it is helpful to consider a further piece of evidence before attempting to select the most suitable inflation ratio.

Table 3.5 extends the series given in table 3.4 into the first three decades of the nineteenth century, while recapitulating the last two decades of the eighteenth century. It shows a striking change in the behaviour of the ratio series compared with the earlier table, since in the early nineteenth century the marriage ratio remained perfectly stable while the baptism, and still more the burial, ratio rose steadily and quite sharply. These changes in pattern are reassuring rather than alarming. Since only Quakers and Jews were exempted from the provisions of Hardwicke's Marriage Act, the number of marriages recorded in Anglican registers ought to be a good measure of the total number of marriages taking place. At the time of the censuses of 1811, 1821, and 1831 incumbents were asked to make returns of marriages in their parishes in each of the preceding 10 years. The national totals built up in this way preserve a virtually unchanging ratio to the number in the aggregative sample of parishes at the same level as that found also in the 1790s. It is likely that the published returns for the early nineteenth century were an accurate reflection of the marriages taking place, so that there seems no reason to resist the conclusion that over the whole period from the 1790s onwards a multiplier of 23.20 is appropriate for converting sample to national totals. For the later eighteenth century the evidence is more ambiguous. Is the rising ratio a reflection of a genuine change in the relationship between the two series? It is difficult to give a confident answer to this question, because the accuracy of Rickman's returns for marriages in 1801 is so much in doubt. It will be seen from table A7.2 that the marriage returns suffer severely from unexplained discrepancies between the published national totals and the totals

9. *1801 Census*, Parish registers, p. [1].
10. See appendix 7, p. 619.

Table 3.5: National and sample totals of baptisms, burials, and marriages, 1780–1829

Period	Baptisms			Burials		
	(1)	(2)	(3)	(1)	(2)	(3)
1780–9	1 969 800	86 603	22.75	1 522 793	67 474	22.57
1790–9	2 189 278	95 910	22.83	1 551 215	67 519	22.97
1800–9	2 425 076	102 565	23.64	1 606 735	67 857	23.68
1810–9	2 763 070	114 553	24.12	1 667 765	68 497	24.35
1820–9	3 190 441	131 510	24.26	1 990 857	79 084	25.17

Period	Marriages		
	(1)	(2)	(3)
1780–9	542 400	23 740	22.85
1790–9	594 749	25 633	23.20
1800–9	658 850	28 051	23.49
1810–9	727 916	31 344	23.22
1820–9	839 350	36 197	23.19

(1) Totals for England without Monmouth and London.
(2) Totals for aggregative sample after reweighting.
(3) Ratio of 1 to 2.

Sources: For national totals up to 1800, table A7.1 modified as described in text; totals for 1801–29, *1811 Census,* Parish registers, pp. 93, 187, 198; *1821 Census,* Parish register abstract, pp.75, 145, 158; *1831 Census,* Parish register abstract, pp. 201, 412, 494.

produced by summing the individual county figures. Some of the discrepancies, like those of 1761, 1790, 1792, and 1797, are evidently due to arithmetic or printing errors, but there are substantial discrepancies for every year 1767–81 which have no obvious cause. There can be no guarantee that eliminating differences between national totals and the sum of county totals removes all errors. In these circumstances there seems no good reason to reject the 'target' ratio of 22.82 for the pre-1801 period as a whole, especially as the 1841 data on which tables 3.2 and 3.3 are based do not suggest any change in the ratio during the eighteenth century.

Table 3.5 also shows that the ratios of the national total to the sample total for baptisms and burials rose steadily and considerably during the early nineteenth century, suggesting at first sight that the close agreement between the observed and the 'target' ratio in the 1780s and 1790s was coincidental and not a safe ground for supposing that it held good over an extended period. But in reality it would have been more surprising if the ratios had remained at the level of the 1790s than that they should have risen, because the returns made by incumbents to Rickman's successive census questions included a growing proportion of unregistered and non-Anglican baptisms and burials. The question addressed to the Anglican ministers had never specified that their returns should be confined to Anglican events. Even the original request of 1801 had asked simply 'What was the number of baptisms and burials in your parish, township or place' (the form of question for marriages was identical). A few returns based on nonconformist registers were included in the 1811 Abstract,[11]

11. The Summary of England refers to the receipt of 99 such returns (*1811 Census*, Parish registers, p. 145).

and larger numbers were included in later years. Rickman appears to have expected that a number of non-Anglican events would be returned by the Anglican incumbents. This is quite explicit in the case of burials. For example in 1831, when a new question about the age of those buried was added to the questions that had been asked previously, he issued a specimen form to be used in tabulating the information. On it there is a space for the entry of burials in the burial grounds of dissenters, Jews, and others, and the totals under this head were added to the Anglican events in the summary at the foot of the form.[12] He also acknowledged in the preface the receipt of returns from secular burial grounds in or near a number of large towns.[13]

The parish register returns themselves, of course, include other direct evidence that incumbents had knowledge of a greater number of events than were recorded in their registers. The returns itemize separately unentered baptisms, burials, and marriages. For England less Monmouth the unentered events formed the following percentages of those entered in 1801–10, 1811–20, and 1821–30 respectively: baptisms 4.90, 6.68, 3.82; burials 5.29, 4.59, 3.56; marriages 0.25, 0.21, and 0.32. Unentered events presumably included such things as baptisms performed at home and burials of unbaptized infants. They appear to have been regarded as separate in general from nonconformist events, since returns from nonconformist sources were also included and were treated as distinct. In some counties unentered events were a very high proportion of those returned. In Middlesex in 1801–10 unentered burials formed over 26 per cent of the total returned. Or again in Northumberland the comparable figure for baptisms was 22 per cent. It is perhaps significant that the percentages of unentered baptisms and burials both fell sharply in the 1820s, a decade that appears to have seen a distinct recovery in the efficiency of Anglican registration.[14] Rickman himself believed that the totals of events returned by incumbents excluded unentered baptisms, burials, and marriages, but in this he may have been mistaken, at least in some instances. Given the imprecision of the main question, this would not be surprising.

Sometimes a pattern suggesting that unregistered or non-Anglican events were included in the parochial returns can be shown locally. For example, if the totals of baptisms in the parishes in the hundred of Edmonton[15] are added together and compared with the totals published in the censuses of 1801 and 1811, a striking difference appears between the period before 1800 and the first decade of the nineteenth century. In the period 1781–1800 the local registers record 7,904 baptisms but the returns published in the 1801 census total only 7,717 during the period, a shortfall of 187 or 2.4 per cent of the 'true' totals. In 6 years out of 20 the published total was too high, in 14 too low. In complete contrast in the decade 1801–10 the total number of baptisms recorded in the several registers of the hundred was 4,873 whereas the figure published in the 1811 census was 5,166, or 6.0 per cent above the 'true' figure. In every year in this decade the published figure is the higher of the two. If further research shows this pattern to be common, it will leave no room to doubt that the rise in the ratios of baptisms and burials shown in table 3.5 came

12. *1831 Census*, Preface, p. xxvi.

13. *1831 Census*, Preface, pp. xxxiv–xxxv.

14. This was Krause's view. See Krause, 'Changes in English fertility and mortality' and 'The changing adequacy of English registration'.

15. The hundred consisted of the parishes of Edmonton, Enfield, Monken Hadley, South Mimms, Tottenham, and Weld Chapel. We are greatly indebted to Mr T. Lewis for carrying out the aggregative tabulations on which the remarks in this paragraph are based.

about because an increasing proportion of all events returned was either unregistered or non-Anglican.

   The foregoing provides good reason to think that the reweighted totals of events from the aggregative sample parishes represent that fraction of the total of Anglican baptisms, burials, and marriages that would be expected from a comparison of the national and sample population totals in 1811. The 'target' ratio of 22.82 seems valid for all three series except that a slightly higher figure of 23.20 is preferable for the early nineteenth century for the marriage series. But there remains, of course, the major question of the scale of the additional inflation needed to take into account the absence of any London parishes from the sample data. Inflating the sample series totals by 22.82 may yield accurate totals for England excluding London, but it is necessary to make a further inflation to produce estimated totals for the country including its capital city.

Table 3.6:   Ratios between national and aggregative sample totals, 1700–1829

Year(s)	Baptisms (1)	Baptisms (2)	Baptisms (3)	Burials (1)	Burials (2)	Burials (3)
1700	21.30	24.20	2.90	21.27	25.64	4.37
1710	22.68	25.86	3.18	21.34	26.16	4.82
1720	22.78	26.33	3.55	21.47	25.62	4.15
1730	22.08	25.36	3.28	21.83	26.05	4.22
1740	21.73	24.58	2.85	22.26	27.89	5.63
1750	21.40	23.91	2.51	22.23	27.09	4.86
1760	22.66	25.22	2.56	22.82	26.98	4.16
1770	22.17	24.78	2.61	22.52	26.69	4.17
1780–9	22.75	25.30	2.55	22.57	26.20	3.63
1790–9	22.83	25.31	2.48	22.97	26.61	3.64
1800–9	23.64	26.08	2.44	23.68	27.13	3.45
1810–9	24.12	26.56	2.44	24.35	27.76	3.41
1820–9	24.26	26.89	2.63	25.17	29.02	3.85

Year(s)	Marriages (1)	Marriages (2)	Marriages (3)
1755–9	21.91	24.70	2.79
1760–9	21.70	25.06	3.36
1770–9	22.37	26.03	3.66
1780–9	22.85	26.54	3.69
1790–9	23.20	27.07	3.87
1800–9	23.49	27.32	3.83
1810–9	23.22	27.04	3.82
1820–9	23.19	27.10	3.91

(1) Ratio of totals for England without Monmouth and London to aggregative sample totals.
(2) Ratio of totals for England without Monmouth to aggregative sample totals.
(3) (2) minus (1).

Source: National totals may be found in table A7.1. See also tables 3.4 and 3.5 and text.

Incorporating London into national estimates

One way of estimating the relative importance of London's contribution to the national totals of events is shown in table 3.6. The table shows the ratios already listed in table 3.4, which express the relationship between the aggregative sample totals and the totals for England without Monmouth less London. Alongside these ratios are shown the comparable ratios when the national totals include London. As might be expected, including London in the national totals produces a much greater increase in the ratios for burials than for baptisms. In the year 1740, for example, London contributed over 20 per cent to the national total of burials but fewer than 12 per cent to the total of baptisms. This was an exceptional year, but throughout the early part of the century the disproportion was marked. Later it became less striking and towards the end of the century marriages replaced burials as the series contributing the largest relative share to the national totals.

Table 3.6 provides clear evidence that the proportional share of London in the national total was much higher early in the eighteenth century than towards its end, but the ratios can only be calculated for every tenth year before the 1780s and it is not possible to tell whether the rather violent fluctuations in the burial figures for London arise because of random fluctuations from year to year, or because there were major short-term fluctuations in the number of deaths.

Fortunately, there is a comparative abundance of evidence about changes in the number of baptisms and burials in London. The bills of mortality collected and published by the Worshipful Company of Parish Clerks provide much valuable information about both burials and baptisms from the sixteenth century onwards. Though the accuracy of the bills has often been impugned, they are helpful in deciding what allowance to make for London in constructing inflation ratios to calculate national totals of events. Moreover, some sources of inaccuracy in the bills can be corrected and we turn first to a discussion of the steps taken to improve upon the published totals from the bills in converting them into estimates of baptism and burial totals. Four correction factors were employed to this end.

First, the bills of mortality and the parish register totals do not agree in the years for which a comparison can easily be made. In 1811 Rickman published the two sets of totals for the bills of mortality area for each year for which he had secured parish register returns in 1801.[16] In general the parish register totals were the higher of the two although it is noteworthy that in the first half of the eighteenth century the burial totals in the bills of mortality were the higher. In the 1710s and 1720s the totals drawn from the bills were as much as 7 per cent the higher. The first step in amending decadal totals drawn from the bills, therefore, was to multiply them by a factor intended to represent the differences observable in Rickman's table. The factor for each decade was taken as the mean of the ratios obtaining for the two years at either end of the decade. Thus the factor for baptisms in the 1720s was 1.074 since the ratios between the figures in the two series was 1.069 in 1720 and 1.079 in 1730. The ratio in 1700 was assumed to hold good for earlier decades.

The second correction factor employed was designed to overcome the problem that London by the end of the eighteenth century covered a larger area than that encompassed by the bills of mortality. Here once more Rickman's tabulations are useful, since in 1801 he published parish register totals for the whole of metropolitan London and in 1811 comparable totals for the bills of mortality area. The difference lies

16. *1811 Census*, Parish registers, p. 200.

in the inclusion in the former of the parishes of St Luke's, Chelsea; Kensington; St Mary-le-Bone; Paddington; and St Pancras. At the beginning of the century there was very little difference between the totals for the two areas. Burials in the 1700s, for example, were only 1.7 per cent higher in the metropolitan area than in the bills of mortality area, but by the 1770s the difference had risen to 11.4 per cent. As with the correction for coverage between the bills and the registers, the ratio for any one decade was taken to be the mean of the ratios for individual years at either end of the decade. Since the bills area constituted almost the whole of the city in 1700, adjustments made for this reason were tapered off to zero shortly before 1700 (the 1690s were the earliest decade to carry an adjustment for this reason).

Two further factors remain. One arises from an uncertainty about whether the parishes of St Ann's, Limehouse, and St Botolph's, Aldersgate, were included in Rickman's 1801 returns. The rehearsal of parishes included in the returns for London given towards the end of the census volume suggests that they were, but they are not listed in the main body of the returns in the Middlesex section of the volume.[17] We have chosen to assume that they were actually missing and have inflated the bills of mortality returns accordingly in the ratio of the population of the two parishes in 1801 to the total population within the bills, or by 1.2 per cent, since it may be presumed that the true figure in the parish registers would have been higher by that amount. The other, and final, correction is an inflation made to permit direct comparison with the totals drawn from the 404 parishes. The latter were corrected for under-registration and we have assumed that the degree of correction found necessary in the aggregative sample is also appropriate for the series in table 3.7.

As an example of the effect of the application of the four correction factors we may observe that in the baptism series the total in the bills of mortality for the 1710s stands at 168,566, and this is multiplied successively by four factors, 1.046, 1.0125, 1.012, and 1.018, listed in the order of our discussion, to produce a revised total of 183,918. It is noteworthy that even after correction by the four factors the corrected burial totals are lower than the original in 1710–9 and 1720–9 because the coverage of the bills was substantially more complete than that of the parish registers. At this stage, however, we seek parish register totals of baptisms and burials rather than true totals of births and deaths.

For the 1780s and 1790s the totals were taken directly from the parish register returns since they cover each year after 1780, but the last two of the four factors just discussed apply to them as well as to the bills of mortality totals and our totals are therefore slightly larger than those of the 1801 parish register returns.

Table 3.7 shows the totals of events recorded in the bills of mortality for London from 1660 to 1800, and the parallel corrected totals of baptisms and burials. The decadal totals resulting from the successive adjustments made to the data drawn from the bills of mortality illustrate the unhealthiness of life in London. This is evident from the absolute surplus of burials over baptisms. It may also be seen in the ratios in the last two columns. The burial ratio is always much higher than that for baptisms, sometimes almost twice as high, an indication of how far London diverged from the rest of England. The true totals of births and deaths in London were greater than the totals recorded in the bills even after making the corrections just described, especially in the eighteenth century, but there is no doubt that the rate of natural increase was

17. *1801 Census*, Parish registers, pp. 443 and 445.

Table 3.7: Decadal totals of baptisms and burials taken from the London bills of mortality and corrected totals, 1660–1799

Period	Baptisms Original	Baptisms Corrected	Burials Original	Burials Corrected	Ratio of corrected totals to totals in aggregative sample series Baptisms	Burials
1660-9	101 729	115 339	242 371	262 538	2.06	4.97
1670-9	122 535	133 335	183 882	194 198	2.45	3.65
1680-9	141 926	155 660	216 419	228 127	2.74	3.91
1690-9	149 955	164 641	204 181	215 515	2.96	4.26
1700-9	155 947	164 474	203 582	205 265	2.85	4.22
1710-9	168 566	183 918	232 139	227 368	3.25	4.53
1720-9	182 392	205 037	266 741	263 332	3.39	4.26
1730-9	170 196	197 042	254 581	257 923	2.99	4.74
1740-9	145 260	172 952	255 139	271 610	2.70	4.85
1750-9	147 792	174 666	202 694	225 744	2.56	4.26
1760-9	159 603	186 943	224 777	254 384	2.56	4.19
1770-9	173 178	206 823	210 342	250 200	2.54	4.16
1780-9	211 160	213 698	233 147	236 420	2.47	3.50
1790-9	227 140	229 870	234 852	238 149	2.40	3.53

Sources: Original totals from the bills of mortality 1660–9 to 1770–9 were taken from Marshall, *Mortality in the metropolis*, pp 67, 70–81. The original burial totals for these decades are those that result after deducting stillborn children and abortives from the overall burial totals. The original totals for 1780–9 and 1790–9 were taken from *1801 Census*, Parish registers, p.448

strongly negative for most of the period, though not perhaps in the closing decades.[18]

The last two columns of table 3.7 show that the size of the addition to the basic inflation ratio of 22.82 necessary in respect of London's contribution to national totals of baptisms and burials varied considerably between the 1660s and the 1790s, rising to a peak in the 1720s in the case of baptisms and in the 1740s in the case of burials. In the main the change from decade to decade was fairly smooth apart from the anomalously high ratio for burials in the 1660s. The preceding century, however, presents greater problems. London's share of the national population rose very rapidly during this period, but the bills of mortality cover only the second half of it. Their use, moreover, is complicated by the fact that the area covered by the bills changed as London grew. And the change in the ratio of London's burial totals to the aggregative sample totals was much less regular because the major outbreaks of plague in London were so severe as to affect decadal totals significantly. In these circumstances the use of a single inflation ratio for a whole decade may be inadequate, and it is necessary to ensure that the timing of plague outbreaks is reflected in the monthly and annual totals of events. We may consider first the plague of 1665 to

18. The trend of events in London in the later years of the eighteenth century is especially difficult to establish with confidence. Public and nonconformist burial grounds developed earlier in London than elsewhere and some of them were large. Anglican coverage of baptisms was also affected by the number and size of the nonconformist congregations, many of which maintained separate baptism registers. A substantial fraction of the final inflation ratios applied to baptisms and burials to produce estimates of total births and deaths, which are described in chapter 5, may be notionally attributed to the necessity of offsetting poor Anglican registration coverage in London.

illustrate our approach to this last problem and then turn to the wider problems of the period before 1660.

The total of burials in 1665 given in the bills of mortality is 97,306, but this total is raised to 101,884 after making the corrections just described. In the decade as a whole the total number of burials was 262,538 (see table 3.7). In the other nine years of the decade, therefore, the corrected total of burials is 160,654, or 17,850 per year. This suggests that if the decade had been free of plague the total number of burials would have been 178,504 and that the basic inflation ratio for the decade should be 3.38, the total of burials in the aggregative sample being 52,785 for 1660–9. The ratio in the plague year, however, rises to 20.14. Some part of this is met, of course, by the basic inflation ratio, but a much higher 'spike' must be introduced into the series of ratios if the totals of the aggregative series are to be made to capture the plague outburst. We have treated each plague outbreak in a highly stylized manner introducing a single 'spike' into the series in the August of each plague year at a level to produce approximately the required totals of burials over the year as a whole. The values of the ratios at either end of each plague year are set at the levels reached by linear interpolation between the basic inflation ratios at 'benchmark' years (see table 3.11 below). This means that the plague peak must be set high enough above the trend line to produce the surplus deaths due to plague in the year in question. In 1665 the basic ratio is 3.38, the full ratio for the year is 20.14, and the August value was therefore set initially at the basic value plus twice the difference between the full and the basic ratios $(3.38 + 2(20.14 - 3.38) = 36.90)$, so that the area of the triangle of plague burials above the basic burial trend line would be approximately equal to the total of plague burials. This method does not produce sufficiently accurate results, however, because there were fewer summer than winter burials in most years in the aggregative series, including 1665, so that plague deaths are too few. The 'spike' ratio was therefore raised enough to offset seasonal influences. In the case of the 1665 plague this meant raising the August value of the ratio to 37.97.

When considering the totals of baptisms and burials in London before 1660, it is convenient to take the two series separately and to deal with the 1640s and 1650s after having considered the rest of the pre-1660 period. In table 3.8 original and corrected totals of baptisms from the bills of mortality are shown for three decades early in the seventeenth century, the earliest decades for which there is full coverage in the bills. The same corrections have been made to the original totals as were made to baptism totals in table 3.7, but in addition a correction intended to offset changes in the area covered by the bills. The original totals shown in table 3.8 cover the city, the Liberties, and the out parishes but exclude the group of distant parishes for which returns were published only from 1636 onwards.[19] To correct for this problem of coverage a series published by Sutherland was used. He provides a population index for London for every fifth year from 1565 to 1665 obtained by linear regression based on baptism frequencies. The index covers a period in which the bills expanded from an initial coverage of the city and Liberties alone to a middle period in which the out parishes were added and latterly to a final period when the distant parishes were covered as well.[20] There is substantial overlap between the early and middle, and the middle and later periods. Thus the earliest period runs from 1565 to 1625, the middle period from 1605 to 1665, and the final period from 1650 to 1665. We calculated the

19. See Sutherland, 'Mortality in London', pp. 290–1.
20. Sutherland, 'Mortality in London', table 6, p. 310.

ratio between the series of events in each pair of overlapping periods at the first year of the overlap and then decayed the ratio linearly to zero working backwards over a 50-year period. For example, the index total of expected baptisms for London when the distant parishes are first included in 1650 is 12,040, but only 10,170 when they are excluded in the figure for the same year given in the middle period series. The ratio between the two is 1.18387. Since the ratio is made to decline linearly to 1.0 in 1600, the ratio for 1635 may be calculated as 1.12871 and so on. The use of a tapering-off period of 50 years is arbitrary and may be a source of inaccuracy. The use of a longer period might have produced greater accuracy, but the final totals would not have been very greatly changed by any reasonable alternative assumptions.

Table 3.8: Decadal totals of baptisms taken from the London bills of mortality and corrected totals, 1610-39

Period	Original	Corrected	Ratio of corrected totals to totals in aggregative sample series
1610-9	73815	86405	1.50
1620-9	80579	97517	1.63
1630-9	96453	121121	1.98

Source: Original totals from Marshall, *Mortality in the metropolis*, p.67. For derivation of corrected totals see text.

The annual baptism series in the bills of mortality begins in 1604 and therefore no decadal totals can be calculated before the decade 1610-9. For the period before the 1610s, therefore, we have used the Sutherland population index to calculate approximate totals of baptisms and hence the relationship between totals of events in London and those in the aggregative sample parishes for certain benchmark years. For example, the annual number of London baptisms for the 1610s was 8,641 after correction (see table 3.8). The Sutherland index figure for 1615 is 7,454 or 7,865 after the correction for coverage described above, while the index figure for 1590 is 4,049, which rises to 4,854 after correction for coverage (the out parishes are excluded from the index figures before 1605). The prevailing level of baptisms in 1590 may therefore be taken to be $8,641 \times 4,854/7,865 = 5,333$, and the ratio between London totals and aggregative sample totals is easily calculated. In this instance it is 1.03. A similar exercise suggests a ratio figure of 0.67 for 1565.

The treatment of London burials is complicated by the periodic heavy incidence of plague. Plague deaths were recorded in many years but if we are guided by Sutherland's relative mortality index there were only seven years during the period when the bills of mortality afford information in which plague caused the number of deaths to rise to more than twice the level that might have been expected in the absence of plague. These were 1563, 1578, 1593, 1603, 1625, 1636, and 1665.[21] In order to accommodate these years individually into an inflation ratio series that incorporates London as well as the rest of England and is derived from a base provided by the aggregative sample series we have treated each in the manner already described for 1665. This involves calculating the base level of mortality at the time of each outbreak and superimposing upon it a sufficiently high peak of mortality in August to bring the total number of burials to the level required for the year as a whole. In table

21. Sutherland, 'Mortality in London', table 3, p. 300.

Table 3.9: Plague year burial totals taken from the London bills of mortality and corrected totals

Year	Original	Corrected
1563	20 732	23 412
1578	7 830	9 456
1593	17 893	23 236
1603	38 876	40 797
1625	54 265	65 143
1636	27 415	28 678
1665	97 306	101 884

Source: The original totals are those published in Sutherland, 'Mortality in London', table 3, p. 300. For derivation of corrected figures see text.

3.9 the original and revised totals of burials in the plague years are shown. As with baptisms, the revised total includes where appropriate a correction for the changing areal coverage of the bills.

The totals of burials in the decades in which major plague outbreaks occurred, excluding plague deaths, are shown in table 3.10. The method used in calculating non-plague burials was explained above for the 1660s. The same method was used for the 1620s and 1630s. Since there was no major outbreak of plague in the 1610s, it was possible to use the burial total for this decade as a base in calculating totals of non-plague burials in earlier decades. The Sutherland population index was employed for this purpose in the same way as for baptisms. The additional mortality occurring

Table 3.10: Decadal totals of burials in London in decades with major plague outbreaks, excluding plague outbreaks

Period	Original	Corrected	Burials other than Plague burials	Ratio of non-plague burials to totals in aggregative sample series
1560–9			33 366	1.00
1570–9			41 793	1.29
1590–9			60 715	1.46
1600–9			74 091	1.89
1610–9	77 390	85 584	85 584	1.82
1620–9	131 375	151 646	96 114	2.04
1630–9	111 474	131 618	115 781	2.26
1660–9	242 371	262 538	178 504	3.38

Note: There was no major plague outbreak in the 1610s but this decade is included in the table for the reason given in the text.

Source: Original totals from Marshall, *Mortality in the metropolis*, p. 67. Abortives and stillborn children were deducted from the overall burial total. In the years before 1629 for which a breakdown of cause of death is not available an estimate of the proportion of stillborn and abortive children was made. The original totals given are those that result after this adjustment. For derivation of other totals see text.

in plague years can then be introduced by the same method as that already described for 1665.

We turn finally to the Civil War and Commonwealth period. Bills of mortality exist for this period but after some experimentation they were ignored, so that the London ratios for this period in both series are obtained by interpolation between the 1635 and 1665 figures. The baptism returns became very defective in the 1640s and 1650s, apparently to an even greater extent than in the country as whole, and since there were no major plague visitations in this period interpolation presents no special problem in the burial series, where coverage probably remained much more complete. There may have been a general deterioration in the completeness of coverage of the bills after the Restoration when compared with the early part of the seventeenth century.[22] The attempt to make some correction for this belongs elsewhere, however.[23] At this stage we are concerned with baptisms and burials rather than births and deaths.

National inflation ratios

Having calculated how large an inflation factor was appropriate from time to time for London, we are now in a position to superimpose it upon the constant figure of 22.82 which was found to hold good for the ratio of the aggregative sample series to the totals of baptisms and burials in England excluding London. These composite national inflation ratios are shown in table 3.11. The ratio figures shown in the table are bench-mark points. Between any two adjacent points the level of the ratio used in any month for the inflation of a monthly total from the aggregative series was obtained by linear interpolation. Since the changes in the London ratios for baptisms took place smoothly over time only 13 points of inflection were necessary to preserve a good fit with the fuller set of ratio figures of tables 3.7 and 3.8. The earliest ratio for 1539 is an impressionistic estimate in both series.

There are many more inflection points in the burial than in the baptism series, partly because the London ratio for burials tended to fluctuate more irregularly than that for baptisms, and partly because of the wish to accommodate plague outbreaks individually rather than englobing them in decadal totals. In addition it seemed worthwhile to have regard to the very striking lack of conformity between burial trends in London and the rest of the country in the late 1720s and early 1730s. In general, years of heavy mortality outside London found some reflection within the capital, as in the late 1650s or the early 1740s, but the exceptionally high mortality experienced in some parts of England between 1727 and 1730 is barely visible in London. If the average number of burials per year in the 1720s is taken as 100, the burial totals for London between 1727 and 1730 are 104, 102, 109, and 98 respectively, while a comparable series for England without London is 111, 126, 140, and 110. To have constrained the pattern of burials in London to follow the trends found in the aggregative sample series would have exaggerated the height of the burials peak considerably and some additional inflection points were therefore added to prevent this happening.

In a lesser degree, of course, distortion will occur in other years because of a lack of parallelism between short-term trends in fertility and mortality in London and those

---

22. See Jones and Judges, 'London population'; Glass, introduction to *London inhabitants*, pp. xxxv–xxxviii; Glass, 'Demography of London'; Finlay, *Population of London*, esp. ch. 2.
23. See ch. 5 below.

Table 3.11: Inflation ratios used in converting totals of baptisms and burials in the aggregative sample series into national totals for England (less Monmouth)

Year and month	Baptisms (1)	(2)	Year and month	Burials (1)	(2)
1539.1	0.48	23.30	*1539.1*	0.70	23.52
1565.1	0.67	23.49	*1563.1*	0.97	23.79
1590.1	1.03	23.85	*1563.8*	12.84	35.66
1615.1	1.50	24.32	*1564.1*	0.99	23.81
1625.1	1.63	24.45	*1565.1*	1.00	23.82
1635.1	1.98	24.80	*1575.1*	1.29	24.11
1665.1	2.05	24.87	*1578.1*	1.32	24.14
1675.1	2.45	25.27	*1578.8*	4.68	27.50
1715.1	3.25	26.07	*1579.1*	1.32	24.14
1725.1	3.40	26.22	*1593.1*	1.44	24.26
1745.1	2.70	25.52	*1593.8*	10.44	33.26
1755.1	2.57	25.39	*1594.1*	1.45	24.27
1800.1	2.44	25.26	*1595.1*	1.46	24.28
			1603.1	1.80	24.62
			1603.8	17.54	40.36
			1604.1	1.85	24.67
			1605.1	1.89	24.71
			1615.1	1.82	24.64
			1625.1	2.04	24.86
			1625.8	22.05	44.87
			1626.1	2.06	24.88
			1635.1	2.26	25.08
			1636.1	2.30	25.12
			1636.8	9.20	32.02
			1637.1	2.34	25.16
			1665.1	3.38	26.20
			1665.8	37.97	60.79
			1666.1	3.41	26.23
			1685.1	3.95	26.77
			1695.1	4.30	27.12
			1705.1	4.35	27.17
			1715.1	4.85	27.67
			1726.1	4.85	27.67
			1726.6	6.03	28.85
			1727.6	4.29	27.11
			1728.6	3.69	26.51
			1729.6	3.55	26.37
			1730.6	4.07	26.89
			1731.6	4.15	26.97
			1732.1	5.24	28.06
			1745.1	4.90	27.72
			1755.1	4.25	27.07
			1775.1	4.20	27.02
			1785.1	3.55	26.37
			1800.1	3.45	26.27

(1) London.
(2) England: in each case the national figure represents the result of adding 22.82 to the London figure.
Note: 1539. 1 indicates January 1539; *1579.8* indicates August 1578, and so on.

found in other parts of England. Indeed, an extended investigation into any such lack of conformity would be likely to prove important and illuminating. Our concern at present, however, is primarily with longer term changes. For this purpose a more sophisticated method of incorporating London into national totals appears unnecessary.

In both the baptism and burial series the final inflation ratio refers to 1800. Thereafter the ratios are maintained at the 1800 level. We have already noted that apparent changes in the ratio for England without London are untrustworthy because Rickman's returns contained many events not under Anglican rites. The same is true of the overall national ratio. The problems to which this gives rise are dealt with at a later stage.[24]

There remains the question of a parallel set of inflation ratios for marriages. The bills of mortality do not unfortunately include marriage returns. Rickman collected annual marriage totals from 1754 onwards in 1801, and London's totals for this period expressed as a ratio to the aggregative sample series may be seen in table 3.6. Rickman's later exercise, summarized in the 1841 census, did not include any separate tabulation for London. Rough indications of the number of marriages in London may be obtained from Rickman's data, however, if the county totals for Middlesex are taken in substitute for London. County totals can be inferred in the same way as the national totals shown in table 3.4 (the total for Middlesex in 1800 obtained in this way is 8,484, which may be compared with the 1800 total of 9,545 for London taken from the 1801 census). The later Rickman returns permit totals of marriages for Middlesex to be calculated for three-year periods centring on 1570, 1600, 1630, 1670, 1700, and 1750. The 1750 figure is extremely low, barely more than a third of the 1800 total, itself a year in which relatively few marriages were celebrated. It presumably reflects the extraordinary impact of Fleet marriages upon the number of marriages celebrated in parish churches.[25] We have chosen to ignore this erratically low figure, but to interpolate instead between the 1700 figure and a figure drawn from the early years after Hardwicke's Act.

The inflation ratios used for marriages are set out in table 3.12. The ratios for 1670 and 1700 were obtained from Rickman's second parish register exercise, carried out in 1836, using the Middlesex totals as a substitute for London. They were derived after adjustment to offset the effect of under-registration correction in the aggregative sample series. Before 1670 it may be progressively more inaccurate to assume that Middlesex and London are broadly equivalent. We have resorted to an arbitrary expedient to provide ratios for earlier dates. On the assumption that relative changes in the marriage ratio will mirror those found in the baptism ratio, it is simple to calculate a figure for marriages at each date for which there is a baptism ratio. The earlier ratios in the marriage series were calculated in this manner using the ratio between the marriage and baptism inflation ratios that obtained in 1670. The two final ratios in the series, for 1765 and 1800, were derived from the London marriage totals published in the 1801 census and shown in table 3.13. The latter were corrected for coverage and under-registration in the way already described for baptisms and burials and they result in the ratios shown in the final column. These are slightly lower than those shown in table 3.6. The difference springs from the fact that the method of

24. See ch. 5 below.
25. See Steel, *National index of parish registers*, 1, pp. 292–320, and Brown, *Clandestine marriages in London*.

Table 3.12: Inflation ratios used in converting marriage totals in the aggregative sample series into national totals for England (less Monmouth)

Year and month	(1)	(2)
1539.1	0.60	23.42
1565.1	0.84	23.66
1590.1	1.29	24.11
1615.1	1.87	24.69
1625.1	2.04	24.86
1635.1	2.47	25.29
1665.1	2.56	25.38
1670.1	2.81	25.63
1700.1	3.75	26.57
1765.1	3.24	26.06
1800.1	3.83	27.03

(1) London.
(2) England: in each case the national figure represents the result of adding 22.82 to the London figure except for 1800 when 23.20 was added to the London figure (see table 3.5 and accompanying text).

Note: *1539.1* indicates January 1539.

calculation used in table 3.6 embodies the assumption that the proportion of parishes that failed to make a return in 1801 was the same in London as elsewhere in the country but in reality the proportion in London was unusually low and this depresses the ratio slightly. After 1800, on the other hand, the ratios in table 3.6 can be accepted as accurate and the 1800 figure in table 3.12 reflects this. The ratios in 1810–9 and 1820–9 are so similar to that of 1800–9 that the last was allowed to stand for the whole period after 1800. The very low ratio for the late 1750s in table 3.13 suggests that marriage registration in London may have taken a little time to reach its 'true' level after Hardwicke's Act. The year 1765 was therefore used as an inflection point and given a value that results in interpolated values in the later decades of the century close to those shown in table 3.13.

The use of the ratios shown in tables 3.11 and 3.12 enables national totals of baptisms, burials, and marriages to be constructed from the aggregative sample

Table 3.13: Totals of London marriages taken from the 1801 returns and corrected totals

Period	Original	Corrected	Ratios of corrected totals to Totals in aggregative sample
1755–9	25 641	26 079	2.73
1760–9	69 583	70 560	3.24
1770–9	76 316	77 310	3.47
1780–9	84 048	84 888	3.58
1790–9	95 580	96 922	3.78

Source: Original totals from *1801 Census*, Parish registers, p. 448.
For derivation of corrected totals see text.

Table 3.14: Sample and national totals of Anglican baptisms, burials, and marriages

Period	Baptisms (1)	(2)	(3)	Burials (1)	(2)	(3)	Marriages (1)	(2)	(3)
1550–9	45 130	1 056 797	23.42	41 970	995 096	23.71	13 262	312 543	23.57
1660–9	56 951	1 374 336	24.13	39 229	1 000 454	25.50	15 560	380 574	24.46
1650–9	55 316	1 374 399	24.85	54 315	1 403 222	25.83	17 746	449 787	25.35
1700–9	57 670	1 491 708	25.87	48 681	1 325 357	27.23	14 820	393 120	26.53
1750–9	68 131	1 730 541	25.40	53 033	1 439 738	27.15	18 541	484 628	26.14
1800–9	102 565	2 590 677	25.26	67 857	1 782 638	26.27	28 051	758 115	27.03
1820–9	131 510	3 321 857	25.26	79 084	2 077 662	26.27	36 197	978 403	27.03

(1) Totals of events in the 404 parishes after population reweighting.
(2) National totals obtained by using the inflation ratios of tables 3.11 and 3.12.
(3) Ratio of 2 to 1.

totals. A selection of the decadal national totals in the three series taken at 50-year intervals is shown in table 3.14. Fuller details of the national totals of baptisms, burials, and marriages may be found in appendix 4.

From the monthly totals of events found in the registers of 404 parishes, national totals of Anglican baptisms, burials, and marriages have been derived by the successive steps described in this chapter and the two preceding it. But these are still totals of ecclesiastical registration, and not estimates of vital events. In the next two chapters, therefore, we turn to the consideration of ways of moving from the former to the latter.

4

From baptisms and burials to births and deaths

I Corrections for nonconformity and late baptism

The conversion of national totals of ecclesiastical registration into totals of vital events involves major changes in the case of baptisms and burials, though not in the case of marriages. Even in the later eighteenth century, when nonconformist baptisms were common and nonconformist or non-denominational burial grounds had ceased to be a rarity, Anglican marriages were still an overwhelming majority of all marriages. Most of this chapter and the next will therefore be taken up with the successive steps taken in converting baptism totals into totals of births and burial totals into totals of deaths.

The necessary changes to baptism and burial totals fall into three groups: those required to take into account the increase of nonconformity; those designed to offset the effects of the lengthening of the interval between birth and baptism; and those intended to cover any remaining gap between the totals produced by earlier changes and the 'true' totals of births and deaths. In all three cases the deficiencies are small or entirely absent at an early date but become increasingly important until by the end of the eighteenth century there is a massive difference between the baptisms and burials recorded in Anglican registers and the totals of births and deaths in England. The first two issues will be discussed in this chapter, leaving to chapter 5 the question of the size of the final inflation ratio.

The growth of nonconformity

Nonconforming congregations increased in number from the late seventeenth century onwards and individual nonconformists became less and less ready to be baptized or buried by an Anglican minister. Since the two tendencies compounded one another their joint effect on Anglican registration coverage increased rapidly during the eighteenth century, and especially in a period beginning in the 1780s and extending to the end of the Napoleonic wars. The estimation of the impact of nonconformity on Anglican coverage presents many problems. Nonconformists comprised a wide diversity of groups, ranging from Roman Catholics to Unitarians, whose attitudes towards record keeping and to Anglican rites varied greatly. The scale of nonconformist activity is difficult to measure directly.[1] Its effect on Anglican baptism, burial, and marriage coverage was unequal. Moreover, because the impact of nonconformity eludes direct measurement, it is difficult to distinguish between its impact and the effect of the presence of an element in the population escaping all ecclesiastical registration, especially the urban slumdwellers, a rapidly growing fraction of the population in the later eighteenth and early nineteenth centuries.

---

1. The problem is discussed by Krause, 'Changes in English fertility and mortality'.

Given the uncertainties surrounding the measurement of the impact of nonconformity, any set of correction factors devised to offset its growing importance must necessarily be arbitrary. There is reason to suppose that the shape of the trend of rising nonconformist abstention from Anglican registration, shown in the following tables, is correct in its general outline but a stronger claim would be hard to substantiate.

The estimates of the totals of nonconformist baptisms shown in table 4.1 are based on the frequency of baptisms recorded in a sample of the nonconformist registers now held in the Public Record Office. A random sample of these registers was drawn for two decades, 1780–9 and 1820–9. The annual frequency of events per register showed no marked or consistent tendency to rise or fall between these two periods and the data were accordingly pooled (similar data from a smaller number of nonconformist registers earlier in the eighteenth century also showed comparable annual means).[2] Trimeans of the decadal frequencies of baptisms and burials per register were calculated, producing a figure of 88.5 for baptisms and 65.5 for burials.[3] Assuming that these are reliable estimates, the national total of nonconformist baptisms and burials can be estimated if the number of chapel registers in use from time to time can be established.

The number of registers in use in each decade has been estimated from the lists of deposited registers. Each register was assumed to have been in continuous use from the earliest listed date. In some cases, of course, chapels went out of existence or ceased to record events but it is probable that this affected only a small proportion of the chapels that responded to the request for deposit made in 1840 and 1857, since their continued existence in the mid century creates a presumption of moderately sustained registration.[4] Often a set of returned registers contains few if any breaks. Nevertheless the assumption is over-simple both in supposing continuous registration for places making a register deposit and in ignoring the registers of chapels that went out of existence. Moreover, some chapels possessed registers not authenticated by the Commissioners and other chapels that maintained registers may have failed to deposit them. The results should be regarded as subject to a margin of error on this score. In table 4.1 the cumulative total of registers at the end of each decade in the Public Record Office lists is shown, together with the midpoint total for each decade.[5] The midpoint total multiplied by the appropriate trimean for each series produces an estimated decadal total of nonconformist baptisms and burials for each decade from 1690–9 to 1820–9.

There was a pronounced jump in the total of baptism and burial registers beginning in the 1780s compared with earlier decades, followed by further growth in the following decades. The steepness of the increase is somewhat masked in the estimated totals of events since these are derived from the cumulative totals of registers, but the build up in the number of nonconformist baptisms and burials recorded went ahead rapidly between the 1770s and 1810s. During this period the number of baptisms

2. There were 28 registers in the 1780s' sample for baptisms and 32 in the 1820s' sample. The corresponding totals of burial registers were 22 and 26. A much smaller sample of 7 registers with coverage of the decade 1740–9 yielded similar annual totals of events.
3. Trimeans were used to reduce the effect of the extreme values in the spread of frequency totals. For the definition of a trimean see appendix 5, fn. 10.
4. The deposit of registers was made under the provisions of 3 and 4 Victoria c.92, and 21 Victoria c.25. See Welch, 'Nonconformist registers'.
5. The nonconformist registers are to be found in the P.R.O. class lists RG4, RG5, and RG8. Most are also listed in *Lists of non-parochial registers and records*.

Table 4.1: Nonconformist baptism and burial registration (England less Monmouth)

	Nonconformist baptism registers			
	Total starting	Cumulative total	Decadal mid-point total	Estimated total of baptisms registered[1]
Before *1690*	27	27		
1690-9	27	54	41	3 629
1700-9	38	92	73	6 461
1710-9	30	122	107	9 470
1720-9	27	149	136	12 036
1730-9	40	189	169	14 957
1740-9	59	248	219	19 382
1750-9	76	324	286	25 311
1760-9	90	414	369	32 657
1770-9	126	540	477	42 215
1780-9	309	849	695	61 508
1790-9	314	1 163	1 006	89 031
1800-9	370	1 533	1 348	119 298
1810-9	513	2 046	1 790	158 415
1820-9	462	2 508	2 277	201 515
1830-9	275	2 783	2 646	234 171

	Nonconformist burial registers			
	Total starting	Cumulative total	Decadal mid-point total	Estimated total of burials registered[2]
Before *1690*	9	9		
1690-9	5	14	12	786
1700-9	12	26	20	1 310
1710-9	3	29	28	1 834
1720-9	2	31	30	1 965
1730-9	7	38	35	2 293
1740-9	11	49	44	2 882
1750-9	18	67	58	3 799
1760-9	18	85	76	4 978
1770-9	34	119	102	6 681
1780-9	155	274	197	12 904
1790-9	86	360	317	20 764
1800-9	82	442	401	26 266
1810-9	123	565	504	33 012
1820-9	175	740	653	42 772
1830-9	93	833	787	51 549

Notes: [1] Decadal midpoint total multiplied by 88.5
[2] Decadal midpoint total multiplied by 65.5.

Source: See text

almost quadrupled from 42,215 to 158,415 while the number of burials quintupled from 6,681 to 33,012.

In table 4.2 the totals of nonconformist baptisms and burials given in table 4.1 are expressed as percentages of the national totals of Anglican baptisms and burials presented in chapter 3. The Anglican totals were first modified to remove the effect of the under-registration corrections described in chapter 1 since it is to be presumed that the same problem troubled nonconformist registration. Reducing Anglican totals in this way indirectly secures a comparable correction for nonconformist registration, though by the eighteenth century the correction factor had become very modest.[6] The rise in the percentage of nonconformist baptisms and burials is, of course, less dramatic than the rise in the cumulative total of nonconformist registers shown in table 4.1 because the number of Anglican baptisms and burials, but especially the former, was rising rapidly in the later decades of the eighteenth century. Nevertheless the percentage of nonconformist baptisms, which did not exceed 2 per cent before the 1770s, shot up to more than 6 per cent in the course of the next half century. The exceptionally rapid growth in the period 1780–1810 stands out clearly.

Table 4.2:   English nonconformist baptism and burial totals expressed as percentages of Anglican national totals

	Baptisms	Burials
1690-9	0.26	0.06
1700-9	0.44	0.10
1710-9	0.65	0.13
1720-9	0.78	0.12
1730-9	0.88	0.15
1740-9	1.19	0.19
1750-9	1.47	0.27
1760-9	1.77	0.30
1770-9	2.05	0.41
1780-9	2.81	0.73
1790-9	3.68	1.17
1800-9	4.63	1.48
1810-9	5.45	1.84
1820-9	6.07	2.06
1830-9	6.68	2.08

Note: The nonconformist totals do not include Quaker births and deaths.

Source: For national totals see table A4.2. They were modified as described in the test; for nonconformist totals see table 4.1.

The Quakers

The nonconformist totals and percentages of tables 4.1 and 4.2 include all sects other than the Quakers. Quaker registration, based on the monthly and quarterly meetings, was very different from that of other nonconformists, and the pattern of Quaker growth and decline was also quite distinct. We have preferred, therefore, to deal separately with the Quakers, taking advantage of the existence of estimates of their total numbers at various dates and making separate estimates of the contribution of Quaker births and deaths to national totals based on a knowledge of the approximate size of the Quaker community. Isichei quotes with approval Rowntree's nineteenth-

6. See tables 1.5 and A4.1 for details of the scale of the correction factor at different periods.

century study of the vicissitudes of the Quaker community. Rowntree estimated that in 1680 when Quaker strength was probably at its height there were 60,000 Quakers in England and Wales but that by 1800 the figure had fallen to 19,800. By 1860, when the first official Quaker returns were made, the number had shrunk to 13,859.[7] If the population of England and Wales is taken as 5.2 million in 1680,[8] the Quakers at that date constituted 1.15 per cent of the population, while by 1800 they were no more than 0.21 per cent. The percentage of Quakers at any time between 1680 and 1800 has been obtained on the arbitrary assumption that their percentage share declined linearly between the two dates. After 1800 further linear decline was assumed from the 1800 level of 0.21 per cent to the 1861 level of 0.07 per cent. Quaker registration began very early. A number of registers contain entries from the 1640s or even earlier[9] and it therefore seems appropriate to begin any correction made in respect of Quaker registration in 1640. Linear growth in the percentage of Quakers was assumed from a zero starting point in 1640 to 1.15 per cent in 1680. Any correction for the presence of Quakers insisting on using their own rites must be applied to marriages as well as baptisms and burials: the Quakers maintained marriage registers from the beginning.

Since Quaker registers record births and deaths rather than baptisms and burials, it would be inappropriate simply to add an estimate of their percentage contribution to national totals to those given in table 4.2 for other nonconformists. The question of making an allowance for the effect of an increasing delay between birth and baptism does not arise in the case of the Quakers. Any inflation of national totals of baptisms and burials made for this reason should therefore not apply to Quakers' births and deaths. But it is convenient to consolidate all adjustments for nonconformity at this stage. To avoid Quaker events being inappropriately inflated because of the delay between birth and baptism when this adjustment is made at a later stage, their percentage contribution at this stage was reduced in such a way that the subsequent inflation for delayed baptism simply restored their appropriate percentage share. For example, as will be seen below, in the 1720s the national baptism total needs to be inflated by about 5 per cent because of the effects of delayed baptism. Quaker births in the 1720s were 0.85 per cent of the national total in that decade (by interpolation between the 1680 and 1810 percentages). The figure of 0.85 per cent was therefore reduced to 0.81 per cent before being added to the figure of 0.78 per cent for other nonconformists (see table 4.2) to produce a total nonconformist figure of 1.59 per cent for the 1720s. The inflation ratios used in increasing Anglican national totals in the three series in respect of all types of nonconformity are shown in table 4.3. The precise inflation ratio applied to individual monthly totals in each series was obtained by linear interpolation between the bench-mark levels shown in the table.

It will be noted that the percentage share of Quaker events in the national totals, based on Rowntree's estimates, have been taken as true five years after the dates to

7. Isichei, *Victorian Quakers*, p. 112.

8. Later in this book we present new estimates of English population totals, but here we use the estimate made by Glass in the course of discussing the reliability of Gregory King's estimate for 1695. Glass, 'Two papers on Gregory King', pp. 203–4.

9. In the index to Quaker registers of monthly and quarterly meetings printed in *Lists of non-parochial registers and records* there are 18 registers in which the first entry is said to date from before 1640, but many of the listed starting dates are inaccurate and it is only in the 1640s that the rapid build up of Quaker registers begins. Fifty-nine registers begin in the 1640s and the cumulative total increases rapidly thereafter until by 1680 a total of 229 had been started. A further nine were begun in the 1690s but there were very few new registers in most subsequent decades. See also Steel, *National index of parish registers*, II, pp. 625–34.

Table 4.3: Inflation ratios applied to national Anglican baptism, burial, and marriage totals in respect of the growth of nonconformity

	Baptisms	Burials	Marriages
1640	1.0000	1.0000	1.0000
1685	1.0111	1.0116	1.0116
1695	1.0129	1.0113	
1705	1.0140	1.0109	
1715	1.0154	1.0105	
1725	1.0159	1.0095	
1735	1.0161	1.0090	
1745	1.0184	1.0086	
1755	1.0204	1.0086	
1765	1.0227	1.0081	
1775	1.0248	1.0085	
1785	1.0316	1.0109	
1795	1.0396	1.0145	
1805	1.0483	1.0169	1.0021
1815	1.0563	1.0203	
1825	1.0623	1.0222	
1835	1.0682	1.0222	1.0014

Source: See text.

which they refer (1685 rather than 1680 and 1805 rather than 1800). This simplifies their amalgamation with the estimates for other nonconformists which refer to whole decades and may therefore be supposed, again for simplicity's sake, to apply to the mid year of each decade. It will also be noted that the estimated percentage share of Quaker events in the national total was adjusted to reflect the fact that an inflation is being made to a total that excludes Quakers. Thus if Quakers were 1.15 per cent of the whole population in 1685 they were 1.16 per cent (1.15/98.85 × 100) of the population excluding the Quakers. Hence the marriage inflation ratio in 1685 in table 4.3 is 1.0116. Finally, we have assumed that the Quaker percentages for England and Wales also hold good for England only.

Some corroborative evidence of the trend in the general growth of nonconformity may be found in the returns of dissenters' places of worship made to the Registrar-General.[10] The returns were made in response to a circular letter sent to the registrar of every bishop and archdeacon, to the clerks of the peace of each county, and to the town clerk of every city or town. Each respondent was asked to make a return of certificates issued to nonconformist congregations licensing them to meet and worship. Some certificates had been lost before the return was requested so that coverage is not complete and some nil returns were made, though often with an explanation that the returns had been made elsewhere so that a nil return was proper. Overall the returns probably give a moderately accurate picture of the scale and timing of nonconformist growth.

The returns were divided into two classes, permanent and temporary places of worship. The latter were often temporary indeed since they included places described as

10. Dissenters Places of Worship, *P.P.* 1852–3, LXXVIII.

forests, forges, gardens, granaries, marquees, cart sheds, stables, and yards. The former, though far less numerous, were much less likely to prove ephemeral. They comprised chapels, churches, edifices, meeting houses, and so on. Table 4.4 shows the growth in the cumulative totals of permanent places of worship and repeats the cumulative totals

Table 4.4:   The growth of nonconformity (England less Monmouth)

	Cumulative totals	
	Baptism registers	Permanent places of worship
Before *1690*	27	143
1690-9	54	175
1700-9	92	216
1710-9	122	237
1720-9	149	264
1730-9	189	285
1740-9	248	309
1750-9	324	363
1760-9	414	434
1770-9	540	575
1780-9	849	853
1790-9	1 163	1 619
1800-9	1 533	2 728
1810-9	2 046	4 990
1820-9	2 508	7 638
1830-9	2 783	10 274

Note : The data for permanent places of worship relate to decades ending a year later than those for baptism registers (e.g. 1691–1700 rather than 1690–9).

Sources: For baptism registers see table 4.1; for permanent places of worship, Dissenters Places of Worship, *P.P.* 1852-3, LXXVIII, pp. 160-1.

of baptism registers given in table 4.1. Until the 1780s there is a steady tendency for the cumulative total of baptism registers to grow more quickly than that for licensed places of worship until in the 1780s the numbers in the two columns agree closely. It appears that the proportion of chapels maintaining an independent register of baptisms grew steadily during the period, though the effect may be partly spurious if the earliest registers of some chapelries had been lost by 1840, causing them to appear to begin to keep a register later than was in fact the case. Nor should it be forgotten that Quaker registers were excluded from table 4.1. Had they been included the agreement between the two series in table 4.4 would have been much closer in the early decades, since the return of permanent places of worship included Quaker meeting houses. Note, for example, that in the 1690s the data of tables 4.2 and 4.3 suggest that non-Quaker baptisms were about 20 per cent of the nonconformist total while table 4.4 shows that non-Quaker nonconformist baptism registers numbered some 30 per cent of the total of all nonconformist permanent places of worship, demonstrating a moderately similar proportion in each case. After the 1780s licensed places of worship increased far more rapidly than did the total of chapels keeping a baptism register. This may be due in part to the very rapid growth of Methodism in the late eighteenth and early nineteenth centuries. Methodists often continued to use the

Anglican church for baptism and burial even though meeting separately for worship.[11]

The inflation ratios of table 4.3 enable Anglican totals to be increased to produce national totals of baptisms and burials recorded in ecclesiastical registers of all types, whether kept by the established church or by rival churches and sects. Both Anglican and nonconformist registration, however, became increasingly incomplete because of changes in baptism custom. As long as baptism followed soon after birth the problems arising under this head are slight. But when parents habitually delayed baptism for many weeks ecclesiastical registration tended to become less satisfactory as a demographic record. The effect of changing custom can, however, be estimated and allowance made for it.

The effects of delayed baptism

If children had been baptized at or soon after birth with provision that a sickly child might be baptized at home when necessary, no problem would arise from the fact that English registers normally record baptism rather than birth.[12] A register of baptisms would contain the same number of events as a register of births, and the date of a baptism would always be very close to the date of birth in cases where the two did not coincide. In some sixteenth-century parishes practice closely followed this ideal, but in later centuries the two drifted further and further apart until by the later eighteenth century there was a median interval of about a month between birth and baptism though with wide variation from parish to parish.[13] When a child died young its death often occurred before baptism, and even in parishes where home baptism was widely practised such baptisms were often not entered in the register unless the child lived long enough to be received into the church by public ceremony.[14] Any count of baptisms therefore falls further and further short of measuring the number of births.[15] Where the burial of unbaptized children is not entered in the burial register, the problem of delay in baptism may occasion a shortfall between deaths and recorded burials as well as between births and recorded baptisms.

11. Interesting evidence of the extent of nonconformist, and especially Methodist resort to the Anglican church for baptism and burial may be found in *Returns of the clergy, 1831*, P.R.O., H.O.71. The return from Southampton, All Saints within Barr for example, remarks that 'The Baptists *hardly ever* and the Methodists *never* bury apart from the Established Church: many also of the Independents and Wesleyan Methodists have their children baptised in the Church': that from Castle Donnington, Leicestershire notes that 'Although there is a numerous body of Dissenters in this parish yet not any one sect keeps any register here. The Baptists register at Nottingham. The Methodists and other sects (Quakers excepted) register chiefly in the parish register here': while at Yarm, Yorkshire, N.R., 'the Roman Catholics bury and marry in the established Church'.

12. In the sixteenth century the Church of England tried to ensure that baptism took place soon after birth. The Prayer Books of 1549 and 1552 enjoined that 'The pastors and curates shall oft admonish the peple that they defer not the Baptisme of Infants any longer than the Sunday, or other Holy day next after the child be borne, unless upon a great and reasonable cause declared to the Curate, and by him approved. And they shall also warn them, that without great cause, and necessity, they baptize not children at home in their houses'. Gibson, *Codex iuris*, p. 446. See also Steel, *National index of parish registers*, I, pp. 41–54.

13. Berry and Schofield, 'Age at baptism'.

14. See Wrigley, 'Births and baptisms', p. 283, fn.9.

15. It is possible, of course, for there to be a long median interval from birth to baptism, and yet for births to be fully recorded, provided that parents were able to anticipate the danger of the early death of their new-born child and ensure that he or she was baptized, while taking a more relaxed attitude and delaying baptism in the case of a healthy child.

There is some evidence that this was indeed the case. In Bedworth, Warwickshire, private baptisms took

The proportion of births that may be lost to a parochial registration system because of the changed timing of baptism is considerable. If the infant mortality rate were 200 per 1,000 live births and one half of all infant deaths occurred in the first month of life, 1 live birth in 10 might be lost to the baptism register if the delay between birth and baptism were one month. The number of registered baptisms would have to be inflated in the ratio 10:9 to offset the effect of delayed baptism. If none of the children who died unbaptized appeared in the burial register, burial totals would also have to be revised to offset the consequent shortfall between deaths and recorded burials.

A method of correction

Table 4.5 shows the correction factors used in inflating totals of baptisms and burials to counter this cause of shortfall between events recorded in parish registers and totals of births and deaths. The technique used in estimating the appropriate factor and the evidence on which its calculation is based has been set out in detail elsewhere,[16] but a brief recapitulation of the method may not be out of place.

Table 4.5:   Inflation factors used to offset the effect of the increasing delay between birth and baptism

	Baptisms	Burials
1550	1.000	
1575	1.020	
1625	1.034	
1675	1.041	1.000
1725	1.051	1.020
1775	1.074	1.045
1825	1.090	1.070

Notes: The ratios given for individual years are based on estimates that refer to the half century of which they are the mid-points. Thus the baptism ratio of 1.020 for 1575 is based on evidence for the half century 1550–99, and so on. Ratio values for years between those given in the table were obtained by linear interpolation. For example, the ratio for 1600 is 1.027 ((1.020 + 1.034)/2 = 1.027). A ratio of 1.090 was assumed to apply uniformly to baptisms after 1825, and a ratio of 1.070 to burials after the same date. Since baptism appears to have taken place very soon after birth in the earliest decades of registration no inflation of baptisms was made before 1550.

It should be noted that the figure added to the total of burials for each year was derived from the *baptism* series since the number of burials unrecorded because of delayed baptism depended on the number of *births* in the year rather than the number of deaths. Thus the number of burials in 1775 was increased by 4.5 per cent on the number of *baptisms* in that year.

Source: Wrigley, 'Births and baptisms', pp. 309–10.

place on a substantial scale in the mid eighteenth century. A total of 96 were registered between 1738 and 1768. Amongst those who were subsequently in observation long enough to be used for the calculation of an infant mortality rate, the rate was 434 per 1,000, compared with an overall rate of just under 200 per 1,000 (this rate was arrived at after the inclusion of children dying unbaptized whose burial was recorded).

Again, in Hillmorton, Warwickshire, in the period 1750–1812, 33 per cent of all infants dying in the first year of life were baptized on the day of their birth and 75 per cent within the first week, compared with 9 and 61 per cent respectively in the case of infants who survived their first year.

We owe this evidence to the kindness of Dr M. Martin in making available to us the results of his recent research.

16. Wrigley, 'Births and baptisms'.

Some years ago Bourgeois-Pichat described a method for estimating levels of endogenous and exogenous infant mortality that could be used wherever infant deaths were tabulated by age at death within the first year of life.[17] The method can be used even though there may be no information about cause of death. It depends upon an empirically demonstrable feature of the distribution of infant deaths by age. If the cumulative total of infant deaths is plotted on a graph in which the axis representing elapsed days since birth has been subjected to an appropriate logarithmic transformation, the points representing the successive monthly totals will be found to lie on or very close to a straight line in the manner shown in the illustrative example in figure 4.1. All deaths above the age of one month may be taken to be exogenously caused (especially where a population lacked modern medical knowledge). Deaths within the first month occur both from exogenous causes and endogenous causes. By projecting the line in the graph leftwards from the point representing mortality at one month to cut the vertical axis, a division between deaths due to endogenous causes (a–b in figure 4.1) and those due to exogenous causes (b–c in figure 4.1) can be made. The

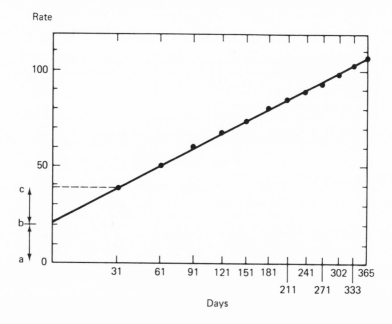

Figure 4.1: Endogenous and exogenous infant mortality. Rural counties of England 1905 (infant deaths per 1000 live births)

Source: 68th Annual Report, pp. cxxx–cxxxi.

technique assumes, of course, that the exogenous mortality curve under one month forms an extension of the line describing its path above one month. It is a property of the Bourgeois-Pichat method that if, say, a quarter of all deaths under one month were not registered, but registration at other ages were complete, the whole of the missing deaths would be concentrated within endogenous deaths, leaving exogenous deaths

17. Bourgeois-Pichat, 'La mesure de la mortalité infantile'.

unaffected because endogenous mortality calculated in this manner is a residual (in figure 4.1 the whole graph would move downwards compressing a–b but leaving b–c unchanged).

It follows that if, say, there were a sharp apparent fall in endogenous infant mortality measured in this way at a time when the exogenous rate did not alter, and when there was independent evidence that the overall level of infant mortality had not changed, the apparent fall in endogenous mortality would be both evidence of registration failure and a measure of its extent. It must imply a deficiency in the registration of deaths and this may in turn be linked to a parallel deficiency in birth registration. The use of the Bourgeois-Pichat technique for sub-dividing infant mortality into two component elements is, therefore, potentially valuable as a measure of under-registration provided that the conditions obtain on which its applicability depends.

In sixteenth- and seventeenth-century England the birth/baptism shortfall can be measured directly. This is feasible because there appears to have been no death/burial shortfall. When an infant was buried the event was recorded in the register whether or not it had been baptized. Infant burials for which there was no preceding baptism can therefore be identified by nominal record linkage either in general reconstitution studies or in *ad hoc* studies.[18] The evidence of 4 reconstitution studies and of 16 special studies is consistent in suggesting that the scale of the birth/baptism shortfall was initially modest but that it rose slowly during the seventeenth century as the customary age at christening changed. The studies also show that the endogenous element within infant mortality was high both absolutely and as a fraction of total infant mortality. Comparison with French data strongly supports the view that burial registration must have been virtually complete during this period.

About 1700 the estimation of the shortfall becomes less straightforward and less precise because the burial of unbaptized children increasingly went unrecorded so that recourse to the burial register no longer provides satisfactory evidence of the birth/baptism shortfall. A form of estimation that depends upon the logic of Bourgeois-Pichat's analytic techniques can, however, be used. In the balance of the parish register period exogenous infant mortality rates derived from parish registers changed little while the total rate based on the same source fell substantially, and the apparent endogenous rate therefore declined very sharply. If it were safe to assume that the true endogenous rate, like the exogenous, had remained at the same level it would be a simple matter to measure the increasing birth/baptism shortfall, and also to make an appropriate adjustment to the total of burials. The problem is complicated by clear evidence that there was a genuine fall in the endogenous infant death rate between the early eighteenth and the mid nineteenth century, so that the apparent fall in the rate was not entirely spurious. Both for this reason and because of the relatively small number of parishes included in the sample of registers studied, the estimates of shortfall shown in table 4.5 are subject to some margin of error. Further work may allow more precise estimation in the future. Nonetheless, the trend of under-registration of this type is hardly in doubt, and it would be surprising if revised estimates changed the absolute figures substantially. The figures for the early nineteenth century are the least solidly based, but by that time there are other ways of

18. See Wrigley, 'Births and baptisms', pp. 285–7 and 290–3, for a description of the methods employed in the two types of study.

estimating the overall shortcomings in ecclesiastical registration, whether caused by baptism delay, nonconformity, or other influences.[19]

Combined results of correcting for nonconformity and delayed baptism

The combined effect of the corrections made for nonconformity and delayed baptism is substantial by the late eighteenth and early nineteenth centuries. In the case of baptisms the combined inflation ratio in 1775 is 1.1006 and in 1825 1.1579. These ratios are obtained, of course, by multiplying together the ratios for the two dates in tables 4.3 and 4.5. It should be noted that the correction ratios for burials made to take account of the effect of delay in baptism are applied to the *baptism* totals and the *burial* totals increased accordingly. Where baptisms exceed burials by a large margin this leads to a more pronounced increase in burial totals than might be expected at first sight. In 1775, for example, the product of the burial ratios in tables 4.3 and 4.5 is 1.0539, but the increase in the total of burials which results from their use is 1.0724, while in 1825 the comparable ratios are 1.0938 and 1.1390. The overall result of the changes in baptisms and burials brought about by correcting for nonconformity and late baptism, therefore, is almost as marked for burial as for baptism totals. The fact that the burial correction ratio for late baptism must be applied to totals of *baptisms* also means that whereas the percentage inflation of baptism totals changes steadily and slowly as the inflation ratio for late baptism alters, the percentage inflation of burials for the same reason fluctuates considerably from year to year round the rising trend because of changes in the relative number of baptisms and burials. For example, in a year in which the burial inflation ratio was 1.050 and the number of baptisms was 50 per cent larger than the number of burials, the number of burials would be increased by 7.5 per cent, but if in the following year the same inflation ratio were used, and the number of baptisms were only 10 per cent higher than the number of burials, the total of burials would be increased by only 5.5 per cent.

Table 4.6 sets out the national totals of baptisms and burials both before correction for nonconformity and delayed baptisms and after these corrections have been made. Totals are given only for a few decades since corrections for nonconformity and late baptism do not complete the process of converting data drawn from ecclesiastical registers into totals of vital events, and these are therefore only intermediate totals.[20] The table shows, however, that there was a much steeper rise in the totals of events in both series in the late eighteenth and early nineteenth centuries than would be suspected from examination of the uncorrected Anglican totals. In the case of burials, indeed, the latter barely changed between the 1780s and the 1810s, whereas the corrected totals grow significantly, if modestly, over the same period. The relative impact of the inflations made to the two series varied considerably over time. The increase in the original Anglican totals produced by the operations described in this chapter was approximately 3½ per cent in the case of baptisms in 1640 when burials were still unchanged. The comparable percentage inflations for baptisms and burials at later

19. Wrigley, 'Births and baptisms' contains a fuller consideration of the issues briefly summarized here. See chapter 5 below for a description of the estimation of overall registration shortfall.

20. It should be unnecessary to reiterate the warning that corrections of the type made in this chapter are at best approximations and at worst may be significantly inaccurate. It is absurd, for example, to suppose that there was no under-registration because of nonconformity before 1640. Many Roman Catholics avoided the use of Anglican rites in Elizabethan and early Stuart England. They were not sufficiently numerous to have made a large difference to the totals of events counted in Anglican registers, but they serve as a reminder of the existence of minor causes of under-registration not covered by the correction factors used.

Table 4.6: National decadal baptism and burial totals (uncorrected and corrected)

	Baptisms			Burials		
	(1)	(2)	(3)	(1)	(2)	(3)
1550–9	1 056 797	1 060 685	1.0037	995 096	995 096	1.0000
1600–9	1 374 336	1 413 371	1.0284	1 000 454	1 000 454	1.0000
1650–9	1 374 399	1 432 100	1.0420	1 403 222	1 408 729	1.0039
1700–9	1 491 708	1 583 653	1.0616	1 325 357	1 357 857	1.0245
1750–9	1 730 541	1 880 254	1.0865	1 439 738	1 513 777	1.0514
1770–9	2 061 324	2 269 774	1.1011	1 618 405	1 727 725	1.0675
1780–9	2 191 060	2 435 282	1.1115	1 784 609	1 917 327	1.0744
1790–9	2 424 025	2 722 732	1.1232	1 775 887	1 939 907	1.0924
1800–9	2 590 677	2 942 940	1.1360	1 782 638	1 976 000	1.1085
1810–9	2 893 591	3 321 235	1.1478	1 799 545	2 034 456	1.1305
1820–9	3 321 857	3 845 005	1.1575	2 077 662	2 368 116	1.1398

(1) Uncorrected national totals of Anglican events
(2) National totals of baptisms and burials after inclusion of nonconformists and correction for delayed baptism
(3) Ratio of (2) to (1)

Index figures of proportionate growth to base 1 000

	(1)	(2)		(1)	(2)	
1600–9/1550–9	1 300	1 333		1 005	1 005	
1650–9/1600–9	1 000	1 013		1 403	1 408	
1700–9/1650–9	1 085	1 106		945	964	
1750–9/1700–9	1 160	1 187		1 086	1 115	
1770–9/1750–9	1 191	1 207		1 124	1 141	
1780–9/1770–9	1 063	1 073		1 103	1 110	
1790–9/1780–9	1 106	1 118		995	1 012	
1800–9/1790–9	1 069	1 081		1 004	1 019	
1810–9/1800–9	1 117	1 129		1 009	1 030	
1820–9/1810–9	1 148	1 158		1 155	1 164	
1820–9/1550–9	3 143	3 625		2 088	2 380	

Source: For uncorrected totals of Anglican events see table A4.1; for the inflation ratios that produce the corrected totals see tables 4.3 and 4.5 and accompanying text.

dates were: 1680s, 5½ and 1; 1700s, 6 and 2½; 1750s 8½ and 5; 1800s 13½ and 11; 1820s, 16 and 14. There was therefore a marked tendency for the relative changes in the two series to become more similar. And indeed the absolute difference in the percentage inflations was much smaller in the early nineteenth century than it had been in the late seventeenth.

The final ratios (1820–9/1550–9) in the bottom half of table 4.6 show that the cumulative effect of the corrections for nonconformity and delayed baptism is very considerable in both series. Nevertheless the corrected totals of baptisms and burials are still far short of the totals of births and deaths that occurred in England, especially in the last half century before civil registration began.[21] Fortunately, for much of this period it is possible to make independent estimates of decadal totals of births and deaths, and so to establish the scale of the residual shortfall between the corrected totals of baptisms and burials and totals of births and deaths. This in turn enables an estimate to be made of the appropriate final correction ratios applicable to baptisms and burials in earlier periods. The calculation of 'true' totals of births and deaths and of final correction ratios forms the subject matter of the next chapter.

21. While much emphasis is properly laid upon the frequency with which Anglican registers failed to include the births, deaths, and marriages occurring in the local parish, it should not be overlooked that aggregative tabulations will also include some overcounting. When a person died and was buried in a 'foreign' parish it was quite common for his burial to be recorded in his home parish as well as in the parish where he died. The same also happened from time to time with baptisms. Or again, where a child was baptized at home and subsequently received into the church, both ceremonies may appear in the register and are easily counted as separate events. Burial registers in the sixteenth and seventeenth centuries often contain entries concerning the burial of abortive or still-born children and these may be included inadvertently in the count of burial totals (on the scale of such entries in a particular parish, see Schofield, 'Perinatal mortality'). And identical entries are sometimes found within the same register, reflecting perhaps the difficulty of achieving perfect accuracy when copying up the register from a notebook. This appears to have been a common habit. It would be likely to happen wherever the register book was not kept in the church. Rickman remarked that because of dampness in church buildings, 'The register book is at present usually kept in custody of the officiating minister, at his own house, if resident on the benefice, otherwise in that of the parish clerk'. *1811 Census*, Preliminary Observations, p. xviii. It is very difficult to quantify the various causes of over-recording and overcounting, but they will have helped to offset equally haphazard causes of under-registration.

5

From baptisms and burials to births and deaths

II Final inflation ratios: offsetting other causes of non-registration

In order to complete the transition from totals of baptisms and burials in a sample of 404 Anglican parishes to estimates of national totals of births and deaths, the scale of residual escape from any form of ecclesiastical registration has to be estimated. There is good reason to suppose that the problem was at its most acute in the late eighteenth and early nineteenth centuries. Krause has argued persuasively that in this period absenteeism and pluralism amongst the Anglican clergy combined with rapid urban growth to cause very serious inadequacies in Anglican registration, in addition to those caused by defection to nonconformist churches.[1] It is therefore a happy coincidence that for much of this period the means exist to calculate the decadal totals of births and deaths with sufficient accuracy to allow the shortcomings of ecclesiastical registration to be followed decade by decade. Before the late eighteenth century the problem of residual escape from ecclesiastical registration becomes progressively less serious until in Tudor and Stuart times it was probably too slight to be a source of serious concern. Some estimate of its extent proves to be feasible, however, from a consideration of the behaviour of the final inflation ratio intended to cover residual loss during the period in which it can be directly measured.

The underlying principle involved in the estimation of the numbers of births and deaths in the early nineteenth century is very simple, though the process of estimation becomes complicated when allowance is made for uncertainties in the data, and when the propriety of some of the assumptions involved in the simplest form of the method of estimation is considered. It is convenient to begin, however, by considering the simplest possible case before turning to the factors that complicate its application.

The use of age data from censuses

In a closed population the sole influence governing the size of any age group at a census point will be the size of the cohort comprising the age group at the last census point and the level of mortality prevailing during the period between the censuses, except in the case of those age groups born during the interval between the two censuses. Thus, if the censuses are taken every 10 years and if the number of people aged 30–4 at the earlier census was 100,000, the number aged 40–4 at the later census will be $100,000 \times {}_5L_{40}/{}_5L_{30}$. If the level of mortality is known, the number in any age group who will survive to the next census point (or to any other point in time) can be predicted. Equally, the numbers who were living in a particular age group at some

1. Krause, 'Changes in English fertility and mortality', and 'The changing adequacy of English registration'.

earlier period can be calculated from the number of those surviving (by multiplying the latter by $_5L_{30}/_5L_{40}$). And further, if the age structure of the population is known at two successive censuses, the probabilities of surviving between any two paired age groups (for example 20–4 to 30–4) can be calculated, and from these in turn the full range of data contained in life tables.[2] But if the mortality characteristics of a population and its age structure are known, the number of births occurring between censuses can also be estimated. Suppose, for example, that the mortality characteristics of a population are known and conform to those of model North level 7 female of the Coale and Demeny regional model life tables,[3] and that the number of those aged 0–9 in the population is 100,000. The ratio of survivors 0–9 to the birth cohort for this mortality regime is known $(_{10}L_0/10l_0)$. It is 0.70532. The number of births associated with the surviving population and occurring in the preceding 10 years will be 100,000/0.70532 = 141780. If, finally, the number of births occurring between two censuses is known, the number of deaths can be calculated. It will be the number of births less the increment of population between the censuses $(B - (P_{t+1} - P_t))$.

The English population in the early nineteenth century was not a closed population, nor did each census provide detailed age data. Any attempt to estimate the number of births and deaths in the manner described, therefore, is fraught with problems. It is possible, however, to obtain estimates of births and deaths in this way that appear to narrow down the range of plausible totals considerably, and so to permit the history of fertility and mortality change over the first four decades of the century to be sketched out with tolerable precision.

Adjusting age data in the 1821 and 1841 censuses

The 1841 census was the first to contain a breakdown of the population into five-year age groups in the manner that has now become conventional. A very small proportion of the population was returned as age unknown, and there is clear evidence of mis-statement of age, yet the data are sufficiently good to allow an age-based exercise to be carried out. We have therefore used the 1841 census as the starting point. Only one earlier census provides age information, that of 1821. In the 1821 census there are totals for each five-year age group up to the age of 20 but above 20 only 10-year divisions are given, and for a substantial fraction of the population no ages were returned. Nevertheless valuable information can be obtained from comparing the paired age groups in the two censuses that sprang from the same birth cohorts (for example, 0–4 and 20–4 in 1821 and 1841 respectively, or 30–9 and 50–9, and so on).

Before making these comparisons, however, it is first necessary to deal with some preliminary points, and to make some adjustments to the census age group totals to offset the absence or distortion of age information.

It is convenient to work almost exclusively with the female population. The early censuses did not cover that part of the male population in the army or navy, though estimates of the numbers in the armed forces were attempted. In 1801 and 1811 the country was at war and large numbers of men failed to appear in the census returns for this reason. Later the proportion of the male population excluded from the census for this reason declined, but since there was no such disturbing influence on female totals, it is best to concentrate upon them. The fact that the English population was not a

2. See, for example, *Methods of using census statistics.*
3. Coale and Demeny, *Regional model life tables.*

closed population points to the same conclusion. Net external migration in the first 40 years of the nineteenth century was not on as large a scale as in the later decades of the century. For much of the period it was probably very slight (net movements within the British Isles probably left England with a positive balance to set against any net negative balance between England and the rest of the world), but whatever net emigration occurred was predominantly male. This consideration also points, therefore, to concentrating upon the female population. We shall proceed initially as if the English female population were closed, but will return later to the question of the scale of net migration.

Table 5.1 sets out the age data for the female population of England in 1821 and 1841. The totals for 1821 are those given in the census but inflated to include all those of unknown age. The inflation was carried out on the assumption that failure to state age was proportionately distributed throughout the whole range of ages. Thus in 1821

Table 5.1: Age structure of the female population of England in 1821 and 1841

1821		1841	
0–4	829 579	0–4	988 163
5–9	728 065	5–9	888 763
10–4	606 455	10–4	794 888
15–9	571 439	15–9	752 462
20–9	967 397	20–4	777 165
30–9	695 285	25–9	631 224
40–9	535 592	30–4	565 942
50–9	375 245	35–9	422 062
60–9	262 722	40–4	425 934
70–9	130 875	45–9	303 887
80–9	37 139	50–4	305 673
90–9	3 286	55–9	187 286
100 and over	124	60–4	213 750
		65–9	128 431
Total	5 743 203	70–4	111 312
		75–9	58 933
		80–4	35 298
		85–9	12 354
		90–4	3 548
		95–9	791
		100 and over	136
		Total	7 608 002

Note: The totals are those recorded for England less Monmouth. Those of age unknown (756 057, or 13.16 per cent, in 1821; 11 132, or 0.15 per cent, in 1841) were distributed in each case in proportion to those whose ages were recorded.

Sources: *1821 Census*, Enumeration abstract, p.429; *1841 Census*, Age abstract, pp. 368–9, 372–3.

no age was given for 13.16 per cent of the total population, and the recorded number in each age group was therefore increased in the ratio 100 : 86.84. In 1841 very few ages were missing. They amounted to only 0.15 per cent of the total and their distribution among the age groups can have only a marginal effect on any final age distribution. In 1821, on the other hànd, more than an eighth of the population was affected and alternative assumptions about the allocation of those of unknown age could clearly produce significantly different final age distributions.

Fortunately, omissions took the form of absence of age data for whole communities rather than groups within them, and it has sometimes been thought reasonable to assume that the age distribution of those omitted was not greatly different from those included, even though it is well known that most of the places failing to make an age return were large cities or parts of an industrial area. Only 394 returns out of a total of 14,374 were missing, or 2.7 per cent, but they included some very large towns. No return was made for Manchester, for example, with a female population of 56,496 (69,815 if Salford is included). Birmingham, Leeds, Bristol, Newcastle, Nottingham, and Brighton were all missing from the 1821 age returns, either completely or in large part. Much of London was affected, including St Andrew, Holborn; Kensington; St George in the East; St George, Hanover Square; St Clement Danes; Camberwell; and Lambeth. Many places in the Black Country failed to make age returns, including Wolverhampton, Sedgley, Walsall, Tipton, Bilston, and Dudley. The same was true of some parts of the industrial West Riding. Given that the missing age returns were predominantly from places whose age structure was likely to be very different from that of the country as a whole, it seemed worthwhile to attempt to devise a means of distributing those for whom no age return was made on some other assumption than that they conformed to the pattern shown elsewhere.

The 1821 census itself is not of great help since the great industrial centres were so seldom covered, but the age data of the 1841 census make possible a rough and ready solution. Age data were published for each hundred, and for a large number of 'principal towns'. It is therefore possible to specify the age distribution in 1841 for many of the places that made no return in 1821. Table 5.2 shows the 1841 age distribution reduced to a base of 100,000 for places whose female population in 1821 amounted to 673,998 out of the total female population of 756,057 for whom no age return was made, or almost 90 per cent of the total missing.[4] The comparable age distribution in 1841 for England, excluding the places covered in the first tabulation, is also shown. If it is assumed that the age structure of the large towns and industrial areas in 1821 differed from the rest of the country in the same way as in 1841, it is then possible to reconstruct their 1821 age structure.

For example, if the 673,998 individuals in the cities and industrial areas had had the same age distribution as those covered by the 1821 age census, there would have been 81,593 aged 30–9. Table 5.2 shows that in this age group in 1841 the ratio of the age structure of those living in these areas to the national age structure was 14,291:12,772. If the population aged 30–9 is inflated in this ratio, its number rises to 91,297. If all age groups are treated similarly the sum of the resultant age group totals

---

4. Of the 394 places for which no age return was made in 1821, it proved possible to obtain age structural data for 168 in 1841. For 111 of the 168 places there was a 'principal town' in 1841 which either consisted of the same unit as a place missed in 1821 or of several 1821 units. In all, 1841 age returns for 76 'principal towns' were used to cover the 111 places missed in 1821 age returns. But sometimes a part of a town was included in the 1821 age returns, though the rest of the town was not covered. In Nottingham, for example, there was no age return for the parish of St Mary in which the female population was 17,420 out of a city total of 21,666, though age returns were made for the rest of the city. In such cases we assumed that the age distribution for the city as a whole was also found in each part (which, though not true for individual instances, is likely to be true on balance over many cases), and so were able to use 1841 age data for the city in question, though weighting the age totals to conform to the relative size of the city or town missed in the 1821 age return. In this way a further 57 places were covered by 1841 age data from 22 'principal towns'.

Table 5.2: Age distribution of the 1841 female population (base 100 000).

	(1)	(2)
0–4	12440	13 062
5–9	10 630	11 844
10–4	9 646	10 572
15–9	9 933	9 878
20–4	11 233	10 044
25–9	9 202	8 145
30–4	8 340	7 289
35–9	5 951	5 483
40–4	6 031	5 532
45–9	3 959	4 005
50–4	3 988	4 031
55–9	2 226	2 506
60–4	2 601	2 851
65–9	1 411	1 739
70–4	1 272	1 501
75–9	606	806
80–4	360	483
85–9	124	170
90–4	39	48
95–9	8	11
100 and over	2	2
Total	100 002	100 002

Column headings

(1) Age distribution of the female population in 1841 living in places that made no age returns in the 1821 census. The 1821 population of these places was 673 998 out of a total of 756 057 in all places missed in the 1821 age census. The 1841 population of these places was 1 042 572. The 1841 population of each place was weighted according to its size in 1821 before calculating the distribution.

(2) Age distribution of the 1841 female population of England (less Monmouth) excluding those places in (1). The distribution covers a population of 6 554 298.

Sources: 1821 Census, Enumeration abstract, *1841 Census*, Age abstract and Enumeration abstract.

is 671,329. Each of the totals was further inflated in the ratio 673,998:671,329 to restore the grand total to its original level. The age group totals arrived at in this fashion were added to the totals of those whose ages were returned in the census, and the operation was completed by distributing the remainder of the population missed in the age returns (82,059 in number)[5] on the assumption that their age distribution followed the pattern found in the 1821 age returns. Since they were chiefly from

5. 756,057 less 673,998.

Table 5.3: Modified female age distribution in 1821

	(1)	(2)	(3)
	Original	Modified	Difference (2)–(1)
0–4	829 579	825 313	−4 266
5–9	728 065	719 610	−8 455
10–4	606 455	600 481	−5 974
15–9	571 439	572 080	641
20–9	967 397	981 918	14 521
30–9	695 285	705 349	10 064
40–9	535 592	538 842	3 250
50–9	375 245	373 235	−2 010
60–9	262 722	258 949	−3 773
70–9	130 875	128 070	−2 805
80–9	37 139	36 026	−1 113
90–9	3 286	3 207	−79
100 and over	124	123	−1
Total	5 743 203	5 743 203	

Source: For original totals see table 5.1; for derivation of modified totals see text.

parishes in rural areas this seems the most reasonable assumption to make. Table 5.3 shows the results of this exercise.

The places missed in the 1821 age census whose age data in 1841 went to make up the age distribution shown in table 5.2 did not all grow at the same pace between 1821 and 1841. In a few cases, such as Knaresborough (Yorks., W. R.), or Bishop's Castle (Shropshire), the female population fell between the two censuses. In others, such as Manchester or Cheltenham, it more than doubled. There is evidently a danger in these circumstances that, since the fastest growing places were a much larger fraction of the total in 1841 than in 1821, and were likely to have a more markedly untypical age distribution than places that grew at a gentler pace, the contrast between the age structure in the group of places as a whole and the rest of England would be greater in 1841 than it had been in 1821. This in turn would cause the modification of the 1821 age structure to be exaggerated. We therefore reweighted the 1841 populations of each place so that each made the same relative contribution to the age distribution as it would have done in 1821 (thus the population of a place that doubled in size between 1821 and 1841 was halved). The age distribution for 1821 shown in table 5.3 was calculated after reweighting in this way, but it is interesting to note that the age distribution after reweighting was virtually the same as that obtained from the unweighted data.

The strengthening of the young adult age groups at the cost of the old and young brought about by estimating the age structure of the population excluded from the age census must represent an age distribution closer to the truth than that obtained by assuming that those excluded had the same age structure as those included, and it represents a sufficiently substantial change to have some effect on the estimation of the number of births and deaths in the first 20 years of the century.

Where age returns were made in 1821 the census authorities of the day believed them to be largely complete. The notes appended to the county summaries of ages, in referring to age coverage in returns that provided age data, usually remark that only a 'small', 'very small', or 'remarkably small' proportion of the returns of ages were deficient, or redundant, or incorrect in the numbers of males and females.[6] There is, however, reason to doubt the accuracy of the age returns and further adjustments to the 1821 age structure will prove to be necessary.

Even at a cursory glance it is evident that the 1841 age data in table 5.1 are also inaccurate. In particular there was a pronounced tendency for the numbers in the first half of each decade of life to be overstated. There were more women returned as aged 20–4 than 15–9, more 40–4 than 35–9, more 50–4 than 45–9, and many more 60–4 than 55–9, a pattern highly unlikely to be found in a rapidly growing population if ages had been correctly returned.

The 1841 census was the first to be based upon householders' schedules delivered to every householder a few days before the census night. These were consolidated by the enumerators on to enumerators' schedules, and the enumerator in so doing was instructed to record the age of every person under 15 as it was stated but above that age to round down the stated age to the next lowest multiple of five years. For example, all those aged 45 to 49 were to be returned as age 45. It would appear either that individual householders tended to return some ages very inaccurately, or that the enumerators were prone to misunderstand their instructions. Since there is some evidence that only 10 years later in 1851 the vast majority of people made an accurate return of age as recorded in the pages of the enumerators' books, the latter possibility seems the more likely.[7] To some extent the problem can be circumvented by consolidating the 1841 data into 10-year age groups, a step that is in any case necessary before inflating the 1841 totals to compare with the 1821 totals for a particular cohort. The tendency of too many women to claim to be aged 20–4 proved a lasting problem in nineteenth-century censuses, producing considerable distortions even in censuses in which age was otherwise accurately returned. We shall return to this problem after first having tackled two further problems posed by the 1841 age data, both commonly found in censuses in all countries. The numbers in the highest age groups were inflated by a marked tendency among the elderly to exaggerate their age, and many children in the first years of life were missed and do not appear in the census return. Both defects, and particularly the first, require some attempt at amendment in order to minimize error in estimating the size of cohorts in an earlier census from the number of survivors at a later date.

We may consider first the problem of understatement of numbers in the age group 0–4. This presents the lesser difficulty of the two. The survivors of those aged 0–4 in the 1841 census were aged 10–4 in 1851, and similarly those aged 5–9 at the earlier census were aged 15–9 at the later. The prevailing mortality during the decade may be presumed to be approximately captured by Farr's third English life table, which was based on all deaths 1838–54. It is therefore a simple matter to calculate the size of the age groups 0–4 and 5–9 in 1841 from the numbers aged 10–4 and 15–9 ten years later ($_5L_0/_5L_{10}$ and $_5L_5/_5L_{15}$). The estimated total for the age group 5–9 agrees well with the enumerated total (884,314 and 888,763 respectively), but there is a substantial discrepancy for the 0–4 age group where the estimated total is 1,024,483 compared with the census figure of 988,163. It seems reasonable to assume that a better figure for the 0–4 age group in 1841 may be obtained by assuming that the ratio between the numbers 0–4 and 5–9 was that implied by the third life table

6. The Westmorland note states that 'ages as returned are rather redundant than deficient' since 51,374 ages were returned for 51,359 people (for women the totals were 25,846 and 25,848). *1821 Census*, Enumeration abstract, p. 354.
7. See Razzell, 'The evaluation of baptisms', and Wrigley, 'Baptism coverage'.

(1,024,483/884,314) and applying it to the enumerated total aged 5–9. This gives a total of 1,029,637 and therefore suggests that the enumerated total was 41,474 too low (4.2 per cent of the census total). The revised total will be used henceforth in place of the enumerated figure.

The correction of totals in the higher age groups can be tackled by a variant of the same method, using information about the size of the birth cohorts from which those in the higher age groups sprang. Before presenting the results of this operation, however, it may be helpful to digress briefly to describe the use made of the third English life table to provide a wider range of life table mortality data. The method employed is set out more fully in appendix 14.

The age structure of English mortality in the mid nineteenth century was broadly similar to that of model North in the Coale and Demeny set of regional model life tables, though having some distinctive features of its own. It seemed valuable to retain these features while moving between a variety of absolute mortality levels. If, for example, mortality were more severe early in the nineteenth century, the third life table would not be directly useful in converting the census totals of those aged 10–9 in 1821 into an estimate of births in the decade 1801–11, but a life table derived from it but embodying higher rates could be deployed with advantage. Expectation of life at birth in the third English life table is very similar to that of level 10 in the North set of Princeton tables. Accordingly, the third life table was defined as level 10 in our 'English' system and the mortality rates for other levels were derived from it using the ratios found in model North. Thus, for example, the ratio of $_5q_{10}$ at level 9 to $_5q_{10}$ at level 10 is identical in Coale and Demeny model North and in our new family of life tables. There is a difference of 2.5 years in expectation of life at birth between any two adjacent levels in the Princeton regional model life tables, and this feature is approximately retained in the family based on the third life table. Thus the level 10 female e_0 is 41.59, while level 9 is 39.10.

The q_xs of the third life table are therefore the source of the set of life tables used in this chapter. The third life table q_xs were, however, modified in one respect. When William Farr constructed the third life table he was aware of the distorting influences upon its construction arising from age-heaping in the census and from the under-reporting of births, and made allowance for them. But he does not appear to have been conscious of the tendency of the elderly to exaggerate their age in the census. Any tendency of relatives to exaggerate the age of elderly decedents was not sufficient to offset this. Later in the century as age reporting at advanced ages improved in the census, death rates in the national life tables rose since deaths were no longer referred to an exaggerated number at risk.[8] Death rates above age 55 were consistently higher in the 1891–1900 life table than in the third life table,[9] even though in the younger age groups there had been a substantial fall in death rates. We have therefore used the life table death rates (q_x) from the 1891–1900 life table in preference to those of the third life table, and it is this hybrid life table that forms level 10 in our 'English' set. We shall see later that the true rates were very probably still higher than those of the 1891–1900 table at advanced ages so that making this modification to the rates of the third life table errs on the conservative side.[10]

8. See *1901 Census*, General report, pp. 51–6 and the related tables of appendix A for a discussion of the inaccuracy of age reporting in the higher age groups in nineteenth-century censuses.
9. See table A14.4.
10. Details of the q_xs above age 55 of the third life table and of the 1891–1900 life table may be found in table A14.4.

Table 5.4 shows the corrected national totals of female baptisms for the cohorts aged 50–9 to 90–4 in 1841 (the totals are those resulting from the operations described in the last chapter: the sex ratio at birth was assumed to be 1.045). Alongside the birth cohorts in the table is shown the numbers of each cohort who would have survived to 1841 at level 9 of female mortality and the numbers

Table 5.4: Female birth cohorts, their survivors in 1841, and the 1841 census totals for females aged 50 and above

Cohort	Age in 1841	(1) Number of births	(2) Survivors in 1841 at level 9 mortality	(3) Census 1841	(4) Ratio (2)/(3)
1781–90	50–9	1 206 593	480 010	492 959	0.974
1771–80	60–9	1 117 244	323 896	342 181	0.947
1761–70	70–9	1 003 650	149 238	170 245	0.877
1751–60	80–9	921 433	33 452	47 652	0.702
1746–50	90–4	444 023	1 908	3 548	0.538

Sources: birth totals are national baptism totals after correction for nonconformity and baptism delay (see ch. 4). The sex ratio at birth was assumed to be 1.045. For level 9 mortality details see appendix 14. Column 3 totals from *1841 Census*. Age abstract, pp. 369, 373, with adjustment for those of unstated age (see note to table 5.1).

enumerated in each age group in the 1841 census. It will be seen that there is a steady and increasingly steep fall in the ratio between the survivors at level 9 mortality and the census totals. The table is not intended as evidence that level 9 mortality accurately describes the mortality history of the cohorts, but as providing strong reason to suppose that elderly people exaggerated their ages in 1841. If we assume that those in their 50s were returning their ages with tolerable accuracy, then it is reasonable to expect that the ratio between the census total 50–9 and the numbers in the later age groups would be similar to that between the total of survivors shown in column 2 for the age group 50–9 and the totals in the parallel age groups lower down the column. For example, the expected total for 60–9 would be $492,959 \times (323,896/480,010) = 332,634$, or 9,547 fewer than the census figure. To proceed in this way assumes, of course, that the same mortality history held for each cohort. This is unlikely to have been the case. Nor is it necessarily true that level 9 is the best choice as a summary of their joint experiences. And the corrected baptism totals fall short of the true birth totals. But it would require extraordinary assumptions about the mortality history of each cohort or about the relation of baptisms to birth totals for the revised totals not to represent a substantial improvement in accuracy over the census totals. It is highly probable that the changes made to the totals in the age groups above age 50 err on the side of modesty. If it were true either that mortality became progressively more severe in earlier cohorts, or that the corrected baptism totals were closer to the true totals of births in the earlier birth cohorts, the reduction in the numbers of the higher age groups in the 1841 census should have been more drastic.

If an expected total is calculated for each age group above 60 in the manner just described for the age group 60–9 the resulting total is 41,685 fewer than those enumerated in the 1841 census. These were allocated between the age groups aged 50 and over in such a way as to preserve the age structure suggested by the model life table; or, to describe the operation in more general terms, the whole female population above age 50 was redistributed to conform to the age distribution jointly determined by the relative sizes of the relevant birth cohorts and the L_xs of level 9. The original and revised census totals are shown in table 5.5. The operation increases the number of women in the 50–9 age group, leaves those aged 60–9 virtually unchanged, and decreases those above 70 more severely with increasing age.

Table 5.5: Census and revised 1841 totals for females aged 50 and above

	(1)	(2)	(3)
	Census	Revised	Difference (2)–(1)
50–9	492 959	513 278	20 319
60–9	342 181	346 345	4 164
70–9	170 245	159 582	−10 663
80–9	47 652	35 770	−11 882
90–9	4 339	2 464[1]	−1 875
100 and over	136	73[1]	−63
Total over 50	1 057 512	1 057 512	

Note: [1] The numbers in the age group 95–9 and 100 and over in table 5.1 were halved (compare 90–4 in table 5.4) before the redistribution of those identified as surplus in the age groups above 60

Sources: For census totals see source note to table 5.4. For derivation of revised totals see text.

The same method of correcting numbers in the older age groups can also be used to revise the census totals in 1821. The results are set out in table 5.6. The only difference between this exercise and the last is that a life table embodying slightly

Table 5.6: Modified and revised 1821 census totals for females aged 50 and above

	(1)	(2)	(3)
	Modified	Revised	Difference (2)–(1)
50–9	373 235	393 778	20 543
60–9	258 949	257 179	−1 770
70–9	128 070	118 947	−9 123
80–9	36 026	27 795	−8 231
90–9	3 207	1 845[1]	−1 362
100 and over	123	66[1]	−57
Total over 50	799 610	799 610	

Note: [1] The numbers in the modified age groups 90–9 and 100 and over were reduced in the same proportion as in the same age groups in 1841 before the redistribution of those identified as surplus in the age groups over 60.

Source: For modified census totals see table 5.3. For derivation of revised totals see text.

more severe mortality rates (level 8 in the family described in appendix 14) gave a better fit between the census population aged 50–9 and its related birth cohort and was used as the basis for the revision set out in table 5.6.[11]

The level of mortality between 1821 and 1841

We may now proceed to an initial comparison of the 1841 and 1821 censuses with a view to discovering the prevailing level of mortality over the two intervening decades.

The third English life table was constructed by William Farr using the deaths recorded during the first 17 years of civil registration in England, 1838–54. It is therefore natural to begin by discovering whether the third life table also captures the mortality experience of the slightly earlier period 1821–41. Table 5.7 sets out the results of inflating the age groups of the 1841 census to provide an estimate of the totals living in the same decennial cohorts 20 years earlier using level 10 of the new set of life tables (that is the modified third English life table). Thus, for example, those women aged 40–9 in 1841 were aged 20–9 in 1821 and it is a straightforward matter to calculate how many would have been living at the earlier date on the assumption that mortality in 1821–41 was at the same level as in 1838–54. The ratio to be used in inflating the 40–9 age group is $_{10}L_{20}$ $_{10}L_{40}$ or 1.2616.

The agreement between the estimated and census totals in 1821 is generally close with the exception of the age groups 0–9 and 20–9. The overall discrepancy totals 99,674, or 1.78 per cent of the census total. The estimated figure is the larger of the two, suggesting that mortality was less severe between 1821 and 1841 than the level of the modified third life table.

The large apparent discrepancies concerning the age groups 0–9 and 20–9 are misleading, for there are strong grounds for supposing that agreement between the estimated and the census totals is closer than would appear at first sight. Both were age groups affected by the misreporting of the age of young women which produced a 'bunching' in the 20s. This inconvenient practice incurred a rather pompous rebuke from George Graham who wrote in 1851 of women choosing 'foolishly, to represent themselves younger than they really were, at the scandalous risk of bringing the statements of the whole of their countrywomen into discredit' [12] The phenomenon was especially marked in 1841. In England and Wales at that census the ratio of females to males in the three age groups 10–9, 20–9 and 30–9 was 0.997, 1.124, and 1.052 respectively. Some rise with age is to be expected from the better life expectancy of women but the second ratio is clearly much higher than would be expected in any smooth progression to a higher ratio.

Fortunately it is feasible to make a further adjustment to the age structure of the 1841 female population in order to overcome the problem of misreporting of age in young adult life. If we assume that the total female population aged 10–39 was correctly reported in 1841 but that it was wrongly distributed between the age groups,

11. Neither the mortality level used in revising the 1841 age structure in table 5.5 nor that used to revise the 1821 age structure in table 5.6 agrees perfectly with the levels over the relevant time periods later found to obtain (see table 7.15). But it seemed desirable to avoid any circularity of argument such as might have been involved if we had revised the calculations just described in the light of our later findings.

12. *1851 Census*, Ages, civil condition, occupations, I, p. xxv. Graham's rebuke may have been misplaced since the distortion of numbers aged 20–9 seems to have been due to overstatement of age rather than to its understatement. See table 5.8 below.

Table 5.7: Comparison of estimated and enumerated decennial age group totals in 1821 (estimates derived from 1841 census data)

	(1) 1841 population	(2) 1821 population Estimated	(3) 1821 population Census modified	(4) Difference (2)–(3)
0–9	1 408 389	1 695 323	1 544 923	150 400
10–9	988 004	1 185 213	1 172 561	12 652
20–9	729 821	920 759	981 918	–61 159
30–9	513 278	689 240	705 349	–16 109
40–9	346 345	549 388	538 842	10 546
50–9	159 582	400 309	393 778	6 531
60–9	35 770	253 992	257 179	–3 187
Total		5 694 224	5 594 550	99 674

Sources: For column 1 totals see tables 5.1 and 5.5; for columns 3 totals see tables 5.3 and 5.6; for derivation of estimated totals see text.

we may improve the distribution while retaining the same overall total by considering the same cohort of women 20 years later in 1861 when they were aged 30–59 (1851 is an unsuitable census to use in this connexion since those aged 10–9 in 1841 were 20–9 in 1851 and this is the age group worst affected by misreporting). If the age groups 30–9 to 50–9 in 1861 are suitably inflated over a 20 year period at level 10 and the resulting totals are then multiplied by the ratio of the 1841 total 10–39 to the sum of the estimated totals, we obtain a revised age distribution for 10–9 to 30–9 in 1841 which is sure to be more accurate than enumerated totals even though the differential impact of net migration may still leave some distortion in the revised figures. The results of this exercise are shown in table 5.8.

Table 5.8: Revised female age structure for age groups 10-9 to 30-9 in 1841

	Enumerated	Revised
10–9	1 547 350	1 630 686
20–9	1 408 389	1 337 214
30–9	988 004	975 843
Total	3 943 743	3 943 743

Source: For enumerated totals see table 5.1; for derivation of revised totals see text.

If the revised age data for 1841 are then used to calculate age group totals in 1821 the comparable figures change as shown in table 5.9. The agreement is now very close with a discrepancy between the total enumerated and estimated populations of only 0.01 per cent. The positive difference between the estimated and census total in the youngest age group 0–9 is probably due at least in part to under-registration of very young children. The problem cannot be tackled using the method adopted for the parallel problem in 1841 because the 1831 census provides no age breakdown. In

Table 5.9: Comparison of estimated and enumerated decennial age group totals in 1821 (revised estimates derived from 1841 census data)

	(1)	(2)	(3)
	1821 population		
	Estimated	Census modified	Difference (1)–(2)
0–9	1 609 647	1 544 923	64 724
10–9	1 170 624	1 172 561	−1 937
20–9	920 759	981 918	−61 159
30–9	689 240	705 349	−16 109
40–9	549 388	538 842	10 546
50–9	400 309	393 778	6 531
60–9	253 992	257 179	−3 187
Total	5 593 959	5 594 550	−591

Note: Compare with table 5.7.

Source: For column 2 totals see tables 5.3 and 5.6; for derivation of estimated totals see text.

view of the fact that the numbers in the age group 20–9 in 1841 have already been corrected to remove the over-reporting in that age group in the census, and that similar calculations generally support the view that the third English life table captures the mortality experience of the period 1821–41 with fair accuracy, it seems reasonable to treat the estimated total of 1,609,647 aged 0–9 in 1821 as close to the truth and to amend the 1821 census figure to agree with it. The addition of 64,724 to the age group represents an increase of 4.2 per cent on the census total 0–9. Most of those missed were probably very small children. If the whole increase related to girls aged 0–4 their number would be raised 7.8 per cent by the addition.

A final adjustment may be made to the 1821 census age distribution to offset the tendency to 'bunch' in the age group 20–9. This is less marked than in 1841, perhaps because the overseers were able to exercise more discretion over reported age than the enumerators were able to do in 1841. Moreover, any redistribution between the age groups makes no difference to the overall balance between the estimated and enumerated totals, since while it involves some changes in age group totals it leaves their sum unaffected. It can be carried out exactly as was done for the parallel operation on the 1841 census totals, but in this case using the revised age group totals 30–9 to 50–9 in 1841 to monitor age distribution 10–9 to 30–9 in 1821.

The end product of the several adjustments made to the census age totals may be seen in tables 5.10 and 5.11. Table 5.10 recapitulates table 5.9 but incorporates the changes arising from the corrections made to the age groups 0–39 in 1821 described in the last two paragraphs. Table 5.11 rehearses the original enumerated age structure of the two censuses and their age structure in its final revised form.

Table 5.10: Comparison of estimated and enumerated decennial age group totals in 1821 (final estimates derived from 1841 census data)

	(1)	(2)	(3)
		1821 population	
	Estimated	Census revised	Difference (1)–(2)
0–9	1 609 647	1 609 647	0
10–9	1 170 624	1 203 968	−33 344
20–9	920 759	946 987	−26 228
30–9	689 240	708 873	−19 633
40–9	549 388	538 842	10 546
50–9	400 309	393 778	6 531
60–9	253 992	257 179	−3 187
Total	5 593 959	5 659 274	−65 315

Note: Compare with tables 5.7 and 5.9.

Source: For column 2 totals see tables 5.3 and 5.6 for ages 40–9 to 60–9; for younger age-groups see text. For derivation of estimated totals see text.

How good is the agreement between the estimated totals in 1821 and the revised census totals shown in table 5.10? How strongly, in other words, do they support the view that the level of English mortality in the period 1821–41 was the same as that of the third life table?

The estimated and census totals for age groups 0–69 differ by 1.15 per cent of the census total with the census figure the higher of the two. The simplest way to gain

Table 5.11: Original and revised age structure of the female population in 1821 and 1841

	1821			1841		
	(1) Revised	(2) Original	(3) Difference (1)-(2)	(1) Revised	(2) Original	(3) Difference (1)-(2)
0-9	1 609 647	1 557 644	52 003	1 918 400	1 876 926	41 474
10-9	1 203 968	1 177 894	26 074	1 630 686	1 547 350	83 336
20-9	946 987	967 397	-20 410	1 337 214	1 408 389	-71 775
30-9	708 873	695 285	13 588	975 843	988 004	-12 161
40-9	538 842	535 592	3 250	729 821	729 821	0
50-9	393 778	375 245	18 533	513 278	492 959	20 319
60-9	257 179	262 722	-5 543	346 345	342 181	4 164
70-9	118 947	130 875	-11 928	159 582	170 245	-10 663
80-9	27 795	37 139	-9 344	35 770	47 652	-11 882
90-9	1 845	3 286	-1 441	2 464	4 339	-1 875
100 and over	66	124	-58	73	136	-63
Total	5 807 927	5 743 203	64 724	7 649 476	7 608 002	41 474

Sources: See table 5.1 for original totals. See tables 5.6 and 5.10 for 1821 revised totals, and tables 5.5 and 5.8 for 1841 revised totals.

some perspective on the closeness of the agreement between the two totals is to repe
the exercise using a different mortality level. The modified third life table represen
an expectation of life at birth for women of 41.59 years. If a more severe mortali
régime is assumed to have characterized the period with expectation of life at birth
39.10 years (level 9 in the life tables set) the inflation exercise produces a populatic
total for the age groups 0–69 of 5,763,648, or 104,374 (1.84 per cent) more than th
revised census figure. Level 10 appears, therefore, to be somewhat closer than level
to describing the mortality of the period with accuracy. It should be noted that th
conclusion is not contingent upon the revisions made to the age structure of the cens
populations in 1821 and 1841. The use of any mortality level more severe than lev
10 in inflating the 1841 age groups would cause overestimation of the 182
population.

The matter is complicated, however, by two further issues, the extent of n
migration, and relative completeness of the two censuses. If there had been n
emigration of women 1821–41, this would produce a shortfall between estimated an
enumerated totals in 1821 even if the correct mortality level were chosen for th
exercise: some of those present in 1821 would still be alive in 1841 but living abroa
On the other hand if enumeration were less complete in 1821 than in 1841, ther
would be an apparent surplus of estimated over enumerated totals on the sam
assumptions.

We have already noted evidence that young children were missed in both censuses
The correction made in 1841 added 4.2 per cent to the original total of girls aged 0–
and 0.5 per cent to the original total of the female population. The comparabl
percentage increases made to the 1821 population were 7.8 and 1.1 per ce
respectively. The larger correction for girls aged 0–4 in the 1821 census suggests th
possibility that coverage was generally less complete in 1821. The inflation of 184
age group totals does not yield any data that can be used to test this directly. Inasmuc
as it shows no evidence of differential under-registration in different age groups (othe
than the age group 0–4), however, it lends no support to the likelihood of significar
shortfall in the census count. Nor has the 1821 census been suspected of gener
under-enumeration by those who have used it in the past. Further work may bring t
light deficiencies not so far revealed, but at present it seems reasonable to accept th
two censuses as tolerably accurate apart from the under-enumeration of smal
children.[13] We may therefore turn to the question of net migration.

Early-nineteenth-century net migration

Migration statistics are few and incomplete for the early part of the nineteent
century. Such as they are, they suggest that net migration was slight. The first perio
for which net migration statistics have been computed is the decade 1841–51. Th
calculation is based on a comparison of the natural increase occurring during th
decade (with allowance for under-registration) with the intercensal increase. It yield
a figure of net emigration for England and Wales of 5 per 10,000 mean population pe

13. Rickman himself was in no doubt about the accuracy of the 1821 census: 'the war having now ceased
there remains no reason to suspect the least deficiency in the Return of 1821. Indeed, the voluntary return o
the ages of persons, an enquiry of far more labour than that of the enumeration of houses, families an
persons, proves, by the extent of the answers, that the Population Act has been carried into effect in the yea
1821, not merely with willingness, but even with zeal, throughout the greatest part of the Kingdom'. *182*
Census, Preliminary observations, p. xxix.

annum.[14] The comparable rate for the United Kingdom was much higher, but the figure for England and Wales was kept low by the immigration of Irish and Scots which largely counterbalanced English movement to North America and Australasia. The net rate for England and Wales remained low throughout the later decades of the nineteenth century, fluctuating between a peak level of 23 per 10,000 in the 1880s and its lowest point in the following decade when at 2 per 10,000 there was almost no net movement.[15] The average level for the last six decades of the century was 11 per 10,000. But if the overall figure was low, the figure for women was lower still. In the late 1870s when for the first time there is a published breakdown for England and Wales of the sex ratio both for emigrants and immigrants, twice as many men as women were involved. Thereafter the ratio showed a gently falling tendency down to the First World War.[16] If the ratio in the 1840s was similar to that of the 1870s, the rate of net outmigration for the female population would have been about 3.5 per 10,000 per annum. If this rate had obtained over the period 1821 to 1841 it would imply a net outmigration of some 40,000–50,000 women. Adding these 'missing' women into the totals obtained by casting back from 1841 would virtually eliminate the surplus of the census over the estimated population in 1821 shown in table 5.10. It is an additional reason for supposing that level 10 does not understate mortality in this period. It is noteworthy that the negative figures in column 3 of table 5.10 arise in the age groups most likely to have been affected by net outmigration between 1821 and 1841. In the older age groups in which net migration was probably trivial the estimated totals tend to exceed those of the census.

Unfortunately, there is no conclusive evidence about the level of net migration before 1841. Data on gross outmigration to extra-European countries exist for both England and Wales and for the United Kingdom from 1825 onwards, and for the latter only from 1815, but the totals are known to be incomplete and they are necessarily a very uncertain guide to net flows.[17] Only two points seem clear from these migration series. The level of gross extra-European outmigration from England and Wales was only a small fraction of the United Kingdom total (125,950 out of 669,314 or 19 per cent in the period 1830–9, for example),[18] and the scale of movement from England and Wales was lower in the 1820s and 1830s than in the 1840s. Over the period 1825–39 recorded outmigration to extra-European countries totalled 149,703, or 9,980 per annum, whereas in the 1840s the comparable figures were 278,381 and 27,838.[19] Given the uncertain quality of the data and the absence of any information about immigration, it seems unwise to attempt to make any firm conclusions about net female migration, other than to suppose that there was probably some net outmigration and that it is unlikely to have exceeded a total of 50,000 women in the two decades. On balance, it seems reasonable to conclude that the third English life

14. Carrier and Jeffrey, *External migration*, p. 14, table 2.
15. Carrier and Jeffrey, *External migration*, p. 14, table 2.
16. Carrier and Jeffrey, *External migration*, p. 102, table 2.
17. Deane and Cole suggest that for England and Wales 'before 1851 the net balance of migration was probably inwards rather than outwards' in the nineteenth century; *British economic growth*, p. 289.
18. Carrier and Jeffrey, *External migration*, p. 90, table B(1) and p. 92, table C(1). These totals should be treated with the greatest reserve. Not only are they known to have been a very imperfect guide to total movements, but the summed totals for England and Wales, Scotland and Ireland do not equal those for the United Kingdom, being in some years less but in others greater.
19. Carrier and Jeffrey, *External migration*, p. 92, table C(1). It should be noted that the statistics refer to movements from ports in England and Wales and may include emigrants who were natives of other parts of the United Kingdom.

table holds good for 1821–41 no less than for 1838–54, and it is therefore possible to estimate birth totals in the 1820s and 1830s using the L_xs from this table.

Mortality levels in the early nineteenth century

The mortality level prevailing in the first 20 years of the nineteenth century can also be investigated by comparison of estimated and enumerated census totals, though the absence of age information in the censuses of 1801 and 1811 introduces greater uncertainty into the calculations. A knowledge of the age structure of the population in 1821, however, makes it possible to calculate age group totals at earlier points in time on any given assumption about the mortality level obtaining during the intervening period. The age groups between 10–9 and 80–9 in 1821, for example, can be used to estimate numbers in the age groups from 0–9 to 70–9 in 1811, while the age groups between 20–9 and 80–9 afford a basis for estimating the population from 0–9 to 60–9 in 1801. It is convenient to consider the two decades 1811–21 and 1801–11 separately so that any significant change in mortality between the two decades may be detected.

In carrying out these exercises we shall again make the assumption that there was neither significant net female migration, nor differential under-enumeration between the censuses. The extent to which these assumptions are justified will be examined later.

The enumerated female population in 1811 was 4,931,924. In the absence of age data any correction for the undercounting of very young girls must be arbitrary. It seems reasonable, however, to make the same proportionate adjustment to the population total as was made in 1821. This increases the total by 55,583 to 4,987,507. The latter total represents the 'target' to be hit. Using the 1821 age data and assuming that level 10 mortality continued during the 1810s produces a total some 59,841, or 1.20 per cent, below the adjusted census figure. The cumulative total for the age groups 0–79 is 4,902,468. On the assumption that the ratio of total population to those aged 0–79 was the same in 1811 as in 1821, the total female population in 1811 may be estimated at 4,927,666 if level 10 mortality had prevailed. The size of the shortfall on this mortality assumption suggests that mortality was probably more severe in the 1810s than in the 1820s and 1830s. Table 5.12 shows the results of an exercise assuming level 9 mortality.

The difference between the estimated and enumerated totals is considerably less than when using level 10 mortality (the estimated total is 12,479 larger than the adjusted census figure). The mortality experience of the decade is clearly better captured by a level 9 mortality schedule than by level 10.

The exercise can be repeated for 1801, and the results are set out in table 5.13. The enumerated total for 1801 was adjusted by the same method as that for 1811 in order to allow for under-registration of the very young. There is again close agreement between estimated and enumerated totals. The same result would, of course, have been produced if the 1811 age data shown in table 5.12 had been used. The estimated total is 29,053 or 0.67 per cent lower than the enumerated figure. If level 9 mortality were assumed to obtain over the period 1811–21 but level 8 over the previous decade ($e_0 = 36.61$) the resulting estimated population total for 1801 exceeds the enumerated figure by 34,973, or 0.80 per cent.

Evidence cast in this form, therefore, suggests that level 9 mortality prevailed during the first 20 years of the century, and level 10 in the second 20-year period,

Table 5.12: Estimates of decennial female cohort totals in 1811 from 1821 census data

	1821 population		1811 population by estimation
10–9	1 203 968	0–9	1 358 813
20–9	946 987	10–9	1 030 381
30–9	708 873	20–9	795 020
40–9	538 842	30–9	619 468
50–9	393 778	40–9	472 068
60–9	257 179	50–9	352 913
70–9	118 947	60–9	231 907
80–9	27 795	70–9	113 844
		Total	4 974 414

Adjustment of estimated total to allow for those aged 80 and over (1821 ratio), 4 974 414 × 5 807 927/5 778 221 = 4 999 986.

Adjusted enumerated total = 4 987 507

Note: The estimation was made using level 9 mortality.

Source: For 1821 population see table 5.11.

1821–41. In the first decade of the century, however, the issue is nicely balanced between level 9 and level 8. The inherent uncertainty of any exercise of this sort suggests that the additional refinement of working to an intermediate mortality level such as 8.5 would be unjustified, and the evidence of the alternative estimates suggests a slight balance in favour of concluding that level 9 best describes mortality between 1801 and 1811. The conclusion is strengthened if a more refined method of estimating the number of women aged 70 and over in 1801 is employed. The adjustment for this group in the female population detailed in table 5.13 was carried

Table 5.13: Estimates of decennial female cohort totals in 1801 from 1821 census data

	1821 population		1801 population by estimation
20–9	946 987	0–9	1 162 900
30–9	708 873	10–9	865 031
40–9	538 842	20–9	694 749
50–9	393 778	30–9	542 702
60–9	257 179	40–9	423 079
70–9	118 947	50–9	318 234
80–9	27 795	60–9	221 957
		Total	4 228 652

Adjustment to estimated total to allow for those aged 70 and over (1821 ratio), 4 228 652 × 5 807 927/5 659 274 = 4 339 724

Adjusted enumerated total = 4 368 777

Note: The estimation was made using level 9 mortality.

Source: For 1821 population see table 5.11.

out on the assumption that those aged 70 and over formed the same proportion of the *total* population in 1801 as in 1821. But this is a crude assumption since age structure is heavily influenced by fertility change. If fertility were exceptionally high between 1801 and 1821, for example, it would have the effect of reducing the proportion of the aged in 1821 compared with 1801, other things being equal. A better estimate may be obtained by noting the relationship between those aged 60–9 and those aged 70 and above in 1821 and using this ratio to calculate the number over 70 in 1801 from the number aged 60–9 in 1801. Such a ratio is, of course, unaffected by fertility changes between 1801 and 1821. Only a sharp change in fertility trends between 1741 and 1761 would be likely to cause the estimate to be misleading. Using this method, the estimated total in 1801 becomes 4,356,945 on level 9 mortality assumptions, 11,832 or 0.27 per cent below the adjusted census total. A similar treatment on level 8 mortality assumptions for the decade 1801–11 results in an estimated total population of 4,425,560, which is 56,783 or 1.30 per cent higher than the adjusted 1801 census figure.

The censuses of 1801, 1811, and 1821

Only two considerations might seriously affect the conclusion that level 9 mortality prevailed in the period 1801–21: the existence of significant female net migration or a marked change in the completeness of enumeration in the first three censuses. The scale of female net migration was probably so slight in these war decades that it can safely be assumed to play no significant part in modifying the estimates already obtained. The problem of the completeness of the first censuses requires further discussion.

Of the two earliest censuses, that of 1801 presents the greater problem, both on general and on particular grounds. As Taylor remarked in his review of the taking of the census in England, ' . . . caution and experience suggest that the first of a series of tables should be held under more suspicion of possible inaccuracy than those which follow' [20] He referred to other statistical series that illustrate the point before remarking of the 1801 census that 'The overseers might well have proved unequal even to the simple task of counting heads; but their conscientiousness and their intimate knowledge of their own localities seem to have carried them through'.[21] After noting the difficulty of measuring any inaccuracy, Taylor concluded that 'a retrospective glance from the surer ground of the second half of the century . . . would suggest the substantial accuracy of this first return. Caution might dictate the assumption of a possible maximum overall inaccuracy of 5 per cent, but this would probably do less than justice to the enumerators of 1801.'[22] Others have reached a similar conclusion on equally general grounds. Krause, for example, suggested that the census totals in 1801, 1811, and 1821 should be inflated by 5, 3, and 1 per cent respectively, to offset under-enumeration.[23]

Rickman himself had suggested that an inflation of the census figures was called for. He suggested that a thirtieth should be added to the census total to produce a best estimate of the size of the population of England and Wales.[24] However he proposed

20. Taylor, 'The taking of the census', p. 718.
21. *Ibid.*, p. 718.
22. *Ibid.*, p. 718.
23. Krause, 'Changes in English fertility and mortality', p. 60.
24. *1811 Census*, Preliminary observations, p.xxv.

the inflation solely as a means of compensating for the very large number of men in the army and navy who were not included in the census. He was emphatic that very few settlements were missed in 1801. 'It was supposed', he wrote, 'that when the Enumeration Returns of 1811 were collected and arranged, a considerable deficiency in those of 1801 would become manifest; but this did not happen, the seeming deficiencies of 1801 so constantly disappearing upon enquiry and explanation as to leave scarcely twenty places additional in 1811, and those among the smallest of the 15,741 which made separate returns.'[25] This is important evidence since Rickman's comparable enquiry into the parish register returns of 1801 revealed very serious omissions and confusion. Rickman therefore suggested that any deficiency in 1801 could arise only from 'a less careful enumeration in 1801 than in 1811', but such tests as he was able to apply caused him to conclude that 'the enumerations of 1801 and 1811 may be equally relied on'.[26]

It might seem *a priori* that the best method of approaching the problem of testing whether the 1801 census was less complete than later enumerations would be to consider the ratio of the total female population to the number of families. Overseers were much less likely to overlook entire families than to miss individuals. If, therefore, their accuracy increased with experience, one might expect the ratio of women to families also to increase, other things being equal. Table 5.14 shows how this ratio changed (the ratio of total populations to total families is too much affected by the fluctuating total of men in the army and navy to be of any significance in this context).

Table 5.14: The number of females per family in the first four censuses (England less Monmouth)

	(1) Families	(2) Female Population	(3) (2)/(1)
1801	1 768 517	4 320 090	2.4428
1811	1 999 848	4 931 924	2.4661
1821	2 332 595	5 743 203	2.4622
1831	2 725 425	6 667 343	2.4464

Sources: 1801 Census, Enumeration. p. 451; *1811 Census*, Enumeration. p. 427; *1821 Census*, Enumeration abstract, p. 427; *1831 Census*, Enumeration abstract, II, p. 832.

If the true ratio had remained the same during the first three censuses, and was correctly reflected in 1811 and 1821, it would be a simple matter to estimate the undercounting in 1801. The corrected census total for 1801 is 4,368,777 (table 5.13). If this is inflated in the ratio 2.4661 : 2.4428 as might be suggested by the data of table 5.14 it produces a revised total of 4,410,447, an increase of 41,670, or less than 1

25. *1811 Census*, Preliminary observations, p. xxvi. Later Rickman returned to the same topic after an exhaustive attempt to produce a full comparative list of the population of all census units in the censuses of 1801 to 1831. On this occasion he found far more missing places in the 1801 census in Great Britain as a whole, a total of 264 places with an estimated population of 73,000, compared with 104 places with a population of 23,000 in 1811, and 25 places with a population of 10,500 in 1821. These are still, however, very small percentages of the total populations. Even the 1801 figure is well under 1 per cent of the British population. *Comparative account of the population of Great Britain*, p. 5.
26. *1811 Census*, Preliminary observations, p.xxvi.

per cent. It is very doubtful, however, whether such a step is justifiable. There are both logical and evidential grounds for hesitation.

First, the 1811 ratio is too high relative to that for 1801. There is a note in the 1801 Middlesex section of the enumeration volume of the census that many lodgers were incorrectly counted as families.[27] This depresses the ratio of females to families since the latter is overstated. The ratio for Middlesex rose from 2.2240 in 1801 to 2.3361 in 1811, but thereafter declined slightly to 2.3330 in 1821 and 2.3147 in 1831. If Middlesex is removed from England the females/families ratio for England without Middlesex becomes 2.4706, 2.4824, 2.4785, and 2.4635 at the first four censuses. Using the first two of these ratios to estimate a corrected census figure for 1801 as was done earlier with the ratios in table 5.14 suggests an inflation of only 20,886, or under one half per cent.

The second is a *ceteris paribus* point. If it were demonstrable that the prevailing levels of fertility and mortality were unchanging in the early nineteenth century and at the same level as had obtained through the latter half of the eighteenth, it would be proper to expect the true ratio between the total female population and the number of families to show little or no change. But there is no reason to make this assumption. Indeed there is strong evidence to suggest that fertility was rising to a peak reached in the 1810s. The 1801 ratio is almost identical to the 1831 ratio on the other side of the peak and is therefore equally acceptable.

In addition there is an evidential problem which takes us to the heart of the general difficulty of assesssing the reliability of the 1801 census. There can be no doubt that the arithmetic of the census clerks and the proof-reading of the printer's galleys left much to be desired. The parish register abstract suffered greatly in this regard. There is accumulating evidence that the counting of baptisms, burials, and marriages was often, perhaps generally, carried out with fair accuracy, but the subsequent tabulations and printing were sadly bungled.[28] The enumeration half of the census also suffered badly. Some of the errors are gross and can be detected very easily. The printed total of families in Wiltshire in 1801, for example, is given as 30,527. In 1811 the comparable total was 41,844. Evidently both cannot be true. If the individual totals for Wiltshire hundreds in 1801 are summed, however, their total proves to be 39,627, and the modest growth that might be expected on general grounds is confirmed. There was no systematic tendency to sum to too low a total. Errors occurred in both directions. The printed total of families for Redbornestoke Hundred in Bedforshire is 2,216 but the sum of the parish totals is 2,016. Sometimes it seems virtually certain that the printed total in the census is wrong but there are no internal inconsistencies that could allow proof of error. It is highly improbable, for example, that the total of families given for Eaton Socon in Bedfordshire in 1801 is accurate. The census figure is 461 families and there were 888 women and girls in these families, an average of 1.93 women per family. In 1811 the comparable figures were 388, 962, and 2.48. Such a radical change in familial structure is most unlikely, though it may fall short of being incredible. Once more instances could be multiplied.

It would be a very laborious matter to rework all the 1801 census tabulations from the parish level upwards, though if this were done while at the same time comparison was made with 1811, and the internal consistency of the data was checked, a much clearer notion of the accuracy of the census would probably be gained. We have

27. *1801 Census*, Enumeration, p. 216.
28. See appendix 7, pp. 597–613; also Wrigley, 'Checking Rickman', and Edwards, 'National parish register data' and 'National marriage data'.

attempted some more cursory checks to try to establish whether any pattern emerges. It would be misleading to claim that this can support a firm conclusion, but it lends greater weight to the view that the 1801 census tended to exaggerate population totals than to the opposite view. The check consisted in glancing through the parish totals in the 1801 census looking for evidence of internal inconsistency in the data (improbable sex ratios, unusual numbers of people per house or per family, and so on). Where there seemed reason to be suspicious, the census return for the same place in 1811 was consulted. A larger number of instances of clear overstatement of population caught the eye than of understatement. Some of the more striking instances of overstatement are shown in table 5.15. The list could be considerably extended. The following parishes, for example, all show evidence of overstatement of population total: in Gloucestershire, Stoke Bishop and Elmore; in Hampshire, Hinton Ampner; in Hereford, Eye; in Northamptonshire, Blisworth and Wilbarston; in Somerset,

Table 5.15: Instances of overstatement of population totals drawn from the 1801 enumeration returns

Year	Population			Inhabited houses	Families
County, Parish	Male	Female	Total		
Devon, Chittlehampton					
1801	1 406	1 597	3 003	281	281
1811	765	807	1 572	323	327
Hampshire, Catherington					
1801	829	370	1 199	92	195
1811	314	293	607	98	126
Hereford, Sellack					
1801	137	343	480	60	60
1811	156	136	292	58	62
Kent, Ebony					
1801	114	237	351	23	28
1811	71	68	139	22	28
Norfolk, Gressenhall					
1801	561	663	1 224	117	117
1811	337	369	706	89	121
Shropshire, Condover					
1801	821	630	1 451	230	241
1811	636	656	1 289	190	269
Staffordshire, Rowley Regis					
1801	2 901	2 126	5 027	731	800
1811	2 492	2 482	4 974	898	1 075
Surrey, Bletchingley					
1801	528	816	1 344	183	185
1811	575	541	1 116	184	227
Westmorland, Over Stavely					
1801	145	179	324	41	42
1811	106	124	230	52	55

Sources: 1801 Census and *1811 Census*, Enumerations.

Ashbrittle; in Wiltshire, Upton Scudamore. In one or two cases there may have been exceptional local circumstances that would serve to explain apparently improbable totals but the bulk of these cases involve an exaggeration of population.[29] There are equally instances where it is clear that numbers were understated. The Woolstanton, Staffordshire, return almost certainly understated the male total by 600, and the male total is also palpably too low for Onsett, Essex. Most of the cases quoted are sufficiently blatant to occasion some surprise that they were not detected at the time. There are also a host of cases where the returns provide some ground for suspicion without being patently unacceptable.

Illustrative evidence of the type given in table 5.15 always falls short of proof. Since the majority of these individual instances of census error appear to involve overstatement, however, they strengthen doubt that it is right to assume that the 1801 census veered to the side of understating numbers. Inexperienced census takers are perhaps as prone to exaggerate numbers as to fall short of the true total. Further work may well establish a firmer basis of judgement. As things stand it seems unwise to impose any inflation on the recorded total apart from the adjustment already made in respect of very young children. Very many errors exist in the 1801 census but there is no firm evidence to show that they produced a general tendency to depress the national total below its true level or to elevate it excessively. The evidence from the ratios in table 5.14 supports the view that the errors tended to cancel one another out. It seems prudent, therefore, to conclude that the early English censuses were tolerably complete and accurate in their coverage of the female population apart from a substantial undercounting of young children, and that there is no reason to suppose that they became progressively more or less complete. In particular there may be more ground for supposing the 1801 census to have erred on the side of overstatement of numbers rather than of understatement, as has been frequently supposed. At a later stage of the argument, however, the effect of adhering to the more conventional view of the completeness of the early censuses will be examined.[30]

Decadal birth and death totals 1801–41

We are now in a position to make estimates of the totals of female births and deaths in England in each of the first four decades of the nineteenth century. Births can be estimated from later census age group totals using an appropriate life table, while an estimate of the number of deaths can be secured by subtracting intercensal increase from the total of births over the same period. The estimates are set out in table 5.16.

Although attention in this chapter has been focussed on the female population, its object has been the estimation of birth and death totals for the two sexes combined. Any discussion of the status of the results obtained in table 5.16, therefore, is most conveniently postponed until after the estimates of female births and deaths have been converted into totals for both sexes. The baptism sex ratio for England (less

29. The first two censuses do not contain the helpful footnotes found in later censuses that seek to explain unusually rapid changes in numbers occurring between any two successive censuses.

In some parishes there were accusations that the 1801 population was overcounted because the scale of payment of the parish officer was geared to the number of persons returned. For example, the rector of Farleigh Hungerford, Somerset, noted in his register in 1811 that the census return for the parish in 1801 was erroneous because the two parish officers concerned had 'increased the number of persons for the sake of a trifling emolument to themselves, which accounts for the apparent increase compared with the return of 1811'.

30. See below, pp. 270–7.

Table 5.16: Decadal female birth and death totals 1801–41 (England less Monmouth)

	Census totals[1]	Corrected census totals[2]		Intercensal increase	Births[3]	Deaths[4]
1801	4 320 090	4 368 777				
1811	4 931 924	4 987 507	1801–11	618 730	1 799 500	1 180 770
1821	5 743 203	5 807 927	1811–21	820 420	2 131 683	1 311 263
1831	6 667 343	6 742 484	1821–31	934 557	2 340 196	1 405 639
1841	7 608 002	7 649 476	1831–41	906 992	2 470 590	1 563 598

Notes: [1] The Census totals are taken from the 1801, 1811, 1821, 1831 and 1841 censuses.

[2] See tables 5.11, 5.12, and 5.13 for 1801, 1811, 1821, and 1841. The 1831 figure was obtained by increasing the 1831 census total in the same ratio as was used for 1821 (the census of 1831 was administered in the same fashion as the earlier nineteenth-century censuses rather than like that of 1841). The 1831 population obtained by estimation from 1841 at level 10 mortality is 6 713 723, using the same conventions as were used in calculating estimated totals for 1811 and 1801. This is 28 761 or 0.43 per cent less than the corrected census figure.

[3] Female birth totals were obtained from the following census age-group totals (table 5.11) and mortality levels: *1801–11*, 10–9 in 1821 (level 9); *1811–21*, 0–9 in 1821 (level 9); *1821–31*, 10–9 in 1841 (level 10); *1831–41*, 0–9 in 1841 (level 10).

[4] Female death totals are the difference between birth totals and intercensal increase in each decade.

Sources: See source note to table 5.14 for census totals 1801–31; for 1841, *1841 Census*, Enumeration abstract, p. 398

Monmouth) in the first three decades of the century 1801–10, 1811–20, and 1821–30 was 103.93, 104.33 and 104.20 respectively (males per 100 females), using the data published in the parish register abstracts of 1811, 1821, and 1831, while the birth sex ratio for England and Wales in the decades 1840–9, 1850–9 and 1860–9[31] was 104.94, 104.62, and 104.28. It might seem likely that the higher level of male compared with female infant mortality would depress a sex ratio based on baptisms if baptism were delayed and many infants died before being christened. But the ratio in the early decades of civil registration was only slightly higher than in the parish register period (the mean of the three decades of baptisms is 104.15; that of the three decades of births 104.61). In view of these data we have used a sex ratio of 104.5 in converting female to total births.

The comparable sex ratios for burials in the parish register period for England (less Monmouth) were 101.34, 101.29, and 103.24 in the first three decades of the century. Civil registration data for England and Wales in 1840–9 and 1850–9 yield ratios for deaths of 102.64 and 103.13.[32] The most obvious explanation of the jump in the sex ratio of burials between the first two decades of the century and the 1820s, to a level that was maintained after civil registration began, is that many men died abroad or at sea because there was almost constant warfare with France during the first 16 years of the century. It is clear that the absence of men in the army and navy did tend to depress the sex ratio for burials. Table 5.17 shows the sex ratios of burials in the three age groups in which there were presumably most men in the armed forces (20–4, 25–9,

Table 5.17: Sex ratio of burials in England and Wales 1813–7 (male burials per 100 female burials)

	15–9	20–4	25–9	30–4	35–9
1813–5	91.94	87.99	83.53	84.14	86.38
1816–7	89.61	92.04	86.37	87.18	87.81
1816–7/1813–5	0.9747	1.0460	1.0340	1.0361	1.0166

Source: 1831 Census, Enumeration abstract, I, Preface, pp. xxxviii–xxxix.

30–4) and the next lower and higher age groups in the last three years of war and the first two years of peace. In the age groups 20–4 to 30–4 the ratio rose appreciably, but much less markedly in the age group 35–9, while in the youngest age group, 15–9, the ratio actually fell slightly. The evidence is more ambiguous than one might wish, however, since the overall sex ratio of burials in England (less Monmouth) in 1817–20 was only 101.11, no higher than in the war years even though by 1817 the number of men in the army and navy had ceased to be inflated by the demands of war. For the period 1801–41, however, we have assumed that the ratio of 103.00 can be used throughout. A ratio of 103.00 is very close to the average of the burial ratio for the 1820s and the death ratio of the 1840s and 1850s (the burial ratio for England and Wales in 1831–40 was 103.67).[33] Adopting it implies a belief that the markedly lower ratio for 1801–20 was chiefly the result of war. In addition to 'normal' male mortality, which went unregistered because of the war, there was also, of course, a substantial

31. Mitchell and Deane, *British historical statistics*, p. 29.
32. Mitchell and Deane, *British historical statistics*, p. 34.
33. Parish register abstract 1841, *P. P.* 1845, XXV, pp. 505–6.

excess of male deaths caused directly or indirectly by the war. We have made no attempt to include this, but have instead made estimates of total deaths which can be used in identifying underlying trends in general mortality.[34]

The use of sex ratios of 104.50 for births and 103.00 for deaths allows the female birth and death totals to be converted into totals for the sexes combined. These are presented in table 5.18.

Table 5.18: Decadal birth and death totals 1801–41 (England less Monmouth)

	Births	Deaths
1801–11	3 679 978	2 396 963
1811–21	4 359 292	2 661 864
1821–31	4 785 701	2 853 447
1831–41	5 052 357	3 174 104

Source: See table 5.16 and text.

The first comment that should be made on the totals of births and deaths shown in table 5.18 is that the superficial appearance of meticulous accuracy conveyed by the absence of rounding in the totals is quite misleading. The justification for printing totals of such apparent precision when calculating projections from census totals to totals of births through a family of life tables and thence to totals of deaths via census totals is not that the results are highly accurate. It is rather to avoid compounding inaccuracies and to make it easier to specify the extent to which estimates reached after a long series of intermediate steps would differ if different assumptions had been made at any stage in the process. The knowledge that the end product of a series of calculations may be subject to a substantial margin of error is an argument for care both in framing and making explicit all assumptions and in carrying out the calculations.

Secondly, the female age groups 0–9 and 10–9 in 1821 and 1841 were used as the basis for calculating the number of births 1801–41 without making any allowance for migration. In the first 20 years of the century the war probably kept net migration to very modest levels and it is possible that the balance of migration was inward because of the movement of Scots, Irish, and Welsh into England. In the next two decades the balance was probably outward but again modest. Throughout it is too uncertain and probably too small in scale to justify any attempt to incorporate it into the calculation of the size of the decennial birth cohorts, especially as the age groups 0–9 and 10–9 must be the least affected by the cumulative effect of any net migration trends. Equally, the calculation of the number of deaths was made as if net migration were nil. If there were net outmigration in the 1820s and 1830s, failure to take this into account would cause the number of deaths to be exaggerated since the intercensal increase is reduced by any net outmigration. We have seen, however, that the net female outmigration in the 20 years before 1841 is unlikely to have been greater than 50,000.[35] In this period there were almost 3 million female deaths, so that the number of deaths would at most be reduced by about 1½ per cent. Once more the lack of clear

34. See below, pp. 224–6, for a further discussion of the sex ratios at burial in the context of sex differential net migration.
35. See above, p. 119.

evidence about the direction and scale of migratory movement, and the probability that it was not sufficiently large to affect the estimation of totals of births and deaths substantially, suggest that it is reasonable to leave it out of account.

Thirdly, the use of model life tables to infer the size of birth cohorts from the numbers surviving to a later census can only give precisely accurate results if the number of births was the same in each year of the cohort. This will never be exactly true of any historical population. Since the English population was growing rapidly in the early nineteenth century it is certain that violating the assumptions on which the model life tables were constructed must involve a penalty of inaccuracy. For example, where birth totals are increasing by 1 per cent each year the effect of calculating a decennial birth cohort *en bloc* from those aged 0–9 rather than making separate calculations for those aged 0–1, 1–4, and 5–9 is to exaggerate the size of the birth cohort by about 0.17 per cent (at level 10 female). This is too small a difference to cause great concern but the number of births is slightly overstated in each decade for this reason.

The census of 1841 was taken in early June 1841, while the census of 1821 was taken in late May.[36] The decennial totals of births and deaths given in table 5.18 may therefore be taken as running between the midpoints of the years quoted. In table 5.19 these totals are compared with the totals of baptisms and burials for the same periods produced by the corrections for nonconformity and delayed baptism described in chapter 4. The comparison enables final inflation ratios to be calculated for the period 1801–31 (the decade 1831–41 calls for separate treatment because civil registration began in 1837, and will be considered later). The table also lists the uncorrected totals of baptisms and burials and the ratios between these totals and those of estimated births and deaths.

The ratios in column 4 indicate how great were the deficiencies in Anglican registration early in the nineteenth century, especially in its second decade, and those of column 5 reveal a substantial shortfall remaining even after making corrections for nonconformity and for delay in baptism. They confirm the pattern of registration failure suspected by Krause.[37] Anglican registration was not uniformly bad. In some rural areas it remained substantially complete throughout this period, but in the urban and industrial areas it must have been seriously defective, and no doubt in many rural parishes also.[38] Krause argued that Anglican registration coverage improved markedly after 1820. The ratios in table 5.19 bear him out in this. The final inflation ratio for burials shows a particularly sharp fall between 1811–21 and 1821–31, and it is of interest to try to discover whether the improvement continued.

Anglican registration in the 1830s

Fortunately, in spite of the dislocation in parochial registration attendant upon the establishment of a civil registration system in 1837, the relative completeness of Anglican coverage can be measured fairly accurately. The year 1837 itself represents the chief problem in marshalling information about the decade preceding the 1841 census. Civil registration began only half way through the year, but Anglican registration was distorted very severely in the months immediately before civil

36. Census night in 1821 was May 27/28. In 1841 it was June 6/7.
37. Krause, 'Changes in English fertility and mortality', esp. pp. 54–9.
38. See on this topic Wrigley, 'Baptism coverage'; Levine, *Family formation*, pp. 153–74, and 'The reliability of parochial registration'; and Razzell, 'The evaluation of baptisms'.

Table 5.19: Comparison of uncorrected and corrected baptism and burial totals and estimated totals of births and deaths 1801–31 (England less Monmouth)

	(1) Uncorrected baptisms	(2) Corrected baptisms	(3) Estimated births	(4) Total inflation ratio (3)/(1)	(5) Final inflation ratio (3)/(2)
1801–11	2 657 323	3 023 437	3 679 978	1.3848	1.2172
1811–21	2 946 897	3 387 237	4 359 292	1.4793	1.2870
1821–31	3 368 809	3 903 270	4 785 701	1.4206	1.2261

	(1) Uncorrected burials	(2) Corrected burials	(3) Estimated deaths	(4) Total inflation ratio (3)/(1)	(5) Final inflation ratio (3)/(2)
1801–11	1 783 993	1 984 667	2 396 963	1.3436	1.2077
1811–21	1 789 106	2 030 752	2 661 864	1.4878	1.3108
1821–31	2 130 598	2 427 270	2 853 447	1.3393	1.1756

Notes:

1 Column 1 figures represent totals after the inflation of the reweighted totals for the sample of 404 parishes but without further correction.

2 Column 2 figures represent totals after correction for nonconformity and delayed baptism.

3 The totals in columns 1 and 2 run July 1801–June 1811, etc.

Source: For estimated births and deaths see table 5.18.

registration was instituted in July 1837. The national totals of baptisms before correction for nonconformity or delayed baptism in the first six months of 1837 were as follows (the average figure for the five preceding years is given in brackets in each case):24,013 (30,185); 41,757 (28,328); 39,723 (31,068); 27,548 (32,374); 35,850 (32,658); 44,898 (31,463). The very high figures for February and March probably arose because it had originally been intended to introduce civil registration in the second quarter of the year. The June figure was again very high in anticipation of the new system. Rather surprisingly burials were also apparently distorted. The comparable monthly figures were: 30,900 (23,713); 44,924 (21,543); 29,536 (23,114); 26,518 (21,769); 25,546 (22,422); and 20,792 (18,898). The February figure is extraordinarily high, although it is true that there was a severe epidemic of influenza in the spring of 1837 which appears to have peaked in February.[39] On only two previous occasions did the February burial total reach a figure even half as high as that of 1837. The January, March, April, and June burial totals were also the highest ever recorded in their respective months, though this was not true of any later month of the year. Monthly totals in late 1836 were not affected in either series.

Since reliable information about 1837 cannot be gleaned either from ecclesiastical or civil registration sources it has to be treated as a residual for which birth and death totals are derived after those for the other years of the decade 1831–41 have been determined.

Table 5.20: Registered and corrected totals of births 1838–41 (England less Monmouth)

	Registered	Corrected	Inflation factor
1838	434 650	508 541	1.170
1839	461 628	530 872	1.150
1840	470 891	534 416	1.135
1841 (Jan.-June)	247 271	276 944	1.120

Source: Totals of registered births from *Annual Reports*.

Civil registration of births was notoriously incomplete in its early years. In table 5.20 the registered totals of births from 1838 to mid 1841 are set out together with the factors used to increase the original totals to 'true' totals. The factors are similar to those suggested by Glass, though slightly higher than his.[40] They were arrived at with the following considerations in mind, which closely constrain any solution. First, the estimated decadal total of births 1831–41 is 5,052,357 (table 5.18). Second, if the population of both sexes aged 0–4 is estimated by the same method used above to make a similar estimate for the female population only,[41] and it is assumed that level 10 mortality held true in this period as in the longer period 1821–41, then the birth cohort born between mid 1836 and mid 1841, from which the census population aged 0–4 sprang, may be calculated as 2,602,566. This in turn implies that there were 2,449,791 births in the first half of the decade and that a final inflation factor of 1.1638

39. There is interesting information about the severity and timing of the influenza epidemic of early 1837 in Creighton, *Epidemics in Britain*, II, pp. 383–8.
40. Glass, 'Population and population movements', p. 234, table 4. Glass makes it clear that he inclines towards higher correction ratios.
41. See above, pp. 109–10.

should be used for baptisms from mid 1831 to mid 1836. The same factor was also used for the second half of 1836. The annual totals for the decade 1831–41 shown in table 5.21 then result. The total for 1837 is obtained by subtracting the total for mid 1831 to 1836 plus the total for 1838 to mid 1841 from the total for the decade as a whole. The birth total for the second half of the decade is 6.2 per cent higher than in the first half.

Table 5.21: Annual totals of births 1831–41 (England less Monmouth)

1831 (July–Dec.)	228 495
1832	472 112
1833	500 219
1834	495 545
1835	495 431
1836	505 473
1837	504 264
1838	508 541
1839	530 872
1840	534 461
1841 (Jan.–June)	276 944
Total *1831–41*	5 052 357

Source: See text.

A similar line of argument may be used to determine the final inflation ratio for converting burial to death totals. Under-registration of deaths in the early years of civil registration is generally agreed to have been very much less than was the case with births. The registered totals of deaths were increased by 2 per cent uniformly from 1838 to mid 1841 and these are the totals shown in table 5.22. In all they number 1,174,742. The decadal total of deaths is 3,174,104, leaving a total of 1,999,362 deaths to be distributed over the years 1831–7. The absence of dependable evidence either from civil or ecclesiastical registration about the number of deaths in 1837

Table 5.22: Annual totals of deaths 1831–41 (England less Monmouth)

1831 (July–Dec.)	149 030
1832	308 540
1833	296 677
1834	307 061
1835	306 697
1836	306 300
1837	325 057
1838	328 119
1839	325 199
1840	344 583
1841 (Jan.–June)	176 841
Total *1831–41*	3 174 104

Source: See text.

entails an arbitrary decision at this point. Adopting a final inflation ratio of 1.0985 for burials produces the annual totals from mid 1831 to 1836 shown in the table and constrains the 1837 total to be 325,057. The total of deaths in the second half of the decade is 1,636,603, or 6.4 per cent more than in the first half. The calculation of annual totals of deaths and the final inflation ratio is less strongly constrained with deaths than with births but a knowledge of the total mortality in the decade as a whole, and of the annual totals from 1838 onwards within a narrow margin of error, together with the likelihood that there were more deaths in the second than in the first half of the decade, implies that only solutions similar to that adopted here are plausible. Indeed, the totals can only be altered by increasing or decreasing the 1837 total somewhat and sharing the difference proportionately over the years 1831–6, so that any change could have only a minor effect on the final inflation ratio.

Table 5.23 shows for the final years of the parish register period the details given in table 5.19 for the decades 1801–31 while recapitulating the data already given. The totals of baptisms and burials collected at Rickman's behest and printed in the parish register abstracts of successive censuses are also given. It is clear that Anglican parish register coverage did improve considerably after the decade 1811–21 even without making any correction for nonconformity or delayed baptism. The improvement is much more clearly marked after correction for these two factors has been introduced. Indeed in the 1830s fewer than 10 per cent of all deaths remained unaccounted for after burials had been corrected. Those who have worked with the returns collected by Rickman have tended to overstate the improvement in purely Anglican coverage because of the inclusion of a growing proportion of non-Anglican events in the returns made by the Anglican clergy and others at census time. The ratio of the Rickman totals to those estimated on the basis of Anglican registers alone (column 1 of table 5.23) rose considerably in the case of both baptisms and burials. In the case of baptisms the successive ratios between 1801–11 and 1831–6 were 1.0340, 1.0554, 1.0668, and 1.0555, while in the case of burials they were 1.0307, 1.0684, 1.1088, and 1.1079.

Finally, it may be noted that there is no comparable problem with marriage in the 1830s. As we have already seen the relation between the aggregative sample totals and those from Rickman's parish register returns was very stable in the early nineteenth century,[42] and there is no reason to suppose that the parish register returns were other than complete or virtually so.[43] Nor was there a sudden surge of marriages in 1837 as was the case with baptisms and burials. Therefore the marriage totals derived from the aggregative sample are used down to and including 1837, and thereafter the Register General's totals.[44] It may be of interest to note that in the period 1831–7 the total number of marriages in England less Monmouth in the parish register abstracts was 775,548, while the total derived from the aggregative sample was

42. See above, table 3.5.

43. Rickman remarked in this connexion that 'The solicitude of the female and her family aided by the precision and severity of the Marriage Act, leaves no occasion to suspect any deficiency in the marriage registry from negligence; and the deficiency from other causes cannot be very important'. *1811 Census*, Preliminary observations, p. xxi.

44. In 1838 there was no published breakdown of marriage totals to enable a total for England less Monmouth to be calculated directly. The total for England and Wales was therefore multiplied by the ratio of the total of marriages for England less Monmouth to the total for England and Wales in the years 1831–7. The parish register abstract totals of marriages for 1754 to 1837 may be found conveniently summarized in *8th Annual Report*, pp. 48–9.

Table 5.23: Comparison of uncorrected and corrected baptism and burial totals and totals of births and deaths 1801–36 (England less Monmouth) together with Rickman's parish register abstract returns (England less Monmouth)

	(1) Uncorrected baptisms	(2) Corrected baptisms	(3) Estimated births	(4) Total inflation ratio (3)/(1)	(5) Final inflation ratio (3)/(2)	(6) Rickman's parish register abstract totals	(7) Ratio (3)/(6)
1801-11	2 657 323	3 023 437	3 679 978	1.3848	1.2172	2 747 715	1.3393
1811-21	2 946 897	3 387 237	4 359 292	1.4793	1.2870	3 110 014	1.4017
1821-31	3 368 809	3 903 270	4 785 701	1.4206	1.2261	3 593 700	1.3317
1831-6	1 991 749	2 317 648	2 697 279	1.3542	1.1638	2 102 300	1.2830

	(1) Uncorrected burials	(2) Corrected burials	(3) Estimated deaths	(4) Total inflation ratio (3)/(1)	(5) Final inflation ratio (3)/(2)	(6) Rickman's parish register abstract totals	(7) Ratio (3)/(6)
1801-11	1 783 993	1 984 667	2 396 963	1.3436	1.2077	1 838 807	1.3035
1811-21	1 789 106	2 030 752	2 661 864	1.4878	1.3108	1 911 475	1.3926
1821-31	2 130 598	2 427 270	2 853 447	1.3393	1.1756	2 362 434	1.2078
1831-6	1 345 464	1 524 175	1 674 305	1.2444	1.0985	1 490 582	1.1233

Notes:

1 Column 1 figures represent totals after the inflation of the reweighted totals for the sample of 404 parishes but without further correction.

2 Column 2 figures represent totals after correction for nonconformity and delayed baptism.

3 The totals in columns 1 and 2 run July 1801–June 1811, etc., but the final totals run from July 1831–December 1836.

4 The totals in the parish register abstracts do not include monthly breakdowns. To preserve comparability with the totals in the first three columns the PRA totals for 1801, 1811, 1821, and 1831 were divided in the same proportion as those in the uncorrected totals of baptisms and burials in column 1. Since the separate totals for Wales were published only for the decade as a whole in 1831–40 and not for individual years, the annual totals for England and Wales were reduced in the proportion obtaining over the decade as a whole.

Source: The PRA totals of column 6 are taken from *1811 Census,* Parish registers, pp. 93, 187; *1821 Census,* Parish register abstract, pp. 75, 145; *1831 Census,* Parish register abstract, pp. 201, 412; Parish register abstract 1841, *P.P.* 1845, XXV, pp. 502–3, 505–6.

769,584. The difference is only about 0.8 per cent, and the maximum difference in any individual year was only 2.7 per cent.

Birth and death totals before 1801

With the information contained in table 5.23 in mind we may now turn to the question of the selection of final inflation ratios for the bulk of the parish register period stretching back in time before 1801. In so doing we pass from a period when the comparatively plentiful information leaves only a relatively small margin of error in estimation to a period where the absence of census information means greater uncertainty. In the case of births a knowledge of the age structure of the population in 1801 is of value, since those aged 0–9 in 1801 must represent the survivors from the birth cohort of 1791–1801, and those aged 10–9 from the cohort of 1781–91. For example, on the assumption that level 9 mortality prevailed in the 1790s, as it did in the period 1801–21, the number of female births in the decade 1791–1801 would have been 1,540,049 and the total number of births 3,149,400 (using the same method of calculation as was used for tables 5.16 and 5.18). The total of corrected baptisms in this decade was 2,709,950, which would mean a final inflation ratio of 1.1622.

As it happens the assumption that mortality in the 1790s was at the same level as in the next two decades produces an estimate of births during the decade that has much to recommend it. Given that the final inflation ratio in the 1830s was 1.1638, and that there is evidence of a very marked peak in the 1810s, it would be most surprising if the ratio were not well below the level of the decade 1801–11 in the preceding decade, and at an absolute level no higher than that of the 1830s. To assume a higher mortality level in the 1790s would run counter to this pattern. Level 8 mortality, for example, implies a birth total of 3,246,237 and a final inflation ratio of 1.1979, implausibly high if our general assumptions hold good.

At this point a further consideration may be introduced. In some measure it is likely to be true that the same forces that produced a growth in nonconformity also tended to increase the proportion of escapes from all ecclesiastical registration. This is plausible in the direct sense that there are many instances of nonconformist congregations in which baptisms were performed either with no written record of the ceremony or with a record but in a form that did not qualify it within the terms of the legislation governing the deposit of nonconformist registers. It is also plausible in a less direct sense. The Anglican church's hold upon rural agrarian society normally appears to have remained strong but where there was much rural handicraft industry, or more generally in towns, its hold was much weaker. These were the settings in which nonconformity was strongest, but in which there was also the most pronounced tendency to eschew all religious ceremonial or to be intermittent and laggard in observance.[45] It is interesting therefore to study the relationship between the percentages by which numbers were increased because of nonconformity and the percentages involved in the final inflation ratio. These are listed in table 5.24.

The ratios given in column 3 of the table constitute a further reason for preferring a level 9 mortality assumption for the 1790s, and hence the figures for the 1790s given in the table, since a higher mortality assumption would cause the ratio to rise in the

45. Levine describes a situation of this type in some detail in 'The reliability of parochial registration', which deals with the framework-knitting parish of Shepshed, Leicestershire, in the late eighteenth and early nineteenth centuries.

Table 5.24: Percentage inflation of baptisms in respect of nonconformity and of residual non-registration

	(1) Nonconformity	(2) Residual non-registration	(3) Ratio (2)/(1)
1791–1801	3.96	16.22	4.10
1801–11	4.83	21.72	4.50
1811–21	5.63	28.70	5.10
1821–31	6.23	22.61	3.63
1831–6	6.82	16.38	2.40

Sources: For nonconformity percentages see table 4.3; for residual non-registration see table 5.23.

1790s compared with the 1800s. For example, level 8 mortality would mean a ratio of 5.00. Indeed, the table suggests a general solution to the problem of estimating the level of the final inflation ratio in earlier decades. The success of the Anglican church in curtailing disregard of baptism after a generation of laxness in the last years of the eighteenth century and the early decades of the nineteenth brought down non-observance to a level about two and a half times that of nonconformist registration by the 1830s. If it is a fair assumption that nonconformity and non-observance had common roots, at least in some degree, it seems reasonable to define the scale of the final inflation ratio as 2.5 times that of the correction made for nonconformity throughout the period before absenteeism and the failure to build churches in areas of rapidly growing population caused a serious slump in Anglican baptism coverage. Krause's work on Anglican registration coverage in the late eighteenth and early nineteenth centuries suggests much the same conclusion. It is equivalent to assuming that by the 1830s the Anglican church had made good its exceptional loss of coverage during the preceding half century and had recovered its earlier position apart from the loss directly or indirectly associated with the continued growth of nonconformity. We have chosen to determine the level of the final inflation ratio in this arbitrary fashion for the decade of the 1770s and earlier.

For the 1780s any solution should involve a ratio between the nonconformity correction factor and the inflation for residual non-registration intermediate between the figure of 2.50 adopted for the 1770s and the figure of 4.10 for the 1790s shown in table 5.24. To assume that level 9 mortality prevailed in the 1780s as in the 1790s produces too small a birth cohort, of 2,644,003, which would imply a final inflation ratio of 1.0651, and since the nonconformity correction factor for the decade was 1.0316, this in turn means that the ratio between the two inflation factors would only be 2.06. The data of table 4.6 also suggest that the 1780s may have been a decade of relatively severe mortality since the number of burials in the 1780s shown in column 2 rose almost 11 per cent above the level of the 1770s, itself a decade that had experienced an even more rapid rise in burials, whereas there was little increase between the 1780s and the 1790s. The argument, however, should not be pressed as it is partially circular.

On the assumption that level 8 mortality characterized the 1780s, the size of the birth cohort is increased to 2,725,300 and the level of the final inflation ratio to 1.0978. At this level it is 3.09 times the level of the nonconformity correction factor which is an acceptable ratio in the light of its level in the decades immediately before and after.

Table 5.25: Final inflation ratios used in converting corrected baptism totals into estimated totals of births

1640	1.0000	1766	1.0568
1686	1.0278	1776	1.0620
1696	1.0323	1781–91	1.0978
1706	1.0350	1791–1801	1.1622
1716	1.0385	1801–11	1.2172
1726	1.0398	1811–21	1.2870
1736	1.0403	1821–31	1.2261
1746	1.0460	1831–6	1.1638
1756	1.0510		

Note: The ratios from 1686 to 1776 represent 2.5 times the percentage increases in respect of nonconformity given in table 4.3 and are intended to relate to the decades centring on the years in question. Later ratios were derived from estimated birth cohorts for the decades shown. For further details see text.

The full set of final inflation ratios for baptisms linked to the schedule of corrections already made for nonconformity is set out in table 5.25. It would be idle to pretend that they they are demonstrably correct. Any such set, particularly before 1801, must be based on a balancing of probablities, rather than inference from indisputable fact. Yet the robustness of the estimates should not be under-estimated. The behaviour of the ratios shown in table 5.24 shows a suggestive regularity. Moreover, the relation between the birth cohorts that the ratios produce for the middle and later decades of the eighteenth century (see table 5.27) and the survivors from these cohorts still living at the time of the 1821 census does not imply any unusual or implausible mortality history in the intervening decades. And the linking of non-observance to nonconformity, while it has been made artificially simple and rigid, probably captures an important element of residual non-registration effectively if arbitrarily. Further work may well, however, suggest improvements. We have deliberately given hostages to fortune in attempting to deal with residual under-registration in this fashion. Some will be redeemed but others may later have to be sacrificed.

Table 5.23 makes a convenient starting point for considering final burial inflation ratios before 1801 no less than for baptism ratios. The ratio for 1831–6 is particularly significant. If fewer than 10 per cent of all deaths remained unaccounted for in the Anglican and nonconformist burial registers in the 1830s, only very modest final inflation ratios should be regarded as acceptable in the eighteenth century. Before the war period civil burial grounds were very uncommon outside London and even in London were probably operating on a considerably smaller scale than during and after the war.[46] Nonconformists, other than the Quakers, were far less likely to have their own burial grounds than to maintain baptism registers, so that nonconformist behaviour is not likely to offer a solution in parallel to that attempted for the baptism inflation ratio. In these circumstances any solution is likely to be highly arbitrary, though if the absolute level of the inflation was low different approaches will tend to produce similar results. We have chosen to assume that the ratio in the 1780s was not

46. See Krause, 'Changes in English fertility and mortality', p. 57.

more than about half its level in the 1830s, or a little less than 1.05.[47] At this level it would also be at about half the level of the baptism ratio for the decade (in the 1830s it was at 60 per cent of the baptism ratio, though in between it rose so sharply that in the 1810s the burial ratio was slightly the higher of the two). In the eighteenth century the two ratios may well have tended to move in parallel since for this period it is a question of trying to capture the effects of a failure to observe ecclesiastical rites at all. We have assumed that the burial ratio was at half the level of the baptism ratio in the 1780s but that in earlier decades it was slightly lower at 40 per cent of the baptism level. By rough interpolation the 1790s ratio was taken to be two thirds of the baptism ratio. The resultant ratios, together with those already given in table 5.23, are set out in table 5.26. The final burial inflation ratio associated in this way with the prevalence of nonconformity is less than 2½ per cent in the 1770s and becomes steadily smaller further back in time.

Table 5.26: Final inflation ratios used in converting corrected burial totals into estimated totals of deaths

1640	1.0000	*1766*	1.0227
1686	1.0111	*1776*	1.0248
1696	1.0129	*1786*	1.0489
1706	1.0140	*1796*	1.1081
1716	1.0154	*1801-11*	1.2077
1726	1.0159	*1811-21*	1.3108
1736	1.0161	*1821-31*	1.1756
1746	1.0184	*1831-6*	1.0985
1756	1.0204		

Note: The ratios given from 1686 to 1796 are intended to relate to the decades centring on the years in question. Later ratios were derived from estimated totals of deaths for the decades shown. For further details see text.

The application of final inflation ratios

The application of the inflation ratios set out in tables 5.25 and 5.26 to the body of monthly totals of baptisms and burials produced by earlier manipulation of the raw parish register data presents no problems in the earlier decades during which the ratio is rising slowly and evenly in both series. Using individual inflation ratios obtained for each month by interpolation between the benchmark points, the overall effect on decadal totals is very close to the level of inflation specified for the mid-point years. Before 1770 the ratios given in tables 5.25 and 5.26 were applied to the January of the year in question with the results shown in table 5.27. After 1770, however, this method is not capable of producing accurate results. To take an extreme example, if the ratios for the first three decades of the nineteenth century in the burial series were used for 1806, 1816, and 1826 respectively (that is 1.2077, 1.3108, and 1.1756), the resultant inflation would be grossly inaccurate for the middle decade 1811–21. The

47. Krause estimated the death/burial ratio in the 1780s to be a little under half its level in the 1830s (1.08 and 1.18). This is a somewhat different measurement, however, since his burials were PRA totals, and he made no separate allowance for nonconformity or delayed baptism. Krause, 'Changes in English fertility and mortality', pp. 57–8.

Table 5.27: Comparison of uncorrected and corrected baptism and burial totals and estimated birth and death totals 1681–1836 (England less Monmouth)

	(1) Uncorrected baptisms	(2) Corrected baptisms	(3) Estimated births	(4) Total inflation ratio (3)/(1)	(5) Final inflation ratio (3)/(2)
1681–90	1 452 044	1 531 772	1 574 047	1.0840	1.0276
1691–1700	1 432 638	1 516 781	1 565 421	1.0927	1.0321
1701–10	1 476 106	1 567 557	1 622 463	1.0992	1.0350
1711–20	1 492 077	1 589 600	1 650 398	1.1061	1.0382
1721–30	1 581 065	1 689 080	1 756 113	1.1107	1.0397
1731–40	1 724 150	1 850 779	1 926 537	1.1174	1.0409
1741–50	1 646 774	1 779 137	1 860 849	1.1300	1.0459
1751–60	1 733 152	1 884 331	1 980 576	1.1428	1.0511
1761–70	1 875 499	2 052 465	2 168 907	1.1564	1.0567
1771–80	2 073 236	2 284 764	2 426 345	1.1703	1.0620
1781–91	2 229 991	2 482 509	2 725 911	1.2224	1.0980
1791–1801	2 408 711	2 709 950	3 149 428	1.3075	1.1622
1801–11	2 657 323	3 023 437	3 680 048	1.3849	1.2172
1811–21	2 946 897	3 387 237	4 359 378	1.4793	1.2870
1821–31	3 368 809	3 903 270	4 786 007	1.4207	1.2262
1831–6	1 991 749	2 317 648	2 697 275	1.3542	1.1638

	(1) Uncorrected burials	(2) Corrected burials	(3) Estimated deaths	(4) Total inflation ratio (3)/(1)	(5) Final inflation ratio (3)/(2)
1681–90	1 542 028	1 565 922	1 583 085	1.0266	1.0110
1691–1700	1 359 051	1 386 526	1 404 284	1.0333	1.0128
1701–10	1 322 802	1 355 599	1 374 619	1.0392	1.0140
1711–20	1 418 369	1 457 942	1 480 218	1.0436	1.0153
1721–30	1 707 778	1 756 893	1 784 779	1.0451	1.0159
1731–40	1 489 135	1 547 129	1 572 450	1.0559	1.0164
1741–50	1 532 966	1 597 388	1 626 629	1.0611	1.0183
1751–60	1 441 436	1 516 458	1 547 466	1.0736	1.0204
1761–70	1 661 122	1 752 469	1 792 183	1.0789	1.0229
1771–80	1 634 885	1 746 277	1 789 501	1.0946	1.0248
1781–91	1 765 115	1 902 385	1 995 527	1.1305	1.0490
1791–1801	1 804 555	1 970 937	2 183 981	1.2103	1.1081
1801–11	1 783 993	1 984 667	2 396 995	1.3436	1.2078
1811–21	1 789 106	2 030 752	2 662 116	1.4880	1.3109
1821–31	2 130 598	2 427 270	2 853 495	1.3393	1.1756
1831–6	1 345 464	1 524 175	1 674 305	1.2444	1.0985

Notes: The totals in columns 1, 2, and 3 run from January 1681 to December 1690, and so on, until the decade 1781–91. In this decade and thereafter the totals run from July 1781 to June 1791, and so on. The total for 1831–6 runs from July 1831 to December 1836. For further details see table A4.1.

overall inflation for that decade would only be approximately 1.2810 because 1816 would be a peak flanked by lower values and the interpolation process would necessarily produce a much lower overall value for the decade. Comparable, if smaller, inaccuracies arise when there is a marked change in the steepness of rise or fall in the ratio.

For the decade 1781–91 and thereafter, therefore, inflection points were introduced every five years and relate to the July of the year in question to make it easier to secure a good fit with estimated decadal totals. Thus, for example, the overall effect of a burial inflation ratio of 1.3108 for 1811–21 is achieved by ratios of 1.2912, 1.3354, and 1.2816 for 1811, 1816, and 1821 respectively.

Comparison of the ratios in column 5 of table 5.27 with the corresponding ratios of tables 5.25 and 5.26 shows a close agreement between the degree of inflation aimed at and achieved when using inflection points in the January of the mid year of the decade. This was the method used down to the 1770s, but in 1781–91 and thereafter the more exact method already described was employed, and the totals run between the mid points of the years shown (for example, July 1781 to June 1791). For earlier decades the inherent uncertainty of the operation made it seem unnecessary to introduce this added refinement. Comparison with table 5.23 for the period after 1801 will show that the totals produced by the final inflation ratios approximate very closely to the estimated 'true' totals. Any remaining differences are negligible. Final inflation ratios are used, of course, throughout the period during which a correction for nonconformity is made and therefore affect totals of births and deaths from the 1640s onwards, though the earliest decades, when the ratios are low, are not included in table 5.27. Fuller details of the effect of each successive change made to the original baptism and burial totals may be found in appendix 4.

Pullout 1 at the end of the volume shows the annual frequencies of births, deaths, and marriages in England in the period 1539–1873, while figure 5.1 shows for each decade the relative share of Anglican events, nonconformist events, the effect of correcting for delayed baptism, and the size of the final inflation intended to cover all other registration escapes. The figure shows only births and deaths since the original Anglican marriage totals are virtually unchanged: only a very small inflation in respect of Quaker marriages was made (see table 4.5).

Assessment of the new estimates

The chain of reasoning that has taken us from the original monthly totals of events in the sample of 404 Anglican registers, which form the empirical base of this book, to the totals of births and deaths shown in appendix 2 has been long and involved. At each stage the solutions adopted to overcome successive problems have been open to argument. As such they represent central estimates within a band of probability rather than precise totals. It is convenient to postpone discussion of the effect of making alternative assumptions about totals of births and deaths until chapter 7 where their demographic implications and internal consistency can be more effectively examined. Then the results of back-projection runs using birth and death totals incorporating different correction factors will be compared with those obtained from the totals whose derivation we have just described.

It may be of interest at this point, however, to compare the estimates of births and deaths obtained in this chapter with previous attempts to construct such series. We may begin by considering the early nineteenth century. For this period a number of

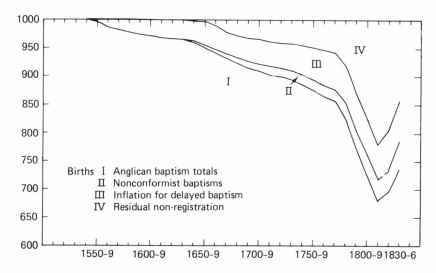

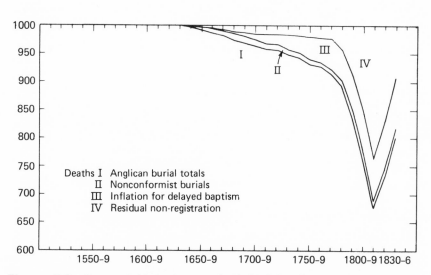

Figure 5.1: Proportionate shares of original Anglican registration and corrections for nonconformity, delayed baptism, and residual non-registration in producing final estimates of decadal birth and death totals 1540 − 9 to 1830 − 6 (base 1000)

Notes: The data shown on the graph all refer to decadal totals from 1540-9 to 1820-9 but the last totals used covered the seven years 1830-6 because 1836 was the last year in which the final totals of births and deaths were derived from the aggregative parish totals. It may be helpful to refer to tables 4.3, 4.5, 5.25, and 5.26 in considering the trends and quantities shown on the graphs.

Source: Table A4.2.

Table 5.28: Decadal birth and death estimates 1801–40 (England less Monmouth)

	Finlaison	Farr	Brownlee	Griffith	Krause	Hollingsworth	Razzell	New estimates
Totals of births ('000s)								
1801–10	3 302	3 448	3 448	3 160	3 656	4 076	3 835	3 680
1811–20	3 735	4 152	3 885	3 577	4 385	4 699	4 486	4 359
1821–30	4 425	4 502	4 502	4 133	4 723	5 181	4 970	4 786
1831–40		4 963	5 165	4 379	5 101	5 299	5 100	5 052
Crude birth rates (per 1 000)								
1801–10	35.6	37.2	37.2	34.1	39.5	44.0	41.4	39.7
1811–20	35.0	38.9	36.4	33.5	41.1	44.0	42.0	40.8
1821–30	35.7	36.3	36.3	33.3	38.1	41.8	40.1	38.6
1831–40		34.9	36.4	30.8	35.9	37.3	35.9	35.6
Birth totals indexed (new estimates taken as 1 000)								
1801–10	897	937	937	859	994	1 108	1 042	1 000
1811–20	857	953	891	821	1 006	1 078	1 029	1 000
1821–30	925	941	941	864	987	1 083	1 038	1 000
1831–40		982	1 022	867	1 010	1 049	1 010	1 000
Ratios of birth totals to Parish Register Abstract baptism totals								
1801–10	1.202	1.255	1.255	1.150	1.330	1.483	1.396	1.339
1811–20	1.201	1.335	1.249	1.150	1.410	1.511	1.442	1.402
1821–30	1.231	1.253	1.253	1.150	1.314	1.442	1.383	1.332
1831–40		1.303	1.356	1.150	1.340	1.392	1.339	1.327
Totals of deaths ('000s)								
1801–10	2 072	2 238	2 196	2 023	2 446	2 946	2 625	2 397
1811–20	2 147	2 529	2 263	2 103	2 800	3 300	2 863	2 662
1821–30	2 602	2 694	2 774	2 599	2 915	3 520	3 162	2 853
1831–40		3 149	3 304	3 064	3 287	3 424	3 286	3 174

Crude death rates (per 1 000)

1801–10	22.4	24.2	23.7	21.8	26.4	31.8	28.3	25.9
1811–20	20.1	23.7	21.2	19.7	26.2	30.9	26.8	24.9
1821–30	21.0	21.7	22.4	21.0	23.5	28.4	25.5	23.0
1831–40		22.2	23.3	21.6	23.1	24.1	23.1	22.3

Death totals indexed (new estimates taken as 1 000)

1801–10	864	934	916	844	1 020	1 229	1 095	1 000
1811–20	807	950	850	790	1 052	1 240	1 076	1 000
1821–30	912	944	972	911	1 022	1 234	1 108	1 000
1831–40		992	1 041	965	1 036	1 079	1 035	1 000

Ratios of death totals to Parish Register Abstract burial totals

1801–10	1.127	1.217	1.194	1.100	1.330	1.602	1.427	1.303
1811–20	1.123	1.323	1.184	1.100	1.465	1.727	1.498	1.393
1821–30	1.102	1.141	1.174	1.100	1.234	1.490	1.339	1.208
1831–40		1.130	1.186	1.100	1.180	1.229	1.179	1.139

Total natural increase *1801–40* (total of births less total of deaths in '000s)

	6 455	6 455	6 463	5 460	6 417	6 065	6 455	6 791

Notes:

1 The population of England less Monmouth in the successive censuses 1801 to 1841 was taken as ('000s): 8 658, 9 868, 11 491, 13 299, 15 113 (see table A6.7). The total population increase 1801–41 was, therefore, 6 455.

2 In calculating crude birth and death rates the population at risk was taken as the midpoint population total in each decade (respectively 9 263, 10 680, 12 395, and 14 206 for 1801–11 to 1831–41).

3 All the quoted estimates of totals of births and deaths referred to England and Wales rather than to England less Monmouth (Finlaison, Farr, Brownlee). The ratio of births in England less Monmouth to all births in England and Wales in 1841–50 was 0.9383. The comparable ratio for deaths was 0.9384. The quoted estimates were therefore adjusted using these ratios to make them comparable with our new estimates.

4 Where estimates were expressed as birth or death rates they also referred to England and Wales rather than England less Monmouth (Hollingsworth, Razzell). We have applied these rates to the decadal midpoint populations listed above to produce birth and death totals, thereby implicitly assuming that the rates in England were the same as in England and Wales.

5 Where birth totals or birth rates were quoted without parallel death totals or rates (Farr, Razzell), death totals were calculated by subtracting

(*cont.*)

Table 5.28: *(Cont.)*

intercensal increase from intercensal birth totals. This explains why in these cases the total natural increase 1801–40 equals the difference between the population in 1801 and that in 1841. (Razzell made a similar calculation but used different census totals and for this reason his death totals and rates were recalculated.)

6   The totals of births and deaths attributed to Griffith were obtained by multiplying the PRA totals for England less Monmouth by 1.15 and 1.10 respectively. These were the factors suggested by Griffith, though he had in mind England and Wales rather than England alone.

7   Hollingsworth's decadal birth and death rates are not given explicitly in all cases. If unspecified they were read off from his graph of birth and death rates 1781–1968. This may involve small errors in the attributed rates but the margin of possible error is slight.

8   Krause committed himself to the view that the birth/baptism ratio (based on PRA totals) was 1.41 in 1811–20 and that the death/burial ratio in that decade lay between 1.45 and 1.48. He accepted a death/burial ratio of 1.18 for 1831–40 though this was 'possibly an overestimate'. He also remarked that Farr's estimated death/burial ratios for 1801–10 to 1831–40 (1.23, 1.33, 1.16, and 1.12) were 'plausible in so far as trend is concerned'. We have assumed a death/burial ratio of 1.465 for 1811–20 and of 1.18 for 1831–40 and obtained ratios for 1801–10 and 1821–30 (1.33 and 1.234) by using the two known ratios and the trends in Farr's figures. This enables death totals to be calculated, and birth totals for decades other than 1811–20 (for which a birth total can be calculated directly) by assuming nil net migration and adding the intercensal death totals to the intercensal natural increase figures.

9   It should be noted that the ratios of births and deaths to PRA totals in 1831–40 are less easy to interpret than those for the three earlier decades because the introduction of civil registration in 1837 severely disturbed the pattern of parochial registration. A huge increase in registered baptisms and burials in the first half of 1837 was later followed by registration coverage that was probably poorer than in the earlier years of the decade.

10   The totals of events are presented as referring to the decades 1801–10, 1811–20, etc. In the case of the new estimates, however, they refer to July 1801–June 1811, July 1811–June 1821, and so on.

Sources:

Finlaison, Letter to Registrar General in *First Annual Report*, pp. 82–6.
Farr, *1871 Census*, General Report, Appendix A, p. 56, table 61.
Brownlee, 'The history of the birth and death rates in England and Wales', p. 221, table viii.
Griffith, *Population problems*, pp. 27–42.
Krause, 'Changes in English fertility and mortality', pp. 57, 69, 70.
Hollingsworth, *Historical demography*, pp. 345–53.
Razzell, 'The evaluation of baptisms', p. 138.

attempts have been made to estimate birth and death rates, though estimates of the absolute number of births and deaths have been less common. Table 5.28 shows how wide the spread of estimates has been for the period 1801–40. As will be clear from the notes to the table a degree of comparability between the estimates has been obtained in several instances only by converting rates into totals or by other devices which might not have carried the full assent of their authors. But the totals of events and the derived statistics make it much easier to place each earlier estimate in relation to the new estimates and to each other. The crude birth and death rates are also shown graphically in figure 5.2.

The third panel of each half of the table makes it easy to appreciate the tendency for the later estimates of both births and deaths to be higher than those made in the nineteenth and early twentieth centuries. Griffith's estimates are conspicuously the lowest of all. His predecessors, Finlaison, Farr, and Brownlee, take widely different views about short-term changes in fertility and mortality but their estimates are uniformly lower than those of later scholars, apart from Brownlee's estimates for the 1830s.

Of the estimates made in the last quarter century our new estimates and those of Krause and Razzell are closely similar for births. The sum of the four decadal birth totals in our estimates and those of Krause and Razzell are respectively (in '000s) 17,877, 17,865, and 18,391. The 40-year total drawn from Razzell is 3 per cent higher than our series, while that of Krause differs by less than a tenth of 1 per cent. Moreover, the fluctuations in decadal birth totals are broadly similar in the three series. If each successive decadal birth total is indexed to its predecessor to the base 1,000 (see table 5.29) the three resulting ratios in our series are 1,185, 1,098, and 1,056, while the comparable ratios from Krause are 1,199, 1,077, and 1,080, and from Razzell 1,170, 1,108, and 1,026. It seems fair, therefore, to describe these three series as substantially alike. Death totals are higher in Krause and Razzell though in Razzell's case the difference was in a sense forced upon him by the assumption of nil net migration made in order to calculate the decadal death totals.

Hollingsworth's estimates are very much higher than any of the other seven. They seem implausibly high. The death totals for 1801–10 and 1811–20 would imply that in the former decade only 62 per cent of all deaths were recorded in Anglican registers or in other registers included in the returns made to Rickman, and in the latter only 58 per cent. Hollingsworth's birth estimates are somewhat closer to those of other scholars than is the case with his death estimates, but even here the differences are substantial. It is probable that some of the assumptions he made in order to simplify his calculations involved distortions that have pushed his estimates some way above the true level. The *relative* changes in Hollingsworth birth totals, however, are very similar to those in the other recent estimates. The successive indexed growth ratios for the three pairs of decades beginning in 1801–10 are 1,153, 1,103, and 1,023.

In respect of their fluctuations from decade to decade, therefore, the more recent estimates of births show strong similarities even in the one case where the absolute numbers involved were aberrantly high. The earlier estimates of Finlaison, Brownlee, and Griffith, however, were not only much lower in absolute numbers but also show a marked difference in trend between adjacent decades. Farr is an exception to this rule. The pattern of changes from one decade to the next in his series is more like that of the estimates made in the last quarter century than those of earlier scholars. In general the same is true of the death estimates, though the pattern is less clear-cut in their case. The relevant data are shown in table 5.29 together with some derived data

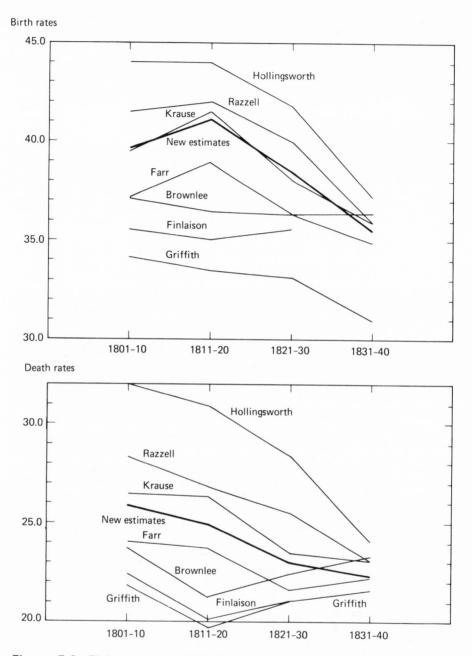

Birth rates

Death rates

Figure 5.2: Eight estimates of English decadal crude birth and death rates 1801 – 10 to 1831 – 40 (rates per 1000 total population)

Source: Table 5.28

Table 5.29: Growth ratio fluctuations in decadal birth and death totals

	(1) Finlaison	(2) Farr	(3) Brownlee	(4) Griffith	(5) Krause	(6) Hollingsworth	(7) Razzell	(8) New estimates
Births								
1811–20/1801–10	1 131	1 204	1 127	1 132	1 199	1 153	1 170	1 185
1821–30/1811–20	1 185	1 084	1 159	1 155	1 077	1 103	1 108	1 098
1831–40/1821–30		1 102	1 147	1 060	1 080	1 023	1 026	1 056
Deviation of the above from the ratio in column 8								
1811–20/1801–10	−54	19	−58	−53	14	−32	15	
1821–30/1811–20	87	−14	61	57	−21	5	10	
1831–40/1821–30		46	91	4	24	−33	30	
Total (ignoring sign)	141	79	210	114	59	70	55	
Deaths								
1811–20/1801–10	1 036	1 130	1 031	1 040	1 145	1 120	1 091	1 111
1821–30/1811–20	1 212	1 065	1 266	1 236	1 041	1 067	1 104	1 072
1831–40/1821–30		1 169	1 191	1 179	1 128	973	1 039	1 113
Deviation of the above from the ratio in column 8								
1811–20/1801–10	−75	19	−80	−71	34	9	−20	
1821–30/1811–20	140	−7	154	164	−31	−5	32	
1831–40/1821–30		56	78	66	15	−140	−74	
Total (ignoring sign)	215	82	312	301	80	154	126	

Note: The ratios were calculated by indexing the total of events in any one decade on the total in the preceding decade which was set to equal 1 000. For example, Finlaison estimated total births in 1801–10 and 1811–20 as ('000s) 3 302 and 3 735. The growth ratio is therefore 1131 = 3735/3302 × 1000.

that may serve to make the pattern of the relative changes easier to grasp.

The figures in the lower half of each panel in the table afford a summary guide to the degree of similarity of relative changes in the totals of births and deaths from decade to decade between the new estimates and those of earlier scholars. Farr, Krause, Hollingsworth, and Razzell form a group in which the pattern of changes is similar to that in the new estimates, while Finlaison, Brownlee, and Griffith form a second group in which the pattern is quite distinct, though within the second group there is a marked similarity of pattern. The reason for the division into two groups is not far to seek. Finlaison, Brownlee, and Griffith all employed either fixed inflation factors or else factors that varied only slightly when converting the Rickman returns into estimates of totals of events. The other estimates, in contrast, reflect a different approach to the problem, usually depending heavily on inferences drawn from the age structure of the censuses of 1821 and 1841. All the latter agree in identifying the second decade of the century as the period when the coverage of vital events in the parish register returns was least complete for both births and deaths.

When the totals of births and deaths in the several estimates are expressed as crude birth and death rates the same patterns of change and level are, of course, visible. The more recent estimates result in higher rates. At the extremes the differences between the highest and lowest estimates are very marked. Hollingsworth's crude birth rate for 1811–20 at 44.0 per 1,000 is more than 10 points higher than Griffith's rate of 33.5. Their estimates of death rates in 1811–20 are even further apart (30.9 and 19.7 per 1,000). More interesting perhaps is the effect of the assumptions on the trends in the rates. Those who used either fixed or virtually fixed correction factors when inflating the Parish Register Abstract returns (Finlaison, Brownlee, Griffith) find little change in the birth rate during the first three decades of the nineteenth century. In contrast, where a different basis of estimation has been used, the second decade invariably has the highest crude birth rate, and thereafter the rate declines rather steeply, falling about 5 points between the 1810s and the 1830s. And there is an equally clear-cut difference between the two groups of estimates in their conclusions about the crude death rate. The first group uniformly identify the 1810s as the decade with the lowest rate, after which there is a rise sufficient to increase the death rate by 2 points by the 1830s. All the other estimates show a reverse pattern with a high death rate in the second decade followed by a steady and significant fall over the two succeeding decades. Trends in the birth and death rates are, of course, tied to one another throughout this period because in a period of slight net migration and a known level of intercensal population increase a high birth rate necessarily implies a high death rate and vice-versa. It is not therefore surprising that the two groups of estimates show internal consistencies of this sort.

There are fewer estimates of birth and death totals for the period before 1801, and they tend to be less secure. All estimates of births and deaths for the eighteenth century are affected by the absence of censuses, which when available provide valuable assistance in identifying the correct relative levels of the two rates by defining the scale of intercensal growth. Before 1780 any estimate linked to the data collected by Rickman in 1801 is further hindered by the fact that totals of baptisms and burials were collected only for every tenth year between 1700 and 1780. Nevertheless, for the sake of completeness, a comparison of available estimates for the last two decades of the eighteenth century is given in table 5.30. The table includes estimates derived from Ohlin's work. Ohlin published estimates of crude rates and population totals throughout the eighteenth century but none for the early nineteenth century.

Table 5.30: Decadal birth and death estimates for the eighteenth century (England less Monmouth)

	Farr	Brownlee	Griffith	Ohlin	Krause	New estimates
Totals of births ('000s)						
1781–90	2 478	2 795	2 551	2 809	2 551	2 726
1791–1800	2 804	3 053	2 792	3 068	3 045	3 149
Birth totals indexed (new estimates taken as 1 000)						
1781–90	909	1 025	936	1 030	936	1 000
1791–1800	890	970	887	974	967	1 000
Totals of deaths ('000s)						
1781–30		2 124	1 930	2 081	1 895	1 996
1791–1800		2 200	2 000	2 161	2 191	2 184
Death totals indexed (new estimates taken as 1 000)						
1781–90		1 064	967	1 043	949	1 000
1791–1800		1 007	916	989	1 003	1 000

Notes:

1   The sources relevant for this table are those listed in table 5.28 except that the source of Ohlin's estimate is given below.

2   Totals for England less Monmouth were obtained from those for England and Wales as described in table 5.28 note 3.

3   The totals attributed to Farr and Brownlee were drawn directly from the sources indicated. Those for Griffith were derived in the way described in table 5.28 note 6. The parish register totals collected by Rickman and published in the 1801 census on which Griffith's totals are based may be found in table A7.1, column 3 and are slightly revised from their original form. Krause leans towards a birth/baptism ratio of 1.10 for 1781–90 but concedes that it might be as high as 1.20. The total in the table for the 1780s was obtained by using a ratio of 1.15 while that for the 1790s was obtained by using an average of the 1780s ratio and that used in table 5.28 for the 1800s ((1.15 + 1.357)/2 = 1.254). Similarly he gives a death/burial ratio of 1.08 for the 1780s and a ratio for the 1790s was calculated as the mean of those for the 1780s and 1800s ((1.08 + 1.33)/2 = 1.205). Ohlin published two sets of birth and death rates which he regarded as equally plausible for each eighteenth-century decade, and parallel estimates of population totals every tenth year. The totals of events given in this table were derived by applying the mean of his birth and death rate estimates for each decade to a population total taken as the mean of the populations totals for the years at either end of the decade (e.g. 1781 and 1791). The decennial population totals used were themselves means of the figures for the year in question from Ohlin's two population totals series.

Source: Ohlin, *The positive and the preventive check*, p. 263.

Any estimates for the period before 1780 have been omitted. Where such estimates involve the use of Rickman's data they are of little interest since they must entail the assumption that the years for which returns were required were representative of the decades in which they occur, which is not the case.[48] Only Farr made estimates on

48. For example, the national burial total in 1730 was 173,592 and 160, 344 in 1740. This might suggest an average annual burial total of 166,969 ((173,592 + 160,344)/2), but the actual figure is 149,459. The totals refer to Old Style years running 1 April to 31 March (see appendix 7 pp. 613–9). If New Style years are assumed to be more appropriate, the lack of agreement is more pronounced since the 1730 and 1740 totals suggest an average of 173,285 compared with the 1730–9 average of 150,779 (the 1731–40 average is 148,914).

other assumptions. He provides decadal birth estimates from the 1740s onwards, but they are patently unrealistic, and have not been reproduced here. They become progressively further and further below the true level moving backwards in time until by the 1740s they are lower than the totals of baptisms recorded in Anglican registers. His estimates are derived from the 1821 and 1841 census age data but he gives no extended description of his method which was complex since he sought to take both mortality and net migration into account. It seems likely that he proceeded on the assumption that the patterns of mortality and net migration found in the mid nineteenth century also obtained earlier. If this is so, it is not surprising that his decadal birth estimates became progressively too small. For example, if the numbers surviving to age 60–9 in 1821 were converted into a birth cohort for 1751–60 on the mortality assumptions of the third English life table, the size of the cohort would be understated to the degree that mortality was actually more severe between 1750 and 1820 than the mortality levels embodied in the life table.

There is less to be said about the pattern of relationship between our new estimates and earlier estimates for the period before 1801 than for the later period. Those who used fixed correction ratios (Brownlee, Griffith) make estimates that must necessarily rise relative to the new estimates as one moves backwards in time since our corrections for nonconformity, delayed baptism, and other causes of under-registration decline steadily from their early-nineteenth-century peak to very much lower values in the early eighteenth century. Ohlin's procedure was more compli-cated but the same comment holds good also for his estimates. Krause's estimates show an opposite trend: although he was conscious of the need to make corrections for nonconformity and for the residual causes of under-registration, which we have tried to capture in the final inflation ratio, he does not appear to have given enough weight to the loss of coverage associated with baptism delay and therefore fails to set his correction factor high enough in the 1780s. Krause suggested a factor lying between 1.10 and 1.20 for baptisms in the 1780s at a time when baptism delay alone would suggest an inflation of about 8 per cent; and a factor of 1.08 for burials when the same consideration suggests an inflation of about 5 per cent (see table 4.5). Farr made estimates of births only. As with his nineteenth-century estimates, his late-eighteenth-century decadal totals fall below the new series.

Retrospect

In a sense the whole of the book so far has been a preparatory exercise designed to provide tolerably reliable totals of births, deaths, and marriages for description and analysis in later chapters. To take up so much space in evaluating, correcting, and testing source material may suggest a disproportionate concern for matters of detail. We are persuaded, however, that the exercise was necessary and worthwhile. The Anglican parish registers contain information of fundamental importance to the understanding of the economic and social history of England, as well as to its population history. But they are very variable in accuracy and completeness. The striking lack of agreement between those who have used them as a source of data for population history is due in part to the wide difference in the assumptions made about their strengths and weaknesses in this regard. It seemed to us proper to make a major effort to investigate both systematic changes in register quality over time, and variations in register coverage that occurred more haphazardly. Such an in-vestigation appeared desirable in its own right but doubly so to match the efforts of so many local historians in laboriously assembling a huge body of new data.

It is now apparent that the general quality of parish registration was relatively high during the first century after its institution, apart from the striking deterioration that took place in Mary's reign. Deficiencies in this period are more often due to later physical damage to registers or to their loss than to a failure to record events in the first instance. After 1640, however, matters are never again so simple. Although mice, mildew, and accident may take a lesser toll, there is evidence of slowly increasing deficiencies due to baptism delay, nonconformity, and a more diffuse disregard of religious observance. The Civil War and Commonwealth, of course, produced a massive and well-known deterioration in register coverage, but the Restoration, though it led to a marked improvement , did not herald a return to the comparative excellence of earlier times. The beneficial impact of legislative action, as for example following the Marriage Duty Act of 1695, is clearly visible in some aspects of registration, but this took place against a background of steady, if slight, decline in the completeness of coverage.

Towards the end of the eighteenth century, and perhaps especially in the 1780s, there was a marked acceleration in the deterioration in Anglican coverage until in the early decades of the nineteenth century Anglican registers afford only limited help in identifying trends in fertility and mortality. At its worst point in the 1810s only 68 per cent of all live-born children received Anglican baptism, and the burial registers contain the names of barely two thirds of those who died during the decade.

Fortunately, during the period when the Anglican registers are at their least reliable the institution of a decennial census enables the true totals of births and deaths to be established with only a relatively small range of possible error. Before 1801 there is no help to be had from censuses and all estimates must be regarded as subject to a greater margin of error. We have attempted to measure the effect of two of the more important causes of under-registration, nonconformity and late baptism, and have added a further correction intended to capture residual causes of incomplete coverage, linked to the prevalence of nonconformity. The end product of the many steps taken to convert monthly totals of Anglican events into totals of births, deaths, and marriages is a national series covering 300 years from 1540 onwards. This is much the longest such series for any European country. Excellent data exist for Sweden from 1749 onwards and less reliable data from 1700.[49] Other Scandinavian countries possess good national data from about the mid eighteenth century. Scholars at the Institut National d'Etudes Démographiques in Paris have estimated French birth and death totals from 1740.[50] And the parish registers of some other countries, perhaps Spain or Germany, might be exploited to provide series comparable to those we have produced. At present, however, the English series are unique.

The new series can be used both for conventional types of description and analysis and also as raw material to which new analytic techniques can be applied. In the later chapters of this book we shall first examine secular demographic trends and then turn to consider short-term changes. In each case we begin by using simple aggregative techniques and later apply more powerful methods of analysis, including some newly developed for the purpose. The new information produced by both old and new

49. See Hofsten and Lundström, *Swedish population history*, ch. 1, and appendix 1.

50. See Blayo, 'Mouvement naturel de la population française de 1740 à 1829', and Henry and Blayo, 'La population de la France de 1740 à 1860'. It is intended ultimately to extend the survey to include the period 1670–1739. Preliminary figures, based on a sample of 51 rural parishes, have been published in Rebaudo, 'La population francaise rurale de 1670 à 1740'.

methods is valuable in its own right, but demographic, economic, and social changes were so closely interwoven in the past that it would be arbitrary and unsatisfactory to consider demographic changes in isolation. This is especially true when the timing and incidence of marriage has a powerful influence on population trends, a prominent feature of English history throughout the early modern period. The second half of the book therefore also includes a description and analysis of the relation between economic and demographic change in both the short and the long term. The lengthy process of trying to turn a sow's ear into a silk purse has reached the stage where a passable imitation of silk has been created but not yet given a coherent shape. Henceforward we turn from questions of the source material, and ways of overcoming or offsetting its defects, to the major substantive issues of English population history between mid-Tudor and early-Victorian times.

II English population history

6

Secular trends: some basic patterns

The task defined

The first part of the book has described how national series of monthly frequencies of births, deaths, and marriages were assembled for the three centuries from the mid sixteenth to the mid nineteenth. The remainder of the volume is devoted to an analysis of the series to discover the course of population change in early modern England. We shall begin by using simple methods to examine those aspects of the story that are most evident from the series themselves. However, it will soon become clear that some of the most important questions about population change cannot be answered directly from aggregate data of this kind. Consequently new and more powerful methods of analysis have been developed in order to identify and measure the components of demographic change and to assess their influence at different times in the past. The methods and the results obtained from them are described in the next chapter. Then we turn to the consideration of short-term variation in the demographic series before attempting in the closing chapters to set the demographic story that emerges in its social and economic context. Clearly within the covers of the present volume it will only be possible to consider a limited number of topics. Since our main aim is to describe the course of national population change, the treatment of other topics, such as regional variation, will have to be deferred until a later occasion.

The first step in interpreting the evidence is to examine its logical status, that is to consider what it is that the series of births, marriages, and deaths represent. Essentially the data record the flows of vital events generated by a population that, before the census of 1801, is invisible and whose size and structure is therefore unknown. The series of births and deaths represent the flows into and out of the population respectively, and the balance between them, usually known as the 'natural increase', largely determines the rate at which the population grows or declines. But birth and death are not the only means of entering or leaving the population: some of those born in the country may leave and die elsewhere, while others, born abroad, may enter the country and die within it. In other words spatial movements supplement the flows of births and deaths, and the balance between these movements, or net migration, supplements the natural increase to produce population growth or decline.

The invisible population that produces the visible flows of events is not an abstract statistical concept but an aggregate of individuals living in a particular area in a specific historical period. The flows of events thus reflect the physical, economic, and political circumstances of the individual members of an historical population as well as the social customs which characterize and influence every aspect of their lives. For example, the flow of deaths reflects not only climate and biological factors but also economic factors such as the kind of agriculture practised, social customs such as those affecting diet or sleeping arrangements, and the distribution of political and economic power which governs the allocation of food, shelter, and wealth amongst individual members of the population.

The importance of context is even more evident in the case of births, for in early modern England as in other societies these events were far from being the product of random sexual encounters between the adult members of the population. The circumstances in which children should be procreated were strictly specified in a tight web of custom, religion, and law. The socially approved institution for procreation was marriage. Hence the importance of the third aggregative series, marriage frequencies, which records the flow of individuals into the reproductive state. It is true that some children were born out of wedlock, but the proportion of illegitimate births, though varying over time, was always low.[1]

One crucial precondition of marriage in England in the past was the expectation that the newly-married couple should command the resources to form an independent unit, both economically and residentially. In these circumstances marriage was dependent upon the availability of the means of earning a livelihood: for peasants a farm, for artisans a craft 'practice', and for labourers a demand for their labour at least at a subsistence wage. Thus the social rules regarding marriage linked the rate of entry into the reproductive state with economic circumstances, thereby raising the possibility that marriage, and hence fertility, could respond to economic change and so enable the population to keep in balance with its economic resources.[2]

The flows of births, deaths, and marriages are therefore the visible outcomes of a complex and inter-related set of biological, social, and economic processes. The essential problem is one of inference, first from the flows of events to the characteristics of the population producing them, and then from the demographic behaviour of the population to the nature of the relationships between social, economic, and demographic change.

The resolution of the first problem of inference, of how to capture the invisible population behind the visible flows of events, has taxed historical demographers for many years. Two devices have commonly been adopted and both are plainly unsatisfactory. The first assumes constant vital rates and makes the population size a simple multiple of the number of vital events recorded.[3] Such a procedure is evidently incapable of discovering changes in vital rates over time, and in so far as the rates did change the method yields erroneous estimates of population size. The second, and more usual, method assumes that the population is closed so that in the absence of migration the size of the population at any date can be calculated by adding or subtracting the balance of births over deaths, or natural increase, between that date and another at which the population has been enumerated. This was the procedure

1. Laslett, *Family life*, fig. 3.1 on p. 113 shows illegitimate baptisms comprising between 0.5 per cent and 5.5 per cent of all baptisms during the parish register period. Laslett also discusses the social context of illegitimate fertility.

2. The classic formulation of the economic concomitants of marriage in western Europe and their demographic consequences is to be found in Malthus's *Essay on population*, especially ch. 4, while the residential independence of married couples is established and discussed in Laslett and Wall, *Household and family*, chs. 1, 4–7. Mackenroth, in his remarkable *Bevölkerungslehre*, published in 1953, makes access to economic resources the lynch-pin of the west European pre-industrial demographic régime. The sociological aspects of the ideas of Malthus and Mackenroth are discussed in Linde, 'Generative Strukturen', and 'Die Bedeutung von T. R. Malthus', and their demographic implications are explored in Schofield, 'Demographic structure and environment'.

3. Rickman used this method in connexion with his two collections of parish register totals of events in 1801 and 1841, the latter being completed after his death. *1801 Census*, Observations on the results, p. 9; *1841 Census*, Enumeration abstract, pp. 34–7.

adopted by those who used Rickman's Parish Register Abstracts to chart the course of population change in the eighteenth century. In this case the size of the population in each decade in the eighteenth century was calculated by a successive subtraction of the decadal natural increase working backwards from one of the nineteenth century censuses.[4] The method is clearly only as good as its assumption that the population was closed. While net migration may have been negligible for some groups at certain dates, as we have argued was the case for females in the early nineteenth century, it is unlikely to have been zero for the whole population over long periods of time. In these circumstances quite small annual rates of net migration can cumulate to reach large totals with the result that estimates of population size calculated on the assumption of no net migration can be seriously wrong.

By way of example, the size of the population in 1695 can be estimated by assuming no migration and simply subtracting the cumulative natural increase between 1695 and the first census enumeration in 1801. In round terms our revised figure for the 1801 population size of England alone is 8.658 million and subtracting from it the cumulative natural increase of 4.259 million accruing over the period yields an estimated population of 4.399 million in 1695.[5] This figure is 784,000 lower than the 5.183 million which Gregory King estimated in 1695 and it is also 233,000 below Glass's substantial downward revision of King's estimate.[6] Either the King estimates are badly wrong, which is not generally thought to be the case, or net migration was on such a scale during the eighteenth century that ignoring it leads to serious error in estimating the population size over the range of a century. Since it is known that large numbers of people left the country to go to the colonies during this period the discrepancy between the population estimates almost certainly points to the inadequacy of the second method of estimating population size, which ignores migration and considers natural increase alone.[7]

Neither of the traditional methods therefore provides an acceptable way of estimating the size of the invisible population. Yet without a knowledge of population size the range of demographic inferences that can be drawn from a series of flows of vital events is severely constrained. Figure 6.1 provides a simple example of the difficulties of interpreting birth and death series when the population that produced them is unknown.

In panel (a) both births and deaths are increasing in number over a 50-year period, with births growing faster than deaths. But it by no means follows that fertility and mortality were rising, for in the absence of emigration the surplus of births over deaths means that the population is increasing. If the population grows at a steeper rate than the slopes of the lines of births and deaths shown in panel (a) then the birth and death rates (i.e. the number of births or deaths per 1,000 population) will decline, as is shown in panel (b). There is therefore no easy inference from the shape of the graph of events in panel (a) to changes in birth or death rates. Nor does the fact that births rose

4. The methods of analysis used in conjunction with the Parish Register Abstracts are discussed in Glass, 'Population and population movements'.

5. For the revised nineteenth-century census population totals used throughout the book see table A6.7. The cumulative natural increase is from January 1696 to 30 June 1801; see tables A2.3–4.

6. Glass's revised total is 4.632 million. These figures are for England only, derived in the manner explained below on pp. 571–2. The equivalent figures as originally estimated for England and Wales by King and Glass are 5.503 and 4.918 million respectively.

7. For the volume of migration to the American colonies in the eighteenth century, a substantial proportion of which came from England, see Potter, 'Growth of population in America', pp. 644–6.

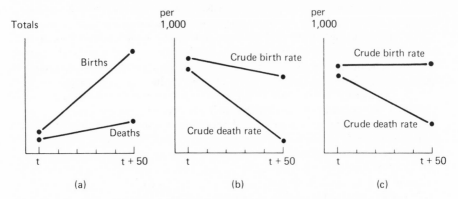

Figure 6.1: Vital events and vital rates

faster than deaths necessarily mean that changes in fertility were more important than changes in mortality over the period. For example, the population may have been growing at exactly the same speed as the number of births recorded, in which case the birth rate would have been constant and the death rate declining (see panel (c)).

Since the discovery of the level, and changes in level, of fertility and mortality is essential to an understanding of the course of population change, we have made a considerable effort to improve on existing methods and find a way to estimate the size of the population during the period when it is invisible before 1801, taking account not only of natural increase but also of net migration. The method we have developed is described in the next chapter, where we also present our population estimates and calculate the levels of fertility and mortality that obtained at different times in the past. While the main discussion of demographic trends must clearly be postponed until then, there are certain features of the course of population change that are quite evident from our series of annual totals of births, deaths, and marriages for the period 1539–1873, and which can conveniently be discussed before embarking upon the additional complications that estimating the size of the population before 1801 entails. In particular there are some very clear patterns in the long-term trends of the three series which point to certain general conclusions about the way population developed, even though the levels of fertility and mortality remain unknown.

The overall pattern of events

The annual frequencies of births, deaths, and marriages are listed in table A2.3 and are drawn with bold lines in pullout 1 at the end of the book. To bring out the long-term trends more clearly the annual figures have also been smoothed by means of a centred 25-year moving average, and the resulting series has been superimposed in lighter type. The vertical scale in pullout 1 has been made logarithmic to ensure that proportional changes in the numbers of events are visually comparable, regardless of the absolute numbers of events concerned. In this way rates of growth at different points in time can be compared directly, simply by inspecting the relative steepness of the pitch of the lines on the graph.

The first feature of the graph to catch the eye is the substantial rise in the number of events in each series over the whole period 1539–1873. It is also evident that there are relatively few years when there were more deaths than births. Since the overall growth in the numbers of events was far greater than could be accounted for by any conceivable increase in the vital rates, we can conclude that generally there was a positive natural increase and that a substantial fraction was retained rather than lost through emigration, producing a large rise in population between the mid sixteenth and late nineteenth centuries.

If we compare the annual numbers of events recorded in a five-year period centred on 1541 with similar figures for a five-year period centred on 1871 we find, in round thousands, that births grew from 111 to 773, deaths from 82 to 471, and marriages from 42 to 180.[8] The growth ratios in the three series between 1541 and 1871 were therefore 6.96, 5.74, and 4.29 respectively. If there were no major differences in the vital rates at the two dates, the three series suggest the population in 1541 was 14 per cent, 17 per cent, and 23 per cent respectively of the population in 1871. Since the latter was 21.635 million, the implied population in 1541 lies between 3.11 and 5.05 million. An assumption of stability in the vital rates is quite likely to be wrong, so these estimates can have no claim to precision. However, the fact that the flows of events increased between four and seven times over the three centuries both provides a rough indication of the order of magnitude of population growth during this period and suggests that the population size in the mid sixteenth century is likely to have been somewhere between 3 and 5 million.

The differences in crude growth ratios between the numbers of events recorded at the beginning and at the end of the period in the series also show that births grew faster than deaths, which in turn grew faster than marriages. In other words, at the end of the period fertility was higher relative to mortality and nuptiality than was the case at the beginning of the period. This may reflect either a faster rise of fertility than of mortality and nuptiality, or a faster fall of nuptiality and mortality than of fertility. We cannot infer which combination of movements in the vital rates produced the observed results without knowing population sizes, but the differences in the rates at which the frequencies of events grew over the period at least tells us that fertility, mortality, and nuptiality did not move in step between the mid sixteenth and mid nineteenth centuries.

Nor were the differences in the growth rates in the three series constant over time. In some periods deaths were increasing faster than births as may be seen on the graph in pullout 1. For example, in the period between 1580 and 1640 the numbers of both births and deaths were increasing, but the latter were growing much faster than the former. After 1640 the numbers of births ceased to grow while the totals of deaths continued for a while on an upward course. Changes in the slopes of the series are also visible at other points on the graph. Clearly the levels of fertility, mortality, and nuptiality changed independently at a number of different dates so that the flows of events reflect the appearance or disappearance of several different configurations of fertility, mortality, and nuptiality between the mid sixteenth and mid nineteenth centuries.

Although the precise identification of these shifts in demographic structure requires a more elaborate style of analysis, a summary consideration of the timing of the main changes of slope of the lines in pullout 1 suggests that the course of population change between the 1540s and the 1870s falls into three rather different phases. The first phase runs from the start of the series up to 1640. With the exception of the first 20

8. Based on the annual frequencies of events for 1539–43 and 1869–73 as shown in table A2.3.

years or so the trend in all three series is strongly upwards and, apart from the years 1556–60, many more births than deaths were recorded, though towards 1640 the gap was closing fast. After 1640 a change occurs: the annual frequencies of both births and marriages fall and then oscillate somewhat until 1710, after which a rising trend clearly sets in again. The end of the first decade of the eighteenth century might seem to mark the end of a relatively stagnant second phase and the beginning of a third which sees the return of sustained growth, continuing until the series end in the 1870s. But the line representing deaths is more erratic and displays a different pattern, for it continues to rise for another 40 years after 1640 before flattening out at the end of the seventeenth century. Furthermore, although deaths, like births and marriages, tend to rise at the beginning of the third phase, their upsurge in the early eighteenth century owes much to some years of exceptionally high mortality in the 1720s and early 1740s, and it is noteworthy that around 1750 the number of deaths sinks back to a level not much higher than had obtained in the last quarter of the seventeenth century.

In gross terms, therefore, the course of the annual frequencies of the three series of events suggests a simple division of the 300-odd years they cover into three periods: 1539–1639, 1640–1709, and 1710–1873. In the two outer periods all three series increase in number and there is a consistent and substantial surplus of births over deaths. By contrast in the central period, spanning the later seventeenth century, the frequencies of events show little tendency to grow, while the number of deaths is much closer to, and often exceeds, the number of births.

Regional variation

The general shape of the patterns traced by the three series over the three centuries from 1539 to 1836 is the sum of the individual experiences of each of the 404 parishes, modified by the addition of events recorded in London and corrected for under-registration arising from a number of sources. Although the graph of events in most parishes bears some resemblance to the aggregate graph in pullout 1, there are some notable differences within the set of parishes. A full study of local demographic variation is no easy task, for some of the causes of under-registration, for example nonconformity and the delay between birth and baptism, varied markedly between parishes and between regions.[9] If no allowance is made for variable correction factors in converting ecclesiastical into vital events there is a danger of mistaking local or regional differences in the inadequacy of Anglican registration for differences in demographic behaviour.[10] A considered examination of local variation would therefore entail the collection and analysis of a great deal of additional evidence on local levels of the major causes of under-registration, and that task is beyond the scope of the present volume. However a rough indication of the range of local variation can be obtained from the distributions of the 404 parishes with regard to one or two summary measures of the patterns of events over time. In view of the limited purpose of this exercise, the problem of local variation in the amount of under-registration will

9. For variation in nonconformity see Whiteman, *Compton census*, for the late seventeenth century, and *1851 Census*, Religious worship, for the mid nineteenth century. Local variation in baptism practice is discussed in Berry and Schofield, 'Age at baptism'.
10. The eighteenth-century regional estimates of population growth, fertility, mortality, and migration, which Deane and Cole calculated from Rickman's county frequencies of ecclesiastical events, are particularly vulnerable to regional differences in the adequacy of registration. Deane and Cole, *British economic growth*, ch. 3.

be ignored, and the distributions of simple frequencies of the *ecclesiastical* events recorded in the parishes will be compared with the aggregate sum of these frequencies contributed by all 404 parishes corrected for the bias in the distribution of the parish population sizes, but not for omissions due to nonconformity or late baptism.

Taking all 404 parishes together, the decade in which the largest number of baptisms was recorded before the mid seventeenth century was the 1640s, and this figure of 62,300 baptisms was not exceeded until the 1730s (in pullout 1 this occurs earlier in the 1700s as a result of the corrections made to counteract under-registration).

Table 6.1: Decade when baptism frequencies first exceeded maximum pre-1660 decadal total

Decade	Parishes	
	No.	Per cent
1660s	56	15
1670s	24	7
1680s	31	9
1690s	18	5
1700s	17	5
1710s	14	4
1720s	18	5
1730s	15	4
1740s	12	3
1750s	16	4
1760s	24	7
1770s	21	6
1780s	12	3
1790s	19	5
1800s	16	4
1810s, or later	49	14
Total	362	100

Note: 42 parishes were excluded because baptism entries were not available by 1610.

Source: Uncorrected parish registers.

Table 6.1 shows the distribution of the parishes according to the decade in which the number of baptisms first exceeded the maximum decadal total recorded in each parish before 1660. In order to give each parish a chance to record a high pre-1660 total those in which baptism registration began after 1609 were excluded from consideration. The scatter of the 362 individual parishes around the aggregate recovery point of the 1730s is very wide, for each decade in the eighteenth century claimed between 3 and 7 per cent of the parishes. The most common outcome (15 per cent of the parishes) was for baptisms to continue to grow without a pause and exceed the pre-1660 maximum at the earliest opportunity in the 1660s. On the other hand there were almost as many parishes, 14 per cent of the total, that by 1800–9 were still not recording as many baptisms as they had produced in their heyday before the mid seventeenth century. Thus the general outline of the course of baptisms in the country as a whole reflects the sum of a rather varied set of experiences amongst the 404 parishes. In some the true growth in births may have been masked by unusually high levels of under-registration, but in others the population may never have regained its early-seventeenth-century level.

The 404 parishes also show considerable variation in the changing relationships between baptisms and burials, which on the national scale are similar in outline to those already described for births and deaths. *In aggregate* the 404 parishes recorded a baptism/burial deficit in only two decades, the 1680s and 1720s, though in the 1550s, 1650s, 1660s, and 1670s the surpluses of baptisms over burials were proportionately very low indeed.[11] Table 6.2 shows for each decade the proportions of the parishes in observation that registered more burials than baptisms. Once more the spread is much wider than was apparent from the aggregate pattern alone. In the

Table 6.2: Parishes with decadal baptism–burial deficits

Decade	Number of parishes in observation	with deficit	Percentage of parishes with deficit
1540s	33	18	55
1550s	61	46	75
1560s	141	7	5
1570s	232	12	5
1580s	261	11	4
1590s	289	20	7
1600s	313	10	3
1610s	349	19	5
1620s	364	16	4
1630s	371	19	5
1640s	377	18	5
1650s	383	36	9
1660s	400	35	9
1670s	404	37	9
1680s	404	46	11
1690s	404	28	7
1700s	404	20	5
1710s	404	25	6
1720s	404	51	13
1730s	404	18	4
1740s	404	26	6
1750s	404	17	4
1760s	404	21	5
1770s	404	11	3
1780s	404	16	4
1790s	404	5	1
1800s	404	4	1
1810s	277	3	1
1820s	274	2	1

Note: The 1830s are complicated by the advent of civil registration and have therefore been excluded.

Source: Uncorrected parish registers.

11. In the national series of births and deaths the 1660s become a decade of deficit due to the large numbers of deaths in the great plague of London in 1665. The impact of London is discussed below.

decades from the 1560s to the 1780s there appears to have been a remarkably steady 'background' proportion of parishes recording baptism/burial deficits. This ran at between 3 and 9 per cent, though the parishes were by no means the same in each decade. In most of these decades the surpluses recorded by other parishes were sufficient to offset these deficits to produce an aggregate surplus for the whole set of 404 parishes. In the two decades when there was an aggregate deficit, the 1680s and the 1720s, only 11 per cent and 13 per cent of the parishes respectively actually recorded deficits, but they were large enough to outweigh the tiny surpluses produced by the 90 per cent or so remaining parishes. In contrast no less than 75 per cent of the 61 parishes in observation recorded deficits in the 1550s, as did 55 per cent of the 33 parishes in observation in the 1540s, yet in both decades the minority of other parishes produced sufficiently substantial surpluses to yield an overall surplus of baptisms over burials.

The final aggregate balance struck in each decade will reflect a number of factors: the proportion of parishes with deficits, the relative sizes of the parishes experiencing deficits or surpluses, the relative degree of under-registration of births and deaths and the combination of levels of fertility and mortality that obtained. Although in these cases the| baptism/burial deficits may be spurious owing to a greater under-registration of births than of deaths, the marked decline in the number of parishes recording deficits between the 1780s and 1790s is likely to be genuine because it took place against a background of a widening differential under-registration in the two series, as was shown in table 5.27. The question of the proportion of parishes suffering heavy mortality at different dates is taken up in chapter 8; but it is already clear from pullout 1 that the aggregate surplus of births over deaths was much more substantial in the mid sixteenth century than in the early eighteenth century and was therefore better able to withstand the ravages of widespread crisis mortality. It is also very evident from table 6.2 that the aggregate balance struck between baptisms and burials at different dates represents an ever-changing mix of the varied experiences of surplus and deficit in individual parishes.

The variation between parishes is brought out more directly in table 6.3 which shows the frequency distribution of parishes according to the numbers of decades in which they recorded decadal baptism/burial deficits, standardizing for the different periods covered by individual registers. Out of a notional three centuries (30 decades) in observation the median parish experience was five decades in which more burials were registered than baptisms; but 34 parishes, or 8 per cent of the total set, had no decade of deficit, while more than a quarter of the parishes had less than three decades and the same proportion had more than seven decades of deficit. A small group of nine parishes, 2 per cent of the total, had burial deficits in more than two out of every three decades. This group comprised marshland parishes (Bradwell, Essex; Milton by Gravesend, Kent; Wyberton, Lincs.), market towns (Sittingbourne, Kent, and Romford, Essex), city-centre parishes in Norwich (St Margaret) and Shrewsbury (St Mary), and the near-London parishes of Edmonton and Putney. Parishes of a similar kind were also prominent in the next group in the table, with between a half and two thirds of the decades recording more burials than baptisms. Although the urban parishes and market towns may have been labouring under the handicap of a greater incidence of nonconformity, which will have depressed the number of baptisms being registered more than the number of burials, the sizes of the deficits involved are generally large enough to suggest that there was a genuine difference between the balance struck between fertility and mortality in these urban and marshland

Table 6.3: Frequency of decades of baptism-
burial deficit by parish

Standardized no. of decades in deficit[1]	Parishes No.	Per cent
0	34	8
1	35	9
2	50	12
3	40	10
4	41	10
5	42	10
6	25	6
7	18	4
8	25	6
9	10	2
10–4	53	13
15–9	22	5
20–30	9	2
All	404	97

Note: [1] Observed number of decades raised to a standard base of 30 decades in observation by multiplying by (30/number of decades actually in observation).

Source: Uncorrected parish registers.

communities and that obtaining in the more isolated and better-drained rural parishes.[12]

London

London constitutes a particularly pronounced example of the urban pattern. Although there are additional difficulties in estimating the number of baptisms and burials occurring in the metropolis it would appear that the latter regularly exceeded the former until around 1802. In part this pattern may reflect a greater differential under-registration between births and deaths than obtained elsewhere, but the baptism/burial deficits are also consistent with London's particular demographic characteristics of massive immigration and high mortality.[13] Since London was growing faster than the population between 1550 and 1750, it had a progressively dampening effect on the natural surplus engendered by the rest of the country. Table 6.4 shows the numbers of baptisms and burials attributed to London and to England as a whole as described in chapter 3, and the final two columns of the table express the numbers of baptisms and burials recorded in London as percentages of the national

12. The comparatively high mortality of marshland and urban parishes was recognized by Short when he published the results of his analysis of a number of parish registers in 1750. Short, *New observations*, pp. 19–20, 63. For an example of a modern study showing differential mortality in wealden, downland, and marshland parishes see Brent, 'Eastern Sussex', pp. 45–6.
13. For the balance between baptisms and burials see *1811 Census*, Parish registers, p. 200. On the level of immigration see Wrigley, 'London's importance', and on mortality Finlay, 'Gateways to death?' and *Population of London*, ch. 5.

Table 6.4: Baptisms and burials in London and England by quarter century

Period	London		England		London as percentage of England	
	Baptisms	Burials	Baptisms	Burials	Baptisms	Burials
1550–74	76 493	111 560	2 694 632	2 098 436	2.8	5.1
1575–99	128 426	155 354	3 047 652	2 288 157	4.2	6.8
1600–24	220 716	239 221	3 504 446	2 744 538	6.3	8.7
1625–49	292 253	376 692	3 796 036	3 280 560	7.7	11.5
1650–74	293 635	520 463	3 457 217	3 564 468	8.5	14.6
1675–99	364 847	546 312	3 557 091	3 645 930	10.3	15.0
1700–24	462 116	593 835	3 767 867	3 504 777	12.3	16.9
1725–49	475 151	679 922	4 124 708	3 953 656	11.5	17.2
1750–74	459 978	612 046	4 578 395	3 890 732	10.1	15.7
1775–99	555 388	601 572	5 680 167	4 370 112	9.8	13.8
1800–24	687 136	598 718	7 115 211	4 556 893	9.7	13.1

Sources: London, see fn. 14.
England, table A4.1, column 5.

frequencies.[14] The London baptism frequencies began at a modest level of 2.8 per cent of the national totals in the period 1550–74, rose progressively until they comprised 12.3 per cent in 1700–24, and then fell back slightly to hold a level of around 10 per cent in the later eighteenth century. London always contributed a higher proportion of the national total of burials, but the build-up over time was broadly similar to the pattern displayed by baptisms. Starting with 5.1 per cent in 1550–74, the London share of the national total of burials grew to reach a maximum of around 17.2 per cent in the period 1725–49 and then declined gently to 13.1 per cent in the first quarter of the nineteenth century. Taking the two columns together it is evident that the unusual conditions obtaining in London had a progressively greater impact on the national balance between baptisms and burials during the seventeenth century and maintained this position throughout much of the eighteenth century.

Table 6.5: Natural increase in London and England by quarter century

25-year period beginning	London	Rest of England	Total	London as percentage of rest of England
1550	−35 067	546 378	511 311	6.4
1575	−26 928	786 423	759 495	3.4
1600	−18 505	778 413	759 908	2.4
1625	−84 439	599 915	515 476	14.1
1650	−227 828	120 577	−107 251	189.0
1675	−181 465	92 626	−88 839	195.9
1700	−131 719	394 808	263 090	33.4
1725	−204 771	375 823	171 052	54.5
1750	−152 068	839 731	687 663	18.1
1775	−46 184	1 356 239	1 310 055	3.4
1800	88 413	2 469 905	2 558 318	3.6

Source: Table 6.4.

The contrast between the shortfall of baptisms continually recorded in London before 1800 and the surpluses produced in aggregate by the rest of the country as represented by the set of 404 parishes is clearly evident in table 6.5 and figure 6.2. The final column of the table shows by how much the surpluses engendered in the countryside were offset by the metropolitan deficits. Before 1625 and after 1775 a combination of substantial surpluses outside London and modest deficits within the capital resulted in relatively small reductions in the non-London surplus of between 2 and 6 per cent. Indeed, in the first quarter of the nineteenth century London returned a modest surplus to increase by 4 per cent the surpluses generated elsewhere. Between 1625 and 1774, however, the London deficits were large and made substantial inroads into the surpluses from other areas. In the 'shoulder' periods of 1625–49 and 1750–74, when these surpluses were still high, the London deficits reduced them by 14 and 18 per cent respectively. In the second half of the seventeenth century the extra-metropolitan surpluses fell precipitately while the London deficits rose so that

14. Pp. 77–83. The quarter-century totals of baptisms and burials in London in table 6.4 were calculated by reversing the process described in chapter 3. The constant 'national' inflation factor of 22.82 was subtracted from the national series of ecclesiastical events and the events contributed by London were obtained as a remainder.

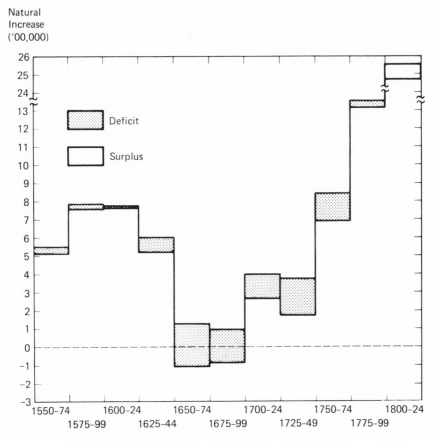

Natural
Increase
('00,000)

Figure 6.2: Natural increase in London and England by quarter
century, 1550–1824

Source: Table 6.5.

the latter were almost exactly double the former, thereby converting the non-London
surplus into a national deficit of almost the same magnitude. In the early eighteenth
century the rest of the country bounced back to record more substantial surpluses, but
the London deficits continued at a high level and reduced the surpluses in the first two
quarters of the century by 33 and 55 per cent respectively.

Overall, London would appear to have had little impact on the national patterns of
events before 1625 and after 1775. In the later seventeenth century its particular
characteristics served to intensify the deteriorating balance between baptisms and
burials already evident in the series of events contributed by the 404 parishes, and its
size relative to the rest of the country was such that it was capable of turning a small
extra-metropolitan baptism surplus into a national deficit of a similar size. In the
eighteenth century London continued to act as a severe drain on the surpluses being
produced elsewhere: even as late as the second quarter of the century it offset about a
half of the national baptism surplus, thereby exercising a strong braking effect on the

national rate of natural increase implied by the totals of baptisms and burials. In terms of the three phases discerned in the national series of births and deaths, London's main contribution was to intensify the stagnation of the second phase between 1640 and 1709, and to reduce and delay the potential for growth in the early years of the third phase beginning in 1710. Indeed, it was the very size and untypicality of London that made it seem advisable to make separate estimates of the numbers of ecclesiastical events occurring there and to incorporate them explicitly in the estimated national totals of events, rather than to include a few London examples in the set of 404 parishes.

Comparison with other studies

If attention is now confined to non-metropolitan England it is encouraging that the aggregate patterns emerging from considerable variations in the individual experiences of the 404 parishes are replicated by two other studies based on substantial sets of parishes.[15] The first study is of a group of parishes in south Yorkshire over the years 1540–1699, while the second draws upon a set of parishes located all over the country, apart from London, during the period 1695 to 1794.[16] In both cases the frequencies recorded are uncorrected ecclesiastical events, so the proper comparison is with the series of baptisms, burials, and marriages from the set of 404 parishes before any corrections have been made to counteract the deficiencies of Anglican registration.[17]

Table 6.6 compares the decadal frequencies of baptisms, burials, and marriages recorded in Morley wapentake, Yorkshire, and in the set of 404 parishes, after being indexed on 1560–9. In both sets of parishes the numbers of events in all three series rose considerably up to 1640, and fell back to remain at a fairly constant level in the later seventeenth century. However the overall pattern is more marked in Morley: the pace of the rise up to 1640 was faster and the later drop in level more pronounced. In

15. Other studies are too restricted either in the time period or area covered to warrant detailed comparison with the national series. For example, Short presented totals of events from the registers of 83 rural parishes and 48 market towns, about half of which came from Yorkshire and Derbyshire, but the time periods spanned by the individual registers were so short and varied that it is impossible to aggregate them into a reasonable series of events. Short, *New observations*, introduction [p. 2], pp. 4–12, 44–9. Chambers collected baptism, burial, and marriage totals for 34 'agricultural' and 26 'industrial' Nottinghamshire parishes for the period 1670–1810, but has only published a graph of the annual totals of events. Neither the figures themselves nor the names of the parishes have ever been publicly revealed. Chambers, *Vale of Trent*, pp. 19–35. The figures were made available to Pentland, who also obtained totals from a further 25 parishes in Worcestershire, Pembrokeshire, and Leeds, but only printed figures of natural increase for the eighteenth century. They nevertheless show a similar pattern to the natural increase (baptisms less burials) of the 404 parishes. See table A4.1 as modified by fn. 17, and Pentland, 'Population and labour growth', pp. 158–60, 173. Finally, there are many studies of individual parishes or of small areas. Several of those published before 1966 are listed in Wrigley, *English historical demography*, pp. 253–63, while work in progress from 1968 to the present has been listed from time to time in *Local Population Studies* (see index to nos. 1–20, covering 1968–78).

16. Drake, 'Elementary exercise', and Krause, 'Population change'.

17. Ideally the aggregate totals of the 404 parishes should have been recomputed by taking the uncorrected figures as recorded in the individual registers and summing them after reweighting to correct for the bias in the distribution of parish population sizes, as outlined in chapter 2. The limited purpose of the present comparison scarcely warranted so great a labour, so average quinquennial deflation factors were calculated from the annual ratios obtaining between the corrected and the uncorrected totals of events summed over all 404 parishes before weighting for population size (table A4.1, cols. 1 and 2). The resulting ratios were used to deflate the re-weighted and corrected aggregate quinquennial totals (derived from table A4.1, col. 4) to obtain a reweighted but uncorrected set of quinquennial totals of events.

Table 6.6: Comparative trends in ecclesiastical events: Morley Wapentake, Yorkshire, and the set of aggregative parishes 1540–1699

| | Index number of frequency of events (1560–9 = 100) | | | | | |
| | Baptisms | | Burials | | Marriages | |
	Morley	Aggregative parishes	Morley	Aggregative parishes	Morley	Aggregative parishes
1540–9	82	89	96	117	81	111
1550–9	84	74	89	112	88	75
1560–9	100	100	100	100	100	100
1570–9	110	102	113	98	106	101
1580–9	115	113	145	117	123	111
1590–9	118	112	169	134	129	108
1600–9	154	125	185	128	151	114
1610–9	163	126	216	155	157	116
1620–9	161	131	248	154	156	108
1630–9	165	134	258	169	165	115
1660–9	136	120	208	168	143	91
1670–9	130	122	223	174	149	94
1680–9	136	126	217	191	148	104
1690–9	116	124	200	167	140	94

Sources: Morley, Drake, 'Elementary exercise', pp. 438–41 (data for 1640–59 lacking); aggregative parishes, table A4.1, column 4, modified as described in fn. 17.

Morley, as well as in the set of 404 parishes, the greater increase in the number of burials than baptisms meant that the mid-sixteenth-century gap between them closed by 1640, after which date the series interlaced, producing alternate periods of deficit and modest natural increase.[18] These results show that the gross patterns evident in the set of 404 parishes as a whole are not just an artefact of the process of aggregation up to the national level, but can reflect the actual experience of a small area such as a wapentake in south Yorkshire.

For the eighteenth century the present series can be compared with quinquennial totals of events collected by Krause for an unspecified set of 200 parishes, taken in equal numbers from each side of a line drawn between the Humber and the Severn.[19] Krause reported quinquennial totals of events for a 'north' and a 'south' group of parishes separately, but the figures have been combined and indexed on 1690–4 to facilitate comparison with the numbers of events recorded in the set of 404 parishes. As is apparent from table 6.7, the fit between the two sets of parishes is remarkably good up to 1760 so far as baptisms and burials are concerned: in few quinquennia are

18. From 1615 data are available for the neighbouring wapentake of Agbrigg and show the same pattern of change over time. Drake, 'Elementary exercise', pp. 438–41.
19. As with the set of 404 parishes no Welsh parishes were included. Apart from 'a few urban parishes in market towns' the sample was a rural one, drawn from printed registers, transcripts, and in a few cases original parish registers and bishops' transcripts. Krause aimed for an even geographical coverage of five parishes per county but only secured a 'few parishes' in Cambridgeshire, Hertfordshire, Huntingdonshire, Northamptonshire, Nottinghamshire, and Rutland. He accordingly boosted the number of Bedfordshire parishes by an unspecified amount and acknowledged receipt of Chambers's Nottinghamshire figures. It is not clear whether the latter, which relate to 60 villages and the town of Nottingham, constitute part of the set of 200 parishes, nor even whether they were added to the totals of events recorded by the 200 parishes and incorporated into the figures that Krause presents. Where burial registers contained entries relating to stillborn or unbaptized children Krause made an addition to the number of baptisms. Krause, 'Population change', pp. 193–4.

Table 6.7: Comparative trends in ecclesiastical events: Krause's 200 parishes and the set of aggregative parishes 1695–1794

	Index number of frequency of events (1690–4 = 100)					
	Baptisms		Burials		Marriages	
	Krause	Aggregative parishes	Krause	Aggregative parishes	Krause	Aggregative parishes
1690–4	100	100	100	100	100	100
1695–9	105	107	100	102	123	130
1700–4	113	113	97	98	136	138
1705–9	106	105	101	103	123	130
1710–4	99	100	100	104	130	140
1715–9	110	112	98	101	145	150
1720–4	112	114	110	117	154	166
1725–9	108	112	132	136	138	161
1730–4	117	122	118	117	168	185
1735–9	123	127	105	108	150	159
1740–4	117	119	120	122	142	157
1745–9	121	124	104	109	151	163
1750–4	125	129	104	106	156	165
1755–9	127	129	108	113	170	176
1760–4	133	137	118	130	189	206
1765–9	134	140	120	125	187	198
1770–4	143	150	116	124	202	204
1775–9	156	160	120	125	210	208
1780–4	153	158	136	145	202	213
1785–9	163	171	128	135	218	228
1790–4	171	182	131	139	219	235

Sources: Krause, 'Population change', p. 195; 'north' and 'south' sets of parishes combined. Aggregative parishes: table A4.1, column 4, modified as described in fn. 17.

the index numbers more than three points apart. In the later eighteenth century, however, there is a tendency for the numbers of events recorded by Krause's set of parishes to grow at a slightly slower rate than the number of events registered in the aggregative sample, possibly because Krause's set contains relatively more small rural parishes with lower rates of growth.[20] In the case of marriages the agreement is in general not so close: in some quinquennia the index numbers of the two sets of parishes approximate each other, while in others they diverge. On the whole the two sets of data tell much the same story about the onset of renewed growth in the eighteenth century. There was little sign of any definitive upward movement before 1710–4 in the case of baptisms and 1715–9 in the case of burials and marriages, but thereafter there was consistent and substantial growth in all three series with a widening gap between baptisms and burials.

The comparisons made between the patterns of events recorded by the 404 parishes and those produced by other sets of parishes and in London have shown that the

20. If the figures from Chambers's 60 Nottinghamshire parishes were added by Krause to those contributed by the set of 200 parishes then the mean annual number of events contributed by, and hence the mean population size of, Krause's set of parishes is about 90 per cent of the mean reweighted size of the set of 404 parishes. If, however, all the events in Krause's data were contributed by 200 parishes, either including or excluding the Nottinghamshire group, then the mean population size of the set of 200 parishes is about 15 per cent larger than the mean size of the 404 parishes, and the explanation given in the text of the slower growth of Krause's group in the late eighteenth century is unlikely to be correct. It is noteworthy that the number of events recorded by Krause's 'northern' parishes grew faster than those recorded by the 'southern' parishes, and faster than those registered by the set of 404 parishes.

general features of the three phases first identified in the national series of births, deaths, and marriages between 1539 and 1836 are also clearly evident in the underlying series of ecclesiastical events. They are therefore unlikely to have been introduced as a result of the corrections made to the ecclesiastical series to overcome under-registration. Indeed, it can be shown that the general patterns followed by both series of events are robust enough in outline to survive the effects of quite substantial changes that might be made to the correction factors to accommodate alternative views about the seriousness of under-registration at different points in time. For example, the early birth frequencies contain a steadily rising increment for delayed baptism that reaches an average of 3.42 per cent in the 1630s, while death frequencies contain no additions to the numbers of burials recorded in the registers.[21] The corrections to the data therefore both increase the rate at which the number of births increased over the first century of registration and enhance the gap between births and deaths over and above the surplus of baptisms over burials. But the increase of 3.42 per cent in the correction factor is negligible compared to the 46 per cent increase in the number of births between the 1540s and the 1630s, while deaths, to which no corrections were made, experienced an even more substantial rise of 53 per cent.[22]

Nor is the marked change in the pattern of events that occurred in 1640 likely to be wrong in its general outline. First of all the failure of the number of births to rise over the period 1640–1709 is despite, rather than because of, the corrections made to the underlying baptism series, for the correction percentage rose from 3.94 in the 1640s to 8.97 in the 1700s. It is true that the increase in deaths owes something to correction factors, which begin to be applied in the 1640s, but even in the 1700s only 3.73 per cent was added to deaths as against the 8.97 per cent added to births.[23] Yet despite the greater inflation given to births this was the period in which deaths rose to the same level as births and in which there were 17 years when they exceeded them.

If no correction had been made for under-registration in the late seventeenth century the series of vital events would have appeared even more stagnant, and there would have been more years in which deaths exceeded births. Alternatively, if a sharper increase had been made in the correction factors applied over the period, with an even greater disparity between the correction factors for births and deaths, there would have been fewer years of deficit. Since the underlying series of ecclesiastical events, once London has been included, record frequent deficits in the second half of the seventeenth century, minor adjustments in the correction factors for under-registration can change the pattern of events to show either a small increase or a more serious decline. But no reasonable correction for under-registration can make the figures show a substantial growth during the period on anything like the scale that occurred in the period before 1640.

In the third period after 1710, even more than in the first period, the sheer scale of the increases in each of the three series, and the size of the gap that opens up between births and deaths from the mid eighteenth century on, are so great that no amount of juggling with correction factors within the bounds of historical and demographic plausibility can make these features disappear. Thus while it is true that alternative assumptions about the scale of under-registration and how it changed over time would modify the rate of growth of the three series and hence the ratios between them, they cannot alter the fundamental pattern, which was one of growth up to 1640, followed

21. See table A4.2.
22. For the decadal totals of events see table A2.1.
23. See table A4.2.

by 70 years of stagnation with births and deaths almost on a par, followed in turn by renewed growth to the end of the series.

Population growth

If the general patterns of change over time in the three series appear to be robust and firmly grounded, is it legitimate to conclude that the periods of growth and stagnation in the series of vital events were also periods of growth or stagnation in the population that produced them? It has already been shown that this need not necessarily be so, for on the one hand changes in the numbers of events being recorded may be produced by vital rates changing while population remains the same size, and on the other hand a stagnant series of vital events may mask changes in population size offset by changes in the vital rates. However, there are limits beyond which it is implausible for vital rates to have strayed, whether for biological or historical reasons. Hence there are limits both to the extent to which numbers of vital events may increase or decrease while remaining compatible with a static population, and to the extent to which a population may change in size while continuing to produce the same numbers of events.

As a first step towards discovering the characteristics of the invisible population we can therefore test how far the changes in the numbers of events recorded are compatible with a static population size. Since *a priori*, thoug.· not necessarily in practice, variation in birth rates is usually more tightly constrained by biological and social factors than is variation in death rates, it will be convenient to work with the series of births. Biological factors effectively limit the maximum level that a crude birth rate of a large population can achieve in normal circumstances to about 55 per 1,000 members of the population.[24] At the lower end of the scale we should not expect to find a crude birth rate lower than 22 per 1,000 in pre-industrial England except as a temporary phenomenon, for this level was not reached nationally until about 1921.[25] In practice most pre-industrial European populations had crude birth rates in the range 28–40 per 1,000, so an increase in the number of births produced by a static population by a ratio of 1.43 (40/28), or a decrease by a ratio of 0.7 (28/40), would imply a shift in fertility across the entire normal pre-industrial European range.[26]

If we now consider the first period in which there was a long-term rise in the number of births, the ratio between the totals for 1540–4 and 1635–9 was 1.455, which, if the population is assumed not to have grown, implies an implausibly large rise in fertility from an implausibly low birth rate in the 1540s. Since deaths grew faster than births over the same period, the rise in mortality would have been even greater.

Furthermore, if the population had failed to grow between 1540 and 1640, it follows that the substantial surpluses of births over deaths, which accumulated to a total of 2.9 million over the period, were not retained but exported. This, in turn, implies an implausibly high level of emigration with an average of 29,000 leaving the country every year, about four times the numbers estimated to have reached the New

---

24. Henry, *Population*, p. 35. Higher crude birth rates are often associated with populations with high proportions of young adults acquired through immigration, for example in cities or in recently settled areas.
25. Mitchell and Deane, *British historical statistics*, p. 30. The crude birth rate fell temporarily below 22 per 1,000 during the First World War.
26. Henry, *Manuel*, p. 53; Reinhard, *Histoire générale*, pt I, chs. 8, 10–3, 15.

World at the height of the wave of emigration in the mid seventeenth century.[27]

Similar arguments can be applied to the third period, from 1710 to 1801, after which date there can be no doubt about the reality of population growth in view of the numbers returned in the decennial censuses. In the eighteenth century, as in the sixteenth, the numbers in all series rose considerably and there were substantial surpluses of births over deaths. Indeed, the quantities involved make the alternative hypothesis of no growth appear even more improbable than it did in the period before 1640. The ratio between the number of births in the quinquennia 1710–4 and 1795–9 is 2.09, which is too great to be produced by a plausible change in the birth rate. Secondly, the cumulative surplus of births over deaths between 1710 and 1799 was 3.795 million. A hypothesis of constant population size would require this large number of people to have emigrated at an average rate of about 42,000 a year, which is about three times more than the probable volume of net emigration in the early nineteenth century.[28]

Finally the population totals from the early censuses both establish the fact of rapid growth in the nineteenth century at a time when the totals of vital events were also increasing sharply, and also, when compared to Gregory King's estimates in 1695, confirm that the population must have grown in size during the eighteenth century. The population of England in 1801 was 8.658 million, some 3.475 million more than the 5.183 million estimated for 1695. Since the cumulative surplus of births over deaths between the two dates was 4.259 million, it would appear that in round terms about 80 per cent of the natural increase accruing during the eighteenth century was retained to swell the population while 20 per cent was exported.[29]

In the first and third periods, therefore, the patterns traced by the series of vital events are sufficiently pronounced for it to be virtually certain that the growth in the numbers of events in each series reflects substantial growth in the size of the population. On the other hand, the lack of any clear movement in the vital series in the intervening period between 1640 and 1709, while incompatible with a marked growth or decline of the population, is consistent either with stagnation or with a modest growth or decline. In the period 1640–84 the natural increase was only 251,609, or 5,591 a year, though in the period 1685–1709 it increased somewhat to 457,829, or 18,313 a year. If all the natural increase had been retained the population would have grown by about 709,000 between 1640 and 1709. But it is known that large numbers of people left the country during this period especially for the American colonies. Indeed, it has been estimated that over the period 1640–99 there were around 309,000 emigrants to North America, which would constitute a loss of 69 per cent of the natural increase over the same period.[30] Since there was also substantial emigration to Ireland it is clearly possible that there was a fall in numbers during the period as a whole or at least for some part of it.[31]

27. For migration estimates see table 6.11 and pp. 219–28 below.
28. The highest rate of net migration implied by the early-nineteenth-century censuses before 1841 was 12,500 a year in the 1820s. See table A6.8.
29. For the 1695 estimate see below pp. 571–2. It is undated within the year, but for convenience has been taken to refer to the population on 30 June 1695, since the census total for 1801 has been standardized to refer to 30 June of that year.
30. Gemery, 'Emigration', table A.5, p. 215, summarized in table 6.11 below. The numbers of emigrants include a small, but unknown, proportion from Wales, Scotland, and Ireland. Natural increase in 1640–99 was 447,509.
31. In the 1670s Reynel estimated that 200,000 had emigrated to Ireland. Reynel, *The true English interest*, in Thirsk and Cooper, *Seventeenth-century economic documents*, p. 758.

In general, therefore, the changes in the numbers of events in each of the three series over time were sufficiently great for it to be possible to draw some general inferences about the presence or absence of population growth during the period. Moreover, a more detailed examination of the timing of changes in the rate of growth of the series of events suggests that it is also possible to discover something about changes in the pace of population growth over time. It is evident from pullout 1 that the series of births and deaths were often growing at divergent rates and that the points of inflexion in the series did not always coincide. Since the series were produced by the same population we can conclude that the balance between fertility and mortality was changing over time leading to considerable variation in the rate of natural increase.[32]

Table 6.8 summarizes the changing relationships between the frequencies of births and deaths in terms of the quinquennial surpluses of births over deaths. The changes in the levels of the surpluses, or natural increase, repeat many of the main features of the demographic story outlined so far. The period before 1640 is characterized by substantial surpluses of births over deaths with the exception of 1555–9 when a large rise in the number of deaths was accompanied by a fall in the number of births. In the seventeenth century the size of the natural increase gradually falls as the numbers of deaths rise to equal the numbers of births, so that in the second half of the century small natural surpluses are interspersed by deficits. The surpluses pick up again in the late 1690s, but natural increase remains relatively low during the first half of the eighteenth century, at about the same level as obtained in the second quarter of the seventeenth century. From the mid eighteenth century the surpluses of births over deaths grow rapidly, first regaining the figures achieved in the later sixteenth century and then far outstripping them.

In order to compare natural increase at different dates the absolute surpluses of births over deaths need to be converted into rates by relating them to the numbers of births and deaths from which they resulted. The figures that appear in the final column of table 6.8 and are plotted in figure 6.3 achieve the desired effect by expressing total births as a ratio to total deaths in each quinquennium. The ratios show the same overall pattern as the absolute levels of natural increase, and if they are compared with the graph of annual frequencies of vital events (in pullout 1) the patterns of change in the rate of natural increase can be related to changes in the constituent series of births and deaths.

First, it should be recalled that the initial 20 years of the series are based on relatively few parishes, but if the data are representative, then one feature that stands out from pullout 1 is the early instability of the series of deaths.[33] Several years in the 1540s record unusually high totals, and although deaths appear to be running at a relatively low and fairly constant level from 1550 to the mid 1580s the series is disturbed by a catastrophic surge of mortality in the late 1550s and by the plague outbreak of 1563. Consequently in the disturbed quinquennia of the 1540s and early 1560s the birth/death ratios were held to just below 1.300 while in 1555–9 the ratio plunged to 0.813, recording the worst deficit in the entire 300-year period. In contrast, the undisturbed mid-century quinquennia (1550–4 and from 1565 to 1584)

---

32. Except in the unlikely event that every change in the rate of natural increase was offset by changes in the volume of net migration, resulting in a constant rate of population growth.
33. For the numbers of parishes in observation each year see table 2.19. Figure 2.3 shows that the registers on which these early figures are based were typical in that the results they yield after 1562 parallel those from the sample of 404 parishes as a whole.

Table 6.8: Natural increase and birth/death ratios by quinquennium, 1540–1869

Quinquennium	Natural increase (births–deaths)	Ratio (births/deaths)	Quinquennium	Natural increase (births–deaths)	Ratio (births/deaths)
1540-4	+104 065	1.245	1705-9	+85 877	1.122
1545-9	+114 701	1.270	1710-4	+38 705	1.053
1550-4	+177 785	1.449	1715-9	+149 370	1.208
1555-9	−112 196	0.813	1720-4	+55 587	1.067
1560-4	+112 357	1.284	1725-9	−68 967	0.926
1565-9	+183 103	1.478	1730-4	+112 679	1.137
1570-4	+140 262	1.349	1735-9	+202 006	1.263
1575-9	+207 608	1.538	1740-4	+39 528	1.046
1580-4	+228 648	1.578	1745-9	+167 429	1.216
1585-9	+154 972	1.323	1750-4	+233 840	1.311
1590-4	+119 408	1.232	1755-9	+197 027	1.249
1595-9	+120 578	1.236	1760-4	+169 703	1.192
1600-4	+177 651	1.348	1765-9	+198 737	1.224
1605-9	+235 266	1.481	1770-4	+279 695	1.318
1610-4	+118 956	1.200	1775-9	+359 459	1.404
1615-9	+162 801	1.286	1780-4	+225 342	1.220
1620-4	+172 209	1.296	1785-9	+428 182	1.439
1625-9	+115 933	1.179	1790-4	+495 349	1.477
1630-4	+193 057	1.329	1795-9	+511 582	1.469
1635-9	+69 419	1.097	1800-4	+506 790	1.429
1640-4	+110 255	1.152	1805-9	+713 222	1.613
1645-9	+165 833	1.273	1810-4	+701 870	1.543
1650-4	+65 571	1.100	1815-9	+894 565	1.654
1655-9	−34 513	0.954	1820-4	+976 163	1.698
1660-4	+62 419	1.094	1825-9	+948 078	1.655
1665-9	−65 045	0.921	1830-4	+919 562	1.620
1670-4	+28 551	1.040	1835-9	+953 209	1.599
1675-9	+7 476	1.010	1840-4	+1 027 713	1.611
1680-4	−88 938	0.895	1845-9	+902 695	1.475
1685-9	+51 600	1.069	1850-4	+1 140 954	1.600
1690-4	+53 012	1.075	1855-9	+1 247 861	1.626
1695-9	+91 288	1.129	1860-4	+1 347 176	1.634
1700-4	+176 052	1.263	1865-9	+1 412 767	1.617

Source: Table A2.2.

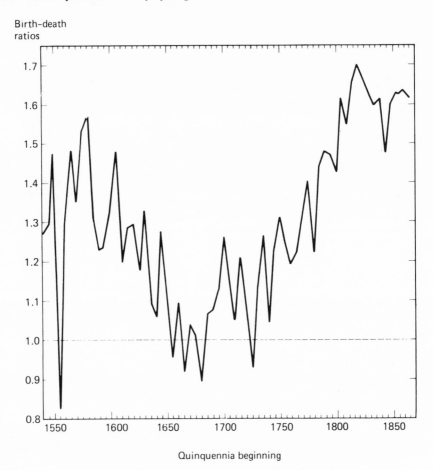

Birth-death
ratios

Quinquennia beginning

Figure 6.3: Quinquennial birth/death ratios 1540 – 1869

Source: Table 6.8.

yielded birth/death ratios between 1.449 and 1.578.[34] The exceptionally high ratios in the period 1575–84 were produced by the number of deaths remaining constant while the number of births began to rise. Between 1585 and 1640 the underlying trend in deaths began to rise more swiftly than that of births and this, coupled with the return of a more disturbed period of mortality, progressively, though unevenly, squeezed the birth/death ratios closer to unity, throttling back the rate of natural increase of the population.

The impression left by the sixteenth-century evidence is of a population with a great potential for growth which was realized if high rates of mortality did not intervene. The violent and frequent upsurges in the number of deaths recorded before 1565 look as if they may have been the last throes of a late-medieval régime of widespread epidemic mortality which, when they subsided in a 20-year period of calm lasting

34. Except 1570–4, when the ratio was slightly lower at 1.349.

from 1565 to 1584, allowed a strong underlying rate of natural increase to break through into the light of day.[35] Although some individual years of heavy mortality returned later, pullout 1 shows plainly enough that it was the inexorable pressure of the underlying trend in the numbers of deaths rising faster than that of births that slowly whittled away the buoyant rates of natural increase of early Elizabethan England.

After 1640 the annual frequencies of births sagged somewhat to 1660 and then drifted slowly back to their 1640 level around 1700, while the underlying trend of deaths continued to rise until the mid 1680s. In consequence the birth/death ratios were close to unity at the best of times, and turned negative as soon as the number of deaths rose above trend. This sometimes occurred as the result of a sudden surge, as in the plague outbreak of 1665, but occasionally the natural deficit was due to a more prolonged increase in the number of deaths, as in the years 1679–85. The trend between 1695 and 1703 suggests that births were about to pull away from deaths but this outcome was delayed, first by a collapse in the number of births over the period 1704–10 and then by a renewed period of disturbed mortality involving first a high plateau of deaths in 1719–24 and then two violent surges in 1727–31 and 1740–2. Indeed 1725–9 was the last quinquennium, and 1741 and 1742 were the last individual years, in which the number of deaths exceeded the number of births.[36] Thus, although the level of the birth/death ratios around 1700 and the pronounced upward trend in births from 1710 might be taken as signs of the onset of powerful population growth, in reality the early-eighteenth-century birth/death ratios, and hence the rates of natural increase, were lower than the ratios recorded in the early seventeenth century, when the sixteenth-century phase of expansion was drawing to a close.[37]

From the mid 1740s, however, births began to pull consistently away from deaths without serious disturbance from short-term fluctuations, so that by the 1770s the birth/death ratios regained sixteenth-century levels. Indeed, in terms of the rate of natural increase, the later eighteenth century looks remarkably like the later sixteenth century. But the gap between births and deaths continued to widen so that in the nineteenth century the rate of natural increase reached unprecedented heights.

Estimating crude rates of natural increase

The quinquennial birth/death ratios bring out very clearly the major changes in the pace of natural increase: accelerating up to the early 1580s, declining to the mid seventeenth century, remaining stagnant in the later seventeenth century with periods of weak growth interspersed by periods of slight decline, rising again to modest levels

35. For the prevalence of epidemic disease in the mid fifteenth century see Gottfried, 'Population, plague'; and *Epidemic disease*. Gottfried points to 1480 as a turning point after which widespread epidemics of bubonic plague were replaced by less frequent epidemics of less lethal diseases, such as typhus, dysentery, and the sweating sickness ('Population, plague', pp. 36–7).
36. Except for war years, deaths did not exceed births again in England until 1976. *Population trends*, x (1977), p. 1.
37. One champion of an early start to population growth argues that 'growth was taking place rapidly between 1690 and 1720 – probably as rapidly as between 1750 and 1780'. Chambers, *Population, economy and society*, p. 114. See also pp. 22–3, 112–3. Chambers cites Tucker, 'Population trends', and Pentland, 'Population and labour growth', as supporting his views. However, Pentland, whose study was largely based on Chambers's Nottinghamshire data, only gives qualified support. He refers to 'the enormous rate of population growth in the first decade of the eighteenth century' (p. 164), but characterizes the first half the century as a period in which 'population grew slowly and erratically' (p. 180).

in the early eighteenth century, regaining late-sixteenth-century levels after 1770, and finally transcending them in the nineteenth century.

Unfortunately the birth/death ratio is not a particularly informative measure of population growth, or more strictly of natural increase, which is conventionally expressed as an annual rate of growth. One way of converting birth/death ratios into annual growth rates lies through linking them to crude birth and death rates, for the difference between these rates yields the annual crude rate of natural increase. Unfortunately the absence of information about population size makes it impossible to calculate crude birth and death rates from the series of events, but the fact that each rate is simply the annual number of events divided by the same, unknown, population size means that the birth/death ratios are also the ratios obtaining between the vital rates. If one of the vital rates is assumed to be constant, then the other rate can be calculated by multiplying the constant rate by the birth/death ratio and the difference between the two vital rates yields the annual crude rate of increase. For example, if the death rate is assumed to be constant, then the birth rate at any date is the death rate multiplied by the birth/death ratio. The annual rate of natural increase is the difference between the two rates and so can easily be calculated by multiplying the constant death rate by the fractional part of the birth/death ratio.[38]

Clearly the absolute levels of the annual rates of natural increase calculated in this way will be scaled according to the level at which the constant death or birth rate is arbitrarily set: the higher the constant vital rate the higher the annual rate of natural increase implied by any birth/death ratio and the greater the change in annual rate of natural increase implied by a given change in the birth/death ratio. Table 6.9 shows

Table 6.9: Birth/death ratios and annual rates of natural increase

(1)	(2)	(3)	(4)
	Annual percentage rate of growth with crude death rate at		
Birth/death ratio	20⁰/oo	25⁰/oo	35⁰/oo
0.8	−0.40	−0.50	−0.70
0.9	−0.20	−0.25	−0.35
1.0	0.00	0.00	0.00
1.1	0.20	0.25	0.35
1.2	0.40	0.50	0.70
1.3	0.60	0.75	1.05
1.4	0.80	1.00	1.40
1.5	1.00	1.25	1.75
1.6	1.20	1.50	2.10
1.7	1.40	1.75	2.45

Note: Columns 2 to 4 obtained by multiplying (column 1–1) by the crude death rate.

38. Let BR stand for the birth rate, DR for the death rate, and B/D for the birth/death ratio. Natural increase = BR − DR. If the death rate is constant then BR = B/D × DR, and by substitution natural increase becomes (B/D × DR) − DR, which simplifies to (B/D − 1) × DR. Alternatively, if the birth rate is constant then DR = D/B × BR, and natural increase becomes BR − (D/B × BR), which simplifies to (1 − D/B) × BR.

the annual percentage growth rates that result from applying the same birth/death ratios to three widely different assumptions about the death rate (20 per 1,000, 25 per 1,000, and 35 per 1,000). The first and last assumptions are probably more extreme than anything to be found in pre-industrial England other than by way of short-term fluctuation. The crude death rate in England and Wales was at about 22 per 1,000 in the mid nineteenth century and rates as low as 20 per 1,000 were not consistently attained until the 1880s. Although death rates as high as 35 per 1,000 were recorded in France and Italy in the past, in other parts of pre-industrial Europe, such as Scandinavia in the mid eighteenth century, the rates were rather lower at about 27 per 1,000.[39]

As is evident from the table, when the birth/death ratios are near to unity, the level of the death rate assumed to be in force makes little difference to the resulting rate of natural increase. For example a birth/death ratio of 1.2 implies an annual rate of natural increase within the fairly narrow range of 0.4 to 0.7 per cent. When the birth/death ratio is higher, the range of possible rates of natural increase implied by different assumptions about the death rate widens, and it is fortunate that the English birth/death ratios rarely exceeded 1.50 before the nineteenth century. But even with the greater discrepancies associated with the higher ratios it is still possible to draw general conclusions. For example, if a birth/death ratio was 1.50, it would be almost certain that the rate of natural increase lay between 1.00 per cent and 1.75 per cent per annum.

Although this method of calculation assumes that the death rate was invariant, it can still provide a fair estimate of changes in the rate of natural increase even if in reality its basic assumption was hopelessly wrong, as would be the case if the changing birth/death ratios had been entirely produced by a shift in the death rate. For example, in round terms the birth/death ratios rose from about 1.20 to 1.50 over the course of the eighteenth century. If the death rate is assumed to have been constant at 25 per 1,000, then according to table 6.9 the rate of natural increase would have risen from 0.5 per cent to 1.25 per cent per annum. If, however, mortality had actually been very high around 1700 and very low around 1800, say with death rates at 35 and 20 per 1,000 respectively, then table 6.9 would still show a rise in the rate of natural increase from 0.7 to 1.0 per cent per annum. Thus even if mortality had improved from one extreme of the range of plausible historical rates to the other, a calculation based on the assumption that it had been constant would still correctly indicate that the rate of natural increase had risen over the period concerned, though it would have exaggerated the scale of the increase.

In reality death rates in pre-industrial England are unlikely to have been as extreme as 20 or 35 per 1,000 except fleetingly in unusual circumstances, so the errors involved in calculating rates of natural increase on the assumption of a constant death rate are unlikely to be substantial. For example, in the first decade of civil registration (1838–47) the crude death rate, corrected for under-registration, was about 22.5 per 1,000, while a rough calculation for 1695, when Gregory King estimated the population to be 5.183 million, yields a crude death rate of 27.3 per 1,000, although a higher figure of 30.9 per 1,000 can be achieved by relating the unusually large

39. Mitchell and Deane, *British historical statistics*, pp. 36–7; Henry and Blayo, 'La population de la France de 1740 à 1860', p. 109; Sundbärg, *Bevölkerungsstatistik Schwedens*, p. 131; Drake, *Population and society in Norway*, p. 49; Jutikkala, 'Finland's population', p. 562. Crude death rates in northern Italy (Lombardy) in the period 1768–1849 seem to have been somewhat higher, in the range 35–40 per 1,000. Cipolla, 'Italian demographic development', pp. 576–7.

numbers of deaths recorded in the 1680s to the same population base.[40] Estimates of the probable death rate in the sixteenth century suffer from the much greater imprecision of estimates of population size at that date, but if 3 million is anywhere near the mark for 1550, the crude death rate will have been around 28 per 1,000 in the 1540s and no more than 33 per 1,000 in the exceptionally mortal 1550s. On this showing the crude death rate can be expected to have varied between 22.5 per 1,000 and about 30 per 1,000. Thus the assumption of a constant death rate of 25 per 1,000 is unlikely to lead to serious error: most of the time the true rate will lie within 10 per cent of the assumed constant rate and even in times of high mortality, when the crude death rate is around 30 per 1,000, it will still be within 20 per cent of the assumed rate. Since the estimated annual rate of natural increase is a simple multiple of the constant death rate, it follows that it too will be subject to an error of up to 10 per cent most of the time, and even when mortality deviates most from the assumed constant level the estimated rate of natural increase will only be about 20 per cent in error.

Table 6.10 and figure 6.4 display the estimated crude rates of natural increase that result from assuming a constant crude death rate of 25 per 1,000 and multiplying it by the fractional part of the birth/death ratios for each decade between the 1540s and the 1860s. The information is presented on a decadal rather than a quinquennial basis in order to iron out some of the sharper short-term fluctuations in mortality which may have taken the crude death rate rather far from the assumed constant level of 25 per 1,000. The final two columns of table 6.10 show by how much the annual growth rate would need to be increased or decreased if the true death rate were 10 per cent or 20 per cent higher or lower than 25 per 1,000. Fortunately in decades with large numbers of deaths when the death rate was likely to have been particularly high, implying that the larger corrections associated with the 20 per cent column of the table would need to be applied, the birth/death ratios were also generally low, so the absolute size of the corrections to be made to the implied rate of natural increase are likely to be small. For example, the second column of the table gives an annual rate of natural increase of 0.17 per cent for the 1550s based on an assumed death rate of 25 per 1,000. If the true death rate had been 20 per cent higher, at around 30 per 1,000, the annual rate of natural increase would have been 0.20 per cent (0.17 per cent + 0.033 per cent), still a low rate of growth. At the other end of the scale, the table shows an annual rate of natural increase of 1.69 per cent for the 1820s. If the death rate had already fallen to 22.5 per cent, as it had by the mid nineteenth century, the assumed death rate would be 10 per cent in error and the true rate of natural increase would be 1.52 per cent per annum.

In practice, therefore, the corrections which need to be made to overcome the unreality of assuming a constant crude death rate of 25 per 1,000 do not significantly alter the general outline of the changes in the estimated rates of natural increase shown in figure 6.4. Indeed, the scale of these changes over time is far greater than the maximum probable error of 20 per cent surrounding each estimate.

Taking decades as the unit of analysis has not altogether removed the depressing effect on growth rates of sudden surges of mortality, and the rates in the 1550s, 1590s

40. The death rate for the first decade of civil registration is based on the figures in Mitchell and Deane, *British historical statistics*, p. 36, inflated to allow for the 2 per cent under-registration of deaths estimated in Glass, 'Note on under-registration', p. 756. The 1695 death rate relates the average annual number of deaths recorded in the 1690s to the population in 1695. The average population in the 1680s may have been slightly lower than it was in 1695, thereby raising the estimated death rate a little higher. See table 6.8, column headed 'Natural increase'.

Table 6.10: Estimated crude rates of natural increase, by decade, 1540–1869 (assuming constant crude death rate of 25 per 1 000)

Period	(1) Birth/death ratio	(2) Percentage annual rate of natural increase	(3) Error limits ± 10 per cent	(4) Error limits ± 20 per cent
1540-9	1.257	0.64	0.064	0.129
1550-9	1.066	0.17	0.017	0.033
1560-9	1.376	0.94	0.094	0.188
1570-9	1.442	1.11	0.111	0.221
1580-9	1.438	1.10	0.110	0.219
1590-9	1.234	0.59	0.059	0.117
1600-9	1.413	1.03	0.103	0.207
1610-9	1.242	0.61	0.061	0.121
1620-9	1.235	0.59	0.059	0.118
1630-9	1.201	0.50	0.050	0.101
1640-9	1.207	0.52	0.052	0.104
1650-9	1.022	0.06	0.006	0.011
1660-9	0.998	−0.01	0.001	0.001
1670-9	1.025	0.06	0.006	0.013
1680-9	0.977	−0.06	0.006	0.012
1690-9	1.102	0.26	0.026	0.051
1700-9	1.190	0.48	0.048	0.095
1710-9	1.130	0.33	0.033	0.065
1720-9	0.992	−0.02	0.002	0.004
1730-9	1.198	0.50	0.050	0.099
1740-9	1.126	0.32	0.032	0.063
1750-9	1.279	0.70	0.070	0.140
1760-9	1.208	0.52	0.052	0.104
1770-9	1.361	0.90	0.090	0.181
1780-9	1.327	0.82	0.082	0.164
1790-9	1.473	1.18	0.118	0.237
1800-9	1.521	1.30	0.130	0.261
1810-9	1.600	1.50	0.150	0.300
1820-9	1.676	1.69	0.169	0.338
1830-9	1.609	1.52	0.152	0.305
1840-9	1.539	1.35	0.135	0.270
1850-9	1.613	1.51	0.151	0.302
1860-9	1.625	1.56	0.156	0.313

Note: Column 2 = (column 1–1) × 2.5

Column 4 may not be exactly twice column 3 because of rounding.

Source: Table A2.1.

and 1720s are markedly below trend for this reason. Otherwise, however, the pattern of change over time is very clear and divides neatly into periods of about half a century. In round terms the birth/death ratios suggest that the rate of natural increase was about 1 per cent per annum in the second half of the sixteenth century. After 1600 it fell precipitately and held to a plateau at around 0.5 per cent per annum during the first half of the seventeenth century. In the 1650s there was a further sharp fall to another plateau at around 0 per cent, on which it remained for most of the second half of the seventeenth century. In the final decade there was a marked rebound in the rate of natural increase, which spent the first half of the eighteenth century in the range 0.25 to 0.5 per cent, a little below the level of the plateau it had occupied in the early

Annual rate
of natural
increase
(per cent)

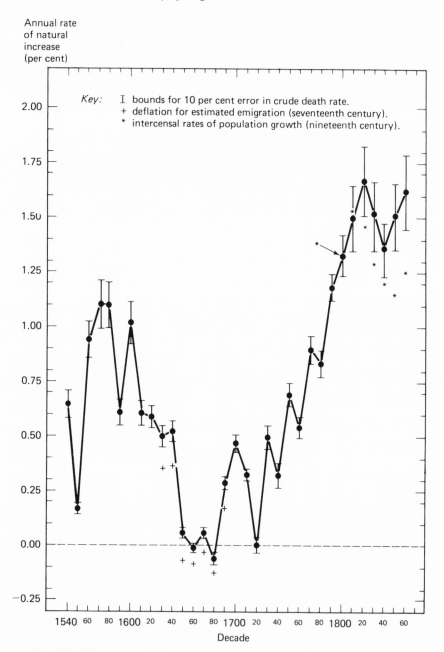

Key: I bounds for 10 per cent error in crude death rate.
       + deflation for estimated emigration (seventeenth century).
       * intercensal rates of population growth (nineteenth century).

Figure 6.4: Estimated crude rates of natural increase by decade,
                1540s to 1860s

Sources: Rates of natural increase, table 6.10; emigration estimates (seventeenth century),
          table 6.11; intercensal rates of population growth (nineteenth century), table 6.12.

seventeenth century. From 1750 the rate grew steadily higher, exceeding 1 per cent in the 1790s and 1.5 per cent per annum in the 1810s.

Since these estimated rates of natural increase are constant multiples of the birth/death ratios, the pattern of rates shown in figure 6.4 naturally repeats the temporal pattern so evident in the birth/death ratios themselves as shown in figure 6.3. The conversion of the birth/death ratios into annual rates of natural increase simply re-expresses in more conventional terms the information the ratios contain about the implications of the underlying rates of fertility and mortality for population growth. But the crude rate of natural increase ignores migration and only if net migration is zero will it be an adequate guide to the rate of population growth. The next step must therefore be to estimate how far the rates of natural increase that have been calculated from the birth/death ratios need to be modified to take account of migration in order to arrive at rates of population growth. Unfortunately it is very difficult to discover how many people moved into and out of the country between the mid sixteenth and mid nineteenth centuries. In the absence of any systematic series of documents from which the volume of migration could be calculated, the most that can be attempted is a rough estimate of the scale of net migration at a few dates, in order to gauge how far it may be necessary to modify the rates of natural increase as measures of the rate of population growth.

Despite the difficulty of quantifying the volume of migration it seems probable that as a general rule losses from emigration and deaths at sea or abroad outweighed the gains from immigration.[41] Thus the correction that needs to be made to take account of migration is equivalent to restoring the missing deaths of the net emigrants, that is it entails lowering the birth/death ratios, and hence the rates of natural increase.

Before emigration to America began on any scale, in the 1630s, net emigration was probably low, so the uncorrected birth/death ratios will only be a little too high and thus the rates of natural increase calculated for this period probably over-estimate population growth in the sixteenth and early seventeenth centuries by only a small margin. From 1630 to 1699 it has been estimated that about 378,000 people left the country.[42] Since the balance of births and deaths was very even over most of this period migration was relatively a more important component of population change, to which, consequently, the rate of natural increase as measured by the uncorrected birth/death ratios is a less reliable guide. An indication of the probable order of magnitude of the impact of migration on the rate of population growth can be obtained by adding the estimated numbers of migrants to the total number of deaths and recomputing the rates of natural increase on the basis of the revised birth/death ratios.[43] Calculations have been made separately for each decade from the 1630s to

41. In the late sixteenth century the numbers of foreigners resident even in the major towns was low; for example 3,760 and 2,513 in London in 1567 and 1581, and 1,132 Dutch refugees in Norwich in 1568. Burn, *History of protestant refugees*, p.6, and Rye, 'Dutch refugees in Norwich', p. 189, respectively. In 1688 a committee of relief claimed to have helped 13,500 refugees in London and 2,000 more elsewhere; Poole, *Huguenots*, p. 81. We are indebted to Mr R. Brown of Churchill College, Cambridge, for these references. In the nineteenth century the censuses imply a net loss through migration; see table A6.8.
42. Gemery, 'Emigration', table A5, p. 215.
43. The calculations assume that migration to other destinations was offset by immigration, so that migration to the New World approximates net migration. It should also be remembered that the figures for the New World refer to immigrants from the British Isles and that towards the end of the century a rising proportion of immigrants came from the Celtic fringe. The increasing persecution of the Huguenots probably increased the volume of immigration in the last decades of the century and as a result the figures for migration to the New World may overstate the volume of net emigration and so reduce the rates of natural increase too severely.

Table 6.11: Revised crude rates of natural increase, by decade, 1630–99

Period	Births	Deaths	Emigrants	Birth/death ratios		Annual rates of natural increase	
				(deaths)	(deaths + emigrants)	(deaths)	(deaths + emigrants)
1630–9	1 565 473	1 302 997	69 100	1.201	1.141	0.50	0.35
1640–9	1 609 745	1 333 657	69 400	1.207	1.147	0.52	0.37
1650–9	1 444 963	1 413 905	71 800	1.022	0.973	0.06	−0.07
1660–9	1 482 753	1 485 379	42 200	0.998	0.971	−0.01	−0.07
1670–9	1 471 113	1 435 086	51 700	1.025	0.989	0.06	−0.03
1680–9	1 564 307	1 601 645	43 100	0.977	0.951	−0.06	−0.12
1690–9	1 558 272	1 414 972	30 300	1.102	1.079	0.26	0.20

Sources: Emigrants: Gemery, 'Emigration', table A.5, p.215. Births and deaths, table A2.1.

the 1690s and are shown in table 6.11, while the revised rates of natural increase are plotted as separate points on figure 6.4. The effect of migration is to drag down the rates of growth in the 1630s and 1640s to around 0.35 per cent per annum and to turn the rates for the four decades from 1650 to 1689 firmly negative, implying a definite population decline.

The wave of emigration to the New World appears to have slackened in the late seventeenth century and then grown substantially during the eighteenth.[44] Since the birth/death surpluses grew with increasing speed over the eighteenth century, the relative importance of migration as a component of population change declined and the rates of natural increase calculated from the birth/death ratios resumed their pre-1630 position as a fair guide to the rate of population growth. Unfortunately the early-nineteenth-century data do not easily permit an estimate to be made of net migration for England alone, but decennial censuses starting in 1801 provide information on the rate of population growth which can be compared with the rates of natural increase calculated from the birth/death ratios. Table 6.12 shows by how much the true rate of population growth fell short of a rate of natural increase based on the birth/death ratio in each of the inter-censal periods from 1801 to 1871.[45] Up to 1821 the birth/death ratios combined with a constant crude death rate of 25 per 1,000 come close to indicating the true rate of population growth, which lies only 2 to 4 per cent below the rate of natural increase they imply. From 1821 to 1871 the rate of population growth lies between 13 and 18 per cent below the estimated rate of natural increase, except that in the period 1851–61 the gap widens to 25 per cent. Since it is known that the crude death rate was about 22.5 per 1,000 after 1841, about 10 per cent of the discrepancy between the rate of natural increase and the true rate of population growth occurring after this date can be ascribed to the 10 per cent error involved in the assumption that the death rate was 25 per 1,000. This leaves a further 4 and 8 per cent

Table 6.12: Intercensal annual percentage rates of natural increase and of population growth

	(1) Natural increase[1]	(2) Population growth[2]	(3) Percentage discrepancy ((1)-(2))/(1) × 100
1801–11	1.338	1.317	2
1811–21	1.594	1.534	4
1821–31	1.693	1.471	13
1831–41	1.479	1.287	13
1841–51	1.392	1.201	14
1851–61	1.533	1.153	25
1861–71	1.536	1.255	18

Notes: [1] Based on the ratio between intercensal births and deaths assuming a constant crude death rate of 25 per 1 000.
[2] Figures are annual percentage compound growth rates with census populations standardized to refer to 30 June.

Sources: Births and deaths, table A2.1; population growth rates, table A6.7.

44. Table 6.11, and Potter, 'Growth of population in America', pp. 644–6.
45. For the date-standardized intercensal rates of growth see table A6.7. The rates of growth calculated from the birth/death ratios are based on the number of events recorded between the standardized date of 30 June in each census year, and so differ slightly from the rates of natural increase given in table 6.10.

discrepancy attributable to the effects of net emigration in the 1840s and 1860s respectively and a more substantial discrepancy of 15 per cent in the 1850s.

The level of net emigration in the 1850s, however, was exceptionally high.[46] In general in the nineteenth century the birth/death ratios provide a reasonable approximation to the true rate of population growth despite the presence of considerable net emigration and despite being based on an assumed crude death rate which is up to 10 per cent too high. Although the true rate of population growth cannot be measured at an earlier date, estimates of the volume of emigration in the mid seventeenth century suggest a modest downward revision of the rates of natural increase. The effect is to deepen the chasm into which the rates of population growth plunge over the course of the seventeenth century and so intensify the contrast between population growth in this and other periods already visible in figure 6.4. Since net emigration is likely to have been less intense at other periods than in the seventeenth and nineteenth centuries the rates of natural increase based on the birth/death ratios are probably a fair approximation to the rates of population growth throughout the period under study.

A full discussion of the significance of changes in the rate of population growth over time will have to await the more rigorous calculations embarked upon in the next chapter, but the present estimates are sufficiently robust to allow one or two general points to be made. First, over most of the three centuries studied, the rate of population growth was rather low. Only before 1600 and after 1770 is it likely that it comfortably exceeded 0.5 per cent per annum, and it probably did not substantially exceed 1 per cent per annum until the 1790s when industrialization was well under way. Although these rates of growth are quite buoyant by pre-industrial west European standards, they are very low by the standards of non-industrial societies today.[47]

Second, the period from the mid sixteenth to the early nineteenth century contains wide fluctuations in population growth rates. Consequently, short-term perspectives may give a misleading impression of the nature of population change at particular points in time. For example, when viewed against the immediate backdrop of the early eighteenth century, the rise in population growth rates after 1750 appears to be substantial, and it is tempting to go on to consider what connexions there may have been between demographic growth and the process of industrialization.[48] Such a line of argument presupposes that the demographic experience of the early eighteenth century was typical of the whole pre-industrial era. But it is abundantly clear from figure 6.4 that the higher growth rates of the later eighteenth century had been paralleled earlier, in the late sixteenth century. Indeed, the clear message of the series of vital events as conveyed through the birth/death ratio is that there was no single long-term rate of population growth in pre-industrial England.[49] Rather there was an

46. See table A6.8.

47. Wrigley, *Population and history*, pp. 152–6, 204–7.

48. There is a large literature on this subject, conveniently and critically appraised in Flinn, *British population growth*.

49. Tucker showed that the early-eighteenth-century rate of growth implied by Griffith's estimates of population size in 1700 and 1750 could not be projected back to 1500 without producing an implausibly high population figure of 4.4 million for that year. But he then assumed a constant rate of growth between a lower figure for 1500 (2.5 to 3.0 million) and 1700, which enabled him to conclude that the rate of growth in the early eighteenth century was 'abnormally low'. He was encouraged to posit a constant long-run rate of growth before 1700 by the fact that it was consistent with Russell's estimate of the size of the population in 1603. However, as is shown in appendix 5 below, this estimate was too low, and there is no warrant for assuming that the rate of population growth was constant during the sixteenth and seventeenth centuries. Tucker, 'Population trends', pp. 208–12.

oscillation from relatively, but not absolutely, high rates of growth in the sixteenth century down to very low and sometimes negative rates in the later seventeenth century, followed by a return to sixteenth-century levels in the later eighteenth century.

For the period between the mid sixteenth and the mid nineteenth century it is clear from the changing relative frequencies of births, deaths, and marriages at different points in time that this flexibility in the rate of population growth reflected a flexibility in each of the vital rates. Even though we are not yet in a position to measure the extent to which fertility, mortality, and nuptiality varied over the centuries, we can at least say that any view of pre-industrial England that regards them as invariant is certain to be mistaken. Furthermore, this flexibility in each of the vital rates, leading to an oscillation in the rates of population growth within quite narrow limits, suggests that the demographic behaviour of the population may have been responding to changes in the physical or economic environment in a regular and structured way. In order to

Table 6.13: Decadal birth/marriage ratios, 1540–1869

Decade	Births/marriages	Decade	Births/marriages
1540-9	2.908	*1710-9*	3.787
1550-9	3.394	*1720-9*	3.654
1560-9	3.374	*1730-9*	3.813
1570-9	3.406	*1740-9*	3.964
1580-9	3.463	*1750-9*	4.051
1590-9	3.535	*1760-9*	3.738
1600-9	3.714	*1770-9*	4.092
1610-9	3.665	*1780-9*	4.182
1620-9	4.074	*1790-9*	4.534
1630-9	3.870	*1800-9*	4.690
1640-9	4.105	*1810-9*	5.018
1650-9	3.200	*1820-9*	4.868
1660-9	3.988	*1830-9*	4.530
1670-9	4.153	*1840-9*	4.425
1680-9	3.989	*1850-9*	4.227
1690-9	4.369	*1860-9*	4.339
1700-9	4.127		

Source: Table A2.1

explore the nature of the interaction between the population and its environment effectively, however, it will be necessary to measure the changing levels of fertility, mortality, and nuptiality with greater precision than is possible with simple methods.

In this context it may be appropriate to give an example of the difficulty of pressing simple aggregative methods too far. The varying ratios between the numbers of births and marriages recorded at different dates appear to offer a simple method of discovering the general outline of changes in fertility. It is clear from table 6.13 and figure 6.5 that the ratios varied considerably, rising from a plateau of about 3.5 births per marriage in the sixteenth century to remain within a fairly narrow range between 3.7 and 4.3 until the 1780s, then rising again rapidly to reach a peak of 5.0 in the 1810s, only to fall back to 4.3 in the 1860s.

Unfortunately the birth/marriage ratio encapsulates a large number of factors affecting the number of marriages as well as the number of births and there is no

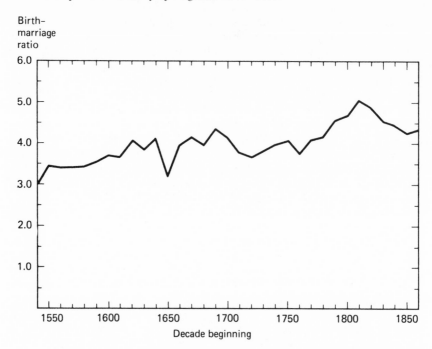

Birth-
marriage
ratio

Figure 6.5: Decadal birth/marriage ratios 1540s – 1860s

Source: Table 6.13.

simple way of converting it into a measure of fertility. Although it appears to measure the average number of children per marriage it will in fact only do so if the population is closed and stationary, and if the three demographic components of fertility, mortality, and nuptiality are constant.[50] Furthermore the birth/marriage ratio can be affected quite powerfully by changes in the proportion of marriages that are remarriages. If adult mortality is high and there is a strong likelihood that a surviving partner will remarry, then the number of marriages will be artificially inflated and the birth/marriage ratio will be measuring the effects of mortality as well as those of fertility and nuptiality. Unfortunately few registers consistently record the marital status of marriage partners so it is difficult to estimate the numbers of remarriages. What little evidence there is at present suggests that in the sixteenth century about 30 per cent of all marriages were remarriages.[51] If this were indeed the case the birth/marriage ratio in table 6.13 would need to be increased by a ratio of 1.429 (100/(100−30)), yielding, for example, figures of 4.154 in the 1540s and 5.050 in the 1590s, which would indicate a considerably higher level of fertility in the sixteenth century.

Finally, data deficiencies also create problems. Marriage registration seems to have been badly affected by the political and religious upheavals of the mid seventeenth

50. If the vital rates are constant, but the population is growing or declining (i.e. if the population is stable), then the mean number of children per marriage can be calculated by taking a weighted average of the totals of marriages in previous years as the denominator in the birth/marriage ratio. See Henry, *Manuel*, p. 78.
51. The evidence about remarriage is discussed on pp. 258–9 below.

century.[52] Even after the Restoration there are signs that a considerable number of marriages were contracted without being registered, a deficiency that may have continued into the early eighteenth century but that had been rectified in most parishes by 1754, when marriage registration was made more rigorous. A consequence of this failure to register a proportion of the marriages is that the birth/marriage ratios for a few decades either side of 1700 are probably too high.[53]

For all these reasons the birth/marriage ratios in table 6.13 and figure 6.5 are unlikely to be a reliable guide to changes in fertility over the long term. Over the short term, however, changes in nuptiality and mortality will not have obtruded so seriously, and pronounced short-run patterns in the ratios may correctly indicate shifts in fertility. For example, the sharp increase and decrease in the birth/marriage ratios over the period 1800–39 may well reflect a corresponding rise and fall in fertility hinging around the maximum ratio recorded in the 1810s.

Since there is no simple way of estimating the levels of fertility, mortality, and nuptiality from the flows of vital events themselves a means must be found of discovering the size and age structure of the population in the period before this information becomes available in the nineteenth-century censuses. This has proved to be the Gordian Knot of English historical demography, and in contrast to its classical prototype there is no analytical parallel to its severance by a clean stroke from Alexander's sword. Rather it has had to be unravelled, an operation that has turned out to be far from simple to perform. So before technical considerations obtrude, it is perhaps worth repeating that the purpose of this chapter has been to show that the main outlines of the course of population change are so firmly etched in the series of births, deaths, and marriages that they are both accessible through the rough and ready methods of analysis employed so far, and proof against radically different assumptions about the accuracy of the data and the scale of the corrections that need to be made to them. While more sophisticated methods will extend and refine the findings of this chapter, some fundamental features of English population history in early modern times emerge straightforwardly from the basic series of births, marriages, and deaths.

52. See table 1.4 and fig. 1.3 above.
53. Wrigley, 'Clandestine marriage'.

7

Secular trends: back-projection estimates of population characteristics and vital rates

The demographic characteristics of a population are most easily calculated where regular censuses are taken and there is continuous vital registration. The fuller the information in both sources, the more elaborate the range of measures that can be employed. Where one source is available but the other is not, there is apt to be greater difficulty in measuring fertility and mortality accurately. In studying the contemporary world and the recent past it is common to dispose of adequate censuses but to lack vital registration data. Methods of estimating fertility and mortality levels from censuses alone have therefore been developed.[1] If the censuses are accurate and the picture is not obscured by large migration flows, satisfactory results are possible.

In studying the behaviour of European populations before the nineteenth century, however, it is more common to have vital registers but no censuses than the reverse, and a different set of problems arises in trying to wring reliable estimates of fertility and mortality from the available data. In chapter 6 we have used a variety of 'traditional' methods of analysing the totals of births and deaths in England between 1540 and 1870. They are informative about demographic change itself and, used in conjunction with economic data, they can begin to reveal the nature of the interplay of economic, social, and demographic variables in early modern England. But they suffer from the shortcomings inherent in all analysis in which the population at risk is unknown. An increase in the number of births, for example, may be a sign of rising fertility, or of unchanged fertility in a growing population, or even of falling fertility if the population is rising faster than the number of births. Totals of births, deaths, and marriages alone may suggest which is the most likely of the three possible trends but such information is very rarely conclusive. The prolonged debate about fertility and mortality trends in the eighteenth century is in part a reflection of the difficulty of making fully effective use of totals of vital events alone. If population totals are used they are usually arrived at either by making assumptions about the level of birth, death, and marriage rates at various periods in the manner begun by Rickman[2], or by a count back from the earliest census, successively subtracting the natural increase accruing in earlier periods. But the first method is circular and the second is only valid where a population is closed.

---

1. The United Nations in the early post-war years sponsored the development of these methods and helped to diffuse a knowledge of Mortara's work in this field, republishing some of his more important articles as *Methods of using census statistics.*
2. See below, pp. 572–7. There have been many attempts to circumvent the difficulties inherent in this approach by more sophisticated manipulation of the data than Rickman employed but none escape from its basic flaws. See, for example, Sogner, 'Aspects of the demographic situation'.

Recent attempts to make fuller use of parish registers

In an attempt to overcome the apparent limitations of vital registers as demographic sources, two new methods of using parish register material have been developed in recent years. The first, family reconstitution, was perfected by Louis Henry.[3] The technique of family reconstitution depends upon the fact that individuals are separately identified in vital registers and it is therefore possible to recapture the life history of an individual by linking together entries in the register concerning his birth, marriage, and death. The history of families can be reconstructed similarly. The novelty of Henry's work lay not in the assemblage of information in this way, which has been the backbone of genealogical work for many generations, but in defining with precision the period during which a particular family might properly be regarded as in observation for the purpose of tabulating its fertility and mortality history.[4] Once this has been done the number of years of exposure to the risk of dying or giving birth can be established and since the number of deaths or births occurring in the period is also known, the information necessary to calculate rates is to hand. By summing the experience of many families the demographic history of a community can be reconstructed. Events can be related to numbers at risk to derive all the main measures of fertility and mortality that might be obtained from a combination of census and registration data in the conventional fashion.

Family reconstitution has proved a very potent weapon in the hands of historical demographers, and its value extends well beyond purely demographic investigations. By providing a skeletal history of every family in a community, which can be fleshed out with information drawn from a wide range of nominal sources, bearing on other aspects of family and community life, it is proving very useful to social and economic historians no less than to demographers.[5] The intricacy and fine detail of family reconstitution, however, which is so valuable in the study of particular communities, is bought at a very high price. Reconstitutions carried out by hand are exceedingly time-consuming. They commonly involve some hundreds of hours of skilled work upon the reconstitution itself before the analysis of the data can begin. And even when satisfactory computerized reconstitution programs are available the cost of each individual reconstitution will continue to be high because of the large volume of data punching involved.[6] In France the reconstitution research being carried out by the *Institut National d'Études Démographiques* covers a sample of only one tenth of one per cent of French parishes (though scores of other reconstitution studies have been made for particular purposes). In England about 35 reconstitutions of English parishes have been completed or are in train (there were about 10,000 ancient parishes in England). Reconstitution has given us a vastly better knowledge of early modern European demography than existed 20 years ago but it is unlikely ever to cover more than a tiny proportion of all parishes. There is also dispute about the representativeness of the rates based on reconstitution since mobile individuals and families tend to

3. Fleury and Henry, *Nouveau manuel*.
4. See Fleury and Henry, *Nouveau manuel*, ch. 7, and Henry, *Manuel*, chs. 5 and 6; see also Wrigley (ed.), *English historical demography*, pp. 147–51, and 'Mortality in pre-industrial England', pp. 549–55.
5. See, for example, Levine, *Family formation*. For a general discussion of the nature and range of sources yielding information that can be integrated with reconstituted families, see Macfarlane, *Reconstructing historical communities*.
6. The number of keystrokes necessary to punch the information contained in the registers of an English parish whose population averaged 1,000 over a period of three centuries will usually range between 1 million and 2.5 million, depending upon the richness of detail contained in the register at different periods.

be under-represented because of the way in which the rules of observation operate.[7] And it is a disadvantage of family reconstitution that it tends to lose track of individuals who remain permanently celibate. It is much more difficult to define the period in observation for an adult who remains single than for a married man or woman. Indeed it is often difficult to establish what proportion of the population never married, a matter of great importance in west European populations.

It is not surprising, therefore, that a second approach to the problem of making the most of vital registers should have been developed. It was pioneered by Ronald Lee,[8] who coined the expression 'inverse projection' to describe it. Most population projections involve making a series of assumptions about the way fertility and mortality will change and converting these into an end product that consists of estimates of the number of births and deaths at some point in the future, together with the population size and age structure at that time. Given a knowledge of population size and age structure in the present and assumptions about the changes in, say, expectation of life at birth and the gross reproduction rate, it is a comparatively straightforward matter to calculate annual totals of births and deaths as far into the future as the assumptions reach. Lee's method of projection is inverse in the sense that the information available is assumed to consist of a continuous series of birth and death totals occurring over a period of time from which the underlying fertility and mortality structure that produced them must be inferred, thus altering the direction of the operation. What is the end product of a conventional population projection becomes the raw material in inverse projection and vice versa. Inverse projection is thus designed to make effective use of totals of vital events such as European parish registers often provide. Lee has demonstrated the value of inverse projection both in relation to national series and to those for individual parishes. The independent evidence of reconstitution studies suggests that the estimates of fertility and mortality derived by inverse projection can be remarkably accurate in favourable circumstances.[9]

Inverse projection, however, suffers from two limitations that restrict its usefulness. First, and more important, it will only produce accurate results where a population is closed, or at least where net migration is negligible. The technique does not generate any independent estimates of net migration. In any population in which there is substantial migration, therefore, estimates of fertility and mortality will tend to become increasingly inaccurate. Second, the program runs forward in time. This means that estimates of population size and age structure must be made for the date at which the series of births and deaths begins, when independent evidence is likely to be least accurate. The initial population size is constrained to be the total resulting from adding all deaths and subtracting all births from a known population total at the end of the birth and death series when a census provides reliable information. If this is not done the population total at the end of the inverse projection run will not agree with the known census total. Deriving an initial population total in this way depends once more on an assumption of population closure, which may be unjustified, leading to inaccurate results. Furthermore, the estimation of the age structure of the initial

7. See, for example, the brief discussion of this issue in Schofield, 'Representativeness and family reconstitution' and other papers published in *Annales de démographie historique*, 1972 in the section entitled *Problèmes de representativité dans les études nominatives*. See also Henry, *Manuel*, ch. 1.
8. Lee, 'Estimating vital rates'.
9. Lee compares inverse projection and reconstitution data for Colyton in 'Estimating vital rates', pp. 498–504.

population must be dependent upon assumptions about the prevailing levels of fertility and mortality at that time, which introduces an element of circularity into the subsequent calculation of these population characteristics.

Aggregative back projection

In order to overcome these two limitations, we have developed an alternative technique which runs backwards in time and produces quinquennial estimates of population size, age structure, and net migration. The technique, which we have called back projection, is incorporated in a computer program. Since the program is complex in detail we have relegated a fuller description of its procedures to appendix 15, where the logical sequence of operations is summarized in flow-chart form in figure A15.6. However, at this stage it may be helpful to explain in outline the general strategy employed.

Since the program runs backwards in time, a starting date can be selected at which the size and age structure of the population is accurately known from a reliable census. At each five-year time step each age group in the current 'census' becomes five years younger, and its size at the previous 'census' can be calculated by adding back the numbers who died, and adjusting for those who entered or left the population as migrants during the quinquennium.

The number of deaths in each age group can be estimated directly by matching the total number of deaths in the quinquennium to a family of mortality tables that is appropriate to the age structure of mortality in the population.[10] Estimating the number of migrants is both more complicated and more indirect. First the life-time net migration is estimated for each age group and then a fixed age-specific schedule is used to discover what proportion of it occurred in the current quinquennium. An age group's life-time net migration is calculated by estimating its mortality history since birth and computing the size of the birth cohort corresponding to the numbers surviving to the current census. If the mortality is accurately specified any discrepancy between the computed size of the birth cohort and the number of births actually recorded in the appropriate quinquennium must represent the age group's life-time net migration up to the date of the current census: emigration if more births were recorded than the mortality history of the survivors would lead one to expect, and immigration in the opposite case.

In order to illustrate the procedures by which the size of an age group is estimated at each step in the back projection, let us take the simplest possible case in which the mortality level prevailing at the beginning of the back projection remains unchanged throughout the lifetime of the whole population living at the time of the initial census. It is now a simple matter to calculate the lifetime net migration total for each age group. For example, in the case of those aged 40–4, the ratio of $_5L_{40}$ to the radix of the population in the appropriate life table will be the ratio between the census population 40–4 and the birth cohort from which it sprang. The estimate of the size of the birth cohort derived in this way can then be compared with the recorded birth total for the period 40–4 years before the census, the difference between the two figures representing that cohort's net migration up to age 40–4. The proportion occurring in the current quinquennium is found by reference to the appropriate part of the age-specific migration schedule. The number aged 35–9 at the previous 'census' five

10. For details of the construction of the life tables used see appendix 14.

years earlier can now be calculated by inflating the number aged 40–4 in the initial 'census' to reflect the combined effect of mortality and migration. Thus the ratio $_5L_{35}/_5L_{40}$ will represent the inflation necessary to offset the effect of mortality in the first five years of the back projection, to which must be added any net migration occurring during the period.

Since the program runs backwards in time, a small number of very elderly people, comprising the 90–4 age group, must be 'born' into the population each time the program advances five years. Eventually, of course, all those living in the population will have been introduced in this way, so that the method used in calculating the size of this new cohort in each step is crucial to the success of the operation as a whole. We have adopted a method of solving this problem that makes the size of the new cohort aged 90–4 (the oldest age group in the system) a function of the absolute size of the current 90–4 age group (about to become 85–9 in the course of the current step), the relative size of the birth cohorts from which the current and new 90–4 age groups sprang, the relative severity of the cohort mortality histories of the two age groups, and their comparative net migration histories.

The success of the program as a whole depends critically upon success in forecasting and measuring mortality since this affects not only the scale of the inflation of population at each step to reflect prevailing mortality, but also the adjustments made to allow for net migration movements, and the size of the new age group 90–4. Assuming, however, that this can be done accurately, it is then a comparatively straightforward matter to specify the size and age structure of the population every five years. This in turn allows the calculation of detailed measures not only of mortality but also of fertility. For example, using an age schedule of fertility, the gross reproduction rate can be estimated. The programs involved and their products are described in greater detail in appendix 15.

Mortality levels fluctuated considerably in the past, of course, and the system of forecasting mortality must be able to cope with this. We have attempted to meet this problem both by the method used to make forecasts during the first pass through the data and also by making further passes in which the output data about mortality from the previous pass are used as input data in the current one, thus introducing an element of 'learning' into the operation of the program. In the first pass mortality is forecast by making estimates of population totals over the period relevant to each cycle of the program by assuming that the rate of net migration currently observable will maintain throughout the period of forecast. Thus if net migration added 0.2 per cent to the population total in the last observed period it is assumed that it will continue to do so as population totals change over the forecast period. This assumption combined with a knowledge of the natural increase occurring in each quinquennium permits the estimate of population totals and from these in turn mortality levels can be calculated from the totals of deaths recorded throughout the forecast period with only a small margin of error. As the first pass progresses initial estimates of mortality for any given period are updated and eventually succeeded by an 'observation' of the mortality level since the program will ultimately reach even the earliest time period and will be able to replace the forecasts by a direct estimate.

A forecast of the level of mortality in any given five-year period has first to be made when the program has reached a point 95 years distant in order to calculate the number of those aged 90–4 to be introduced at the top of the age pyramid of the population. It is likely to be least accurate at so great a distance in time and will tend to improve in accuracy each time the forecast is revised as the program moves nearer to the five-year period in question. The discrepancies between the level first forecast and the level found when the program reached the period were reassuringly small. The average *absolute* difference was 0.78 of a mortality level, which is equivalent to a difference in expectation of life at birth of just under 2 years (a unit difference in mortality level is approximately 2½ years). But there was no systematic tendency for initial estimates to be above or below the level later found, and the average discrepancy between forecast and result *when sign is taken into account* reduces to only 0.025 of a level or under one tenth of a year in terms of expectation of life.[11]

After the initial forecast of mortality made at a distance of 95 years the next critical phase in forecasting begins at 45 years, the age before which our age-specific schedule constrained migration to occur. Consequently it is this and subsequent forecasts that determine the level of net migration. Since the forecasting period is now much shorter, the forecasts become more accurate. The average absolute difference between the forecast and found mortality level was 0.41 of a level at 45 years distance, and, taking sign into account, the figure drops to 0.007, a negligible difference. At 95 years distance the forecast figure taking sign into account was on average slightly higher than that later found; at 45 years fractionally lower.

Close agreement between the levels forecast and the levels found is not proof of the accuracy of the forecast, of course, since it is possible that the initial forecasts affect the behaviour of the system sufficiently to cause the two sets of levels to agree well together, but lack of agreement would give cause for concern.

In the second and any subsequent passes, the program is able to function without making forecasts of population totals from which to derive mortality-level estimates. The mortality levels observed in the previous pass can be used as forecasts of mortality in the current pass. The migration output data from any one pass may also be used as input to the next pass, and if both migration and mortality data are used in this way the system quickly converges upon a set of results that will not subsequently vary if further passes are made. Any incompatibility between mortality and migration estimates can also be reduced and eventually eliminated by successive passes.

Only three types of information are required by the program as input data: the population at the starting date divided by age into the conventional five-year age groups (though with the first age group subdivided 0–1 and 1–4); an estimate of the level of net migration at the starting date; and quinquennial totals of births and deaths, so ordered that the latest five-year group ends at the date of the census. The starting point for the English back projection was the 1871 census whose data were adjusted to the mid-point of the year. Births and deaths were therefore grouped mid 1866 to mid 1871, and so on. The current level of net migration was assumed to be that prevailing in the decade 1861–71 as estimated from revised census and vital registration data (table A6.8). As the program moves backwards in time in five-year steps, every fifth year it provides a census (the population total divided into age groups) and a net migration total. The quinquennial census data taken from the final pass, together with the quinquennial totals of vital events centred on the census dates (1869–73, 1864–8, etc.), are input to a separate demographic program that yields quinquennial estimates of the gross reproduction rate, expectation of life at birth and other life table data, and associated measures such as the net reproduction rate and dependency ratios. Annual

11. The most extreme individual difference between the forecast mortality level and that later found was 2.3. The forecasts of mortality in the two quinquennia of the severest mortality crises, 1556–61 and 1726–31, were respectively 1.1 and 1.6 levels under-estimated at a distance of 95 years.

crude rates of birth, death, marriage, and natural increase may also be derived.[12]

It should be noted that because the size of the age group 90– 4 introduced at each step of the program is in part a function of the relative size of the birth cohort from which it sprang and that of the next younger age group, either the program must stop when 90 years from the end of the known series of births and deaths, or an estimated series of births 95 years long must be added to the empirical data. The same has to be done for deaths since the mortality experience of those aged 90– 4 must also be compared with that of the next younger age group. We have chosen the latter alternative even though it entails a growing margin of error in the findings of back projection as the program approaches the end of the observed data in 1538. Details of the assumptions made about quinquennial birth and death totals before 1541 may be found in appendix 15.

The program is complex and there are some stylized elements in its construction that mean that even where the data used are perfectly accurate it will not produce results that would exactly replicate the demographic characteristics of past populations, assuming these were available for checking purposes. For example, adopting a fixed age-specific schedule of net migration inevitably means that the *timing* of surges in migration will not be accurately captured when the schedule varies even if the *total* net migration were correctly estimated. Since the age schedule probably altered quite sharply from time to time as the volume of migration fluctuated, the totals produced by the program may often be substantially at variance with the true totals of individual quinquennia. Or again, if there were a radical change in the *relative* levels of mortality at different ages at some period in the past, the use of a family of life tables derived from a mortality schedule appropriate for a later period must produce some inaccuracy. We have used a family of life tables linked to Farr's third English life table,[13] which reflects English mortality in the period 1838– 54, and there is reason to believe that the relative mortality levels it embodies (though not, of course, the absolute levels) approximate quite well to English experience from the mid nineteenth century back until the later seventeenth century, at least in infancy and childhood. But there is also reason to doubt whether the same was true of the sixteenth and early seventeenth centuries.[14]

The maximum likely extent of any inaccuracies in the findings of back projection due to the type of mortality schedule adopted can be investigated by using the same data but a different family of life tables. In the same way the effects of varying the age-specific cohort migration schedule can be tested. Again, simulated data sets can be created to discover how sensitive the results of back projection are to changes in the totals of births and deaths used in the main run. And the effects of differing assumptions about the size of the age group 90– 4 in the starting population can be examined. The last two sections of this chapter are devoted to describing the results of these sensitivity tests. In general the tests are reassuring. So too were the results of tests on Scandinavian data where detailed demographic measures are available from the mid eighteenth century. For example, using only the series of births and deaths for Sweden back projection produces results that agree closely with the published Swedish population totals, age structural details, net migration totals, gross reproduction rates, and estimates of expectation of life at birth over a period of two centuries from 1750 to 1950. It also proves capable of equal success using data for

12. See appendix 15.
13. For details of their derivation see appendix 14.
14. See Schofield and Wrigley, 'Infant and child mortality'.

Stockholm alone, a more searching test, since the relative importance of net migration was much greater in the city than in the country as a whole.[15] Nevertheless it is proper to emphasize that the results obtained by back projection should be regarded as estimates which may subsequently be improved upon rather than as definitive findings, and that the results are subject to a margin of error which is in general larger in the earlier decades than in the later.

A comparison of nineteenth-century census data and the results of back projection

Having briefly described the functioning of back projection we may shortly turn to a consideration of the results it produces using the birth and death totals whose derivation was described in the first five chapters of the book. We shall consider first the movement of total population, and then turn to age structure, net migration, and fertility and mortality.

Before considering the data yielded by back projection generally, however, it is convenient first to compare the results of back projection with population data drawn from the censuses of 1801 to 1871 since they afford a valuable check upon the precision of back-projection results. Table 7.1 sets out the English population totals at the first eight censuses. The totals given are those arrived at after making additions to the recorded totals to offset the absence from the census of men in the army, navy, and merchant marine. The census totals have also been modified to make them all refer to

Table 7.1: English population totals in the censuses of 1801 to 1871 and those derived from back projection

Year	(1) Census	(2) Back projection	(3) Ratio (2)/(1)
1871	21 635 388	21 500 720	0.9938
1861	19 097 878	18 937 536	0.9916
1851	17 030 076	16 736 084	0.9827
1841	15 113 000	14 970 372	0.9906
1831	13 298 585	13 283 882	0.9989
1821	11 491 346	11 491 850	1.0000
1811	9 868 286	9 885 690	1.0018
1801	8 658 265	8 664 490	1.0007

Note: The population totals refer to 30 June in each year indicated.

Sources: Census totals, table A6.7; back-projection totals, table A3.1.

the mid-point of the year and to make good the under-recording of young children. Details of the adjustments made may be found in appendix 6. The totals arrived at by back projection are given in parallel with the census totals. Both are given in the reverse of the normal order since back projection works backwards in time. The first back-projection totals are somewhat lower than the census totals. This occurs because those excluded from the 1871 census totals as a result of their membership of the armed forces or merchant navy are also excluded from the age-group totals of 1871 which

15. We hope to publish separately the results of these and other experiments designed to test the program. See appendix 15, pp. 733–6 for some details of the Stockholm back projection.

represent the starting data for the back-projection program. Their numbers and age distribution are not known with the same degree of accuracy as those of the population resident in England, and, since deaths occurring among them were not included in the Registrar General's returns, to have included them would have meant a slight underestimation of mortality levels.

In the course of time, however, those seamen and soldiers who were abroad in 1871 are reintroduced into the population by the back-projection program. From the point of view of the program they are like any other group of emigrants and are slowly built back into the population through the estimated totals of net emigration because they were born in England though they did not die there in the period covered by back projection. We should therefore expect the census and back-projected totals to converge in a manner reflecting both the age distribution of seamen and soldiers abroad in 1871 and the age schedule of net migration. The former is set out in table 7.2 and the latter in table 7.3.

Table 7.2: Age distribution of English merchant seamen, sailors, and soldiers abroad in 1871

	(1)	(2)
		(1) expressed to the base of 10 000
under 15	618	46
15–9	17 129	1 280
20–4	36 645	2 739
25–9	31 666	2 367
30–4	23 320	1 743
35–9	12 613	943
40–4	5 814	434
45–9	3 325	248
50–4	1 727	129
55–9	664	49
60–4	229	17
65 and over	75	5
	133 825	10 000

Note: The totals given in the census are for England and Wales. Those given in this table are the census totals multiplied by 0.93, the approximate share of England in the total for England and Wales in the national population.

Source: *1871 Census*, General Report, appendix A, p.142, table 160

The age schedule of net migration is an important element in back projection and it is therefore unfortunate that so little is known about it for English populations at any period before 1871. We have constructed a schedule derived from Swedish data for the later nineteenth century for use in the back projection, preferring an arbitrary

Table 7.3: Age schedule of
cohort net migration used
in back projection

	(1)	(2)
	Schedule	Cumulative totals of (1)
0-1	0.013	0.013
1-4	0.052	0.065
5-9	0.045	0.110
10-4	0.040	0.150
15-9	0.065	0.215
20-4	0.200	0.415
25-9	0.280	0.695
30-4	0.200	0.895
35-9	0.075	0.970
40-4	0.030	1.000

Note: See appendix 15 for further
details of the operation of the schedule.

Source: Hofsten and Lundstrom,
Swedish population history, pp. 77-80
(and see accompanying text).

solution of this type to guesswork from scattered and fragmentary English material.[16]
The Swedish data show very clearly how great are the changes in age-specific cohort
net migration proportions even over the course of half a century.[17] There is no reason to
doubt that the fluctuations were equally marked in English experience in the
nineteenth century, and every reason to suppose that in earlier centuries the age
schedules were substantially different. In the later seventeenth century, for example,
when emigration to North America included a high proportion of indentured labour, it
is almost certain that the proportion of cohort net migration occurring in the age band
15-24 should be much higher than that shown in table 7.3.[18]

16. The earliest systematic English data begin in 1877 but they are tabulated on a current, not a cohort
basis, and are gross rather than net figures. In the first full decade of such data, 1881-90, there were about
twice as many adult male as adult female emigrants, and children formed about a sixth of all emigrants.
(Carrier and Jeffery, *External migration*, p. 102). Glass quotes some broad age breakdowns for the mid
nineteenth century, but these are also for gross emigration, have only partial coverage, and are concerned
only with dividing children from adults (Glass, 'A note on under-registration', p. 83, table 8).
    The subdivision of age-specific cohort migration shown in table 7.3 represents a stylized approximation
to the average of the late-nineteenth-century Swedish schedules taken from Hofsten and Lundström,
Swedish population history, pp. 78-9, figures 4.2 and 4.3.
17. For example, in the birth cohort most heavily depleted by net emigration, that of 1861-5, more than
two thirds of the total loss occurred in the age groups 15-19 to 25-9, where as in the birth cohort of 1851-5
the comparable proportion was under one half.
18. For example, 74 per cent of indentured servant emigrants leaving via London in 1683-4 were in the
age group 15-24 (calculation by Mr D. Souden of Emmanuel College, Cambridge, from data on 785
servants published in Nicholson 'Some early emigrants to America' and Wareing 'Some early emigrants to
America, 1683-1684. A supplementary list'). More general lists from earlier in the century also suggest a
heavy predominance of emigrants in this age group. Mr Souden analysed a total of 4,669 cases of emigrants
from London in 1635 whose ages were stated (comprising the vast majority of all those listed) and found
that 56 per cent were aged 15-24. The lists are to be found in Hotten, *Original lists of emigrants*,
pp. 35-145.

Any failure to specify age-specific cohort net migration accurately affects the timing of migration but should not distort the final total significantly when measured over substantial periods of time, unless the *average* age distribution in the various cohorts is very different from the schedule used.[19] In considering the slow convergence of the census and back-projection totals to closely similar totals in 1831 and earlier this point should be borne in mind. Not only were the back-projection totals inevitably lower than the census totals in the first decades of the exercise because of the problem of the overseas army and navy in 1871, but also, and more importantly, the use of a fixed net migration schedule necessarily prevents accurate identification of big short-term surges or recessions of migration. For example, there was an exceptionally high level of net emigration from England in the 1850s, which reached a total of at least 365,000 in that decade. In the 1840s there was very little net emigration, perhaps less than 90,000, and in the 1860s the total was approximately two thirds that of the 1850s, or about 245,000.[20] The cohorts aged from 20 to 60 in 1871, therefore, were much more heavily depleted by emigration in the 1850s than in either of the other two decades but the back-projection program, though it may correctly identify the total in each five-year cohort in the 1871 census lost by emigration at that date, will distribute them according to the schedule shown in table 7.3, whereas in reality the true schedule was probably quite different during the decades of very high emigration. The combined effects of failure to time migration accurately and the problems caused by seamen and soldiers in 1871, therefore, kept the back-projected population below the census totals back to 1841 but not thereafter.

Over the four censuses 1801–1831 the back-projected and census totals never differ by more than 0.18 per cent. In this period net migration was at a modest level and the problem of a fixed migration schedule is therefore minimized. Census and back-projected totals should and do agree closely.

By 1801 all those aged 25 and over belong to cohorts no longer represented in the population by the time of the 1871 census, but instead introduced successively into the highest age group at each cycle of the program. Thus, for example, those aged 50–4 in 1801 were first introduced as a small number of people aged 90–4 in 1841, and gradually made younger and increased in number as the program moved backwards towards 1801. The overall success of back projection is heavily dependent upon achieving accuracy in determining the size of each successive group of 90–4 year olds. If the totals introduced in this way are too high, population totals will be exaggerated and the age structure of the population will also be distorted; if too low, there will be comparable problems.[21] It is therefore instructive to examine this aspect of the functioning of back projection, taking advantage of the earliest available census data on age structure given in the 1821 census. If this is replicated with tolerable accuracy by back projection it will be clear that the methods used to calculate the number of those aged 90–4 at each cycle are working well and, equally, that their subsequent rejuvenation is being carried out satisfactorily.

Unfortunately, the test cannot be made straightforwardly because elderly people frequently exaggerated their age in nineteenth-century censuses, as we have already seen.[22] All age groups above age 50 appear to have been affected by the tendency, though the worst distortion is found in the highest age groups. Age misstatement is a

19. For a fuller discussion of this point see pp. 277–81 below.
20. See table A6.8 for the net migration estimates quoted here.
21. See below, pp. 282–3.
22. See above, pp. 109–13.

problem affecting both the starting population in 1871 and all earlier censuses in which ages were stated. For example, in table 7.4 the original age distribution of the 1871 population is shown, together with the revised distribution intended to be used in back projection. The numbers in the age groups above age 50 were redistributed as if their relative size had been determined solely by the relative size of the birth cohorts from which they sprang and the effects of mortality at level 10 in the 'English' life table set.[23] This produces a more nearly accurate age distribution than that found in the

Table 7.4: Original and revised census age distribution of the population of England in 1871

	(1) Original	(2) Revised	(3) (1) expressed to the base 100 000	(4) (2) expressed to the base 100 000
0-1	645 141	676 089	3 029	3 144
1-4	2 233 711	2 344 203	10 487	10 902
5-9	2 533 670	2 541 983	11 895	11 822
10-4	2 269 926	2 261 090	10 657	10 516
15-9	2 043 681	2 066 670	9 595	9 612
20-4	1 884 037	1 870 576	8 845	8 700
25-9	1 675 924	1 701 065	7 868	7 911
30-4	1 467 626	1 449 804	6 890	6 743
35-9	1 262 152	1 288 931	5 926	5 995
40-4	1 157 683	1 109 021	5 435	5 158
45-9	988 866	1 044 572	4 643	4 858
50-4	887 059	894 545	4 165	4 160
55-9	670 600	736 458	3 148	3 425
60-4	580 945	573 525	2 727	2 667
65-9	412 253	421 982	1 935	1 963
70-4	302 290	275 044	1 419	1 279
75-9	168 455	156 382	791	727
80-4	81 854	66 738	384	310
85-9	26 661	18 692	125	87
90-4	5 933	3 462	28	16
95 and over	1 214	731	6	3
Total	21 299 683	21 501 563	99 998	99 998

Notes: The revised total is arrived at after taking into account correction for the under-registration of children aged 0-4 and adjusting to 30 June 1871 (see appendix 6). Since there was a marked tendency in the original age reporting to exaggerate the proportion in the first half of each decennium of age (e.g. to exaggerate the numbers 40-4 relative to 45-9), in each decennium from 10-9 to 40-9 the numbers in the two five-year age groups were determined by taking the number in the decennium as a whole and dividing it according to the relative size of the respective birth cohorts and the effect of level 10 mortality. For the treatment of age groups aged 50 and over see text.

Source: 1871 Census, Ages, civil condition, etc., Summary tables, pp. xii–xiii.

census, but it is unlikely to be perfectly accurate. Nor would it be possible to demonstrate that any particular set of totals corresponded exactly with the true age distribution in, say, 1871.

Some preliminary reallocation of population totals between the age groups in

23. A similar exercise is described above on pp. 111–2. See pp. 113–8 and p. 589 fn. 2 for evidence that mortality at approximately level 10 appears to have obtained throughout the half century before 1871.

earlier censuses is also necessary before they can be used to check the results of back projection. Table 7.5 shows the original and revised age structures of those aged 40 and over in 1821 for comparison with the results obtained by back projection. The total in the age group 40–9 is unchanged but above age 50 the totals were redistributed in column 2 on the assumption that their sizes were the product of the relative sizes of the birth cohorts involved and mortality at level 9. In column 3 the redistribution was carried out in the same way but assuming level 8 mortality, which being more severe reduces the numbers in the higher age groups still more radically.[24] Those aged 40 and over in 1821 include those who were in the age group 90–4 in 1871 and all those introduced at the top of the age pyramid subsequently.

Table 7.5: Original and revised census age distributions of the population of England aged 40 and over in 1821 compared to the results obtained by back projection

	(1) Original	(2) Revised (level 9)	(3) Revised (level 8)	(4) Back projection
40–9	1 065 538	1 065 538	1 065 538	1 070 155
50–9	737 793	778 366	797 937	779 302
60–9	500 552	502 470	501 586	506 223
70–9	246 754	225 090	213 333	217 079
80–9	65 786	48 242	41 710	42 622
90–4	4 565	1 743	1 345	1 393
Total 40–94	2 620 988	2 621 449	2 621 449	2 616 774

Notes: The totals shown in column 1 have been adjusted from those listed in the census in the following ways:

(i) those whose age was not stated have been distributed among the age groups on the assumption that they had the same age distribution as those whose age was given but with the modifications shown in table 5.3 for the female population and here applied to both sexes

(ii) the totals have been adjusted to 30 June 1821 (see appendix 6)

(iii) since the age group 90–9 was not divided in the census the total 90–4 was obtained by assuming the same proportional division between 90–4 and 95–9 as may be found in the 1841 census

(iv) those excluded from the census because of their membership of the armed forces or merchant navy were distributed on the assumption that their age distribution was the same as in 1851

(v) strictly speaking the total in column 3 should be very slightly larger than that in column 2 because adopting a more severe mortality assumption would slightly reduce the total population aged 95 and over but in modifying the level 9 distribution this refinement was ignored.

Source: Column 1, *1821 Census*, Enumeration abstract, pp. 428–9 (but see notes)

Early runs of the back-projection program soon showed that the original revised total for the 90–4 age group in 1871 based on level 10 mortality was slightly too high because it produced too large a population in the early decades of the century. A redistribution of the 1871 age pyramid based on level 9 mortality, on the other hand,

24. See pp. 120–2 above for evidence that mortality was probably in the neighbourhood of levels 8 and 9 in the decades before 1821.

produced a total for the 90–4 age group that led to an undershooting of the census totals early in the century by a larger margin. Using a compromise total of 3,350 people aged 90–4 in 1871, instead of the total of 3,462 shown in table 7.4, while keeping all other age group totals as shown in the table, produced the results shown in table 7.5, which appear tolerably good, having regard to the difficulty of knowing the target totals with precision. The age-group totals produced by back projection consistently lie between the census totals revised on level 8 and level 9 assumptions with only one exception, and the overall total 40–94 agrees very closely with the census total. There is also a good fit in the younger age groups 0–39 which formed the age groups 50–89 in 1871 as may be seen in table 7.6.

Table 7.6: Revised census age distributions of the population of England aged 0–39 in 1821 compared with the results obtained by back projection

	(1) Revised census totals	(2) Back projection
0–4	1 788 752	1 785 194
5–9	1 445 225	1 468 780
10–4	1 237 326	1 251 962
15–9	1 135 227	1 134 021
20–9	1 882 022	1 841 574
30–9	1 380 776	1 393 545
Total 0–39	8 869 328	8 875 076

Notes: The totals shown in column 1 have been adjusted from those listed in the census in the following ways:

(i) those whose age was not stated have been distributed among the age groups on the assumption that they had the same age distribution as those whose age was given but with the modification shown in table 5.3 for the female population and here applied to both sexes

(ii) the totals have been adjusted to 30 June 1821 (see appendix 6)

(iii) the numbers in the age group 0–4 have been increased to offset under-registration (see appendix 6)

(iv) those excluded from the census because of their membership of the armed forces or merchant navy were distributed among the age groups on the assumption that their age distribution was the same as in the 1851 census.

Source: Column 1, *1821 Census*, Enumeration abstract, pp. 428–9 (but see notes).

The second earliest date at which the census provides an age breakdown, and therefore an opportunity to check the results obtained by back projection, is 1841. Table 7.7 sets out this comparison which also merits a brief discussion. The census population above age 50 has been revised using the same method as has already been described for 1871 and 1821 and on the assumption that level 10 was the appropriate mortality level to use. Since only 30 years separate 1841 from 1871 only those aged 60 or more in 1841 belonged to the 90–4 age group in 1871 or to still older cohorts introduced at 90–4 in later steps of the program. But because the effects of age

Table 7.7: Original and revised census age distributions of the population of England aged 50 and
over in 1841 compared to the results obtained by
back projection

	(1) Revised census totals	(2) Back projection
50–4	563 674	566 020
55–9	444 358	446 418
60–4	376 533	367 247
65–9	278 887	277 549
70–4	185 545	181 205
75–9	106 966	100 527
80–4	45 474	42 731
85–9	14 381	13 416
90–4	2 582	2 253
Total 50–94	2 018 400	1 997 366

Notes: The totals shown in column 1 have been adjusted from those
listed in the census in the following ways:

(i) those whose age was not stated have been distributed among the
age groups on the assumption that they had the same age distribution
as those whose age was given

(ii) the totals have been adjusted to 30 June 1841 (see appendix 6)

(iii) those excluded from the census because of their membership of
the armed forces or merchant navy were distributed among the age
groups on the assumption that their age distribution was the same
as in the 1851 census.

Sources: Column 1, *1841 Census*, Age abstract, pp. 368–9 and
372–3 (but see notes).

mis-statement appear to affect all age groups above 50, it is convenient to consider
the 1841 population in this age range.[25] Below age 50 the back-projection age-group
totals are smaller than those in the census (the respective totals 0–49 are 12,973,006
and 13,093,882), largely because of the inability of the program to pick up the timing
of migration movement with a fixed cohort migration schedule, to which reference
has already been made.

The same shortfall between back-projected and census totals is visible over age 50.
The back-projected total for the age-range 50–94 is 1,997,366 whereas the census
total comes to 2,018,400, or 1.0 per cent more. The comparatively small overall
difference conceals differences of opposite sign in the several age groups. Their
import is not easy to assess because both sets of age-group totals are much influenced
by the assumption of level 10 mortality made in correcting the census age-group totals
found in the 1841 and 1871 censuses.[26]

25. See above, pp. 109–13.
26. For example, if the age group totals for 80–4 and 85–9 in 1871 were slightly higher in reality than the
revised totals given in table 7.4 and these had been used in back projection, this would have had the effect of
increasing the back-projected totals in the age groups 50–4 and 55–9 in 1841, and since these provide the
two largest age group totals contributing to the overall total for the age range 50–94, the back-projected
total would then be larger than the census total above 50. Again, varying the level 10 mortality assumption
in revising the 1841 age totals, though it could not alter the overall total over 50, would modify its age
distribution and so alter the pattern of relative sizes of population totals in the two columns of table 7.7.

In general the evidence of the census totals 1801–71 and the more detailed age breakdowns of 1821 and 1841 suggests that back projection performs well over the period during which its performance can be checked effectively. There is virtual identity in overall population totals from back projection and census in each of the four censuses 1801 to 1831, which encourages the belief that the 1871 input age data must have been modified correctly. The more detailed comparisons of the two sources for 1841 and 1821 also tend to sustain the view that the program is following the right path during the first 70 years of back projection. Before 1801 it moves into the pre-census age when its progress can no longer be monitored in the same way in the absence of reliable independent information about the size or structure of the English population.

Estimates of population size

The population totals estimated by back projection at five-year intervals between 1541 and 1871 are shown in table 7.8 and figure 7.1.[27] The vertical scale is logarithmic to enable comparisons to be made of the rate of population change regardless of absolute level. In round terms the course of population change as shown in the figure can be summarized fairly simply. When first 'visible', in 1541, the

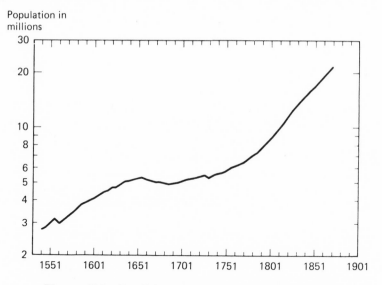

Figure 7.1: English population totals 1541 – 1871

Source: Table A3.1

27. The difference between any two successive population totals equals the difference between the quinquennial birth and death totals plus the net migration total for the period. Thus, for example, the population in 1601 was 4,109,981, while that in 1606 was 4,253,325, a difference of 143,344. The natural increase of the period was 179,330 (703,918 births less 524,588 deaths), and the net emigration was 35,988. Adding these two totals gives the intercensal difference almost exactly (179,330 – 35,988 = 143,342). The difference of 2 arises because of small rounding errors in the allocation of deaths by age group.

Table 7.8: Quinquennial English population totals 1541–1871

1 Population total
2 Increase since last total
3 Percentage increase since last total
4 Compound annual percentage growth rate since last total

	(1)	(2)	(3)	(4)
1541	2 773 851			
1546	2 853 711	79 860	2.88	0.56
1551	3 011 030	157 319	5.51	1.08
1556	3 158 664	147 634	4.90	0.96
1561	2 984 576	−174 088	−5.51	−1.13
1566	3 128 279	143 703	4.81	0.94
1571	3 270 903	142 624	4.56	0.90
1576	3 412 722	141 819	4.34	0.85
1581	3 597 670	184 948	5.42	1.06
1586	3 805 841	208 171	5.79	1.13
1591	3 899 190	93 349	2.45	0.49
1596	4 011 563	112 373	2.88	0.57
1601	4 109 981	98 418	2.45	0.49
1606	4 253 325	143 344	3.49	0.69
1611	4 416 351	163 026	3.83	0.76

	(1)	(2)	(3)	(4)
1711	5 230 371	48 364	0.93	0.19
1716	5 275 978	45 607	0.87	0.17
1721	5 350 465	74 487	1.41	0.28
1726	5 449 957	99 492	1.86	0.37
1731	5 263 374	−186 583	−3.42	−0.69
1736	5 450 392	187 018	3.55	0.70
1741	5 576 197	125 805	2.31	0.46
1746	5 634 781	58 584	1.05	0.21
1751	5 772 415	137 634	2.44	0.48
1756	5 993 415	221 000	3.83	0.75
1761	6 146 857	153 442	2.56	0.51
1766	6 277 076	130 219	2.12	0.42
1771	6 447 813	170 737	2.72	0.54
1776	6 740 370	292 557	4.54	0.89
1781	7 042 140	301 770	4.48	0.88

Year	Population	Change	%	%		Year	Population	Change	%	%
1616	4 509 865	93 514	2.12	0.42		1786	7 289 039	246 899	3.51	0.69
1621	4 692 975	183 110	4.06	0.80		1791	7 739 889	450 850	6.19	1.21
1626	4 719 684	26 709	0.57	0.11		1796	8 198 445	458 556	5.92	1.16
1631	4 892 580	172 896	3.66	0.72		1801	8 664 490	466 045	5.68	1.11
1636	5 058 102	165 522	3.38	0.67		1806	9 267 570	603 080	6.96	1.35
1641	5 091 725	33 623	0.66	0.13		1811	9 885 690	618 120	6.67	1.30
1646	5 176 571	84 846	1.67	0.33		1816	10 651 629	765 939	7.75	1.50
1651	5 228 481	51 910	1.00	0.20		1821	11 491 850	840 221	7.89	1.53
1656	5 281 347	52 866	1.01	0.20		1826	12 410 995	919 145	8.00	1.55
1661	5 140 743	−140 604	−2.66	−0.54		1831	13 283 882	872 887	7.03	1.37
1666	5 067 047	−73 696	−1.43	−0.29		1836	14 105 979	822 097	6.19	1.21
1671	4 982 687	−84 360	−1.66	−0.34		1841	14 970 372	864 393	6.13	1.20
1676	5 003 488	20 801	0.42	0.08		1846	15 933 803	963 431	6.44	1.26
1681	4 930 385	−73 103	−1.46	−0.29		1851	16 736 084	802 281	5.04	0.99
1686	4 864 762	−65 623	−1.33	−0.27		1856	17 763 920	1 027 836	6.14	1.20
1691	4 930 502	65 740	1.35	0.27		1861	18 937 536	1 173 616	6.61	1.29
1696	4 961 692	31 190	0.63	0.13		1866	20 166 624	1 229 088	6.49	1.27
1701	5 057 790	96 098	1.94	0.38		1871	21 500 720	1 334 096	6.62	1.29
1706	5 182 007	124 217	2.46	0.49						

Note: The totals refer to 30 June of each year indicated.

Source: Table A3.1.

population of England was 2.774 million. It then grew continuously, though with a temporary set-back from 3.159 to 2.985 million in the late 1550s, to reach 4.110 million in 1601 and 5.281 million in 1656. Next followed a period of decline down to 4.865 million in the mid 1680s, succeeded by a slow recovery which brought the population back to 5.350 million by 1721 and beyond the 6 million mark in 1761, although interrupted by a further temporary setback from 5.450 to 5.263 million in the quinquennium 1726–31. In the later eighteenth and early nineteenth centuries the population continued to grow at an accelerating pace, reaching 8.664 million in 1801 and 11.492 million in 1821. Thereafter the rate of growth slackened slightly but the population continued to increase and reached a total of 21.501 million in 1871.

Population-size estimates from back projection have already been compared with the population totals enumerated in the nineteenth-century censuses. The outcome was reassuring. In the period before the first census the population totals found by back projection generally fall within the admittedly rather wide range of earlier estimates arrived at by various scholars using many different sources and methods. They confirm some features of population history, such as the growth in the sixteenth and eighteenth centuries, that have been firmly ensconced in the textbooks for many years. The distinctive contribution of the present series of quinquennial population totals is that they make it possible to calculate the rate of growth more precisely and on a finer time scale, pinpointing its variations over time.

A fuller comparison between the present and previous estimates is presented in appendix 5, but it may be noted here that of the many different earlier figures available back projection agrees fairly well with Rickman's average national estimates for the period 1600–1670 published in the 1841 census, and with King's contemporary estimates in 1695. On the other hand back projection found faster rates of population growth in the century 1540–1640 than were apparent from earlier estimates of population size, and discovered a fall in the size of the population between 1656 and 1686 which previous estimates had been unable to reveal. Earlier estimates of population size in the eighteenth century have been based on the totals of baptisms and burials in every tenth year which Rickman published in the 1801 census, and have assumed that the population was closed. In contrast we have birth and death totals for every year and back projection generates estimates of net migration. As a result our results show more growth in the early eighteenth century than is evident in the more highly regarded of earlier estimates. In appendix 5 we explore the degree to which errors in each of the component elements of the earlier estimates (baptism and burial inflation ratios, lack of provision for migration, and reliance on data from untypical years) have obscured the true course of population change in the eighteenth century.

The general pattern of change in the size of the population found by back projection corresponds closely to the conclusions drawn from the application of the simpler methods of analysis of the flows of vital events described in chapter 6. Both approaches found substantial population growth up to the mid seventeenth century, followed by a decline in the later seventeenth century, modest growth in the early eighteenth century and thereafter accelerating growth until the early nineteenth century.

In the first phase, from 1541 to 1656, the population grew from 2.774 to 5.281 million, almost doubling (× 1.90) in 115 years, an increase equivalent to an average growth rate of 0.56 per cent per annum. The decline that then ensued, relieved only temporarily in the early 1670s, coupled with the slow recovery in the early eighteenth century, meant that the 5.5 million mark, representing a doubling of the 1541 population, was not in fact reached until 1741. Thus the cessation of population growth in the mid seventeenth century ensured that the first doubling of the population after 1541 took exactly 200 years to achieve. Thereafter growth accelerated and the population next doubled within a period of 80 years to exceed 11 million in 1821 at an average rate of growth of 0.90 per cent per annum. It continued to grow, at a slightly faster rate, and had almost doubled again to reach 21.5 million in 1871, after a further half century (a rate of growth of 1.26 per cent per annum). The period between the mid seventeenth and mid eighteenth centuries therefore stands out as an apparently anomalous interlude of stagnation between two periods of substantial population growth.

In reality, the division between the three phases was not as sharp as this summary might imply, as is clear from the gradual change in the slope of the population-size curve in figure 7.1. A fuller insight into the change in the rates of growth of the population is provided by the compound annual growth rates for each quinquennium, tabulated in table 7.8 and shown graphically in figure 7.2. In general the annual growth rates are similar to those calculated by the crude short-cut methods employed

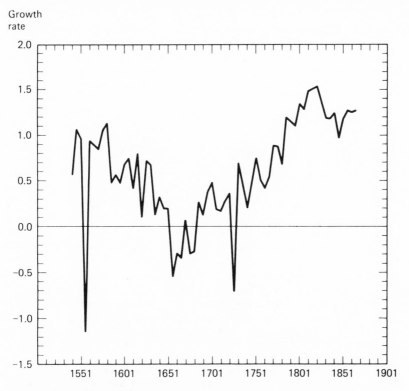

Figure 7.2: Compound annual growth rates of the population of England 1541 – 1871

Note: Each point represents the compound annual growth rate over the five-year period beginning at the date indicated (1541-6, 1546-51, and so on).

Source: Table 7.8.

in chapter 6 (see table 6.10 and figure 6.4). Taking account of net migration, as back projection does, only marginally lowers the rates calculated in chapter 6 assuming a constant death rate and a closed population. It has little impact on the general shape of the course of population growth over time, although it does produce some temporary differences.

In the middle of the sixteenth century the population was growing rapidly at an average rate exceeding 0.85 per cent per annum, apart from the late 1550s when the combination of a surge in deaths and a sharp drop in births produced a fall of 5.5 per cent in the size of the population over the quinquennium.[28] Between 1561 and 1586 growth rates averaged almost 1.0 per cent per annum, but when higher mortality supervened in the last 15 years of the century the rate of growth halved. The seventeenth century began with a slight recovery in growth rates, but after 1621 growth became weaker and more irregular, and after 1656 it turned negative as the population entered on a 30-year period of decline. The rate of decline was never very marked, but its cumulative effect, relieved by five years of modest growth in the early 1670s, was a population total in 1686 that was 7.9 per cent lower than what it had been in 1656.[29]

After 1686 the population began to grow again, but slowly and hesitantly at first, not exceeding 0.5 per cent per annum in any quinquennium until 1731–6. Furthermore, in the late 1720s, as in the late 1550s, soaring deaths and plunging births cut the population total substantially. It fell by 3.4 per cent between 1726 and 1731, wiping out the growth that had been accumulated since 1711, and reducing the population size to a figure somewhat below its mid-seventeenth-century peak.

The late 1720s was the last quinquennium in which the population fell, and it was followed by a period of 40 years in which, with the exception of the early 1740s, growth rates were between 0.40 and 0.75 per cent per annum. It was only in the last 15 years of the eighteenth century that the rate of population growth equalled and then exceeded late-sixteenth-century levels, while in the early nineteenth century it rose further to reach a maximum of 1.55 per cent per annum in the quinquennium 1821–6. Thereafter the rate of growth fell back to about 1.2 in the 1830s and apart from a temporary dip down to 0.99 in the late 1840s, it remained between 1.2 and 1.3 per cent per annum until 1871.

The picture of population growth that emerges from back projection is therefore one of strong and sustained increase in the later sixteenth century which became progressively more heavily trimmed after 1621 until it ceased altogether in 1656. It was succeeded by a decline in the size of the population between 1656 and 1686, followed by such slow and interrupted growth that the size of the population in 1731 was less than it had been in 1656. When consistent population growth finally returned in the mid eighteenth century it did so initially at a level that was modest by sixteenth-century standards. Indeed the rate of population growth in the later

---

28. The possibility that these unusual years produced a temporary but sizeable drop in the population with repercussions on the levels of wages and prices was first emphasized by Fisher, who claimed that the leap in the numbers of wills proved in the late 1550s suggested an increase of 150 per cent in the death rate, which would imply a fall of 20 per cent in the size of the population assuming birth and death rates of 35 and 31 per 1,000. Back projection suggests that average rates were 38 and 28 per 1,000 in the mid sixteenth century (1545–54) which would imply a more modest drop of 15 per cent. This is still, however, much higher than the fall found by back projection, very probably because adult death rates rose by a greater percentage than overall rates. Fisher, 'Influenza and inflation', p. 127.

29. The implied annual average rate of decline over the period 1656–86 is 2.7 per 1,000.

eighteenth century only reached sixteenth-century levels after 1771 and it was not until after 1786 that Elizabethan rates of growth were exceeded.

English population growth rates can be compared with rates recently calculated for France and Sweden in the eighteenth and nineteenth centuries. In France population totals have been estimated by Henry and Blayo for the period 1740–1860, while in Sweden official population counts beginning in 1749 can be supplemented by

Table 7.9: Annual growth rates of the populations of England, France, and Sweden in the eighteenth and nineteenth centuries

Quinquennium beginning	France	Sweden	England
1700		0.59	0.49
1705		0.39	0.19
1710		0.68	0.17
1715		0.68	0.28
1720		0.68	0.37
1725		0.68	−0.69
1730		0.68	0.70
1735		0.10	0.46
1740	0.00	0.04	0.21
1745	−0.01	0.75	0.48
1750	0.40	1.04	0.75
1755	0.55	0.53	0.51
1760	0.31	0.53	0.42
1765	0.38	0.66	0.54
1770	0.30	−0.21	0.89
1775	0.40	0.95	0.88
1780	0.07	0.30	0.69
1785	0.32	0.35	1.21
1790	0.00	0.83	1.16
1795	0.70	0.57	1.11
1800	0.27	0.63	1.35
1805	0.34	−0.21	1.30
1810	0.20	0.56	1.50
1815	0.61	0.95	1.53
1820	0.69	1.40	1.55
1825	0.58	0.83	1.37
1830	0.42	0.93	1.21
1835	0.52	0.74	1.20
1840	0.45	1.11	1.26
1845	0.36	0.98	0.99
1850	0.36	0.89	1.20
1855	0.16	1.17	1.29
1860		1.28	1.27
1865		0.26	1.29

Notes: The uniformity of the growth rates in Sweden 1710–35 is a function of the assumptions made by Widén. The English rates refer to 1701–6, 1706–11 etc., and to the mid point of the year in each case.

Sources: France, Henry and Blayo, 'La population de la France de 1740 à 1860', p. 97; Sweden, Hofsten and Lundstrom, *Swedish population history*, p. 172 for 1700 to 1750; and *Historisk Statistik*, pp. 44–6 for later data; England, table A3.1.

Widén's estimates for the period 1700–50.[30] The annual rates of growth in France from 1740 to 1860, and in England and Sweden from 1700 to 1870, are tabulated in table 7.9 and shown graphically in figure 7.3. The French population was stationary in the 1740s, then grew at about 0.4 per cent per annum from 1750 to 1780, lost momentum in the next 15 years, but recovered to grow by almost 0.5 per cent per annum on average from 1795 to 1840. Thereafter the rate of growth declined once more to reach 0.16 per cent in 1855–60. The Swedish growth rates fluctuated considerably in response to occasional severe mortality crises, but averaged slightly above 0.5 per cent per annum from 1700 to 1815, and then rose sharply to reach an average of 1 per cent per annum over the next half century.

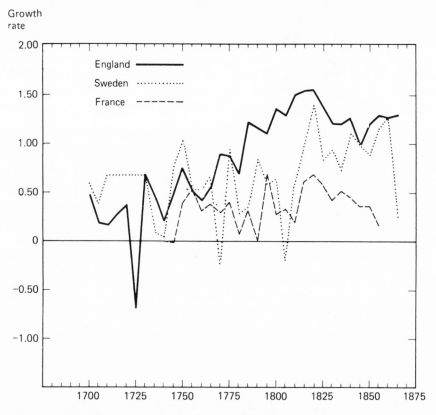

Figure 7.3: Compound annual growth rates of the populations of England, France, and Sweden in the eighteenth and nineteenth centuries

Note: Each point represents the compound annual growth rate over the five-year period beginning at the date indicated. The English rates, however, refer to 1701–6, 1706–11, and so on, rather than 1700–5 and so on.

Source: Table 7.9.

30. France: Henry and Blayo, 'La population de la France de 1740 à 1860', p. 95. Sweden: Hofsten and Lundström, *Swedish population history*, p. 172 and Sundbärg, *Bevölkerungsstatistik Schwedens*, p. 75.

In contrast the English growth rates were at a low level at the beginning of the century but then rose so that by the middle of the century they were similar to the rates of growth obtaining in France and Sweden. From 1770 the English annual growth rates began to rise powerfully and pulled well away from both France and Sweden over the period 1770 to 1815. By the latter date English rates of growth had risen to a point at which they were about twice and three times the trend values of the Swedish and French rates respectively. Thereafter both the English and the French rates of growth tended to fall while the Swedish rates continued to rise, so that by 1860 the English and Swedish populations were growing at about the same rate while the French population was growing far less quickly.

The differences in the changing population growth rates of the three countries reflect differences in the changing balance of fertility and mortality to be found in each of them. Later in this chapter we take up the question of how far it was movements in fertility or in mortality that caused the patterns of population growth rates just described. At this point we would emphasize that in pre-industrial England the rate of population growth was far from constant. Population growth cannot have been the product of a balance struck between a constant level of mortality and a traditional level of fertility determined by inflexible social rules concerning marriage and reproduction. Nor do the growth rates betray much sign of the applicability of the 'crisis' model which is sometimes thought appropriate to traditional societies.[31] According to this model a traditional society normally experiences a steady rate of population growth until the population becomes too large for its available resources, whereupon it is suddenly and savagely cut back by a great surge in the death rate. Although England suffered two major falls in population caused by high mortality in the late 1550s and again in the late 1720s, there was no regular cycle with a constant growth rate being periodically interrupted by brief spells of abrupt population decline. Rather the long-term oscillation in growth rates which was so marked a feature of early English population history (figure 7.2) suggests that demographic behaviour may have been responding slowly and systematically to secular change in its economic, social, biological, or physical environment. We consider the nature of the relationship between secular demographic and economic change in chapter 10 below. Meanwhile it may be noted that annual growth rates in England, France, and Sweden, even at their height, never approached the levels commonly found in the Third World today.[32]

The age structure of the population

In addition to crude totals of population aggregative back projection also generates estimates of the number of people in each five-year age group every fifth year from 1871 back to 1541. The age structures emerging from back projection reflect changes in mortality (which determine the scale of inflation of each age group in each quinquennial step), fluctuations in fertility (through the linking of the size of the group of 90–4 year olds introduced in each step at the top of the age pyramid to the size of the corresponding birth cohorts), and changes in the estimated level and

31. Cipolla, *Economic history of world population*, pp. 76–7.
32. For example, Keyfitz recently published estimates of the intrinsic rates of natural increase for many countries, chiefly referring to the mid 1960s. The rate was above 3 per cent per annum in 5 African populations out of 12 (maximum 3.57); in 4 South American populations out of 10 (maximum 3.76); and in 3 Asian populations out of 19 (maximum 4.76). The corresponding figures for rates of growth above 2 per cent per annum were 9, 7, and 15. Keyfitz, 'Changes in birth and death rates', table B, pp. 676–9.

direction of migration. Since back projection uses fixed age-schedules it is insensitive to any changes in the age-specific patterns of mortality and migration that may have occurred in the past. Consequently the age structures it produces cannot capture the temporary occurrence of unusual age profiles such as might have arisen during severe epidemics of certain diseases or during times of unusually heavy migration.

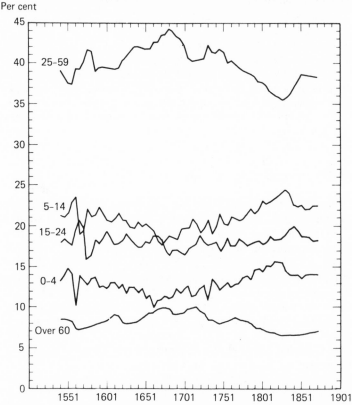

Figure 7.4:   The changing age structure of the English population 1541 – 1871 (percentages in five age groupings)

Source: Table A3.1.

The age structures found by back projection are set out in table A3.1 and are here presented graphically in figure 7.4. The data have been summarized into five age groups corresponding to life-cycle stages, namely infancy (0– 4), childhood (5–14), young adulthood (15–24), when most people were unmarried and many left home to go into service, and adulthood (25–59), when most people were married, and 'old age' (age 60 and above).[33]

33. These age distributions represent a compromise between historical life-cycle stages and the conventional five-year groups. The canon law tradition ended infancy in the seventh, childhood in the fourteenth, and adolescence in the twenty-eighth year, implying age groupings of 0–6, 7–13, 14–27. Lyndwood, *Provinciale*, pp. 34, 40 (in a gloss on 'adulti'). In practice the age at which children left home to go into service or apprenticeships varied considerably, as did age at marriage. Some social structural aspects of life-cycle stages are discussed in Laslett, *Family life*, especially chs. 1–2, 4–5.

In the nineteenth century, between 1806 and 1871, the age structure found by back projection did not change greatly. Where it can be checked against census returns, the agreement is close, once the latter have been corrected for under-registration and mis-statements of age.[34] During this period the population was relatively young; between 36 and 40 per cent were under age 15 and only 6.5 to 7.0 per cent were over age 60. Indeed 1826 represents the point at which the population was at its youngest. Infants comprised 15.5 per cent of the population and children a further 24.1 per cent, making 39.6 per cent of the population under age 15. Young adults made up 18.5 per cent of the population, adults 35.4 per cent, and the elderly the final 6.5 per cent.

Tracking back through the eighteenth century the population becomes progressively older: the proportions of infants and children decline while those of adults and the elderly increase until in 1676 and 1681 the age structure reaches its oldest configuration. If the age structures in 1826 and 1676 are compared it is apparent that the greatest relative changes occurred in the smallest groups at either extreme of the age range. Thus the proportion of infants fell by almost a third from 15.5 to 11 per cent, while the proportion of the elderly rose by a third from 7 to 10 per cent. The proportion of children also fell, but by about a quarter from 24 to 18 per cent, and that of adults rose by the same proportion from 35 to 44 per cent. The proportion of young adults in the population, on the other hand, remained more nearly constant, falling from 18.5 to 17 per cent.

Before 1671 the age structure of the population became younger again, until in the mid sixteenth century it resembled the pattern that obtained in the mid nineteenth century. However, it should be emphasized that as back projection moves between 1640 and 1540 the age structures it finds become gradually more dependent upon assumptions about the size of the quinquennial birth cohorts before 1540. Since these cohorts pre-date the beginning of the parish register data, the birth totals are unknown and the figures used in back projection are guesses based on some stylized assumptions about the rates of growth of the population and the relative changes in fertility and mortality. Thus in the 1580s, for example, the shape of the younger end of the age structure, i.e. the under-40s, is based on the quinquennial birth cohorts recorded in the parish registers, but the age structure of the over-40s is partially a function of the size of estimated pre-1541 birth cohorts. It follows that as back projection approaches 1540 the age structures it finds become more and more conjectural.[35]

Although some uncertainty surrounds the results obtained for the sixteenth century, the age profiles found later are more firmly based. The relatively old age structure that back projection recovers for the later seventeenth century is of particular interest since this is the period in which Gregory King estimated the age distribution of the population, and in the absence of other information King's estimate has often been taken as a guideline for the whole pre-industrial period. Table 7.10 compares King's estimates with the age structure found by back projection in 1696. King has a somewhat higher proportion of the elderly in the population (10.7 as against 9.2 per cent), but his figure of 38.4 per cent for the proportion of infants and children (aged

34. For example, in 1821 the percentages of the total population found in the age groups 0–4, 5–14, and over 60 in the census were 15.6, 23.3, and 6.8 compared with back-projection results for the same age groups of 15.5, 23.7, and 6.7 respectively. It should be noted that age group percentages at the extremes of life are those most likely to fluctuate considerably. The figure of 6.8 for those over 60 in the census is that obtained using level 9 mortality assumptions. At level 8 the figure is 6.6 (see table 7.5).
35. See appendix 15 for a discussion of the pre-1541 birth and death totals.

Table 7.10: Comparison of Gregory King's estimate of the age structure of the English population with that obtained by back projection (percentage distributions)

	(1)	(2)
	King 1695	Back projection 1696
0–4	14.90	11.67
5–9	12.73	10.53
10–4	10.73	9.08
15–9	9.45	8.36
20–4	8.36	8.23
25–9	7.13	7.62
30–4	6.35	7.04
35–9	5.33	6.11
40–4	4.56	6.56
45–9	3.84	5.75
50–4	3.16	5.49
55–9	2.73	4.37
60 and over	10.73	9.18
Total	100.00	100.00

Sources: Column 1, Glass, 'Two papers on Gregory King', p. 212; Column 2, detailed age breakdown from back-projection output not printed in this volume.

0–14) is much higher than the 31.3 per cent found by back projection. He also appears to have underestimated seriously the proportion of the population in later middle age (14.3 as against 22.2 per cent aged 40–59). King's age structure is therefore much too young for the later seventeenth century. Indeed, as Glass has observed, it is similar to that recorded in the census of 1821.[36] Since back projection indicates that the population was almost at its youngest in 1821 it follows that King's age structure is a poor guide to most of the pre-industrial period, with the possible exception of the mid sixteenth century.

King's figures have therefore misled scholars into over-estimating the numerical importance of infants and children in pre-industrial England. One consequence has been the adoption of exaggerated inflation ratios when calculating the size of the total population from the numbers of adults enumerated in sources such as lists of communicants. Another has been too pessimistic a view of the level of the dependency ratio, that is of the numbers of dependents supported by the adult population. Indeed seventeenth-century age structures have been likened to those obtaining in the developing world today.[37] But the latter commonly have over 40 per cent of the population under age 15 and are therefore younger than any age structure to be found in the English historical record, and very much younger than that of late-seventeenth-century England, when only 28 to 31 per cent of the population was aged under 15 years. The dependency burden in England in the recorded past was

36. Glass, 'Two papers on Gregory King', pp. 214–6.
37. For example, 'in the economies of the so-called "mercantilist" era the proportion of the young in the population was only a little less than in the backward communities of the present day'. Coleman, 'Labour in the English economy', p. 284.

therefore lighter than in traditional societies today.[38] The size of the burden and the economic implications of changes in the age structure over time will be discussed in chapter 10 below.

Estimates of net migration

Though their accuracy must be subject to strong reservations, the net migration totals produced by back projection deserve careful consideration. Quinquennial net migration totals and annual migration rates in each quinquennium are set out in table 7.11 and the rates are graphed in figure 7.5.

Table 7.11: English net migration totals and rates 1541–1871

(1) Quinquennium beginning	(2) Total	(3) Rate per 1 000 per annum	(1) Quinquennium beginning	(2) Total	(3) Rate per 1 000 per annum
1541	18 095	1.27	1706	26 959	1.03
1546	20 378	1.40	1711	27 539	1.05
1551	21 757	1.42	1716	27 615	1.03
1556	19 244	1.27	1721	28 104	1.04
1561	17 038	1.12	1726	25 981	0.97
1566	18 502	1.15	1731	24 193	0.91
1571	20 992	1.26	1736	24 780	0.90
1576	23 279	1.33	1741	25 865	0.94
1581	26 360	1.42	1746	27 773	0.98
1586	30 791	1.61	1751	31 378	1.07
1591	34 743	1.77	1756	35 004	1.16
1596	36 214	1.81	1761	35 306	1.14
1601	35 988	1.73	1766	31 326	0.99
1606	34 130	1.57	1771	26 325	0.80
1611	29 741	1.33	1776	22 017	0.64
1616	24 877	1.09	1781	17 213	0.48
1621	22 081	0.93	1786	15 429	0.41
1626	24 055	1.00	1791	18 211	0.46
1631	31 250	1.26	1796	22 644	0.54
1636	39 912	1.58	1801	28 324	0.64
1641	49 246	1.92	1806	33 539	0.70
1646	57 637	2.21	1811	40 747	0.80
1651	63 076	2.41	1816	50 370	0.91
1656	62 195	2.41	1821	62 648	1.05
1661	55 222	2.16	1826	77 847	1.21
1666	45 209	1.79	1831	90 284	1.32
1671	34 815	1.39	1836	101 501	1.40
1676	25 807	1.02	1841	115 068	1.49
1681	19 365	0.79	1846	123 678	1.52
1686	18 061	0.74	1851	121 525	1.41
1691	19 581	0.79	1856	109 456	1.19
1696	22 143	0.88	1861	101 575	1.04
1701	25 014	0.97	1866	117 292	1.12

Source: Table A3.1

Note: Positive figures represent net outflow. The rates were obtained by relating the average annual migration total for each quinquennium to its mid-point population total.

38. For modern data see Shryock and Siegel, *Methods and materials of demography*, pp. 132–3.

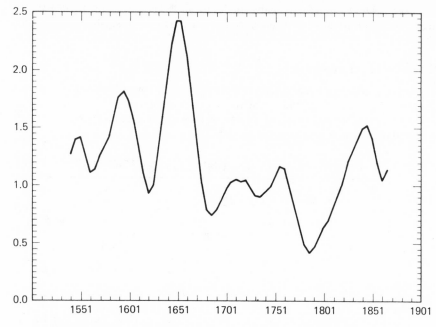

Figure 7.5: English annual net migration rates 1541 – 1871

Note: The rates refer to five-year periods beginning in the year shown (1541-6, 1546-51, etc.); rates per 1000 total population.

Source: Table 7.11.

It must be emphasized that not only are the net migration totals on which the table and figure are based necessarily imprecise for reasons already touched upon, but also that they. do not measure what is normally understood by net migration. They are derived solely from the comparison of observed birth cohorts with hypothetical birth cohorts constructed by inflating individual age groups at a point in time by the mortality obtaining over the period intervening between that date and the dates of their several birth cohorts. Any difference between the estimated and observed birth cohorts is treated as net migration and a fraction of this difference is allocated to each five-year time period using a standard age-specific schedule of cohort migration. It follows, therefore, that not only will those who leave to settle abroad be treated as migrants but so also will those who leave to fight abroad and fail to return, and those who take service at sea and whose ships founder taking them with them, or those vagrants who died on the road and whose burial went unrecorded. Missing deaths, in short, appear as emigrants. At all periods of early modern English history loss of life at sea was considerable, and at some periods, most notably during the Napoleonic wars, loss of life in the armed forces, whether abroad or at sea, was substantial.

Three further points must also be borne in mind. First, these are totals of *net* migration. Throughout the bulk of the early modern period it is likely that more Scots, Welsh, and Irish entered England than Englishmen went to settle elsewhere in the British Isles. It is therefore quite possible for there to have been a substantial emigration of Englishmen, say to the North American colonies, while net migration was modest. Nineteenth-century migration estimates underline the potential importance of the point.[39] Second, the most that can be expected of net migration estimates produced by aggregative back projection is that the total migration over a period will be approximately correct. It is impossible that its *timing* should be accurately captured unless the net migration experienced by every cohort in the past had in fact followed the fixed age schedule imposed by back projection. In reality migration tends to fluctuate markedly in the short term, but this feature is lost by the allocation of cohort migration to individual time periods according to a fixed age-schedule. Third, the net migration figures for the period before 1586 suffer from the additional disadvantage that they may have been affected by errors in estimating the sizes of the birth cohorts before 1541.[40]

Subject to these reservations, the positive net migration totals in table 7.11 show that the balance of migration was always outward. However, both the absolute numbers of migrants and the annual net migration rates derived from them were usually low. In the later sixteenth and early seventeenth centuries back projection estimates a fairly constant net loss of between 1.00 and 1.80 per 1,000 of the population. In the quinquennium beginning in 1581, for example, when the population was about 3.6 million and the rate was 1.42, the absolute number of net emigrants was estimated at about 5,000 a year, a small enough figure for a considerable proportion to be reasonably attributable to deaths at sea and similar losses.[41] In the seventeenth century the net migration rate rose steadily from 1621 to reach a peak of around 2.41 per 1,000 in 1651–61 followed by a sharp fall to a low level of 0.74 per 1,000 in the quinquennium beginning in 1676. Thereafter the rate remained mainly about 1.00 until the 1760s. From the mid 1760s there was a further fall and the rate fell as low as 0.41 in 1786 but it recovered steadily from then on to reach 1.52 in 1846–51, though it declined to little more than 1.00 during the next 20 years.

39. For example, the rates of net emigration for the different countries of the British Isles in the later nineteenth century have been estimated as follows (rates per 10,000 mean population per annum)

	England and Wales	Scotland	Ireland North	South
1841–51	−5			
1851–61	−17			
1861–71	−10	−37	−169	
1871–81	−7	−28	−119	−127
1881–91	−23	−58	−108	−163
1891–1901	−2	−13	−55	−118

Carrier and Jeffery, *External migration*, p. 14.

40. The fixed age schedule of net migration allows no migration to occur in age groups above 40–4 (see table 7.3).

41. The Registrar General of Seamen provided the Registrar General with information about loss of life among merchant seamen in the 1850s and 1860s. In the 18 years 1852–69 a total of 68,531 deaths occurred, or an average of 3,807 annually, a rate of 21 deaths per 1,000 merchant seamen per annum. The great majority of the deaths was due to drowning and accident rather than disease. In addition there were in the years 1858–69 an average of 1,582 deaths of natives of England and Wales in the army abroad, *32nd Annual Report*, pp.xxxv and xxxvii. The number of seamen in earlier periods is not known accurately, though already by the later seventeenth century it must have been very substantial. Gregory King estimated that there were 50,000 common seamen in 1688 (Laslett, *The world we have lost*, pp. 32–3), and in the early eighteenth century estimates of the numbers of seamen engaged in the coal trade alone range between 5,000 and 15,000 (Nef, *British coal industry*, II, pp. 141–2). It seems very likely that the death rate among sailors would have been higher in earlier centuries than in the nineteenth, and that the absolute total would have constituted a substantial part of all net emigrants.

It will be recalled that the totals of births and deaths for the period 1801–41 were obtained by estimating the size of the decennial female birth cohorts from their survivors at later censuses and assuming that net female migration was nil over this period. Since census totals are available from 1801 onwards this made it possible to derive totals of female deaths, and overall totals of births and deaths were then calculated after determining the probable birth and death sex ratios.[42] This procedure limits the scale of net migration by restricting it to males. They will have been the larger element in the true net migration total, but to the degree that the assumption of closure in the female population is unjustified the net migration totals for these decades and for a brief period before 1801 may be artificially depressed. On the other hand, emigration during the early decades of the nineteenth century was at a low ebb because of the Napoleonic war, and it is entirely possible that the influx of women from Ireland and Scotland may have been on a scale to justify the assumption that female emigration and immigration was in balance.

After 1801 decadal net migration totals can also be obtained from the census totals and the decadal balance of births and deaths. Between 1801 and 1841 these estimates are subject to the same reservations arising from the assumption of female population closure as those taken from back projection, but back projection with its reliance on a fixed cohort age schedule of migration is less well able to capture the sharp fluctuations in net migration totals than the more orthodox method, and the alternative set of migration totals and rates for the nineteenth century given in table 7.12 are to be preferred for this reason. It should be noted, however, that they are heavily affected by the accuracy of the totals of intercensal population increase. If either the original census counts or the corrections made to them contain inaccuracies, the migration

Table 7.12: Net migration totals and rates 1801–71: comparison of back-projection data with estimates based on census totals and vital events

	Totals		Rates per 1 000 per annum	
	Back projection	Census and vital events	Back projection	Census and vital events
1801–11	61 863	73 032	0.67	0.79
1811–21	91 117	74 202	0.85	0.69
1821–31	140 495	125 273	1.13	1.01
1831–41	191 785	63 838	1.35	0.45
1841–51	238 746	87 367	1.49	0.54
1851–61	230 981	364 606	1.28	2.02
1861–71	218 867	244 530	1.07	1.20
Total	1 173 854	1 032 848		

Notes: All dates refer to 30 June of the years in question. Rates relate migration totals to the mean of the census population totals at either end of the relevant 10-year period (table 7.1).

Sources: Back projection, table A3.1; census and vital events, tables A2.3, A2.4, and A6.8.

42. See above, pp. 126–36.

estimates will be distorted.[43] It is possible, for example, that the net migration total for the 1830s was in reality higher than in the previous decade.[44]

The back-projection migration totals for the whole period 1801–71 exceed those obtained by the more conventional method by 141,006, a substantial discrepancy. Most of this, however, arises because in the latter calculations the full revised census total for 1871 was used (21,635,388), whereas in back projection the 1871 total used excluded seamen and soldiers abroad (21,500,720). Given that net migration is taken to be the difference between the decadal surplus of births over deaths and the intercensal increase, this necessarily depresses the migration total using the conventional method by 134,668 (21,635,388−21,500,720) compared with the total derived by back projection. The true discrepancy in the 70-year net migration totals produced by the two methods is therefore reduced to 6,338 (141,006− 134,668), or about 0.6 per cent. This is a satisfactory agreement bearing in mind the degree to which the timing of migration in back projection is controlled by its fixed cohort age schedule.

There are few sources of value for testing the accuracy of the net migration estimates produced by back projection. Neither England nor the English colonies kept a record of all migrant movements in the seventeenth and eighteenth centuries. Some migrant flows were apparently fully recorded, notably the movement of convicts sentenced to transportation to the North American colonies in the eighteenth century.[45] Others were covered either intermittently or incompletely. There are, for example, surviving lists of indentured servants leaving major ports such as Bristol, London, or Liverpool for North America or the West Indies for various periods, though continuous coverage is usually restricted to a relatively short period.[46] But even in the nineteenth century many people left England whose departure was never recorded, and in other cases, though a record may have been made at the time, it was subsequently lost or destroyed.[47] Equally, many people entered England, for example from the Celtic fringe or in the wake of the persecution of the Huguenots, but their numbers are uncertain in the absence of adequate records.[48]

Comparison of the net migration estimates produced by back projection during the period 1801–71 with alternative estimates derived by more conventional procedures suggested that while back projection obtained approximately the right total of net migration it was not very successful at apportioning it correctly between decades. A similar comparison with an independent estimate of the volume of migration to the

43. See appendix 6 for a description of the method used to derive the estimates.
44. See p. 596 below for a discussion of the sensitivity of migration estimates to very slight changes in census coverage.
45. Smith, *Colonists in bondage*, pp. 116–7 and 311–2.
46. Some summary data may be found in Smith, *Colonists in bondage*, pp. 307–37.
47. Series of data are available on the numbers of passengers from United Kingdom ports to extra-European countries from 1815, and of passengers to United Kingdom ports from extra-European countries from 1855. Mitchell and Deane, *British historical statistics*, pp. 47–9. The early data are discussed in Carrier and Jeffery, *External migration*.
48. The numbers of Scots, Irish, and Welsh entering England cannot be determined until information on place of birth becomes available in the 1841 census. Even after that date migration estimates involve crude assumptions about mortality rates and are considered by their authors to be 'very unreliable'. Flinn, *Scottish population history*, pp. 441–4. For an impressionistic account of Celtic immigration in the nineteenth century see Redford, *Labour migration*, pp. 134–49, and for an example of figures of earlier immigration from abroad see ch. 6, fn. 41. Some of the problems which arise in attempting to estimate both internal and external migration from nineteenth-century British census data are discussed in Baines, 'The use of published census data in migration studies'.

New World in the seventeenth century points to a similar conclusion. In the 70 years between 1630 and 1699 the number of migrants to the New World has been estimated by Gemery to have been 378,000 (table 6.11). Back projection found 544,000 net emigrants over the same period (table 7.11). It is not easy to make an effective comparison of the cumulative totals in the two series. Gemery's estimates refer to gross migration from all parts of the British Isles to North America and the West Indies. The back projection estimates are of net migration to all destinations from England only. To make a direct comparison, therefore, Gemery's total would need to be reduced to allow for the migration of Scots, Welsh and Irish to America, and by whatever proportion is appropriate to convert his figure to a net basis. The back projection figure should be reduced to eliminate any net migration to destinations other than America and to take account of the loss of life at sea other than in passage to North America (Gemery includes mortality at sea in his gross migration estimate) and in wars abroad which are included in the net migration estimates because of the way in which back projection operates. While it would be hazardous to attempt to quantify the effects of the several factors which make a direct comparison difficult, it is reasonable to suppose that Gemery's estimates and those derived from back projection are in surprisingly close agreement when allowance has been made for their differing bases of calculation. It is important to note in this connexion that there appears to have been a substantial English migration to Ireland in this period. In the early 1670s Reynel, in commenting on the reasons for England's 'want of people', attributed it in large part to emigration, remarking that 200,000 people had been 'wasted in repeopling Ireland', the same number as he believed to have departed for the plantations.[49]

It is widely agreed that migration to the North America colonies fell to much lower levels after the decades of heavy outflow in the mid seventeenth century. The rate found by back projection fell from a peak of 2.41 per 1,000 in the 1650s to about 0.80 in the last 15 years of the century and remained at or a little above this rate throughout the first three quarters of the eighteenth century before dropping further in the half-century after 1771, during which it averaged only 0.64. The eighteenth century boasts even fewer estimates of net migration than the seventeenth.[50] Fortunately, however, there is a persuasive and independent piece of evidence concerning emigration in the eighteenth century against which to measure the findings of back projection.

When Rickman requested baptism and burial totals from incumbents in 1801, he asked that separate counts of males and females should be made in both categories of events.[51] The totals and the sex ratios derived from them are shown in table 7.13 along with similar data for the first three decades of the nineteenth century. It will be seen that the sex ratio at baptism varied very little over time. The average of the eight individual ratios for 1700 to 1770 was 104.2, while in the 1780s and 1790s the ratios were 104.3 and 104.1. In the first full decade of civil registration, 1841–50, the ratio at birth was 104.8. The slightly lower level of the ratio in the eighteenth century may

49. The passage comes from Reynel's *The true English interest* published in 1674. It is reproduced in Thirsk and Cooper, *Seventeenth century economic documents*, p. 758.
50. Potter ventured an estimate of 350,000 immigrants to America between 1700 and 1790 as 'a shot in the dark' (the total excluded slaves). This figure covered all Europe rather than England or Britain, but he also quoted an estimate of C. A. and M. R. Beard of 750,000 for the period 1660 to 1770. Potter, 'Growth of population in America', p. 645.
51. *1801 Census*, Parish registers, unnumbered first page, 'Questions'.

Table 7.13: Sex ratios at baptism and burial in Rickman's returns, 1700–1830

	Baptisms			Burials		
	M	F	Sex ratio	M	F	Sex ratio
1700	70 680	67 611	104.5	59 849	60 937	98.2
1710	63 955	61 706	103.6	64 660	63 975	101.1
1720	71 808	68 472	104.9	74 913	72 850	102.8
1730	74 499	71 559	104.1	81 340	80 142	101.5
1740	78 628	74 414	105.7	77 175	76 827	100.5
1750	82 963	79 858	103.9	70 974	71 607	99.1
1760	86 117	82 882	103.9	71 363	71 288	100.1
1770	95 464	92 613	103.1	78 637	81 193	96.9
1780–9	1 065 739	1 021 950	104.3	833 362	850 172	98.0
1790–9	1 181 694	1 135 495	104.1	859 831	860 429	99.9
1801–10	1 385 762	1 333 379	103.9	928 790	916 482	101.3
1811–20	1 576 136	1 510 714	104.3	956 902	944 694	101.3
1821–30	1 824 465	1 750 845	104.2	1 187 588	1 150 300	103.2

Note: The sex ratio is taken as 100 (M/F).

Source: *1801 Census*, Parish registers. pp. 184 and 373; *1811 Census*, Parish registers. pp. 93 and 187; *1821 Census*, Parish register abstract, pp. 75 and 145; *1831 Census*, Parish register abstract, pp. 201 and 412.

well have been due to the delay in baptizing infant children, since the higher level of male infant mortality would depress the sex ratio at baptism below its level at birth.[52] The baptism sex ratio leaves little doubt that the incumbents were conscientious and accurate in their division of all baptisms between the sexes. It is therefore significant that the sex ratio at burial should have been so much lower. The average level of the ratio for the eight decadal years 1700 to 1770 is almost exactly 100, while in the 1780s and 1790s the average figure was lower still at 99. In the first two decades of the nineteenth century the burial sex ratios were a little higher at 101.3, while in the 1830s the ratio rose to 103.2, drawing close to the sex ratio at baptism.

All those who are born must die, but they need not, of course, die in their country of birth. If England in the eighteenth and early nineteenth centuries had been a closed population the sex ratio at death or burial would have been about 104. The fact that it was well below this level most of the time implies both that there was substantial net migration and that it was sex selective. A burial sex ratio of 100, such as obtained in the eighteenth century, implies that the deaths of 4 males out of 204 male and female births, or 1.96 per cent, were missing. Since the crude birth rate was about 32 per 1,000 in the first half of the eighteenth century, the net surplus of male over female emigration was equivalent to about 0.63 per 1,000 of the population (32 × 0.0196).[53] If the sex ratio of net emigrants is taken as three males to each female, the burial sex ratio would imply that the overall net emigration rate was about 1.20 per 1,000, a level similar to that found by back projection (an emigration sex ratio of 3:1 implies that there would be 2 surplus male emigrants for each matched pair

52. Male death rates are generally higher than female during the first year of life unless cultural influences intervene: Shryock and Siegel, *Methods and materials of demography*, pp. 228–9 and bibliography there listed. Family reconstitution studies covering some 20 English communities also consistently show higher male infant mortality than female.
53. The calculation is necessarily crude because it takes no account of the age patterns of migration or death, the latter differing somewhat between the sexes.

of male and female emigrants and that therefore the figure for the surplus of male over female emigrants should be doubled to obtain the overall emigration rate). A higher sex ratio among emigrants would imply a lower overall emigration rate, while a more even sex balance among emigrants points to a higher overall rate. There is no reliable evidence about the eighteenth century sex ratio among emigrants,[54] but it was probably high even among true emigrants and higher still among the group regarded as emigrants by back projection, since this included military losses abroad and deaths among sailors, both of which groups were exclusively male. The evidence afforded by Rickman's data, therefore, lends support to the emigration rates obtained by back projection.

In a period when a preponderance of emigrants was male, fluctuations in the rate of net emigration would produce opposite movements in the sex ratio at burial. For example, a fall in emigration would cause the ratio to rise nearer to the sex ratio at birth. The impact would not, of course, be immediate since the cohorts whose sex composition was affected by emigration would be depleted by death over several decades after the peak years of migration had passed. If, for example, the median age at emigration were 25, at the mortality levels prevailing in the eighteenth century the greatest impact on burial sex ratios would occur about 40 years later. It is therefore of interest to note that the rise in burial sex ratios that occured in the early nineteenth century had been preceeded by a dip in net emigration rates 30 years earlier (table 7.11).

The least reliable net migration figures produced by back projection are those for the sixteenth century, especially before 1580, since they involve the use of data about birth cohorts before 1541 whose size is a matter of guesswork. The sixteenth-century rates suggest a level of net emigration slightly above that of the early eighteenth century, except that after 1581 the rate increases substantially for some 30 years. The rise may be related in part to the considerable movement to Ireland occurring late in the sixteenth and early in the seventeenth century and to the foreign wars of the period.[55] Further work on sex ratios at burial in the sixteenth and seventeenth centuries may throw more light on the validity of the back-projection figures but at present there is no convenient test of their accuracy.

A major difficulty in interpreting the net migration estimates produced by back projection is to know what allowance to make for deaths of merchant seamen and of those serving in the army and navy abroad, or indeed for deaths of men fighting at home in the Civil War whose bodies may have been buried but not entered in any register. The back-projection totals must always tend to exaggerate the true level of net emigration. The difference between the apparent and true net totals may have been considerable. In the 1850s and 1860s the number of deaths at sea or abroad of merchant seamen and soldiers was equivalent to about 0.25 per 1,000 per annum of the English population living at the time.[56] It is scarcely possible to estimate the rate at

54. Amongst indentured servants leaving London for the New World in the early eighteenth century only about 6 per cent were female. Galenson, 'British servants and the colonial indenture system', p. 43.
55. Dr R. Hunter, of the New University of Ulster, who is currently working on English settlement in Ireland in the early seventeenth century, suggests that during the reign of James I a total of some 12,000 adult English males, exclusive of soldiers, settled in Ireland, though he emphasizes the tentative and preliminary nature of the estimate. Many men were caught up in military ventures abroad. Clark estimates that between 1591 and 1602 some 6,000 men were involved in this way in the county of Kent at a time when the total population of the county may have been about 130,000. Many died abroad. Clark, *English provincial society*, p. 226.
56. See above, p. 221, fn. 41.

earlier periods, and the rate itself no doubt fluctuated widely between times of peace and times of war, but it would be unwise to assume that it was on average lower than 0.25 and may well have been higher, perhaps as high as 0.50. In considering the rates in table 7.11 it would be prudent to make a tentative subtraction of this order of magnitude from the printed figures, taking them one with another.

Although the rates of net migration were never very high, their cumulative effect over three centuries was substantial. For example, the surplus of births over deaths in the 260 years between 1541 and 1801 was 7.411 million. Subtracting this total from the census figure of 8.658 million in 1801 suggests a population of only 1.247 million

Table 7.14: Net migration and population growth 1541–1871

1 Natural increase
2 Net migration
3 Compound annual percentage rate of population growth
4 Compound annual percentage rate of natural increase
5 Impact of net migration on annual growth rate (4)–(3)

	(1)	(2)	(3)	(4)	(5)
1541–51	275 652	38 473	0.82	0.95	−0.13
1551–61	14 547	41 001	−0.09	0.04	−0.13
1561–71	321 867	35 540	0.92	1.03	−0.11
1571–81	371 038	44 271	0.96	1.08	−0.12
1581–91	358 671	57 151	0.81	0.95	−0.14
1591–1601	281 748	70 957	0.53	0.70	−0.17
1601–11	376 488	70 118	0.72	0.88	−0.16
1611–21	331 242	54 618	0.61	0.73	−0.12
1621–31	245 741	46 136	0.42	0.53	−0.11
1631–41	270 307	71 162	0.40	0.54	−0.14
1641–51	243 639	106 883	0.27	0.47	−0.20
1651–61	37 533	125 271	−0.17	0.07	−0.24
1661–71	−57 625	100 431	−0.31	−0.11	−0.20
1671–81	8 320	60 622	−0.11	0.02	−0.13
1681–91	37 543	37 426	0.00	0.08	−0.08
1691–1701	169 012	41 724	0.26	0.34	−0.08
1701–11	224 554	51 973	0.34	0.44	−0.10
1711–21	175 248	55 154	0.23	0.33	−0.10
1721–31	−33 006	54 085	−0.16	−0.06	−0.10
1731–41	361 796	48 973	0.58	0.67	−0.09
1741–51	249 856	53 638	0.35	0.44	−0.09
1751–61	440 824	66 382	0.63	0.74	−0.11
1761–71	367 588	66 632	0.48	0.58	−0.10
1771–81	642 669	48 342	0.89	0.95	−0.06
1781–91	730 391	32 642	0.95	0.99	−0.04
1791–1801	965 456	40 855	1.13	1.18	−0.05
1801–11	1 283 063	61 863	1.33	1.39	−0.06
1811–21	1 697 277	91 117	1.52	1.60	−0.08
1821–31	1 932 527	140 495	1.46	1.57	−0.11
1831–41	1 878 275	191 785	1.20	1.33	−0.13
1841–51	2 004 458	238 746	1.12	1.26	−0.14
1851–61	2 432 433	230 981	1.24	1.37	−0.13
1861–71	2 782 051	218 867	1.28	1.38	−0.10

Note: The natural increase figures were obtained by adding the net migration totals to the difference between successive 'census' totals found by back projection.

Sources: Column 1, table A2.4; column 2, table 7.12.

in 1541, a figure well under half the total found by back projection (2.774 million). Table 7.14 shows the impact of net migration on population growth at different points in time in two ways: first by listing the numbers of migrants and the natural increase for each decade, and secondly by showing how far the rate of population growth is reduced when net migration is taken into account.

It is apparent from the table that over most of the period studied the volume of net emigration was low compared to the surplus of births over deaths and that consequently net emigration reduced the rates of population growth by a relatively small amount. Between the mid seventeenth and mid eighteenth century, however, natural increase was low and even occasionally negative and in these circumstances net migration exerted a more powerful influence on population growth rates. For example, between 1656 and 1686 the population fell from 5.281 million to 4.865 million, a fall of 0.416 million, and of this about 58 per cent was due to net emigration (in the back-projection sense of the term) and the remainder to an adverse balance of births over deaths. It is also noteworthy that the low rates of population growth found by back projection in the early eighteenth century occurred because the relatively small surpluses of births over deaths were subject to substantial proportionate reductions from net emigration.

There were times, therefore, when the balance of net migration influenced national population trends. Nevertheless, changes in fertility and mortality played a much larger part in determining rates of population growth.

Fertility and mortality

Disagreement about the relative importance of changes in fertility and mortality in determining the rate of population growth, especially in the eighteenth and early nineteenth centuries, has constituted the prime point of argument amongst demographic historians for many years. At one extreme McKeown has long maintained that there is no reason to suppose that there were significant changes in fertility before the last third of the nineteenth century and that therefore a fall in mortality must be the explanation of the acceleration in population growth.[57] Hollingsworth took a similar line, suggesting that fertility was constant and very high between 1635 and 1820, with a crude birth rate of 44 per 1,000 and that the changes in population growth rates were therefore solely the result of mortality changes.[58] On the other hand Habakkuk, Ohlin, and Krause were all led to a very different conclusion. While not denying that a fall in mortality occurred in the eighteenth and early nineteenth centuries, they stressed the likelihood that fertility rose significantly and may even have been the more important influence on growth rates.[59]

The main fertility and mortality findings of back projection are set out in table 7.15

---

57. McKeown has recently restated his view in *The modern rise of population*. Chapter 2 contains a succinct summary of his line of argument.
58. Hollingsworth, *Historical demography*, pp. 350–1.
59. Habakkuk, for an example, remarked that 'Few generalisations are so well established in the books as that which ascribes the increase in the population of England and Wales in the second half of the eighteenth century to a fall in the death rate caused primarily by improvements in medicine, medical skill, and public health' but later stressed that 'There is contemporary warrant for the view that the acceleration of population growth was to a very large extent the result of a high birth rate, and that this in turn was the result of the economic developments of the period'. Habakkuk, 'English population in the eighteenth century', pp. 269 and 281. See also Ohlin, *The positive and the preventive check*, especially ch. 9; and Krause, 'Changes in English fertility and mortality'.

and figure 7.6. They show the gross reproduction rate (GRR) and expectation of life at birth (e_0) for each quinquennium in the period 1541 to 1871.[60] Each figure relates to the quinquennium centred on the date shown. The same information is presented on a cohort basis in table A3.2. Annual crude birth and death rates may be found in table A3.3.

The secular pattern of fertility change is simple. Fertility was high in the mid sixteenth century when the GRR was about 2.8, then fell abruptly to about 2.4 and thereafter tended to fall further but only slowly and slightly until it sagged suddenly to a nadir of about 1.9 for 30 years after 1650. A sharp recovery to late-sixteenth-century levels followed and then for 70 years the GRR showed a gently rising trend to reach 2.3 by 1756. In the late eighteenth century the increase accelerated to reach a peak value of 3.06 in 1816. After 1816 there was an abrupt fall in the GRR to only 2.37 in 1846, followed by a renewed, if modest, rise until 1866 when it stood at 2.55. The final figure in the series, that for 1871, already suggests a resumed fall which rapidly accelerated in the final decades of the nineteenth century. The broken line on figure 7.6 continues the history of the falling GRR to 1901, using estimates published by Glass.

Splicing Glass's estimates onto the GRR figures derived from back projection exaggerates the true fall in fertility because of deficiencies in both sets of figures; the former underestimate its true level while the latter overestimate it. Glass made no allowance for the under-registration of births, and so underestimated the true level of fertility.[61] On the other hand, although back projection takes into account the effect of sex differential mortality in determining the number of women of child-bearing age, it makes no allowance for the sex differential impact of net emigration. Since more males than females left the country the proportion of women to the total in the child-bearing age groups is understated and the GRR therefore overestimated. When these distorting effects are taken into consideration, it is interesting to note that the agreement between the two sets of estimates in the period of their overlap between 1841 and 1871 is very close, as may be seen in table 7.16. Any remaining discrepancies probably arise because of differences in the unit concerned (Glass's figures refer to England and Wales rather than England only); in the length of periods to which the estimates refer (Glass used data for three years centring on the date shown rather than for five years); and the use of different fertility schedules in distributing births by age group.[62]

Throughout the whole fertility series there were very few marked short-term departures from the trend line, but rather a steady progression towards and between the major turning points about 1660 and 1815. There was a sudden drop in fertility in the late 1550s at the same time that mortality reached an exceptionally high level, and a fairly sharp fall between 1566 and 1571, but no other dramatic short-term movements, except for the curious period from 1641 to 1686 when fertility passed through a marked trough. This period appears to be the most unusual of the whole three-century-long series. Fertility fell sharply between 1646 and 1651, remained at a very low level until 1681, and then returned abruptly to the level of the early decades of the century.

60. For an account of the methods used to calculate e_0 and the GRR see appendix 15.
61. At a later date Glass published estimates of the extent of under-registration in late-nineteenth-century Britain. Glass, 'A note on under-registration'. His estimates and Teitelbaum's are discussed in appendix 8.
62. See Glass, 'Changes in fertility in England and Wales', pp. 162–5; and appendix 15, pp. 730–2, for details of the fertility schedules used.

Table 7.15: Changes in English fertility and mortality 1541–1871: quinquennial GRRs and e_0s

	GRR	e_0		GRR	e_0		GRR	e_0
1541	2.87	33.8	1651	1.85	37.8	1761	2.37	34.2
1546	2.66	32.5	1656	2.01	34.1	1766	2.39	35.0
1551	2.80	38.0	1661	1.81	35.7	1771	2.50	35.6
1556	2.31	30.7	1666	1.98	31.8	1776	2.53	38.2
1561	2.32	27.8	1671	1.90	33.2	1781	2.49	34.7
1566	2.48	38.0	1676	1.91	36.4	1786	2.62	35.9
1571	2.13	38.2	1681	1.94	28.5	1791	2.77	37.3
1576	2.18	40.3	1686	2.17	31.8	1796	2.76	36.8
1581	2.32	41.7	1691	2.16	34.9	1801	2.69	35.9
1586	2.35	38.3	1696	2.18	34.1	1806	2.93	38.7
1591	2.36	35.5	1701	2.34	37.1	1811	2.87	37.6
1596	2.24	37.7	1706	2.25	36.4	1816	3.06	37.9
1601	2.35	38.1	1711	2.05	35.9	1821	2.98	39.2
1606	2.34	40.8	1716	2.25	37.1	1826	2.86	39.9
1611	2.19	37.3	1721	2.27	32.5	1831	2.59	40.8
1616	2.15	36.8	1726	2.21	32.4	1836	2.53	40.2
1621	2.23	40.0	1731	2.20	27.9	1841	2.49	40.3
1626	2.11	34.0	1736	2.37	35.6	1846	2.37	39.6
1631	2.11	38.7	1741	2.22	31.7	1851	2.40	39.5
1636	2.09	36.1	1746	2.27	35.3	1856	2.44	40.4
1641	2.15	33.7	1751	2.34	36.6	1861	2.51	41.2
1646	2.09	38.5	1756	2.32	37.3	1866	2.55	40.3
						1871	2.54	41.3

Source: Table A3.1

Note: The data refer to five-year periods centring on the years indicated.

Figure 7.6: Changes in English fertility and mortality 1541–1901: quinquennial GRRs and e_o s

Sources: Table A3.1. The fertility data for the period after 1871 are taken from Glass, 'Changes in fertility in England and Wales', p. 168 (see also table 7.16). The post-1871 mortality data are calculated from the Registrar-General's life tables for 1871–80, 1881–90, 1891–1900, and 1901–10. The points for 1881, 1891, and 1901 were taken to be the means of the e_0s for 1871–80 and 1881–90, 1881–90 and 1891–1900, and so on.

Note: The data are centred on the years indicated.

Table 7.16: Gross reproduction rates: a comparison of estimates of Glass with those derived from back projection

	Estimate		*1841*	*1851*	*1861*	*1871*	*1881*	*1891*	*1901*
Original:	Glass	(1)	2.107	2.195	2.256	2.344	2.278	2.043	1.725
	Back projection	(2)	2.492	2.403	2.507	2.537			
Corrected:	Glass	(3)	2.363	2.318	2.351	2.402			
	Back projection	(4)	2.386	2.304	2.372	2.403			
Ratio:	(3)/(4)	(5)	0.990	1.006	0.991	1.000			

Sources: (1) Glass, 'Changes in fertility in England and Wales', p. 168.
(2) Table A3.1.
(3) Corrections for birth under-registration, table A8.5.
(4) Corrections for sex distribution in age group 15–49, *1841 Census*, Age abstract, pp. 368 and 372; *1851 Census*, Ages, civil condition, etc., vol. I, Summary tables, pp. cxcii–cxciii; *1861 Census*, Ages, civil condition, etc., part I, Summary tables, pp. x–xi; *1871 Census*, Ages, civil condition, etc., Summary tables, pp. xii–xiii.

Given the exceptional nature of the behaviour of the GRR in the mid seventeenth century, it is natural to ask whether the apparent changes are real, especially as the early part of the period coincides with the Civil War and Commonwealth. During this period registration was notably defective. In the worst year, 1651, the total of registered baptisms was increased by 26:4 per cent because of defective registration.[63] Is it therefore likely that the apparent fall in fertility in these years was spurious? The possibility that the totals of registered baptisms was not sufficiently inflated cannot be entirely dismissed but there are considerations that make it rather improbable that there is any serious distortion of the true birth totals in this period. First, fertility remained equally low for 20 years after the Restoration when the level of under-registration was radically lower than between 1640 and 1660.[64] Second, if there were a serious failure to correct baptisms sufficiently it is likely that burials would also be affected. Yet during the middle decades of the century mortality tended to worsen and was more severe in the quinquennium centred on 1681 than at any other during the period covered by figure 7.6 except for those centred on 1561 and 1731. Third, any increase in totals of births in these decades would raise the totals of net emigration, already at a high level for the period. The balance of probability is against this.

The last point, however, does raise another consideration. In a period of heavy net emigration in which the majority of emigrants were men, back projection causes the number of women of child-bearing age to be underestimated and so fertility will be overstated, other things being equal, because the program assumes that women will form that fraction of the population of child-bearing age suggested by the mortality experience of the cohorts comprising it. However, the same feature which suggests that the true level of fertility was even lower than the estimated GRR, may also help to explain why it fell so low. The sexual imbalance in emigration was very marked, with indentured labour comprising the bulk of the emigrants. This would tend to reduce

63. See table A4.1.
64. The average amount by which the totals of baptisms were inflated to offset under-registration in the years 1640–59 was 18.9 per cent, whereas in the years 1660–79 the average was only 4.6 per cent (see table A4.1).

marriage opportunities for women, and result either in a later age at marriage or a higher proportion remaining unmarried, or both, with a consequent reduction in the GRR. We shall see later that throughout the period of very low general fertility there was a high age at first marriage for women and a high proportion never marrying, so that it is possible that the dip in the GRR between 1651 and 1681 was in part an indirect result of the migration history of the period.

One further gloss upon the GRRs listed in table 7.15 is called for. They were calculated by using a fertility schedule with a mean age at maternity of 32 years.[65] Data from reconstitution studies suggest that this may be approximately correct for early modern England as a whole (see tables 7.26 and 7.27).[66] But they also suggest that the mean age at maternity may have fluctuated by about two years between its maximum and minimum levels, bearing in mind that female age at first marriage fell by about three years from its high point in the seventeenth century to its low point in the early nineteenth century. It is therefore reasonable to suppose that although mean age at maternity may have averaged 32 years, it probably ranged between 31 and 33 years. In figure 7.7 the effect of using fertility schedules with mean ages of 31 and 33

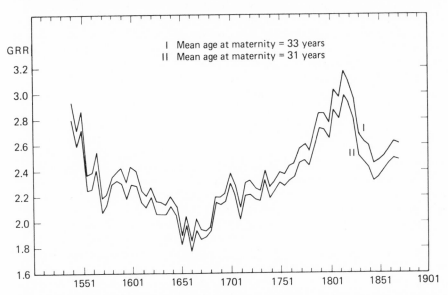

Figure 7.7: Alternative estimates of English quinquennial GRRs with mean ages of maternity of 31 and 33 years

Note: The data are centred on the years indicated. For further details see text.

65. See table A15.3.
66. In considering the evidence about age at marriage and marital fertility rates contained in these two tables, it should be remembered that the average age at maternity for illegitimate births was considerably lower than for legitimate births. For example, the median age of women at the birth of a first illegitimate child in the four parishes of Colyton (Devon), Hawkshead (Lancs.), Alcester (Warwicks.), and Aldenham (Herts.) in the early modern period as a whole was about 25 years only. The great majority of illegitimate births were first births.

may be seen.[67] Using the schedule associated with a mean age at maternity of 31 always produces a lower estimate than using the alternative schedule, because it shifts a greater share of the burden of child-bearing into younger age groups less depleted by mortality.

The 'true' GRR will have been closer to the upper bound of the band lying between the two sets of estimates during the period when the GRR was low in the seventeenth century, and closer to the lower bound in the early nineteenth century, because age at first marriage was high in the former period but had fallen considerably by 1800. The 'true' rate was probably about 1–2 per cent higher than in table 7.15 in the middle decades of the seventeenth century but 2–3 per cent lower than the level shown in the table a century and a half later. Or, to put it more concretely, when expressed as a 5-point moving average, as shown in figure 7.8, the GRR reached its lowest point in 1671 (1.91) and its higher point (2.94) in 1816, suggesting that it rose by 54 per cent between the two dates. It would probably be more accurate to set its low point a little higher at, say, 1.95, and reduce its high point rather more substantially to, say, 2.85, suggesting a somewhat smaller overall rise of 46 per cent. The effect of introducing this complication into the consideration of secular fertility changes in early modern England is to suggest that it is probable that the results presented earlier slightly exaggerate the absolute magnitude of the changes, but otherwise to leave the picture unaltered. It should be noted, incidentally, that the close agreement between our estimates of the GRR and those of Glass for the period 1841–71 strongly suggests that the mean age at maternity in these decades was close to 32 years (table 7.16).

Mortality changes also follow a fairly clear-cut overall trend though with more violent short-term fluctuations. Expectation of life at birth was exceptionally high in the later sixteenth and early seventeenth centuries, varying in the period between 1566 and 1621 from a high point of 41.7 years in 1581 to a low of 35.5 years in 1591, and averaging over 38 years. The best years lay between the mid 1560s and the mid 1580s,[68] when mortality was less severe than it was again to be until after the end of the Napoleonic wars. This was a period that the graph of deaths in pullout 1 shows to have been almost entirely free from significant mortality crises and that contained the highest individual figure for expectation of life recorded during the whole period down to 1871. Interestingly, this unusually low mortality did not pass unremarked by contemporaries, for it was in 1584 that Hakluyt made his much quoted reference to 'our long peace and seldom sickness'.[69] But immediately before this golden interlude the late 1550s are a grim reminder of the perils that had faced populations in earlier generations, for shocks of this magnitude or greater had probably occured intermittently, and at times quite frequently, throughout most of the later medieval period. The e_0 figures for 1556 and 1561 in table 7.15 tend to cloak the degree of severity of the crisis. The crude death rate in 1556, 1557, and 1558 was 42.5, 53.9, and 47.3 per 1,000 respectively, and the population of England fell by almost 200,000 between 1556 and 1560, from 3.159 to 2.964 millions, or by 6 per cent.[70] The 1540s and early 1550s, on the other hand, being free of such major crises, experienced mortality levels comparable to those of later periods in early modern England.

67. The schedules used are those published by Coale and Demeny, *Regional model life tables*, p. 30.
68. Between 1564 and 1586 the crude death rate was never higher than 26.3 per 1,000 (table A3.3).
69. Hakluyt, 'Discourse of western planting', p. 234.
70. See table A3.3.

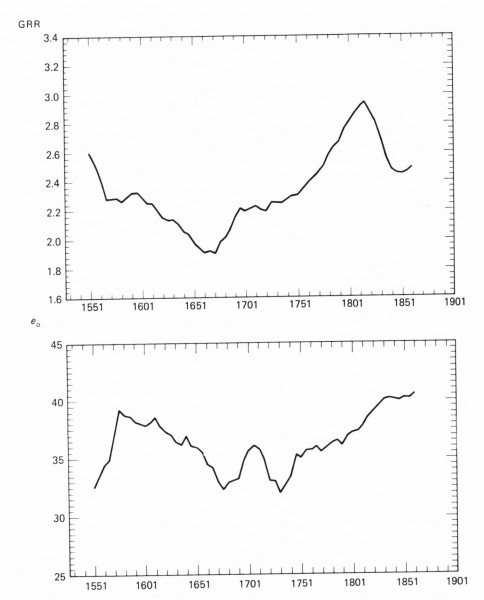

Figure 7.8: Five – point moving averages of English quinquennial
GRRs and e_0 s 1551 – 1861

Note: The data are centred on the years indicated (each reading
covers a 25-year period).

Source: Table A3.1.

From the end of the sixteenth century for three quarters of a century mortality grew steadily worse, expectation of life falling by seven years from 39.3 years in the 25-year period centring on 1576 to only 32.3 years in the quarter century centring on 1676. In the five-year period centring on 1681 e_0 was only 28.5 years, even though there was no single year of exceptional death rates (the crude death rates in the years 1679–83 were 37.2, 33.8, 38.9, 35.0, and 31.8 per 1,000 respectively).[71] In the century between Elizabeth's reign and the Restoration England had passed from a mortality régime that may have been unusually mild by the general standards of early modern Europe to one that was probably much closer to the norm. Family reconstitution studies throw some light on the changes in age-specific mortality which caused the rise in mortality and these are discussed briefly later in this chapter.

The last years of the seventeenth century and the early years of the eighteenth saw a considerable but short-lived improvement in mortality, but there was already a sharp fall in the e_0s in 1721 and 1726 while the e_0 for 1731, 27.9 years, was the second lowest in the entire series. The late 1720s, like the late 1550s, contained several successive bad years. The crude death rates in the worst years, 1727–31, were 35.5, 39.8, 44.7, 36.2, and 34.1 per 1,000 respectively, compared with an average of 28.8 and 28.0 for the five-year periods on either side (1722–6 and 1732–6).[72] As with the crisis of the 1550s the quinquennial phasing cloaks the severity of conditions in the worst period since the highest death rates do not all fall in one quinquennium.[73]

After 1731 there was recovery and fairly steady improvement, though the early 1740s, the 1760s and the early 1780s were all periods of relapse from the rising trend in expectation of life. Thereafter there was a decline in the scale of fluctuations in the quinquennial estimates of e_0, and between 1781 and and 1826 expectation of life at birth improved from about 35 years to 40 years, though after this there was no significant change for a further half-century. Even in the period 1820–70 e_0 was only about two years higher than in the reigns of Elizabeth and James I. The average e_0 in the 50 years covered by the 10 figures for 1826–71 was 40.4 years, while in the 60 years 1566–1621 the comparable figure was 38.6 years. Figure 7.8, which uses the same data as those of figure 7.6 but expresses them as a five-point moving average, may serve to bring out more clearly the gross changes in fertility and mortality.

The determinants of the intrinsic growth rate

Presentation of the fertility and mortality findings of back projection separately from each other is, however, in many respects less illuminating than considering them in conjunction. It is important to be able to distinguish the relative importance of each in affecting the intrinsic growth rate of the population, so that the question that has intrigued two generations of economic and demographic historians can be more conclusively answered. Is a rise in GRR from 2.5 to 3.0, for example, more important than a rise in e_0 from 35 to 40 years in affecting growth rates?

It is convenient to begin by considering the determinants of the net reproduction rate, which measures the proportionate increase per generation in a stable population.

$$NRR = p(\bar{m}).GRR$$

71. See table A3.3.
72. See table A3.3.
73. See below pp. 664–7.

where $\overline{m}$ is the mean age at maternity and p is the probability of surviving to that age. The net reproduction rate, therefore, is the simple product of the GRR and the probability of surviving to the mean age at maternity.[74] It follows that if the GRR and $p(m)$ are plotted on the two axes of a graph, both of whose scales are logarithmic, all combinations of GRR and $p(m)$ that produce a given level of NRR will lie on a straight line running between the two axes and cutting them at points equidistant from their common origin, as may be seen in figure 7.9.

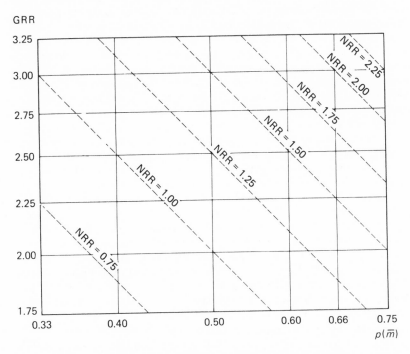

Figure 7.9: The relation between the GRR, the proportion surviving to the mean age at maternity, and the NRR

The intrinsic growth rate, r, measures the annual rate of growth of a stable population, and is closely linked to the NRR. It can be derived from NRR if t, the mean generation length, is known, since $r = \log_e \text{NRR}/t$. The mean generation length and the mean age at maternity are not identical but they are linked to one another since

$$t \doteq \overline{m} - \sigma^2 \frac{\log \text{GRR}}{2\overline{m}}$$

74. Note, however, that the NRRs published in table A3.1 were not calculated by this approximation but by a method that takes advantage of the fuller range of data available from back projection; for details see appendix 15, pp. 730–2.

where σ^2 is the variance of the fertility function $m(a)$. Coale remarks that it is safe to assign a fixed value of 50 to σ^2 in this connexion.[75]

If t were invariant any given level of NRR would be uniquely associated with a particular level of r and it would be possible to replace the diagonals showing NRRs in figure 7.9 by another set of diagonals representing all the combinations of GRR and $p(\bar{m})$ that result in intrinsic growth rates of 1 per cent per annum, 2 per cent per annum, and so on, and the successive diagonals would be equidistant. But t is not invariant, changing as a function of $\bar{m}$ and the GRR. A high GRR, for example, is only attainable with a relatively low mean age at maternity $\bar{m}$, and the two will act conjointly to depress t. Where marriage is late, on the other hand, the mean age at maternity will be higher, the GRR lower, and t is necessarily larger.

At some cost to precision, however, a graph can be constructed that displays r rather than the NRR. We have already noted that the assumption of a fixed fertility schedule with a mean age at maternity of 32 years when calculating GRRs involved some sacrifice of accuracy.[76] Similarly, assuming that t is constant at 31.5 years introduces a degree of inaccuracy, but the penalty is not severe.[77] A further complication arises from the need to convert the measure of mortality furnished by back projection (that is, e_0) into the probability of survival to the mean age at maternity. In any given family of life tables the two quantities will be uniquely associated, and the present graphs display scales of both e_0 and $p(\bar{m})$ whose relative positions have been calculated on the basis of the female model North Princeton life tables.[78] A different set of life tables, representing a different age structure of mortality, would, of course, produce a slightly different relation between the two. Any change over time in this regard cannot therefore be captured on the graph, but equipping the horizontal mortality axis with two scales in this fashion has the great advantage of enabling a direct comparison to be made of the relative importance of changes in the GRR and e_0 in altering r, the intrinsic growth rate.

Assessing the joint effect of changes in fertility and mortality in this way, therefore, involves crudities. Rather as a map, being flat, does only rough justice to the earth's surface, so a graph in this form is a somewhat crude way of analysing the impact of changes in fertility and mortality; but as a representational device its countervailing virtues are substantial. In such a graph, as may be seen in figure 7.10, any combination of GRR and $p(\bar{m})$ can be plotted as a point, and, by plotting a succession of such points, change over time can be traced. Any vertical movement between two

75. Coale, *The growth and structure of human populations*, p. 25. The three formulae given in the text are taken from Coale's discussion of stable population characteristics (Coale, *ibid.*, pp. 16–25).

76. See above, pp. 233–6.

77. When the NRR is close to 1.0 the level of t makes little difference to r (at NRR = 1.0, of course, the level of t is irrelevant). Even when the NRR is very high by the standards of pre-industrial western Europe, r does not vary very greatly given that t is constrained within fairly narrow margins by the relatively high age at first marriage. For this reason t is unlikely to have varied by more than a maximum of 3 years. If, therefore, a value of t is selected in the mid-point of its range, no observed t will be more than 1.5 years distant from its assumed value. For example, if the true range of the value of t were between 30 and 33 years, and it was assumed to be constant at 31.5, the maximum possible error in calculating r with the NRR at the high level of 1.5 is the difference between a rate of increase of 1.287 per cent per annum (where $t = 31.5$) and either 1.352 or 1.229 per cent per annum (where $t = 30$ and $t = 33$ respectively). These differences are not trivial but neither are they dramatically large. Over a 50-year period of growth, for example, the final population would be about 3 per cent above or below the figure calculated from $t = 31.5$ on the two extreme assumptions. And the true value of t would normally have been much less than 1.5 years distant from the assumed value.

78. The model North tables display a strong similarity to those used in back projection. See table A14.1.

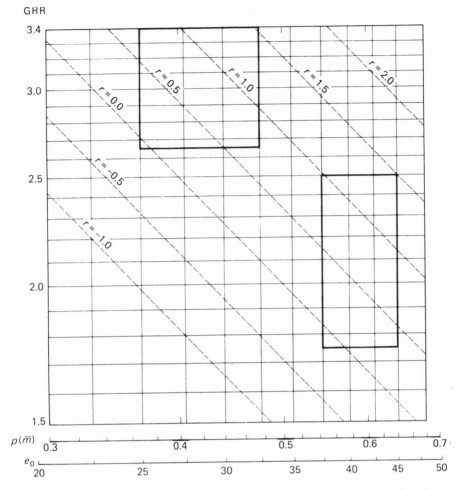

Figure 7.10: The relative importance of changes in GRR and e_0 in influencing intrinsic growth rates

points represents a change in fertility; any horizontal movement a change in mortality. Since the two axes are isometric with respect to the intrinsic growth rate, the relative scale of movement in the two directions will show the relative importance of the contributions made by changes in fertility and mortality to any change in the rate.

This valuable visual feature of the graph derives from the definition of the NRR, and hence indirectly the intrinsic growth rate, as the simple product of GRR and $p(\bar{m})$. From this algebraical relationship it follows that a proportionate increase or decrease in either the GRR or $p(\bar{m})$ will have exactly the same impact on r as the same proportionate change in the other variable. In view of the occasional misunderstanding of this point, it must be stressed that in this respect fertility and mortality are on an equal footing; there is no *theoretical* reason why changes in mortality should have a greater leverage than changes in fertility in determining changes in the intrinsic growth rate, or vice versa. Whether in reality it was fertility or mortality that experienced the greater proportional change and so exerted the greater influence on the intrinsic growth rate is a matter for empirical verification. In addressing the question it should be remembered that the fact that it is *proportional* not absolute changes that are in question means that the magnitude of the effect of a unit change in either variable on the intrinsic growth rate depends upon the existing level of that variable, for it is this that determines whether the change is proportionately large or small. And in this connexion it needs to be borne in mind that mortality enters into the picture through its inverse, survivorship. Thus if high fertility is offset by high mortality, small absolute changes in mortality have great leverage in changing growth rates because they represent large poportional increases in the *low* survivorship entailed in high mortality. If, on the other hand, a population has a régime of low fertility balanced by low mortality, the high survivorship associated with the latter means that small changes in mortality have little effect on the intrinsic growth rate and that unit changes in fertility have proportionately greater effect than they exert when mortality is high.

Consider the two boxes drawn on figure 7.10. Both enclose terrains in which GRR varies by 0.75 (1.75 to 2.50 and 2.65 to 3.40) and the e_0 by 7.5 years (37.5 to 45.0 and 25.0 to 32.5), and both range between situations in which r is slightly negative to others where r is approximately 1.5. But whereas the 'high-pressure' box is slightly wider than it is high, the height of the 'low-pressure' box is more than twice its width. Since a movement of unit length along either the survivorship or fertility axes will have the same effect on the intrinsic growth rate, it will be immediately clear, as we have already noted, that unit changes in mortality exercise a considerable influence on intrinsic growth rates in a 'high-pressure' régime where the GRR is high and e_0 is low, but that unit changes in fertility are disproportionately influential in a 'low-pressure' situation where the GRR is low and e_0 relatively high.

Figure 7.10 also makes it easy to assess the implications of some of the more extreme views that have been expressed about the causes of the acceleration in English population growth in the eighteenth century. The intrinsic growth rate of the English population reached a peak early in the nineteenth century when it was roughly 1.5 per cent per annum. Expectation of life at birth at the time was no higher than 40 years. If it were true that changes in mortality alone had caused intrinsic growth rates to rise from zero at the beginning of the eighteenth century to 1.5 per cent per annum just over a century later, it will be clear from figure 7.10 that expectation of life at birth must have been no higher than about 24 years in 1700 (the GRR needed for $r = 1.5$ when $e_0 = 40.0$ is about 2.75 and the point of intersection between the horizontal representing GRR = 2.75 and the diagonal representing $r = 0$ implies an e_0 of about 24 years). Such a change of 16 years in expectation of life at birth would imply an extraordinary improvement in mortality for which there seems to be no warrant.

Early modern England was a land in which both fertility and mortality were low by the standards of many traditional societies. In figure 7.8, representing a five-point moving average of the quinquennial e_0s, the graph never falls as low as 32 years. In only three of the individual quinquennial periods shown in figure 7.6 did expectation of life fall below 30 years. At the other extreme no individual reading reached 42 years, and the five-point moving average did not exceed 41 years. The extreme figures, moreover, were rare aberrations. Between 1541 and 1871 out of 67 e_0s 60 lay between 31 and 41 years, as may be seen in table 7.17. Within this range the impact of

Table 7.17: Distribution of individual quinquennial e_0s 1541-1871

	e_0		e_0
27 –	2	36 –	6
28 –	1	37 –	11
29 –	0	38 –	7
30 –	1	39 –	5
31 –	3	40 –	7
32 –	3	41 –	3
33 –	4		
34 –	5	Total	67
35 –	9		

Source: Table 7.15.

mortality upon the intrinsic growth rate is limited at the maximum to about 0.80 per cent per annum.

In contrast fertility had a substantially greater relative impact. In figure 7.8, the values of the GRR vary between a minimum of 1.91 and a maximum of 2.94. Of the individual readings 61 out of 67 lie between 1.9 and 2.9, a range sufficient to change the intrinsic growth rate by about 1.3 per cent per annum, or more than half as large again as the comparable mortality figure. The spread of individual GRR readings is shown in table 7.18.

Table 7.18: Distribution of individual quinquennial GRRs 1541-1871

1.8 –	3	2.6 –	3
1.9 –	3	2.7 –	3
2.0 –	4	2.8 –	3
2.1 –	10	2.9 –	2
2.2 –	9	3.0 –	1
2.3 –	14		
2.4 –	5	Total	67
2.5 –	7		

Source: Table 7.15.

The history of the combined effect of changes in GRR and e_0 is shown in figures 7.11 and 7.12. In the former the data are those of table 7.15 while in the latter the same data have been converted into five-point moving averages to make overall trends easier to identify (thus the GRR and e_0 for 1551 represent the averages of the individual readings for 1541, 1546, 1551, 1556, 1561, and so on). The e_0s in table 7.15 refer, of course, to the sexes combined but to construct figures 7.11 and 7.12 female e_0s are needed. In the Princeton model North life tables the difference in expectation of life between the sexes is always close to three years over the range of e_0s experienced in early modern England. English mid-nineteenth-century mortality, reflected in the third life table, resembled model North, and accordingly in constructing the two figures the female e_0 was assumed always to be 1.5 years greater than the figure for the sexes combined. This may do some violence to precision since the difference between male and female e_0 in the third life table was only two years, and the *r* s in table A3.1 were obtained using a family of female life tables that follow

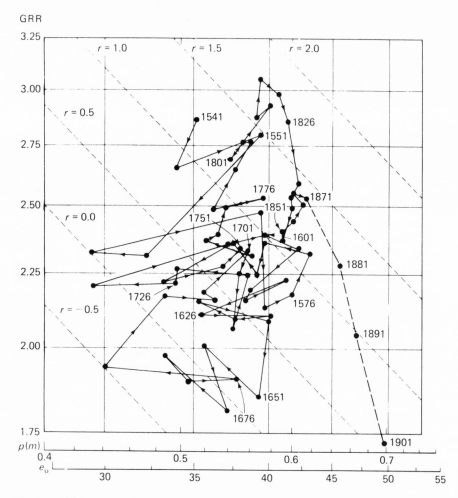

Figure 7.11: The combined effect of English fertility and mortality changes in determining intrinsic growth rates 1541 – 1871 (quinquennial data)

Notes: The years shown are the central years of the five-year periods to which each point relates. For further details see text.

Source: Table A3.1.

the 'English' model (see appendix 14, pp. 710–3). The solution adopted in constructing figures 7.11 and 7.12, however, lessens the inevitable arbitrariness involved in making international comparisons (figure 7.13), and makes only marginal differences to the outcome. Some of the very slight discrepancies between the r values plotted in figure 7.11 and those listed in table A3.1, however, arise for this reason.

We may begin by considering figure 7.12 since the overall pattern of change is more easily visible in this figure. The line connecting the individual points at first

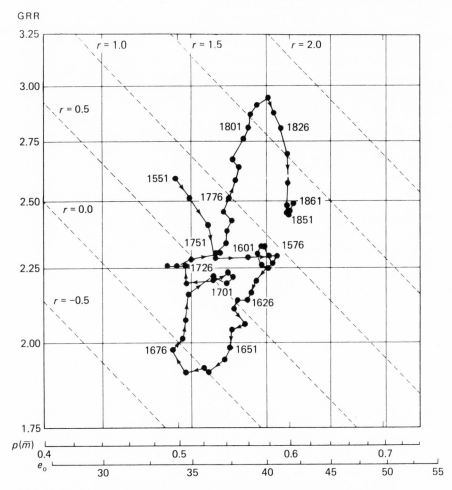

Figure 7.12: The combined effect of English fertility and mortality
changes in determining intrinsic growth rates 1551 – 1861
(5 – point moving averages of quinquennial data)

Note: The years shown are the central years of the 25-year periods to which
each point relates. For further details see text.

Source: Table A3.1.

moves sharply down the graph from the high point reached in the earliest years as
fertility fell rapidly. It then moves out to the right in the golden period of low mortality
in the later sixteenth century and there is a cluster of neighbouring points from 1571 to
1611, a period of relatively stable fertility and mortality when the intrinsic growth rate
was about 0.85. Thereafter, fertility fell steadily and mortality worsened until in 1661
the intrinsic growth rate fell to zero, remaining at this level or lower for four
successive readings on the graph.

Fertility and mortality contributed equally to the steady fall in r from 1611 to 1671, though fertility was again dominant during its subsequent rise to 1691. Between 1691 and 1751, however, there was a long period in which horizontal movement predominated over vertical movement, reflecting the greater importance of mortality change, with rapid improvement between 1691 and 1706, followed by a very sharp deterioration down to 1731 and recovery in the next 15 years. After the mid eighteenth century fertility once more proved dominant as the graph rose almost vertically to reach a very high level in the early nineteenth century, swaying slightly to the right as it rose, before plunging equally rapidly to 1841 when the fall levelled off to be replaced by a slight recovery after 1851. Mortality improvement continued to push the graph fractionally to the right in the first half of the nineteenth century as it had done in the later eighteenth century but this movement was modest compared with the movements up and down engendered by fertility changes.

The period between 1691 and 1751 when mortality was most clearly the more important influence on growth rates includes, of course, one of the two most severe mortality episodes in the early modern period with very high death rates in the period 1727–31, but also the benign years about the beginning of the eighteenth century when the e_0 rose to a higher average level than for many years on either side.[79] Even so, it is interesting to note that the two most extreme points within this period shown in figure 7.12 were only sufficiently far apart to have raised or depressed r by about 0.4 per cent per annum with constant fertility. In contrast in the period next following of equal length, 1751–1811, the change in fertility with constant mortality was enough to raise the growth rate by 0.8 per cent.

In considering the relative importance of fertility and mortality changes in altering the intrinsic growth rate it is convenient to divide the period as a whole into two parts of unequal length. It seems fair to characterize the period from 1551 to 1751 as one in which the two variables were of roughly equal importance. The vertical distance between the highest and lowest levels of fertility (1551 and 1671) is substantially greater than the horizontal distance between the highest and lowest levels of mortality (1731 and 1576) but the pattern varied over time. At different periods during these two centuries the relative importance of the two influences on the intrinsic growth rate changed considerably. The pattern after 1751 forms a striking contrast with the earlier period. Although mortality improved almost without interruption throughout the ensuing century, its influence on growth rates was swamped by sweeping changes in fertility. Vertical movement, both up and down, dominated the behaviour of the graph. The vertical spread of points was more than twice the horizontal spread.

In figure 7.11 the behaviour of the graph inevitably conveys a more hectic impression since it lacks the dampening effect introduced by the use of a moving average to produce the data points of figure 7.12, but it reveals points of importance concealed in figure 7.12. The most striking difference is to be found in the location of the points representing 1561, 1681, and 1731. Each involved a very sharp horizontal movement leftwards in the graph. These were the three most severe quinquennia of high mortality in early modern English history. Two were caused by exceptional epidemic outbursts, those of 1557–9 and 1727–31.[80] In both cases figure 7.11

---

79. The average crude death rate in the five years 1727–31 was 38.0 per 1,000; in the 17 years 1702–18 it was only 26.8 per 1,000, even though the period included an isolated year of high mortality in 1705 and above average death rates in 1711–12 (see table A3.3).
80. The annual crude death rates in these two periods were as folows: 1557–9, 42.5, 53.9, 47.3; 1727–31, 35.5, 39.8, 44.7, 36.2, 34.1 (table A3.3).

somewhat masks the true severity of the surge in mortality because the years ending in '7' and '8' fell in one quinquennium while the others fell in the next (thus explaining why the points representing 1556 and 1726 are also both well out to the left). The third case, 1681, is displaced to the left because there was a prolonged period of high mortality in the late 1670s and 1680s and not because of a single major epidemic outburst.[81] The three brief episodes of very high mortality represent such a sharp departure from normal mortality that even when their effect is muffled by inclusion in a five-point moving average they impose a considerable lateral spread upon the graph in figure 7.12. When they are shown as isolated events, as in figure 7.11, it is easier to appreciate the general dominance of fertility over mortality change in determining the intrinsic growth rate, apart from the three short periods when death rates were far above normal. If these three periods are ignored, the extreme fertility readings in the period down to 1751 (1541 and 1661) are separated by a vertical distance almost twice as great as the horizontal distance between the two mortality extremes (1741 and 1581). In the period between 1751 and 1871, on the other hand, the ratio of the fertility and mortality extremes is much the same as in figure 7.12: that is, fertility movement is about twice as great as mortality movement measured between the extreme values recorded.

In the period after 1751 expressing the relative importance of changes in fertility and mortality in this fashion understates the dominance of fertility in changing the intrinsic growth rate since between 1751 and 1871 fertility first climbed from a low point in 1751 to its peak in 1816 and then fell so substantially that by 1846 it was almost down to its mid-eighteenth-century level, whereas mortality tended to improve throughout. There were times when it worsened somewhat from one quinquennium to the next but in general changes were modest and predominantly rightwards on the graph. In consequence, between any two successive points the vertical displacement was usually much larger than the horizontal displacement, especially after 1781.

In the first two centuries the pattern was less clear cut. Strategically, so to speak, fertility was the more influential factor, as we have seen; its extremes were further apart than those of mortality if the three exceptional mortality episodes are ignored. But tactically, the change in the intrinsic growth rate from one quinquennial reading to the next was often more affected by mortality than by fertility change. Short-term mortality changes, as might perhaps be expected, were often sharper than those in fertility but the cumulative effect of the secular shifts in fertility, even in the earlier period, tended to outweigh those in mortality.

This tendency continued after 1871. A few points to represent changes between 1871 and 1901 have been incluued in figure 7.11. They are joined by broken lines.[82] Although mortality began to fall rapidly after 1871 and the graph therefore moves out to the right, the fall in fertility was so rapid that fertility continued to exercise a dominant influence on the trend in the intrinsic growth rate, which by 1901 was back at a level typical of much of English early modern history but at lower levels of both fertility and mortality.

81. The crude death rate from 1679 to 1686 was never lower than 31 per 1,000 but also never as high as 39 per 1,000.
82. The GRRs used to plot the points 1881 to 1901 were taken from Glass, 'Changes in fertility in England and Wales', p. 168. The e_0s used were taken from the English life tables of 1871–80, 1881–90, 1891–1900, and 1901–10. The 1881 figure was taken as the mean of the figures for 1871–80 and 1881–90; and so on.

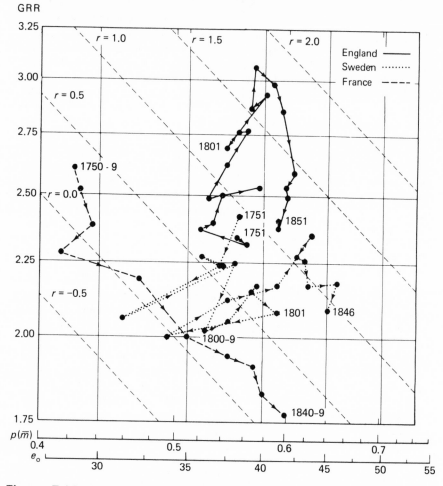

Figure 7.13: A comparison of English, French, and Swedish fertility and mortality data 1750 – 1850

Sources: France. Mortality: Blayo, 'La mortalité en France de 1740 à 1829', p.141 (1740-9 to 1820-9) and Bourgeois-Pichat, 'The general development of the population of France', p.505 (1830-9 and 1840-9). The figure for 1830-9 represents the average of the e_o s given for 1830-2, 1835-7, and 1840-2; and that for 1840-9, the average of 1840-2, 1845-7, and 1850-2. Fertility: Bourgeois-Pichat, *ibid*, p.506 (1771-1850). Each decadal figure used in the graph represents the average of two quinquennial periods (for example, 1771-5 and 1776-80). For the decades before 1770 the GRRs were estimated using the crude birth rates given in Henry and Blayo, 'La population de la France de 1740 à 1860', p.109. The CBR for 1770-5 (37.2) was equated with the GRR given by Bourgeois-Pichat for 1771-5 (2.40) and earlier GRRs calculated on the assumption that they changed proportionately to changes in the CBR.

Sweden. Mortality: Hofsten and Lundström, *Swedish population history*, p.54 (the e_o s were taken from fig. 38). Fertility: *Historisk statistik*, p.105, table 34. GRRs were taken as the total fertility rate divided by 2.05. The data points of the graph refer to the five-year periods beginning at the dates indicated.

England. See figure 7.11.

Although English demographic trends in the eighteenth and early nineteenth centuries were largely determined by fertility changes, as might be expected in a 'low-pressure' régime, it does not follow that English experience was paralleled elsewhere in western Europe. Indeed, Sweden and France, two other countries for which details of GRR and e_0 are available for much of the period, neatly exemplify other possible demographic régimes. In figure 7.13 English, Swedish, and French experience is contrasted over the period 1750–1850 (it should be noted that the French data are decennial, while those for Sweden and England are quinquennial).

In Sweden the bulk of the acceleration in intrinsic growth rates between 1750 and 1850 is attributable to declining mortality rates, without which there would have been no consistent and significant change in growth rates. Fertility fluctuated considerably between a GRR of 2.0 and 2.4 but without any clear trend, whereas mortality, though moving erratically, showed marked improvement (the average GRR for 1751–1800 was 2.19 and for 1801–50, 2.17, but female e_0 improved from 37.0 to 41.7 years in the two half-centuries). The lateral spread of the Swedish graph is, however,

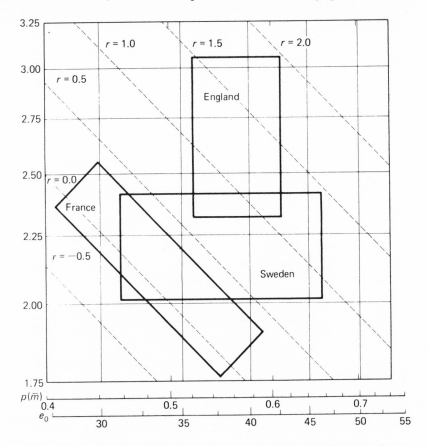

Figure 7.14: Simplified representation of the demographic terrain covered by England, France, and Sweden 1750–1850

Source :   See figure 7.13 and text

exaggerated by the exceptional mortalities reflected in the quinquennial points centring on 1771 and 1806. The behaviour of the Swedish graph represents a stark contrast with that of England over the same period, and it may in part explain the preference often shown by English demographic historians for a falling death rate as the main cause of English population growth. The Swedish data have long been available, and in the absence of conclusive English evidence it has been tempting to assume that England followed the Swedish pattern.[83] France represented a compromise between the English and Swedish extremes. The intrinsic growth rate in France was never far above zero, and, unlike either of the other two countries, it showed no tendency to rise, but the lack of change in r did not mean a lack of change in fertility and mortality. Rather the two declined in a manner which ensured that the changes in one were almost exactly offset by changes in the other so that France slid down the diagonal representing $r = 0$, instead of moving out towards $r = 1.0$ or higher in the fashion of England or Sweden.

To make the nature and extent of the contrasts between the three countries easier to appreciate, the points shown in figure 7.13 have been 'boxed' in figure 7.14. Clearly the demographic history of western Europe in this period includes a wide variety of individual national experience.

Back projection and family reconstitution

The existence of a substantial number of completed family reconstitution studies is of value both as a check upon the results of back projection and because reconstitution data help to suggest the proximate causes of some of the gross changes in fertility and mortality observed in back projection. The reconstitution data used here are drawn from 12 parishes, all of which possessed registers sufficiently full and complete to allow reconstitution to begin before 1600 and to be carried forward into the nineteenth century. The parishes in question are: Alcester (Warwicks.), Aldenham (Herts.), Banbury (Oxon.), Colyton (Devon), Gainsborough (Lincs.), Gedling (Notts.), Hartland (Devon), Methley (Yorks., W.R.), Shepshed (Leics.), Southill and Campton with Shefford (Beds.), Terling (Essex), and Willingham (Cambs.).[84] The parishes form part of a larger group of parishes that will provide the material to be used in a later Cambridge Group publication. Here the results are presented chiefly in the form of simple averages of the individual rates or other measures found in the several parishes. The 12 are widely scattered in location, vary substantially in size, and were very different from one another in their socio-economic characteristics. Consequently the averages quoted in the following pages are derived in many cases by combining very different absolute rates. Since the 12 parishes do not constitute a random sample, the average measures are unlikely to be representative of the country as a whole, and so cannot profitably be compared in level with measures derived from back projection. However, the amplitude and timing of changes can be compared

83. McKeown, for example, is inclined to use Swedish data as a pointer to what happened elsewhere. McKeown, *The modern rise of population*, especially pp. 30 and 41, but generally in ch. 2. Habakkuk, influenced by Ohlin and Utterström, has also done so from time to time, as, for example, in 'The economic history of modern Britain', pp. 498–9.

84. We are deeply indebted to the following for carrying out these reconstitutions: Mr J. D. Asteraki (Southill and Campton with Shefford), Mrs L. Clarke (Gainsborough), Mrs P. Ford (Alcester), Dr D. Levine (Shepshed, Terling), Mr W. Newman Brown (Aldenham), Miss G. Reynolds (Willingham), Mrs S. Stewart (Banbury, Hartland), Professor M. Yasumoto (Methley), Mrs J. D. Young (Gedling).

with changes in parallel measures taken from back projection, especially if the patterns in the reconstitution data are widespread among the individual parishes.

It is convenient to begin by considering the light thrown by reconstitution data on mortality trends before turning to fertility and nuptiality. It will be recalled that back projection involves the use of age schedules of mortality which are determined by the family of life tables used,[85] and can therefore only provide independent estimates of mortality in the form of overall measures, such as expectation of life at birth.[86] Reconstitution, on the other hand, provides evidence both of overall mortality trends and of any differential trends at different ages.

Table 7.19: Infant and child mortality rates ($1\,000q_x$) from 12 reconstitution studies (simple means)

	1550-99		1600-49		1650-99		1700-49		1750-99	
	M	F	M	F	M	F	M	F	M	F
0-1	143	127	142	123	154	133	168	148	135	122
1-4	65	59	88	81	96	102	97	95	87	87
5-9	29	30	42	37	38	45	38	44	31	30
0-9	222	203	250	224	264	256	277	263	235	222

Source: Cambridge Group reconstitutions.

Table 7.19 shows infant and child mortality rates prevailing in the 12 parishes in tne five successive half-centuries between 1550–99 and 1750–99. Although the absolute levels varied considerably from parish to parish,[87] the *pattern* of change shows a surprising regularity considering the strikingly different social and economic histories of the parishes.[88] Table 7.20 shows for each time period and age group the number of parishes in which the mortality rate was at its highest level of the 250-year period. In 7 of the 12 parishes infant mortality was higher in the period 1700–49 than in any of the other four half-centuries. The table therefore makes it clear that in general infant mortality was at its worst early in the eighteenth century. This was also

Table 7.20: Number of parishes experiencing a peak value in their mortality series for the age groups 0-1, 1-4, and 5-9 in five time periods (rates for the sexes combined)

	1550-99	1600-49	1650-99	1700-49	1750-99	Total
0-1	2	1	1	7	1	12
1-4	1	0	5	4	2	12
5-9	1	2	4	5	0	12

Source: Cambridge Group reconstitutions.

85. See appendix 14.
86. The relative mortality rates at different ages at all overall levels of mortality are prescribed by the assumptions built into the family of life tables used.
87. In the period 1700–49, for example, the male and female infant mortality rates in Gainsborough stood at 284 and 245 per 1,000 respectively, while those in Hartland were only 85 and 75.
88. This point is explored in Schofield and Wrigley, 'Infant and child mortality'.

a period of high child mortality rates but 1700–49 was no worse in this respect than the preceding half-century.[89]

Reconstitution does not yield estimates of mortality in adolescence and early adulthood because of the problems of defining periods in observation within the parish for people in this age range, but the mortality of married adults can be studied, though with a substantial margin of error arising from the presence in each cohort of a proportion of husbands and wives whose date of death is unknown.[90] The figures

Table 7.21: Expectation of life at age 30: simple means of data from 12 parishes

	M	F
1550–99	29.2	30.2
1600–49	29.8	29.6
1650–99	28.4	28.9
1700–49	30.4	30.2
1750–99	32.1	32.4

Source: Cambridge Group reconstitutions.

given in table 7.21 represent the expectation of life at age 30. Their absolute level should be viewed with reserve, especially in the case of the last period, 1750–99.[91] The table shows that adult mortality worsened a little between the late sixteenth and late seventeenth centuries (though the male figure actually improved slightly between 1550–99 and 1600–49). During this period, therefore, adult mortality was moving in parallel with infant and child mortality, but whereas infant and child mortality continued to deteriorate in the early eighteenth century, there was a sharp improvement in adult mortality between 1650–99 and 1700–49. Once more there was a notable uniformity of behaviour in the 12 parishes. As may be seen in table 7.22 there was a scattering of the peaks in adult mortality throughout the first three half-centuries, but only one peak occurred after 1700. Adult mortality appears to have experienced widespread improvement in the cohort marrying 1700–49.

Inferences drawn from a comparison of the timing of the peaks in adult mortality with those in infant and child mortality (tables 7.22 and 7.20) should, however, be made with caution. The latter refer to children *born* in the periods indicated and

89. The uniformity of pattern in the peaks of infant mortality rates is even more marked than might appear at first sight in the sense that some of the anomalies are readily explicable. The parish with a peak in 1750–99 was Gedling which at this time was experiencing a very rapid growth in the framework knitting industry. In all probability the worsening mortality was linked to this (the two parishes in which mortality at age 1–4 peaked in 1750–99 were Gedling and Shepshed, both framework knitting parishes: for a discussion of the probable links between this industry and increased mortality, see Levine, *Family formation*, pp. 67–71).

90. The method of calculation and the margins of error involved are described in Wrigley, 'Mortality in pre-industrial England', pp. 551–5, but the programs currently in use involve slightly different assumptions from those set out in the article. They will be described in our forthcoming book to be devoted to the description of a number of reconstitution studies.

91. In the cohort married in this period some men and women survived beyond the terminal dates of the reconstitutions. There is therefore a higher proportion of unknowns and a wider margin of uncertainty.

Table 7.22: Number of parishes experiencing a peak of adult mortality in five time periods (male and female e_{30} considered separately)

	M	F	Total
1550–99	6	2	8
1600–49	2	4	6
1650–99	4	5	9
1700–49	0	1	1
1750–99	0	0	0
	12	12	24

Source: Cambridge Group reconstitutions.

almost all their deaths occur within the same half-centuries. The former refer to couples *marrying* in the periods shown and many of their deaths will have taken place in the following half-century.[92] Despite this difficulty the tables strongly suggest a divergence of trends in adult mortality rates on the one hand and infant and child rates on the other between the mid seventeenth and mid eighteenth centuries.[93]

These changes in the relative levels of mortality at different ages can be brought out more clearly by re-expressing the information given in earlier tables in terms of level

Table 7.23: The mortality levels found in reconstitution studies expressed in terms of the Princeton life tables

North

	1550–99	1600–49	1650–99	1700–49	1750–99
$_1q_0$	11.5	12	11	10	12
$_4q_1$	15	13	12.5	12	13
$_5q_5$	14.5	12.5	12	12.5	14.5
e_{30}	6.5	6	5.5	7	9

West

	1550–99	1600–49	1650–99	1700–49	1750–99
$_1q_0$	12.5	13	12	11	13
$_4q_1$	14	12	11.5	11	12
$_5q_5$	10	7	6.5	6.5	9.5
e_{30}	7.5	7.5	6.5	8	10

Sources: Tables 7.19 and 7.21 and Coale and Demeny, *Regional model life tables*.

92. For example, at level 8 of the model North female tables the distribution of deaths in a cohort from age 30 onwards is such that approximately 60 per cent of all deaths would have taken place outside the half century in which the cohort was married, assuming that the marriages were evenly spread through the half century.

93. There are notable similarities between the changing age pattern of mortality found in reconstitution studies and that found by Hollingsworth in his peerage studies. Hollingsworth, 'Mortality in the British peerage families', p. 327.

North and level West of the Princeton model life tables. The levels shown in table 7.23 were obtained by finding for each sex and age group the level in the model tables closest to the q_x or e_{30} in question, and averaging the separate readings for males and females. For example, the male infant mortality for 1550–99 shown in table 7.19 is nearest level 12 in the North tables, but the female rate is nearest level 11, and therefore the level shown in table 7.23 is 11.5. Similarly, the male e_{30} in 1550–99 was nearest to level 7 North, the corresponding female e_{30} was nearest to level 6, and the resulting level in the table is 6.5.

The table suggests that mortality early in life conformed to the North pattern reasonably well apart from the earliest half-century but that adult mortality was very much more severe than might have been expected from the infant and child rates in model North terms. In model West terms the picture is different. The earliest period is once more anomalous but thereafter the rates $_1q_0$ and $_4q_1$ were homogeneous, as were $_5q_5$ and e_{30} but at much more severe mortality levels. In both model West and model North terms the anomalies were growing less striking in the final half-century.

The changing age patterns of mortality suggested by table 7.23 bring out the unreality of the assumption incorporated in back projection that the age pattern of mortality of the third English life table, which was basically model North in character and on which the family of life tables used in back projection was based, obtained at all times in the past. Later in this chapter we explore the issue of how sensitive the results of back projection are to changes in the age schedule of mortality. Here we shall consider whether the changes in estimates of e_0 obtained from back projection are consistent with the mortality trends revealed in reconstitution studies despite the inability of the former to reflect changing age patterns of mortality.

In order to make this comparison the information summarized in table 7.23 must be converted into an estimate of expectation of life at birth. To attempt this must entail making some heroic assumptions, and we have deliberately adopted a very rough-and-ready solution to the problem. Clearly the *absolute* level of the mean expectation of life taken from a dozen parishes is not comparable with the results of back projection since there is no reason to suppose that the parishes are a representative sample. What is at issue is rather the question of the timing and amplitude of any changes in the e_0s derived from reconstitution and back projection, and for this purpose a refined calculation is unnecessary.

Table 7.24 compares the estimates of e_0 based on the reconstitutions with cohort

Table 7.24: Expectations of life at birth derived from reconstitution studies compared with those taken from back projection

	Reconstitution	Change on previous cohort	Back projection	Change on previous cohort
1550–99	42.5		36.8	
1600–49	41.9	−0.6	36.4	−0.4
1650–99	39.5	−2.4	33.9	−2.5
1700–49	39.5	0.0	34.5	0.6
1750–99	45.0	5.5	36.5	2.0

Note: See text for derivation of reconstitution e_0s. The back-projection figure for 1750–99 is based on only seven readings since no complete e_0 can be calculated for any cohort after 1781.

Sources: Tables 7.23 and A3.2.

e_0s from the back projection. The latter represent the means of the individual quinquennial figures for the period shown. The former were calculated from within the model West levels in table 7.23 stylized as follows:[94] in 1550–99 mortality in the age group 0–4 was at level 13 and at level 8 for all later ages; in 1600–49 that the comparable levels for the same age groups were 13 and 7.5; in 1650–99 levels 12 and 6.5; in 1700–49 levels 11 and 7.5; and in 1750–99 levels 13 and 10. In order to calculate l_xs and L_xs for the sexes combined it was assumed that the sex ratio at birth was 105.

The reconstitution e_0s are considerably higher than those obtained from back projection. This is not surprising. Mortality levels varied greatly from parish to parish. The worst, like Gainsborough, were far less healthy than the nation as a whole, though the 12 included a sufficiently high proportion of healthy parishes to produce an average mortality less severe than that experienced in England generally. The back projection, moreover, was based on birth and death totals that included estimates for London where mortality was much higher than in the rest of the country.

The pattern of change in expectation of life from one half-century to the next, however, which proved to be stable within the group of reconstitution parishes, also turns out to be similar between the reconstitution results and those of back projection. In the reconstitution parishes there was a fall of about three years in expectation of life between 1550–99 and 1650–99, little change in the succeeding half-century, and very sharp improvement of over five years in the final cohort. In back projection the results were very similar with a fall of 2.9 years over the first century, very little change in the next half-century, and a rise of two years in the final period. Cohort e_0s can only be calculated down to the cohort of 1781, however, and the continued improvement in mortality after 1781 makes it certain that if figures were available for cohorts born in the last two decades of the eighteenth century, they would increase the figure for 1750–99 somewhat. Even taking this consideration into account, the improvement in expectation of life in the last cohort is much greater in the reconstitution set. This discrepancy may be due in part to the greater margin of error in the final reconstitution cohort to which reference has already been made,[95] but it may also be due in part to a deterioration in Anglican registration coverage, to offset which the data used in back projection were, of course, extensively modified. Although the problem is likely to have been less serious in the data used for reconstitution since some causes of under-registration, such as late baptism or nonconformity, affect reconstitution calculations in a lesser degree, it is still true that under-registration in the late eighteenth and early nineteenth centuries was much more widespread than at other times and may well have tended to cause mortality to be underestimated in the reconstitution results. In general, however, reconstitution evidence confirms the overall national trends in mortality discovered by back projection, though it also suggests that the national trends conceal important differences in the mortality levels of different communities, and it reveals that there were changes in the age structure of mortality over time which back projection cannot detect.

The fertility and nuptiality evidence from reconstitution is even more helpful and

94. Model West tables were used chiefly because there is a much better agreement between $_5q_5$ and e_{30} in model West than in model North in table 7.22, which reduces any possible error due to selecting an inappropriate mortality level for adolescence and the early adult years, but also to maximize the contrast with the age pattern of mortality assumed by back projection.
95. See above, p. 250, fn. 91.

illuminating when placed in conjunction with the back-projection results. In the first place, as may be seen in table 7.25, the reconstitution studies strongly suggest that any change in marital fertility probably had only a minor impact on the level of gross reproduction rates between the late sixteenth and the early nineteenth centuries. There

Table 7.25. Age-specific marital fertility rates (live births per 1 000 woman-years lived): means of 12 reconstitution studies

	20–4	25–9	30–4	35–9	40–4	Cumulative marital fertility 20–44 (live-born children)
1550–99	348	324	274	234	125	6.53
1600–49	384	346	303	245	127	7.03
1650–99	376	347	295	241	125	6.92
1700–49	382	352	287	224	108	6.77
1750–99	411	338	283	234	118	6.92
Mean	380	341	288	236	121	6.83

Source: Cambridge Group reconstitutions.

was remarkably little change in the age-specific marital fertility rates obtained by averaging the individual rates in the 12 parishes. The cumulative marital fertility over the age groups 20–44 varied only between 6.53 and 7.03 children, the latter being only 8 per cent higher than the former. The only changes of apparent significance were in the age group 20–4. The rate for 1550–99 was substantially lower than those in later years while that for 1750–99 was somewhat above the average. Rates in this age group are sometimes based on rather small numbers of births because of the high age of first marriage, and they are more likely to vary for this reason. They are also sensitive to changes in the level of prenuptial pregnancy, and it is likely that the higher rate in this age group in 1750–99 reflects the very sharp rise in prenuptial pregnancy in the later eighteenth century.[96] The marital fertility rates in individual parishes

96. Hair, 'Bridal pregnancy' and 'Bridal pregnancy .... further examined'. In the 12 reconstitution parishes the proportion of all first births (or more strictly first baptisms) that occurred within 9 months of marriage varied as follows (simple means of individual parish rates per 1,000 first births):

	Period since marriage (in months)		
	0–8	0–7	8
1550–99	255	203	52
1600–49	228	170	58
1650–99	162	102	60
1700–49	213	167	46
1750–99	299	255	44
1800–49	342	301	41

The figures show a very clear cut pattern of change with relatively low levels of prenuptial pregnancy in the later seventeenth century, a substantial rise in the next half century, and a still larger increase in the later eighteenth century. The rate went even higher in the early decades of the nineteenth century when it was more than double the rate in 1650–99 (the great majority of the birth intervals relating to the period 1800–49 came from the first two decades of the century). It is interesting to note that the rate for the ninth month varied very little (a proportion of these births were in any case post-nuptially conceived), and that therefore the rate for the period 0–7 months varied much more sharply than that for 0–8 months (by a factor of 3 between trough and peak). The period when prenuptial pregnancy was at its nadir was also the period when illegitimacy was rare and age at first marriage high, and vice versa. It would appear that social influences on fertility had a notable and consistent effect on all aspects of behaviour affecting fertility.

fluctuated more from cohort to cohort than did the average rates shown in the table, and there were substantial differences in their absolute level from place to place, but nothing to suggest that the lack of change in the average rates was adventitious. It seems reasonable to conclude, provisionally at least, that the wide swings in the level of the gross reproduction rate that took place between 1541 and 1871 owed very little to changes in marital fertility.

Reconstitution data on age at first marriage, on the other hand, suggest that nuptiality changes were highly important in influencing fertility changes in the early modern period. The changes are shown in table 7.26. They go far towards explaining how the gross reproduction rate came to vary as it did.

Table 7.26: Mean age at first marriages: means of 12 reconstitution studies

	1600–49	*1650–99*	*1700–49*	*1750–99*	*1800–49*
Male	28.0	27.8	27.5	26.4	25.3
Female	26.0	26.5	26.2	24.9	23.4

Note: The data were cohorted by date of marriage.

Source: Cambridge Group reconstitutions.

Although all 12 reconstitutions begin in the sixteenth century they provide very little usable marriage data before 1600. Since age at marriage is discovered by linking a baptism and a marriage record, in the early years of a reconstitution those who married young and whose baptism occurred within the parish register will appear in a tabulation of marriage ages, while those who married later in life will not. There will therefore be a downward bias in age at marriage calculated from parish registers until a sufficient time has elapsed for those who married late to have their baptism records within the file. In the circumstances it is prudent to use only marriages taking place 50 years or more after the beginning of registration in the parish and the table consequently begins with the half-century 1600–49. Male marriage age was then at its peak, declining slightly in the next two half-centuries before falling more markedly in the period after 1750. The pattern of change for women was not dissimilar but in their case the average age at first marriage was slightly higher in the period 1650–99 than in any other, and in 1700–49 still marginally higher than in 1600–49. After 1750 there was a rapid fall in female marriage age. Between 1650–99 and 1800–49 age at first marriage for women fell by 3.1 years. Since marriage age had fallen little in 1700–49, and most of the marriages represented in the 1800–49 cohort took place early in the century (some reconstitutions stopped in 1812 and very few went beyond 1837), most of the fall must have occurred during the second half of the eighteenth century.

The pattern of change was once more fairly uniform in the 12 parishes. The movements of the overall average were not dominated by the behaviour of a few 'rogue' parishes. Table 7.27 sets out the distribution of the periods of peak marriage age amongst the parishes. The table suggests that the data of table 7.26 may be somewhat misleading in that the near plateau in male marriage age may have ended by 1700 rather than extending into the early eighteenth century: only one of the parishes experienced a peak in male marriage age after 1700. The table also tends to reinforce

Table 7.27: Distribution of peak ages at first marriage in 12 parishes over five half-century periods

	1600–49	1650–99	1700–49	1750–99	1800–49	Total
Male	5	6	1	0	0	12
Female	4	5	3	0	0	12

Source: Cambridge Group reconstitutions.

the probability that the peak age at marriage for women came at a later date than for men since three parishes reached a peak value in 1700–49 compared with one for men, while only four peaked in 1600–49 compared with five in the case of men. The difference between the two sexes may possibly be bound up with the very heavy net emigration of the seventeenth century which must have reduced the male population of marriageable age far more than the female.

Too much should not be read into the relatively small movements in marriage age before the eighteenth century. Twelve parishes are too few to give confidence that small changes in marriage age countrywide were the same as those shown in table 7.26, but tables 7.26 and 7.27 between them provide strong evidence of a major fall in marriage age between the late seventeenth and the early nineteenth centuries. Given stability in marital fertility rates, a change in female marriage age as marked as that which appears to have occurred between 1650–99 and 1800–49, will cause a marked rise in the gross reproduction rate. It is safe to assume that the drop of three years in age at first marriage for women between the two half-centuries understates the extent of the fall from peak to trough since the marriage cohorts used embrace long and arbitrary time periods. Let us assume, however, for the sake of simplicity, that female marriage age fell from 26.5 to 23.5 years between the mid seventeenth and early nineteenth centuries. At the overall mean rates of marital fertility given in table 7.25 the increase in cumulative marital fertility achieved by age 45 is about 25 per cent (from 4.42 to 5.50 children). If the scale of the fall in marriage age in the 12 parishes is representative but the absolute ages in the country as a whole were higher (say, 27.5 and 24.5 years) the proportionate effect on fertility would be greater; if lower, less. As a first approximation, however, we may assume that the fall in marriage age increased fertility by about a quarter.

Over the period during which the change in marriage age was occurring the gross reproduction rate rose from about 2.0 in the second half of the seventeenth century to about 2.9 in the first quarter of the nineteenth century. Earlier marriage alone would therefore account for more than half of the rise in the GRR. But there were other changes directly or indirectly linked to changing marriage age which between them suggest that a full understanding of the behaviour of the marriage market in England would go far towards explaining changes in overall fertility, and thus in turn population trends generally, since we have already seen that fertility changes dominated the demographic scene in eighteenth-century England. The collective impact of the several factors associated with changing marriage patterns is most easily appreciated by constructing a simplified model to identify their relative importance, covering not only age at marriage but also proportions never marrying, illegitimacy ratios, and mean age at maternity. Information about changing levels of illegitimacy is to hand, and changes in mean age at maternity can be estimated roughly from a knowledge of changes in marriage age, but the question of the proportions never marrying calls for some prior consideration.

Proportions never marrying

The incidence of marriage is closely related to its timing. There is a general tendency in western societies for early marriage to be associated with low levels of permanent celibacy (remaining single throughout life), and for late marriage to go with a higher level of permanent celibacy. It is therefore most unfortunate that there is no direct and general evidence about the detailed incidence of marriage in England before the census of 1851. Nor is it possible to make the type of indirect estimates from reconstitution studies that have proved possible in France or in other countries in which marital status and age are routinely recorded in burial registers.[97] Such information is too sporadic to be useful in English registers.

Other types of indirect estimation are, however, possible. Livi-Bacci, for example, in discussing a variety of demographic measurements that can be attempted even when only aggregate data are available, suggested a method of tackling the problem.[98] He argued that there is a close correlation between the number of births occurring in any given 10-year period and the number of marriages taking place 25 years later, and that the difference between the two totals must represent the combined effect of death or migration before marriage on the one hand, and permanent celibacy on the other. However his procedure for calculating the proportion never marrying involved the assumptions that fertility was constant and that net migration was zero, which back projection has shown to be inappropriate for early modern England.

The estimates of proportions never marrying shown below in table 7.28 were obtained, therefore, in a manner designed to exploit the fuller information afforded by back projection. For each five-year birth cohort an estimate can be made of the number of marriages involving its members by using a fixed age schedule to divide up marriages occurring in quinquennial blocks between 15 and 40 years later, allocating a share of each five-year total to the birth cohort in question.[99] The marriage total for

97. See, for example, Gautier and Henry, *Crulai*, pp. 74–6.
98. Livi-Bacci, 'Can anything be said about demographic trends?'.
99. Since back projection makes no distinction between the sexes, the age schedule used in allocating marriages to birth cohorts was derived from reconstitution data to reflect the mean experience of the 12 parishes for the sexes combined. Note that a quinquennial birth cohort is aged approximately 2.50 years on average at the *end* of the quinquennium. Thus its average age will be 12.50 years at the beginning of the quinquennium starting 15 years after the *beginning* of the birth cohort quinquennium, and 17.49 years at the *end* of the quinquennium. Similarly its average age will be 37.50 years at the beginning of the quinquennium starting 40 years later and 42.49 years at its end. Since very few first marriages occurred to men and women aged more than 42.50 years, the age schedule was constrained to ensure that all marriages occurred by this age.

The following table shows the proportional split of marriages by age for each quinquennium starting between 15 and 40 years after the beginning of the birth cohort quinquennium.

Age group at end of quinquennium	Range of mean ages	Proportion of marriages
15–9	12.50–17.49	.0275
20–4	17.50–22.49	.3325
25–9	22.50–27.49	.3750
30–4	27.50–32.49	.1575
35–9	32.50–37.49	.0725
40–4	37.50–42.49	.0350

The procedure is unreal in that it takes no account of changing age at marriage. This point is discussed further below, pp. 261–3.

the cohort as a whole will therefore be made up of separate sub-totals entering marriage in successive five-year age groups. Each such age group sub-total of married persons is then reduced to reflect the mortality experience of the cohort between the age group of marriage and the age group 40– 4 using the cohort life tables provided by back projection. If these totals of surviving married persons are cumulated, the number of surviving married persons aged 40– 4 is obtained. Subtracting this total from the total number aged 40– 4 given by back projection yields an estimate of the number never marrying in the cohort.

Four points should be borne in mind in considering the results produced by this method. First, the estimated number of surviving married persons aged 40– 4 is a function of marriage totals and general mortality rates only. The calculation therefore assumes that the mortality of married people was the same as that of the population as a whole. This assumption cannot be tested for lack of suitable historical evidence, though since a high proportion of adults married overall mortality is unlikely to be very different from that of the married population. It is also implicitly assumed that there was no net migration of married people, whereas the population totals with which the totals of married people are compared reflect, of course, the joint effect of migration and mortality. It is highly probable that married people migrated much less freely than single persons, but there may at times have been sufficient net emigration among the married population to affect the estimated proportions never marrying and in such circumstances the estimated proportions will be too low. Second, as has been mentioned elsewhere, it is probable that the total of marriages in the later seventeenth century is too low, being affected by the prevalence of clandestine marriage,[100] and that in consequence the estimated total of married people aged 40– 4 will also be too low, causing the proportion of 'never-married' people to be overestimated. Third, the results are sensitive to the assumptions made in specifying the schedule that allocates marriages to individual birth cohorts, especially in periods when the number of marriages was rising fast (see below, pp. 261–3). Finally, and by far the most important point, the calculation of the numbers never marrying requires the elimination of those marriage partners who were not marrying for the first time, otherwise double counting will lead to serious errors. Unfortunately, English marriage registers provide only very sporadic and incomplete evidence about the proportion of those marrying who were widows or widowers. From such scraps of evidence as exist it appears clear that a far higher proportion of all marriages were remarriages in earlier periods than in the nineteenth century. Perhaps as many as 30 per cent of all those marrying were widows or widowers in the mid sixteenth century, a situation that may owe much to mortality crises.[101] By the mid nineteenth century, in contrast, it is clear

100. See above, pp. 28–9, 190–1.

101. Very few English parish registers consistently record the marital status of brides and grooms in the period before the coming into effect of Hardwicke's Marriage Act in 1754, but there are occasional exceptions to this rule. Information drawn from two parishes is tabulated below. The percentages refer to the proportion of all brides and grooms who were widowed.

	Percentage of all those marrying who were widows or widowers	Number of marriages
Landbeach, Cambs.		
1595–1694	28.6	251
1695–1794	19.2	202
Beccles, Suffolk		
1608–41	22.7	429
1662–1700	26.4	492

from civil registration returns that the comparable proportion was much lower at 11.27 per cent.[102]

In the absence of dependable and representative evidence about remarriage before the nineteenth century any solution to this problem must at present be arbitrary. We have assumed that the proportion of all brides and grooms who were widowed declined linearly from 30 per cent in 1541 to 11.27 per cent in 1851, even though it is, of course, improbable that change took place smoothly over so long a period.

The resulting estimates are set out in table 7.28. The proportions listed are five-point moving averages of those for individual cohorts. Thus the figure of 84 given for 1556 refers to the five cohorts born 1541–6 to 1561–6, and so on. The individual figures fluctuate more widely than those shown, being subject in some instances to major distortions from mortality crises with which a fixed age schedule of marriage is too inflexible to deal satisfactorily.[103]

We may begin by considering the accuracy of the results obtained in the middle of the nineteenth century when they can be compared with census data. The proportion of those never married at age 45–54 in the censuses of 1851, 1861, and 1871 was 11.9, 11.2, and 10.9 per cent respectively.[104] These figures may be compared with the proportions listed in the table for the cohorts aged 40–4 in 1841, 1851, and 1861 (9.6, 11.0, and 10.7 per cent). This is the most appropriate comparison to make even though the census figures are 10 years later in each case because the schedule by which marriages were distributed among the cohort age groups constrains all marriages to take place by the time the cohort is aged 40–4, whereas in reality a small number of first marriages occur at a later age, so that the census proportions at a slightly higher age give a better estimate of the proportion of those who never marry. The agreement between the estimates and the census proportions is very close in two of the three cases, but less good in the third. In view of the fact that the estimates in table 7.28 are five-point moving averages, and that the census data should probably be

1701–54	21.2	789
1754–80	17.8	458
1781–1809	17.4	570

Hollingsworth's study of the British peerage also shows a considerable fall in the proportion of remarriages. The percentages of remarriages for the sexes combined for the five successive half-centuries 1600–49 to 1800–49 were 19.7, 19.8, 14.3, 14.0, and 10.7. These figures were derived by giving an equal weight to the percentages for men and women taken separately, and represent the data for the *cohorts* born 1575–1624 to 1775–1824 (that is, it was assumed that the *current* proportion of remarriages could be estimated satisfactorily by offsetting the cohort figures by a quarter century). Hollingsworth, 'Demography of the British peerage', p. 14, table 4. Similar but slightly higher percentages are obtained if the alternative data set given by Hollingsworth is used (p. 21, table 13).

In Worcestershire the mortality crisis of the late 1720s raised the percentage of widows and widowers amongst marriage partners from 15 to 25 over a two-year period. Johnston, 'The impact of the epidemics of 1727–30', p. 291.

102. This figure represents the average proportion during a 15-year period centring on 1851 (data from the Registrar-General's *Annual Reports*).

103. For example, the individual figure for the 1556–61 cohort is −197 and that for 1726–31 is −32. Such negative figures arise because the age schedule of marriage allocates too many marriages to the severely depleted birth cohorts in question, but the effect is offset by compensating effects in adjoining cohorts.

104. The percentages relate to England less Monmouth. Source references to the sections of the 1851, 1861, and 1871 censuses containing details of marital status by age may be found at the foot of table 10.3.

Table 7.28: Estimated proportions of people never marrying by cohort (per 1 000 aged 40–4) in England: five-point centred moving averages

(1) Year in which cohort aged 0–4	(2) Year in which cohort aged 40–4	(3) Proportion never marrying	(1) Year in which cohort aged 0–4	(2) Year in which cohort aged 40–4	(3) Proportion never marrying
1556	1596	84	1691	1731	128
1561	1601	67	1696	1736	131
1566	1606	42	1701	1741	112
1571	1611	57	1706	1746	96
1576	1616	135	1711	1751	107
1581	1621	147	1716	1756	107
1586	1626	174	1721	1761	73
1591	1631	205	1726	1766	86
1596	1636	229	1731	1771	77
1601	1641	241	1736	1776	46
1606	1646	242	1741	1781	36
1611	1651	236	1746	1786	62
1616	1656	214	1751	1791	49
1621	1661	188	1756	1796	52
1626	1666	171	1761	1801	68
1631	1671	181	1766	1806	72
1636	1676	208	1771	1811	65
1641	1681	241	1776	1816	63
1646	1686	270	1781	1821	71
1651	1691	270	1786	1826	78
1656	1696	267	1791	1831	75
1661	1701	249	1796	1836	82
1666	1706	230	1801	1841	96
1671	1711	191	1806	1846	102
1676	1716	185	1811	1851	110
1681	1721	176	1816	1856	119
1686	1726	147	1821	1861	107

Source: Back-projection tabulations.

Notes: For details of the method used in constructing the series see text. The readings are five-point moving averages centred on the years shown.

regarded as subject to a margin of error,[105] the comparison of the estimates and the census returns is reassuring.

It is convenient at this point to enlarge upon an issue mentioned briefly above, which bears upon the assessment of the results contained in table 7.28, and any comparison between them and other sources of information about proportions never marrying. The schedule used in dividing up marriages occurring in each quinquennium between the cohorts aged 15–9 to 40–4 at the end of the quinquennium was obtained from reconstitution data and represents a distribution with a mean age at first marriage for men of 26.9 years, and 25.9 years for women. It was selected because it represents approximately the average age at marriage found in the 12 reconstitution parishes over the whole 300-year period.[106] But it is also clear that age at marriage varied over time, and in particular that it fell sharply during the eighteenth century (table 7.26). Any change in marriage age will alter the proportionate allocation of marriages between the cohorts of marriageable age, and as may be seen in figure 7.15 this may cause substantial changes in the estimated proportions never marrying.

Any change in the age schedule of marriage that increases the proportion allocated to the younger age groups must increase the estimated proportion never marrying because the marriages allocated to any particular cohort will be exposed longer on average to the wasting effect of mortality. But the effect will be much stronger during a period in which the number of marriages is rising rapidly than when there is little change in the total of marriages from one quinquennium to the next. In figure 7.15 the heavy line represents the estimates already given in table 7.15, while the upper and lower lines represent respectively the estimates that result if average age at first marriage is taken to be 24.4 years (male 25.1, female 23.7) and 27.5 years (male 28.1, female 26.9).[107] Since the number of marriages did not rise very greatly until the end of the seventeenth century, the upper and lower lines remain close to the main

---

105. For example, the percentages of those never married given by Mitchell and Deane, and drawn from the nineteenth-century censuses of England and Wales, reveal occasional oddities. The female percentages never married in the cohorts aged 45–54 in the censuses of 1851 to 1871 show a tendency to fall with increasing age, but in the comparable cohorts of the censuses of 1881 to 1901 the percentages reported as never married are higher when the cohorts have reached the age group 75–84 than they were when the same cohorts were aged 45–54. It seems improbable that the relative mortality of single, married, and widowed women could have changed so greatly as to have produced this change in pattern, and more likely that there was a change in the accuracy of reporting marital status. There was no comparable change in male percentages. Mitchell and Deane, *British historical statistics*, pp. 15–6.

106. The data refer to Banbury which had an average marriage pattern over the whole reconstitution period from the late sixteenth to the early nineteenth centuries.

107. The 'young' pattern was derived from marriage data in the parish of Gedling in the period 1800–49; the 'old' pattern from Hartland in the period 1725–74.

The proportional distributions of marriages between the age groups (to be compared with the 'standard' distribution set out in fn. 99) were as follows:

Age group at end of quinquennium	Proportion of marriages	
	'Young'	'Old'
15–9	.0850	.0125
20–4	.5100	.2150
25–9	.2650	.4125
30–4	.0975	.2225
35–9	.0250	.0925
40–4	.0175	.0450

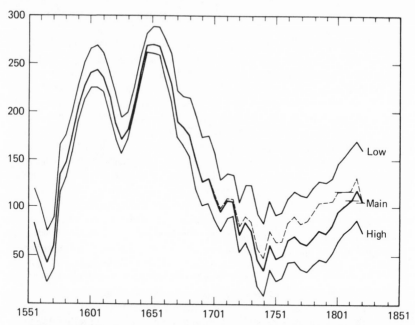

Figure 7.15: Estimated proportions never marrying on various assumptions about age at marriage

Notes: See text for details of the assumptions lying behind the estimates relating to low, central, and high age at marriage alternatives. The data refer to the proportion never marrying per 1000 surviving to the age group 40-4 in cohorts born in the quinquennial periods ending at the dates indicated. Each reading represents a 5-point moving average of such proportions. The three horizontal bars drawn at 1801, 1811, and 1821 represent the proportions never married in the appropriate comparable mid-nineteenth-century cenuses. The broken line represents a modified estimate (for details see text).

estimate for more than a century, but thereafter the upper and lower bounds diverge much more substantially from the main estimate. The broken line which begins in 1701 and continues through to 1821 shows the degree to which the main run estimates might be changed on reasonable if arbitrary assumptions about changing age at marriage. Guided by the evidence of table 7.26 we assumed that between 1701 and 1791 the marriage age schedule moved linearly from the schedule used in the main run to a schedule representing a 60 per cent shift towards the very young age at first marriage embodied in the upper bound estimate. Between 1791 and 1821 the schedule was assumed to move linearly back towards the main run assumption about marriage age. Modifying the marriage age schedule in this way reflects the view that marriage age fell sharply during the eighteenth century but rose again early in the next century.[108] It is probable that the dotted line represents a closer approximation to the

108. The year 1791 was chosen as the turning point having it in mind that the low age at first marriage figures for men and women in the period 1800– 49 in table 7.26 refer principally to the first two decades of the century since some reconstitutions finished in 1811 and most of the remainder in 1837. The birth cohort to which the low point might notionally refer, therefore, would consist of those born in the last years of the eighteenth century. There is as yet very little direct evidence that age at marriage began to rise in the second quarter of the nineteenth century, as implied in figure 7.15, but strong indirect evidence is presented below in figure 10.11.

truth than the main run results and it is interesting to note that the new estimates suggest that the percentages never marrying in the cohorts aged 40–4 in 1841, 1851, and 1861 were 11.7, 12.0, and 10.7, compared with figures of 9.6, 11.0, and 10.7 in the main run and comparable census figures of 11.9, 11.2, and 10.9 respectively. Clearly all estimated proportions never marrying should be regarded as lying within a probability band rather than as precise figures.

Despite their necessary lack of precision there appears to be little difficulty in accepting the broad accuracy of the pattern of change revealed in table 7.28 and figure 7.15 between, say, the cohorts born in the 1680s and the end of the series in the nineteenth century. The proportion never marrying begins at a high level in the 1680s cohorts when it was about 16 per cent but thereafter falls steadily to bottom out at a very low level, about 4–7 per cent, in the cohorts born in the 1730s and 1740s (and therefore marrying chiefly in the 1750s and 1760s). Thereafter there is very little change until the cohorts born in the 1780s. In these and the subsequent cohorts, however, the proportion never marrying begins to rise to reach 10–2 per cent in the most recent cohorts. These changes accord well with the changes in age at first marriage revealed by reconstitution studies (table 7.26). Marriage age fell steadily and substantially throughout the eighteenth century. If both series are reliable guides to marriage behaviour they suggest that changes in the proportions marrying tend to antedate somewhat those in age at marriage.[109]

The cohorts born in the late sixteenth and the first three quarters of the seventeenth century present a greater challenge to interpretation. In the earliest cohorts shown in table 7.28 the proportions never marrying are not very different from the proportions found in the mid eighteenth century, 4–8 per cent. After the first five readings, however, the figures rise steeply to reach about 24 per cent among the cohorts born about the turn of the sixteenth century, and, after a substantial fall a quarter of a century later, they rise even higher to about 27 per cent in the cohorts born in the mid century and therefore marrying in the 1670s and 1680s (it is plausible, however, to assume that the lower bound estimates in figure 7.15 are to be preferred to those in the table since age at marriage was high in the later seventeenth century). A rise in the proportion never marrying during the later sixteenth and early seventeenth centuries is not surprising in view of the very steep fall in real wages during the period, though the very high absolute level reached may come as a surprise. For the later decades of the seventeenth century it is also misleading. In the Restoration period clandestine marriage was widespread. Where this resulted in a marked fall in the number of marriages recorded in an individual parish, it will have been corrected by the program designed to detect under-registration,[110] but where the fall was modest or gradual it will have escaped correction.[111] The second wave of high proportions never marrying, beginning with the cohort born in 1636, therefore, may safely be regarded as exaggerating the phenomenon.

The earlier wave may be thought to represent a greater puzzle. It may be genuine: the highest figures coincide with the period in which real wages were at their lowest

109. There is further discussion of the joint effect of changes in the timing and incidence of marriage as reflected in corrected crude marriage rates in chapter 10 below, especially pp. 428–9.
110. See pp. 20–3 above and appendices 12–3.
111. It is indicative of the continued effect of clandestine marriage on marriage totals that the birth/marriage ratios in the Restoration period should be relatively high, even though fertility was low. For example, the ratio over the four decades 1660–99 was 4.12 compared with 3.83 in the next 40 years 1700–39 (table A2.1) though fertility rose considerably between the two periods.

point in the 700-year span covered by the Phelps Brown and Hopkins index.[112] High figures have been recorded in other countries suffering from comparable stresses. For example, the percentages of men and women who had never married in the age group 45–9 in Sweden in 1900 were 13.5 and 19.4 respectively, having risen from much lower levels earlier in the century before population pressure had built up to the degree experienced later in the century (in 1800 the comparable figures were 6.9 and 11.7). In post-famine Ireland, too, very high figures were recorded. In 1911, for example, the male and female percentages never married in the age group 45–54 were 29 and 24 respectively (in 1851 the comparable percentages were only 12 and 11).[113] Remarkable increases in the proportions never marrying can also be shown to have occurred in the British peerage in the seventeenth century. Hollingsworth's gross nuptiality tables for this elite group suggest that the proportion of each cohort remaining permanently single rose very steeply between the cohort born 1550–74, when only 4 per cent of the males and 9 per cent of the females never married, and the cohorts born towards the end of the seventeenth century, when the percentage for both sexes rose to well over 20.[114] On the other hand, it is also possible that the proportion of remarriages is overestimated and the percentage never marrying therefore exaggerated. For example, the assumption of linear decline between 1541 and 1851 in the percentage of all marriages that were remarriages produces an estimated level of about 25 per cent for the cohort born in 1601. If, however, remarriage was less frequent than has been assumed, and first marriages comprised 80 rather than 75 per cent of all marriages in this cohort, the proportion never marrying would fall from 24 to 19 per cent. The evidence of the Beccles marriage register suggests that this possibility should be taken seriously (see fn. 101).

It is worth noting that the fall in the proportions never marrying visible in the cohorts born between 1616 and 1636 comes about largely because of the high level of the marriage rate during the period of civil marriage under the Commonwealth. Assuming that registration of marriage became for a time complete in the 1650s, this may suggest the extent of the distortion of the level of celibacy because of clandestine marriage later in the century.[115]

It is also worth noting how important changes in the incidence of marriage may well have been in influencing movements in the GRR during the seventeenth century. Table 7.26 suggests that there were no major changes in age at marriage during the century[116] but table 7.28 and figure 7.15 show that there were probably major changes in proportions never marrying, though interpretation of the data is complicated by the problem of clandestine marriage. If, however, it is assumed that the proportions never marrying rose throughout the later sixteenth century to reach a peak amongst the cohorts born in the first decade of the seventeenth century and thereafter tended in general to fall during the rest of the century, it seems clear that changes in the

112. See table A9.2 and figure 10.9.
113. Sundbärg, *Bevölkerungsstatistik Schwedens*, pp. 96–7: Kennedy, *The Irish*, p. 144. The proportions never marrying rose even higher in Ireland to reach a peak in the 1930s and 1940s.
114. Hollingsworth, 'Demography of the British peerage', p. 17.
115. It may be of interest to note that Hardwicke's Marriage Act a century later does not appear to have made a very marked difference to the completeness of marriage registration. This is partly because the prevalence of clandestine marriage appears to have declined very greatly in the early eighteenth century except in London, and partly because the London marriage totals are estimated indirectly (see p. 30 above).
116. The half-century periods of table 7.26 are so long that they might conceal important changes in age at marriage (e.g. a peak in the middle of the century flanked by lower levels at its beginning and end), but sub-division into quarter-century blocks also shows no significant variation in marriage age.

incidence of marriage might account for a substantial part of the long term changes in the GRR show in figure 7.8 *Ceteris paribus* a rise in the proportion never marrying from, say, 8 to 24 per cent, such as took place between the cohorts born before 1570 and those born early in the seventeenth century, would reduce overall fertility by 17 per cent, which is about the percentage by which the GRR fell in the first half of the seventeenth century (with a mean age at maternity in the early 30s, of course, the maximum effect on measures of current fertility such as the GRR of changes in the incidence of marriage in a given birth cohort will occur some 30–5 years later). Equally, a subsequent fall in the proportion never marrying would have a commensurate but opposite effect.

The method we have used to try to identify changes in the incidence of marriage among cohorts born between the Elizabethan and Victorian periods is only capable of producing estimates subject to a substantial margin of error. Nevertheless the patterns that emerge are bold in outline and it seems safe to conclude that marriage incidence varied considerably over time and in a manner likely to reinforce the effect of changes in age at marriage on total fertility.[117] When age at first marriage was high in the later seventeenth century, the proportion of those never marrying was also high, and by the later eighteenth century, when age at first marriage had fallen by about three years, the proportion never marrying had also fallen considerably. It seems conservative to assume that the proportion fell from 15 to 7 per cent over much the same period that age at first marriage for women was falling from 26.5 to 23.5 years.

For all its imperfections the information contained in table 7.28 is also important in providing valuable supporting evidence of the general accuracy of back projection. It will be recalled that the totals of marriages found in the parish registers were subjected to very few alterations because of supposed deficiencies. Apart from a very slight adjustment in respect of Quaker marriages, registration was assumed complete. In the early nineteenth century when the inflation factors applied to baptisms and burials to produce totals of births and deaths were as high as 1.513 and 1.516 respectively, the comparable inflation factor for marriages was only 1.002.[118] If the totals of births and deaths used in back projection were significantly inaccurate, or if the logic of the back projection program were faulty, it is unlikely that estimates of the total of married persons aged 40–4 made by combining a knowledge of marriage totals with cohort mortality data and age structure estimates derived from back projection would produce results that square with the nineteenth-century censuses and are generally plausible at other periods, except by an extraordinary sequence of offsetting errors. Since estimated proportions never marrying are always quite low they are vulnerable to relatively small errors in each of the components of the calculation. The exercise of calculating the proportions therefore constitutes a severe independent test of the reliability of the corrections made to the original series of events and of the accuracy of the estimates of mortality and of the age structure of the population produced by back projection.

A simple model of the changes in the components of fertility that led to population growth in the eighteenth century

The scale of the changes in the timing and incidence of marriage in the early modern

117. This issue is discussed in a different context in chapter 10 below, especially pp. 421–30.
118. The peak inflation ratio for births occurred in the year 1816, for deaths in 1815. The marriage ratio quoted applied to each year between 1800 and 1830. See table A4.1.

period have now been examined. In order to construct a model of the combined effect of changes in the several factors affecting fertility, however, it is first necessary to discuss the scale of changes in the level of illegitimacy and in the mean age at maternity.

There is much empirical evidence about the close relationship between age at marriage and illegitimacy ratios. It might seem natural to expect illegitimacy to be common when marriage was late because many men and women would be sexually mature but unmarried. In certain circumstances, like those to be found in Bavaria in the early nineteenth century,[119] this may be so, but it is often the case that when marriage is late illegitimacy ratios are low. Nor is this necessarily surprising. Rules of social conduct that have sufficient strength to prevent the young from marrying until their later twenties, and that keep a significant minority unmarried for life, are also likely to be effective in preventing less permanent unions. Conversely, where marriage is early and almost universal, sanctions against intercourse outside marriage may be weak.

At all events there was a major rise in the illegitimacy ratio between the mid seventeenth and early nineteenth centuries. It moved in sympathy with changes in marriage age and was on a sufficient scale to have substantial impact on overall fertility.[120] In the second half of the seventeenth century the ratio stood at about 1.5 per cent, but by the early nineteenth century had risen to about 6 per cent.[121] The ratio rose only moderately until the mid eighteenth century but then shot up rapidly, mirroring the opposite trend in age at first marriage.[122]

A further factor connected to change in marriage age and affecting population growth rates is the mean age at maternity. A fall in marriage age will reduce the mean age at maternity, other things being equal, and this in turn will boost fertility by ensuring that a larger proportion of women survive to reproduce. Mean age at maternity is most conveniently derived from a general fertility schedule. Reconstitution studies provide information about marital fertility by age, but not about general fertility, which will, of course, be affected by the proportions married in each age group, and by the distribution of illegitimate births by age, no longer a negligible element in the total picture by the early nineteenth century. However, bearing in mind the evidence of table 7.25 about marital fertility rates by age, and on the assumption that female age at first marriage fell from 26.5 to 23.5 years, it is reasonable to suppose that mean age at maternity would fall from about 33 to 31 years. Assuming further that mortality was constant at level 8 of the Princeton North tables (female $e_0 = 37.5$ years), the proportion of women surviving to the mean age at maternity would rise from 0.5381 to 0.5506.

The cumulative effect on population growth rates of the four factors we have discussed (age at marriage, proportions marrying, illegitimacy levels, and the mean age at maternity) may be grasped by considering table 7.29. The table is designed to represent in a stylized form the impact of changes in marriage behaviour between the

119. See Knodel, 'Law, marriage and illegitimacy'
120. The illegitimacy ratio measures the proportion of all births that are illegitimate. It is simple to calculate but a crude measure, the deficiencies of which are discussed by Drake, 'Norway', especially pp. 301–2.
121. See Laslett, *Family life*, ch. 3, 'Long term trends in bastardy in England' and especially figure 3.2 on p. 115.
122. Prenuptial pregnancy percentages displayed trends very similar to those found in the illegitimacy ratios and further emphasize the power and consistency of social influences on fertility behaviour in early modern England. See fn. 96, p. 254 above.

later seventeenth and early nineteenth centuries, holding mortality and marital fertility constant. The comparison is made by calculating gross and net reproduction rates and the intrinsic growth rates that each set of circumstances implies.

Table 7.29: Two models designed to illustrate the effect of changes in the components of fertility in changing intrinsic growth rates

Model	(1) Total marital fertility	(2) Correction for celibacy	(3) Correction for illegitimacy	(4) Convert to GRR	(5) Convert to NRR	(6) Convert to intrinsic growth rate
I	4.42	3.76	3.81	1.86	1.00	0.0000
II	5.50	5.12	5.44	2.65	1.46	0.0126
I	100	100	100	100	100	
II	124	136	143	143	146	

Notes: Column 1   Marital fertility rates in both models as shown in table 7.25 (average for all periods of 12 reconstitution parishes); female mean ages at first marriage 26.5 years (model I) and 23.5 years (model II).

Column 2   Proportion never marrying 0.15 (model I) and 0.07 (model II).

Column 3   Illegitimacy ratio 1.5 per cent (model I) and 6.0 per cent (model II).

Column 4   Sex ratio at birth 105 males per 100 females (i.e. column 4 = column 3 × 100/205).

Column 5   Mortality in both models as in Princeton model North female tables, level 8 (e_0 = 37.5 years). Mean age at maternity 33 years (model I), 31 years (model II). NRR = $p(\bar{m})$. GRR.

Column 6   Intrinsic growth rate $r = \log_e$ NRR/t.

Mean generation length, $\quad t = \bar{m} - \sigma^2 \dfrac{\log \text{GRR}}{2\bar{m}}$

For further details see text.

It will be recalled that the net reproduction rate is the product of the probability of reaching the mean age at maternity, $\bar{m}$, and the gross reproduction rate; that r, the intrinsic growth rate, can be derived from the NRR if t, the mean generation length, is known; and that t can be estimated from a knowledge of $\bar{m}$ and the level of the GRR.[123] If, therefore, the GRR can be determined, the other elements necessary to calculate the NRR and r are to hand. In table 7.29 an estimated GRR was obtained by assuming that each woman who married for the first time did so at the mean age at first marriage and that she then experienced the marital fertility rates shown in table 7.25 as representing the average experience of the 12 reconstitution parishes over the early modern period as a whole. The resulting cumulative fertility totals were then modified to reflect the effects of the proportion never marrying and of the illegitimacy ratio. These in turn were multiplied by the ratio of female births to all births to provide an estimated GRR. And, finally, net reproduction rates and intrinsic growth rates were derived using the formulae set out earlier in the chapter.[124]

Twenty years ago Habakkuk, in the course of a general survey of the relationship between demographic and economic change in early modern Britain, remarked with

123. See above, pp. 236–8.
124. See above, pp. 236, 237.

commendable caution: 'We obviously need to find out much more about age at marriage and nuptiality, but I am not convinced that we must at this stage reject the possibility that a fall of two or three years in age at marriage, plus some increase in nuptiality, *could* have caused an acceleration of the rate of growth of the sort we observe in the later eighteenth century'.[125] By considering the behaviour of the two model populations in table 7.29, we can look again at this issue in the light of the findings of back projection.

Since mortality and marital fertility were held constant in the two model populations, the impact of other factors, all of which were directly or indirectly connected to the timing and incidence of marriage, is made easily visible and their relative importance can be gauged. Taken together, as in column 5 of table 7.29, the changes raise the net reproduction rate very considerably from 1.00 to 1.46, implying an increase in the intrinsic growth rate from zero to 1.26 per cent per annum. According to back projection the average level of the net reproduction rate in England in the second half of the seventeenth century was almost exactly 1.00, but during the first quarter of the nineteenth century it was on average about 63 per cent higher.[126] Thus almost three quarters of this rise is attributable to changes in the marriage-related phenomena incorporated in table 7.29. Relaxing the assumption that mortality was constant enables the balance of the increase in the NRR to be accounted for, since mortality improved substantially in the course of the eighteenth century. For example, if, following the mortality estimates from back projection, e_0 is allowed to improve by five years from level 8 (model I) to level 10 (model II), the NRR rises to 1.63, which is the same as the average level found by back projection in the first quarter of the nineteenth century.[127]

Assuming that the differences between model I and model II capture adequately, if crudely, the scale of the changes in nuptiality that occurred in England between the Restoration and the end of the Napoleonic Wars, it is remarkable that although back projection identifies a rise in fertility as the principal agent of population growth, in doing so it proves to be paying tribute to the primacy of nuptiality in directing the course of events, even though, ironically, it makes no use of marriage totals. In the event Habakkuk's foresight in wishing to retain the possibility of changes in marriage as the prime cause of population growth in the eighteenth century has proved amply justified. A little earlier Mackenroth had expressed the view that marriage was the key variable in determining population trends in pre-industrial Europe, and he too has been vindicated in the case of early modern England.[128] Mackenroth argued forcefully that marriage was crucial precisely because it was a socially defined and

125. Habakkuk, 'The economic history of modern Britain', p. 493.

126. Table A3.1.

127. Expectation of life at birth improved by five years (two mortality levels) between the 25-year periods covered by the quinquennia centred on the years 1676 to 1696 and those centred on 1806 to 1826 (table A3.1), though the absolute levels of expectation of life were slightly less than levels 8 and 10 of model North.

128. Mackenroth, *Bevölkerungslehre*. After having remarked that mortality was high in pre-industrial Europe and that marital fertility was also high, he stressed the key rôle of marriage in facilitating an accommodation between population size and the productive potential of a country or community at the prevailing level of material technology. '*So bleiben Heiratsalter und Heiratshäufigkeit die Variablen des generativen Verhaltens. Uber sie vollzieht sich die Anpassung von Bevölkerungsvorgang und Wirtschaftsvorgang*' (p. 120). Mackenroth's general point has a special force where mortality is *not* high for then changes in age at marriage exert a relatively greater influence on fertility levels. See Crafts and Ireland, 'A simulation of the impact of changes in age at marriage'.

controlled act, the means by which an accommodation could be reached between a population and its economic circumstances.

We discuss this issue and related questions further in chapter 10, but turn now to an examination of the sensitivity of the findings of back projection described in this chapter to alternative views about the totals of vital events that occurred in the past and to alternative assumptions about critical variables in the internal procedures of estimation.

Sensitivity tests: alternative data sets

Although the national totals of births and deaths used in back projection were calculated to the last digit, we have stressed that they can never be more than best estimates, each subject to a margin of error. Indeed, even if by good fortune precisely accurate totals had been obtained, there would be no way in which their accuracy could be established. It is therefore prudent to try to discover whether the fertility and mortality findings of back projection are sensitive to changes in the data of the scale that would be produced by different assumptions about Anglican registration coverage or about the appropriate level of correction needed, especially in the early nineteenth century when parochial registration was least comprehensive. In particular it is desirable to find out whether changes in results induced by alterations in the data tend to become cumulatively greater over so long a period of time as the three centuries covered in back projection. Having discussed the implications of alternative data sets, we shall also look briefly at the extent to which alternative assumptions about cohort migration schedules and mortality schedules and the accuracy of the initial age structure might have affected the empirical results obtained from back projection.

To have investigated every aspect of the question of alternative data sets would have occupied much space. We have chosen to concentrate on a limited range of possibilities which might be thought to embody the thinking of those whose considerations of defects in parochial registration or of coverage in the early censuses has led them to different conclusions from those reached in the first five chapters of this book. This means considering the effect of different degrees of inflation of the basic series over long periods of time. We have not investigated more esoteric alternatives such as the possibility, say, that there was a massive deterioration in coverage limited to a brief period: for example, that birth totals in the 1700s should be raised 20 per cent relative to those for the 1690s and 1710s.[129] It is important to remember in this connexion the close correspondence between the reweighted totals of events derived from the 404 parishes in the aggregative sample and the totals found in Rickman's national survey of the 1830s (see tables 3.1 and 3.2). This tends to restrict reasonable alternative assumptions to different percentage inflations of the same basic totals of ecclesiastical events.

Six new data sets were constructed as follows.

1. Assume that the number of births was never less than 10 per cent greater than the number of Anglican baptisms, and the number of deaths never less than the 5 per cent greater than the number of Anglican burials. The national totals of Anglican baptisms

---

129. The data used in the main back-projection run do themselves embody, of course, the view that between about 1780 and 1830 there was a very great deterioration in Anglican parish register coverage, and the under-registration detection program resulted in a very large increase in baptism and burial totals in periods like the Civil War (table A4.1).

and burials were therefore multiplied by 1.1 and 1.05 respectively and wherever the resulting total was larger than in our national estimate it was substituted. This meant increasing the birth total for each quinquennium earlier than 1706, and the death total for each quinquennium earlier than 1726. In this and other new data sets that involved changes affecting totals back to 1541 (sets 1, 2, 4, and 6) the manufactured totals of births and deaths stretching back for a century before 1541 were also modified.[130] The birth totals were increased by the ratio used in 1541 and the death totals were raised by the same absolute amount as the birth totals, so that with no net migration the population in the mid fifteenth century would differ from that of 1541 by the same amount as in the main back projection.

2. Assume that birth and death totals were correct for the period 1781–1871 but that totals in both series should be raised by 1 per cent in 1776–81, 2 per cent in 1771–6, 3 per cent in 1766–71, 4 per cent in 1761–6, and 5 per cent in all earlier quinquennia. All the changes were made by inflating appropriately the totals used in the main run. These totals reflect the view that the existence of age data in the early-nineteenth-century censuses permits the true totals of births and deaths to be estimated with fair precision from about 1781 onwards but that before 1781 escapes from registration due to nonconformity or other reasons were more serious than allowed for in the main data set and that the two series were equally affected. For pre-1541 totals see simulation 1 above.

3. Assume that the total of females enumerated in the 1811 census was still understated by 1 per cent even after the correction made to offset the under-registration of young children. The earlier correction had added 1.1 per cent to the registered total. Similarly, assume that in 1801 there was a more serious undercounting of the total female population requiring the total to be increased by a further 3 per cent in addition to the correction for under-registration of young children (which had also added 1.1 per cent to the census total). It has been widely assumed that coverage was incomplete in the early censuses, and that it was worst in the first and thereafter improved.[131] Assuming greater deficiencies of coverage in 1801 and 1811 than in 1821 has the effect of raising estimates of births and deaths in 1801–11 and 1811–21 considerably because the survivors recorded in the 1821 census have to be increased in a greater proportion to 'hit' the totals in the two earlier censuses. The necessary additional inflation will be greater for 1801–11 than for 1811–21 because the argument assumes the 1801 census deficiency to have been larger than that in 1811. Moreover, the proportional inflation necessary to reach appropriate totals of deaths will be substantially higher than that for births because the total of deaths is obtained by subtracting the intercensal increase in total female population from the intercensal total of female births (making allowance for the changes in the size of intercensal population increases brought about by the changed population totals). The *absolute* increase in the totals of deaths will therefore be similar to that for births and the relative increase much larger. The conversion of female totals of births and deaths to totals for the two sexes combined was made in exactly the same way as for the totals used in the main run.

The revised total of births for the decade 1811–21 was 3.1 per cent greater than that used in the main run, and for 1801–11 4.6 per cent greater, while the corresponding percentage increases in deaths were 8.9 and 13.9. The percentage increase in the final

130. Details of the totals used in the main back-projection run may be found in appendix 15.
131. This was Krause's view. Krause, 'Changes in English fertility and mortality', p. 60.

inflation ratio, intended to capture residual non-registration, as implied by the revised totals of births and deaths in 1801–11, was then applied to all other final inflation ratios before 1801, which meant increasing birth and death totals back to 1640.[132]

4. In this simulation the totals used in simulation 3 were adopted when larger than those of simulation 2; otherwise those of simulation 2 were used. In the case of births this meant using simulation 2 totals for all periods before 1776; in the case of deaths for all periods before 1771. Simulation 4 represents what might be termed a maximal view of under-registration, involving both a very substantial increase in the totals of events in the late eighteenth and early nineteenth centuries, and considerable increases throughout all earlier periods.

5. Since much hinges on the completeness of the registration of young children in the 1821 and 1841 censuses for the estimation of 'true' totals of births and deaths (and hence correction factors for baptism and burial totals), one limiting assumption would be that the registration of young children in the censuses of 1821 and 1841 was complete and that therefore no correction for under-registration is needed. This assumption necessarily reduces totals of births and deaths, just as the assumption on which simulation 3 was based necessarily increases them. The totals of female births in the decades 1811–21 and 1831–41 were reduced in the same proportion that the original census totals of those aged 0–9 in 1821 and 1841 had been increased in respect of under-registration.[133] Revised final inflation ratios were calculated for 1811–21 and 1831–41. A revised birth total for 1821–31 was obtained by using a final inflation ratio for the decade equal to the mean of those for 1811–21 and 1831–41. The final inflation ratio for 1751–61 (and all earlier decades) was assumed to be accurate and ratios for decades between 1751–61 and 1811–21 were obtained by linear interpolation. Deaths for the decades 1801–41 were obtained by subtracting revised intercensal population increases from the new decennial birth totals. For the decades 1761–71 to 1791–1801 revised totals were obtained in the same way as for births 1761–71 to 1801–11 (i.e. linear interpolation between an unchanged final inflation ratio for 1751–61 and the revised ratio for 1801–11).

As with simulation 3 deaths are proportionately more affected than births by the changes just described. The greatest change in births occurs in the decade 1811–21 when their number is reduced by 3.2 per cent compared with the total used in the main run. In the same decade deaths are reduced by 4.6 per cent. In other decades the percentage changes are smaller except that the 1831–41 total of deaths falls by 5.6 per cent. The large percentage change in this decade occurs because the 1831 census total is more affected than that of 1841 by the removal of the correction for under-registration of young children, which increases the intercensal increase figure and thereby depresses the total of deaths.

6. Finally, it seemed useful to test the effect of a small and simple change in the balance of births and deaths made consistently over a long period, and at the same time to investigate how far migration and mortality were, so to speak, interchangeable, an increase in deaths causing a fall in net migration, or vice versa. Accordingly, in this run all deaths totals from 1751 back to the beginning (and including the period before 1541) were increased by 1 per cent while births were left unchanged.

It would be possible, of course, to present a mass of detail from the results obtained from the six simulation exercises, but since their purpose was limited to establishing

---

132. See tables 5.25 and 5.26.
133. The percentage reductions were 2.2 and 3.2 respectively (table 5.11).

how sensitive the results obtained from the main run were to modified data sets, it would be otiose to do so. Instead, results of the simulation runs are presented in summary graphical form in figures 7.16, 7.17, and 7.18. They deal respectively with population totals, net migration totals, and the level of the crude birth rate. These three indicators were chosen because the first is the most general measure of the effects of changes made to the data, the second is the most volatile of the demographic measures derived from back projection since it is in a sense a residual, while the third is a simple measure of fertility which may serve to indicate the degree to which fundamental demographic indices were affected by changing the totals of vital events. In each case the results are presented as deviations from a line representing the total or rate found in the main back-projection run. Thus, in figure 7.16 the line representing simulation 5 shows that in 1541 the population was just over 98 per cent of the total in the main run at that date.

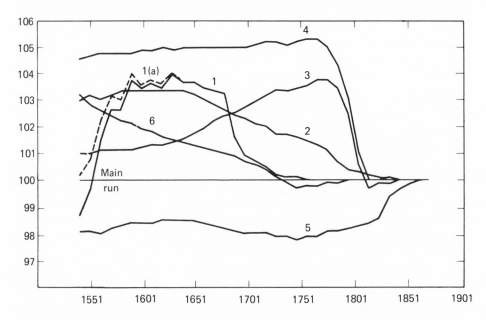

Figure 7.16: Population totals from six simulation exercises
(main back-projection run = 100)

Note: For details of birth and death totals used in the simulations see text.

It will be clear at a glance that none of the simulations produced striking changes in the back-projection results, and that the main outlines of English demographic history would not be greatly changed under any of the assumptions embodied in the simulations. In all cases the secular swings in fertility and mortality which were discussed earlier in this chapter would remain with only minor modification to their magnitude and timing. Population totals never vary by more than a maximum of just over 5 per cent from the totals found in the main run. Birth rates are equally stable. Where birth totals in the simulation runs were higher than in the main data set, the percentage increases in rates were normally less than the percentage increase in

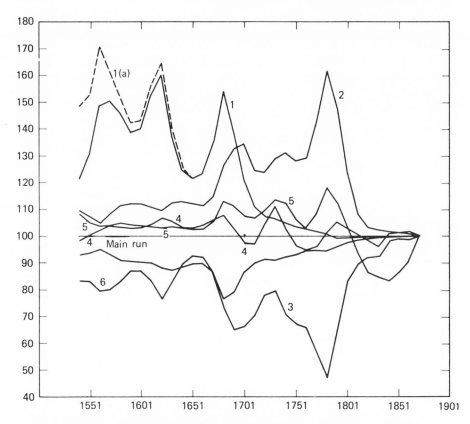

Figure 7.17: Migration totals from six simulation exercises (main
back-projection run = 100)

Notes: For details of birth and death totals used in simulations see text. The migration totals
relate to the five-year periods following the dates shown: only every other reading
has been plotted (i.e. 1541, 1551, 1561, etc.).

births, because the population totals were also higher. Crude birth rates never differed
by more than 4 per cent from those of the main run (except in the mid sixteenth century
in simulation 1), and in general the differences were less than 2 per cent.[134] Net
migration figures changed far more, even by as much as 50 per cent when compared
with main back-projection run, but in view of their method of derivation this was to be
expected.

The various simulations fall into distinct categories so far as their effects upon
population characteristics are concerned. Simulations 3 and 5, for example, form a
similar pair. The first, it will be recalled, involved increasing births and deaths
considerably in the late eighteenth and early nineteenth centuries and more modestly
back to the mid seventeenth century. The second reduced both, and over a shorter

134. Crude death rates in simulations 3 and 5 would vary rather more than the crude birth rates because, as
we have just seen, there were greater percentage changes in death totals, especially in the early nineteenth
century.

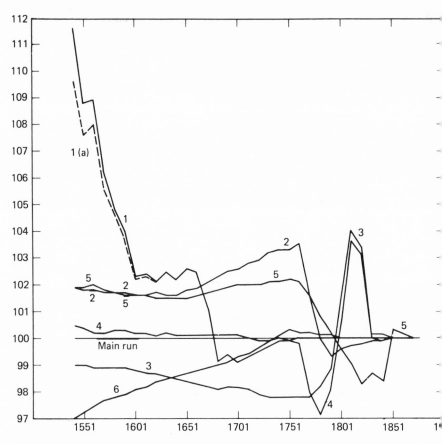

Figure 7.18: Crude birth rates from six simulation exercises (main back-projection run = 100)

Notes: For details of birth and death totals used in the simulations see text. The birth rates relate to five-year periods centring on the dates shown: only every other reading has been plotted (i.e. 1541, 1551, 1561, etc.).

period lasting from 1761 to 1841. In both cases the quinquennial birth and death total before 1641 and 1761 respectively were left unaltered. The results are clear and simple, and come close to representing a mirror image of one another. Population totals are raised in simulation 3 by a proportion that reached a maximum in the 1770 and 1780s when it was 3.7 per cent. Although birth and death totals before 1641 were not changed in this simulation it was not until 1581 that the ratio between simulation population totals and those from the main run ceased to alter. Before 1581 the simulation 3 totals settle down to a level just over 1 per cent greater than those of the main run. Simulation 5 population totals describe a similar path but on the opposite side of the line representing the main run, and because the alteration of the origina totals goes back less far, a stable ratio between simulation 5 and main run totals i achieved quicker and so obtains over a longer period.

The crude birth rates associated with simulation 3 and 5 are also a mirror image of one another. In the period when birth totals were substantially raised in simulation 3 the birth rate is higher than in the main run but at other times it is lower because the population totals were consistently higher. Equally, in simulation 5 birth rates are generally higher in virtue of the lower population totals it produces, except that in the period in which birth totals were sharply reduced the rate is lower than in the main run. And the migration output from the two simulations is once more very similar but of opposite sign. In simulation 3 the substantial increase in death totals, especially in the late eighteenth and early nineteenth centuries, causes a marked reduction in net migration levels compared with the main run. The difference gradually reduces, however, moving back in time until by 1600 emigration is at about 90 per cent of the level of the main run. The same description applies to simulation 5 as to simulation 3 except that simulation 5 net emigration totals are proportionately closer to those of the main run, and that they are always above rather than below them. The two simulations, therefore, show that if substantial changes are made to the data series but the changes affect only a limited period, population totals, migration, and crude rates are all affected in the short term. The long term effects, however, are limited. After a period of adjustment the simulations develop a very stable relationship to the results from the main run.

Simulations 1 and 6 also have much in common because the relative size of births and death totals is changed and the difference maintained over a long period of time. This produces a tendency for the characteristics measured in the three figures to drift further and further away from the patterns found in the main run.

We may first consider the very simple case of simulation 6. Here the only change made to the main run totals was to increase all deaths before 1751 by 1 per cent. This has the effect of slightly but steadily increasing the population total until, after two centuries, in the mid sixteenth century it is about 3 per cent greater than that of the main run. Since birth totals are unchanged, this depresses the birth rate commensurately. Migration totals are somewhat reduced as more people are, so to speak, killed rather than exported. (It may be noted that if births rather than deaths had been increased by 1 per cent in every year before 1751 and deaths had been left unaltered, the result would be almost exactly a mirror image of that just described, with a decrease in population totals, an increase in net migration, and higher birth rates compared with the main run.)

In simulation 1 both birth and death totals are increased, but the former by a larger percentage than the latter. A significant discrepancy between totals of births and deaths in simulation 1 and those of the main run begins only about 1700 but becomes more and more pronounced moving backwards in time towards the mid sixteenth century. By then the totals used in the main run were no longer increased by corrections for nonconformity, late baptism, or residual non-registration, so that the 10 and 5 per cent inflations of baptisms and burials used in simulation 1 could take full effect. As with simulation 6 there is a slow tendency for the demographic characteristics of the population to drift further and further from those of the main run. By 1600 the population total had reached a level about 4 per cent higher than that of the main run but was showing a tendency to stabilize at this level of discrepancy. The birth rate was 2.5 per cent above the main run level and net emigration was more than 40 per cent higher. The percentage change in the birth rate is the lowest of the three because the increase in the total of births is partially offset by the greater population size. The large and progressive increase in net emigration compared with the main run occurs because the increase in births in this simulation is greater than that of deaths, which forces up the migration total since every person who is born must at some later stage of life either die or leave the country. In order to judge the plausibility of the net migration results it is necessary, of course, to consider not only the relative change but also the absolute totals involved, which are not presented here (though they can easily be calculated from the totals listed in table A3.1). But it is worth noting that the plausibility of the migration totals affords one way of assessing the validity of the assumptions contained in the various simulations. While there is no reliable independent information about the true levels of migration totals in pre-industrial England, simulation 1 may be thought to exceed the limits of plausibility in the sixteenth century. Consequently the view that baptisms should always attract a 10 per cent inflation while burials are increased by 5 per cent may be rejected.

It will be noticed that in simulation 1 there is a very marked change in trend in all three figures before about 1580. In this context the changes should be ignored. They arise because of a very sharp falling off in the relative level of net migration, which causes the relative level of total population to fall so greatly as to take the absolute total below that of the main run in 1541 and to elevate the birth rate abruptly in sympathy. The change in net migration levels in turn is produced by the artificiality of the assumptions made about pre-1541 birth and death totals. Because the *absolute* difference between the totals is made the same as in the main run the *relative* increase in deaths is larger in simulation 1 than in the other simulations because the inflation of births is greater. This means that the program forecasts more severe mortality before 1541 and migration totals are accordingly more and more severely reduced for periods before about 1580. Moreover, the same influence affects population size by progressively reducing the size of the age group 90–4 introduced at the top of the age pyramid at each five-year cycle of the program. To a lesser extent the other simulations are similarly affected (except for simulation 6).[135]

The lines labelled 1(a) in figures 7.16, 7.17, and 7.18 show the sensitivity of the early years to pre-1541 totals of births and deaths. The data used were the same as in simulation 1 except that the pre-1541 totals of deaths were those of the main run increased by 5 per cent. This has the anticipated effect in causing migration totals to be less severely depressed than in simulation 1 with consequential changes to population totals and crude birth rates, though it does not greatly change the overall pattern.

Finally, simulations 2 and 4 also display broadly similiar features, at least in the sixteenth and seventeenth centuries, which is to be expected since they use the same birth and death totals for the whole period before the 1770s. In this period both embody the view that further corrections are necessary in addition to those made for the data in the main run. As in simulation 1, totals of events in both series are increased all the way back to the start, but the proportionate increase is the same for both births and deaths. The simulations both produce larger population totals than those of the main run, but in each case the increase stabilizes after a period of adjustment. In simulation 2 population totals rise slowly to about 3 per cent above those of the main run, moving backwards in time. This level is reached about 1650 but thereafter the difference varies only between 3.0 and 3.3 per cent. In simulation 4, influenced by sharing the birth and death totals of simulation 3 in the late eighteenth and early nineteenth centuries, the percentage increase over the main run totals rises

135. See p. 271 above.

very rapidly to about 5 per cent by 1781 but thereafter scarcely changes, though tending to decline very gradually to 4.5 per cent in the sixteenth century. In both simulations birth rates are closely similar to those of the main run. Indeed, in the case of simulation 4 the birth rate is barely distinguishable from that of the main run except in the early nineteenth century under the influence of assumptions taken over from simulation 3 about birth totals at the time of the early censuses. Migration totals, too, in general resemble those of the main run, especially in the case of simulation 4. In simulation 2 they settle down to a level about 10 per cent higher than that found in the main run after a more severe initial discrepancy, which occurred in the late eighteenth century when the discrepancy briefly rose to more than 50 per cent. This is a large percentage deviation but at this period net migration in the main run was at an exceptionally low absolute level so that the absolute size of the discrepancy is not large. Simulations 2 and 4, therefore, suggest that increasing birth and death totals by the same percentage implies an increase in population totals but only modest changes in birth rates and migration totals.

Reviewing the simulations as a whole, it seems reasonable to draw the following conclusions. First, making a significant change to birth and death totals over a restricted period, while it continues to affect population totals and birth rates outside the period in which totals of events are changed, does not have a marked or cumulative long-run influence on the characteristics of the population (simulations 3 and 5). Second, increasing birth and death totals by unequal proportions produces a drift away from the results obtained from the original data set, and exerts a powerful leverage on migration totals (simulations 1 and 6). In the case of the early modern English data used in back projection, this suggests that the ratio of births to deaths must be roughly correct since to make a greater percentage increase in births than deaths would drive up net emigration to improbable levels (and there would be equally striking implausibilities in the results obtained after increasing deaths proportionately more than births). Third, increasing birth and death totals in the same proportion leads to larger population totals but little change in migration levels or in birth rates (simulations 2 and 4). Thus, so far as fertility and mortality are concerned, the trends found in the main back-projection runs would hardly change at all if, say, the totals of births and deaths used were consistently 5 per cent too low in the first two and a half centuries of the period covered, and a revised data set was substituted for them. Indeed, given the constraint on data changes imposed by the necessity of keeping net migration totals at plausible levels, it is not easy to imagine any data changes that would be both plausible and likely to alter significantly the path of fertility and mortality change revealed by the main back-projection exercise.

Sensitivity tests: migration and mortality schedules

The results obtained by back projection are not only subject to modification if the birth and death totals are changed, but also if different assumptions are made about migration and mortality schedules while birth and death totals remain unaltered. To test their sensitivity on this score a simple, if crude alternative was used in each case. The cohort age schedule of migration used in the main run represents a rough average of the experience of a number of Swedish quinquennial cohorts in the later nineteenth century.[136] The Swedish data themselves show how artificial it is to use an unchanging schedule since even over a period of half a century there were very

136. See above, pp. 200–1.

substantial changes from cohort to cohort.[137] Since the schedule used in the main run was relatively elderly (with 48 per cent of the cohort total leaving in the age group 25–34), for the purpose of establishing the sensitivity of the results to a change in schedule, an alternative schedule was specified with 80 per cent of net migration occurring in the age groups 10–24. The two schedules are set out in table 7.30.[138] An equally crude solution was adopted in order to test the influence of an alternative mortality schedule. The schedule used in the main run consists of a family of life

Table 7.30: Alternative age schedules of cohort net migration

	(1) An adolescent schedule	(2) Cumulative totals of (1)	(3) The main run schedule	(4) Cumulative totals of (3)
0–1	0.000	0.000	0.013	0.013
1–4	0.000	0.000	0.052	0.065
5–9	0.000	0.000	0.045	0.110
10–4	0.100	0.100	0.040	0.150
15–9	0.300	0.400	0.065	0.215
20–4	0.400	0.800	0.200	0.415
25–9	0.150	0.950	0.280	0.695
30–4	0.050	1.000	0.200	0.895
35–9	0.000	1.000	0.075	0.970
40–4	0.000	1.000	0.030	1.000

Note: See table 7.3 and accompanying text for notes on the derivation of the main-run schedule from Swedish data.

tables based on the third English life table.[139] As an alternative the Princeton model West tables were used. It is quite clear that model West is an inappropriate selection for England in the mid nineteenth century, since it describes the age pattern of mortality then prevailing much less well than model North. In this context, paradoxically, this constitutes a recommendation since its use will tend to produce a large contrast with the results obtained in the main run.[140]

The population and migration totals from the two simulations are shown in figures 7.19 and 7.20 in the same way as the results of the earlier simulation were shown in figures 7.16 to 7.18. A graph of crude birth rates was not made in this instance since it would have been a mirror image of the population totals graph. In contrast with the earlier simulations, the number of births was the same as in the main run, and the birth rates therefore vary from those of the main run solely as a function of the different population totals. Where the population total in the simulation is 5 per cent greater than the main run, the birth rate will be approximately 5 per cent lower, and so on.

It is convenient to consider first the results obtained from the simulation using a different cohort age schedule of migration. Population totals throughout are lower

137. See fn. 17, p. 201 above.
138. See fn. 18, p. 201 above for scattered evidence that at times an age schedule as extreme as that given in table 7.30 may have been appropriate for some classes of English emigrants.
139. See appendix 14.
140. In carrying out this exercise no attempt was made to modify the 1871 age structure of the population in accordance with model West mortality patterns. Had this been done the result would probably have been to reduce substantially the extent of the contrast between the results of the main run and the test run.

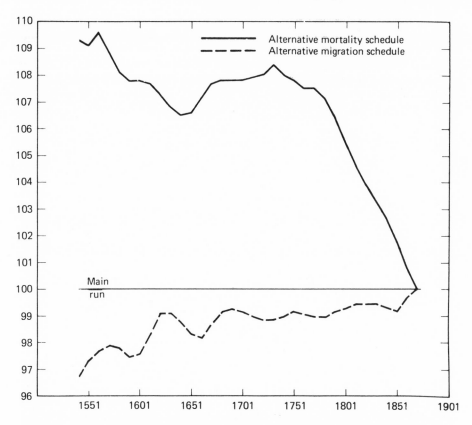

Figure 7.19: Population totals from two simulations using alternative migration and mortality schedules (main back-projection run = 100)

Notes: For details of the alternative schedules used see text.

than in the main run, and the percentage difference shows an irregular tendency to grow larger moving backwards in time from the origin in 1871. The initial difference occurs, as may be seen in figure 7.20, because net emigration is markedly smaller in the 1850s and 1860s in the simulation than in the main run. By 1851 the population total in the simulation is 136,000 smaller than in the main run. Thereafter for a time the net migration totals in the simulation were larger than in the main run so that by 1821 the difference in total population had shrunk to 52,000, but the initial tendency to a lower population total was never fully made up. Indeed the absolute difference between the simulation and main run population totals thereafter fluctuated only within fairly narrow margins, reaching a minimum of 35,000 in 1691 and a maximum of 99,000 in 1601 and showing no long-term trend. As the total population became smaller the relative shortfall in the size of the simulation population became more pronounced. For example, the absolute difference between the main run and simulation population was much the same in 1541 as in 1661 (91,000 in both instances) but in figure 7.19 the index level in 1541 is 96.7 compared with 98.2 in

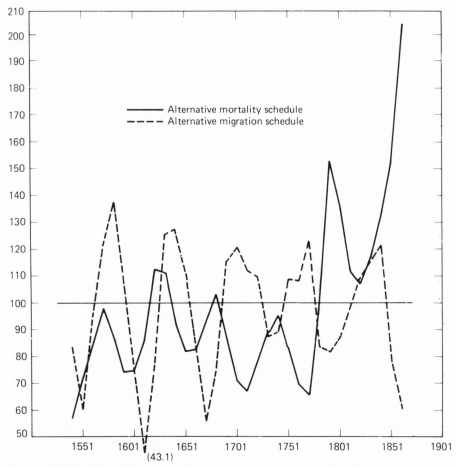

Figure 7.20: Migration totals from two simulations using alternative migration and mortality schedules (main back-projection run = 100)

Notes: For details of the alternative schedules used see text. The migration totals relate to the five-year periods following the dates shown: only every other reading has been plotted (i.e. 1541, 1551, 1561, etc.).

1651. It is therefore broadly true to say that adopting an exceptionally young cohort migration schedule sharply reduces net emigration in the early decades of the run in the mid nineteenth century; and that the consequent small reduction in total population compared with the main run is never recovered; the difference does not grow in absolute size but it becomes relatively more pronounced as population totals decrease. None of the changes induced by the change of migration schedule is on a scale to make a significant difference to the fertility and mortality trends reported for the main run.

Adopting model West mortality schedules results in a more pronounced divergence from the path taken by the main run. Yet there are similarities between the two simulations, since in both cases it is principally a very marked difference between the main run and simulation totals of migration in the first few decades of the back projection that establishes the divergence. It has already been pointed out that model West mortality schedules are inappropriate for mid-nineteenth-century England. When they are linked to the 1871 age structure they produce massively higher levels of net emigration in the 1840s, 1850s, and 1860s, so that the population in 1841 is already 394,000 higher than the total from the main run at that date (and 250,000 higher than the 1841 census total: table 7.1). By 1781 the absolute difference rises to 498,000. Thereafter, however, the absolute difference falls slowly but with fair regularity until in 1541 it is only 259,000. Since the total population in the sixteenth century was much lower than in the eighteenth century the ratio between the simulation and main run populations shown in figure 7.19 still shows some tendency to rise but during the period of 240 years from 1541 to 1781 it always lies within a narrow band about 7 to 10 per cent higher than the main run. After the initial period in which the level of emigration is well above that found in the main run, the model West simulation almost always results in lower migration totals than in the main run. Often the margin of difference is substantial.

During the sixteenth, seventeenth, and early eighteenth centuries the model West simulation results in significantly lower levels of fertility and mortality compared to those of the main run because the population is considerably larger, but it does not greatly alter the main demographic trends of the period since the ratio of the population totals drawn from the two series is fairly stable. After the middle of the eighteenth century the slightly slower rate of growth in the simulation population implies a somewhat faster rise in birth and death rates. Once again, however, the overall pattern of demographic fluctuations in pre-industrial England is not greatly altered even though a markedly different age structure of mortality is assumed.

It is worth stressing that whatever inaccuracies may have resulted from the assumptions embodied in the migration and mortality schedules used in the main program, they must be far less than might be suggested by the results obtained using the alternative schedules just described. It is demonstrable that model West is a very poor choice to characterize English mortality in the middle of the nineteenth century and probably equally bad for the preceding two centuries.[141] And it is ludicrous to suppose that the alternative migration schedule captured English experience in the nineteenth century, though it may have come nearer to doing so in the seventeenth. The alternative mortality schedule is suspect also for another reason. It results in a population of 9.137 million in 1801 compared with the main run figure of 8.664 million, and a census figure in that year of 8.565 million (this includes an estimate for those in the armed forces and merchant marine, and an adjustment to bring the population to the mid-year point for more exact comparison with the back-projection results).[142] It is thus 6.7 per cent larger than the adjusted census figure (and more than 10 per cent higher than the unadjusted figure). To accept it would imply a greater

141. See table A14.1 for evidence of the poorness of fit between the third English life table and model West. In earlier centuries neither model West nor model North provides a good fit with English reconstitution data, primarily because adult mortality was relatively much more severe than infant and child mortality in terms of either of the two models. Model North, however, fits English early modern infant and child mortality data better than model West (table 7.23). See also Schofield and Wrigley, 'Infant and child mortality'.

142. See table A6.7.

inaccuracy in the 1801 census than has normally been thought likely. In 1821 the comparable figure is over 5 per cent and since the 1821 census has not normally been suspected of significant under-registration, this is probably the more telling statistic.

Considering the effect of altering birth and death totals, or of modifying migration and mortality schedules does not exhaust the range of sensitivity tests that might be made, or of related issues that might be examined. In principle, for example, it is desirable to consider the joint effect of modifying, say, both birth totals and the mortality schedule. We have not done so because there seemed no reason to expect the results to do other than underline the robustness of the main run results to any but the most extreme combinations of improbabilities. A more important potential source of error lies in the age structure of the starting population in 1871, and especially in the size of the age group 90–4. It is not difficult to show that the age structure reported in the 1871 census was inaccurate in several respects, and adjustments can be made that must at least reduce the extent of the error.[143] Such errors as remain may have some effect on the estimation of mortality levels and on the timing of migration in the mid nineteenth century but will not greatly affect earlier periods, apart from any inaccuracy in the estimation of the initial age group 90–4. Inaccuracies in other age groups are, in a sense, cured by the passage of time as they disappear from the population, but an inaccuracy in the highest age group has a permanent effect because at each quinquennial step of the program the size of the new age group introduced at the top of the age pyramid is in part a function of the size of its predecessor.[144]

If the 1871 age group 90–4 is made 10 per cent larger than the total used in the main back-projection run,[145] the result is to increase population totals throughout. The effect is initially slight but by the time the whole population consists of cohorts introduced initially at age 90–4 (that is by 1781) the discrepancy has grown to almost 5 per cent, and thereafter continues to rise slowly to 6.6 per cent in 1731. Between 1731 and 1641 the ratio of the two populations shows a slight, irregular tendency to decrease. The absolute difference falls steadily and, since population totals changed very little in this period, the ratio declines to just under 6 per cent. Before 1631 the absolute difference again continues to fall but the absolute population totals fall more quickly, so the ratio begins to rise once more and by 1541 the simulated population total is almost 9 per cent larger than that of the main run.

The reporting of age by the very old is so inaccurate in early censuses that the total for the 90–4 age group used in any back-projection exercise is bound to be greatly changed from the census total; and while it is not difficult to improve upon the reported age totals by making the size of the older age groups consistent with the size of the birth cohorts from which they sprang and the mortality levels to which they were subject,[146] it would be dangerous to rely solely upon these considerations in arriving at a figure for those aged 90–4. Hence the importance of ensuring that any back projection starts not from the earliest date at which there is a census that provides details of age structure but with a census whose forerunners provide data against which the implications of any initial total selected for the age group 90–4 can be checked. For example, by 1821 all those aged 40 or more had first been introduced at the top of the age pyramid. The 1821 census provides useful if incomplete age data

143. See above, pp. 202–3.
144. See appendix 15, especially pp. 722–30 for a description of the method used to calculate each new 90–4 age group.
145. See above, pp. 204–5.
146. See above, pp. 202–5.

and therefore allows the size of the age group 90–4 in 1871 to be calibrated effectively. The overall population totals of all the early censuses are also valuable in this regard.[147] As a result the total in the age group 90–4 in 1871, which would have been 3,462 from the consideration of birth cohort size and intervening mortality alone, was amended to 3,350, a reduction of 3.2 per cent in the original total.

The selection of the correct total for the initial 90–4 age group is clearly vital to the success of any back-projection exercise. Relatively small inaccuracies in this total can have a marked effect throughout the entire run, especially if the population decreases substantially moving back in time. But, provided that the back projection is started late enough in time for its findings to be checked against age data drawn from earlier censuses, establishing the correct initial total for the 90–4 age group does not appear to present intractable problems.

Before concluding this discussion of sensitivity testing, it may be of interest to touch upon a closely related issue. It has been pointed out on several occasions that the results obtained by back projection become increasingly subject to error as the program approaches 1541 because the results obtained are more and more influenced by the arbitrarily selected pre-1541 birth and death totals.[148] It will be clear from the results of the sensitivity tests which have just been reported that the effects of the pre-1541 birth and death totals on back-projection results will not be confined exclusively to the 95-year period after 1541, which must be directly affected by the quinquennial totals of events before that date. The indirect effects will also be felt in the period after 1636 because of the way in which in successive passes through the data the output of an earlier pass affects the findings of subsequent passes. Thus, an estimated mortality level in, say, 1590, which was partially determined during the first pass by pre-1541 data, will in turn exercise an influence on results in the second and subsequent passes throughout most of the seventeenth century.[149]

The scale of the effects of pre-1541 data on results for periods later than 1636 may be discovered by carrying out a back projection that stops in 1636 and therefore makes no use of data before 1541 but is in other respects identical to the main back-projection run. The results provide reassuring evidence that the post-1636 results from the main run are not seriously affected by the indirect influence of assumptions about totals of events before 1541. The greatest difference between the 'census' totals from the two parallel sets of results is found at the earliest date, 1636, as might be expected, but even then the difference is only 6,018 in a total population of just over 5 million, or just over one tenth of one per cent (the main run total is the larger of the two). The age structure of the two populations is virtually identical. The differences between the two sets of 'census' totals rapidly diminish at later dates. By 1651 they are already reduced to 331, and soon become negligible, though they never disappear completely and even in the nineteenth century tiny differences remain, though the absolute difference never exceeds 20 persons after 1801.

Conclusive evidence that the results of the main run back projection described in this chapter are accurate is unattainable. Indeed, if such evidence existed it would have made some of the substantive work and much of the testing unnecessary, since the

147. See above tables 7.5 and 7.6 and pp. 203–5 for a comparison of the 1821 census age data with the results of back projection; and table 7.1 and pp. 199–202 for a comparison of population totals drawn from the census with those obtained by back projection.
148. The totals are listed in table A15.5
149. Further details of the ways in which these effects arise may be found in appendix 15 which describes the operations entailed in back projection by means of a simplified example.

existence, say, of unimpeachable evidence about the size of the English population in 1550 would provide a 'target' to hit, and would immediately eliminate many of the alternatives that must otherwise be considered. Sensitivity testing does, however, show clearly that the results that have been described are robust, and that some of the alternatives suggested from time to time imply levels of net migration so implausible that they may be dismissed. While there will remain room for argument about the precise levels of fertility and mortality at a given period, the trends in overall population totals and the wide secular swings in gross reproduction rates and expectation of life revealed by back projection appear to be too firmly established to be easily doubted.

In any pre-industrial society it is natural to expect that there will be important links between secular demographic trends and secular changes in economic variables such as prices and real wages. The way is now open for a new consideration of many of the topics so often discussed under this head since the demographic results obtained by back projection enable them to be analysed with greater rigour than in the past. These issues form the subject of chapter 10, but before devoting attention to them we turn in the next two chapters to a consideration of short-term demographic fluctuations to parallel that given to secular demographic change in this chapter and the last.

8

Short-term variation: some basic patterns

The previous two chapters have discussed the inferences that can be drawn from the estimated national series of births, deaths, and marriages for several aspects of long-term population change. However, a glance at the graph of the series in pullout 1 at the end of the volume reveals that they were also subject to short-term fluctuations which were occasionally of considerable size. This chapter and the next will examine the nature of the short-term variation in the series of events and, as with chapters 6 and 7, the first will adopt a simple approach to the subject while the second will pursue the analysis further, making use of more demanding methods.

In the present chapter two main aspects of short-term variation will be considered. First, the seasonal pattern of births, deaths, and marriages will be examined. Such patterns are not, of course, visible in pullout 1 which shows only annual fluctuations, but short-term fluctuations within the year were as marked as those occurring between years, and, as with the annual data, the pattern of seasonal fluctuations reveals much concerning the social, economic and physical environment. In all three series the seasonal patterns were clearcut, some proving remarkable stable over more than three centuries, though others changed radically. Second, the amplitude of annual fluctuations in each of the series will be described and the problematical subjects of the nature and significance of the relationships obtaining between them discussed. Since considerable interest attaches to the responsiveness of fertility, mortality, and nuptiality to short-term fluctuations in economic conditions, the covariation between each of the series and annual movements in a real-wage index will also be studied. Mortality crises, which have received much attention from economic and demographic historians, represent a further element in our treatment of short-term fluctuations. In this case the year is in some respects a clumsy unit of time to employ, and we shall therefore briefly discuss the monthly patterns of mortality in crisis periods as well as examining the distribution and severity of crisis years. Other aspects of mortality crises, including their geographical distribution, are examined in appendix 10.

It will be abundantly clear by the end of the chapter that although simple methods suffice to lay bare the overall patterns of covariation between the annual fluctuations in the series, the interpretation of the results is far from straightforward and calls for more sophisticated methods of analysis. These are provided in the next chapter, contributed by Ronald Lee, where both monthly and annual fluctuations are considered, and data on temperature and rainfall are also taken into account. Overall the results of the more complex analyses confirm the patterns described in this chapter and, as was the case when the results of back projection were compared to those obtained by simpler methods, it is evident that the more powerful techniques can probe deeper into the ways in which birth, death, and marriage fluctuations affected each other or responded to changes in the physical or economic environment.

Seasonal patterns

The monthly totals of events in table A2.4 show that there was a consistent pattern of seasonal fluctuation in each of the three series. To help bring out these patterns more clearly and to show how they changed over time, the numbers of events recorded in each of the 12 months in each half-century have been expressed as index numbers.[1] In calculating the index numbers, 100 represents the total that would be expected on the basis of an 'even split' of the events between the 12 months, after paying attention to the different number of days in each month.[2] Thus, for example, an index number of 112 indicates that a month obtained 12 per cent more events than average. It is important to note that the seasonal patterns reflect the monthly distributions in the *ecclesiastical* events recorded in the set of 404 parishes, for the enhancements of the original data made to convert them into national series of vital events involved inflation factors which increased linearly over time and therefore added no further information on seasonality.[3] It should also be borne in mind that England retained the Julian calendar until September 1752, by which time the date was lagging behind the solar cycle by 11 days. For example, events recorded in May 1752 in fact occurred between 12 May and 11 June, properly reckoned. Thus the seasonality of events falling in the period before the mid eighteenth century needs to be moved forward mentally by about a third of a month.[4]

The index numbers calculated for baptisms are shown in table 8.1 and figure 8.1. The table contains two further statistics which summarize the range of seasonal variation in each half century: the ratio between the maximum and minimum monthly index, and the mean absolute deviation of the 12 monthly index numbers from 100. In general the lines on the figure follow a pronounced but smooth wave pattern which rises from the start of the year to reach an apogee in March and then descends to a nadir in July, finally recovering to reach a plateau in the last three months of the year. This pattern is consistently present over time though the sharpness of the wave flattens considerably, especially after 1750. In the two centuries before 1750 taken together, when the seasonal pattern in baptisms is at its clearest, between 10 and 20 per cent more baptisms occured in the first four months of the year than would have been expected on the basis of an even split between the months. Each of the remaining months scored under par, the summer months recording between 10 and 20 per cent fewer, but the autumn and early winter months only slightly fewer, events than would be expected on the basis of an even split between the months. The traditional seasonal pattern of baptisms therefore divided the year into three equal parts: a late winter and spring (January–April) with above average numbers, a deficient summer (May–August), and an autumn and early winter (September–December) in which numbers were only a little below expectation.

---

1. To avoid a possible disturbance from the imminent prospect of civil registration the final 'half-century' was terminated in 1834. For an example of such a disturbance see Schofield, 'Comment on age at baptism', p. 52.
2. To take account of leap years, February was considered to contain 28.25 days, and the year was taken to be 365.25 days long. The inaccuracies involved in these approximations are negligible.
3. The index numbers were calculated on the aggregate parish monthly totals after correcting deficient periods of registration and after weighting by parish population size. The seasonality of events in London is not included. The data, therefore, correspond to the stage reached at the end of chapter 2, and to the annual totals in table A4.1, col.4.
4. The re-alignment with the solar cycle was achieved by stepping from 2 September to 14 September in 1752. Thereafter England followed the Gregorian calendar. Cheney, *Handbook of dates*, pp. 10–1.

Table 8.1: Monthly indexes of baptisms by half-century

(100 = all events × number of days in month/365.25)

Period	(B)	(C)	Baptism (B) or Conception (C)												Ratio max./min.	Mean absolute deviation
	Jan.	Feb	March	April	May	June	July	Aug.	Sept.	Oct.	Nov.	Dec.		
	April	May	June	July	Aug	Sept.	Oct.	Nov.	Dec.	Jan.	Feb.	March		
1540-99	111	123	123	111	89	81	78	89	105	100	101	91	1.58	12.2
1600-49	110	125	124	112	92	82	77	88	97	100	99	97	1.63	11.7
1650-99	108	119	122	118	97	85	82	84	96	99	97	96	1.49	10.9
1700-49	107	117	117	114	100	91	86	86	95	97	95	97	1.36	9.0
1750-99	103	108	110	115	104	101	94	87	94	95	90	98	1.32	7.4
1800-34	96	98	103	113	106	106	99	96	100	96	90	96	1.26	4.8
Percent of parishes at:														
Maximum	4.7	33.4	42.1	15.1	0.2	0.0	0.0	0.2	2.5	1.2	0.2	0.2		
Minimum	0.5	0.0	0.2	0.0	3.2	25.7	42.3	22.8	0.7	0.7	1.5	2.2		

Notes: February allocated 28.25 days. Percentages of parishes at maximum and minimum values calculated on period 1601-1720 (see text).

Source: Monthly frequencies of events in set of 404 parishes after weighting for population size (except for max. and min. distributions). Corresponding annual totals are given in table A4.1, column 3.

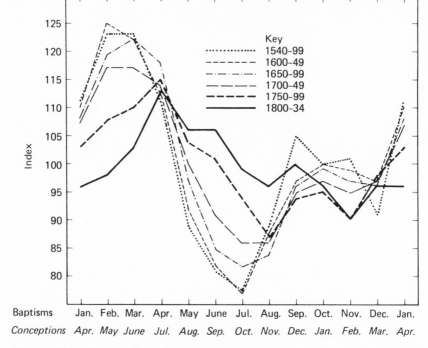

Figure 8.1: Seasonality of baptisms

Source: Table 8.1

The seasonality of baptisms, shown in aggregate in table 8.1 and figure 8.1, was also followed by the overwhelming majority of individual parishes. Monthly indexes were calculated for each of the 404 parishes and the proportional spread of the maximum and minimum parish indexes across the months is shown on the last two lines of table 8.1. The calculation was based on baptisms recorded in the period 1601–1720 in order to ensure that all but a few parishes were in observation during the whole period studied and in order to minimize problems arising from the growing divergence between parishes in the age at which infants were baptized, a complication discussed below. No less than 75.5 per cent of the parishes experienced a baptism peak, and only one parish a baptism minimum, in February and March, the two months with the highest monthly indexes aggregated over all the parishes. Over the first four months of the year when the aggregate monthly indexes were above average, 95.3 per cent of the parishes returned maximum figures as against only 0.7 per cent with baptisms at a minimum. Furthermore, the trough in the aggregate monthly indexes from May to August was accompanied by an almost exact reversal of the percentages of parishes experiencing maximum and minimum baptismal frequencies, and the last four months of the year, which in aggregate produced average monthly indexes, witnessed few maximum or minimum values amongst individual parishes.

Although this near homogeneity in the seasonal patterns of baptism among the 404 parishes holds good for a lengthy central period, 1601–1720, the aggregate monthly indexes displayed in table 8.1 and figure 8.1 reveal a considerable evening-up of baptism seasonality between the sixteenth and the nineteenth centuries. Of the surpluses that formerly accrued to the early months in the year only those of April held to anything like their former level, and of the summer deficits those of May and June turned into surpluses while those of July and August withered away. Although this flattening of the seasonal curve in the figure is particularly marked after 1750, the last two columns of the table show that this was a process which had been going on since the sixteenth century. In the period 1540–99 the month in which baptisms were at a maximum (February) claimed 58 per cent more events than the month (July) in which they were at a minimum. The ratio of maximum to minimum increased slightly in the next half-century, but then fell in each successive half-century until, in the period 1800–34, the maximum month claimed only 25 per cent more births than the minimum month. If the variation of all the months is taken into account, the average monthly deviation from an even split across the year fell from 12 per cent in the sixteenth century to just under 5 per cent in the early nineteenth century, with most of the reduction in seasonal variation occurring after 1700.

In interpreting these patterns the first question that needs to be tackled is whether the seasonal distribution of baptisms can be taken as an indication of the seasonal distribution of births. If baptisms always took place soon after birth, then the question would not arise and the monthly distribution of baptisms would be a good guide to the seasonality of births. If this was not the case, then there are two ways in which the interval between birth and baptism could produce differences between the seasonal distributions of baptisms and births. First, if all children were baptized at the same age, say three months, the seasonal patterns of baptisms would simply echo that of births lagged by the appropriate number of months. Second, the greater the spread of the ages at which children were baptized, the more diffuse the monthly distributions of baptisms would be compared to the seasonal distribution of births.

There is little evidence for the age at baptism in the sixteenth century, but what there is points to a nearly universal custom of baptizing shortly after birth. Thereafter a great variety of practice developed: in some places the sixteenth century pattern persisted into the nineteenth century, while in others children were not baptized until they were several weeks, or even several months old, though the appearance of these very late ages at baptism was largely confined to the period after 1750. The increasing variation in the age at baptism pushed up the average interval between birth and baptism: in the late seventeenth century the median interval was still only 8 days, but by 1800 it had risen to 30 days.[5]

The pattern of baptism visible in the sixteenth century therefore probably accurately represents the seasonal distribution of births. However, it is clear from figure 8.1 that the baptism distribution flattened out over time, gradually at first, but at a faster pace and with a shift of about one month to the right in the whole distribution after 1750. These developments are consistent with the increase and the greater variation in the age at baptism and with the addition of 11 days to the date accompanying the adoption of the Gregorian calendar in 1752. Consequently, the underlying seasonal distribution of births may have been constant over time. Unfortunately it is not possible to test this hypothesis precisely, because when the

---

5. Berry and Schofield, 'Age at baptism'. The median figures refer to the median age at baptism in the median parish of the set investigated. The interquartile ranges in the median parish in the late seventeenth century, and around 1800, were 6 and 21 days respectively. The median intervals for the earliest and latest baptizing parish in the two periods were 1 and 19 days (1650–99), and 3 and 114 days (1791–1812).

Table 8.2: Quarterly indexes of baptisms and births compared

Period	Jan.–March	April–June	July–Sept.	Oct.–Dec.
(100 = all events × number of days in quarter/365.25)				
Baptisms				
1540–99	119	93	91	97
1600–49	119	95	86	98
1650–99	115	99	86	97
1700–49	113	101	88	96
1750–99	106	106	91	94
1800–34	99	108	98	94
Births				
1838–45	105	103	96	96

Note: February allocated 28.25 days.

Sources: Baptisms, table 8.1; births, *8th Annual Report of the Registrar General*, pp. 126-7.

civil registration of births began in 1837 the Registrar General only reported the seasonal distribution of registrations of birth by quarter.[6]

Table 8.2 compares quarterly index numbers of births for the period 1838–45 with equivalent figures for baptisms for each 'half-century' from 1540–99 to 1800–34. Although the interval between birth and civil registration is not known, a local study in a parish with late baptism suggests that it may only have been a little shorter on average, though less variable, than the interval between birth and baptism. Indeed the quarterly seasonal distribution of birth registrations in table 8.2 is similar to that of baptisms in the early nineteenth century, though it peaks somewhat earlier in the year. Both are much flatter than the quarterly distribution of baptisms, and hence presumptively of births, in the sixteenth century. But in the absence of any direct information on the seasonality of the occurrence of births it is difficult to tell whether the gradual evening out of the seasonal distribution of baptisms over time as shown in table 8.1 reflects a similar trend in the seasonal distribution of births or the effects of an increasing variation and delay in age at baptism that also afflicted the registration of births in the mid nineteenth century. However, in Scotland births had to be registered within three weeks, and the *monthly* distribution of birth registrations was similar to that of baptisms in England in the early nineteenth century. This lends support to the view that there had been a substantial flattening in the seasonal distribution of births in England since the sixteenth century.[7]

Not only was the general outline of the seasonal pattern of baptisms persistent over a long period of time in England, it can also be found over much of north-west Europe. Although there are some differences of detail, in general the early months in

6. Monthly figures were not published for the period covered by this volume.
7. In England births had normally to be registered within 42 days: 6 & 7 William IV c. 86, ss. 18–20. A check on the civil and parish registers of Colyton, Devon in the period 1837–51 found the mean interval between birth and civil registration to have been 20 days compared to 33 days until baptism. The standard deviations of the two sets of intervals were 13 and 36 days respectively. Scottish registration was regulated by 17 & 18 Victoria c. 80. The monthly index numbers in 1856–60 were 103, 101, 104, 108, 107, 103, 98, 94, 94, 97, 95, 98. *Annual Reports of the Registrar-General of births, deaths and marriages in Scotland*, 1856–60 in *P.P.*, 1857 (sess. 1) IV, p. 371; 1857–8, XXIII, p. 237; 1859 (sess. 1), XII, p. 579; 1860, XXIX, p. 819; 1861, XVIII, p. 549. Figures for 1855 were evidently deficient and were disregarded.

the year have also been found to have recorded most baptisms or births, and those of high summer the least, in a number of individual parishes in Denmark, France, and Germany in the eighteenth century, in north Holland and western Belgium in the seventeenth and eighteenth centuries, and nationally in Sweden in the period 1749 to 1855.[8] This seasonal pattern had the advantage of minimizing the number of births occurring during the period of crop-gathering over the summer months when female labour was in great demand, but it also suffered from the drawback that most births occurred in the cold months of the late winter and early spring when the climate was particularly favourable to the spread of respiratory infections.

Seasonality in births entails seasonality in conceptions, and in table 8.1 and figure 8.1 the corresponding months have been indicated as lying nine months before each month of baptism. The resulting seasonal cycle in conceptions is likely to be more diffuse than the true pattern, because variation in the period of gestation results in only 66 per cent of conceptions in a calendar month issuing in a birth nine months later.[9] Moreover its accuracy rests on two assumptions: that the interval between birth and baptism was short, as indeed was generally the case before 1750, and that there was no intervening seasonality in foetal mortality. Not surprisingly historical data on the latter point is exceedingly hard to find, but *a priori* it could be argued that unless the seasonal effect were concentrated at a particular stage of foetal development the ensuing negative effect on the seasonality of births, averaged over the nine months gestation period, would be very weak. In Sweden in the mid nineteenth century the seasonal distribution of stillbirths was quite close to that of live births which suggests that there was little special seasonality in the incidence of late foetal mortality.[10] Although parallel evidence is lacking for England, the seasonality of deaths in the first year of life was similar to that of stillbirths in Sweden.[11] Thus, unless there was some pronounced seasonality in early foetal mortality, it would seem to be reasonable to treat the seasonality of births, set back nine months, as indicating, if somewhat diffusely, the seasonal cycle of conceptions.[12]

If we take the traditional seasonal pattern before it becomes obscured by high and variable ages at baptism in the later eighteenth century, we find that conceptions were at their highest in the late spring and early summer (April to July) and at their lowest in the late summer and autumn (August to November). The annual seasonal pattern of conceptions may reflect several factors, both biological and social, though little is

8. Denmark: 26 sample parishes reported in Johansen, *Bevolkningsudvikling*, p. 100; France: 16 scattered parishes reported in Guillaume and Poussou, *Démographie historique*, p. 172; and national sample of parishes reported in Houdaille, 'Mouvement saisonnier des conceptions', p. 453; Germany: Giessen and 8 nearby parishes reported in Imhof, 'Die nicht-namentliche Auswertung', p. 248; north Holland: van der Woude, *Het Noorderkwartier*, III, pp. 788–90; West Belgium: Dalle, *De bevolking van Veurne-Ambacht*, p. 127; Sweden: national tabulations of births summarized and printed by Fåhraeus, 'Om förhållandet', p. 233. The equivalent monthly index numbers for Sweden (Jan. to Dec.) were 106, 106, 106, 101, 94, 89, 89, 92, 116, 104, 100, 102. The anomalously high figure for September is discussed below.

9. Leridon, *Natalité*, pp. 18–9.

10. Monthly indices for stillbirths in Sweden during the period 1831–55 (Jan. to Dec.) were 109 109, 107, 101, 96, 92, 89, 88, 102, 101, 101, 106. The anomalously high figure of 102 in September echoes the peak in live births in that month. Fåhraeus, 'Om förhållandet', p. 233. The seasonality of still-births was also the same as that of live births in mid-twentieth-century France, Leridon, *Natalité*, p. 76.

11. Schofield and Wrigley, 'Infant and child mortality', pp. 88–9.

12. Little is known about the seasonality of inter-uterine mortality. Modern data from New York show that conceptions in January to March suffer most and conceptions in October and November least, but the patterns are too slight to affect the seasonality of births. Leridon, *Natalité*, p. 76.

known of their relative strength.[13] It is often supposed that sexual intercourse was more frequent in the late spring and early summer, reaching a seasonal apogee much celebrated in literature. Family reconstitution studies show that the only group of conceptions that deviated from the prevailing pattern was that of first births conceived in marriage which betrayed some influence of the seasonality of marriage. First births conceived before marriage, on the other hand, which were free from this constraint, followed the general seasonal cycle of conceptions as did those of higher order births to married couples.[14]

The fall in conceptions between August and November was so steep that it would appear that other factors may have intervened to intensify the decline from the early summer peak. Since conceptions in this period issued in births in the crop-gathering months of May to August in the subsequent year, their relative infrequency throughout north-west Europe suggests that there may also have been an economic dimension, whether consciously recognized or not, to the seasonal patterning of sexual activity throughout the year. However, the connexion with the seasonal demands of agriculture is clearly not an entirely satisfactory explanation for the same seasonal pattern of births can be found in London in the early seventeenth century.[15]

One interesting minor anomaly from the general seasonal distribution of baptisms is the relatively high monthly index for September that occurs only in the sixteenth century. The same feature can be found in the eighteenth century in certain protestant parishes around Giessen, in Lutheran Denmark and Sweden, and in some, but not all, communities both protestant and catholic in Holland in the seventeenth and eighteenth centuries. However, it is not visible in France or in west Belgium.[16] In Swedish national data September had the highest monthly birth index from 1749 to 1855, and it still had the second highest as late as 1900.[17] With an average period of gestation of 268 days the corresponding peak in conceptions falls between 5 December and 5 January. In Sweden Christmas and the New Year were celebrated by two weeks of heavy eating and drinking from 24 December to 6 January.[18] Moreover a recent local study of seasonality analysed on a weekly basis for 19 widely scattered

---

13. For example, the seasonality of births is similar over the whole of North America despite large differences in seasonal variations in the climate. Leridon, *Natalité*, pp. 73–5. After reviewing the evidence Leridon concludes that the influence of 'natural' and 'mechanistic' factors on the seasonality of births in the past has been exaggerated, *ibid.*, p. 83.

14. The results from family reconstitution will be reported in a forthcoming volume. No data are available for the seasonality of illegitimate births in England. In Sweden in the mid nineteenth century the seasonal pattern of illegitimate births was the same as that of legitimate births in a slightly more accentuated form. Fåhraeus, 'Om förhållandet', p. 233. This was also the case in west Belgium in the seventeenth and eighteenth centuries, Dalle, *De bevolking van Veurne-Ambacht*, pp. 126–7, and in France in 1948–51, Leridon, *Natalité*, p. 81.

15. Finlay, *The population of London*, p. 181, tabulating baptisms in six central London parishes in the period 1581–1640. Geneva exhibited the same seasonal pattern of births which gradually became more even during the eighteenth century, as was the case generally in England. Perrenoud, *La population de Genève*, I, p. 408. Many small towns in Europe appear to have followed the rural seasonal pattern of births, though some did not. Bardet, 'La démographie des villes', p. 123. Strassburg presents an interesting example of a town that followed the rural pattern in the later sixteenth century, but acquired a different seasonality of births in the seventeenth. Kintz, 'Aspekte einer städtetypischen demographischen Beispiel', pp. 1,051–3. Kintz notes that the seasonal pattern changed when the population of Strassburg passed the 25,000 mark, but the example of London shows that size did not necessarily entail a change in seasonality.

16. See note 8, above.

17. 1749–1855: see note 8 above; 1900: *Bidrag till Sveriges officiela statistik, A) Befolkningsstatistik*, XLII:1, 1900, pp. 34–5.

18. Bringéus, *Årets festseder*, pp. 33–90.

English parishes in the period 1580–1620 finds a peak in conceptions in the same fortnight.[19] The greater seasonal conviviality of this time of year may have led to an increase in the frequency of sexual activity, producing a surge of births in the following September. An explanation related to better nutrition over the festival period is only plausible if conceptions in other months were reduced by malnutrition, but this is unlikely in view of the continuance of the pattern in Sweden until the end of the nineteenth century. Whether England in the sixteenth century possessed a similar tradition of extended celebrations at Christmas and the New Year is not known, but the implied peak in conceptions in this season, which disappeared on a national level in the early seventeenth century, is an intriguing forerunner of a pattern clearly evident at a later date in other countries.[20]

If we now turn our attention to the seasonal pattern of burials as shown in table 8.3 and figure 8.2, it is striking not only how similar it is in its general outline to the seasonal pattern of baptisms but also how little it changed over time. Since the interval between death and burial was always very short, with the overwhelming majority of burials occurring within three days of death, the monthly distribution of burials can

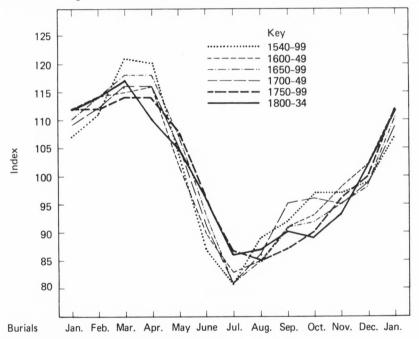

Figure 8.2: Seasonality of burials

Source: Table 8.3

19. Dyer, 'Seasonality of baptisms', figure 1.
20. A number of customs, including wassailing, are documented for the more recent past in Wright, *British calendar customs: England,* II, pp. 209–93; III, pp. 1–91, but they fall far short of the sustained communal conviviality typical of traditional Sweden. Some parishes maintained high monthly index figures for September baptisms into the nineteenth century, and in 10 parishes September was the month with the highest monthly index over the whole parish register period. There does not seem to be any pattern in the distribution of these parishes to suggest the preservation of an earlier tradition, along regional or other lines.

Table 8.3: Monthly indexes of burials by half-century

(100 = all events × number of days in month/365.25)

Period	Jan.	Feb.	March	April	May	June	July	Aug.	Sept.	Oct.	Nov.	Dec.	Ratio max./min.	Mean absolute deviation
1540–99	107	111	121	120	99	87	81	89	92	97	97	99	1.50	9.8
1600–49	112	114	115	116	102	90	83	85	91	93	98	102	1.40	10.1
1650–99	110	114	118	118	107	93	81	85	91	92	95	98	1.46	11.0
1700–49	109	112	116	116	105	91	81	86	95	96	95	99	1.44	9.6
1750–99	112	112	114	114	108	96	87	85	87	90	96	100	1.34	9.9
1800–34	112	114	117	110	105	96	86	87	90	89	93	102	1.36	9.9
Percent of parishes at:														
Maximum	10.4	16.8	23.5	31.2	8.7	0.7	0.0	1.5	2.0	1.7	1.7	1.7		
Minimum	0.7	0.2	0.0	0.2	1.7	7.9	39.6	18.6	11.9	8.4	5.7	5.0		

Notes: See table 8.1.

Source: See table 8.1.

be taken as a nearly perfect proxy for the seasonality of deaths.[21] While burials, like baptisms, occurred more frequently in the first four months of the year and relatively infrequently in the summer, usually reaching a minimum in July, the annual cycles of the two series differed a little in that burials built up to a maximum later in the spring (in March–April rather than February–March), and recovered more slowly from the summer trough. Although infant mortality was relatively high in the past and about one half of infant deaths occurred within the first month of life, the seasonal pattern of burials was not simply a reflection of the seasonal pattern of baptisms.[22] Family reconstitution studies show that the seasonal pattern of burials early in the first year of life indeed followed a cycle close to that of baptisms, but that burials of other infants under one displayed a pattern very like the inverse of the temperature curve, while burials of older children followed a radically different monthly pattern which peaked in the summer and was at a minimum in the late winter. Moreover, adult burials comprised a substantial majority of the total, and it was their monthly distribution, which was quite different from that of either infants or children, that determined the general seasonal pattern.[23]

The last two lines of table 8.3, which for comparability with baptisms are also based on burials registered between 1601 and 1720, confirm that this aggregate pattern was shared by the overwhelming majority of individual parishes. About one half of the parishes experienced a seasonal maximum in March and April and 82 per cent returned a maximum monthly index that fell within the first four months of the year. Conversely burials were at a minimum in 78 per cent of the parishes in the four summer months from June to September, when the aggregate monthly indexes were also at their lowest. Amongst the small group of anomalous parishes with burial peaks in the late summer and autumn, or troughs falling in the winter months, the urban parishes of Ipswich, Norwich, and Shrewsbury are particularly conspicuous. The experience of London in the period 1581–1650 shows that the seasonal pattern of mortality could be very different in an urban environment, even in years undisturbed by bubonic plague. London lacked both the burial peak in the late winter and early spring and the mid-summer trough. Instead it suffered excess mortality in August, September, and October with monthly index figures of 109, 120, and 115 respectively.[24] A similar pattern obtained in Geneva in the same period, the late summer peak in burials being caused by a high level of mortality amongst children.[25] It would therefore seem that the combination of high density and imperfect sanitation that was typical of towns in pre-industrial Europe magnified the normal seasonal prevalence of fly-borne diseases such as dysentery, which particularly affected children, to such an extent that the overall seasonal pattern of mortality was substantially altered.

The two final columns of table 8.3 show how little change there was in the seasonal pattern of burials over time, much less than was the case with baptisms. Between the sixteenth and nineteenth centuries the ratio between the maximum and minimum

21. Berry and Schofield, 'Age at baptism', p. 453.
22. The proportion of deaths at various ages under stable population conditions are conveniently tabulated in Coale and Demeny, *Regional model life tables*. For the proportion of infant deaths in the first month of life see Wrigley, 'Mortality in pre-industrial England', pp. 567–8.
23. Schofield and Wrigley, 'Infant and child mortality', pp. 88–92.
24. The figures are simple averages of the monthly indexes presented for six central London parishes in Finlay, *The population of London*, p. 138.
25. Perrenoud, *La population de Genève*, I, pp. 429–31.

month (March and July) fell from 1.50 to 1.36, while with baptisms the ratio fell from 1.58 to 1.26. Again, in contrast with the mean absolute deviations of the monthly baptism indexes which fell consistently over time, those of burials remained almost constant over the centuries. Nonetheless there are one or two changes in the relative positions of individual months which can be observed. In the sixteenth century the March–April peak was more pronounced than subsequently, while the index figures for January and May–June were relatively low. The relative share of annual mortality accruing in June rose over time counterbalancing a fall in the index figures for April. October also appears to have been unusually mortal in the sixteenth century, but this was the result of unusually large clusterings of autumn deaths in certain years. The subsequent fall in the index numbers for October therefore reflects a diminution in the incidence of autumn epidemics, except in the early eighteenth century when high mortality in the 1720s drove up the October index almost to its sixteenth century level. In any one year, of course, the impact of a mortality 'crisis' might produce a radically different seasonal pattern of deaths, and the seasonality of crisis mortality is discussed in appendix 10.

The salient feature of the seasonal pattern of mortality presented here, however, is its stability over very long periods of time.[26] Furthermore, as was the case with births, the English experience was similar to that of other parts of north-west Europe. For example in the villages around Giessen in Germany, in parts of Belgium, and in Denmark and Sweden in the eighteenth century, deaths reached a maximum in the spring and a minimum in July or August.[27] Indeed, when data become available nationally for a number of countries in the mid nineteenth century the same seasonal pattern of deaths can be seen in Scandinavia, Scotland, the Low Countries, Switzerland, Austria, Hungary, and Romania.[28] Table 8.4 presents monthly index numbers for a selection of countries ranged according to latitude. In general the further north the country the later the spring peak.[29]

Further south in Europe, however, a different seasonal pattern prevailed: in Italy and Spain, for example, relatively few deaths occurred in the spring and most deaths were recorded in the summer months from July to September, precisely when mortality in northern Europe was generally at a minimum.[30] France and Germany followed an intermediate pattern with both the north European spring peak and an additional, slightly lower, peak in August and September.[31] These geographical

26. There is some sign of a slight shift to the right in the seasonal cycle after 1750, which may be due to the advancement of the calendar in 1752.

27. Giessen area: Imhof, 'Die nicht-namentliche Auswertung', p. 250; Belgium: Bruneel, *La mortalité dans les campagnes* [Brabant], II, pp. 60–1, and Dalle, *De bevolking van Veurne-Ambacht*, p. 156; Denmark: Johansen, *Bevolkningsudvikling*, p. 117. The monthly index numbers for Sweden in the period 1749–1855 (Jan.–Dec.) were 109, 113, 116, 120, 111, 95, 84, 86, 88, 87, 93, 98; Fåhraeus, 'Om förhållandet', p. 234.

28. The data spanning various time periods for 18 countries and 5 capitals within the date range 1841–77 are tabulated in Berg, 'Årstidernas inflytelse', pp. 118–9.

29. In Iceland, for example, the peak in deaths was delayed until May, June, July, which recorded index numbers of 113, 148, and 120, respectively.

30. This pattern was also present in a number of Italian parishes in the seventeenth century. Corsini, 'Problemi di utilizzazioni', pp. 125, 129.

31. In the eighteenth century there was no sign of the late summer peak in the parishes around Giessen. Imhof, 'Die nicht-namentliche Auswertung', p. 250. However, out of 16 French parishes reported by Guillaume and Poussou (*Démographie historique*, p. 142), only Crulai in Normandy lacked a late summer burial peak. On p. 143 they cite an eighteenth-century observation to the effect that 'Les mois de septembre et d'octobre sont, en France, les plus mortels et le mois de juillet celui qui l'est le moins'. Moheau, *Recherches et considérations*, p. 230.

Table 8.4: Monthly indexes of deaths in selected European countries

Country	Period	Jan.	Feb.	March	April	May	June	July	Aug.	Sept.	Oct.	Nov.	Dec.	Ratio max./min.	Mean absolute deviation
Finland	*1859–74*	104	113	116	124	127	109	90	83	77	80	87	92	1.65	15.3
Scotland	*1855–75*	113	117	113	106	100	95	90	88	85	87	98	108	1.38	9.5
Netherlands	*1860–75*	111	113	114	106	91	96	96	95	92	87	91	99	1.31	8.1
N. Germany	*1872–76*	102	110	111	104	98	91	96	109	102	91	93	95	1.22	6.2
France	*1853–68, '72*	106	110	110	104	94	87	90	105	108	98	94	95	1.26	7.1
Spain	*1863–70*	95	90	88	86	82	94	117	123	118	110	101	96	1.50	11.5

Source: Berg, 'Årstidernas inflytelse', pp. 118–9.

differences in the seasonality of mortality probably reflected the influence of climate on the prevalence of different forms of disease, with respiratory infections more frequent in the north and intestinal infections in the south. The last two columns of the table show that the further north or south a country was situated, the more pronounced the seasonal pattern became. The English evidence presented here is of some interest because it shows that the seasonal pattern of mortality, which was later widespread throughout north Europe, can be traced back to the mid sixteenth century, and may well be much older than this.

Table 8.5 and figure 8.3 show the seasonal pattern of marriages in England and how it changed over time. The monthly seasonality of marriages was not only quite different from that of births and deaths, it was also more pronounced, and changed more markedly between the sixteenth and nineteenth centuries. In its overall shape, however, it remained the same, with peaks in the early summer and autumn separated by a late summer trough and a chasm in March. In the sixteenth century this pattern was particularly sharp: although the early summer peak in June and the trough in August were modest in amplitude, the autumn peak was immense, with October and November returning indexes of 184 and 201 respectively, and the chasm in March plunged to an index of 8. At this date the deficiency of marriages in March extended, though to a far lesser degree, into April and May, reflecting the variable timing of the ancient ecclesiastical prohibitions on marriage in Lent and Rogationtide. The third prohibited period, Advent, considerably reduced the frequency of marriages in December.[32]

Although the prohibited periods ceased to be part of the law of the Church of England after the Reformation it seems that habits changed slowly.[33] While April and May emerged as two of the most popular months for marriage by the mid seventeenth century, December increased its share of marriages more slowly, but it did so consistently and by the early nineteenth century it had acquired the third highest monthly index. March, on the other hand, still languished at the bottom of the monthly league table and had only achieved an index of 73 in the early nineteenth century. The peak in marriages in January in the sixteenth century seems to have been a consequence of the reluctance to marry in December rather than of an anticipation of marriages which would otherwise have been solemnized during Lent, for the January peak was very marked in the 1540s and 1550s when the December index was very low, and it declined consistently during the later sixteenth century as the December index rose.[34]

---

32. Lyndwood's fifteenth-century digest of canon law mentions three prohibited seasons: Advent, Lent, and Rogationtide, the dates of which varied with Easter. Advent began between 27 November and 3 December and the prohibition was lifted on 13 January, a period of six to seven weeks. The Lenten ban ran for 10 weeks from Septuagesima to the first Sunday after Easter. At its earliest this period stretched from 18 January to 29 March and at its latest from 21 February to 2 May. The third prohibited period comprised the three weeks from Rogation to Trinity Sunday, which ranged from 26 April–17 May to 30 May–20 June. Lyndwood, *Provinciale*, p. 274 as cited in Burn, *Ecclesiastical law*, II, p. 467. The prohibition applied to the solemnization, not to the contracting, of marriages. For the date ranges of ecclesiastical festivals see Cheney, *Handbook of dates*, tables 1 to 36.
33. In 1575 Convocation required the bishops to publicize in every parish church a statement that marriages might be solemnized at all times of the year, but Queen Elizabeth rejected the Article concerned. Despite the lack of any legal basis for the prohibited seasons after the Reformation, bishops and other church officers continued to issue licences of exemption for a fee. Burn, *Ecclesiastical law*, II, pp. 467–8.
34. These developments are also visible in the monthly national totals of marriages in table A2.4.

The autumn peak in marriages was never again so pronounced as it had been in the sixteenth century. By the mid seventeenth century it fell to index numbers in the region of 125–46, where it remained until the nineteenth century, with October taking over the lead from November after 1700 as the most popular month for marriage. The subsidiary peak in the early summer, which in the sixteenth century had been confined

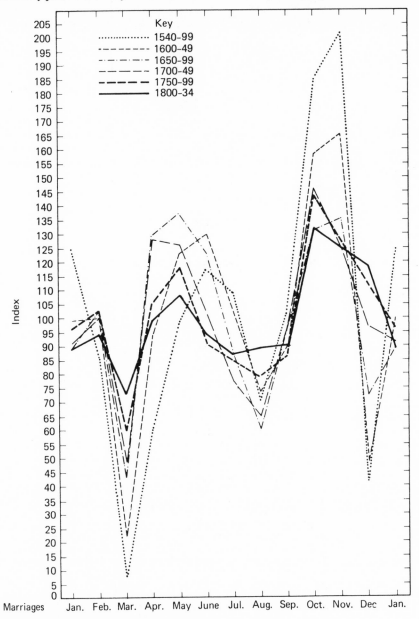

Figure 8.3: Seasonality of marriages

Source: Table 8.5

Table 8.5: Monthly indexes of marriages by half-century

(100 = all events × number of days in month/365.25)

Period	Jan.	Feb.	March	April	May	June	July	Aug.	Sept.	Oct.	Nov.	Dec.	Ratio max./min.	Mean absolute deviation
1540–99	124	86	8	61	98	117	109	70	102	184	201	41	25.13	39.4
1600–49	99	100	22	93	123	129	103	73	89	158	165	48	7.50	28.7
1650–99	89	102	43	129	137	123	87	60	96	131	135	72	3.19	25.8
1700–49	91	100	48	128	126	103	77	65	96	146	125	97	3.04	21.2
1750–99	96	102	60	105	117	91	84	79	86	143	127	112	2.38	17.5
1800–34	89	94	73	99	108	94	87	89	90	132	125	119	1.81	14.1
Percent of parishes at:														
Maximum	1.5	5.2	0.0	8.2	15.6	7.7	0.5	0.0	0.2	38.4	22.3	0.5		
Minimum	1.2	0.0	86.9	0.0	0.0	0.2	0.7	7.4	0.2	0.0	0.0	3.2		

Notes: See table 8.1.

Source: See table 8.1.

to June, grew both in height and in extent, reaching its maximum in the later seventeenth century when April, May, and June had indexes of 129, 137, and 123 respectively and May temporarily displaced November as the most popular month. From 1700, however, the peak both narrowed and subsided until in the early nineteenth century only May was left with an index over par (108).

This emergence and disappearance of an early summer peak encompasses several rather different courses followed by the constituent months, as can be seen from tables 8.5 and A2.4. The rise and fall of the number of marriages in June was a gradual one, building up during the sixteenth century to reach and maintain a high level from 1600 to 1699, and then declining rapidly. May reached its maximum plateau a little later, in the mid seventeenth century, which it maintained until 1750, after which a less rapid decline set in. With April, on the other hand, the rise to prominence was very fast around 1650 and the decline after 1750 was almost as rapid as June's subsidence earlier in the century. In aggregate, therefore, the growth of the early summer peak was a slow process spread over a period of about two centuries until by the later seventeenth century the early summer had become as popular as the autumn. But the process then went into reverse so that after 1750 the autumn regained its former absolute dominance in the seasonal pattern of marriages. The summer trough in marriages between these two peaks showed relatively little change over time, though it widened as July and September lost their earlier importance, and became shallower in the years after 1750.

Both the unevenness of the seasonal distribution of marriages and the scale of its reduction over time are clearly apparent in the summary statistics in the two final columns in table 8.5. The very high ratio of the maximum to the minimum month of 25.13 in the sixteenth century reflects the extraordinary deficiency of marriages in March more than their superfluity in November. But although the ratio fell as March gained in popularity, it was still at 1.81 in the early nineteenth century, higher than the equivalent ratios for baptisms and burials had ever been at any date. The mean absolute deviation of the monthly indexes is a more sensitive measure of changes in seasonality, for it is less dominated by the very low values in March and it also captures the relative movements of the early summer and autumn peaks as well as the changes in the summer trough discussed above. This statistic fell steadily over time from a very high figure of 39.4 in the sixteenth century to 14.1 in the early nineteenth century. And once more this last figure represents a greater seasonal variation than either baptisms or burials had ever experienced at any date.

The last two rows of table 8.5 show that marriages also differed from baptisms and burials in the degree to which individual parishes followed, or diverged from, the aggregate pattern. In order to maintain comparability with the other two series the maximum and minimum monthly indexes were calculated over the period 1601–1720, when the Lenten trough had somewhat abated and when the early summer peak was at its fullest extent. So far as the minimum month was concerned, the distribution of marriage seasonality across the parishes was even more homogeneous than with the other series. A very high proportion, 87 per cent, of the parishes recorded fewest marriages in March, and of the other months only August was recorded by more than a handful of parishes.[35] In contrast the maximum incidence of marriage seasonality was more widely spread than was the case with either baptisms or burials. A majority of

---

35. Parishes in Bedfordshire and Cambridgeshire were particularly prominent amongst those with an August minimum.

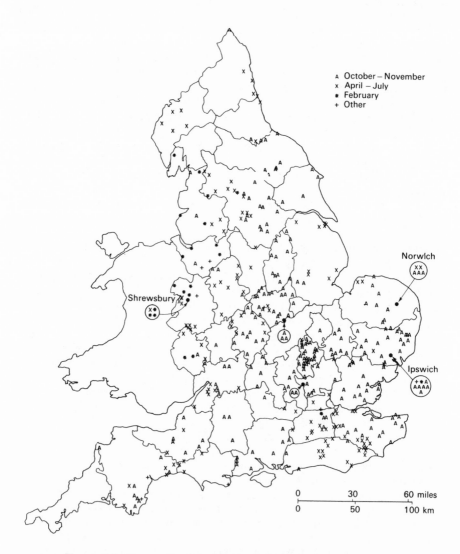

Figure 8.4: Geographical distribution of peak marriage seasons

Source: Monthly frequencies of marriages in set of 404 parishes

parishes (61 per cent) recorded most marriages in either October or November; but 31 per cent experienced a seasonal maximum in the early summer months of April to June. February was the only other month which represented a peak in marriage seasonality for more than a negligible number of parishes.

With marriages, as with baptisms and burials, the same general seasonal pattern can be found in outline over much of north-west Europe, but marriage is a more purely social event and hence the seasonal patterns of marriage reflect more markedly regional or national differences in social customs and religion. In catholic Italy, France, and west Belgium, for example, a continuing ban on marriages in Advent and Lent produced a peak in the intervening months of January and February to add to the more usual peaks in the early summer and autumn.[36] In the eighteenth century the Lutheran parishes around Giessen, and the Lutheran countries of Denmark and Sweden, shared the same general seasonal pattern as England but without any signs of a disinclination to marry in March or December.[37] In Denmark and Sweden the clustering of marriages in the autumn was particularly pronounced. In the period 1749–95 the latter recorded monthly indexes of 217, 166, and 185 in October, November, and December, making an autumn peak roughly equivalent to the highest recorded in England in the sixteenth century.[38]

But despite their differences of emphasis, these seasonal patterns of marriage in north-west Europe exhibit a common basic structure which reflects the exigencies of the changing seasonal demand for labour in agriculture.[39] The summer trough in marriages coincided with the major crop-gathering period of the year, and the autumn and early summer peaks fell in the slack seasons after the gathering of the 'harvests' of crops, and young animals, respectively. In England the two peak periods for marriage also coincided with the seasons in which 'hiring fairs' were usually held.[40] These were periods of change and mobility when young living-in farm servants often received much of the wages due to them and left to seek new masters or new opportunities.[41] They were natural times to break with the past, to cast off the old status of dependency and assume the social responsibilities and rewards of marriage.

In this context the geographical distribution of parishes with a marriage peak in either the autumn or the early summer may be of some interest. Figure 8.4 shows the geographical distribution of parish marriage peaks in the period 1601 to 1720 tabulated in table 8.5. Parishes with a peak in the early summer (April to June) are marked 'X' while autumn peaks (October and November) are denoted by an 'A', February peaks by a '*', and peaks at other times of the year by a '+'. Autumn marriage peaks clearly predominated over most of south-east England, with the

36. Italy: di Comite, 'I matrimoni nel XVII secolo', pp. 7–48; France: Guillaume and Poussou, *Histoire démographique*, p. 184; in west Belgium the peak occurred in February and April, Dalle, *De bevolking van Veurne-Ambacht*, pp. 135–7.

37. Imhof, 'Die nicht-namentliche Auswertung', p. 246; Johansen, *Bevolkningsudvikling*, p. 82. Fåhraeus, 'Om förhållandet', p. 232.

38. The monthly index numbers for Sweden (including Finland) from Jan. to Dec. were 78, 66, 67, 84, 72, 97, 62, 36, 83, 217, 166, 185. Fåhraeus, *ibid.*

39. The economic basis for the summer trough is particularly clear in mid-twentieth-century France (1927–38): in arable areas the summer minimum occurred in August while in the wine-growing regions in the south it fell in September. Bourgeois-Pichat, 'Le mariage', pp. 637–8.

40. A study of settlement examinations in eight counties from the seventeenth to the nineteenth centuries showed 90 per cent of hirings beginning on May Day (1 May), Michaelmas (29 September), or Martinmas (11 November). Kussmaul, *Servants in husbandry*, pp. 103–5.

41. Kussmaul, *ibid.*, pp. 73–7.

exception of Surrey, Sussex, and parts of west Kent. Further north and west the early summer peaks were more prominent. The February peak seems to have been very largely confined to certain parishes in a western strip of counties running from Lancashire down through Cheshire and Shropshire to Herefordshire. The regional distribution between the two main marriage seasons in early summer and the autumn appears to reflect the balance between pastoral and arable farming, and this impression is confirmed when the agricultural characteristics of each parish are taken into account. Table 8.6 shows that the predominantly arable parishes had most marriages in the autumn, while those that were more pastoral in character were more likely to experience a marriage peak in the early summer. Consequently, the national temporal pattern noted above, in which the early summer peak rose to an apogee in the later seventeenth century and then declined, may have reflected changes in the relative importance of pastoral and arable agriculture. Urban parishes, in contrast, although mainly experiencing a marriage peak in the autumn, were also more likely than the rural parishes to produce a seasonal maximum in a season other than the autumn or early summer.[42]

Table 8.6: Maximum month of marriage seasonality by farming type

| Farming type | Percentage | | | |
	April–June	Oct.–Nov.	Other	No. of parishes
Arable	19	77	4	215
Wood pasture	44	52	4	86
Open pasture	52	30	18	86
Urban	18	53	29	17
All	31	61	8	404

Key: Arable = 'Mixed farming types' and 'stock-keeping with corn-growing, sometimes with dairying'.
Wood pasture = 'Dairying and pig-keeping', 'stock fattening and pig-keeping', 'stock rearing and pig-keeping'.
Open pasture = All 'open pasture' types.

Sources: Marriage seasonality: see table 8.1; farming types: Thirsk, 'Farming regions', p. 4.

Although the seasonal pattern of marriages appears to have followed the rhythm of the agricultural year, it is important to remember that in England the event recorded in the parish registers was the 'solemnization of matrimony', a religious occasion which was not necessarily synchronous with the establishment of a stable sexual union. Indeed the high proportion of first births conceived prenuptially (between 20 and 40 per cent) shows that sexual relationships had often preceded the solemnization of marriage according to the rites of the Church of England.[43] Furthermore, the tendency, noted above, for prenuptial conceptions to follow the same seasonal pattern as that of later births indicates that for many couples sexual expression followed a

42. In Europe towns sometimes shared the seasonal marriage pattern of the surrounding countryside, and sometimes departed from it. Bardet, 'La démographie des villes', p. 123. In Geneva the seasonality of the marriages of immigrants was more in tune with rural patterns than that of the marriages of long-standing inhabitants of the town. Perrenoud, *La population de Genève*, 1, pp. 383–92.
43. Hair, 'Bridal pregnancy'.

general seasonal cycle and was not constrained by ideals of virginity before marriage. It does not, of course, follow that the establishment of a sexual relationship, even of a continuing kind, necessarily led to regular cohabitation, for the latter was a social act involving the expectation of economic and residential independence, conditions which made its feasibility dependent upon the availability of material resources.[44] Thus while the seasonal pattern of cohabitation, or household formation, cannot be observed, it is perhaps more likely that it followed the seasonality of marriage rather than that of sexual activity as implied by the seasonality of conceptions. For the peak seasons of marriage occurred at the points in the agricultural year when there was not only the leisure to celebrate in church and at table, but also a relative abundance of material wealth after the 'harvest', whether of crops or livestock.

Annual variation and co-variation

Just as the seasonal movements of births, deaths, and marriages throw some light on the relationship between the demography of early modern England and its social and economic context, so too do the annual fluctuations in the three series. In turning to consider the latter, it is convenient to begin by reviewing some of the circumstances which may have helped to produce the annual movements so evident in pullout 1. The disturbances visible in the graphs may have been generated within the demographic system itself, or they may have originated in shocks emanating from the wider world. To take the latter category first, variations in climate or in the price of food may have had an impact on each of the three demographic variables. For example, in a society where fuel was scarce and the insulation of dwellings poor, extreme winter temperatures might be expected to increase mortality from respiratory infections, reduce fertility either through the death of pregnant women or through the impact of infection on foetal wastage, and reduce nuptiality through the dislocation of normal activities caused by extreme cold.[45] High summer temperatures might have a similar effect on mortality and fertility, through an increase in water- and food-borne diseases. Again, food was necessary for survival, and the yield of the harvest each year therefore of major significance. As Davenant remarked in the late seventeenth century, fluctuations in the amount of grain available were reflected in more than proportionate movements in its price.[46] If alternative foodstuffs were not available, there would be an even more disproportionate impact on the division of the reduced supply of food amongst individuals because of their differing ability to pay the higher price. Already by the sixteenth century there was a significant section of the population dependent on the market for the satisfaction of all or most of its food requirements.[47] Since expenditure on food comprised a large proportion of the oudgets of ordinary people, harvest fluctuations had an immediate and striking impact on the standard of living.

---

44. For a summary of the social and economic correlates of marriage see Laslett, *The world we have lost*, ch. 4, and *Family life*, ch. 1.
45. Some of these possibilities are discussed below in this chapter and chapter 9. For the impact of climatic variation and infection on fertility, see Leridon, *Natalité*, pp. 46–8.
46. Davenant, 'An essay', II, pp. 224–5. Davenant derives some figures on the volume of agricultural production from Gregory King but presents these calculations as his own. Tooke in his *Thoughts and details on high and low prices*, part 3, p. 90, attributes them to King, and other scholars have followed suit. See Slicher van Bath, *Agrarian history*, pp. 118–9, where other formulations of the harvest/price relationship are given.
47. Everitt, 'Farm labourers' and 'Marketing'.

If Malthus was right in his observation that the rule of economic independence at marriage was accompanied in the minds of those contemplating matrimony by expectations of a minimum standard of living consonant with their station in life, then nuptiality may also be expected to have varied in the short run in response to fluctuations in the harvest.[48] Variations in the standard of living, and above all in nutrition may also have affected fertility, through changes in the frequency of sexual intercourse, in the proportion of anovulatory menstrual cycles, or in foetal wastage.[49] Mortality, too, might be affected by the prevailing level of nutrition. When food was scarce mortality might rise either from outright starvation or through a lowered resistance to disease.[50] The responsiveness of both fertility and mortality to fluctuations in the price of food, however, will have depended on how near the population was to the margins of subsistence, and the degree to which there was effective social intervention to protect the poor from the consequences of high food prices, for example through communally financed grain provision, or through price-linked relief benefits as under the Speenhamland system.[51]

Thus the ways in which fertility, mortality, and nuptiality may be found to have responded in the short term to fluctuations in external influences can illuminate several aspects of the social and economic structure in the past. But each of the three demographic processes may also have responded to variations in the other two series. For example, the high probability that infants might die in the days and weeks soon after birth makes it likely that the fluctuations in fertility were echoed by fluctuations in mortality.[52] Conversely fluctuations in mortality may have been reflected in counter-movements in both nuptiality and fertility as the number of potential marriage partners, and of pregnant women and the embryos they were carrying, varied inversely with the death rate. On the other hand, mortality fluctuations may also have found a positive echo in fertility as variations in the survivorship of breast-fed young children shortened or prolonged the average period of lactation and so affected fecundity.[53]

In addition to these biological links between the demographic processes there are others that were mediated by the social or economic structure. For example, with illegitimacy comparatively uncommon, and with a late age at marriage and relatively high adult mortality combining to limit the average number of children per marriage, first-born legitimate children comprised a significant fraction (about a quarter) of all

48. Malthus, *Essay on population*, pp. 67–8.
49. See, for example, Bongaarts, 'Does malnutrition affect fecundity?', for a discussion of the probable effects of poor nutrition in modern populations.
50. The relationship between nutritional level and resistance to disease is a disputed one. Writers emphasizing the connexion include McKeown, *The modern rise of population*; Scrimshaw, Taylor, and Gordon, *Interactions of nutrition and infection*. Contrary views are expressed in Keys *et al.*, *The biology of human starvation* and Hocking, *Starvation*. Moreover, a pathogen such as bubonic plague is so toxic that the level of nutrition of the patient scarcely affects the outcome. Biraben, *Les hommes et la peste*, 1, p. 147.
51. For a sixteenth-century example of communal purchases by an urban authority see Dyer, *Worcester*, p. 167. Government policy directives to justices of the peace, codified in the Book of Orders, are described in Leonard, *English poor relief* and their implementation discussed in Everitt, 'Marketing', pp. 577–86. For a discussion of the relationship between poor-relief expenditures and food prices in the period 1790–1834 see Baugh, 'Cost of poor relief'.
52. The distribution of deaths over the first year of life is studied in detail in Bourgeois-Pichat, 'La mesure de la mortalité infantile'.
53. Knodel, 'Breast feeding', pp. 1,113–4.

births.[54] Consequently one might expect that fluctuations in nuptiality would have been echoed by movements in fertility. Furthermore, fluctuations in nuptiality may themselves have reflected prior fluctuations in mortality. In a society where marriages entailed economic and residential independence the opportunity to marry depended upon the availability of housing, and on the means of earning a livelihood from a landholding, a craft practice, or from the demand for one's labour. The supplies of these 'ecological niches' could not be expanded rapidly in the short run, so *fluctuations* in the opportunity to marry will have depended largely on fluctuations in the mortality of those who already occupied them.

The co-variations in the fluctuations in the demographic series and in external factors may have been simultaneous or lagged by a number of months or years. The speed of response will have depended upon the biological, social, or economic mechanisms linking the variables and can therefore be a valuable indicator of which of several possible connexions was dominant in any particular instance. For it is evident even from this brief discussion that there was a dense network of possible relationships between fluctuations in fertility, mortality, and nuptiality both internally within the framework of the demographic processes themselves, and between them and external factors. Sometimes the direction of the movements in a pair of series, whether similar or contrary, can indicate the nature of the process linking them; but more often the interpretation of the patterns of co-variation in the series is problematical, with several possible links, both direct and indirect, between them.

The picture is further complicated by the internal structure which may be present in each series. The nature of the underlying process generating an observed series may be such that a fluctuation from the trend value in a given year entails sympathetic or compensatory movements in subsequent years in that series. For example, a sudden rise in mortality may anticipate the deaths of people who would normally have died soon afterwards and thus be followed by a period in which the numbers of deaths were unusually low. Compensatory fluctuations of this kind occur because of the effect of an initial fluctuation in a demographic rate on the stock of people normally at risk to experience the event in question. Thus fluctations in the birth rate affect the stock of fecundable women and fluctuations in nuptiality the stock of young people not already married. It is therefore probable that each of the three demographic series possessed an internal structure in which each fluctuation was followed by a compensatory echo. On the other hand, other series may contain a positive rather than a negative echo. For example, both the consumption of seed corn in years of deficient harvest and the ability to store grain in abundant years could have prolonged the influence of a harvest fluctuation and so forged a positive link between fluctuations in food prices in adjacent years.

A fluctuation at any given time in each of the series may therefore comprise not only the deviation from trend occurring at that moment because of a prior or simultaneous fluctuation in another series but also the echo of earlier fluctuations within the same series. In order to study the relationships between the fluctuations in a pair of series it is obviously essential to remove the contaminations arising from the internal structure linking the fluctuations within each of the series. Otherwise there is a

---

54. Family reconstitutions of 3,932 families in observation from marriage to the death of a spouse, drawn from 14 parishes over the period 1550–1840, produce an average of 3.97 births per family. Parishes as described on p. 248 above, omitting Colyton and adding Bottesford (Leics.), Earsdon (Northumbs.), and Hawkshead (Lancs.). The ratios in table 6.13, although unsatisfactory in some respects, also suggest about four births per marriage.

risk of mistakenly claiming that there is a systematic relationship between the fluctuations in two series when it may be a spurious artefact of similarities in their internal structures. Conversely, offsetting internal structures that have not been removed from the series may mask a genuine relationship between their short-run fluctuations.

It is evident that the potential interest of short-term fluctuations in fertility, mortality, and nuptiality is matched by the complexity of their dynamic relationships both to each other and to variations in the environment. In short, the subject is not an easy one; it poses problems that are both logically and technically demanding, and in such circumstances a casual or naïve approach can be disastrous. Unfortunately, despite the long-standing interest in the subject, few investigations have approached the data with the degree of rigour required by the nature of the questions posed. Usually the only structure removed from a series is a trend, which is often calculated as a simple moving average and then subtracted from the original data to yield a series of 'fluctuations'. Such a procedure leaves behind all the internal structure in the series derived from the 'echo' effects of earlier fluctuations and may therefore lead to spurious conclusions about relationships between them.[55] Even less justifiably, many studies have been quite unsystematic in their approach, relying upon a 'casual and sometimes entirely fallacious inference from raw demographic series'.[56] The casual approach typically involves the piling up of mounds of instances, preferably of a dramatic kind. Such an exercise is futile from a scientific point of view, because the issue is not whether individual examples of particular co-variations can ever be found in the historical record, for in long and variable series some examples of any particular relationship are likely to occur by chance. The issue is rather one of the strength and consistency of the relationships.

Such questions can only be answered by a systematic study, and one that is alert to the realities of the demographic and economic processes underlying the series. The most important technical problem is the isolation of pure fluctuations by removing both trend and the influences of earlier fluctuations, but this is by no means straightforward. In general, simple methods are limited both in their ability to remove the structure in the series and in the depth of the analysis that can be attempted. On the other hand, while more sophisticated methods can in principle identify and remove the structure more effectively, and can probe deeper into the relationships between fluctuations both within and between series, they make strong assumptions about the properties of the underlying processes. If these are mis-specified, and it is often difficult to be sure this is not the case, the apparently precise and detailed results may well be spurious.

This dilemma has persuaded us to adopt several approaches, ranging from the very simple to the more advanced. Where all methods agree, we can be reasonably confident that we have identified some genuine and robust features of short-term variation in the past. Where they differ, an assessment must be made of which of the methods is the most likely to produce correct results. In the event there turns out to be a substantial area of common ground between the results obtained by the different approaches. This is a fortunate outcome because there are some aspects of short-term

55. Unless the effects of internal structure are specifically estimated and controlled for, as in chapter 9. Furthermore, in transforming series using moving averages it is possible to generate periodicities, a point that needs to be borne in mind when interpreting the results. See, for example, table 9.1, and the discussion in Granger and Hughes, 'A new look at some old data'.

56. The quotation is from Lee, 'Methods and models', pp. 337–8.

variation that can only be analysed through the use of more complicated techniques. The fact that in the areas of overlap the latter tell the same story as other simpler methods increases our confidence in their correctness in those regions which only they can reach.[57]

We shall begin by casting an eye over the annual series of births, deaths, and marriages graphed in pullout 1 to identify some of the general features of short-term variation, and how they changed over time. We shall then attempt a more systematic analysis of the relationships obtaining between annual fluctuations in fertility, mortality, and nuptiality, both generally and in the years when fluctuations in each series were most extreme, at the same time investigating the relationships between fluctuations in the demographic variables and fluctuations in a series of real wages. Special attention will be given to periods of crisis mortality.

Annual fluctuations

The annual totals of events graphed in pullout 1 are the outcomes of the processes of birth, death, and marriage occurring within the population. Since in normal circumstances the size of the population changed only slowly over time, almost all the annual fluctuations on the graph are produced by variations in the processes, that is in fertility, mortality, and nuptiality, rather than by changes in the size of the population to which they relate. The graphs have been drawn to a logarithmic vertical scale so that a direct comparison can be made of the amplitude of the fluctuations in different years within the same series, or between the series.

Some features of short-term variation in fertility, mortality, and nuptiality are immediately apparent from the graphs. First, fluctuations in mortality were the most severe, and those in fertility the least, with nuptiality occupying an intermediate position. Second, fluctuations in both mortality and fertility were far from symmetrical around the long-term trend in each series. The greatest disturbances in mortality were surges above the normal level, while, in contrast, the biggest fluctuations in fertility were in a downward direction. Contrary movements (i.e. downward fluctuations in mortality and upward fluctuations in fertility) were more modest. Fluctuations in nuptiality, on the other hand, were fairly symmetrical in size above and below trend.

These differences in the amplitude and symmetry of the fluctuations are consistent with some of the features of short-term variation that have already been noted. The asymmetry of the fluctuations in mortality is consistent with the periodic exposure of the population to epidemic disease and the lack of any countervailing mechanism capable of producing a comparable reduction in mortality. This may at the same time account for the asymmetry in the fluctuations in fertility, since a sharp rise in mortality could have depressed fertility through maternal or foetal mortality. Other factors may also have operated asymmetrically. For example, nutrition appears to depress fecundability only when it falls below a threshold level. Above the threshold improvements in nutrition would be unlikely to produce any positive echo in fertility. It is also possible that frequency of sexual intercourse may have responded

57. We have also obtained similar results using Box-Jenkins (autoregressive integrated moving average methods). These techniques are flexible, but complex, so the analyses are not reported here. Other approaches to the analysis of short-run fluctuations include spectral analysis: see for example, Lee, 'Methods and models', 'Models of pre-industrial population dynamics', and 'Natural fertility and spectral analysis'.

asymmetrically, being more likely to fall below a normal level when conditions such as climate, nutritional level, or social or economic circumstances were unfavourable than to rise above it when conditions were exceptionally favourable.

The graphs in pullout 1 also demonstrate another feature of the fluctuations in the underlying demographic processes, for the fluctuations followed certain patterns rather than being random or unstructured. For example, there are some conspicuous examples of compensatory movements in the series of deaths, particularly in the years following major mortality crises in the late 1550s, the 1590s, the mid 1640s, and the late 1720s.[58] Compensatory movements can also be found in the series of births and marriages; for example, there is a particularly marked trough followed by a recovery in both series in the years 1799–1805. Conversely, the graphs also show that a fluctuation in a series was often positively related to the fluctuation in the previous year. Many of the examples of counter-swings just cited occurred after periods in which the numbers of events had been above or below trend consistently for a number of years. Indeed most of the major disturbances to the series extended over a period of more than one year. There are several possible reasons for this pattern. For example, in the case of mortality it may have been related to the length of time it took an epidemic disease to spread across the country. The same consideration may also explain the periods of several years with below-average numbers of births, in view of the links between mortality and fertility that have already been discussed. Alternatively the fluctuations in social and economic conditions that influenced short-run change in all three series may have tended to move in a similarly clustered way.

The more striking periods of disturbance readily visible on the graphs also provide many examples of the possible relationships between fluctuations in the series discussed earlier. There were several periods, such as the late 1550s, the late 1590s and the late 1720s, when surges in mortality were accompanied by falls in nuptiality and fertility. On other occasions, as in 1692–3 and 1799–1801, there was a positive association between fluctuations in nuptiality and fertility independent of mortality. The real issue, however, is whether such patterns in the co-movements of the fluctuations in the series were sufficiently frequent, either in extreme circumstances or more generally across the whole range of fluctuations large and small, that they can be taken to constitute evidence of the existence of a coherent relationship between short-term variations in the series in question.

Crude birth, death, and marriage rates

It is therefore time to turn to a more systematic examination of the fluctuations in demographic behaviour, and in so doing turn from totals of events to demographic rates. Totals of births, deaths, and marriages are not ideal indicators of fluctuations in the underlying demographic processes because they are unable to reflect sudden and relatively sharp changes in population size. Population size usually changed rather slowly, by 1.5 per cent per annum at most, but occasionally there were more dramatic changes. For example in two four-year periods of very high mortality accompanied by very low fertility in the late 1550s and the late 1720s the population fell by 6.2 and 4.0

---

58. In such years the population may well have been reduced, so a fall in the number of deaths does not necessarily entail a fall in mortality. This point will be discussed below.

per cent respectively.[59] In such circumstances the absolute numbers of births, marriages, and deaths in the years after the crisis will be lower than normal even though the vital rates may have returned to their pre-crisis level. Thus fluctuations in the numbers of events exaggerate compensatory downswings in the death *rate* after a crisis, while flattening compensatory upswings in the birth and marriage *rates*. It is therefore more satisfactory to investigate the fluctuations in the vital rates rather than those in the totals of events. Annual crude birth, death, and marriage rates are given in table A3.3, and their derivation is described in the accompanying text.

The annual crude rates reveal a degree of short-term variation that was concealed when the data were aggregated into five-year blocks for back projection as discussed in the previous chapter. For example, the expectation of life at birth (e_0') calculated for 1556 was based on deaths from the years 1554–8, and deaths from 1559–63 were used for the next quinquennium centring on 1561 (see table 7.15). They yielded e_0's of 30.7 and 27.8 years respectively. This suggests a whole decade of high mortality. The crude death rates show that this was not so. Rather there was a major crisis in the years 1557–9 when the rates were 42.5, 53.9, and 47.3 per 1,000 respectively, while in only two other years of the decade 1554–63 did the rate exceed 30 (in 1560 and 1563) and in three years it was below 25. In contrast, the unusually low e_0s for 1681 and 1686 (28.5 and 31.8 years) were caused by continuously high mortality throughout the decade 1679–88, when the crude death rate was never lower than 28.9 nor higher than 38.9 per 1,000.

Annual crude rates are the most widely used of all demographic measures, and it may be useful to summarize the distribution of each of the vital rates over the 331 years being studied as a background to a consideration of their short-term variation. It should be borne in mind in this connexion that they were influenced by secular changes in fertility, mortality, and nuptiality as well as by short-term fluctuations.

The median crude death rate was 25.9; it never fell below 19.2 (1583) and it attained its highest value (53.9) in 1558. Half of the years had death rates that fell within a fairly narrow range from 23.5 to 28.4, while 80 per cent of the annual rates lay between 22.0 and 31.6. It is noteworthy that despite the existence of violent fluctuations in mortality, only six years (1557–9, 1625, 1665, and 1729) recorded rates in excess of 40 per 1,000 (42.5, 53.9, 47.3, 41.6, 43.0, and 44.7 respectively).

Although the level of the crude birth rate was higher than that of the death rate, its spread was similar in absolute terms, with the rates of half of the years in the period also falling in a band of five points (from 31.6 to 36.1, around a median of 34.1), and 80 per cent of the annual rates lying within a range of 10 points (from 29.3 to 39.1). Since the median crude birth rate was higher than the median death rate, it follows that in relative terms the distribution of birth rates was more tightly bunched than that of the death rates. The lowest rate recorded was 22.9 (in 1659) and the highest was 44.3 (in 1815).

The crude marriage rate was, of course, much lower than either the birth or the death rate, but in relative terms the distribution was similar to that of the birth rate.

59. From 1556 to 1560 and from 1727 to 1731. The greatest annual reductions occurred in 1558–9 (3.2 per cent) and 1728–9 (1.7 per cent). The population also fell, though less dramatically, in 1544–6, 1587–8, 1592–3, 1596–8, 1623–6, 1638–9, 1649–50, 1652–4, in all but five years between 1657 and 1686, 1689–90, 1693–4, 1710–2, 1719–21, 1741–3 and 1762. After this date the population did not fall again (other than in war time) until 1974–5. Table A3.3, 1541–1871; Mitchell and Deane, *British historical statistics*, pp. 9–10, 1871–1940; *Registrar-General's Statistical Review of England and Wales*, 1940 to date.

The median rate was 8.4 and the central half of the 331 years had rates lying between 7.9 and 9.0, while 80 per cent of the annual rates fell in the range 7.3 to 10.1. The lowest rate recorded was 5.5 (in 1648) and the highest was 15.1 (in 1548). The highest marriage rates occurred in the mid sixteenth century, probably because remarriage was more common at that date.[60] The extreme lower end of the distribution was dominated by years from the later seventeenth century, a period when nuptiality was generally low and when registration was imperfect on account of the practice of clandestine marriage.[61]

The question of how far annual fluctuations in the vital rates followed fluctuations in the standard of living has attracted much attention. The most important factor in determining the level of the standard of living in the short run was the price of food. Many annual food-price series therefore cover harvest years beginning in September or October, but there is evidence to suggest that prices in the summer months began to reflect expectations about the harvest to be gathered in the autumn, which could be estimated with growing confidence as the year progressed.[62] Thus, if there was a connexion between demographic behaviour and food prices, one would expect the vital rates in the late summer to be responsive to the food prices of the next harvest year, rather than those of the harvest in the previous autumn. We have therefore calculated an alternative set of vital rates running from 1 July to 30 June as a more appropriate series for comparison with fluctuations in the standard of living than the calendar year rates contained in table A3.3, and our subsequent discussion of annual fluctuations is based exclusively on these rates.[63] To avoid ambiguity we refer to individual years by specifying the calendar years they span (e.g. 1541/2 runs from 1 July 1541 to 30 June 1542). Since the first and last dates for which population estimates have been calculated are 1 July 1541 and 1 July 1871, the series of vital rates run from 1541/2 to 1870/1, and therefore cover 330 years.

The Phelps Brown and Hopkins real-wage data, as revised in appendix 9, provide a convenient measure of annual fluctuations in living standards. They refer to years running from 1 October to 30 September, and are cited here according to the calendar years they span (e.g. 1596/7). The series relates prices of a basketful of consumables to money wages, but as the latter changed very slowly, the short-term fluctuations in the real-wage index are largely determined by variations in consumables prices, which in turn are dominated by fluctuations in the price of food.[64] Although by no means everyone in the past depended for their survival on market purchases, nor are wage rates necessarily a good guide to earnings, the real-wage index may still be regarded as an approximate guide to fluctuations in the overall standard of living.

In this connexion the following points may be borne in mind. First, although in times of shortage consumers may have 'traded down' to cheaper grains, at least until the late seventeenth century the price of all grains tended to move in sympathy with

60. See chapter 7, fn. 101.

61. For nuptiality see table A3.1 and figure 10.9. The imperfections of marriage registration in this period are discussed on pp. 28–9 above.

62. The behaviour of prices in response to expectation about the coming harvest is extensively chronicled and discussed by Tooke. See, for example, his treatment of cereal prices in the months before the harvests of 1795 (poor) and 1796 (good). *History of prices*, I, pp. 181–3, 187, 390.

63. The totals of events occurring in the years running July to June are given in table A2.3. The corresponding population totals can be obtained by simple interpolation from the calendar year totals in table A3.3.

64. Food (and drink) accounted for 80 per cent of the basket of consumables. Phelps Brown and Hopkins, 'Seven centuries of the prices of consumables', p. 180.

one another.[65] Second, although a proportion of the population consisted in self-sufficient farmers producing food for their own consumption and so apparently immune from movements in the real-wage index, the more severe a harvest deficiency the higher the proportion of this group that would be forced into the market as purchasers of food. Third, in an economy where expenditure on food accounted for a high proportion of all consumption, fluctuations in food prices caused large proportional variations in the relatively small amount of purchasing power available for other goods and services. Those who provided these goods and services were therefore subjected to exaggerated fluctuations in the demand for their labour, which diminished their earnings in times of high food prices, though the opposite happened, of course, when food was cheap. Agricultural labourers experienced the same contrary movements since deficient harvests both diminished the demand for their labour, and raised the price of food, while abundant harvests produced the opposite effect.

In so far as agricultural wage labourers and producers of other goods and services were not cushioned from the effects of poor harvests by direct access to food from their own plots of land, the real-wage index will therefore tend to understate the size of the annual fluctuations in their standard of living. In contrast, farmers who had a surplus for sale even in bad years may have sometimes enjoyed an increased income in years of general suffering. Their standard of living would then have tended to vary inversely with the real wage. However, both the increasing prevalence of wage labour in agriculture and the growth of the non-agricultural sector of the economy between the sixteenth and the nineteenth centuries will have meant that a rising proportion of the population was adversely affected by high food prices both as consumers and as producers.

Annual percentage deviations from trend in vital rates and real wages

In order to examine the relationship between short-term variation in the series of real wages and vital rates we first need to remove the primary influences of the secular trends so as to isolate the fluctuations. Accordingly we have re-expressed the rates and real-wage index number for each year as a percentage deviation from a 25-year unweighted moving average of each series centred on the year in question. This procedure has the further advantage that because the amplitudes of the fluctuations in individual years are proportional to trend they are comparable both within each series, and between the series.[66] Both the original annual values and the 25-year moving averages of the series are plotted in figure 8.5, the lighter line representing the moving average. Since the vertical scale of the graph is logarithmic, the distances between the heavy and lighter lines, which represent the deviations of the annual values from trend, are also directly comparable from year to year and between the series.

Before we examine the relationships between the series it may be useful to consider the degree of variation within each of them and the changes which occurred over time. To help bring out the patterns implicit in the figure more clearly the data have been summarized by averaging the annual percentage deviations from the 25-year moving means for each decade and quarter century. The results are displayed in table 8.7 and

65. Appleby, 'Grain prices and subsistence crises', pp. 876–81.
66. A similar procedure is adopted in chapter 9 where the series are divided by a centred 11-year moving average.

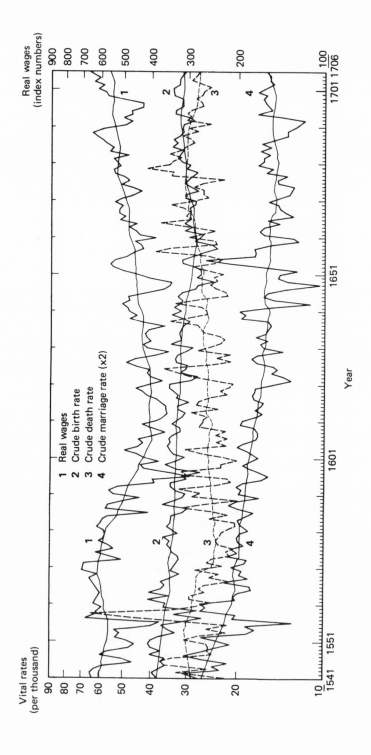

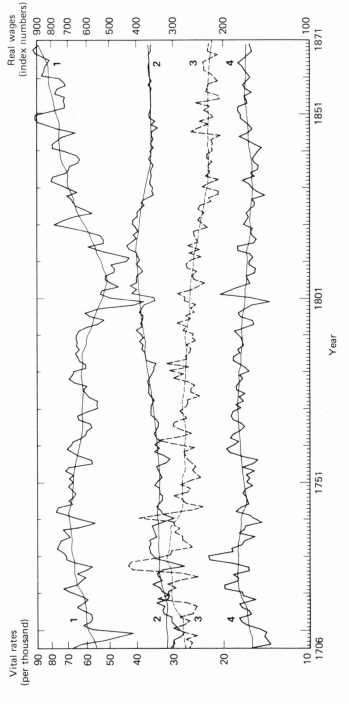

Figure 8.5: Deviations from trend in annual vital rates (July–June) and real wages (October–September)

Note: The trend lines represent a 25-year moving average of the annual values.

Source: See text.

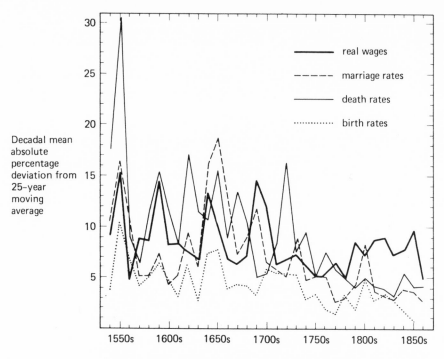

Figure 8.6: Decadal percentage deviations from trend in vital rates and real wages

Source: Table 8.7.

the decadal figures are graphed in figure 8.6. Several features of the variation in the series deserve comment.

First, annual fluctuations in mortality were almost always more pronounced than variations in nuptiality and fertility, the last being the most stable of the three demographic series. The pronounced variability of mortality in the short run has inclined some scholars to believe that it was also the most variable component of demographic change in the long run and therefore the one most responsible for changes in the rate of population growth. Such an inference is not only logically fallacious but also, as is clear from the results of the previous chapter, empirically incorrect. Most of the time the degree of variation in nuptiality was intermediate between fertility and mortality, but in some decades, notably the 1640s, 1650s, 1690s, and 1800s, nuptiality was more variable than mortality. Second, the variability of each of the three demographic series declined over time. In the first full quarter century (1550/1–1574/5) the average absolute proportional deviation of the annual crude death rate from trend was 17.7 per cent, while the comparable figures for the marriage and birth rates were 12.2 and 8.0 per cent. By the mid nineteenth century (1850/1–1870/1) the average percentage deviations had declined to 4.0, 3.1, and 0.8 respectively.

Several historians have noted the 'stabilization' of mortality in the early modern period and have described it primarily in terms of the disappearance of the major

Table 8.7: Mean absolute percentage deviations from 25-year moving average

Decade[1]	Real wage	CDR	CMR	CBR	Decade[1]	Real wage	CDR	CMR	CBR
1540s[2]	9.1	17.6	10.5	3.8	1710s	6.3	8.3	5.7	5.5
1550s	15.3	30.3	16.3	10.4	1720s	6.6	16.1	5.2	5.3
1560s	4.8	9.0	10.4	6.9	1730s	7.3	7.2	8.9	5.3
1570s	8.8	6.3	5.0	4.2	1740s	5.8	9.4	4.7	2.9
1580s	8.6	11.6	5.1	4.9	1750s	5.1	5.1	5.4	3.4
1590s	14.4	15.3	7.3	6.4	1760s	5.3	7.5	5.2	1.9
1600s	8.2	11.7	4.3	4.7	1770s	6.5	5.7	2.6	1.5
1610s	8.4	8.4	5.3	3.1	1780s	5.0	5.0	3.1	3.2
1620s	7.4	17.0	9.3	6.3	1790s	8.5	4.0	4.3	2.0
1630s	6.7	11.4	6.0	3.6	1800s	7.2	4.9	8.3	4.7
1640s	13.2	10.6	16.1	7.3	1810s	8.8	4.2	3.7	2.6
1650s	10.2	15.1	18.6	7.7	1820s	8.9	3.9	3.2	3.4
1660s	6.9	8.9	9.4	3.9	1830s	7.2	3.1	2.9	2.6
1670s	6.3	13.3	7.2	4.3	1840s	7.7	5.5	3.9	1.5
1680s	7.2	10.4	9.0	4.2	1850s	9.6	4.0	3.7	0.8
1690s	14.5	5.0	11.7	3.3	1860s	4.9	4.1	2.7	0.7
1700s	11.9	5.3	6.5	5.8					

Quarter centuries[1]	Real wage	CDR	CMR	CBR	Quarter centuries	Real wage	CDR	CMR	CBR
1550/1–1574/5	10.5	17.7	12.2	8.0	1725/6–1749/50	6.6	12.3	6.5	4.7
1575/6–1599/1600	9.9	11.9	5.6	5.1	1750/1–1774/5	5.8	6.1	4.7	2.4
1600/1–1624/5	7.7	11.3	6.0	4.8	1775/6–1799/1800	6.3	4.8	3.5	2.4
1625/6–1649/50	9.9	12.3	10.3	5.1	1800/1–1824/5	9.6	4.2	5.4	3.7
1650/1–1674/5	8.3	12.0	12.6	5.5	1825/6–1849/50	6.7	4.4	3.4	2.2
1675/6–1699/1700	9.8	9.1	9.8	3.8	1850/1–1870/1	6.8	4.0	3.1	0.8
1700/1–1724/5	8.3	6.2	5.9	5.2					

Notes: [1] Years run from 1 July to 30 June (vital rates) and 1 September to 31 August (real wages). Decades run from year 0/1 to year 9/0. [2] 1541/2–1549/50.

Sources: Real wages, table A9.2; crude vital rates calculated from table A2.3 (events, July–June) and table A3.3 (interpolated to obtain populations for July–June).

surges in mortality due to epidemic disease or starvation, concluding that the death rate fell as a result.[67] But it is possible, of course, for mortality to 'stabilize' at a higher level, an outcome that is difficult to detect if only the totals of deaths are known. The evidence contained in table 8.7, together with the figures of the expectation of life at birth presented in table 7.15, shows that the 'stabilization' of mortality over the first 75 years of the seventeenth century was accompanied by a deterioration, rather than an improvement, in the 'background' level of mortality. This pattern is consistent with the view that there were long-term changes in the relationships between micro-organisms and their human hosts, whereby an initial phase of sporadic but widespread and lethal encounters, characterized by infrequent and massive increases in mortality (epidemics), gave way to a less hectic, endemic phase, in which the relationship was more continuous and the general level of mortality consequently higher. Later still, a mutual accommodation might occur, with the micro-organisms becoming less lethal and the host more tolerant, so that a long-term fall in mortality ensued.[68] On a less sweeping time scale, however, the variability of mortality was often positively related to the level attained by the death rate. The large changes of level in the expectation of life at birth which occurred in the late sixteenth century, and in the century after 1675, parallel the changing variability of mortality as shown in table 8.7 and figure 8.6.

But it was not only mortality that stabilized between the mid sixteenth and mid nineteenth centuries. There was a considerable decline in the mean annual proportional deviations from trend in all three vital rates. If fluctuations in fertility, nuptiality, and mortality were interconnected, then a dampening in the variability of one of the processes could have helped to stabilize the others. Alternatively the demographic processes may have stabilized because environmental influences became less volatile or the population less sensitive to them. Data on climate are only available from the later seventeenth century (temperature from 1659 and rainfall from 1697), but they betray no signs of any changes in variability during the period studied.[69] On the other hand, there were several changes in economic and social life that may have lessened the impact of fluctuations in the environment. For example, one consequence of improvements in the standards of the construction of houses and in the supply of fuel may have been to put less strain on the body's energy reserves in periods of extreme cold, thereby reducing the probability that such periods would be ones of high mortality and low fertility.[70] Or again, improvements in agricultural

67. Helleiner, 'The vital revolution reconsidered', p. 85. Chambers also emphasizes the importance of the decline in epidemic mortality in the eighteenth century, *Population, economy and society*, pp. 87–106, 150–1. Flinn, however, although arguing for a reduction in the frequency and severity of crises, is guarded on the question of a fall in the general level of mortality. 'The stabilisation of mortality', pp. 315–7.
68. For a detailed exposition of this thesis, with historical examples, see McNeill, *Plagues and peoples*. It is also considered, and rejected, for England by McKeown, mainly because it would imply the existence of considerable migration and a *rise* in mortality at some date before the nineteenth century, phenomena that are excluded *a priori* in McKeown's schematic view of history. McKeown, *The modern rise of population*, ch. 7. Long term trends in mortality are discussed in ch. 7, above, and the evidence on migration patterns in the period before 1750 is summarized in Clark, 'Migration in England'.
69. Data were taken from Lamb, *Climate*, II, pp. 572–5, 620–3, and analysed by Box-Jenkins (ARIMA) methods. Although the annual rainfall figures became more stable around 1800 they regained their former variability in the course of the nineteenth century. Interpretation of the data is complicated by the increase in the number of stations contributing to the composite series.
70. Medieval houses were impermanent structures. The distribution of first-building dates for permanent houses built to higher standards rises sharply from 1550 reaching a maximum in the period 1660–1720. Machin, 'The great rebuilding', pp. 39, 55. The increase in availability of coal in inland areas via canals

production, storage, and distribution would have helped to lessen the impact of climatic variation on the food supply, and with the 'standard of living' less subject to violent fluctuations, the variability of fertility, mortality, and nuptiality may also have diminished. Furthermore, the institutionalization of communal responsibility for individual survival through the poor law may have secured a more equitable distribution of food in times of crisis than would have occurred if allocation had been left to market forces tempered by individual charity.[71]

In this context it is instructive to consider the changes in the variability of the real-wage index over time, which are also included in table 8.7 and figure 8.6. Fluctuations in the index are dominated by the price of food, and so the variability of the index reflects the variability of the weather mediated by the system of agricultural production and distribution. Over most of the period, from the 1540s to the 1750s, the real-wage index experienced the same modest reduction in variability as the three demographic series. There was also a close similarity between real wages and the demographic series in some of the major exceptions to this common trend. The 1550s, the 1590s, and the 1650s, for example, were decades of great fluctuation in real wages as well as in fertility, nuptiality, and mortality. The existence of a common pattern in the 1550s and 1650s is reassuring because it suggests that the great variability of the demographic series was not an artefact of the particularly defective registration in these two decades.[72] The increased variability of the demographic series in the 1620s, however, was not paralleled in real wages, and the extreme fluctuations in the latter in the 1690s were reflected only in the marriage series, the crude birth and death rates being more stable than usual in this decade of very high food prices. From the 1690s onwards the real-wage series was much less subject to massive, temporary increases in variability and decades of unusually high variability in the demographic rates occurred quite independently of fluctuations in the standard of living.

After 1750 the long-term trends in the variability of the economic and demographic series part company, for while the latter continued to become more stable, the variability of real wages tended to increase until the mid nineteenth century. The decline in the long-term trends in the variability of all the series in the period before 1750 would be consistent with the hypothesis that improvements in agricultural production, storage, and distribution stabilized food prices and lessened the impact of climatic variation on the population. But the subsequent rise in the variability of food prices poses a problem of explanation, since it suggests that trends in the variability of fertility, mortality, and nuptiality were independent of that in food prices. Indeed, even in the period before 1750 the lack of a perfect correspondence between the decades of unusually high variability in the four series suggests that the variation in

and railways is discussed by Wrigley, 'Supply of raw materials in the industrial revolution'. For the biological effects of extreme cold see Royal College of Physicians, *Report of the Committee on Accidental Hypothermia*. The connection between daily temperature change and mortality, particularly amongst the elderly, in Britain to-day is described in Bull and Morton, 'Relationship of temperature with death rates' For the relationship between reproductive efficiency and stored body energy see Frisch, 'Nutrition, fatness and fertility', especially pp. 99–101.

71. The traditional medieval principles underlying individual and social responsibility for the poor are discussed in Tierney, *Medieval poor law*. These principles were codified into an administrative system in 1598 and 1601 (39 Elizabeth I, c.3 and 43 Elizabeth I, c.2). There are few thorough studies of the actual operation of the old poor law. But see, for example, Hampson, *The treatment of poverty in Cambridgeshire*; Beier, 'Poor relief in Warwickshire', and Baugh, 'Cost of poor relief'.

72. See figures 1.1 and 1.2.

real wages was neither a necessary nor a sufficient cause of variation in each of the three demographic processes.

The summary measures of variability contained in table 8.7 and figure 8.6 therefore afford only rather inconclusive indications of the nature of the relationship between short-term variation in the series. In order to pursue the problem further a more systematic exploration of the connexions between the fluctuations in each pair of series is required. *A priori* one might expect such connexions to be most apparent when the fluctuations in either series were at their greatest. We shall therefore begin by concentrating on the 20 years in each series when the percentage deviations of the annual values from the 25-year moving average were most extreme.[73] Since, in this preliminary analysis, only a limited number of exceptional, single years are under consideration no attempt has been made to remove the internal structure in each of the series.

Extreme fluctuations

To help bring out the relationship between the extreme fluctuations in each series and fluctuations in the other series, table 8.8 displays both the magnitudes of the 20 greatest fluctuations in each direction in each series and the sizes of the percentage deviations of the other series in the same years. The first column in each panel of the table shows that these years were not spread evenly throughout the whole period, a result consistent with the reduction in the variation of the series over time discussed above. If, for convenience, three 'centuries' are distinguished, beginning in 1541/2, 1640/1, and 1745/6, the long final period contains only 9 of the 40 years of extreme fluctuation (20 high + 20 low) in the real-wage series, and only 3, 2, and 1 extreme fluctuations in the series of marriages, births, and deaths, respectively.[74] Extreme fluctuations in the death rates were more frequent in the first century than in the second, in the ratio of 22 to 17, while the series of marriage rates and real wages experienced more extreme fluctuations in the second period in the ratios of 14:23 and 13:18 respectively. The greatest deviations in the birth rate were fairly evenly split between the two periods in the ratio 20:18. The results of an analysis of extreme fluctuations will therefore largely reflect the relationships obtaining between the series in the period before 1745.[75]

By way of example of the use to which the data in table 8.8 can be put, we can test the hypothesis that there was a connexion between low real wages and high death rates. To give the hypothesis the greatest possible chance of success we shall make the rather weak requirement that in the years when real wages were proportionately most below trend the death rate need only be above average. The second panel of table 8.8 shows that in the years when real wages fell most below trend the death rate was sometimes, but by no means always, above average. The first line of the panel, referring to 1596/7, provides a striking example of the expected pattern, for real

73. In the case of the vital rates these years are almost exactly the same as those in which they attained their highest and lowest values. The pronounced secular trend in real wages, however, meant that most of the lowest values occurred in the period around 1600 and most of the highest values in the nineteenth century, so the years of greatest fluctuation from trend do not correspond to those with the most extreme values.
74. The boundaries correspond approximately with periods of major change in the variability of the series and in secular trends in population and real wages. They are also used later in this chapter and in chapter 9.
75. The analyses presented later in this chapter and in chapter 9 show that the relationships between the series were generally strongest before 1745, and in some cases weakened considerably after that date.

Table 8.8: Twenty greatest annual deviations above and below a 25-year moving average in each series, with contemporaneous deviations in other series

Real wages	Annual percentage deviation above or below (−) moving average			
ABOVE	Year	Real wage	Death rate	Marriage rate	Birth rate
	1821/2	27.55	−1.68	5.64	5.93
	1654/5	22.88	−11.60	36.05	9.28
	1690/1	22.04	−8.40	−10.95	−1.08
	1557/8	20.75	60.54	−5.00	−25.75
	1850/1	20.58	−3.85	6.17	1.60
	1706/7	20.38	−3.62	0.67	−3.20
	1653/4	19.61	6.58	1.79	−2.38
	1603/4	19.47	21.04	3.73	5.88
	1627/8	19.16	−18.56	6.52	4.56
	1851/2	19.04	−1.71	5.60	1.74
	1849/50	18.75	8.04	2.60	−3.24
	1689/90	18.02	4.80	−11.29	2.01
	1822/3	17.30	2.86	3.02	6.08
	1704/5	16.71	7.09	0.82	3.34
	1655/6	16.68	−16.91	67.52	10.33
	1592/3	15.92	29.80	3.65	1.10
	1643/4	14.80	29.27	−30.59	4.14
	1722/3	14.44	−3.32	12.19	3.08
	1833/4	14.23	−7.80	8.31	−2.53
	1570/1	13.91	7.28	−6.35	−1.15
BELOW	1596/7	−35.78	20.86	−15.33	−4.38
	1556/7	−33.66	7.30	−41.78	−12.79
	1710/1	−29.84	1.22	−12.21	−12.70
	1800/1	−29.43	4.94	−18.05	−11.16
	1555/6	−28.36	−28.18	−15.52	1.41
	1649/50	−24.55	−11.91	−15.29	−17.00
	1799/1800	−23.70	−4.56	−5.32	−2.93
	1648/9	−23.57	−6.07	−35.01	−5.84
	1597/8	−22.80	25.61	−9.10	−17.72
	1697/8	−22.06	−5.41	4.50	−1.57
	1545/6	−21.64	26.55	−14.53	−0.91
	1586/7	−21.56	1.46	−8.18	−6.69
	1698/9	−21.40	−3.26	8.17	−0.98
	1812/3	−21.10	−5.65	−4.34	−0.87
	1550/1	−20.51	−14.75	−11.18	10.97
	1709/10	−20.21	−10.07	−9.79	−9.97
	1647/8	−19.10	−11.04	−17.98	−4.32
	1740/1	−18.50	0.19	−15.30	−2.87
	1661/2	−18.47	6.52	−16.97	−4.07
	1630/1	−18.11	7.27	−14.66	−4.78

(cont.)

Table 8.8: (cont.)

Death rates	Annual percentage deviation above or below (−) moving average			
ABOVE	Year	Real wage	Death rate	Marriage rate	Birth rate
	1558/9	124.23	9.64	−7.09	−6.68
	1557/8	60.54	20.75	−5.00	−25.75
	1625/6	42.99	0.23	−9.42	−3.81
	1657/8	42.93	0.35	12.03	−7.49
	1728/9	41.23	−13.70	−7.91	−18.67
	1727/8	37.19	−9.89	−8.75	−3.30
	1680/1	36.47	2.41	3.23	−0.44
	1741/2	36.29	−8.56	−9.39	−12.43
	1729/30	35.39	−1.75	4.01	−8.88
	1638/9	35.08	−0.34	−1.09	−4.97
	1665/6	31.69	−6.81	−8.32	7.89
	1592/3	29.80	15.92	3.65	1.10
	1587/8	29.47	12.47	4.50	−10.34
	1643/4	29.27	14.80	−30.59	4.14
	1624/5	26.61	2.43	−5.81	0.97
	1545/6	26.55	−21.64	−14.53	−0.91
	1597/8	25.61	−22.80	−9.10	−17.72
	1658/9	25.14	−7.36	13.98	−16.69
	1762/3	24.21	6.48	1.12	−3.27
	1544/5	23.33	1.28	−4.38	−5.39
BELOW	1555/6	−28.18	−28.36	−15.52	1.41
	1553/4	−28.09	−8.85	−19.95	−9.72
	1677/8	−28.08	−7.65	−1.64	−1.48
	1567/8	−25.61	6.71	9.89	8.23
	1541/2	−19.73	5.90	4.02	−0.02
	1600/1	−19.65	−13.64	−0.97	−0.11
	1621/2	−18.72	1.05	−9.13	9.15
	1627/8	−18.56	19.16	6.52	4.56
	1589/90	−18.46	1.11	7.27	1.32
	1725/6	−18.08	−7.77	−0.53	1.64
	1629/30	−18.03	−6.40	4.43	2.68
	1547/8	17.97	4.40	23.52	8.74
	1646/7	−17.62	−7.19	−3.00	5.58
	1645/6	−17.39	8.13	1.13	7.96
	1655/6	−16.91	16.68	67.52	10.33
	1692/3	−16.44	−8.22	−19.94	−2.25
	1733/4	−16.38	12.56	5.60	8.10
	1717/8	−16.07	7.99	3.78	2.37
	1549/50	−16.01	−17.16	0.35	8.96
	1633/4	−15.90	−6.94	−1.14	−0.30

Table 8.8: (cont.)

Marriage rates	Annual percentage deviation above or below (−) moving average			
ABOVE	Year	Marriage rate	Real wage	Death rate	Birth rate
	1655/6	67.52	16.68	−16.91	10.33
	1654/5	36.05	22.88	−11.60	9.28
	1561/2	29.93	9.60	−15.41	1.48
	1641/2	28.17	10.98	−0.05	3.65
	1731/2	27.38	5.17	−2.62	5.22
	1730/1	26.30	6.58	9.37	1.91
	1559/60	25.66	6.64	18.13	−22.59
	1639/40	24.31	12.13	15.23	1.76
	1547/8	23.52	4.40	−17.97	8.74
	1802/3	22.83	3.07	11.22	6.87
	1560/1	21.93	1.57	−2.42	2.74
	1640/1	20.98	5.40	−0.18	11.47
	1542/3	20.01	7.95	12.93	5.33
	1683/4	16.94	−2.47	14.81	−3.96
	1552/3	14.67	−5.80	−7.42	3.08
	1701/2	14.10	5.75	−5.30	8.90
	1658/9	13.98	−7.36	25.14	−16.69
	1685/6	13.91	8.12	4.88	0.29
	1695/6	13.73	−15.07	6.03	4.01
	1803/4	13.64	2.01	−1.12	1.67
BELOW	1556/7	−41.78	−33.66	7.30	−12.79
	1648/9	−35.01	−23.57	−6.07	−5.84
	1643/4	−30.59	14.80	29.27	4.14
	1554/5	−23.52	−4.29	−15.87	−2.86
	1693/4	−23.27	−13.81	4.08	−10.59
	1652/3	−21.83	11.11	−2.72	−6.99
	1622/3	−21.09	−9.27	−1.84	−8.63
	1660/1	−20.49	−2.27	−13.87	1.32
	1553/4	−19.95	−8.85	−28.09	−9.72
	1692/3	−19.94	−8.22	−16.44	−2.25
	1800/1	−18.05	−29.43	4.94	−11.16
	1647/8	−17.98	−19.10	−11.04	−4.32
	1661/2	−16.97	−18.47	6.52	−4.07
	1691/2	−16.53	10.74	−0.69	−1.02
	1667/8	−15.76	3.35	5.25	3.49
	1555/6	−15.52	−28.36	−28.18	1.41
	1596/7	−15.33	−35.78	20.86	−4.38
	1740/1	−15.30	−18.50	0.19	−2.87
	1649/50	−15.29	−24.55	−11.91	−17.00
	1623/4	−15.15	−0.28	18.31	−13.49

(cont.)

Table 8.8: (cont.)

Birth rates	Annual percentage deviation above or below (−) moving average			
ABOVE	Year	Birth rate	Real wage	Death rate	Marriage rate
	1564/5	18.36	1.56	−6.94	−2.62
	1562/3	18.00	6.91	2.66	−1.64
	1640/1	11.47	5.40	−0.18	20.98
	1550/1	10.97	20.51	−14.75	−11.18
	1588/9	10.54	12.13	4.92	13.11
	1642/3	10.33	11.08	4.08	2.25
	1655/6	10.33	16.68	−16.91	67.52
	1686/7	10.06	4.92	1.21	4.02
	1599/1600	9.71	−1.02	−9.48	4.13
	1620/1	9.62	13.68	−15.78	5.06
	1718/9	9.52	1.65	−9.48	4.33
	1654/5	9.28	22.88	−11.60	36.05
	1702/3	9.24	13.25	−10.10	5.46
	1621/2	9.15	1.05	−18.72	−9.13
	1549/50	8.96	−17.16	−16.01	0.35
	1701/2	8.90	5.75	−5.30	14.10
	1632/3	8.78	−0.18	−12.96	4.96
	1547/8	8.74	4.40	−17.97	23.52
	1551/2	8.64	−14.53	1.55	0.22
	1567/8	8.23	6.71	−25.61	9.89
BELOW	1557/8	−25.75	20.75	60.54	−5.00
	1559/60	−22.59	6.64	18.13	25.66
	1728/9	−18.67	−13.70	41.23	−7.91
	1597/8	−17.72	−22.80	25.61	−9.10
	1649/50	−17.00	−24.55	−11.91	−15.29
	1658/9	−16.69	−7.36	25.14	13.98
	1623/4	−13.49	−0.28	18.31	−15.15
	1556/7	−12.79	−33.66	7.30	−41.78
	1710/1	−12.70	−29.84	1.22	−12.21
	1741/2	−12.43	−8.56	36.29	−9.39
	1659/60	−12.12	−6.17	−15.25	1.46
	1800/1	−11.16	−29.43	4.94	−18.05
	1693/4	−10.59	−13.81	4.08	−23.27
	1587/8	−10.34	12.47	29.47	4.50
	1801/2	−10.29	−5.54	3.97	−5.96
	1709/10	−9.97	−20.21	−10.07	−9.79
	1631/2	−9.90	−3.45	−5.58	0.98
	1553/4	−9.72	−8.85	−28.09	−19.95
	1679/80	−9.31	1.82	10.29	9.43
	1729/30	−8.88	−1.75	35.39	4.01

Sources: See table 8.7.

wages fell 35.8 per cent below trend (the most violent downward fluctuation in the table) and the death rate rose 20.9 per cent above trend. Furthermore, the subsequent year (1597/8) witnessed the ninth largest downward fluctuation in real wages, 22.8 per cent below trend, a fall matched by a rise in the death rate of 25.6 per cent above trend.

It is conspicuous examples such as these that have led some historians to suggest that there was a close relationship between a fall in the real wage and an increase in the death rate, with the implication that the population was living so close to the level of subsistence that a deficient harvest could have lethal consequences on a grand scale.[76] However, there are other years listed in the second panel of the table in which the real wage fell savagely yet the death rate either scarcely rose above trend (e.g. 1586/7, 1710/1, 1800/1) or was actually below average (e.g. 1555/6, 1649/50, 1799/1800). Indeed the years 1709/10 and 1710/1, which witnessed the 16th and 3rd most severe downward fluctuations in real wages, provide a strong counter-example to 1596/8. This episode has been cited by other historians arguing for the relative immunity of the population to fluctuations in the harvest, for despite the dire plunge in living standards the death rate was 10.1 per cent *below* trend in 1709/10 and only 1.2 per cent above trend in 1710/1.[77]

Clearly, argument by selection of specific instances is an unsatisfactory way to proceed. What is at issue is not whether a sharp fall in real wages ever coincided with a rise in the death rate, but how far this was a typical feature of life in the past. From the second panel of table 8.8 it can readily be seen that 10 of the set of 20 years that witnessed the greatest downward fluctuations in real wages were indeed years in which the death rate was above average, but in the remaining 10 years the death rate was below average.

In order to evaluate this result more effectively we need to know how often we should expect the death rate to be above or below trend regardless of the state of real wages. Because of the asymmetry in the series of death rates caused by the fact that fluctuations above trend were more extreme than fluctuations below, the rates were above and below trend in 43 and 57 per cent of the years respectively. If there were no connexion between fluctuations in the death rate and real wages we should expect to find the death rate above trend on 8.6 occasions in any set of 20 years (0.43 × 20). The probability of 10 or more years with above average death rates occurring entirely by chance is approximately 1 in 3.[78] It would therefore be unwise to claim on the basis of this evidence that extreme downward fluctuations in real wages were linked with above-average death rates.

Table 8.8 also enables us to reverse the perspective and investigate whether the years in which mortality fluctuated furthest above trend were also years of below average real wages. This turns out to have been the case in 9 of the 20 years, but in the remaining 11 years real wages were higher than usual. In view of the relative

76. The sensitivity of mortality to fluctuations in food prices is more often implied than stated explicitly. For example: 'With so many people living near the borderline of starvation, the difference made by good harvests and warm winters was incalculable'. Hill, *Reformation to industrial revolution*, p. 254. Holderness notes 'the coincidence of many great epidemics with phenomenally bad harvests', *Pre-industrial England*, p. 12. In contrast, for seventeenth-century France Goubert states categorically 'L'ampleur et la fréquence des pointes cycliques du prix des grains provoquent l'ampleur et la fréquence des crises démographiques'. 'En Beauvaisis', p. 463.

77. See, for example, Chambers, *Population, economy and society*, pp. 87–96.

78. The probability (0.34) was calculated from the cumulative terms of the binomial distribution.

frequency of the fluctuations above and below trend in the real-wage series we would expect on the basis of chance alone to find 9.6 occasions in any set of 20 years with below-average real wages.[79] The observed result is very close to this figure and the conclusion must be that there was no systematic connexion between the highest peaks in the death rate and lower than normal real wages. It will be recalled, however, that the death rate was very variable in the sixteenth and seventeenth centuries, so it is possible that a connexion between real wages and mortality may have existed but that it was overlaid by other factors, such as epidemic disease. This supposition will be examined further below when all years, and not just those of exceptional price or mortality fluctuations, are considered.

Table 8.8 further shows that even when the fluctuations of the dependent series were in the expected direction there was no simple relationship between the magnitudes of their deviations: very low real wages might be associated with either very high or quite modest deviations above average in the death rate, and very high death rates coincided with both large and small deviations below trend in real wages. However, the connexion between low real wages and high death rates is only one side of the relationship between fluctuations in the two series, and it is possible that extremely high real wages may have been associated with low death rates, and vice versa. Consider the first and fourth panels of table 8.8. They show that in 10 of the 20 years of extreme upward fluctuations in real wages the death rate was indeed below trend as expected, but that in the other 10 years the death rate was above trend, counter to expectation. Similarly, in the 20 years when the death rate was furthest below trend the real-wage series was above and below trend in equal proportions. The lack of a systematic relationship between fluctuations in real wages and death rates was therefore an all-round one, failing to appear when either series experienced extreme fluctuations in either direction.

Even though there is no clear evidence of an immediate impact of real-wage fluctuations on mortality, it is possible, of course, that such a relationship existed but was not a simultaneous one, that the effect of fluctuations in food prices became apparent only in the following year. Despite the obscurity of the biological or epidemiological mechanisms that might produce such an effect, the possibility is clearly one that should be investigated. Moreover, we also need to examine the relationships obtaining between extreme fluctuations in real wages and births and marriages, and between the series of births, marriages, and deaths themselves.

In order to abbreviate the discussion, the information contained in table 8.8 has been summarized in table 8.9, which reports the number of occasions on which a responding series was above or below trend during the 20 years in which an initiating series experienced its greatest proportional fluctuations either side of trend. To help evaluate the observed frequencies an indication is given of the statistical significance of the results: a single asterisk indicates that the probability of obtaining the observed, or even more extreme values through chance alone is less than 5 per cent, and a double asterisk denotes a probability of less than 1 per cent.[80] In the latter case it is highly likely that there was a systematic relationship between the series, while in the former there are reasonable grounds for believing that such a relationship existed. On the

79. In the real-wage series 52 per cent of the years were above trend, and 48 per cent below trend.
80. Calculated from the cumulative terms of the binomial distribution. The expected proportions of frequencies occurring above trend in the responding series of deaths, marriages, and births were 0.43, 0.49, 0.53, respectively. The expected proportions occurring below trend can be obtained from the complements of these figures.

other hand figures without an asterisk are insufficiently removed from a chance result to provide reliable evidence of a connexion between the series. Results are given for relationships between the fluctuations in the series occurring simultaneously and at a lag of one year.[81]

Table 8.9: Above and below average deviations in a responding series in the 20 most extreme years of fluctuation in an initiating series

Initiating series	Responding series No. of occasions (out of 20) in which series moved as predicted in same (+), or opposite (−), direction					
Real wages	Death rates		Marriage rates		Birth rates	
	(−)	(−)	(+)	(+)	(+)	(+)
Direction of extreme fluctuations	Lag 0	Lag 1	Lag 0	Lag 1	Lag 0	Lag 1
Above	10	12	15*	13	13	13
Below	10	13*	18**	13	18**	18**
Death rates	Marriage rates		Birth rates			
	(−)	(+)	(−)	(−)		
Direction of extreme fluctuations	Lag 0	Lag 1	Lag 0	Lag 1		
Above	13	12	16*	12		
Below	11	12	14	7		
Marriage rates	Birth rates					
	(+)	(+)				
Direction of extreme fluctuations	Lag 0	Lag 1 Expected				
Above	17**	14				
Below	16**	14*				
Birth rates	Death rates					
	(+)	(+)				
Direction of extreme fluctuations	Lag 0	Lag 1				
Above	5	4*				
Below	5**	7*				

Note: *denotes a result significant at the 5 per cent level, and ** a result significant at the 1 per cent level.

Sources: Lag 0, table 8.8. Lag 1, annual deviations calculated from data as described in sources for table 8.7.

Table 8.9 is arranged according to the initiating series. Only 7 of the 12 possible pairs are shown, since only in these cases is a relationship plausibly to be expected. The layout of the table reflects the presumptive direction of causation. Strictly speaking, of course, it is impossible to tell the direction of causation when the relationship is simultaneous, but on general grounds it is altogether more probable that movements in real wages are the stimuli, and movements in the vital rates the responses, than vice versa. In the case of simultaneous movements between the death rate and the marriage or birth rates, the relative frequencies associated with each of the two possible signs for the relationships give a powerful indication of which is likely to be stimulus and which response, as a moment's reflection will reveal. With contemporaneous co-variations in the marriage and the birth rates, however, the sign provides no help; but it is in general more likely that movements in the marriage rate provoked a sympathetic movement in the birth rate rather than the other way round.

Thus the first panel of the table takes the two sets of 20 years when real wages

81. Lags of two years were investigated but no significant results were obtained.

experienced their greatest proportional fluctuations above and below trend and reports the frequencies of deviations above and below trend in the responding series of birth, marriage, and death rates. The first column of the panel summarizes the lack of any systematic relationships between the years of extreme fluctuations in either direction in real wages and simultaneous movements in the opposite direction in the death rate which has already been discussed at length. The second column reveals that such a relationship was more likely to occur in the year following an extreme downward fluctuation in the real wage. The figure of 13 such occasions out of 20 is significant at the 5 per cent level. In this respect the English experience would seem to have been unlike the classic subsistence crises in France, for there the death rate responded quickly to a rise in food prices and declined abruptly once prices returned to normal.[82]

The table also shows a clear positive relationship between fluctuations in real wages and marriage rates in the same year, followed at a lag of one year by a rather weak connexion which failed to reach the 5 per cent level of significance. Furthermore the simultaneous relationship between the two series was stronger when real wages were very low than when they were very high. Indeed in no less than 18 out of the 20 years when real wages were furthest below trend marriage rates were also below trend. This is one of the strongest relationships in the table, only equalled by the comparable relationship between real wages and the birth rate, both simultaneously and at a year's lag. Moreover, reference back to table 8.8 shows that the magnitude of the response in the birth rate in the current year was more directly related to the size of the fluctuation in real wages than was the case with either marriages or deaths. The figures for the response of the birth rate to *upward* fluctuations in real wages and for the lagged responses of the marriage rate to movements in real wages in either direction are in the expected direction but fail to attain the 5 per cent level of statistical significance.

The most definite conclusions to emerge from the first panel of the table are therefore that extreme downward fluctuations in real wages were accompanied by marriage rates below trend in the same year and by birth rates below trend both in the same and the following year. Extreme fluctuations in real wages had no effect on death rates in the current year, but there is reasonable evidence of connexion between very low real wages and higher than average death rates in the following year. Thus in England in the past the classic *crise de subsistance*, insofar as it was captured by the real-wage series, affected nuptiality and fertility much more than mortality.

If the death rate is taken to be the initiating series, as in the second panel in the table, it can be seen that there was a tendency for extreme movements in the death rate to be associated with contrary movements in the marriage rate in the same year and with sympathetic movements in the following year. Such a pattern is consistent with the contrary action of mortality in interrupting marriages about to be contracted while opening up later opportunities for remarriages or first marriages. However the figures in the table provide only weak evidence for the existence of these associations and none were significant at the 5 per cent level.

On the other hand the second panel furnishes clear evidence that years of extreme upward fluctuations in mortality were occasions when the birth rate was below average, and rather less persuasive evidence that downward fluctuations in the death rate were accompanied by above-average birth rates. Reference back to the third

82. 'La crise adopte comme limites chronologiques celles de l'année agricole', Goubert 'En Beauvaisis', p. 468. See also the quotation from the same source in fn. 76, above.

panel of table 8.8 shows that in many of the years in which the death rate was far above average the fall in the birth rate in the same year was also likely to be extreme. It is also evident from the same panel that in these 16 years of extreme counter-movements in the births and deaths real wages were as likely to be above average as below. Thus without independent evidence of the movement of food prices a 'scissors' movement in the birth and death rates can scarcely be accepted as evidence of a subsistence crisis, as has sometimes been claimed.[83] Indeed the existence of such scissors movements in the rates in years of *lower* than average food prices suggests that maternal mortality and morbidity may have been powerful influences in reducing fertility in years of epidemic disease.

In this connexion it is interesting that there was a weak, and statistically insignificant, tendency for extremely high fluctuations in the death rate to be accompanied by below-average birth rates in the following year (12 cases out of 20). Such a relationship would be consistent with the affect of mortality on the stock of pregnant women, or the action of morbidity on fecundity, reducing conceptions or causing early foetal wastage and so reducing the birth rate in the following year as well as simultaneously. This negative relationship failed to materialize, however, following years of very low mortality, when birth rates were more often below than above average (13:7). In this case a positive pattern may have predominated, without attaining statistical significance, because the expected consequences of low mortality on the stocks of pregnant mothers and on fecundity may have been more than offset by the effect of an above-average birth rate associated with the extreme downward fluctuation in the death rate in the preceding year. For this will have raised the proportion of the married female population protected by post-partum amenorrhea, thereby reducing the numbers of conceptions, and hence the birth rate, in the following year.

The third panel in the table shows that when fluctuations in the marriage rate were extreme in either direction there was a strong tendency for the birth rate to move sympathetically in the same year and a similar though weaker tendency for it to respond positively in the following year.[84] This result does not altogether accord with general expectations since the normal delay between marriage and first birth would cause the major impact on births of an increase or decrease in marriages to occur after a lag of one year. But this is a complex issue which is best examined with the more sophisticated methods employed in chapter 9.

Finally, the fourth panel of table 8.9 examines the relationship between extreme fluctuations in the birth rate and movements in the death rate. In view of the high levels of infant mortality in the past, which resulted in between 18 and 31 per cent of all deaths being infant deaths, one might have expected the relationship to have been a positive one.[85] However, the table shows that positive relationships were so rare that the figures constitute good evidence that the relationship between the two series was

83. For example, Appleby writes 'If it can be established that plague was definitely not present, amenorrhea becomes confirming evidence of famine'. 'Disease or famine?', p. 423. Rogers accepts this opinion and regards a drop in conceptions as evidence that famine was the cause of the heavy mortality in parts of Lancashire in 1623. *The Lancashire population crisis of 1623*, p. 26.

84. The lagged relationship after extremely high marriage rates was not significant at the 5 per cent level.

85. The lower figure is obtained with a combined-sex e_0 of 33.5 and a GRR of 1.81, and the higher figure with an e_0 of 38.5 and a GRR of 3.00, approximately the conditions obtaining in 1661 and 1816, respectively (table 7.15). Coale and Demeny, *Regional model life tables*, pp. 305, 309, 401, 405 (model North, levels 7 and 9).

actually negative.[86] We have already observed that there was a simultaneous negative relationship between birth rates and death rates when the latter were experiencing extreme fluctuations. Thus the present result extends the relationship to the occasions when the birth rate was subject to extreme fluctuations. This would suggest that the factors causing extreme fluctuations in either series were also tending to make the other series move in the opposite direction. As has already been argued, the lack of any systematic relationship between extreme fluctuations in the death rate and the level of real wages suggests that the cause of these counter-movements at the extremes of the two series lies elsewhere, probably in the activities of micro-organisms which raised both mortality and morbidity, thereby reducing fertility. The negative relationship with the death rate at one year's lag is more difficult to explain in terms of biological, social, or economic factors. Possibly it is a statistical artefact, reflecting the tendency, which can be seen in figure 8.6, for years of extreme fluctuations in the birth rate to be followed by other years departing from trend in the same direction and for these groups of years to be periods when the death rate also consistently departed from trend in the opposite direction.

So far we have been considering the effect of extreme fluctuations in the initiating series on the level of the responding series. We shall now reverse the perspective and examine the question of how far extreme fluctuations in the responding series were associated with above- or below-average fluctuations in each of the series thought to be influencing them. It is important to take this further step because a relationship that obtains between extreme fluctuations in one series and the direction of fluctuations in another may not necessarily hold when the series are reversed. For example, it was discovered that in almost every year when real wages were furthest below trend the birth rate was also below trend. But it does not necessarily follow that the years in which the birth rate was *most* below trend were also years when real wages were below trend. For major downward fluctuations in the birth rate may have been produced by other factors, such as disease, which may have been independent of fluctuations in real wages. We therefore need to investigate how far the relationships we have established for extreme fluctuations in the initiating series also obtained for extreme fluctuations in the responding series.

Table 8.10 is constructed along the same lines as the previous table but shows for each set of the 20 most extreme fluctuations either side of trend in the responding series how often the initiating series was above or below trend in the same year, and in the previous year. A comparison with the corresponding panels in table 8.9 soon reveals that most of the relationships between the series were symmetrical: the figures in the cells are similar no matter whether the connexion is viewed from the perspective of the initiating or the responding series. Sometimes the strength of a relationship is increased or diminished, but the overall patterns remain the same. This is the case with the links between real wages and each of the series of vital rates: not only were extreme fluctuations in real wages associated positively with above- or below-average fluctuations in birth rates and marriage rates, but extreme fluctuations in each of the vital rates were also associated positively with movements in the real wage in both the same and the previous year. Similarly, the general lack of association between extreme fluctuations in the real wage and movements in the death rate was paralleled by the absence of any relationship between extreme fluctuations in the

86. Only the link between very high birth rates and low death rates in the same year failed to reach the 5 per cent level of significance.

Table 8.10: Above and below average deviations in an initiating series in the 20 most extreme years of fluctuation in a responding series

Responding series	Initiating series No. of occasions (out of 20) in which series moved as predicted in same (+), or opposite (−), direction					
Death rates	Real wages		Birth rates			
	(−)	(−)	(+)	(+)		
Direction of deviations	Lag 0	Lag −1	Lag 0	Lag −1		
Above	9	9	4*	5*		
Below[1]	10	12	6	7		
Marriage rates	Real wages		Death rates			
	(+)	(+)	(−)	(+)		
Direction of deviations	Lag 0	Lag −1	Lag 0	Lag −1		
Above	16**	14	11	15**		
Below	16**	15*	9	18**		
Birth rates	Real wages		Marriage rates		Death rates	
	(+)	(+)	(+)	(+)	(−)	(−)
Direction of deviation	Lag 0	Lag −1	Lag 0	Lag −1	Lag 0	Lag −1
Above	15*	14	16**	17**	15	14
Below	16**	18**	13	17**	15**	12

Notes: [1] One of the 20 largest annual deviations below trend in the death rate (1541/2) was the first year in the series and so no comparison could be made with a birth rate in the preceeding year. The 21st largest annual deviation below trend, which occurred in 1554/5, was taken instead. See notes to table 8.9.

Sources: See table 8.9.

death rate and movements in the real wage. Indeed, while the previous table provided evidence of a fairly strong link between extreme downward movements in the real wage and above-average death rates in the following year, the present table shows that when extreme upward movements in the death rate are considered there was no relationship with below-average real wages in either the same or the previous year. Thus while very high food prices appear to have had some effect on death rates in the following year, very high death rates were not significantly associated with above-average food prices.

Most of the relationships between the vital series remained as they were in the previous table. However the rather weak, and statistically insignificant, negative relationship between extreme fluctuations in the death rate and movements in the marriage rate in the same year disappeared, while a similarly weak positive relationship with the marriage rate in the following year became much stronger, and highly significant, when extreme fluctuations in the marriage rate were made the focus of attention. In particular, almost all the years when the marriage rate was exceptionally far below trend were preceded by a year in which the death rate was also below trend (18 out of 20), though years when the death rate was furthest above trend were not so frequently followed by an above-average marriage rate in the subsequent year (12 out of 20).

Reversing the perspective also modifies the relationship between below average death rates and the level of the birth rate in the following year. When extreme fluctuations in the death rate were considered, birth rates were found to have been negatively related to them, with the exception of the birth rate in the year after an extremely low death rate, which anomalously proved to be more likely to be below, rather than above, average. When the connexion is examined from the point of view of the birth series, however, the anomaly disappears, and the relationship with movements in the death rate in both the same and the previous year is consistently negative, though only the link between sharply lower birth rates and above-average death rates in the same year is sufficiently clear-cut for there to be virtually no doubt about its reality.

Mortality crises

Many of the most spectacular extreme fluctuations in the three demographic series occurred during periods of crisis mortality. Since these episodes have received a great deal of attention from historians, it may be of interest to examine their characteristics in early modern England more fully before going on to examine the links between the fluctuations in the series in normal as well as extreme circumstances. In order to do this we shall broaden the definition of a mortality crisis to include a larger number of years, and examine how their intensity and frequency changed over time; the monthly distribution of mortality during crisis periods; and how closely English crises coincided with those elsewhere in western Europe. Further aspects of crisis mortality are examined in appendix 10 where the characteristics of local crises in the 404 parishes constituting the aggregative set are analysed. Appendix 10 covers such questions as the geographical distribution of crisis mortality; the seasonality, severity, and duration of local crises; and the susceptibility of parishes to crises in relation to location, agricultural type, proximity to a market town, and so on.

It must be emphasized that any discussion of crisis mortality entails an arbitrary decision as to what constitutes a crisis. Making a simple dichotomy (crisis and non-crisis) must mean producing a pattern whose characteristics are dependent upon the criteria that determine where the line should be drawn. On the national level a crisis may be defined in terms either of a specified level of the death rate or of an upward fluctuation above trend of a certain magnitude. Although the former alternative has its attractions, it suffers from the disadvantage that not every year has an equal chance of attaining it, because of the secular changes in mortality which alter the level of the prevailing death rate. We have therefore preferred to adopt the second alternative and have employed the same measure of the magnitude of excess mortality used previously, namely the percentage deviation of the annual crude death rate from a centred 25-year moving average. Any year in which the death rate was at least 10 per cent above the moving average was taken to be a crisis year. This criterion singles out 45 years of crisis mortality, about 14 per cent of the 330 years being studied.[87]

Table 8.11 displays the percentage deviations from trend, and the corresponding level of the death rate, in each of these years, arranged in descending order of

87. Eleven of these years were not amongst the set of 45 years within highest death rates. In descending order of severity they were 1596/7, 1623/4, 1766/7, 1779/80, 1639/40, 1613/4, 1802/3, 1590/1, 1609/10, 1846/7, and 1845/5, and ranked 53rd to 55th, 57th, 68th, 70th, 77th, 79th, 112th, 162nd, and 205th, respectively. They were replaced by 1730/1, 1556/7, 1685/6, 1689/90, 1683/4, 1723/4, 1721/2, 1720/1, 1669/70, 1731/2, and 1667/8. The highest death rate (1558/9) was 64.84 per 1,000, and the 45th highest death rate (1667/8) was 30.56 per 1,000.

Table 8.11: Years with an annual crude death rate more than 10 per cent above trend

Year	Per cent above trend	Crude death rate	Year	Per cent above trend	Crude death rate
1558/9	124.23	64.84	*1559/60*	18.13	33.63
1557/8	60.54	46.99	*1590/1*	18.07	28.85
1625/6	42.99	36.48	*1783/4*	16.73	31.48
1657/8	42.93	38.93	*1684/5*	15.65	34.85
1728/9	41.23	43.24	*1639/40*	15.23	29.27
1727/8	37.19	41.78	*1670/1*	15.15	34.49
1680/1	36.47	41.38	*1846/7*	15.11	25.99
1741/2	36.29	39.67	*1681/2*	14.81	34.85
1729/30	35.39	42.23	*1742/3*	14.64	32.61
1638/9	35.08	34.46	*1546/7*	14.15	33.45
1665/6	31.69	37.43	*1781/2*	14.05	30.80
1592/3	29.80	32.01	*1613/4*	13.71	29.25
1587/8	29.47	31.41	*1719/20*	13.55	34.17
1643/4	29.27	33.21	*1542/3*	12.93	32.54
1624/5	26.61	32.18	*1678/9*	12.44	34.32
1545/6	26.55	36.93	*1682/3*	11.80	33.86
1597/8	25.61	31.41	*1802/3*	11.22	28.98
1658/9	25.14	34.72	*1609/10*	10.79	27.33
1762/3	24.21	33.81	*1854/5*	10.65	24.96
1544/5	23.33	35.84	*1779/80*	10.53	29.93
1603/4	21.04	30.64	*1766/7*	10.38	30.04
1596/7	20.86	30.11	*1679/80*	10.29	33.69
1623/4	18.31	30.04			

Notes: Years run from 1 July to 30 June. Trend is calculated as a 25-year unweighted moving average of the annual crude death rates.

Sources: See table 8.7.

severity. The first 20 of these years will, of course, be familiar from the third panel of table 8.8.

The year 1558/9 stands out as having experienced by far the worst mortality, in terms both of the deviation from trend and of the level of the death rate attained. The previous year stands second in both measures, though falling well behind the first. Then follow 9 further years in which the death rate was 30 per cent or more above trend, 11 years in which it was between 20 and 30 per cent above trend, and 23 years in which it was between 10 and 20 per cent above trend. If we take these three groups, and for convenience call them 3-star, 2-star, and 1-star crises, respectively, we can use them to provide an indication of the changing relative frequency of crises of different degrees of severity.

Table 8.12 divides the 45 crisis years into 25-year periods.[88] The 11 most severe crises comprising the 3-star category all occurred before 1750. Two fell in the late 1550s, and three in the late 1720s, underlining the exceptionally high mortality of these periods. A further group of five 3-star crises occurred between 1625/6 and 1680/1, while the final crisis in this category occurred in 1741/2, making a fourth year of very severe mortality in the second quarter of the eighteenth century, the largest number in any sub-period. The first column of the table also shows that 3-star crises

88. The first period extends over 34 years (1541/2 to 1574/5) and the final period over 21 years (1850/1 to 1870/1).

Table 8.12: National crisis years by degree of severity

Quarter century	3-star	2-star	1-star
1541/2–74/5	1557/8, 1558/9	1544/5, 1545/6	1542/3, 1546/7, 1559/60
1575/6–99/1600		1587/8, 1592/3, 1596/7, 1597/8	1590/1
1600/1–24/5		1603/4, 1624/5	1609/10, 1613/4, 1623/4
1625/6–49/50	1625/6, 1638/9	1643/4	1639/40
1650/1–74/5	1657/8, 1665/6	1658/9	1670/1
1675/6–99/1700	1680/1		1678/9, 1679/80, 1681/2, 1682/3, 1684/5
1700/1–24/5			1719/20
1725/6–49/50	1727/8, 1728/9, 1729/30, 1741/2		1742/3
1750/1–74/5		1762/3	1766/7
1775/6–99/1800			1779/80, 1781/2, 1783/4
1800/1–24/5			1802/3
1825/6–49/50			1846/7
1850/1–70/1			1854/5

Note: Years run from July to June.

Source: Table 8.11.

were absent for two fairly long periods: for 65 years between 1559/60 and 1624/5, and for 45 years between 1681/2 and 1726/7. The second column of the table shows that in the first of these periods the absence of 3-star crises was offset by the presence of many 2-star crises, for 6 out of the 11 crises of this severity occurred in the late sixteenth and early seventeenth centuries. Two of these fell in the well-known years of dearth in the mid 1590s, and it is noteworthy that despite their prominence in the text books, the years 1596/7 and 1597/8 do not rank as 3-star crises. Of the five other years with 2-star crises, two were adjacent years in the 1540s, two fell in the mid seventeenth century, of which one (1658/9) followed on from a 3-star crisis year, and the last occurred very much later in 1762/3. Thereafter there was no year in which the death rate rose as much as 20 per cent above normal.

In contrast, 1-star crises were spread more evenly, the last occurring in 1854/5. Several preceded or followed years that ranked as 2- or 3-star crises, though others occurred in isolation, as in 1542/3, 1590/1, 1609/10, 1613/4, 1670/1, 1719/20, and in several years from 1766/7 on. One period stands out. The seven years from 1678/9 to 1684/5 contain only one year, 1683/4, which was not a 1-star crisis and also include a 3-star crisis in 1680/1. Since the general level of mortality was very high in this period (see fig. 8.6), this long sequence of years well above trend is the more remarkable. Thereafter there was never more than one 1-star crisis in a 25-year period except in the last quarter of the eighteenth century. In the early 1780s there were three such years, in 1779/80, 1781/2, and 1783/4. The three 1-star crises in the nineteenth century occurred when the prevailing level of mortality was relatively low, so that the resulting death rates (ranging between 25.0 and 29.0 per 1,000), though high for their period, were modest by the standards of the later seventeenth century.

There is therefore little evidence of a diminution in the frequency of 1-star crises over time. The major change lay rather in the reduced incidence of the more pronounced crises, which were mainly confined to the period before 1666. Apart from the heavy mortalities in the late 1720s, there were very few further major crises. Thus the marked decline in the overall variation in mortality from the third quarter of the seventeenth century that was noted earlier in the chapter was in part due to the virtual disappearance of 2- and 3-star crises.

It has already been emphasized that any categorization of crises is arbitrary, but the present approach, though crude, is consistent, and this helps to bring out the overall patterns. This is no small gain, for the literature is replete with a bewildering array of descriptions of crisis mortality in many localities at different points in time, based on a variety of definitions or on none.[89] The information in table 8.12 on the prevalence and severity of national outbreaks makes it possible to distinguish crises reported in local studies that were of national importance from those that were not. For example, the epidemics of the late 1720s were widespread and produced a national mortality crisis, but of the nineteenth-century cholera outbreaks only that of 1854/5 saw an upward fluctuation in the overall death rate sufficiently marked to place it even in the 1-star category. In other cholera years mortality, even though severe, was very

---

89. Compendious notes can be found in Short, *New observations* (1750) and *Comparative history* (1767) and in Creighton's monumental *Epidemics in Britain* (1894). Plague is treated exhaustively in Shrewsbury, *Bubonic Plague*. Modern regional studies include Appleby, 'Disease or famine?' (Cumbria); Oswald, 'Epidemics in Devon'; Slack, 'Mortality crises' (Devon and Essex); Jones, 'Parish registers: north Shropshire'; Palliser, 'Dearth and disease in Staffordshire'; and Brent, 'Eastern Sussex'. Crisis mortality features in innumerable studies of single parishes or small areas.

localized.[90] Airborne infections of influenza-like diseases were more widespread, though normally less lethal, and were more likely to result in a substantial increase in the national death rate. Although inferences about the cause of crisis mortality must be drawn cautiously, this type of infection appears to have been largely responsible for the crisis years identified in the later eighteenth and nineteenth centuries, with the exception of 1854/5 and 1846/7.[91]

Mortality crises and monthly death rates

Although convenient, the year is a clumsy unit of time to use when attempting to identify mortality crises, since severe epidemics are often over in a matter of weeks in any one place, and even at a national level their effect may be visible only for a few months out of the twelve. Occasionally, an epidemic of great severity may sweep the whole country, raising the *monthly* death rate far above its normal level, and yet depart again so swiftly that the *annual* rate is only slightly raised. We have therefore calculated monthly death rates by referring the monthly totals of deaths as given in table A2.4 to monthly estimates of the population size. The latter have been interpolated between the quinquennial population estimates derived from back projection in a manner analogous to that described in appendix 3 for annual estimates of population size.

Two limitations of series of monthly death rates should be noted. First, the national monthly totals of deaths were based on the burials recorded in the 404 parishes inflated up to a national level and corrected to allow for the exceptional character of mortality in London. In plague years the large numbers of extra burials recorded in London were distributed in an artificial manner rising smoothly from January to an August peak and then falling away smoothly again to the end of the year.[92] Since the overwhelming bulk of plague deaths in London occurred between July and October the national monthly totals of deaths, and hence the monthly rates, give too flat an impression of the true incidence of mortality in these years, exaggerating the death rates in the first half of the year and underestimating them in the months from July to October. The years whose true monthly rates have been distorted in this way are 1563, 1578, 1593, 1603, 1625, 1636, and 1665. Second, monthly death rates can only be calculated for the period covered by the data available from the 404 parishes. Civil registration began in July 1837 and the Registrar General published quarterly but not monthly totals of deaths. Most of the 404 aggregative tabulations stop in 1837, but we have taken advantage of the fact that the data for 83 of the parishes continue into the period of civil registration to extend the series of monthly death rates up to June 1839. Here, as with the annual rates, it should always be remembered that the data are based on a diminishing number of parishes the further one moves earlier than 1662 or later than 1811, between which dates all 404 parishes were fully in observation.[93]

90. See, for example, the lists of places affected in 1831–2 and 1849 in Creighton, *Epidemics in Britain*, II, pp. 821–2, 843–4.
91. Creighton, *ibid.*, II, *passim*. Although influenza was present in 1846/7 it was overshadowed by the heavy mortality associated with the Irish famine fever, variously described as typhus, typhoid, dysentery, and diarrhoea. *9th Annual Report*, pp. 150–2, *10th Annual Report*, pp. viii, xx.
92. See above, p. 80.
93. The frequency distribution of the dates at which burial registration began and ended is similar to the distribution for baptism registration detailed in table 2.19.

The series of monthly death rates reflect not only the underlying secular trends in mortality and the specific monthly disturbances that are the present object of attention, but also the regular seasonal variation in the incidence of mortality. To eliminate this component the rates for each month (January, February etc.) were taken separately and treated as if each constituted an independent annual series of 'readings'. A relative measure of the size of the fluctuations was then calculated in the same manner as for the series of annual rates by expressing each annual 'reading' as a percentage deviation from a 25-year moving average of the appropriate monthly series. However, since the monthly rates are based on a lower level of aggregation of the data, they are inherently more unstable than the annual rates and the 10, 20, and 30 per cent cut-off points used to categorize the latter would have been inappropriate. Instead we have used deviations of 25, 50, and 100 per cent above trend as comparable indicators of increasingly severe monthly mortality rates. The two most severe categories (50–99 and over 100 per cent above trend) are indicated by one and two asterisks respectively in the list of all crisis months given in table 8.13. Despite the different criteria adopted in constructing the table it can be used to throw light on the rough classification of the annual death rates in table 8.12.

First, it is evident that there was a close correspondence between the severity of the annual death rate and the number of months in the year that were individually picked out as having unusually high mortality: in the 3-star crisis years most of the months feature in table 8.13 but in the 1-star crisis years fewer months appear in the table. In some of the major 3-star crises, such as 1557/8 and 1558/9, almost every month was at a 'crisis' level. In such years even the months that do not appear in the table were often well above their expected trend values. The same is true of the 2-star crisis of 1596/7. Only January, March, May, and June in 1597 are picked out in table 8.13, but in fact the heavy mortality began in November 1596 when the monthly rate was 21 per cent above trend, and it remained more than 20 per cent above trend until June 1597. The appearance of a gap in the table, therefore, does not necessarily imply that mortality was unremarkable in the period in question, simply that it did not rise to 25 per cent above trend. For a fuller appreciation of the gradations in the monthly fluctuations in mortality the table needs to be read in conjunction with table A2.4 which contains the underlying monthly totals of deaths.

Table 8.13 not only provides an indication of the timing of the most severe mortality within the major crisis periods, but also reveals the existence of isolated months of heavy mortality which were too brief in duration to have had a major impact on the annual death rate. A conspicuous example can be found in the midsummer of 1551 when a lethal infection known contemporaneously as 'the sweat' pushed the July and August death rates 105 and 34 per cent above trend.[94] Other short, but less violent, visitations occurred several times in the 20 years from 1565 to 1584. This was a period of exceptionally low mortality with no national crises on an annual basis, yet it was by no means immune from crisis mortality. Similarly, other periods with few or no annual crises also experienced a sharp rise in the death rate in the occasional month, as in February 1837 when an outbreak of influenza raised the monthly death rate 82 per cent above trend.[95] Table 8.13 therefore sharpens and supplements the

94. Typically a visitation of the disease lasted only a few days: Creighton, *Epidemics in Britain*, I, pp. 259–64; and Slack, 'Mortality crises', pp. 25–7, who notes the modest impact of the disease on the annual death rate. Earlier outbreaks of sweating sickness are discussed in Gottfried, 'Population, plague', pp. 17–27, where the disease is said to be predominantly autumnal in its incidence.
95. The death rate was above trend in the surrounding months: by 28 per cent in January and 22 per cent in

Table 8.13: National crisis months

Months with death rate at least 25 per cent above trend[1]

1542 (Dec.)	1652 (Oct.)
1543 (Jan.–Feb.*, Apr.–May*, Oct.)	1654 (Feb.)
1544 (Jul., Oct.*, Nov.–Dec.)	1657 (Aug.*, Sep., Nov.–Dec.*)
1545 (Jan., Sep.–Oct.*, Nov.)	1658 (Jan.–Apr., May*, Jun., Sep.*, Oct.–Nov., Dec.*)
1546 (May, Jun.–Jul.*)	1659 (Mar.)
1547 (Feb., May, Jun.*)	1665 (Apr.–May, Jun.–Jul.*, Aug.**, Sep.–Nov.*)
	1667 (Aug.)
1550 (Jul.)	1669 (Oct.*)
1551 (Jul.**, Aug., Dec.)	1670 (Aug.–Oct.)
1556 (Sep., Dec.)	
1557 (Jun.–Jul., Aug.–Oct.*, Nov.**, Dec.*)	1678 (Oct.)
1558 (Jan.–Feb.*, Mar.–Apr., Jul., Aug.–Dec.**)	1679 (Mar., Aug.–Sep., Dec.)
1559 (Jan.–Apr.**, May*)	1680 (Sep., Oct.*, Nov., Dec.*)
1560 (Mar., May–Jun.)	1681 (Jan.–Jul.)
1563 (Apr.–May, Jun.–Jul.*, Aug.–Oct.)	1682 (Dec.)
1564 (Oct.)	1684 (Aug.–Sep.)
1566 (Apr.)	1685 (Mar.–Apr.)
1570 (Sep., Oct.)	1692 (Feb.)
1571 (Jan.)	1693 (Nov.)
1573 (Mar.)	
1574 (Feb.)	1705 (Jun.)
	1719 (Aug.*, Sep.)
1578 (Mar.)	1720 (Sep.)
1579 (Jan.)	
1580 (May, Jul.)	1727 (Aug.–Nov.*, Dec.)
1584 (Sep.)	1728 (Jan.–Apr., Aug.–Sep.*, Dec.)
1587 (Aug.–Dec.)	1729 (Jan.–Feb., Mar.*, Apr., May*, Sep.–Oct., Nov.–Dec.*)
1588 (Jan.–Feb.*, May)	1730 (Jan.–Feb., May)

1590 (Aug.*, Oct.)	1731 (Apr.)
1591 (Mar.-Apr., Aug.)	1733 (Feb.)
1592 (Sep., Dec.)	1737 (Nov.)
1593 (Jan.-Aug.)	1741 (Aug.-Dec.)
1597 (Jan., Mar., May*, Jun., Jul.*, Sep.-Dec.)	1742 (Jan.*, Mar., May-Jun., Aug.)
1598 (Jan., Feb.)	1743 (Apr.-May)
	1748 (Jan.)
1603 (May-Jul., Aug.-Oct.*, Nov.)	
1610 (Mar., Jul.-Aug., Oct.)	1762 (Aug.)
1612 (Sep.)	1763 (Jan.-Feb., Jun.)
1614 (Mar., May)	1766 (Oct.)
1616 (Jan.*, Aug.)	1768 (Jan.)
1622 (Dec.)	
1623 (Jul.-Aug., Oct.-Dec.)	1775 (Dec.)
1624 (Oct.)	1780 (Feb.)
	1781 (Sep., Oct.)
1625 (Feb.-Mar., Apr.-Jul.*, Aug.-Oct.**, Nov.-Dec.)	1783 (Aug., Sep.*)
1636 (Jun.-Jul.)	1784 (Feb.)
1638 (Jan., Aug.-Oct.*, Nov.)	1797 (Mar.)
1639 (Jan., Mar.-Jun., Oct.)	
1640 (Apr.-May)	1803 (Apr.)
1643 (Jul.-Oct., Nov.*, Dec.)	1814 (Jan.)
1644 (Feb., Jul., Oct.)	
	1834 (Oct.)
	1837 (Jan., Feb.*)
	1839 (May)

Notes: [1] To remove seasonal effects a trend is calculated for each month separately (e.g. the series of January totals of deaths). A single asterisk denotes a monthly death rate 50–99 per cent above trend, and a double asterisk a monthly death rate 100 or more per cent above trend.

Sources: Monthly deaths: table A2.4; population sizes interpolated from quinquennial totals in table A3.1.

picture conveyed by the annual data in table 8.12, yet the overall pattern of the incidence of crisis mortality over time remains essentially the same. Not only does the frequency of months with unusually high deaths decline apart from the familiar exceptional periods, as in the early eighteenth century, but the amplitudes of the fluctuations in the monthly death rate also diminish. With the exception of the special cases of the London plagues of 1625 and 1665, fluctuations of 100 per cent or more above trend were confined to the 1550s. Moreover both the absolute and the relative frequencies of the fluctuations of between 50 and 99 per cent, identified by a single asterisk in table 8.13, also fell over time.

The timing of mortality crises in England and abroad

For many purposes, however, fluctuations in the annual death rate provide an adequate indication of the incidence of crisis mortality, and it is on this basis that we shall compare the English experience with that of a number of neighbouring areas for which data are readily available.

Comparative evidence is available for Scotland and Brabant from the early seventeenth century. Both these areas show heavy mortality in the years following the disastrous harvests of 1622 (Scotland in 1623 and 1624, Brabant in 1624 and 1625).[96] Although the harvest was not especially deficient in England in 1622 (real wages for 1622/3 as shown in table A9.2 were only 9 per cent below trend) 1622/3 was a 1-star crisis year, and it was followed by a 2- and then a 3-star crisis year. It is apparent from the monthly death rates that mortality was not uniformly high over this three-year period and the different periods of crisis mortality were probably due to different causes. Figure A10.7 below shows that the local crises occurring in the months after the poor harvest of 1622 were mainly concentrated in the north, where food prices appear to have risen severely as in Scotland in clear contrast with the milder course taken by prices in the south on which the real-wage calculations were chiefly based.[97] In 1624 and 1625, however, local crises occurred mainly in the south-east.

As the seventeenth century progresses it is also possible to compare the timing of crisis mortality in England with that in northern Holland (from 1650) and France (from 1670) as well as in Scotland and Brabant.[98] In this way it can be seen how far the major epidemics or famines were shared by several regions in north-west Europe.[99] There is no sign of a common pattern in the mid seventeenth century. From the 1630s to the 1660s none of the crisis years in England are years of heavy mortality elsewhere, while crisis years in Brabant (1635–6) and Scotland (1636–7 and 1660–1) are not

March. The epidemic is discussed by Creighton, *op. cit.*, II, pp. 384–8, who notes that it was 'remarkably simultaneous, sudden and brief' (p. 387).

96. Flinn, *Scottish population history*, appendix A, pp. 483–8, lists annual mortality indices, where 100 represents the average annual burial total over the whole period 1615–1854. The indices for 1623 and 1624 were 413 and 118. For Brabant see Bruneel, *La mortalité dans les campagnes*, pp. 214, 218–307. In 1624 and 1625 both plague and dysentery contributed to the heavy mortality (pp. 222–6).

97. Appleby, *Famine in Tudor and Stuart England*, p. 146.

98. Holland; van der Woude, *Het Noorderkwartier*, I, pp. 203–8 and III, pp. 635–9. France: Rebaudo, 'La population française rurale de 1670 à 1740', p. 597 and Blayo, 'La mortalité en France de 1740 à 1829', pp. 52–3.

99. There are several other studies of crisis mortality in north-west Europe, covering rather smaller areas and so not considered here. The timing of crises in southern Europe was very different. See, for example, del Panta and Livi-Bacci, 'Chronology, intensity and diffusion of mortality in Italy', pp. 70–1.

paralleled in England.[100] In the 1670s and 1680s, on the other hand, there is a better correspondence; the 1-star crisis in 1670/1 is echoed in Scotland and north Holland, and that of 1678/9 in Brabant, though mid-decade crises in 1672/4 (north Holland), 1675 (Scotland), and 1676 (France and Brabant) are not matched in England. In 1679/80, however, England embarked upon a six-year period of high mortality which reached crisis level in every year except 1683/4. Each of the other four countries suffered high mortality in 1680. In France and Scotland it extended into 1681 (Scotland also experiencing heavy mortality in 1685), while in north Holland large numbers of deaths were recorded over the period 1679 to 1682.

In several years in the 1690s harvests were deficient and food prices high over much of north-west Europe. Heavy mortality can be found in Scotland in 1694 and from 1696 to 1699, in north Holland in 1690–4, and in France and Brabant in 1693 and 1694. In England the price of consumables was high from 1692/3 to 1699/1700, driving the real-wage index down to figures between 8 and 22 per cent below trend. Indeed the years 1697/8 and 1698/9 were the tenth and thirteenth most extreme fluctuations below trend in the entire series from 1541 to 1870. Yet the annual death rate in England in the 1690s was remarkably unresponsive, never rising by more than 6 per cent above trend (1695/6), and actually falling below trend in three years, including those of the lowest real wages in 1697/8 and 1698/9. Even the more volatile monthly death rate only rose significantly above average in November and December 1693 (by 26 and 22 per cent).[101] England's prominent exemption from the common experience of north-west Europe probably reflects her exceptional degree of development in agricultural production and marketing.[102]

England was also free from crises in the early eighteenth century in years when other countries were afflicted: for example 1709–10 (France), 1714 (north Holland), 1716 and 1722–3 (Scotland), and 1723 (Brabant). England's one crisis in this period, a 1-star surge in 1719/20, was echoed only in north Holland, where it was exceptionally severe.[103] North Holland also shared the heavy mortality which struck England in the form of three consecutive 3-star crisis years in the late 1720s, but interestingly it was absent in Scotland and Brabant, and only affected France in 1729. England's next crisis, again a severe one, fell in 1741–3 and comprised a 3-star crisis in 1741/2 followed by a 1-star crisis in 1742/3. Once again the heavy mortality was shared by some, but not all, of England's neighbours: on this occasion north Holland and most of France escaped while Brabant, Britanny, and Normandy suffered in 1741, Scotland in 1740–2, and the Paris basin in 1743. For the remainder of the eighteenth century there was a general lack of correspondence between crisis years in England and elsewhere, as had been the case in the mid seventeenth century and in the period from the 1690s to the mid 1720s. The only exceptions to this general rule were

100. Comparison on an annual basis is complicated by the offsetting of the year (July to June) adopted for the English data. In the case of 1636, June and July feature as crisis months in table 8.13, but this reflects the arbitrary allocation of London plague deaths in that year.
101. Accordingly November, but not December, appears as a crisis month in table 8.13. There was little evidence of governmental concern at the level of food prices in the 1690s, in marked contrast to the mid 1590s when high food prices coincided with upward fluctuations in the death rate. Outhwaite, 'Food crises in early modern England'.
102. The contrasts between price movements and agricultural developments in England and France in this period are discussed in Appleby, 'Grain prices and subsistence crises'.
103. Although the years 1704/5 and 1705/6 were unremarkable, June 1705 appears as a crisis month in table 8.13 and the death rate in the calendar year 1705 was more than 10 per cent above trend (see table A3.3). 1705 was a crisis year in France but not elsewhere.

the crises of 1762/3 and those falling in the period from 1779 to 1784, which were also years of high mortality in north Holland (in the last year there was also a crisis in Brabant). The majority of the mortality crises in England, therefore, were not shared with neighbouring countries, nor was England afflicted by many of the crises experienced abroad. Not surprisingly the coincidence in the timing of crises was greatest with north Holland an area possessing close trading links with England.[104]

The analysis of co-movements

The analysis of mortality crises was based on the annual proportional deviations from trend, as was the earlier examination of the relationships between extreme fluctuations in the demographic series and an index of real wages. Although this investigation confirmed the existence of many, though by no means all, of the 'expected' connexions, it is possible that the relationships may only have obtained in extreme circumstances. We turn now, therefore, to the question of how far they held good generally.

It will be recalled that a study of the relationships between the fluctuations in a pair of series requires the elimination not only of the underlying trend, but also of any structure in the series relating fluctuations in a given year to past fluctuations. The annual proportional deviations from trend considered so far eliminate the trend but leave the internal structure in the series. Since dealing with the latter usually involves rather complex procedures, we have preferred to adopt a simple nonparametric approach that nonetheless takes account of this problem, leaving a more sophisticated analysis to the next chapter.

Here, we shall be testing the existence of a general relationship between the short-term fluctuations in each pair of series by observing how often the series moved in the same, or opposite, directions. If, for example, fluctuations in real wages were positively associated with fluctuations in marriage rates, we should expect to find that upward or downward movements in the first series were associated with movements in the second series in the same direction. Conversely negative relationships would imply movements in opposite directions in the two series. These positive or negative co-movements in the series might occur simultaneously or be offset by one or more years if the response were lagged. If the relationship between the fluctuations in the two series were perfect then a movement in one of the series would always be accompanied by a movement in the other series in the expected direction. If there were no relationship between the two series, on the other hand, the movements in one series would be random with respect to movements in the other.

Table 8.14 illustrates the point in diagrammatic form. The four cells in the table represent the four possible combinations of direction of movement in the two series: both rise, both fall, or one rises and the other falls. The marginal totals at the end of the rows and at the foot of the columns represent the overall frequencies of upward and downward movements in the series regardless of the direction of the movement in the other series. For example, the marginal total of the first row of the figure sums the upward movements in the first series ($u_1 = u_1 u_2 + u_1 d_2$). The marginal totals can be used to estimate how often we would expect the two series to move in the same or opposite directions purely by chance in the absence of any relationship between them. If the probability of an upward or downward movement in either series is independent

104. Wilson, *England's apprenticeship*, pp. 271–2.

of the direction of movement in the other series we can obtain the expected frequencies for each of the four combinations of movements in the series, and so fill in expected values for each of the four cells in table 8.14, by multiplying together the corresponding marginal totals and dividing by the total number of movements in the series.[105] Thus, for example, the number of times we would expect two independent series to move upwards at the same time (u_1u_2) is calculated by multiplying the number of times the first series moves upwards (u_1) by the equivalent figure for the second series (u_2) and dividing the product by the total number of time-intervals in the series (N).

Such calculations provide a yardstick against which to compare the observed frequencies of positive and negative co-movements in the two series and make it possible to estimate how likely it is that there was a systematic non-random relationship between them. If the two series turn out to have moved, either in the same or in opposite directions, far more often than would be expected on the basis of chance alone, we can conclude that there was some systematic relationship between them. On the other hand, if the observed frequencies in each of the four cells in table 8.14 are not very different from the frequencies that would arise by chance we shall be unable to reject the possibility that the series were unrelated. The greater the divergence of the observed results from the expected, the more unlikely it is that they were produced by two independent series.

The standard method of estimating the likelihood that the frequencies in a table, such as table 8.14, were produced by two independent variables is to calculate the chi-square statistic. Furthermore, a measure of the strength of the association between the variables (phi) can be calculated from the chi-square value.[106] Unfortunately this simple approach is not directly applicable to the series of births, deaths, marriages, and real wages, for it assumes that each observation in each series is independent of previous observations in the series and, as has already been pointed out, this was not

Table 8.14: Schematic 2 × 2 table of co-movement frequencies in two series

1st series movements	2nd series movements		
	Up	Down	Total
Up	$u_1 \, u_2$	$u_1 \, d_2$	u_1
Down	$d_1 \, u_2$	$d_1 \, d_2$	d_1
Total	u_2	d_2	N

105. The probability of an event (e.g. an upward movement) is best estimated by the proportion of outcomes in which the event occurred (i.e. the appropriate marginal total divided by the grand total). Under conditions of independence the joint probability of the occurrence of the two events is the product of the individual probabilities (i.e. the product of the marginal totals divided by the square of the grand total). The corresponding *number* of events is obtained by multiplying the joint probability by the number of outcomes at risk (= the grand total), thus the expected number of events is the product of the marginal totals divided by the grand total.

106. Phi = $\sqrt{(\text{chi-square}/N)}$. It is zero when the variables are completely independent, and attains a value of unity when they are completely associated.

so.[107] However it is possible to allow for the autocorrelation in the upward and downward movements within each series by calculating an alternative statistic, known as z.[108] Because of the importance of avoiding contamination from the internal structure within the series, we shall assess the relationship between co-movements of pairs of series in terms of z rather than use the more familiar measures of chi-square and phi. The higher the value of z, the less likely it is that the patterns of co-movements could have been produced by two independent series.

Conveniently, the statistic z is normally distributed with zero mean and unit variance, so the probability of obtaining any given result can easily be found in standard tables of the normal distribution. The values of z corresponding to the conventional 5 per cent, 1 per cent, and 0.1 per cent significance levels are 1.7, 2.3, and 3.1 respectively. Thus a z value of more than 3.1 would indicate that the likelihood of the series being independent of each other was less than 1 in 1,000, while with a z value of less than 1.7 there would be more than a 1 in 20 chance that the pattern of co-movements could have arisen from two unrelated series. In the latter case it would be imprudent to claim that there was a systematic relationship between the movements in the two series, while in the former case the risk of error in claiming that the series were related would be negligible.

This approach to studying the relationship between short-term fluctuations in two series has the advantage of being simple and robust; moreover it is easy to calculate and the technique makes no great assumptions about the nature of the variables whose behaviour is being investigated. On the other hand, the reduction of each series to a simple dichotomy (an upward or downward movement) disregards much of the information contained in the data. The technique measures only the *consistency* of the relationship between the *directions* of the movements in a pair of series; no attention is paid to the magnitude of the movements in either series. Thus relationships that may be very strong but that only occur when one or other series experiences a major fluctuation may fail to show up in a high z value precisely because such occasions are rare. Conversely a high z value indicates a consistent relationship between the directions of the movements in the two series, but the magnitude of the fluctuations in the two series may bear little relationship to each other. The estimation of the general relationship between the magnitudes of the fluctuations in a pair of series is a complex matter and will be postponed until the next chapter.

Internal structure within the series

Before we analyse the patterns of co-movements it may be of interest to consider the nature of the serial correlation in the movements in each of the series. Since they extend over a period of 330 years in which considerable changes occurred both in the demographic régime and in the economy, it is likely that both the internal structure of the series and the nature of the co-variance between them also changed over time. Accordingly, we shall distinguish three sub-periods, beginning in 1541/2, 1640/1,

107. The dichotomization of the series into directions of movement (up or down) removes the primary effects of trend but not those of serial correlation.

108. The technique is taken from Goodman, 'Tests based on movements and co-movements', and enables the effect of serial correlation in the series of movements to be calculated over any number of time steps. The greater the degree of serial correlation the more the z statistic is reduced, and the more the conventionally calculated chi-square statistic underestimates the probability that the observed pattern of co-movements in the series could have arisen by chance.

and 1745/6, as in the analysis of extreme fluctuations. This rather arbitrary subdivision allows certain differences over time to emerge, but the proper identification of the dates when the structure of internal variation in the series changed significantly would repay further investigation.

Table 8.15 summarizes the internal co-movements in the series in each of the three sub-periods. Each annual movement occurs between two annual values and, for brevity, is labelled according to the first year of the pair (e.g. the movement in '1581/2' occurs between the annual values for 1581/2 and 1582/3). The table reports the z values which measure the probability that movements within each series 1, 2, and 3 years apart are unrelated to each other.[109]

The signs of the z values are almost all negative, which indicates that a rise in a series in a given year tended to be followed by falls in the three following years, or conversely that a fall tended to be followed by a run of rises. Since the relationship is symmetric with respect to time the negative values also mean that a movement in a given year tended to be preceded by counter-movements in the preceding years.

The major exception to this overall pattern is to be found in the column of z values for the movement in real wages in the adjacent year, which are all positive. The z values for the first two periods are so small that the patterns of co-movements they represent may well have arisen by chance but from 1745/6 on there appears to have been a significant positive 'carry over' in movements in real wages from one year to the next. Since annual fluctuations in real wages were chiefly due to fluctuations in the prices of consumables, which in turn were dominated by prices of food, this pattern might have been an indirect effect of climatic characteristics, but the relationships between the movements in successive years of the annual rainfall series and the series of summer and winter temperatures all proved to have been strongly negative.[110] It is therefore probable that the presence of a positive relationship reflects some features of the agricultural or marketing systems which permitted a 'carry over' in the direction of movements in prices from one year to the next.

Two possibilities are the necessity to retain a proportion of the annual crop as seed corn for the next year and the development of storage facilities which would make the harvest yield in one year a factor in the determination of the price of grain in the next. Since yields rose between the sixteenth and late eighteenth centuries one would expect the seed-corn effect to have declined in strength from the first to the third period.[111] The low z values in table 8.15 for the first two periods suggest that before 1745/6 the necessity to retain seed corn did not *as a general rule* induce a systematic positive relationship between the direction of the movements in food prices from one year to the next, though it may well have done so under extreme conditions. The high positive z value at a lag of one year in the period after 1745/6 suggests that improvements in storage and marketing arrangements may have begun to forge a link between adjacent years in the direction of movement in food prices.

At lags of two and three years, however, the signs of the z values are negative for

109. *Ex hypothesi* the test is made under the assumption of independence between the annual values.
110. Rainfall series (from 1697) and temperature series (from 1659) from Lamb, *Climate*, II, pp. 572–5, 620–3. The z values for co-movements within the rainfall, winter, and summer temperature series at one year's lag over the period 1697–1871 were −5.7, −4.8, and −4.8, respectively.
111. A recent summary of the evidence concludes that 'wheat output in relation to the seed-corn used increased from about 1:3 or 1:4 to 1:8 or 1:10, between the thirteenth and eighteenth centuries, but the timing of the improvements is still very much in dispute'. The major increase probably occurred early because an average ratio of 1:8 is cited for the mid seventeenth century, and productivity is thought only to have risen by 10 per cent during the eighteenth century. Holderness, *Pre-industrial England*, p. 73.

Table 8.15: Co-movements within series, by period (z values)

Period	Real wages Lags (years)			Death rates Lags (years)			Marriage rates Lags (years)			Birth rates Lags (years)		
	1	2	3	1	2	3	1	2	3	1	2	3
1541/2–1639/40	0.1	−3.3**	−0.5	−1.9*	0.0	−0.9	−1.5	−2.0*	−3.0**	−1.7*	−1.8*	−1.0
1640/1–1744/5	0.3	−1.0	−1.5	−0.9	−1.4	−1.1	−0.5	−1.0	−1.5	−0.9	−1.8*	−0.3
1745/6–1870/1	2.1*	−1.2	−3.4**	−4.0**	−0.1	0.9	−0.4	−3.0**	−2.0*	−2.2*	−1.2	−0.2

Notes: *denotes statistical significance at the 5 per cent level
       **denotes significance at the 1 per cent level.

Sources: See table 8.7.

every period, indicating that the real-wage series was characterized by counter-movements immediately after the 'carry over' effect in the adjacent year. The evidence for such a counter-movement is particularly strong at a distance of two years in the period up to 1639/40, and at three years from 1745/6. This might reflect a factor such as an over-reaction on the part of farmers to earlier movements in prices leading to an expansion or reduction in the area of land sown.

Amongst the vital rates negative z values (i.e. compensatory swings) predominate at all lags. Such a pattern may reflect genuine short-run counter-movements in the probabilities of birth, marriage, and death, or it may be the direct result of the effect of a rise or fall in a vital rate in a given year upon the stock of susceptible persons in subsequent years. An effect of this kind is easy to envisage in the case of births, where the constraints of physiology and socially determined practices such as breastfeeding imposed an average interval between births of about 2.5 years.[112] Table 8.15 shows that in general there is strong evidence for the existence of counter-movements in the series of birth rates at lags of one and two years, and little evidence of a systematic counter-movement at a lag of three years.

So far as mortality is concerned, the table shows that in the first period up to 1640 there was a moderate negative relationship between the movement of the death rate in a given year and the direction of movement in the adjacent year, but little if any relationship at greater lags. In the middle period, 1640/1 to 1744/5, the compensatory movement in the adjacent year was much weaker but a small negative relationship emerged in the second and third years. In the final period, from 1745/6 to 1870/1, the compensatory movement in the adjacent year was particularly pronounced but it disappeared in the second year and became positive rather than negative in the third year. With the exception of the period 1640/1 to 1744/5, therefore, a movement in the series of death rates was characterized by a moderate to strong counter-movement in the year next following. Once again such a pattern may reflect a genuine 'saw-toothed' behaviour of the death rates in the first and third periods, in which the probability of dying rose and fell in alternate years, or it may be an indirect result of the effect of a prior movement in the death rate on both the size and age-composition of the surviving pool of susceptibles.[113]

In the series of marriage rates, in contrast, the main counter-movements occurred two or three years apart, with the point of greatest impact shortening from three to two years between the first and third periods. Since at all times marriage took place at a relatively advanced age it is unlikely that the stock of young unmarried people became seriously depleted or enlarged by annual fluctuations in the marriage rate, so it is not immediately obvious why a movement in the rate should have provoked a compensating movement two to three years later. It is, of course, possible that the pattern may have arisen from changes in the opportunities for marriage. In so far as these were linked positively to fluctuations in deaths (through access to landholdings and craft 'practices'), or more generally to the real wage, then the internal structure in the series of marriage rates may have reflected the internal structures of these other

112. From 23.3 months with no breastfeeding to 39.0 months with prolonged breastfeeding. Knodel, 'Breast feeding', p. 1,114.
113. Where endemic mortality fell disproportionately heavily on age-groups that were normally subject to high mortality, such as the very young or the very old, the reduction in the pool of susceptibles would have a particularly marked depressive effect on the death rate in the years immediately following. For examples of such an age-incidence in outbreaks of bubonic plague see Schofield, 'An anatomy of an epidemic', pp. 109–18.

series. This latter point will be considered later, but it has already been shown that the evidence of compensating movements in the death rate at a distance of two or three years was weak, so it is unlikely that any reaction in marriages at this lag was induced in this way unless the response of marriages to mortality was much delayed. Nor was the timing of the counter-movements in the series of real wages aligned with the counter-movements in the marriage rates, for although there were strong compensatory movements in the real-wage series, they preceded the movements in marriages by one year in the first period, but, even more awkwardly, they trailed it by one year in the third period.

Whatever may be the explanation for the internal structures in the movements of the series of vital rates there is no doubt that compensating movements were the dominating feature of all series in each period. It occurred soonest with deaths and was most delayed in the case of marriages. The pattern was less pronounced in all three series in the period from 1640/1 to 1744/5. This was a period in which population growth rates were low and the long-term trend in real wages was upwards, while the evidence for the existence compensatory movements in real wages was relatively weak. Although the issue is evidently too complex to be grasped adequately by the simple methods employed in this chapter, it is possible that the relatively light pressure of population on food supplies in this period may have eased the 'carry over' problems from harvest to harvest and so reduced the amount of compensatory fluctuation in the real-wage series. If the vital rates were responsive to movements in real wages, then the attenuation in the compensatory pattern in the series of vital rates may also have owed something to this feature of the internal structure of the real-wage series.

Co-movements between the series

Such an argument presupposes that the movements in the series of real wages and vital rates were related to each other in a systematic manner. We shall now test whether this was the case, and whether there were systematic links between the co-movements in the vital series themselves, taking a pair of series at a time. Table 8.16 shows the z values for the relationships between co-movements in each associated pair, arranged according to the initiating series. As in the analysis of extreme fluctuations in table 8.9, only the results for the 7 most plausible of the 12 possible pairs are shown. And, as before, the layout of the table reflects the presumptive direction of causation even though, strictly speaking, this cannot be known from the data alone when the co-movements are simultaneous.

When the relationship between the movements in the two series is lagged by one or more years, of course, the direction of the causal flow is no longer a problem. Calculations were made up to lags of three years, but those relating to lags of more than one year generally indicated no systematic relationships between the series, and so are not reported here. The method of calculating z values took account of the serial correlations in the series lagged up to four steps back, by which point the effect was very small and had a negligible influence on the z value. It must, however, be emphasized that the relationships between the movements in each pair of series were studied without any attempt to hold constant other variables that may have been influencing them. As will become clear, each pair is part of a wider network embracing all four series, and an accurate appreciation of the true nature of the relationships between each pair requires the elimination of contaminating influences from other relationships in the network. This would be an essential part of a complete analysis, but it is much better accomplished by the more sophisticated methods to be adopted in the next chapter. Here we shall be considering only the more simple, robust relationships obtaining between pairs of series.

Table 8.16: Co-movements between series, by period (*z* values)

| Real wages and | Death rates | | Marriage rates | | Birth rates | |
Period	Lag 0	Lag 1	Lag 0	Lag 1	Lag 0	Lag 1
1541/2-1639/40	0.4	−1.3	3.5**	1.6	2.3*	3.0**
1640/1-1744/5	−2.4**	−0.8	2.4**	−0.5	2.3*	2.6**
1745/6-1870/1	0.7	0.4	1.1	2.1*	1.7*	2.0*

| Death rates and | Marriage rates | | Birth rates | |
Period	Lag 0	Lag 1	Lag 0	Lag 1
1541/2-1639/40	−1.9*	3.2**	−0.6	−0.5
1640/1-1744/5	−2.6**	1.2	−0.6	−3.3**
1745/6-1870/1	−1.1	1.4	−0.9	−0.3

| Marriage rates and | Birth rates | |
Period	Lag 0	Lag 1
1541/2-1639/40	1.1	2.5**
1640/1-1744/5	0.6	2.8**
1745/6-1870/1	3.1**	−1.4

| Birth rates and | Death rates | |
Period	Lag 0	Lag 1
1541/2-1639/40	−0.6	0.1
1640/1-1744/5	−0.6	−1.0
1745/6-1870/1	−0.9	3.2**

Notes: *denotes statistical significance at the 5 per cent level
**denotes significance at the 1 per cent level.

Sources: See table 8.7.

Table 8.16 provides strong evidence of systematic positive relationships between movements in real wages and movements in both nuptiality and fertility in all three periods, and of a strong negative relationship with movements in the death rate, but only in the period 1640/1 to 1744/5.[114] The relationship between real wages and the marriage rate was an 'instantaneous' one before 1745/6, but was stronger at a lag of one year from the date on.[115] The earlier pattern of co-movements between the series is consistent with the prescription of economic independence that characterized

114. The results of the econometric analysis summarized in table 9.8 indicate a stronger relationship between food prices and mortality in the period 1541–1639. The analysis both controls for fluctuations in fertility and takes the relative amplitudes of the fluctuations into account, whereas the present analysis only considers the relative frequency of co-movements in an opposite direction in the two series. The econometric analysis confirms the appearance of a relationship between the series of the 'wrong' sign in the period from 1745, as in table 8.16.
115. According to the econometric analysis in chapter 9 the instantaneous relationship was not so strong in the period 1640–1744 as it had been before 1640, nor did it decline in strength after 1745 (table 9.8).

marriage in England.[116] The lagged response in the marriage rate, visible from 1745/6, occurs at a time when the ratio of illegitimate to legitimate births and the proportion of prenuptial conceptions were rising, which suggests that there may have been a longer interval between the formation of a stable sexual union and the 'solemnization of matrimony' in church that gave rise to the register entries comprising the marriage series.[117] If this were so, cohabitation may still have been immediately responsive to movements in the real-wage series.

The latter were also positively related to movements in the birth rate both in the same year and at a lag of one year. The z values are a little lower in the period after 1745, but, in general, the evidence of the influence of movements in the real wage on births in the same year and the next is clear-cut and consistent. In each period the z values are a little higher when the birth rate lags real wages by one year.[118] This suggests that the impact of fluctuations in the real wage at, or soon after, conception was stronger than in the later stages of pregnancy. The consistently strong relationships suggest that the nutritionally based mechanisms outlined earlier in the chapter were operating throughout the period under study.[119] The positive relationship between movements in real wages and in the birth rate, especially when lagged by one year, may also have reflected an indirect link by way of the strong connexion between movements in real wages and the marriage rate, which has already been discussed. Once again, the unravelling of these multiple possibilities is better left for the more sophisticated methods used in the next chapter, which also take advantage of monthly data to explore the nature of the relationships between fluctuations in real wages and in the vital rates in greater detail.

The method of studying co-movements used here, it will be remembered, measures only the frequency of the upward and downward movements in the series and is therefore insensitive to relationships that may have been strong but occurred infrequently. Thus the lack of any *general* systematic relationship between movements in real wages and in the death rate, except in the period 1640/1 to 1744/5, does not necessarily mean that mortality was never sensitive to fluctuations in food prices, but rather that the relationship was not a general one. Indeed, we have already seen that the analysis of extreme fluctuations in the series revealed a relationship between exceptionally sharp falls in real wages and above average death rates in the following year, albeit a rather weak one. This lagged relationship only shows up in the co-movements of the two series in the period before 1640/1 and even then the evidence for its existence is very weak, despite the fact that real wages fell to very low levels during this period. However, mortality was very variable at the time (table 8.7), and any relationship between mortality and real wages may have been obscured because the death rate was heavily subject to variation from other influences, such as epidemic disease. The very strong evidence for a negative link between movements in real wages and the death rate that emerges for the period 1640/1 to 1744/5 suggests that as the variability of mortality lessened over time the underlying relationship between the series became more apparent, even though real wages experienced a

116. The relationship between secular changes in real wages and nuptiality are discussed below in chapter 10.
117. Illegitimacy ratios: Laslett, Oosterveen and Smith, *Bastardy*, table 1.1 and fig. 1.2. Prenuptial conceptions: Hair, 'Bridal pregnancy', pp. 237–40, and 'Bridal pregnancy further examined', pp. 60–1.
118. The econometric analysis finds the same lagged pattern, but no decline in the strength of the relationships after 1745. See table 9.8 below.
119. See fn. 49, above.

secular rise to attain relatively high levels by the mid eighteenth century. However, the general relationship between the movements in the series that emerged in this period was simultaneous, not lagged by one year as in the case of extreme fluctuations.[120] From 1745/6 the link between movements in real wages and mortality disappears, a development that may have been related to the generally higher level of real wages or to social intervention in the market such as price-indexed relief payments for the poor, which would tend to reduce the proportion of the population vulnerable to changes in the price of food.[121]

The simple analysis of co-movements in real wages and mortality, therefore, has shown that overall they were very much weaker than the relationships obtaining between real wages and either nuptiality or fertility, a result confirmed by the more detailed analysis reported in the next chapter. Inasmuch as fluctuations in the latter two series were linked to real wages through social customs and through biological changes much less dramatic than those required to induce death, their greater responsiveness to short-term changes in the price of food need occasion no surprise.

Changes in mortality, however, may also have influenced the movements in both marriage and birth rates. For example, when the death rate was high, the number of marriages may have been temporarily reduced either because the potential partners had died, or due to a more general dislocation accompanying the high mortality. However, after a burst of high mortality an above average number of farms and craft 'practices' will have become vacant which could have led to a rise in the marriage rate. This would imply a negative relationship between the movements in the death and marriage rates in the same year and a positive relationship in the following year. These patterns were present in years of extreme fluctuations in the death rate, and table 8.16 shows that they obtained generally regardless of the size of the fluctuations. The simultaneous counter-movement in the rates was particularly marked in the years from 1640/1 to 1744/5. The death rate was then moving counter to real wages and the marriage rate was moving in sympathy with them, so it is possible that the opposite movements in the death and marriage rates at this time reflected a common origin in fluctuations in real wages. But the same relationship also obtained in the earlier period when short-run movements in real wages and the death rate were not related.

The first period also provides the strongest evidence for a sympathetic movement in the marriage rate in the year following a movement in the death rate. Some of these marriages may have been between bachelors and spinsters, but in this period it is likely that between a quarter and a third of all marriages were remarriages, and remarriage tended to take place fairly quickly. The close relationship between movements in the death rate and the marriage rate a year later therefore occurred at a time when there was much remarriage. The weakening of this relationship after 1640 was accompanied by a reduction in the proportion of marriages that were remarriages, and a lengthening of the remarriage interval.[122] Moreover, long drawn out and

120. However, the econometric analysis finds the strongest relationships between the *levels* of the series with deaths lagging real wages by one and two years. See below, tables 9.7, 9.10, and 9.12.

121. The real-wage series experienced a secular decline from the mid 1740s to the mid 1810s (table A9.2). However the z values for the co-movements in real wages and the death rate in the period of decline (1745 to 1812) at both zero and 1 year lags were of the wrong sign (1.0 and 0.13) and similar in magnitude to the z values in table 8.16 for the period 1745/6 to 1870/1 as a whole.

122. The econometric analysis confirms the existence of negative and positive relationships between the series at zero and one year lags respectively independent of the movement in real wages (food prices). See table 9.8, below. The high level of mobility prevents a full investigation of remarriage intervals in England.

profound changes in the structure of the economy were diminishing the importance of access to land or a craft 'practice' as a means of meeting the prerequisite of economic independence at marriage as an increasing fraction of the population became dependent upon the sale of its labour power. Indeed, in the period after 1745/6 not only was the evidence of the lagged relationship between movements in the death and marriage rates weaker but there was also less sign of the simultaneous counter-movements in the two series.

The next section of the second panel of table 8.16 shows that there was generally a very weak negative relationship between movements in the death rate and movements in the birth rate, both in the same year and at a lag of a year. The lagged relationship, however, became very strong in the period 1640/1 to 1744/5, only to weaken again thereafter. A negative relationship between movements in the two series could have been produced by the death of pregnant women, or by foetal mortality moving in sympathy with the death rate. The relationship might be simultaneous or lagged depending on the stage in pregnancy at which the survival of the mother or child was most affected by the fluctuations in mortality. Alternatively, fecundity might be impaired through morbidity, leading to a lagged relationship between birth and death rates. The generally low z values, however, make it difficult to claim the existence of a systematic general relationship in the *movements* of the two rates (except in the middle period at one year's lag). This is an interesting result, because a fairly strong negative relationship between the series was found when *extreme* fluctuations were considered, a pattern confirmed for fluctuations of all sizes by the econometric analysis reported in the next chapter.[123] It would therefore appear that while there was a negative relationship between the relative *positions* of the death and birth rates above or below trend, the *directions* of the annual movements in the series were unrelated, except in the period 1640/1 to 1744/5 when the evidence for a negative link between the movements, with birth rates lagging death rates by one year, was very strong. If this connexion between the movements in the rates were due to morbidity, then it may be indirect evidence that the higher level of the death rate in this period may have been due to a greater prevalence of infectious disease.[124]

Another reason why the negative simultaneous relationship between fluctuations in mortality and fertility appears to be weak may be that it was partially offset by a positive relationship between the two series arising from the high levels of mortality obtaining in infancy. At zero lag the positive and negative effects are confounded, and it is perhaps a tribute to the strength of the simultaneous negative links between fluctuations in the death rate and fertility that they consistently outweigh the positive links between fluctuations in the birth rate and mortality. With a one year lag, however, the effects of the two series on each other can be separated. Although the structure of infant mortality is such that most deaths attributable to an annual birth cohort occur in the same year, about 30 per cent fall in the subsequent year so it would be reasonable to expect a positive relationship between movements in the birth rate

A study of 423 men and 295 women who remarried in the same parish in which they were bereaved in the period 1600–1799 found that for men the mean interval to remarriage rose from 22.9 to 31.2 months between 1600–49 and 1750–99, and for women from 26.6 to 40.3 months. The main increases occurred around 1750 for men, and 1700 for women. Schofield and Wrigley, 'Remarriage intervals', tables 2 and 3. For the frequency of remarriages see chapter 7, fn. 101.

123. See below, table 9.8. The relationship is not produced by a few large fluctuations in the death rate but holds for fluctuations of all sizes. See figure 9.13.

124. For secular changes in mortality see table 7.15 and figure 7.6, above.

and movements in the death rate, lagged one year. The final panel of table 8.16 shows that there was no such relationship between movements in the birth rate and movements in the death rate in the first period, followed by a weak negative link in the second period, and then a strong positive link in the period beginning in 1745/6. As may be seen in table 8.7 the death rate became much more stable in the mid eighteenth century, and therefore the emergence of a systematic positive lagged relationship may be due to a reduction in other causes of variation in the death rate which had previously obscured the link between short-run movements in the birth and death rates.[125]

Finally, table 8.16 affords strong evidence of a positive relationship between movements in the marriage rate and the birth rate, confirming the pattern already evident in the years of extreme fluctuations in either series. Up to 1744/5 this occurred with the birth rate lagging nuptiality by one year, but thereafter the positive movements in the two rates were simultaneous. The earlier, lagged relationship accords with the general expectation that fluctuations in nuptiality would be reflected in fertility through conceptions occurring soon after marriage, and the shortening of the response time might appear to reflect the rise in proportion of first births conceived before marriage in the eighteenth century.[126] But the analysis of this relationship undertaken in the next chapter, while confirming its strength, also shows that the explanation is by no means as straightforward as appearances might suggest.

Summary

We have used two complementary methods to investigate the connexions between the short-run variations in the three underlying demographic processes, and between each of them and variations in the standard of living as expressed by the real wage. We have examined the patterns of co-variation when the fluctuations in each of the series were at their most extreme, and we have tested the general consistency of the direction of the movements in the series regardless of the size of the fluctuations. The methods of analysis have been selected because of their simplicity, and while this has its advantages it has also become apparent that the identification and interpretation of the patterns of short-run variation in the series is a task of some complexity. For example, since the series were all interconnected in varying degrees, the interpretation of the relationships between any pair of series has been clouded by the inability of these simple methods of analysis to allow for the existence of alternative, indirect connexions between them running through other series in the network. Nor has any attempt been made to control for the effects of external factors impinging on each of the constituent series of a pair.

Nevertheless the two very different approaches adopted here yielded substantially the same results and it would therefore seem possible to draw some simple and robust conclusions about the nature of short-term variation in the series under consideration. First, the death rate was highly variable and, apart from the period 1640/1 to 1744/5, its fluctuations seem to have been largely independent of short-run movements in any

125. This would also explain the absence of a significant positive relationship in years of extreme fluctuation in either series in tables 8.9 and 8.10, since few such years fell in the period after 1745.

126. On the other hand the interval between birth and baptism grew longer in this period, which would have a delaying effect on the immediacy of the response of the birth rate. The median birth–baptism interval of the median of a group of parishes lengthened from 8 to 30 days between 1650–1700 and 1791–1812. Berry and Schofield, 'Age at baptism', p. 458.

of the other series, both generally and when fluctuations were most marked. In the period 1640/1 to 1744/5, however, there was strong evidence that movements in real wages were systematically associated with simultaneous movements in the death rate in the opposite direction, and when the real wage fell very far below trend there was a weak tendency for the death rate to rise above the average in the following year. In general, however, short-run fluctuations in the death rate appear to have been very largely determined by variations in factors unrelated to harvest plenty or failure, amongst which those determining the prevalence of lethal micro-organisms, though multifarious and for the most part unobservable, may have been the most significant.[127]

The fact that when using national data the impact of high food prices on death rates appears limited and uncertain is not to deny, of course, that much more clear-cut examples of the devastating effect of food shortages may be found locally or regionally.[128] It is conceivable that some of the widespread epidemics that caused sharp rises in national death rates may have spread from small areas badly affected by food shortages, in which a weakened population was attacked by diseases that later spread more widely killing people who were not undernourished. And it is true, of course, that the statistical base of the real-wages index is partial, limited, and fragile. Yet examination of the major fluctuations in the national annual death rates seems to support the same conclusion as was reached in relation to secular mortality change: the dominant influences on mortality trends appear to have been exogenous to the economic system, or at least not to have been regularly and substantially affected by changes in living standards.

Marriage and birth rates, on the other hand, were more closely associated with short-run variations, both in real wages and in the other vital rates. Marriage rates followed movements in the real wage both in the current and previous year; they were also positively related to fluctuations in the death rate in the previous year but negatively related to movements in the death rate in the current year. Extreme fluctuations in marriage rate followed the same pattern, except for the absence of a negative link to the death rate in the current year. These connexions with short-run movements in economic conditions and in mortality are consistent with two aspects of marriage in the past: the requirement of economic independence and the preference for nuclear households headed by a single married couple.[129]

Short-run movements in the birth rate reflected fluctuations in both economic conditions and the other series of vital rates. The connexion with fluctuations in real wages was general and strong, and was in evidence throughout the period studied. In particular when real wages plunged far below trend they were almost certain to depress the birth rate. But fluctuations in the birth rate were also positively associated with fluctuations in the marriage rate and negatively associated with movements in the death rate, the latter relationship emerging particularly clearly when the fluctuations were extreme. Since, overall, there appears to have been little relationship between fluctuations in death rates and movements in real wages, either generally or at the extremes, the inverse relationship between birth rates and death rates underlines the

127. Van der Woude comes to a similar conclusion about north Holland, remarking that there is no unambiguous instance of a mortality crisis linked to high food prices from the middle of the seventeenth century onwards. *Het Noorderkwartier*, 1, p. 207.
128. See, for example, Appleby, *Famine in Tudor and Stuart England*, chs. 7–9. Gooder, 'The population crisis of 1727–30'.
129. The social and economic correlates of marriage are discussed in Laslett, *Family life*, ch. 1.

independent and double importance of disease as a factor behind short-run demographic variation in the past.

The observed inter-relationships between the vital series may have been due to direct interactions between them through social and biological mechanisms, or they may have reflected a sympathetic variation in each of the series in response to fluctuations in external variables. In order to take the analysis further we need to find ways of disentangling the web of possible relationships between the present variables, and of measuring the influence of fluctuations in each upon every other, uncontaminated by the effects of other links in the network. To achieve this aim we shall need both to increase the power of the lens by examining short-run variation on a monthly rather than an annual basis, and to widen its angle by broadening the range of variables considered so as to include others, such as rainfall and temperature, which may have had an independent influence on the short-term varations in fertility, mortality, and nuptiality. These tasks will be undertaken in the next chapter where the methods of analysis will more closely match the complexity of the problems to be resolved.

9

Short-term variation: vital rates, prices, and weather

Ronald Lee

In this chapter we investigate the economic, demographic, and meteorological causes of short-run fluctuations in English vital rates over the three centuries from 1540 to 1840. The monthly series of births, deaths, and marriages stretching over this period constitute an unusually long and detailed set of data which, with the help of some econometric techniques little used in this context, make it possible to explore the relationships in some detail. There are a number of interesting questions that can be posed: for example, did high food prices cause high mortality, and if so, how soon? Were runs of bad harvests particularly lethal? Did high food prices reduce fertility, and if so, was it due to increased foetal loss, or to reduced conceptions? Were fertility and mortality affected by temperature? Did mortality crises depress fertility, and if so how? Did increased mortality lead to new marriages by opening up opportunities for the survivors? These are among the issues discussed in this chapter.

The data

The demographic data used in the analysis are the monthly series of births, marriages, and deaths as listed in table A2.4. The large number of vital events making up the series is particularly important, because when the number of events is small, as is the case with a single parish, year to year changes in numbers of events are dominated by pure chance, and the problem is of course much worse for monthly changes.[1] In such circumstances statistical attempts to determine the causes of change are unlikely to be successful, even with very long series. Conversely, when the base population and average number of events are large, the influence of pure chance becomes negligible and the systematic aspects of changing rates are more easily studied. In this chapter the data are used both in their monthly form and by harvest year, aggregated from October to September.

In addition to the demographic data, series of wheat prices, temperatures, and rainfall are also used. A series of wheat prices by harvest year was based on the following sources: before 1650, the Bowden series; 1650 to 1682, the average of the Eton and Winchester series; 1683 to 1789, the Navy Victualling series, from London and Portsmouth; 1790 to 1840, the Gayer, Rostow, and Schwartz series.[2] All splices in forming the continuous series were based on a 20-year overlap. Starting in 1683, the series were available on a monthly basis.[3] Monthly temperatures for central

1. Lee, 'Methods and models', pp. 343–7, and Spencer, 'Variability of demographic data'.
2. Bowden, 'Agricultural prices, farm prices and rents', pp. 818–21; for Eton and Winchester, Mitchell and Deane, *British historical statistics*, p. 486; for Navy Victualling, Beveridge, *Prices and wages*, pp. 566–9 and 584–7, and Gayer, Rostow, and Schwartz, *Growth and fluctuations*, microfilmed supplement to vols I and II, table 26, pp. 650–1.
3. The two monthly series agreed very closely during the period of overlap. In the Navy Victualling series the numerous monthly gaps were filled by imposing the normal seasonal pattern on the annual figures.

England from 1659 to 1840 were taken from Manley, and rainfall data, which were unfortunately available only on an annual basis, were taken from Glasspoole for 1727 to 1840.[4]

The use of wheat prices as the sole indicator of economic conditions requires some explanation, despite their traditional role in studies of this kind. We are really interested in short-run changes in real income, measured in terms of food, and the question is whether wheat prices can be used as a proxy for this variable. As a first step it needs to be shown that wheat prices are a good proxy for food prices in general. Numerous statistical analyses were carried out relating short-run variations in wheat prices to those of other grains, livestock, animal products such as eggs and milk, and a general food price index, using the annual price series for the period 1450 to 1650 published by Bowden. There were no systematic leads or lags, and changes in the series were closely associated with one another. Certainly consumers substituted less expensive foods for more expensive ones when prices rose, but since all prices tended to move together in the short run, any distortion should be constant over the period. Of course, a segment of the population grew and consumed its own food, without recourse to the market. But high prices corresponded to times of generally poor harvest, and so should reflect the condition of subsistence farmers.

Ideally, we should have an independent measure of income. For the long run, nominal wage series are available, but these contain almost no short-run variation, and so a real-wage index constructed by combining them with the wheat price series adds nothing to the analysis of short-run fluctuations. Furthermore, different segments of the population were affected differently by an agricultural price increase; presumably labourers with no plot of their own, and no compensation in kind, fared the worst.[5] The present approach is insensitive to sectional differences of this kind and therefore a strong reaction to prices by part of the population appears as if it were a weak or moderate reaction by the whole population.

Methods of analysis

The first step in analysing short-run fluctuations is to remove the longer run variation from the series. For the demographic series, this effectively removes all the influence of population size and age structure; the remaining variance in births, deaths, and marriages corresponds closely to variance in fertility, mortality, and nuptiality.[6] For prices, this removes most of the influence of secular inflation and secular real-income change, leaving behind variance closely related to short-run changes in real income. In the case of the annual death series, an additional adjustment was made to eliminate the purely demographic effect of fluctuations in prior births, operating through infant and child mortality. This was done by subtracting from deaths the expected deviation arising from fluctuations in births in the current and previous four years, given the average level of infant and child mortality in each period.[7] A similar adjustment of

4. For the temperature series, Manley, 'Central England temperatures': for rainfall, Glasspoole, 'Two centuries of rainfall'.
5. Mendels, in 'Industry and marriages', analysed separately nuptiality in agricultural and protoindustrial populations in Flanders, and found quite different responses to agricultural and industrial price fluctuations.
6. Lee, 'Methods and models' and 'Natural fertility and spectral analysis'.
7. Estimates of the average infant mortality rate for each half century from 1550 to 1799 were taken from data for twelve English parishes (those listed on p. 248 above); for 1800 to 1840 the rate was taken to be 0.150. Of course, only a fraction of infant deaths occur in the same calendar year as the birth of the infant;

births for the influence of past variations in nuptiality could have been made, but we have preferred to make allowances for this effect when interpreting the estimated coefficients, rather than beforehand.

Long-run fluctuations and trends in the series were removed by dividing each series by a centred moving average of itself, with a length of 11 years, 41 quarters, or 121 months, depending on the series in question. The difference in the lengths of these three cases arises from the decision to include a five-year period on either side of the central unit. Such moving averages effectively remove the longer fluctuations of more than 15 or 20 years duration, associated with changes in the size or age structure of the population, as may be seen in table 9.1.

If we are using annual data, the series are now ready for analysis. If, however, we are using quarterly or monthly data, a further transform to remove seasonal patterns

Table 9.1: Proportion of variance remaining after division by an 11-year moving average

Period of fluctuation (years)	Proportion of original variance remaining in a transformed series
2	1.190
3	1.190
4	0.826
6	1.190
8	1.487
11	1.000
15	0.456
20	0.182
30	0.042
40	0.014
60	0.003

Note: This table shows the approximate squared gain of the transformation, which is the proportion of the variance in a series that remains after the transformation, at each frequency or period of fluctuation. The values were calculated from the equation derived in the appendix of Granger and Hughes, 'A new look at some old data'.

this fraction is known as the 'separation factor' and must be calculated. To do this, it was necessary first to estimate the distribution of infant deaths over the first year of life. The proportion of infant deaths in the first month of life was taken to be 50 per cent from 1540 to 1700, and thereafter to decline linearly to 33 per cent in 1850. Deaths in the remaining 11 months of the first year of life were distributed according to Bourgeois-Pichat's biometric formula (see Pressat, *Demographic analysis*, pp. 90–4). Suitable summation of the monthly rates then yielded separation factors, which ranged from 0.735 to 0.675. Mortality in the first to fourth calendar years after birth was calculated from the Princeton model North female life table with life expectancy of 37.5 years, with appropriate allowance for the fraction of infant mortality not occurring in the calendar year of birth. If we denote the resulting adjustment coefficients for the ith year after birth by Q_i, and births and deaths in year t by B_t and D_t, then the adjusted death series, D_t^*, is given by:

$$D_t^* = D_t - \sum_{i=0}^{4} Q_{i,t}(B_{t-i} - \bar{B}_t)$$

where $\bar{B}_t$ is the average number of births occurring in the 11 years centred on year t. When B_t is constant or changes steadily over time, $B_{t-i} - \bar{B}_t$ will be very close to zero, and so no adjustment will be made and $D_t^* = D_t$. Similarly, over the long run, the average value of D_t^* will equal the average value of D_t. When B_t fluctuates, however, they will diverge. D_t^* will be referred to as 'adjusted deaths' or 'adjusted mortality'.

may be desirable; and in this chapter such series have been appropriately 'differenced' for this purpose, as described in appendix 16.

The form of econometric analysis used here is based on distributed lag models. These allow both contemporaneous and previous levels of a variable such as prices to affect the level of another variable, such as fertility or mortality. This is appropriate because not all reactions are instantaneous, and some of the demographic variables have delayed 'echo' responses to a perturbation. Often it is necessary to 'smooth' the estimated distributed lag effects, and here two different methods have been used: one is to form a moving average of the estimated coefficients, the other is to use polynomial distributed lags, also known as 'Almon lags'. Since the two methods give similar results the latter are reported only when they diverge significantly from those smoothed by a moving average. The estimates reported in this chapter have also been corrected for auto-correlated errors, though with data series as long as these this has little effect on the results. For further details of the econometric procedures adopted see appendix 16.

The general strategy of the analysis is to begin by estimating linear relationships among fluctuations in the variables, relationships which are assumed to hold over the entire three-century period, and for the whole range of amplitudes. In this way the general patterns are established. Later the assumption of global uniformity is relaxed and we look for changes in the relationships by sub-period, for threshold effects, for the effects of runs of bad harvests, and so on. This both solidifies the earlier analysis by confirming or rejecting its assumptions, and gives a more detailed picture of the relations among the series.

Once the relationship between two series has been estimated, it is necessary to interpret the results. Often interpretation is clarified by considering some theoretical hypotheses about the relationships between the series, and these will be discussed separately in each relevant section. It is also often helpful to formalize some purely demographic relationships that affect the results. For example, given the age structure of mortality in the past, a certain percentage increase in mortality will normally result in the death of a calculable percentage of pregnant women, and thereby reduce births. Similarly, information on the propensity to remarry allows the expected effects of a mortality crisis on the subsequent number of remarriages of widows and widowers to be derived in advance. A comparison of purely demographic effects of this kind with the coefficients estimated from the analysis of the series of vital events can sharpen the evaluation of some of the more interesting hypotheses linking short-run variations in economic and demographic variables.

Nuptiality and mortality

It is often asserted that high mortality opened opportunities for the single, thereby encouraging marriages and helping to replenish the depleted married population.[8] Inspection of plotted marriage and burial series has tended to confirm the hypothesis. Here we shall examine how far more formal statistical procedures lead to the same conclusion when using English data. First, however, let us consider the hypothesis more carefully.

There are several ways in which high mortality might affect nuptiality. When death

8. See, for example, Habakkuk, 'English population in the eighteenth century' and Ohlin, 'Mortality, marriage and growth'.

claims married people, it creates widows and widowers, many of whom remarry. Again, deaths create economic opportunities for those who are as yet unmarried, allowing them to marry. Both these effects will boost the number of marriages. On the other hand, there are also negative effects of mortality on nuptiality. The number of marriages per month or year is partly a function of the size of the population at risk to marry, and this marriageable population would be reduced by increased mortality. Moreover, numerous marriages may be postponed in the year of the crisis, either because of the death of a relative, the illness of a betrothed, or a general sense that the time was not propitious. Postponement, however, should, by definition, have little long run effect on the number of marriages.

It is possible to attach approximate numerical values to two of these effects *a priori*. The influence of normal remarriage patterns on nuptiality is easily calculated, and so is the effect of mortality-induced variation in the number of potential brides and grooms. These can be charted by month following a change in the base month's mortality.[9] If we consider the sum of these effects over the five-year period following a mortality change, we can get a sense of their contribution to the long-run compensating reaction of marriages. For each 1 per cent increase in mortality, remarriage would raise marriages by about 0.29 per cent of the normal monthly number over the next five years (which is the sum total over the first 60 months of all the remarriage probabilities), while depletion of the marriageable population would lower marriages by about 0.045 per cent ($0.00075 \times 60 = 0.045$; see fn. 9). The net effect would, therefore, be to increase marriages by roughly 0.25 per cent. The postponement effect should be close to zero, cumulated over five years. Only the mortality stimulus to marriages in which both partners are marrying for the first time remains unquantified. By comparing an empirical estimate of the cumulative

9. Let D_t be the number of deaths in month t, and let M_{t+i} be the number of marriages occurring i months after month t. We want to find the elasticity of M_{t+i} with respect to D_t, denoted $E_{M_{t+i} \cdot D}$, defined as $(\partial M_{t+i} / \partial D_t)$ (D/M) where D and M are the long-run average numbers of deaths and marriages, respectively. First consider the contribution of remarriages. Let $D_{M,t}$ be the number of deaths of married people in month t, with average value D_M. Let rM_i be the proportion of widows or widowers normally remarrying after a duration of i months of widow(er)hood, available from reconstitution studies. Then $rM_i = \partial M_{t+i} \partial D_M$. Now let us assume that the deaths of married people vary in proportion to all deaths, so that $\partial D_{M,t} \partial D_t = D_{M,t}/D_t$. Also note that D_M must be approximately equal to M, since the flows into and out of the population of married *couples* must be roughly offsetting, and one death suffices to break a marriage. Then the elasticity of M_{t+i} with respect to D_t will be given by:

$$E_{M_{t+i} \cdot D_t} = (\partial M_{t+i} / \partial D_{M,t}) (\partial D_{M,t} / \partial D_t) (D/M) \text{ which is equal to } rM_i (D_M/D) (D/M)$$

which is roughly equal to rM_i. So we have: $E_{M_{t+i} \cdot D_t} = rM_i$.

To this must be added the effect of mortality on the population at risk of marriage, say S_t. Let deaths to this population be $D_{S,t}$, and note that $\partial S_t / \partial D_{S,t} = -1$. Assume that $D_{S,t}$ varies in proportion to all deaths, D_t, so that $\partial D_{S,t} / \partial D_t = D_{S,t}/D_t$. The elasticity of the marriageable population with respect to total deaths is then:

$E_{S_t \cdot D_t} = (\partial S_t / \partial D_{S,t}) (\partial D_{S,t} / \partial D_t) (D/S)$ so $E_{S_t \cdot D_t} = -D_S/S$, which is just the average death rate of the marriageable population. Since marriages will be proportional to S, this is also the elasticity for M_t, and it will be the approximate elasticity for subsequent months of M_{t+i}.

Putting these together we have: $E_{M_{t+i} \cdot D_t} = rM_i - (D_S/S)$. For the Princeton model North female life table with $e_0 = 37.5$, the annual death rate for ages 20–9 is 0.009, which should be about right for D_S/S. The monthly rate would then be 0.00075. Values of rM_i were calculated from Colyton data, assuming that half of broken marriages resulted from the death of the husband, and that 43 per cent of widowers and 25 per cent of widows eventually remarried (see Henry, 'Etude de la nuptialité', pp. 5–12, and Gautier and Henry, *Crulai*, pp. 85–9); these latter figures are particularly subject to error.

elasticity to the derived figure of 0.25, we can assess the contribution of this last, and most interesting, response. It will also be useful to bear in mind that a fully compensating response would require a cumulative elasticity of unity; this would imply that the number of married couples automatically returned to its original level within five years after a mortality variation.

Empirical estimates of the relation of mortality and nuptiality, using harvest year data from 1548 to 1834, are set out in table 9.2. It should be noted that here and throughout this chapter any mention of marriages, deaths, births, or prices *refers to the ratios of these variables to 11-year or 121-month moving averages*. To get a clear picture of the effect of mortality on nuptiality it is necessary to take into account the influence of prices on nuptiality as well; therefore both mortality and prices were included as explanatory variables, each with lags of from zero to four years. This explains why the results presented in Table 9.2 refer to the period 1548 to 1834. The use of moving average data means that the first 'reading' is for the sixth year after the beginning of the demographic series in 1539 (i.e. 1544) and that the last is 1834, while the wish to study the effect of explanatory variables upon a dependent variable over a four-year period implies that the first year in which their impact can be estimated is 1548. Comparable considerations govern the dating of other tables and figures in this chapter. It may be noted in this connection that the moving average for monthly data is slightly shorter than for annual data.

The estimated coefficients expressing the effect of mortality on nuptiality are given in table 9.2 (in this and other tables in this chapter a double asterisk after a coefficient indicates that it is significantly different from zero at the 0.01 per cent level based on a two-tailed test; a single asterisk indicates the 0.05 per cent level; and a dagger the 0.10 significance level). The coefficients measure elasticities, that is, the ratio of the induced percentage change in marriages to original percentage change in deaths.

Table 9.2: The net effect of adjusted mortality on nuptiality, estimated from harvest year data 1548–1834

Lag in years	Estimated coefficient
0	−0.100**
1	0.194**
2	0.159**
3	0.022
4	0.036

The simplest way to interpret the lagged coefficients is to imagine a situation in which mortality was normal every year, except for one year in which it increased, say, by 100 per cent. Then the estimated coefficients describe the reaction of marriages to this mortality crisis in the year of the crisis (0 lag) and in each of the next four years (lags 1 to 4). In the year of the crisis, marriages would be 10.0 per cent below normal (100 per cent times − 0.100 is − 10.0 per cent); this is due primarily to postponement, since deaths of potential couples would account only for − 0.9 per cent. In the next four years, marriages would be about 19, 16, 2, and 4 per cent above normal, respectively. These increases reflect the making-up of marriages postponed in the first year, the remarriages of widows and widowers, and perhaps some marriages where neither partner had been married before.

The sum of the effects over the five years is 0.311. This is fairly close to the 0.25 that was derived *a priori*, and we can conclude that these estimates do not provide evidence that mortality stimulated marriages where neither partner had been previously married. The positive response of the *flow* of marriages is only about a third the size that would be needed to replace the negative effect of mortality on the *stock* of marriages. It is worth adding that although this discussion has spoken of 'mortality crisis', the estimation procedure assumed that elasticities were equal for mortality fluctuations large and small, positive and negative, so the results should hold best for the typical deviation in mortality, and might not characterize well the response to a crisis. This possibility will be explored in a later section.

The pattern of delay in the response of marriages to deaths (called the 'lag structure') can be estimated in greater detail using monthly data, but at the expense of not controlling for price-level variations. The estimated coefficients are again elasticities, and they have exactly the same interpretation as the annual coefficients, but with 'months' substituted for 'years'. To be consistent with the annual coefficients, the estimated monthly coefficients should be about one twelfth as large as the annual ones.

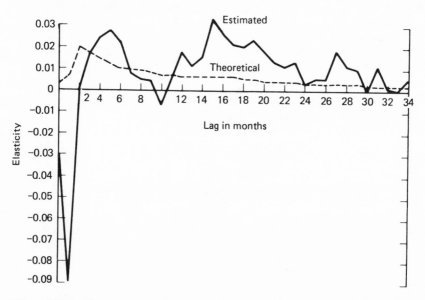

Figure 9.1: The theoretical and observed reaction of nuptiality following a variation in mortality, by elapsed months (estimated from monthly data 1547–1834)

> *Notes:* The solid line shows a 5-point moving average of the coefficients, except for the first four points which were not averaged. The dotted line shows the theoretical elasticities implied by remarriage frequencies based on Colyton data, and by the mortality assumptions described in fn. 9.

The estimated coefficients are plotted against lag in figure 9.1. The solid line shows a five-point moving average of the individual estimated coefficients, which are extremely erratic in an unsmoothed form. Recalling the interpretation of the annual lagged coefficients, the plotted monthly coefficients can be viewed as the path of nuptiality following an isolated month of mortality at double its usual level. We see that nuptiality begins to decline before the crisis, reaches its trough one month following the crisis, and then rebounds strongly. The stretch of increased nuptiality has two humps, one centred at about 5 months, and the other at about 15 months. Figure 9.1 also shows the elasticities that would have been expected on the basis of depletion of the marriageable population, and the Colyton remarriage distributions (for details, see fn. 9). The first hump in the estimated elasticities is fairly well explained; the second hump, however, is unexpected. The latter apparently reflects the making-up of postponed marriages after a delay of a year or more, and may also include some marriages that were first marriages for both partners. The cumulated sum of the estimated elasticities for the first 36 months is 0.27 which is in good agreement with cumulated annual elasticities for the first three years, 0.25.

Fertility and mortality

A reduction in the number of baptisms during or following a mortality crisis, and a subsequent increase of baptisms, is a widely noted aspect of demographic crises in pre-industrial Europe. Typically, however, these phenomena have been studied on an episodic rather than statistical basis, and there have been few efforts to disentangle their demographic, biological, and behavioural aspects.[10] The availability of monthly data series makes it possible to resolve some open issues.

It will be useful to begin by cataloguing the effects that might be present:

1 Because neonatal mortality was very high (about half of infant deaths occurred in the first month of life), a positive association of births and deaths at zero months' lag is to be expected – here causality runs from births to deaths, and *not* from mortality or morbidity to fertility. The annual death series has been adjusted to remove this effect.

2 A mortality increase kills a certain number of pregnant women, and also a certain number of women who would have become pregnant in subsequent months. When life expectancy at birth is 37.5 years, this contributes an elasticity of -0.0009 for monthly series at all lags.[11]

3 A mortality crisis also kills husbands of women who would have become pregnant subsequently; this contributes an additional -0.0009 for each month lag after the ninth.

4 From 8 to 10 months' lag, there will be additional reductions in births due to fewer conceptions, resulting from the influence of the conditions – famine or epidemic – causing the high mortality. This reduction could be due to famine amenorrhea or stress amenorrhea,[12] to voluntary control, to a decline in libido, to short-run migration, or to a negative association of morbidity and fecundity.[13]

10. See Lee, 'Methods and models'.
11. This assumes that deaths of reproductive-age women increase in proportion to total deaths. Using a model North female life table with $e_0 = 37.5$, the annual death rate to women aged 20 to 39 would be 0.0106, which implies a monthly rate of about 0.0009.
12. See Ladurie, 'Famine amenorrhoea' and articles in Mosley, *Nutrition and human reproduction*.
13. See Leridon, *Human fertility*, pp. 46–9.

5   The reduction in conceptions in the crisis month will be echoed by an increase in succeeding months, as an atypically large proportion of women is in the fecundable state. This positive effect can be calculated once the negative effect of which it is the consequence is estimated.[14]

6   From 10 months on, there may be positive effects due to lactation interruption and child replacement, in turn due to infant deaths. Tentative values may be assigned to these.[15]

7   From zero to nine months' lag, but particularly from six to nine months, there may be increased foetal mortality due to epidemic disease.[16]

8   From nine months on, there are initially negative and later positive effects flowing from the effect of the crisis on nuptiality, as estimated in the previous section. These will offset the negative effects discussed under points 2 and 3 above, and can be explicitly evaluated using the estimated mortality–nuptiality effects together with a schedule of fertility by marriage duration.[17]

Now let us turn to the empirical estimates of the association, beginning with annual data, and looking at fertility–mortality associations net of the influence of price variations. Once again the estimation procedure assumes that the elasticities will be the same for small or large fluctuations, and positive or negative ones. The results, therefore, will refer to a typical mortality variation, and not specifically the effect of a crisis.

Table 9.3: The net effect of adjusted mortality on fertility, estimated from harvest year data 1548–1834

Lag in years	Estimated coefficient
0	−0.183**
1	−0.124**
2	0.050*
3	−0.040†
4	−0.012

Because births conceived in one year mostly take place in the next, all the effects discussed above will be blurred in these annual regressions. Nonetheless, it is possible to discern strong negative effects at lag zero and one, and a substantial positive echo at lag two. These effects are consistent with the discussion. The cumulative effect after five years amounts to − 0.309, so a doubling of mortality in one year would lead to the long-run loss of about 31 per cent of the normal annual number of births, spread over the next five years.

A more detailed picture is available from the monthly data, again at the cost (which is probably quite low) of not controlling for the influence of prices. There is also some danger that the variable delay between birth and baptism, particularly after the middle

14. See Henry, *Human fertility*, pp. 57–9.
15. As, for example, in Lee, 'Methods and models', p. 359.
16..As has been argued by Hotelling and Hotelling, 'Causes of birth rate fluctuations'.
17. Henry, *Human fertility*, pp. 57–9.

of the eighteenth century, may distort the analysis.[18] Estimated monthly coefficients are plotted in figure 9.2 and can be interpreted exactly as were those for nuptiality and mortality: they depict the perturbed stream of births following an isolated variation in mortality.

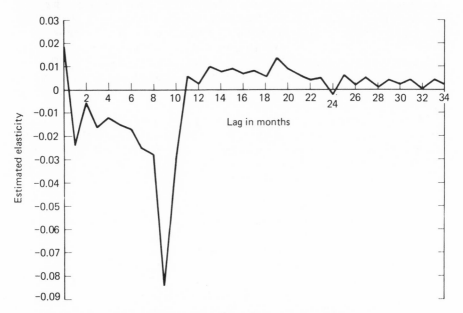

Figure 9.2: The reaction of fertility following a variation in mortality by elapsed months (estimated from monthly data 1547–1834)

Note: The figure shows a 5-point moving average of the coefficients, except for points at lags of 0, 1, 8, 9, 10, and 11 months which were not averaged.

A comparison of the estimated coefficients with expectations based on theoretical considerations suggests the following points. The positive effect at zero lag is exactly what would be expected, in both sign and magnitude (see point 1 above).[19] Between one month and seven months lag, the negative effect is about 10 times too large to be attributed to mortality of pregnant women, and therefore must be due primarily to foetal loss. In order for this to be so, foetal mortality would have to have been very responsive to the underlying causes of the mortality variation, since under modern conditions normal foetal mortality in the later months of pregnancy is only about 0.003 per live birth.[20] Lags of 8 to 10 months represent effects on births that normally

18. Berry and Schofield, 'Age at baptism'.
19. The expected magnitude can be derived from the variance of fertility, the variance of mortality, the neonatal mortality rate, and the monthly death rate of reproductive age women. The calculation is complicated. Alternatively, the estimated positive coefficient, together with all the other information just listed except the neonatal death rate, can be used to calculate the implied neonatal death rate. The result is 0.11, and implies that 11 per cent of infants born died in the same month in which they were baptized.
20. Leridon, *Human fertility*, p. 81.

would have been conceived close to the month of the mortality variation. The striking negative peak in the coefficients at nine months lags could, therefore, be due either to unusually high foetal mortality in the first month of pregnancy, or to a reduction in conceptions, as discussed earlier. After the tenth month, there is a strong positive rebound, tapering off toward the last of the estimated coefficients, at a lag of 36 months. This also agrees well with the earlier theoretical discussion; it represents the making-up of earlier non-occurring births, births to new marriages stimulated by the mortality variation, and a negative effect due to the loss of husbands and wives. Once again it must be stressed that these results are not specifically for a crisis. They also imply, for example, that a reduction in mortality would be associated with a reduction in births in that month, an increase in births in the next 10 months, and then a decline in births in the next 24 months.

It is also of interest to consider the *total* effect of the mortality variation on births, by summing all the individual monthly effects. This results in a figure of -0.103 from the monthly estimates, which does not agree very well with the result of -0.26 from the first three annual coefficients.

Fertility and nuptiality

It has often been noted that birth and marriage series show a pronounced tendency to move together in the short run, and it is natural to attribute this to the obvious link between new marriages and first births. In this instance, however, the natural explanation is not the correct one, as has already been shown on several occasions.[21] The point can be made again here in a particularly clear way, by comparing the regression coefficients for births on marriage found for harvest year data with a set of theoretical coefficients calculated on the basis of information on the monthly distribution of births by duration of marriage taken from English family reconstitution studies.[22] These theoretical coefficients allow for a substantial amount of premarital

Table 9.4: The relation of nuptiality and fertility, estimated from harvest year data 1548–1834

Lag in years	Estimated coefficient	Theoretical coefficient
0	0.24**	0.07
1	0.20**	0.13
2	0.07*	0.10
3	0.07*	0.08
4	0.05	0.08

21. See Ohlin, *The positive and the preventive check*, pp. 155–64, Carlsson, 'Fertility oscillations', pp. 418–22, and Lee, 'Natural fertility and spectral analysis', pp. 298–9.

22. The theoretical coefficients were calculated for the first two years by using distributions of first births by duration of marriage, from 12 reconstitution studies, combined with the aggregate monthly distribution of marriages within the harvest year, averaged over the whole period. The result for the first two years was then multiplied by 0.26, the approximate proportion of all births that were first births; this converted the figures into elasticities. For the subsequent three years, the coefficients were derived from Crulai data (Gautier and Henry, *Crulai*, pp. 257–64) on births of all orders by duration of marriage, and then divided by the birth-marriage ratio to obtain elasticities. Use of Crulai data was necessitated by the unavailability of English data on higher order births.

pregnancy in England; some 26 per cent of first births were premaritally conceived in the sample used here.[23] It is clear from table 9.4 that the estimated coefficients greatly exceed the theoretical ones in the first two years. Before discussing these results further, however, let us also consider the monthly data.

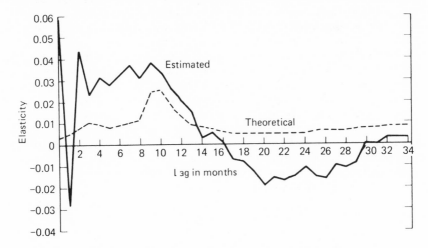

Figure 9.3: The theoretical and observed association of nuptiality and fertility, by elapsed months following a nuptiality variation (estimated from monthly data 1547–1834)

Notes: The solid line shows a 5-point moving average of the coefficients, except for the points at 0, 1, and 2 months lag which are not averaged. The theoretical elasticities are calculated for the first 16 months from reconstitution data from 10 English parishes, giving births by duration of marriage, and including the influence of premarital conceptions. For the remaining months, they are derived from a biometric fertility model.

The monthly coefficients are plotted in figure 9.3, together with the theoretical monthly coefficients derived as for table 9.4.[24] The discrepancy between the estimated and theoretical curve is striking. The estimate shows no strong peak around nine months; indeed the association of births and marriages is quite similar at all lags from two to ten months, while at one month there is a peculiar chasm, and at zero months a high peak (note, however, that these two points were not smoothed by averaging). Putting aside this anomalous result for the first two coefficients, how can the general strength of the association of births and marriages over the first nine months be explained?

One hypothesis might be that many brides were premaritally pregnant and therefore gave birth from zero to eight months after marriage. But this is already taken into account by the theoretical coefficients. Indeed, by summing the estimated monthly

23. This figure results from counting all births in months 0 to 7, and half those in month 8, as premaritally conceived. The figure is consistent with Hair, 'Bridal pregnancy' and 'Bridal pregnancy . . . further examined', who found a trend in premarital pregnancy from 20 to 40 per cent of first births over this period.
24. Except that for monthly data, we do not need to take account of the seasonal distribution of marriages.

coefficients for lags of zero to eight and a half months,[25] we find that fully 90 per cent of brides would have to be pregnant to account for the results, and the number of additional births beyond eight and a half months would still be unaccounted for. Alternatively, we may sum the estimated coefficients from month zero to month 11. These are found to imply that on the average each additional marriage led to 1.4 additional births within a year, which is physiologically impossible.

The only possible explanation is that the estimated association is spurious, not causal; some common influence affects both marital fertility and nuptiality. Calculation shows that more than half (about 56 per cent) of the incremental births must be due to women *already* married, who experience higher than usual marital fertility. It is also clear that the conception rate of married women responds several months more quickly than nuptiality to a common influence, whatever it may be.

To test whether nuptiality and fertility were both responding to variations in real incomes or mortality, a regression was run of births on marriages, using harvest year data, and controlling for the lagged effects of deaths and prices, in the expectation that the previous association between births and marriages would disappear. In the event, the association at zero lag remained unchanged although at a lag of one year the association was substantially reduced. The lack of any change at zero lag shows that neither prices nor mortality is likely to be the common influence affecting nuptiality and marital fertility, and the puzzle remains.

Vital rates and wheat prices

We have already discussed the notion that mortality opened opportunities for the single and thereby stimulated marriages. Similarly, a good harvest, low agricultural prices, and high real wages could help provide the material basis for marriage, and thus encourage nuptiality. Whether prices might affect only the timing of marriages, or whether they might affect the cumulative number as well, is a matter for empirical analysis.

The estimated effects of wheat prices on nuptiality, net of the effect of mortality are presented in table 9.5. There is a strong negative association in the year of high prices

Table 9.5: The net effect of wheat prices on nuptiality, estimated from harvest year data 1548–1834

Lag in years	Estimated coefficient
0	−0.131**
1	−0.057**
2	−0.028
3	−0.002
4	0.000

25. Because these coefficients are elasticities for the births of all orders, we must multiply them by the reciprocal of the proportion of all births that are first births, or by $3.85 = 1/0.26$.

a smaller negative association persisting in the next year, and a still smaller one in the third year; then marriages return to normal levels. It is perhaps surprising that there is no positive rebound of marriages after the high prices have receded, and postponed marriages are made up, and conversely following low prices. The cumulative effect is -0.218; that is, a doubling of prices in one year would lead to an apparently permanent loss of 22 per cent of the normal annual number of marriages.

For the period 1691 to 1834 it is possible to use monthly data to estimate the lag pattern in detail. The estimates are therefore based on roughly the second half of the period used for the harvest year data. The estimated monthly coefficients are plotted in figure 9.4. Even after considerable smoothing they remain highly erratic, but a pattern is nonetheless discernible. They show a rather strong negative reaction throughout the first 13 months following a price change, followed by a weak positive rebound, absent from the annual coefficient estimates. The sum of the coefficients over 36 lags is -0.041, which does not agree well with the -0.216 from annual data. Results of a later section indicate that the discrepancy cannot be explained by the different periods of the annual and monthly data.[26] Given the erratic character of the monthly estimates, the annual results should be regarded as more reliable.

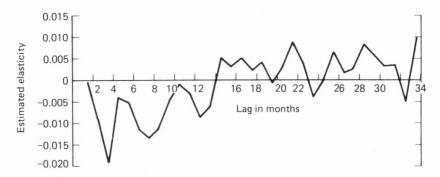

Figure 9.4: The reaction of nuptiality following a variation in wheat prices, by elapsed months (estimated from monthly data 1691–1834)

Notes: The individual coefficients were smoothed by a 9-point moving average followed by a 2-point moving average, except for the first few points shown which were averaged over fewer coefficients. The coefficients were estimated by a regression corrected for second order autoregressive disturbances.

Fertility might also co-vary with wheat prices either as a consequence of the relation of nuptiality to prices, or because marital fertility itself was responsive to price changes. Using the results of the previous section, it is easy to show that the effect of prices on fertility operating through nuptiality must be relatively inconsequential.[27] Any substantial effect found must be a direct one.

26. See below, pp. 373–7.
27. For example, a doubling of prices in a given year would reduce marriages by 14 per cent, as estimated above. This would lead to a 0.02 times 14 per cent or 0.28 per cent reduction in fertility that year, and about 1.4 per cent in the next year. These effects (0.0028 at zero lag, and 0.014 at one-year lag) may be compared to the estimates to be presented below.

There are a number of reasons why marital fertility might be responsive to prices. Couples might consciously restrict their fertility in hard times; harvest failure might prompt the absence of the husband in search of work; poor nutrition might lead to famine amenorrhea, or trying times to stress amenorrhea.[28] There is some evidence that caloric consumption must fall below 1,500 calories daily before conceptions are affected, and that even then there is a lag of about two months before the decline in conceptions occurs.[29] It is also worth noting that if prices do affect marital fertility, then we should expect to find a positive echo effect reflecting the natural periodicity of the reproductive cycle.

Evidence concerning the the association of births and prices, net of deaths, is given in table 9.6 revealing a strong negative relationship, with a cumulative elasticity of

Table 9.6: The net effect of wheat prices on fertility, estimated from harvest year data 1548–1834

Lag in years	Estimated coefficient
0	−0.073**
1	−0.086**
2	0.047**
3	−0.029**
4	−0.003

− 0.144. It is particularly striking that it should be evident with zero lag, since only three months' worth of conceptions could be affected. This suggests that foetal mortality could be a factor, a possibility that can be investigated in more detail using monthly data.

The estimated monthly coefficients for 1691 to 1834 are plotted in figure 9.5. There is a clear negative effect, followed by a positive echo after the expected interval. As with the monthly regression of births on marriages, the coefficients suggest a periodicity of roughly 30 months, which is consistent with an inter-birth interval of about this length. The effect on marital fertility becomes negative at least by the third month lag, and perhaps sooner, suggesting that prices affected foetal mortality through at least the first two trimesters of pregnancy, and perhaps the third.[30] The maximum effect occurs between seven and twelve months after the crisis, but there is no dramatic spike corresponding to nine months lag as there was for the fertility–mortality relation. Of course, the birth–baptism lag may distort the results, but not much more than it did for the fertility–mortality relation. Summing the coefficients over all lags yields a cumulative elasticity of − 0.109 from monthly data, which is only slightly lower than the − 0.112 from the first three lags with harvest year data.

28. Ladurie, 'Famine amenorrhoea'.
29. Leridon, *Human fertility*, pp. 93–4.
30. The Almon lag estimates, while generally agreeing closely with the others, show negative effects from lag zero.

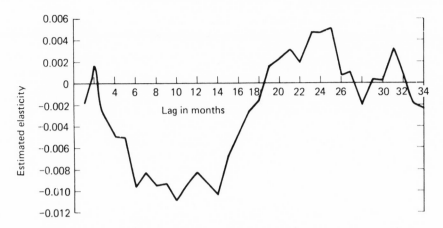

Figure 9.5: The reaction of fertility following a variation in wheat prices, by elapsed months (estimated from monthly data 1691–1834)

Notes: The individual coefficients were smoothed by a 5-point, then a 3-point moving average, except for the second and third points which were smoothed by 3-point and 5-point moving averages respectively. The coefficients were estimated by a regression corrected for second order autoregressive disturbances.

The question of the relation of short-run fluctuations in mortality and grain prices is a popular one and has attracted dozens of studies, despite its tenuous link to the broader issue of the relation between mortality and living standards.[31] There are, of course, a number of ways in which wheat prices might affect mortality. Outright starvation was probably uncommon, but it is likely that high prices led to a gradual physical weakening of segments of the population, as they were first forced to draw upon financial or food reserves, then on bodily reserves. And a population so weakened might well be more vulnerable to disease and death, although this latter link does not receive strong support from the medical literature. Another possibility is that harvest failure prompted short-term migration of people in search of food and work, and that this mobility may have helped spread disease.

With the present data, and with more flexible econometric techniques, it is possible to ascertain not only the broad outlines of the relationship between mortality and grain prices, but also some of its more subtle detail. Much of this will be described in later sections, as with fertility and nuptiality; here we consider only the general relationships obtaining between prices and deaths based on fluctuations of every kind occurring over the whole period.

The estimated coefficients for harvest year data are shown in table 9.7. Several points call for comment. First, the relationship is very weak, and explains only 16 per cent of the variance in mortality, less than is explained by prices in the case of fertility or nuptiality. Second, the relationship is nonetheless highly significant statistically;

31. The following is a small sample: Appleby, 'Disease or famine?' and 'Nutrition and disease'; Chambers, *Population, economy and society*; Lee, 'Models of pre-industrial population dynamics'; and 'Methods and models'; Mirowski, 'The disease–dearth nexus'; Thomas, *Swedish population movements*.

Table 9.7: The effect of wheat prices on adjusted mortality, estimated from harvest year data 1544–1834

Lag in years	Estimated Coefficients
0	0.048
1	0.090**
2	0.096**
3	−0.028
4	−0.079**

the probability that the estimated coefficients comprise a freak sample and that the relationship really is zero is less than one in a thousand. There can be no doubt that variations in prices were indeed followed by variations in mortality. Third, the major effect occurs not in the year of high prices, but in the two subsequent years. This suggests that the quality of the harvest affected the long-run health and resistance of the population, rather than causing outright starvation. Further discussion of this surprisingly long lag will be postponed until later sections. Fourth, there is a strong negative echo of the price-induced mortality increase, for the fourth and fifth coefficients are negative, suggesting that the effect of high prices was primarily to advance by a few years the deaths of the weak, who would in any case have died soon, rather than to strike down those who would otherwise have lived many years more. For the first three years during and following a price variation, the cumulated elasticity of deaths is 0.234; for the next two years, however, the elasticity is − 0.107, leaving a net effect of only 0.127 cumulated over five years. Similar estimates, which allow for more distributed lag terms, show that mortality returned to normal levels at lags of five and six years.[32]

Analyses of the mortality–grain price relation that do not allow for distributed lag effects are bound to be seriously misleading. Furthermore, one could not expect to detect this relationship by visually scanning plots of burials and prices; it is weak, and its effects are too dispersed in time. It will be shown later that there are non-linear effects operating; that the pattern of response to a large increase in price is different from the response to a small one; and that the nature of the relationship changed substantially over time.

Analysis of the monthly mortality and price data poses a problem. Monthly price data are available only from 1683 on, but later analysis by sub-period will show that for harvest data from 1746 to 1834, the mortality–price relation is very weak, and of the 'wrong' sign. Thus, for most of the period that can be studied using monthly data, the relationship may no longer exist, or exist in a changed form. We should not be surprised, then, if the monthly results are inconsistent with those reported for the harvest year analysis, which spanned the full three centuries.

The estimated monthly coefficients are plotted in figure 9.6. The explained proportion of variance is very small (0.069) but nonetheless the association of the

32. When the analysis is done, instead, with the unadjusted death series, the coefficients are: 0.028, 0.066, 0.089, − 0.031, and − 0.081.

series is very highly significant (at beyond the 0.001 level).[33] The coefficients depict positive and lagged effects of prices on mortality, and show a peak effect at 16 months. It is peculiar that the coefficients at lags of zero and one month are strongly negative (-0.038 and -0.039 respectively), but this may merely reflect the unreliability of the unsmoothed estimates. If we cumulate the coefficients over the 36 months, we find 0.116, a somewhat higher figure than the cumulated sum of 0.098 for the first three years of the annual estimates averaged for the last two periods (see table 9.8).

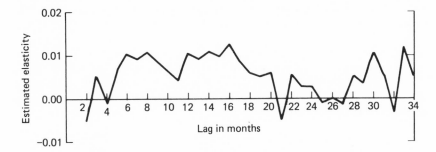

Figure 9.6: The reaction of mortality following a variation in wheat prices, by elapsed months (estimated from monthly data 1691–1834)

Notes: The individual coefficients were smoothed by a 9-point moving average reduced to a 5-point moving average at either end of the series. The coefficients were estimated by a regression corrected for second order autoregressive disturbances.

Analysis by sub-period

So far, the entire three-century period has been treated as if it were a homogeneous whole, which we could understand as well by looking at its first century or its last. It is now time to confront the obvious importance of structural change over this period, which witnessed the beginnings of the industrial revolution, along with urbanization, major shifts in the occupational distribution, a decline in the relative importance of agricultural production, and improvements in transportation with consequent reductions in regional price differences. These changes may well have altered the relationships we have so far been studying, and it is therefore important to examine sub-periods separately.

The century from 1548 to 1640 was a period of generally rapid population growth, low mortality, and falling real wages. The century from 1641 to 1745 was one of relative demographic stagnation, higher mortality, and rising real wages. The century from 1746 to 1834 includes the early stages of the industrial revolution, and excludes the last major mortality crisis of 1741–3; it was a period of renewed rapid population growth and social change. A division into three sub-periods, therefore, each roughly one century long, seems both convenient and sensible.

33. The dependent variable is deaths in each month minus deaths 12 months previously; the variance explained is of this differenced data, not the original monthly data.

It was shown in the previous chapter that the variability of each of the three vital series lessened over time, most strikingly in the case of mortality. The mean absolute annual deviations of births and marriages in the early nineteenth century were about one half as high as they had been in the mid sixteenth century, while that of deaths had fallen to below a third of its earlier value. The variability of prices also diminished over time; the standard deviation of the fluctuations of the annual price series around the 11-year moving average was 0.25 in the period 1540 to 1640, 0.24 in the period 1641 to 1745, and 0.19 in the century after 1746.

The relationships between fluctuations in vital rates and prices, and, where appropriate, to adjusted mortality have been estimated separately for each sub-period following the same methods as were used for the period as a whole. The estimated coefficients for different lags are given in table 9.8, and plotted in figure 9.7. The diagram for fertility shows a striking homogeneity across sub-periods; there is virtually no change in fertility's pattern of response to prices, and only in the last period does the relation to mortality weaken. If we sum the coefficients over all lags to get an estimate of the cumulative elasticity between births and prices, we find − 0.134, − 0.131, and − 0.184, which are very similar. For the response of fertility to

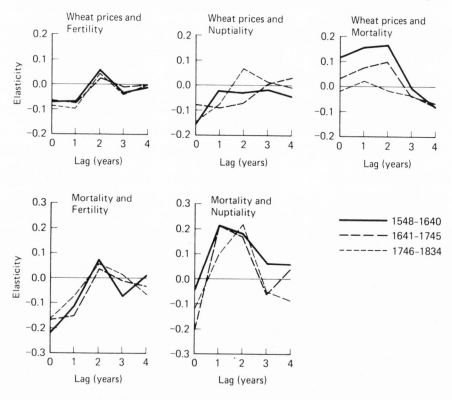

Figure 9.7: The relation of vital rates to mortality and wheat prices by sub-period (estimated from harvest year data 1548 – 1640, 1641 – 1745, and 1746 – 1834)

Source: The estimated elasticities are taken from table 9.8.

mortality we find -0.322, -0.303, and -0.218. In this context mortality is used as a proxy for morbidity; the fall in its variance in the third period may have been paralleled by a change in the diseases it reflected, and this may account for its somewhat reduced association with fertility.

Table 9.8: The net effects of adjusted mortality and wheat prices on vital rates by sub-period, estimated from harvest year data 1548–1834

Explanatory Variable and lag	1548–1834	1548–1640	1641–1745	1746–1834
		Fertility		
Constant	1.453**	1.457**	1.432**	1.404**
Price 0	−0.073**	−0.071**	−0.066**	−0.088**
1	−0.086**	−0.070**	−0.077**	−0.097**
2	0.047**	0.056**	0.024	0.040*
3	−0.029**	−0.034†	−0.011	−0.037*
4	−0.003	−0.015	−0.001	−0.002
Deaths 0	−0.183**	−0.217**	−0.163**	−0.160**
1	−0.124**	−0.114**	−0.148**	−0.074
2	0.050*	0.070*	0.040	0.065
3	−0.040†	−0.072*	−0.004	0.014
4	−0.012	0.011	−0.028	−0.063
R^2	0.64	0.69	0.60	0.67
		Nuptiality		
Constant	0.906**	0.813**	1.042**	1.106**
Price 0	−0.131**	−0.162**	−0.079†	−0.150**
1	−0.057**	−0.021	−0.089*	−0.077**
2	−0.028	−0.033	−0.070†	0.066**
3	−0.002	−0.020	0.001	0.010
4	0.000	0.045†	0.031	−0.004
Deaths 0	−0.100**	−0.052	−0.207*	−0.126
1	0.194**	0.215**	0.218*	0.093
2	0.159**	0.185**	0.172†	0.214**
3	0.022	0.065	−0.064	−0.048
4	0.036	0.060	0.040	−0.082
R^2	0.41	0.66	0.31	0.64
		Adjusted mortality		
Constant	0.876**	0.657**	0.899**	1.136**
Price 0	0.048	0.117†	0.037	−0.016
1	0.090**	0.155*	0.073†	0.020
2	0.096**	0.165*	0.098*	−0.016
3	−0.028	−0.008	−0.039	−0.038
4	−0.079**	−0.082	−0.066	−0.083**
R^2	0.16	0.22	0.17	0.15

Notes: The regressions are corrected for second order autoregressive disturbances using the iterative Cochrane–Orcutt procedure. The regressions for adjusted mortality are for 1544 on. The R^2 was calculated for the untransformed variables.

The pattern of response of nuptiality to prices and mortality changed a little more over time, but not to any great extent, as the shapes of the curves in figure 9.7 remain fairly similar in the three periods. The cumulated elasticities of nuptiality with respect to prices are -0.281, -0.206, and -0.155. This diminishing cumulative effect conceals a largely offsetting movement in the values for lags zero and one, so that the bulk of difference in the cumulated effect is due to lags two, three, and four following the price increase. One interpretation of these results might be that in the earliest period high prices led to permanent cancellation of many marriages, while in the latest period they were more frequently made up after a few years postponement.

The cumulative elasticities of nuptiality with respect to mortality are 0.473, 0.159, and 0.051. This is a very striking difference, suggesting that in the later two sub-periods remarriage may have been later or less frequent. In fact, reconstitution studies do show a lengthening of remarriage intervals. One might speculate that this reflected the diminishing importance of land holdings as a basis for marriage.

Mortality presents the clearest contrast across sub-periods. In the first, there is a cumulative elasticity in relation to prices of 0.347. In the second, the shape of the distributed lag coefficients remains similar, but the level is lower, and the cumulative elasticity is only 0.103. By the third period, every estimated coefficient but one is negative and the cumulative elasticity is -0.133. It will be seen later that this unexpected result is weakened when weather is included in the analysis.

It is tempting to suppose that wheat prices became less relevant as an indicator of real income over the course of these three centuries, as fluctuations in money incomes from industrial sources became more important. If true, this might account for the declining impact of wheat prices on mortality. However, the effect of prices on fertility actually became slightly more pronounced over the three centuries, which is at odds with the hypothesis. There are a number of other possible explanations which merit consideration. Perhaps the effect on mortality of fluctuations in real income depended on the general level of real income, and was less pronounced when living standards were higher. But this does not help, since the third period did not have particularly high real incomes compared to the preceding periods, at least according to the Phelps Brown and Hopkins real-wage index.[34] Nor is it clear that the distribution of income had become more even. The improvement of transport must have reduced the impact of local harvest failures, and this may have been an important factor. It is also possible that the declining influence of price variations was due to the declining variability of mortality in general. If prices had always acted merely to intensify fluctuations which were primarily of independent epidemiological origin, then the great reduction in such independent fluctuations in the last period would also have reduced the impact of prices on mortality.

The R^2 values also merit discussion. These give the proportion of the variance in the dependent variable explained jointly by all the independent variables. For fertility the R^2s indicate that 60 to 70 per cent of the variance is explained in each sub-period. However, this similarity of R^2s across sub-periods masks a sharp decline in both the numerator and the denominator of the R^2 measure. Because of this, it is useful also to look at another statistic: the proportional change in fertility caused jointly by all the independent variables in a typical year.[35] In the first sub-period, fertility would

---

34. See appendix 9.
35. This was calculated as $\sqrt{SSR/T}$ where T is the number of observations and SSR is the regression sum of squares.

typically deviate 5.1 per cent from its mean due to prices and mortality; in the second sub-period this had declined to 4.2 per cent, and in the last to 2.8 per cent. Because variation in fertility from all other sources was likewise declining, the R^2 remains similar.

For nuptiality, the R^2 is similar in the first and last sub-periods at 0.66 and 0.64, but it was less than half that in the middle sub-period, at 0.31. On the other hand, the typical variations due to prices and mortality were 7.3, 6.1, and 4.1 per cent respectively. This shows that the lower R^2 for 1641 to 1745 was due principally to an increase in the unexplained variation in nuptiality, not to the small decline in explained variance.

For mortality, the R^2 declines steadily but not dramatically over time. This gives a somewhat misleading impression, since the typical price-induced variation declines very sharply, from 7.8 per cent in the first period to 4.3 per cent in the second and only 2.1 per cent in the third. It is also worth noting that although the R^2s for fertility and nuptiality are much higher than for mortality, this is *not* because prices had less influence on mortality, but rather because the variability from other sources was greater.

Runs of high prices, threshold effects, and other nonlinearities

So far, all the relationships have been assumed to be of a general linear nature, so that a given level of prices was taken to have the same additive effect whether it occurred in winter or summer, whether it was very high or very low, and whether it followed a period of high or low prices. But this restrictive assumption may be untrue, and it is now time to relax it and search for various nonlinear effects of prices on vital rates.

It seems plausible to suppose that mortality would be particularly badly affected by a *run* of high prices and that its effect would be greater than the sum of effects of comparable but isolated instances of high prices. To test for this possibility, the number of consecutive years in which prices were at least 22 per cent (one standard deviation) above normal was included as a variable, along with its square, in a regression that also included linear lagged price variables. However, in this regression the 'consecutive years' variables contributed almost nothing to the explained variance, and the hypothesis that runs of years of high prices were especially lethal was rejected.

It is also plausible to suppose that the effects of prices on mortality might differ by season. For example, a shortage of customary staple foods in the summer months could perhaps be compensated for by foraging, but in the winter this option might not be open, so that high prices might have more severe effects in winter than in summer. To test this hypothesis, separate regressions were run of deaths on lagged prices for each of the four seasonal quarters, and an F-test was used to compare these to the previous pooled regressions. The hypothesis that the association between variations in prices and mortality differed by season was rejected.

It is sometimes suggested that price increases might have had different effects on vital rates than price decreases, an hypothesis supported by Mendels's work on marriage fluctuations in Flanders.[36] However, analysis of the English data, after allowing for such differential responses at all lags, led to rejection of the hypothesis.

A final hypothesis, that will be discussed in considerable detail, is that the effect on

36. Mendels, 'Industry and marriages'.

vital rates of a variation in prices depended on the initial level of prices. For example, it would not be surprising if variations in prices in the neighbourhood of the average price level had little effect, while increases in prices above some threshold level had a major effect. There are numerous statistical procedures for examining this kind of nonlinearity. One simple method is to introduce squared terms of prices in the equations. Another is to try alternate functional forms; the so-called 'Box-Cox' procedure can be used actually to solve for the best functional form as part of the estimation procedure. A further possibility, which requires estimating more coefficients, and therefore puts greater demands on the data, is to break the price variable into categories by level. This method provides the richest and most flexible description of the relationships and so has been used here, although experiments were also made with other methods, which yielded generally consistent results.

Table 9.9: Categorical wheat price variables

Category label	Price range	Number	Frequency
Very low	< 0.78	39	0.134
Low	0.78 to 0.99	127	0.436
High	1.00 to 1.21	86	0.296
Very high	1.22 to 1.44	30	0.103
Extremely high	> 1.44	9	0.031

The price variable has a mean value of unity by construction, since it is measured as a ratio to a moving average. Its standard deviation is 0.22, with a minimum value of 0.45 and a maximum of 2.01 over the 291-year period 1544–1834. For present purposes, the standard deviation was used to define five categories of price level, as shown in table 9.9. It should be noted that 73.2 per cent of prices fall within one standard deviation of the average price, in the categories 'low' and 'high', and that the 'extremely high' category includes only nine cases, or 3.1 per cent of the sample.

Table 9.10: The effect of categorical wheat price variables on adjusted mortality, estimated from harvest year data 1544–1834

Price category	Estimated coefficient at each lag in years				
	0	1	2	3	4
Very low	−0.008	−0.017	−0.020	−0.009	0.033
Low	−0.006	−0.012	0.009	0.006	0.017
High	0.001	0.011	0.014	−0.001	−0.025
Very high	0.008	0.026	0.029	0.005	−0.044
Extremely high	0.069	0.052	0.067	−0.036	0.001
R^2 = 0.18					

Notes: The estimates were corrected for second order autoregressive disturbances by the iterative Cochrane–Orcutt procedure. The 'Very low' category was excluded in the original regression, and the estimated coefficients were re-expressed in the above form by constraining the weighted sum of the coefficients, including the 'Very low' category, to be zero at each lag. The R^2 given is for the transformed regression and is therefore not comparable to those in table 9.8.

Regressions were run for fertility, mortality, and nuptiality on these categorical price variables, using harvest year data for 1544 to 1834, and allowing for effects with lags of zero to four years. We will first consider the results for mortality. Table 9.10 presents the basic regression results, on which the next three interpretative diagrams are based. In figure 9.8 a separate curve for each level of prices plots the coefficients by lag. Consider the initially highest line, labelled 'Eh' for 'extremely high'; it shows the path of mortality in the years during and following a hypothetical isolated episode when the price level is at least 44 per cent above average. Mortality would be 6.9 per cent above average in the base year, fall slightly to 5.2 per cent above average the following year, rise slightly to 6.7 per cent above average in the next year, and then drop sharply to 3.6 per cent *below* average in the third year following the high prices, and finally return to the average level. Similarly, the curve labelled 'Vl' for 'very low' prices (at least 22 per cent below average) shows that following an hypothetical isolated episode, mortality would be below average for the first four years, then rebound to above average in the last year. Careful inspection of figure 9.8 supports the following observations. Only extremely high prices produce a substantial response of mortality in the base year; otherwise the peak effect occurs in the first or second year following the price change. The delayed effects of prices on mortality are evident at all five levels, and therefore the reality and importance of these effects are strongly confirmed. There is also strong confirmation of the rebound of mortality in the third and fourth years following a price variation, for every price level.

Now consider figure 9.9, which again shows the coefficients of table 9.10, but this time plots mortality as a function of price level, with a separate curve for each lag. This format facilitates consideration of nonlinearities and threshold effects. Under the assumption of linearity, each of the curves in figure 9.9 would be forced into a straight line with slope equal to the regression coefficient.[37] Inspection of the line for lag zero (the year of the price variation) shows that in this instance linearity would be a poor assumption. Going from very low prices through to very high prices, there is only a 1.6 per cent increase in mortality; between very high prices and extremely high prices, however, mortality rises dramatically by 6.1 per cent. For the base year, then, we might well speak of a 'threshold effect'. At lags one and two, the assumption of linearity would be quite reasonable, as can be seen by attempting to pass a straight line through the points on the curves labelled 1 and 2. For lags three and four, nonlinearities are again present, since the rebound after extremely high prices occurs earlier and ends earlier than for other price categories. Figure 9.9 also shows how regular and systematic are the estimated effects of price on mortality. At lags of zero, one, and two years the ordering of mortality level is perfect across all price levels.

A summary picture of these effects can be obtained by cumulating them over all lags. For example, to find the total or net effect of extremely high prices we can add together the effects at lag zero, lag one, and so on. The results of doing this are presented in figure 9.10. The broken line represents the sum over the first three years, before the inverse echo effect occurs. This line shows a very regularly increasing effect of prices on mortality; it clearly reveals nonlinearity, but does not suggest a threshold effect. The dotted line shows the strength of the echo, given by the sum of the last two lags, and we observe that it is negative when prices are high, and positive when they are low, and that it is nonlinear. The solid line shows the total effect over the five years, including the compensating echo. Of course, since everybody dies sooner or later, price variations can only affect the timing of deaths, and a sum of the

37. On the horizontal axis each price category is centred on its mean value.

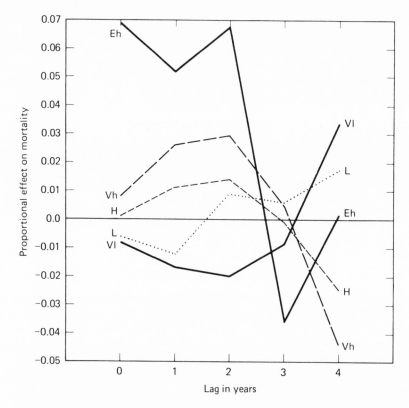

Figure 9.8: Lag patterns in the relation of mortality to categorical wheat price levels (estimated from harvest year data 1544 – 1834)

Notes: The vertical scale indicates the proportional deviation of mortality from its mean associated with prices in a given category and at a given lag, if prices at all other lags are distributed according to their sample frequencies.
Abbreviations: Vl, very low; L, low; H, high; Vh, very high; Eh, extremely high.
For definition of the price categories see table 9.9.

Source: The estimated coefficients are given in table 9.10.

coefficients over enough lags would always have to be zero. However, it is noteworthy that for every price level except extremely high, the solid line is close to zero, indicating that within five years the compensation is complete; the price variations merely advance or retard the timing of deaths for those with a foot already in the grave.

These estimates show clearly that the association of mortality and prices is real, and not the spurious result of a few coincidental harvest failures and mortality crises. The patterns revealed are too regular and persistent at all levels of prices for that to be the case.[38] On the other hand, the relationships are revealed to be very, very weak. Even a

38. It is true that the few episodes of extremely high prices explain the lion's share of mortality–price association. In one set of regressions, the linear model accounted for 11.4 per cent of mortality's variance;

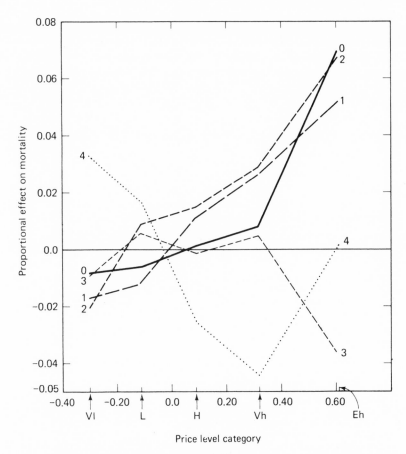

Figure 9.9: The relation of adjusted mortality to categorical wheat price level by lag (estimated from harvest year data 1544–1834)

Notes: The vertical scale indicates the proportional deviation of mortality from its mean associated with prices in a given category and at a given lag, if prices at all other lags are distributed according to their sample frequencies. The price categories are located on the horizontal axis at their category means.
For definition of the price categories see table 9.9.

Source: The estimated coefficients are given in table 9.10.

when the 'extremely high' price variable was added this went up to 12.5 per cent; and when extremely high prices alone were used 6.2 per cent of the variance was explained. Thus, the nine instances of extremely high prices account for more than half the variance explained by the mixed 'linear–extremely high' model, and they also account for almost half the variance explained by the full categorical price model. Nonetheless, the smaller positive and negative price variations still show a regular and statistically significant relation to mortality.

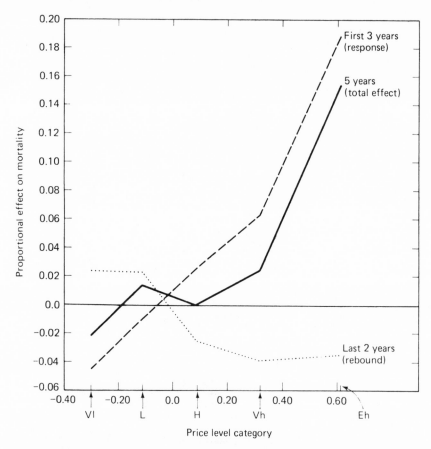

Figure 9.10: The cumulated effect of wheat price level on adjusted mortality (estimated from harvest year data 1544 – 1834)

Notes: The vertical scale indicates the summed proportional deviations of mortality from its annual mean level, following a year of prices at the given category, if prices in all other years are distributed according to their sample frequencies. The price categories are located on the horizontal axis at their category means.
For definition of the price categories see table 9.9

Source: See table 9.10 for the individual coefficients summed in this figure.

year of 'extremely high' prices, such as occurred only a few times a century, would raise mortality by a mere 19 per cent (of the average annual number of deaths), an effect spread over three years, and then partially compensated for by unusually low mortality in the following year. Even if the association of variations in prices and mortality can now be regarded as quite well established, the question of *causality* must remain open, at least until we determine whether that association derives solely from a common link to the weather.

Since the results for fertility and nuptiality are less complex than those for mortality, they will be discussed in less detail and only the cumulative effects will be

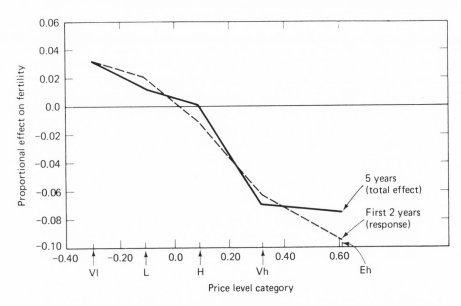

Figure 9.11: The cumulated effect of wheat price level, net of mortality, on fertility (estimated from harvest year data 1548–1834)

Notes: The vertical scale indicates the summed proportional deviations of fertility from its annual mean level, following a year of prices at the given category, if prices in all other years are distributed according to their sample frequencies. The price categories are located on the horizontal axis at their category means.
For definition of the price categories see table 9.9.

presented. Figure 9.11 shows these for fertility, estimated net of lagged mortality. The broken line is the sum of the effects in the first two years, since the echo in this instance occurs in the third year. The broken line shows a consistent and quite linear pattern of effects; abnormally low prices raise fertility and abnormally high ones depress it. The solid line shows the total effect over five years, and is quite similar to the broken line. The amount of 'compensation' in the last three years after a price variation is clearly quite small, except for extremely high prices.

Figure 9.12 shows the results for nuptiality, again cumulated over two and five years. The impact of prices on nuptiality is shown to be quite linear in the first two years, but the next three years give a jagged appearance to the total five-year effect.

The results for fertility and nuptiality suggest that systematic nonlinearity is not an important feature of the relation of fertility or nuptiality to prices; departures from linearity appear to be random.

Finally, we may consider the possibility of nonlinearities in the relations of fertility and nuptiality to mortality. Figure 9.13 shows the cumulated effects of mortality on fertility, by category, revealing a strongly linear pattern with no notable deviations.

Figure 9.14, relating nuptiality to mortality, reveals a different pattern, suggesting that only extremely high or very low mortality had a marked effect on nuptiality. This result is difficult to explain, since the remarriage mechanism should produce a proportional response to any change in mortality, large or small. Inspection of the estimated coefficients (not included here) shows that the apparent nonlinearity derives

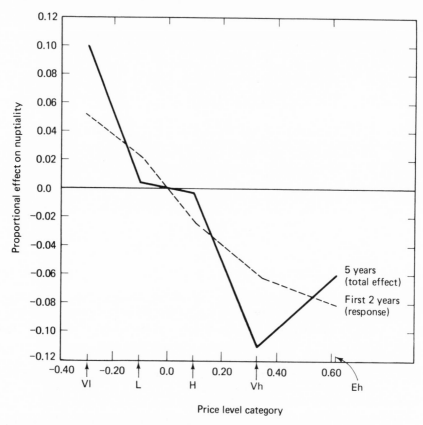

Figure 9.12: The cumulated effect of wheat price level, net of mortality, on nuptiality (estimated from harvest year data 1548 – 1834)

Notes: The vertical scale indicates the summed proportional deviations of nuptiality from its annual mean level, following a year of prices at the given category, if prices in all other years are distributed according to their sample frequencies. The price categories are located on the horizontal axis at their category means.

For definition of the price categories see table 9.9.

almost entirely from a large negative coefficient at lag zero for very high mortality. This does not disprove the result by any means, but it suggests that we exercise caution in interpreting it.

Weather and vital rates

There have been highly important secular changes in the prevailing level of mortality in pre-industrial Europe, which do not appear to have had any obvious social or economic causes. For example, mortality was high in the later fourteenth and fifteenth centuries, low in the late sixteenth century, high again in the seventeenth century, and

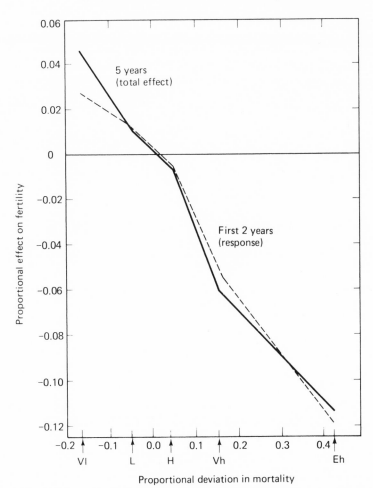

Figure 9.13: The cumulated effect of adjusted mortality, net of prices, on fertility (estimated from harvest year data 1548–1834)

Notes: The vertical scale indicates the summed proportional deviations of fertility from its annual mean, following a year of prices at the given category, if prices in all other years are distributed according to their sample frequencies. The mortality categories are located on the horizontal axis at their category means.

For definition of the price categories see table 9.9.

then from the mid eighteenth century embarked upon a secular decline.[39] These apparently exogenous mortality changes had a profound effect on population growth and hence on living standards, relative prices, and many other aspects of the society and economy.[40] But what accounted for the mortality changes themselves?

39. Material in this volume documents some of these changes; for a review of other evidence see Lee, *Econometric demographic history*, pp. 66–8 and 234–60.

40. See, for example, Lee, 'Models of pre-industrial population dynamics' and 'Population in pre-industrial England'.

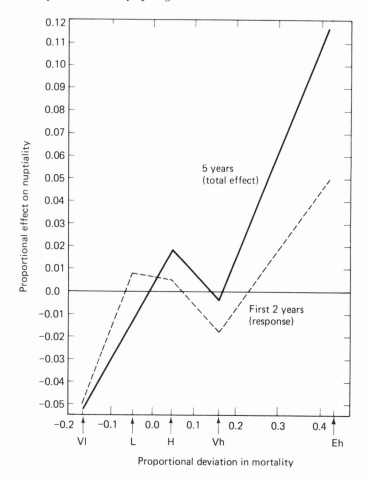

Figure 9.14: The cumulated effect of adjusted mortality, net of prices, on nuptiality (estimated from harvest year data 1548–1834)

Notes: The vertical scale indicates the summed proportional deviations of nuptiality from its annual mean, following a year of prices at the given category, if prices in all other years are distributed according to their sample frequencies. The mortality categories are located on the horizontal axis at their category means.
For definition of the price categories see table 9.9.

One possible explanation, attracting increasing attention lately, is epidemiological change – due in part to voyages of exploration, in part to co-evolution of people and parasites, and in part to more fortuitous factors such as natural periodicities in some diseases.[41] Another important hypothesis is that climatic changes were responsible.[42]

41. See, for example, Chambers, *Population, economy and society*; Durand, 'World population'; Helleiner, 'The vital revolution reconsidered', and McNeill, *Plagues and peoples*.
42. See, for example, Braudel, *Capitalism and material life*, Ladurie, *Histoire du climat*, and Utterström, 'Climatic fluctuations and population'.

Studies of secular change in climate and mortality have not yet been fruitful, although there is a substantial medical literature on the effects of climate on health.[43] But the study of the relation between short-run variations in weather and mortality fluctuations is a more tractable subject which yields substantive findings of interest in their own right as well as suggesting the possible order of magnitude of long-term effects, though inference from the causes of short-run change to secular trend is at best a very speculative business.

The basic meterological data for England are monthly mean temperatures since 1659, and annual rainfall since 1727. These were first detrended as described above,[44] and then used in conjunction with data on births and deaths for the appropriate periods to study the relationship between weather variations and changes in vital rates. The existence of monthly temperature data permits the effect of heat and cold to be considered in detail, and the bulk of this section will be devoted to the analysis of these data.

It was clearly necessary to allow each calendar month's temperature to exert a different effect on mortality or fertility, since, for example, a high winter temperature might have quite different consequences from a high summer temperature. For this reason a separate equation was estimated for deaths occurring in each calendar month, as influenced by the temperature in that month and in each of the three preceding months. Put differently, a calendar month's temperature was considered to affect not only the current month's deaths, but also those in the following three months. Similarly, each calendar month's births were considered to be influenced by temperature from seven to eleven months previously.

It was also necessary to prevent the seasonality of vital events and temperature from influencing the analysis, since otherwise possibly spurious correlations might have been found. For example, we were interested in learning whether an *unusually* cold January would lead to *unusually* high mortality, not whether mortality was typically high in typically cold months. Analysing each calendar month's mortality separately abstracts from the normal seasonal patterns, and so avoids this problem. Both fertility and mortality can be considered in this fashion and we turn first to mortality.

The estimated equations for mortality, one for each calendar month, are shown in table 9.11. For every month, the joint effect of temperature variables is highly significant, as shown by F-tests (not included in the table). The coefficients are scaled in such a way that they indicate the proportional change in a month's deaths resulting from a change of one degree centigrade in a month's temperature. Thus, an increase of one degree in July's temperature would increase deaths in August by about 4.2 per cent.

The pattern of effects is difficult to discern in the table, but becomes clearer when the estimated coefficients are plotted as in figure 9.15. In the table each regression shows the effects of the four preceding months' temperatures on a month's mortality, for each of the 12 calendar months. In figure 9.15 this information is rearranged so as to look at the effect of a single calendar month's temperature on deaths over the succeeding four months. For example, the frame for January shows the effects of January temperatures on mortality in January (zero months' lag), and also on mortality in February, March, and April (at one, two, and three months' lag, respectively). Thus each frame plots estimated coefficients from four different regressions equations of table 9.11.

43. Tromp, *Medical biometeorology*.
44. See above, pp. 357–9.

Table 9.11: The effect of temperature on mortality by calendar month, estimated from data 1664–1834

Independent variable: Temperature	Dependent variable: mortality in the month of											
	Jan.	Feb.	March	April	May	June	July	Aug.	Sept.	Oct.	Nov.	Dec.
Lagged 0 months	−0.032**	−0.024**	−0.030**	−0.023**	−0.008	0.003	0.008	0.026**	0.005	0.004	−0.011	−0.019**
Lagged 1 month	−0.003	−0.005	−0.004	−0.012†	−0.012*	−0.010†	0.002	0.042**	0.037**	0.047**	0.010	0.003
Lagged 2 months	0.015*	0.001	−0.001	−0.001	−0.014*	−0.004	−0.002	0.020*	0.034**	0.005	0.030**	0.021**
Lagged 3 months	0.011†	0.011†	−0.001	−0.003	0.000	−0.010*	−0.008	−0.007	0.000	0.011	0.000	0.016*
R^2	0.31	0.18	0.18	0.14	0.11	0.08	0.05	0.25	0.17	0.12	0.08	0.20

Notes: A maximum likelihood method was used to correct for second order autoregressive errors. Neither the estimated autoregressive parameters nor the constant term is shown in this table. The R^2 includes the explanatory power of the autoregressive coefficients. The coefficients have been scaled to show the proportional change in a month's deaths resulting from a change of one degree centigrade in temperature.

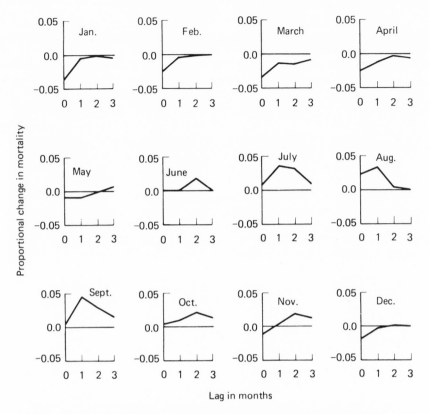

Proportional change in mortality

Lag in months

Figure 9.15: The effect of monthly temperature on mortality in subsequent months (estimated from calendar month data 1664–1834)

Notes: The vertical scales measure the proportional change in monthly mortality from its mean level following an increase of 1° Centigrade in the temperature of the base month. Each frame shows the effect of the given month's temperature on mortality in the same month (lag 0) and each of the three succeeding months (lags 1 to 3).

Source: Table 9.11.

Certain patterns emerge clearly from the figure. Temperature in winter and early spring has a strong *negative* effect on mortality (coefficients less than zero), showing that colder weather is associated with higher mortality. This holds for December to May, at nearly all lags, so that a cold April is linked with higher mortality even as late as July, for example. Temperature in the summer has a strong positive effect on mortality; hotter weather is associated with higher mortality. This holds for June to November at almost all lags. When separate analyses were done for 1664 to 1745 and 1746 to 1834 the same pattern was found in each sub-period.

Figure 9.15 also reveals an important pattern in the lag with which temperature affects mortality. When temperature is negatively related to mortality, as in December to May, the strongest effect occurs immediately in the same month as the temperature change, and the estimated coefficients then taper off rapidly toward zero as the lag increases from one to three months. In the months whose temperatures are positively related to mortality, on the other hand, the strongest effect is on mortality in the months *following* the temperature change: for example, a hot July has its greatest effect on mortality in August. The estimated coefficients peak at one or two months lag, and then decline towards zero. The same lag pattern was found within each sub-period, which tends to confirm its reality.

The patterns of seasonality and lag structure can be brought into still sharper relief by further manipulation of the coefficients of table 9.11. To observe the different monthly effects more clearly we can sum the coefficients of each calendar month's temperature over all lags; this is equivalent to adding up all the coefficients within each frame of figure 9.15. The results are shown in figure 9.16. The strongest positive effects are for January to April, and the strongest negative effects are for July to October. Mortality was evidently more sensitive to temperature change in the summer than the winter. However, since winter temperatures were roughly twice as variable as summer temperatures (a standard deviation of two degrees for January and only one degree for August), mortality was equally influenced by actual variations in winter and summer temperatures.

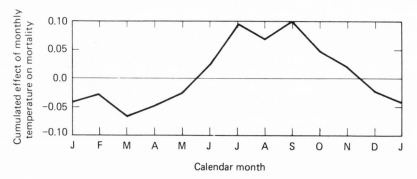

Figure 9.16: The cumulated effect of monthly temperature on mortality (estimated from calendar month data 1664–1834)

Note: The coefficients were cumulated over lags of 0 to 3 months and express the cumulated effect of an increase in temperature of 1° Centigrade.

Source: Table 9.11.

To observe the different winter and summer lag patterns more generally we can sum all the coefficients at a given lag over all the winter or summer months. The results are shown in figure 9.17, with the scale for summer inverted to facilitate comparison with winter. The immediate impact of winter temperature is shown by the strong peak at lag 0. The delayed impact of summer temperature is shown by the low value at lag 0, and high values at lags of 1 and 2 months. This pronounced difference between the winter and summer months may be due to the age- and cause-specific pattern of mortality by season. In the winter months cold weather may be killing the older population through pneumonia, bronchitis, influenza, and other respiratory tract diseases, which are rapidly lethal. In the summer hot weather may be killing infants and young children through digestive tract diseases, which are debilitating,

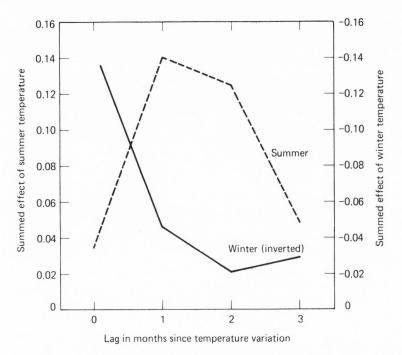

Figure 9.17: Lag patterns of the effect of temperature on mortality by season (estimated from calendar month data 1664 – 1834)

Notes: Summer refers to the period from June to November; winter, December to May. The vertical scales measure the sum of all the estimated coefficients at each indicated lag. The winter scale has been inverted to facilitate comparison with summer.

Source: Table 9.11.

but take longer to kill. This is speculative, but it is consistent both with the age pattern of deaths in eighteenth-century London, where the older people had their highest death rates in the winter, but children in the summer and early autumn, and with the generally more rapid transmission of airborne infections, such as those affecting the respiratory tract, than of digestive tract diseases, which spread more slowly as food or water become contaminated either by human or by insect vectors.[45]

It is also informative to sum the coefficients over both months and lags, to get single measures of the effects of winter and summer temperatures. These totals can then be divided by 12, to give the effect of a one degree change in winter or summer temperature on the *annual* number of deaths. In this way we find that a one degree increase in winter temperature would reduce annual mortality by 1.9 per cent, and a one degree increase in summer temperature would raise annual mortality by 2.9 per cent. Of course such calculations assume away a host of complications, but they will

45. For London see Bradley, 'Enquiry into seasonality'. For a modern example of the impact of temperature changes on the death rate lagged according to the cause of death concerned, see Bull and Morton, 'Relationship of temperature with death rates'.

nevertheless provide a basis for comparison with regressions using annual data, to be considered next.

Regressions based on annual data allow us to consider the effects of wheat prices and rainfall together with those of temperature, and thereby to determine whether the relation observed earlier between prices and mortality was spurious, and merely reflected the common influence of weather on both variables. These regressions will also allow us to see whether the effects of monthly temperature on monthly deaths are sufficiently strong to survive aggregation to the level of annual data. Based on the monthly analysis summarized in figure 9.16, an average winter temperature variable (December to May) was constructed, and likewise an average summer temperature variable (June to November). Since the deaths are summed on a harvest year basis (October to September), annual deaths will be affected by both the current and the previous year's summer temperature, and therefore a lagged value was included. For symmetry, a lagged value of winter temperature was included, but there was no reason to expect much effect.

A regression including temperature, prices, and rainfall was estimated for 1733 to 1834, and the rainfall coefficient was found to be small and insignificant. Regressions including interactions between temperature and rainfall were also tried, but no significant effects were found, so neither cold, wet winters nor hot, wet summers appear to have been particularly mortal. There would be more reason for confidence in this finding, however, if rainfall data had been available on a monthly rather than an annual basis.

The results of regressions of mortality on temperature and prices are shown in table 9.12. The first three columns refer to the whole period of data availability, 1665 to 1834. The similarity of the temperature coefficients in columns 1 and 3, regardless of whether prices are included in the equation, suggests that the effects of temperature were direct, and did not operate through agricultural production. In the same way, by comparing columns 1 and 2, we can conclude that the relation of mortality to temperature did not obscure the estimated relation of prices to mortality for the period as a whole.

The coefficients for temperature agree surprisingly well with the results of the monthly regressions. The zero lag winter coefficient is -0.023, compared to -0.019 for monthly data; the coefficient at one year's lag is small and insignificant. For summer temperature, both coefficients are substantial, and they must be summed for comparison to the monthly results, giving a figure of 0.041 for annual data compared to 0.029 for monthly data. A comparison of the amount of variance explained by temperature alone versus prices alone shows that prices explained a somewhat greater proportion over this period (17 per cent versus 12 per cent).

Columns 4 to 9 give similar results by sub-period. These show that at zero lag the effects of neither winter temperature nor summer temperature changed much from one sub-period to the next, while the effects of summer temperature on deaths in the next harvest year became much less severe, dropping from 0.039 to 0.008. It is particularly interesting to note from the R^2 values in the table that in the first period prices alone explained substantially more variance in mortality than did temperature alone, while in the second period temperature alone explains rather more of the variance than prices. Furthermore, the inclusion of temperature in the second period considerably reduces the perverse negative association of prices and mortality estimated for 1746 to 1834. The coefficient at lags zero to two become positive, and the summed coefficients drop from -0.133 to -0.074 when temperature is included.

Table 9.12: The effects of temperature and prices on adjusted mortality, estimated from harvest year data 1665–1834 and by sub-period

Dependent variable: adjusted mortality

Independent variable	1665–1834			1665–1745			1746–1834		
	Temp. and price	Price only	Temp. only	Temp. and price	Price only	Temp. only	Temp. and price	Price only	Temp. only
	(1)	(2)	(3)	(4)	(5)	(6)	(7)	(8)	(9)
Constant	0.440*	0.866**	0.605**	0.124	0.717**	0.427	0.856**	1.136**	0.710**
Winter temp. (0)	-0.023**		-0.023**	-0.022		-0.021**	-0.021**		-0.023**
Winter temp. (-1)	0.004		0.003	-0.001		-0.001	0.011†		0.009
Summer temp. (0)	0.017†		0.017†	0.020		0.019	0.014†		0.018*
Summer temp. (-1)	0.024**		0.024**	0.039*		0.037*	0.008		0.013
Price (0)	0.044	0.027		0.076	0.069		0.014	-0.016	
Price (-1)	0.084**	0.092**		0.112*	0.124*		0.007	0.020	
Price (-2)	0.086**	0.076*		0.144**	0.142**		0.006	-0.016	
Price (-3)	-0.022	-0.011		-0.041	-0.013		-0.029	-0.038	
Price (-4)	-0.026	-0.047		-0.017	-0.031		-0.072*	-0.083**	
R²	0.28	0.17	0.12	0.37	0.26	0.12	0.31	0.15	0.16

Notes: The price coefficients are elasticities. For temperature the coefficients are scaled to show the proportional change in adjusted annual deaths due to a change of 1 degree Centigrade in temperature. Winter temperature represents the average of monthly temperatures from December to May; summer temperature that from June to November. The equations were corrected for second order autoregression in disturbances. The R^2 was calculated for the untransformed variables.

By contrast, the price coefficients for the period 1665 to 1745 are very little affected by the inclusion of temperature; the cumulated elasticity drops from 0.291 to 0.274.

It is instructive to compare the estimates for the entire sub-period 1641 to 1745, given in table 9.8, with those for 1665 to 1745 given in column 5 of table 9.12. All the regression coefficients are more positive in table 9.12, and the cumulative elasticity is much higher at 0.291 versus 0.103. The R^2 is also higher at 0.26 versus 0.17. This suggests that the relation of mortality to prices was very different in the 24 years 1641 to 1664 than in the rest of the sub-period. Omitting these years, there would be very little change between 1544 to 1640, and 1665 to 1745. The cumulated elasticities were 0.347 versus 0.291, and the R^2s were 0.22 versus 0.26. The structural change in the relation of mortality to prices, therefore, appears not to have occurred until after 1745. It should be added that a comparison of estimates for fertility and prices shows no such discrepancy between 1641 to 1745 and 1665 to 1745.

We may now turn to the relation of temperature to fertility. As with mortality, it is convenient to begin with the analysis of monthly data. Because the estimated effects were all weaker than for mortality, they will not be presented or discussed in such detail. Equations were estimated for births in each calendar month as a function of the temperature 7 to 11 months previously, thus allowing for effects impinging before, during, and after the time of potential conception. For every estimated equation the F-test showed significant effects of temperature on births, but the proportion of variance explained was generally quite low.

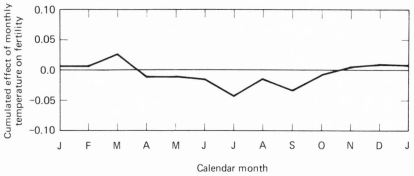

Calendar month

Figure 9.18: The cumulated effect of monthly temperature on fertility (estimated from calendar month data 1665–1834)

Note: The coefficients were cumulated over lags of 7 to 11 months and express the cumulated effect of an increase in temperature of $1°$ Centigrade.

In order to summarize the cumulative effect of each calendar month's temperature, the coefficients at all lags were summed, as was done earlier for mortality. The results are presented in figure 9.18. It will be seen by comparison with figure 9.16 that the effects of temperature on fertility are much weaker than on mortality. Warm winters and cool summers lead to more births. On the whole, those months in which higher temperature promotes fertility are the same ones in which it reduces mortality; and, similarly, those in which lower temperatures boost fertility also lower mortality.

The lag patterns can be examined by summing the coefficients at each lag over all the summer or winter months, as was done earlier for mortality. The results are shown in figure 9.19, with the curve for summer inverted for easier comparison to winter. First consider the winter months. The coefficients are close to zero for lags of 7 and 8 months, so cold weather apparently did not lead to miscarriages in the second and third months of pregnancy. The peak coefficient occurs at a 9-month lag, which could reflect either miscarriages or conceptability, since it seems unlikely that cold weather would reduce coital frequency. In view of the fact that the coefficients at 10- and 11-month lag are still substantial it seems quite likely that cold temperatures caused morbidity (recall that they sharply raised mortality) which in turn reduced fecundability and increased miscarriages.

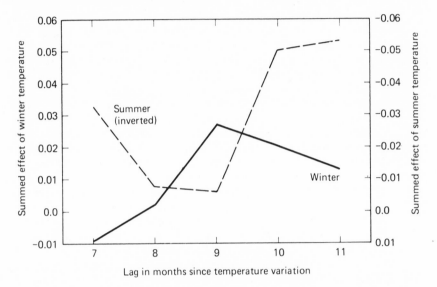

Figure 9.19: Lag patterns of the effect of temperature on fertility by season (estimated from calendar month data 1665–1834)

Notes: Summer refers to the period from April to October; winter, November to March. The vertical scales measure the sum of all the estimated coefficients at each indicated lag. The summer scale has been inverted to facilitate comparison with winter.

In the summer months, we observe a moderate adverse effect of hot weather on births 7 months later. This suggests an effect on miscarriages in the second to third month of pregnancy. Such a finding is plausible, since this is a time when the cerebral cortex is being formed, and when hot summer weather has been shown to lead to various disorders in foetuses that survive to birth.[46] At 8 and 9 months' lag the coefficients are very close to zero, suggesting that hot weather did *not* cause a reduction in coital frequency, and therefore that, in this temperate climate at least, the 'comfort factor' was of no importance.[47] The strongest effects are at lags of 10 and 11 months, and again this suggests that hot weather increased morbidity which in turn reduced fecundability and perhaps raised miscarriages. On this interpretation, the delayed effect on summer conceptions as opposed to the immediate effect on winter

46. Tromp, *Medical biometeorology*, pp. 401, 535, 569, and 570.
47. Parkes, 'Environmental influences on fertility'.

conceptions is entirely consistent with the results for mortality. It is possible that we are reading too much into the lag structure, given the variable delay between birth and baptism; however, the consistency of these results with those for mortality is reassuring, since there was virtually no delay between death and burial.

The estimated coefficients may be summed over all lags and all months for summer and winter separately, to get measures of the impact of average summer and winter temperatures on annual deaths. The results suggest that a one degree increase in winter temperature would raise annual births by only 0.5 per cent, while a one degree decrease in summer temperature would raise them by 1.1 per cent. The effects are only a quarter to a third the size of those for mortality.

Annual data were also analysed, using prices and winter and summer temperatures as independent variables, for the period 1665 to 1834, and for two sub-periods. Since, given the hypothesized lags, births in a harvest year would be affected by the current as well as the lagged winter temperature, both were included. For fertility, the contemporaneous summer temperature would be expected to have virtually no effect, but it was included for symmetry, along with the lagged value.

The estimated equations are reported in table 9.13. They show that entering temperatures in the equations has a negligible effect on the coefficients of prices, in each of the periods. The regressions also show that temperature had substantially less explanatory power than prices in the earlier period, and that the discrepancy became even more strongly marked in the later period. The effect of winter temperature may be found by summing the coefficients at lags zero and one; this yields 0.010, which is twice as large as the 0.005 obtained from monthly data. The estimates also show that the influence of winter temperatures declined by about half from the first to the second sub-period. For summer temperatures, the theoretically relevant coefficient is for lag one, and that is −0.010 which is very close to the −0.011 found with monthly data. This effect is nearly the same in the two sub-periods.

In summary, the results of this analysis have been surprisingly rich, particularly since the English climate is so moderate. Temperature emerges as a variable with explanatory power usually weaker than grain prices, but substantial nonetheless. As was expected, warmer winters and cooler summers were more healthy, with a favourable influence on both mortality and fertility. Less expected, however, was the robust result that the influence of winter temperatures on health was immediate, while the influence of summer temperatures was delayed by one or two months. The simultaneous consideration of temperature and prices does little to change their estimated effects, except on mortality in 1746 to 1834, when the anomalous negative effect was substantially reduced. Rainfall was found to have no effect on mortality.

It is interesting to consider the implications of these results for long-term changes in fertility and mortality. Before doing so, however, we must warn that the medical literature stresses the effects of the *variability* of temperature as opposed to its level, and that it may, therefore, be quite inappropriate to apply these results for short-run fluctuations to the consideration of long-run trends. However, the close agreement of results from the monthly data with those from the annual lends some support to extrapolation. It has been suggested that the climate in north-western Europe alternated between the 'maritime' pattern, moderated by the influence of the ocean, and the 'continental' pattern, reflecting the influence of large land masses.[48] According to de Vries, there was a shift from the continental to the maritime pattern

48. De Vries, 'Histoire du climat'.

Table 9.13: The effects of temperature and prices on fertility, estimated from harvest year data 1665–1834 and by sub-period

				Dependent variable: fertility					
	1665–1834			1665–1745			1746–1834		
Independent variable	Temp. and price	Price only	Temp. only	Temp. and price	Price only	Temp. only	Temp. and price	Price only	Temp. only
	(1)	(2)	(3)	(4)	(5)	(6)	(7)	(8)	(9)
Constant	1.128**	1.137**	0.954**	0.980**	1.138**	0.811**	1.246**	1.158**	1.042**
Winter temp. (0)	0.003		0.005*	0.004		0.004	0.004		0.006†
Winter temp. (−1)	0.007**		0.009**	0.010**		0.013*	0.004		0.007*
Summer temp. (0)	0.007†		0.008†	0.015†		0.015†	0.000		0.004
Summer temp. (−1)	−0.010**		−0.010*	−0.008		−0.006	−0.010*		−0.011†
Price (0)	−0.049**	−0.054**		−0.033	−0.048*		−0.086**	−0.086**	
Price (−1)	−0.090**	−0.094**		−0.076**	−0.077***		−0.098**	−0.098**	
Price (−2)	0.012	0.014		−0.015	−0.015		0.043	0.043	
Price (−3)	−0.036	−0.011		0.010	0.006		−0.023	−0.030†	
Price (−4)	0.042	0.007		−0.008	−0.007		0.007	0.015	
R^2	0.45	0.40	0.11	0.41	0.32	0.18	0.64	0.61	0.05

Notes: The price coefficients are elasticities. For temperature the coefficients are scaled to show the proportional change in annual births due to a change of 1 degree Centigrade in temperature. Winter temperature represents the average of monthly temperatures from November to March; summer temperature that from April to October. The equations were corrected for second order autoregression in disturbances. The R^2 was calculated for the untransformed variables.

around 1698, with a switch back to the continental pattern around 1758. The maritime pattern was characterized by winter temperatures that were warmer by roughly one degree Centigrade, and summers that were cooler by a somewhat smaller amount.[49] For the sake of discussion, let us consider the effects on mortality, fertility, and natural increase of a one degree warming of winters and cooling of summers. Using the monthly estimates, we find that mortality would drop by about 5 per cent (an increase of about two years in life expectancy) and fertility would increase by almost 2 per cent.[50] If crude birth and death rates were at about 30 per 1,000, this would imply an absolute increase in the population growth rate of about 0.20 per cent per year. This is not a large effect, but it is far from negligible. Furthermore, if the switch from continental to maritime climates was accompanied by a reduction in the variance of temperatures within each season the effects would be still larger.

Concise summary of conclusions

This chapter has tackled a number of questions concerning the short-run fluctuations in the vital series and their relationships with similar fluctuations in prices and the weather, using a variety of analytical techniques. It may, therefore, be convenient to draw together the various conclusions that have emerged at different points in the analysis. It should be remembered that, unless otherwise stated, the relationships summarized here refer to linear effects calculated over the whole range of variation in the series and over the whole period, except for monthly price and temperature effects, which can only be studied from dates in the late seventeenth century.

A   Mortality fluctuations

   1   Weather

     a   Mortality was increased by cold temperatures in 'winter' (December to May) and by hot temperatures in 'summer' (June to November). Every calendar month's mortality was significantly affected by temperature.

     b   The main effect of winter temperature was contemporaneous, but for summer temperature the effect was delayed one or two months.

     c   A one degree Centigrade warming of winter would reduce annual mortality by about 2 per cent; a one degree Centigrade cooling of summer would reduce annual mortality by about 4 per cent. Combined, these changes would raise period life expectancy by about two years.

     d   All these generalizations hold, in broad outline, for the two sub-periods 1665 to 1745 and 1746 to 1834. Prices explain a greater proportion of the variance in annual mortality from 1665 to 1834 than does temperature. Prices dominate from 1665 to 1745, but temperature was equally important from 1745 to 1834.

     e   Annual rainfall was not associated with mortality.

---

49. De Vries, 'Histoire du climat'.
50. See above, pp. 391, 396. Using annual data a similar estimate results. The warming of winter would lower mortality by 1.9 per cent ($-2.3 + 0.4$) and raise fertility by 1.0 per cent ($0.3 + 0.7$). The cooling of summer would lower mortality by 4.1 per cent ($1.7 + 2.4$), and raise fertility by 1.0 per cent if we ignore the zero lag estimate of 0.7, which could only result from an implausibly strong effect of temperature on stillbirths in the last trimester (tables 9.12 and 9.13). The total effect is to lower mortality by 6.0 per cent, and raise fertility by 2.0 or 1.3 per cent, depending on whether we include the zero lag summer term.

2 Prices
   a Price variation accounts for only a small proportion of the variance in mortality, about 16 per cent for annual data. Nonetheless, in statistical terms it is a very significant association.
   b Following a price variation, mortality responded positively over the following two or three years, and there was then a compensating negative reaction. The net or cumulated effect over five years was essentially zero, except when prices were extremely high (more than 44 per cent above average). This suggests that most price variations merely altered by a couple of years the timing of deaths which would in any case soon have occurred.
   c Cumulated over three years, the initial positive relation of mortality to prices is smoothly increasing and upward curving in a nonlinear manner. There is, however, no threshold effect; even prices far below average bear a positive relation to mortality.
   d Only extremely high prices had a contemporaneous (same year) effect on mortality; the peak effect for most price levels was delayed one or two years. In a linear model, the peak effect is delayed two years.
   e In the periods 1544 to 1640 and 1641 to 1745 there was a positive but weakening relation between prices and mortality; in 1746 to 1834 the relation becomes negative and very weak.
   f Including summer and winter temperature in the regression leaves unchanged the positive mortality–price relation for 1665 to 1745, and weakens the negative one for 1746 to 1834.
   g Runs of high prices had no significant additional effects on mortality.
   h The effect of prices on mortality did not differ significantly by season.
   i Increases and decreases in prices had symmetric effects on mortality.

B Marital fertility fluctuations

   1 Mortality and associated morbidity
      a From 1 to 8 months after a mortality variation there is a weak negative effect due in part to deaths of pregnant women, but primarily to foetal loss.
      b At precisely 9 months there is a very strong negative effect which could reflect early foetal mortality, or fewer conceptions.
      c After 10 months there is a strong positive effect due to the echo of the low fertility, and to new marriages; this slowly diminishes over the next 26 months.
      d Analysis of annual data shows that these relations hold in broad outline for all three sub-periods; however, they are somewhat weaker in the last sub-period.
      e Analysis of annual data shows that the relation of fertility to mortality was linear.
   2 Prices
      a There is a strong negative association, beginning after a lag of about 3 months, and peaking at 9 or 10 months. This suggests that foetal loss may have played an important rôle.
      b There is a positive echo centred at about 24 months' lag, as biometric models of birth intervals would predict.

    c   The cumulated effect over five years is strongly negative.

    d   The relation is slightly nonlinear. Responses to increases and decreases in prices were symmetric.

    e   The relation is very similar in each of the three centuries, but is noticeably stronger in the last sub-period.

    f   The indirect effect of prices on fertility, operating through nuptiality, is of negligible importance.

3   Temperature

    a   Allowing for lags of 7 to 11 months, cold temperatures in 'winter' (December to May) and warm temperatures in 'summer' (June to November) reduced fertility; these effects are symmetric to those for mortality, but only about a quarter to a third as strong.

    b   The main effect of winter temperature on fertility was 9 months later, while the effect of summer temperature was mainly 10 and 11 months later. This is consistent with the immediate effect of winter temperature on mortality, and delayed effect of summer temperature on mortality. It also establishes that summer temperature did not effect fertility through coital frequency.

    c   A one degree Centigrade warming of winter temperatures would raise annual fertility by about 1 per cent, as would a one degree cooling of summer temperature. Combined with the effects on mortality, these temperature changes, which are characteristic of a shift to a maritime climate, would raise the rate of natural increase by an absolute increment of about 0.20 per cent per year.

    d   These generalizations hold in broad outline for the two sub-periods (1665 to 1745 and 1746 to 1834. Over the whole period, and in each sub-period, price explains more of the variance in fertility than temperature.

4   Nuptiality

    a   There is a close association of births and marriages, particularly at lags of 0 to 9 months.

    b   Most of the association is *not* due to births resulting from the new marriages, even after allowing for bridal pregnancy.

    c   Therefore, some unobserved set of variables has a strong influence both on nuptiality and on the fertility of pre-existing marriages, causing a spurious association of the two series. Deliberate control of fertility within marriage would be consistent with this finding, but other explanations cannot be ruled out.

C Nuptiality fluctuations

1   Mortality

    a   In a month of increased mortality, nuptiality is low, and reaches a trough in the next month; thereafter it rises above average for about two years.

    b   The total effect is strongly positive, but can be almost entirely accounted for by the effect of mortality on remarriages.

    c   Analysis of annual data shows that the relation holds in broad outline in each sub-period, but that it declines dramatically in strength.

    d   Analysis of annual data suggests that the relation might hold only for extremely high or very low mortality, but this finding is shaky.

2 Prices
   a There is a negative effect, strongest in the first year.
   b The relationship is quite linear at all lags.
   c In the last century (1746–1834) there appears to be a positive echo, weakening the cumulative effect of prices.

10

The economic setting of long-term trends in English fertility and mortality

In the course of the three centuries from 1541 to 1871 the population of England grew seven-fold despite the fact that there were bursts of heavy migration in the seventeenth and nineteenth centuries. Yet, though the overall growth was so substantial, it was far from uninterrupted. The combination of low fertility, heavy emigration, and relatively high mortality in the second half of the seventeenth century reduced numbers quite sharply, and the peak population total of 5.281 million reached in 1656 was not again surpassed until 1721. Growth was rapid in the first and last centuries of the period, but in the intervening century it was never more than faltering and often failed completely. During these 300 years of demographic vicissitude England was radically transformed from a rural, agrarian country into the first nation to be reshaped by the industrial revolution. In this chapter we turn from the intricacies of short-term fluctuations to consider the relationship of secular demographic trends to some aspects of the sweeping economic changes of the early modern period. We shall first consider population growth trends and the long-term changes in prices and real wages and then turn to fertility and mortality changes in the same context.

Population growth, prices, and real wages

When Robert Malthus wrote his *Essay on the principle of population* he made the tension between population growth and food production the central thesis of the work. Increase in food production could only be secured with difficulty and slowly except in lands of recent settlement. If, as Malthus thought only too apt to happen, population rose without a commensurate increase in food production, each man's ability to satisfy his wants would be jeopardized and the price of food must rise. As he put it, when there was 'An increase of population without a proportional increase of food . . . . The food must necessarily be distributed in smaller quantities, and consequently a day's labour will purchase a smaller quantity of provisions. An increase in the price of provisions would arise, either from an increase of population faster than the means of subsistence; or from a different distribution of the money of society'.[1]

Figure 10.1 provides suggestive evidence of the justice of Malthus's assertion over the 250 years preceding the appearance of his *Essay* in 1798. It plots the fluctuations in population totals and the changes in a 25-year moving average of the price of a basket of consumables using the series constructed by Phelps Brown and Hopkins. Between 1541 and 1656 the population of England almost doubled while the price series more than tripled. The two series peaked at the same time in 1656 and thereafter both dipped for a period of about 30 years. After 1686 there was a resumption of

1. Malthus, *Essay on population*, p. 82.

402

population growth, but on a modest scale, and the recovery was sharply interrupted in the late 1720s so that it was only after 1731 that steady and increasingly rapid population growth reappeared. The price index, though moving without clear trend, tended to fall rather than rise until after the resumption of uninterrupted population growth. Indeed, only after 1750 did the index rise to a level higher than the peak reached a century earlier.

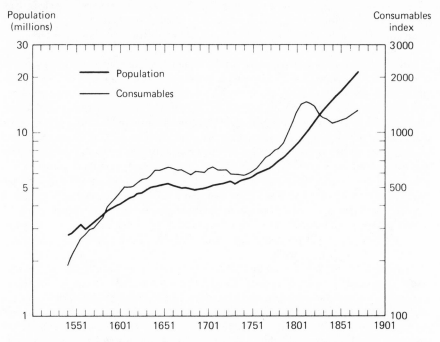

Figure 10.1: English population totals compared to a 25-year moving average of a basket of consumables index

Note: The consumables index represents a 25-year moving average of the index figures centred on the dates shown.

Sources: Population totals table A3.1; consumables index Phelps Brown and Hopkins, 'Seven centuries of the prices of consumables', pp. 194-6.

When population growth was once more rapid and continuous, however, the same relationship between the two series supervened as was visible in the late sixteenth and early seventeenth centuries. Between 1731 and 1811 the population once again almost doubled while the price index rose two and a half times. Under pressure of population growth prices rose rapidly, in both periods outstripping the pace of the rise in population.

If there was a notable uniformity in the behaviour of the two series relative to each other until the beginning of the nineteenth century, however, there was a remarkably clean break with the past thereafter. Between 1811, when the price index turned down, and 1871 population doubled yet again, maintaining an even higher rate of growth than in the preceding 60-year period, but the price of the consumables basket first fell and then levelled out. The historic link between population growth and price rise was broken; an economic revolution had taken place. And by an ironic coincidence Malthus had given pungent expression to an issue that haunted most pre-industrial societies at almost the last moment when it could still plausibly be represented as relevant to the country in which he was born.

The movements in the PBH index of the price of a basket of consumables were dominated by food price fluctuations.[2] Since the vagaries of the seasons and of plant and animal diseases caused the quantity and quality of the harvest to change sharply in the short run, a smoothing device is required to enable long-term price trends to be picked out. Hence the use of the 25-year moving average for the consumables index in figure 10.1.

Using the same method of damping out the influence of weather and mischance, the information incorporated in figure 10.1 can be re-expressed in the form shown in figure 10.2. Here rates of growth in the two series are plotted against one another. Each point on the graph records the compound annual rates of growth of population and of the 25-year moving average of the PBH consumables index over a period of 25 years. Thus, the placing of the point for 1781 shows that between 1781 and 1806 the 25-year moving average of the price index was rising by 2.24 per cent annually while population over the same quarter century was growing each year by 1.10 per cent.

Representing price and population movements in this way once again brings out the striking uniformity of experience over two and a half centuries during which the elasticity of response of food prices to population change was approximately 3:2. If population over a quarter-century period was rising by 1 per cent per annum food prices rose by about 1.5 per cent per annum. Equally, during the period of falling population, food prices tended to fall slightly faster. Indeed, the underlying relationship between population and price movements may have been even closer than is suggested by figure 10.2 since it was at times somewhat distorted by the effect of extraneous factors. For example, the first three points in the series suggest exceptionally high rates of price increase at a time of comparatively modest population growth. But their location reflects the effect of the 'Great Debasement' of 1544–51 which exaggerated the price rises that would otherwise have occurred. Again, the stresses of financing a prolonged war and the large issue of paper currency after the suspension of specie payments in 1797 may account for the unusually rapid price rises reflected in the positioning of the points representing price movements in the quarter-century periods beginning in 1771, 1776, and 1781.

The contrast between the pre-industrial pattern and later trends stands out even more starkly in figure 10.2 than in figure 10.1. In spite of a population growth rate higher than that of any earlier period, varying between 1.15 and 1.45 per cent per annum, the price of food and other basic commodities did not increase. Since food imports supplied only a modest proportion of English food needs until well into the nineteenth century,[3] the graph is a remarkably vivid tribute to the increase in the productive capacity of English agriculture in the period after about 1780.

Thinking men of the day, once they were convinced that population was rising fast, had been apprehensive about the future. The blind Sir John Call collected information

2. In constructing the consumables index Phelps-Brown and Hopkins gave food prices a weighting of 80 out of a total of 100 (farinaceous 20, meat and fish 25, butter and cheese 12½, drink 22½). Phelps-Brown and Hopkins, 'Seven centuries of the prices of consumables', p. 180.
3. Deane and Cole estimated that in the 10-year periods centring on the years 1770, 1780, 1790, 1800, 1810, and 1820 imports of grain formed the following percentages of gross domestic output respectively: 1.4, 1.3, 3.4, 6.2, 4.9, and 7.6. *British economic growth*, table 17, p. 65.

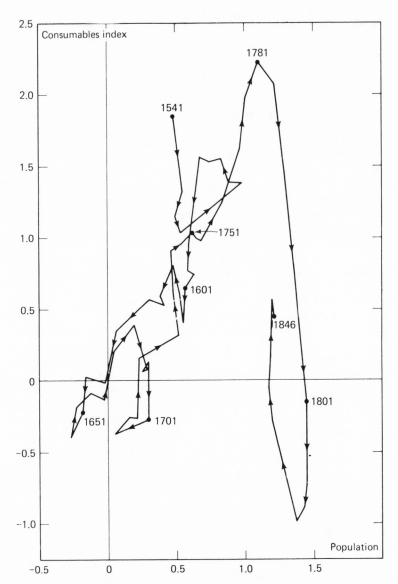

Figure 10.2: Annual rates of growth of population and of a basket of consumables index

Note: The population growth rate was measured between any given 'census' date and the 'census' 25 years later. The rate of growth of the price of consumables was measured using the readings on a 25-year moving average of the index for the same dates as for population totals. Where a date is indicated it shows the beginning date of a 25-year period.

Sources: See figure 10.1.

about totals of baptisms and burials from four parishes in every county in England and Wales for the years 1788 to 1797, and, discovering that the former outnumbered the latter in the proportion of 3 to 2, communicated both his findings and his alarm to the Board of Agriculture in 1800. Sir John had been provoked into collecting parish register material by his concern about the high prices of corn and meat in 1795 and 1796. 'Bearing these things in mind . . . I deliberated in what manner I should satisfy myself, whether an increased population had not been the principal cause of the scarcity which had happened, and whether a progressive increase of the same nature might not keep us in annual expectation of the like event'.[4] Having argued that the population had risen from 8 million to 10.5 million between 1788 and 1800, he added, 'Let everyone, therefore, who considers this subject, form his conclusion of what our situation will be ten years hence, unless some proper measures are taken to meet the exigence'.[5] He advocated easier enclosure of the waste and of common fields as a solution. Like Adam Smith and Malthus he had no doubt that all prosperity sprang from a productive agriculture.[6] 'Were the subject new', he wrote, 'it might easily be shown how much the riches, the comfort, the strength, the exertion of ingenuity, the superior excellence of manufactures, the extension and protection of commerce, depended on the cultivation of the soil possessed by any nation, so as to produce a reasonable and competent supply of the necessaries of life'.[7] Sir John's forebodings proved groundless, but they were certainly not irrational for at any earlier period of English history they would have been justified.

If allowance is made for the exceptional factors at work during the mid sixteenth and late eighteenth centuries, the grouping of the individual points in figure 10.2 is surprisingly close round a straight line running through the origin and rising or falling by three units in the vertical axis for every two on the horizontal. The closeness of fit is surprising both because of the long period of time involved and perhaps also because it might have been expected that if population pressure were the cause of the rise in the consumables index, a high rate of population growth would have caused a disproportionately rapid rise in the index as productive capacity in agriculture more and more signally failed to match the demand for food. If this had been the case, the cluster of points would have lain in a curved rather than a straight band.

Although the overall impression of linearity of relationship is marked, there were two periods before the major break about 1800 when the positioning of the points suggests that the usual relation of prices to population growth was modified. In each 25-year period from that starting in 1561 until that starting in 1581 the rate of growth of prices was very close to 1.5 per cent per annum, showing no tendency to fall even though population growth rates were declining steadily and quite quickly in the successive quarter-century periods. This may possibly represent the close approach to a threshold level of population pressure sufficient to modify the linear relationship between the two variables, of the type just touched upon. Again, there is a cluster of five points, 1701–21, representing 25-year periods spanning almost the whole of the first half of the eighteenth century, in each of which the price index was falling gently even though population was rising, though only very slowly. These points stand some way below their 'expected' position, and, to a lesser degree, the three points immediately preceding (1686, 1691, and 1696) and the point next following (1726)

4. Call, 'An abstract of baptisms and burials', p. 479.
5. Call, 'An abstract of baptisms and burials', p. 483.
6. This issue is explored further in Wrigley, 'The process of modernisation'.
7. Call, 'An abstract of baptisms and burials', p. 483.

also stand away from the main belt of points. Their positioning is a tribute to the advance in agricultural productivity in England secured during the seventeenth century which enabled a substantial export of grain to take place while at the same time prices on the home market tended to fall.[8]

Nevertheless, the comparative uniformity of relationship between price rise and population change from the mid sixteenth to the late eighteenth century is notable and the exceptions not very prominent, especially bearing in mind the limitations of the PBH index.[9] Phelps Brown and Hopkins themselves, reviewing their price series, raised a number of questions, and concluded by writing, 'For a century or more, it seems, prices will obey one all-powerful law; it changes, and a new law prevails; a war that would have cast the trend up to new heights in one dispensation is powerless to deflect it in another. Do we yet know what are the factors that set this stamp on an age; and why, after they have held on so long through such shakings, at last they give way, quickly and completely, to others?'[10] They were reviewing a much larger period even that that considered in this book but within the period 1541–1871 it seems fair to conclude that prices behaved in a less wayward fashion than they supposed. Beneath the short-term movements in prices there was a striking regularity of response to population trends apart from the total break with earlier patterns that took place about 1800.

During this very long period, however, the level of money wage's changed considerably, and we may therefore now turn to consider whether there was a comparable uniformity of pattern in the relation between real-wage trends and population growth.

Any real-wage index based on the PBH wage data must be regarded with even more reserve than the price index since any inaccuracies or imbalance in the latter are compound by the shortcomings of their measure of nominal wages. These are well known, stemming from the problem that throughout the early modern period the wage data refer only to one group of trades.[11] And there are other problems inherent in any index series of such length. For example, the changing nature of the components in the price series make any comparison of the absolute level of the index at widely spaced points in time meaningless. Nor, therefore, is it prudent to draw inferences about relative living standards in periods that are far apart. For example, the index stood at about 400 at one low point in the early seventeenth century compared with a level of about 500 at another low point early in the nineteenth century, but it would be unwise to suppose that this affords a dependable guide to the relative severity of the two troughs. There is undoubtedly urgent need to construct a better-based wage series. At present, however, the PBH index is the only available series covering the whole period and we have chosen to treat it as if it were reliable while recognizing that the subsequent argument might need to be modified in some degree if a better real-wage

8. Kerridge estimated that English food production doubled between 1540 and 1700. Kerridge, *Agricultural revolution*, p. 332. On the subject of English grain exports see Ormrod, 'Dutch commercial and industrial decline'.

9. The consumables index contains no element that might measure changes in the cost of buying or renting accommodation. From time time, moreover, Phelps Brown and Hopkins were obliged to rely upon substitute commodities or guesswork to make good breaks in the price series of a particular commodity. And there are unavoidable problems with any index maintained over many centuries when a new basic foodstuff, such as the potato, comes into general use.

10. Phelps Brown and Hopkins, 'Seven centuries of the prices of consumables', p. 189.

11. The trades represented varied over time. Phelps Brown and Hopkins, 'Seven centuries of building wages', pp. 168–74.

index existed. For the very general purposes of the present discussion the index is probably sufficiently reliable to sustain the argument. It should be noted that in their original article Phelps Brown and Hopkins did not publish real-wage figures for some runs of years in the sixteenth, seventeenth, and eighteenth centuries. Appendix 9 describes the method used to calculate a complete series based on PBH data.

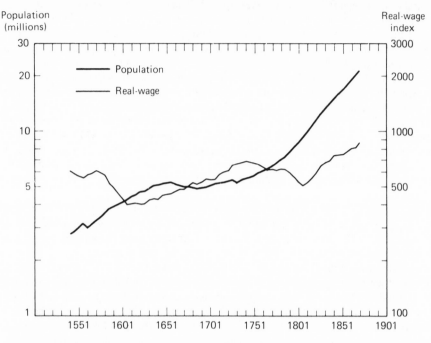

Figure 10.3: English population totals compared to a 25-year moving average of a real-wage index

Note: The real-wage index represents a 25-year moving average of the index figures centred on the dates shown.

Sources: Population totals table A3.1; real-wage index table A9.2.

In figure 10.3 the graphs of population growth and real-wage trends are compared. The wage index is once again a 25-year moving average of the annual figures. It falls steeply during the period of rapid population growth in the late sixteenth century, though the fall was not perfectly regular. The effect of the exceptionally bad harvests and high prices of the middle 1550s is not damped out completely even by a 25-year average and so there is a fall in the earliest period followed by a recovery over the next two decades. After 1571, however, the index fell rapidly and without interruption until 1606. The slowing of population growth in the early seventeenth century was accompanied by a bottoming out in the fall in real wages, and as population growth ceased and was followed by a fall in numbers, a hesitant recovery in real wages began after 1626 and was confirmed from about 1640 onwards. The rise continued without significant interruption until population growth resumed in earnest in the mid eighteenth century, after which real wages fell until 1806, though there was a 20-year period from 1766 to 1786 during which the fall was arrested. Finally, after 1806, and in spite of the continued rapid population growth, the wage index turns up once more to rise by 1871 to a higher level than at any earlier point in the series during the period under review.[12]

As with prices and population, the nature of the relation between real wages and population is perhaps more easily grasped when changes in the two series are expressed in terms of rates of change over quarter-century periods than when shown as changing totals. In figure 10.4 this relation is set out in the same manner as was used for prices and population in figure 10.2, with the annual rate of population growth over a 25-year period plotted against the comparable rate of growth in real wages using a 25-year moving average of the wage data.

The overall pattern is again fairly straightforward. Until the radical change at the end of the eighteenth century, rapid population growth, at a rate of 0.5 per cent per annum or more, entailed falling real wages, whereas periods of slight population growth or of population decline were associated with rising real wages. Towards the end of the eighteenth century, however, although population was growing at more than 1 per cent per annum, and significantly faster than at any earlier period, real wages, which had been falling sharply, recovered and began to rise also, reaching a rate of growth higher than any previously experienced in spite of the rapidity of population growth. For the first time since the land was fully settled swiftly rising numbers proved consonant with rising real wages. The meaning of the industrial revolution is visible in the figure.

But if an overall pattern is visible, there are refinements within the pattern that make figure 10.4 in some respects more informative than figure 10.2. First, the graph suggests that the early modern English economy was capable of sustaining a population growth rate of about 0.5 per cent per annum without depressing real wages, and, equally significant, that a zero rate of population growth was associated with an annual rate of growth in real wages of about 0.5 per cent. About a third of all the individual points on the graph before the great change in the late eighteenth century fall within a box bounded by the horizontal lines representing a rate of growth of real wages of between 0.0 and 0.75 per cent per annum and the vertical lines representing annual population growth rates of between 0.0 and 0.55 per cent. Within this box the positioning of the individual points, though by no means perfectly linear, suggests, assuming that the factor share of wages in total national income may be taken to have changed little, that the economy was growing by about 0.5 per cent annually and that the degree to which wage earners benefitted from this growth was dependent upon the rate of population growth.

Outside the box the graph suggests a second conclusion which both supplements and extends the first. The growth rate of the economy, at least as measured through the PBH real-wage index, does not appear to have been very responsive to population growth rates, particularly in the sixteenth and seventeenth centuries. When the rate of population growth rose above 0.5 per cent per annum for a prolonged period in the late sixteenth century real wages declined catastrophically, reaching a rate of fall of almost 1.5 per cent per annum in the quarter century starting in 1581. The behaviour of the graph, indeed, suggests that a rate of annual population growth of one half per cent represented a threshold which once crossed brought about a precipitous fall in real wages. But if there was a marked difficulty in achieving a rate of growth in the economy as a whole at a rate higher than an annual one half per cent, there may also

12. The index had been at an even higher level in the fifteenth century, but as we have already noted, comparisons of the absolute level of the index at dates :parated by centuries can have little meaning.

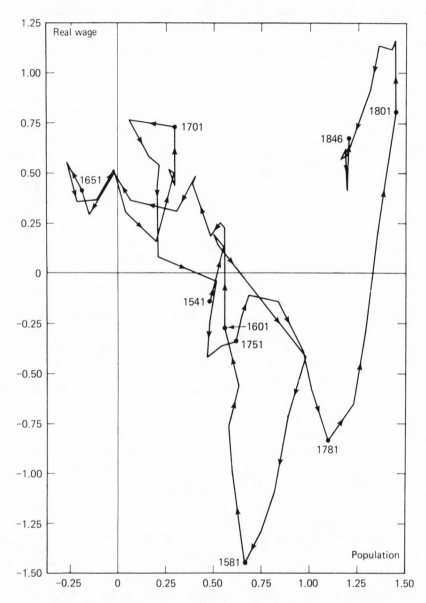

Figure 10.4: Annual rates of growth of population and of a real-wage index

Note: The population growth rate was measured between each given 'census' date and the 'census' 25 years later. The rate of growth of real wages was measured using the readings on a 25-year moving average of the index for the same dates as for population totals. Where a date is indicated it shows the beginning date of a 25-year period.

Sources: See figure 10.3.

have been a comparable difficulty in periods without population pressure in increasing individual productivity at more than about the same rate. The group of points from 1636 to 1676 (covering the quarter-century periods 1636–61 to 1676–1701), during which population growth rates varied from about 0.0 to − 0.30 per cent per annum, all lie fairly close to a line representing an annual rate of wage rise of about 0.4 per cent, and there seems little indication that the lowest rates of population growth were associated with the highest rates of real-wage rise.[13]

There is a third feature of the graph which calls for comment. In the periods covered by the points from 1541 to 1681 the boomerang shape of the belt of points that formed the basis for the discussion of the previous paragraph is fairly clearly visible. If it is justifiable to assume that the PBH index is a reliable guide to real wage trends in this period, the graph appears to substantiate the view both that population growth rates above 0.5 per cent per annum courted savage falls in real wages, and that the benefit to real wages brought about by modest population growth rates petered out when the growth rate had fallen to zero.

For a few decades in the later sixteenth century population growth rates averaged almost 1.0 per cent per annum. The economy was clearly incapable of making effective use of the additional labour coming onto the market and real wages suffered a drastic fall. Only when the growth rate had fallen below 0.5 per cent per annum did the rate of fall begin to diminish. Then, however, wages recovered rapidly, re-entering the 'box' in which further moderation in population growth rates was associated with modest improvements in the real wage, until, when population ceased to grow, real wages were growing by about one half per cent annually. When population growth rates turned negative, however, there was no further rise in the rate of growth in real wages, and the graph moves out horizontally.

After 1681, however, there was a century when the pattern changes somewhat, though remaining very clearly pre-industrial and quite different from the last phase. The band of points occurring in this period tends to move out to the right and straighten, suggesting both that the underlying growth rate of the economy had improved and that when population growth rates exceeded one half per cent per annum they no longer produced a change in the shape of the relation between the two variables. Real wages were still very adversely affected but a broadly linear relationship between rates of change in the two variables was maintained, whereas in the sixteenth century the relationship had been curvilinear, producing the lower half of the 'boomerang'. It would be mistaken, however, to suppose that the period after 1681 presents more than a hint of a change of pattern. It is true that all the points from 1686 to 1721 lie above and to the right of the curve of points from 1541 to 1681 (other than those for 1621 and 1626) and the same is true of the points for 1761 to 1781 at the end of the middle period. It is also possible that the PBH real-wage index is especially fallible as a guide to the intervening period 1726 to 1756 whose points are interlaced among those for the first period. The 25-year moving average of the index reaches its peak value in 1741. But the series depends solely upon the wages of building craftsmen in Maidstone at this period. It misses entirely the effect on wages in the new industrial areas in northern England of the prosperity of the middle third of the

13. English early modern economic history does not appear to lend support to Boserup's view that population growth in a pre-industrial economy tended to spark off changes in agricultural techniques which would allow productivity per head in agriculture to be maintained, albeit at the cost of longer hours of work, while at the same time encouraging changes elsewhere in the economy that would lead to a rise in output per head overall. Boserup, *Conditions of agricultural growth*, p. 118.

century, and the fact that they comprised a rapidly growing fraction of the total labour force. It is therefore conceivable that a better wage index would keep an even higher proportion of the points in the second period above the band of points forming the 'boomerang' in the period before 1681.[14]

Nevertheless the possibility that the period before 1800 can be subdivided should not be allowed to obscure its general uniformity of experience, nor the decisive nature of the break occuring during the industrial revolution, a change so decisive that it must reflect a dramatic rise in the rate of growth in the economy as a whole, whatever changes there may have been in the factor share of labour in national income, and whatever the deficiencies of the PBH index as a measure of real wages. Perhaps for the first time in the history of any country other than a land of recent settlement rapid population growth took place concurrently with rising living standards. A basic feature of the human condition had changed. Figure 10.4 shows one cycle in the changing relation of population and economy which was probably typical of much earlier history. Rapid population growth in the sixteenth century provoked a sharp fall in living standards which in turn was followed by a falling away in the rate of population growth so pronounced as to produce a 30-year period during which population fell and a much longer period lasting 65 years during which population was below the peak total reached in 1656. In this middle period real wages rose steadily. After the early decades of the eighteenth century, however, the population growth rate accelerated and real wages first grew more slowly and then declined, paralleling closely events 200 years earlier. Past experience would have suggested a repetition of the later phases of earlier cycles – a slowing down in population growth followed eventually by a recovery in real wages. Instead England crossed a threshold into a new era.

Before 1800 matters fell out much as Malthus had insisted they must. The faster population grew, the faster the price of food rose, and since the impact of rising food prices was only partially cushioned by rising money wages, the faster population grew, the lower the standard of living and the grimmer the struggle to exist.[15] After 1800 poverty was, so to speak, no longer inevitable and the stage was set for the high indignation about poverty so characteristic of many nineteenth-century reformers. Some spent much energy in excoriating Malthus. Perhaps now it can be seen that both Malthus and his successors were right in their generations, for the world viewed by a man of Marx's generation had changed fundamentally from that which Malthus surveyed two generations earlier. The tension between population growth and living standards that had pinned men down in poverty gave way before a change in productivity so profound that an increase in poverty was no longer the price of an increase in numbers.

Mortality fluctuations and real-wage trends

Malthus had no doubt that the very slow increase in the population of European

14. Many years ago Gilboy directed attention to the importance of regional differences in wage movements in the eighteenth century. Gilboy, 'The cost of living and real wages' and *Wages in eighteenth century England*, especially ch. 8. The range of measures of price and real-wage trends for the period 1750–1850 is discussed in Flinn, 'Trends in real wages' and in von Tunzelmann, 'Trends in real wages revisited'. See below, pp. 431–3 for a further discussion of the question of the timing of the eighteenth-century real-wage peak, which concludes that it was probably not reached until about 1780.
15. The real-wage index is almost a mirror image of the consumables price series. Phelps Brown and Hopkins, 'Seven centuries of the prices of consumables', pp. 183, 186.

countries was caused in large measure by the operation of the positive check that linked poverty and high mortality. He was prepared to concede that the preventive check achieved by delaying marriage operated to some degree at all levels in society,[16] but he placed greater stress upon the positive check whose effect he thought to be confined largely to 'the lowest orders of society'.[17] He supposed that the children of the poor both in towns and in the country suffered from malnutrition to a degree that undermined their health and stunted their growth,[18] and that high mortality resulted. The bulk of chapter 5 of the *Essay on population*, in which Malthus dealt with the positive check in England, is given over to an attack upon the poor laws, but he made clear his view that the subjection of the poor to want was beyond human resolution. 'The truth is, that the pressure of distress on this part of a community is an evil so deeply seated, that no human ingenuity can reach it'.[19] If Malthus's view of the forces that combined to keep population growth at modest levels were just, therefore, it would be expected that falling real wages would cause a rise in mortality and vice-versa. We have already seen that economic distress appears to have influenced mortality levels only slightly and uncertainly in the short term.[20] What of the relation in the longer term?

In figure 10.5 long-term changes in English mortality are set out in the form of a series of figures of expectation of life at birth based on deaths occurring during the five-year period centring on the dates shown, while the PBH real-wage index is reproduced as an 11-year moving average.

Although there are three periods in which the line representing the e_0 plunged sharply downwards (1556 and 1561; 1681; and 1731), and also frequent sharp, if limited, deviations from trend, there is also a clear general pattern to be observed. The middle years of Elizabeth's reign formed a period of remarkably mild mortality. They were free from any serious epidemic visitations[21] and expectation of life was then higher than at any subsequent period until after the Napoleonic Wars. For the next century conditions worsened and expectation of life fell by about 10 years to reach a nadir in 1681. The early 1680s experienced a series of moderate crises, so the overall level of mortality was high, though these were not years of high prices. Sixty years later, in the 1740s there began a steady secular improvement in mortality which had by the 1820s advanced expectation of life to a level equalling its previous best, though for the last half century to 1871 there was little further change. The sixty years after the end of the long deterioration and before the almost equally long period of improvement presents no clear pattern of change. In the 1690s expectation of life rose sharply and the improvement was maintained in the next 15 years, but in the 1720s e_0 fell as quickly as it had previously risen, and in 1731 reached the second lowest single point in the whole series.[22] There was dramatic improvement immediately thereafter but a sudden reversal with the bad years of the early 1740s before the period of secular amelioration supervened.

16. Malthus, *Essay on population*, p. 63.
17. Malthus, *Essay on population*, p. 71.
18. Malthus, *Essay on population*, pp. 72–3.
19. Malthus, *Essay on population*, p. 95.
20. See above, pp. 320–32, 349–51, 371–3, 378–82.
21. Between 1564 and 1586 the crude death rate never rose higher than 26.3 per 1,000. See table A3.3.
22. The quinquennial e_0s shown in figure 10.5 are not, of course, a sensitive guide to the relative severity of individual epidemic crises. Two or three moderately bad years within the quinquennium may produce a lower e_0 than a single year of the most acute crisis if the latter occurs in isolation. Moreover, the bounds of the quinquennial periods are arbitrary and may divide a period of peak mortality. In considering the three

Real-wage
index

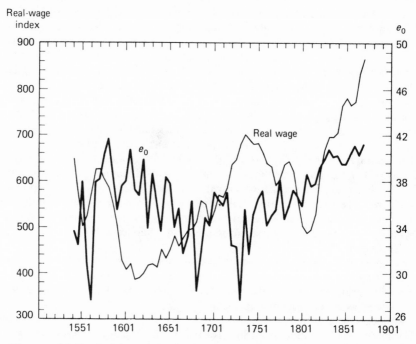

Figure 10.5: Quinquennial expectation of life at birth data compared
with an 11-year moving average of a real-wage index

Note: The e_0 graph represents mortality in the five-year period centring on the years shown.
The real-wage graph is an 11-year moving average centring on the years shown.

Sources: Real wages table A9.2; e_0s table A3.1.

It is not easy to detect any sign of a pattern linking mortality fluctuations with those
in the real wage. The very high death rate of the late 1550s occurred soon after two
harvest years of exceptionally high prices in 1555 and 1556. The real wage and
expectation of life graphs plunge almost together as a result. Both recovered sharply
but thereafter tended to fall, yet expectation of life, though declining, was still at a
relatively high level when the graph of real wages fell to its lowest point. And for a full
half century after real wages had begun their long and sustained rise mortality
continued to deteriorate. The switchback period of rapid mortality fluctuations

---

quinquennia of especially high mortality in figure 10.5, therefore, it is important to bear in mind the level of
death rates in the years that composed the quinquennia and in the years adjoining them. They were as
follows (crude death rates per 1,000: table A3.3):

	1556	24.4		1678	26.7		1726	27.7
	1557	42.5		⎧1679	37.2		1727	35.5
	1558	53.9	1681	⎪1680	33.8		1728	39.8
	⎧1559	47.3	quinquennium	⎨1681	38.9		⎧1729	44.7
1561	⎪1560	31.6		⎪1682	35.0	1731	⎪1730	36.2
quinquennium	⎨1561	25.9		⎩1683	31.8	quinquennium	⎨1731	34.1
	⎪1562	24.2		1684	33.6		⎪1732	29.8
	⎩1563	34.6		1685	33.3		⎩1733	29.0
	1564	26.3		1686	31.5		1734	26.0
				1687	28.9			

between 1680 and 1740 occurred when the real-wage curve was still rising steadily to a high peak. And the final period of mortality improvement took place against a background of falling real wages for a substantial part of the time.[23]

If, therefore, one were to scan early modern English history in the expectation that it would yield evidence that economic conditions had a significant long-term impact on mortality, there would be little to confirm the expectation in the real-wage and mortality data of figure 10.5. The usual assumption is, of course, that periods of economic stress when wages are low will tend to raise mortality levels, that there will be evidence of the operation of the Malthusian positive check.[24] Of this there is almost no sign.

Alternative assumptions are conceivable. It is reasonable to suppose that in certain circumstances improving living standards will tend to raise mortality rather than reduce it. If higher real wages, by changing the structure of demand in ways that increase the relative importance of industry and services, thereby concentrate more people in cities, higher death rates may well result. The rapid growth of London in the seventeenth century will have played some part in the rising mortality of the period. For example, a crude calculation shows that if the expectation of life at birth in the countryside was 40 years, but only 20 years in London, then an increase in the proportion of the national population living in London from 5 to 10 per cent would cause the expectation of life in England as a whole to fall by about one year.[25] Urban growth in smaller places, which also occurred in the seventeenth century, would also tend to raise mortality.[26]

To the degree, therefore, that rising real wages may justly be linked to urban growth, they exerted an influence upon mortality, though in the opposite direction to that which is usually assumed to exist. Again, the absence of any improvement in mortality in the second and third quarters of the nineteenth century at a time of rapidly improving real wages is certainly due in part to the very rapid growth in the percentage of the population living in towns where death rates were high. There were thus links between higher wages, the changing demand structure, and rapid urban growth. Better wages *in the same economic and social environment* may reduce mortality, but since better wages may also involve moving to a less healthy environment, there was

23. The relation between short-term economic and demographic change (which shows only a very modest influence of price changes on mortality levels) is summarized above, pp. 389–401.

24. McKeown is an unusually trenchant defender of this viewpoint. 'When death rates are high, as in developing countries today and in all countries in the recent past, mortality is due largely to a high incidence of infectious diseases. The level of infection is determined mainly by the standard of living, and even modest improvements are reflected rapidly in a lower death rate'. McKeown, *The modern rise of population*, p. 35. See also p. 161.

25. A discussion of the rapid growth of London and of some implications of its growth may be found in Wrigley, 'London's importance'.

26. Urban growth appears to have continued strongly during the seventeenth and early eighteenth century even though the total national population fell for a time after 1656 and did not permanently surpass the total attained in 1656 until the 1730s. This forms a marked contrast with the sixteenth century when there may have been urban regression rather than advance (apart from London) during much of the period of rapid population growth. On the latter point see Phythian-Adams, 'Urban decay'. On the former see Daunton, 'Towns and economic growth in eighteenth-century England', p. 247, table 1. Patten has provided a wealth of information about the development of the urban system as a whole in the seventeenth century: Patten, *English towns 1500–1700*. Not all towns suffered such high mortality as London, but they were much less healthy than the countryside. The empirical relation between population density and mortality level which Farr formulated in the nineteenth century (that mortality varied as the 12th root of the density of population: Farr, *Vital statistics*, pp. 173–6) may not have been equally applicable in the seventeenth century but some comparable formulation would be appropriate.

sometimes a negative rather than a positive relationship between wealth and health.

It is doubtful, however, whether the course of real wages was ever the dominant influence on mortality trends. A slowly changing balance between infective parasites and their human host was probably a weightier factor, a balance which tilted to and fro largely outside the consciousness of men and, with few exceptions, quite outside their power to influence.[27] Within these larger movements quite violent swings in mortality could occur regardless of economic conditions. For example, the period between the 1680s and the 1740s was a time of generally improving real wages but quinquennial death rates rose and fell haphazardly despite this.

There were particular parishes, especially in the highland areas of England in the sixteenth century, in which the 'classic' pattern of poor harvests and numerous deaths can be found,[28] and individual men, women, and children throughout the early modern period died from the effects of malnutrition. Many burial registers carry occasional references to 'a wandering hunger-starved boy', 'a poor starveling child found in John Adams' barn', and the like. Occasionally, and most evidently in the periods of high prices in the later 1550s and 1597, there was a strong apparent link between the exceptional poverty which necessarily accompanied dear food and an upsurge in deaths. But there is no warrant in the English evidence for the view that *long-term* movements towards lower wages provoked higher general mortality, nor that a steady rise in real wages brought a saving of life.

Tudor and Stuart governments were deeply concerned about the implications of bad harvests and the unrest they could provoke. At times high food prices, which in a pre-industrial economy is a synonym for low real wages, caused great and widespread suffering. But there is no sign of the population approaching a Malthusian ceiling and finding its growth rate reduced further and further by rising mortality, except perhaps for a few decades at the beginning of the seventeenth century, and even then the apparent connexion may well be only coincidence since the deterioration in mortality continued long after real wages had started to advance again.

The lack of evidence that long-term economic trends caused marked differences to mortality levels in early modern England does not necessarily imply the lack of important influences in the reverse direction. The changes in mortality between the mid seventeenth and mid eighteenth centuries, which drove death rates up to a level high by English standards, helped to prevent population from registering any significant growth during this period. If the lack of pressure from growing numbers enabled economic growth not only to 'widen' but also to 'deepen' and so strengthen the gathering impetus of economic change, then mortality played a significant, if subordinate part in securing the pause. But the reasons for the higher mortality appear to have been largely exogenous to the socio-economic system, or at least not to have operated through the real wage.[29]

27. There were, of course, important exceptions to this rule. For example, success in establishing *cordons sanitaires* had a substantial effect at times in reducing the severity of plague epidemics, as in the case of the outbreak at Marseilles in 1720. Biraben, *Les hommes et la peste*, I, pp. 245–51; also, for a more general discussion of the same issue, *ibid*, II, p. 183. The great difficulty of establishing effective control of the movement of individuals, or of isolating those who were infected or had been in contact with disease carriers, emerges vividly in Cipolla's account of the plague visitation in Prato in 1630–1. Cipolla, *Cristofano and the plague*.
28. See Appleby, *Famine in Tudor and Stuart England*.
29. It is possible to imagine indirect links between the socio-economic system and mortality which may have been important. For example, if the rise in mortality during the seventeenth century were due to the

The absence of a connexion between real wage and mortality trends that could serve to moderate or revive population growth in accord with economic circumstances lends an added interest to the examination of secular changes in fertility. If the positive check was unimportant in this regard, what of the preventive check?

Fertility fluctuations and real-wage trends

The discussion of the results of back projection in chapter 7 showed that during most of early modern English history changes in fertility outweighed those in mortality in determining growth rates. Their predominance is especially clear in accounting for the acceleration in growth rates between the late seventeenth and early nineteenth centuries. But were fertility fluctuations linked to changes in the real wage, or were they like mortality fluctuations, largely independent of economic circumstances?

The findings of chapter 7 immediately suggest the likelihood of a link between real-wage changes and fertility because the fluctuations in fertility that occurred were shown to have been produced very largely by changes in marriage age and in other fertility variables that moved in sympathy with such changes.[30] Marriage is a deliberate act in all societies, and in a society in which marriage is not tied by custom to physical maturity it must be responsive to the actors' appreciation of their circumstances. The actors include the bride and groom, their parents, and on occasion other kin, and in a more diffuse sense the community in which they live. The decisions taken will reflect the actors' assessment of their individual experience and that of the community perhaps over a period of many years, and also of their expectations for the future. If personal experience and community wisdom join in viewing the remembered past as a period of deteriorating conditions when it was increasingly difficult to maintain accustomed standards of food, clothing, and shelter, and if there is recognition that, in marrying, a couple are declaring a belief that they have attained a sufficient command of resources to be able to maintain accustomed standards, then in such circumstances it is to be expected that marriage will be delayed to a later date or may be foregone completely. Conversely, in improving times marriage may be ventured upon earlier. To the degree that all these assumptions hold good they should give rise to changes in fertility which reflect prior changes in a measure of individual prosperity such as the real wage mediated through alterations in the timing and intensity of marriage. Back projection unfortunately yields no direct evidence about nuptiality more refined than the crude marriage rate, though this measure can prove illuminating. Before discussing the evidence of changing marriage behaviour in England, however, we shall first consider the fertility fluctuations revealed in the current and cohort gross reproduction rates derived from back projection.

Figure 10.6 shows the pattern of changes in the PBH real-wage index expressed as an 11-year moving average and in the quinquennial gross reproduction rates. When shown in this way the influence of years of exceptionally high or low prices is still sufficient to cause substantial short-term variations in the real-wage series. The very

---

introduction and spread of new diseases, and the subsequent fall in mortality to an accommodation between host and parasite, then the speed of adjustment may have been linked to the frequency of exposure because of its selective effect. This in turn might be in part a function of the level and type of migratory movements, which brings the issue back within the workings of the socio-economic system. On this range of issues see McNeill, *Plagues and peoples*, especially pp. 5–14, 218–24, 235–56.
30. See above, pp. 265–9.

poor harvests of the 1550s and the 1690s, for example, have an evident effect in depressing the wage graph. Equally, the run of favourable years in the 1730s pushed the graph up to a marked peak beyond the trend line. Disregarding such temporary effects, there were three major turning points in the real-wage graph, occurring in about 1610 when the precipitous fall in wages of the late sixteenth century was at last halted, about 1750 when almost a century and a half of rising living standards came to an end, and about 1805 when the benefits of the agricultural and industrial revolution became so marked as to overcome the traditional problems that went with rapid population increase.

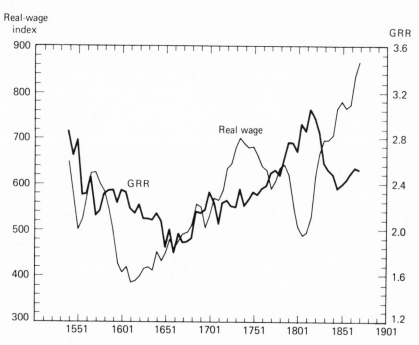

Figure 10.6: Quinquennial gross reproduction rates compared with an 11-year moving average of a real-wage index

Note:　The GRR graph represents fertility in the five-year period centring on the years shown. The real wage graph is an 11-year moving average centring on the years shown.

Sources: GRRs table A3.1; real wages table A9.2.

There were also three major turning points in the graph of quinquennial GRRs. In each case the fertility change was in the same direction as that in real wages, but in each case also the fertility change took place about half a century later than that in real wages. There was a first turning point in the GRR about 1660 when fertility reached its nadir after more than a century of decline from the relatively high levels of the mid sixteenth century. The second turning point came about 1815 following a century and a half of rising fertility. Finally, fertility reached a second low point in the mid 1840s, and thereafter the GRR rose for 20 years before the onset of the great fall of fertility which ushered in a totally different demographic regime. The third turning point in fertility was the least clear-cut because it was much sooner reversed than were the earlier turning points.[31]

The turning points in the fertility graph therefore appear to have occurred approximately 50, 65, and 40 years after the comparable changes in the real-wage graph, though the greater length of the second interval may be spurious if the unrepresentive nature of the PBH wage data in the eighteenth century affected real-wage trends in the way suggested earlier.[32] In view of this and of the more general uncertainty about the exact timing of any major turning point in series with many brief, erratic fluctuations it might seem foolhardy to make great play with the question of the length of the lag between turning points in the two series. Yet, on the other hand, since fertility as measured by GRRs calculated on current birth totals does appear to have echoed major changes of direction in the real-wage graph it is not a phenomenon to be ignored. The wide swings in the absolute level of real wages were later mirrored by similar major rises and falls in fertility. The two vertical scales on the graph have a common origin, and it will be seen that the fluctuations in the two series are of the same order of magnitude (though physiological constraints upon fertility set an upper limit, of course, to the height that can be reached by the GRR so that fertility could not match the levels reached by the real wage early in the sixteenth or late in the nineteenth centuries).

It is also true that the poor quality of the real-wage data implies a margin of uncertainty about the length of the lag between real-wage and fertility changes. It is even conceivable that the existence of the pattern described would be cast into doubt with better wage data, but on present evidence it appears highly likely that fertility did fluctuate in sympathy with prior changes in real wages and that there was a long lag between them.[33]

If a causal connexion between real wages and fertility is hypothesized to exist, it is natural to ask whether there can be any plausible explanation for such a long lag between the two series. In contemporary industrialized societies where birth control is widely practised a swift response to changing circumstances is easily secured. The tempo of fertility can be increased or moderated by the decisions of couples who are already married. In earlier times when the chief method of altering the general level of fertility was through the timing and incidence of marriage rather than by reducing or increasing fertility within marriage, it was less easy to achieve an immediate response to any change in the prevailing economic or social climate.[34] Assuming that such responses were made primarily through changes in marriage decisions, there must necessarily have been a longer delay between any alteration of economic circumstances and evidence of its full impact on a measure of fertility such as the gross reproduction rate. The delay would be especially marked if a change in marriage practice took place only when any one generation came to perceive its circumstances as significantly better or worse than those of its predecessor, leaving it unresponsive to the early stages of a change in secular trend which are never easy to distinguish from short-term fluctuations.

31. See below, pp. 435–8 for further discussion of fertility changes in the second half of the nineteenth century.
32. See above, pp. 407–8, 411–2 and also below pp. 430–5, 638–41.
33. For further discussion of this issue see below, pp. 430–5.
34. There was, of course, as we have seen, a positive association between annual movements in real wages (pushed up or down by price changes in the wake of harvest fortunes) and short-term fertility movements, but this was superimposed on the prevailing general level of fertility and left no longer term mark upon it. See above, pp. 350–3, 370, 372–7, 382–3.

With this in mind it is instructive to consider the relation between the major, secular trends in the PBH real-wage index and changes in the *cohort* GRRs. These may be seen in figure 10.7. Cohort GRRs measure the reproductive experience of successive

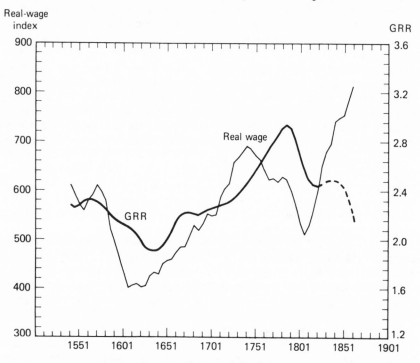

Real-wage index

GRR

Figure 10.7: Cohort gross reproduction rates compared with a 25-vear moving average of a real-wage index

Notes: The cohort GRR graph represents the fertility of generations born in the five–year period preceding the years shown. The real-wage graph is a 25-year moving average centring on the years shown. Since the cohort GRRs are very closely similar in level to a 5-point moving average of the current GRRs 30 years later, the directly calculated set of cohort GRRs has been extended using appropriate values from the set of current GRRs supplemented by Glass's estimates of the current GRR for 1881, 1891, and 1901 suitably adjusted to remove the 'jump' between his series and that produced by back projection (see ch.7, fn.82). The estimated cohort GRRs are shown by a broken line.

Sources: Cohort GRRs table A3.2; real wages table A9.2.

five-year birth cohorts, following the history of each cohort throughout its reproductive life. They are therefore less subject than current rates to marked fluctuations (compare the GRR graphs in figures 10.6 and 10.7), representing instead a weighted average of age-specific current rates over a period of 35 years.[35] Since the cohort GRRs are specified by year of birth the fertility graph of figure 10.7 differs

35. Cohort GRRs were constructed by selecting appropriate diagonal sets of rates from the matrix of current rates formed to calculate current GRRs. They therefore suffer from the same limitation as current GRRs in that age-specific fertility rates are not observed directly but conform to a shape imposed by a fertility schedule chosen to reflect an assumed mean age at maternity. See appendix 15.

from that of figure 10.6 not only in being much smoother but also in having been shifted substantially to the left. The real-wage graph in figure 10.7 also differs from that of figure 10.6. It is shown as a 25-year rather than an 11-year moving average to match the dampening effect upon the fertility graph caused by the change to a cohort GRR.

The turning points in the real-wage and fertility graphs are much more nearly coincident in figure 10.7 than was the case in figure 10.6. Those of the mid seventeenth and early nineteenth centuries, indeed, are now only about 15 years apart, though there is a much longer lag in the third turning point which took place in the eighteenth century. We have already seen that the peak level of the PBH series in this period is displaced to the left by the effect of the exceptional harvests of the 1730s in boosting real wages to a level above the trend line, and also that it is probable that the PBH index may be an especially fallible guide to national real wages in the middle third of the eighteenth century. There is some reason, therefore, to think that with better information about real wages the relation between the turning points in the two series in the eighteenth century would prove to be similar to that obtaining in the other two cases.[36]

In considering the implications of the data summarized in figures 10.6 and 10.7 it is important to distinguish between two separable issues: the extent and nature of any causal connexion between real-wage changes and fertility trends; and the significance of the relatively long time lag between changes in the secular trend of real wages and those in *current* fertility levels. The former in the present state of knowledge entails an element of speculation, but whatever the most satisfactory model to 'save the phenomena' in this connexion, the significance of the lack of synchronism in real-wage and fertility swings remains and may be considered independently.[37]

Marriage behaviour and real-wage trends

Although the argument for a link between real-wage trends and changes in marriage practice leading to fertility changes rests at present largely upon grounds of inherent likelihood and lacks direct evidence it would be over-cautious to dismiss the parallelism of movement in the PBH index and the cohort GRR as coincidence, since plausible, if still speculative reasons for the existence of the observed pattern can be adduced. The argument hinges upon the central importance of marriage both as an expression of economic independence and as an influence on fertility.

Setting up an independent household, which was expected of a newly married couple in early modern England, requires command of or access to substantial resources, and if those marrying wish to live no less well than their parents (or if their parents control marriage decisions and have the same wish) they must postpone, or even avoid marriage in worsening circumstances, but may approach it earlier than the older generation if times are getting better. Precisely because marriages last for a long time it is not simply short-term prospects which affect marriage decisions but an appreciation of the probable course of events over half a lifetime. The powerful influence of short-term influences on the timing of marriage has often been stressed and is clearly visible in early modern England.[38] Whatever the secular trend in marriage age and incidence, seasons of plenty encouraged marriage, while hard times

36. See below, pp. 431–4.
37. See below, pp. 438–43.
38. See above, pp. 349–50, 368–9, 374–5, 383–4.

led to their postponement. But underlying such short-term fluctuations in marriage frequency, in the tactics of marriage as it were, there was a working out of strategy. The strategic situation will favour a move towards earlier and more universal marriage, on this argument, only if the prospect over the likely term of the marriage matches some standard in the actors' minds, and this in turn may hinge on their reaction to trends over a preceding period of some length. Discussing marriage behaviour in these terms invites ridicule if it is taken to imply a knowledge of trends in real wages and a conscious attempt to adjust behaviour accordingly. Such knowledge did not exist. Yet, mediated by conventions about the timing and incidence of marriage, the impact of changing real wages on marriage patterns over a period of time may be similar to that which would be produced by conscious calculation.[39]

In this general context there are several possible mechanisms that might produce a lag between real-wage and fertility changes of the type visible in figure 10.7. For example, suppose either that marriage decisions were actually made predominantly by the parental generation rather than the bride and groom, or that the younger generation came unconsciously to perceive their prospects largely through the eyes of their parents. A parental generation brought up in the latter stages of a downward phase in the real-wage cycle might spend much of their married lives after the trend had turned upwards without ever reaching the standard of living they had known in childhood and early youth. If as a result they viewed their life-cycle experience pessimistically and communicated this view to the next generation, an 'appropriate' change in marriage behaviour would be very slow to appear. Or again, suppose that the social mechanisms that translated the pressure of economic circumstances into changing marriage practice were insensitive to slight changes in the trend of real wages (which are not easily distinguishable from the constant flux of short-term changes). If this were so, it would only be after the new trend in real wages was well established (when, for example, real wages had risen 10 per cent from a low point or fallen 10 per cent from a high point) that marriage patterns would respond. This hypothesis is plausible in the sense that short-term fluctuations in real wages were so violent that society 'ought' to have been insensitive to any but a firmly set change in trend. It is interesting to note in this connexion that the mean proportional annual fluctuation in real wages was 8–10 per cent until the early eighteenth century, falling to about 6 per cent thereafter (table 8.7). Other possible chains of connected circumstances might be adumbrated that could result in a long lag between real-wage and fertility movements, and of course the various possibilities need not be mutually exclusive, but there is too little evidence at present to make an informed judgement about them. It seems clear that the existence of a long lag between movements in the two series does not preclude the possibility of a causal link between them but only when detailed work based on family reconstitution studies becomes available will it be possible to distinguish more satisfactorily between the several possible hypotheses.

It is, however, already possible to use summary data from family reconstitution studies to discover whether changes in marriage age conformed to the pattern that would be expected if marriage were the intervening variable through which real-wage changes had an impact on fertility trends. In figure 10.8 changes in male and female age at marriage and cohort GRRs are plotted for quarter-century periods from 1550–74 to 1775–99. The marriage age information is also given in table 10.1. The fertility graph is plotted upside down so that the degree of parallelism of movement in

39. See Wrigley, 'Fertility strategy' for a discussion of related issues.

the three graphs is easier to assess. The age at marriage data are for birth cohorts originating from the periods indicated. For this reason the latest quarter century covered is 1775–99.[40] The reconstitution data are drawn from the same 12 parishes used in chapter 7.[41]

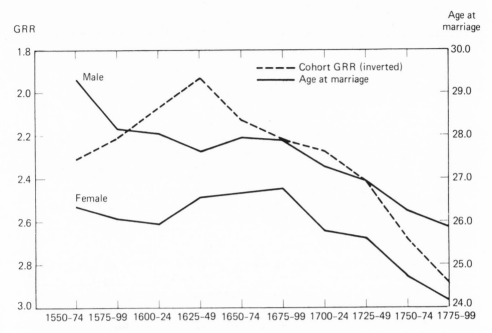

Figure 10.8: Trends in age at marriage and cohort gross reproduction rates

Note: The cohort GRRs are the averages of the quinquennial figures given in table A3.2 for 1551 to 1571, 1576 to 1596, etc. The GRR scale has been inverted

Sources: Age at marriage table 10.1; cohort GRRs table A3.2.

Male marriage age was at its highest point in the earliest cohort, fell to about 28 in the second cohort (1575–99), and thereafter scarcely changed for the next century. After the cohort of 1675–99, however, the average male age at marriage fell steadily until in the final cohort (1775–99) it was just under 26. From the last seventeenth century cohort onwards the pattern for women was similar, though the fall was somewhat greater, reducing age at first marriage from 26¾ to barely 24 years. At an earlier date, on the other hand, female marriage age had shown a tendency to rise throughout the seventeenth century cohorts, and it fell less in the two earliest intervals than did male marriage age.

40. In order to avoid a downward bias in age at marriage data when cohorting by date of birth, an individual is accepted by the tabulation program only if his or her date of birth is 50 years or more before the end of the period covered in the reconstitution. All reconstitutions ended before 1850 so that the latest quarter-century cohort is that of 1775–99, and since the commonest date of ending reconstitutions was either 1837 or 1840, the bulk of those included in the final quarter-century cohort were born in the first half of the period.
41. The parishes are listed on p. 248.

Table 10.1: Age at first marriage cohorted by date of birth (means of data taken from 12 reconstitution studies)

	M	F
1550–74	29.3	26.4
1575–99	28.2	26.1
1600–24	28.0	26.0
1625–49	27.6	26.6
1650–74	28.0	26.6
1675–99	27.9	26.8
1700–24	27.3	25.8
1725–49	26.9	25.6
1750–74	26.2	24.7
1775–99	25.9	24.1

Note: The 12 parishes from which the data used in this table were drawn are listed in chapter 7, fn. 84. The figures given above represent the averages of the individual figures for the 12 parishes, except for 1775–99 when they are based on 10 parishes (Gainsborough and Methley yield no data for the last quarter century because an individual is accepted by the age at marriage tabulation program only if his or her date of birth is more than 50 years before the date of end of observation in the parish in order to avoid a downward bias in age at marriage data. The reconstitution of both Gainsborough and Methley finished before 1825 so that no individuals are accepted from the birth cohort of 1775–99).

Source: Cambridge Group reconstitutions.

　　In view of the earlier discussion of marriage and fertility,[42] it is not surprising that figure 10.8 shows a generally close agreement between changes in female marriage age and changes in the cohort GRR. The agreement is not perfect. Female marriage age was still rising in the birth cohort of 1675–99 when the cohort GRR had already begun to increase, and although changes in marriage age and fertility were modest in the two earliest cohorts, they were in opposite directions. In part this may be due to the small number of parishes involved. Every parish was, of course, subject to local influences, so that while a small sample of this type may pick up major changes, it would not be surprising if minor changes which might be visible in national data were not fully reflected in the sample parishes. Again, age at marriage is only one aspect of marriage behaviour. Both the proportions never marrying and the level of illegitimacy could make an important contribution to the overall impact of marriage behaviour, in the broad sense, upon fertility.[43] For example, if the birth cohort whose behaviour was first affected by improving living standards in the seventeenth century used its good fortune, so to speak, to reduce the proportion of those never marrying rather than to reduce age at marriage, then the anomaly between marriage age changes and changes in the GRR in the later seventeenth century might disappear. We have earlier seen that such estimates of proportions never marrying as can be derived by combining back-projection data with marriage totals tends to lend weight to this possibility, though the precision of the estimates, especially before the eighteenth century leaves much to be desired.[44] However, it is possible to capture the effects both of changes in the timing of marriage (age at marriage) and of changes in its incidence (the proportion of each generation who marry) by calculating a crude marriage rate whose behaviour can be compared with movements in the real wage.

42. See above, pp. 253–7, 265–9.
43. See above, pp. 257–67.
44. See above table 7.28 and the discussion on pp. 258–64.

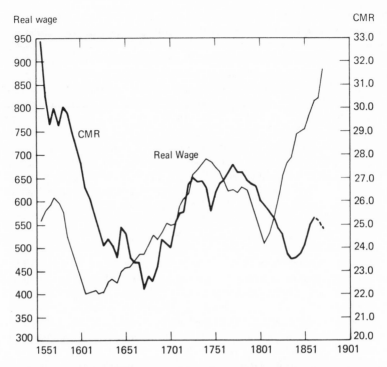

Figure 10.9: Crude marriage rates (marriages per 1000 persons aged 15 – 34) compared with a real-wage index(both 25-year moving averages)

Notes: Table A3.1 contains only broad age divisions of the population. The totals of those aged 15-34 at each 'census' were taken from more detailed, unpublished output tables. The marriage rate per 1000 aged 15-34 in the quinquennium 1869-73 obtained from Mitchell and Deane was 25.26 compared with 25.53 from the back-projection data. The later rates based on Mitchell and Deane were adjusted upwards by the difference between the two figures (0.27) to ensure a good 'fit' between the two series. The 25-year moving averages are centred on the dates shown. The CMR values which depend in part on data drawn from Mitchell and Deane are shown by a broken line.

Sources: Crude marriage rates table A3.1; real wages table A9.2. The marriage rates after the quinquennium 1869-73 refer to England and Wales and were obtained from the census data and crude rates in Mitchell and Deane, *British historical statistics,* p.12 and pp. 45-6.

The relation between secular swings in real wages and in the crude marriage rate may be seen in figure 10.9. Both series consist of 25-year moving averages, which were used in order to damp out short-term influences. The absolute level of the CMR shown in the figure will appear unusual. Marriage totals were related to the population aged 15–34 rather than the whole population, as would be done conventionally. The highest likelihood of marriage occurs in this age group, which however forms a changing fraction of the total population. Calculating a rate related to those of an age most likely to marry provides a different and better guide to marriage behaviour than the normal crude rate. The rate begins at a very high level in the mid sixteenth century, sweeps down rapidly until 1641, recovers slightly, but then sags further to its lowest point in 1671. Thereafter it rises steadily until 1726, dips briefly before rising to a peak in 1771, and then enters a 60-year period of decline until 1836, before a final period of increase down to 1861.

In considering the behaviour of the marriage rate graph it should be remembered that the marriage totals include remarriages. Remarriages formed a higher proportion of all marriages in the earlier part of the period than later, and this explains the exceptionally high rates found in the sixteenth century.[45] And there were short-term as well as secular effects resulting from the mixing of marriages and remarriages. The hump in the marriage rate graph between 1721 and 1741 is produced by the exceptional number of remarriages that took place in the wake of the mortality crisis of the late 1720s.[46] Had the proportion of remarriages in these years been normal the hump would disappear.[47] It should also be remembered that the prevalence of clandestine marriage in the half-century following the Restoration makes Anglican marriage registration a defective guide to marriage totals in the later seventeenth century.[48]

Bearing these points in mind it may be seen that figure 10.9 tends to repeat the pattern already observed when comparing real-wage trends with current and cohort fertility data, while at the same time making it clear that marriage rate data, like age at marriage evidence, strongly suggest that alterations in the incidence and timing of marriage were the means by which the fertility fluctuations were brought about. This may also be seen in figure 10.10 in which quinquennial readings of the 25-year moving averages of the CMR and current GRR are plotted. On general grounds it is to be expected that turning points in the timing and incidence of marriage will slightly precede those in the GRR. The two nineteenth-century turning points in the two series conform to this expectation. In each case the CMR changes trend 10–15 years before a change of trend in the GRR. The same may also have happened in the mid seventeenth century when allowance is made for the probable influence of clandestine marriage in depressing the CMR in the years following the Restoration. And there are lesser respects in which the two graphs show similarity of behaviour. In both, for example, there was a lengthy pause in the sixteenth century downswing lasting for two decades after 1560. But there is also a major anomaly; the CMR reached its eighteenth-century peak in 1771 whereas the corresponding peak in the GRR occurred only in 1816, a much longer gap than is found between any other major changes of trends in the two series.

In order to consider the anomaly more effectively, and also as a first step towards the fuller examination of the timing of turning points in all the series we have been considering (GRR, CMR, and PBH real wage), it is convenient to attempt a rough and ready correction to the CMR graph to remove the distortion due to the declining importance of remarriage as time passed. In figure 10.11 the CMR graph shown in figure 10.10 has been tilted downwards on a 'hinge' in 1851. It will be recalled that in

45. See above, pp. 258–9.
46. See above, p. 258, fn. 101.
47. The CMR for the five-year period centring on 1731 is about 4 points higher than the local average level, and therefore increases the level of the graph in the years 1721, 1726, 1731, 1736, and 1741 by about 0.8 (the graph represents a five-point moving average). If the CMR in 1731 had been free from the influence of the very large proportion of remarriages it would have remained close to the local average level.
48. See above, pp. 28, 258–63.

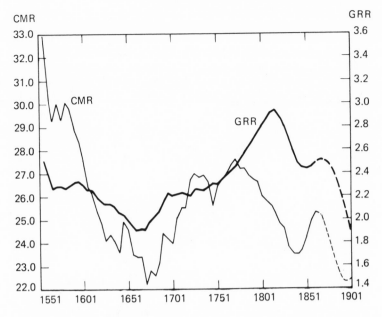

Figure 10.10 Crude marriage rates (marriages per 1000 persons aged 15 – 34) compared with gross reproduction rates (both 25 year moving averages)

Notes: See note to figure 10.9 for details of marriage rate calculations. The 25–year moving averages are centred on the dates shown. See note to figure 10.7 for source of GRR data after 1871.

Source: Table A3.1.

the mid nineteenth century 11.27 per cent of all those marrying were making a remarriage. We have assumed here, as previously in chapter 7, that the remarriage percentage in 1541 was 30 per cent, and that the percentage declined linearly from 1541 to 1851. After 1851 the percentage can be measured directly.[49] It is then a simple matter to calculate a first marriage rate for the whole period. There is little evidence as yet about the absolute level of remarriage before the beginning of civil registration and still less about the timing of changes in the remarriage proportion,[50] but it is safe to assume that the revised CMR graph shown in figure 10.11 is a better guide to changes in the timing and incidence of first marriage than that shown in figure 10.10.

The general parallelism between movements in the CMR and GRR is more easily visible in figure 10.11, and the two anomalies appear somewhat differently. The timing of the seventeenth-century nadir in nuptiality is less easy to identify with confidence because when the whole CMR graph is tilted down from its hinge in 1851 earlier points are depressed more than later ones. The entire period 1641–81 now appears as an irregular trough. If the effect of the exceptionally high marriage rates of

49. From the Registrar-General's *Annual Reports.*
50. But the trends in two parishes may be seen in ch. 7, fn. 101 and the general problem is discussed on pp. 258–9 above.

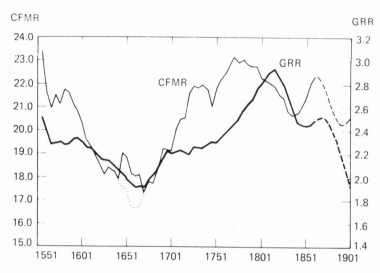

Figure 10.11: Estimated crude first – marriage rates (marriages per 1000 persons aged 15 – 34) compared with gross reproduction rates (both 25-year moving averages)

Notes: See note to figure 10.9 and text for details of marriage rate calculations. The 25-year moving averages are centred on the dates shown. See note to figure 10.7 for source of GRR data after 1871.

Source: Table A3.1.

the years of civil registration during the Commonwealth is removed,[51] the probability that the turning point occurred about 1660 is easier to appreciate (see the dotted line in figure 10.11: five points on the graph are affected because it represents a 25-year moving average). Inasmuch as the prevalence of clandestine marriage was related to the rise of nonconformity,[52] it may be that the overall shape of the marriage graph in the mid seventeenth century is best assessed after removing the effect of the brief period of civil marriage when, presumably, the marriages of those of all religious persuasions would have been more likely to have been recorded. If this is a fair assumption, the mid-seventeenth-century troughs in the CMR and GRR display the same relation to each other as would be expected on general grounds.

The late-eighteenth-century anomaly also looks somewhat different on the CMR graph in figure 10.11. Instead of a peak in 1771 followed by an increasingly rapid decline, the period 1771 to 1796 appears as a virtual plateau in the marriage rate, though 1771 remains the highest single point. Only after 1796 is there an unambiguous decline. Even 1796, however, is still 20 years before the GRR peak in 1816, and fertility, unlike nuptiality, comes to a sharp peak rather than having a plateau-like summit.

51. By the simple expedient of giving the CMR for the quinquennium centred on 1656 (1654–8) a value equal to the average of the rates for the quinquennia on either side.
52. Mrs J. Lawley's further work on those who were clandestinely married in Tetbury, Gloucestershire, in the late 1690s shows clearly the close connexion between nonconformity and clandestine marriage in the parish (private communication). For a discussion of the extent of clandestine marriage in Tetbury see Wrigley, 'Clandestine marriage'.

Three factors deserve to be considered in connexion with this apparent anomaly. First, during a period in which age at marriage is falling fast, there will be a 'telescoping' effect which will increase crude marriage rates to a level above that implied by the new, lower marriage age once the fall has ceased. If therefore, marriage age fell rapidly in the later eighteenth century but the fall had begun to decelerate before its end, the CMR would experience a sharp rise during its period of most rapid fall due in part to the pace of change rather than the change of marriage habit itself. The evidence from reconstitution studies is not sufficiently detailed or broadly based to allow the period of most rapid fall in marriage age to be pinpointed with confidence, but it is perfectly possible that, if this factor were better documented, it would suggest that the 'true' nuptiality peak came at the end of the 'plateau', in 1796 rather than 1771. The evidence about age at marriage given in table 10.1 tends to support this interpretation. Both for men and women there was a marked deceleration in the rate of decline in age at first marriage between the cohorts born in 1750–74 and those born in 1775–99. This relates, however, only to age at marriage and not to the proportions marrying, whereas the CMR is affected by both aspects of nuptiality.

The same 'telescoping' effect would, of course, also affect fertility, though the effect would be spread over a longer period of time because the cohorts affected would continue to bear children for many years after the 'telescoping' of marriage had ended. Both the scale and timing of the effect are very difficult to estimate in the absence of detailed information about the timing of the fall in marriage age in the later eighteenth century, but it is certainly likely that the effect would be more pronounced in this period than at other comparable turning points in the series since changes in marriage age appear to have been much greater in this period than at any other time in early modern English history.

Second, the possibility of a rise in marital fertility cannot be excluded. In one respect, indeed, there is clear evidence that it took place. We have seen that the proportion of women who were pregnant at marriage increased dramatically between the late seventeenth and the early nineteenth centuries.[53] In the 12 reconstitution parishes from which data on age at marriage were drawn the proportion of brides who were certainly pregnant at marriage increased from 10 per cent in 1650–99 to 30 per cent in 1800–49.[54] There was a substantial increase in each successive intervening half-century period, and there is some indication that the rise in prenuptial pregnancy increased the level of marital fertility among women aged 20–4, the age group whose fertility level was most likely to have been affected. The average marital fertility rate for women aged 20–4 rose from 376 in 1650–99 to 411 in 1750–99 in the 12 reconstitution parishes.[55] It may well have risen further in the early decades of the nineteenth century but the marital fertility rates for 1800–49 in the 12 parishes are based on very small numbers of events and do not yield trustworthy data.[56] Assuming

53. See above, p. 254, fn. 96.
54. These percentages refer to women whose first child was baptized before the end of the eighth month of marriage. A proportion of those baptized in the ninth month would also, of course, have been prenuptially conceived.
55. See table 7.24.
56. Some of the reconstitutions ended in 1812 and the others mainly in 1837. In a high proportion of cases, therefore, the marriages formed after 1800 were still in being at the end of the period of observation and so cannot be used for marital fertility tabulations because, unless the date of the end of the marriage is known, the period during which the wife was at risk cannot be defined. This date is seldom known with certainty until both partners to a marriage have died, especially from 1812 onwards when, under the provisions of Rose's Act, the normal form of entry in the burial register consisted simply of the name and age of the deceased.

that the rise in marital fertility rates due to increasing prenuptial pregnancy continued after 1800, this would have helped to produce a further rise in the GRR. It is, however, rather artificial to describe such a change as a rise in marital fertility. It would perhaps be more accurate to regard it as a concealed continuation in the fall in marriage age. Marital fertility in the strict sense may also have increased, but as yet there is no evidence from family reconstitution studies to lend support to the possibility.

A third factor complicating the interpretation of changes in the CMR and GRR towards the end of the eighteenth century is the rapid growth in the ratio between illegitimate and legitimate births. Between 1750 and 1810 the ratio roughly doubled from about 3 to 6 per cent.[57] In 1751 the GRR in figure 10.11 stood at 2.30; in 1816 at 2.94. But for the increase in the illegitimacy ratio, however, the 1816 figure would have been significantly lower at 2.85. The illegitimacy ratio appears to have risen fairly steadily throughout the period, but there is no reason to suppose that the fertility peak would have been at a different time if the ratio had not risen, although it would have been less marked.[58]

The timing of turning points in the real-wage, nuptiality, and fertility series

The relative timing of the turning points in the secular trends in real wages, nuptiality, and fertility holds a special interest since it helps both to test the existence of a connexion between economic and demographic change, and to suggest its nature. So far the three variables have been considered only in pairs, and it is now convenient to consider their joint behaviour.[59]

In table 10.2 the dates of major changes of trend in the three series are set out, together with the lags between them. There are three turning points common to all three series, and a fourth in the two demographic series in the later nineteenth century when nuptiality and fertility finally ceased to conform to the old pattern in their relationship to real-wage trends. The first two columns of the table contain some alternative dates in square brackets and where this affects the calculation of intervals between dates the corresponding alternative intervals are also shown in brackets in the lower half of the table. The bracketed dates represent revised views about the dating of turning points where there is good reason to think that the dates arising directly from calculations using the data printed in tables A3.1 and A9.2 may be misleading. We have already discussed our reasons for wishing to alter two dates on the line listing turning points in the CFMR. Before turning to a consideration of the table as a whole,

---

57. Laslett, *Family life*, p. 115, figure 3.2.
58. Two other points related to the height and shape of the peak in the GRR may be borne in mind. First, as we have previously noted (see above, pp. 233–4), the assumption of an unchanging fertility schedule linked to a mean age at maternity of 32 years will have caused the rise in the GRR from its low point in the later seventeenth century to its peak in the early nineteenth to be exaggerated. On the assumption that mean age at maternity fell from 33 to 31 during the period, the GRR at its peak would be some 2.7 per cent lower than the level shown in figure 10.11 (2.86 rather than 2.94). Second, the apparently sharp peak in 1816 is a rather misleading product of the long moving average used. The individual GRRs for the five-year periods centring on 1806, 1811, 1816, and 1821 were 2.93, 2.87, 3.06, and 2.98 (table A3.1). This represents a nearly flat 20-year plateau of high fertility. The high figure in 1816 occurs because there was a 'baby-boom' at the end of the Napoleonic War period. The crude birth rate in 1815 reached 44 per 1,000 and in 1816 it was 42 per 1,000, the two highest annual figures in the whole series (table A3.3).
59. The cohort GRR is, from the method of its construction, bound to reach peaks and troughs about 30 years before the current GRR and is therefore ignored in this discussion.

Table 10.2: The major turning points in 25-year moving averages of the PBH real-wage index, the estimated crude first marriage rate (per 1 000 persons aged 15–34), and the gross reproduction rate.

		Trough	Peak	Trough	Peak
(1)	PBH	*1621*	*1741 [1781]*	*1806*	
(2)	CFMR	*1671 [1661]*	*1771 [1796]*	*1836*	*1861*
(3)	GRR	*1661*	*1816*	*1851*	*1871*
Intervals (in years)					
(2) – (1)		50 [35]	30 [15]	30	
(3) – (2)		−10 [0]	45 [20]	15	10
(3) – (1)		40	75 [35]	45	

Note: For explanation of the dates and intervals given in square brackets see text.

Sources: Tables A3.1 and A9.1.

it is convenient to discuss the alternative dating of the eighteenth-century peak in the PBH series.

As we have frequently emphasised the PBH data, and hence any index of real wages based upon them, are very far from meeting the requirements of a reliable guide either to price or to wage movements, but especially to the latter. They have been used *faute de mieux*. No other series covering the whole early modern and industrial periods at present exist. If fully satisfactory series were somehow to be conjured into being it is quite possible that the timing of all the major turning points in real wages would be changed, but while it is improbable that the first or third would be greatly altered,[60] it is likely that the second would be moved substantially. The trend of real wages during the industrial revolution has, of course, been a perennially fascinating and controversial topic amongst economic historians for many years. Partly for this reason more attention has been given to the construction of wage series after 1750 than to the preceding period. Recently, von Tunzelmann has used principal component analysis of both price and wage data in an attempt to establish some bounds to what it is reasonable to hold about the trends in real wages between 1750 and 1850.[61]

Von Tunzelmann's analysis shows that on present evidence (new wage or price series might alter the picture) there is relatively little uncertainty about real-wage movements between the late 1760s and the early 1810s. During this half century there is a local peak about 1780 and a very steep-sided trough about 1800. This pattern is mirrored, of course, in the PBH real-wage series: PBH data are among the series used by von Tunzelmann. Between 1750 and the late 1760s, however, the upper and lower bounds established by principal component analysis diverge so considerably that it is

60. More uncertainty attaches to the early-seventeenth-century turning point than to that in the early nineteenth. The 25-year moving average in 1606 was virtually identical with that in 1621 (indeed fractionally lower). An 11-year moving average of the same data reaches its lowest point in 1611 (see figure 11.5), while the data collected by Bowden suggest that the real wages of agricultural workers showed no clear tendency either to rise or fall throughout the half century 1590–9 to 1640–9. Bowden, 'Agricultural prices, farm prices, and rents', p. 865, table XVI.

61. Von Tunzelmann, 'Trends in real wages revisited'.

possible at one extreme to view the period as one of a substantial fall in real wages, and at the other as one in which a very sharp rise occurred. The divergence does not arise because the price series are in disagreement, but because workers in the north of England enjoyed rapidly rising money wages while money wages in the south changed very little.

The degree of distortion which may arise through dependence on regional wage data at this period may be appreciated by considering figure 10.12. The lower graph represents the annual values of the PBH real-wage series plotted as a 25-year moving

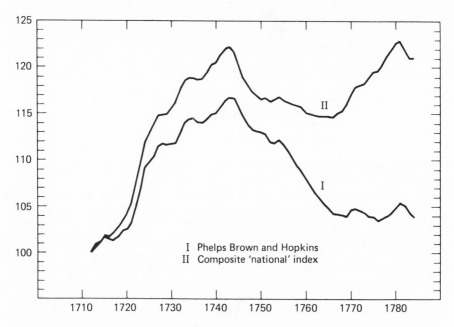

Figure 10.12: Two real-wages indices: Phelps Brown and Hopkins and a composite 'national' index (both 25-year moving averages)

Note: For method of construction of composite 'national' index see text.

Sources: Phelps Brown and Hopkins table A9.2; composite 'national' index table A9.2 and Gilboy, 'The cost of living and real wages', p.140.

average. The PBH wage data are, of course, drawn entirely from the south, and the real-wage series therefore shows a substantial fall from a peak reached in the early 1740s to a much lower level in the mid 1760s, after which the decline is arrested for 20 years before beginning to dip once more after 1781, the beginning of a steep descent to a very low level in the early nineteenth century (see figure 10.9). The upper graph represents an attempt to obtain a better balanced estimate of real-wage changes by combining northern and southern data. It was derived by splicing together the PBH data and Gilboy's annual real-wage estimates for Lancashire which were based on the wages paid to building labour in the county. Her series runs from 1700 to 1796 which explains why the 25-year moving averages shown in the figure begin in 1712 and end in 1784.[62] The relative contribution of the northern and southern data to the composite index of 'national' real-wage trends was determined by using the county population estimates of Deane and Cole. They published estimates for 1701, 1751, 1781, and 1801.[63] The share of northern England[64] in the national total for England less Monmouth increased from 34.17 per cent in 1701 to 36.20 per cent in 1751, 38.89 per cent in 1781, and 41.00 per cent in 1801. The relative weight of the northern and southern real-wage series for any individual year was calculated on the assumption that the percentage share of the north changed linearly between the dates listed. Both the composite and PBH series were indexed to 100 in 1712.

The composite 'national' series traces out a significantly different path from that of the PBH series, especially in the period between about 1750 and 1775. Both series rise almost without interruption from 1712 to a peak in 1743, though the 'national' series advances somewhat faster; and both fall sharply thereafter until 1750. In 1750 the composite series stood at 116.5 compared with the PBH figure of 112.9, a relatively modest difference. By 1775, however, the index figure in the PBH series had fallen back to 103.8 while the composite figure had risen to 119.4. The gap between the two series had widened from 3.6 to 15.6 points. Moreover, by 1780 the composite series had risen to a level slightly higher than the peak of the early 1740s, whereas the PBH series was languishing about 10 per cent below its earlier peak. Whereas the one series suggests unambiguously a peak in the early 1740s, the other presents a more complex picture with twin peaks some 40 years apart.[65]

In table 10.2 we have indicated a preference for the year 1781 as a turning point in the real-wage series by putting it in brackets beside 1741. As is evident from figure 10.12 the issue does not appear clear-cut even in the composite 'national' real-wage series. It is appropriate, however, to emphasize how much the high level of real wages at and near the 1740s peak was the result of the favourable harvests of the period, especially in the 1730s. The exceptional nature of the period may be illustrated from an analysis of the PBH consumables index. In the 25-year period centring on 1743 (the peak year in the real-wage series) the index was below its own 25-year moving average in only five years, and in two of these five the discrepancy was minimal (less than a tenth of 1 per cent in each case). The behaviour of the index was largely determined by food prices movements, and in a period of remarkably steady money wages such a high concentration of favourable years could scarcely fail to produce a marked local peak in real wages. The underlying trend in the 'national' series may therefore be regarded as fairly flat in the middle decades of the century before a brief period of further advance down to 1781. Thereafter the evidence of individual series and of more sophisticated analysis such as that of von Tunzelmann points unanimously to a sharp and marked fall in real wages for a generation or more.

62. Gilboy, 'The cost of living and real wages', p. 140, table 2.

63. Deane and Cole, *British economic growth*, p. 103, table 24. Deane and Cole published two sets of estimates for 1781. We have used the (b) alternative.

64. Northern England was assumed to comprise Lancashire, Cheshire, Yorkshire, Cumberland, Westmorland, Durham, Northumberland, Derbyshire, Nottinghamshire, Staffordshire, Leicestershire, Warwickshire, Shropshire, and Worcestershire This is a slightly more restricted list than that of Deane and Cole who also included Lincolnshire, Herefordshire, and Rutland in the north. Our list was intended to include only those counties that were either unambiguously in the north or were affected in some measure by industrial growth during the eighteenth century.

65. The question of real-wage trends in the eighteenth century was discussed by Deane and Cole, *British economic growth*, pp. 18–22. Their conclusions, though very cautiously expressed, are consonant with those presented here.

In view of the foregoing it is perhaps unnecessary to stress once more that all th dates given in table 10.2 must be regarded as rough approximations at best. From th method of its construction estimates of the level of the GRR are available only fc quinquennial periods. The 25-year moving average is thus a moving average of fiv such periods and its peaks and troughs must all fall in years ending in '1' or '6'. Th CMR was similarly constructed and although the PBH real-wage series is annual th same restricted set of dates was used. Even if all the data used in compiling the thre series had been perfectly accurate, therefore, the dating of turning points would not b accurate to less than five years. Thus, an interval between turning points in two of th series which appeared to be of 20 years in length might be as little as 15 or as much a 25 years in length. But this necessary inaccuracy is compounded by any defec inherent in the data and by the clumsiness of a device like a 25-year moving average a a tool for identifying turning points. Moreover, since there are only three majc turning points common to all three series there is an evident risk that coincidenc might give rise to patterns that would not appear if *more* evidence had been availab over a longer period of time. All these considerations point to caution, but it would b to carry caution to excess to eschew any attempt to find a pattern in the relationship c the turning points in the three series. Since we have given reasons for preferring th bracketed dates to those calculated directly from the data we shall use them rather tha the originals in discussing the evidence set out in table 10.2.

If any consistent pattern existed between turning points in the three series, it woul be expected that a change of trend in real wages would first produce a change i nuptiality and that this in turn would lead to a change in fertility. This sequence visible in the intervals between the turning points shown in the table. The first of th intervals (real wage to nuptiality change) averaged about 25 years in length (35, 1: and 30 years respectively); the second (nuptiality to fertility change) averaged 10 to 1 years (0, 20, and 15 years respectively); while the overall interval (real wage t fertility change) was in each case about 40 years (40, 35, and 45 years respectively In the case of the second interval there was also a fourth instance in the mid nineteent century when the interval was 10 years. Despite the inherent imprecision of an attempt to measure the relative timing of major secular changes of trend in the thre series, the dates listed in table 10.2 may be said to lend support to the view that secula fertility trends were responsive to prior changes in real wages because the timing an incidence of marriage was affected by them, but that real-wage changes took som time to produce this response, presumptively because changes in the trend of rea wages must initially have been difficult to distinguish from the random annua fluctuations in real wages produced by the varying fortunes of the harvest. I considering this issue the length of the first interval shown in table 10.2 (real wage t nuptiality change) should be recognized to be somewhat deceptive. With th advantage of *ex post facto* knowledge it is possible to detect turning points in th real-wage graph which must necessarily have been obscure at the time. Only the slov accumulation of new readings over a period of years after the retrospectivel identified turning point can have provided the 'information' needed to convince th 'system' that a change of trend had occurred. Therefore the interval between 'perceived' change in real wages and a change in secular nuptiality trend must i reality have been considerably shorter than the 25 years or so shown in the table

In general it is a rather noticeable feature of the long-term trends in the PBH index the CMR, and the GRR shown in figures 10.9 and 10.11 that using an average as lon, as 25 years results in broad sweeping movements between the major turning points

But there is one exception to the rule. In all three series the long sixteenth-century decline, which, at least in the case of the PBH index, had begun early in the century, was interrupted for a time in the 1560s and 1570s. The PBH index rose between 1556 and 1571, the CMR from 1566 to 1581, and the GRR from 1566 to 1596. The timing of the minor peaks which ended this brief period of recovery represents a telescoped version of that found with the major peaks, 25 years separating the peak in the PBH index (1571) from that in the GRR (1596). The earlier trough was even more severely telescoped. The episode was both brief and involved relatively small changes in the values of the three variables (though in the case of the PBH index especially, a very marked departure from trend). In these circumstances a very long moving average is an unwieldy analytical tool to use,[66] and it may therefore be best to regard the behaviour of the three series in the mid-Elizabethan period as supplementary evidence of the close relationship obtaining between trends in real wages, nuptiality, and fertility rather than as a further instance of a major change in secular trend, comparable to those already discussed.

Overall the evidence set out in table 10.2 and depicted in figures 10.9 and 10.11 constitutes a strong case for supposing that the institution of marriage in early modern England functioned effectively in matching nuptiality, and so at one remove fertility, to secular changes in economic opportunity. Within the welter of short-term movements in the marriage rate, responding to good or bad seasons, more fundamental alterations in nuptiality gradually became established when underlying economic circumstances changed. As each generation grew up and crossed the threshold into adult life the marriage conventions of society, reflecting its underlying economic condition, acted like a filter. At times young men and women were allowed to pass relatively freely into the married state, but at other times the mesh tightened, ponding back the flow so that many had long to wait before they passed through, while others spilled round, moving forward into middle life single and excluded from marriage.

Though the case is strong, however, it will fall short of being conclusive until more is known about the factors that governed marriage decisions; too much is at present inferential. Confidence would also be increased if it were possible to find reliable regional data, especially for the eighteenth century when the divergent trends in real wages in the north and south would afford an excellent test of the rôle of marriage as the social institution linking fertility to economic opportunity.

Nuptiality and fertility in the later nineteenth century

We have already noted that nuptiality and fertility responded in the 'traditional' way to the recovery in real wages early in the nineteenth century. The 25-year moving average of the CMR began to rise after 1836 and the GRR followed suit after 1851,

---

66. For example, the behaviour of the CMR 25-year moving average is very much affected by the extremely low rate found in the quinquennium centring on 1556. When this had been left behind for the first time by the average (in 1571), the value of the average recovered quite sharply when viewed against its trend. But for this single reading the downward tendency of the graph would have been much less conspicuously interrupted. The same point applies, though with less force, to the real-wage graph. The influence of the exceptionally bad harvests of 1555 and 1556 (and of other unfavourable years in the late 1540s and early 1550s) is visible even in a very long moving average, though even if harvests had been normal there would have been a conspicuous interruption in its earlier rapid fall. Real wages in the 1560s and early 1570s rivalled those a quarter of a century earlier.

but both turned down again after a brief rise lasting about 20 years and thereby broke their long-standing link to the real-wage series, which continued to rise.[67] It may be of interest to comment briefly on the subsequent relation of trends in nuptiality and fertility down to the end of the century.

Between 1871 and 1911 the English GRR fell by more than a third.[68] This was the period during which for the first time fertility within marriage began to be controlled deliberately by a substantial and growing proportion of married couples, but there were also changes in the timing and incidence of marriage which exercised a significant independent influence in depressing fertility, especially in the early decades of its decline. As may be seen in figure 10.11 the 25-year moving average of the CMR fell very sharply between its peak in 1861 and 1891, though thereafter it began to rise once more. What were the changes in marriage behaviour that caused the CMR to fall so substantially in the last third of the nineteenth century and how greatly did they depress fertility?

Statement of the ages of the bride and groom on marriage was not compulsory in England, so that the annual marriage returns published by the Registrar General cannot be used with confidence to follow changes in marriage age in the later nineteenth century. A rising proportion of brides and grooms chose to state their age as time went on, but information drawn from a sample with a constantly changing composition presents difficulties of interpretation.[69] However, from 1851 onwards the census returns permit the singulate mean age at first marriage to be calculated.[70] The results of such a calculation are shown in table 10.3. Female age at first marriage fell by about half a year between 1851 and 1871 but rose thereafter by more than a year between 1871 and 1901. Male trends were broadly similar. The fall in marriage age between 1851 and 1871 *ceteris paribus* would explain a significant part of the rise in the GRR over the same period. Similarly, the rise in marriage age between 1871 and 1901 would, in the absence of any change in marital fertility, have reduced the completed fertility of women surviving to the end of the child-bearing period by about 7 per cent. Overall fertility would have fallen by a greater margin.[71]

Furthermore, there were changes in the proportion of men and women who never married which considerably reinforced the changes in marriage age and provide further help in explaining the substantial changes in the CMR during the later nineteenth century shown in figure 10.11. As may be seen in table 10.4 the proportion

67. Glass brought to light the extent of the fluctuations in marriage rates in the later nineteenth century in 'Marriage frequency and economic fluctuations'.

68. Glass estimated the GRR for England and Wales as 2.344 in 1870–2 and 1.469 in 1910–2. Glass, 'Changes in fertility in England and Wales', p. 168, table II.

69. Glass even found a small proportion of missing ages at marriage in a sample study based on marriage certificates relating to the year 1951. Glass, *Numbering the people*, p. 192.

70. This measure was devised by Hajnal, and is described by him in 'Age at marriage'. Crafts reports the result of his recent work on the singulate mean age at marriage in England and Wales in 1861 in 'Average age at first marriage'.

71. The figure of 7 per cent is intended only as a rough approximation. It was obtained as follows. The successive age-specific marital fertility rates per 1,000 for the age groups 25–9 to 40–4 in the 12 reconstitution parishes were 341, 288, 236, and 121 respectively (table 7.25). At these rates the cumulative total of marital fertility would fall by 7 per cent if age at marriage increased from 25 to 26 years (the reconstitution data were used because no age-specific fertility data were collected by the Registrar General until after the passage of the Population (Statistics) Act in 1938). The fall in fertility must have been greater than suggested by this calculation because death claimed an increasing fraction of women in each successive age group so that the effective rates were all lower than those shown but the later by a greater margin than the earlier. A rise in marriage age would therefore cut fertility by a larger margin than suggested on the implicit assumption that all survived to age 45.

Table 10.3: Singulate mean age at marriage 1851–1911 (England less Monmouth)

	M	F
1851	26.94	25.77
1861	26.39	25.39
1871	26.43	25.13
1881	26.60	25.30
1891	27.06	25.96
1901	27.31	26.27
1911	[27.65]	[26.25]

Notes: Since the later nineteenth century censuses do not always give 5-year age divisions in tabulating the number of single men and women, the calculation of singulate mean age at marriage was always based on the cumulation of years lived single up to age 45 rather than age 50 and the percentage never marrying was taken to be the percentage single in the age group 45–54. In those years in which the results of these calculations can be compared with the results obtained by the more conventional cumulation to age 50 the differences are trivially small (in 1861, for example, the results using the more conventional formula are 26.40 for men and 25.41 for women).
The 1911 figures were obtained by assuming that the figures for England only would bear the same proportion to those for England and Wales combined as was the case in 1901. The 1911 census published no tabulations for Wales and Monmouth as a unit, and it would have been excessively tedious to have cumulated the separate breakdowns for all the Welsh counties.

Sources: *1851 Census*, Ages, civil condition, etc., I, Summary tables, pp. cxcii–cxciii·
        1861 Census, Ages, civil condition, etc., part I, Summary tables, pp. xiv–xv, xxi–xxii
        1871 Census, Ages, civil condition, etc., Summary tables pp. xvi–xvii, xxv–xxvi
        1881 Census, Ages, condition as to marriage, etc., Summary tables, p.v. and pp. 463, 478
        1891 Census, Ages, condition as to marriage, etc., Summary tables, p.v. and pp. 491, 501
        1901 Census, Summary tables, pp. 162–3, 168–9, 172, 179–81
        1911 Census, Ages and condition as to marriage, Tables, pp. 1–2.

of men and women who were still single at age 45–54, and who may therefore be regarded as never marrying, varied substantially in the successive censuses from 1851 to 1911. The male proportion fell considerably from 1851 to 1881 before rising in the later decades of the century until in 1911 the figure was slightly higher than in 1851.

Table 10.4: Proportions single at age 45–54, 1851–1911 (England less Monmouth)

	M	F	Sex ratio 45–54 (males per 1 000 females)
1851	11.36	12.36	958
1861	10.44	12.07	944
1871	9.60	12.18	926
1881	9.52	12.05	901
1891	9.85	12.53	909
1901	10.86	13.78	921
1911	[11.91]	[15.97]	[918]

Note: For 1911 figures see note to table 10.3.

Sources: See table 10.3.

The pattern for women is more like that of men than might appear at first sight. The final column shows the sex ratio in the age group 45–54. It will be seen that the ratio fell steeply between 1851 and 1881,[72] reducing the likelihood of marriage for women. This largely explains the flatter trend in the female proportion single between 1851 and 1881, but thereafter the proportion of permanently single women rose sharply in spite of the rising sex ratio. The proportion of men and women still single at age 45–54 reflects, of course, the conditions prevailing in the marriage market some 20 years earlier rather than the current situation. The CMR was at a low level in the 1830s and rose to a peak in the 1860s before falling again to a very low level in the 1890s (figure 10.11). The fluctuations in the proportions single in table 10.4 therefore correspond closely to the earlier changes in the CMR. The increase in the proportion of women never marrying from 12 to 16 per cent between 1881 and 1911 would have reduced the female GRR by between 4 and 5 per cent, *ceteris paribus*. It seems therefore that the combined effect of a rising marriage age and a rising proportion never marrying in the later nineteenth century would have sufficed to reduce the GRR by between 10 and 15 per cent from its 1871 peak, quite apart from fall in marital fertility occurring in the same period.

Neither improving standards of living nor the possibility of limiting fertility within marriage persuaded late-Victorian men and women to embark on marriage younger or more generally. They turned away from the marriage patterns of earlier generations, throttling back fertility by changes in behaviour which all tended to produce the same effect – later marriage, a rising proportion never marrying, fertility control within marriage, even a fall in illegitimate fertility;[73] and all this during a period when real incomes were rising steadily in secular trend. The whole represents a clear break with the nuptiality and fertility patterns of earlier centuries, a demographic revolution to match the economic revolution three quarters of a century earlier.

The lag between real-wage and fertility changes

Although the nature and functioning of the social and economic institutions that produced the long lag between a change in the trend of real wages and a corresponding change in fertility will not be fully understood without much further work, the fact that there were wide slow oscillations in fertility which broadly mirrored the real-wage fluctuations but with a time lag of about 40 years is of the greatest interest in itself. Fertility responded to real-wage changes and vice-versa as if the system were operating homeostatically but with very slow feedback between the two components, resulting in a wide, leisurely swings about a notional equilibrium point.[74]

To gain some insight into the implications of the relation between real wages and fertility changes which have been described earlier we may begin by considering a simplified scheme in which mortality is assumed to remain at a constant level so that changes in the population growth rate are a function of the fluctuating level of fertility.

72. The fall in the sex ratio between 1851 and 1881 presumably reflects the sex differential impact of net migration and the rise in its scale from a low level in the 1830s and 1840s to a much higher level in the next two decades.
73. The illegitimacy ratios, expressed as a percentage of all births, in England and Wales for the quinquennia centring on the years 1851, 1861, 1871, 1881, 1891, and 1901, were as follows: 6.68, 6.44, 5.50, 4.84, 4.35, and 3.94. Mitchell and Deane, *British historical statistics*, pp. 29–30. On the deficiencies of the ratio as a measure of the phenomenon, however, see Drake, 'Norway', pp. 299–306.
74. The range of feedback mechanisms connecting a pre-industrial population and its economy is discussed in Schofield, 'Demographic structure and environment'.

We have already noted that the early modern English economy appears to have been able to sustain a population growth rate of about 0.25–0.50 per cent per annum without adversely affecting real wages.[75]

In the prolonged period of falling real wages in the sixteenth and early seventeenth centuries fertility was also falling but for most of the period it remained sufficiently high to cause a population growth rate above the level at which real wages could be sustained or increased. Then, from about the time of Charles I's accession until after the Restoration real wages were rising because fertility had fallen sufficiently to bring population growth rates down to a very modest level, but fertility was still falling because its response to any real-wage change was so dilatory. For most of Charles II's reign, indeed, the intrinsic growth rate was actually negative with fertility at a very low absolute level. During this period, therefore, there was no renewed population pressure to check whatever beneficial effects might flow from rising real wages, which may be presumed both to have increased the volume of demand and to have changed its structure. Moreover, even after fertility had begun to rise again there was a further period of about half a century when the GRR, though rising, was still at a modest level and intrinsic growth rates were low, posing no threat to the continued rise in real wages. Only towards the middle of the eighteenth century did the acceleration in the population growth rate cause pressure on real wages, producing for a time a situation that began to resemble that found in the later sixteenth century.

For about a century therefore, the economy was able to profit from the advantages that flow from a rising level of real income and to undergo structural change in consequence without provoking a population rise fast enough to threaten further progress.[76] The unusual length of this benign period was in part the gift of the economic/demographic régime which characterized early modern England. A régime in which the demographic response to changed economic circumstances was faster might well have experienced much greater difficulty in acquiring a sufficient momentum of growth and change to take advantage of a conjuncture of other factors and so permit an industrial revolution to take place. The mere existence of the régime was certainly not sufficient in itself to secure such a profound change. It may well have existed in England in earlier secular cycles without producing an industrial revolution, and it is possible that similar régimes may have existed elsewhere in Europe. Other equally necessary predisposing conditions were required if rapid economic development was to occur.[77] But the fact that the rolling adjustment between economic and demographic fluctuations took place in such a leisurely fashion, tending to produce large if gradual swings in real wages, represented an opportunity to break clear from the low-level income trap which is sometimes supposed to have inhibited all pre-industrial economies. A long period of rising real wages, by changing the structure of demand, will tend to give a disproportionately strong boost to demand for commodities other than the basic necessities of life, and so to sectors of the economy whose growth is especially important if an industrial

75. See above, pp. 409–12 and figure 10.4.
76. This process, which Coleman recently described as 'the divergence of England' to mark the contrast between English and continental experience (Coleman, *The economy of England*, ch. 11), was reflected in the material possessions of men as well as in the production techniques in use. The connexion between these two related developments is discussed in Machin, 'The great rebuilding'. The article contains persuasive evidence of the great increase in the resources devoted to house construction and improvement during the century between 1640 and 1740, a period when population growth was very slight, and real wages were rising substantially.
77. These are reviewed in Wrigley, 'The process of modernisation .

revolution is to occur. The 'iron law of wages' did not apply to early modern England, where on the contrary the magnitude of the fluctuations in real wages is striking.[78]

The régime of economic and demographic fluctuations appears to have been symmetrical so that there were prolonged periods of deepening distress and falling real wages, such as took place in Elizabethan England, no less than of rising prosperity. Eventually a downturn in real wages was followed by a fall in fertility, and the fertility fall of the sixteenth and seventeenth centuries supervened early enough to avoid the worst miseries of Malthus's positive check. Indeed, as we have seen, mortality was not greatly increased even when real wages were at their lowest. But the delayed response to altered circumstances nonetheless caused two or three generations to suffer from sharply falling standards of living.

A similar malign period began in the later eighteenth century as the country moved towards the opposite extreme of the long cycle begun in the early seventeenth century. The continued rise in the GRR caused the population to begin to grow at a rate above that at which the prevailing level of real wages could be sustained. The equilibrium rate of economic growth was probably itself a little higher than in the sixteenth century,[79] but not high enough to match the late-eighteenth-century population growth rate. Real wages in consequence turned down after more than a century of steady growth, but fertility remained on a rising trend, reflecting the behaviour of real wages half a century earlier. Thus the difficulties experienced by the labouring masses in England at the time of the revolutionary and Napoleonic wars did not arise simply because of the special stresses of the war itself, nor as a result of the dislocations of the early decades of the industrial revolution, but were also a 'normal' result of their position in the economic/demographic cycle of early modern England. The period of immiseration in the half century ending about 1815 is what might have been expected in view of previous *pre-industrial* national experience, and did not represent a new or unlooked for turn of events. Throughout the early modern period fertility responded sluggishly to changes in the trend of real wages, and population growth was peculiarly liable to outstrip the growth in national income for several decades after the onset of a decline in real wages.

Very early in the new century, however, and at a time when population was growing rapidly, the real-wage curve turned up once more after a relatively short period of decline. This is vivid testimony to the marked acceleration in the rate of economic growth. To have sustained both a rising real wage and a rate of population growth of 1½ per cent per annum would have been far beyond the capacity of any pre-industrial economy. A radical break with the past had occurred. For a time, however, fertility change followed the long-established pattern. Given that there had been a downturn in real wages in the later eighteenth century it was to be expected that fertility would start to fall soon after 1800. As it happened real wages began to rise once more at much the same time that the GRR began to fall. If demographic data were available only, say, from the mid eighteenth century it would be tempting to

---

78. Ricardo contended that the 'natural price of labour' depended on 'the price of food, necessaries and conveniences required for the support of the labourer and his family'. He remarked that 'It is not to be understood that the natural price of labour, estimated even in food and necessaries, is absolutely fixed and constant', and he conceded that it depends in part on 'the habits and customs of the people', but he did not envisage major changes in the level of real wages and supposed that 'In the natural advance of society, the wages of labour will have a tendency to fall' because the supply of labour would tend to outrun demand. Ricardo, *Political economy*, pp. 115, 118, 121.

79. See especially, pp. 411–2.

suppose that the rise in real wages and the contemporary fall in fertility were related to one another. But it is probable that the coincidence was fortuitous; that the fertility change was not the result of the change of trend in the wage index about 1810 but rather of the change of trend in the opposite direction 30 years earlier. Viewed in a longer perspective, it seems evident the positive but lagged relation between real-wage and current-fertility trends continued well into the nineteenth century. Seen in this light the rise in real wages at the beginning of the nineteenth century should be linked to the modest rise in fertility that occurred in the 1840s and continued into the 1860s, rather than to the fall in fertility beginning in the 1810s.

The oddity of the century after 1750 did not lie in a change in the relation between the real wage and fertility but in the fact that the fall in real wages was reversed after less than half a century, a much briefer period than had previously occurred in the long swings of the economy since 1500. The reversal of trend took place because of the massive economic changes of the industrial revolution, but the traditional relation to prior changes in the real wage appears to have continued to govern changes in fertility trends until the 1860s, though the recovery in fertility from the mid 1840s to the mid 1860s was perhaps more muted than might have been expected from past experience. After the 1860s, however, the demographic revolution was as striking as the earlier economic changes that accompanied the industrial revolution. According to the canons of the traditional system the continued rise in real wages should have pulled fertility back up to the very high levels of the early nineteenth century. Instead after the mid 1860s it began the steady, long-continued decline which by the 1930s had taken the GRR below 1.00.

Much of the foregoing is oversimplified. The rate of population growth was never simply a function of fertility changes. Mortality changes may often have been less influential than those in fertility but they were substantial. And the volume of net migration was at times large enough to modify significantly the rates of population growth that would otherwise have occurred. Both mortality and migration, for example, were important in securing an exceptionally long period of rising real wages between the early seventeenth and mid eighteenth centuries. Expectation of life fell during most of the seventeenth century to reach a low point about 1680, and between 1630 and 1680 there was also a large net emigration from England which involved the loss of almost half a million from the population.[80] Had there been no worsening of mortality or rise in emigration during this period, population growth would have been slight because of the low fertility, but it would have remained positive. The level of population reached in 1656 was not again permanently surpassed for a further 80 years. This helped to ensure that the rising trend in real wages which began in the second quarter of the seventeenth century as population growth moderated was able to continue well into the eighteenth century. The unusual length of this benign period, therefore, cannot be explained without reference to mortality and migration trends even though the general pattern of economic/demographic changes was set by the response of fertility to real-wage trends.

Furthermore, to treat the PBH real-wage index as a reliable measure of the changing fortunes of the nation is to carry over-simplification to the point of caricature. For lack of an alternative it has been used in the argument of the chapter as if it were both reliable and representative of the trend in real income not only of the wage-paid minority but also of the population at large. We have previously

80. See above table 7.11.

stressed the defects of the index as a measure of wage trends.[81] It is proper also to emphasize that, even if it were a perfect wage index, it would not necessarily be a good guide to the trends in living standards generally. Especially in the earlier centuries a large proportion of the population was either not dependent upon wages for income or was dependent upon them only to a limited extent. Since the incomes of the owners of land and capital might move inversely with the incomes of those dependent upon the sale of their labour, the PBH index is necessarily an imperfect measure of changes in incomes as a whole. Furthermore, ideally one might wish to have a measure of family income rather than of the individual male adult wage. The two measures might diverge substantially with the spread or decay of by-employment in the household. And the PBH index can be only a guide to the wages of those in work, and will not reflect the prevalence of unemployment or underemployment. But it would be no less foolish to dismiss the index as an unsafe guide than to suppose it fully satisfactory. Its value in the context of our discussion of the relation between economic and demographic trends lies in its ability to reflect economic opportunity, and its various inadequacies as a measure of personal or family real income can be tolerated if it serves in this regard. The price paid for labour in the market must be powerfully influenced by the scale of opportunities to earn income in other ways, and it is therefore probable that a rough index of adult male wage rates answers, adequately if imperfectly, the needs of the argument just presented.

Our examination of the implications of the reciprocal relation between economic and demographic change is intended only as a plausible paradigm of the working of a central feature of English society in the past. It requires, and will benefit from, much further testing and modification. Its value lies in the different perspective that it can give to familiar problems. For example, it suggests that the threat to living standards, and perhaps at one remove to the gathering momentum of the industrial revolution, posed by the increasingly rapid population growth of the late eighteenth century would repay closer consideration. The magnitude of the growth in the productive powers of a society that could cope with the pace of population increase and still permit rising living standards after about 1810 needs no stressing. Real wages in the 1770s and 1780s were probably little more than stationary in the face of an annual population growth rate of less than 1 per cent. Fifty years later real wages were rising by perhaps 1 per cent per annum even though the annual population growth rate had risen to 1.5 per cent. Unless there was a remarkable change in the factor share of wages in national income in the interim, this suggests that the annual rate of growth in national income had risen from no more than 1 per cent to not less than 2.5 per cent.[82]

But if the achievement was spectacular it may nevertheless have been precarious. The volume, and especially the structure of home demand was under threat as long as the population growth rate was so far above the normal maximum rate of expansion of pre-industrial economics. The evidence of figure 10.3 suggests that until the end of the eighteenth century England was in danger of repeating the painful experience of the sixteenth century, to which for a time the later eighteenth bore an ominous resemblance. Only a major rise in the rate of growth of agricultural productivity could avert the danger.

Or again, it is noteworthy that the fact that a growing fraction of the workforce in

81. See above, pp. 407–8, 411–2.

82. There seems no reason to suppose that the factor share of wages changed greatly in this period, though precise information is lacking. The issue is reviewed in Deane and Cole, *British economic growth*, pp. 300–1.

the eighteenth century came to depend chiefly or solely upon wages for a livelihood does not appear to have undermined the long-standing relation between real-wage and fertility trends. It is perhaps surprising that a wage-paid proletariat should not have distorted the pattern set long ago by yeomen, husbandmen, and craftsmen. Possibly when there is better direct evidence about the behaviour of individual socio-economic groups, there will prove to be a variety that is concealed in the national aggregate, and this tentative conclusion will need to be modified. It may well be, moreover, that the very marked fall in marriage age in the eighteenth century and the consequent rise in fertility to an exceptionally high level owes something to the prevalence of early marriage among wage earners, whose share in the total population was growing.[83] But it is also possible that the response of wage earners to secular economic trends was not greatly dissimilar to that of other major elements in the population. The fall in fertility after about 1815 set in at much the same time as might have been expected in earlier centuries following a comparable, preceding change in real wages, and then continued for more than a generation, in spite of the rapid further growth of wage-dependent labour and the fact that real wages were rising. Malthus expressed fears about the 'irresponsibility' of agricultural labourers, corrupted by the malign effects of the Speenhamland system, but their large families do not appear to reflect failure to make an appropriate response to economic difficulties so much as a customary slowness in responding to changes in real income. The next generation behaved differently.

Age structural changes and the dependency ratio

Changes in fertility levels affected the living standards of the population not only through their impact on population growth rates, but also by modifying the age structure of the population. Population age structure is largely determined by fertility[84] and therefore the substantial changes in fertility levels occurring in early modern England necessarily entailed considerable alterations in the ratio of dependents to those of working age. Details of the changing age structure were given in chapter 7.[85] We look now at the economic consequences of changing fertility levels as they affected the dependency ratio.

Conventionally the dependency ratio is taken to be the number under 15 and over 65 per 1,000 people aged 15–64.[86] Given the relatively small proportion of people aged 65 and over in the past we have preferred to treat the number of those under 15 and over 60 per 1,000 people aged 15–59 as the dependency ratio. Since the proportion of the population under 15 was always so much greater than the proportion over 60, it is not surprising that the dependency ratio was determined by the former more than by the latter, and that consequently it was highest in 1826, following a period of very high fertility, and lowest in 1671 after the period of low fertility in the mid seventeenth century. As may be seen in figure 10.13 the ratio follows a bow-shaped curve through time, starting at about 780 dependents per 1,000 adults in the mid sixteenth century, falling to reach 624 in 1671, and then rising again to a peak of 857 in 1826, after which it fell back to about 760 in the mid nineteenth century. It

83. See Loschky and Krier, 'Income and family size' for evidence that points to this conclusion, albeit based on very slender empirical foundations.
84. See Coale, 'The effects of changes in mortality and fertility' for a discussion of this point.
85. See figure 7.4 and table A3.1.
86. Shryock and Siegel, *Methods and materials of demography*, pp. 133–4.

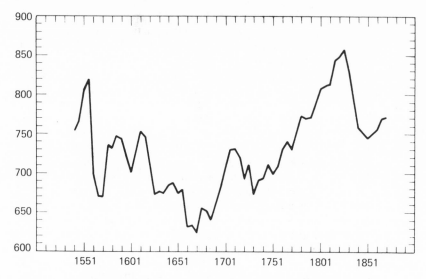

Figure 10.13: The dependency ratio 1541 – 1871

Note: The dependency ratio is taken as the number of those aged 0-14 and 60 or over per 1000 persons aged 15-59.

Source: Table A3.1.

was markedly affected by major mortality crises, and especially that of the late 1550s. In such periods the characteristic fall in the ratio was probably less in reality than appears on the graph because in times of crisis mortality the age structure of mortality changes and the use of a set of life tables intended to reflect the long-rather than short-term age structure of mortality may have caused the loss of child life to be exaggerated. It should also be noted that the dependency ratio in the mid sixteenth century is affected by the assumptions made about the size of birth cohorts before 1541. These are at best based on informed guesses, and the reconstruction of the age structure of the population in this period is therefore more uncertain than in later times.

The difference between the dependency burden in the late seventeenth century on the one hand and in the early nineteenth or mid sixteenth centuries on the other, appears large. In a period of rapid population growth adults had up to two fifths as many dependents again to support as they had in a period of stationary or falling population such as the later seventeenth century. Thus the period immediately before industrialization appears particularly fortunate in its age structure, while the process of industrialization itself seems to take place against the background of a steadily deteriorating ratio between dependents and adults. However, the dependency ratio in its crude form exaggerates the economic consequences of changes in the age structure, for children and old people both consumed less than adults and also contributed something to production. If age-specific schedules of production and consumption could be estimated, therefore, it would be possible to obtain a better measure of the effect of changes in the age-structure of the population on the total amount of production and consumption, and hence on the balance between them.

To prepare age-specific production and consumption schedules over a period of 350 years would be to embark upon a substantial research topic in its own right. Since, however, the present purpose is limited to improving upon the conventional dependency ratio as a guide to the economic consequences of changes in the age structure, a standard set of age-schedules of production and consumption, prepared for the study of contemporary peasant societies, has been taken as a basis for calculation.[87] The schedules are held constant over time so that changes in the total amounts of production and consumption simply reflect changes in the age structure of the population. The procedure is unreal in that it makes no allowance for changes that may have occurred historically either in the age-specific patterns or in other factors affecting production and consumption, but it is well suited to the present purpose which is to isolate and measure the impact of changes in age structure.

Table 10.5: Model age schedules of production and consumption

	Production units			Consumption units		
Age	Male	Female	Sexes combined	Male	Female	Sexes combined
0–4	0.000	0.000	0.000	0.320	0.320	0.320
5–9	0.000	0.000	0.000	0.520	0.480	0.500
10–4	0.150	0.090	0.120	0.820	0.680	0.750
15–9	0.750	0.280	0.515	1.000	0.800	0.900
20–54	1.000	0.300	0.650	1.000	0.800	0.900
55–9	0.600	0.130	0.365	0.900	0.720	0.810
60–4	0.600	0.130	0.365	0.800	0.640	0.720
65 and over	0.350	0.050	0.200	0.700	0.560	0.630

Source: Mueller, 'Economic value of children' p. 107 ('medium' consumption), and p. 118 ('standard' production).

Table 10.5 gives the basic model age schedules scaled so that an adult male both consumes and produces one unit. Amongst males consumption at ages 0–4 is about a third of adult consumption and increases rapidly through childhood; in contrast it falls relatively little in old age. Female infants consume as much as males, but from age 10 upwards their consumption is set at 80 per cent of that of males of an equivalent age. Children under age 10 contribute nothing to production and those aged 10–4 contribute very little. Amongst males there is a marked jump in production in the 15–9 age group which attains 75 per cent of the adult level. Full adult production is held until age 55, after which it falls to 60 per cent of the adult level over the next 10 years, and from age 65 it drops still further to about one third of the level attained by those aged 20–54. Female production is always low, reflecting the sex-specific allocation of 'non-productive' tasks such as housekeeping and child rearing.

Back projection makes no distinction between the sexes so in keeping with the approximate nature of the exercise a simple average was taken of the male and female age schedules.[88] In order to bring out the relative impact of changes in the age

87. Mueller, 'Economic value of children', discusses a range of age-specific production and consumption schedules appropriate to peasant societies. The schedules adopted here are Mueller's 'standard' production and 'medium' consumption schedules, since they seemed most appropriate for pre-industrial England.
88. It was assumed that there were equal numbers of males and females in each age group. With a model North pattern of mortality the sex ratios of children (0–14) and adults (15–59) varies between a maximum

structure, the production and consumption schedules have been scaled so that when they are applied to the least favourable age structure in 1826 the total amount of production and consumption each sums to 1,000 units. If these schedules are now applied to the populations found by back projection at different dates it is possible to observe by how much the total volumes of production and consumption per head changed relative to 1826 as a result of changes in the age structure. The results of this calculation along with the ratio between consumption and production at each date are shown in table 10.6 and figure 10.14.

Since the population was at its youngest in 1826 consumption per head was at its lowest and the figures for consumption at all other dates are above the 1826 level of 1,000, reaching a maximum of 1,053 in 1661, when the population was almost at its

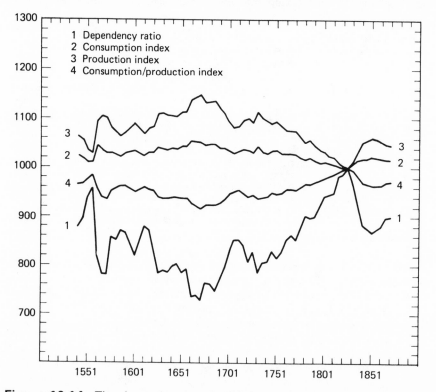

Figure 10.14: The dependency ratio, the consumption/production ratio, and indices of the effects on production and consumption levels of changes in the age structure of the population, 1541–1871 (1826 = 1000)

Note: The derivation of the ratios and indices shown is given in the notes to table 10.6.

Source: See table 10.6.

of 1,015 and a minimum of 955 (males per 1,000 females) across the range of mortality experienced between 1541 and 1871 (levels 5 to 10). The sex ratio of the elderly was 781 at level 5 and 841 at level 10. Coale and Demeny, *Regional model life tables*, pp. 224–9.

oldest. The same is true of production per head, but the older age structures of the pre-industrial period increased production proportionately more than consumption so that the production index reached a maximum of 1,146 in 1671 (1826 = 1,000).

Table 10.6: Dependency ratios, consumption/production ratios, and indices of the effects on production and consumption levels of changes in the age structure of the population, 1541–1871

(1) Dependency ratio
(2) Consumption index
(3) Production index
(4) Consumption/production ratio

	(1)	(2)	(3)	(4)		(1)	(2)	(3)	(4)
1541	878	1 023	1 062	964	1711	852	1 033	1 083	954
1546	895	1 018	1 055	966	1716	840	1 037	1 095	947
1551	938	1 009	1 034	976	1721	807	1 035	1 099	941
1556	957	1 010	1 027	984	1726	829	1 030	1 091	944
1561	815	1 045	1 093	956	1731	785	1 043	1 113	937
1566	781	1 035	1 104	938	1736	806	1 032	1 100	938
1571	780	1 028	1 101	934	1741	808	1 029	1 094	940
1576	857	1 028	1 080	951	1746	830	1 034	1 090	949
1581	851	1 025	1 071	957	1751	815	1 034	1 093	946
1586	871	1 020	1 062	961	1756	827	1 028	1 084	948
1591	866	1 027	1 069	961	1761	852	1 028	1 076	955
1596	844	1 031	1 078	956	1766	863	1 028	1 075	956
1601	818	1 033	1 088	950	1771	852	1 026	1 075	955
1606	848	1 027	1 077	954	1776	879	1 020	1 062	961
1611	879	1 023	1 067	959	1781	902	1 017	1 051	967
1616	870	1 029	1 079	954	1786	898	1 020	1 056	966
1621	829	1 030	1 082	952	1791	900	1 014	1 045	971
1626	784	1 040	1 108	939	1796	922	1 010	1 037	975
1631	789	1 038	1 109	936	1801	942	1 011	1 032	980
1636	786	1 035	1 105	937	1806	946	1 008	1 024	984
1641	797	1 038	1 105	939	1811	949	1 006	1 021	986
1646	802	1 037	1 103	939	1816	983	1 002	1 010	992
1651	785	1 042	1 111	937	1821	989	1 000	1 003	997
1656	792	1 042	1 113	937	1826	1 000	1 000	1 000	1 000
1661	736	1 053	1 136	927	1831	986	1 008	1 013	995
1666	739	1 052	1 142	921	1836	927	1 016	1 033	983
1671	728	1 050	1 146	916	1841	884	1 019	1 051	970
1676	764	1 044	1 131	923	1846	875	1 019	1 055	966
1681	761	1 046	1 133	923	1851	868	1 022	1 061	964
1686	747	1 046	1 134	923	1856	874	1 020	1 059	964
1691	770	1 039	1 120	927	1861	881	1 018	1 054	965
1696	793	1 038	1 110	935	1866	898	1 016	1 048	970
1701	826	1 033	1 092	946	1871	900	1 016	1 046	972
1706	852	1 028	1 081	951					

Notes: The dependency ratio is taken as the number of those aged 0–14 and 60 or over per 1 000 persons aged 15–59. The least favourable (highest) ratio occurred in 1826. Ratios at all other dates were indexed on 1826 (1 000). The age schedules of production and consumption from which the production and consumption indices were derived are given in table 10.5. Both were at their least favourable in 1826 because of the very high proportion of children under 15 at that date. Other values in both series are indexed on 1826 (1 000). The consumption/production ratio was obtained by dividing the consumption index figure by the production index figure at each date.

Source: Table A3.1.

Because the production index moved more favourably than the consumption index between 1826 and any other date the balance between the two indices as expressed by their ratio was always better (lower) at other dates than in 1826. In the mid sixteenth century, when the population was also comparatively young, the consumption/production ratio was about 970, implying an improvement of 3 per cent as compared with 1826. There was relatively little change in the age structure of the population between 1561 and 1621 and the consumption/production ratio remained on a plateau showing a surplus of 4–5 per cent relative to 1826. Then the ratio of consumption to production improved rapidly as the population became older, until in 1671 it reached 916, implying a gain of over 8 per cent when compared to 1826. This advantage was whittled away as the population became younger again during the eighteenth and early nineteenth centuries. The reduction was temporarily arrested during the early eighteenth century and in 1756 the consumption/production ratio was still 5 per cent more favourable than in 1826. Thereafter the movement towards a younger population gathered momentum and the relative advantage enjoyed by earlier populations was quickly extinguished. After 1826 the return towards a slightly older age-structure made up some of the ground lost in the early nineteenth century. By 1871 the consumption/production ratio had improved by 3 per cent since its least favourable point.[89]

Figure 10.14 also shows that changes in the age structure of the population affected the balance between production and consumption far less than is suggested by the dependency ratio. Both indices are at a minimum in 1671, and at a maximum of 1,000 in 1826, but the difference between the minimum and maximum values of the consumption/production ratio (8½ per cent) is only one third of the corresponding difference for the dependency ratio (27 per cent). Yet, although taking age-specific differences in consumption and production into account produces a less dramatic picture of the economic impact of changes in the age structure, the effect is still far from negligible in terms of the relative proportion of production that was surplus to consumption at different dates. The changing age structure of the population tended to reinforce the general implications of fertility fluctuations for living standards in early modern England. Periods of high fertility meant high population growth rates and declining real wages, but they also entailed a youthful age structure which produced an unfavourable consumption/production ratio. Conversely, the benefit to real wages brought about by low fertility and the absence of population growth was reinforced by an older age structure and the lower consumption/production ratio that accompanied it.

89. The results concerning the consumption/production ratio given here are not sensitive to alternative assumptions about the age schedules involved. For example, Professor Yasumoto has kindly made available to us data enabling an age-specific production schedule to be constructed for a farm belonging to the Earl of Mexborough in the parish of Methley in the West Riding of Yorkshire in the years 1792–4 and 1797–1801. The information is obtained by merging information drawn from the farm's wage books with family reconstitution details. Yasumoto, 'Industrialisation and population change', pp. 17–22.

The age weightings of the production schedule for the age groups 10–4 to 65 and over are as follows (expressed in such a way as to sum to 1.00): 0.088, 0.169, 0.211, 0.182, 0.175, 0.175. They are very different from the age weightings of table 10.4 when similarly expressed (0.054, 0.233, 0.293, 0.165, 0.165, 0.090), and it is not hard to suppose that they were far from representative of early modern England. Yet when these weightings are used with the same consumption schedules the changes in the results reported in table 10.6 are relatively minor. For example the consumption/production ratios for 1551, 1601, 1651 . . . 1851 in table 10.6 are as follows: 976, 950, 937, 946, 946, 980, and 964. The comparable ratios with Methley weightings are 967, 945, 931, 934, 944, 979, and 971. The Methley figures are lower with one exception, but the mean difference between parallel figures in the two series is only 6.

The changes in the balance between production and consumption summarized in figure 10.14, which sprang from the changing age structure of the population, may have been accompanied by changes in consumption patterns which carried similar implications. Generally speaking the younger the population the greater the proportion of consumption that is directed towards agricultural produce.[90] Thus the respite in the pressure of demand for agricultural produce afforded by the cessation of population growth in the later seventeenth century was reinforced by the relatively old age structure of the population, while as population growth accelerated in the later eighteenth century, the rising proportion of young people would have tended to cause demand for food to grow disproportionately quickly.

From the point of view of the non-agricultural sector of the economy, the years 1626–96 stand out as the period in which the age structure of the population was most favourable to demand; the rather low proportion of children allowed a higher proportion of consumption to be directed towards non-agricultural goods, producing more favourable balance between production and consumption which in turn provided a greater potential for saving and investment. The later sixteenth and early eighteenth centuries were a little less favourable, while during the late eighteenth and early nineteenth centuries the increasing proportion of children in the population both reduced the relative surplus of production available for saving or investment and swung the direction of consumption back towards the agricultural sector. Industrialization, therefore, occurred not only in the face of mounting population pressure, which for a time drove up agricultural prices and depressed real wages, but also in despite of a changing age structure which, as it grew younger, became progressively less favourable to a surplus of production over consumption and to the generation of a demand for non-agricultural goods. In *pre-industrial* terms this aspect of the demographic background to industrialization was far from propitious. The problems posed by an increased rate of population growth were aggravated by the age structural changes that accompanied it.

The significance of the absolute level of the dependency ratio and of any changes in its level has received much attention in recent discussions of the interaction of economic and demographic variables in relation to economic growth, but there are other aspects of the changing age structure of English population in the past that also merit attention. For example, as a result of the low level of fertility in the later seventeenth century there was a lengthy period when the proportion of the population aged 60 or over hovered just below 10 per cent, a very high figure for a pre-industrial society. Indeed, the national figure did not again exceed this level until 1931. By the early nineteenth century the percentage had fallen by a third to about 6.5 per cent (see figure 7.4 and table A3.1). The social implications of these changes warrant further investigation. During the period when the over-60s constituted almost 10 per cent of the population the ratio of those aged 25–59 to those aged 60 and over lay between 4:1 and 4.5:1. In the mid nineteenth century it rose above 5.5:1 for a time. Since the overwhelming bulk of the married population were to be found in the 25–59 age group, the relative burden of the care of the elderly, in so far as it fell upon individual married couples, was substantially greater in the seventeenth than in the nineteenth century, even though the overall dependency ratio was more favourable in the earlier period. And the difference in the ratios understates the true extent of the contrast

90. *Determinants and consequences of population trends*, 1, pp. 438–40. On the general issues discussed in this section see also Spengler, 'Demographic factors and early modern economic development'.

considerably since age at marriage and the proportions never marrying were both higher in the late seventeenth century than in the mid nineteenth.

Again, the age groupings used to calculate the conventional dependency ratio are arguably inappropriate in some respects for pre-industrial England. If we assume, for example, that those aged 15–24 were commonly out in service and had ceased either to burden their families of origin or to contribute to their budgets, and, for simplicity's sake, that they also made no *net* contribution to the budgets of the families with whom they were in service, then a special interest may attach to the ratio of those aged 0–14 (dependent children) to those aged 25–59 (the married population which would have to support them). The ratio varied quite dramatically over time, for whereas in 1826, when the population was at its youngest, there were 1,120 children under 15 for every 1,000 adults between 25 and 60, in 1671 the comparable figure was only 657. This represents an even more striking contrast than the opposite change in the ratio of the elderly to those aged 25–59 which we have already noted. The overall dependency. ratio, if calculated in relation to the 25–59 age group rather than the 15–59 age group, is also more volatile than the conventional dependency ratio, but the overall ratio is something of an abstraction. The young and the old deserve separate consideration. They entail different social and psychological stresses and rewards. Moreover, in pre-industrial England many of the old lived in their own households or even in institutional care, whereas young children outside the parental household were a rarity. That the ratio of dependent children to the married population should have fluctuated so greatly in the past is a fact whose implications are likely to reward further study and analysis.

Conclusion

In any agricultural economy in which productivity per man and per acre is either stationary or rises only very slowly, rapid population growth spells disaster unless there are still large areas of virgin land to be taken up. This was the truism to which Malthus directed attention so effectively. He himself, even in the first edition of the *Essay on the principle of population*, was cautious in drawing conclusions about the implications of the tension between population growth and prosperity. But to others it has seemed clear that there was a pattern in pre-industrial demography arising from its basic characteristics. Fertility was high, and mortality could not be other than high also, its high level being maintained not by matching fertility year in year out but by intermittent, savage mortality spasms which pruned the population back sharply.[91] In most years, according to this view, there are surpluses of births and the population may grow quite rapidly but, since the productive capacity of the community cannot match its power of demographic increase, each such interlude of growth is terminated by a mortality surge which may wipe out the gains of a generation in a matter of months. This was the characteristic cycle of events portrayed by Goubert in the

91. 'However poor, the material available tends to suggest that any agricultural society . . . tends to adhere to a definite set of patterns in the structure and movements of birth and death rates. Crude birth rates are very high. . . . Death rates are also very high, but *normally* lower than birth rates. . . . The population of an agricultural society is characterised by a normal rate of growth of 0.5 to 1.0 per cent per year. . . . throughout the demographic history of agricultural societies, death rates show a remarkable tendency to recurrent, sudden dramatic peaks that reach levels as high as 150 or 300 or even 500 per thousand . . . . The intensity and frequency of the peaks controlled the size of agricultural societies'. Cipolla, *Economic history of world population*, pp. 76–7.

Beauvaisis.[92] Anyone who lived to old age in a community of this type could expect to have survived two or three periods in which the deprivation and disease brought on by poor harvests killed anything up to a fifth or more of the population in a single season of mortality. Since such times of stress were usually local or regional, the pattern would be less clear-cut nationally, but even averaged out across a country the existence of local crises would ensure a high and fluctuating death rate. This was the high-pressure equilibrium between population and resources that trapped most men in poverty and misery.

Early modern England, no less than other pre-industrial economies, was constrained by the difficulty of achieving rapid increases in productivity. The major improvements in agricultural technique introduced during the sixteenth and seventeenth centuries may have allowed more rapid economic progress to be made in England than was common elsewhere but growth was still very modest by the standards of the post-industrial world. Yet England patently did not conform to the high-pressure paradigm. An accomodation between population and resources was secured not by sudden, sharp mortality spasms, but by wide, quiet fluctuations in fertility, which in their downward phase reduced fertility levels to the point where population growth ceased even though mortality was still low by the standards of other pre-industrial societies. In contrast to the mortality-dominated high-pressure equilibrium sometimes regarded as generally present in all pre-industrial societies, England experienced a fertility-dominated low-pressure system. It was a system capable of achieving a balance between population and resources, but it is perhaps misleading to describe it as an equilibrium system since one of its most striking features was the remarkable slowness of response between economic (real-wage) and demographic (fertility) changes. There were slow but substantial oscillations in both fertility and the real wage, reminiscent of a graph of room temperature in a house in which there is a very long delay between a change in the reading on a room thermostat and a reaction in the central-heating boiler. England displayed what might be termed dilatory homeostasis, winning the war of adjustment, but doing so by employing a strategy appropriate to yesterday's circumstances. Indeed, the operation of the 'English' system only becomes visible with the benefit of a wide-angle lens covering several centuries. In close-up only the lack of adjustment may be visible, a perspective that explains Malthus's concern at the end of the eighteenth century.

The existence of a pattern connecting changes in fertility and the real wage, and the absence of such a pattern in the case of mortality seems clear at the national level, but one might have greater confidence in the general validity of this conclusion if it could be verified regionally. It would be particularly interesting, if and when regional fertility and real-wage data become available, to find out whether the timing of fertility changes was different in those areas, like Lancashire, where real-wage trends diverged from the national pattern in the early decades of the industrial revolution.[93] Similarly, it would be instructive to discover whether the absence of sympathetic secular changes in mortality in response to real-wage changes, which is so striking in the case of national data, is equally hard to find, say, in the north-west in the first

---

92. Goubert, *Beauvais et le Beauvaisis*, 1, pp. 45–59.
93. Deane and Cole have attempted 'highly tentative' estimates of the level of county birth rates for the periods 1701–50, 1751–1800, and 1801–30, but their estimates are based on Rickman's data and Brownlee's correction factors applied uniformly to all counties. It is unlikely that the results represent a reliable guide to regional fertility trends. Deane and Cole, *British economic growth*, p. 131, table 29, and more generally pp. 106–35.

century of parochial registration, for in this part of the country subsistence crises continued to occur from time to time at least until 1623.[94]

Furthermore, an international setting is as important as regional data for a better assessment of the significance of the findings about English historical demography in relation to its economic environment. We need to know how far English experience diverged from that of other European countries, and in particular whether comparable time lags in adjustment may have characterized other countries.

Other solutions to the tension between population growth and economic resources are possible, apart from the worst rigours of the positive check. In later eighteenth-century France, for example, a new means of securing low levels of general fertility began to appear quite widely. This was the deliberate restriction of fertility within marriage, a solution adopted more and more widely in the nineteenth century. Though subsequently much regretted by French writers with populationist views, the deliberate limitation of fertility within marriage was capable of securing great benefits to a pre-industrial society continually menaced by the tendency of population growth to outstrip any growth in productive capacity. It was also likely to involve less time lag in adjustment than the system that obtained in England. Had the economic constitution of western Europe remained largely unchanged, it might have been of substantial advantage to the French people as the nineteenth century wore on and other parts of Europe moved towards an 'Irish' fate.

The adoption of a new method of fertility control in France may have been connected with a lack of previous success in securing a satisfactory economic/demographic balance. Sauvy once calculated that the optimum population of France in the late eighteenth century was 10 to 12 million at a time when her actual population was 24 million.[95] If this were so, it suggests that older mechanisms of adjustment were comparatively ineffective. If, as Goubert once suggested, grain prices were a barometer of mortality in early modern France,[96] any equilibrium attained must have been uncomfortably close to the high-pressure end of the spectrum. If adjustment took place primarily through an increase in mortality as conditions deteriorated, and if this was the case not just in short-term crises but in secular trend also, French conditions must have been harsher than English. Certainly, mortality was much higher in France than in England,[97] but this is not conclusive evidence in itself since mortality levels were affected by many factors other than the standard of living. Only if mortality levels showed a clear tendency to be affected by secular changes in real income would the case be established.

The absence of any pattern linking economic conditions and mortality in England is no less striking than the presence of a clear pattern in the case of fertility. There is no clearly discernible relation between secular real-wage trends and mortality changes, and indeed mortality only fluctuated within a comparatively modest range. If the individual figures of expectation of life shown in figure 10.5 are expressed as a

94. The regional patterning of mortality crises is discussed on pp. 670–85.

95. Sauvy, *Théorie générale de la population*, 1, pp. 186–7.

96. Goubert, *Beauvais et le Beauvaisis*, 1, pp. 75–6.

97. See figure 7.13. Duvillard's estimate of expectation of life at birth for the sexes combined was 29 years, and it is believed to refer to a period about 1770 (Bourgeois-Pichat, 'The general development of the population of France', pp. 480, 494). His table was published in 1806, but modern scholarship has arrived at a very similar conclusion. Blayo, for example, concludes that in the period 1740–89 expectation of life at birth for men was under 27 years and for women just over 28 years (Blayo, 'La mortalite en France de 1740 a 1829', p. 137). During the same period expectation of life at birth in England averaged 36 years for the sexes combined, a marked difference (table A3.1).

five-point moving mean (i.e. represent data covering 25-year periods), they never drop below 32 years nor rise higher than 41 years. They contradict both the view that pre-industrial mortality was always high and that it had fallen between Elizabethan times and the mid eighteenth century. There were a few brief periods, especially 1557–9, 1679–86, and 1727–31, when the relative tranquility of English mortality was severely disturbed, and a scattering of other isolated years when the death rate was well above its normal level, but such occasions were probably less common and less severe in England than elsewhere in western Europe. And periods of high mortality usually occurred because of the independent and unpredictable visitations of infectious disease. They were rarely related to economic conditions.[98] Endemic infectious diseases made infancy and early childhood dangerous, but during most of English history between Elizabethan and Victorian times a young man or woman of 20 could look forward on average to a further 35– 40 years of life.

In spite of the several intriguing features of English mortality history revealed by back projection, however, it seems proper to lay prime stress on the remarkable features of the history of nuptiality and fertility in England when reviewing the 250-year period before the onset of the industrial revolution. Given that there were very substantial fluctuations in the gross reproduction rate during this period, and that the fluctuations appear to have borne a close relation to secular economic trends; and given further that this relation both helped to secure the country from periods of misery dominated by the positive check, and at times made possible a sustained rise in real wages, it is natural to wonder how far the peculiarities of the English marriage system, whose operation caused the fluctuations in fertility, may have served to initiate or facilitate the economic changes that culminated in the industrial revolution. The issues are complex and any attempt to resolve them may prove premature. But population trends, productivity, and economic growth were so intimately linked and so fundamental to the constitution of pre-industrial societies that the issues merit a fuller discussion. We shall attempt to examine some of them in the next chapter.

98. See above, table 8.8 and pp. 320– 32.

11

Conclusion: a dynamic model of the relationship between population and environment in early modern England

This is a large book but it leaves much unfinished, indeed barely begun. In this concluding chapter we shall first attempt to establish the status of our earlier findings, pointing to the deficiencies of knowledge and method of which we are conscious, and then go on to place the findings in their wider setting, and to suggest some possibilities for further work.

The reliability of the results presented earlier in the volume

The book is subtitled a *reconstruction* of the population history of England. The choice of title was deliberate. The source materials available are far too imperfect for any such history to be based directly upon demonstrably reliable and complete data. Parish registers, from which the bulk of the useful information must be gleaned, are defective guides to the totals of vital events that occurred in the past. And even if this had not been so, the absence of censuses before the nineteenth century would have posed a serious problem since what can be inferred from a knowledge of the total of vital events alone is very limited using conventional techniques of analysis. Much of the book has therefore been taken up with a description of the complex series of steps taken to convert totals of baptisms and burials in a non-random sample of 404 Anglican parish registers into national estimates of births and deaths; and with an exposition of the technique of aggregative back projection devised to make the best possible use of the national birth and death totals once these had been derived.

As we have stressed at several previous junctures, the final outcome of the processing, correction, inflation, and demographic analysis of the original parish register data is necessarily subject to a margin of error. Totals of births, deaths, and marriages are printed to the final digit even when the totals themselves may run into hundreds of thousands, and the measures of fertility and mortality based upon them may be taken to the third decimal place. This was done to avoid the loss of information and cumulation of errors which rounding at each successive stage would have entailed, but the appearance of accuracy conveyed by results reproduced in this form is, of course, deceptive. When the best efforts of the modern bureaucratic state are unable to ensure precision in the demographic data that it collects,[1] it is not to be expected that uncertainty can be eliminated from estimates of fertility and mortality relating to a period beginning more than 400 years ago. But an exaggerated scepticism about the results presented is equally uncalled for.

To substantiate this claim it is convenient first to consider back projection as a

---

1. For example, the U.S. census of 1950 appears to have returned a figure for the total population of the country about 1.4 per cent lower than the true total, with much greater inaccuracies in certain sub-categories: Hansen *et al.*, 'The accuracy of census results', p. 420.

technique, and then to review the effects of possible data errors. We may note first that back projection has exact internal accounting. All the births and deaths taking place in each quinquennium are 'used', and the final (earliest) population total will be equal to the initial (latest) population total after subtracting the total of births occurring between the two dates and adding the totals of deaths and the estimated totals of net migration. It is true that the accuracy of the results obtained is not solely a function of the precision with which birth and death totals were previously estimated. The results are also influenced by the structure of the family of life tables employed in allocating deaths to individual age groups, by the age-specific schedule of net migration used, by the decision made about the size of the age group 90–4 introduced at the top of the age pyramid of the starting population, and by the way in which data from earlier passes are used as the program makes further passes through the data. Fortunately, the extent of the potential inaccuracies introduced by these factors can be estimated by carrying out simulations in which the effects of making extreme assumptions about alternative possibilities are examined. It can be shown that their influence, though not insignificant, could not be such as to change the results obtained in a way that would modify any major findings other than marginally.[2] Moreover, the fact that there are censuses available as a check upon the operation of back projection during the first 70 years 1801–71, and that by this criterion it performs very well, gives additional confidence in its general accuracy.[3]

To claim that back projection is a robust technique whose results would not be greatly changed by altering the assumptions made about the range of parameters necessary to its functioning is not, of course, to claim that the results obtained cannot be improved upon. It is known, for example, that the age structure of mortality in England changed between the sixteenth and seventeenth centuries,[4] but the age structure embodied in the family of life tables used in the present generation of back-projection runs is invariant.[5] Although it can be shown that even a drastic change in the age structural assumptions used does not make a radical difference to the findings of back projection,[6] a future version of the program that incorporated a facility for progressively modifying the age structure of the life tables used would represent a useful advance. It would make only small differences to fertility and mortality estimates, but might improve the precision of estimates of both the scale and timing of net migration.

The best and most sophisticated technique cannot, of course, be proof against serious defects in the empirical data. The original data, consisting of monthly totals of the baptisms, burials, and marriages recorded in Anglican parish registers, were so greatly in need of correction to offset various causes of under-registration, and so far from constituting a random sample of the country's 10,000 ancient parishes, that the whole of the first part of the book was given over to a description of the measures taken to try to overcome these problems. It would be remarkable if the operation as a whole had been entirely successful: nor would the success be demonstrable even if it had been achieved. But here, too, sensitivity tests carried out using alternative data sets proved most illuminating in indicating the scale of changes in the final results that

2. See above, pp. 277–84.
3. See above, pp. 199–202.
4. See Schofield and Wrigley, 'Infant and child mortality'.
5. See appendix 15.
6. See above, pp. 277–84.

different corrections to the original totals of baptisms and burials would entail.[7]

The tests showed that any assumption about the inadequacy of the corrections made to the original data that involved increasing the number of births used in the main back-projection run by a greater proportion than the number of deaths would force up totals of net emigration to implausible levels unless the differential inflation of totals of events were modest. To make the opposite assumption (that death totals should be increased proportionately more than births), unless again the differential were modest, would produce net immigration, another implausible result. Increasing both births and deaths by similar proportions would increase the estimates of total population size but would leave the estimates of levels of fertility and mortality very little altered, and so would not affect, for example, discussions of the relationship between changes in real wages and changes in fertility and mortality. It is also possible by simulation to establish the effects of changing totals of births and deaths over a limited period of time while leaving totals at other periods unchanged.[8] All tend to show, however, that the findings of the main back-projection run are robust. Neither changes in the input parameters, nor changes in totals of events that have any claim to plausibility, appear likely to make a sufficiently big difference to the results to require major modifications to the results or arguments presented in the second half of the book.

There are other reasons for considering that the results obtained by back projection are broadly reliable. First, they accord very well with the findings of chapter 6 in which the same data were used in conjunction with simpler methods of analysis. Back projection makes possible a more extensive and sophisticated analysis of demographic trends, but there is no conflict between results derived in this way and those obtained by other techniques. A second weighty reason supporting the general accuracy of back projection is that shown indirectly in figure 7.15. This figure shows the results of attempting to estimate changes in the proportions never marrying between the sixteenth and nineteenth centuries. The method used can only produce plausible results if the totals of births and marriages bear a true relation to one another, and if the totals of deaths are generally correct and have been converted successfully into accurate estimates of the prevailing mortality level. If any of these conditions fail it is very unlikely that offsetting errors would produce a plausible result. There are special factors (especially the influence of differential net migration and the changing percentage of all marriages that were remarriages) that further complicate the exercise, and introduce some distortions that need to be allowed for in interpreting the results,[9] but the internal coherence between the three demographic series (births, deaths, and marriages) is nonetheless reassuring. This is especially so when it is remembered that marriage totals were used virtually unchanged whereas both birth and death totals were extensively corrected for various causes of under-registration. Third, it is reassuring that when a back projection was run using Swedish data for the city of Stockholm there was close agreement between the results obtained and independent measures of population size, age structure, and net immigration which are available for Stockholm for a period of two centuries.[10]

The reliability of the back-projection results is probably least in the sixteenth century and particularly before about 1580. This is partly because some types of

7. See pp. 269–77 and figures 7.16, 7.17, and 7.18.
8. See above, pp. 270–1, where simulation 3 is of this type.
9. See above, pp. 257–65.
10. See below, pp. 733–6.

mistakes both in input parameters and in data can produce errors of estimation which cumulate, and since such mistakes must be present in some degree their impact will tend to be greater in the earliest period. But it is mainly because in order to obtain estimates of population size and demographic rates back to 1541, it is necessary to invent birth and death totals for the period 1446–1541.[11] The totals used were arrived at by taking a consensus view of the size of the English population in the mid fifteenth century and the phasing of population growth between then and 1541, to which was added an assumption of nil net migration. Clearly the resulting totals of births and deaths are far less securely founded than those derived from the parish registers for the period after 1541, and since their effect on the outcome of back projection becomes more and more pronounced as the program nears 1541, the results obtained grow less and less secure *pari passu*.

Back projection has tended to take pride of place in discussing the use made of the data obtained originally from the 404 parish registers forming the aggregative sample. The technique is new and has proved a powerful tool, but it would be unfortunate if its discussion were allowed to obscure the importance and dependability of the results obtained using other methods of analysis, and especially those concerning short-term rather than secular demographic trends. For the first time an exhaustive study of short-term fluctuations in each of the three demographic series has been possible. Their relation to each other and to economic and meteorological fluctuations has been examined. Because of the great length of the series it has been possible to distinguish changes over time both in the variance of the series themselves and in their relation to each other and to external factors. Related questions such as the seasonal patterning of events, and the intensity, prevalence, and duration of epidemic outbreaks have also been considered.

The studies of short-term variation were chiefly based on residual values after the trends in the series had been removed. Since the corrections made to the original data to offset the several causes of under-registration changed only slowly over time, their effect is limited to *trends* in the series. They have no bearing on the measurement of short-term variation. The results obtained would have been the same whatever the scale of the inflation factors applied to the original data. And the size of the raw totals of events taken from the parish registers before any corrections had been made to them was such as to reduce the influence of random fluctuations to a comparatively negligible level except in the earliest decades in the mid sixteenth century when few registers were in observation. Thereafter each original monthly total of baptisms or burials consisted of several hundred events, a reassuringly substantial number.

Modelling the setting of pre-industrial populations

Understanding flows from success in bringing different aspects of reality into a common framework within which their influence upon one another can be assessed. In general in the search for understanding there is a constant tension between clarity and comprehensiveness. If one is to be attained, the other must be sacrificed in some degree. And in the flux of history a framework that may prove adequate for one period is often irrelevant to another.

The three centuries between 1541 and 1871 include one of the most fundamental of all changes in the history of society. To describe the events of the late eighteenth and

11. See appendix 15 for details of the totals used.

early nineteenth centuries in England as an industrial revolution may be a misnomer in that the changes were spread over many decades, but the extent and significance of the changes were so great that there can be no doubt that their cumulative impact was revolutionary. The creation of more extensive and precise demographic information covering the whole period 1541–1871 by means of aggregative back projection opens up the possibility of examining demographic change in relation to economic change both before and during the industrial revolution and of finding a satisfactory framework within which the mutual accommodation between the two can be better understood. Models of such processes can be framed with greater confidence and tested more effectively, as we shall try to show.

It may be helpful to begin by considering a range of possible systems for keeping population and economy in balance that appear to have relevance for the description of pre-industrial west European experiences. A similar set of models has already been described elsewhere,[12] but the models need some modification and extension to serve as an appropriate point of entry for the discussion of the implications of the findings of back projection. They are set out diagrammatically in figures 11.1 to 11.5, presenting sets of relations between the demography of a community and its economic characteristics in a highly schematic fashion.

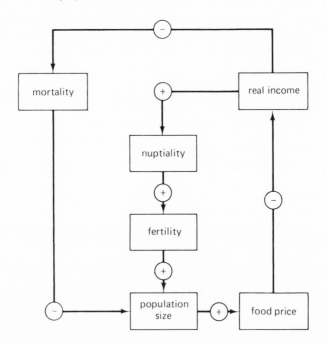

Figure 11.1: The positive and preventive checks

Malthus's view of the question is summarized in figure 11.1. Rapid population growth continuing over a long period of time was impossible because agricultural production could not be expanded commensurately. Malthus envisaged two sets of

---

12. See Schofield. 'Demographic structure and environment'.

relationships that might serve to keep a population in balance with its food base, or more generally with its economic resources. These were the positive and the preventive checks, and they are shown in figure 11.1 as outer and inner negative feedback loops.[13] In both cases an increase in population is associated with a rise in food prices and hence with a fall in real incomes. Since the supply of cultivable land is fixed, at some point there must be diminishing returns to both capital and labour if attempts are made to expand production further. Therefore the prices of all agricultural products will tend to rise if population increases, at least beyond some threshold level (or, in an economy in which there is slow improvement in technology, some threshold rate).

Where the positive check operates this causes mortality to rise and so moderates, halts, or reverses the rise in population. But the fall in real incomes may also depress nuptiality and through it fertility, thus achieving the same effect on population size by a different mechanism, which Malthus called the preventive check. Both may, of course, operate simultaneously. A fall in population will produce symmetrical but opposite changes in food prices and in the demographic variables which in turn will cause population numbers to be restored to a higher level.

Though both keep population and resources in balance, the implications of the two systems of the positive and the preventive check are substantially different, as may be seen from a consideration of figure 11.2. If the preventive check is entirely in abeyance and fertility levels do not vary with population size, the reduction in population growth rates and the eventual attainment of an equilibrium population comes about as a result of rising mortality and will cause the equilibrium population total to be higher than would be the case if the preventive check were also operating. As a result real incomes will be lower than they might otherwise have been. Where the preventive check also exists an equilibrium population will be reached at a lower absolute size of population and with higher real wages. It may be noted that the absolute level of fertility may be as important in determining real incomes as its sensitivity to the growth of population. If fertility is relatively low (fertility 2 in figure 11.2), the level of real incomes will benefit even though fertility is insensitive to population size. Thus in pre-industrial west European societies where fertility levels were modest because age at marriage was high (the classical form of the preventive check) the resulting equilibrium population for this reason alone would be lower and real incomes higher than would be possible under an 'Asiatic' régime where fertility was at a high absolute level. The equilibrium population P_2 will enjoy higher living standards than that at P_1.

The operation of the preventive check, however, is not necessarily confined to producing a lower general fertility level. It may also vary fertility levels in response to prevailing conditions. Population P_{2a} is still more favourably placed than population P_2. In this population not only are fertility levels always relatively modest but they also fall when population rises beyond a certain level. In those west European populations in which marriage took place some years after sexual maturity and was also responsive in timing or incidence to economic circumstances and prospects the equilibrium population might occur quite close to the optimum. The graph of fertility

13. Negative feedback may be said to exist when a change in one element within a system sets in train changes elsewhere in the system that tend to restore the original equilibrium state. Positive feedback, in contrast, denotes a set of relationships such that an initial change becomes accentuated by the changes elsewhere in the system that it provokes.

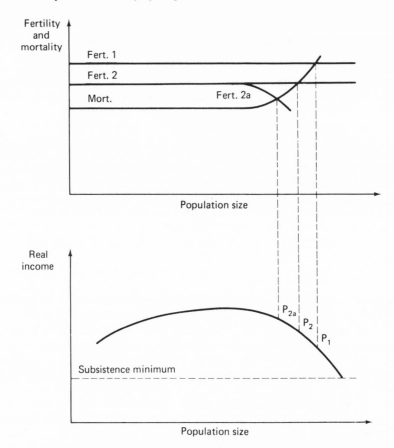

Figure 11.2: Fertility, mortality, and real income

2a as drawn in figure 11.2 cuts the mortality graph just after mortality has begun to rise; both display sensitivity to increasing population pressure before their combined changes bring population growth to a halt. But it is quite possible, of course, to envisage circumstances in which fertility would be more responsive than mortality to growing numbers and population growth would stop before mortality had begun to rise. In such a case the preventive check alone would determine the point at which population growth ceased.

How frequently the various theoretical possibilities occurred in reality it is not as yet possible to assess except in the case of early modern England. But it seems clear that where the preventive check was inadequate to prevent rising numbers the increase in food prices and the consequent fall in living standards must at some point cause the death rate to rise and so restore the balance between mouths and available food. In such cases the positive check loop was, so to speak, the court of last resort for overcoming the problem of population growth. Where the preventive check did not exist at all it was also the court of first resort. Even where the preventive check operated powerfully the positive check might come into play from time to time, since the preventive check, operating slowly through nuptiality, is incapable of securing abrupt and substantial short-term adjustments between a population and its available resources, such as may be necessary in time of famine. In the wake of harvest failure a rise in mortality may be the only way of achieving what a fall in nuptiality or the direct physiological effects of malnutrition on fertility could not achieve. Where the preventive check did not exist both long- and short-term adjustments had to be made by varying the level of mortality, combined with whatever effect undernourishment had upon the level of fertility.

It is characteristic of the Malthusian system that the factors affecting its operation are all endogenous to it. But this is a very restrictive assumption, and other systems have been suggested in which exogenous influences have a powerful influence. A very simple ecological niche system is shown in figure 11.3. In it mortality is exogenously determined. It would capture certain key relations in a community in

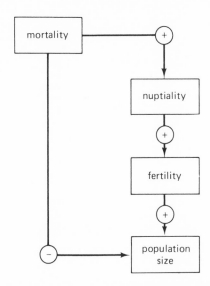

Figure 11.3: A system of ecological niches

which the possibility of marrying was contingent upon securing access to a peasant holding or craft workshop following the death of an existing household head, and where the number of such niches was fixed. The system ensures an almost constant ratio between a population and its resource base without invoking economic factors such as food prices or real incomes. An increase in mortality, by causing deaths among existing niche-holders, creates marriage opportunities which will raise fertility sufficiently to offset the higher mortality; and, equally, a reduction in the prevailing mortality level will depress fertility by restricting marriage opportunities. It can be shown that changes in the timing and incidence of marriage within the range commonly found in pre-industrial western Europe were large enough to offset the changes in mortality level commonly experienced.[14] Since a death in the older generation and a marriage in the younger are linked events, age at marriage will be approximately the same as expectation of life at the mean age at paternity. The system

14. Ohlin, 'Mortality, marriage and growth'.

need not create such severe difficulties for younger sons as might appear at first sight because many men will die without direct heirs and many more without male heirs, thus creating marriage opportunities for men who might have no expectations at their fathers' deaths.[15] Since the number of niches is assumed to be fixed, the number of married couples is also invariant and, in its pure form, a system of this type will regulate population very effectively. It is reminiscent of the situation found among some species of birds which breed only after gaining control of an individual territory.[16]

Mortality may also be exogenously determined in a less simplistic system than that of figure 11.3. And another exogenous force may also powerfully influence the operation of the system if demand for labour is in part exogenously determined. In figure 11.4 both these possibilities are represented. The system is kept in balance by

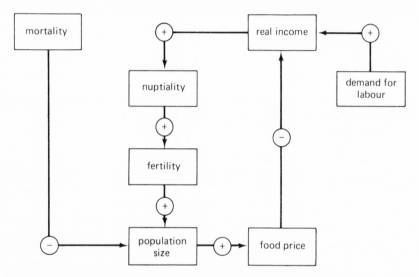

Figure 11.4: Exogenous influences on a preventive check system

the preventive check. It embodies the assumption that there are conventional prerequisites of marriage whose character will influence the rate at which marriages are formed, and that the ability to meet the prerequisites is a function of the level of real incomes. For example, the convention that each newly married couple should begin life in a separate dwelling and should command the resources to equip it to accepted standards might provide the necessary discipline. In times of high incomes the required saving might be achieved by the early twenties, but in harsher times a longer delay would be inevitable, and might also mean that an increased proportion of men and women would never marry. If exogenously determined mortality and the demand for labour do not vary, the level of real incomes will oscillate about the same average level (the equilibrium real wage), with wide variations if the feedback system operates sluggishly but with little variation if adjustment is rapid.

15. See Wrigley, 'Fertility strategy'.
16. See Wynne-Edwards, *Animal dispersion*, pp. 145–51.

Both exogenous factors, however, may impinge severely upon the operation of the system. For example, if mortality became more severe (perhaps because of the introduction of new and virulent diseases), a new equilibrium position would in time appear with both fertility and real incomes at a higher level than previously (see figure 11.2). Equally, the level of real incomes may be affected by influences external to the local or even to the national system. The box showing 'demand for labour' in figure 11.4 represents demand from a distance, international demand, whose level is not determined by the functioning of the local system. The demand may arise because of the existence of foreign markets for any type of product, agricultural or industrial, but the box may stand especially for the type of demand for industrial goods, notably cloth or other textile products, which is met by workers, sometimes called proto-industrial,[17] who may no longer own their productive equipment, nor even the raw materials upon which they work. The existence of such demand may sustain demand for labour and hence real incomes at a relatively high level, and so provoke population growth, for far longer than would be possible within a locally closed system, but it does not, of course, represent a final escape from the negative feedback of the simpler situation. The larger system, just like the smaller, is subject to the overall constraints of any pre-industrial economy. Connexion to the larger whole makes for more dizzying alternations in fortune, with wider fluctuations in the level of real wages, but it does not afford any general relief. Indeed, if international demand should fail after a long period of prosperity, the process of contraction will entail greater miseries than would arise within a local system.

So far we have concentrated on characteristics of pre-industrial economies that promoted negative feedback, and on the possible effects of demographic or economic factors exogenous to the local system. It is clearly proper to give first attention to the elements within the system whose relationship promotes negative feedback since by definition they must predominate in a pre-industrial economy. What is meant, indeed, by a pre-industrial economy is a system in which movements of incipient expansion cannot fructify in a sustained exponential growth, but rather tend to provoke changes that will make continued growth more and more difficult to secure.[18] But elements of positive feedback were never wholly absent, and it is also true by definition that during the industrial revolution they came to predominate over the forces that had always previously restrained or reversed growth. To these positive elements therefore, we now turn.

We may begin by noting that even within the web of relations already considered there are latent possibilities of positive feedback. For example, it is natural to expect that if there is a link between the real income and mortality it will be negative. High real incomes, other things being equal, will lower death rates, and vice versa. But higher real wages may produce other changes that work in the opposite sense, and may outweigh the direct effect, which in any case is unlikely to be marked unless real incomes are very low. Where real incomes are high and rising, they will powerfully stimulate demand for industrial goods since the income elasticity of demand for such goods is relatively high. They will also cause a sharp increase in demand for tertiary services. Both types of demand are likely to be met chiefly by town dwellers, and

17. See, for example, Mendels, 'Proto-industrialisation'; Levine, *Family formation*; Medick, 'The proto-industrial family economy'.
18. See Wrigley, 'The process of modernisation'.

towns will therefore grow rapidly.[19] But in pre-industrial societies high population densities normally meant high death rates so that through this chain of connexion the effect of a rise in real incomes may tend to slacken population growth rather than to increase it, as may be seen in figure 11.5. The possibility is not purely theoretical. Holland in the later seventeenth century appears to have experienced a cessation in population growth which may be accounted for at least in part in this way.[20] It is a conjunction of circumstances that may serve to keep real incomes at a stable and relatively high level, though it is not the type of relation that could initiate sustained growth over a long period.

Figure 11.5 is intended to summarize the discussion so far by incorporating all the links already discussed, and to extend it to include some positive feedback loops which may tend to destabilize the system. The two negative loops form an inner and an outer circle in the centre of the figure and have already been described. This area of the figure, however, also contains a new path. Changes in net migration, which here denotes immigration less emigration, are shown as tending to be positive when real incomes rise and labour is likely to be attracted in, but negative when the opposite is the case. The possibility of important exogenous influences on mortality and the demand for labour is indicated in each case by an arrow from a circular rather than an oblong box. The figure differs from those shown earlier, however, chiefly because there are positive as well as negative feedback pathways within it.

One such positive feedback loop involving urban mortality has already been described. A more important potential loop is shown in the top right corner of the figure. There a rise (or fall) in real income is shown as tending to become intensified by stimulating (or reducing) the demand for the goods and services produced by secondary and tertiary industry, which by boosting (or depressing) the demand for labour, reinforces the trend in real wages. The presence of such a set of relations is a logical consequence of the assumption that income elasticity of demand for industrial products is above unity. As long as the preventive- or positive-check cycles remain vigorous, of course, the effects of the 'industrial' loop are likely to be limited, but its existence suggests one possible path of escape from the typical pre-industrial situation.

Any possibility that in a period of rising real incomes the 'industrial' loop might find sufficient momentum to break clear from the classic pattern, however, was long nullified not only by the strength of the negative feedback loops elsewhere in the system but also by the raw material supply constraints that typically plagued industry and made rising product prices hard to avoid in periods of expansion. The constraints existed because the supply of industrial raw materials, like the supply of food, depended primarily upon the productivity of the land. Almost all industrial raw materials were organic, or, if inorganic, could only be converted into a useful form by

19. A growth in demand for industrial products need not necessarily create urban rather than rural employment, of course. The cheapness of rural labour and the comparative freedom of the countryside from gild restrictions sometimes meant a disproportionately rapid growth in rural rather than urban industry. The overcrowded rural industrial parish might almost be regarded as the *locus classicus* of proto-industrial growth, as in the case of the framework knitting industry at Shepshed in Leicestershire (Levine, *Family formation*). The same might happen in areas other than Europe. In eighteenth-century Japan, for example, a similar development took place. See Smith, 'Pre-modern economic growth'. Any growth in trade, commerce, administration, the professions, or other forms of tertiary employment tended to be more unambiguously urban.

20. Wrigley, 'London's importance'; de Vries, *Dutch rural economy*, pp. 115–7. But a contrary view has recently been advanced: Sharlin, 'Natural decrease in early modern cities'.

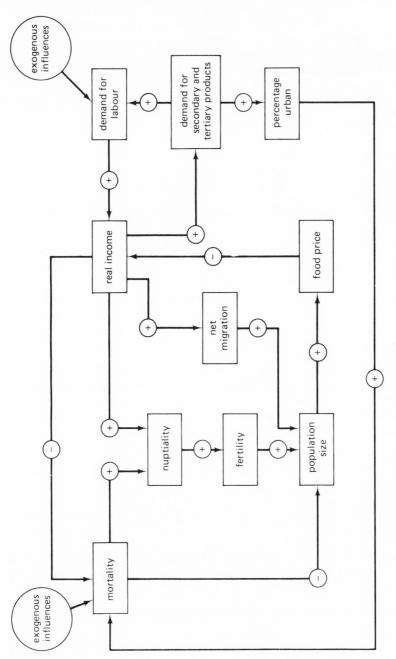

Figure 11.5: A fuller system with positive feedback possibilities

Note: Net migration = immigration less emigration.

the use of organic materials (as in the smelting of metals by charcoal made from wood). Energy shortage before the application of coal as a source of energy or power in more and more industrial processes was also a major handicap, both as a restriction on the scale of production that could be attained and because it tended to keep productivity per worker at a low level.[21] When technological change finally removed the supply bottleneck, however, there was a stronger possibility that positive feedback within this area of the diagram might prove powerful enough to dominate the system as a whole. If the rate of growth of production could outstrip the rate of growth of the population in which the changes were taking place an industrial revolution might occur.

The same process of technological change in other aspects of the economy may also weaken or even remove sections of the negative feedback loops within the system. Particularly strategic in this regard would be any development that served to weaken the characteristic tendency of food prices to rise as numbers grew in pre-industrial economies. Over-rapid population growth in relation to food production formed the Achilles' heel of the traditional world. Unless and until a way was found of preventing the effects of population growth from raising food prices and thus depressing real wages, an economy in the incipient stages of growth could not be made proof against the stresses its development entailed.

English experience viewed in model terms

The construction of simple models of the sort just described entails some sacrifice of comprehensiveness to clarity. Pre-industrial communities rarely displayed such simplicity and regularity in their behaviour.[22] A large national economy was particularly unlikely to do so, even though comparatively 'pure' instances of certain patterns might be found in small communities within it. Nevertheless it may be instructive to discover how far the use of the range of models whose features are summarized in figure 11.5 illuminates the changing relations between English demographic structure and its social and economic environment.

Illustrations of all the sets of relationships described in the last section may be found in English history between Elizabethan and Victorian times, many of them indeed co-existing at the same time. But whereas some were always of peripheral importance at best, others were powerful and stable for centuries at a time. None, however, stood unaffected by the flux of events throughout the entire period, except for certain links such as those between fertility or mortality and population size which are logically necessary and do not depend upon the circumstances of the day. All the other relationships either disappeared or changed drastically in importance; though in one or two cases the change was just beginning in 1871 and only became fully evident later in the last quarter of the nineteenth century.

In order to facilitate the identification of the changes taking place over time, it is helpful to increase the information conveyed in the system diagrams by allowing the

21. See Wrigley, 'Raw material supply in the industrial revolution'. For an interesting discussion of the importance of peat as an energy source in the development of the Dutch economy in the seventeenth century see de Zeeuw, 'Peat and the Dutch Golden Age'.

22. Some approach it, however. The Austrian village of Heidenreichstein may be a case in point. A simple agricultural economy combined with impartible holdings and socio-economic customs that maintained a largely invariant labour force on each holding ensured this. Berkner, 'The stem family and the developmental cycle of the peasant household'.

strength of the relationship between any two boxes to be indicated by the thickness of the line connecting them. A broken line indicates a weak connexion, or one with very little significance in the system as a whole, a thin line indicates a firm but not especially powerful link, while a thick line is intended to show that the link in question was strong and influential over the behaviour of the whole system. Lines of intermediate thickness are also used. Finally, the three links whose status cannot change because they are logically rather than empirically validated (those that show that higher fertility, lower mortality, and immigration all tend to increase the size of the population, and vice-versa) are shown as broad but hollow lines.

Figure 11.6 is meant to represent the general situation of Elizabethan England. The negative feedback cycle between population size, food prices, real wages, nuptiality, and fertility, which we have termed the preventive-check cycle, dominates the system as a whole, and the lines linking population size through food price to real wages are shown as especially thick. The evidence presented in chapter 10 leaves no doubt that the dominant feature of the situation was the steep fall in real wages. Nor is there much reason to doubt that the principal reason for the fall was population growth (see figures 10.1 and 10.2). The trends in the crude marriage rate suggest that real-wage changes may have had a marked effect on nuptiality (see figure 10.9), which would in turn affect fertility and so complete the circle back to population size. But while the relationships existing between this inner circle of factors may have met the logical requirements of negative feedback, their operation seems to have involved a considerable time lag. The evidence of the turning points in nuptiality behaviour relative to those in the real wage suggests that adjustments were sluggish so that while the system continued to be dominated by these relationships, it would only be near to the notional point of equilibrium quite infrequently,[23] as the long slow swings about the equilibrium point took place.

At the other extreme from the massively strong links between population size, food price, and the real wage were those shown dotted in figure 11.6. There is some slight evidence that real wages affected mortality directly in the short-term. In one period of near-famine following the very poor harvest of 1596 the death rate rose sharply and during the decades in which real wages were plunging to their nadir expectation of life was falling slightly, though still at a fairly high absolute level. But this last may well have been no more than coincidence, and even years of high prices bore an uncertain relation to high death rates.[24] Overall the short-term relationship between the real wage and mortality was very weak and the secular relationship was even more uncertain so that it might have been just as realistic to have suppressed the link.

Much the same is true of the indirect link between the real wage and mortality running round the bottom of the figure, by which trends in real wages influence the proportion of the population living in an urban environment and thus have a positive effect on mortality levels. But towns in the sixteenth century experienced very mixed fortunes, and in many cases their fortunes appear to have had little to do with purely economic factors,[25] so that the status of these links is doubtful and any effect slight, though the rapid growth of London against a background of falling real wages forms a conspicuous exception to the general rule.

The third dotted link is that between mortality and nuptiality. In one sense this was probably quite a strong link. Any period of unusually high mortality produced a surge

23. See above, pp. 438–43.
24. See above, table 8.8.
25. Phythian-Adams, 'Urban decay'.

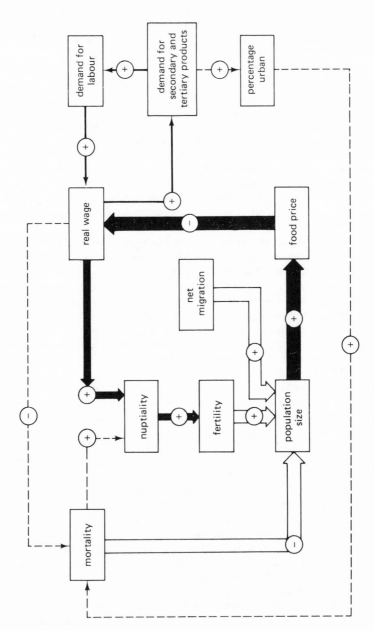

Figure 11.6: England in the late sixteenth century

Note: Net migration = immigration less emigration

in marriages, but a high proportion of these were remarriages and the simplicity of the diagram cannot do justice to the complications this implies since in this instance a rise in nuptiality need not always have been followed by higher fertility.[26] A widow who remarried may not have had any more children than she would have had if her late husband had not died. The effects of secular mortality changes upon nuptiality are as yet too unclear to clarify this aspect of the link between the two boxes.

A cluster of links containing the elements of positive feedback is shown in the top right-hand corner of the figure connecting the real wage, the demand for secondary and tertiary products, and the demand for labour. The links are shown as firmly existing but not especially powerful. Direct, empirical evidence of their relative strength is, however, slight. In a period of falling real wages the presence of a positive feedback loop of this sort will, of course, tend to exaggerate the problem and exert a further downward pressure on real wages. It may have played a part in aggravating the problem of the sturdy beggar, of which both local and central government were so vividly aware; the problem of men who possessed skills and were in good health, but who could find no employment for lack of demand for their services.

Since there was some international migration in Elizabethan times, such as the refugees from the southern Netherlands who came to East Anglia, the existence of these movements is shown in the figure. It bore no apparent connexion to the rest of the system, however, and so is left without incoming links.

In the preliminary discussion of simple models of demographic structure and environment, attention was drawn to the possibility of exogenous influences on mortality and demand for labour which might affect the functioning of the system but were external to it. One of the most striking features of the middle decades of Elizabeth's reign was their remarkable freedom from epidemics and the modest background level of mortality which raised expectation of life at birth as high as 40 years for a short period.[27] This may be regarded as an exogenous circumstance which tended, *ceteris paribus*, to increase the growth rate of the population, and so, through the web of relationships already discussed, to act as another factor increasing the downward pressure on real wages. The other element in the system that might be partially determined exogenously, demand for labour, was probably too little affected by changes in the overseas demand for English goods and services to have had much destabilizing effect overall in this period, though in some areas employment experienced violent swings as a result of the vicissitudes of the cloth trade which were closely bound up with its fortune in foreign markets.[28]

If we now move forward in time approximately a century to try to capture the functioning of the system in the seventeenth century, several changes are apparent and are shown in figure 11.7. One link has disappeared, one changed status, and one new one has appeared.

The heart of the system remains the preventive-check cycle. Indeed, the cycle is strengthened by the appearance of a link between the real wage and net migration which reinforces its operation. Probably about 300,000 emigrants left England for North America and the West Indies between 1630 and 1690 and there was also at

26. See above, pp. 363–6.
27. Table 7.15.
28. Fluctuations in the exchange rates in the 1540s and 1550s and temporary closures of the major overseas market of Antwerp in the early 1560s and 1570s led to great instability in the volume of cloth exports, with the third quarter of the century witnessing a contraction of some 25 per cent. Fisher, 'Commercial trends', pp. 153–6, 159–60.

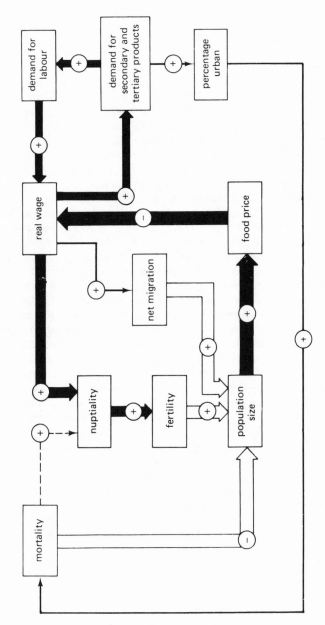

Figure 11.7: England in the seventeenth century

Note: Net migration = immigration less emigration

times substantial movement to Ireland.[29] Poverty, or lack of a suitable economic niche in England, was not, of course, the sole reason for emigration. Many left to gain a greater freedom to worship as they wished, and in individual cases there was no doubt a vast miscellany of motives, but the economic circumstances of the country had much to do with securing a large flow of indentured servants to the colonies and also with its later drying up. The demand for labour on the other side of the Atlantic did not disappear in the later seventeenth century, but its supply price rose in England to the point where the importation of slaves became a more and more attractive alternative.[30] As with other aspects of the preventive-check cycle the time lag between real-wage and migration trends was considerable. There was inertia within the system. Real wages were already at their nadir when movement across the Atlantic first attained a high volume, and had improved considerably before it ended. The peak level of emigration to the colonies probably occurred in the 1640s and 1650s,[31] but it continued at a substantial, if declining level for a further generation or more. However, long-distance migration requires an institutional framework and a network of formal and informal contacts, of a complexity to suggest that it is neither easy to bring into existence nor to bring to an end abruptly.

Elsewhere within the cycle of preventive checks adjustment was also slow. We have already examined at some length the relation between real-wage movements, marriage behaviour, and fertility change, and need do no more here than to repeat that the turning point in *current* fertility levels occurred several decades after the corresponding changes in real wages, though *cohort* fertility changes were much more nearly simultaneous with those in the real wage.[32] In the seventeenth century, taken broadly as the period from about 1630 to about 1730, however, the effects of the functioning of the preventive-check cycle were very different from those of the preceding period. Population growth was slight and at times negative. The underlying improvement in agricultural productivity caused food prices to tend to fall in secular trend, and real wages were rising steadily if slowly as a result. The operation of the cycle therefore switched from depressing fertility to allowing it to rise, but the slowness of response between real wage and fertility changes meant that the return to population growth was sluggish.

The delay in a return to rising population totals was made more pronounced and the subsequent growth restrained by the behaviour of mortality in the period. In so far as mortality was exogenously determined the fates conspired to reduce the likelihood of population growth. The secular trend in mortality was steadily upwards until the 1680s, though real wages had been rising for several decades, and for a further half-century thereafter mortality moved very erratically and showed no sustained tendency to fall.[33] This circumstance represented the reverse of the situation in the late sixteenth century. Then the remarkably modest level of mortality tended to quicken and prolong population growth with an inevitable and deleterious effect on real wages. In the seventeenth and early eighteenth centuries, on the other hand, mortality trends brought benefit to real wages by inhibiting population growth.

Furthermore, the exogenous mortality changes were exaggerated by the strengthening of the positive link between the proportion of the population living in

29. See above, p. 224.
30. Menard, 'From servants to slaves'.
31. See tables 6.11, 7.1, and figure 7.5 for details of the changing net migration totals of the period.
32. Figures 10.6 and 10.7.
33. Figure 7.6.

towns and mortality. In the sixteenth century the relation between the demand for industrial products or tertiary services and urban growth had been uncertain, for although London grew, other towns experienced mixed fortunes. Urban population overall may well have increased but it is also possible that the percentage of the population living in towns fell since national population as a whole grew so markedly. Since real wages were declining this is what 'should' have happened. In the seventeenth century the pattern is clearer. Real wages were rising and towns of all sizes grew in spite of the virtual cessation of overall population growth. In particular, London became a dominant feature of national social and economic life. In spite of the disappearance of plague, latterly almost entirely an urban disease, urban death rates were generally much higher than those in the countryside, and were probably higher in big cities than in small towns. On the most conservative assumptions, London alone contained well over a tenth of the population of England before the end of the seventeenth century, and its growth acted as a brake checking any incipient tendency to renewed population increase. The conditions for a relatively high-level equilibrium trap were beginning to become apparent in late-seventeenth-century England.[34]

The links to the mortality box in figure 11.7 also differ in one other respect from those of figure 11.6. The dotted line carrying a negative link between real wages and mortality is removed. From what has already been remarked it will be clear that the seventeenth century retained no vestige of the positive check. Nor did it ever return in England. There may have been times in earlier English history, for example in the late thirteenth and early fourteenth centuries, when this link would have dominated the working of the whole system, when the negative feedback loop between population size, food prices, real wages, and mortality was its prime determinant, but if so such times were long past by 1700.

Another difference between the two last figures lies in the positive feedback loop involving real wages, the demand for secondary and tertiary products and the demand for labour. This is shown as having strengthened somewhat. The evidence for such a change is slender and impressionistic, but towards the end of the period the development of rural domestic industry suggests that the effect represented by this part of the figure was being widely felt. Industries such as framework knitting, glove making, small metal wares, pottery, and glass were feeling the beneficial effect of rising living standards. The examination of inventories reveals the extent to which the household was acquiring as a matter of course utensils and furnishings that had until recently been luxuries.[35] The building industry also received a fillip.[36] The demand for labour strengthened in consequence and both primary employment and by-employment were more plentiful. By the end of the century Defoe's 'topping workmen' were living well and finding employment easier to obtain.[37] Nevertheless, the degree of any strengthening in this component of the system is necessarily a matter for conjecture in the absence of comparative, quantifiable data from the two periods. Equally difficult to quantify is the extent of the exogenous element in demand for

34. Wrigley, 'London's importance'.
35. See, for example, Marshall's clear evidence of this tendency even in a district as relatively remote and economically retarded as Cumbria: Marshall, 'Social structure and wealth'. More general evidence for the country as a whole may be found in Thirsk, *Economic policy and projects*, especially chaps. 5 and 7.
36. Machin, 'The great rebuilding'.
37. Defoe was writing in 1705 about the high earnings of journeymen and the comparative ease with which they could maintain their families in decent comfort. The passage containing his comment is quoted at length in George, *London life*, p. 157.

labour arising from overseas demand for English industrial goods, though it is perhaps safe to assume that it had strengthened, thus constituting an additional reason for emphasizing the links in this section of the diagram.

Figure 11.7 then is intended to depict English demographic structure and its environment not long before the industrial revolution took hold. It represents a system no longer showing any trace of the positive-check cycle, the more drastic form of negative feedback which could serve to keep a pre-industrial population in balance with its resources. Instead the balance was maintained by the preventive-check cycle. If a preventive-check cycle is able by itself to achieve a balance between a population and its resources without even occasional resort to the positive check, that population is necessarily more fortunately placed than régimes of high mortality. It constitutes a 'low-pressure' rather than a 'high-pressure' solution to the problem of overcoming the tension between the potential capacity of a pre-industrial society to grow more rapidly demographically than economically. But in this instance English good fortune was compounded by special factors which both pushed prosperity to heights unusual by pre-industrial standards and prolonged the period of prosperity beyond the common span.

In a pre-industrial economy, however, good times alternate with bad. Although the resumption of population growth was long delayed, it was gathering momentum in the eighteenth century and, by the end of its third quarter, had reached a rate as high as any in the sixteenth. And as population growth quickened, the preventive-check cycle, whose strength seemed undiminished, began to produce some of the characteristic changes that constitute the other half of the slow-moving cycle. Food prices rose, real wages fell, and for a time there could be no prospect of relief arising from a fall in fertility because of the slow response in this section of the cycle. Had the evolution of this phase of the cycle followed the same pattern that had obtained in the past, there would have been a period of severe impoverishment followed by a braking of the pace of population growth as the elements within the system slowly altered in level in such a way as to restore the balance between population and resources. The penalty for failure to adjust by means of the preventive-check cycle would have been, of course, a resort to the severer discipline of the positive check. The example of Ireland is eloquent testimony to the continued danger of relapse into this form of control. Ireland was saved from its worst rigours only by the comparative ease with which in the nineteenth century the links between real wages, net migration, and population size could be used to short circuit the full savagery of the positive check. The escape from death by migration also probably saved many lives in Scotland in the 1840s.[38]

In England, however, history did not repeat itself, and in figure 11.8 an attempt is made to identify the changing structure of relations that had emerged by the early decades of the nineteenth century.

The most striking single difference between this figure and its predecessors is the complete disappearance of the positive link between population size and food prices, one of the most fundamental and strongest of all the features of the classic pre-industrial system. Had it not disappeared, the continued existence of the rest of the preventive-check cycle would have forced down real wages, and would presumably have caused the fall in fertility, which in any case occurred between 1815 and 1840, to have continued until population growth was halted, as had happened in

38. See Flinn, *Scottish population history,* pp. 430–8.

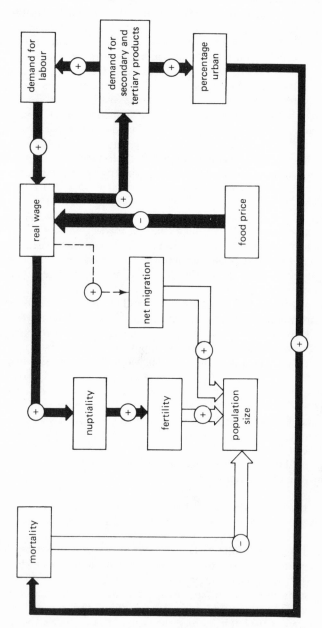

Figure 11.8: England in the early nineteenth century

Note: Net migration = immigration less emigration

the early seventeenth century in comparable circumstances. But food prices, though they still had a controlling influence on real wages, which had fallen to a very low level in the early nineteenth century, were no longer affected by high rates of population growth in the early nineteenth century. The strikingly close positive link between them which had been maintained at all phases of the cycle during the preceding 250 years had vanished.[39] In practice after a marked fall from the very high levels of the Napoleonic War period, food prices thereafter showed little change in the next half century, apart from the short-term variations associated with the fortunes of the harvest. English agriculture was able to raise production broadly in step with population, in spite of its exceptionally high rate of growth, until, later in the century, food imports began to supplement home production on an increasingly substantial scale.

A second contrast between figure 11.8 and its predecessors is the further strengthening of the positive feedback loop connecting real wages, the demand for the products of secondary and tertiary industry, and the demand for labour. Again it would be reassuring to have much more complete information about any changes in the income elasticity of demand for different types of product during the period, and of real income trends amongst different socio-economic groups. The substantial fall in real production costs achieved by many industries during the early decades of the industrial revolution, however, must have tended to reinforce the strength of demand.[40] Nevertheless, until about 1810 real wages were tending to fall rather than rise which would have had very serious implications for employment assuming that the figure correctly captures this aspect of the functioning of the English economy. It is likely, therefore, that the fact that demand for labour, like mortality, was always likely to be determined in part exogenously was of great importance at this period, since it may have helped to ensure that demand for labour remained tolerably strong in circumstances in which it might otherwise have been expected that the demand would weaken seriously. Once real wages had again started to rise, of course, the problem became less acute.

The positive link between the percentage of the population living in cities and mortality is also shown as having strengthend in figure 11.8. From the later eighteenth century onwards towns and cities grew apace, and the attendant public health problems were too great to be countered by the local government authorities and medical profession of the day. Later in the century Farr suggested that an empirical law could be stated which related population density and the death rate.[41] He was tireless in stressing the vast difference between expectation of life in the countryside and that in cities such as Liverpool or Manchester, and there can be little doubt that the rapid rise in the proportion of the population living in cities had much to do with the absence of any significant improvement in expectation of life between 1820 and 1870.[42]

Any vestigial link that may have existed between mortality and nuptiality is shown

39. Figure 10.2.
40. 'The maintenance of money wages, and a rise in money wages in some areas, then gave a strong boost to internal markets. . . . Once innovations had allowed cost-reducing techniques and a rising productivity to become established, then the circle became a self-reinforcing process'. Mathias, *The first industrial nation*, pp. 18–9.
41. Farr considered that the level of mortality varied as the twelfth root of the density of the population. Farr, *Vital statistics*, pp. 173–6.
42. Figure 7.6.

as having disappeared in figure 11.8. The same connexion between real wages and net migration is shown as in the previous figure but this time as an uncertain link. It is no doubt justified in the sense that lack of economic opportunity was a prime motive for many emigrants, and the timing of emigration was influenced by economic fluctuations.[43] But the secular tendency of real wages and that of net migration bore no relation to one another.

If, finally, we move forward into the last quarter of the nineteenth century, to a point in time at or just after the end of the period covered by our aggregative back-projection exercise, we find that the classic pre-industrial system is on the point of disintegration, as may be seen in figure 11.9. The system as a whole is now dominated by the connexion between rising real incomes and growth in the secondary and tertiary sectors, but, because a means had been found of overcoming the problem of declining marginal returns in agriculture, the logical foundation of the traditional system of demographic regulation, the other feedback relationships had been ruptured or reduced to inconsequence. Agriculture, indeed, was becoming an industry like any other, rather than an industry *sui generis*. The constraints imposed by the fact that the supply of cultivable land cannot be significantly increased ceased to pose a problem from the point in time when technological progress could secure rises in the yield from unit inputs of capital and labour that matched or exceeded population increase. And any transitional difficulties were eased by the huge increase in the area of cultivated land in countries of recent settlement which ensured that any potential problems on the supply side from the inadequate pace of technological change would prove stillborn.

Elsewhere in the system the logical links remained, of course, unchanged, but all empirical links either disappeared or were of reduced strength. The link between population size and food prices had already disappeared early in the century, but now a further link in the preventive check cycle disappeared. Whereas in the past real-wage changes were positively linked to nuptiality, though with a long time-lag, now the two moved independently. The steady secular rise in real wages which had begun early in the century would in the past have tended to encourage earlier and more universal marriage after a suitable interval. For a time expectation was fulfilled. From about 1840 until 1870 the changes in age at marriage and proportions marrying were in the expected direction though perhaps less pronounced than might have been expected, but thereafter couples proved less willing to embark on marriage despite improving material circumstances.[44] Moreover, the old link between marriage and fertility was losing its strength as a slowly rising proportion of married couples took steps to limit the number of their children. And the final link in the old preventive-check cycle, though still present, was less prominent than in the past. The level of food prices was still a very powerful influence on real wages because food was a large fraction of the average household budget, but each further upward shift in real wages tended to reduce the relative importance of food compared to other items, and so slowly weakened the link between the two. Even the link between urban growth and mortality was of much reduced importance. The gap between urban and rural death rates had begun to close, and in the early decades of the twentieth century disappeared entirely.

43. See, for example, Cairncross, *Home and foreign investment*, ch. 8, and, for an analysis with a different emphasis, Thomas, *Migration and economic growth*.
44. See above, pp. 435–8.

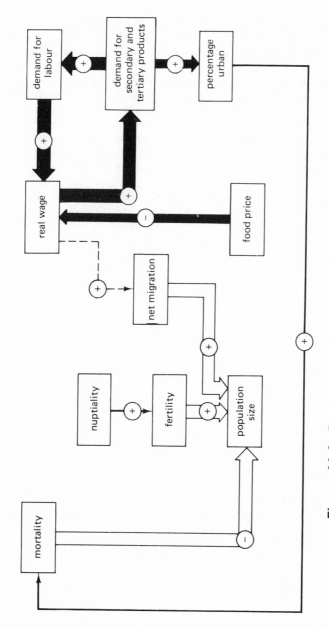

Figure 11.9: England towards the end of the nineteenth century

Note: Net migration = immigration less emigration

Viewed in the very abstract way encouraged by the use of diagrammatic models, the most important single change occurring between the early eighteenth century, when England was still a clear example of one variant form of the preventive-check cycle, and the late nineteenth century, when the industrial age was firmly established, was the breaking of the positive link between population size and food prices. Although in the later eighteenth century growth in the industrial sector was gathering momentum, and the strength of the demand for industrial labour might possibly have induced sufficient positive feedback in the system as a whole to have overcome the tendency for real wages to fall, it is more likely that the traditional dominance of the preventive-check cycle would have continued. Indeed, as long as the cycle remained unbroken the maintenance of real wages at a high level, by tending to promote population growth, would have forced food prices up further and must eventually have caused very grave problems. Once food prices no longer responded to population growth, however, England was free from this danger and the opportunity existed for new configurations to gain command within the system.

It is of particular interest that the other elements in the preventive-check cycle, consisting of the links that caused a positive relation between real wages and population size, did not immediately decay when their *raison d'être*, so to speak, was removed. The response of nuptiality and fertility had always been somewhat sluggish when the preventive-check cycle was operating in full vigour, and remained so as it fell into decay. Just as there had typically been a lag of up to half a century between a turning point in the secular trend of real wages and a sympathetic change in the trend of the gross reproduction rate, so there was a similar lag after the decay of the old link between population size and food prices before the dying out of the traditional links further round the cycle. Thus fertility fell for a generation or so after reaching a peak about 1815, reflecting the earlier fall in real wages, but recovered thereafter as the effect of the improvement in real wages, which began early in the century, made itself felt within the traditional system. But the recovery was brief and hesitant and by 1870 at the latest it had ceased, giving way to a new era in which the secular trend in real wages no longer provided any clue to the trends in nuptiality and fertility a few decades later.

It is intriguing to reflect on the difference between English and French fertility history between the late eighteenth and late nineteenth centuries. French fertility began to decline before the eighteenth century ended and had already reduced the gross reproduction rate by 1850 to about 1.7, a level not reached in England until 1900.[45] Fertility and mortality declined almost exactly in step so that the intrinsic growth rate changed little, remaining very low throughout the whole period.[46] The fall in French fertility is often discussed as if it were the first instance of a new pattern of behaviour which was only adopted more tardily elsewhere in western Europe. But in many ways French behaviour appears much more like the development of a novel variant of a long-established pattern than the first appearance of a new one. Early-eighteenth-century France was still a country in which the positive-check cycle was a major feature of the mechanisms keeping numbers and resources in balance. Living

45. The French GRR in 1846–50 was 1.73, in 1851–5 it had fallen slightly to 1.69: Bourgeois-Pichat, 'The general development of the population of France', p. 506. The English GRR in 1900–2 was 1.725: Glass, 'Changes in fertility in England and Wales', p. 168.
46. Figure 7.13.

standards were low and much of the population vulnerable to short-term shocks.[47] Crude birth and death rates were about 40 per 1,000, and were therefore extremely high by English standards. The developments of the next century and a half may be seen as a successful transfer from the positive- to the preventive-check cycle (see figures 11.1 and 11.2) with one important original feature – that instead of the link between real income and fertility being chiefly indirect through nuptiality, it became increasingly a direct link which by-passed nuptiality.

Several features of French demographic history during this period suggest the extent of the differences between development in France and later changes in England. In France there was a strikingly close correspondence between the onset of family limitation within marriage and a fall in marriage age as might be expected in the context of the preventive-check cycle: one method of control could be relaxed when another had short-circuited it.[48] In England on the other hand, as we have seen, nuptiality declined considerably just when family limitation was first becoming widespread (see figure 10.10). In France there were substantial regional differences in the timing of the start of the practice of family limitation; in England its onset was almost simultaneous throughout the whole country.[49] Once family limitation had begun in England fertility fell without interruption whereas between 1850 and 1870 there was a period of stability and even slight recovery of fertility in France after the initial fall and before the downward tendency was renewed.[50] In general the control of fertility in marriage started first among the upper echelons of society in England, percolating slowly down to groups such as coalminers and agricultural workers much later; but in France the rural peasantry in some areas were among the first to reduce their marital fertility.[51]

The techniques used to secure a fertility fall may have been the same in both countries, but similarity of method does not necessarily imply any further similarities. By the late eighteenth or early nineteenth century France had achieved a rough

---

47. The scale of the short-term shocks is visible in the data recently presented by Rebaudo based on a national sample of rural French parish registers and covering the period 1670 to 1740: Rebaudo, 'La population française rurale de 1670 à 1740'. Their causation was no doubt various, but Goubert remarks of the mortality peaks that, 'In the seventeenth century, and especially between 1640 and 1740, they are usually connected with the high price of grain': Goubert, 'French population between 1500 and 1700', p. 471.

48. There is an interesting examination of this complex question in Lesthaeghe and van de Walle, 'Economic factors and fertility decline'.

49. For a discussion of departmental variations in the timing of the onset of the fertility fall in France and a review of related literature, see van de Walle, 'Alone in Europe'. The remarkable homogeneity of English experience emerges clearly in Teitelbaum, *The British fertility decline*.

50. The GRR in France fell regularly from about 2.0 in 1800 to 1.69 in 1851–5 but then rose marginally and was still 1.70 in 1866–70. Thereafter the fall was resumed and by 1900 the rate was down to about 1.4. Van de Walle has provided measures of overall and marital fertility in terms of the Princeton measures I_f and I_g. I_f rose from 0.271 to 0.282 and I_g from 0.478 to 0.494 between 1851 and 1871. Bourgeois-Pichat, 'The general development of the population of France', p. 506: van de Walle, *The female population of France*, p. 127.

51. Wrigley, *Population and history*, pp. 186–7 provides some summary evidence of national patterns of fertility fall by socio-economic group. In France crude birth rates in large regions, notably in Normandy and Aquitaine, had already fallen to very low levels by 1800 (in the department of Calvados in Normandy, for example, in 1801–10 it was only 21.4 per 1,000: van de Walle, *The female population of France*, p. 259). Some of the lowest rates occurred in overwhelmingly agricultural areas; and in some areas in which fertility in general remained quite high there were nevertheless clear signs of family limitation from an early date in individual settlements, as in the case of Boulay in the department of Moselle: Houdaille, 'La population de Boulay'.

balance of fertility and mortality, with a crude birth rate of about 33 per 1,000 and a crude death rate of about 30 per 1,000, a position resembling that in England in, say, 1700.[52] She was well on the way to replacing a 'high-pressure' with a 'low-pressure' system of relationships between the country's demography and economy, having made a smooth transition between the two (set out diagrammatically in figure 7.13). She was achieving by fertility control within marriage what England had achieved by regulating the timing and incidence of marriage.[53] The context of change in late-nineteenth-century England was entirely different. The preventive-check cycle had become obsolete long before the 1860s. The old link between population size and food prices had disappeared two generations earlier and other features of the cycle decayed thereafter. The practice of *coitus interruptus* may have been common to both cases, and the changes in age- and duration-specific marital fertility rates may have displayed similarities, but the spread of family limitation in England occurred in response to circumstances radically different from those in France a century earlier.

The limitations of models

Highly stylized models create problems both in what they show and in what they conceal. They introduce a quite unreal simplicity into the relations they depict, and render invisible much that was important. This, of course, is the price that must be paid for any benefits they confer. Their clarity, as we have emphasized, inhibits comprehensiveness, and it is timely to stress this point by giving some instances of their limitations.

It is clearly improper, for example, to treat the movement of real *wages* as if it always accurately captures national trends in real *income*, even supposing that Phelps Brown and Hopkins were successful in tracing the course of real wages. Other sources of income were always important in the aggregate total of income, and their fluctuations affected a large proportion of the population. It is unlikely that a more complete measure of real income would have followed exactly the same path as a real-wage index based on Phelps Brown and Hopkins, yet it is the former which would have been the more appropriate to use in examining the effects of income on nuptiality and fertility.[54] Still better would have been a measure of real income related to the family unit rather than the individual. In default of data to meet these ideal requirements over long periods of time, however, the use of the PBH wage index was unavoidable.

Again, there is no reason in principle to expect income changes to have the same effect on nuptiality and fertility behaviour in different socio-economic groups. It would be surprising, indeed, if there were uniformity in this respect, but all the models represent national behaviour as if it were uniform. Probably different groups responded in different ways to similar situations. For example, rising real wages are shown as positively related to the demand for secondary and tertiary products. Globally such a relation may be presumed to have existed, but there may well have

52. Bourgeois-Pichat estimated a crude birth rate of 32.0 per 1,000 and a crude death rate of 29.8 for France in 1801: Bourgeois-Pichat, 'The general development of the population of France', p. 506. In England the comparable figures for the 15-year period centring on 1701 were 32.0 and 27.6 (table A3. 1).
53. It may be noted that there were also significant changes in both the timing and incidence of marriage in France as the eighteenth century progressed. Age at marriage was rising and more men and women were remaining permanently single. Henry and Houdaille, 'Célibat et âge au mariage'.
54. For a fuller discussion of the weaknesses of the price and wage data published by Phelps Brown and Hopkins see pp. 407–8, 411–2, 430–5 and appendix 9.

been sub-groups within the population with virtually fixed consumption patterns whose reaction to a rise in, say, daily wage rates would have been to work less,[55] and such groups may well have comprised large numbers of men and women at times. The degree of homogeneity in national experience and behaviour can be tested in some respects,[56] but in others much is unknown or known only very imperfectly.

The models used also tend to obscure modifications to basic patterns that were not sufficiently great to have reversed or annulled a relation shown in the model, but which may have figured prominently at the time. For example, the gross reproduction rate reached an exceptionally high absolute level in the early nineteenth century. In general trend its behaviour at this period conformed to the pattern that had long held good, and therefore fits the model, but it may nevertheless have been boosted by special factors to a level higher than it would otherwise have reached, and the timing of the peak may also have been affected somewhat. If, for example, proto-industrial employment and unusually high fertility are associated with each other, the high level of fertility prevailing in the later eighteenth century may be, in part at least, a reflection of this feature of the English economy of the period. Or, equally plausibly, and the two possibilities are not mutually exclusive, the process whereby an increasing proportion of the workforce, both in industry and in agriculture, became purely wage-paid may have tended to result in generally earlier marriage and hence higher fertility as institutional forms like service in husbandry or apprenticeship became practised less widely. Underlying any such special circumstances the relations captured by the model appear to have continued to hold sway, but to concentrate on them alone may mean missing much else of interest.

The details that are lost to view in summary models may be of vital importance to the success of its functioning as a whole. It would be valuable, for example, to incorporate more explicitly other features of the advantages stemming from the centrality of age at marriage and proportions marrying to the operation of the preventive-check cycle. As we have seen, marriage trends appear to have been relatively slow to respond to changes in the secular trend of real wages (though it should be remembered that such changes were necessarily difficult to detect at the time given the amplitude and erratic nature of short-term fluctuations in food prices and hence in real wages, so that it may be that only in retrospect does the response appear slow). But on the other hand, changes in the timing and incidence of marriage, when they do occur, have a very rapid effect upon birth rates and rates of population growth, acting faster than changes in marital fertility in this regard.[57] Moreover, a relatively late age at marriage entails a high mean age at maternity and this helps to keep intrinsic growth rates low and to ensure that there is no great demographic momentum in the society even in periods of growth.[58]

Late marriage was also the crucial element in the 'low pressure' equilibrium which characterized early modern England. This brought substantial economic benefits both because the resultant age structure of the population imposed only a relatively light dependency burden, and because low fertility meant that fewer resources were wasted

---

55. This issue is discussed in Coleman, 'Labour in the English economy'.
56. There is, for example, evidence of a remarkable uniformity in the changing age structure of mortality in a scattering of parishes from all over England in the sixteenth and seventeenth centuries: Schofield and Wrigley, 'Infant and child mortality'.
57. Lesthaeghe, 'Nuptiality and population growth'.
58. There is a succinct discussion of some aspects of this question in Ryder, 'Stationary populations', pp. 5–8.

on children who died before contributing to production than would have been the case if the equilibrium had been one of 'high pressure' where both fertility and mortality were high. These features are lost in diagrammatic representation, but they are part of the reason why pre-industrial England was more fortunately circumstanced than traditional societies in eastern Europe or Asia.

The services that appropiate models can perform are nevertheless notable. By setting a number of aspects of the demography and economy of societies in the past in an intelligible relationship to one another, they should make it easier to identify the major special features of a particular period or place, precisely because they stand outside the model. If the fertility history of England in the late eighteenth and early nineteenth centuries requires more for its understanding than is to be found in figures 11.8 and 11.9, the status of the special features of the period will be thrown into relief once the 'normal' pattern has been clarified. Again, the use of models should suggest a series of hypotheses to be tested. Some of the relations shown in the series of figures in this chapter have a firm empirical base. It seems indisputable, for example, that secular trends in population and food price movements were very closely linked in England throughout the sixteenth, seventeenth, and eighteenth centuries, and some of the demographic linkages have also been extensively tested in earlier chapters. But it would greatly strengthen the set of models as a whole if the links between real-wage movements and the demand for goods and services outside the primary sector could be much more thoroughly investigated. In particular it would be very helpful to know whether the income elasticities of demand changed significantly over the three centuries covered by the figures, and how great was the relative importance of the exogenous component in the demand for labour at different periods.

Finally, the functioning of the national aggregate will never be well understood unless analyses or relations that appear to characterize the national entity are paralleled by similar work on a local scale. Only in this way can those aspects of English demographic and economic history in which there was homogeneity of behaviour throughout the country be distinguished from those where the national aggregate reflects an average condition that may prove to have been true of few individual communities, and that may therefore tend to lead to misguided conclusions about the relations between demographic and economic behaviour in the past. The local content has not been entirely excluded from this book. It figures to some degree, for example, in the discussion of the regional patterning of outbreaks of epidemic disease in appendix 10, but in a full and balanced treatment of demographic structure and environment it should figure as prominently as the national setting.

Some relevant material already exists. For example, while there is a considerable similarity in mortality trends between the peerage and the general populace at least until the eighteenth century, there is a striking contrast in the history of nuptiality between the two. Age at first marriage of the brides of peers climbed steadily from a level well below that of the population as a whole in the late sixteenth century to a level well above the common run by the late eighteenth.[59] There is, perhaps not surprisingly, no trace amongst the peers of the pattern of relation between real wages and marriage trends that was so characteristic of England when treated as a national

---

59. Female mean age at marriage among the children of British peers rose from 20 to 25 between 1600 and 1800 while in the general population it fell from 26 to 24 if the reconstitution studies carried out so far are representative of the country as a whole. Hollingsworth, 'Demography of the British peerage', p. 25 and table 7.26.

unit. But the peers were not exempt from general mortality trends, which seem to have been in large measure exogenously determined.

Much, however, remains to be done. For example, the striking absence of evidence that changes in real wages exert any considerable influence upon either short- or long-term national mortality fluctuations, which has been stressed in this book, deserves extensive local and regional study to test the possibility that such influences may have been present locally but have been masked by aggregation. We hope to remedy the lack of microcosmic studies to match those of national patterns, in part at least, when the volume to be devoted to parish reconstitutions is published, but there is scope for very many studies at all levels of aggregation. They will take on a new significance now that the national picture has grown clearer.

Concluding remarks

It is perhaps in the nature of historical research of the type we have pursued in this book that the appetite should grow by what it feeds upon. Success in uncovering the main trends in English fertility and mortality back to 1541 sharpens the hunger for still longer series to study, and for similar data from other countries. Models, like other methods of attempting to distinguish the particular from the general, require extensive testing if confidence in their accuracy is to grow. So slow moving were the long cycles of pre-industrial life that the two centuries from the mid sixteenth to the late eighteenth century only span one full cycle, and that one the last before the old relationships that produced such cycles fell into decay one by one, until by the end of the nineteenth century they remained only as logical possibilities and not as parts of observable reality, like the fading grin on the proverbial Cheshire cat. In such circumstances, there is an obvious danger, perhaps even a likelihood, that models will be imperfectly framed and may remain uncorrected for lack of sufficient evidence to constitute a searching test. If, for example, French or Swedish evidence stretched back in comparable detail over a similar span of time, or if English evidence could be gleaned for the fourteenth and fifteenth centuries, it would be far easier to point with confidence both to the general patterns of the pre-industrial past, and to the ways in which England differed from her neighbours before and during the industrial revolution.

The fascination of work on population history stems from its central position in the fabric of social and economic life in the past. Because the source materials for its study are abundant but problematic a great part of this book has been given over to a critical evaluation of the evidence and to a description of the methods by which we have arrived at national series of births, deaths, and marriages. We have also explained at length the new technique of back projection by which it is possible to derive estimates of population totals, age structure, and vital rates from the totals of births and deaths. Back projection provides tolerably reliable series covering most major aspects of national demographic behaviour over a period of 330 years, yielding data from the mid sixteenth century onwards of a range and quality not available for any other country until the mid eighteenth century.

Creating reliable series of fertility and mortality data, however, though a valuable exercise in its own right, was undertaken chiefly because it was a necessary preliminary to a reconsideration of the interconnexion between demographic, social, and economic change. Armed with results which clearly invalidated some views on these issues that have attracted wide support,[60] or which forced an intensive reworking of other hypotheses, we have suggested a new interpretative framework which, though crude, appears to 'save the phenomena' as they are at present known.

Since demographic and socio-economic change are inextricably intertwined a fully satisfactory interpretation of population history must embrace a wide spectrum of related topics and techniques. It will include at one extreme matters like the structure of demand, or the terms of trade between industry and agriculture; and at the other, residence conventions at marriage, suckling habits, or provision for old age. It will require an alertness for opportunities to quantify historical evidence and to make effective use of statistical techniques, but it will be equally alive to the importance of studying the attitudes of individuals and groups wherever possible. The family is the prime institutional form in population history, and the births, marriages, and deaths of its members were affected by their behavioural conventions and beliefs as well as by their social and economic circumstances.

Needless to say, our present enterprise falls well short of encompassing such a wide range of topics. It has been devoted to statistical rather than to attitudinal studies, neglecting the individual in favour of the mass. Given the nature of the available sources, this was perhaps the easier task, though we considered that it also held logical priority. But if our own hunger has been whetted for a more comprehensive understanding of population history, it may not be too much to hope that others in reading this book will have felt the same pangs, and may be moved to carry out the work needed to satisfy them.

---

60. For example, the view that mortality played the dominant rôle in determining changes in population growth rates, whose most recent champion has been McKeown, must now be set aside so far as English demographic history in early modern times is concerned. McKeown, *The modern rise of population*, pp. 152–4.

Appendix 1

A list of the aggregative sample parishes and of the names of those who carried out the aggregative tabulations

The following is a list of the 404 parishes forming the sample from which national totals of births, deaths, and marriages were derived. Where the parish name is asterisked, this indicates that the tabulation includes totals taken from the registers of a chapelry or chapelries within the parish.

Bedfordshire
  Ampthill
  Blunham
  Bolnhurst
  Campton with Shefford
  Chalgrave
  Clophill
  Cranfield
  Felmersham
  Flitwick
  Harlington
  Kempston
  Maulden
  Millbrook
  Milton Ernest
  Northill
  Pavenham
  Pulloxhill
  Riseley
  Sandy
  Souldrop
  Southill
  Stevington
  Studham
  Thurleigh
  Tingrith
  Toddington
  Woburn
  Wootton
Berkshire
  Harwell
  Sonning

Winkfield
Buckinghamshire
  Aylesbury
  Princes Risborough
  Wing
Cambridgeshire
  Fowlmere
  Haddenham
  Linton
  Melbourn
  Orwell
  Sawston
  Waterbeach
  Willingham
Cheshire
  Bunbury
  Chester Holy Trinity
  Frodsham
  Gawsworth
  Nantwich
  Sandbach
  Wilmslow
Cumberland
  Bridekirk
  Crosthwaite
  Dalston
  Greystoke
  Wigton
Derbyshire
  Dronfield*
  Wirksworth*
Devonshire

Berry Pomeroy
Blackawton
Branscombe
Chardstock
Colyton
Hartland
Hemyock
Ilsington
Modbury
Offwell
Paignton
Staverton
Stoke Gabriel
Topsham
Widecombe in the Moor
Dorsetshire
Swanage
Symondsbury
Thorncombe
Durham
Darlington
Middleton St George
Whitburn
Essex
Ardleigh
Bradwell juxta Mare
Dedham
Dengie
Great Baddow
Great Burstead
Great Sampford
Great Yeldham
Hadleigh
Little Sampford
Maldon All Saints and St Peters
Romford
Stanford Rivers
Stow Maries
Thaxted
White Notley
Wickford
Gloucestershire
Avening
Bishops Cleeve
Cam
Dymock
Eastington
Fairford
Horsley

Minchinhampton
North Nibley
Stroud
Tetbury
Westbury on Trym
Winchcombe
Wotton under Edge
Hampshire
Aldershot
Boldre
Ellingham
Fordingbridge
Headley
Meonstoke
Odiham
Ringwood
Romsey
Selborne
Herefordshire
Bromyard
Eaton Bishop
Ledbury
Lugwardine
Wigmore
Yarkhill
Hertfordshire
Aldenham
Barley
Berkhampstead St Mary
Berkhampstead St Peter
Hemel Hempstead
Hitchin
Hunsdon
Rickmansworth
Watford
Huntingdonshire
Great Stukeley
Kent
Ashford
Benenden
Biddenden
Bromley
Chiselhurst
Cranbrook
Eastry
Eltham
Goudhurst
Gravesend
Herne

Hythe
Lenham
Milton next Gravesend
Newenden
Reculver
Sandhurst
Sevenoaks
Sittingbourne
Speldhurst
St Nicholas at Wade
Staplehurst
Sundridge
Tenterden
Tonbridge*
Westerham
Wickhambreux
Wye
Yalding
Lancashire
Ashton under Lyne
Chorley
Deane
Hawkshead
North Meols
Radcliffe
Rochdale
Torver
Tunstall
Warton
Leicestershire
Ashby de la Zouche
Ashfordby
Bottesford
Breedon on the Hill
Castle Donnington
Coleorton
Desford
Enderby
Great Bowden
Hinckley
Husbands Bosworth
Kibworth Beauchamp
Kirby Muxloe
Kirkby Mallory
Little Bowden
Long Clawson
Loughborough
Market Bosworth
Market Harborough

Medbourn
Melton Mowbray
Prestwold
Saddington
Shepshed
Wigston Magna
Wymondham
Lincolnshire
Holland
Wrangle
Wyberton
Kesteven
Grantham
Leasingham
Quarrington and Old Sleaford
Ropsley
Lindsey
Clee
Frodingham
Gainsborough
Great Grimsby
Haxey
Irby on Humber
Scartho
Middlesex
Edmonton
Northolt
Norfolk
Banham
Docking
Kenninghall
North Elmham
Norwich St Benedict
Norwich St Giles
Norwich St James with Pockthorpe
Norwich St Margaret
Norwich St Saviour
Sculthorpe
Sedgeford
Shipdham
Swaffham
Wells
Wymondham
Northamptonshire
Aynho
Northumberland
Berwick upon Tweed
Earsdon
Felton

Tynemouth
Woodhorn
Nottinghamshire
  Arnold
  Blyth
  Burton Joyce
  Cropwell Bishop
  Darlton
  Edwinstowe*
  Fledborough
  Gedling
  Warsop
Oxfordshire
  Banbury
  Chinnor
  Chipping Norton
  Standlake
  Wootton
Rutland
  Oakham
Shropshire
  Alberbury
  Albrighton
  Baschurch*
  Bitterley
  Bromfield
  Ercall Magna*
  Ludlow St Lawrence
  Onibury
  Oswestry
  Pontesbury
  Shrewsbury St Alkmund
  Shrewsbury St Chad
  Shrewsbury St Julian
  Shrewsbury St Mary
  Stanton Lacy
  Wem*
  Westbury*
Somersetshire
  Bridgewater
  Bruton
  Congresbury
  Crewkerne
  Martock
  Milborne Port
  North Cadbury
  North Petherton
  Pitminster
  Wedmore

Staffordshire
  Alstonefield
  Audley*
  Barton under Needwood
  Burslem
  Eccleshall
  Ellastone
  Rocester
  Sedgley*
  Stone*
  Stowe by Chartley
  Tatenhill
Suffolk
  Cavendish
  East Bergholt
  Eye
  Framlingham
  Fressingfield
  Hadleigh
  Horringer
  Ipswich St Clement
  Ipswich St Lawrence
  Ipswich St Mary Elms
  Ipswich St Mary Stoke
  Ipswich St Matthew
  Ipswich St Nicholas
  Ipswich St Peter
  Ipswich St Stephen
  Lavenham
  Laxfield
  Marlesford
  Mendlesham
  Mildenhall
  Peasenhall
  Rattlesden
  Saxmundham
  Sibton
  Stradbroke
  Wickhambrook
  Woodbridge
  Wortham
  Yoxford
Surrey
  Abinger
  Beddington
  Carshalton
  Cobham
  Cranley
  Gatton

Limpsfield
Nutfield
Putney
Reigate
Walton on the Hill
Wimbledon
Wotton
Sussex
Ardingley
Bolney
Brede
Cowfold
East Grinstead
Felpham
Frant
Hailsham
Harting
Hurstpierpoint
Northiam
Pevensey
Salehurst
Woodmancote
Worth
Warwickshire
Alcester
Budbrooke
Chilvers Coton
Curdworth
Dunchurch
Edgbaston
Harbury
Kenilworth
Kingsbury
Mancetter*
Monks Kirby
Napton
Polesworth
Rowington
Tanworth
Tredington
Wiltshire
Bishops Cannings
Bromham
Wishford Magna
Worcestershire

Kings Norton
Worcester St Helen
Yorkshire
East Riding
Bridlington
Bubwith
Etton
Hunmanby
North Riding
Easingwold*
Gilling
Kirkdale
Marske in Cleveland
Oswaldkirk
Sessay
Stainton in Cleveland
Yarm
West Riding
Addingham
Almondbury*
Adel
Bolton Percy
Brodsworth
Burnsall
Carlton juxta Snaith
Clapham
Conisborough
Darfield
Dewsbury
Emley
Farnham
Gisburne*
Guiseley*
Hartshead
Horbury
Ilkley
Kippax
Ledsham
Otley*
Skipton
Thornhill with Flockton*
Thornton in Lonsdale
Waddington
Wath upon Dearne*

The work of counting and recording the monthly totals of baptisms, burials, and marriages in the 404 parishes was carried out by a total of 230 local historians who volunteered to give assistance in the enterprise. Their names are given below. Further details may be found in successive issues of *Local Population Studies*, where the name and address of each volunteer is given when each aggregative tabulation is listed. We are, of course, equally grateful to many other volunteers whose tabulation does not form part of the sample of 404 parishes either because it did not meet the tests for inclusion or because the work arrived too late to be included.

Mr J. Addy
Rev. R. Appleton
Mrs M. E. Armstrong
Mr J. D. Asteraki
Mr B. Ayre
Dr A. R. H. Baker
Mrs P. Baker
Mrs R. R. Barker
Miss B. K. Barnardiston
Mr F. A. Barnett
Miss D. M. Bartholomew
Mr. P. Batham
Mr W. de B.-P. Batty Smith
Mr F. W. Baty
Mr. J. Benson
Mrs S. W. Bell
Rev. R. G. Bircham
Mr P. C. Birtchnell
Mrs B. Board
Mr J. Bones
Mr K. P. Boulton
Mr W. S. B. Bowring
Rev. J. W. Bransom
Mr C. A. Brown
Mr K. J. Bruce
Miss A. Buck
Mrs P. J. Bunker
Mr R. O. Calver
Mr G. Carrick
Mrs K. M. A. Carter
Mr J. J. Chadwick
Mr C. Charlton
Mr J. Charnock
Mrs M. Codling
Miss F. B. Collins
Mrs I. Cooper
Mr G. Cornwall
Mr W. Couth

Mrs J. Cowley
Mrs M. Cowley
Col. J. M. Cowper
Mrs P. Crabbe
Mrs E. M. Crane
Mrs B. Crawley
Miss M. M. H. Cross
Mrs M. Cule
Miss A. Cunningham
Mr G. C. S. Curtis
Mr G. M. R. Davies
Dr S. Davies
Miss W. L. Davis
Mr P. Dickenson
Miss J. Edwards
Mr C. A. Ellwood
Dr and Mrs F. G. Emmison
Mrs K. A. Emmison
Mr M. G. Emmison
Mr R. E. Emms
Mr K. Evans
Rev. L. E. C. Evans
Mr F. H. Erith
Mrs V. C. Findlay
Mr A. J. Fletcher
Dr J. M. Fletcher
Mrs P. Ford
Mrs J. E. Fox
Mrs D. A. Frost
Mr A. Gaydon
Mr J. S. W. Gibson
Mrs J. Goadby
Dr. A. Gooder
Mr H. E. Gough
Mrs K. M. Gow
Mr F. R. Grace
Mr J. E. Gryspeerdt
Mr W. E. Gryspeerdt

Mr R. M. B. H. Hackman
Mrs J. Hammond
Miss G. Hanks
Mr T. R. Harris
Mrs A. Harrison
Mr R. Harrison
Mr L. C. Hayward
Mrs B. Hazlewood
Mr T. Hedley Barry
Miss W. Herrington
Mr G. E. Hewlett
Mr A. R. Higgott
Mrs J. B. Hodgkiss
Mrs E. Hodgson
Mr J. T. Hopkins
Miss C. Howden
Mr J. R. Howe
Dr W. G. Howson
Mr M. C. W. Hunter
Rev. L. B. Hutchings
Mr and Mrs F. T. Jackson
Mr S. Jacques
Mr I. I. Jeffries
Mrs J. E. Jones
Mr C. H. Keene
Miss M. J. Kennedy
Mrs E. Key
Mr R. Laslett
Dr D. F. Lawton
Mrs J. Lawley
Mr G. Lea
Mrs A. Leach
Mr E. Legg
Mrs K. Leonard
Mr P. A. Little
Mr L. C. Lloyd
Mrs B. Ludlow
Mrs B. Maltby
Rev. R. A. Marchant
Mr F. Marston
Miss J. B. Martin
Mr D. McCallum
Mrs E. McLaughlin
Dr L. McMurdo
Miss G. A. Mc Neill
Mrs L. McWilliam
Miss M. G. Meades
Miss O. M. Meades
Mr R. N. Middlewick

Miss P. Miller
Dr D. Mills
Mr H. P. Mills
Mrs P. Moll
Mrs J. Moore
Dr V. Morgan
Mr E. L. Morley
Rev. F. W. Moyle
Mrs F. Neale
Mrs A. Newman
Mr W. Newman-Brown
Miss P. A. Nicklin
Mr A. H. Noble
Mr P. Northeast
Mrs B. Nuttall
Miss S. Ogley
Miss K. J. Oosterveen
Miss M. Ory
Brigadier J. J. Packard
Mr A. F. Pallister
Mr D. O. Pam
Mrs K. K. Patey
Mr G. M. Pearce
Mrs K. Percy
Miss S. T. Percy
Mrs M. F. Pickles
Mrs M. E. Pickup
Mr L. Pierce
Mr R. F. Pinfold
Mr W. H. Place
Mr F. W. Popham
Miss J. M. Potter
Mr M. Potter
Dr H. E. Priestley
Mr A. Pritchard
Mrs P. A. Puddifoot
Mr A. Purvis
Mr A. J. Pye
Mr P. Quiddington
Mrs A. Raistrick
Miss S. Ratcliffe
Mr J. Ravensdale
Miss E. Reader
Mr M. Reed
Rev. E. V. Rees-Thomas
Mr and Mrs H. Reid
Mr J. N. Rhodes
Mr W. J. Richardson
Miss O. W. Riches

Mr J. Ridgard
Mr D. T. Roberts
Mr M. Robson
Miss V. C. Roope
Mr R. H. Rose
Rev. P. Rowley
Mrs R. K. Serjeant
Mr R. Sharpe France
Miss L. Shenton
Miss M. Sheppard
Mr H. R. Shute
Miss M. A. Siviter
Mr I. M. Slocombe
Mrs P. Smedts
Mr E. W. Sockett
Mr R. Speake
Mrs D. Squires
Mr F. S. Stancliffe
Mr B. Stapleton
Mr R. L. Stevens
Mr J. E. Stoney
Mr T. H. Storey
Mr G. A. Tatchell
Mr E. G. Thomas
Mr J. P. Toomey
Mrs M. Tonkin
Mr K. S. S. Train

Mr R. W. Trubridge
Mr C. W. Turner
Mr D. Turner
Mr A. G. Veyey
Mrs P. G. Wain
Mr J. Wakelin
Mr M. L. Walker
Mr D. G. Ward
Mr J. W. Wardell
Mr M. A. Watkinson
Mr R. Watson
Mr F. West
Mrs E. Welby
Mrs Y. Welsh
Miss N. Wenham
Lt. Col. P. White
Mr G. C. Whitehouse
Mr J. C. Wilkerson
Mr J. W. J. Wilkins
Miss R. Willan
Mr A. L. Wood
Mrs E. M. Wood
Mrs J. Woodall
Mrs I. M. Woods
Mrs M. Woods
Mrs J. D. Young

Appendix 2

Monthly, annual, quinquennial, and decennial totals of births, deaths, and marriages (England less Monmouth)

From 1539 to 1836 (1837 in the case of marriages) the totals printed in table A2.1 to A2.4 below were derived from national totals of Anglican baptisms, burials, and marriages.[1] The national totals of Anglican events themselves come ultimately from a non-random sample of 404 parish registers. The original totals required extensive processing to offset periods of defective registration and to counteract the fact that registration did not begin or end at the same date in all tabulations. Furthermore, it proved necessary to re-weight the raw totals of events in the sample because comparison of the parish characteristics profile of the aggregative sample parishes with the profile of a random sample revealed some important differences between them. When the aggregative sample totals had been re-weighted they were multiplied by an empirically derived ratio to provide national totals of events. These operations are described in chapters 1 to 3. Once totals of Anglican events had been obtained, they were further corrected for nonconformity, delay in baptism, and residual non-registration as appropriate, to translate ecclesiastical into the required demographic totals. This second set of changes is described in chapters 4 and 5. The effect of each step between the raw data and the final totals may be seen by consulting table A4.1.

From 1837 onwards the *Annual Reports* of the Registrar General are available as a source of information, but his published totals of births, deaths, and marriages also needed correction. The estimation of totals of events for the period 1837–41 is described in chapter 5, and the final 40 years, 1841–71, are covered in appendix 8.

The data are listed in increasing order of detail beginning with decennial totals in table A2.1 and ending with monthly totals in table A2.4. The latter run only until 1836 (1837 in the case of marriages). The Registrar General did not publish totals for periods shorter than the quarter except for special purposes. Annual totals are printed both for the calendar year and for the year beginning 1 July. For certain purposes the latter may be the more useful unit of time. Totals of both births and deaths tended to reach a low point about the middle of the year, so that, for example, the impact of a winter epidemic on the annual death rate may be easier to gauge from a series based on the year beginning 1 July than from one based on the year beginning 1 January. The former also corresponds well to the food-price year since prices by the mid summer were already influenced by the harvest prospect and the harvest itself would then largely control prices until the approach of its successor. Annual totals for calendar years are taken to 1873 since the calculation of quinquennial rates centred on census years meant using births, deaths, and marriages for the years 1869–73 when

---

1. The inception of civil registration in 1837 caused a very marked distortion of the monthly frequencies of both baptisms and burials so that parish register data are an unreliable guide to the monthly distribution of the annual total of events in 1837, but there was no similar distortion of monthly marriage totals.

calculating rates for the five-year period centring on the census total corrected to 30 June 1871.

A semi-logarithmic graph of the annual totals of births, deaths, and marriages is provided in pullout 1 at the end of the volume. Although the data are listed in their most summary form first (decennial totals in table A2.1), they were built up from the individual monthly totals listed last (in table A2.4). In the various stages involved in transforming the raw parish register data into national estimates of births, marriages, and deaths, the monthly totals were held in long precision decimal form for intermediate operations, but rounded to whole numbers before being summed to form annual totals.

Table A2.1: Decennial totals of births, deaths, and marriages 1540-9 to 1860-9 (England less Monmouth)

Decade	Births	Deaths	Marriages
1540 – 9	1069069	850303	367599
1550 – 9	1060685	995096	312543
1560 – 9	1118907	813447	331630
1570 – 9	1135326	787456	333364
1580 – 9	1259177	875557	363571
1590 – 9	1266583	1026597	358314
1600 – 9	1413371	1000454	380574
1610 – 9	1444280	1162523	394052
1620 – 9	1516788	1228646	372296
1630 – 9	1565473	1302997	404545
1640 – 9	1609745	1333657	392173
1650 – 9	1444963	1413905	451549
1660 – 9	1482753	1485379	371831
1670 – 9	1471113	1435086	354217
1680 – 9	1564307	1601645	392142
1690 – 9	1558272	1413972	356706
1700 – 9	1638671	1376742	397065
1710 – 9	1632637	1444562	431063
1720 – 9	1754363	1767743	480115
1730 – 9	1904851	1590166	499633
1740 – 9	1848574	1641617	466349
1750 – 9	1975263	1544396	487563
1760 – 9	2138729	1770289	572228
1770 – 9	2409290	1770136	588714
1780 – 9	2652706	1999182	634293
1790 – 9	3134369	2127438	691379
1800 – 9	3563320	2343308	759763
1810 – 9	4258687	2662252	848739
1820 – 9	4770338	2846097	980007
1830 – 9	4946417	3073646	1091983
1840 – 9	5514120	3583712	1246173
1850 – 9	6283310	3894495	1486537
1860 – 9	7172372	4412429	1652852

Table A2.2: Quinquennial totals of births, deaths, and marriages 1540–4 to 1865–9 (England less Monmouth)

Quinquennium	Births	Deaths	Marriages	Quinquennium	Births	Deaths	Marriages
1540 – 4	529147	425082	184930	1700 – 4	846128	670076	204535
1545 – 9	539922	425221	182669	1705 – 9	792543	706666	192530
1550 – 4	573848	396063	167878	1710 – 4	766531	727826	207806
1555 – 9	486837	599033	144665	1715 – 9	866106	716736	223257
1560 – 4	552607	430250	180542	1720 – 4	866596	931009	245191
1565 – 9	566300	383197	151088	1725 – 9	867767	936734	234924
1570 – 4	541715	401453	162054	1730 – 4	933746	821067	267718
1575 – 9	593611	386003	171310	1735 – 9	971105	769099	231915
1580 – 4	624437	395789	176459	1740 – 4	906323	866795	230338
1585 – 9	634740	479768	187112	1745 – 9	942251	774822	236011
1590 – 4	635187	515779	186793	1750 – 4	986021	752181	236989
1595 – 9	631396	510818	171521	1755 – 9	989242	792215	250574
1600 – 4	688498	510847	188833	1760 – 4	1054513	884810	291541
1605 – 9	724873	489607	191741	1765 – 9	1084216	885479	280687
1610 – 4	713024	594068	199111	1770 – 4	1160571	880876	291036
1615 – 9	731256	568455	194941	1775 – 9	1248719	889260	297678
1620 – 4	753770	581561	177942	1780 – 4	1249260	1023918	305183
1625 – 9	763018	647085	194354	1785 – 9	1403446	975264	329110
1630 – 4	779905	586848	197771	1790 – 4	1530071	1037722	342460
1635 – 9	785568	716149	206774	1795 – 9	1601298	1089716	348919
1640 – 4	836248	725993	208181	1800 – 4	1686800	1180010	379638
1645 – 9	773497	607564	183992	1805 – 9	1876520	1163298	381125
1650 – 4	722863	657292	195652	1810 – 4	1995505	1293635	406498
1655 – 9	722100	756613	255897	1815 – 9	2263182	1368617	442241
1660 – 4	725134	662715	191049	1820 – 4	2375157	1398994	480625
1665 – 9	757619	822664	180782	1825 – 9	2395181	1447103	499382
1670 – 4	734112	705561	179871	1830 – 4	2401836	1482274	535191
1675 – 9	737001	729525	174346	1835 – 9	2545581	1591372	556792
1680 – 4	762127	851065	201070	1840 – 4	2709272	1681559	582737
1685 – 9	802180	750580	191072	1845 – 9	2804848	1902153	663436
1690 – 4	758591	705579	157454	1850 – 4	3043592	1902638	742374
1695 – 9	799681	708393	199252	1855 – 9	3239718	1991957	744163
				1860 – 4	3471164	2123988	800612
				1865 – 9	3701209	2238441	852240

Table A2.3: Annual totals of births, deaths, and marriages 1539–1873 (by calendar year January–December, and by year July–June: totals refer to England less Monmouth)

	Calendar year			Year beginning July			
Year	Births	Deaths	Marriages	Births	Deaths	Marriages	Year
1539	113857	67442	56918	114502	78736	47610	1539
1540	111615	100161	36525	94966	99687	33331	1540
1541	94167	72256	38957	106084	64321	38140	1541
1542	113752	71019	42286	112431	91782	43977	1542
1543	108371	97056	35093	107300	71248	32444	1543
1544	101242	84590	32069	101585	102478	34734	1544
1545	105256	102792	30229	105846	105461	30675	1545
1546	107647	95018	36206	101604	95499	37848	1546
1547	97919	83457	39982	116138	69439	43631	1547
1548	116675	79954	43693	107629	73440	38657	1548
1549	112425	64000	32559	118380	73491	35501	1549
1550	123206	80321	35047	121757	75947	31480	1550
1551	119350	83887	33844	120026	91847	35479	1551
1552	114460	82340	37790	114382	84747	40451	1552
1553	113921	81297	40492	100676	66702	28131	1553
1554	102911	68218	20705	109012	79023	26689	1554
1555	111986	80383	29822	114727	67117	29332	1555
1556	111327	77094	23933	98845	100859	20172	1556
1557	86159	133887	22910	82819	146564	32250	1557
1558	96146	166387	34026	100965	196801	30561	1558
1559	81219	141282	33974	81872	100040	40101	1559
1560	102383	93735	41825	107694	82775	38079	1560
1561	110637	77340	40041	106674	72303	40276	1561
1562	114505	73081	35064	124252	88195	30680	1562
1563	108786	105536	31376	104888	89408	31649	1563
1564	116296	80558	32236	124808	79722	30671	1564
1565	121367	73644	28945	114549	84803	27689	1565
1566	111404	81042	26493	112160	81286	28396	1566
1567	112301	79527	32731	117895	65285	35490	1567
1568	120203	72924	31151	109305	79880	29166	1568
1569	101025	76060	31768	102779	74391	32053	1569
1570	111172	85203	31823	111406	91579	31312	1570
1571	108830	81854	30680	109341	73107	34434	1571
1572	110311	76599	33141	108397	84391	31203	1572
1573	105562	79298	31098	106458	81448	30811	1573
1574	105840	78499	35312	108456	70787	36497	1574
1575	111475	76031	34783	114123	74233	33812	1575
1576	118130	71307	34606	117521	70289	36126	1576
1577	119425	73984	31900	122420	80322	33009	1577
1578	121832	83929	37513	121179	83302	34870	1578
1579	122749	80752	32508	128617	81854	35604	1579
1580	121440	88691	38666	115265	81007	35240	1580
1581	121524	71852	33759	123106	78237	33089	1581
1582	125779	80262	32589	129580	74282	34664	1582
1583	126153	70947	34090	127188	75417	36567	1583
1584	129541	84037	37355	128460	93783	37315	1584
1585	130292	89868	38176	128779	80867	35217	1585
1586	125217	83183	33364	117786	93624	33487	1586
1587	111902	107981	34670	113813	119904	37931	1587
1588	126541	109101	40881	140615	97192	41060	1588
1589	140788	89635	40021	129722	76672	39040	1589

Table A2.3: *(cont.)*

	Calendar year			Year beginning July			
Year	Births	Deaths	Marriages	Births	Deaths	Marriages	Year
1590	122085	91266	35223	122027	112432	32731	1590
1591	115466	110688	36169	119055	105304	38709	1591
1592	128182	110606	37391	130141	124988	37856	1592
1593	129299	121259	38793	135184	94193	39537	1593
1594	140155	81960	39217	136578	83126	38054	1594
1595	131022	83956	34942	120836	87070	33072	1595
1596	121788	96575	33703	126319	120771	31330	1596
1597	116624	133155	29204	108058	125554	33342	1597
1598	116132	105307	35259	133348	91384	36116	1598
1599	145830	91825	38413	146058	92533	38871	1599
1600	138567	86702	38270	133384	82294	37151	1600
1601	128787	84079	34949	125925	93771	35094	1601
1602	128529	100783	36171	139814	111629	36684	1602
1603	148915	142069	39511	144386	127481	38926	1603
1604	143700	97214	39932	147661	91514	42185	1604
1605	148789	90959	40716	146132	100193	40149	1605
1606	144029	97722	37955	149263	92719	36991	1606
1607	149899	94851	36219	146585	103181	36833	1607
1608	140967	104503	38346	138993	95649	37236	1608
1609	141189	101572	38505	140110	119775	38237	1609
1610	144424	126840	40109	150820	117291	43206	1610
1611	150901	108430	43873	144870	116588	42619	1611
1612	143408	123317	39739	139677	113448	38700	1612
1613	133250	115976	37974	136441	130447	36595	1613
1614	141041	119505	37416	145816	104548	39092	1614
1615	149379	112264	38863	147587	126103	37616	1615
1616	139870	131004	37228	134320	123945	36869	1616
1617	142268	116527	35738	149623	114353	39993	1617
1618	145193	107631	41750	148522	99164	40643	1618
1619	154546	101029	41362	155727	106121	40377	1619
1620	163253	104483	40889	163743	100368	40649	1620
1621	162078	99976	38795	165111	98149	35518	1621
1622	153682	101488	32035	139362	118742	31097	1622
1623	133281	144374	29687	131611	143114	33179	1623
1624	141476	131240	36536	153160	152987	36399	1624
1625	152016	197455	34112	145292	172752	34735	1625
1626	141067	118805	37086	143006	119670	35985	1626
1627	149684	109141	40081	158520	100728	41207	1627
1628	161333	106892	41342	160501	114702	43337	1628
1629	158918	114792	41733	159421	102680	41779	1629
1630	160118	116649	37895	148876	135597	34224	1630
1631	135377	131278	36611	141106	121757	39920	1631
1632	157524	114674	41281	170951	113774	41504	1632
1633	165607	112062	40359	157665	110962	39386	1633
1634	161279	112185	41625	160572	116000	43744	1634
1635	159375	123061	42464	162389	133422	40388	1635
1636	164627	145896	38377	162020	136844	39873	1636
1637	160995	129751	41460	157759	141629	39094	1637
1638	153977	159899	37628	150240	174609	39662	1638
1639	146594	157542	46845	159764	147884	49641	1639
1640	175242	142584	48392	174311	129593	47885	1640
1641	164071	132364	51131	161956	131462	50770	1641
1642	167389	132607	45389	172858	138125	41110	1642
1643	172173	163338	32184	163541	170352	28777	1643
1644	157373	155100	31085	161255	141894	38559	1644

Table A2.3: *(cont.)*

	Calendar year			Year beginning July			
Year	Births	Deaths	Marriages	Births	Deaths	Marriages	Year
1645	168614	123449	42714	168486	112171	42287	1645
1646	166437	107473	42938	164314	114918	41098	1646
1647	157007	125047	38696	148199	124799	34749	1647
1648	144687	121481	28607	145395	131507	27317	1648
1649	136752	130214	31037	127285	123815	35354	1649
1650	133961	131398	37308	146906	127517	38154	1650
1651	150658	116054	38027	141748	117992	37609	1651
1652	140650	130763	34829	141786	134930	32623	1652
1653	138433	135831	34844	147909	150186	41922	1653
1654	159161	143246	50644	165245	125375	55517	1654
1655	168375	123059	63615	166915	119181	68234	1655
1656	164110	124181	56356	150183	135124	46337	1656
1657	143571	169530	46642	138683	204185	45663	1657
1658	128444	197801	43334	122428	179569	45611	1658
1659	117600	142042	45950	127559	121869	40312	1659
1660	144477	125177	35636	147652	124170	31696	1660
1661	145953	143038	31071	140198	153630	33303	1661
1662	131949	137186	37931	135907	136486	41749	1662
1663	148419	128669	42759	158814	123002	43430	1663
1664	154336	128645	43652	147570	156341	41706	1664
1665	154350	219601	38560	158935	190440	36461	1665
1666	153812	142335	36319	148942	147771	40222	1666
1667	148629	150797	37554	150794	154414	32634	1667
1668	150035	144977	33507	148575	149449	34763	1668
1669	150793	164954	34842	150011	155786	36143	1669
1670	146494	162505	35296	142467	172522	36517	1670
1671	137397	150616	39860	140815	143197	39182	1671
1672	153310	133288	37229	153727	126916	36062	1672
1673	150913	128210	34922	154667	132401	33234	1673
1674	145998	130942	32564	138568	131439	32813	1674
1675	138004	145470	32087	146537	144745	32125	1675
1676	155413	137360	34426	155244	132410	36614	1676
1677	155384	124979	37735	151777	112024	36899	1677
1678	149528	135015	35083	146058	172971	34134	1678
1679	138672	186701	35015	139220	168665	40372	1679
1680	145500	168413	41583	151695	205220	37644	1680
1681	148385	191805	40102	144899	171293	42028	1681
1682	150430	171336	38598	155748	165701	40073	1682
1683	159808	155526	43542	159705	154047	39836	1683
1684	158004	163985	37245	156610	170030	37859	1684
1685	152580	162200	38485	151920	154068	40889	1685
1686	162880	153218	39146	166946	148893	37642	1686
1687	161776	141154	41340	160080	139003	40753	1687
1688	164319	143447	38527	167087	143307	36550	1688
1689	160625	150561	33574	158390	155529	33176	1689
1690	155240	149853	34485	154594	136564	33500	1690
1691	158209	134681	32366	155645	146896	31586	1691
1692	153796	135705	30244	155065	123292	30333	1692
1693	151849	135748	29902	142311	151088	29169	1693
1694	139497	149592	30457	148872	144789	34802	1694
1695	159379	152029	40778	165319	150377	42748	1695
1696	166309	143395	39699	165623	144814	38019	1696
1697	159507	140102	37911	156224	132256	39185	1697
1698	158351	134121	40248	157003	135087	40468	1698
1699	156135	138746	40616	157712	141504	41172	1699

Table A2.3: *(cont.)*

	Calendar year			Year beginning July			
Year	Births	Deaths	Marriages	Births	Deaths	Marriages	Year
1700	162389	140165	41705	170239	134898	39994	1700
1701	173149	135260	41871	172384	133174	43482	1701
1702	173244	128446	41722	173836	126821	40932	1702
1703	171952	127079	41273	166181	138473	38840	1703
1704	165394	139126	37964	166544	151069	40164	1704
1705	166599	162851	40698	166003	146182	40180	1705
1706	163776	137966	40573	158210	136018	41477	1706
1707	154691	130849	39006	155668	134098	35832	1707
1708	158635	140883	36581	157086	141711	36627	1708
1709	148842	134117	35672	148045	129465	37750	1709
1710	146181	138042	39379	144025	146423	37158	1710
1711	151272	148843	38176	150927	157794	39384	1711
1712	149841	157222	40061	155121	142824	43270	1712
1713	157516	134752	44289	159887	136951	45705	1713
1714	161721	148967	45901	159562	150007	46456	1714
1715	164368	137218	45516	171091	135868	42275	1715
1716	175871	139639	42001	173465	133872	43277	1716
1717	169171	132020	42638	171629	132648	46173	1717
1718	175748	136617	48766	185301	145148	47497	1718
1719	180948	171242	44336	168560	183414	41462	1719
1720	163942	173698	43663	165887	167657	45979	1720
1721	169205	168109	45971	176802	168205	46359	1721
1722	180182	158951	50307	180192	157108	53427	1722
1723	189477	168266	54024	191530	169086	53424	1723
1724	183790	161985	51226	177946	153884	48460	1724
1725	179207	137091	47907	184168	134762	48429	1725
1726	187376	150890	51094	188352	152805	50926	1726
1727	187774	194438	45538	178170	227813	44482	1727
1728	157187	215690	44718	147909	232652	44149	1728
1729	156223	238625	45667	162708	223938	49086	1729
1730	165692	190734	57582	180889	181422	59086	1730
1731	191566	179238	58792	186737	161508	59727	1731
1732	187232	157675	54260	192804	161453	49361	1732
1733	194562	154169	49276	195470	137742	50296	1733
1734	194694	139251	47808	194379	143675	46742	1734
1735	196793	145334	48167	197823	151627	46162	1735
1736	192455	153167	43785	188377	152888	42336	1736
1737	190115	167423	46236	191877	163525	48983	1737
1738	193709	150924	46072	194695	157478	47064	1738
1739	198033	152251	47655	198495	165465	46758	1739
1740	187378	173018	45343	183023	166525	41015	1740
1741	173969	193553	40705	165493	220048	43699	1741
1742	169959	202158	45031	180783	179849	45169	1742
1743	186667	159559	49654	184005	143244	50504	1743
1744	188350	138507	49605	192280	131450	48926	1744
1745	190988	141249	46002	189609	153133	46050	1745
1746	187268	157372	44969	185660	157236	46909	1746
1747	185592	161520	49408	185948	169063	47425	1747
1748	191219	162130	48234	191391	152048	48914	1748
1749	187184	152551	47398	191370	149219	48279	1749
1750	199653	158030	48127	201641	163041	45837	1750
1751	197265	151506	46880	197701	153328	48358	1751
1752	191727	147644	46789	192098	140439	47390	1752
1753	198625	145402	48541	197500	147425	49335	1753

Table A2.3: *(cont.)*

	Calendar year			Year beginning July			
Year	Births	Deaths	Marriages	Births	Deaths	Marriages	Year
1754	198751	149599	46652	201587	152093	46222	1754
1755	203002	149762	49775	205960	149185	51579	1755
1756	201401	154206	51398	190770	156166	47702	1756
1757	190765	157547	44576	186309	161763	45927	1757
1758	189592	165150	48990	196620	165260	52730	1758
1759	204482	165550	55835	212607	166935	58174	1759
1760	204966	161100	59892	206218	153958	60207	1760
1761	213587	162678	60128	215378	181748	57042	1761
1762	212467	193250	54601	204599	208560	54630	1762
1763	206057	199535	58108	214592	175074	58974	1763
1764	217436	168247	58812	218144	160413	57808	1764
1765	221115	163163	55913	215282	176677	54734	1765
1766	211101	188088	55194	212975	188822	53242	1766
1767	213126	185804	51994	213207	187586	54836	1767
1768	213155	175716	57083	219513	170062	59058	1768
1769	225719	172708	60503	229663	175734	60371	1769
1770	235144	182994	60342	231603	182697	59783	1770
1771	226894	175401	57762	232212	175995	56437	1771
1772	232010	177662	58169	232833	174227	59294	1772
1773	236297	180825	56899	230563	175796	56190	1773
1774	230226	163994	57864	238917	161009	58612	1774
1775	243847	173041	57508	246174	174794	56493	1775
1776	242978	165654	58958	248126	176186	61259	1776
1777	251571	178228	61514	250552	172548	61963	1777
1778	253945	177954	60983	255791	183597	60647	1778
1779	256378	194383	58715	252779	208555	60056	1779
1780	252199	202359	62522	250604	193180	62098	1780
1781	250187	209350	59875	247480	217293	57479	1781
1782	246670	200399	58948	248108	187019	59723	1782
1783	248266	208538	61985	246021	224593	62486	1783
1784	251938	203272	61853	269453	193297	66681	1784
1785	270689	197046	70771	272634	197383	67181	1785
1786	280424	194906	65206	276818	192172	64267	1786
1787	274808	190471	64490	286709	192713	66340	1787
1788	291543	199962	65262	286688	202373	63967	1788
1789	285982	192879	63381	298750	190193	65532	1789
1790	301289	197275	67547	293250	198491	66857	1790
1791	297011	196442	66577	303803	197986	69446	1791
1792	316921	202918	71089	318049	219584	72622	1792
1793	311117	225051	70981	306369	214967	67033	1793
1794	306733	216036	66266	314518	234719	63129	1794
1795	311267	235676	60714	312515	211236	64868	1795
1796	310336	206040	69693	314975	223756	72357	1796
1797	329823	225671	72216	329670	211539	74613	1797
1798	329981	209346	76518	325964	219588	71647	1798
1799	319891	212983	69778	323885	213907	68456	1799
1800	315010	229891	63680	299680	236699	59494	1800
1801	293780	243178	59974	305299	235912	68632	1801
1802	339925	235950	84718	368608	254507	90639	1802
1803	365127	251024	88531	357263	229551	85075	1803
1804	372958	219967	81735	383758	219987	79696	1804
1805	372976	218154	75730	369545	213116	74217	1805
1806	374781	215055	74401	376022	236826	76923	1806
1807	376791	244848	80367	378268	243571	78878	1807
1808	379576	246600	76544	366977	237714	74614	1808

Table A2.3: *(cont.)*

Year	Calendar year			Year beginning July			Year
	Births	Deaths	Marriages	Births	Deaths	Marriages	
1809	372396	238641	74083	378546	260027	75167	1809
1810	385489	272767	75565	395762	265784	80028	1810
1811	394990	262006	83475	391457	258960	80955	1811
1812	391257	247742	79649	401882	240711	79800	1812
1813	407295	242277	78216	411281	269595	82718	1813
1814	416474	268843	89593	442714	250183	92751	1814
1815	464302	263372	94719	460880	282086	94665	1815
1816	449663	276783	89310	449982	264116	84110	1816
1817	453762	268530	83413	439374	271629	83801	1817
1818	448392	282159	89270	457334	280673	88091	1818
1819	447063	277773	85529	444393	285974	90383	1819
1820	449847	271304	93234	460081	258189	90315	1820
1821	469453	269024	92682	482518	274047	98943	1821
1822	489990	275524	98452	489551	289727	98178	1822
1823	484953	292116	98153	477854	287407	98436	1823
1824	480914	291026	98104	488018	283943	101421	1824
1825	484533	296920	105969	482275	303304	100301	1825
1826	489633	300328	97865	469673	301252	97605	1826
1827	468368	285826	92754	491324	277559	98610	1827
1828	490940	277741	109033	479961	290539	102413	1828
1829	461707	286288	93761	456605	271389	93524	1829
1830	466050	271424	95967	468228	274328	100831	1830
1831	467910	298572	104744	471461	316907	106482	1831
1832	472112	308540	108632	487785	303625	110056	1832
1833	500219	296677	114002	492184	284234	117997	1833
1834	495545	307061	111846	494643	320132	107894	1834
1835	495431	306697	109360	503795	312603	112759	1835
1836	505473	306300	114738	507103	319877	108065	1836
1837	504264	325057	106262	502898	322939	108562	1837
1838	508541	328119	111113	522180	317646	113490	1838
1839	530872	325199	115319	537000	336006	116439	1839
1840	534461	344583	114900	533308	340135	114917	1840
1841	538231	329194	115087	542198	327321	114038	1841
1842	539238	334563	111475	535060	333900	112020	1842
1843	544273	331620	116675	554443	335641	120736	1843
1844	553069	341659	124600	549843	345448	128667	1844
1845	550790	334416	135439	562847	323590	139549	1845
1846	574911	372148	136542	565333	415803	130187	1846
1847	541158	402012	127477	544078	394888	127770	1847
1848	562242	378221	130704	579348	366339	131853	1848
1849	575747	415356	133274	567910	398883	138213	1849
1850	589332	346280	143421	603803	358607	145218	1850
1851	608969	370367	145011	613004	372396	146763	1851
1852	616265	381363	149510	615472	398957	151789	1852
1853	604042	394442	154616	616276	383823	152872	1853
1854	624984	410186	149816	622867	435108	143845	1854
1855	624839	398756	142392	635257	363234	146592	1855
1856	646089	365787	149045	644063	371031	151486	1856
1857	650802	393241	148902	649602	415956	144400	1857
1858	642553	421193	146520	653224	415807	153612	1858
1859	675435	412880	157304	680690	418758	158839	1859
1860	668891	395963	160147	669007	391984	156969	1860
1861	680163	408402	154224	689189	409001	153674	1861
1862	695022	409765	154188	702203	425540	158697	1862
1863	707928	444748	162940	713204	457550	165462	1863

Table A2.3: *(cont.)*

	Calendar year			Year beginning July			
Year	Births	Deaths	Marriages	Births	Deaths	Marriages	Year
1864	719160	465110	169113	723673	461771	169215	1864
1865	725435	460767	174195	726770	470517	177701	1865
1866	729755	469952	176491	734137	450876	172578	1866
1867	742438	442154	168429	748506	426501	168619	1867
1868	758960	451117	166659	749570	472101	165469	1868
1869	744620	464451	166466	760844	476520	168543	1869
1870	761930	483693	170702	762750	478429	172676	1870
1871	766666	483471	179110				
1872	794046	462237	189141				
1873	797768	462476	192850				

Table A2.4: Monthly totals of births, deaths, and marriages 1539–1837 (England less Monmouth)

Births

Year	Jan.	Feb.	Mar.	Apr.	May	Jun.	Jul.	Aug.	Sep.	Oct.	Nov.	Dec.
1539	8595	12576	12649	17334	4083	6870	8154	7984	11106	6850	10757	6899
1540	14611	9532	14957	7407	11312	4933	8349	6795	6643	7680	13625	5771
1541	6229	11832	9245	7163	4999	6635	11027	5608	6188	9733	9906	5602
1542	9341	12380	8201	10904	9132	8062	7249	9356	7603	10675	12554	8295
1543	9033	11590	10301	11847	8253	5675	7540	9675	11282	9216	7638	6321
1544	11294	9397	10691	8918	9584	5744	9416	6968	8474	7545	5182	8029
1545	8557	7683	13434	9831	7021	9445	6709	8876	12817	6087	7605	7191
1546	7778	11238	12144	9704	9799	5898	7276	7822	10232	7771	8407	9578
1547	8801	11459	8914	7018	6164	8162	6156	7683	8697	9338	6311	9216
1548	9864	14462	9398	13606	8903	12504	9351	5952	7186	6613	8378	10458
1549	9775	13575	13577	8726	8635	5403	7895	7200	10259	10520	9678	7182
1550	10344	15486	14787	10424	6251	8354	9592	7963	6932	12109	12959	8005
1551	13199	10142	15469	9497	8931	6959	6878	9822	10372	10376	10465	7240
1552	9563	13936	13035	9789	9743	8807	6993	8418	9305	8600	6306	9965
1553	13982	9075	12658	11541	8456	9083	7704	5707	6029	13689	10570	5427
1554	8339	10473	12434	7553	6869	5882	9264	6538	10514	11921	6965	6159
1555	12477	9153	10493	8149	6728	10651	4472	7586	16728	8172	9942	7435
1556	10197	11324	11005	10225	9732	7909	5529	8453	9242	6551	10863	10297
1557	9517	8487	9406	9334	5995	5171	4517	4208	7617	9555	6528	5824
1558	8984	8095	8511	8420	7229	3331	6165	8973	7771	8072	8517	12078
1559	10241	9979	10634	9275	5867	3393	3727	4135	4993	5429	6621	6925
1560	6321	6834	9791	10655	7131	9310	6916	7475	10349	8197	9180	10224
1561	9307	9907	13266	8349	8261	6263	7744	12184	8477	8582	10147	8150
1562	8167	8750	11692	8034	7576	7171	9789	10040	10582	10265	10899	11540
1563	11625	9791	12153	9048	11263	7257	6565	8700	7678	8503	8547	7656
1564	10426	9268	11527	9397	8318	8303	8363	8194	10805	10891	11034	9770
1565	11653	10129	13043	12786	9539	8601	9664	8716	10017	10006	9072	8141
1566	10935	11159	12279	9227	7655	7678	7636	8087	10076	9828	8704	8140
1567	10276	9299	13522	9410	8046	9136	6710	8928	8920	9850	9609	8595
1568	13222	12918	12512	9583	8891	8157	7276	9793	11282	10166	7834	8569
1569	9016	9303	10007	9701	8960	7398	6549	7430	9378	9220	7404	6659

Table A2.4: *(cont.)*

Births

Year	Jan.	Feb.	Mar.	Apr.	May	Jun.	Jul.	Aug.	Sep.	Oct.	Nov.	Dec.
1570	9054	8730	9382	12011	7853	9109	8872	9186	9222	10920	8357	8476
1571	10763	11422	9564	10636	7564	6424	6924	9755	9555	8727	8679	8817
1572	9023	9848	12281	9198	8698	7836	5504	9758	8902	8407	11420	9436
1573	9654	9074	11415	9893	8592	6342	6097	9366	9702	8382	8994	8051
1574	11237	11086	8982	9118	9747	5696	6498	7949	9853	9447	7727	8500
1575	9648	11042	12235	10337	7838	7382	9242	7613	10369	8011	9134	8624
1576	12048	11864	11579	9747	8226	7666	7882	8149	11010	8712	10788	10459
1577	9830	10916	11645	10936	8515	8679	7106	8989	10801	10861	9738	11409
1578	12014	11029	13440	10447	7962	8624	6533	9267	10121	10799	10905	10691
1579	11005	11492	11763	9757	10596	8250	6943	9218	10575	10186	12037	10927
1580	12009	12252	13346	13148	10324	7652	8627	7920	8349	9780	9140	8893
1581	11665	12413	11649	11474	7342	8013	8346	8731	10239	10274	11250	10128
1582	10874	11768	11458	12757	8499	8782	8358	8229	13330	10354	10947	10423
1583	11879	12557	14832	9986	9957	8728	7607	8546	10707	10338	10952	10064
1584	11139	13119	14303	11541	10563	8309	7658	11142	10888	9658	11089	10132
1585	12936	13177	13580	10138	9751	8311	8142	12128	11492	11801	10017	8819
1586	11154	12723	13149	11446	9158	8750	7924	10132	10151	12476	8710	9444
1587	11050	10554	10819	11860	8515	6151	6855	8770	8616	9766	9604	9342
1588	10320	10943	12057	10383	8518	8639	7397	10158	12512	12161	10281	13172
1589	13233	13043	15262	12622	10992	9782	9042	12519	12075	10511	12096	9611
1590	12085	10938	11347	10541	11679	7278	8018	9765	9262	10494	10969	9709
1591	13015	12681	13256	9897	8005	6956	6161	9704	10302	9854	8523	7112
1592	11489	12566	13374	12478	9401	8091	8377	9210	11575	11776	9324	10521
1593	10314	12686	13305	13942	10217	8894	9971	9370	11398	9281	10625	9296
1594	11166	14150	13613	13566	11152	11596	10893	9696	12516	11423	8854	11530
1595	11448	13158	14148	13401	9612	9899	8251	10483	11429	8918	10659	9616
1596	10255	10873	11783	10688	9126	8755	8160	9856	10353	11034	10899	10006
1597	13919	12562	12763	10017	10116	6634	7914	8435	9434	8251	7720	8859
1598	9173	10205	10377	11709	8577	7404	8425	7996	9483	10350	10050	12383
1599	13791	13607	13327	13349	10576	10011	10328	10312	14709	10798	12132	12890
1600	13802	14530	14336	12229	9309	10683	8652	11609	9767	10593	11371	11686
1601	11326	12695	15338	11201	9688	9458	8379	10029	10014	11795	9714	9150
1602	11356	11800	12651	13349	9659	8029	8508	10998	9515	11031	10697	10936
1603	13400	13759	17366	11768	11754	10082	10865	10411	10994	13648	12681	12187
1604	13634	12359	14075	13364	11063	9105	10198	10773	12494	11761	11342	13532
1605	14077	14500	15240	12947	10155	10642	8986	11861	12939	13281	11730	12431
1606	11906	14391	15317	12111	10937	10242	9766	11673	11962	11345	13529	10850
1607	13792	15290	15683	13184	12819	9370	10730	11309	11901	11973	13140	10708
1608	14294	14559	14844	11806	11304	10017	8603	10230	11302	12749	10890	10369
1609	14225	12798	14637	13424	10514	9252	9323	8957	10076	11778	12248	13957

Table A2.4: *(cont.)*

Births

Year	Jan.	Feb.	Mar.	Apr.	May	Jun.	Jul.	Aug.	Sep.	Oct.	Nov.	Dec.
1610	13038	13965	14296	14616	10049	7807	10146	10046	13114	12893	11463	12991
1611	13533	14293	17756	12707	10711	11167	9650	9944	12381	12110	10801	15848
1612	13487	13597	15653	11858	10252	9289	9583	12881	11159	12406	12693	10550
1613	13230	13697	13634	10835	11061	7948	8657	10028	10535	12238	11661	9726
1614	14135	13694	13579	12904	10680	8604	9564	9498	12340	14920	10279	10844
1615	12704	13434	14989	14236	12424	10584	10456	10968	11905	13926	11644	12109
1616	14770	14604	15004	12239	9181	10781	7445	10606	11957	10502	10180	12601
1617	12162	12849	14107	11358	9082	11471	8697	11913	12489	12254	14515	11371
1618	12729	13628	17028	12776	13019	9204	8736	11379	11321	11948	12609	10816
1619	14425	15329	15613	13361	12713	10272	8938	12021	12542	14460	13158	11714
1620	15325	13473	15880	15738	11619	10859	11467	10461	13244	15115	14487	15585
1621	13566	16663	14805	15330	11386	11634	11005	11270	14468	13359	14228	14364
1622	15362	14116	16996	15415	13505	11023	8717	9721	11806	11600	12264	13157
1623	12422	13133	16161	12192	9489	8700	8539	9465	8057	12147	10953	12023
1624	11168	14793	12834	11285	11342	9005	8775	11341	12826	14317	11849	11941
1625	16421	14933	15944	14344	11583	8886	10678	12229	11872	13012	11063	11051
1626	15596	12740	15220	13549	10153	8129	9649	9779	10975	12968	10836	11473
1627	12642	13214	15851	15120	12003	8496	10438	10472	13253	12350	13232	12613
1628	13458	15147	17823	14607	13265	11862	10294	12200	12361	12332	14803	13181
1629	14781	14932	16640	14336	13723	10918	9788	12399	12728	12809	13534	12330
1630	16188	16764	16779	12969	12733	10400	9454	13864	11200	14035	13820	11912
1631	14863	14980	13730	11611	11240	8167	9508	8492	9774	11726	10915	10371
1632	13148	13644	15919	16645	10493	10471	10271	10473	13410	14339	13070	15641
1633	14500	16197	21467	14777	13644	13162	9853	10138	13352	12792	11594	14131
1634	14126	14694	17725	14838	12647	11775	9365	11958	12292	12530	15028	13801
1635	15264	15344	16738	12725	14850	10177	10243	12030	12898	12163	14113	12830
1636	16421	17279	15634	13938	14111	10729	10617	11643	13232	14988	12627	13408
1637	14991	15399	15904	16057	11988	11166	10556	12485	11469	13358	13402	14220
1638	16344	16161	15481	13629	9953	10701	11038	11390	12627	11697	12304	12652
1639	13709	14133	19083	13575	8622	9410	8354	9449	13371	11670	12550	12668
1640	13232	14948	19553	16103	16380	11486	11095	14857	14614	13886	15399	13689
1641	15623	13688	18550	15542	15500	11868	11036	13085	11784	13979	12221	11195
1642	15034	16072	15746	14467	16659	10678	11246	12031	12518	16173	13128	13637
1643	16659	17295	17055	18069	12854	12193	13393	12357	12633	14049	13885	11731
1644	14690	16411	17516	13057	11957	10965	9167	10449	13782	13551	11818	13113
1645	16329	15022	18214	15186	13372	12667	10190	13234	14153	13246	14079	14337
1646	14683	14942	18939	16713	13746	10598	10806	11094	12499	13353	16467	12971
1647	15456	17556	16365	13591	11042	10410	8785	13480	11622	13261	9829	12906
1648	15554	13253	15397	14349	11170	8721	8798	10472	11806	12029	11777	11489
1649	13123	14351	15104	15875		9401	8987	8059	10050	10578	9323	10731

Table A2.4: (cont.)

Births

Year	Jan.	Feb.	Mar.	Apr.	May	Jun.	Jul.	Aug.	Sep.	Oct.	Nov.	Dec.
1650	9914	10652	15334	13749	10003	9905	8526	10401	12376	11269	11158	10674
1651	14109	12686	17785	15180	11126	11616	10536	11064	11403	12689	11572	10892
1652	11038	13857	16049	14236	10323	8089	9323	11177	10926	12091	11415	12126
1653	15318	12341	16045	11573	11651	7800	9203	7349	10896	13750	11498	11009
1654	13066	16278	15903	15722	12825	10410	12101	10631	13954	12585	12300	13386
1655	14903	14639	17381	16668	13765	12933	12393	11786	14567	13951	12919	12471
1656	15279	14058	17378	17124	12522	12467	11211	11843	12805	12408	13230	13785
1657	13877	12884	16259	11569	11430	8882	9515	12251	11606	12426	11034	11838
1658	12342	12778	15324	12350	9231	7988	9105	8226	10840	10700	9222	10338
1659	9944	11258	13536	11211	10905	7143	8128	7366	9805	9838	9213	9253
1660	11534	13547	13710	14612	10752	9801	10068	11609	13162	12946	10683	12053
1661	12769	12752	15663	14002	11799	10146	10331	9812	12121	11720	11497	13341
1662	12513	13253	12941	13286	10892	8491	8192	10038	9799	11516	10761	10267
1663	11652	13151	13799	13816	12636	10280	10687	11778	12708	12250	13133	12529
1664	13915	15521	15552	15225	14662	10854	10946	10031	11722	11698	12596	11614
1665	13758	13136	14769	14553	12316	10431	12008	11306	13609	13376	12371	12717
1666	14872	14926	15227	14935	13050	10538	9521	10155	12732	13719	11643	12494
1667	13205	14616	16129	12259	12688	9781	9765	9441	12310	12560	12763	13112
1668	13979	15258	15930	13811	12359	9496	9615	10839	11062	12105	13323	12248
1669	13507	13206	15767	13270	12682	10951	10913	11896	10934	13543	12196	11928
1670	14413	11778	15435	15557	12405	9013	9647	9989	11548	11803	12554	12352
1671	13338	14414	14224	13797	10254	8547	8533	7876	11202	12610	11163	11439
1672	13335	12559	16290	13390	11886	12532	10798	10839	13220	14145	12302	14014
1673	13659	13118	15136	14559	11293	10644	10634	13500	10227	11862	13799	12482
1674	14483	13721	16990	13883	13776	9310	9017	10390	10854	12718	11469	9387
1675	11721	12229	13060	14429	12775	10519	9830	10212	9963	11610	11117	10539
1676	14886	13775	15176	15277	12828	11324	10125	11639	10180	13553	13811	12833
1677	15569	13382	14643	15606	12314	11583	11822	10735	12804	12460	12340	12126
1678	12632	13029	17388	13956	12320	10165	9993	10241	13095	13095	10527	13087
1679	11579	13666	17942	13023	10538	9272	8494	9908	11801	11694	10005	10750
1680	13239	13910	14720	13303	11554	9842	9532	9775	11351	12115	13338	12821
1681	15385	14567	15478	14487	14020	8826	9160	8597	12037	12729	12422	10677
1682	12562	13425	14619	15044	13244	10383	11316	9762	11279	13288	12584	12924
1683	14296	13703	15930	15213	13380	12073	11313	11909	14075	12914	11275	13727
1684	13551	14845	16086	15245	12977	11788	10854	12838	12241	12971	11894	12714
1685	14353	15063	16440	13947	12890	10405	9323	10864	11860	11718	12382	13335
1686	15462	12941	15064	15503	13440	10045	10255	11551	14609	14213	14426	15388
1687	16773	14405	17113	13746	14322	10145	11673	11510	12934	13984	13143	12028
1688	13635	16010	14064	16167	13230	11702	12843	11448	14930	13724	11842	14724
1689	13703	14800	14956	16167	14137	13813	11589	10332	12566	13659	11755	13148

Table A2.4: *(cont.)*

Births

Year	Jan.	Feb.	Mar.	Apr.	May	Jun.	Jul.	Aug.	Sep.	Oct.	Nov.	Dec.
1690	14341	13915	16496	16961	11860	11768	10995	11145	10585	12224	12331	12619
1691	14273	14552	15425	15623	13347	11475	9229	11935	13400	12167	12575	14208
1692	13735	14990	17214	12880	11931	11381	11786	10337	10672	13551	12566	12753
1693	14883	13352	16053	14395	13178	11539	11750	10032	10689	12648	10421	12909
1694	12788	12371	13977	14225	11890	8611	9155	9010	11626	12687	12175	10982
1695	14332	12570	16568	14824	13024	11919	11230	11273	13222	12793	13410	14214
1696	14787	16370	15918	17022	12888	12192	11273	11790	12367	14717	13564	13421
1697	14427	17137	15544	16288	13510	11585	10350	11680	10564	13704	11586	13132
1698	15657	14858	16964	13531	13839	10359	12617	12115	10509	13788	10995	13119
1699	15163	15113	14368	15670	12589	10957	12315	11115	11203	13189	11571	12882
1700	14874	13658	16434	15221	12656	12594	12336	11665	12430	14280	12497	13744
1701	15134	15688	19378	16110	13724	13253	10884	12785	12481	14379	16497	12836
1702	14408	15277	20579	16672	13739	11847	11182	12782	12809	13948	14000	16001
1703	17502	15876	17543	15648	14341	12204	11711	13088	13574	13693	12408	15549
1704	16378	15305	16785	15197	13031	10647	12700	12091	14713	14005	12652	13029
1705	15257	15398	15512	15540	15049	11737	12312	11554	13389	14285	12400	12842
1706	14407	16970	17388	14464	12947	11721	11542	11413	10305	14227	10778	14530
1707	13244	16605	14787	12286	13194	12215	10269	12601	11875	12515	13053	13617
1708	14802	15856	14126	14337	12908	11279	10865	13806	13000	13121	12951	12709
1709	14069	13080	15328	13976	14227	11079	11225	10913	9342	13923	10667	11013
1710	13127	13557	15114	16125	13484	9555	10923	9239	10050	12044	11321	11642
1711	13261	12709	14275	15326	12920	10315	11921	11260	12581	12098	12436	12170
1712	13018	13554	15898	13116	11930	10945	11548	11214	11741	12533	12168	12176
1713	13188	14736	15672	15543	14765	10837	10805	12274	13237	12106	12846	12507
1714	13296	14111	19277	14575	13886	10967	11637	11819	12978	13704	11963	13508
1715	15834	15358	14485	14267	12838	11171	14687	12486	13019	13894	13229	13100
1716	14139	15592	17502	17892	14285	11266	14807	11888	14585	13844	14530	15541
1717	13959	15355	17359	13988	13513	14096	12064	12246	15080	13818	13198	14495
1718	15194	15895	17155	17320	12866	12298	12524	14545	13122	14483	14537	15809
1719	16419	17527	19327	15687	17307	14014	11961	13644	12675	14082	13320	14985
1720	17240	16887	16577	14539	12864	9786	10938	11716	13801	14035	12876	12683
1721	15517	15177	16845	17478	13742	11079	12890	12284	12997	14967	11863	14366
1722	15596	16578	18704	17351	16141	13065	12849	11770	13865	14910	14695	14645
1723	16024	15436	18350	16561	15527	15547	12137	13577	16210	16356	15630	17410
1724	18694	16547	17819	16617	15838	13983	12903	14141	14175	14749	14369	14721
1725	16277	16684	16213	14330	17219	12931	14465	12113	14085	15660	15496	15296
1726	16347	18444	16685	16792	16376	13971	13703	14414	14475	15419	13985	16003
1727	18437	16451	17813	17349	15990	13551	13000	13312	14251	16159	15623	15135
1728	15302	16292	18892	16085	12170	11246	9636	9413	11132	13132	11681	12206
1729	12872	14442	17353	14067	11500	10475	10761	12881	13187	12673	13548	12464

Table A2.4: *(cont)*

Births

Year	Jan.	Feb.	Mar.	Apr.	May	Jun.	Jul.	Aug.	Sep.	Oct.	Nov.	Dec.
1730	12613	13418	17062	16015	16107	11979	11005	11568	11493	14568	15597	14267
1731	17628	16126	17529	18877	17041	15190	14325	14008	14765	16733	14037	15307
1732	17214	14698	17853	18295	15590	13912	12484	13672	14548	16319	15428	17219
1733	19232	15969	17355	18623	17919	14036	15727	14296	18415	14310	13391	15289
1734	16528	18604	20316	17098	15192	16304	13232	14258	16549	16173	15310	16930
1735	20526	17756	17424	17820	15531	14670	15219	14592	16346	16345	16008	14556
1736	19898	18170	18442	18225	16407	13615	12148	15508	14771	16506	13943	14822
1737	18108	16775	17702	17716	16493	13885	15685	11999	14684	16732	15090	15246
1738	17486	17353	18154	17916	16205	13330	14780	11737	15023	16855	13608	19265
1739	17764	17763	17955	19625	16173	14147	15594	13490	14326	16813	16854	17529
1740	17480	15589	19025	19611	17182	15002	14281	13894	12777	13785	15271	13481
1741	15741	16241	19284	17698	16996	13574	12456	11380	12510	12487	13033	12569
1742	16535	13746	16616	14862	14925	14374	13374	13818	12438	13910	12002	13359
1743	16954	16967	16695	18844	19203	13219	13751	12113	13573	15538	14676	15134
1744	17110	15835	18324	16590	16622	14739	15480	12667	16714	14763	14752	14754
1745	17839	16224	18455	17931	15899	16802	13210	12434	15763	15299	14452	16680
1746	16062	16322	19089	16665	17220	16413	12946	13819	14977	13778	15215	14762
1747	17327	15995	19183	16553	16845	14260	12500	14565	13973	14904	14461	15026
1748	19405	16636	15489	17602	16552	14835	14704	14640	14132	16707	13967	16550
1749	16928	16809	19443	17694	16073	13744	15799	12564	13022	15012	14454	15642
1750	16418	16339	18068	22007	15409	16636	14891	13171	18024	15841	14601	18248
1751	18275	18260	20495	18571	16444	14820	13076	13607	15295	14726	15669	18027
1752	16423	17297	21487	19807	18502	13785	15144	14437	8036	16274	14028	16507
1753	17747	16386	19111	22156	16006	16266	15947	12732	16657	15522	14025	16070
1754	18507	16108	20408	17491	14949	19084	15185	14282	15956	16041	15720	15020
1755	18080	16340	20860	18296	18936	16871	15252	15683	15334	15319	16009	16022
1756	18470	19795	18349	19039	18759	17929	14034	14837	13719	16828	14167	15475
1757	17304	15521	17428	18135	18999	14323	16782	14078	14002	17191	13837	13165
1758	15479	15420	17156	18067	16996	14136	15950	14204	14515	17191	14229	16249
1759	17218	17541	16849	20127	17142	15405	18254	14253	17669	16785	13933	19306
1760	19395	19090	18049	19048	19926	16899	15614	15816	14661	15226	14745	16497
1761	20263	18030	21225	16974	20943	16224	16526	16410	15714	16681	17283	17314
1762	21841	18018	18692	20356	19425	17118	15724	15310	16726	17947	15770	15540
1763	19101	15990	16330	19357	19799	17005	18198	15493	14335	19409	14310	16730
1764	18355	17555	20597	24173	17723	17714	17954	14979	16774	16692	15980	18940
1765	17934	17395	21039	20787	19136	20534	16136	15658	19754	17986	16579	18177
1766	17980	18127	20913	18264	18247	17461	16263	18146	14684	16937	16942	17137
1767	16711	19122	20959	18766	16925	19383	17378	17358	14292	16644	19384	15204
1768	20188	16685	18426	20331	20705	16612	19571	15253	14767	17540	15945	17132
1769	20171	18831	22852	20447	18805	18199	18764	16051	16701	19025	16386	19487

Table A2.4: *(cont.)*

Births

Year	Jan.	Feb.	Mar.	Apr.	May	Jun.	Jul.	Aug.	Sep.	Oct.	Nov.	Dec.
1770	19312	19118	19097	26009	18240	21473	20450	16284	20632	16972	16991	20566
1771	17811	19021	22082	20320	20758	19716	19178	16493	19644	16869	16558	18444
1772	18047	18772	21660	22802	20860	22885	18920	17650	15059	17884	18284	19187
1773	21981	19602	21442	23185	22073	17566	17147	16860	17297	21442	17340	20362
1774	21036	17859	18557	21880	22762	18021	21303	16225	17115	20814	16803	17851
1775	22672	19187	21944	26012	19286	19705	20964	15923	16876	21355	17195	22728
1776	16905	21953	24730	21998	21903	23644	17912	17336	18008	19044	17177	22368
1777	20891	20555	27909	21604	22301	23021	19414	20689	19099	19093	19120	22875
1778	21949	19730	24233	26437	21921	20992	19689	20816	18634	18811	20267	20466
1779	23510	23947	23068	24965	23560	18058	17752	19932	19189	22237	18183	21977
1780	24356	22047	25110	21657	21362	18977	20634	17964	16539	21026	19176	23351
1781	21229	21631	22009	25433	19325	22287	21618	15322	22337	19483	17731	21782
1782	21025	21476	22829	21979	22135	19763	18891	16555	20837	18473	17645	25062
1783	22072	19749	21981	22431	20657	23755	19219	18647	20124	19749	20674	19208
1784	20866	22749	21314	23065	22061	18105	20564	20296	18438	24137	18503	21600
1785	24373	21052	25744	23461	29803	21482	24162	18786	21741	23649	17980	18456
1786	24405	22439	21719	30764	23442	25091	26756	19335	19260	24824	18159	24230
1787	23274	22010	22974	28741	25037	22218	22484	19414	23809	20992	19476	24379
1788	24844	24949	30928	22814	26652	25968	22031	22550	24061	21651	21830	23265
1789	23117	24406	26492	28699	23645	24941	21452	22947	19108	23347	24557	23271
1790	31686	26249	26265	28951	30020	20897	22446	22853	19935	24500	22717	24770
1791	26620	22958	25145	29212	25743	26351	26288	21777	23843	25715	20650	22709
1792	30099	24396	24963	31903	27139	24321	29053	22606	25794	23248	23818	29581
1793	25868	23828	30029	27862	27534	28828	22940	20874	27623	24079	22026	29626
1794	25716	24453	28725	29836	22108	28363	24337	23431	23878	23702	25758	26426
1795	24335	25136	32006	29146	32941	23422	22837	26320	22659	26282	24761	21422
1796	28326	24864	29854	25054	34048	26088	26418	20990	22048	25257	23105	24284
1797	30306	29085	27983	30343	26814	28342	28558	25634	23194	26813	23213	29538
1798	24668	28102	27665	36608	29841	25836	30494	23817	27819	23076	24208	27847
1799	27577	22164	35533	25462	29595	28372	24117	24063	26064	25233	22501	29210
1800	23009	26312	31226	32004	25296	34850	25213	26694	23092	24270	22379	20665
1801	24814	22588	25966	28457	29562	25980	21833	22962	22384	21772	22490	24972
1802	27231	23072	28469	27684	30747	31683	28453	28118	29732	30890	24959	28887
1803	34129	28306	30744	38170	37042	29178	32865	26186	28741	30650	24332	24784
1804	32332	29637	28243	38318	33298	27877	33410	27990	32130	29736	27335	32652
1805	27327	29754	34870	38521	29847	40186	29084	26810	29784	28599	27590	30604
1806	28343	31280	31591	37988	35853	32019	28454	30377	28411	29673	29791	31001
1807	31940	27901	40602	28344	38982	30546	29503	30897	28425	29897	29909	29845
1808	36441	27799	30155	35258	34477	35662	36482	27324	29199	33171	26801	26807
1809	30646	26884	30792	36085	33106	29680	35000	28211	27439	33961	27438	33154

Table A2.4: (cont.)

Births

Year	Jan.	Feb.	Mar.	Apr.	May	Jun.	Jul.	Aug.	Sep.	Oct.	Nov.	Dec.
1810	30749	27813	31757	37411	29562	36051	36360	30125	34281	30382	25902	35096
1811	30519	28846	35772	36575	28990	42914	32785	28660	37337	29915	30278	32399
1812	32162	31906	36298	30960	38860	29897	32824	33544	29645	28632	33138	33391
1813	38341	30741	31534	34952	36598	38542	34036	34542	32266	33005	31178	34834
1814	29579	36146	34179	37849	45710	31231	40536	33190	35526	36817	28413	30558
1815	38452	33965	44289	43423	43839	36966	41986	35694	37613	40700	30567	38895
1816	37981	34293	42565	43562	34469	44642	35568	34611	35353	37042	31749	35568
1817	33930	32206	45678	42986	40801	42230	35288	39197	34695	33911	35929	36253
1818	35887	31664	40207	36512	44200	34973	34774	41607	38080	34090	39926	39857
1819	43526	33187	37231	40701	43424	34316	33224	38502	38495	38915	31370	34587
1820	39718	32250	35129	49390	41090	32138	40998	36416	34274	38884	30507	39053
1821	37016	35999	41094	49348	33835	42657	42419	37132	38678	39072	33213	38990
1822	37772	38064	42514	47841	43770	43053	37710	40990	43449	32999	37362	44466
1823	35606	36764	52900	38574	43749	44982	38271	41831	37365	38688	39201	37022
1824	36002	41843	40381	44010	40301	42939	40749	44990	36397	40520	35345	37437
1825	43328	36026	37865	48749	51504	35108	43494	35717	37854	44819	33664	36405
1826	43297	38563	45066	41837	45002	36557	42997	37245	37767	42077	34045	45180
1827	33111	34135	35538	51062	34629	41887	42745	35410	44418	38014	35367	42052
1828	34724	37854	46574	46679	44503	42984	37709	44422	40806	39616	37356	37713
1829	31067	37591	49093	42226	42187	40175	39052	41923	36406	34637	35134	32216
1830	35598	36308	38462	41242	44904	40723	35059	46369	36907	43657	31009	35812
1831	41140	35069	38331	41095	48502	35278	41563	38857	36428	44655	33014	33978
1832	44826	36482	39916	45303	35833	40606	39835	32898	46155	34820	31335	44103
1833	42336	34943	42606	45765	47442	45547	40118	39721	46265	37939	36648	40889
1834	46890	36434	46256	39592	43484	47948	36497	46760	41639	39922	40805	39318
1835	35197	37473	45351	45675	44166	41840	39826	48901	39531	39933	38723	38815
1836	45119	46484	36238	42882	50229	37114	46298	42611	43332	44938	33326	36902

Table A2.4: *(cont.)*

Deaths

Year	Jan.	Feb.	Mar.	Apr.	May	Jun.	Jul.	Aug.	Sep.	Oct.	Nov.	Dec.
1539	6882	3514	5648	7998	6052	4055	7734	6822	4406	4174	4098	6059
1540	6171	2989	11860	12460	5844	6079	5324	8681	10449	12664	7942	9698
1541	6537	7492	9109	7720	8407	5664	1814	3894	8327	4795	5820	2677
1542	6969	4880	5925	9159	4797	5264	5609	4582	6000	4599	5132	8103
1543	10515	10026	7941	12947	11805	4523	4177	7118	6368	8919	7320	5397
1544	3775	5957	7873	5086	3967	5311	7477	7894	6763	12446	9676	8385
1545	10363	5485	8846	9527	8459	7157	5855	7225	11127	11181	9525	8042
1546	6661	7626	9455	6803	10869	11092	9255	8070	3849	7035	8543	5760
1547	7439	8559	6745	9111	10385	10748	2269	3776	6159	6997	4793	6476
1548	5337	7310	7196	6684	7815	4627	5695	7694	7537	6769	5225	8065
1549	5554	3292	7412	5297	7241	3659	3967	6291	6481	3507	5378	5921
1550	6617	5167	6990	9394	8305	5473	7617	8814	4784	5131	7292	4737
1551	8087	7350	8878	3895	4293	5069	12350	9698	4471	6326	4048	9422
1552	7735	5501	8250	9802	7204	7040	5788	6589	6351	6339	6147	5594
1553	6271	6393	11010	8483	8867	6915	5899	5409	5378	5672	4569	6431
1554	5660	5420	6980	4677	5601	5006	3822	5232	5217	5358	8230	7015
1555	6257	5359	11183	10493	5265	5592	7489	4360	5254	5970	7328	5833
1556	5973	6702	7492	3140	3710	3866	6058	8972	9587	5980	5400	10214
1557	7813	8798	10690	10723	7982	8642	7964	12121	11096	14839	18556	14663
1558	13914	12551	11925	12202	9364	7369	8565	19401	18072	17519	18954	16551
1559	18960	20186	19106	20601	11416	7470	5161	8034	7376	7534	7051	8387
1560	9565	8633	11591	9329	9072	8307	4870	5768	5637	6461	7080	7422
1561	7555	5754	9331	8914	7376	6607	5735	5893	4699	4841	5442	5193
1562	7293	7036	7420	7081	6318	5347	4264	4498	4891	5024	5485	8419
1563	9940	6126	8545	11567	9404	10032	9209	8741	8107	9459	8025	6381
1564	7247	5726	6028	7617	6431	6437	6098	6851	5923	10300	6438	5462
1565	7202	6836	6788	6121	6367	5336	3975	5753	5421	7603	6213	6029
1566	8410	6695	10201	11647	7379	5477	3218	5201	4650	5064	4990	8110
1567	7800	8725	9657	10715	7107	6049	5173	4195	4715	3950	5994	5447
1568	5325	5681	6650	6903	6363	4889	4727	5575	6316	6015	7555	6925
1569	6304	5754	7546	9725	6239	7199	5548	5307	5668	6310	5104	5356
1570	6361	5257	7481	7324	8861	5814	4935	7304	8072	9005	7682	7107
1571	11357	8212	7435	8679	6033	5758	4311	5954	6316	4859	5621	7319
1572	7118	6769	7114	6899	5771	5056	5623	5524	6085	6091	7763	6786
1573	7375	6257	10903	8295	8206	5483	4011	5342	5239	5249	5579	7359
1574	7895	9279	9216	8825	6461	6993	6301	4513	4285	4523	4464	5744
1575	7016	7312	7730	7133	5656	6110	4559	6211	7007	5848	5940	5509
1576	5400	6118	6408	6067	8619	6547	5248	4327	5342	6334	6008	4889
1577	5954	4715	7496	6447	7279	6250	6705	5678	6067	6015	5693	5685
1578	7413	5412	11145	6854	7518	6137	6214	6945	5797	7348	6426	6720
1579	9759	7038	6791	7275	7480	5509	5583	6029	5938	7978	5420	5952

Table A2.4: *(cont.)*

Deaths

Year	Jan.	Feb.	Mar.	Apr.	May	Jun.	Jul.	Aug.	Sep.	Oct.	Nov.	Dec.
1580	6033	6381	8084	9781	9171	5504	7837	7092	5538	7348	9259	7663
1581	6977	6577	7110	6870	4669	5067	5415	4036	5647	6550	6901	6033
1582	7231	5775	8587	8110	6571	7381	4370	6327	5703	7784	6760	5663
1583	5844	7428	6808	6137	6427	5031	5056	6506	5181	5046	5866	5617
1584	6857	6923	8944	8255	5389	5777	6288	6399	8633	7636	6836	6050
1585	8851	8906	9540	9996	7994	6604	6870	5984	6533	5839	6607	6144
1586	7954	6987	7243	7497	6663	6546	6004	5839	6660	7167	6252	8371
1587	8101	9271	9835	9564	8306	8254	7372	8612	8974	9704	10343	9645
1588	13210	12400	10123	10055	11485	7981	7027	6661	6476	7856	7584	8243
1589	9303	8212	10149	10109	8216	7356	5526	6589	5534	5046	6175	7420
1590	6797	6445	7796	7441	6369	5534	7444	10402	7388	9936	6539	9175
1591	8456	10220	13849	12299	8248	8476	6942	9230	7869	8599	7557	9943
1592	9300	10369	10683	10476	8457	7879	6736	7067	10793	9324	9068	11454
1593	12214	11559	12238	14150	10850	9535	9225	9789	8987	7615	7967	7130
1594	7506	8567	7584	7492	6849	5482	5578	5922	5954	6573	6092	9361
1595	7675	5739	8365	10260	7210	5397	6415	5692	6221	7324	6046	7612
1596	7411	9196	9250	8393	6840	6670	7669	6899	7097	7300	9284	10566
1597	12125	11184	14423	12092	13072	9060	10326	8328	9407	10596	10164	12378
1598	12325	11878	11620	10949	9458	8125	6058	6887	6335	6264	6677	8731
1599	8903	8698	9530	9199	8131	5971	6338	6125	6947	7216	7295	7472
1600	8893	8760	9204	10618	8228	5437	5873	4595	5714	6139	6299	6942
1601	8484	7181	8365	9002	7559	6141	6407	5324	5431	5507	7802	6876
1602	8414	9491	11514	10693	8530	7782	6333	7418	6703	6896	8016	8993
1603	10449	10885	10884	11534	13222	10296	10349	13733	15325	15445	11391	8566
1604	7607	8791	9736	10003	8958	7587	6683	7770	8231	5743	7624	7481
1605	8119	8348	6784	8245	8408	7078	6295	6848	6919	8166	6823	8926
1606	10522	9246	10151	9454	8978	7865	5668	5616	6650	8291	7203	8078
1607	9441	7843	10294	10428	7377	6830	5650	6193	4963	8401	8743	9688
1608	11954	9170	9817	11763	9951	6888	7738	6883	7654	7850	7137	7698
1609	7900	8421	9896	8778	8990	6704	6012	7736	8338	9155	10073	9569
1610	11763	11530	13469	12648	10914	8568	10173	9782	9443	10643	9139	8768
1611	11877	9483	9902	9506	9416	9159	6634	6651	8154	9156	9938	9554
1612	12654	11035	11757	12171	11016	8868	7949	8589	11542	9914	9075	8747
1613	10708	10041	12206	8740	8246	7691	6682	7805	10024	10436	11411	11986
1614	10361	11609	15233	12411	12514	9971	8617	7875	7609	7150	7489	8662
1615	9937	10669	11171	8411	8875	8083	7850	9756	8923	9838	9211	9540
1616	16403	11867	11842	10404	11992	8477	7392	11616	10726	9962	9786	10537
1617	10601	11271	11064	10756	11789	8445	8518	7632	9559	9092	9002	8798
1618	11511	10719	12613	11452	8094	7363	7099	6861	7729	7260	9176	7754
1619	7869	9800	8959	9674	8481	8502	6917	6697	7325	8162	9751	9892

Table A2.4: *(cont.)*

Deaths

Year	Jan.	Feb.	Mar.	Apr.	May	Jun.	Jul.	Aug.	Sep.	Oct.	Nov.	Dec.
1620	9974	9809	8875	11801	10433	7485	7564	6219	6540	7134	9343	9306
1621	9620	10371	8745	9052	7379	9095	7233	5783	6739	7305	8303	10351
1622	11658	7634	9402	7713	8023	8005	6366	5914	7230	7131	9185	13227
1623	12226	12111	12212	12915	11558	8667	11012	11453	10344	12541	14135	15200
1624	13293	13379	11124	13544	8813	8276	7350	9385	9982	12909	11905	11280
1625	11537	14085	17246	18097	15559	13652	15249	21053	22546	19790	14372	14269
1626	12813	12141	13188	10432	8373	8526	8420	6912	8293	9120	10558	10029
1627	11554	8922	12292	14148	11757	7665	7116	5921	6969	7928	7161	7708
1628	10290	9810	10047	9424	9878	8476	9378	7429	6788	7867	7847	9658
1629	11564	13677	13208	10698	9529	7059	7951	7725	6945	8035	8539	9862
1630	8533	9259	10625	9585	7873	7748	8696	10878	8743	10258	11765	12686
1631	13880	12912	13043	12097	11684	8955	10602	9447	8263	10590	9081	10724
1632	10916	10096	11666	11048	10369	8955	8445	9083	7999	7490	8396	10211
1633	9355	10260	11536	11301	10437	9261	7787	7397	7121	7980	8883	10744
1634	10799	9692	11050	10759	10182	8568	9090	7698	6964	7215	10154	10014
1635	12862	9960	10827	10610	9784	10822	8961	9600	9009	8933	10002	11691
1636	10404	12449	14906	12066	12777	12624	13460	12121	11585	12056	9960	11488
1637	11690	9245	10581	11877	12311	10547	10674	11283	9263	8749	11101	12507
1638	15884	12926	12243	14141	12311	10547	9789	14912	15949	15338	13366	12493
1639	17206	12870	16867	17916	15921	11982	10528	9226	10480	12457	10872	11217
1640	11385	11978	15342	17264	16078	11057	9558	9566	9718	9891	9295	11452
1641	14372	11138	13520	12475	9973	8635	9473	8435	10890	10122	12430	10901
1642	10405	11820	12503	12254	12125	10104	11351	9351	9579	8701	12445	11969
1643	12591	11570	12511	12642	13892	11523	13262	14558	13650	15174	16373	15592
1644	14505	14979	14183	14178	13068	10810	13113	12071	10615	13328	11673	12557
1645	12528	9357	12040	14363	11736	8513	7768	8726	8766	8423	9603	11626
1646	11545	8755	9041	10314	9689	7915	7340	10012	8315	8109	8977	7461
1647	9806	11342	12137	11678	10243	9498	8847	9643	10462	9908	10921	10562
1648	10135	10413	11606	11844	11468	8990	7884	6843	7601	9925	10623	14149
1649	12589	9675	12872	14306	13435	11605	9523	9570	10131	8212	9244	9052
1650	10573	8943	16375	10953	11132	10107	11201	12469	10918	9948	8264	10515
1651	12396	10018	11438	11999	10719	7632	8382	7571	7469	9778	8830	9822
1652	12225	9699	10849	11802	12136	9429	7274	9116	11594	14640	11423	10576
1653	11367	11811	14515	12548	11590	8476	8069	9921	11110	10761	10995	14668
1654	14268	15710	14931	14210	13708	11765	9021	8902	10524	10230	10512	9395
1655	12446	10840	11591	11341	11106	9467	8035	8560	8995	10677	8757	11244
1656	12212	10796	10424	9998	9662	9821	8414	9474	11265	10037	10520	11558
1657	13147	12421	14291	13447	11663	8887	9475	20700	15261	13888	18355	17995
1658	19123	16157	20117	17926	21126	14062	9048	11464	19076	15571	15226	17905
1659	14386	14319	19256	16359	15697	10262	8284	8083	8271	8614	8061	10450

Table A2.4: (cont.)

Deaths

Year	Jan.	Feb.	Mar.	Apr.	May	Jun.	Jul.	Aug.	Sep.	Oct.	Nov.	Dec.
1660	12619	13268	12812	12877	10413	8117	8550	9610	7677	10200	10079	8955
1661	9785	10625	11517	12734	13472	10966	12026	13719	11258	10837	13377	12722
1662	12986	13561	14100	14985	13910	10149	8409	9652	9167	8964	8885	12418
1663	12641	13907	13801	16453	12724	9465	9397	7188	7122	9046	7960	8965
1664	11352	11864	13110	13712	13248	10038	9552	9699	8724	8465	8880	10001
1665	13630	13378	16971	18292	19496	19253	19485	24963	21841	22056	17340	12896
1666	11198	11667	12926	11037	12656	12375	12340	12701	12300	9618	11925	11592
1667	12419	10918	14322	13579	14165	11892	10552	15737	12819	10921	12094	11379
1668	13222	13857	13624	15649	12941	11619	10429	9127	10442	11593	10960	11514
1669	15858	13088	14388	15899	13520	12631	10463	10801	12691	19387	13765	12463
1670	14717	14263	13437	12958	10779	10062	9139	14341	17080	16595	13875	15259
1671	14452	14015	16956	15471	14273	11066	10348	9640	10435	11169	11616	11175
1672	11190	13510	13941	13057	14532	12584	9804	9235	7918	8271	8683	10563
1673	10528	11594	13447	14083	12589	10205	8677	7800	7778	9329	11315	10869
1674	11354	13169	15790	12944	14427	10787	10540	8261	8914	7656	8781	10157
1675	11126	10978	14440	14948	13335	11211	11320	9893	8493	9066	14160	15408
1676	11940	12297	11990	14781	12632	12062	10161	8801	9313	10296	10070	12314
1677	13717	11267	11930	13032	12632	8877	7776	9152	8277	8824	10669	8826
1678	10124	9141	9502	10016	10305	9412	9742	11139	13268	14984	13617	13765
1679	17695	15853	19029	17359	15491	11029	11300	15498	16304	14540	14022	18581
1680	13725	14983	14753	11852	12606	10501	9558	10409	14141	17948	17701	20236
1681	18562	19404	22191	19373	19479	16218	13001	11614	12330	14131	13254	12248
1682	15734	16343	18130	18042	15681	10785	11610	11007	12986	11539	13212	16267
1683	15068	14096	17540	15784	14475	12117	10686	10769	9900	12425	10916	11750
1684	16090	14909	15152	16479	13622	11349	11226	14116	13614	12476	13100	11852
1685	16192	13370	18490	18257	14919	12418	11471	10663	10550	10979	11840	13699
1686	14444	13215	15843	15543	14156	12313	12426	10015	10288	10472	11961	11894
1687	15894	13148	14574	14271	13040	10262	10798	10051	10944	8294	9572	10306
1688	12254	14500	15564	12641	11713	12366	11452	10077	10263	10401	10807	11409
1689	14735	11748	13028	12976	14247	12164	12118	10710	10468	10838	14449	13080
1690	15832	11189	15007	16813	14271	10754	11085	10799	10437	11862	10343	11461
1691	13335	11208	11307	12200	12150	10377	9385	10942	10576	10009	11199	11993
1692	16795	16662	12805	13105	11718	11707	8129	7770	8775	9621	7718	10900
1693	10810	11225	14925	11826	12105	9488	8695	8773	9326	9793	14082	14700
1694	15475	13675	15308	16874	13283	11104	10549	9158	9414	12187	11686	10879
1695	15797	12016	12854	13751	13384	13114	11346	11752	11751	10871	11212	14181
1696	12016	12548	14626	14494	13111	12469	9433	10597	11788	9439	10088	12786
1697	13668	12826	13425	15517	12704	12543	10695	9324	9480	9147	10020	10753
1698	12758	11406	13730	10532	13627	10784	9672	10610	9332	10285	11308	10077
1699	12491	10992	14293	13759	11704	10564	11657	10940	9997	10571	10348	11430

Table A2.4: *(cont.)*

Deaths

Year	Jan.	Feb.	Mar.	Apr.	May	Jun.	Jul.	Aug.	Sep.	Oct.	Nov.	Dec.
1700	12019	12785	13166	14052	12132	12407	10458	8887	10283	11771	10100	12105
1701	11779	10117	13380	13381	12098	10539	10577	11176	10548	10405	10315	10945
1702	11264	10365	12309	13199	12105	9966	10419	7735	9144	10358	9967	11615
1703	12665	10273	12271	11509	11815	9050	8782	8274	9977	11178	9534	11751
1704	14308	13022	14969	13729	12711	10238	9167	9374	10559	11135	9616	10298
1705	15435	12597	17263	15280	15434	14911	11276	11443	12848	11386	12704	12274
1706	12957	11527	13776	13149	11947	10895	9956	11054	10761	10960	10471	10513
1707	12720	10733	13521	12756	12689	9884	9451	9722	9287	10530	9074	10482
1708	12265	14832	12928	12562	12517	10448	10258	9624	11065	11788	10185	12411
1709	13842	12054	15198	12379	12333	10574	9235	9105	10802	9702	9179	9714
1710	12198	11617	12752	12210	12817	10134	12016	10580	9375	11859	11324	11160
1711	14900	15217	13942	13963	11944	10143	11492	10718	11218	12019	10783	12504
1712	16258	15325	17582	15334	12902	11659	11748	12112	11102	11019	10441	11740
1713	13424	9835	12611	14629	13429	10734	9466	10067	9779	9603	10377	10798
1714	11858	11209	13328	14171	13788	12507	10552	10986	12054	12294	12248	13972
1715	13142	12295	13690	13740	13212	11822	10935	8203	8371	9635	9474	12699
1716	14490	11041	13068	13396	13512	11044	9668	9382	10369	9975	11073	12621
1717	12547	11591	13646	10844	11721	10435	9227	10727	9627	9771	10915	10969
1718	12309	12232	11617	13088	12814	9352	9403	10704	9983	12098	10469	12548
1719	13116	12179	15477	15093	13609	10469	10395	19412	16567	15426	14285	15214
1720	14196	15762	17495	17449	15566	11647	9537	12814	19117	15788	13330	11997
1721	12111	16121	18483	13654	13938	11767	11873	10542	15832	15820	14050	13918
1722	16161	12563	14910	16180	14081	12275	11908	9515	12458	13459	11820	13621
1723	15038	12835	12758	15492	14644	13560	13299	12298	13563	16015	14442	14322
1724	16097	14376	16059	15020	12940	10655	10703	11774	13101	13526	13074	14654
1725	12033	13381	14957	12782	12531	11362	9914	10193	9467	8997	10850	10624
1726	11939	11842	13122	14107	12586	11121	10641	12611	11989	14251	12494	14187
1727	15542	12498	14090	12351	11098	11053	10160	19333	23526	23981	20507	20299
1728	20590	19908	21903	20943	14353	12310	13029	22404	20252	16727	14781	18497
1729	21421	20500	26803	22820	21841	13584	12329	15630	19512	20729	21639	21817
1730	20625	20045	19969	18999	18092	14552	11632	11775	12238	14300	14215	14292
1731	17681	17522	16382	19619	17350	14416	12287	12554	12452	12781	11512	14682
1732	13850	12094	14448	16351	14894	13603	10342	11071	11536	12739	11592	15155
1733	14982	19762	16228	13351	12775	11920	9092	10806	13200	11730	9741	10582
1734	11362	11486	12211	12183	13498	11851	9054	10114	11576	13196	10089	12631
1735	14199	12224	13878	13283	12787	10644	9788	10697	10648	12543	12654	11989
1736	14214	15089	15493	14199	13567	10746	10328	11285	12419	12998	10577	12252
1737	15453	15057	15834	13662	12885	12138	11457	12359	11550	16773	19597	12658
1738	14206	12059	15172	13059	14478	10157	10364	12753	10749	10910	13364	13653
1739	15293	12962	17352	15199	13110	11769	11247	10667	10602	10365	12093	11592

Deaths

Year	Jan.	Feb.	Mar.	Apr.	May	Jun.	Jul.	Aug.	Sep.	Oct.	Nov.	Dec.
1740	16730	15044	15780	17967	17968	15410	11909	11290	11668	11639	13486	14127
1741	12409	14506	16940	16832	18063	13656	13696	15470	15734	18356	18172	19719
1742	22740	17687	22840	18752	19146	17736	12480	13995	14098	14194	14354	14136
1743	13185	12736	16509	21171	20422	12569	11136	8912	10943	11611	9926	10439
1744	14359	12555	15089	13608	14344	10322	9011	9368	9479	9420	10058	10894
1745	12059	13051	14827	10952	11565	10766	10641	7854	9846	12349	12504	14835
1746	13487	14219	15108	15549	14201	12540	11735	11166	11750	13266	12268	12083
1747	15051	13441	14654	15852	13502	12468	12437	12722	13292	12575	11097	14429
1748	19327	16310	16529	16093	13244	11008	10650	9808	10987	13494	12822	11858
1749	13630	12948	14216	14306	14722	12607	10555	11118	11469	11825	11553	13602
1750	13315	12258	13684	14621	13931	11288	10892	11322	11135	14523	15587	15474
1751	13538	14310	14053	14681	14652	12874	10306	11090	10158	10024	12680	13140
1752	14420	13647	15373	15473	14552	12465	10241	9735	7327	10895	12152	11364
1753	13518	13424	13536	13997	13783	10467	10813	9374	9707	9442	13178	14163
1754	13595	12075	14048	15277	13318	12435	11025	9394	10071	11847	11535	14979
1755	14309	14802	14931	13606	14621	10973	9872	10331	10253	10414	13028	12622
1756	12173	13475	14782	13743	15274	13218	11656	9976	11073	11018	13813	14005
1757	16360	12266	13574	13820	15131	13474	12013	10988	12127	13232	11751	12811
1758	13975	14964	16617	15806	14775	12614	12110	10561	11202	13928	13425	15083
1759	14556	13552	15962	16862	14639	13380	12249	13231	12737	12690	12295	14397
1760	16667	14928	16426	14118	16064	12133	11830	11279	10153	12048	13020	12434
1761	14231	12923	14399	15591	14292	11758	12185	11579	13116	13749	15153	13702
1762	15265	15496	17320	18387	18913	16883	13553	16233	14232	14436	15656	16876
1763	23185	19233	20065	18379	19523	17189	12790	13136	12668	14821	13703	14843
1764	15858	14530	17442	16430	15937	13016	13634	13343	11818	12363	11492	12494
1765	13822	13498	16895	13712	14253	13099	12846	11802	12883	13573	12531	14249
1766	16911	16311	17285	15595	16772	15919	14361	14337	14717	16565	14336	14979
1767	17661	15253	17089	16895	18017	14612	13772	12780	12535	14633	15628	16929
1768	21004	14517	16838	17361	17911	13678	12930	12524	11139	12158	12800	12856
1769	16074	15719	16323	16681	16120	14738	12930	12741	13586	11917	12007	13872
1770	15544	14450	17782	17964	18074	14867	15695	14119	12291	14298	14333	13577
1771	15713	15245	17095	17503	17433	15395	13033	13687	11816	12139	12381	13961
1772	16453	15745	18070	16469	17516	14725	12434	12741	13156	12543	13357	14453
1773	16817	14046	16110	16681	18155	13734	13398	14089	13910	15102	15043	15332
1774	16665	14189	16450	14876	14830	13504	12591	11581	10865	12059	13203	13181
1775	15719	12113	15093	15594	14974	14036	11858	13745	11553	12957	16000	19399
1776	17714	15418	15259	14592	14051	12248	12780	12631	10670	12680	12715	14896
1777	17722	15575	18623	16529	17128	14237	14295	12025	12250	13418	12621	13805
1778	16649	14843	19094	16620	14821	12107	12228	12729	14134	14912	14607	15210
1779	19712	15251	17705	15554	16781	14774	13715	14957	14248	17392	15887	18407

Table A2.4: (cont.)

Deaths

Year	Jan.	Feb.	Mar.	Apr.	May	Jun.	Jul.	Aug.	Sep.	Oct.	Nov.	Dec.
1780	21922	20687	19193	20450	17152	14545	13507	13286	15354	15189	14488	16586
1781	18455	17245	18511	18837	16084	15638	14721	16558	17509	21209	16447	18136
1782	17579	18437	20779	18726	18975	18217	16458	12518	12665	14059	15659	16327
1783	17411	14045	17852	16528	17024	16473	15000	18338	22751	17696	16359	19061
1784	21126	20711	21930	19089	19057	13475	14674	14130	12933	15940	14760	15547
1785	16266	16342	20289	18395	18667	15454	14284	15099	14471	15421	16137	16221
1786	19023	14488	20001	18775	18187	15276	14653	13345	13961	15634	14349	17214
1787	16926	17032	17337	17895	18746	15080	13941	14142	13361	14447	14761	16803
1788	17651	18384	20478	17414	16075	15256	14129	14053	16246	14550	16201	19525
1789	19883	16060	20521	19807	16266	15132	13645	13160	11785	14346	15481	16793
1790	17723	15868	18677	18490	18240	15985	17672	12523	13360	13484	17392	17861
1791	18883	16850	17308	17271	18601	17286	14216	14549	14053	15433	14738	17254
1792	19930	16636	18868	18506	18027	15776	15839	15735	14949	14661	15682	18309
1793	21130	20255	21028	23263	19034	19699	16845	15206	17588	16418	16286	18299
1794	23096	20244	19945	17592	17955	15493	16030	18170	16013	16329	16878	18291
1795	23866	21938	23746	22930	21418	19110	17946	17109	16557	17224	17970	15862
1796	17550	16480	21309	17551	18160	17518	17335	15206	14451	15937	16428	18115
1797	22047	17967	27120	23309	19980	15861	17664	15770	14876	15667	17945	17465
1798	17654	19111	21150	20358	17451	16428	14807	16391	15676	16213	16697	17410
1799	22348	20868	20966	21158	18599	18455	15231	14830	12446	13945	14546	19591
1800	20797	20628	23040	20268	20623	17962	16671	16614	18505	17945	18372	18466
1801	22550	23056	22080	21440	21822	19178	18385	17744	17768	18942	18848	21365
1802	22954	18452	23262	18938	19985	19269	18259	16519	18096	20070	19281	20865
1803	22735	22202	26779	26879	23777	19045	16821	16343	17612	19597	19546	19688
1804	20882	17963	20700	22358	18193	17848	16718	15169	17183	17069	14432	19452
1805	21046	18973	20763	19270	20759	19153	16436	14544	15152	16466	17663	17929
1806	18350	18536	21427	20194	18941	17478	16004	15513	15521	16233	17642	19216
1807	21821	21891	26103	26110	22092	18680	18178	19223	18000	15730	17701	19319
1808	22958	21004	26684	24154	24218	18402	18831	18253	18474	17395	18978	19249
1809	23278	16767	22506	22967	21945	19071	17232	17324	17733	19336	18423	22059
1810	24600	24736	24811	25671	25125	22977	20486	20006	19295	22208	20173	22679
1811	25647	22520	26540	23392	22487	20351	18471	18612	18560	19381	21541	24504
1812	24124	21611	26717	23015	23715	18709	19116	16246	16788	16987	20719	19995
1813	22494	22149	23139	19944	22933	20201	16546	17595	17007	17484	18318	24467
1814	34932	24830	29778	22368	26288	19982	18292	17071	19152	19173	17196	19781
1815	24055	23450	25733	23048	23105	20091	20373	20347	19579	19486	19878	24191
1816	25673	26669	30633	27806	23569	23882	19481	18186	17831	18868	19732	24453
1817	23752	21576	26182	25004	24567	24484	19305	21426	19111	21797	19351	22975
1818	25997	23497	28111	25207	24099	21753	20673	22918	23645	20285	20379	25595
1819	27875	22658	26690	25590	22933	21432	18105	18916	22740	20689	23042	27103

Table A2.4: *(cont.)*

Deaths

Year	Jan.	Feb.	Mar.	Apr.	May	Jun.	Jul.	Aug.	Sep.	Oct.	Nov.	Dec.
1820	28438	23956	30489	26679	25606	20211	20176	17252	18586	17788	19072	23051
1821	24227	22760	26282	25475	22391	21129	19444	17685	22376	24533	20587	22135
1822	25464	22142	27327	25041	24270	23043	20381	20273	21275	20675	20614	25019
1823	28753	26619	29446	26246	27283	23143	22262	21451	19354	22410	21468	23681
1824	25705	25930	28541	26963	25740	23902	21862	22383	20582	24052	22036	23330
1825	24104	25944	27226	25634	24102	22688	22672	23011	25631	26639	24215	25054
1826	33236	25050	27756	23749	24168	22123	22009	25119	24674	24239	21982	26223
1827	25908	28960	27969	26346	23557	24266	21508	19012	20651	20227	24423	22999
1828	23479	24622	28554	25720	23716	22648	21229	23829	20808	21340	21375	20421
1829	25704	25569	32059	28853	27392	21960	21357	19920	19246	18878	21225	24125
1830	26955	27130	23614	21949	24727	22263	18756	20913	19950	21007	19584	24576
1831	25707	24124	26811	24978	24597	23325	25466	25672	25936	23401	24246	24309
1832	30598	31078	28975	28036	24430	24760	21295	25228	26315	20544	21026	26255
1833	28605	24210	26873	26045	32376	24853	21669	23609	22228	20240	20057	25912
1834	23542	22479	27454	25638	26956	24450	21398	27796	25233	28495	24341	29279
1835	31594	27461	29547	27098	26234	21656	21192	21946	22563	23829	27149	26428
1836	31185	27353	29675	28688	29297	23298	24773	21446	21767	21065	22712	25041

Marriages

Year	Jan.	Feb.	Mar.	Apr.	May	Jun.	Jul.	Aug.	Sep.	Oct.	Nov.	Dec.
1539	7662	2713	0	3123	1709	10252	4454	665	3808	4721	15444	2367
1540	6180	616	0	2078	3197	4080	3251	1801	1834	4702	8645	141
1541	5897	2087	0	271	2297	2405	7006	3957	515	3804	9422	1296
1542	4945	513	0	694	2325	3663	2987	3904	2739	5794	14644	78
1543	5872	409	0	2342	3803	1405	4875	3765	2978	4756	4479	409
1544	2686	2258	226	2277	2381	1354	4301	1994	2964	5537	5926	165
1545	4760	957	313	1446	3172	3199	2595	1256	4046	3805	3614	1066
1546	3646	3251	870	60	4445	2021	3214	877	2813	6524	8365	120
1547	5531	1493	0	210	5030	3671	5734	3622	2495	6666	5472	58
1548	4934	1620	338	3011	2853	6828	4972	1274	3858	8174	4974	857
1549	2561	5195	547	392	2452	3401	3927	878	2901	4415	5295	595
1550	4187	2391	88	3432	2064	5328	3516	1531	2114	6212	3698	486
1551	3052	3958	0	2209	3216	1488	2539	2425	2766	6600	4538	1053
1552	4632	4497	29	322	2794	3284	2456	1657	3784	6214	5787	2334
1553	5542	1620	132	2022	2473	6430	3443	3803	4275	5324	4230	1198
1554	1323	58	0	1556	1766	1155	2541	690	2828	4027	4600	161
1555	2743	2327	51	747	4016	1958	3502	733	1904	5555	6210	76
1556	4063	975	0	1409	1179	3726	1436	999	1978	4027	4141	0
1557	3094	1350	25	796	1280	1046	1323	1044	1963	5413	4853	723
1558	5063	3520	24	1165	3432	3727	4067	786	2501	4441	4231	1069
1559	4051	1348	36	2719	1631	3681	4875	2494	2431	5091	4465	1152
1560	4397	4203	230	1551	4245	4967	4255	1654	5092	4373	5212	1646
1561	4263	2775	72	1522	3372	3843	3958	2638	3737	6276	5889	1696
1562	4733	1492	321	2881	2972	3683	2540	2037	2372	6815	4545	673
1563	2809	1504	57	1105	3009	3214	3124	1329	4748	4909	4840	728
1564	3796	923	151	1816	2242	3043	3760	1478	2850	5446	5981	750
1565	2624	2386	201	340	2592	2596	3828	1404	1679	5004	5000	1624
1566	2120	1387	115	912	2165	2451	2053	832	3420	4826	5155	1057
1567	2923	1204	0	2152	1796	2978	2502	1431	2139	5337	5473	4796
1568	3270	3279	477	798	2699	3289	2728	2001	3233	4217	4401	759
1569	2685	1481	33	1737	2131	3760	3318	2008	2171	5773	5927	744
1570	3130	1010	388	2829	1982	2773	2992	1623	3147	5717	5235	997
1571	2364	2124	306	891	2746	3170	2965	1669	2408	5544	4986	1607
1572	3881	1673	72	1568	3098	5063	2202	2039	2198	4658	5774	915
1573	4578	674	571	1787	3218	2589	2903	1787	2284	3677	6279	751
1574	3438	2949	148	1070	3799	3307	4016	2303	2798	5250	6621	1194
1575	3692	1437	47	1895	2613	3445	3041	1884	2839	5076	6295	1333
1576	2847	3620	299	935	2886	3030	3323	3104	2128	5040	5839	1828
1577	4571	2486	98	1277	4133	3546	2648	1473	2730	4416	4879	890
1578	2907	1649	20	3267	2459	3997	2971	2024	3194	5984	5315	2052
1579	2771	3156	333	624		3987	2675	2450	2074	5832	4500	1647

Marriages

Year	Jan.	Feb.	Mar.	Apr.	May	Jun.	Jul.	Aug.	Sep.	Oct.	Nov.	Dec.
1580	3905	2375	53	2775	3702	3616	2796	2114	2894	5971	6519	1946
1581	3676	965	457	2273	2675	2954	2992	1790	2730	5601	5889	1757
1582	2836	2794	108	1392	2617	2583	3210	1300	3355	4903	5913	1578
1583	3873	2347	249	2245	2255	3436	2754	1758	3121	4678	5346	2028
1584	2916	3266	1185	1085	4101	4329	3311	1761	3084	5301	5193	1823
1585	3022	3843	180	1968	3291	4538	3255	2126	2305	4741	7461	1446
1586	3129	2262	255	2602	3062	2573	3173	2574	2732	3743	5710	1549
1587	2637	3500	310	1253	3455	2851	2429	1813	2739	6001	5448	2234
1588	3063	3039	105	2682	3761	4617	3675	1820	3383	6127	6440	2169
1589	4393	1918	152	3364	3518	4101	3399	2078	2554	5980	7172	1392
1590	2948	3607	1001	1236	4043	3630	2640	1857	4150	4404	4178	1529
1591	3148	2177	175	1928	3448	3097	2882	2634	3868	4952	6079	1781
1592	4476	1871	618	3078	3266	3204	3179	2425	3274	4585	5701	1714
1593	3134	4070	212	1395	3553	4614	3865	2268	3518	4326	5885	1953
1594	3710	2510	534	3018	4444	3506	3368	2185	2237	6378	4751	2576
1595	3661	3864	1052	1189	3567	3226	2597	1969	2936	4585	4655	1641
1596	2338	3698	142	1999	3550	2962	2552	2586	2512	5001	4541	1822
1597	2626	1430	419	2452	3135	2254	2244	1155	2781	4355	4491	1862
1598	2877	4154	146	2169	3587	3521	2675	1838	2752	4430	4624	2486
1599	2913	3888	190	2742	3557	4021	3135	2211	3168	5785	4787	2016
1600	3537	1810	1112	3229	4085	3996	3549	2120	2854	5012	5579	1387
1601	3147	3251	109	1938	3467	4738	2487	2171	3219	4536	4763	1123
1602	3033	2362	232	2446	4124	4598	2885	2229	2622	5299	4796	1545
1603	2733	4296	1097	681	4629	3872	3290	2410	2460	6278	6255	1510
1604	3583	3275	386	3067	3563	2849	3814	2083	2834	6594	5949	1935
1605	4664	3058	317	3603	3650	3684	3395	2179	4256	5503	4505	1902
1606	3201	3490	1527	1562	3730	4899	2547	2014	3235	4795	5441	1514
1607	3229	2970	200	3138	2945	4963	3372	2059	2560	4061	5444	1278
1608	4447	1614	536	4029	3821	3612	3069	2599	2096	5551	5783	1189
1609	2806	3943	200	2295	3908	3797	3553	2300	2485	5821	5694	1703
1610	3471	3182	367	2324	3210	4127	4800	1751	3343	6057	6017	1460
1611	4708	2359	624	4078	4109	3900	4813	2796	3292	5848	5458	1888
1612	2506	4224	321	2643	2802	6028	3466	2349	3035	4929	6086	1350
1613	3529	3387	287	2923	3597	3762	2642	2407	2352	5116	5986	1986
1614	2633	3730	1368	886	4280	3209	3310	2433	2005	6024	6351	1187
1615	3438	2650	569	2337	3634	5154	2812	2589	2748	5753	5499	1680
1616	3191	2500	401	3051	4147	3245	2961	1947	3462	4781	5444	2098
1617	2470	3302	888	1793	4374	3349	3585	2249	2395	4663	5164	1506
1618	3777	3548	164	3384	3552	6006	3208	2493	3194	6790	4394	1240
1619	2929	2131	385	4280	4552	5047	3450	2808	2766	5523	6186	1305

Table A2.4: *(cont.)*

Marriages

Year	Jan.	Feb.	Mar.	Apr.	May	Jun.	Jul.	Aug.	Sep.	Oct.	Nov.	Dec.
1620	3654	4845	184	1942	4507	3207	4174	2531	2432	5868	5968	1577
1621	3073	2317	171	4076	4318	4144	3976	2738	2308	5106	4911	1657
1622	2765	3348	683	1454	2943	3629	3023	1742	1831	5469	3814	1334
1623	2361	3512	531	2046	2520	2914	2038	1873	2043	4993	3914	942
1624	3166	2414	580	4065	3657	3494	2722	2099	3565	5199	4580	995
1625	2665	3311	633	2151	3562	4917	3058	1611	2190	3857	5009	1148
1626	2391	3580	188	3237	3696	4770	2304	2097	1914	7120	4748	1041
1627	3669	1239	573	4106	3326	3848	3928	2687	2771	5832	6005	2097
1628	2801	3886	562	2539	3406	4693	4355	2657	3324	4903	6675	1541
1629	4039	3417	311	3712	3631	4772	3653	2475	2992	5285	6408	1038
1630	4175	2145	718	4219	3757	4914	2942	1840	2998	4612	4346	1229
1631	2668	2831	385	2888	3567	3918	3108	2546	3996	4546	5010	1148
1632	3868	2224	924	3958	5050	3542	3922	3351	2455	4778	5433	1776
1633	3400	3932	653	1835	6194	3775	2759	3369	2383	5732	5313	1014
1634	3725	2259	458	4273	3557	4544	3709	2567	3117	5507	6676	1233
1635	4039	2331	601	5596	4159	4209	3749	2768	2436	5271	6292	1013
1636	3292	4303	489	2518	4970	3687	3819	1907	2745	5263	4808	976
1637	3688	2637	597	3682	4970	4781	2930	2862	3641	4891	5137	1644
1638	3792	1480	989	4563	3302	3863	3440	1549	3436	4757	4945	1512
1639	3973	3714	956	2368	4155	4857	4336	3283	3629	6186	7942	1446
1640	4125	2968	618	5672	4029	5407	3512	4552	3194	6158	6559	1598
1641	3329	5161	1518	777	6929	4598	4361	2984	4193	5685	9876	1720
1642	3538	3454	606	3172	4745	6436	4398	3283	3056	4693	6589	1419
1643	3830	1881	622	3828	4262	3249	2743	1362	1664	3507	3530	1706
1644	1982	2482	1749	2440	3132	2480	3927	1739	1802	2815	4059	2478
1645	3732	3846	1448	3350	5782	3581	3482	3515	3191	4759	4440	1588
1646	2647	3400	2654	2825	5986	3800	2328	2393	2837	6085	4035	3948
1647	3289	2991	2012	2345	4415	4420	1955	2621	2882	5861	3696	2209
1648	1430	3087	1262	2300	4098	3348	2997	2539	751	2361	2735	1699
1649	2761	1738	1082	2110	4278	2266	3003	2075	1808	3520	3997	2399
1650	2434	2985	1722	4500	4179	2732	3472	3033	1534	4821	3106	2790
1651	2830	3201	823	4284	5045	3215	2748	3144	2739	3024	4399	2575
1652	3281	2782	1734	3173	4086	3924	2480	1626	2917	1725	3803	3298
1653	1727	4127	1535	3734	2807	2844	1918	1401	9884	714	1913	2240
1654	2313	2585	4288	4171	6118	4377	4480	2946	4282	5740	5212	4132
1655	2832	4664	3179	5770	6024	6256	5542	4102	4859	7696	6734	5957
1656	4159	5249	3783	5943	9364	4846	4277	3154	4087	4460	3311	3723
1657	2154	3184	3174	4282	5449	5082	4429	1869	4089	4792	3651	4487
1658	1876	3515	2019	4553	5961	4422	3323	2706	3736	4240	4429	2554
1659	2908	3035	1882	5608	6402	4788	3557	2093	3169	4460	4754	3294

Table A2.4: (cont.)

Marriages

Year	Jan.	Feb.	Mar.	Apr.	May	Jun.	Jul.	Aug.	Sep.	Oct.	Nov.	Dec.
1660	3231	2099	2145	3515	3015	4980	2437	2236	1761	2667	5089	2461
1661	2491	3321	517	2857	3450	2409	2674	1173	3062	3760	3258	2099
1662	2858	2378	915	3620	4493	3013	3221	1294	3003	5982	5490	1664
1663	2441	4242	1558	3173	4934	4747	3473	2934	3073	4568	5495	2121
1664	3330	4436	787	4119	5150	3944	4039	1505	4377	5177	5080	1708
1665	3348	2535	1827	3965	4660	3485	3316	1648	2657	4940	4714	1465
1666	2850	4083	568	3089	2860	4271	3005	1582	2402	4700	4949	1960
1667	3718	2913	540	4872	5148	4433	2601	1080	2466	4182	3623	1978
1668	2887	1143	2111	3264	4044	3255	2611	1533	2225	3943	4512	1979
1669	2223	3776	580	3399	3752	4230	2834	1984	2786	4075	3963	1240
1670	2752	2786	401	5016	4897	3409	2336	1512	2407	3467	4582	1731
1671	3007	2841	1838	2854	5891	4051	2797	2019	2040	4723	5263	2536
1672	2868	3625	465	4977	4048	3821	2827	1611	2359	4451	4239	1938
1673	3390	2161	857	5038	4355	2836	2538	1839	2353	3688	4406	1461
1674	2564	2871	1646	2061	3486	4321	2143	1667	2505	2683	4385	2232
1675	2479	2085	400	4310	3901	4023	2012	1748	2348	3087	4231	1463
1676	3105	1428	1292	4243	4106	3062	2747	1294	2804	4144	4815	1386
1677	2765	3038	916	3529	4265	4911	2989	1664	1955	4831	5003	1869
1678	2703	2203	533	5315	4828	3006	2744	1473	2347	3755	4023	2153
1679	2789	3136	2040	2399	3462	3813	2643	1896	2797	4518	3539	1983
1680	3213	4595	893	4461	4294	5540	2990	2061	3160	4275	4465	1636
1681	3019	2993	533	4679	4228	3605	3318	2062	2631	4247	6206	2581
1682	3072	3298	893	4705	3805	5210	2464	1381	2675	4369	4293	2433
1683	3748	3105	1253	4888	5124	4340	2905	2053	3286	5673	4788	2379
1684	2979	1918	1511	5240	3725	3379	2987	2066	3070	3808	5006	1556
1685	3377	3147	1627	3632	4150	3433	2585	1742	3195	4586	5093	1918
1686	3586	2169	597	6202	5243	3973	1771	1863	2611	4282	5088	1761
1687	4230	2144	1701	4251	4744	3196	2640	1903	3561	4948	5160	2862
1688	2656	4376	875	4121	3944	3707	3017	2311	2643	4418	3690	2769
1689	2586	2350	740	4860	3513	3653	1873	1339	2451	4310	3989	1910
1690	2410	2399	1737	3347	3982	3429	2731	1331	2638	4219	4565	1697
1691	2433	2608	810	3213	3581	3674	1938	1386	2368	4362	3924	2069
1692	2630	1952	1948	3155	3424	2430	2573	1578	2203	2835	3288	2328
1693	2945	2864	1034	2739	2754	3292	2574	1422	2210	3730	2867	1471
1694	1989	2229	463	3416	3617	3181	1930	1455	2143	4099	3606	2329
1695	3460	1923	2135	3626	4444	3652	3384	2543	2744	4944	4999	2924
1696	3136	3524	870	5111	3600	4969	2126	2592	2718	4382	4078	2593
1697	2999	2432	652	5216	4643	3588	2054	2196	2828	4473	4599	2231
1698	3175	3728	1971	2700	5671	3559	2488	2195	2708	4896	4294	2863
1699	3638	3520	832	5242	4371	3421	2530	1840	3450	4604	4951	2217

Table A2.4: (cont.)

Marriages

Year	Jan.	Feb.	Mar.	Apr.	May	Jun.	Jul.	Aug.	Sep.	Oct.	Nov.	Dec.
1700	4029	2578	863	6194	4271	3645	2178	2092	3284	5351	5053	2167
1701	2852	3228	1561	3775	4667	3786	2767	1929	3051	5442	5653	3160
1702	3566	3495	844	6144	3931	3500	3181	1649	3125	4977	4800	2510
1703	3095	3146	2363	4425	3992	3669	2967	2216	2998	4846	4535	3021
1704	2644	3537	1194	3646	3712	3524	1981	2562	2875	5637	4262	2395
1705	3071	3294	467	4851	5416	3358	3362	1978	3331	5093	3698	2779
1706	3886	1869	2729	4299	3811	3345	2145	2162	3131	5291	4903	3002
1707	2698	4266	633	4877	3636	4733	2759	1250	3292	4654	3303	2905
1708	2440	2702	844	4350	4193	3140	2536	2359	3238	4522	3762	2495
1709	2223	2965	2436	2853	3633	3605	2169	2514	2351	3396	4550	2977
1710	2281	3276	1282	4647	4800	3507	2468	1590	2474	5867	4136	3051
1711	3226	2248	670	4092	4469	2867	2201	2021	3345	4706	4776	3555
1712	2768	3004	2018	3467	3981	3542	2669	1875	3792	5325	4343	3277
1713	3485	3166	751	5247	5155	4185	2682	2573	3847	5541	3449	4208
1714	4289	3161	2206	4392	5550	3807	2478	2442	3490	5058	5359	3669
1715	3617	4128	1329	4938	4920	5028	2813	2567	3469	4992	3686	4029
1716	3204	2787	859	6009	4463	3397	2705	2072	3208	5737	4498	3062
1717	3410	3952	1715	4004	4501	4383	2713	1870	3630	4958	4118	3354
1718	4173	4747	1598	5195	4944	4873	3150	2961	3402	5110	4656	3957
1719	4208	3529	3235	4890	4488	3911	2480	2266	2661	4414	5179	3075
1720	3259	4708	1500	4926	3579	3415	3082	2545	3438	4830	4680	3701
1721	4091	3869	1118	4716	5971	3938	2626	2103	3359	5585	4300	4295
1722	5392	2982	3018	4507	4723	3469	3421	2875	3761	7213	5041	3905
1723	3967	6070	1222	5531	5801	4620	2864	2850	4259	6718	5977	4145
1724	4096	3968	1347	6450	5604	5146	3128	2577	3987	5601	4958	4364
1725	3352	3436	2973	4583	5695	3806	2398	3520	3719	5206	5372	3847
1726	2979	4355	1356	5517	5374	4786	3113	3023	4236	5567	6027	4761
1727	3713	4063	1214	5637	6083	3489	3257	2476	3167	5476	3860	3103
1728	3640	4134	2951	3869	4494	4055	3488	2154	3007	5320	4022	3584
1729	3351	4570	1348	5133	4596	3576	2838	2576	3679	5619	4524	3857
1730	4050	3664	3328	4114	6318	4519	4184	3510	4656	6683	6564	5992
1731	3661	4200	3358	5909	5563	4806	3554	3557	5222	6960	6852	5150
1732	4562	4908	1457	7299	5665	4541	3534	2564	4691	5804	4883	4352
1733	3800	3148	3571	4508	5374	3132	2802	3108	3962	6981	4955	3935
1734	4589	5997	1014	4863	4265	3825	3103	2699	3184	5996	4376	3897
1735	3401	3492	1842	5533	5177	4042	3022	2304	3513	6128	5333	4380
1736	3451	3062	3315	3482	4289	3883	2334	2792	3160	5272	4920	3825
1737	3249	3511	1347	3821	4251	3854	2632	2836	4054	6553	4950	4178
1738	3046	3252	1322	5906	5580	3674	2990	2834	3913	5413	4488	3654
1739	4243	2986	2867	4620	5094	3962	3634	2543	3550	6010	3879	4267

Table A2.4: *(cont.)*

Marriages

Year	Jan.	Feb.	Mar.	Apr.	May	Jun.	Jul.	Aug.	Sep.	Oct.	Nov.	Dec.
1740	4021	3918	998	5766	4639	3533	3328	2721	3620	4757	4621	3421
1741	2532	3607	2228	3316	3954	2910	2535	2060	3977	5395	4483	3708
1742	3637	3715	2530	3753	4043	3863	2757	2302	3939	5764	5106	3622
1743	3507	3594	949	4369	5322	3938	3636	2621	4049	8098	5402	4169
1744	4101	3067	3205	3912	4986	3258	3988	2479	4144	6956	4344	5165
1745	3125	4290	914	4659	4471	4391	3572	2854	3507	5979	3867	4373
1746	3806	3220	2966	4435	4526	2945	3165	2532	4011	5998	3039	4326
1747	4341	3451	2884	5050	3907	4205	3389	2193	3920	5905	6034	4129
1748	3223	4090	841	4185	5410	4106	3574	2825	4319	6501	4864	4296
1749	3363	3092	3735	3984	5535	2826	3084	3119	3789	6169	4803	3899
1750	4011	5038	1809	4427	3808	4323	2522	2970	4582	5359	4944	4334
1751	3297	3639	1107	4843	4865	3375	2931	2445	3599	6695	4863	5221
1752	4030	3349	3083	3655	5101	3386	2925	2839	2116	6189	5152	4964
1753	4237	3399	2966	4280	4289	4034	3245	2426	3426	5735	5363	5141
1754	4286	6264	2713	2632	4293	3811	2764	3359	2770	5081	4606	4073
1755	3441	4065	2248	4213	5379	4223	3409	3573	3868	6417	4897	4042
1756	3834	4654	3391	4046	4263	5185	3428	3535	2927	5717	5887	4531
1757	3930	4019	1759	4361	4887	2721	2873	2790	2504	5608	5211	3913
1758	4022	3212	3104	3862	5269	3559	3386	2965	3596	6981	4826	4208
1759	5243	5578	1592	4727	4720	4908	3865	3121	4232	7546	5655	4648
1760	4644	5185	1506	6249	7093	4430	4665	3061	4048	6792	6833	5386
1761	5629	2889	4193	5251	6740	4720	3824	3493	3934	7668	6358	5429
1762	4345	5473	1433	5058	5751	4276	3773	3280	4638	6415	5446	4713
1763	3944	3765	1878	6088	6391	4299	4961	4934	3803	6993	6085	4967
1764	4525	4729	3737	4101	5259	4880	4644	3325	3999	7637	6116	5860
1765	4472	5286	2228	5765	5037	3439	5103	2851	4644	6505	5094	5489
1766	4666	3499	2668	5433	5301	3481	3883	4384	3899	6996	5817	5167
1767	3580	3202	3010	4208	4550	4546	3778	3794	3366	6040	6039	5881
1768	4077	4104	1501	5985	6382	3889	3899	4243	3744	6568	6156	6535
1769	5704	3621	4084	3792	6496	4216	4531	4023	3993	7390	7027	5626
1770	4789	5203	1998	4498	6311	4982	4616	4104	4032	8083	6036	5690
1771	4682	4000	1960	6416	6332	3832	4162	4069	3787	6699	5936	5887
1772	3840	4040	3336	4668	4873	5140	3836	3780	4242	7044	7767	5602
1773	4439	5098	2215	5388	5397	4485	3836	4201	4153	6928	5993	4766
1774	4465	4591	2045	5417	5700	4095	4232	4279	3362	7503	6693	5482
1775	5300	5345	2091	4787	4600	4938	3405	4320	4286	7971	5906	5559
1776	4068	4477	1957	6176	5704	3664	4129	4352	4040	7453	6760	6178
1777	5193	4083	3141	5640	5487	4803	4211	4147	4259	7624	7229	5697
1778	4836	4967	4251	5539	4338	4865	4760	3847	4072	7517	6313	5678
1779	4846	4587	2060	6649	6348	3970	4007	3879	4330	7201	5627	5211

Table A2.4: *(cont.)*

Marriages

Year	Jan.	Feb.	Mar.	Apr.	May	Jun.	Jul.	Aug.	Sep.	Oct.	Nov.	Dec.
1780	5250	4885	4006	4977	6067	4616	3992	3587	4439	8636	6576	5491
1781	6133	5725	2499	5474	5179	4367	4031	3184	4224	8449	5483	5127
1782	5384	4123	2517	5023	6349	3585	3634	4124	4207	7498	6677	5827
1783	4330	4034	4117	4757	5080	5438	4370	3612	5312	7387	6974	6574
1784	4866	5158	2033	4926	6688	4586	3690	4371	4232	7464	7730	6109
1785	5898	5150	4875	5121	7423	4618	4977	4887	4913	8562	7316	7031
1786	5684	5507	2747	4603	5721	5233	4600	4184	4881	8345	7360	6341
1787	5143	4947	2381	5125	6866	4094	5750	3999	4555	8751	6849	6030
1788	4940	4808	4962	4830	6388	4478	4571	4005	5238	7812	6339	6891
1789	4544	6199	3091	5232	4788	5257	4536	5335	3895	7555	6779	6170
1790	6412	5364	3589	5861	5873	4163	4806	4814	3935	8917	7787	6026
1791	5139	4100	4608	5079	6340	5306	5418	5405	4651	7571	6654	6306
1792	5631	6068	2704	7084	7866	4088	5156	4437	5610	9508	6865	6072
1793	5638	5905	3749	7975	7437	4270	5954	4081	4568	7922	6857	6625
1794	4768	4982	4739	4522	5691	6324	4643	4116	5821	6995	6823	6842
1795	3988	3988	3705	5796	6623	3789	4648	3912	4239	6941	7136	5949
1796	5568	5240	3999	5108	6761	5130	5198	5035	4401	9668	7780	5568
1797	6022	6680	3863	5705	6726	5711	5318	4991	4714	8203	7577	6706
1798	6173	6846	3801	7073	7848	5363	5273	4597	5350	10705	6810	6679
1799	5696	3802	5237	5438	7037	5023	4638	4531	5136	9283	7168	6789
1800	4952	5035	3511	6141	5343	5929	4200	3415	5036	8144	5977	5997
1801	5200	4438	3023	4812	5251	4001	3927	4456	3638	7919	7224	6085
1802	5075	5484	4779	6379	6136	7530	6522	7345	5932	10637	10149	8750
1803	6570	7550	4685	7695	8864	5940	6828	7296	6252	11084	8233	7534
1804	6856	6353	3684	8247	7320	5388	5658	5188	6597	10269	8332	7843
1805	6379	6040	4183	6619	6687	5901	6034	4861	5421	9193	7024	7388
1806	5622	5448	3948	6256	7395	5627	5726	4660	5664	9131	7537	7387
1807	6088	5220	5521	5746	7900	6343	6023	5617	6565	9206	8271	7867
1808	5624	6214	4189	5380	6503	7419	5343	5615	6092	9550	7215	7400
1809	5747	5333	3200	7342	6851	4926	5319	5544	5028	8664	7357	8772

Table A2.4: (cont.)

Marriages

Year	Jan.	Feb.	Mar.	Apr.	May	Jun.	Jul.	Aug.	Sep.	Oct.	Nov.	Dec.
1810	5387	4772	5776	6429	5931	6188	5836	5220	5492	8733	8165	7636
1811	6717	6268	4330	7634	6624	7373	6596	5231	6179	9360	8469	8694
1812	6240	4826	6573	5924	7363	5500	5458	6378	5153	8923	10123	7188
1813	5026	6822	5689	6795	6229	6016	5871	6515	5322	8730	8254	6947
1814	6745	7274	4094	7031	9942	5993	5700	6536	6867	10634	9693	9084
1815	7607	6466	7577	6364	8908	7315	7217	6727	6521	11586	9204	9227
1816	6635	8075	4869	8794	7233	8577	6369	6367	6312	9313	7385	9381
1817	7465	5525	4096	6991	8207	6699	5640	5613	7253	8487	9287	8150
1818	5994	5213	7744	6196	7670	6554	6133	6325	6807	10689	10481	9464
1819	5901	7290	4812	6559	7930	5700	6099	6352	5919	9691	10189	9087
1820	6912	6042	4802	8700	9680	6910	7195	6655	5941	10470	9723	10204
1821	5855	5528	6135	6778	7087	8744	7165	7000	6676	11572	9867	10275
1822	7108	7914	4820	9525	10373	6648	7279	11351	5245	9106	9683	9400
1823	6711	6781	7942	7475	9624	7581	8101	7526	7463	10328	8492	10129
1824	6892	7762	6943	7728	9111	7961	7240	7889	6315	10431	9313	10519
1825	8344	6793	5225	9582	13123	6647	7308	8553	8786	11283	9711	10614
1826	7934	5437	7775	6643	9827	6430	7619	6648	6952	12424	10023	10153
1827	6448	9073	4931	7466	8099	7769	6676	6309	8206	9566	8746	9465
1828	8132	7855	5969	8488	11255	7943	8744	8308	8649	11110	10875	11705
1829	7188	6380	6529	7452	7521	7952	6044	7786	6601	10139	10521	9648
1830	6611	6717	5459	7848	8379	7771	6603	6975	8069	11140	11174	9221
1831	7955	6550	6553	9202	10196	7193	7728	7575	8651	12162	10023	10956
1832	8428	8099	7465	9060	7615	8720	7746	8326	8484	12745	10485	11459
1833	7579	7543	6635	9678	10979	8397	10283	7254	8906	12777	11817	12154
1834	7872	9273	8786	8559	11555	8761	7712	8661	8360	10875	11063	10369
1835	8419	8201	8134	7320	9267	9513	8403	9102	9149	10373	9857	11622
1836	8542	9133	7002	9562	12198	7816	8161	10066	8487	11679	11773	10319
1837	5958	8665	7030	7106	10674	8147	6964	5924	10644	13973	8645	12532

Appendix 3

Back-projection results: population and net migration totals; age structure; natural increase; net-migration and population growth rates; fertility, mortality, and crude vital rates

The data used in back projection are described in chapter 7 and listed appendix 2. The technique itself is set out in appendix 15 and described more generally in chapter 7. Appendix 15 also gives details of the techniques used in converting the output of back projection into estimates of fertility and mortality. In this appendix the results of back projection are reproduced more fully than elsewhere in the book, though even so they are substantially compressed compared to the original print-out. For example, space does not permit the printing in full of the age structure of the population at each quinquennial 'census', though the calculation of a detailed age structure is, of course, an integral part of the operation of the back-projection program itself.

The back-projection results are set out in three tables. In table A3.1 quinquennial data are given. They are all current rates or proportions. In table A3.2 some cohort fertility and mortality data may be found, while in table A3.3 annual crude rates and population totals are listed.

In consulting table A3.1 the following notes may prove helpful:

1 The population totals all refer to 30 June of the years in question.

2 Compound annual growth rates refer to the five-year period from one 'census' to the next. Similarly, the annual net migration totals represent the average net migration between one 'census' and the next.

3 The gross and net reproduction rates, the intrinsic growth rates, the expectation of life figures and the crude rates (birth, death, marriage, and natural increase per 1,000 total population) all refer to five-year periods centring on the dates shown.

4 The age-group data are the percentages of the total population falling within the age group shown.

5 The dependency ratio is the total of those aged under 15 or over 60 divided by the total of those aged 15–59 and multiplied by 1,000.

The cohort data given in table A3.2 are all derived from the same tabulations as those given in table A3.1. The cohort GRRs and e_0s are built up from the age-specific current rates by taking appropriate diagonals through the tables of current rates. The cohorts all notionally refer to the five-year periods centring on the dates shown. Thus, the last cohort GRR for 1826 refers to those born in the years 1824–8. In 1841, when the cohort would be aged 15 on average, it is given the age-specific rate for the age group 15–9 taken from the set of rates used in making up the current GRR for that year; in 1846 the rate for 20–4, and so on. Similarly, the last e_0 notionally refers to the cohort born 1779–83 and the cohort life table is built up from the grid of current rates until in 1871 the rate for the age group 90–4 is used (the family of life tables used in back projection do not go beyond age 95 and therefore no one survives to a greater

527

Table A3.1: Quinquennial demographic data produced by back projection: population totals, growth rates, net migration, age structure, fertility, and mortality

Key: Pop.: Population total; CGR: Compound annual growth rates; Mig.: Average annual net migration total; e_0: Expectation of life at birth; GRR: Gross reproduction rate; NRR: Net reproduction rate; ITR: Intrinsic growth rate; CBR: Crude birth rate; CDR: Crude death rate; CRNI: Crude rate of natural increase; CMR: Crude marriage rate; DR: Dependency ratio.

Year	Pop.	CGR	Mig.	e_0	GRR	NRR	ITR	CBR	CDR	CRNI	CMR	0–4	5–14	15–24	25–59	60+	DR	Year
1541	2773851	0.57	3619	33.75	2.869	1.452	1.20	39.84	29.41	10.43	15.13	13.25	21.24	17.96	39.09	8.47	753	1541
1546	2853711	1.07	4076	32.50	2.655	1.298	0.84	37.06	31.24	5.81	12.77	13.89	21.04	18.35	38.25	8.47	767	1546
1551	3011030	0.96	4351	37.99	2.795	1.576	1.46	38.75	26.03	12.72	11.94	14.69	21.54	17.87	37.54	8.35	804	1551
1556	3158664	-1.13	3849	30.73	2.311	1.072	0.22	32.20	33.30	-1.10	8.32	13.96	22.93	17.55	37.39	8.16	820	1556
1561	2984576	0.94	3408	27.77	2.322	0.977	-0.07	34.68	32.90	1.78	12.21	10.21	23.63	19.57	39.30	7.29	699	1561
1566	3128279	0.89	3700	37.97	2.477	1.396	1.07	37.18	24.79	12.39	9.69	14.00	18.90	20.65	39.24	7.21	670	1566
1571	3270903	0.85	4198	38.22	2.130	1.207	0.60	32.83	24.40	8.43	9.69	13.29	19.47	19.77	40.15	7.32	669	1571
1576	3412722	1.06	4656	40.26	2.176	1.292	0.82	33.80	22.49	11.31	10.20	12.78	22.10	15.98	41.66	7.49	735	1576
1581	3597670	1.13	5272	41.68	2.322	1.422	1.13	34.34	21.82	12.52	9.54	13.53	21.08	16.37	41.44	7.59	730	1581
1586	3805841	0.48	6158	38.31	2.353	1.337	0.93	32.77	24.92	7.85	9.69	13.64	21.30	18.28	38.98	7.80	746	1586
1591	3899190	0.57	6949	35.51	2.358	1.251	0.72	32.61	26.85	5.76	9.62	12.40	22.29	17.86	39.52	7.93	743	1591
1596	4011563	0.48	7243	37.65	2.243	1.255	0.73	31.20	24.98	6.22	8.59	12.53	21.38	18.45	39.58	8.08	723	1596
1601	4109981	0.69	7198	38.12	2.354	1.331	0.92	33.61	24.60	9.01	9.12	12.30	20.63	19.35	39.45	8.27	701	1601
1606	4253325	0.75	6826	40.82	2.339	1.406	1.09	34.20	22.82	11.39	9.08	13.02	20.45	18.51	39.40	8.62	727	1606
1611	4416351	0.42	5948	37.27	2.194	1.216	0.62	32.30	26.03	6.21	9.07	13.05	20.84	17.75	39.28	9.08	753	1611
1616	4509865	0.80	4975	36.79	2.153	1.179	0.53	31.83	26.03	5.80	8.47	12.25	21.57	17.85	39.43	8.90	746	1616
1621	4692975	0.11	4416	39.95	2.229	1.315	0.87	32.68	23.50	9.18	7.79	12.78	20.74	18.16	40.29	8.02	711	1621
1626	4719684	0.72	4811	33.96	2.107	1.207	0.22	31.59	28.10	3.48	8.02	11.61	20.68	18.97	40.84	7.90	672	1626
1631	4892580	0.67	6250	38.71	2.105	1.207	0.60	31.78	24.12	7.69	8.09	12.45	19.87	18.19	41.46	8.03	676	1631
1636	5058102	0.13	7982	36.14	2.094	1.129	0.39	31.64	26.52	5.12	7.97	12.40	19.73	17.72	42.03	8.12	674	1636
1641	5091725	0.33	9849	33.70	2.152	1.088	0.27	32.42	28.61	3.81	8.80	11.83	20.48	17.34	42.08	8.27	683	1641
1646	5176571	0.20	11527	38.47	2.089	1.191	0.56	30.68	24.44	6.24	7.11	12.25	19.90	17.36	41.91	8.59	687	1646
1651	5228481	0.20	12615	37.82	1.852	1.040	0.12	26.79	24.64	2.15	6.73	11.06	20.24	18.06	41.72	8.92	673	1651
1656	5281347	-0.54	12439	34.11	2.008	1.026	0.08	28.92	28.70	0.22	9.87	11.38	19.78	17.80	41.75	9.28	679	1656
1661	5140743	-0.29	11044	35.71	1.810	0.965	-0.11	26.78	26.30	0.48	7.52	9.91	19.37	18.73	42.58	9.40	631	1661
1666	5067047	-0.34	9042	31.79	1.977	0.946	-0.18	30.04	31.04	-0.99	7.48	10.86	18.18	18.65	42.58	9.73	633	1666
1671	4982687	0.08	6963	33.18	1.899	0.944	-0.18	29.66	29.69	-0.03	7.31	10.92	17.63	18.13	43.43	9.89	624	1671
1676	5003488	-0.29	5161	36.37	1.906	1.033	-0.10	29.75	26.93	2.82	6.87	11.29	18.36	16.83	43.58	9.95	655	1676
1681	4930385	-0.27	3873	28.47	1.939	0.836	-0.57	30.13	35.44	-5.31	8.07	11.03	18.74	16.28	44.24	9.71	652	1681
1686	4864762	0.27	3612	31.77	2.170	1.038	0.12	32.87	31.41	1.46	8.01	11.37	18.57	17.06	43.90	9.10	640	1686
1691	4930502	0.13	3916	34.87	2.159	1.127	0.38	31.63	28.66	2.97	6.51	12.31	18.37	16.97	43.28	9.06	660	1691
1696	4961692	0.38	4429	34.13	2.184	1.117	0.35	31.56	28.99	2.57	7.62	11.67	19.61	16.59	42.95	9.18	680	1696

Table A3.1: *(cont.)*

Year	Pop.	CGR	Mig.	e_0	GRR	NRR	ITR	CBR	CDR	CRNI	CMR	0–4	5–14	15–24	25–59	60+	DR	Year
1701	5057790	0.49	5003	37.11	2.337	1.290	0.82	33.09	26.48	6.61	8.19	12.28	19.81	16.35	42.18	9.38	708	1701
1706	5182007	0.19	5392	36.44	2.245	1.219	0.63	31.23	27.47	3.76	7.52	12.64	19.76	17.19	40.60	9.81	730	1706
1711	5230371	0.17	5508	35.93	2.052	1.100	0.30	28.82	27.26	1.56	7.55	11.34	20.88	17.58	40.22	9.97	730	1711
1716	5275978	0.28	5523	37.10	2.245	1.239	0.69	32.10	26.33	5.78	8.52	11.61	20.17	17.81	40.33	10.08	720	1716
1721	5330465	0.37	5621	32.51	2.266	1.108	0.33	33.03	31.41	1.63	8.91	12.32	19.12	18.70	40.40	9.46	692	1721
1726	5449957	-0.70	5196	32.41	2.213	1.079	0.24	32.86	31.56	1.29	8.83	12.71	19.73	17.88	40.58	9.11	711	1726
1731	5263374	-0.70	4839	27.88	2.202	0.930	-0.23	34.02	34.98	-0.96	10.09	11.08	20.73	17.55	42.23	8.41	673	1731
1736	5450392	0.46	4956	35.64	2.366	1.259	0.74	35.51	27.74	7.77	8.52	13.50	20.73	17.77	41.37	8.35	691	1736
1741	5576197	0.21	5173	31.70	2.218	1.059	0.18	32.85	31.58	1.27	8.19	12.91	19.90	17.87	41.21	8.11	693	1741
1746	5634781	0.48	5555	35.34	2.273	1.200	0.58	33.49	27.00	6.48	8.46	12.06	21.50	16.72	41.73	8.11	711	1746
1751	5772415	0.75	6276	36.57	2.339	1.274	0.78	33.76	26.16	7.60	8.24	12.61	21.51	17.47	41.39	7.99	699	1751
1756	5993415	0.51	7001	37.29	2.315	1.284	0.80	32.82	25.90	6.92	8.06	13.04	20.09	18.48	40.02	8.37	709	1756
1761	6146857	0.42	7061	34.23	2.370	1.216	0.63	33.89	28.70	5.19	9.39	12.51	21.08	17.52	40.29	8.60	730	1761
1766	6277076	0.54	6265	35.04	2.392	1.254	0.72	34.28	28.07	6.21	9.89	12.85	20.91	17.57	39.91	8.76	740	1766
1771	6447813	0.89	5265	35.60	2.501	1.329	0.91	35.86	27.59	8.27	9.11	13.06	20.63	18.39	39.41	8.50	730	1771
1776	6740370	0.88	4403	38.17	2.581	1.433	1.15	36.28	25.48	10.79	8.81	13.70	20.92	17.94	39.07	8.36	754	1776
1781	7042140	0.69	3443	34.72	2.488	1.293	0.82	35.61	28.83	6.78	8.58	13.84	21.53	17.48	38.92	8.24	773	1781
1786	7289039	1.20	3086	35.93	2.623	1.406	1.09	37.57	27.04	10.53	8.99	13.40	22.12	17.83	38.69	7.97	769	1786
1791	7739889	1.15	3642	37.33	2.767	1.536	1.38	39.08	26.22	12.86	8.77	14.60	21.54	18.04	38.41	7.41	771	1791
1796	8198445	1.11	4529	36.76	2.764	1.513	1.33	38.74	26.66	12.08	8.43	14.70	22.07	18.14	37.72	7.37	790	1796
1801	8664490	1.35	5665	35.89	2.693	1.442	1.18	37.71	27.08	10.63	8.46	14.32	23.08	17.73	37.60	7.26	807	1801
1806	9267570	1.29	6708	38.70	2.931	1.680	1.67	40.51	24.70	15.81	8.39	15.09	22.70	18.03	37.20	6.99	811	1806
1811	9885690	1.49	8149	37.59	2.868	1.602	1.52	39.48	25.56	13.92	7.91	14.98	22.98	18.66	36.49	6.89	813	1811
1816	10651629	1.52	10074	37.86	3.056	1.718	1.74	41.92	25.53	16.39	8.38	15.58	23.28	18.23	36.04	6.83	843	1816
1821	11491850	1.54	12530	39.24	2.981	1.730	1.76	40.75	24.12	16.63	8.15	15.53	23.68	18.27	35.84	6.68	848	1821
1826	12410995	1.36	15569	39.92	2.855	1.683	1.67	38.91	23.40	15.51	8.12	15.52	24.10	18.45	35.39	6.54	857	1826
1831	13283882	1.20	18057	40.80	2.588	1.555	1.42	35.65	22.00	13.65	7.79	14.39	24.41	18.96	35.70	6.54	829	1831
1836	14105979	1.19	20300	40.15	2.531	1.499	1.30	35.58	22.31	13.27	7.85	13.94	23.75	19.61	36.12	6.58	794	1836
1841	14970372	1.25	23014	40.28	2.492	1.480	1.26	35.92	22.25	13.65	7.66	13.93	22.60	20.00	36.89	6.58	758	1841
1846	15933803	0.98	24736	39.56	2.374	1.388	1.05	34.92	22.95	11.97	8.22	13.96	22.34	19.41	37.72	6.57	750	1846
1851	16736084	1.19	24305	39.54	2.403	1.404	1.09	35.78	22.80	12.98	8.67	13.53	22.48	18.68	38.66	6.66	744	1851
1856	17763920	1.28	21891	40.39	2.444	1.456	1.20	35.91	22.40	13.51	8.29	14.01	22.04	18.59	38.58	6.80	749	1856
1861	18937536	1.26	20315	41.19	2.507	1.519	1.34	36.20	21.88	14.32	8.33	14.08	22.07	18.48	38.50	6.87	755	1861
1866	20166624	1.28	23458	40.32	2.553	1.518	1.34	36.45	22.70	13.75	8.48	14.13	22.42	18.11	38.41	6.93	769	1866
1871	21500720	–	–	41.31	2.537	1.541	1.39	35.95	21.92	14.03	8.36	14.05	22.45	18.14	38.32	7.05	771	1871

Note: Owing to rounding the CRNI does not in all cases equal the difference between the CBR and the CDR.

age). Further details of the calculation of cohort rates may be found in appendix 15. Table A3.3 provides annual population totals and the crude birth, death, marriage,

Table A3.2: Cohort demographic data produced by back projection: fertility and mortality

Key: GRR: Gross reproduction rate; NRR: Net reproduction rate; e_0: Expectation of life at birth.

Year	GRR	NRR	e_0	Year	GRR	NRR	e_0
1541	2.282	1.157	34.64	1701	2.250	1.203	35.89
1546	2.259	1.143	34.36	1706	2.262	1.188	35.48
1551	2.273	1.245	37.15	1711	2.279	1.186	35.25
1556	2.306	1.133	33.04	1716	2.289	1.205	35.69
1561	2.324	1.107	31.82	1721	2.308	1.135	33.26
1566	2.320	1.315	38.03	1726	2.337	1.147	33.14
1571	2.302	1.312	38.20	1731	2.372	1.093	30.93
1576	2.280	1.336	39.24	1736	2.414	1.270	35.52
1581	2.246	1.332	39.65	1741	2.459	1.225	33.56
1586	2.202	1.245	37.71	1746	2.508	1.330	35.83
1591	2.167	1.180	36.23	1751	2.561	1.384	36.60
1596	2.146	1.205	37.34	1756	2.619	1.424	36.92
				1761	2.685	1.399	35.39
1601	2.126	1.201	37.57	1766	2.746	1.455	36.02
1606	2.107	1.221	38.58	1771	2.793	1.501	36.57
1611	2.082	1.150	36.60	1776	2.848	1.580	37.89
1616	2.044	1.125	36.35	1781	2.908	1.543	36.19
1621	1.986	1.129	37.55	1786	2.937	1.600	--
1626	1.937	1.016	34.55	1791	2.907	1.624	--
1631	1.917	1.068	36.88	1796	2.816	1.568	--
1636	1.912	1.018	35.36				
1641	1.922	0.988	34.21	1801	2.691	1.494	--
1646	1.952	1.066	36.61	1806	2.571	1.486	--
1651	2.002	1.068	35.99	1811	2.490	1.420	--
1656	2.075	1.046	34.02	1816	2.445	1.403	--
1661	2.155	1.104	34.65	1821	2.434	1.423	--
1666	2.204	1.070	32.61	1826	2.453	1.447	--
1671	2.221	1.117	33.59				
1676	2.221	1.165	34.95				
1681	2.206	1.025	30.71				
1686	2.198	1.096	32.95				
1691	2.217	1.159	34.68				
1696	2.241	1.157	34.37				

and natural increase rates for the calendar year in question. Net migration rates are also given. Since the totals of net migration can only be estimated for five-year periods, annual migration rates cannot be calculated. The rates shown are average rates applying to a five-year period and are calculated by relating the annual migration total for the period to its mid-point population. Thus, the net migration rate printed against 1541 (1.3) represents the rate prevailing during the period 1541–6 and is calculated from the annual average migration total (3,619) and the population at the beginning of 1544 (the printed population totals all refer to 30 June of the year in question and the mid-point population is therefore the mean of the printed totals for 1543 and 1544). The annual population totals between each quinquennial 'census' total were obtained by assuming that the quinquennial migration total was evenly divided between each of the five years in question and modifying the annual totals of natural increase accordingly when moving from one annual total to the next.

Table A3.3: Annual crude rates produced by back projection: birth, death, marriage, natural increase, and net migration (rates per 1 000 total population)

Key: Pop.: Population total; CBR: Crude birth rate; CRNI: crude rate of natural increase; CDR: Crude death rate; CMR: Crude marriage rate; Mig. Rate: Net migration rate (positive figures indicate emigration).

Year	Pop.	CBR	CDR	CRNI	CMR	Mig. Rate
1541	2773851	34.0	26.1	7.9	14.0	1.3
1542	2811994	40.5	25.3	15.2	15.0	
1543	2829024	38.3	34.3	4.0	12.4	
1544	2861457	35.4	29.6	5.8	11.2	
1545	2856945	36.8	36.0	0.9	10.6	
1546	2853711	37.7	33.3	4.4	12.7	1.4
1547	2855740	34.3	29.2	5.1	14.0	
1548	2898363	40.3	27.6	12.7	15.1	
1549	2928476	38.4	21.9	16.5	11.1	
1550	2969289	41.5	27.1	14.4	11.8	1.4
1551	3011030	39.6	27.9	11.8	11.2	
1552	3034857	37.7	27.1	10.6	12.5	
1553	3060140	37.2	26.6	10.7	13.2	
1554	3089762	33.3	22.1	11.2	6.7	
1555	3115399	36.0	25.8	10.1	9.6	
1556	3158664	35.2	24.4	10.8	7.6	1.3
1557	3152801	27.3	42.5	-15.1	7.3	
1558	3085207	31.2	53.9	-22.8	11.0	
1559	2985522	27.2	47.3	-20.1	11.4	
1560	2963505	34.6	31.6	2.9	14.1	1.1
1561	2984576	37.1	25.9	11.2	13.4	
1562	3015539	38.0	24.2	13.7	11.6	
1563	3048188	35.7	34.6	11.7	10.3	
1564	3060260	38.0	26.3	11.7	10.5	
1565	3101938	39.1	23.7	15.4	9.3	1.2
1566	3128279	35.6	25.9	9.7	8.5	
1567	3155452	35.6	25.2	10.4	10.4	
1568	3204361	37.5	22.8	14.8	9.7	
1569	3230085	31.3	23.6	7.7	9.8	
1570	3254772	34.2	26.2	8.0	9.8	1.3
1571	3270903	33.3	25.0	8.3	9.4	
1572	3302938	33.4	23.2	10.2	10.0	
1573	3322745	31.8	23.9	7.9	9.4	
1574	3343556	31.7	23.5	8.2	10.6	
1575	3377026	33.0	22.5	10.5	10.3	
1576	3412722	34.6	20.9	13.7	10.1	1.3
1577	3455298	34.6	21.4	13.2	9.2	
1578	3492740	34.9	24.0	10.9	10.7	
1579	3525961	34.8	22.9	11.9	9.2	
1580	3568068	34.0	24.9	9.2	10.8	1.4
1581	3597670	33.8	20.0	13.8	9.4	
1582	3637267	34.6	22.1	12.5	9.0	
1583	3687293	34.2	19.2	15.0	9.3	
1584	3733792	34.7	22.5	12.2	10.0	
1585	3763197	34.6	23.9	10.7	10.1	
1586	3805841	32.9	21.9	11.0	8.8	1.6
1587	3823844	29.3	28.2	1.0	9.1	
1588	3811594	33.2	28.6	4.6	10.7	
1589	3848858	36.6	23.3	13.3	10.4	
1590	3895749	31.3	23.4	7.9	9.0	1.8
1591	3899190	29.6	28.4	1.2	9.3	
1592	3905992	32.8	28.3	4.5	9.6	
1593	3904196	33.1	31.1	2.0	9.9	
1594	3938238	35.6	20.8	14.8	10.0	
1595	3984741	32.9	21.1	11.8	8.8	
1596	4011563	30.4	24.1	6.3	8.4	1.8
1597	4009868	29.1	33.2	-4.1	7.3	
1598	3985129	29.1	26.4	2.7	8.9	
1599	4019850	36.3	22.8	13.4	9.6	

Table A3.3: *(cont.)*

Year	Pop.	CBR	CDR	CRNI	CMR	Mig. Rate
1600	4066132	34.1	21.3	12.8	9.4	
1601	4109981	31.3	20.5	10.9	8.5	1.7
1602	4134937	31.1	24.4	6.7	8.8	
1603	4155924	35.8	34.2	1.7	9.5	
1604	4165631	34.5	23.3	11.2	9.6	
1605	4214580	35.3	21.6	13.7	9.7	
1606	4253325	33.9	23.0	10.9	8.9	1.6
1607	4303043	34.8	22.0	12.8	9.4	
1608	4339621	32.4	24.1	8.4	8.8	
1609	4376139	32.3	23.2	9.1	8.8	
1610	4389648	32.9	28.9	4.0	9.1	
1611	4416351	34.2	24.6	9.6	9.9	1.3
1612	4438684	32.3	27.8	4.5	9.0	
1613	4458964	29.9	26.0	3.9	8.5	
1614	4459009	33.2	26.8	6.4	8.4	
1615	4494328	33.2	25.0	8.3	8.7	
1616	4509865	31.0	29.1	2.0	8.3	1.1
1617	4515264	31.5	25.8	5.7	7.9	
1618	4545558	31.6	23.7	8.1	9.2	
1619	4589940	33.7	22.0	11.7	9.0	
1620	4634570	35.5	22.5	12.7	8.8	
1621	4692975	34.5	21.3	13.2	8.3	0.9
1622	4755520	32.3	21.3	11.0	6.7	
1623	4771723	27.9	30.3	-2.3	6.2	
1624	4755803	32.0	27.6	2.2	7.7	
1625	4751559	32.0	41.6	-9.6	7.2	1.0
1626	4719684	29.9	25.2	4.7	7.9	
1627	4738209	31.6	23.0	8.6	8.5	
1628	4791190	33.7	22.3	11.4	8.6	
1629	4832178	32.9	23.8	9.1	8.6	
1630	4884108	32.8	23.9	8.9	7.8	
1631	4892580	27.7	26.8	0.8	7.5	1.3
1632	4905679	32.1	23.4	8.7	8.4	
1633	4956606	33.4	22.6	10.8	8.1	
1634	4997059	32.3	22.5	9.8	8.3	
1635	5035381	31.7	24.4	7.2	8.4	1.6
1636	5058102	32.6	28.8	3.7	7.6	
1637	5075295	30.3	25.6	6.2	8.2	
1638	5083442	31.5	31.5	-1.1	7.4	
1639	5051090	29.0	31.2	-2.2	9.3	
1640	5054987	34.7	28.2	6.5	9.6	
1641	5091725	32.2	26.0	6.2	10.0	1.9
1642	5112369	32.7	25.9	6.8	8.9	
1643	5137252	33.5	31.8	1.7	6.3	
1644	5120591	30.7	30.3	0.4	6.1	
1645	5130102	32.9	24.1	8.8	8.3	
1646	5176571	32.2	20.8	11.4	8.3	2.2
1647	5214439	30.1	24.0	6.1	7.4	
1648	5226311	27.7	23.2	4.4	5.5	
1649	5228671	26.2	24.9	1.3	5.9	
1650	5220613	25.7	25.2	0.5	7.2	
1651	5228481	28.8	22.2	6.6	7.3	2.4
1652	5239621	26.8	25.0	1.9	6.7	
1653	5233861	26.5	26.0	0.5	6.7	
1654	5218968	30.5	27.5	3.1	9.7	
1655	5246222	32.1	23.5	8.6	12.1	2.4
1656	5281347	31.1	23.5	7.6	10.7	
1657	5283967	27.2	32.1	-4.9	8.8	
1658	5206026	24.7	38.0	-13.3	8.3	
1659	5136446	22.9	27.7	-4.8	9.0	
1660	5129697	28.2	24.4	3.8	7.0	
1661	5140743	28.4	27.8	0.6	6.0	2.2
1662	5116266	25.8	26.8	-1.0	7.4	
1663	5104642	29.1	25.2	3.9	8.4	
1664	5129409	30.2	25.1	5.0	8.5	
1665	5109593	30.4	43.0	-12.8	7.6	1.8
1666	5067047	28.1	28.1	-0.4	7.2	
1667	5059176	29.7	29.8	-0.4	7.4	
1668	5046514	29.7	28.7	-1.0	6.6	
1669	5035598	29.9	32.8	-2.8	6.9	
1670	5021781	29.2	32.4	-3.2	7.0	
1671	4982680	27.6	30.2	-2.6	8.0	1.4
1672	4973342	30.8	26.8	4.0	7.5	
1673	4993190	30.2	25.7	4.6	7.0	
1674	5008493	26.1	26.1	3.0	6.5	
1675	5008659	27.6	29.0	-1.5	6.4	
1676	5003488	31.1	27.5	3.6	6.9	1.0
1677	5021160	31.6	24.7	6.1	7.5	
1678	5055751	29.6	26.7	2.9	6.9	
1679	5023676	27.6	37.2	-9.6	7.0	

Table A3.3: (cont.)

Year	Pop.	CBR	CDR	CRNI	CMR	Mig. Rate
1680	4989069	29.2	33.8	-4.6	8.3	
1681	4930385	30.1	38.9	-8.8	8.1	0.8
1682	4900118	30.7	35.0	-4.3	7.9	
1683	4886292	32.7	31.8	0.9	8.9	
1684	4888077	32.3	33.6	-1.2	7.6	
1685	4870784	31.3	33.3	-2.0	7.9	
1686	4864762	33.5	31.5	2.0	8.1	0.7
1687	4879202	33.2	28.9	4.2	8.5	
1688	4896666	33.6	29.3	4.3	7.9	
1689	4916833	32.7	30.6	2.1	6.8	
1690	4916081	31.6	30.5	1.1	7.0	
1691	4930502	32.1	27.3	4.8	6.6	
1692	4935334	31.2	27.5	3.7	6.1	0.8
1693	4963190	30.6	27.4	3.2	6.0	
1694	4950496	28.2	30.2	-2.0	6.2	
1695	4950662	32.2	30.7	1.5	6.2	
1696	4961692	33.5	28.9	4.6	8.0	
1697	4978072	32.0	28.1	3.9	7.6	0.9
1698	4997611	31.7	26.8	4.9	8.1	
1699	5015098	31.1	27.7	3.5	8.1	
1700	5026877	32.3	27.9	4.4	8.3	
1701	5057790	34.0	26.7	7.5	8.3	
1702	5091997	34.0	25.2	8.8	8.2	
1703	5134009	33.5	24.8	8.7	8.0	1.0
1704	5156714	32.1	27.0	5.1	7.4	
1705	5167186	32.6	31.5	0.7	7.9	
1706	5182007	31.6	26.5	5.0	7.8	
1707	5198807	29.8	25.2	4.6	7.5	1.0
1708	5214985	30.4	27.0	3.4	7.0	
1709	5224968	28.5	25.7	2.8	6.8	
1710	5238156	27.9	26.4	1.6	7.5	
1711	5230371	28.5	28.5	0.5	7.3	
1712	5217996	28.7	30.1	-1.4	7.7	1.1
1713	5224785	30.2	25.8	4.4	8.5	
1714	5242213	30.9	28.4	2.4	8.8	
1715	5246260	31.3	26.0	5.2	8.7	
1716	5275978	33.3	26.5	6.9	8.0	1.0
1717	5310048	31.9	24.9	7.0	8.0	
1718	5343506	32.9	25.6	7.3	9.1	
1719	5378136	33.7	31.8	1.8	8.2	
1720	5357759	30.6	32.4	-1.8	8.2	1.0
1721	5350465	31.6	31.4	-0.2	8.6	
1722	5354441	33.7	29.7	4.0	9.4	
1723	5370904	35.3	31.3	4.0	10.1	
1724	5387727	34.1	30.0	4.1	9.5	
1725	5406168	33.2	25.4	7.8	8.9	
1726	5449957	34.4	27.7	6.7	9.4	1.0
1727	5480307	34.3	35.5	-1.2	8.3	
1728	5425467	29.0	39.8	-10.8	8.2	
1729	5335527	29.3	44.7	-15.4	9.6	
1730	5269100	31.5	36.2	-4.7	10.9	
1731	5263374	36.4	34.1	2.3	11.2	0.9
1732	5283764	35.4	29.8	5.6	10.3	
1733	5310276	36.6	29.0	7.6	9.3	
1734	5363165	36.4	26.0	10.3	8.9	
1735	5409030	36.4	26.9	9.5	8.9	
1736	5450392	35.3	28.1	7.2	8.0	0.9
1737	5480925	34.7	30.6	4.1	8.4	
1738	5504321	35.2	27.4	7.8	8.4	
1739	5536582	35.8	27.5	8.3	8.6	
1740	5564656	33.7	31.1	2.6	8.2	
1741	5576197	31.2	34.7	-3.5	7.3	0.9
1742	5516469	30.8	36.7	-5.8	8.2	
1743	5512230	33.9	29.0	4.9	9.0	
1744	5547818	34.0	25.0	9.0	8.9	
1745	5603475	34.1	25.2	9.0	8.2	
1746	5634781	33.2	27.9	5.3	8.7	1.0
1747	5657650	32.8	28.6	4.3	8.5	
1748	5668980	33.7	28.6	5.1	8.3	
1749	5702768	32.8	26.8	6.1	8.3	
1750	5739364	34.8	27.5	7.3	8.4	
1751	5772415	34.2	26.3	7.9	8.1	1.1
1752	5810512	33.0	25.4	7.6	8.1	
1753	5855895	33.9	24.8	9.1	8.3	
1754	5899694	33.7	25.4	8.3	7.9	
1755	5942912	34.2	25.2	9.0	8.4	1.2
1756	5993415	33.6	25.7	7.9	8.6	
1757	6021018	31.7	26.2	5.5	7.4	
1758	6038563	31.4	27.4	4.1	8.1	
1759	6062922	33.7	27.3	6.4	9.2	

Table A3.3: (cont.)

Year	Pop.	CBR	CDR	CRNI	CMR	Mig. Rate
1760	6101593	33.6	26.4	7.2	9.8	
1761	6146857	34.8	26.5	8.3	9.8	
1762	6173425	34.4	31.3	3.1	8.8	1.1
1763	6162402	33.4	32.4	1.1	9.4	
1764	6194858	35.1	27.2	7.9	9.5	
1765	6245527	35.4	26.1	9.3	9.5	
1766	6277076	33.6	30.0	3.7	9.0	
1767	6294963	33.9	29.5	4.3	8.8	1.0
1768	6314318	33.8	27.8	5.9	8.3	
1769	6357503	35.5	27.2	8.3	9.5	
1770	6405166	36.7	28.6	8.1	9.4	
1771	6447813	35.2	27.2	8.0	9.0	
1772	6498765	35.7	27.3	8.4	9.0	0.8
1773	6552106	36.1	27.6	8.5	8.7	
1774	6601608	34.9	24.4	10.6	8.8	
1775	6674251	36.5	25.9	10.6	8.6	
1776	6740370	36.1	24.6	11.5	8.8	0.6
1777	6807906	37.0	26.2	11.0	9.0	
1778	6881506	36.9	25.9	11.0	8.9	
1779	6949296	36.9	28.0	8.9	8.5	
1780	6989116	36.1	29.0	7.1	9.0	
1781	7042140	35.5	29.7	5.8	8.5	0.5
1782	7068884	34.9	28.4	6.6	8.3	
1783	7126530	34.8	29.3	5.6	8.7	
1784	7144515	35.3	28.5	6.8	8.7	
1785	7217228	37.5	27.3	10.2	9.8	0.4
1786	7289039	38.5	26.7	11.7	9.0	
1787	7370599	37.3	25.8	11.4	8.8	
1788	7461509	39.1	26.8	12.3	8.8	
1789	7542738	37.9	25.6	12.3	8.4	
1790	7648209	39.4	25.8	13.6	8.8	0.5
1791	7739889	38.4	25.4	13.0	8.6	
1792	7842063	40.4	25.9	14.5	9.1	
1793	7936885	39.2	28.4	10.8	8.9	
1794	8024644	38.2	26.9	11.3	8.3	0.5
1795	8100800	38.4	29.1	9.3	7.5	
1796	8198445	37.9	25.1	12.7	8.5	
1797	8285135	39.8	27.2	12.6	8.7	
1798	8398737	39.3	24.9	14.4	9.1	
1799	8500584	37.6	25.1	12.6	8.2	
1800	8606033	36.6	26.7	9.9	7.4	0.6
1801	8664490	33.9	28.1	5.8	6.9	
1802	8728212	39.0	27.0	11.9	9.7	
1803	8836648	41.3	28.4	12.9	10.0	
1804	8958695	41.6	24.6	17.1	9.1	
1805	9116801	40.0	23.9	17.0	8.0	
1806	9267570	40.4	23.2	17.2	8.6	0.7
1807	9400058	40.1	26.1	14.0	8.0	
1808	9528047	39.8	25.9	14.0	8.0	
1809	9650602	38.6	24.7	13.9	7.7	
1810	9762413	39.5	27.9	11.6	7.7	
1811	9885690	40.0	26.5	13.5	8.4	0.8
1812	10010037	39.1	24.8	14.3	7.7	
1813	10163058	40.1	23.8	16.2	7.7	
1814	10296594	40.5	24.1	14.3	8.7	
1815	10480975	44.3	25.1	19.2	9.0	
1816	10651629	42.2	26.0	16.2	8.4	0.9
1817	10827421	41.9	24.8	17.1	7.7	
1818	10985092	40.8	25.7	15.1	8.1	
1819	11151679	40.1	24.9	15.2	7.7	
1820	11300024	39.8	24.0	15.8	8.3	
1821	11491850	40.9	23.4	17.4	8.1	1.1
1822	11687791	41.9	23.6	18.4	8.4	
1823	11875085	40.8	24.6	16.2	8.3	
1824	12053002	39.9	24.3	15.3	8.1	
1825	12244547	39.6	24.2	15.3	8.7	
1826	12410995	39.5	24.2	15.3	7.9	1.2
1827	12563846	37.3	22.8	14.5	7.4	
1828	12762041	38.1	21.8	16.7	8.5	
1829	12935893	35.7	22.1	13.6	7.3	
1830	13105539	35.6	20.7	14.9	7.3	
1831	13283882	35.2	22.5	12.8	7.9	1.3
1832	13420379	35.2	23.0	12.2	8.1	
1833	13586482	36.8	21.8	15.0	8.4	
1834	13776375	36.0	21.3	13.7	8.9	
1835	13932829	35.6	22.0	13.6	7.9	
1836	14105979	35.8	21.7	14.1	8.1	1.4
1837	14272904	35.3	22.8	12.6	7.5	
1838	14432562	35.2	22.7	12.5	7.7	
1839	14616795	36.3	22.3	14.1	7.9	

Table A3.3: *(cont.)*

Year	Pop.	CBR	CDR	CRNI	CMR	Mig. Rate
1840	14797488	36.1	23.3	12.8	7.8	
1841	14970372	36.0	22.0	14.0	7.7	1.5
1842	15162235	35.6	22.1	13.5	7.4	
1843	15340381	35.5	21.6	13.9	7.6	
1844	15536169	35.6	22.0	13.6	7.6	
1845	15717550	35.0	21.3	13.8	8.0	
1846	15933803	36.1	23.4	12.7	8.6	
1847	16058597	33.7	25.0	8.7	7.9	1.5
1848	16183051	34.7	23.4	11.4	8.1	
1849	16371324	35.2	25.4	9.8	8.1	
1850	16515615	35.7	21.0	14.7	8.7	
1851	16736084	36.4	22.1	14.3	8.7	1.4
1852	16952384	36.4	22.5	13.9	8.8	
1853	17144592	35.2	23.0	12.2	9.0	
1854	17352736	36.0	23.6	12.4	8.6	
1855	17516176	35.7	22.8	12.9	8.1	
1856	17763920	36.4	20.6	15.8	8.4	1.2
1857	18015056	36.1	21.8	14.3	8.3	
1858	18226800	35.3	23.1	12.1	8.0	
1859	18442320	36.6	22.4	14.2	8.5	
1860	18682352	35.8	21.2	14.6	8.6	
1861	18937536	35.9	21.6	14.4	8.1	1.0
1862	19197408	36.2	21.3	14.9	9.0	
1863	19453744	36.4	22.9	13.5	8.4	
1864	19689072	36.5	23.6	12.9	8.6	
1865	19930656	36.4	23.1	13.3	8.7	
1866	20166624	36.2	23.3	12.9	8.8	
1867	20426416	36.4	21.7	14.7	8.3	1.1
1868	20724960	36.6	21.8	14.9	8.0	
1869	20978960	35.5	22.1	13.4	7.9	
1870	21239824	35.9	22.8	13.1	8.0	
1871	21500720	35.7	22.5	13.2	8.3	

Note: Owing to rounding the CRNI does not in all cases equal the difference between the CBR and the CDR.

Appendix 4

From parish register data to estimated national totals of births, deaths, and marriages (England less Monmouth)

The tables printed in this appendix show the totals of baptisms, burials, and marriages taken from the 404 parish register tabulations returned to the Cambridge Group, and the effects of the steps taken to convert them into national totals of births, deaths, and marriages. Table A4.1 sets out the stages leading to the establishment of national annual totals of baptisms, burials, and marriages and also the final annual totals of births, deaths and marriages. Table A4.2 shows the effect of the several operations by which baptism totals were changed to birth totals, and burial totals to death totals (i.e. the derivation of column 6 from column 5 in table A4.1). These data are given for decades rather than annually since the inflation ratios that produced them change smoothly without sudden, erratic movements from year to year.

The first six columns in table A4.1 show the effect of successive corrections and contain the following data:

1 Raw annual totals of events in the 404 tabulations making up the aggregative sample.
2 Annual totals after correction for deficient registration (see chapter 1 and appendices 12 and 13).
3 Annual totals after re-weighting to offset the untypical population size distribution of the parishes in the aggregative sample (see chapter 2).
4 Annual totals after inflation in the periods before 1662 and after 1811 to compensate for the fact that parish tabulations begin and end at different dates, though all are in observation in the period 1662–1811 (see chapter 2).
5 Annual totals after the inflation of aggregative sample totals by a factor designed to convert them into national totals (see chapter 3).
6 Annual totals after the totals of Anglican events have been increased by factors intended to offset the effects of the growth of nonconformity, of the increasing delay between birth and baptism, and of all residual causes of non-registration in order to produce national totals of births, deaths, and marriages (see chapters 4 and 5).

The next five columns of the table contain a series of ratio figures, calculated to a base of 1,000, intended to make the effects of the successive changes in the data easier to appreciate. It may be noted that the ratios in this column are not always precisely those that might be expected in view of the ratios listed in tables 3.11 and 3.12. For example, the baptism ratio for the year 1539 is 23.293 while in table 3.11 the ratio applicable to the baptism totals in January 1539 is 23.30, rising linearly to 23.49 in January 1565. Since the lowest monthly inflation ratio in 1539 is 23.30 and each later ratio is slightly higher, it might seem logical to expect that the ratio for the year as a whole given in table A4.1 would be higher than 23.300. Minor discrepancies of this

Table A4.1: The conversion of parish register data into estimated national totals of births, deaths, and marriages (England less Monmouth)

Births

Year	(1)	(2)	(3)	(4)	(5)	(6)	(7) (2)/(1) x1 000	(8) (3)/(2) x1 000	(9) (4)/(3) x1 000	(10) (5)/(4) x1 000	(11) (6)/(5) x1 000	(12)	Year
1539	572	590	321	4888	113857	113857	1031	544	15227	23293	1000	9175	1539
1540	708	738	482	4788	111615	111615	1042	653	9934	23311	1000	8990	1540
1541	679	702	434	4037	94167	94167	1034	618	9302	23326	1000	7814	1541
1542	990	1033	713	4879	113752	113752	1043	690	6843	23315	1000	8706	1542
1543	1032	1054	688	4646	108371	108371	1021	653	6753	23326	1000	8813	1543
1544	972	1024	651	4338	101242	101242	1053	636	6664	23338	1000	8398	1544
1545	916	1026	700	4509	105256	105256	1120	682	6441	23344	1000	7869	1545
1546	1004	1099	733	4611	107647	107647	1095	667	6291	23346	1000	8075	1546
1547	1056	1134	693	4191	97919	97919	1074	611	6048	23364	1000	7913	1547
1548	1269	1396	837	4991	116675	116675	1100	600	5963	23377	1000	9388	1548
1549	1268	1431	816	4809	112425	112425	1129	570	5893	23378	1000	9222	1549
1550	1214	1447	893	5265	123162	123206	1192	617	5896	23393	1000	9324	1550
1551	1169	1344	887	5097	119213	119350	1150	660	5746	23389	1001	8631	1551
1552	1131	1310	869	4884	114240	114460	1158	663	5620	23391	1002	8282	1552
1553	1124	1372	864	4854	113611	113921	1221	630	5618	23406	1003	8673	1553
1554	864	1309	780	4378	102547	102911	1515	596	5613	23423	1004	8273	1554
1555	806	1484	862	4760	111502	111986	1841	581	5522	23425	1004	8987	1555
1556	862	1409	872	4726	110758	111327	1635	619	5420	23436	1005	8321	1556
1557	843	1207	698	3654	85650	86159	1432	578	5235	23440	1006	6469	1557
1558	968	1391	837	4073	95497	96146	1437	602	4866	23446	1007	6933	1558
1559	1572	2037	982	3439	80617	81219	1296	482	3502	23442	1007	6343	1559
1560	2874	3186	1456	4328	101530	102383	1109	457	2973	23459	1008	8060	1560
1561	3276	3513	1664	4672	109631	110637	1072	474	2808	23466	1009	8482	1561
1562	3919	4250	2068	4830	113371	114505	1084	487	2336	23472	1010	8789	1562
1563	4101	4310	2083	4584	107629	108786	1051	483	2201	23479	1011	8343	1563
1564	4351	4679	2352	4894	114966	116296	1075	503	2081	23491	1012	8737	1564
1565	4820	5103	2615	5102	109886	121367	1059	512	1951	23498	1012	9083	1565
1566	4552	4893	2439	4675	109959	111404	1075	498	1917	23521	1013	8582	1566
1567	4508	4954	2493	4708	110758	112301	1099	503	1888	23525	1014	8442	1567
1568	4949	5369	2689	5031	118455	120203	1085	501	1871	23545	1015	9074	1568
1569	4319	4602	2314	4223	99481	101025	1066	503	1825	23557	1016	7638	1569

Table A4.1: *(cont.)*

Births

Year	(1)	(2)	(3)	(4)	(5)	(6)	(7) (2)/(1) x1 000	(8) (3)/(2) x1 000	(9) (4)/(3) x1 000	(10) (5)/(4) x1 000	(11) (6)/(5) x1 000	(12)	Year
1570	4705	5155	2585	4642	109383	111172	1096	501	1796	23564	1016	8440	1570
1571	4710	4989	2616	4538	106994	108830	1059	524	1735	23577	1017	7860	1571
1572	5170	5531	2689	4591	108364	110311	1070	486	1707	23604	1018	8534	1572
1573	4993	5271	2670	4387	103618	105562	1056	488	1707	23619	1019	8133	1573
1574	4851	5093	2672	4395	103810	105840	1050	525	1645	23620	1020	7804	1574
1575	5347	5623	2873	4622	109276	111475	1052	511	1609	23643	1020	8402	1575
1576	5858	6160	3069	4896	115768	118130	1052	498	1595	23645	1020	9158	1576
1577	5673	6007	3118	4942	117003	119425	1059	519	1585	23675	1021	8854	1577
1578	5749	6094	3199	5037	119328	121832	1059	525	1575	23690	1021	8957	1578
1579	6095	6466	3221	5072	120198	122749	1060	498	1575	23698	1021	9503	1579
1580	6270	6536	3189	5014	118883	121440	1061	488	1572	23710	1022	9587	1580
1581	6094	6332	3197	5013	118930	121524	1042	505	1568	23724	1022	9263	1581
1582	6512	6797	3423	5182	123062	125779	1039	504	1514	23748	1022	9637	1582
1583	6636	6944	3531	5194	123391	126153	1044	508	1471	23756	1022	9622	1583
1584	6789	7243	3672	5330	126674	129541	1046	507	1452	23766	1023	9859	1584
1585	6956	7419	3732	5356	127372	130292	1067	503	1435	23781	1023	9960	1585
1586	6804	7133	3619	5142	122378	125217	1067	507	1421	23800	1023	9435	1586
1587	6080	6405	3234	4591	109335	111902	1048	505	1420	23815	1023	8464	1587
1588	6712	7049	3654	5186	123603	126541	1053	518	1419	23834	1024	9313	1588
1589	7564	7964	4081	5764	137482	140788	1050	512	1412	23852	1024	10508	1589
1590	6680	7145	3535	4995	119184	122085	1070	495	1413	23861	1024	9430	1590
1591	6190	6660	3340	4721	112694	115466	1067	502	1413	23871	1025	8787	1591
1592	7045	7520	3732	5234	125069	128182	1045	496	1402	23895	1025	9843	1592
1593	7173	7499	3766	5275	126126	129299	1030	502	1401	23910	1025	9773	1593
1594	7506	7731	4078	5712	136677	140155	1054	527	1401	23928	1025	10077	1594
1595	7161	7547	3869	5334	127738	131022	1046	513	1379	23948	1026	9686	1595
1596	6928	7247	3595	4953	118701	121788	1046	496	1378	23965	1026	9283	1596
1597	6453	6692	3484	4737	113636	116624	1037	521	1360	23989	1026	8394	1597
1598	6575	6877	3502	4711	113126	116132	1046	509	1345	24013	1027	8514	1598
1599	8240	8647	4457	5911	142018	145830	1049	515	1326	24026	1027	10576	1599
1600	8192	8412	4409	5611	134910	138567	1027	524	1273	24044	1027	10209	1600
1601	7610	7980	4156	5211	125350	128787	1049	521	1254	24055	1027	9642	1601
1602	7856	8278	4223	5192	125066	128529	1054	510	1229	24088	1028	9760	1602
1603	8939	9287	5155	6011	144863	148915	1039	555	1166	24100	1028	10791	1603
1604	8984	9438	4995	5793	139753	143700	1051	529	1160	24124	1028	10926	1604
1605	9104	9533	5173	5993	144663	148789	1047	543	1159	24139	1029	11022	1605
1606	8891	9437	5031	5793	139998	144029	1061	533	1151	24167	1029	10818	1606
1607	9431	9866	5238	6025	145664	149999	1046	531	1150	24177	1029	11289	1607
1608	9170	9523	4996	5660	136946	140967	1038	525	1133	24195	1029	10841	1608
1609	8837	9194	5004	5662	137123	141189	1040	544	1131	24218	1030	10450	1609

Table A4.1: *(cont.)*

Births

Year	(1)	(2)	(3)	(4)	(5)	(6)	(7) (2)/(1) x1000	(8) (3)/(2) x1000	(9) (4)/(3) x1000	(10) (5)/(4) x1000	(11) (6)/(5) x1000	(12)	Year
1610	9203	9559	5120	5786	140228	144424	1039	536	1130	24236	1030	10826	1610
1611	9511	9882	5352	6040	146477	150901	1039	542	1129	24251	1030	11171	1611
1612	9273	9605	5103	5733	139167	143408	1036	531	1123	24275	1030	10854	1612
1613	8461	8864	4763	5323	129274	133250	1048	537	1118	24286	1031	9934	1613
1614	9029	9463	5085	5627	136795	141041	1048	537	1107	24310	1031	10511	1614
1615	9276	9826	5397	5955	144842	149379	1059	549	1103	24323	1031	10873	1615
1616	9212	9652	5083	5571	135587	139870	1048	527	1096	24338	1032	10561	1616
1617	9433	9856	5236	5661	137870	142268	1045	531	1081	24354	1032	10609	1617
1618	9770	10164	5345	5772	140671	145193	1040	526	1080	24371	1032	10927	1618
1619	10046	10546	5684	6139	149690	154546	1050	539	1080	24383	1032	11338	1619
1620	10680	11110	6000	6481	158079	163253	1040	540	1080	24391	1033	11944	1620
1621	10849	11252	5960	6429	156899	162078	1037	530	1079	24405	1033	12071	1621
1622	10265	10807	5647	6092	148731	153682	1053	523	1079	24414	1033	11592	1622
1623	8598	9094	4893	5279	128954	133281	1058	538	1079	24428	1034	9756	1623
1624	9331	9755	5204	5598	136846	141476	1045	533	1076	24446	1034	10431	1624
1625	9952	10450	5586	6008	147008	152016	1050	535	1076	24469	1034	11174	1625
1626	9354	9858	5200	5568	136403	141067	1054	527	1071	24498	1034	10487	1626
1627	9854	10286	5507	5899	144715	149684	1044	536	1071	24532	1034	10941	1627
1628	10648	10953	5957	6348	155955	161333	1029	544	1066	24568	1034	11598	1628
1629	10823	11159	5866	6242	153600	158918	1031	526	1064	24607	1035	11771	1629
1630	10323	10824	5901	6280	154740	160118	1049	545	1064	24640	1035	11417	1630
1631	9072	9605	4982	5301	130810	135377	1059	519	1064	24676	1035	10133	1631
1632	10449	10925	5796	6158	152191	157524	1046	531	1062	24714	1035	11471	1632
1633	11022	11634	6084	6465	159978	165607	1056	523	1063	24745	1035	12215	1633
1634	10742	11203	5916	6286	155775	161279	1043	528	1063	24781	1035	11762	1634
1635	10619	11208	5840	6207	153916	159375	1055	521	1063	24797	1035	11766	1635
1636	10936	11397	6036	6409	158967	164627	1042	530	1062	24803	1036	11937	1636
1637	10730	11289	5905	6267	155440	160995	1052	523	1061	24803	1036	11817	1637
1638	10084	10508	5646	5990	148646	153977	1042	537	1061	24816	1036	10999	1638
1639	10109	10421	5378	5702	141495	146594	1031	516	1060	24815	1036	10879	1639
1640	11559	12161	6436	6813	169061	175242	1052	529	1059	24814	1037	12674	1640
1641	10543	11491	6019	6374	158134	164071	1090	524	1059	24809	1038	11976	1641
1642	10501	11858	6134	6494	161169	167389	1129	517	1059	24818	1039	12360	1642
1643	10041	11990	6311	6672	165615	172173	1194	526	1057	24822	1040	12443	1643
1644	8936	10920	5762	6092	151229	157373	1222	528	1057	24824	1041	11334	1644
1645	9200	11626	6167	6520	161870	168614	1264	530	1057	24827	1042	12068	1645
1646	9138	11260	6081	6430	159622	166437	1232	540	1057	24825	1043	11687	1646
1647	8862	10785	5731	6060	150435	157007	1217	531	1057	24824	1044	11194	1647
1648	8010	9813	5275	5579	138492	144687	1225	538	1058	24824	1045	10185	1648
1649	7539	9319	4981	5266	130770	136752	1236	534	1057	24833	1046	9671	1649

Table A4.1: *(cont.)*

Births

Year	(1)	(2)	(3)	(4)	(5)	(6)	(7) (2)/(1) x1 000	(8) (3)/(2) x1 000	(9) (4)/(3) x1 000	(10) (5)/(4) x1 000	(11) (6)/(5) x1 000	(12)	Year
1650	7336	9107	4885	5153	127970	133961	1241	536	1055	24834	1047	9425	1650
1651	8017	10135	5501	5788	143785	150658	1264	543	1052	24842	1048	10449	1651
1652	7888	9804	5142	5398	134100	140650	1243	524	1050	24843	1049	10081	1652
1653	7743	9529	5090	5309	131860	138433	1231	534	1043	24837	1050	9792	1653
1654	9447	11028	5969	6095	151452	159161	1167	541	1021	24849	1051	11248	1654
1655	10449	11776	6356	6442	160059	168375	1127	540	1014	24846	1052	11868	1655
1656	10221	11617	6194	6271	155855	164110	1137	533	1013	24853	1053	11697	1656
1657	8980	10428	5413	5481	136215	143571	1161	519	1013	24852	1054	10500	1657
1658	7908	9266	4838	4899	121745	128444	1172	522	1013	24851	1055	9330	1658
1659	7410	8769	4436	4480	111358	117600	1183	506	1010	24857	1056	8803	1659
1660	8693	10204	5444	5497	136671	144477	1174	534	1010	24863	1057	10244	1660
1661	9270	10345	5494	5550	137935	145953	1116	531	1010	24853	1058	10385	1661
1662	8922	9524	5010	5010	124578	131949	1067	526	1000	24866	1059	9524	1662
1663	10263	10657	5630	5630	139990	148419	1038	528	1000	24865	1060	10657	1663
1664	10876	11219	5847	5847	145433	154336	1032	521	1000	24873	1061	11219	1664
1665	10701	11132	5837	5837	145300	154350	1040	524	1000	24893	1062	11132	1665
1666	10477	10950	5804	5804	144658	153812	1045	530	1000	24924	1063	10950	1666
1667	10221	10804	5592	5592	139645	148629	1057	518	1000	24972	1064	10804	1667
1668	10014	10570	5631	5631	140829	150035	1056	533	1000	25010	1065	10570	1668
1669	10366	10970	5645	5645	141401	150793	1058	515	1000	25049	1066	10970	1669
1670	9991	10576	5470	5470	137238	146494	1059	517	1000	25089	1067	10576	1670
1671	9672	10078	5116	5116	128590	137397	1042	508	1000	25135	1068	10078	1671
1672	10726	11006	5698	5698	143341	153310	1026	518	1000	25156	1069	11006	1672
1673	10733	10967	5593	5593	140965	150913	1022	510	1000	25204	1070	10967	1673
1674	10016	10188	5396	5396	136244	145998	1017	530	1000	25249	1071	10188	1674
1675	9424	9595	5089	5089	128655	138004	1018	530	1000	25281	1072	9595	1675
1676	10593	10738	5721	5721	144735	155413	1014	533	1000	25299	1073	10738	1676
1677	10970	11114	5710	5710	144558	155384	1013	514	1000	25317	1074	11114	1677
1678	10358	10510	5485	5485	138967	149528	1015	522	1000	25336	1075	10510	1678
1679	9771	9960	5077	5077	128748	138672	1019	510	1000	25359	1076	9960	1679
1680	10147	10353	5317	5317	134948	145500	1020	514	1000	25380	1077	10353	1680
1681	10366	10556	5415	5415	137486	148385	1018	513	1000	25390	1078	10556	1681
1682	10512	10703	5478	5478	139233	150430	1018	512	1000	25417	1079	10703	1682
1683	11004	11253	5808	5808	147760	159808	1023	516	1000	25441	1080	11253	1683
1684	10800	11185	5733	5733	145946	158004	1036	513	1000	25478	1082	11185	1684
1685	10322	10637	5526	5526	140794	152580	1031	520	1000	25494	1083	10637	1685
1686	10879	11249	5890	5890	150162	162880	1034	524	1000	25522	1084	11249	1686
1687	11066	11396	5839	5839	149025	161776	1030	512	1000	25536	1085	11396	1687
1688	10955	11315	5923	5923	151247	164319	1033	515	1000	25559	1086	11315	1688
1689	10710	11117	5780	5780	147729	160625	1038	520	1000	25559	1087	11117	1689

Table A4.1: *(cont.)*

Births

Year	(1)	(2)	(3)	(4)	(5)	(6)	(7) (2)/(1) x1 000	(8) (3)/(2) x1 000	(9) (4)/(3) x1 000	(10) (5)/(4) x1 000	(11) (6)/(5) x1 000	(12)	Year
1690	10244	10574	5578	5578	142662	155240	1032	528	1000	25576	1088	10574	1690
1691	10390	10760	5675	5675	145273	158209	1036	527	1000	25599	1089	10760	1691
1692	10275	10671	5507	5507	141105	153796	1039	516	1000	25623	1090	10671	1692
1693	10122	10486	5430	5430	139206	151849	1036	518	1000	25636	1091	10486	1693
1694	9193	9453	4981	4981	127781	139497	1028	527	1000	25654	1092	9453	1694
1695	10708	10899	5681	5681	145875	159379	1018	521	1000	25678	1093	10899	1695
1696	11403	11528	5921	5921	152120	166309	1011	514	1000	25692	1093	11528	1696
1697	10535	10637	5669	5669	145819	159507	1010	533	1000	25722	1094	10637	1697
1698	10650	10788	5620	5620	144680	158351	1013	521	1000	25744	1094	10788	1698
1699	10356	10530	5535	5535	142577	156135	1017	526	1000	25759	1095	10530	1699
1700	10818	10923	5749	5749	148202	162389	1010	526	1000	25779	1096	10923	1700
1701	11596	11641	6122	6122	157935	173149	1004	526	1000	25798	1096	11641	1701
1702	11581	11622	6117	6117	157932	173244	1004	526	1000	25819	1097	11622	1702
1703	11440	11497	6063	6063	156669	171952	1005	527	1000	25840	1098	11497	1703
1704	11471	11501	5824	5824	150609	165394	1003	506	1000	25860	1098	11501	1704
1705	11413	11437	5859	5859	151615	166599	1002	512	1000	25877	1099	11437	1705
1706	11235	11294	5751	5751	148956	163776	1005	509	1000	25901	1099	11294	1706
1707	10610	10732	5425	5425	140599	154691	1011	505	1000	25917	1101	10732	1707
1708	10720	10818	5554	5554	144087	158635	1009	513	1000	25943	1101	10818	1708
1709	10023	10174	5206	5206	135104	148842	1015	512	1000	25952	1102	10174	1709
1710	9660	9877	5105	5105	132600	146181	1022	517	1000	25986	1102	9877	1710
1711	10002	10212	5277	5277	137126	151272	1021	517	1000	26018	1103	10212	1711
1712	9922	10081	5217	5217	135738	149841	1016	518	1000	26030	1104	10081	1712
1713	10487	10685	5478	5478	142593	157516	1019	513	1000	26060	1105	10685	1713
1714	10825	11046	5614	5614	146303	161721	1020	508	1000	26080	1105	11046	1714
1715	10784	10998	5698	5698	148604	164368	1020	518	1000	26092	1106	10998	1715
1716	11624	11805	6091	6091	158926	175871	1016	516	1000	26105	1107	11805	1716
1717	11612	11775	5854	5854	152816	169171	1014	497	1000	26119	1107	11775	1717
1718	11877	12045	6076	6076	158701	175748	1014	504	1000	26134	1108	12045	1718
1719	12078	12306	6250	6250	163336	180948	1019	508	1000	26155	1108	12306	1719
1720	11194	11430	5656	5656	147934	163942	1021	495	1000	26166	1109	11430	1720
1721	11212	11471	5833	5833	152627	169205	1023	508	1000	26187	1109	11471	1721
1722	12036	12291	6204	6204	162466	180182	1021	505	1000	26190	1109	12291	1722
1723	12584	12792	6521	6521	170787	189477	1017	510	1000	26211	1110	12792	1723
1724	12349	12607	6318	6318	165602	183790	1021	501	1000	26213	1110	12607	1724
1725	12157	12411	6157	6157	161196	179207	1020	496	1000	26169	1111	12411	1725
1726	12712	12969	6445	6445	168662	187376	1020	497	1000	26143	1111	12969	1726
1727	12463	12653	6462	6462	168936	187774	1015	511	1000	26098	1112	12653	1727
1728	10755	10850	5416	5416	141347	157187	1009	499	1000	26063	1112	10850	1728
1729	10281	10375	5387	5387	140404	156223	1009	519	1000	—	1113	10375	1729

Table A4.1: *(cont.)*

Births

Year	(1)	(2)	(3)	(4)	(5)	(6)	(7) (2)/(1) x1 000	(8) (3)/(2) x1 000	(9) (4)/(3) x1 000	(10) (5)/(4) x1 000	(11) (6)/(5) x1 000	(12)	Year
1730	11254	11324	5719	5719	148838	165692	1006	505	1000	26025	1113	11324	1730
1731	12942	13019	6618	6618	171999	191566	1006	508	1000	25990	1114	13019	1731
1732	12582	12778	6473	6473	168019	187232	1016	507	1000	25957	1114	12778	1732
1733	12764	12968	6730	6730	174513	194562	1016	519	1000	25931	1115	12968	1733
1734	13218	13308	6740	6740	174540	194694	1007	506	1000	25896	1116	13308	1734
1735	13211	13313	6820	6820	176317	196793	1008	512	1000	25853	1117	13313	1735
1736	12908	12961	6672	6672	172276	192455	1004	515	1000	25821	1119	12961	1736
1737	12753	12831	6592	6592	169971	190115	1006	514	1000	25784	1120	12831	1737
1738	12987	13032	6719	6719	172974	193709	1003	516	1000	25744	1121	13032	1738
1739	13234	13295	6870	6870	176620	198033	1005	517	1000	25709	1121	13295	1739
1740	12581	12708	6499	6499	166921	187378	1010	511	1000	25684	1123	12708	1740
1741	11550	11618	6035	6035	154793	173969	1006	519	1000	25649	1124	11618	1741
1742	11408	11444	5900	5900	151039	169959	1003	516	1000	25600	1125	11444	1742
1743	12483	12537	6476	6476	165687	186667	1004	517	1000	25585	1127	12537	1743
1744	12710	12822	6538	6538	166979	188350	1009	510	1000	25540	1128	12822	1744
1745	12753	12826	6627	6627	169114	190988	1006	517	1000	25519	1129	12826	1745
1746	12722	12802	6494	6494	165631	187268	1006	507	1000	25505	1131	12802	1746
1747	12907	12938	6434	6434	163967	185592	1002	497	1000	25484	1132	12938	1747
1748	13092	13102	6624	6624	168751	191219	1001	506	1000	25476	1133	13102	1748
1749	13283	13347	6481	6481	165009	187184	1005	486	1000	25460	1134	13347	1749
1750	13292	13423	6908	6908	175804	199653	1010	515	1000	25449	1136	13423	1750
1751	13408	13549	6823	6823	173512	197265	1011	504	1000	25430	1137	13549	1751
1752	12926	13039	6627	6627	168456	191727	1009	508	1000	25420	1138	13039	1752
1753	13532	13596	6860	6860	174321	198625	1005	505	1000	25411	1139	13596	1753
1754	13690	13766	6862	6862	174238	198751	1005	498	1000	25392	1141	13766	1754
1755	13687	13744	7002	7002	177766	203002	1004	509	1000	25388	1142	13744	1755
1756	13856	13899	6942	6942	176158	201401	1003	499	1000	25376	1143	13899	1756
1757	12919	12949	6567	6567	166655	190765	1002	507	1000	25378	1145	12949	1757
1758	12883	12931	6517	6517	165427	189592	1004	504	1000	25384	1146	12931	1758
1759	13908	13985	7023	7023	178204	204482	1006	502	1000	25374	1147	13985	1759
1760	13849	13930	7034	7034	178415	204966	1006	505	1000	25365	1149	13930	1760
1761	14337	14340	7319	7319	185692	213587	1000	510	1000	25371	1150	14340	1761
1762	14423	14448	7273	7273	184495	212467	1002	503	1000	25367	1152	14448	1762
1763	13774	13816	7048	7048	178713	206057	1003	510	1000	25357	1153	13816	1763
1764	15040	15075	7429	7429	188355	217436	1002	493	1000	25354	1154	15075	1764
1765	14866	14915	7545	7545	191313	221115	1003	506	1000	25356	1156	14915	1765
1766	14310	14346	7194	7194	182437	211101	1003	501	1000	25360	1157	14346	1766
1767	14358	14424	7257	7257	183981	213126	1005	503	1000	25352	1158	14424	1767
1768	14262	14337	7252	7252	183799	213155	1005	506	1000	25345	1160	14337	1768
1769	15122	15283	7670	7670	194412	225719	1011	502	1000	25347	1161	15283	1769

Table A4.1: *(cont.)*

Births

Year	(1)	(2)	(3)	(4)	(5)	(6)	(7) (2)/(1) x1 000	(8) (3)/(2) x1 000	(9) (4)/(3) x1 000	(10) (5)/(4) x1 000	(11) (6)/(5) x1 000	(12)	Year
1770	15667	15749	7983	7983	202302	235144	1005	507	1000	25342	1162	15749	1770
1771	15386	15430	7693	7693	194987	226894	1003	499	1000	25346	1164	15430	1771
1772	15687	15689	7861	7861	199160	232010	1000	501	1000	25335	1165	15689	1772
1773	15794	15800	7999	7999	202610	236297	1000	506	1000	25329	1168	15800	1773
1774	15782	15785	7786	7786	197183	230226	1001	493	1000	25325	1169	15785	1774
1775	16416	16431	8235	8235	208584	243847	1002	501	1000	25329	1171	16431	1775
1776	16290	16329	8194	8194	207542	242978	1002	502	1000	25329	1172	16329	1776
1777	17130	17156	8473	8473	214584	251571	1001	494	1000	25326	1174	17156	1777
1778	16899	16913	8544	8544	216304	253945	1002	505	1000	25316	1176	16913	1778
1779	17384	17433	8615	8615	218068	256378	1003	494	1000	25313	1177	17433	1779
1780	17005	17013	8463	8463	214214	252199	1000	497	1000	25312	1177	17013	1780
1781	17188	17188	8380	8380	212075	250187	1000	488	1000	25307	1180	17188	1781
1782	16595	16610	8205	8205	207696	246670	1001	494	1000	25313	1188	16610	1782
1783	16440	16501	8198	8198	207467	248266	1004	497	1000	25307	1197	16501	1783
1784	16525	16576	8259	8259	208948	251938	1003	498	1000	25299	1206	16576	1784
1785	17829	17856	8807	8807	222839	270689	1002	493	1000	25302	1215	17856	1785
1786	17978	18013	9058	9058	229143	280424	1002	503	1000	25297	1224	18013	1786
1787	17961	17997	8826	8826	223261	274808	1002	490	1000	25296	1231	17997	1787
1788	18429	18499	9317	9317	235583	291543	1004	504	1000	25285	1238	18499	1788
1789	18284	18342	9090	9090	229834	289822	1003	496	1000	25284	1244	18342	1789
1790	18968	18988	9525	9525	240856	301289	1001	502	1000	25287	1251	18988	1790
1791	18730	18735	9339	9339	236096	297011	1000	498	1000	25281	1258	18735	1791
1792	19903	19910	9891	9891	250034	316291	1000	497	1000	25279	1268	19910	1792
1793	19554	19558	9634	9634	243540	311117	1000	493	1000	25279	1277	19558	1793
1794	19106	19147	9427	9427	238251	306733	1002	492	1000	25273	1287	19147	1794
1795	18977	19010	9494	9494	239926	310036	1007	499	1000	25271	1297	19010	1795
1796	18879	19007	9392	9392	237366	310267	1005	494	1000	25273	1307	19007	1796
1797	19919	20028	9907	9907	250326	329823	1004	495	1000	25268	1318	20028	1797
1798	19961	20027	9836	9836	248532	329981	1003	491	1000	25268	1328	20027	1798
1799	19334	19407	9465	9465	239099	319891	1004	488	1000	25261	1338	19407	1799
1800	18628	18707	9252	9252	233694	315010	1004	495	1000	25259	1348	18707	1800
1801	17122	17188	8567	8567	216393	293780	1004	498	1000	25259	1358	17188	1801
1802	19975	20067	9876	9876	249449	339925	1005	492	1000	25258	1363	20067	1802
1803	21613	21705	10576	10576	267168	365127	1004	487	1000	25262	1367	21705	1803
1804	21658	21759	10772	10772	272071	372958	1005	495	1000	25257	1371	21759	1804
1805	21700	21843	10741	10741	271287	372976	1007	492	1000	25257	1375	21843	1805
1806	21824	21924	10758	10758	271717	374781	1005	491	1000	25257	1379	21924	1806
1807	22212	22308	10754	10754	271653	376791	1004	482	1000	25261	1387	22308	1807
1808	22061	22155	10769	10769	272012	379576	1004	486	1000	25259	1395	22155	1808
1809	21898	22021	10501	10501	265233	372396	1006	477	1000	25258	1404	22021	1809

Table A4.1: *(cont.)*

Births

Year	(1)	(2)	(3)	(4)	(5)	(6)	(7) (2)/(1) x1 000	(8) (3)/(2) x1 000	(9) (4)/(3) x1 000	(10) (5)/(4) x1 000	(11) (6)/(5) x1 000	(12)	Year
1810	22080	22242	10805	10805	272909	385489	1007	486	1000	25258	1413	22242	1810
1811	22366	22475	10995	10995	277760	394990	1005	489	1000	25262	1422	22475	1811
1812	15379	15532	7697	10761	271786	391257	1010	496	1398	25257	1440	22032	1812
1813	15752	15752	7826	11054	279215	407295	1000	497	1412	25259	1459	22933	1813
1814	16180	16180	7899	11156	281810	416474	1000	488	1412	25261	1478	23553	1814
1815	17581	17581	8693	12278	310162	464302	1000	494	1412	25262	1497	25594	1815
1816	16840	16840	8330	11765	297205	449663	1000	495	1412	25262	1513	24515	1816
1817	16587	16587	8394	11927	301290	453762	1000	506	1421	25261	1506	24379	1817
1818	16605	16623	8359	11878	300035	448392	1001	503	1421	25260	1494	24434	1818
1819	16916	16916	8398	11934	301419	447063	1000	496	1421	25257	1483	24862	1819
1820	17165	17165	8412	12101	305679	449847	1000	490	1439	25261	1472	25699	1820
1821	17656	17659	8844	12724	321376	469453	1000	501	1439	25257	1461	26439	1821
1822	18691	18700	9268	13332	336768	489990	1000	496	1438	25260	1455	27997	1822
1823	18658	18661	9203	13238	334403	484953	1000	493	1438	25261	1450	27940	1823
1824	18483	18483	9156	13173	332717	480914	1000	495	1439	25257	1445	27672	1824
1825	18806	18811	9257	13318	336377	484533	1000	492	1439	25257	1440	28163	1825
1826	18786	18800	9397	13516	341442	489633	1001	500	1438	25262	1434	28148	1826
1827	18454	18454	9084	13067	330071	468368	1000	492	1438	25260	1419	27630	1827
1828	19518	19518	9632	13857	349989	490940	1000	493	1439	25257	1403	29222	1828
1829	18453	18456	9165	13184	333035	461707	1000	497	1439	25261	1386	27632	1829
1830	18583	18618	9364	13469	340258	466050	1002	503	1438	25262	1370	28773	1830
1831	19177	19177	9504	13670	345333	467910	1000	496	1438	25262	1355	28712	1831
1832	18656	18681	9560	13813	348899	472112	1001	512	1445	25259	1353	28165	1832
1833	18150	19697	10123	14625	369465	500219	1085	514	1445	25263	1354	29698	1833
1834	18535	19515	9988	14481	365809	495545	1053	512	1450	25261	1355	29588	1834
1835	19460	19481	9976	14474	365616	495431	1001	512	1451	25260	1355	29594	1835
1836	19073	19074	9761	14768	373029	505473	1000	512	1513	25259	1355	30152	1836

Table A4.1: *(cont.)*

Deaths

Year	(1)	(2)	(3)	(4)	(5)	(6)	(7) (2)/(1) x1 000	(8) (3)/(2) x1 000	(9) (4)/(3) x1 000	(10) (5)/(4) x1 000	(11) (6)/(5) x1 000	(12)	Year
1539	362	362	219	2865	67442	67442	1000	605	13082	23540	1000	5377	1539
1540	649	662	423	4254	100161	100161	1020	639	10057	23545	1000	7793	1540
1541	565	585	328	3070	72256	72256	1035	561	9360	23536	1000	6442	1541
1542	579	604	418	3015	71019	71019	1043	692	7213	23555	1000	5459	1542
1543	677	700	576	4117	97056	97056	1034	823	7148	23574	1000	6246	1543
1544	918	977	528	3587	84590	84590	1064	540	6794	23582	1000	8308	1544
1545	1044	1113	668	4358	102792	102792	1066	600	6524	23587	1000	8699	1545
1546	866	961	625	4025	95018	95018	1110	650	6440	23607	1000	7316	1546
1547	825	876	571	3534	83457	83457	1062	652	6189	23615	1000	6272	1547
1548	874	949	582	3384	79954	79954	1086	613	5814	23627	1000	6154	1548
1549	795	858	466	2706	64000	64000	1079	543	5807	23651	1000	5564	1549
1550	832	973	584	3396	80321	80321	1169	600	5815	23652	1000	6308	1550
1551	913	1055	629	3545	83887	83887	1156	596	5636	23663	1000	6812	1551
1552	956	1107	628	3478	82340	82340	1158	567	5538	23675	1000	6992	1552
1553	863	1055	644	3431	81297	81297	1222	610	5328	23695	1000	6557	1553
1554	570	862	540	2878	68218	68218	1512	626	5330	23703	1000	5358	1554
1555	628	985	645	3392	80383	80383	1568	655	5259	23698	1000	5922	1555
1556	854	1191	641	3250	77094	77094	1395	538	5070	23721	1000	6826	1556
1557	1649	2096	1153	5643	133887	133887	1271	550	4894	23726	1000	10962	1557
1558	2255	2798	1667	7007	166387	166387	1241	596	4203	23746	1000	12796	1558
1559	3333	3731	1853	5950	141282	141282	1119	497	3211	23745	1000	11339	1559
1560	2483	2805	1390	3946	93735	93735	1130	496	2839	23754	1000	7076	1560
1561	2342	2543	1202	3254	77340	77340	1086	473	2707	23768	1000	6219	1561
1562	2639	2900	1419	3074	73081	73081	1099	489	2166	23774	1000	5773	1562
1563	3317	3633	1730	3583	105536	105536	1095	476	2071	29455	1000	6791	1563
1564	2626	3150	1693	3381	80558	80558	1200	537	1997	23827	1000	5711	1564
1565	2863	3264	1592	3090	73644	73644	1140	488	1941	23833	1000	5674	1565
1566	3139	3624	1803	3398	81042	81042	1155	498	1885	23850	1000	6225	1566
1567	2888	3498	1781	3330	79527	79527	1211	509	1870	23882	1000	5974	1567
1568	2824	3328	1641	3049	72924	72924	1178	493	1858	23917	1000	5646	1568
1569	3101	3481	1786	3177	76060	76060	1123	513	1779	23941	1000	5723	1569

Table A4.1: *(cont.)*

Deaths

Year	(1)	(2)	(3)	(4)	(5)	(6)	(7) (2)/(1) ×1000	(8) (3)/(2) ×1000	(9) (4)/(3) ×1000	(10) (5)/(4) ×1000	(11) (6)/(5) ×1000	(12)	Year
1570	3651	3976	2032	3553	85203	85203	1089	511	1749	23981	1000	6513	1570
1571	4047	4233	2040	3410	81854	81854	1046	482	1672	24004	1000	6648	1571
1572	3590	3736	1931	3186	76599	76599	1041	517	1650	24042	1000	5765	1572
1573	3745	3919	2007	3297	79298	79298	1046	512	1643	24052	1000	6025	1573
1574	3673	3919	2031	3258	78499	78499	1067	518	1604	24094	1000	6021	1574
1575	3562	3763	2022	3153	76031	76031	1056	537	1559	24114	1000	5582	1575
1576	3441	3650	1916	2957	71307	71307	1061	525	1543	24115	1000	5375	1576
1577	3647	3924	1993	3066	73984	73984	1076	508	1538	24130	1000	5750	1577
1578	3831	4076	2121	3261	83929	83929	1064	520	1537	25737	1000	5974	1578
1579	4087	4370	2185	3343	80752	80752	1069	500	1530	24156	1000	6373	1579
1580	4284	4538	2408	3672	88691	88691	1059	531	1525	24153	1000	6588	1580
1581	3781	3943	1954	2974	71852	71852	1043	496	1522	24160	1000	5714	1581
1582	4197	4381	2259	3321	80262	80262	1044	516	1470	24168	1000	6117	1582
1583	3880	4121	2071	2935	70947	70947	1062	503	1417	24173	1000	5568	1583
1584	4468	4738	2467	3476	84037	84037	1060	521	1409	24176	1000	6381	1584
1585	4862	5224	2662	3713	89868	89868	1074	510	1395	24204	1000	6927	1585
1586	4511	4931	2476	3436	83183	83183	1093	502	1388	24209	1000	6489	1586
1587	6146	6541	3222	4460	107981	107981	1064	493	1384	24211	1000	8559	1587
1588	6391	6664	3254	4502	109101	109101	1043	488	1384	24234	1000	8720	1588
1589	5194	5430	2704	3699	89635	89635	1045	498	1368	24232	1000	7037	1589
1590	5210	5574	2775	3765	91266	91266	1070	498	1357	24241	1000	7189	1590
1591	6228	6638	3365	4567	110688	110688	1066	507	1357	24236	1000	8561	1591
1592	6627	7005	3393	4560	110606	110606	1057	484	1344	24256	1000	8947	1592
1593	6271	6672	3189	4280	121259	121259	1064	478	1342	28332	1000	8491	1593
1594	5169	5385	2516	3376	81960	81960	1042	467	1342	24277	1000	6856	1594
1595	4856	5274	2579	3454	83956	83956	1086	489	1339	24307	1000	6694	1595
1596	5540	5880	2961	3967	96575	96575	1061	504	1340	24345	1000	7462	1596
1597	8684	9091	4108	5461	133155	133155	1047	452	1329	24383	1000	11375	1597
1598	6166	6498	3304	4311	105307	105307	1054	508	1305	24428	1000	8007	1598
1599	5379	5700	2900	3753	91825	91825	1060	509	1294	24467	1000	6945	1599
1600	5205	5420	2789	3538	86702	86702	1041	515	1269	24506	1000	6539	1600
1601	5085	5376	2735	3426	84079	84079	1057	509	1253	24541	1000	6451	1601
1602	6222	6593	3317	4096	100783	100783	1060	503	1235	24605	1000	7781	1602
1603	7385	7698	3659	4404	142069	142069	1042	475	1204	32259	1000	9026	1603
1604	6643	6932	3345	3938	97214	97214	1044	483	1177	24686	1000	8095	1604
1605	5870	6163	3162	3682	90959	90959	1050	513	1164	24704	1000	7104	1605
1606	5958	6372	3404	3955	97722	97722	1069	534	1162	24708	1000	7329	1606
1607	5921	6237	3313	3842	94851	94851	1053	531	1160	24688	1000	7155	1607
1608	6658	6955	3712	4232	104503	104503	1045	534	1140	24694	1000	7935	1608
1609	6494	6884	3609	4116	101572	101572	1060	524	1140	24677	1000	7854	1609

Table A4.1: *(cont.)*

Deaths

Year	(1)	(2)	(3)	(4)	(5)	(6)	(7) (2)/(1) x1 000	(8) (3)/(2) x1 000	(9) (4)/(3) x1 000	(10) (5)/(4) x1 000	(11) (6)/(5) x1 000	(12)	Year
1610	8201	8565	4521	5140	126840	126840	1044	528	1137	24677	1000	9707	1610
1611	6775	7140	3873	4394	108430	108430	1054	542	1135	24677	1000	8079	1611
1612	8080	8383	4427	5001	123317	123317	1037	528	1130	24658	1000	9476	1612
1613	7705	7926	4179	4704	115976	115976	1029	527	1126	24655	1000	8910	1613
1614	7972	8282	4357	4851	119505	119505	1039	526	1113	24635	1000	9214	1614
1615	7320	7637	4103	4554	112264	112264	1043	537	1110	24652	1000	8468	1615
1616	8408	8801	4804	5311	131004	131004	1047	546	1106	24666	1000	9693	1616
1617	8078	8389	4341	4718	116527	116527	1038	517	1087	24698	1000	9098	1617
1618	7253	7570	4010	4356	107631	107631	1044	530	1086	24709	1000	8199	1618
1619	6639	7060	3760	4085	101029	101029	1063	533	1086	24732	1000	7647	1619
1620	7254	7616	3885	4219	104483	104483	1050	510	1086	24765	1000	8249	1620
1621	7077	7446	3722	4035	99976	99976	1052	500	1084	24777	1000	8039	1621
1622	6964	7428	3775	4090	101488	101488	1067	508	1083	24814	1000	8020	1622
1623	9954	10748	5369	5816	144374	144374	1080	500	1083	24824	1000	11594	1623
1624	9017	9535	4876	5283	131240	131240	1057	511	1083	24842	1000	10286	1624
1625	10056	10619	5278	5707	197455	197455	1056	497	1081	34599	1000	11433	1625
1626	8034	8498	4430	4773	118805	118805	1058	521	1077	24891	1000	9116	1626
1627	7527	7831	4066	4382	109141	109141	1040	519	1078	24907	1000	8401	1627
1628	7621	7894	3983	4287	106892	106892	1036	505	1076	24934	1000	8438	1628
1629	8084	8341	4305	4601	114792	114792	1032	516	1069	24949	1000	8859	1629
1630	7924	8242	4375	4670	116649	116649	1040	531	1067	24978	1000	8724	1630
1631	9111	9467	4925	5250	131278	131278	1039	520	1066	25005	1000	9991	1631
1632	8179	8499	4318	4582	114674	114674	1039	508	1061	25027	1000	8950	1632
1633	8161	8498	4216	4476	112062	112062	1041	496	1062	25036	1000	8948	1633
1634	7829	8227	4216	4476	112185	112185	1051	512	1062	25064	1000	8665	1634
1635	8195	8766	4619	4903	123061	123061	1070	527	1061	25099	1000	9230	1635
1636	9319	9706	4831	5124	145896	145896	1042	498	1061	28473	1000	10192	1636
1637	9299	9702	4862	5153	129751	129751	1043	501	1061	25180	1000	10184	1637
1638	10836	11167	5983	6340	159899	159899	1031	536	1060	25221	1000	11722	1638
1639	10702	10985	5886	6240	157542	157542	1026	536	1060	25247	1000	11531	1639
1640	9619	10251	5323	5638	142554	142554	1066	519	1059	25284	1000	10750	1640
1641	8860	9907	4931	5225	132269	132364	1118	498	1051	25315	1001	10391	1641
1642	8620	10172	4969	5223	132446	132607	1180	488	1051	25358	1001	10562	1642
1643	9489	12262	6121	6418	163053	163338	1292	499	1049	25406	1002	12677	1643
1644	8593	11413	5801	6084	154756	155100	1328	508	1049	25437	1002	11798	1644
1645	7030	9355	4608	4836	123115	123449	1331	493	1049	25458	1003	9671	1645
1646	6151	8336	4004	4198	107131	107473	1355	480	1048	25520	1003	8617	1646
1647	6596	9103	4650	4879	124583	125047	1380	511	1049	25535	1004	9410	1647
1648	6525	8978	4508	4728	120968	121481	1376	502	1049	25585	1004	9280	1648
1649	6634	9470	4823	5058	129603	130214	1427	509	1049	25623	1005	9790	1649

Table A4.1: *(cont.)*

Deaths

Year	(1)	(2)	(3)	(4)	(5)	(6)	(7) (2)/(1) x1000	(8) (3)/(2) x1000	(9) (4)/(3) x1000	(10) (5)/(4) x1000	(11) (6)/(5) x1000	(12)	Year
1650	5956	9137	4867	5093	130715	131398	1534	533	1046	25666	1005	9418	1650
1651	5829	8439	4290	4490	115394	116054	1448	508	1047	25708	1006	8692	1651
1652	6525	9201	4824	5051	129953	130763	1410	524	1047	25728	1006	9482	1652
1653	6996	9663	5002	5237	134923	135831	1381	518	1047	25763	1007	9961	1653
1654	8769	10278	5361	5511	142222	143246	1172	522	1028	25807	1007	10453	1654
1655	7746	9203	4641	4725	122117	123059	1188	504	1018	25845	1008	9310	1655
1656	7763	9051	4679	4758	123166	124181	1166	517	1017	25886	1008	9145	1656
1657	9960	11455	6375	6484	168060	169530	1150	557	1017	25919	1009	11572	1657
1658	11189	13372	7468	7552	195994	197801	1195	558	1011	25953	1009	13423	1658
1659	8813	10348	5358	5414	140678	142042	1174	518	1010	25984	1010	10378	1659
1660	7660	9047	4713	4760	123912	125177	1181	521	1010	26032	1010	9073	1660
1661	8732	10011	5374	5427	141516	143038	1146	537	1010	26076	1011	10037	1661
1662	9250	10006	5196	5196	135664	137186	1082	519	1000	26109	1011	10006	1662
1663	8765	9413	4865	4865	127180	128669	1074	517	1000	26142	1012	9413	1663
1664	8918	9319	4855	4855	127092	128645	1045	521	1000	26178	1012	9319	1664
1665	9976	10402	5058	5058	216834	219601	1043	486	1000	42870	1013	10402	1665
1666	10351	10841	5352	5352	140475	142335	1047	494	1000	26247	1013	10841	1666
1667	10492	11042	5663	5663	148752	150797	1052	513	1000	26267	1014	11042	1667
1668	9723	10307	5435	5435	142944	144977	1060	527	1000	26301	1014	10307	1668
1669	10761	11363	6174	6174	162557	164954	1056	543	1000	26329	1015	11363	1669
1670	10711	11336	6072	6072	160062	162505	1058	536	1000	26361	1015	11336	1670
1671	10046	10562	5621	5621	148283	150616	1051	532	1000	26380	1016	10562	1671
1672	9479	9978	4966	4966	131157	133288	1053	498	1000	26411	1016	9978	1672
1673	8915	9404	4769	4769	126096	128210	1055	507	1000	26441	1017	9404	1673
1674	9353	9842	4864	4864	128722	130942	1052	494	1000	26464	1017	9842	1674
1675	10364	10761	5395	5395	142905	145470	1038	501	1000	26488	1018	10761	1675
1676	9476	9949	5081	5081	134812	137360	1050	511	1000	26533	1019	9949	1676
1677	8298	8767	4616	4616	122537	124979	1057	527	1000	26546	1020	8767	1677
1678	9264	9764	4975	4975	132266	135015	1054	510	1000	26586	1021	9764	1678
1679	11950	12609	6871	6871	182850	186701	1055	545	1000	26612	1021	12609	1679
1680	11269	11745	6185	6185	164766	168413	1042	527	1000	26640	1022	11745	1680
1681	12549	12968	7034	7034	187550	191805	1033	542	1000	26663	1023	12968	1681
1682	10862	11335	6269	6269	167349	171336	1044	553	1000	26695	1024	11335	1682
1683	10460	10925	5677	5677	151712	155526	1044	520	1000	26724	1025	10925	1683
1684	11112	11741	5974	5974	159857	163985	1057	509	1000	26759	1026	11741	1684
1685	11127	11604	5900	5900	158017	162200	1043	508	1000	26783	1026	11604	1685
1686	10422	11012	5559	5559	149106	153218	1057	505	1000	26822	1028	11012	1686
1687	9482	10040	5110	5110	137239	141154	1059	509	1000	26857	1029	10040	1687
1688	9603	10149	5182	5182	139386	143447	1057	511	1000	26898	1029	10149	1688
1689	9915	10561	5432	5432	146276	150561	1065	514	1000	26929	1029	10561	1689

Table A4.1: *(cont.)*

Deaths

Year	(1)	(2)	(3)	(4)	(5)	(6)	(7) (2)/(1) x1 000	(8) (3)/(2) x1 000	(9) (4)/(3) x1 000	(10) (5)/(4) x1 000	(11) (6)/(5) x1 000	(12)	Year
1690	10055	10669	5398	5398	145536	149853	1061	506	1000	26961	1030	10669	1690
1691	9190	9631	4839	4839	130618	134681	1048	502	1000	26993	1031	9631	1691
1692	8889	9361	4868	4868	131570	135705	1053	520	1000	27028	1031	9361	1692
1693	8962	9421	4862	4862	131547	135748	1051	516	1000	27056	1032	9421	1693
1694	9808	10304	5356	5356	145079	149592	1051	520	1000	27087	1031	10304	1694
1695	10051	10373	5428	5428	147236	152029	1032	523	1000	27125	1033	10373	1695
1696	9467	9784	5112	5112	138680	143395	1033	522	1000	27128	1034	9784	1696
1697	9373	9683	4993	4993	135453	140102	1033	516	1000	27129	1034	9683	1697
1698	9349	9582	4775	4775	129557	134121	1025	498	1000	27132	1035	9582	1698
1699	9402	9618	4938	4938	134026	138746	1023	513	1000	27142	1035	9618	1699
1700	9594	9717	4983	4983	135285	140165	1013	513	1000	27149	1036	9717	1700
1701	9474	9584	4800	4800	130325	135260	1012	501	1000	27151	1038	9584	1701
1702	8522	8645	4552	4552	123603	128446	1014	527	1000	27154	1039	8645	1702
1703	8827	8963	4499	4499	122213	127079	1015	502	1000	27164	1040	8963	1703
1704	9227	9258	4931	4931	133968	139126	1003	533	1000	27169	1039	9258	1704
1705	10365	10410	5774	5774	157031	162851	1004	555	1000	27196	1037	10410	1705
1706	9662	9709	4871	4871	132714	137966	1005	502	1000	27246	1040	9709	1706
1707	8962	9031	4609	4609	125808	130849	1008	510	1000	27296	1040	9031	1707
1708	9334	9443	4954	4954	135477	140883	1012	525	1000	27347	1040	9443	1708
1709	9214	9388	4708	4708	128933	134117	1019	501	1000	27386	1040	9388	1709
1710	9585	9750	4838	4838	132730	138042	1017	496	1000	27435	1040	9750	1710
1711	10348	10500	5207	5207	143126	148843	1015	496	1000	27487	1040	10500	1711
1712	10805	10938	5492	5492	151245	157222	1012	502	1000	27539	1040	10938	1712
1713	8907	9070	4682	4682	129167	134752	1018	516	1000	27588	1043	9070	1713
1714	9672	9862	5167	5167	142894	148967	1020	524	1000	27655	1043	9862	1714
1715	9273	9460	4747	4747	131334	137218	1020	502	1000	27667	1045	9460	1715
1716	9545	9727	4823	4823	133462	139639	1019	496	1000	27672	1046	9727	1716
1717	9310	9408	4555	4555	126082	132020	1011	484	1000	27680	1047	9408	1717
1718	9220	9322	4712	4712	130403	136617	1011	505	1000	27675	1048	9322	1718
1719	10919	11076	5927	5927	164019	171242	1014	535	1000	27673	1044	11076	1719
1720	11132	11494	6022	6022	166637	173698	1028	524	1000	27671	1042	11494	1720
1721	10971	11177	5821	5821	161049	168109	1019	521	1000	27667	1042	11177	1721
1722	10450	10588	5488	5488	151878	158951	1013	518	1000	27675	1047	10588	1722
1723	11066	11226	5810	5810	160738	168266	1014	518	1000	27666	1047	11226	1723
1724	10737	10944	5589	5589	154656	161985	1019	511	1000	27671	1047	10944	1724
1725	9436	9639	4712	4712	130396	137091	1022	489	1000	27673	1051	9639	1725
1726	10280	10488	5079	5079	143621	150890	1020	484	1000	28277	1051	10488	1726
1727	13249	13409	6851	6851	186003	194438	1012	511	1000	27150	1045	13409	1727
1728	15189	15242	7804	7804	207253	215690	1003	512	1000	26557	1041	15242	1728
1729	16901	17034	8675	8675	229573	238625	1008	509	1000	26464	1039	17034	1729

Table A4.1: *(cont.)*

Deaths

Year	(1)	(2)	(3)	(4)	(5)	(6)	(7) (2)/(1) x1 000	(8) (3)/(2) x1 000	(9) (4)/(3) x1 000	(10) (5)/(4) x1 000	(11) (6)/(15) x1 000	(12)	Year
1730	13323	13402	6806	6806	182611	190734	1006	508	1000	26831	1044	13402	1730
1731	12366	12416	6281	6281	170786	179238	1004	506	1000	27191	1049	12416	1731
1732	10514	10648	5340	5340	149772	157675	1013	502	1000	28047	1053	10648	1732
1733	10253	10429	5213	5213	146111	154169	1017	500	1000	28028	1055	10429	1733
1734	9383	9463	4696	4696	131475	139251	1009	496	1000	27997	1059	9463	1734
1735	9414	9473	4907	4907	137280	145334	1006	518	1000	27976	1059	9473	1735
1736	10448	10505	5186	5186	144926	153167	1005	494	1000	27946	1057	10505	1736
1737	11494	11567	5687	5687	158773	167423	1006	492	1000	27919	1054	11567	1737
1738	9971	10022	5110	5110	142488	150924	1005	517	1000	27884	1059	10022	1738
1739	9929	9953	5150	5150	143565	152251	1002	517	1000	27877	1061	9953	1739
1740	11778	11931	5890	5890	163959	173018	1013	494	1000	27837	1055	11931	1740
1741	13419	13494	6624	6624	184197	193553	1006	491	1000	27808	1051	13494	1741
1742	13772	13835	6930	6930	192576	202158	1005	501	1000	27789	1050	13835	1742
1743	10823	10928	5422	5422	150537	159559	1010	496	1000	27764	1060	10928	1743
1744	9093	9205	4684	4684	129884	138507	1012	509	1000	27729	1066	9205	1744
1745	9551	9621	4780	4780	132372	141249	1007	497	1000	27693	1067	9621	1745
1746	10707	10782	5359	5359	148060	157372	1007	497	1000	27628	1063	10782	1746
1747	10959	11027	5517	5517	152033	161520	1006	500	1000	27557	1062	11027	1747
1748	11016	11064	5542	5542	152360	162130	1004	501	1000	27492	1064	11064	1748
1749	10258	10316	5214	5214	143045	152551	1006	505	1000	27435	1066	10316	1749
1750	10457	10543	5405	5405	147902	158030	1008	513	1000	27364	1068	10543	1750
1751	10308	10382	5183	5183	141517	151506	1007	499	1000	27304	1071	10382	1751
1752	10047	10143	5060	5060	137816	147644	1010	501	1000	27236	1071	10143	1752
1753	9887	9931	4980	4980	135317	145402	1004	501	1000	27172	1075	9931	1753
1754	10360	10420	5137	5137	139281	149599	1006	493	1000	27113	1074	10420	1754
1755	10275	10320	5142	5142	139202	149762	1004	498	1000	27072	1076	10320	1755
1756	10712	10807	5301	5301	143463	154206	1009	491	1000	27063	1075	10807	1756
1757	11138	11181	5431	5431	146938	157547	1004	486	1000	27055	1072	11181	1757
1758	11885	11909	5701	5701	154256	165150	1002	479	1000	27058	1071	11909	1758
1759	11557	11574	5693	5693	154046	165550	1001	492	1000	27059	1075	11574	1759
1760	11038	11064	5528	5528	149600	161100	1002	500	1000	27062	1077	11064	1760
1761	11055	11088	5572	5572	150731	162678	1003	503	1000	27052	1079	11088	1761
1762	12695	12734	6665	6665	180326	193250	1003	523	1000	27056	1072	12734	1762
1763	13564	13619	6896	6896	186529	199535	1004	506	1000	27049	1070	13619	1763
1764	11630	11718	5754	5754	155653	168247	1008	491	1000	27051	1081	11718	1764
1765	11725	11796	5565	5565	150464	163163	1006	472	1000	27038	1084	11796	1765
1766	13099	13150	6466	6466	174869	188088	1004	492	1000	27044	1076	13150	1766
1767	12646	12743	6379	6379	172452	185804	1008	501	1000	27034	1077	12743	1767
1768	12329	12441	6011	6011	162544	175716	1009	483	1000	27041	1081	12443	1768
1769	11736	11857	5882	5882	159037	172708	1010	496	1000	27038	1086	11857	1769

Table A4.1: *(cont.)*

Deaths

Year	(1)	(2)	(3)	(4)	(5)	(6)	(7) (2)/(1) x1 000	(8) (3)/(2) x1 000	(9) (4)/(3) x1 000	(10) (5)/(4) x1 000	(11) (6)/(5) x1 000	(12)	Year
1770	12620	12658	6235	6235	168517	182994	1003	493	1000	27028	1086	12658	1770
1771	12356	12362	5967	5967	161338	175401	1000	483	1000	27038	1087	12362	1771
1772	12493	12498	6039	6039	163201	177662	1000	483	1000	27025	1089	12498	1772
1773	12499	12502	6142	6142	165962	180825	1000	491	1000	27021	1090	12502	1773
1774	11516	11524	5542	5542	149771	163994	1001	481	1000	27025	1095	11524	1774
1775	11906	11920	5850	5850	157844	173041	1001	491	1000	26982	1096	11920	1775
1776	11631	11666	5592	5592	150568	165654	1003	479	1000	26926	1100	11666	1776
1777	12316	12364	6040	6040	162222	178228	1004	489	1000	26858	1099	12364	1777
1778	12274	12301	6034	6034	161690	177954	1002	491	1000	26796	1101	12301	1778
1779	13527	13559	6633	6633	177292	194383	1002	489	1000	26729	1096	13559	1779
1780	13679	13716	6938	6938	184997	202359	1003	506	1000	26664	1094	13716	1780
1781	13881	13948	7201	7201	191546	209350	1005	516	1000	26600	1093	13948	1781
1782	13328	13406	6865	6865	182173	200399	1006	512	1000	26536	1100	13406	1782
1783	13738	13842	7133	7133	188804	208538	1008	515	1000	26469	1105	13842	1783
1784	13726	13781	6914	6914	182632	203272	1004	502	1000	26415	1113	13781	1784
1785	13705	13719	6633	6633	174888	197046	1001	483	1000	26366	1127	13719	1785
1786	13280	13301	6506	6506	171483	194506	1002	489	1000	26358	1137	13301	1786
1787	12895	12928	6327	6327	166779	190471	1003	489	1000	26360	1142	12928	1787
1788	13470	13484	6612	6612	174199	199962	1001	490	1000	26346	1148	13484	1788
1789	12929	12956	6345	6345	167108	192879	1002	490	1000	26337	1154	12956	1789
1790	13111	13138	6449	6449	169789	197275	1002	490	1000	26328	1162	13138	1790
1791	13422	13454	6397	6397	168406	196442	1002	475	1000	26326	1166	13454	1791
1792	13446	13481	6542	6542	172186	202918	1003	485	1000	26320	1178	13481	1792
1793	14712	14776	7265	7265	191161	225051	1004	492	1000	26313	1177	14776	1793
1794	14273	14314	6905	6905	181655	216036	1003	482	1000	26308	1189	14314	1794
1795	15513	15527	7514	7514	197622	235576	1001	484	1000	26301	1193	15527	1795
1796	13368	13475	6454	6454	169707	206040	1008	479	1000	26295	1214	13475	1796
1797	14226	14292	7036	7036	184880	225671	1005	492	1000	26276	1221	14292	1797
1798	13176	13267	6434	6434	169086	209346	1007	485	1000	26280	1238	13267	1798
1799	13569	13643	6523	6523	171395	212983	1005	478	1000	26275	1243	13643	1799
1800	14665	14753	7036	7036	184870	229891	1006	477	1000	26275	1244	14753	1800
1801	15337	15466	7452	7452	195750	243178	1008	482	1000	26268	1242	15466	1801
1802	14435	14524	7069	7069	185464	235950	1006	487	1000	26267	1271	14524	1802
1803	14608	14708	7440	7440	195464	251024	1007	506	1000	26272	1284	14708	1803
1804	13172	13249	6365	6365	167190	219967	1006	480	1000	26267	1316	13249	1804
1805	12962	13039	6242	6242	163993	218154	1006	479	1000	26273	1330	13039	1805
1806	12815	12891	6073	6073	159564	215055	1006	471	1000	26274	1348	12891	1806
1807	14067	14151	6889	6889	180980	244848	1006	487	1000	26271	1353	14151	1807
1808	14280	14354	6817	6817	179086	246600	1005	475	1000	26271	1377	14354	1808
1809	13564	13651	6474	6474	170058	238641	1006	474	1000	26268	1403	13651	1809

Table A4.1: *(cont.)*

Deaths

Year	(1)	(2)	(3)	(4)	(5)	(6)	(7) (2)/(1) x1 000	(8) (3)/(2) x1 000	(9) (4)/(3) x1 000	(10) (5)/(4) x1 000	(11) (6)/(5) x1 000	(12)	Year
1810	15113	15196	7344	7344	192950	272767	1005	483	1000	26273	1414	15196	1810
1811	14227	14305	6900	6900	181296	262006	1005	482	1000	26275	1445	14305	1811
1812	9739	9820	4648	6438	169115	247742	1008	473	1385	26268	1465	13672	1812
1813	9036	9057	4481	6206	163031	242277	1002	495	1385	26270	1486	12984	1813
1814	10114	10114	4982	6900	181256	263843	1000	493	1385	26269	1483	14499	1814
1815	9781	9805	4774	6613	173699	263372	1002	487	1385	26266	1516	14056	1815
1816	10376	10376	5037	6973	183239	276783	1000	485	1384	26278	1511	14875	1816
1817	10058	10058	4862	6769	177827	268530	1000	483	1392	26271	1510	14542	1817
1818	10523	10523	5181	7212	189491	282159	1000	492	1392	26274	1489	15214	1818
1819	10464	10466	5130	7142	187641	277773	1000	490	1392	26273	1480	15133	1819
1820	10249	10263	5007	7001	183932	271304	1001	488	1398	26272	1475	14925	1820
1821	10400	10401	4978	6960	182849	269024	1000	479	1398	26271	1471	15127	1821
1822	10593	10593	5174	7236	190084	275524	1000	488	1399	26269	1449	15404	1822
1823	11382	11382	5639	7884	207161	292116	1000	495	1398	26276	1410	16554	1823
1824	11760	11760	5735	8017	210684	291026	1000	488	1398	26280	1381	17103	1824
1825	12082	12082	5985	8369	219843	296920	1000	495	1398	26269	1351	17572	1825
1826	12474	12474	6177	8639	226927	300328	1000	495	1399	26268	1323	18142	1826
1827	12083	12083	5952	8323	218646	285826	1000	493	1398	26270	1307	17573	1827
1828	11760	11760	5800	8110	213062	277741	1000	493	1398	26272	1304	17103	1828
1829	12442	12442	6073	8545	224474	286288	1000	488	1407	26270	1275	18271	1829
1830	11855	11855	5785	8140	213847	271424	1000	488	1407	26271	1269	17411	1830
1831	13463	13463	6499	9144	240213	298572	1000	483	1407	26270	1243	19774	1831
1832	13718	13718	6744	9489	249285	308540	1000	492	1407	26271	1238	20148	1832
1833	13203	13203	6417	9029	237208	296677	1000	486	1407	26272	1251	19391	1833
1834	13350	13350	6674	9390	246706	307061	1000	500	1407	26273	1245	19605	1834
1835	13423	13423	6639	9380	246389	306697	1000	495	1413	26267	1245	19865	1835
1836	13139	13146	6389	9345	245492	306300	1001	486	1463	26270	1248	20028	1836

Table A4.1: *(cont.)*

Marriages

Year	(1)	(2)	(3)	(4)	(5)	(6)	(7) (2)/(1) x1 000	(8) (3)/(2) x1 000	(9) (4)/(3) x1 000	(10) (5)/(4) x1 000	(11) (6)/(5) x1 000	(12)	Year
1539	133	133	108	2430	56918	56918	1000	812	22500	23423	1000	3076	1539
1540	194	194	120	1559	36525	36525	1000	619	12992	23428	1000	2710	1540
1541	184	189	136	1663	38957	38957	1027	720	12228	23426	1000	2430	1541
1542	222	231	183	1802	42286	42286	1041	792	9847	23466	1000	2389	1542
1543	215	225	163	1495	35093	35093	1047	724	9172	23474	1000	2280	1543
1544	197	208	156	1365	32069	32069	1056	750	8750	23494	1000	1972	1544
1545	229	246	151	1288	30229	30229	1074	614	8530	23470	1000	2211	1545
1546	257	291	188	1541	36206	36206	1132	646	8197	23495	1000	2489	1546
1547	311	368	216	1701	39982	39982	1183	587	7875	23505	1000	2948	1547
1548	335	377	240	1858	43693	43693	1125	637	7742	23516	1000	2923	1548
1549	282	323	181	1384	32559	32559	1145	560	7646	23525	1000	2430	1549
1550	265	338	195	1490	35047	35047	1275	577	7641	23521	1000	2543	1550
1551	274	342	196	1439	33844	33844	1248	573	7342	23519	1000	2561	1551
1552	284	360	222	1605	37790	37790	1268	617	7230	23545	1000	2644	1552
1553	268	337	238	1719	40492	40492	1257	706	7223	23556	1000	2477	1553
1554	173	263	121	878	20705	20705	1520	460	7256	23582	1000	1932	1554
1555	196	295	181	1265	29822	29822	1505	614	6989	23575	1000	2060	1555
1556	152	239	154	1015	23933	23933	1572	644	6591	23579	1000	1623	1556
1557	202	269	153	970	22910	22910	1332	569	6340	23619	1000	1628	1557
1558	288	407	243	1440	34026	34026	1413	597	5926	23629	1000	2297	1558
1559	640	720	320	1441	33974	33974	1125	444	4503	23577	1000	2769	1559
1560	1088	1149	517	1772	41825	41825	1056	450	3427	23603	1000	3127	1560
1561	992	1027	544	1695	40041	40041	1035	530	3116	23623	1000	2668	1561
1562	1109	1160	570	1482	35064	35064	1046	491	2600	23660	1000	2509	1562
1563	1020	1073	540	1328	31376	31376	1052	503	2459	23627	1000	2175	1563
1564	1090	1143	584	1363	32236	32236	1049	511	2334	23651	1000	2216	1564
1565	1081	1147	547	1224	28945	28945	1061	477	2238	23648	1000	2130	1565
1566	1033	1140	505	1120	26493	26493	1104	443	2218	23654	1000	2096	1566
1567	1099	1243	631	1381	32731	32731	1131	508	2189	23701	1000	2271	1567
1568	1117	1243	602	1313	31151	31151	1113	484	2181	23725	1000	2264	1568
1569	1156	1252	637	1337	31768	31768	1083	509	2099	23761	1000	2217	1569

Table A4.1: *(cont.)*

Marriages

Year	(1)	(2)	(3)	(4)	(5)	(6)	(7) (2)/(1) x1 000	(8) (3)/(2) x1 000	(9) (4)/(3) x1 000	(10) (5)/(4) x1 000	(11) (6)/(5) x1 000	(12)	Year
1570	1175	1281	659	1339	31823	31823	1090	514	2032	23766	1000	2240	1570
1571	1290	1351	656	1288	30680	30680	1047	486	1963	23820	1000	2281	1571
1572	1356	1416	722	1393	33141	33141	1044	510	1929	23791	1000	2325	1572
1573	1382	1476	706	1306	31098	31098	1068	478	1850	23812	1000	2348	1573
1574	1466	1544	826	1482	35312	35312	1053	535	1794	23827	1000	2427	1574
1575	1571	1638	819	1450	34783	34783	1043	500	1780	23857	1000	2545	1575
1576	1532	1590	828	1450	34606	34606	1038	521	1751	23866	1000	2462	1576
1577	1369	1455	768	1334	31900	31900	1063	528	1737	23913	1000	2226	1577
1578	1446	1568	905	1570	37513	37513	1084	577	1735	23894	1000	2395	1578
1579	1533	1594	784	1360	32508	32508	1040	492	1735	23903	1000	2437	1579
1580	1691	1754	936	1614	38666	38666	1037	534	1724	23957	1000	2669	1580
1581	1590	1626	820	1410	33759	33759	1023	504	1720	23943	1000	2459	1581
1582	1569	1620	806	1360	32589	32589	1033	498	1687	23962	1000	2403	1582
1583	1728	1790	876	1420	34090	34090	1036	489	1621	24007	1000	2561	1583
1584	1802	1874	979	1554	37355	37355	1040	522	1587	24038	1000	2626	1584
1585	1865	1929	1004	1587	38176	38176	1034	520	1581	24055	1000	2681	1585
1586	1580	1673	884	1387	33364	33364	1059	528	1569	24055	1000	2317	1586
1587	1700	1770	926	1440	34670	34670	1041	523	1555	24076	1000	2427	1587
1588	2097	2166	1091	1696	40881	40881	1033	504	1555	24104	1000	2972	1588
1589	1965	2064	1076	1661	40021	40021	1050	521	1544	24095	1000	2825	1589
1590	1841	1919	946	1460	35223	35223	1042	493	1543	24125	1000	2627	1590
1591	1758	1843	972	1497	36169	36169	1048	527	1540	24161	1000	2523	1591
1592	1934	2003	1013	1547	37391	37391	1036	506	1527	24170	1000	2715	1592
1593	2061	2124	1055	1605	38793	38793	1031	497	1521	24170	1000	2851	1593
1594	2030	2145	1067	1619	39217	39217	1057	508	1517	24223	1000	2874	1594
1595	1775	1901	965	1440	34942	34942	1071	497	1492	24265	1000	2509	1595
1596	1688	1789	932	1388	33703	33703	1060	521	1489	24282	1000	2356	1596
1597	1591	1641	812	1202	29204	29204	1031	495	1480	24296	1000	2136	1597
1598	1827	1898	1060	1450	35259	35259	1039	558	1368	24317	1000	2434	1598
1599	2117	2200	1162	1580	38413	38413	1039	528	1360	24312	1000	2789	1599
1600	2045	2146	1206	1572	38270	38270	1049	561	1303	24345	1000	2700	1600
1601	1874	1972	1106	1432	34949	34949	1052	561	1295	24406	1000	2470	1601
1602	1994	2088	1163	1480	36171	36171	1047	557	1273	24440	1000	2564	1602
1603	2175	2260	1294	1620	39511	39511	1039	573	1252	24390	1000	2759	1603
1604	2426	2510	1354	1634	39932	39932	1035	539	1207	24438	1000	3030	1604
1605	2286	2352	1402	1665	40716	40716	1029	596	1188	24454	1000	2794	1605
1606	2262	2337	1312	1550	37955	37955	1055	550	1181	24487	1000	2822	1606
1607	2248	2347	1253	1477	36219	36219	1044	534	1179	24522	1000	2767	1607
1608	2163	2262	1325	1562	38346	38346	1046	586	1179	24549	1000	2667	1608
1609	2152	2284	1336	1568	38505	38505	1061	585	1174	24557	1000	2676	1609

Table A4.1: *(cont.)*

Marriages

Year	(1)	(2)	(3)	(4)	(5)	(6)	(7) (2)/(1) ×1 000	(8) (3)/(2) ×1 000	(9) (4)/(3) ×1 000	(10) (5)/(4) ×1 000	(11) (6)/(5) ×1 000	(12)	Year
1610	2180	2356	1395	1631	40109	40109	1081	592	1169	24592	1000	2747	1610
1611	2464	2587	1527	1784	43873	43873	1050	590	1168	24592	1000	3010	1611
1612	2165	2262	1389	1614	39739	39739	1045	614	1162	24621	1000	2629	1612
1613	2161	2274	1328	1541	37974	37974	1052	584	1162	24642	1000	2635	1613
1614	2146	2266	1311	1515	37416	37416	1056	579	1156	24697	1000	2622	1614
1615	2323	2428	1375	1574	38863	38863	1045	566	1145	24691	1000	2774	1615
1616	2217	2336	1323	1505	37228	37228	1054	566	1138	24736	1000	2645	1616
1617	2149	2250	1283	1446	35738	35738	1047	570	1127	24715	1000	2529	1617
1618	2356	2478	1509	1688	41750	41750	1052	609	1119	24733	1000	2760	1618
1619	2423	2573	1494	1671	41362	41362	1062	581	1118	24753	1000	2866	1619
1620	2302	2501	1476	1649	40889	40889	1086	590	1117	24796	1000	2786	1620
1621	2311	2468	1399	1563	38795	38795	1068	567	1117	24821	1000	2750	1621
1622	2005	2141	1158	1292	32035	32035	1068	541	1116	24795	1000	2374	1622
1623	1780	1897	1073	1193	29687	29687	1066	566	1112	24884	1000	2102	1623
1624	2129	2315	1320	1469	36536	36536	1087	570	1113	24871	1000	2565	1624
1625	2097	2211	1234	1370	34112	34112	1054	558	1110	24899	1000	2440	1625
1626	2278	2392	1346	1488	37086	37086	1050	563	1105	24923	1000	2631	1626
1627	2405	2538	1452	1605	40081	40081	1055	572	1105	24973	1000	2791	1627
1628	2544	2656	1469	1655	41342	41342	1044	553	1127	24980	1000	2913	1628
1629	2602	2731	1509	1664	41733	41733	1050	553	1103	25080	1000	2983	1629
1630	2259	2405	1368	1510	37895	37895	1065	569	1104	25096	1000	2628	1630
1631	2084	2213	1320	1457	36611	36611	1062	596	1104	25128	1000	2414	1631
1632	2537	2687	1488	1640	41281	41281	1059	554	1102	25171	1000	2932	1632
1633	2339	2470	1454	1600	40359	40359	1056	589	1101	25224	1000	2688	1633
1634	2433	2667	1497	1648	41625	41625	1096	561	1101	25258	1000	2901	1634
1635	2433	2615	1534	1677	42464	42464	1075	587	1093	25321	1000	2838	1635
1636	2374	2498	1387	1518	38377	38377	1052	555	1094	25281	1000	2706	1636
1637	2357	2551	1503	1639	41460	41460	1082	589	1090	25296	1000	2751	1637
1638	2230	2364	1364	1487	37628	37628	1060	577	1090	25305	1000	2550	1638
1639	2704	2866	1700	1851	46845	46845	1060	593	1089	25308	1000	3086	1639
1640	2677	3002	1765	1911	48392	48392	1121	588	1083	25321	1000	3206	1640
1641	2587	3074	1864	2022	51113	51131	1188	606	1085	25278	1000	3284	1641
1642	2092	2784	1660	1792	45360	45389	1331	596	1080	25313	1001	2962	1642
1643	1427	2072	1178	1269	32157	32184	1452	569	1077	25340	1001	2195	1643
1644	1361	2009	1149	1227	31048	31085	1476	572	1068	25304	1001	2126	1644
1645	1580	2540	1578	1685	42654	42714	1608	621	1068	25314	1001	2686	1645
1646	1573	2576	1587	1693	42868	42938	1638	616	1067	25321	1002	2723	1646
1647	1325	2346	1429	1525	38622	38696	1771	609	1067	25326	1002	2478	1647
1648	1069	1748	1056	1128	28544	28607	1635	604	1068	25305	1002	1848	1648
1649	1029	1831	1146	1221	30963	31037	1779	626	1065	25359	1002	1936	1649

Table A4.1: *(cont.)*

Marriages

Year	(1)	(2)	(3)	(4)	(5)	(6)	(7) (2)/(1) x1 000	(8) (3)/(2) x1 000	(9) (4)/(3) x1 000	(10) (5)/(4) x1 000	(11) (6)/(5) x1 000	(12)	Year
1650	1056	2274	1379	1470	37212	37308	2153	606	1066	25314	1003	2399	1650
1651	1062	2334	1405	1497	37917	38027	2198	602	1065	25329	1003	2461	1651
1652	1119	2149	1287	1371	34718	34829	1920	599	1065	25323	1003	2265	1652
1653	1237	2098	1287	1369	34727	34844	1696	613	1064	25367	1003	2213	1653
1654	2786	3479	1899	1991	50454	50644	1249	546	1048	25341	1004	3586	1654
1655	3232	4281	2421	2500	63360	63615	1325	566	1033	25344	1004	4352	1655
1656	3299	4189	2147	2213	56118	56356	1270	513	1031	25358	1004	4251	1656
1657	2581	3295	1780	1832	46432	46642	1277	540	1029	25345	1005	3336	1657
1658	2008	2869	1653	1701	41127	43334	1429	576	1029	25354	1005	2904	1658
1659	1744	2848	1757	1802	45722	45950	1633	617	1027	25373	1005	2877	1659
1660	1405	2294	1362	1399	35447	35636	1633	594	1027	25537	1005	2318	1660
1661	1502	2032	1194	1217	30900	31071	1353	588	1019	25390	1006	2049	1661
1662	1855	2401	1486	1486	37715	37931	1294	619	1000	25380	1006	2401	1662
1663	2241	2740	1674	1674	42503	42759	1223	611	1000	25390	1006	2740	1663
1664	2356	2723	1709	1709	43379	43652	1156	628	1000	25383	1006	2723	1664
1665	2271	2591	1507	1507	38309	38560	1141	582	1000	25421	1007	2591	1665
1666	2229	2526	1417	1417	36073	36319	1133	561	1000	25457	1007	2526	1666
1667	2286	2635	1463	1463	37290	37554	1153	555	1000	25489	1007	2635	1667
1668	2169	2387	1300	1300	33262	33507	1101	545	1000	25586	1007	2387	1668
1669	2205	2406	1351	1351	34580	34842	1091	562	1000	25596	1008	2406	1669
1670	2239	2435	1366	1366	35021	35296	1088	561	1000	25638	1008	2435	1670
1671	2256	2547	1540	1540	39542	39860	1129	605	1000	25677	1008	2547	1671
1672	2286	2567	1436	1436	36919	37229	1123	559	1000	25710	1008	2567	1672
1673	2123	2336	1346	1346	34623	34922	1100	576	1000	25723	1008	2336	1673
1674	1854	2049	1251	1251	32277	32564	1105	611	1000	25801	1009	2049	1674
1675	1859	2037	1232	1232	31797	32087	1096	605	1000	25809	1009	2037	1675
1676	2150	2335	1322	1322	34104	34426	1086	566	1000	25797	1009	2335	1676
1677	2176	2402	1444	1444	37374	37735	1104	601	1000	25882	1010	2402	1677
1678	2065	2276	1341	1341	34739	35083	1102	589	1000	25905	1010	2276	1678
1679	2114	2317	1338	1338	34662	35015	1096	577	1000	25906	1010	2317	1679
1680	2460	2686	1585	1585	41154	41583	1092	590	1000	25965	1010	2686	1680
1681	2305	2488	1525	1525	39677	40102	1079	613	1000	26018	1011	2488	1681
1682	2352	2582	1468	1468	38182	38598	1098	569	1000	26010	1011	2582	1682
1683	2414	2626	1654	1654	43060	43542	1088	630	1000	26034	1011	2626	1683
1684	2194	2409	1411	1411	36823	37245	1098	586	1000	26097	1011	2409	1684
1685	2300	2507	1459	1459	38045	38485	1090	582	1000	26076	1012	2507	1685
1686	2398	2591	1481	1481	38699	39146	1080	572	1000	26130	1012	2591	1686
1687	2516	2760	1562	1562	40873	41340	1097	566	1000	26167	1011	2760	1687
1688	2369	2589	1454	1454	38093	38527	1093	562	1000	26199	1011	2589	1688
1689	2028	2204	1265	1265	33201	33574	1087	574	1000	26246	1011	2204	1689

Table A4.1: *(cont.)*

Marriages

Year	(1)	(2)	(3)	(4)	(5)	(6)	(7) (2)/(1) x1 000	(8) (3)/(2) x1 000	(9) (4)/(3) x1 000	(10) (5)/(4) x1 000	(11) (6)/(5) x1 000	(12)	Year
1690	1954	2141	1298	1298	34102	34485	1096	606	1000	26273	1011	2141	1690
1691	2004	2201	1217	1217	32011	32366	1098	553	1000	26303	1011	2201	1691
1692	1951	2138	1135	1135	29913	30244	1096	531	1000	26355	1011	2138	1692
1693	1899	2085	1123	1123	29579	29902	1098	539	1000	26339	1011	2085	1693
1694	1790	1986	1142	1142	30128	30457	1109	575	1000	26382	1011	1986	1694
1695	2369	2584	1527	1527	40343	40778	1091	591	1000	26420	1011	2584	1695
1696	2444	2617	1485	1485	39280	39699	1071	567	1000	26451	1011	2617	1696
1697	2260	2396	1416	1416	37514	37911	1060	591	1000	26493	1011	2396	1697
1698	2444	2575	1504	1504	39828	40248	1054	584	1000	26481	1011	2575	1698
1699	2524	2658	1514	1514	40196	40616	1053	570	1000	26550	1010	2658	1699
1700	2627	2726	1553	1553	41274	41705	1038	570	1000	26577	1010	2726	1700
1701	2723	2792	1561	1561	41443	41871	1025	559	1000	26549	1010	2792	1701
1702	2827	2900	1556	1556	41301	41722	1026	537	1000	26543	1010	2900	1702
1703	2729	2805	1540	1540	40859	41273	1028	549	1000	26532	1010	2805	1703
1704	2637	2692	1416	1416	37585	37964	1021	526	1000	26543	1010	2692	1704
1705	2597	2651	1518	1518	40298	40698	1021	573	1000	26547	1010	2651	1705
1706	2521	2583	1516	1516	40176	40573	1025	587	1000	26501	1010	2583	1706
1707	2472	2540	1458	1458	38626	39006	1028	574	1000	26492	1010	2540	1707
1708	2489	2547	1368	1368	36230	36581	1023	537	1000	26484	1010	2547	1708
1709	2408	2484	1334	1334	35328	35672	1032	537	1000	26483	1010	2484	1709
1710	2447	2541	1471	1471	39008	39379	1038	579	1000	26518	1010	2541	1710
1711	2464	2524	1428	1428	37816	38176	1024	566	1000	26482	1010	2524	1711
1712	2518	2595	1501	1501	39686	40061	1031	578	1000	26440	1009	2595	1712
1713	2924	3041	1657	1657	43880	44289	1040	545	1000	26482	1009	3041	1713
1714	2919	3045	1719	1719	45480	45901	1043	565	1000	26457	1009	3045	1714
1715	2853	2964	1704	1704	45101	45516	1039	575	1000	26468	1009	2964	1715
1716	2836	2943	1573	1573	41620	42001	1038	534	1000	26459	1009	2943	1716
1717	2904	3010	1598	1598	42257	42638	1037	531	1000	26444	1009	3010	1717
1718	3021	3108	1830	1830	48336	48766	1029	589	1000	26413	1009	3108	1718
1719	2823	2904	1662	1662	43945	44336	1029	572	1000	26441	1009	2904	1719
1720	2868	2947	1639	1639	43283	43663	1028	556	1000	26408	1009	2947	1720
1721	2981	3079	1726	1726	45576	45971	1033	561	1000	26406	1009	3079	1721
1722	3247	3346	1888	1888	49876	50307	1030	564	1000	26417	1009	3346	1722
1723	3407	3513	2031	2031	53565	54024	1031	578	1000	26374	1009	3513	1723
1724	3329	3417	1926	1926	50795	51226	1026	564	1000	26373	1008	3417	1724
1725	3146	3237	1801	1801	47507	47907	1029	556	1000	26378	1008	3237	1725
1726	3163	3256	1922	1922	50672	51094	1029	590	1000	26364	1008	3256	1726
1727	2929	3000	1714	1714	45164	45538	1024	571	1000	26350	1008	3000	1727
1728	2807	2849	1683	1683	44353	44718	1015	591	1000	26354	1008	2849	1728
1729	3025	3065	1720	1720	45302	45667	1013	561	1000	26338	1008	3065	1729

Table A4.1: *(cont.)*

Marriages

Year	(1)	(2)	(3)	(4)	(5)	(6)	(7) (2)/(1) x1 000	(8) (3)/(2) x1 000	(9) (4)/(3) x1 000	(10) (5)/(4) x1 000	(11) (6)/(5) x1 000	(12)	Year
1730	3748	3789	2169	2169	57126	57582	1011	572	1000	26337	1008	3789	1730
1731	3773	3841	2216	2216	58331	58792	1018	577	1000	26323	1008	3841	1731
1732	3553	3631	2046	2046	53839	54260	1022	563	1000	26314	1008	3631	1732
1733	3246	3294	1858	1858	48899	49276	1015	564	1000	26318	1008	3294	1733
1734	3261	3303	1802	1802	47444	47808	1013	546	1000	26329	1008	3303	1734
1735	3159	3233	1818	1818	47805	48167	1023	562	1000	26295	1008	3233	1735
1736	2851	2906	1652	1652	43459	43785	1019	568	1000	26307	1008	2906	1736
1737	2984	3029	1748	1748	45895	46236	1015	577	1000	26256	1007	3029	1737
1738	3138	3184	1742	1742	45733	46072	1015	547	1000	26253	1007	3184	1738
1739	3130	3223	1801	1801	47312	47655	1030	559	1000	26270	1007	3223	1739
1740	2737	2840	1715	1715	45019	45343	1038	604	1000	26250	1007	2840	1740
1741	2689	2795	1539	1539	40418	40705	1039	551	1000	26263	1007	2795	1741
1742	2900	2977	1704	1704	44717	45031	1027	572	1000	26242	1007	2977	1742
1743	3241	3329	1880	1880	49311	49654	1027	565	1000	26229	1007	3329	1743
1744	3360	3437	1879	1879	49262	49605	1023	547	1000	26217	1007	3437	1744
1745	3095	3184	1744	1744	45691	46002	1029	548	1000	26199	1007	3184	1745
1746	3038	3100	1704	1704	44668	44969	1020	550	1000	26214	1007	3100	1746
1747	3229	3300	1873	1873	49082	49408	1022	568	1000	26205	1007	3300	1747
1748	3312	3347	1831	1831	47918	48234	1011	547	1000	26170	1007	3347	1748
1749	3311	3366	1798	1798	47093	47398	1017	534	1000	26192	1006	3366	1749
1750	3255	3315	1828	1828	47820	48127	1018	551	1000	26160	1006	3315	1750
1751	3326	3378	1780	1780	46582	46880	1016	527	1000	26170	1006	3378	1751
1752	3289	3331	1778	1778	46498	46789	1013	534	1000	26152	1006	3331	1752
1753	3523	3564	1844	1844	48244	48541	1012	517	1000	26163	1006	3564	1753
1754	3439	3486	1773	1773	46372	46652	1014	509	1000	26155	1006	3486	1754
1755	3722	3762	1895	1895	49478	49775	1011	504	1000	26110	1006	3762	1755
1756	3731	3762	1955	1955	51093	51398	1008	520	1000	26135	1006	3762	1756
1757	3394	3425	1696	1696	44316	44576	1009	495	1000	26130	1006	3425	1757
1758	3671	3682	1866	1866	48708	48990	1003	507	1000	26103	1006	3682	1758
1759	4188	4202	2126	2126	55517	55835	1003	506	1000	26113	1006	4202	1759
1760	4250	4267	2282	2282	59558	59892	1004	535	1000	26099	1006	4267	1760
1761	4372	4391	2292	2292	59797	60128	1004	522	1000	26089	1006	4391	1761
1762	4065	4085	2084	2084	54303	54601	1005	510	1000	26057	1005	4085	1762
1763	4507	4524	2217	2217	57799	58108	1004	490	1000	26071	1005	4524	1763
1764	4538	4548	2245	2245	58503	58812	1002	494	1000	26059	1005	4548	1764
1765	4252	4262	2133	2133	55622	55913	1002	500	1000	26077	1005	4262	1765
1766	4182	4190	2105	2105	54914	55194	1002	502	1000	26087	1005	4190	1766
1767	3833	3842	1979	1979	51732	51994	1002	515	1000	26140	1005	3842	1767
1768	4145	4167	2170	2170	56801	57083	1005	521	1000	26176	1005	4167	1768
1769	4478	4522	2300	2300	60208	60503	1010	509	1000	26177	1005	4522	1769

Table A4.1: *(cont.)*

Marriages

Year	(1)	(2)	(3)	(4)	(5)	(6)	(7) (2)/(1) x1 000	(8) (3)/(2) x1 000	(9) (4)/(3) x1 000	(10) (5)/(4) x1 000	(11) (6)/(5) x1 000	(12)	Year
1770	4546	4565	2292	2292	60052	60342	1004	502	1000	26201	1005	4565	1770
1771	4352	4367	2190	2190	57491	57762	1003	501	1000	26252	1005	4367	1771
1772	4390	4401	2204	2204	57900	58169	1003	501	1000	26270	1005	4401	1772
1773	4382	4388	2153	2153	56638	56899	1001	491	1000	26307	1005	4388	1773
1774	4322	4333	2189	2189	57601	57864	1003	505	1000	26314	1005	4333	1774
1775	4463	4473	2173	2173	57253	57508	1002	486	1000	26347	1004	4473	1775
1776	4581	4590	2224	2224	58704	58958	1002	485	1000	26396	1004	4590	1776
1777	4610	4619	2320	2320	61251	61514	1002	502	1000	26401	1004	4619	1777
1778	4589	4610	2296	2296	60728	60983	1005	498	1000	26449	1004	4610	1778
1779	4566	4573	2210	2210	58473	58715	1002	483	1000	26458	1004	4573	1779
1780	4638	4648	2351	2351	62271	62522	1002	506	1000	26487	1004	4648	1780
1781	4624	4626	2250	2250	59639	59875	1000	486	1000	26506	1004	4626	1781
1782	4493	4493	2212	2212	58719	58948	1000	492	1000	26546	1004	4493	1782
1783	4689	4689	2321	2321	61751	61985	1000	495	1000	26605	1004	4689	1783
1784	4761	4762	2316	2316	61623	61853	1000	486	1000	26608	1004	4762	1784
1785	5183	5183	2649	2649	70513	70771	1000	511	1000	26619	1004	5183	1785
1786	4866	4866	2438	2438	64972	65206	1000	501	1000	26650	1004	4866	1786
1787	4957	4957	2408	2408	64267	64490	1000	486	1000	26689	1003	4957	1787
1788	4841	4842	2432	2432	65041	65262	1000	502	1000	26744	1003	4842	1788
1789	4876	4879	2363	2363	63172	63381	1001	484	1000	26734	1003	4879	1789
1790	4855	4888	2516	2516	67329	67547	1007	515	1000	26760	1003	4888	1790
1791	5080	5114	2477	2477	66369	66577	1007	484	1000	26794	1003	5114	1791
1792	5342	5392	2642	2642	70870	71089	1009	490	1000	26824	1003	5392	1792
1793	5244	5256	2636	2636	70765	70981	1002	502	1000	26846	1003	5256	1793
1794	4945	4952	2459	2459	66075	66266	1001	497	1000	26871	1003	4952	1794
1795	4665	4688	2248	2248	60542	60714	1005	480	1000	26931	1003	4688	1795
1796	5185	5202	2579	2579	69502	69693	1003	496	1000	26949	1003	5202	1796
1797	5506	5527	2671	2671	72020	72216	1004	483	1000	26964	1003	5527	1797
1798	5518	5535	2829	2829	76318	76518	1003	511	1000	26977	1003	5535	1798
1799	5166	5172	2576	2576	69601	69778	1001	498	1000	27019	1003	5172	1799
1800	4723	4759	2352	2352	63525	63680	1008	494	1000	27009	1002	4759	1800
1801	4543	4567	2215	2215	59831	59974	1005	485	1000	27012	1002	4567	1801
1802	6282	6297	3127	3127	84524	84718	1002	497	1000	27030	1002	6297	1802
1803	6559	6599	3268	3268	88333	88531	1006	495	1000	27030	1002	6599	1803
1804	6046	6082	3019	3019	81558	81735	1006	496	1000	27015	1002	6082	1804
1805	5753	5764	2795	2795	75571	75730	1002	485	1000	27038	1002	5764	1805
1806	5698	5711	2747	2747	74246	74401	1002	481	1000	27028	1002	5711	1806
1807	5934	5952	2966	2966	80202	80367	1003	498	1000	27040	1002	5952	1807
1808	5800	5821	2826	2826	76391	76544	1004	485	1000	27031	1002	5821	1808
1809	5675	5747	2736	2736	73934	74083	1013	476	1000	27023	1002	5747	1809

Table A4.1: *(cont.)*

Marriages

Year	(1)	(2)	(3)	(4)	(5)	(6)	(7) (2)/(1) x1 000	(8) (3)/(12) x1 000	(9) (4)/(3) x1 000	(10) (5)/(4) x1 000	(11) (6)/(5) x1 000	(12)	Year
1810	5681	5782	2789	2789	75418	75565	1018	482	1000	27041	1002	5782	1810
1811	6179	6202	3083	3083	83313	83475	1004	497	1000	27023	1002	6202	1811
1812	4377	4404	2159	2941	79497	79649	1006	490	1362	27031	1002	5951	1812
1813	4127	4140	2118	2890	78064	78216	1003	512	1364	27012	1002	5800	1813
1814	4766	4771	2426	3308	89423	89593	1001	508	1364	27032	1002	6684	1814
1815	4987	4990	2565	3499	94543	94719	1001	514	1364	27020	1002	6990	1815
1816	4687	4692	2419	3298	89146	89310	1001	516	1363	27030	1002	6574	1816
1817	4276	4378	2248	3079	83264	83413	1024	513	1370	27043	1002	6183	1817
1818	4593	4731	2406	3297	89109	89270	1030	509	1370	27027	1002	6680	1818
1819	4581	4705	2303	3160	85379	85529	1027	489	1372	27019	1002	6647	1819
1820	4736	4857	2497	3443	93073	93234	1026	514	1379	27033	1002	6916	1820
1821	4785	4857	2482	3423	92520	92682	1015	511	1379	27033	1002	6917	1821
1822	5012	5066	2637	3637	98287	98452	1011	521	1379	27029	1002	7213	1822
1823	5256	5282	2629	3624	97991	98153	1005	498	1378	27024	1002	7521	1823
1824	5175	5175	2628	3623	97940	98104	1000	508	1379	27039	1002	7369	1824
1825	5474	5477	2839	3915	105798	105969	1001	518	1379	27033	1002	7799	1825
1826	5121	5122	2622	3614	97706	97865	1000	512	1378	27035	1002	7293	1826
1827	4974	4979	2482	3426	92609	92754	1001	498	1380	27031	1002	7099	1827
1828	5516	5540	2917	4027	108864	109033	1004	527	1381	27034	1002	7898	1828
1829	4953	4961	2509	3465	93615	93761	1002	506	1381	27017	1002	7073	1829
1830	5176	5178	2568	3547	95823	95967	1000	496	1381	27015	1001	7382	1830
1831	5431	5468	2803	3870	104588	104744	1007	513	1381	27025	1001	7796	1831
1832	5515	5516	2907	4012	108472	108632	1000	527	1380	27037	1001	7862	1832
1833	5861	5870	3051	4213	113843	114002	1002	520	1381	27022	1001	8368	1833
1834	5879	5891	2993	4134	111689	111846	1002	508	1381	27017	1001	8401	1834
1835	5822	5824	2922	4038	109206	109360	1000	502	1382	27045	1001	8336	1835
1836	5720	5779	2868	4240	114576	114738	1010	496	1478	27023	1001	8543	1836
1837	1208	1275	579	3925	106112	106262	1055	454	6779	27035	1001	8209	1837

sort arise because of the rounding of monthly totals originally calculated in long precision decimal form which are then aggregated together to form the annual totals. Since slight inaccuracies on either side of the true ratio are equally likely to occur, however, no general bias or imprecision arises.[1]

The twelfth column contains annual totals comparable to those in column 4, but without re-weighting for parish size (the step represented by the figures in column 3).

Table A4.2 shows the proportionate share of the several successive changes made to national totals of baptisms and burials in order to convert them into birth and death totals. For example, the sum of baptisms for 1820–9 in table A4.1 is 3,321,857,

Table A4.2: Proportionate shares of final decadal birth and death totals derived from Anglican parish register totals, and from corrections for nonconformity, delayed baptism, and residual non-registration (base 10 000)

(1) Anglican baptism or burial totals
(2) Nonconformist baptism or burial totals
(3) Inflation for delayed baptism
(4) Residual non-registration
(5) Final totals

	Births					Deaths				
	(1)	(2)	(3)	(4)	(5)	(1)	(2)	(3)	(4)	(5)
1540-9	10 000	0	0	0	10 000	10 000	0	0	0	10 000
1550-9	9 963	0	37	0	10 000	10 000	0	0	0	10 000
1560-9	9 882	0	118	0	10 000	10 000	0	0	0	10 000
1570-9	9 810	0	190	0	10 000	10 000	0	0	0	10 000
1580-9	9 777	0	223	0	10 000	10 000	0	0	0	10 000
1590-9	9 750	0	250	0	10 000	10 000	0	0	0	10 000
1600-9	9 724	0	276	0	10 000	10 000	0	0	0	10 000
1610-9	9 698	0	302	0	10 000	10 000	0	0	0	10 000
1620-9	9 673	0	327	0	10 000	10 000	0	0	0	10 000
1630-9	9 658	0	342	0	10 000	10 000	0	0	0	10 000
1640-9	9 606	12	353	29	10 000	9 976	12	0	12	10 000
1650-9	9 512	35	364	89	10 000	9 924	39	0	37	10 000
1660-9	9 418	58	375	149	10 000	9 876	64	0	60	10 000
1670-9	9 327	80	386	207	10 000	9 823	89	4	84	10 000
1680-9	9 233	102	401	264	10 000	9 748	109	37	106	10 000
1690-9	9 158	117	418	307	10 000	9 684	109	82	125	10 000
1700-9	9 103	128	433	336	10 000	9 627	105	131	137	10 000
1710-9	9 045	139	450	366	10 000	9 584	100	167	149	10 000
1720-9	9 007	143	469	381	10 000	9 570	92	182	156	10 000
1730-9	8 956	147	506	391	10 000	9 482	86	272	160	10 000
1740-9	8 860	163	543	434	10 000	9 436	82	304	178	10 000
1750-9	8 761	179	579	481	10 000	9 322	80	400	198	10 000
1760-9	8 658	196	614	532	10 000	9 276	77	427	220	10 000
1770-9	8 556	217	648	579	10 000	9 143	80	537	240	10 000
1780-9	8 260	262	658	820	10 000	8 927	98	566	409	10 000
1790-9	7 734	306	647	1 313	10 000	8 348	119	652	881	10 000
1800-9	7 270	352	637	1 741	10 000	7 607	130	696	1 567	10 000
1810-9	6 795	381	623	2 201	10 000	6 759	136	747	2 358	10 000
1820-9	6 964	433	663	1 940	10 000	7 300	160	861	1 679	10 000
1830-9	7 372	495	708	1 425	10 000	8 014	178	894	914	10 000

1. The effect of rounding may be clearly seen in the column 10 ratios for marriages from 1800 to 1837. The 'target' ratio (see table 3.12) is 27.030 throughout this 38-year period. The annual ratio varies from 27.009 to 27.045, but the average figure of 27.028 is very close to the 'target'.

while the sum of births for the same years is 4,770,338 (columns 5 and 6). The ratio figure in column 1 of table A4.2 for 1820–9 is 6,964 (3,321,857/ 4,770,338 × 10,000), and the figures in columns 2 to 4 show the relative importance of corrections for nonconformity, delayed baptism, and residual non-registration during the decade in converting the baptism total into a total for births. Comparable data for marriages are not given since only very minor changes in respect of Quaker marriage registration were made to the original Anglican totals (see table 4.3). In considering the data in table A4.2 it will be helpful to refer to tables 4.3, 4.5, 5.25, and 5.26 in which are shown the inflation ratios that produced the changes summarized in table A4.2.

Appendix 5

National population totals: the results of back projection compared with earlier estimates

The technique of back projection was born from a dissatisfaction with earlier attempts to estimate the size of the population. Where its results can be checked, as for example against the English nineteenth-century censuses and the Swedish population counts back to 1749, back projection proves to be a reliable method of estimating population size.[1] Furthermore sensitivity tests have shown that while alternative assumptions about the scale of the inflation required to overcome the deficiencies of Anglican registration produce very different series of births and deaths, the population totals which back projection calculates on the basis of these alternative series differ less than might be expected *a priori* and all lie within 5 per cent of the main results presented in chapter seven.[2] The population totals that back projection derives from our preferred national series of births and deaths therefore seem to be robust and it may be of some interest to compare them with earlier estimates of population size produced by other means. In considering the latter a convenient distinction may be drawn between the eighteenth century and the period before 1700. The eighteenth century is dominated by estimates based on the totals of baptisms and burials collected by Rickman in 1801 and generally known under the title of the Parish Register Abstracts (hereafter abbreviated to PRA). The earlier period is served by a similar, though more limited, exercise that Rickman carried out in the 1830s, and by modern estimates based on enumerations of sections of the population that the civil and ecclesiastical authorities made on a number of occasions in the past.

Population estimates before 1700

To move from an enumeration of a part of the population to a figure for the population as a whole, it is necessary to estimate both the completeness of the count and the fraction of the total population that the enumerated proportion comprised. The difficulties and uncertainties that such procedures entail are very apparent in the case of the first population estimate of this kind that can be made in the period under study. In the mid 1540s counts were made of communicants in a number of parishes in connexion with the dissolution of the chantries.[3] The total number of parishes covered is too small for a national estimate to be based directly on the numbers of communicants enumerated, but many years ago Russell had the ingenious idea of constructing an estimate by finding the ratios between the parish totals of

1. See above, pp. 199–202 and below, pp. 733–6.
2. See above, pp. 269–77.
3. The dissolutions were ordered by two acts of parliament in 1545 and 1547 (37 Henry VIII c. 4 and 1 Edward VI c. 14). The commissioners' surveys date from 1546 and 1548 and are in the Public Record Office, class E301. Surveys for some counties have been printed, see Russell, *British medieval population*, p. 20, n. 5.

communicants and the numbers of taxpayers assessed in the same places for the poll tax of 1377.[4] Since a national estimate of the number of taxpayers can be made from the 1377 poll-tax returns, a national estimate of the number of communicants can be obtained for the mid 1540s by multiplying the earlier total by the average ratio found between the parish totals enumerated at the two dates. This procedure assumes that parishes with chantries in the 1540s comprised a representative cross-section of all parishes so far as population growth in the later middle ages is concerned. Russell believed that this was not the case, asserting that chantries were located in more prosperous parishes which, he alleged, grew faster than others in the late middle ages.[5] However, he proceeded to compare the numbers listed in the poll tax and chantry certificates and produced a preliminary estimate of 'about 5 million' for the size of the population in 1545, but rejected this estimate as too high and assumed instead that a constant rate of population growth obtained between two estimated population sizes of 2.75 million in 1430 and 3.78 million in 1603. He thus arrived at a population total of 3.22 million for 1545 by simple interpolation.[6]

It is apparent from the evidence Russell cites in his tables that some of the ratios between the parish totals enumerated in the 1377 poll tax and in the chantry certificates are implausibly high. Some of the discrepancies are due to the fact that the poll tax was levied on the civil unit of the vill while the chantry certificates referred to the ecclesiastical parishes, areas that might not coincide, especially in the north where parishes might include several vills.[7] A revision of Russell's data, correcting erroneous figures, omitting misidentified settlements and adding further vills from the poll-tax returns to make up the area designated by the equivalent parish names in the 1540s, produces a median parish ratio between the poll-tax returns and the chantry certificates of 1.538, a figure close to the ratio that Russell ultimately preferred.[8]

If the 122 parishes from 11 counties on which this figure is based were representative of the national rate of growth, then they would have comprised the same proportion of the national population in the mid 1540s as they did in 1377. Thus if the national total of taxpayers in 1377 is multiplied by the average parish growth ratio between the two dates an estimate can be obtained of the national number of communicants in the mid 1540s.[9] In making this calculation the trimean of the parish ratios has been used because it gives a more representative picture of the distribution of the parish ratios than does the median, without being influenced by extreme values as is the case with the arithmetic mean.[10] Multiplying a national total of 1.417 million taxpayers in 1377 by a trimean of 1.645 produces a national total of communicants in

4. *Ibid.*, pp. 19–22, 270–81. The poll tax assessments are in the Public Record Office, class E179. See Beresford, 'Poll taxes'.

5. Russell, *British medieval population*, p. 22.

6. *Ibid.*, pp. 22, 270–2.

7. Russell was aware of this difficulty, *ibid.*, p. 279.

8. *Ibid.*, pp. 279–81. If a further 60 parishes which could not be checked conclusively are taken into account the median ratio becomes 1.57. Russell calculated ratios for 201 parishes from 18 counties. Beresford comments on the 'elementary misreadings of the original documents' which undermine Russell's figures: 'Poll taxes', n. 7. We are grateful to Professor Beresford for the loan of transcripts of some of the 1377 poll tax assessments.

9. Note that this calculation does not require any estimate of the national *population* in 1377, and it avoids the problems of the under-enumeration of taxpayers in 1377 and of changes in the age structure by incorporating them in the parish growth ratios.

10. The trimean is defined as the arithmetic mean of the median and the first and third quartiles with the median given double weight, i.e. $(q_1 + 2q_2 + q_3)/4$. It is therefore effectively an arithmetic mean of the central half of the distribution. Tukey, *Exploratory data analysis*, pp. 46–7.

the mid 1540s of 2.331 million.[11] Since the chantry certificates occasionally returned highly rounded numbers of communicants, this national estimate must be regarded as a very approximate figure indeed.[12]

The next step is to estimate the proportion of the population too young to have been counted as communicants in the mid 1540s, in order to arrive at a figure for the total population. Russell thought that the age of communion was 14, but the medieval tradition, reflected in the standard English fifteenth-century canon law commentary, was that full participation in spiritual life began when a child had reached years of discretion at the age of 7.[13] After the reformation the Church of England required some evidence of knowledge and understanding as a precondition for receiving communion, for example the royal injunctions of 1538 specified the need to be able to recite the 'articles of faith' and the 'pater' in English.[14] In 1560–1 the 'Interpretations' of the bishops ruled 'that children be not admitted to the Communion before the age of 12 years', and the Canons of 1571 both tried to ensure that this knowledge was acquired at a young age by laying a penalty of 10 shillings on parents whose children of age 10 and over were not being catechized, and required knowledge of the articles of faith, the Lord's prayer, and the ten commandments by age 14 on pain of excommunication.[15] Although neither the 'Interpretations' nor the Canons of 1571 had any legal status they appear to have been enforced by some bishops.[16]

If we take the range 12–4 as the age at which children were beginning to attend communion in some numbers after several years of effort by the Edwardian and the early Elizabethan reformers, then it seems likely that in the last years of the reign of the theologically conservative Henry VIII the age of communion may not have risen much above the canonical age of 7 of pre-reformation days. A convenient compromise would be to take the age of 10 as constituting the point at which the chantry commissioners in the mid 1540s may have counted a child as one of the 'howsling people'.

If we now make use of the results of back projection we find that 24.9 per cent of the population was under age 10 in 1546, the year in which the majority of the chantry

11. The national total of taxpayers is as estimated by Russell after making an allowance of 5 per cent for exemptions and deficiencies, *British medieval population*, p. 146. If the 60 unchecked parishes are included, the trimean becomes 1.638 and the national total of communicants falls very slightly to 2.321 million. The ratio between the total numbers of people enumerated in the chantry and poll tax returns summed over all the 122 checked parishes is 2.249, which suggests that the larger parishes did indeed experience greater growth, as Russell alleged. In view of the dangers of this bias and of the distortion in the overall ratio which can be caused by one or two very large parishes, the trimean probably provides the most stable and representative indication of the rate of growth between 1377 and the 1540s.

12. The method of calculation is rather sensitive to inaccuracies in the numbers of communicants returned by the chantry commissioners.

13. By the Constitutions of Peccham (1281) communion was only given to those who had been confirmed, and by the constitutions of Walter (1322) boys ('pueros') were to be confirmed. Lyndwood in his fifteenth century commentary glosses 'pueros' as 'qui est major septennio', i.e. has reached age seven in modern, elapsed-year reckoning. The text of the constitutions are printed in Gibson, *Codex iuris*, pp. 454, 457, and the gloss is in Lyndwood, *Provinciale*, p. 34.

14. Frere and Kennedy, *Visitation articles*, II, p. 37.

15. For the 'Interpretations' see *ibid*, III, p. 62. The text of the 1571 Canons (nos LI and XLVIII respectively) is given in Strype, *Annals of the reformation*, I, part 2, pp. 567–8.

16. The Canons were devised by the bishops and were neither voted by the Lower House of Convocation nor allowed by the queen. Bishop Guest's 1565 injunctions for the diocese of Rochester prohibited attendance at communion before age 13 or 14, while Archbishop Grindal's 1571 injunctions for the province of York required attendance from the age of 14. Frere and Kennedy, *Visitation articles*, III, pp. 161, 287.

returns were made, and was therefore too young to be included in the numbers of communicants. Multiplying the estimated total of 2.331 million communicants by 100/(100–24.9) we obtain an estimated population total of 3.104 million, or about 9 per cent higher than the 2.854 million found by back projection, as shown in table A3.3. Considering the approximate nature of the estimate based on the chantry certificates and the uncertainties attending the back-projection estimates in the mid sixteenth century, the fit is reasonably good. The figure of 3.104 million also lies part way between Russell's own preferred estimate of 3.22 million and a revised total of 2.8 million that Cornwall derived 'employing only the more plausible-looking estimates'.[17] The agreement between back projection and Cornwall's revised total is very close.

The convergence on a figure of about 3 million for the size of the population in the mid 1540s throws some further light on the course of population change in the later middle ages. If Russell's estimate of a population size of 2.232 million in 1377 is accepted as a reasonable starting point, then the population in 1546 was about 28 per cent higher than it had been in 1377, which implies a slow but by no means negligible compound annual rate of growth of 0.15 per cent per annum over the intervening 169 years.[18] Most scholars, however, believe that the population was stagnant until well into the fifteenth century: some point to the 1480s as a turning point while others favour the 1510s.[19] If the population had indeed remained stagnant until the mid 1480s or the mid 1510s the resulting average annual rates of growth up to the mid 1540s would have been about 0.41 and 0.82 per cent respectively. The latter figure is very similar to the average annual rate of growth of 0.87 per cent that back projection finds between 1541 and 1556. If, therefore, the mid-century growth rate had prevailed during the quarter century before 1541 it would imply a late date for the beginning of renewed population growth. Since the population of Wales is likely to have been in the region of 0.207 million it would also suggest that the lower bound of the estimate of 2.5 to 3 million, which has often been repeated but never substantiated, for the population of England and Wales in 1500 was not far wide of the mark.[20]

It is, of course, simplistic to argue in terms of stagnation from 1377 to about 1510 and a constant rate of growth from then until the mid sixteenth century, especially in view of the changes in the rate of population growth so evident after 1541. Fortunately it is possible to make an independent estimate of the population size in the mid 1520s

17. Cornwall, 'English population in the early sixteenth century', pp. 32–3.
18. Russell's 1377 total involves the assumption that 33 per cent of the population was under age 14. Given the high level of mortality in 1377 fertility was probably also fairly high (otherwise the population decline would have been precipitous) and in these conditions Russell's figure of 33 per cent under age 14 is not unreasonable. Russell's population figure is in *British medieval population*, p. 146. His mortality figures have been revised by Ohlin in 'No safety in numbers', pp. 61–70.
19. The evidence is reviewed in Hatcher, *Plague, population*, pp. 63–7.
20. For example, Clapham refers to 'an opinion often expressed, which is perhaps near the truth', Chambers to 'most medievalists' view', and Clarkson to 'most historians'. Clapham, *Concise economic history*, p. 78; Chambers, *Population, economy and society*, pp. 111–2, Clarkson, *Pre-industrial economy*, p. 26. The estimate of 0.207 million for the population of Wales is calculated by multiplying 2.232 million by 0.09288, the proportion of the population of England and Wales comprised by Wales in the 1603 communicants returns. See Figure A5.1. Alternative estimates can be based on the Welsh proportions in the 1690 hearth-tax returns (0.05907) and the 1801 census (0.06617), which yield Welsh populations in 1507 of 0.132 and 0.148 million respectively. See Glass, 'Two papers on Gregory King', p. 218 and Hollingsworth, *Historical Demography*, pp. 83–4. Russell used the Welsh clerical poll-tax returns and laity/clergy ratios from neighbouring English shires to estimate the population of Wales in 1377 at 0.125 million, *British medieval population*, pp. 328–9.

that can be compared with the 2.854 million estimated for 1546 and so enable a calculation to be made of the rate of population growth in the two decades before the parish registers begin. But the sources concerned, the muster rolls of 1522 and the tax assessments of 1524–5, raise many problems of interpretation which leave considerable doubts about the precision of the estimate of population size based upon them.

First of all, while the muster rolls in principle covered all males between the ages of 16 and 60, the tax returns only listed those over age 16 who were wealthier than a minimum exemption limit.[21] It is not easy to discover how many were too poor or too elusive to be recorded on the tax lists. A comparison with the muster rolls in a few rural hundreds in five counties, which included people with no possessions whatsoever, suggests that about 6 per cent of the eligible population escaped notice in the tax assessments, while comparison with total population estimates in three towns indicates that between 33 per cent and 48 per cent of the eligible urban population were too poor to be taxed.[22] Cornwall, who used the muster and tax returns to estimate the national population size, compared successive annual returns and found that a number of names only occurred on one list. He concluded that evasion was rife and based his count on the total number of names occurring in the documents.[23] Such a procedure assumes that there was neither mortality nor migration, but a document for Towcester hundred in Northamptonshire shows that about 2 per cent of the tax payers died and 15 per cent moved in the course of the year between tax assessments. Thus the overcounting implicit in Cornwall's method rather more than offsets the 6 per cent or so of countrymen who were too poor to feature in the tax lists.[24]

A further difficulty lies in determining what proportion of the total population those listed in the sources comprised. Cornwall assumed that there were an equal number of adult females who were not enumerated, and that the under-16s comprised 40 per cent of the population.[25] This is a high proportion and one that according to back projection was only attained in the early nineteenth century when fertility was at its highest with

21. For the muster records see Cornwall, 'English country towns', and for the tax returns see Sheail, *Lay subsidy returns of 1524–5*, i, pp. 9–81.
22. 12,451 persons were listed in the muster returns as opposed to 11,730 in the tax assessments for Berks. (Kintbury Eagle and Faircross hundreds), Bucks. (Ashendon and Chiltern hundreds), Norfolk (South Erpingham, West Flegg, Happing, and Tunstead hundreds, and Yarmouth), Rutland, and Wilts. (Rammesbury, Selkley, Kingbridge, and parts of Highworth, Cricklade, and Staple hundreds). The percentages omitted ranged from 2.0 (Wilts.) to 11.0 (Berks.) with considerable variation from vill to vill. Muster returns: PRO E315/464 (Berks.), Bodleian MS Eng. Hist. e. 187 (Bucks.), PRO E36/25 (Norf., except S. Erpingham in E101/61/16 ff. 14d et seq.), E36/55 (Rutland), E179/259/17 (Wilts.). Tax assessments: PRO E179/73/121 (Berks.), E179/78/93, 96 (Bucks.), E179/150/210, 215, 250, 263 (Norf.), E179/165/110, 113 (Rutland), E179/197/16 (Wilts.). For the urban percentages escaping assessment see Hoskins, 'Early Tudor towns', p. 17.
23. Cornwall, 'English population in the early sixteenth century', pp. 33–6. He included the few women taxed even though his subsequent calculations assumed that only men were assessed.
24. Out of 278 taxpayers assessed in Towcester hundred in April 1524, 6 (2 per cent) were said to have died and 41 (15 per cent) had 'removyd' when the next assessment was made in January 1525. Those stated to have 'removyd' came overwhelmingly from those paying the lowest rate of tax of 4d. Of this group, who by virtue of their assessment were most likely to have been servants, 36 per cent had left the hundred between April and the following January. PRO E179/155/131. Hollingsworth subjects some of Cornwall's data to algebraic analysis and shows that the best fit is obtained with no under enumeration and an annual loss through death and migration of 11 per cent amongst the rich and 26 per cent amongst the poor, rather than with the combination of under-enumeration and no migration that Cornwall assumed. Hollingsworth, *Historical demography*, pp. 49–52.
25. Cornwall, 'English population in the early sixteenth century', p. 36.

a GRR of about 3.00. In the first 15 years covered by back projection, the GRR was somewhat lower at about 2.75, and the proportion of the population under 16 was only 37 per cent. However, if fertility had risen suddenly at the beginning of the sixteenth century, as it did around 1800 then a figure of 40 per cent of the population under age 16, although high, would not be unreasonable. Finally the tax data Cornwall used only covered six counties (Berks., Bucks., Rutland, Suffolk, Sussex, and Worcs.), but he argued that the proportion of the national population that these counties comprised was fairly stable over the long term. Slightly amending his calculations, it was 12.60 per cent in the poll tax of 1377 and 10.86 per cent in the hearth-tax returns of 1689. Since the mid 1520s lie almost exactly half way between the two dates, the mean of these two proportions (11.51 per cent) may perhaps be taken as the most likely basis on which to arrive at a national total.[26]

Thus Cornwall's estimate of 78,005 adult male taxpayers in the six counties, when inflated by a factor of 100/11.51 to refer to England as a whole, and further inflated by a factor of 10/3 to refer to people of both sexes and all ages, yields a total population size for the mid 1520s of 2.259 million, compared to Cornwall's own mean estimate of a national population of 2.348 million.[27] This figure implies that there had been little, if any, growth since 1377 (2.232 million), and then a rapid expansion of the population to reach, in 1541, the 2.774 million found by back projection. The assessments underlying the population estimate for the early 1520s were made between mid 1522 and January 1525.[28] Taking account of the numbers assessed at each date, the weighted average date of assessment was in late February 1524, some 17.35 years before the earliest back-projection population estimate in mid 1541. The implied rate of population growth during the intervening period is 1.2 per cent per annum, faster than that recorded at any subsequent period until the early nineteenth century.

Thus if the muster and tax returns are considered a reasonable guide to the number of adult males, it would appear that the most striking feature of the recovery from the long stagnation since 1377 was a period of exceptionally rapid population growth in the 1520s and 1530s which then slackened off somewhat after 1541 when the course of population change can be observed more effectively. Alternatively, it might be argued that the estimate of population size in the mid 1520s is vulnerable on a number of counts, perhaps the most serious being an uncertainty about the proportion of the population too poor or too elusive to be taxed. For example, if the average rate of population growth of 0.87 per cent per annum that obtained between 1541 and 1556 is projected backwards, the population total in February 1524 would have been 2.384 million. The assessments could produce a population figure of this size if the rate of omission of adult males had been 6 per cent over and above those whose omission was offset by Cornwall's ignoring of the effects of migration. In view of the uncertainties involved, and of the sensitivity of the final result to quite modest errors in the estimation procedure, the tax and muster returns cannot be held to provide decisive

26. Cornwall, *ibid.*, p. 39, has 11.31 per cent for 1377 and 10.85 per cent for 1689. The former figure is a miscalculation from Russell's data obtained by relating a national total of taxpayers, which included the clergy and a 5 per cent inflation for the poor, to county totals which lacked both these additional elements. Russell, *British medieval population*, pp. 132–3, 146. Cornwall seems to have truncated his figure for 1689 rather than rounding it to 2 decimal places. A further complication lies in the fact that the tax lists for Berkshire and Worcestershire did not cover the whole county so that Cornwall had to make an additional estimate of appropriate inflation factors to obtain the county totals of taxpayers. *Ibid.*, pp. 37–9.
27. Cornwall, 'English population in the early sixteenth century', p. 39.
28. *Ibid.*, p. 33.

evidence about the point at which the late medieval population had begun to grow. However, unless the adult male population was very seriously under-enumerated in the mid 1520s, it can at least be said that the 15 years before 1541, like the 15 years after that date, witnessed relatively rapid population growth.

Similar problems of estimation and interpretation beset the partial enumerations of the population made at several dates after 1541. In general, the taxation and muster records become progressively less reliable and no modern scholars have used them as a basis for population estimates.[29] In the late eighteenth century Chalmers claimed that the numbers of fighting men in the muster returns of 1575 and 1583 provided a basis for estimating the population of England and Wales at 4.688 million which implies a population of 4.253 million for England alone.[30] Considering the under-enumeration attending these sources at this date, Chalmers's unspecified method of correcting the original data must have been over-generous to have produced so high a population total since table A3.3 shows that back projection finds a population of only 3.526 million in 1579, the mid-point of the period from which Chalmers's data came.

In the absence of suitable state records, historians have generally turned to ecclesiastical surveys as a means of estimating the size of the population. The first of these, a survey of households taken in 1563, has survived for only 11 dioceses and historians have preferred to work with the national coverage afforded by a survey of communicants, non-communicants, and recusants taken in 1603 which listed a total of 2.091 million persons.[31] Sixteen is generally taken to be the age at communion in the seventeenth century, and back-projection results for 1601 indicate that 35.0 per cent of the population was too young to be enumerated in the survey. If this proportion is added to the 2.091 million counted in the documents, the national population total comes to 3.217 million, only 77 per cent of the 4.156 million found by back projection in 1603. It would therefore appear that the communicants survey missed between a quarter and a fifth of the adult population. The only way in which the figure of 2.091 million adults found by the survey can be reconciled with a total population of 4.156 million is for the under-16s to have comprised almost a half (49.7 per cent) of the population. This is highly improbable, because a population as young as this implies very high fertility with a GRR of about 4, a much higher level than the figure of 2.35 found by back projection in 1601, and one not even attained today in countries of high fertility where marriage occurs soon after puberty.[32]

29. Schofield, *Parliamentary lay taxation*, pp. 326–42.
30. The English population is calculated by assuming the Welsh population comprised the same proportion of the total population of England and Wales (0.09288) as in 1603. Alternative proportions based on data from 1690 and 1801 would yield English population totals based on Chalmers' figures of 4.411 and 4.378 million respectively. See fn. 20 above. Chalmers, *Comparative strength of Great Britain*, p. 34.
31. The original returns for 1563 are in the British Museum, Harleian MSS 594–5, 618, while the 1603 survey returns are in Harleian MSS 280, ff. 157–172v. The figure of 2.091 million has been calculated by omitting the Welsh dioceses and revising the totals for the dioceses of Gloucester and Winchester as suggested by Hollingsworth, *Historical demography*, pp. 82–4.
32. The highest contemporary GRRs (1966–74) are to be found in parts of Africa, Asia, and the Middle East and lie in the range 3.0 to 3.5. United Nations, *Demographic Yearbook 1975*, pp. 518–27. A gross reproduction rate of 4 implies a total fertility rate of 8. This is only attainable if the population has the highest age-specific fertility rates ever recorded (that of the present-day Hutterites in North America). Historical European populations usually have lower fertility rates than this. Scott Smith, 'A homeostatic demographic régime', pp. 22–3. Hollingsworth's estimate of about 4 million for the population of England and Wales implies a population for England alone of 3.628 million which in turn implies a gross

This conclusion about the serious incompleteness of the 1603 returns does not augur well for the success of the next survey of communicants, the Compton Census, as a basis for estimating the national population in 1676. The national figures from this survey have long been available in a summary printed by Dalrymple in 1773 but assigned to the year 1688.[33] However, recent research into the detailed parish totals has shown that in some areas the returns referred only to male communicants while in others errors were made in the opposite direction and figures for the total population rather than the numbers of communicants were certified.[34] The figures printed by Dalrymple, therefore, are not strictly speaking the count of communicants that they purport to be. Indeed an estimate based on them as if they referred to communicants, and therefore inflated to cover the population under 16 (back projection suggests that 31.2 per cent of the population was under 16 in 1676) yields a population total of 3.852 million.[35] This figure is 77 per cent of the population total of 5.003 million estimated by back projection for 1676, a shortfall of exactly the same magnitude as occurred in 1603, implying that it was under-enumeration rather than the prevalence of nonconformity in the later seventeenth century that was the chief cause of the deficiency in the returns.

If, however, attention is confined to those parishes in the random sample, discussed in chapter 2, in which the numbers returned in the Compton Census appear to refer strictly to communicants, a different picture emerges. The ratio between the size of the population of these parishes in 1676 and in 1811 is 2.37, using the age structure data of back projection for 1676. Applying this ratio to the national census total of 9.477 million in 1811 implies a population of 4.236 million in 1676, or 85 per cent of the back-projection figure.[36] But the national growth ratio of 2.37 is affected by the presence of a small number of very large and rapidly growing parishes in the random sample. If the growth ratio of parishes whose population was greater than 1,500 in 1811 is modified to reflect the growth experience of the much larger total of parishes in this category in the *aggregative* sample (see table 2.1) the overall ratio is reduced to 1.927. This causes the estimated population size in 1676 to rise to 4.918 million, a total that differs by only 2 per cent from the 5.003 million found by back projection.

---

reproduction rate of about 3.0, rather higher than that found by back projection. Hollingsworth, *Historical demography*, pp. 83–4. Russell estimated the population at 3.78 million, *British medieval population*, p. 270.

33. Dalrymple, *Memoirs of Great Britain and Ireland*, II, appendix, pp. 11–5, cited and discussed in Hollingsworth, *Historical demography*, pp. 81–8. The identification of the 1688 list as a summary of the Compton Census was made by Whiteman, 'The census that never was'. Russell refers to the returns as dating from 1690, *British medieval population*, p. 270.

34. Private communication from Dr A. Whiteman of Lady Margaret Hall, Oxford, who is preparing a critical edition of the Compton Census.

35. This is a maximal estimate based on Hollingsworth's observation (*Historical demography*, p. 85) that the province of York, which was missing from the Compton returns, had 27.5 per cent of the houses of the province of Canterbury in the 1690 Hearth Tax lists. Using Whiteman's figures ('The census that never was', p.1) this gives a total of 2,650,542 communicants in England alone. Dalrymple's 1688 document makes a lower estimate for the missing province of York at 16.7 per cent of the Canterbury total. On this basis the national total of communicants would be reduced to 2,409,130 and the estimated total population would fall to 3.502 million. Hollingsworth does not offer a personal estimate for the Compton census returns but tries to reconcile them with Gregory King's estimate of 5.5 million for the 1690s, *Historical demography*, pp. 85–8. Russell estimates the population of England at 4.08 million on the basis of Dalrymple's list, *British medieval population*, p. 270. A contemporary estimate (*c*. 1670) based on an average of 80 families of seven persons in 9,725 parishes yielded a population size of 5.446 million. Chamberlayne, *Angliae notitia*, I, p. 56, cited in Hollingsworth, *Historical demography*, p. 125.

36. Tables 2.1, 7.8, and A6.7.

The last estimate of the size of the population before 1700 to be based on a partial enumeration is the best known and probably most securely founded of all. Gregory King took as his starting point Davenant's list of the number of houses in the Hearth Tax Office in 1689, inflated them by 5.1 per cent to bring them forward to 1695 and then proceeded to draw upon his vast collection of information about matters social and demographic to estimate the number of empty houses and the average numbers of persons per house in London, market towns, and villages, and so arrive at a total population of England and Wales of 5.503 million. Glass has scrutinized each stage in King's reasoning, taking into account both the information in King's own notebooks and the results of modern research on households in London in the later seventeenth century, and provided an alternative and lower estimate for England and Wales of 4.918 million.[37]

Figures for England alone have had to be derived somewhat circuitously because the only stage at which it is possible to separate England and Wales is in Davenant's original list of the numbers of houses. Since London had a much higher ratio of persons per house than other communities, the Welsh element in the population was calculated by finding the proportion that houses in Wales (77,921) comprised of the total number of houses *excluding* London (1,212,663), namely 6.4256 per cent.[38] On the assumption that household size was on the average the same in Wales as in non-metropolitan England, this percentage for Wales was subtracted from King's figure for the total population excluding London (4.898 million) to yield a figure of 4.583 million. King's estimate of the population of London (585,000) was then added back in to reach a national household population estimate of 5.108 million. To this was added a further 75,000 vagrants on the assumption that King's total of 80,000 should be split between England and Wales in proportion to the numbers of houses in Davenant's list. The result was a figure of 5.183 million as King's estimate of the population of England in 1695. Glass's revision of King's original estimate for England and Wales was concerned with improving the calculations based on Davenant's list of houses, so the same percentage reduction was made to the equivalent element in the estimates for England alone, that is to the 5.108 million household population, and to this was added the estimated 75,000 vagrants, yielding a total revised population of 4.632 million.

The population estimate for 1695 produced by back projection was 4.951 million which falls neatly between King's estimate of 5.183 million and Glass's revised total of 4.632 million, though it is rather closer to the former than to the latter. In view of the considerable element of doubt surrounding many aspects of population estimates of this kind the fit with King's original figure is remarkably good. Although there are reasons for reducing King's figures, as Glass has argued, particularly so far as London is concerned, there may be others that would offset them and leave King's estimate nearer to its original figure than Glass's calculations suggest. For example, in the 1660s, when detailed Hearth Tax returns were made to the exchequer, it can be shown that the central records omitted a proportion of the houses exempt from the tax, and in the later eighteenth century, when evidence is more plentiful, it appears that the size

37. Glass, 'Two papers on Gregory King', pp. 183–204. Davenant's list of houses by county is printed on p. 218.
38. Unfortunately London is amalgamated with Westminster and Middlesex in Davenant's list. From King's workings, as shown in Glass, *ibid.*, p. 201, fn. 49, London had 105,000 out of King's revised total of 1,300,000 houses so this ratio was applied to Davenant's total of 1,319,215 houses to find the number of houses attributable to London for exclusion from Davenant's list.

of the household was negatively rather than positively associated with the size of the village as King had assumed.[39] Since the bulk of the population lived in small settlements, King's population estimate is particularly sensitive to the accuracy of his ratio of 4.04 persons per house in the 'villages and hamlets', and it may well be that this ratio should be increased.

Thus of the pre-1700 population estimates based on partial enumerations it is the first and the last, the chantry certificates and King's manipulation of the Hearth Tax returns, that agree most closely with the figures produced by back projection. A further set of population estimates for this period has been made using the totals of baptisms, burials, and marriages recorded in parish registers. In 1836 Rickman wrote to incumbents with registers extending back at least to 1600 and asked them to return to him the numbers of baptisms, burials, and marriages during a number of three-year periods centred on 1570, 1600, 1630, 1670, 1700, and 1750.[40] In the 1841 census, which appeared after Rickman's death, the totals of events were converted into population estimates by the simple expedient of calculating for each county the ratios between the numbers of events recorded in 1800 in the parishes included in the survey and the county population in the 1801 census and then applying the same ratio to the numbers of events recorded in the sample years back to 1570. In this way at each date three estimates of the population of each county could be made, based on the numbers of baptisms, burials, and marriages respectively, and the county populations summed to provide three estimates of the national population.[41] An alternative set of national estimates was made directly by calculating ratios between the number of events in the whole set of parishes in 1800 and the national population in 1801, but was never published.[42]

For these population estimates to be correct three conditons need to be fulfilled: the parishes with registers back to 1570 must be a continuously representative cross-section of the country, the three-year periods must not be ones in which untypically high or low numbers of vital events occurred, and the ratios between the baptism, burial, and marriage totals in the registers and the population size must be constant at all dates. The tests carried out on the set of 404 parishes established a close correspondence with Rickman's national totals of events and showed that amongst the 404 parishes there was no demographic bias associated with the date at which registration began.[43] Consequently the first condition of representativeness is likely to have been met by Rickman's own group of early-registering parishes. Furthermore, table A5.1 shows that each of the three-year periods selected by Rickman was reasonably typical of the decade in which it was situated so far as the number of events recorded in each series in the set of 404 parishes is concerned, thereby fulfilling the second condition of temporal representativeness.[44] The third condition, however, is

---

39. For the omission of exempt households in the 1660s see Patten, 'Hearth taxes, 1682–9', pp. 18–21; and for the relationship between the size of household and size of settlement see Wall, 'Mean household size in England', p. 195.

40. Rickman knew which parishes had early registers from a previous survey which he had published in the *1831 Census*, Parish register abstract. The accuracy of the 1836 returns is discussed on pp. 66–71, and in appendix 7, pp. 624–9.

41. *1841 Census*, Enumeration abstract, pp. 34–7. The figures for England and Wales were given wider currency by being quoted with approval by Griffith in *Population problems*, p. 12.

42. See above, pp. 70–1.

43. See above, pp. 56–62 (for start of registration) and pp. 66–71 (for agreement with Rickman's totals).

44. The low index of 86 in table A5.1 for burials in the years 1599–1601 reflects the unusually high

Table A5.1: Representativeness of Rickman's sample years, 1569–1751

Years[1]	Baptisms	Index (100 = average of reference decade) Burials	Marriages	Reference decade
1569-71	97	104	102	*1565-74*
1599-1601	103	86	102	*1595-1604*
1629-31	97	96	98	*1625-34*
1669-71	97	103	102	*1665-74*
1699-1701	101	99	102	*1695-1704*
1749-51	92	101	101	*1745-54*

Note: [1] April to March.

Source: Tables A2.3 and A2.4.

more problematical. It is clear from back projection that Rickman's assumption of constant vital rates was badly mistaken and that these rates varied considerably between each of the sample three-year periods and the reference year of 1800.[45] This failure of the method might at first sight appear to prove fatal to the validity of the results. However, Rickman failed to estimate the vital rates correctly in his reference year. Although his figures for 1800 incorporated some nonconformist baptisms and burials, they were based on registered church ceremonies and so omitted a considerable proportion of the true number of births and deaths.[46] Consequently the reference ratios between the numbers of births and deaths on the one hand and the size of the population on the other, were substantially underestimated. At earlier periods the Anglican registers gave a better picture of the number of births and deaths occurring and it is conceivable that the true birth and death rates could have risen over time along with the incidence of nonconformity. Thus a deterioration in registration coverage could have offset real movements in fertility or mortality and produced constant rates in relation to the numbers of baptisms and burials recorded in the Anglican registers. Such a possibility prevents an *a priori* rejection of Rickman's assumptions of constancy in the Anglican rates; but in reality, as back projection shows, changes in the vital rates were not offset by changes in registration coverage.[47]

   The 1841 census published national population totals for each of the three-year periods based on baptisms, burials, and marriages separately, and table A5.2 shows the range of estimates at each date. From 1630 burials consistently yield the highest population totals and the discrepancy between the series is greatest in 1670, a period when the relative levels of fertility and mortality were very different from what they were to be in 1800. These discrepancies were evident in 1841 and a preferred estimate of population size was calculated by taking the arithmetic average of the totals based on the three series. The resulting set of population estimates incorporates a much weaker assumption concerning the constancy of vital rates, for it only requires the average of the three rates to have been constant over time.[48] This is much more realistic since movements in the death rates tended in general to offset rather than

mortality of 1597–8 and 1602–3 which were included in the reference decade. It is these years, rather than Rickman's sample years of 1599–1601, that were untypical.

45. See table A3.3.
46. See pp. 74–6 and 625, and table 5.27.
47. For vital rates see appendix 3 and for under-registration see tables 5.25 and 5.26.
48. This point was stressed in Deane and Cole, *British economic growth*, p. 100.

Table A5.2: National population totals from Rickman's 1836 survey (England less Monmouth), and from back projection (in millions)

	(1)	(2)	(3)	(4)	(5)	(6)
	Population totals based on sum of counties				National figures	
Period	Baptisms	Burials	Marriages	Average	Average	Back projection[1]
1569–71	3.587	3.830	3.979	3.798	3.721	3.255
1599–1601	4.500	4.001	4.797	4.433	4.352	4.066
1629–31	5.098	5.371	5.117	5.196	5.131	4.884
1669–71	4.897	6.706	4.494	5.366	5.279	5.022
1699–1701	5.364	6.208	5.307	5.626	5.522	5.027
1749–51	5.869	6.296	5.938	6.034	5.922	5.739

Note: [1] Totals refer to centre year of period (e.g. 1570, 1600).

Sources: Cols. (1) to (4) *1841 Census*, 'Enumeration abstract', p. 37.
Col. (5) General Register Office Library, M74.10, MS notebook as described in appendix 7, fn. 10.
Col. (6) table A3.3.

reinforce movements in the birth and marriage rates.[49] The 'average' population estimates are also shown in table A5.2 along with the parallel set of unpublished average estimates which were calculated on the basis of national rather than county vital rates, and both are compared with the population totals found by back projection. The back-projection estimates are always below Rickman's average figures, and generally below even the lowest of the estimates based on individual series, but apart from 1570 and 1700 the percentage differences are small. Even at their worst Rickman's averages are generally superior to estimates based on other methods and sources.

Figure A5.1 brings together the several different estimates of population size discussed in the preceding pages, and shows how they compare with the quinquennial totals produced by back projection. The figures plotted form the basis of the statements about population size to be found in a large number of articles, monographs, and general textbooks, and the wide range of choice on offer in the secondary literature reflects the considerable discrepancies between the several estimates as is evident in figure A5.1.[50] It is also clear from the figure that the estimates of population size based on the returns of communicants in 1603 and 1676 are substantially lower than those derived from any other source.

Overall the earlier estimates form a wide band of points through which the results of back projection steer a fairly middling course. Starting in the mid 1540s in general agreement with the revised figures from the chantry certificates, the back-projection estimates pass below all but a few of the lowest ranges of Rickman's estimates and well above the figures based on the returns of communicants to conclude with a population size in 1696 very close to what Gregory King estimated it to have been at the time. Apart from 1570 and 1700, back projection confirms the broad accuracy of Rickman's estimates of population size averaged over baptisms, burials, and marriages and published as long ago as 1841, even though they are from 5 to 8 per cent

49. See tables A3.1 and A3.3.
50. In several cases the figures cited in the literature refer to England and Wales while those presented and discussed here refer to England alone. For the ratios between the populations of the two countries at various dates see fn. 20 above and the references cited there.

Population
(millions)

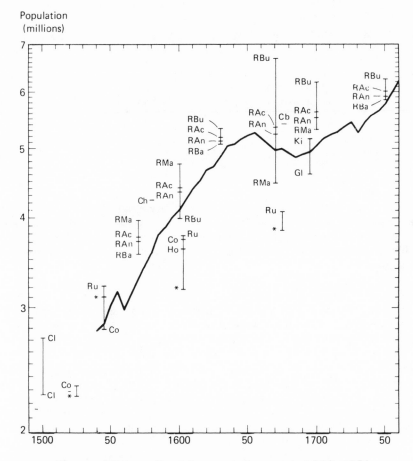

Figure A5.1:   English population totals 1500–1751

Key and sources:

Cb	Chamberlayne, *Anglia notitia*, ɪ, p.56 cited in Hollingsworth, *Historical demography*, p.125.
Ch	Chalmers, *Comparative strength of Great Britain*, p.34.
Cl	Clapham, *Concise economic history*, p.78.
Co	Cornwall, 'English population in the early sixteenth century', p.44.
Gl	Glass, see text and fn.37.
Ho	Hollingsworth, see text and fn.32.
Ki	King, see text and fn.37.
RAc	Rickman (1841), average of county estimates, see table A5.2.
RAn	Rickman (1841), national average, see table A5.2.
RBa	Rickman (1841), estimate based on baptisms, see table A5.2.
RBu	Rickman (1841), estimate based on burials, see table A5.2.
RMa	Rickman (1841), estimate based on marriages, see table A5.2.
Ru	Russell, *British medieval population*, (1545) p.272, (1603, 1676) p.270.

(*cont.*)

Figure A5. 1:   *(cont.)*

*	For amendments to estimates in 1524, 1545, 1603, and 1676, see text.
⌐	Back projection.
Notes:	Only the maximum and minimum of Rickman's estimates based on individual series are shown.
	Certain estimates were originally made for England and Wales and have been reduced to refer to England alone as follows:
	1500, 1579, 1603 (Hollingsworth): England and Wales figure multiplied by 0.90712, the ratio of the number of communicants in England to the number in England and Wales in 1603. Hollingsworth, *Historical demography*, pp.83-4.
	1695: see text.

too high. These figures were born of what on the face of it should have been a fatal combination of a serious miscalculation of vital rates for the year 1800 and a false assumption of demographic constancy over time. That despite this handicap they should have come so near to the mark furnishes a classic example of historical serendipity.

Population estimates after 1700

Unfortunately the same cannot be said of an earlier set of population estimates for the eighteenth century which Rickman made in 1801.[51] In this case the estimates were based on the numbers of baptisms, burials, and marriages recorded nationally in the parish registers every tenth year from 1700 to 1780 and then annually until 1800.[52] There are problems with the unrepresentativeness of some of the years sampled in the early eighteenth century, which will be considered below, but the main reason for the unsatisfactoriness of the series of population estimates Rickman published in the 1801 census is that they were calculated by applying a constant vital rate to the series of baptism totals alone. Once more the rate was that obtaining in 1800, but on this occasion there was no opportunity of rescue from further offsetting errors amongst the other two series of events. As a result Rickman's baptism-based population estimates are in general too low by comparison with back projection up to 1720, but too high thereafter.[53] The overall effect is to exaggerate the rate of population growth particularly in the 1760s.

The national totals of baptisms, burials, and marriages that Rickman collected in 1801 have formed the basis of several further attempts to estimate the size of the population at 10-year intervals during the eighteenth century. But instead of following Rickman in applying fixed vital rates to the numbers of events recorded, later scholars have preferred to adopt a more complicated approach. First they have estimated correction factors to convert Rickman's figures of baptisms and burials into totals of births and deaths, and then, on the assumption that the population was closed, they have calculated population sizes by working backwards from the population total given in the 1801 census, successively subtracting the surplus of births over deaths occurring in each intervening decade. All start from the same basic data and all share the assumption that there was no net migration. But they differ in

51. *1801 Census*, Observations on the results, p. 9.
52. Annual totals of marriages were returned from 1754. The data are discussed extensively in appendix 7.
53. However, Rickman's figure for 1700 is above that found by back projection.

Table A5.3: Population estimates for England (1701–1801) based on
the Parish Register Abstracts;[1] and on present data (in millions)

	Parish Register Abstracts						Present data	
	Rickman[2]	Finlaison[2]	Farr[2]	Brownlee[2]	Griffith[2]	Ohlin	Lee and Schofield	Back projection
	(1801)	(1831)	(1861)	(1916)	(1926)	(1955)		
1701	5.112	4.795	5.716	5.440	5.449	4.90	4.94	5.058
1711	4.893	4.675	5.838	5.585	5.615	5.11	5.15	5.230
1721	5.197	4.991	5.839	5.604	5.648	5.16	5.29	5.350
1731	5.412	5.312	5.774	5.553	5.610	5.15	5.22	5.263
1741	5.663	5.444	5.746	5.534	5.615	5.18	5.55	5.576
1751	6.039	5.640	5.917	5.734	5.839	5.45	5.79	5.772
1761	6.290	6.051	6.276	6.134	6.224	5.90	6.18	6.147
1771	6.936	6.750	6.680	6.535	6.653	6.41	6.51	6.448
1781	7.427	7.298	7.073	7.033	7.080	6.90	7.07	7.042
1791	8.101	7.976	7.710	7.701	7.672	7.64	7.67	7.740
1801	8.561	8.579	8.585	8.550	8.561	8.55	8.55	8.664

Notes: [1] With the exception of the final two columns the estimates were originally made for
England and Wales and have been deflated by 0.93383 to obtain figures relevant to England
(less Monmouth). The deflation factor has been based on 1801 population figures for England
and Wales (8 872 980) and England less Monmouth (8 285 852), i.e. excluding armed forces and
others temporarily abroad. In the case of Rickman, Finlaison, and Griffith the estimates refer
to 1700, 1710, etc., rather than 1701, 1711, etc.
[2] Figures for England and Wales printed in Glass, 'Population and population movements',
p. 240.

Sources: Rickman, *1801 Census*, Observations on the results, p. 9.
Finlaison, *1831 Census*, Enumeration abstract, p. xlv.
Farr, *1851 Census*, Ages, civil conditions, etc., I, p. lxviii.
Brownlee, 'The history of birth and death rates in England and Wales', p. 228.
Griffith, *Population problems*, p. 18.
Ohlin, *The positive and preventive check*, p. 263.
Lee and Schofield, 'British population in the eighteenth century'.
Back projection, table A3.1.

their calculations of the numbers of births and deaths that the registered totals of
baptisms and burials imply, obtain different surpluses of births over deaths in each
decade, and hence arrive at different estimates of population size.[54]

The resulting range of population totals at different points in the eighteenth century
can be seen in table A5.3 and figure A5.2. The two earliest sets of calculations based
on Rickman's data after those of Rickman himself provide the most extreme estimates
of population size, at least over the first few decades of the century. Finlaison, in
1831, began by calculating that burials in the mid nineteenth century needed to be
inflated by 7.9 per cent to yield the number of deaths. He then assumed that there was
no net migration between the censuses of 1821 and 1831 so that the intercensal
increase in the size of the population was entirely due to the surplus of births over
deaths. Having calculated the number of deaths by multiplying the number of
registered burials by 1.079 he deduced that the number of registered baptisms needed
to be increased by 24 per cent in order to arrive at the right total of births between 1821
and 1831. These two inflation ratios (1.24 for baptisms and 1.079 for burials) were
then applied to Rickman's totals of events at all dates. The gap between the two

54. For a critical discussion of methods applied by various scholars to the PRA data see Glass, 'Population
and population movements'. The numbers of vital events they severally estimate for the period 1700–1840
are discussed and compared with our own estimates on pp. 142–52 and in tables 5.28 to 5.30.

Population
(millions)

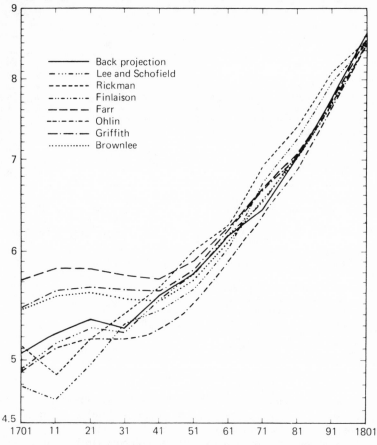

Figure A5.2: English population totals 1701–1801

Source: Table A5.3

inflation ratios (16.1 per cent) was rather larger than that used by subsequent scholars and it had the effect of producing larger decadal totals of natural increase which, when successively subtracted from the 1801 population total, furnished very low estimates of population size in the early eighteenth century.[55]

Farr, on the other hand, appears to have taken a quite different course, starting with the observation that in the first decade of the nineteenth century the excess of baptisms over burials needed to be increased by 'nearly one third part' in order to attain the amount of population growth that occurred between the censuses of 1801 and 1811. He then assumed that the same relative degree of under-registration obtained in the

55. *1831 Census*, Enumeration abstract, p. xlv. The description of the method is unclear, and it should be noted that it is difficult to reconcile these inflation ratios and the PRA returns with Finlaison's population totals.

eighteenth century and increased the decadal surpluses of baptisms over burials by 33 per cent back to 1740. Between 1710 and 1740 burials exceeded baptisms, so Farr made a further assumption that the shortfall was entirely due to missing baptisms. He calculated that in the 1740s this was equivalent to about 2.5 per cent of the numbers of baptisms recorded, and proceeded to add 2.5 per cent to the baptisms recorded in each decade before 1740.[56] This is equivalent to postulating a gap of 2.5 per cent between the inflation ratios to be applied to baptisms and burials, and it is interesting to note that Farr's procedure of multiplying the decadal baptism – burial surpluses after 1740 by 1.33 is equivalent to postulating a wider gap of about 5 per cent in the inflation ratios of the two series in most of the later decades of the century, and one of about 11 per cent in the 1790s. These figures are much lower than Finlaison's constant gap of 16.1 per cent between the inflation ratios for the two series, and it is scarcely surprising that Farr obtained much lower decadal totals of natural increase, and hence much higher population estimates. Indeed Farr's figures are the highest of all in the first four decades of the century.[57]

Early in the twentieth century two further attempts were made to derive estimates of population size from the totals of baptisms and burials in the Parish Register Abstracts. Both Brownlee and Griffith used the transition from ecclesiastical to vital registration in the 1830s, along with data from the censuses, to estimate the shortfall between baptisms and births and between burials and deaths. They differed in their methods, Brownlee's approach being considerably the more complex, and so arrived at rather different results (Brownlee favouring 1.243 and 1.200, and Griffith 1.15 and 1.10, as inflation ratios for baptisms and burials respectively).[58] However they obtained almost the same difference between the inflation ratios for baptisms and burials (4.3 per cent with Brownlee and 5.0 per cent with Griffith), figures that were close to Farr's in the later eighteenth century and well below Finlaison's difference of 16.1 per cent between the baptism and burial inflation ratios. Consequently, Brownlee and Griffith obtained similar and relatively low totals of natural increase, leading to similar estimates of population size, which in the first half of the century were much closer to Farr's high figures than to Finlaison's low estimates of population size.

More recently Ohlin has reworked Rickman's data, but his results have only been published in summary form. Ohlin began with two fixed points, the population as enumerated in the 1801 census and a figure of 5.25 million for England and Wales in 1701 based on Glass's revision of Gregory King's near-contemporary estimate.

56. Farr is but one of three signatories to the section of the 1851 census that contained these estimates, but he is usually credited with authorship. In discussing the procedures adopted for the period before 1740 the census report states that 'by referring back to the probable deficient registration of baptisms in the earlier period the series is carried back to 1701'. *1851 Census*, Ages, civil conditions etc., p. lxviii, reprinted in *1861 Census*, General report, p. 22 and appendix A, p. 56, table 61. Ohlin established that Farr in practice added 2.5 per cent to baptisms before 1740 and that the 'earlier period' cited in the census report was probably the 1740s when one third of the excess of baptisms over burials equalled 2.54 per cent of the number of baptisms. Ohlin, *The positive and preventive check*, pp. 234–6.

57. In 1871 Farr published details of a method of estimating the shortfall between baptisms and births back to 1740, similar to that adopted here in chapter 5, but the resulting figures do not appear to have been incorporated in his estimates of natural increase and population size. *1871 Census*, General report, pp. xiii–xiv, 54–6. Farr's calculations are discussed in Glass, 'Population and population movements', pp. 225–8 and his estimated decadal totals of births are tabulated on p. 227.

58. Brownlee, 'The history of birth and death rates in England and Wales', pp. 218–22; Griffith, *Population problems*, pp. 15–7. Brownlee's methods are discussed extensively in Glass, 'Population and population movements', pp. 228–37.

Assuming that there was no net migration, he then compared the excess of baptisms over burials implied by Rickman's PRA returns with the natural increase implied by the two population totals, and calculated that for the former to equal the latter the inflation factor applied to baptisms would have to be about 7 or 8 per cent higher on average than the inflation factor applied to burials. He used early-nineteenth-century data to obtain an inflation ratio of 1.20 for burials and hence a factor of 1.27 for baptisms, and provided a lower alternative pair of average ratios of 1.15 and 1.23 on the assumption that burials must have been under-registered by at least 10 per cent in 1700. The resulting estimates of population size were virtually identical and the figures discussed here are Ohlin's preferred series obtained with the constant baptism and burial inflation ratios of 1.27 and 1.20 respectively.[59]

In 1974 Lee published a new and more sophisticated method of extracting information on fertility and mortality, as well as on the size and age structure of a population, from totals of births and deaths. Lee's technique, which he called 'inverse projection', is analogous to the method of back projection outlined in appendix 15, but differs from it in that it runs forward in time and assumes the population to have been closed. Lee tried his technique on the eighteenth-century PRA data by starting in 1701 with a population of 5.826 million (Brownlee's figure) to which he assigned an age structure suitable for a population with an expectation of life at birth of 30 years and that was growing at 0.5 per cent a year. The projection was then made on the basis of decadal totals of births and deaths which Lee calculated from the PRA returns in the manner of Brownlee. Although new estimates of fertility and mortality were obtained, the decadal population totals found by inverse projection were almost exactly the same as Brownlee's figures and so will not be further commented on here.[60] Inverse projection has also been applied to national series of births and deaths based on the set of 404 parishes, which differ only marginally from those presented in appendix 2. Not surprisingly the resulting estimates of population size are closer to the totals found by back projection than to estimates based on the PRA returns. However, inverse projection finds rather lower population sizes in the early eighteenth century. This is partly because the projection worked from a lower 1801 population total, partly because it assumed population closure, and partly because the surplus of births over deaths was smaller.[61]

The validity of the various sets of estimates of population size derived from Rickman's totals of baptisms and burials depends upon three factors: the representativeness and accuracy of the data, the appropriateness of the inflation factors by which baptisms are converted into births and burials into deaths, and the reality of the assumption that net migration in England was zero throughout the eighteenth century. On the first point appendix 7 shows that the PRA data are marred by inaccuracies in the figures returned by individual incumbents and by some slipshod aggregation of the parish totals into county and national aggregates.[62] A more serious failing from the present point of view, however, lies in the unrepresentativeness of the years for which Rickman collected the totals of baptisms and burials, particularly in the first half of the

59. Ohlin, *The positive and the preventive check*, pp. 254–5, 260–4. His population totals have been incorporated in a figure in Reinhard, Armengaud, and Dupâquier, *Histoire générale*, p. 203.
60. Lee, 'Estimating vital rates', esp. p. 505.
61. Lee and Schofield, 'British population in the eighteenth century'. Between the two projections further work was done on the nineteenth-century censuses and this resulted in slightly higher inflations of the numbers of births and deaths from about 1775 onwards.
62. See pp. 597–619.

eighteenth century. It was shown in chapter 3, and particularly in table 3.4, that there was a close agreement between the PRA totals and the numbers of baptisms and burials recorded in the same sample years in the set of 404 aggregative parishes.[63] The annual totals of events available for the latter can therefore be used to test the typicality of the years included in the PRA returns. Table A5.4 indexes the number of events recorded in each of the PRA sample years on the annual average frequency of the 'decade' of which each PRA year forms the centre.[64] For example, an index of 100

Table A5.4: Representativeness of the Parish Register Abstract sample years (annual average of surrounding decade = 100)

Year[1]	(1) Baptisms	(2) Burials	(3) Ratio (1)/(2)
1700	101	99	102
1710	93	103	90
1720	91	112	81
1730	96	103	93
1740	100	104	96
1750	106	104	102
1760	100	96	104
1770	104	103	101
1780	101	106	95

Note: [1] Individual years run from April until following March from 1700 to 1750, and from January to December thereafter. Up to 1750 the bounds of the surrounding decade are October ('year − 5) to September ('year' + 5), from 1760 the bounds run from July ('year' − 5) to June ('year' + 5).

Source: Estimated national totals of baptisms and burials: annual totals, table A4.1, col. 5; monthly totals unpublished.

for baptisms in 1760 would signify that the number of events recorded for that year equalled the annual average of events recorded in the decade running from July 1755 to June 1765. Since most incumbents appear to have followed the Old Style year, in totalling events for the years before 1753 the individual 'years' in the table run from April to March and the bounds of the surrounding decades are adjusted to run from October to September.[65] It is clear from the table that in picking the first year in each decade Rickman alighted upon years which tended to record below-average numbers of baptisms in 1710, 1720, and 1730 and above-average numbers in 1750 and 1770. At the same time all except two of the sample years (1700 and 1760) recorded above-average numbers of burials, with 1720 standing out as exceptionally mortal. If the index scores of baptisms and burials are considered together and expressed as a ratio the PRA sample years are well below average in the ratio of baptisms to burials

63. See pp. 66–76.
64. The figures tabulated are estimated national totals of ecclesiastical events, including corrections for defective registration, population size bias, and the omission of London, but excluding any corrections to convert the data into series of vital events. Annual totals of these series of baptisms and burials are given in table A4.1.
65. See pp. 613–9. In practice the Old Style year usually began, as in principle it should, on 25 March. As the data were tabulated by calendar month the year was split on the March–April border.

between 1710 and 1740, and again in 1780, with 1720 standing out as markedly untypical of its 'decade'. On the other hand 1700, 1750, and 1770 were reasonably representative, while 1760 recorded an above-average ratio between baptisms and burials.

The typicality of the ratios between baptisms and burials in the sample years is crucial to the calculation of population size from the PRA totals because these ratios determine the amount of natural increase occurring over a whole decade. Since no net migration is permitted, the ratios therefore also effectively determine the rate of population growth. The index numbers given in table A5.4 do not augur well for the representativeness of the sample years, and table A5.5 shows the extent to which they give a true or false picture of the size of the surplus of baptisms over burials at different points in the eighteenth century. The first column in the table gives the baptism – burial surplus in each decade, following the most usual method adopted by scholars who rely on the PRA totals, whereby the decadal surplus is calculated from the averages of the baptisms and burials in the two sample years bounding the decade.[66] Thus the surplus recorded for 1720, for example, contributes towards the calculation of two decadal surpluses, 1710–20 and 1720–30, having equal weight with the surpluses recorded in the years 1710 and 1730 in the respective calculations. The second column of the table shows the actual surplus in each decade when

Table A5.5: Decadal baptism-burial surpluses calculated from Parish Register Abstracts sample years and from all years (thousands).[1]

Decade	(1) PRA years	(2) All years	(3) PRA deficiency (2) – (1)
1700s	57.5	166.4	108.9
1710s	−148.8	92.3	241.1
1720s	−191.6	−111.6	80.0
1730s	−58.2	198.3	256.5
1740s	183.7	88.9	−94.8
1750s	298.8	290.8	−8.0
1760s	313.0	209.4	−103.6
1770s	315.0	442.9	127.9

Notes: [1] 'PRA years' 1700, '10, '20, '30, and '50 run April to subsequent March; 1760, '70, and '80 run January to December. Decadal surplus calculated as average of surpluses in the two boundary years (e.g. 1700 and 1710).

'All years' include all events in the ten calendar years January 1700 to December 1709, etc.

Source: Estimated national totals of baptisms and burials: annual totals, table A4.1, col. 5; monthly totals unpublished.

66. Thus Farr, Griffith, and Ohlin; though Griffith rather curiously states that he took the PRA years to be 'representative of the decade of which they are the centre'. Griffith, *Population problems*, p. 18. Brownlee interpolated through groups of years by means of 'mechanical quadrature' but notes that this method produced results not greatly different from those obtained by taking a mean of the terminal frequencies of each decade; Brownlee, 'The history of birth and death rates in England and Wales', p. 228. Finlaison's procedures remain obscure.

baptisms and burials for all years are taken into account and the third column gives the amount by which the PRA-based estimates exceed or fall short of the true decadal totals.[67]

It is evident from table A5.5 that the PRA sample years give a very misleading impression of the balance between baptisms and burials over most of the eighteenth century. In the first four decades, and again in the 1770s, they understate the size of the baptism surplus (or exaggerate the burial surplus), while in the intervening period they exaggerate the size of the surplus in the 1740s and 1760s, but get it about right in the 1750s. The years from 1710 to 1740, which emerged from table A5.4 as being markedly untypical in one or both series, wreak havoc on the decadal baptism – burial surpluses in the first half of the century. For example, in both the 1710s and the 1730s the PRA sample years 'lose' about a quarter of a million events and so turn large decadal surpluses into serious deficits. As a result the PRA totals substantially underestimate the amount of natural increase before 1740 and slightly overestimate it in the mid century. This consistent bias is reflected in almost all of the estimates of population size based on natural increase calculated from the PRA returns, for they show little, if any, growth up to 1740 followed by considerable rises between 1740 and 1780. In contrast, population totals calculated from a full set of annual totals of baptisms and burials might be expected to show more signs of growth in the early eighteenth century and greater sluggishness in the period 1740–80.

After 1780 the PRA totals were collected for each year, so their representativeness is not at issue. However the two other factors that affect the validity of the population -size estimates, namely the inflation ratios to be applied to baptisms and burials to convert them into totals of births and deaths, and the assumption of zero net migration, are relevant throughout the century. Since it is the sizes of the decadal totals of natural increase that determine population size, the critical figure in this context is the difference between the inflation ratios to be applied to baptisms and burials. It will be remembered that although Brownlee and Griffith selected rather different inflation ratios for baptisms and burials the difference between them was in each case very similar at 4.23 and 5.00 per cent respectively. With Ohlin baptisms were inflated 7 per cent more than burials, while with Finlaison the gap was much wider at 16.1 per cent. Only Farr allowed for a varying difference in the inflation ratios, rising from 2.5 per cent before 1740 to 5 per cent in the later eighteenth century, and 10.8 per cent in the 1790s. The present set of national series of vital events also incorporates a changing difference in the inflation ratios, since the testimony of family reconstitution, the internal consistency of the early-nineteenth-century censuses, and the history of dissent all suggested that the escape from Anglican registration both differed as between baptisms and burials and was far from constant over time.[68]

The varying inflation ratios applied to baptisms and burials have been tabulated on a decadal basis in table 5.27, but here it may be noted that the difference between the ratios for the two series lay at around 6 per cent in the first four decades of the century, rose a little to about 7 per cent in the 1740s and 1750s, 7.5 per cent in the 1760s and 1770s, and then reached 9.2 and 9.7 per cent in the last two decades of the century. These differences are therefore always higher than those applied to the PRA totals by Farr, Brownlee, and Griffith (except Farr in the 1790s) and always lower than those

---

67. A *very* small part of the discrepancy is due to the fact that from 1700 to 1750 inclusive the PRA totals were collected on the basis of the Old Style calendar, a feature preserved in column 1 of table A5.5.
68. See chs. 4 and 5.

applied by Finlaison. Up to 1780 they are close to the constant difference of 7 per cent adopted by Ohlin. If the present set of inflation ratios is accepted as broadly correct then it would appear that Finlaison always over-inflated baptisms relative to burials, thereby producing exaggerated totals of natural increase, particularly in the early eighteenth century. By the same standard Farr, Brownlee, and Griffith under-inflated baptisms relative to burials so that their figures for natural increase were always too low and became more seriously under-stated as the century progressed. Ohlin, on the other hand, got the relative inflation of baptisms to burials about right up to 1780 but a little too low after that date.

Although scholars have differed over the amount by which the baptisms and burials enumerated in the PRA returns should be inflated in order to arrive at totals of vital events, they have agreed in considering the population to have been closed. Consequently their estimates of population size at different dates have been entirely determined by the amount of natural increase that their respective inflations of the PRA returns produced. But the assumption that there was no net migration from England during the eighteenth century is implausible in view of the numbers leaving for the Americas, not to mention those dying abroad or at sea.[69] If the estimates produced by back projection are taken as a reasonable indication of the level of migration and other losses, then over most of the century there was a net loss of about 1 per cent of the population in each decade.

If the three potential sources of error affecting the validity of population estimates based on the PRA returns are considered together it can be seen that they sometimes offset and sometimes reinforced each other. Since all estimates are based on the PRA sample year totals and all share the assumption of a closed population it will be convenient to begin by taking these two factors together. Tables A5.4 and A5.5 showed that many of the sample years were untypical and that they understated the amount of natural increase in the first four decades of the eighteenth century and in the 1770s. On the other hand the PRA returns overstated natural increase in the 1740s and 1760s, and recorded it correctly in the 1750s and in the last two decades of the century. In order to arrive at population growth totals all figures of natural increase need to be reduced by the net outmigration that occurred during the eighteenth century. The general failure to make this reduction by assuming a closed population therefore helped to offset the PRA's understatement of natural increase in the first four decades of the century and in the 1770s, but led to an overstatement of population growth in the 1750s, 1780s, and 1790s (when the PRA returns recorded the natural increase correctly), and exaggerated even further the PRA's overstatement of natural increase in the 1740s and 1760s.

Superimposed on this common pattern are the effects of the different relative inflation ratios for baptisms and burials favoured by individual scholars. In general, Finlaison's ratios, which boost natural increase far more than would appear warranted, have the same effect as the failure to take account of migration – that is they offset the understatement of population growth in the early eighteenth century inherent in the PRA returns and exaggerate it at other times. In contrast, the ratios of Farr, Brownlee, and Griffith understate natural increase and so work in the opposite direction, reinforcing the understatement of population growth in the early part of the century, but offsetting the exaggeration of growth later in the century consequent upon the failure to take account of outmigration.

69. See pp. 224–6, above.

Table A5.6 shows how far the different quantities involved in each of the three potential sources of error combined in practice to produce similar or different growth rates in each of the sets of population estimates based on the PRA returns. So far as Farr, Brownlee, and Griffith are concerned, the varying amounts of error inherent in each of the three sources offset each other in five of the decades in the century (the 1700s, 1740s, and 1750s, and the 1780s and 1790s) so that they obtained about the same rates of population growth that were found by back projection. However the distortion introduced by the unrepresentativeness of the PRA sample years between 1710 and 1740 was so great that other errors and omissions were unable to save these scholars from substantially underestimating the extent both of the growth in population in the 1710s and 1730s and of the decline in the 1720s. In addition the under-assessment of natural increase in the 1770s and its over-assessment in the 1760s in the PRA returns was reflected in a corresponding under- and over-assessment by these scholars of population growth in these decades.

Table A5.6: Decadal population growth (1701-1801): rates per 1 000 starting population

Decade	Rickman	Finlaison	Farr	Brownlee	Griffith	Ohlin	Lee and Schofield	Back projection
1701-11	−43	−25	21	27	30	43	43	34
1711-21	62	68	0	4	6	10	27	23
1721-31	41	64	−11	−9	−7	−1	−13	−16
1731-41	46	25	−4	−3	1	6	63	59
1741-51	66	36	30	36	40	52	43	35
1751-61	42	73	61	70	65	83	67	65
1761-71	103	115	64	74	69	86	53	49
1771-81	71	81	59	68	64	76	86	92
1781-91	91	93	90	96	84	107	85	99
1791-1801	57	76	113	110	116	119	115	119

Source: Table A5.3.

Finlaison's population estimates are based on inflation ratios that exaggerate the amount of natural increase by the standard of the inflation ratios adopted here. Unfortunately it is difficult to compare Finlaison's figures with other population estimates because of the obscure way in which he calculated decadal totals of events from the PRA sample years. Nevertheless, as expected, he obtains growth rates in the first four decades of the century much higher than those estimated by any other scholar.[70] By the standards of back projection he grossly exaggerates the amount of growth in the 1710s, and even points to a similar growth rate in the 1720s when back projection indicates that the population was falling. On the credit side he alone detects the existence of substantial population growth in the 1730s, and his growth rates from the 1740s onwards are more or less consistent with back projection, except that he understates the rate of growth in the 1790s and wildly exaggerates the rate of population growth in the 1760s.

Since Ohlin's results were obtained by applying inflation ratios that boosted baptisms relative to burials by almost the same amount as was the case with the present data, his population growth figures illustrate rather neatly the combined

70. The heavy fall in the population in the 1700s is an egregious exception.

effects of an erroneous assumption that the population was closed and the unrepresentativeness of the PRA sample of years. In general his results are similar to those obtained by Farr, Brownlee, and Griffith and he too fails to capture the full extent of population change between 1710 and 1740. However, he consistently records higher growth rates than these other scholars and so rather overestimates the amount of population growth between 1740 and 1770.

Lee's population totals are of particular interest since they were based on data that differed only very slightly from the present estimated national series of vital events and were derived by applying a method of estimation which is analogous to back projection. Since the major difference between 'inverse' and 'back' projection lies in the former's assumption of a closed population, a comparison between the two sets of results brings out very clearly the consequences of ignoring migration when charting the course of population growth in the eighteenth century. Not surprisingly in view of their common basis in the same vital data, the two sets of population estimates show a similar pattern in their changing decadal population growth rates (table A5.6). But Lee's assumption of no net migration entails retaining all natural increase within the population. Consequently his population growth rates are consistently higher than those of back projection until the 1770s when differences in the data cause back projection to find greater rates of increase. As a consequence of his higher rates of growth Lee's population estimate of 4.94 million in 1701 is the third lowest of all, some 0.118 million below the population total found by back projection.

Figure A5.2 (p. 578) brought together the various population-size estimates which have been based either on the PRA returns or on the present estimated national series of events and which have been tabulated in table A5.3. If Rickman's egregious figures based on a constant baptism rate are ignored, the sets of estimates tell much the same story at the end of the century between 1771 and 1801. In the middle of the century, from 1741 to 1761, the population totals are spread over a wider range, while before 1740 the estimates based on the PRA returns have suggested anything from population stagnation (Farr, Brownlee, Griffith, and Ohlin) to quite substantial growth (Rickman and Finlaison).

Back projection treads a fairly middling path finding a population of 5.058 million in 1701, part way between the estimates of Brownlee and Griffith on the one hand, and Ohlin and Lee on the other, but nearer to the latter. However, back projection goes on to find more evidence of population decline in the 1720s than in any other set of estimates followed by substantial growth in the 1730s. This was a controversial decade in which Rickman and Lee adumbrated the back-projection result, while Finlaison found modest growth and Farr, Brownlee, Griffith, and Ohlin recorded stagnation or decline. The present series of vital events therefore show that the PRA returns badly obscured what really happened in the 1730s and restore strong, but not overwhelming, population growth to a decade which saw the lowest food prices and highest real wages since the 1520s, the latter at a level not to be surpassed until the 1840s (appendix 9). Consequently, despite its relatively modest start in 1701, the population total that back projection finds for 1741 is near the centre of the range of earlier estimates (5.576 million).

In the mid-century decades all sets of estimates record generally similar rates of growth except that in the 1760s back projection falls behind the rest, largely because it takes cognizance of some years of heavy mortality (1762–3 and 1766–7) which escaped the PRA returns, and so its population total for 1771 is a little below that of most other sets of estimates. At the end of the century back projection produces faster rates of growth than anyone except Ohlin and its population estimate for 1801 (8.664 millions) is about 1 per cent higher than the total enumerated in the 1801 census, which is the point of departure of most other series of estimates.[71]

In general, therefore, the present population totals based on back projection differ most from previous estimates in the course they chart in the period 1701 to 1741. Starting the century with a population total that lay towards the lower end of the range of earlier estimates, back projection traces a more lively course with a falling population in the 1720s and a decade of particularly marked growth in the 1730s. With the advantage of totals of events for every year, and not merely for every tenth year, back projection is able to bring to light hitherto hidden aspects of population change both during the first 40 years of the eighteenth century and, less dramatically, in the 1760s. The combination of full annual data, variable inflation ratios, and attention to net migration makes little difference to the course of population change after 1751 plotted by earlier scholars, but before that date it reveals a new outline of clear, if modest and interrupted, population growth between 1701 and 1751. The rise, at 14 per cent, is larger than that in any earlier estimates with the exception of those made by Rickman and Finlaison.

Thus in the eighteenth century, as in earlier periods, the population totals produced by back projection thread their way through a band of earlier estimates calculated by a wide variety of methods. As has been shown above, back projection appears to be a robust method of estimating population size.[72] It would therefore appear that almost any reasonable correction of the deficiencies inherent in parish registration would leave the course of population change very much as depicted here and firmly within the range of expectation generated by earlier estimates.

For some readers the results of back projection may have proved disappointing in that they lack the excitement of the wholly unexpected. But while some features of the story told here, for example the growth of population in the sixteenth and eighteenth centuries, have long been familiar, the precise size of the population at any date and the rates of growth that obtained at different points in time before 1801 have been matters of considerable debate.[73] In the event, the effect of the use of back projection has been rather like the scraping away of layers of old varnish from a picture: the shapes of some previously obscure outlines have become more distinct and some unsuspected features have been revealed. The uncertainty and the scope for debate is now greatly diminished.

---

71. Some scholars adjusted their population size estimates to mid-year values, for example Farr to mid 1801 and Finlaison to mid 1800. See sources cited at foot of table A5.3.
72. See above, pp. 269–83.
73. See, for example, Habbakuk, 'The economic history of modern Britain', pp. 488–91; Tucker, 'Population in history', and 'Population trends'; and Flinn, *British population growth*. One scholar, at least, has felt that the quest for knowledge was hopeless: 'any attempt to estimate the total population at any period [before 1801] must always involve a confidence in a multiplicator which none but the wilfully deluded can feel'. Rich, 'Population of Elizabethan England', p. 247.

Appendix 6

English population totals 1801—71

The population totals returned in the nineteenth-century English censuses should only be compared with one another with some caution since they were subject to a number of distorting influences which affected the different censuses in varying degree. In this appendix we attempt to reduce the difficulties of direct comparison by proposing modifications to the published totals designed to offset three distorting influences: the fact that census night varied from early March to early June; the under-registration of young children; and the failure of the census to include men in the armed forces and the merchant marine. It was necessary to undertake this exercise in order to monitor more accurately the success of aggregative back projection both in relation to population totals and to net migration.

Table A6.1 shows the published totals for England less Monmouth at the first eight censuses, the dates of each census, and a revised total for 30 June in each census year. The revised totals were obtained by assuming that compound daily growth occurred between any two adjacent censuses and obtaining a total at 30 June by interpolation. Thus the 1801 census fell 112 days before 30 June 1801 and the 1811 census fell 34 days before 30 June 1811. The number of days in a full decade may be taken as $365.25 \times 10 = 3,652.5$ days, and the interval between the 1801 and 1811 censuses as $3,652.5 + (112 - 34) = 3,730.5$ days. The ratio of the 1811 to the 1801 census total is

Table A6.1: Nineteenth-century population totals adjusted to 30 June of each census year (England less Monmouth)

Census	Date	Total (sexes combined)	Total adjusted to 30 June
1801	10 March	8 285 852	8 319 325
1811	27 May	9 476 700	9 491 364
1821	28 May	11 198 604	11 204 711
1831	30 May	12 992 875	13 007 663
1841	6/7 June	14 860 783	14 872 281
1851	30/1 March	16 764 470	16 811 848
1861	7/8 April	18 779 811	18 833 694
1871	2/3 April	21 299 683	21 369 569

Note: See text for method of adjustment.

Sources: 1801 Census, Enumeration, p. 451; *1811 Census*, Enumeration, p. 427; *1821 Census*, Enumeration abstract, p. 427; *1831 Census*, Enumeration abstract, II, p. 832; *1841 Census*, Enumeration abstract, p. 398; *1851 Census*, Numbers of inhabitants, I, p. clxviii; *1861 Census*, General report, appendix, p. 79; *1871 Census*, General report, appendix A, p. 14.

9,476,700/8,285,852 = 1.1437206, and the ratio by which the 1801 census total should be increased to give an estimated total for 30 June 1801 is therefore the antilog of (log 1.1437206 × 112/3730.5) or 1.0040398. This produces the revised total of 8,319,325 shown in table A6.1.

It is, of course, arbitrary to obtain estimated populations on 30 June of each census year by assuming uniform population growth rates in intercensal periods. Birth and death rates show a regular seasonal pattern, as well as irregular short-term fluctuations. More accurate adjustments might have been obtained by exploiting a knowledge of birth and death totals between the census dates and 30 June in each census year but this alternative was not pursued.

Under-registration of young children is a source of inaccuracy in most censuses and affected all nineteenth-century English censuses, though in varying degree. We have used two methods of estimating the extent of under-registration, one for the first four censuses which were not based on individual household schedules, the other for the censuses of 1841 and later where such schedules were used and detailed census age tabulations were published. It is convenient to consider the latter first.

In appendix 8 estimates are presented of the totals of births occurring in the five-year periods immediately preceding the censuses of 1851, 1861, and 1871. Similar estimates for the comparable period before the 1841 census were given in the course of chapter 5.[1] It is probable that throughout the middle decades of the nineteenth century mortality was at or very close to that defined by the third life table,[2] and it is therefore possible to obtain a rough estimate of the number of children who would survive from the birth cohort to form the population aged 0–4 at census time ($_5L_0/5l_0$). The totals in question are set out in table A6.2. They must be too large, however, by the extent to which the birth cohort was depleted by net emigration as well as death. Decadal net emigration totals may be calculated by subtracting the intercensal increase figures from those for natural increase. The latter may be calculated from the data in table A.8.5, while the former are derived from table A6.7 of this appendix, using population totals that exclude the correction made for children aged 0–4 to avoid circularity. The resulting net emigration totals for 1831–41 to 1861–71 are 45,384, 59,751, 377,351, and 263,253. In deriving from these the net emigration totals shown in column 3 of table A6.2, the same assumption was made about the age distribution of migration and the allocation of its impact on census age groups as was made to cope with a similar problem in appendix 8. The ratios given in column 7 suggest that enumeration of young children improved between the censuses of 1841 and 1851 but did not change significantly in the next two censuses held in 1861 and 1871.

1. See table 5.28.
2. This is clear from the work done by William Farr in connexion with what would have been the fourth English life table. The third life table was based on deaths registered over the 17 years 1838–54. After a further 17 years had elapsed, Farr collected data for a new life table which was to have reflected mortality over the full 34 years, but he concluded that it was pointless to carry out a full tabulation because 'the mortality at the several ages having been calculated for each of the 34 years 1838–71, the mean of the rates was found to agree so closely with the mean rates on which the Life Table was based that a new construction became unnecessary. The law of mortality had fluctuated from year to year, but had as yet remained constant; so that the persistence of the force of death as it affects different ages is beyond doubt'. *Supplement to the 35th Annual Report*, p. xxvi. Farr published a summary mortality table to show why he thought it unnecessary to proceed further and from this a life table for 1855–71 can be derived with only a small possible margin of error. It suggests an expectation of life at birth (sexes combined) of 41.33 years, less than half a year greater than that of the third life table (see appendix 14). Evidence for supposing that the third life table also captures the mortality experience of the 1830s is given in chapter 5, pp. 113–8.

590 The Population History of England 1541–1871

Table A6.2: Under-registration of children aged 0–4 in the censuses of 1841–71 (England less Monmouth)

	(1) Births	(2) Survivors aged 0–4	(3) Net emigration	(4) Estimated census population 0–4		(5) Enumerated census population 0–4	(6) Difference (4)–(5)	(7) Ratio (4)/(5)
1836–41	2 602 489	2 095 722	719	2 095 003	1841	1 966 861	128 142	1.065
1846–51	2 860 473	2 303 470	1 120	2 302 350	1851	2 201 824	100 526	1.046
1856–61	3 296 588	2 654 633	5 974	2 648 689	1861	2 535 419	113 270	1.045
1866–71	3 755 806	3 024 460	4 168	3 020 292	1871	2 888 298	131 994	1.046

Note: The totals of column 5 have been adjusted to 30 June in the manner described for total populations. In 1851 age group totals were given for registration counties but not for ancient counties. The 1851 total, therefore, was further adjusted to offset the lack of agreement between the Monmouthshire population totals on the two different bases.

Sources: For column 1 totals see table A8.5. The quinquennial periods begin on 1 July and end on 30 June (the totals for the first six months of 1846, 1856, and 1866 are 295 733, 336 592, and 376 741 respectively; the comparable figures for 1836–41 may be found in table A2.3. For net emigration totals see text. Column 5 totals were taken from the censuses of 1841 to 1871 modified as indicated above: 1841 Census, Age abstract, pp. 368, 372; 1851 Census, Ages, civil condition, etc., I, p. cxcii; 1861 Census, Ages, civil condition, etc., Summary tables, p. x; 1871 Census, Ages, civil condition, etc., Summary tables, p. xii.

Any estimate of the degree of under-registration of the very young in censuses before 1841 is inevitably less reliable than that for the later censuses. Only the 1821 census provides any age data, and it will be remembered that we concluded in another connexion that estimation from 1841 data suggested that the female population aged 0–9 was 64,724 larger than the census total after those of unknown age had been distributed between the several age groups.[3] This represents 1.127 per cent of the total female population of 5,743,203 in 1821. An estimate of under-registration based on the female population is likely to be more accurate than one based on the male population when calculating back from an early adult age group because of the lesser scale of female net migration compared with male. It is therefore better to arrive at an overall inflation factor for the whole population through the female population only rather than by a calculation based on both sexes, provided that the sex ratio of those under 10 in 1821 is not implausible. If, for example, boy children were more completely counted than girl children, an estimate based on girls alone would exaggerate the scale of the shortfall. But it would also lead to an unusual sex ratio among the census population in the young age groups.

Fortunately, the sex ratio among young children in the 1821 census is exactly what one would be led to expect from a consideration of model life tables. Table A6.3 shows the totals of males and females aged 0–4 and 5–9 in 1821 after distributing those of unknown age in each sex to conform with the age distribution of those for whom an age return was made. A higher percentage of the male population had been the subject of an age return than of the female (87.62 compared with 86.84) so that there was a larger increase in female than in male numbers following the allocation of those of unknown age. The sex ratios of male to female children for both age groups lie between those found in level 9 and level 10 of the Princeton model North life

Table A6.3: Sex ratios among young children in England less Monmouth in 1821 and in two model life tables

Age	(1) Male	(2) Female	(3) Sex ratio (1)/(2)	(4) Sex ratio level 9	(5) Sex ratio level 10
0–4	838 750	829 579	1.01106	1.01043	1.01366
5–9	731 743	728 065	1.00505	1.00429	1.00806

Note: In deriving sex ratios from the L_xs of the model life tables a sex ratio at birth of 1.045 was assumed.

Source: Male and female totals from *1811 Census* Enumeration, pp. 428–9, modified as described in the text. See Coale and Demeny, *Regional model life tables* for L_xs from model North used for the ratios shown in columns 4 and 5.

tables, a finding that mirrors expectation for the early decades of the nineteenth century. Therefore, the combined population of both sexes was increased by 1.127 per cent in 1821, and the same percentage increase was made for 1801, 1811, and 1831. There is no direct evidence of the scale of under-registration of young children in the three last censuses, but each was conducted by the parish overseers without the regular use of schedules delivered to each house, and to use the same inflation factor is reasonable, if arbitrary. The results are shown in table A6.4.

3. See pp. 115–6.

Table A6.4: Corrections for under-registration of young children in the censuses of 1801 to 1831

	(1) Census population adjusted to 30 June	(2) Column 1 totals × 1.01127	(3) Difference (2)–(1)
1801	8 319 325	8 413 084	93 759
1811	9 491 364	9 598 332	106 968
1821	11 204 711	11 330 988	126 277
1831	13 007 663	13 154 259	146 596

Note: See text for reason for selection of inflation factor shown at head of column 2.

Source: See table A6.1 for column 1 census totals.

A third respect in which the raw census totals can prove deceptive lies in the omission from the main census counts of men serving in the army and navy or on merchant shipping. Every census, however, includes an estimate of the total number of men falling into these categories. At the height of the Napoleonic wars those excluded formed a far higher proportion of the male population than in times of peace. Failure to make allowance for the armed forces and merchant marine can therefore result in misleading estimates of intercensal growth rates if one census was conducted in war time and the other after its end. The matter is complicated by the fact that the men excluded in the earliest censuses included certain categories present in the main returns in later censuses. Initially all those in the navy, army, or regular militia, as well as all seamen, were excluded. In 1841 only those abroad or in ports of the United Kingdom, but not those ashore, were missing from the main returns, while in 1851 and thereafter only those abroad were counted separately.

In 1851 the Registrar General attempted to consolidate information from the earlier censuses. He divided the totals for the whole United Kingdom from earlier censuses on the assumption that the proportion coming from each constituent country had been

Table A6.5: Men excluded from the main census returns because of service in the army, navy, or merchant marine

	England and Wales	England less Monmouth
1801	263 635	245 181
1811	290 273	269 954
1821	172 428	160 358
1831	155 189	144 326
1841	121 050	112 577
1851	126 561	117 702
1861	162 273	150 914
1871	143 898	133 825

Note: For derivation of totals for England less Monmouth see text.

Source: For England and Wales totals see *1851 Census*, Numbers of inhabitants, Report, p. xxiii; and *1871 Census*, General Report, p. 142, table 158.

the same in earlier years as it was in 1851.[4] The totals for England and Wales from this source are reproduced in table A6.5, together with the comparable totals from the censuses of 1861 and 1871. An estimated total for England less Monmouth has been made by multiplying the England and Wales total for each year by 0.93 since England less Monmouth formed about 93 per cent of the England and Wales population total throughout this period. It should be noted that the Registrar General made one exception to his simple rule for apportioning totals in the first five censuses. In 1821 Rickman had drawn attention to the very large numbers of foreigners manning British merchant ships in 1811 and had guessed that they might number 100,000 at that time.[5] In 1851 the Registrar General adopted this estimate, and made some further arbitrary adjustments to the totals which would have been produced by his usual method of sub-division between the constituent countries of the United Kingdom in order to arrive at a round total of 374,000 for Great Britain as a whole.[6]

To act in this way seems arbitrary and might be expected to distort comparisons of 1801 and 1811 since at the time of the first census the country was also at war and therefore might equally be expected to have employed an exceptionally large proportion of foreigners in merchant shipping. Whether by accident or good judgement, however, the allocations made by the Registrar General in 1851 appear to be very close to the truth. This is most readily apparent from a consideration of the sex ratios in the overall population in the early censuses.

In table A6.6 the column 6 ratios suggest a remarkable stability in the sex ratios of the English population during the early nineteenth century once the main returns for the male population have been increased by the estimated numbers of men in the armed forces and merchant navy taken from table A6.5. If the column 6 ratios had fluctuated, and particularly if the ratio for 1811 seemed implausible, it would have been tempting to devise new estimates of the number of men omitted from the main returns but table A6.6 suggests that the procedure adopted in 1851 yields reliable results, at least for England. If, for example, it were assumed that the overall ratio in 1821 was reliable and this were used as a means of estimating the 'true' totals of men missing at sea or in the army in 1801 and 1811 the resulting totals (251,696 and 269,980) are so closely similar to those given in table A6.6 that there appears to be no justification for amending them.[7]

Table A6.7 consolidates the results of the three steps taken in correcting the original returns of the censuses from 1801 to 1871, and shows the changes in growth rates implied by the corrections, while table A6.8 presents the net migration totals implied by the revised census totals. The ratios given in column 8 of table A6.7 show that the cumulative effect of the successive corrections varies considerably between the censuses, adding almost 4.5 per cent to the 1801 original total but only slightly over 1.5 per cent to the totals in the censuses of 1841 to 1871. Comparison of the annual growth rate figures of column 1 and column 6 shows that growth rates in the

4. *1851 Census*, Numbers of inhabitants, Report, pp. xxii–xxiii.
5. *1821 Census*, Preliminary observations, p. viii.
6. *1851 Census*, Numbers of inhabitants, Report, p. xxiii, fn.
7. The estimates quoted were obtained by the following method. If the overall sex ratio, including men in the forces and at sea, was 0.976243 in 1821, then the expected male total in 1801 and 1811 will be the female population multiplied by the ratio, from which in turn the number of men missed in the main census count can be estimated. For example, in 1801 the female total is 4,320,090 and the estimated male total is therefore 4,217,548 (4,320,090 × 0.976243). The main census return gives a male total of only 3,965,762, so that the implied total of men in the army, navy, and on merchant ships is 251,786 (4,217,548 − 3,965,762).

Table A6.6: Sex ratios in the male and female populations 1801–31 (England less Monmouth)

	(1) Male Main returns	(2) Male Armed forces etc.	(3) Total (1) + (2)	(4) Female total	(5) Ratio (1)/(4)	(6) Ratio (3)/(4)
1801	3 965 762	245 181	4 210 943	4 320 090	0.917981	0.974735
1811	4 544 776	269 954	4 814 730	4 931 924	0.921502	0.976238
1821	5 446 401	160 358	5 606 759	5 743 203	0.948321	0.976243
1831	6 325 532	144 326	6 469 858	6 667 343	0.948374	0.970380

Sources: Column 1 and column 4 totals see source note to table A6.1; column 2 totals from table A6.5.

Table A6.7: Corrected population totals 1801–71 (England less Monmouth)

Census	(1) Original total	(2) Corrected to 30 June	(3) Difference (2)–(1)	(4) Corrected for under-registration of children 0–4	(5) Difference (4)–(2)	(6) Corrected for armed forces and merchant marine	(7) Difference (6)–(4)	(8) Ratio (6)/(1)
1801	8 285 852	8 319 325	33 473	8 413 084	93 759	8 658 265	245 181	1.0449
1811	9 476 700	9 491 364	14 664	9 598 332	106 968	9 868 286	269 954	1.0413
1821	11 189 604	11 204 711	15 107	11 330 988	126 277	11 491 346	160 358	1.0270
1831	12 992 875	13 007 663	14 788	13 154 259	146 596	13 298 585	144 326	1.0235
1841	14 860 783	14 872 281	11 498	15 000 423	128 142	15 113 000	112 577	1.0170
1851	16 764 470	16 811 848	47 378	16 912 374	100 526	17 030 076	117 702	1.0158
1861	18 779 811	18 833 694	53 883	18 946 964	113 270	19 097 878	150 914	1.0169
1871	21 299 683	21 369 569	69 886	21 501 563	131 994	21 635 388	133 825	1.0158

Compound annual growth rates per cent

	(1)	(2)	(4)	(6)
1801–11	1.352	1.327	1.327	1.317
1811–21	1.675	1.673	1.673	1.534
1821–31	1.505	1.503	1.503	1.471
1831–41	1.352	1.349	1.322	1.287
1841–51	1.213	1.233	1.207	1.201
1851–61	1.142	1.142	1.142	1.153
1861–71	1.267	1.271	1.273	1.255

Sources: For totals in columns 1 and 2 see table A6.1; for totals in column 5 see tables A6.2 and A6.4; for totals in column 7 see table A6.5.

Table A6.8: Natural increase, intercensal increase, and net migration 1801-71 (England less Monmouth)

	(1) Natural increase	(2) Intercensal increase	(3) Net emigration (1)–(2)
1801-11	1 283 053	1 210 021	73 032
1811-21	1 697 262	1 623 060	74 202
1821-31	1 932 512	1 807 239	125 273
1831-41	1 878 253	1 814 415	63 838
1841-51	2 004 443	1 917 076	87 367
1851-61	2 432 409	2 067 802	364 607
1861-71	2 782 039	2 537 510	244 529

Source: For natural increase see tables A2.3 and A2.4; the totals run from mid year to mid year (for example, July 1801 to June 1811). For intercensal increase see table A6.7, column 6.

early decades of the century are reduced. The fall is particularly marked for the decade 1811–21, which remains the decade with the highest rate of population growth but with a much smaller margin compared with 1821–31, though the growth rate of the latter is also reduced.

The most striking feature of the net migration figures is the massive difference between the 1850s and the earlier decades of the century. The lower growth rate of the 1850s which is a striking feature of table A6.7 is explained by the very large net emigration taking place in the decade. The low net emigration total for the 1840s no doubt reflects the influx of Irish people in the later years of the decade following the Irish famine. The low figure for the 1830s is slightly surprising. It may reflect the arbitrariness of assuming the same proportionate correction for under-registration of young children in the first four censuses. If, for example, there had been a deterioration of a third in the coverage of young children between 1821 and 1831 (implying an increase in the 1831 figure in column 5 of table A6.7 of about 50,000) the net emigration figure for 1821–31 would be reduced to about 75,000, while that for 1831–41 would rise to over 110,000. Equally, any general improvement in enumeration coverage between 1831 and 1841 would have the same effect. Since the 1841 population was over 15 million even an improvement of as little as one tenth of 1 per cent makes a difference of 15,000 to the size of the intercensal increase figure and depresses the net emigration figure by the same margin.

Appendix 7

Rickman's Parish Register Returns of 1801 and 1841

The reliability of the 1801 national totals

One of the questions addressed to the incumbent and overseers of the poor of each parish at the time of the first national census ran as follows: 'What was the number of baptisms and burials in your parish, township or place, in the several years 1700, 1710, 1720, 1730, 1740, 1750, 1760, 1770, 1780 and each subsequent year to the 31st day of December 1800, distinguishing males from females?' A similar request was made for marriage totals for each year from 1754 to 1800 inclusive.

The returns made in response to these questions have been the basis of the great bulk of all subsequent work on the growth of English population in the eighteenth century.[1] The original returns were seriously inaccurate, both because many parishes failed to make a return and because there was some duplication of returns. The Abstract of Answers and Returns notes that returns had been obtained from 9,701 parishes[2] in England but that 952 returns were missing. The comparable figures for Wales were 790 and 191, making combined totals of 10,491 and 1,143. The Parish Register volume of the census was ordered to be printed on 21 December 1801. At a later date 'when the printing of the foregoing Abstract was in considerable forwardness' an attempt was made to remedy the defects of the original returns, and the results were published in a Supplement bound in with the main volume.

The Supplement remarked that the total number of returns 'probably wanting' had been raised to 1,164 for England and Wales but that 389 of these were chapelries which had been found to have been included in the returns for the mother churches in the original survey. Of the 775 remaining, returns for 495 were said to have been received, leaving the comparatively small number of 280 still missing.[3] The additional returns and the parishes still missing were listed county by county in the Supplement.

There is evidence of administrative incompetence in the original returns,[4] but any

---

1. There is a convenient summary of these writings in Glass, 'Population and population movements'. See also Deane and Cole, *British economic growth*, ch. 3 and Flinn, *British population growth*. Flinn's discussion reflects the increasingly jaundiced view taken recently of the Parish Register Abstracts. 'For many reasons, results drawn from the PRA, whether in the form of totals of population or of vital rates, are built on such shifting sand as to make them virtually unacceptable for the purposes of modern scholarship'. Flinn, *ibid.*, p. 20.

2. Throughout this appendix the term 'parish', when used without qualification, is intended to denote any ecclesiastical unit, whether a rectory, vicarage, or chapelry, that maintained a register of baptisms, burials, and marriages, or any of the three.

3. *1801 Census*, Parish registers, p. 449.

4. For example, the parishes of Brean, Burnham, Mark, and Weare are listed under the hundred of Bath Forum, Somerset, and again under Bempstone. Comparison with the 1811 returns suggests that there was also double counting in the totals of baptisms, burials, and marriages. Serious spelling errors abound as, for example, Fontagel for Tintagel in Cornwall, or Binleston for Burleston in Dorset. Sometimes the two types of error are compounded. Trentham in the hundred of Pirehill in Staffordshire appears again in the same hundred as Frentham.

shortcomings in these returns are dwarfed by the astonishing defects in the supplementary returns.[5] Rickman was acutely aware of their inadequacy and made a great effort to remedy matters when the 1811 census was published. He was especially concerned to produce revised totals of events for the eighteenth century so that they could be compared with the new returns of baptisms, burials, and marriages for the years 1801–10. He concluded that this could be achieved by increasing the final totals in the 1801 Abstract (i.e. the totals from the original returns plus the totals for the supplementary return) by one thirty-second in the case of baptisms, one twenty-ninth in the case of burials, and one fiftieth in the case of marriages. He published revised totals for England and Wales combined, but not for the two separately nor for individual counties. The new figures are those that have been most widely used by those interested in eighteenth-century population history.

In view of the well-known deficiencies in the 1801 data it may seem pointless to embark upon further study of them. Even if the returns had been perfectly accurate and had been handled with precision by the census clerks, the totals of baptisms and burials would still be of very limited direct use in estimating totals of births and deaths. Our reason for examining Rickman's work once more does not spring from a belief that it was of higher quality than has been generally supposed. Indeed it will be seen that the list of deficiencies in the material he published can be extended further. It is rather that some further assessment of the 1801 returns is needed in order to be able to make the most of more recently collected data from parish registers. No subsequent exercise has covered more than a tiny fraction of the parish registers for which returns were made in 1801. Any description and discussion of the results of such an exercise, like that presented in chapter 3, must therefore include a comparison with Rickman's findings. This in turn required that the strengths and weaknesses both of the original returns and of Rickman's subsequent manipulation of the data should be considered.

It is convenient to begin by discussing what might be termed Rickman's strategy – his handling of the general problems of inaccuracies and deficiencies in the 1801 returns – before turning to discuss the internal consistency of his published data and the reliability of the parish returns upon which the whole edifice was constructed.

We may consider first how Rickman sought to rectify the errors and omissions of 1801 considered generally. He noted in 1811 that much of the confusion had arisen from two causes: the mode of distribution of the printed schedules, and the lack of any list of parishes and chapelries that currently maintained separate registers. Two schedules were sent to every overseer of the poor, one for his own use as an enumerator and the other for the minister of the parish to use in making a parish register return. In large parishes with several townships this meant that the incumbent received a number of forms.

Where there were also several chapelries in the parish, each maintaining a separate register, he would find good use for them. But if the parish were undivided for registration purposes he was sometimes tempted to divide the entries in his register between the townships in the parish. Thus several returns might be made from the

---

5. There are three instances of parishes listed both as having provided a return in the Supplement and as still missing (Beechamwell, Norfolk; Marlesford, Suffolk; High Worsall, Yorkshire). These errors are particularly glaring since the duplications occur cheek by jowl on the printed page. But they are of small consequence compared with the other types of mistakes in the Supplement. For example, in England (excluding Monmouth) a total of 432 new returns were listed in the Supplement. Of these 117 are also to be found in the original returns. Similarly, of the 260 returns said to be still outstanding, 72 may be found in the original returns.

same registering unit. This increased the apparent number of returns, though without necessarily distorting the total number of recorded events. The lack of a reliable list of parishes not only caused confusion about the number of parishes missed. It also produced a spurious inflation in the total of events. This occurred when the supplementary returns were sought. The *Liber Regis* of Bacon was used to help in identifying parishes from which no return had been received. But the spelling of place names in the *Liber Regis* had changed greatly since its publication. As a result of the confusion this caused, returns were requested from many parishes that had already made a return. Rickman was able to identify and attempt to measure these sources of error because he took far more care in 1811 to compile an accurate list of parishes. After sending over 2,000 letters to incumbents in an attempt to clarify any obscurities he concluded that the total number of parishes (registering units) was 11,159 in 1811, and believed that this figure must have been within three or four of the true total. Comparison of the 1801 and 1811 returns led him to conclude that the total number of returns really obtained in 1801 was 10,643, or 343 fewer than he had supposed 10 years earlier.[6]

After summarizing the results of a comparison of the two sets of returns, Rickman then turned to the question of the correction of the aggregate totals of baptisms, burials, and marriages published in 1801. He believed that 141 of the 1801 returns had been duplicated, that 516 parishes had been genuinely missed, and that 281 of the places listed in the 1801 returns as having registers in fact possessed none. He obtained totals of baptisms, burials, and marriages in the period 1801–10 for the first two of these three groups of parishes, deducted the former from the latter, and expressed the remainder as a proportion of the total number of events in the same period in each of the three series. Thus the net 'weight' of the registration deficiency in each series was established and Rickman argued that by inflating the eighteenth-century totals in the three series in like proportion he had created series that were comparable to the data for 1801–10 collected at the time of the 1811 census.

It is not possible directly to check several aspects of Rickman's work summarized in the 1801 and 1811 censuses but it is possible to make independent estimates of the extent of the deficiency in the eighteenth-century data collected in 1801, and to extend the work Rickman carried out in 1811.

Rickman's own later work is an indispensable aid to any assessment or extension of the results he published in 1811. In particular the material which he collected in 1831 is of the utmost value. The Parish Register Abstract published in the census of that year contains details of the registers surviving in each parish down to 1812, often with a considerable amount of additional information.[7] It is usually clear, for example,

6. In 1811 Rickman remarked that the number of parish register returns supposed to have been received from England and Wales in 1801 (including the Supplement) was 11,065 (*1811 Census*, Preliminary observations, p. xviii). This is one of many instances where it is impossible to reconcile his statements at different periods from the printed census, and one must suppose either that he was referring to material on which further work had been done after the publication of the census, or that his arithmetic failed him. The 1801 census suggests a figure of 10,986 (9,701 English parishes in the original returns, 790 Welsh parishes in the original returns, and 495 parishes in England and Wales in the supplementary returns).

7. Concern to know more about the older parish registers was not new. Rose's Act of 1812 (52 George III, c. 146, s. 19) provides 'That the rector, vicar, curate or officiating minister of every parish and chapelry in England ... shall transmit to the Registrar of the Diocese in which the parish or chapelry shall be situated, before the first day of June 1813, a list of all registers which now are in such parish or chapelry respectively, stating the periods at which they respectively commence and terminate, the periods (if any) for which they are deficient, and the places where they are deposited'. It would be interesting to know if any

whether all three types of events were recorded in the parish registers or whether, as often happened in chapelries, only baptisms were recorded, with the mother church still being used for other events. With chapelries it is often possible to tell from the returns at what date registration began in each series. Registration was not always maintained uninterrupted from the date at which a particular series began. In a number of chapelries, for example, marriages ceased to be celebrated after the passing of Hardwicke's Marriage Act of 1753 because of uncertainty about the validity of marriages celebrated in chapelries. In some instances, too, the returns make it clear that from a certain date registration ceased entirely in one church and was absorbed into the registers of a neighbouring church.[8]

Had he possessed this information in 1811, Rickman might well have adopted a different approach to the problem of correcting the 1801 returns for he would have known how many of the parishes missed in that census were not registering units throughout the eighteenth century. His method of correction, employing fixed inflation ratios to correct the 1801 returns, implicitly assumed that all the parishes missed in 1801 were registering events throughout the eighteenth century, whereas rather more than a fifth of all the parishes missed in the original returns of 1801 did not exist as registering units in 1700. An unchanging inflation ratio, therefore, tends to exaggerate the proportion of events missed in earlier years since in most cases the baptisms, burials, and marriages of people of living in such parishes before the inception of local registration were recorded in the registers of a parish that *was* included in the 1801 returns.

The simplest way of checking Rickman's revised figures for eighteenth-century registration totals is to attempt to identify the parishes missed in the original return of 1801, and then to make some estimate of the shortfall this occasioned. We have preferred to work from the original returns of 1801, and to ignore the supplementary returns partly because the work done on them was so hasty and partly because they are not placed within their appropriate hundreds as was the case with the original returns and this increases identification difficulties. Parishes missed in 1801 were identified by comparing the list of parishes in each hundred for which a return was made in 1801 with the similar list of 1811, while also consulting the 1831 Parish Register Abstract, and indeed other census volumes (especially the Enumeration Abstract of 1841) where parish sub-divisions and boundaries are at issue. This is laborious and can never be entirely satisfactory. Parishes in 1801 were often in a different hundred from the hundred in which they appeared in 1811. Occasionally there was a change of county also. Frequently there is a change of spelling or of name.[9] In some cases a

---

lists made under the Act survive. Rickman, in 1831, wrote that the Act proved 'incompetent to the attainment of this desirable purpose'. *1831 Census*, Preface, p. xxviii. Rickman made a further attempt to elicit the information when asking for the parish register returns published in the 1831 census, suggesting that a copy of the 1813 return would suffice. This finally produced the information he sought.

8. For example, in Sussex the two parochial chapelries of Durrington and Heene had both maintained registers of baptisms, burials, and marriages for an early date (from 1627 or earlier in Durrington; from 1594 or earlier in Heene). Both abandoned marriage registration in 1754 in the wake of the uncertainties created by Hardwicke's Act, and both gave up the registration of baptisms and burials in 1792. In all cases registration was taken up by the mother church of West Tarring.

9. Thus Herberbury in 1801 becomes Harbury in 1811 (Warwickshire, Knightlow Hundred). Such cases do not occasion much difficulty. More awkward are cases, common in 1801, where either the census clerk or the compositor appears to have misread names. Thilnwick in 1801 becomes, correctly, Kilnwick in 1811 (Yorkshire, East Riding, Harthill Wapentake, Bainton Beacon). But there can also be complete changes of name. For example, the chapelry called Billington in 1801 was called Lango in 1811 (Lancashire,

place listed in 1801 is not a registering unit and an informed guess must be made about its identity.[10] This operation resulted in a list of 632 missing parishes for England excluding Monmouth.

It is not easy to decide how closely this total agrees with Rickman. In the original return of 1801 he supposed that 919 parishes were missing for England less Monmouth. When the supplementary return was made up this figure had fallen to 692 because many of the parishes originally supposed to be missing were found to be chapelries whose returns proved to have been included with those of the mother churches[11]. The latter figure suggests a reasonably close agreement. However, 189 of the 692 parishes can be shown to have been included in the original return and many of the places listed as missing in the Supplement were not registering units (81 cases).[12] This implies a much less good agreement.

Rickman returned to this issue amongst others in 1811. There are difficulties in obtaining comparable figures from his Preliminary Observations because he gives no information for any unit other than England and Wales combined and because he gives little detail. Moreover, his figures can be accepted only with some reservation even in 1811 since they are not fully consistent. For example, the figure for the number of duplicates among the supplementary returns is first given as 150 and later as 141.[13] His new conclusion, as we have seen, was that 516 parishes had been missed. The supplementary returns had contributed 354 (495 returns less 141 duplicates) to the 1801 total. Rickman therefore implies that for England and Wales as a whole the true number of missing parishes in the original returns of 1801 was 870 (516 + 354). He provided no separate figure for England. If the number of missing were proportional to the total of parishes in England compared with England and Wales combined (10,189 c.f. 11,159), the number missing for England alone would be 794.

It is fair to assume that the proportion missing in Wales was much higher than in England. In the original 1801 returns, for example, missing parishes formed 8.7 per cent of the total in England, whereas in Wales the comparable figure was 20.1 per cent. This probably overstates the true disproportion in missing parishes because uncertainties over the spelling of Welsh place names inflated the Welsh figure excessively. On the assumption that the disproportion is not overstated, however, the number of missing English parishes would fall to 713, still a substantially larger figure than the 632 found by the method used in this appendix, but the difference is much reduced.

Since it is not clear how Rickman tackled the problem of discovering misnamed, duplicated, and missing parishes, it is impossible to account satisfactorily for the discrepancy between his figures and ours. It seems probable that there were

Blackburn Hundred). Sometimes the notes to the 1811 census are helpful in cases of this sort but in other cases only the use of the 1831 Parish Register Abstract, or the fuller footnotes of the 1841 Enumeration Abstract, or a gazetteer can resolve the uncertainty. Even with these aids some decisions were probably mistaken.

10. Where a parish consisted of several townships, for example, it may appear in 1801 under the name of one of the constituent townships. If there are no chapelries within the parish to complicate matters, it is reasonable to suppose that the 1801 return refers to the parish as a whole.

11. 692 is the total number of parishes listed either as found or as still missing in the supplementary returns (432 found plus 260 still missing).

12. See fn. 5.

13. *1811 Census*, Preliminary observations, pp. xviii and xix.

intermediate steps involved in his work not directly based on a comparison of the 1801 and 1811 census materials.

It is, however, possible to make alternative estimates of the inflation ratios to be used in amending the baptism, burial, and marriage totals published in 1801 and to compare them with those Rickman published in 1811. Moreover, what can be done for the country as a whole can also be done for each county. The proportion of parishes missed varied greatly from county to county, and it had always been a drawback of the 1811 inflation ratios that Rickman provided only national estimates. In table A7.1 the successive columns show the total number of events from the original 1801 returns for England; the same inflated by the ratios which Rickman proposed in 1811 but modified to reflect the better original coverage in England; and estimates made in the course of the present exercise (columns 1, 2, and 3).

The following steps were taken in increasing the totals in the 1801 original returns to produce the column 2 totals, which should be understood as an attempt to provide for England less Monmouth the totals that Rickman himself would have arrived at using his method of correcting the original returns if he had made a separate estimate. First, the proportion of the supplementary returns attributable to England alone was calculated by summing the burial total in 1800 for the English parishes in the supplementary returns and expressing this as a fraction of the burial total for England and Wales combined. Only the burial totals are subdivided in this way. Otherwise all data given by Rickman are for England and Wales combined. Therefore this estimate has to be based on burials only. The English percentage was 85.6 (the absolute total of burials for England and Wales in the supplementary returns is given as 6,004 in the summary table, whereas the sum of the county totals is 5,966, another instance of imprecision in handling of the data). Thus the baptism total for England in the 1801 original returns, 226,276, is increased by 7,028 (0.8558 times the total of 8,212 baptisms in the supplementary returns) to 233,304. The totals derived in this way were then further increased not by the inflation ratios used by Rickman in 1811 but by slightly smaller ratios intended to reflect the fact that registration coverage was better in England than in Wales, and also to correct an astonishing lapse on Rickman's part when he came to calculate the ratios in 1811.

His intention was to tabulate the total number of events occurring on average in 1801–10 in the parishes missing both from the original and supplementary returns of 1801 and to relate them to the total number of events recorded on average over the same period in the whole country. In this way an inflation ratio could be derived and used to correct the totals in the final summary of eighteenth-century baptisms, burials, and marriages published in the first census. He gives the average for baptisms in the missing parishes as 9,181, for burials as 6,250, and for marriages as 1,626 and asserts that they represent 1 in 32, 1 in 29, and 1 in 50 respectively of the totals for England and Wales.[14] The annual national averages for the decade published later in the volume are 287,891, 195,019, and 83,209 respectively.[15] He remarks that 'The annual average number of such additional baptisms . . . is as one in thirty-two to the average number of baptisms from 1801 to 1810' (he also gives figures for burials and marriages).[16] It is not, therefore, clear whether he appreciated the importance of expressing the averages for the missing parishes as a fraction of the national averages

14. *1811 Census*, Preliminary observations, p. xx.
15. *1811 Census*, Parish registers, p. 196.
16. *1811 Census*, Preliminary observations, p. xx.

less the missing parish totals, or whether he simply used the gross figures, though the latter is the more likely. In neither case do the ratios he published square with the ratios that may be calculated from the data published in 1811. His ratios were 1 in 32, 1 in 29, 1 in 50. The ratios it would be proper to use are 1 in 30.36, 1 in 30.20, and 1 in 50.17 respectively; while the ratios resulting from using the gross national figures are 1 in 31.36, 1 in 31.20, and 1 in 51.17.[17] In calculating a revised Rickman series for table 1 we have used the second of the three sets of ratios just quoted. They suggest that the original returns should be multiplied by 1.03294, 1.03311, and 1.01993 for baptisms, burials, and marriages respectively. These proportions were then reduced to reflect the fact that the registration coverage was better in England than in Wales. The reductions were calculated by using the data on the percentages of missing parishes given above (see p. 601). If 20.1 per cent of Welsh parishes were missed in the original returns compared with 8.7 per cent in England, this suggests that the inflation percentage in England should be only 89.8 per cent of the figure for England and Wales combined (English parishes constituted 91.3 per cent of the total of parishes but only 82.0 per cent of all missing parishes were English).[18] Therefore the final ratios for further inflation are 1.02958, 1.02973, and 1.01790 for baptisms, burials, and marriages. For example, the figure of 233,304 baptisms for 1800 (original return figure of 226,276 plus 7,028 from the supplementary returns) becomes 240,205 when multiplied by 1.02958.

The new estimates in column 3 of table A7.1 were calculated upon a different basis using the following method. First, the population of the 632 missing parishes was tabulated (using the 1811 rather than the 1801 census since the earlier census is seriously inaccurate for some places). This yielded a total of 426,113 compared with the English total of 9,476,700. It suggests that the total of events tabulated by Rickman in the original returns of 1801 should be increased by 4.708 per cent: 100(426,113/(9,476,700−426,113)). To do this involves the implicit assumption that baptism, burial, and marriage rates in the missing parishes were the same as in the rest. Rickman's method (tabulating the actual frequency of events in 1801–10 in missing parishes, and comparing this to national total frequencies to derive an inflation ratio) is probably to be preferred, but the data he used have been destroyed and his method is therefore impracticable.

As will be seen from the table the differences between the two sets of estimates are in general relatively small. Yet there are also a number of striking discrepancies between totals for the same year taken from columns 2 and 3. These occur because the national totals frequently fail to equal the sum of the county totals in the 1801 census. Rickman

17. If Rickman had used more accurate inflation ratios based on the figures he published in 1811 it would have had the effect of slightly increasing his estimates of baptisms and reducing those of burials, and would therefore have increased all natural increase figures. For example his published figures for baptisms and burials in England and Wales in 1800 are 254,870 and 208,063 giving a surplus of 46,807. Using his data but calculating the inflation ratios more accurately these figures become 255,288, 207,788, and 47,500. The effect of using more accurate ratios is, however, slight. At the birth and death rates prevailing in the eighteenth century the use of more accurate ratios would boost the rate of increase by about 0.1 per 1,000 per annum.

18. The total number of parishes in England and Wales is given in 1811, when Rickman's knowledge of their number had greatly improved, as 11,159. The total for England only is 10,189 or 91.3 per cent of the total. If 8.7 per cent of the 91.3 per cent of English parishes were missing compared with 20.1 per cent of the 8.7 per cent of Welsh parishes, this implies that 82.0 per cent of all missing parishes were English and as many as 18.0 per cent were Welsh. Therefore the overall inflation ratio for England and Wales combined should be reduced in the ratio of 82.0 to 91.3, or 0.898 (and the Welsh inflation ratio, incidentally, should be increased in the ratio of 18.0 to 8.7 or 2.069).

Table A7.1: Estimates of numbers of baptisms, burials, and marriages

	Baptisms			Burials		
	(1)	(2)	(3)	(1)	(2)	(3)
1700	138 291	146 851	143 535	120 786	127 853	125 205
1710	125 661	133 482	130 535	128 635	136 001	133 461
1720	140 280	148 898	145 997	147 763	156 280	153 666
1730	146 058	155 118	152 234	161 482	171 140	168 155
1740	153 042	162 528	159 055	154 002	163 827	160 657
1750	162 821	173 150	170 325	142 581	151 031	148 835
1760	168 999	179 628	177 386	142 651	151 400	149 156
1770	188 077	199 806	197 784	159 830	169 246	166 410
1780	200 537	213 140	210 583	176 674	187 198	184 795
1781	203 506	216 241	212 956	174 329	184 486	182 343
1782	198 148	210 521	207 350	165 449	175 483	173 025
1783	194 638	207 003	209 754	165 702	175 859	179 805
1784	202 585	215 117	211 999	170 617	180 848	178 468
1785	215 753	229 113	225 778	169 747	179 618	177 558
1786	214 435	227 769	223 686	164 475	174 264	172 047
1787	216 418	229 690	226 611	164 738	174 306	172 322
1788	220 976	234 408	231 324	166 618	176 465	174 346
1789	220 693	234 480	231 415	165 185	174 937	172 872
1790	226 790	240 787	237 411	164 905	174 588	171 508
1791	225 731	239 858	236 302	166 396	176 173	174 993
1792	238 559	253 217	249 723	167 688	177 614	175 467
1793	233 788	248 218	244 728	181 097	191 621	189 498
1794	226 846	240 931	237 985	176 766	187 041	184 167
1795	225 583	239 475	236 189	187 563	198 753	195 240
1796	227 336	241 323	237 982	169 229	179 374	177 148
1797	237 109	251 584	249 305	170 271	180 362	177 211
1798	239 427	254 098	250 677	167 101	176 963	174 906
1799	236 020	250 548	246 901	169 244	179 015	176 334
1800	226 276	240 205	238 056	185 279	196 078	193 282

Column headings
(1) Rickman's totals from 1801 original returns.
(2) Revised estimates based on Rickman's 1811 data.
(3) New estimates.

Note: For full explanation of the derivation of the totals in columns 2 and 3 see text.

Source: Col. 1, *1801 Census*, Parish registers, pp. 189, 373.

based all his inflations upon the published national totals for England and Wales printed at the end of the parish register volume of the 1801 census, where a table representing the sum of the original and supplementary returns is printed. But these totals included many trivial errors and a smaller number of serious mistakes made in cumulating the county totals. The source of the error is easy to establish in some cases. For example, the baptism and burial totals for Surrey in 1783 were omitted from the national totals of that year. The nature of the error is easy to detect in this

1700–1800 (England less Monmouth)

	Marriages		
	(1)	(2)	(3)
1755	43 946	45 993	45 685
1756	45 451	47 606	47 251
1757	43 090	45 064	44 796
1758	45 258	47 337	47 051
1759	49 504	51 780	50 804
1760	51 551	53 914	53 593
1761	48 909	51 182	53 965
1762	50 513	52 768	52 521
1763	55 793	58 296	58 006
1764	56 841	59 379	58 263
1765	52 923	55 287	55 021
1766	51 029	53 351	53 053
1767	47 270	49 454	50 404
1768	50 844	53 190	54 118
1769	54 045	56 537	57 535
1770	54 724	57 319	58 252
1771	52 889	55 345	56 345
1772	52 500	55 055	56 198
1773	52 125	54 507	55 677
1774	52 823	55 249	56 230
1775	54 485	56 935	58 058
1776	56 722	59 327	60 495
1777	56 720	59 325	60 459
1778	54 722	57 245	58 395
1779	55 487	58 088	59 093
1780	56 100	58 741	59 678
1781	55 606	58 172	59 253
1782	56 494	59 066	58 747
1783	59 656	62 201	62 036
1784	62 119	64 768	64 597
1785	64 019	66 934	66 686
1786	61 755	64 485	64 220
1787	62 998	65 980	64 587
1788	61 772	64 492	64 341
1789	63 393	66 273	65 946
1790	67 517	70 459	66 074
1791	65 456	68 287	68 092
1792	68 597	71 624	71 359
1793	65 561	68 486	68 201
1794	64 611	67 448	67 233
1795	61 993	64 747	64 490
1796	65 850	68 791	68 501
1797	67 339	70 358	72 134
1798	71 859	74 935	74 755
1799	70 215	73 093	73 046
1800	63 155	65 875	65 700

instance since adding the county totals (5,802 baptisms, 6,198 burials) to the published national figure produces an exact agreement with the sum of the county totals in the case of burials and leaves a difference of only three in the case of baptisms. In other cases simple, if massive, arithmetic errors appear to explain the discrepancies. Rickman's national marriage total in 1761 falls exactly 3,000 short of the sum of the county totals, for example, while his marriage total for 1790 is 4,000 too large. There were many smaller discrepancies ending in one or two noughts which

Table A7.2: Years in which the published national totals

	Baptisms			
	(1)	(2)	(3)	(4)
1750	162 821	0	163 121	300
1760	169 722	723	169 722	723
1770	188 077	0	189 077	1 000
1780	200 437	−100	201 237	700
1781	202 506	−1 000	203 506	0
1783	200 443	5 805	200 443	5 805
1785	215 752	−1	215 752	−1
1786	214 431	−4	213 831	−604
1787	213 627	2 791	216 627	209
1789	221 063	370	221 063	370
1793	233 988	200	233 788	0
1794	227 346	500	227 346	500
1795	225 587	4	225 623	40
1797	238 116	1 007	238 116	1 007
1798	238 427	−1 000	239 427	0
1799	235 820	200	235 820	−200
1800	227 372	1 096	227 372	1 096

	Burials			
	(1)	(2)	(3)	(4)
1700	120 736	−50	120 736	−50
1710	127 627	−1 008	128 627	−8
1730	161 410	−72	161 410	−72
1760	142 751	100	142 751	100
1770	159 830	0	159 142	688
1782	165 419	−30	165 419	−30
1783	171 900	6 198	171 900	6 198
1785	168 747	−1 000	169 747	0
1789	165 210	25	165 210	25
1790	164 905	0	163 905	−1 000
1791	166 396	0	167 396	1 000
1794	176 767	1	176 767	1
1795	187 563	0	186 563	−1 000
1797	169 303	−968	169 303	−988
1799	169 244	20	168 464	−780
1800	184 657	−622	184 657	−622

suggest arithmetic error. Other inaccuracies are more puzzling. The published national marriage totals were consistently too low between 1767 and 1781, by amounts varying between 1,200 and 1,500, a figure which suggests that a county the size of Hampshire was consistently missed during this period. But the differences do not match the totals for any county and the reason for the run of errors remains uncertain.

Table A7.2 contains details of those years in each series in which the sum of the county totals differs from the published national total given in column 1 of table A7.1. A column of 'true' totals is also shown, because in some instances county totals are themselves clearly inaccurate and do not equal the sum of the totals for individual hundreds within the county. For example, the county burial total for Devon in 1795 is given as 8,753, compared with 6,531 in the previous year. It was a year of

of baptisms, burials, or marriages in the 1801 census are inaccurate

		Marriages		
	(1)	(2)	(3)	(4)
1759	48 868	−636	48 868	−636
1761	51 909	3 000	51 909	3 000
1762	50 518	5	50 518	5
1764	56 841	0	56 041	800
1767	48 482	1 212	48 482	1 212
1768	52 053	1 209	52 053	1 209
1769	55 341	1 296	55 341	1 296
1770	56 029	1 305	56 029	1 305
1771	54 205	1 316	54 205	1 316
1772	53 786	1 286	54 054	1 554
1773	53 536	1 411	53 536	1 411
1774	54 066	1 243	54 066	1 243
1775	55 824	1 339	55 824	1 339
1776	58 169	1 447	58 169	1 447
1777	58 134	1 414	58 134	1 414
1778	56 149	1 427	56 149	1 427
1779	56 823	1 336	56 823	1 336
1780	58 388	2 288	57 388	1 288
1781	56 978	1 372	56 978	1 372
1785	64 019	0	64 129	110
1787	63 008	10	62 108	−890
1788	61 872	100	61 872	100
1790	63 517	−4 000	63 517	−4 000
1792	67 597	−1 000	68 597	0
1794	64 631	20	64 631	20
1797	69 338	2 000	69 338	2 000
1799	70 216	1	70 216	1

Column headings

(1) Sum of county totals.
(2) Column 1 total minus the total given in the 1801 census.
(3) 'True' total (see text).
(4) Column 3 total minus the total given in the 1801 census.

exceptionally high mortality but an increase of more than a third over the total for 1794 is a suspiciously large rise compared with those in other counties. The sum of the Devon hundred totals, however, proves to be 7,753, representing a much more modest rise in burials of about 19 per cent over the previous year. The error of 1,000 between the two totals is probably another example of faulty arithmetic. In other cases errors in county totals are more likely to have been printer's mistakes, since the *national* total tallies with the sum of the correct county totals. The national total of burials in 1798, for example, is 1,000 greater than the sum of county totals but the national total is the more accurate because the printed county total for Northampton-shire (2,407) is 1,000 less than the sum of the hundred totals.

The corrections made to the national totals cover inaccuracies arising from failure to add up county totals with precision, and some of the more conspicuous defects in the county totals themselves, but no attempt was made to check *all* county totals against the totals of the hundreds within each county. Sometimes even a rapid scrutiny of county totals suggests serious errors. For example, the baptism total for Worcestershire in 1780 is given as 3,189, made up of 1,290 male and 1,899 female baptisms. The male figure proves to be a misprint for 2,090. It is abundantly clear that a systematic check of this sort would bring to light many more errors (see pp. 612–4 below). The 'true' totals shown in table A7.2, therefore, though significantly more accurate than the totals Rickman printed could be improved upon if they were built up from hundred rather than county totals as the prime units of information.[19]

Another point of difference between the series shown in the second and third columns of table A7.1 may be noted. The rate of growth in each series is slightly higher in the new estimates than in the revised Rickman series. For example, the number of baptisms rises by 73.1 per cent between 1700 and 1798 in the Rickman series, but by 74.7 per cent in the new series (1798 rather than 1800 was chosen because it is the latest year in the baptism series not affected by arithmetic error in Rickman's series). This happens because Rickman used a fixed inflation ratio, which was inevitable on the information available to him at the time but is clearly wrong in principle since many of the missing returns were for chapelries that began registration part way through the eighteenth century. Where the returns for the mother church are included in the 1801 returns it is to be supposed that at the point at which registration began in any particular chapelry, the chapelry's contribution to any inflation ratio will fall abruptly and totals in the original returns should be raised in a diminishing proportion.[20]

The parish register returns published in the 1831 census make it feasible to estimate the degree to which any inflation ratio should be reduced between 1800 and 1700 since they list the time periods covered by surviving registers before 1812 and in the case of chapelries often record when registration began. Since the population of the registering units in 1811 is known, their 'weight' in the total population of missing parishes is also known and the effect of the disappearance of any one parish upon the inflation ratio can therefore be calculated. The information necessary for such calculations is shown in table A7.3. In this table the figure for marriages in 1800 (15.00) indicates that in parishes containing 15 per cent of the total population of the missing parishes there was no registration of marriage in 1800. Marriages of people living in these parishes must have taken place elsewhere and should have been included in the returns. Therefore the inflation ratio for the marriage series in that year should be reduced by 15 per cent. The percentage reduction in the inflation ratio tends

19. Rickman's revised totals for England and Wales which were printed in the 1811 census have been widely used and reproduced, but it has been clear for a very long time that they contained serious arithmetic errors. In the *8th Annual Report* George Graham, in the course of his discussion of marriage fluctuations as a barometer of economic conditions, produced a revised set of marriage totals from 1754 onwards, having noted that the 1801 returns were 'disfigured by a few arithmetical errors' (*8th Annual Report*, p. 7 and pp. 48–9). He also appears to have proceeded by substituting the sum of county totals for the printed national total wherever the two differed.

Rickman's proneness to haphazard error, incidentally, persisted beyond 1801. In 1811 the table that contains the original and inflated totals of baptisms, burials, and marriages for the eighteenth century includes the following serious printing error in the calculation of a revised marriage total for 1787 arrived at by adding 1/50 to the 1801 figure: $69,067 + 1,381 = 76,448$ (*1811 Census*, Preliminary observations, p. xx).

20. It is, of course, also probable that in most cases the populations of chapelries were growing faster than those of their mother churches and that therefore the inflation ratios should be reduced moving backwards in time even before separate registration ceased, but this is a refinement we have ignored.

to rise in all three series moving backwards in time, but it should be noted that it can fall as well as rise because parishes missing from the 1801 return may maintain registers for a period but then cease registration in one or more series for a time, and during the period when there is no registration in the parish in question, registration coverage will improve. That this can occur on a considerable scale may be seen from the marriage series, which was already high in 1800 and rose to 16.85 by 1754 moving backwards in time. It then fell to a low of 14.05 in 1743 before rising once more to 23.26 by 1701.[21] The period of fall is an indirect reflection of the uncertainty

Table A7.3: Percentage by which the total inflation ratio is reduced to take account of registration coverage in missing parishes

	Baptisms	Burials	Marriages		Baptisms	Burials	Marriages
1800	0.18	0.79	15.00	1751			15.33
1796	0.52	1.13	15.08	1750	6.53	7.10	15.62
1795		1.24		1748	6.56		
1794	0.60	1.52		1747			14.93
1791	0.52	1.44		1745	6.72	7.25	14.39
1790		1.51		1743	7.83	8.37	14.05
1789	0.53	1.52		1742	7.86	8.40	14.07
1788			15.86	1741	8.02	8.55	14.23
1787	1.27	2.29		1738	8.04	8.58	14.25
1785	1.32	2.33	15.91	1737		8.60	
1783	1.37	2.39	15.94	1736	8.24	8.71	14.27
1782	1.40	2.41		1735	9.89	10.35	15.91
1781		2.43	15.85	1733		10.97	16.54
1779	1.53		15.77	1732	10.55	11.64	
1778	1.56	2.46	15.72	1731	10.61	11.70	16.60
1777	1.80	2.54		1729			16.76
1776		2.77		1728	10.65	11.74	16.80
1775	1.86	2.86	15.67	1727	10.76		
1774		2.84		1724		12.21	17.27
1772			16.43	1723	12.08	13.53	17.82
1771	2.22	3.12		1722	12.70	13.93	18.43
1770	2.27			1721	13.39	14.67	
1769	2.72	3.56	16.45	1720	14.01	15.81	18.99
1768	2.83			1719	14.40	16.21	19.26
1766	2.86	3.60		1718	15.51	16.70	19.83
1765	4.11	4.85	16.48	1717	15.78	17.04	20.18
1764	4.14	4.88	16.44	1716	17.93	19.19	21.00
1763	4.16			1715		20.69	
1762	4.23		16.51	1712	18.01		21.06
1759	4.95	5.14		1711	18.09	20.77	21.14
1758			16.55	1710	18.38	21.06	21.42
1757	5.01	5.58		1708	18.40		
1755			16.65	1707	19.01		22.03
1754	5.06	5.63	16.85	1703	20.17	22.23	23.19
1753	6.11	6.68	16.50	1702	20.22		
1752	6.24	6.81	15.51	1701	20.29	22.30	23.26

Notes: The table should be read backwards in time; thus, the figure in the baptism column for 1800, 0.18, holds good for 1799, 1798, and 1797 but is replaced by 0.52 in 1796.

See text for fuller explanation.

21. Rickman's marriage data in the 1801 returns only extend back to 1754 but in table A7.3 the percentage reduction figures for marriages are taken back to 1700 as for baptisms and burials.

about the status of marriages celebrated in chapelries brought about by Hardwicke's Act. This induced incumbents to cease to allow marriages to take place in many chapelries. The effect appears to be spread over a decade only because the last recorded marriage in such parishes may have taken place some time before the Act came into force. In general in compiling the information used in this table we have assumed, unless the 1831 return explicitly states otherwise, that any parish that was a vicarage or rectory was maintaining registration even though the earliest surviving register book in 1831 was of a late date (that is we have assumed that registers existed but had been lost by 1831). In the case of chapelries we have made the opposite assumption, that even where the 1831 return does not explicitly state that registration only began at a certain date it is assumed to have begun only at the time of the earliest recorded register. It follows that chapelries account for almost all of the changes shown in table A7.3.

Another noteworthy feature of table A7.1 is that the new estimates given in column 3 are always lower than those in column 2 representing the revised Rickman series, except where Rickman's additions were faulty. We return later to the question of the evidence for the supposition that Rickman's figures were too high, but it is convenient at this point to touch on another aspect of the relationship between the two series. It is natural to suspect that the method used to generate the new estimates would tend to produce too high a figure. The method is based on the assumption that the number of events in the 'missing' parishes was proportional to their population. Since many were very small and a disproportionate number were chapelries it is reasonable to suppose that some were missed initially because very few if any events were being registered. In the case of very small parishes the incumbent would usually live elsewhere and the local celebration of the Anglican rites might present difficulties. In the case of chapelries the mother church might still attract a greater share of total events than the population of the chapelries would suggest. In both cases using the population of the 'missing' parish as a guide to the extent of correction needed would result in an overestimate. Rickman's reliance on the actual frequency of events registered in 'missing' parishes in 1801– 10 as a proportion of total events avoids this danger. It also affords a rough and ready means of discovering whether the new estimates are over-inflated.

We have seen that Rickman appears to have believed in 1811 that 713 English

Table A7.4: New estimates of numbers of baptisms, burials, and marriages and 'expected' totals

		(1) New estimates	(2) 'Expected' totals'	(3) Difference (1)–(2)
Baptisms	*1700*	143 535	144 339	804
	1750	170 325	171 679	1 354
	1800	238 056	239 696	1 640
Burials	*1700*	125 205	125 603	398
	1750	148 835	149 539	704
	1800	193 282	194 154	872
Marriages	*1755*	45 685	45 458	227
	1800	65 700	65 204	496

Sources: New estimates, table A7.1, column 3. For derivation of 'expected' totals see text.

parishes were missed in the original returns compared with a total of 632 thrown up in the course of the present study. Since a large number of parishes are common to both lists it is probable that the frequency of events registered in the two groups of parishes was roughly proportionate to the number of parishes in each group. If 'missing' parishes normally registered fewer events than their population would suggest, the new estimates would tend to be higher than the base figure of column 1 plus the difference between the totals of column 2 and column 1 multiplied by 632/713. For example, if there were 100,000 events in a given year in column 1, and 106,000 in column 2, the 'expected' figure in column 3 would be 100,000 + (6,000 × 632/713) = 105,318. Table A7.4 presents some examples of the application of this method of discovering whether the new estimates given in column 3 of table A7.1 are too high when compared with an 'expected' figure derived in the manner just described. The 'expected' figures have been modified to allow for the changes in the inflation percentage during the century. Allowance has also been made for the effect of arithmetic errors in Rickman's original totals.[22]

Only in the case of marriages are the new estimate figures higher than the 'expected' totals, suggesting that there were disproportionately few marriages in the 'missing' parishes. Where the 'missing' parishes were chapelries that did not celebrate marriages the absence of events is taken into account in calculating an inflation percentage (see table A7.3). But it may be that even in chapelries in which some marriages were celebrated a substantial number of couples preferred to use the mother church. This would produce the observed effect. The 'expected' baptism and burial totals, on the other hand, are consistently lower than the new estimates. The most reasonable explanation, by symmetry with the explanation for the discrepancies in the marriage totals, is that the chapelries within the 'missing' parishes were places where the age structure of the population produced high birth rates, which would also tend to mean high death rates given the high proportion of all deaths accounted for by the very young. But the most important of the steps that Rickman took in correcting his original 1801 returns, the addition of totals shown in the Supplement, is impossible to check satisfactorily, and it is therefore equally likely that the explanation of the discrepancies lies in part in the difficulty he experienced in identifying duplicate returns. This might well have affected baptisms and burials more than marriages since many chapelries did not celebrate marriages and so caused no risk of double counting. It may be significant in this regard that burials occupy a position between baptisms and marriages in the relative extent and direction of the discrepancies in table A7.4, and that they also occupied an intermediate position in chapelry registration – more chapelries recorded baptisms than burials, but marriages were less often registered than either. Viewed as a whole the test does not suggest that the new estimates tend to produce figures which are too high.

Having considered the way in which Rickman manipulated the national totals of events in an attempt to overcome the defects of the original returns of 1801, we may now work down from the general to the particular, from the methods used in

---

22. For example, the original Rickman figure for burials in 1700 is 120,786 (col. 1, table A7.1). The revised Rickman figure (col. 2) is 7,067 larger. The first step in deriving an 'expected' figure for col. 3 is to reduce 7,067 in the ratio 632/713, or 6,264. But this figure is still too high since the col. 3 figure in table A6.1 was derived after taking account of the fact that 22.3 per cent of the parishes missing in 1800 were not registering units in 1700 (see table A7.3). Therefore 6,264 should be reduced proportionately (i.e. multiplied by 0.777) to 4,867. Finally, the original Rickman total was discovered to be 50 too high when compared with the sum of the county totals, so that the final 'expected' figure is 120,786 – 50 + 4,867 = 125,603.

correcting national totals to the original returns from individual parishes upon which the whole structure rested. We have already seen several instances of the ineptitude of Rickman or of his staff in tabulating and aggregating the returns. It is not surprising that the enterprise should have encountered difficulties. Tabulation of the original returns to provide totals for each hundred by aggregating parish totals, and for each county by aggregating hundred totals, represented an immense labour since the work was all done by hand. If error was to be avoided, some form of cross tabulation designed to ensure that row and column totals both summed to the same figure would have been necessary. It seems clear that this was not done in 1801. Even the final stage of summing the county totals produced many serious errors, as we have already seen. The earlier stages of summation involved similar errors.

In table A7.5 the published county baptism totals for Suffolk are compared with the totals produced by adding together the individual figures for the 24 hundreds within

Table A7.5: Suffolk baptism totals from 1801 parish register returns

	(1)	(2)	(3)
1700	4 342	4 337	5
1710	3 910	3 816	94
1720	3 900	3 915	15
1730	4 196	4 205	9
1740	4 337	4 341	4
1750	4 448	4 452	4
1760	4 713	4 714	1
1770	5 382	5 379	3
1780	5 386	5 288	98
1781	5 390	5 395	5
1782	5 001	4 907	94
1783	5 526	5 630	130
1784	5 339	5 343	4
1785	5 801	5 808	7
1786	5 969	5 973	4
1787	6 069	5 973	96
1788	6 018	6 025	7
1789	5 952	5 948	4
1790	6 190	6 200	10
1791	6 208	6 205	3
1792	6 446	6 453	7
1793	6 238	6 242	4
1794	6 156	6 260	104
1795	5 804	5 830	26
1796	5 970	5 964	6
1797	6 429	6 338	91
1798	6 528	6 339	189
1799	6 190	6 094	96
1800	6 051	6 059	8
TOTAL	159 889	159 433	

Column headings

(1) Sum of the totals for the individual hundreds.
(2) Published county totals.
(3) (1)–(2)

Source: 1801 Census, Parish registers, pp. 288–300.

the county. In no case do the two totals agree. Usually the differences are small: 17 were under 10, 3 between 10 and 26, 7 between 91 and 104, and 2 were rather larger at 130 and 189. The total of the differences ignoring sign is 1,102, or about 0.7 per cent, while the net difference of 456 amounts to only 0.3 per cent of the total of baptisms in the 29 years covered. In some individual years the differences are much more substantial, ranging up to almost 3 per cent. No doubt similar checks would reveal the same general pattern in other counties but a complete survey of this type, though very desirable is outside the scope of this appendix.

Table A7.6 contains the result of a similar exercise to that set out in table A7.5 but in table A7.6 the aggregation of hundred totals to make up county totals is tested for all counties at a single date rather than for the same county at all dates (the choice of 1730 for table A7.6, like the choice of Suffolk for table A7.5, was quite arbitrary). The inaccuracies revealed by table A7.6 are less frequent and in the main less serious than those of table A7.5. In 27 cases the totals in columns 2 and 3 agree, in 4 cases the difference is under 10, in 8 cases between 10 and 30, and in the 3 remaining cases the differences are 72, 100, and 270. The total of the differences ignoring sign is 628 (0.4 per cent) and the net difference is 320 (0.2 per cent). It may be noted that the sum of the totals of column 3 (161,410) does not agree with the national total in the 1801 census which is 161,482 (see table A7.1). Undoubtedly there are a multitude of similar errors, small and larger, which could only be picked up by a systematic reworking of the successive stages of aggregation in the census.

The accuracy of the original returns themselves is an even larger topic. The only way to test the matter adequately would be to take a number of hundreds for which the registers listed in the 1801 returns still exist and parallel the work of the incumbents of the day, comparing the result with the published totals in the census. This is beyond the scope of this appendix.[23]

In a few cases, however, some checking is easy to carry out because occasionally a single parish constituted a whole hundred. Table A7.7 contains some details about six such parishes. For each parish there are, of course, 29 individual annual totals of baptisms and burials (every tenth year 1700 to 1770 and every year 1780 to 1800), and 46 such totals for marriages (each year 1755 to 1800, ignoring 1754 which was not a full year in Rickman returns).

The six parishes are Aylesbury (Buckingham), Berwick upon Tweed (Northumberland), Bridgwater (Somerset), Bishop's Cleeve (Gloucester), Ludlow (Shropshire), and Romford (Essex). All annual totals in the Cambridge Group's aggregative tabulations are made on the New Style calendar with each year beginning 1 January. In the parish registers before the introduction of the New Style calendar in 1752 the year usually (though not invariably) begins on 25 March. Before discussing the general accuracy of Rickman's figures, therefore, it is convenient to consider how incumbents interpreted the request made to them for parish register returns for years before 1752. The request itself, quoted in the first paragraph of the appendix, is ambiguous.

The bottom half of table A7.7 and the summary information given in table A7.8 show that five of the six incumbents in the small sample available used the O.S. calendar before 1752. In the sixth parish, Romford, it is very probable that the incumbent recalculated to the N.S. convention. This emerges most clearly in the

---

23. Materials for a fuller examination of this question are, however, being assembled. See also Wrigley, 'Checking Rickman' which deals with the returns made for the five parishes of Cliston Hundred, Devon.

Table A7.6: County burial totals for 1730

	(1)	(2)	(3)	(4)
Bedford	10	1 758	1 758	0
Berkshire	25	2 237	2 226	11
Buckingham	10	2 469	2 569	100
Cambridge	16	2 226	2 226	0
Chester	9	3 480	3 480	0
Cornwall	11	4 033	4 033	0
Cumberland	7	1 629	1 629	0
Derby	7	2 556	2 563	7
Devon	33	6 637	6 617	20
Dorset	12	2 499	2 499	0
Durham	8	3 300	3 300	0
Essex	24	5 217	5 217	0
Gloucester	31	4 521	4 542	21
Hampshire	13	3 093	3 093	0
Hereford	12	1 576	1 552	24
Hertford	10	2 343	2 345	2
Huntingdon	5	1 213	1 213	0
Kent	17	5 492	5 492	0
Lancashire	10	6 754	6 754	0
Leicester	7	2 068	2 068	0
Lincoln	33	5 934	5 912	22
Middlesex	10	12 779	12 779	0
London and Westminster	3	12 206	11 936	270
Norfolk	33	6 260	6 242	18
Northampton	22	3 136	3 136	0
Northumberland	8	2 333	2 261	72
Nottingham	11	2 415	2 415	0
Oxford	16	2 281	2 281	0
Rutland	5	359	359	0
Shropshire	16	3 485	3 509	24
Somerset	39	5 879	5 879	0
Stafford	8	3 695	3 695	0
Suffolk	24	4 568	4 568	0
Surrey	14	6 074	6 074	0
Sussex	9	2 740	2 710	30
Warwick	8	3 226	3 226	0
Westmorland	6	932	932	0
Wiltshire	31	3 688	3 683	5
Worcester	9	2 720	2 720	0
Yorkshire E.R.	17	2 366	2 366	0
Yorkshire N.R.	14	2 574	2 572	2
Yorkshire W.R.	12	6 979	6 979	0
TOTAL		161 730	161 410	

Column headings

(1) Number of hundreds in county.
(2) Sum of totals for individual hundreds.
(3) Published county totals.
(4) (2)–(3)

Source: Cols. 2 and 3, *1801 Census*, Parish registers.

burial register where the total for 1720 agrees with the Group figure exactly using the N.S. year but is out by 21 using the O.S. year. Accordingly in table A7.8 on the B lines the Romford data is taken using the N.S. year. Comparison of lines A and B in the lower half of table A7.8 shows how large an improvement in agreement between the two series is obtained if the Rickman returns are assumed to follow the O.S. year until 1752 with the exception of Romford. Comparison of lines B and C suggests that with this adjustment the returns from the first half of the eighteenth century are as accurate as those from the second half when allowance is made for the fact that the Group's returns can only be adjusted from a year beginning 1 January to a year beginning 1 April rather than 25 March since the unit of recording is the calendar month. This explains why the B series is initially lower than the C but catches up with it at discrepancies of 4 or more. If the Group totals could be adjusted to the O.S. year exactly there would in all probability be a sharp rise in the percentage of 0 and 1 discrepancies by transfer from the higher values.[24]

The top halves of tables A7.7 and A7.9 show the result of comparing the tabulations published by Rickman in the 1801 census with Group aggregative tabulations over the second half of the century. Some of the discrepancies are more apparent than real. These are indicated in the table and all such months have been excluded from the summary shown in table A7.9 and from the totals of events in table A7.7. They probably occur because the incumbents making the returns appear to have had more complete registers than have survived to the present,[25] or if the registers were already defective in 1801, to have had an alternative source of information,[26] or possibly to have interpolated to make good missing months. The large number of asterisked figures in the line referring to marriages in Berwick occur for a different reason. The Group totals are frequently the larger from 1773 to 1791 because of the inclusion of marriages recorded as having been performed in Scotland 'and dues paid', which the incumbent appears to have excluded from his return.

Tables A7.7 and A7.9 show only the size of discrepancies between parallel series without distinguishing the sign of the discrepancy. It will be seen, however, that there is no strong tendency for the discrepancies to be consistently of the same sign since the totals obtained by summing the events in comparable series are usually very close to each other whether considered separately for each parish or amalgamated as in table A7.9. The differences between the totals are always far smaller than the sum of the individual discrepancies. In table A7.9, for example, the sum of the discrepancies in baptisms amounts to 365 compared with a difference of 41 in the totals, while the

---

24. We have been able to make this further adjustment of the Ludlow returns with the following results for baptisms and burials combined (i.e. 12 annual comparisons in all).
Discrepancy between annual totals

	0	1	2	3	4	5	6	7	8	9	10	>10	Mean discrepancy
A		1	2	1	3		1		1			3	5.9
B		4	2	2	1			1	1		1		3.6
C	3	2	3	2		1		1					2.3

A. Rickman's returns compared with N.S. totals
B. Rickman's returns compared with O.S. totals (1 April – 31 March)
C. Rickman's returns compared with O.S. totals (25 March – 24 March)

25. An illustration of the way in which spurious discrepancies may arise occurred in the course of preparing the data. There were initally large discrepancies between the Group's figures for baptisms and burials in Aylesbury in 1783 and 1784 and those in the Rickman returns. In each case there were several blank months in the Group's return. Further work on the Aylesbury register led to the discovery of entries for the blank months on a separate sheet in an earlier register. With the addition of these months the two sets of totals tallied closely.

26. Many incumbents are believed to have made up parish registers (and no doubt also Bishop's Transcripts) from rough note books used at the time of the ceremony in church.

Table A7.7: Comparison of annual totals of events in the 1801 parish register returns with comparable totals drawn from Cambridge Group tabulations

	No. of years	No. of events Census	Group	Mean (approx.)	0	1	2	3	4	5	6	7	8	10	10
Baptisms 1760–1800															
Aylesbury	23	2 136	2 180	93	3	5	5	1	3	1	2	1			2 (12,16)
Berwick	23	2 078	2 176	92	0	5	2	4	4	3	3				1 (19)
Bridgwater	23	2 657	2 601	114	2	7	5	2	1	1	1		1	1	2 (13,14)
Cleeve	23	822	809	35	14	7	1						1		
Ludlow	23	2 546	2 534	110	11	6	4						2		
Romford	23	1 900	1 880	86	5	7	2	4			1		1	1	1 (25*)
Burials 1760–1800															
Aylesbury	23	1 837	1 801	78	6	6	4	3						1	3 (12,17,29)
Berwick	23	4 015	4 004	174	22		4								1 (11)
Bridgwater	23	2 217	2 180	98	7	6	4			1		1	1		3 (13,19,15)
Cleeve	23	561	561	24	21	2									
Ludlow	23	1 886	1 877	82	14	6	2	1							
Romford	23	1 984	1 962	90	5	10	4				1			1	1 (15*)
Marriages 1755–1800															
Aylesbury	46	1 001	1 006	22	36	7	1*	3*	1*	3*	1*	1*			
Berwick	46	827	821	32	19*	4	1*	3*	1*	4*	4*	1*			
Bridgwater	46	1 520	1 499	33	26	13	3	2	1						
Cleeve	46	430	430	9	44	2								1	
Ludlow	46	903	896	20	31	15									
Romford	46	802	819	18	32	10		2					1		10 (11*,12*,15*,16*,16*,19*,20*,20*,22*,27*)

Baptisms *1700–50*

		6													
Aylesbury	(a)	6	419	429	71			2			1	2			1 (14)
	(b)			435		1	2	1			2				
Berwick	(a)	6	550	582	103	1	1	1	1						2 (28*,26)
	(b)			554		1	1	3		1					2 (37*,12)
Bridgwater	(a)	6	506	515	85	1			1	2					1 (11)
	(b)			491			2		1		1				1 (12)
Cleeve	(a)	6	143	144	24	1	2	3		1					
	(b)			149		1	1	1		1					
Ludlow	(a)	6	409	433	70		1	1	2		1				
	(b)			409			2	2	1					1	
Romford	(a)	6	327	326	54	2	2	1	1		1		1		
	(b)			329		2	2	2	2						

Burials *1700–50*

		6													
Aylesbury	(a)	6	420	435	71		3			2	1				
	(b)			437			2	1	1	2					
Berwick	(a)	6	561	569	94	1	2	1	1	2	1	1			
	(b)			559		2	2		1	2		2			
Bridgwater	(a)	6	481	529	84	1	2	1	1	1	1		2		1 (27)
	(b)			486				1	1		1				
Cleeve	(a)	6	142	141	24	2		2	1	2	1	1			
	(b)			143			3			1					
Ludlow	(a)	6	447	414	72		1	1	1	1		1			3 (11,12,13)
	(b)			432			2	2	1						
Romford	(a)	6	477	481	80	3	1		1	1		1			1 (21)
	(b)			450		1				2	2				

(a) Group totals for years running 1 January to 31 December.

(b) Group totals for years running 1 April to 31 March.

*Discrepancy not evidence of inaccuracy (where the figure asterisked refers to more than one year some of the discrepancies may be genuine).

Sources: 1801 *Census* Parish registers, pp. 20, 97, 103, 223, 251, 272, and Cambridge Group aggregative tabulations.

Table A7.8: Effect of Old Style calendar on totals of events (annual totals of baptisms and burials)

		No. of annual totals	Discrepancy between comparable totals											
			0	1	2	3	4	5	6	7	8	9	10	>10
1700-50	A	71	5	10	14	6	10	6	6	2	1	1	2	8
1700-50	B	71	13	25	10	4	7	1	5	2	1	0	1	2
1760-1800	C	274	110	67	33	16	8	6	8	2	5	5	2	12
		Same expressed as cumulative percentages												
	A		7	21	41	49	63	72	80	83	85	86	89	100
	B		18	54	68	73	83	85	92	94	96	96	97	100
	C		40	65	77	82	85	88	91	91	93	95	96	100

A Rickman's totals compared with Group totals for year beginning 1 January.
B Rickman's totals compared with Group totals for year beginning 1 April (except Romford where the year beginning 1 January has been used — see text).
C Rickman's totals compared with Group totals for year beginning 1 January.
Source: Table A7.7.

Table A7.9: Comparison of corrected annual totals of events in the 1801 parish register returns for Aylesbury, Berwick, Bridgwater, Cleeve, Ludlow, and Romford with the comparable totals drawn from Cambridge Group tabulations

		No. of years	No. of events Census	Group	Discrepancy between comparable totals										
					0	1	2	3	4	5	6	7	8	9	10	>10
Baptisms	*1760-1800*	137	12 139	12 180	35	37	19	11	8	5	7	1	5	3	1	5
Burials	*1760-1800*	137	12 500	12 385	75	30	14	5	0	1	1	1	0	2	1	7
Marriages	*1755-1800*	257	5 483	5 471	186	51	4	5	4	2	3	0	1	0	1	0

Source: Table A7.7.

comparable figures for burials are 235 and 115, and for marriages 136 and 12.

Discrepancies are fewest and smallest in the marriage series partly because the number of events was fewer and partly no doubt also because the printed marriage registers which came into general use after Hardwicke's Act made for easy counting. Seventy-two per cent of the comparable pairs of annual marriage totals in table A7.9 were identical while a further 20 per cent differed by only one. The comparable figures for burials are 55 and 22 per cent, while for baptisms they are 26 and 27 per cent. The average annual frequency of events in both the baptism and burial series was about 90 (Cleeve was much smaller than the other five parishes which averaged about 100). In the baptism series 20 per cent of the comparable annual totals showed discrepancies of 5 or more; in the burial series 9 per cent showed discrepancies in this size range. Individual parishes varied considerably. The incumbent of Berwick must have been meticulously accurate in counting burials since 22 of the 23 annual totals agree exactly with the Group totals even though this was the largest of the six parishes, recording an average of 174 burials per annum. In view of this it is odd that his baptism totals were frequently slightly fewer than those in the Group's tabulation, conceivably because it is very easy with baptisms to count the number of entries without checking each entry to see if it refers to twins.

Some of the observed discrepancies are probably due to transcription errors on the part of Rickman's clerks. These are almost impossible to avoid in any large body of data. Others no doubt reflect inaccuracies on the part of the local volunteers who were kind enough to carry out the tabulations for the Group.[27] The evidence of table A7.9 suggests, however, that the basic operation of data collection was carried out conscientiously by the incumbents to whom Rickman sent his request. The differences in the overall totals in table A7.9 between Rickman's returns and the Group returns amount to 0.34 per cent for baptisms, 0.92 per cent for burials, and 0.22 per cent for marriages. None of these is large enough to be a cause for misgiving about the parish register returns in the 1801 census if it is safe to assume that the six parishes are representative of the mass of parishes in general.

Many registers, however, even in the eighteenth century, contained gaps or years of deficient registration and this occasions some additional uncertainty about the reliability of Rickman's data. Rickman was conscious of this problem and made some effort to overcome it, but it is likely that he was only partially successful both because defective years were not always noted and because his method of correcting returns for defective years may not always have been adequate. Inasmuch as such years were commoner in the early part of the century than in its later decades this would tend to cause the apparent rate of growth in the frequency of events to be overstated.

On the page at the front of the volume of parish register returns of 1801 on which the questions addressed to incumbents and overseers are listed, there is the following footnote: 'In cases where the returns are stated to be in some years "defective", such defects have been supplied, in every instance, by an average number of baptisms, burials, and marriages (or of either) taken from the returns of the same parish, in such of the years specified in the respective tables as are immediately preceding and subsequent to such defect'. In the returns for the six parishes none of the incumbents seems to have drawn attention to defective years and indeed there is no year that was unambiguously defective in these series, but in another parish hundred, Ottery St Mary, not included in the foregoing tables, the incumbent must have described the baptisms and burials in 1710 and again in 1730 as defective since the totals of events in Rickman's series are much inflated compared with the totals in the Group's returns. The Group's figures for the years 1700, 1710, 1720, 1730, and 1740 run 54, 27, 58, 4, 48 for baptisms, and 54, 3, 53, 22, 39 for burials. In Rickman's series both the low baptism figures have been changed to 52 while the two low burial figures are both given as 44 (the other figures in both series are the same in the Rickman and Group series or differ only slightly). The interpolated figures are interesting since they are not averages of the two adjacent years but lower, and lower also than the average for the series as a whole. The fact that the same figure was used twice over in each series also suggests rough and ready adjustments. If the method used for Ottery was widely used in correcting defective years it would lead to some understatements of the 'true' totals even after adjustment.

County estimates

The revised Rickman series and the new estimates in table A7.1 differ relatively little except where Rickman's additions were faulty. Using the Rickman method

---

27. The method used in checking the accuracy of Group tabulations where possible is described in appendix 11, and more summarily on pp. 16–8 above. Berwick, Bishop's Cleeve, and Ludlow were tested, but not the other three parishes.

produces somewhat higher totals of events in all three series, and, because the inflation ratio is fixed, it implies a slightly lower overall growth over the century as a whole. But the differences are too small to support any major change in the interpretation of eighteenth-century population growth. At the county level, however, it is another story. Table A7.10 shows the number of parishes missed in each county in Rickman's original 1801 returns and their population as a percentage of the county total in 1811. It also shows the total number of parishes in each county and expresses the number missing as a percentage of this figure[28] (a parish being defined once more, of course, as a vicarage, rectory, or chapelry maintaining a separate registration).

There are substantial differences in registration coverage between the counties. At one extreme almost 19 per cent of all Hampshire parishes were missed (with 8 per cent of the county population) and almost 11 per cent of Wiltshire's population lived in parishes that failed to make a return. At the other extreme all the Westmorland parishes appear to have been included. Westmorland contained only 61 parishes and a population of less than 50,000, but some large and populous counties were also very well covered, notably Lincolnshire, the county with the second largest number of parishes, where as few as 13 parishes out of a total of 607, containing only 1 per cent of the population of the county, were missed. Moreover, among the counties least well covered there were some where the degree of omission was virtually constant throughout the century, but others where many of the missing parishes were chapelries that began registration during the century so that coverage was much better in 1700 than in 1800. Hampshire is an example of the former type. In Hampshire 8.25 per cent of the population in 1800 lived in parishes not included in the 1801 original returns. The baptism figure given in the returns should therefore be increased by 100/91.75 (from 6,594 to 7,187). The figure for 1700, however, should be increased by almost as great a margin, 100/91.84, or from 3,376 to 3,676, because the only parishes missing in 1801 that began registration during the century were three tiny chapelries, each with a population of less than 100.

In the West Riding of Yorkshire, on the other hand, there were far more striking changes in registration coverage during the century. In 1800 the baptisms returned should be increased in the ratio 100/91.35, or from 15,334 to 16,790, to make good the missing returns. In 1700, however, the comparable ratio falls to 100/96.08, or an increase from 6,628 to 6,898. Whereas the 1801 returns suggest that the baptism total in the West Riding rose by 231 per cent, the revised figures suggest a rise of 243 per cent, and the final figure is higher, of course, than would be obtained by applying a national inflation ratio to the original 1801 return (16,308).

It is outside the scope of this appendix to discuss in full the implications of table A7.10 since to present revised estimates for each county in all three series for each year in the eighteenth century for which Rickman collected returns would occupy much space; and to examine them in detail much more. It may be of interest, however, to point to one of the uses to which the information may be put, especially as this

28. The total of 10,141 parishes for England as a whole may be compared with the figure of 10,189 given in the 1811 census and 10,327 in the 1831 census (including nine parishes that failed to make a return). The growth in numbers is to be expected because of the increase in the number of chapelries that began to act as separate registering units. The three Ridings of Yorkshire show how much the growth in parishes was tied to the increase and redistribution of population. The number of parishes in the East, North, and West Ridings in 1801 and 1831 (1831 shown in brackets) was the following: 234(234). 225(227), 278(307).

throws light not only upon the accuracy of the 1801 returns but also those sought by Rickman more than 30 years later and published in 1841.

Table A7.10: Registration coverage in 1801 by county

County	(1)	(2)	(3)	(4)	(5)	(6)
Bedford	6	124	2 127	70 213	4.8	3.0
Berkshire	10	158	3 519	118 277	6.3	3.0
Buckingham	11	205	7 079	117 650	5.4	6.0
Cambridge	5	172	3 140	101 109	2.9	3.1
Cheshire	16	122	15 303	227 031	13.1	6.7
Cornwall	8	201	4 285	216 667	4.0	2.0
Cumberland	5	135	644	133 744	3.7	0.5
Derby	12	181	7 422	185 487	6.6	4.0
Devon	25	468	15 944	383 308	5.3	4.2
Dorset	16	258	5 471	124 693	6.2	4.4
Durham	4	99	3 820	177 625	4.0	2.2
Essex	12	403	6 898	252 473	3.0	2.7
Gloucester	13	332	9 806	285 514	3.9	3.4
Hampshire	57	307	20 228	245 080	18.6	8.3
Hereford	16	222	4 690	94 073	7.2	5.0
Hertford	15	131	7 967	111 654	11.5	7.1
Huntingdon	1	97	201	42 208	1.0	0.5
Kent	23	395	16 588	373 095	5.8	4.5
Lancashire	17	190	50 471	828 309	9.0	6.1
Leicester	10	251	7 074	150 419	4.0	4.7
Lincoln	13	607	2 438	237 891	2.1	1.0
Middlesex	10	190	18 317	953 276	5.3	1.9
Norfolk	34	687	12 846	291 999	5.0	4.4
Northampton	17	292	7 753	141 353	5.8	5.5
Northumberland	3	92	1 150	172 161	3.3	0.7
Nottingham	23	214	10 327	162 900	10.8	6.3
Oxford	8	223	1 874	119 191	3.6	1.6
Rutland	1	50	57	16 380	2.0	0.4
Shropshire	15	230	8 278	194 298	6.5	4.3
Somerset	34	476	10 830	303 180	7.1	3.6
Stafford	13	177	18 036	295 153	7.3	6.1
Suffolk	30	500	16 143	234 211	6.0	6.9
Surrey	12	143	12 615	323 851	8.4	3.9
Sussex	7	297	3 992	190 083	2.4	2.1
Warwick	13	208	6 493	228 735	6.3	2.8
Westmorland	0	61	0	45 922	–	–
Wiltshire	39	309	20 725	193 828	12.6	10.7
Worcester	9	197	6 138	160 546	4.6	3.8
Yorkshire E.R.	30	234	15 132	167 353	12.8	9.0
Yorkshire N.R.	8	225	3 633	152 445	3.6	2.4
Yorkshire W.R.	31	278	56 659	653 315	11.2	8.7
ENGLAND	632	10 141	426 113	9 476 700	6.2	4.5

Column headings

(1) Number of parishes missed in the original 1801 parish returns.
(2) Total number of parishes in 1801.
(3) Population of missing parishes in 1811.
(4) County population in 1811.
(5) (1)/(2) × 100.
(6) (3)/(4) × 100.

Sources: Col. 3, *1811 Census*, Enumeration; Col. 4, *ibid.*, p. 427.

Table A7.11: County baptism, burial, and marriage rates in 1800 (per 1 000 total population)

County	(1) 1801 Population	(2) Baptisms 1801	(2) Baptisms 1841	(3) Burials 1801	(3) Burials 1841	(4) Marriages 1801	(4) Marriages 1841	(5) Baptism rates 1801	(5) Baptism rates 1841	(6) Burial rates 1801	(6) Burial rates 1841	(7) Marriage rates 1801	(7) Marriage rates 1841	(8) Percentage of county population covered 1841
Bedford	63 393	1 785	1 828	1 219	1 210	483	415	19.2	19.1	28.2	28.8	7.6	6.5	52.6
Berkshire	109 215	3 251	3 261	2 398	2 269	633	594	22.0	20.8	29.8	29.9	5.8	5.4	50.0
Buckingham	107 444	3 088	3 060	2 376	2 265	828	812	22.1	21.1	28.7	28.5	7.7	7.6	50.1
Cambridge	89 346	2 751	2 634	1 995	1 948	701	773	22.3	21.8	30.8	29.5	7.8	8.7	52.0
Cheshire	191 751	5 276	4 747	4 411	4 247	1 489	1 420	23.0	22.1	27.5	24.8	7.8	7.4	73.2
Cornwall	188 269	5 905	5 673	3 086	3 213	1 322	1 247	16.4	17.1	31.4	30.1	7.0	6.6	45.1
Cumberland	117 230	2 863	2 313	2 426	1 733	770	549	20.7	14.8	24.4	19.7	6.6	4.5	25.5
Derby	161 142	4 584	4 349	3 302	3 018	1 141	1 058	20.5	18.7	28.4	27.0	7.1	6.6	31.5
Devon	343 001	9 998	9 574	7 546	6 404	3 249	2 256	22.0	18.7	29.1	27.9	9.5	6.6	42.2
Dorset	115 319	2 837	3 189	2 021	2 171	812	796	17.4	18.8	24.6	27.7	7.0	6.9	35.6
Durham	160 361	4 316	2 950	4 028	2 407	1 234	819	25.1	15.0	26.9	18.4	7.7	5.1	53.7
Essex	226 437	6 488	6 424	5 119	5 081	1 558	1 464	22.6	22.4	28.7	28.4	6.9	6.5	52.2
Gloucester	250 809	6 764	6 765	5 120	5 089	1 845	2 125	20.4	20.3	27.0	27.0	7.4	8.5	50.1
Hampshire	219 656	7 187	6 782	5 466	4 741	2 107	2 144	24.9	21.6	32.7	30.9	9.6	9.8	30.2
Hereford	89 191	2 316	2 404	1 367	1 437	467	428	15.3	16.1	26.0	27.0	5.2	4.8	40.9
Hertford	97 577	2 719	2 743	2 097	2 022	596	628	21.5	20.7	27.9	28.1	6.1	6.4	61.1
Huntingdon	37 568	1 088	1 196	805	932	323	386	21.4	24.8	29.0	31.8	8.6	10.3	48.7
Kent	307 624	10 617	11 040	9 208	9 564	2 633	2 477	29.9	31.1	34.5	35.9	8.6	8.1	56.8
Lancashire	672 731	20 918	18 157	16 997	15 019	5 849	5 097	25.3	22.3	31.1	27.0	8.7	7.6	37.6
Leicester	130 081	3 788	3 160	2 838	2 611	970	909	21.8	20.1	29.1	24.3	7.5	7.0	61.9
Lincoln	208 557	6 543	6 911	4 029	4 538	1 590	1 602	19.3	21.8	31.4	33.1	7.6	7.7	52.5
Middlesex	818 129	20 856	23 176	27 656	26 698	8 682	8 486	33.8	32.6	25.5	28.3	10.6	10.4	39.1
Norfolk	273 371	8 917	8 232	6 339	5 818	2 151	1 961	23.2	21.3	32.6	30.1	7.9	7.2	53.4
Northampton	131 757	3 264	3 500	2 628	2 897	1 016	981	19.9	22.0	24.8	26.6	7.7	7.4	56.1
Northumberland	157 101	3 235	3 766	2 826	3 018	973	1 161	18.0	19.2	20.6	24.0	6.2	7.4	30.2
Nottingham	140 350	4 745	4 311	2 728	2 406	1 218	1 068	19.4	17.1	33.8	30.7	8.7	7.6	41.9
Oxford	109 620	3 069	2 957	2 212	2 098	735	622	20.2	19.1	28.0	27.0	6.7	5.7	40.9
Rutland	16 356	479	519	302	289	127	151	18.5	17.7	29.3	31.7	7.8	9.2	50.8
Shropshire	167 639	4 798	3 961	3 619	3 197	1 132	893	21.6	19.1	28.6	23.6	6.8	5.3	47.6
Somerset	273 750	7 180	7 210	5 417	5 544	1 878	1 810	19.8	20.3	26.2	26.3	6.9	6.6	36.9
Stafford	239 153	7 145	7 348	5 946	5 512	1 876	1 705	24.9	23.0	29.9	30.7	7.8	7.1	46.7
Suffolk	210 431	6 507	6 292	4 082	4 028	1 652	1 500	19.4	19.1	30.9	29.9	7.9	7.1	63.9
Surrey	269 043	7 116	8 351	7 624	7 977	2 065	2 134	28.3	29.7	26.4	31.0	7.7	7.9	47.0
Sussex	159 311	5 263	5 216	3 085	3 248	1 248	1 110	19.4	20.4	33.0	32.7	7.8	7.0	61.0
Warwick	208 190	5 825	5 255	4 474	4 673	1 786	2 079	21.5	22.4	28.0	25.2	8.6	10.0	39.8
Westmorland	41 617	1 100	957	850	719	242	219	20.4	17.3	26.4	23.0	5.8	5.3	25.6
Wiltshire	185 107	4 685	4 567	3 627	3 568	1 209	1 182	19.6	19.3	25.3	24.7	6.5	6.4	47.6
Worcester	139 333	4 121	4 105	3 289	3 161	904	876	23.6	22.7	29.6	29.5	6.5	6.3	58.1
Yorkshire	858 892	24 825	24 996	18 569	18 823	6 168	7 138	20.5	21.9	28.9	29.1	7.2	8.3	57.7
ENGLAND	8 285 852	238 212	235 318	193 116	185 355	65 662	62 774	23.3	22.4	28.7	28.4	7.9	7.6	47.3

Notes:

1 Each 1801 based total of baptisms, burials, or marriages was calculated by inflating the total given in the original 1801 returns to allow for parishes missed in the county concerned. For example, the number of baptisms returned for Bedford was 1731 and 3.03 per cent of the county population lived in parishes that made no return. $1731 \times 100/96.97 = 1785$

2 The derivation of the 1841 based totals is given in the text.

3 It will be noticed that the national figures for the 1801 based totals of baptisms, burials, and marriages differ slightly from those given in column 3 of table A7.1. The differences are due to small rounding errors in the individual county totals which were taken to fewer decimal places than were used in the table A7.1 calculations. The totals given here differ from those of table A7.1 as follows: baptisms + 156; burials   166; marriages   38.

Sources: 1801 Census, Enumeration, p 451, and Parish registers; *1841 Census*, Enumeration abstract; and see footnote 30.

Comparison of the 1801 and 1841 returns

Table A7.10 makes possible estimates on a county basis of the totals of baptisms, burials, and marriages in 1800, and from these baptism, burial, and marriages rates can be derived by relating the totals to the county populations in 1801. In 1836 Rickman again collected baptism, burial, and marriage totals for 1800 and certain earlier years for a large sample of parishes in each county. This body of material provided the base for the estimates of county population totals published in the 1841 census for widely spaced years from 1570 onwards.[29] His method was to use the information collected earlier and published in 1831 to identify parishes in which registration started early, and then ask the incumbents of these parishes to return to him a form on which they were to record the number of events recorded in their registers for the years 1569–71, 1599–1601, 1629–31, 1679–81, 1699–1701, 1749–51, and 1800. He stressed in a covering note that 'A correct return of the baptisms, burials and marriages for the year 1800 is peculiarly requisite as being the connecting link of the above series of parish registers with the enumerated population of 1801 and subsequent enumerations'.[30]

For the parishes included in this later survey, therefore, there is an independent count of the number of baptisms, burials, and marriages in the year 1800 which must in almost every case have been carried out by a different incumbent from the one approached in 1801.

Rickman's notes[31] give the total of baptisms, burials, and marriages returned for 1800 for the parishes in each county that had registers extant from 1600 onwards, together with the total population of these parishes in 1801. It is therefore possible to calculate baptism, burial, and marriage rates for each county from the sample of parishes included in Rickman's survey. For England as a whole the population of these parishes in 1801 was 3,916,390 or 47.3 per cent of the English total in the case of baptisms. Coverage in individual counties varied considerably but was always a large enough percentage of the total to justify an initial expectation that demographic rates for the parishes covered would be close to those for the county as a whole since there is no reason to expect that the parishes excluded would differ greatly from those included.

Table A7.11 contains a comparison of county baptism, burial, and marriage totals and rates in 1800 derived from the 1841 Rickman material with the totals and rates obtained by inflating the original 1801 returns by the same method used to calculate the new estimates shown in table A7.1. The inflation ratios may differ between the three series for the same county for reasons discussed in connexion with table A7.3. Thus the ratios for all three are the same in Kent (1.047), but in Lancashire the ratios for baptisms, burials, and marriages are 1.065, 1.065, and 1.052 respectively.

---

29. Rickman himself was, of course, dead by 1841 and the final work on these estimates must have been done by other hands, but the project was conceived by him and is usually regarded as part of his immense contribution to the development of population statistics in England.

30. Printed circular letters of inquiry were issued in October and November 1836. The form on which the annual totals were to be recorded is reproduced in manuscript form in a fair copy of what appears to have been the final version of Rickman's working, later published in summary form in the 1841 census. The notebook is in the library of Somerset House and is entitled *List of parishes in each county of England and Wales possessing registers extant in 1570 and 1600 with the populations of the same parishes in 1801* (M74.10). The injunction to take special care over the totals for 1800 is reproduced beneath the form on which the annual totals were to be recorded.

31. See fn. 30.

In considering the data of table A7.11 it is convenient to begin by reiterating a point already made in chapter 3 when discussing the parish register material published in the 1801 and 1841 censuses. The fact that the national totals derived from the later exercise are always lower than those based on 1801 data suggests that incumbents in 1801 included some non-Anglican events in their returns, or else included events relating to Anglicans that were not entered in the register, such as the baptism of children at home, or the burial of unbaptized children.[32] Table A7.12 shows the several totals of baptisms, burials, and marriages for 1800 deriving from the calculations made for this appendix and compares them with the national totals derived from the aggregative set of 404 parishes. The ratios in the table also underline the probability that the attempt to collect supplementary returns in 1801, and then to correct for such parishes as were still missing in 1811, led Rickman to an overestimation of the number of events.

Table A7.12: Totals of events in 1800 calculated on several bases

	(1)	(2)	(3)	(4)
Baptisms	233 694	235 318	238 212	240 205
Burials	184 870	185 355	193 116	196 078
Marriages	63 525	62 774	65 662	65 875
	(2)/(1)	(3)/(1)	(4)/(1)	
Baptisms	1.0069	1.0193	1.0279	
Burials	1.0026	1.0446	1.0606	
Marriages	0.9882	1.0336	1.0370	

Column headings

(1) Totals derived from inflation of aggregative sample of 404 parishes to national levels (see chapter 3).
(2) Totals based on returns made to Rickman in 1836 and published in the 1841 census (table A7.11).
(3) Totals based on reworking of original returns made to Rickman in 1801 (table A7.11).
(4) Totals estimated by Rickman in 1811 by inflation of original and supplementary returns of 1801 (table A7.1).

The fact that national burial and marriage rates based on 1841 data are relatively lower when compared with 1801 data than is the case with baptism rates is surprising, since escapes from registration were greater in the case of baptisms than in the other two series. It is possible that it may also be partly spurious. The 1801 population of the parishes within each county for which returns were obtained in 1836 was separately stated for baptisms, burials, and marriages and was normally higher for baptisms than burials and for burials than marriages. In calculating the rates shown in table A7.11, however, we have always used the 'baptism' population as the denominator. This was done because the discrepancies between the three totals almost certainly arise in the main from the presence of chapelries that had registers recording baptisms but not burials, or baptisms and burials, but not marriages. In these circumstances it seems clearly proper to use the 'baptism' population for all three calculations since the

32. See pp. 74–6.

burials and marriages arising in chapelry populations are recorded in other registers and will therefore appear in due proportion elsewhere within the sample. If, however, the alternative population base had been used for burials the 1841-based national rate would rise from 22.4 to 22.6 and the marriage rate from 7.6 to 7.8.

The number of baptisms in 1800 was unusually low, with totals well below the trend line for baptisms in the 1790s, so that it is interesting to note a number of county baptism rates above 30 per 1,000, whether based on the 1801 or 1841 data – Hampshire, Kent, Lincolnshire, Norfolk, Nottinghamshire, and Sussex. This does not, of course, necessarily indicate that the birth rate was higher in these counties than elsewhere, but it does suggest that crude birth rates as high as 40 must have been widespread. The crude *baptism* rates in both Kent and Sussex in 1798, a year of high fertility, must have been 37 per 1,000 or higher.

The most interesting feature of table A7.11, however, lies in the pattern by county of the relation between baptism, burial, and marriage rates derived from the 1801 returns and those based on the material collected in 1836. This can be most easily appreciated if the counties are regrouped, as may be seen in table A7.13.

Group 1 in table A7.13 consists of those counties in which the 1841 baptism and burial figures are both lower than those of 1801 and one or both are lower by 1.5 per

Table A7.13: Comparison of county baptism, burial, and marriage rates in 1800 derived from the 1801 returns and Rickman's 1836 inquiry published in the 1841 census

Differences between rates per 1 000 (bold type when the 1841 rate is higher)

	Baptism	Burial	Marriage		Baptism	Burial	Marriage
Group 1				*Group 3*			
Durham	8.5	10.1	2.6	Surrey	**4.6**	**1.4**	**0.2**
Shropshire	5.0	2.5	1.5	Northumberland	**3.4**	**1.2**	**1.2**
Leicester	4.8	1.7	0.5	Dorset	**3.1**	**1.4**	**0.1**
Cumberland	4.7	5.9	2.1	Huntingdon	**2.8**	**3.4**	**1.7**
Lancashire	4.1	2.0	1.1	Northampton	**1.8**	**2.1**	**0.3**
Westmorland	3.4	3.1	0.5	Lincoln	**1.7**	**2.5**	**0.1**
Nottingham	3.1	2.3	1.1	Kent	**1.4**	**1.2**	**0.5**
Cheshire	2.7	0.9	0.4	Hereford	**1.0**	**0.8**	**0.4**
Norfolk	2.5	1.9	0.7	Yorkshire	**0.2**	**1.4**	**1.1**
Hampshire	1.8	3.3	**0.2**	Somerset	**0.1**	**0.5**	**0.3**
Derby	1.4	1.8	0.5				
Devon	1.2	3.3	2.9	*Group 4*			
				Warwick	2.8	**0.9**	**1.4**
Group 2				Stafford	0.8	**1.9**	**0.7**
Cambridge	1.3	0.5	**0.9**	Rutland	2.4	**0.8**	**1.4**
Oxford	1.0	1.1	1.0	Middlesex	2.8	**1.2**	**0.2**
Suffolk	1.0	0.3	0.8				
Wiltshire	0.6	0.3	0.1	*Group 5*			
Essex	0.3	0.2	0.4	Cornwall	1.3	**0.7**	**0.4**
Buckingham	0.2	1.0	0.1	Sussex	0.3	**1.0**	**0.8**
Worcester	0.1	0.9	0.2	Berkshire	0.1	**1.2**	**0.4**
Gloucester	0.0	0.1	**1.1**	Hertford	**0.2**	0.8	**0.3**
				Bedford	**0.6**	0.1	1.1

Column headings
Note: For definition of the groups see text. See also table A7.11.

Source: Table A7.11.

1,000 or more (in every case except one the 1841 marriage figure is also the lower of the two). There are 12 counties in group 1. Group 2 contains 8 further counties showing the same pattern but with less extreme differences between 1801 and 1841 rates. In group 3, on the other hand, there are 9 counties that show an opposite pattern with higher 1841 baptism and burial rates. The 4 counties in group 4 have substantial but conflicting discrepancies between baptism and burial rates based on the two sources, while group 5 consists of the 5 remaining counties in which the similar discrepancies exist but at a low level.

Up to a point the grouping is intelligible. Northern counties with very big parishes, and those where industry or nonconformity were strongly represented, figure prominently in group 1 as might be expected if incumbents in 1801 tried conscientiously to report baptisms and burials known to them but not always recorded in their registers. Such events would necessarily escape the notice of their successors 35 years later. Within group 1 there is a solid block of 9 counties stretching from Leicestershire and Shropshire at its southern end through Nottingham, Derby, and Cheshire to Lancashire and thence northward to Cumberland, Westmorland, and Durham. The tendency for this pattern to appear more strongly in the west and centre than in the east is suggested by the presence of other counties in group 2 that extend the area displaying this pattern of relationship between 1841 and 1801 data. Wiltshire, Worcester, Gloucester, Oxford, and Buckingham fall into this category. Devon and Hampshire are firmly in the same camp, and Warwick, Stafford, Berkshire, and Cornwall tend in the same direction in that although the baptism and burial differences point in opposite directions, the larger anomaly is of the type found in group 1 and group 2. There is also a block of East Anglian counties sharing the same characteristics: Norfolk, Suffolk, Cambridge, and Essex.

In some instances the 1841 rates within these 23 counties are so low that it is reasonable to doubt whether the 1836 returns were accurate, or, if accurate, were related to too large a population at risk. Durham and Cumberland illustrate the problem. Anglican baptism rates of 18.4 and 19.7 per 1,000 respectively, and still more burial rates of 15.0 and 14.8 are suspiciously modest, especially in a year of rather high mortality. The likelihood that the 1841 rates are at fault in some counties of this type is strengthened if the parish register returns for the 1790s and earlier are consulted. If the higher level of the 1801 figures were explicable on the grounds that many known but unregistered events were being returned, it might be expected that totals in earlier years would be much lower since they would be increasingly outside the knowledge of the incumbent in 1801. There is, however, no trace of this in counties such as Durham, Shropshire, Leicester, Cumberland, and Lancashire where the phenomenon is most pronounced. On the other hand detailed examination of the build up of the populations at risk sometimes suggests an explanation for some at least of the discrepancies. For example, in Durham the returns include the parishes of Jarrow, Houghton-le-Spring, and Chester-le-Street. Their populations were taken as 15,624, 6,414, and 11,665 respectively. These were the total populations of the three parishes in the 1801 census. But South Shields chapel in Jarrow had its own registers and a population of 8,108. Similarly Penshaw chapelry in Houghton-le-Spring had a population of 1,399, and Lamesley chapelry in Chester-le-Street had a population of 1,705. All 3 chapelries should have been excluded in building up the county total at risk. Their combined population of 11,212, if excluded, would have reduced the county population at risk by 13 per cent and would have increased baptism, burial, and marriage rates significantly. No doubt very many similar cases might be found with sufficient patience, although in general Rickman was careful to exclude chapelry populations.

A mistake of a different sort helps to explain the very low rates in Shropshire. One of the parishes in Rickman's Shropshire sample was Halesowen, a parish that does not appear in the 1801 enumeration under that name. Rickman working on the 1836 returns attributed to it a population of 11,000, although in 1811 and 1821 its population was only 6,888 and 8,187 (these totals relate to that part of Halesowen which is in Shropshire; a part lies in Worcester but there is a separate chapelry, Cradley, in this part of the parish). It is unlikely that Halesowen's population in 1801 was more than 6,000, so that the population at risk in Shropshire is overstated by 5,000, enough to change the baptism rate to 25.2, the burial rate to 20.3, and the marriage rate to 5.7 and thereby considerably reduce the difference between the 1801 and 1841 derived rates.

At the other extreme there are several counties in group 3 where 1841 baptism and burial rates were considerably higher than the 1801 rates. Discrepancies of this type are far harder to explain on general grounds. In some instances these 1841 rates were based on rather a small proportion of the parishes in the county, or the county itself was so small that the presence or absence of individual parishes in the sample might make a marked but meaningless difference to the resultant rates. This almost certainly explains Northumberland's presence in this group when all its near neighbours are in group 1. The Northumberland data are drawn from only 8 parishes out of the total of 92 in the county, and 4 of the 8 containing well over half the population of the sample were the 4 Newcastle parishes. It is not surprising that rates should be higher in these city parishes if Anglican coverage of events in the city was good. In a few instances the 1841 rates, though higher than those of 1801, were not sufficiently different to raise a problem. Such explanations might account for Huntingdon, Hereford, Somerset, and possibly Dorset, but there remain 5 counties even if these counties are removed from the group: Surrey Northampton, Lincoln, Kent, and Yorkshire. To these Middlesex should probably be added since there is a large difference between the 1801 and 1841 baptism rates, similar to that found in Surrey.

With these counties there is again some evidence of geographical grouping. Middlesex and Surrey are metropolitan counties flanked by Kent, while Yorkshire and Lincolnshire are also neighbours. Coverage in 1841 was average or good in all these counties except for Middlesex which is at the lower end of the distribution. There are two factors which may help to explain the existence of a small group of counties with higher 1841 than 1801 rates. First, the work of the 1801 census clerks was demonstrably very careless. Second, even though the 1841 rates should normally be lower than those of 1801, parishes with early registers, though half or more of the county total of parishes, may have represented a sufficiently non-random selection in a few counties to produce anomalies of the sort observed. As with some of the counties in other groups particular explanations probably account for the observed pattern in individual cases. In Middlesex, for example, although only 39 per cent of the population was living in the parishes included in the sample, almost exactly one half of the parishes (94 out of 190) were involved. The sample included relatively few of the bigger parishes and it is quite likely that Anglican baptism coverage was especially poor in the larger parishes.

As might be expected, the effect of decisions made by Rickman or his clerks is frequently very hard to establish. The parish of Halifax, for example, contained a total population of 63,434 in 1801. There were four subdivisions of the parish regarded as chapelries by the census authorities – Elland, Heptonstall, Rastrick, and Sowerby. Rickman excluded all four from the total of population at risk in Halifax, thereby reducing the population to 50,738. He was right to have excluded the first two since returns from these two chapelries were also part of his West Riding sample but the Halifax registers included events from all the chapelries in the parish except Elland and Heptonstall.[33] It therefore seems that by excluding Rastrick and Sowerby as well as Elland and Heptonstall, Rickman must have understated the population at risk and in consequence overstated the baptism, burial, and marriage rates. As it happens this would be a premature conclusion. Halifax parish contained a total of 11 chapels in 1800 (St Ann's, Sowerby Bridge, Sowerby, Illingworth, Lightcliffe, Rastrick, Elland, Ripponden, Luddenham, Heptonstall, and Crostone), even though the subdivisions of the parish were mainly called townships, not chapelries.In order to clarify the complex question of the size of the populations served by the chapels (and to emphasize that the existing provision was inadequate) the 1811 parish register returns gave details which enable the populations served by the chapels at Elland and Heptonstall to be more accurately known.[34] Elland served the township of Stainland as well as Elland itself, while Heptonstall was the chapel for Wadsworth, Erringden, and part of Stansfield in addition to Heptonstall. The combined populations served by the two chapels was 15,460 and the population covered by the registers of the mother church and therefore at risk in 1800 was 47,974. Thus the effect of the decision about the population at risk in Halifax, made by Rickman or his assistants, had the effect of depressing rather than raising the Yorkshire rates, if only marginally. Few parishes present such a complicated picture as Halifax but the example of Halifax will serve to show how many minor errors, and no doubt a few major mistakes, crept into the 1841 workings.

The remaining five counties (Sussex, Berkshire, Hertford, Bedford, and Rutland) do not call for comment since either their 1801 and 1841 rates were very similar, or in the case of Rutland, the discrepancies are probably a function of the small size of the country.

In general the comparison of 1801 and 1841 may be said to strengthen confidence in the accuracy of the work done by incumbents for Rickman. Where there are differences they do not necessarily signify carelessness since many events known to an incumbent but not recorded in his register could not have been known to a rector or vicar in the same parish 35 years later. Anomalies remain, however, and their origin could in many cases be clarified by further work.

Summary

It may be helpful briefly to recapitulate the main points which emerge from a consideration of Rickman's excursions into demographic history.

1 Where it is possible to check the accuracy of the original returns made by incumbents in 1801, the results suggest that they achieved a high standard of accuracy in general. It should be noted, however, that most ministers appear to have used the Old Style year when casting up annual totals of events for the years before the advent of the New Style calendar in 1752.

2 The handling of the parochial returns by the census clerks in 1801 superimposed a

---

33. *1831 Census*, Parish register abstract, p. 402.
34. *1811 Census*, Parish registers, p. 183.

host of errors, some of them very serious, upon whatever inaccuracies there may have been in the parochial returns. There are many identifiable errors made in aggregating from the hundred to the county, and from the county to the country. No doubt there were similar errors in aggregating from the parish to the hundred.

3 Rickman was not successful in identifying the parishes missed in the 1801 returns when he first attempted to do so in the 1801 census. When he returned to the matter in 1811 he was more successful, but in attempting to make allowance for the missing parishes to produce a revised set of baptism, burial, and marriage totals for the eighteenth century he made arithmetic errors so that his inflation ratios are inaccurate. Moreover, his method involved the assumption that all parishes that were registering units in 1811 had been registering units throughout the eighteenth century, but this was not so. It therefore seemed worthwhile to attempt to construct a revised set of national totals of baptisms, burials, and marriages using his data but avoiding such of his errors as can be identified and corrected (see table A7.1).

4 Rickman only attempted to produce a revised set of totals of events for England and Wales as a whole, but it is also possible to produce revised totals for each county. If this is done it reveals wide variations in the completeness of the 1801 returns on a county basis.

5 There is suggestive evidence that incumbents in 1801 included in their returns for 1800 and other recent years events that were known to them but not recorded in their registers (as they well might in view of the form of the question addressed to them).

6 The 1836 returns which formed the basis for the county estimates of population published in the 1841 census can be translated into baptism, burial, and marriage totals for the years covered by the inquiry. The totals for 1800 may be compared with the totals for the same year derived from the 1801 returns. In general they tend to offer mutual confirmation to each other and afford evidence to support points 1 and 5 above. Where there are discrepancies between the two sets of totals, reasons for them can in some cases be advanced.

Appendix 8

English birth and death totals 1841–71

Although civil registration began in 1837, estimates of fertility in the middle decades of the nineteenth century based on the published totals of births will be too low because there was substantial under-recording of births. To a much smaller degree deaths were probably also under-recorded. Only after the 1874 Act,[1] which imposed penalties for failure to report births and deaths, did coverage improve to the point where it may be regarded as tolerably complete. This poses a problem for any attempt to juxtapose findings about fertility and mortality in the last years of the parish register period with data for the early years of civil registration. Since we wished to follow changes in fertility and mortality down to 1871, it was necessary either to adopt an existing set of revised birth and death totals or to produce a new set. We adopted the latter alternative, partly because totals were needed for England less Monmouth rather than for England and Wales, and partly because existing estimates differed significantly in some decades from those produced by the method of estimates with which we experimented.

The new estimates were made by estimating birth totals from the age groups 5–9 and 10–4 in suitable censuses. Thus the estimate of total births for 1841–6 was derived from the age group 5–9 in 1851, that for 1846–51 from the age group 10–4 in 1861, and so on. The age groups 5–9 and 10–4, unlike the age group 0–4, are not thought to have been subject to serious under-registration in the mid-nineteenth-century censuses and afford a reasonably secure base from which to attempt to carry out the calculation. Table A8.1 shows the results of such an exercise. The ratios used in inflating the age groups to convert them into birth cohorts are the ratios $5l_0/{}_5L_5$ and $5l_0/{}_5L_{10}$ from the third English life table,[2] except in the case of the last birth cohort based on the age group 10–4 in 1881 for which the ${}_5L_{10}$ was obtained from the q_x s of the third life table to age five and thereafter the q_x s of the 1871–80 life table.[3] Using the third life table for the whole period 1841–71 may involve small inaccuracies, but they are unlikely to be important for the reasons given by Farr in discussing the mortality of the period 1855–71.[4]

That there was a substantial under-registration of births throughout the period is immediately clear from the table, but the estimated birth cohorts are too low inasmuch as they take no account of the loss of young children through net emigration.

---

1. An act to amend the law relating to the registration of births and deaths in England. 37 & 38 Vict. c. 88. This act made it the duty of the parents of a child to register its birth and provided for a fine to be levied for failure to comply with the act. The nearest relatives of a deceased person were likewise requested to register the death under threat of the same penalty (40 shillings fine). The development of legislation about birth and death registration is described in Glass, *Numbering the people*, esp. ch. 4.
2. See appendix 14. The ratio $5l_0/{}_5L_5$ is 1.386997, while the ratio $5l_0/{}_5L_{10}$ is 1.440258.
3. The resulting ratio $5l_0/{}_5L_{10}$ is 1.416170.
4. See appendix 6, p. 589, fn. 2.

Table A8.1: Quinquennial birth cohorts 1841–71 estimated from the census totals in age groups 5–9 and 10–4 (England less Monmouth)

Census	Age group	Population (sexes combined)	Estimated birth cohort		Registered births
1851	5–9	1 956 750	2 714 007	*1841–6*	2 507 666
1861	10–4	1 972 447	2 840 833	*1846–51*	2 691 567
1861	5–9	2 198 212	3 048 914	*1851–6*	2 948 956
1871	10–4	2 277 374	3 280 006	*1856–61*	3 152 548
1871	5–9	2 541 983	3 525 723	*1861–6*	3 425 618
1881	10–4	2 630 918	3 725 827	*1866–71*	3 651 535

Notes: The populations have been corrected to 30 June of each census year (see appendix 6). The estimated birth totals and those for registered births cover periods beginning on 1 July and ending on 30 June. Since the 1851 and 1881 censuses provide no age details for the ancient counties, but only for registration counties, and since the population of England less Monmouth (ancient counties) is slightly different from the total of England and Wales less Wales and Monmouth (registration counties), the age totals for the latter area in 1851 and 1881 were adjusted in the ratio of the former to the latter. In all cases, therefore, the population totals and the birth totals refer to England less Monmouth (ancient counties). The total of registered births, however, is necessarily for England less Monmouth as defined by registration county. The difference between the population of the two slightly different areas is, however, negligibly small. The annual totals from which the quinquennial totals were derived are given in table A8.5 (though the totals for the first six months of 1846, 1856, and 1866 which enter into the quinquennial totals are not separately listed in table A8.5: they are 276 386, 320 869, and 364 617 respectively).

Unfortunately there is no reliable independent evidence of the scale of net migration in this period, still less of its distribution by age. We have therefore resorted to some arbitrary expedients to make good the deficiency.

The overall level of net migration in each decade may be estimated by taking the difference between the natural increase and the intercensal increase. With the decadal estimated birth totals shown in table A8.1 the net emigration figures for the three decades 1841–51, 1851–61, and 1861–71 are approximately 10,000, 300,000 and 200,000.[5] These are, of course, the lowest possible figures to take since any further amendment to birth totals in respect of net emigration would increase them by increasing the total of natural increase, but on the other hand to have used higher totals which took emigration into account would have introduced an element of circularity into the argument. It appears safe to assume that these net emigration totals are conservative, and that any amendment to birth totals derived by taking them into consideration will err by being too low rather than too high.

Using the net emigration figures just quoted, and pursuing a policy of heroic simplification, improved birth cohort totals can be estimated by a process of iteration. If the overall decadal emigration totals can be apportioned by age group, revised census age group totals for 5–9 and 10–4 can be obtained. These in turn can be used to calculate decadal natural increase totals once more, and from these in turn new net emigration totals, thus enabling the cycle to be repeated. In practice the emigration estimates rapidly coverage so that by the fourth cycle the process can be halted with the results shown below in table A8.2.

5. The exact figures are 9,728, 306,807, and 204,409. For decadal death totals see table A8.5. The intercensal increase figures were taken from table A6.7, but excluding the additions made for under-registration of those aged 0–4 since this would have introduced an element of circularity into the calculation.

To enable the impact of emigration on census age group totals to be assessed, some notion of the age structure of net emigration is needed. Glass quotes data that suggest that in the 1840s just over a fifth of all emigrants were children under 12 and that thereafter down to 1871 the proportion fell slightly to just under a fifth.[6] Information about the age profile of gross emigration is not necessarily a good guide to the age profile of net emigration, but in the absence of other information we have assumed the same proportions to hold good for the latter as for the former. If the percentage of children under 12 amongst net emigrants is taken to be 22.5 in the 1840s and 19.0 in the period 1851–71, it follows that in the three successive decades 1841–71 the number of child emigrants under 12 was 2,250, 57,000, and 38,000 respectively, using the figures for net emigration given above.

The use to which these estimates of child migration was put is most easily grasped by representing the problem in Lexis diagram terms as shown in figure A8.1. We have assumed that net emigration was evenly spread over each decade, and evenly distributed in each of the first three five-year age groups 0–4, 5–9, and 10–4. Moreover, we have assumed that migration continued at the same pace over the 3

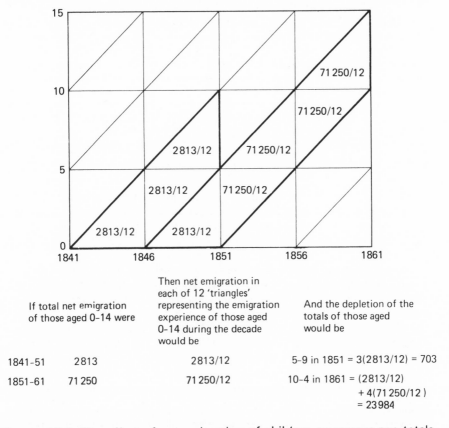

If total net emigration of those aged 0–14 were		Then net emigration in each of 12 'triangles' representing the emigration experience of those aged 0–14 during the decade would be	And the depletion of the totals of those aged would be
1841–51	2813	2813/12	5–9 in 1851 = 3(2813/12) = 703
1851–61	71 250	71 250/12	10–4 in 1861 = (2813/12) + 4(71 250/12) = 23 984

Figure A8.1: The effect of net emigration of children on census age totals

6. Glass, 'A note on under-registration', p. 83, table 8.

years 12–14 as over the 12 years 0–11, so that, for example, the total number of net emigrants 1851–61 aged 0–14 is the total for 0–11 raised in the proportion 15/12 (57,000 × 15/12 = 71,250). If these assumptions are made the calculation of the degree to which each age group in 1851 and 1861 had been affected by net emigration may easily be determined. The birth cohort of 1841–6 on its way to constituting those aged 5–9 in 1851 occupied 3 of the 12 triangles in the Lexis diagram making up the life history of those aged 0–14 in the decade 1841–51. This means that those aged 5–9 were 703 fewer in number in 1851 than would have been the case in the absence of any net migration (2,813 × 3/12 = 703). Similarly, those aged 10–4 in 1861 had lost 23,984 members of their birth cohort to net emigration ((2,813 × 1/12) + (71,250 × 4/12) = 23,984). It will be appreciated that, since the size of the birth cohort 1866–71 was estimated from the age group 10–4 in 1881, it is necessary to make an estimate of net emigration for the decade 1871–81 in the same way as for the decades 1841–71.[7]

Once the revision of the age groups 5–9 and 10–4 shown in table A8.1 had been carried out, the iteration already described could begin making use of the output of any one cycle as input for the next. The effect of this process may be seen in table A8.2, which shows how the estimates of decadal net migration change and rapidly converge. The change between the third and fourth cycles is so modest that the iteration was halted after the fourth cycle.

Table A8.2: Net emigration estimates 1841–71 (England less Monmouth)

	Original estimate	1st cycle	2nd cycle	3rd cycle	4th cycle
1841–51	10 000	45 486	56 568	59 463	59 964
1851–61	300 000	356 062	366 822	369 734	370 500
1861–71	200 000	250 400	256 789	258 817	259 052

Note: For the derivation of the original estimates and the subsequent iterations see text.

While it is likely, for the reasons already mentioned, that the final net emigration totals are still somewhat below their true levels, there appears to be no way of improving upon them in the absence of accurate independent evidence of the scale of net English emigration without an element of circularity being introduced into the argument.

Using the net emigration totals given in table A8.2 and revising the census age group totals of table A8.1 appropriately results in the revised estimates of birth cohort size given in table A8.3. The degree of inflation necessary to convert registered births into the new estimates of total birth falls from 8.5 to 3 per cent between 1841–6 and 1866–71. The fall is not quite regular, however, since the ratio for 1856–61 is marginally higher than that for 1851–6. The sequence as a whole suggests that the estimates based on the 10–4 age groups are relatively rather higher than those based

7. This total was obtained by estimating total births 1871–6 by back projection from 1881 using the 1871–80 life table after adjusting the 1881 total for the age group 5–9 to 30 June, and adding the registered birth total 1876–81 multiplied by 1.01. The addition of 1 per cent to the registered total 1876–81 was made because of the evidence brought to light by Teitelbaum that a modest degree of under-registration continued down to 1911. Teitelbaum, 'Birth under-registration', p. 332. The decadal death total was then subtracted from the birth total to yield a total of natural increase which proved to be 250,042 larger than the intercensal increase.

Table A8.3: Quinquennial birth cohorts 1841–71 estimated from modified census totals in age groups 5–9 and 10–4 (England less Monmouth)

Census	Age group	(1) Population (sexes combined)	(2) Estimated birth cohort		(3) Registered births	(4) Ratio (2)/(3)
1851	5–9	1 960 931	2 719 806	*1841–6*	2 507 666	1.0846
1861	10–4	2 003 112	2 884 998	*1846–51*	2 691 567	1.0719
1861	5–9	2 220 165	3 079 363	*1851–6*	2 948 956	1.0442
1871	10–4	2 305 182	3 320 057	*1856–61*	3 152 548	1.0531
1871	5–9	2 557 350	3 547 037	*1861–6*	3 425 618	1.0354
1881	10–4	2 657 566	3 763 565	*1866–71*	3 651 535	1.0307

Note: See text for derivation of modified census totals. The unmodified totals are given in table A8.1.

on the 5–9 age groups. It is very likely that this arises because the assumption made about the age structure of net migration is unrealistic. If a smaller proportion of total net emigration occurred in the age group 10–4 than was assumed, and a higher proportion in the age groups 0–9, the anomaly would disappear. Since each decade consists of one estimate based on a 5–9 age group and one on a 10–4 age group, any offsetting errors of this type will be greatly reduced by considering decades as a whole. The results of this are given in table A8.4, together with some comparable estimates made by others who have studied the problem.

Table A8.4: Estimated and registered decadal birth cohorts 1841–71

	(1) Estimated	(2) Registered	(3) Ratio (1)/(2)	Farr	Glass	Teitelbaum
1841–51	5 604 804	5 199 233	1.0780	1.065	1.078	1.061
1851–61	6 399 420	6 101 504	1.0488	1.029	1.042	1.028
1861–71	7 310 602	7 077 153	1.0330	1.018	1.020	1.019

Notes: For totals of columns 1 and 2 see table A8.3. These refer to England less Monmouth. The ratios of Farr, Glass, and Teitelbaum all refer to England and Wales. Farr's ratios are drawn from one of several exercises he carried out. They are listed and discussed in Glass, 'A note on under-registration', p. 71. For Glass's own ratios, Glass *ibid.*, p. 86, table 12. Teitelbaum's ratios may be found in Teitelbaum, 'Birth under-registration', p. 338, table 5.

The new estimates involve higher correction ratios than those made earlier, except that Glass's ratio for 1841–51 is the same as that produced by the present exercise. The differences are especially marked in the decade 1861–71. Two considerations tending to support a relatively high inflation ratio for the 1860s may be advanced. First, the 1874 Act was intended to improve registration coverage. As long as there was no legal obligation laid upon parents to register a birth, the situation was thought to be unsatisfactory in this respect. In this general sense it would be surprising if the percentage of children whose births went unregistered were negligible before 1874. But, second, there is evidence that even after 1874 registration was less than complete. Teitelbaum estimates that an inflation ratio of 1.016 is needed to convert

Table A8.5: Registered and revised totals of births and deaths 1841–71 (England less Monmouth)

	Births			Deaths	
Year	Registered	Revised	Year	Registered	Revised
1841	480 563	538 231	1841	322 680	329 134
1842	485 800	539 238	1842	328 003	334 563
1843	494 794	544 273	1843	325 118	331 620
1844	507 403	553 069	1844	334 960	341 659
1845	509 991	550 790	1845	327 859	334 416
1846	537 300	574 911	1846	366 287	372 148
1847	506 655	541 158	1847	397 245	402 012
1848	528 324	562 242	1848	375 219	378 221
1849	542 492	575 747	1849	413 701	415 356
1850	556 814	589 332	1850	346 280	346 280
1851	576 948	608 969	1851	370 367	
1852	584 581	616 265	1852	381 363	
1853	573 694	604 042	1853	394 442	
1854	594 317	624 984	1854	410 186	
1855	594 915	624 839	1855	398 756	
1856	615 909	646 089	1856	365 787	
1857	621 172	650 802	1857	393 241	
1858	614 061	642 553	1858	421 193	
1859	646 287	675 435	1859	412 880	
1860	640 823	668 891	1860	395 963	
1861	652 435	680 163	1861	408 402	
1862	667 873	695 022	1862	409 765	
1863	681 488	707 928	1863	444 748	
1864	693 534	719 160	1864	465 110	
1865	700 836	725 435	1865	460 767	
1866	706 271	729 755	1866	469 952	
1867	719 835	742 438	1867	442 154	
1868	737 176	758 960	1868	451 117	
1869	724 550	744 620	1869	464 451	
1870	742 730	761 930	1870	483 693	
1871	748 697	766 666	1871	483 471	
1841.1–6	247 271	276 944	1841.1–6	173 373	176 841
1851.1–6	296 368	312 816	1851.1–6	191 852	
1861.1–6	335 165	349 410	1861.1–6	214 728	
1871.1–6	385 590	394 844	1871.1–6	243 375	

	Decadal totals		
	Registered	Revised	Ratio revised/registered
Births			
1841–51	5 199 233	5 604 863	1.0780
1851–61	6 101 504	6 399 463	1.0488
1861–71	7 077 153	7 310 845	1.0330
Deaths			
1841–51	3 555 831	3 600 420	1.0125
1851–61	3 967 054		
1861–71	4 528 806		

Note: The decadal totals run from 1 July to 30 June. The annual totals are those published by the Registrar General in his *Annual reports* multiplied by a factor that represents the proportion of all births for the decade in which the year falls that occurred in England less Monmouth. The factors for births for the decades *1841–50, 1851–60,* and *1861–70* are 0.93831, 0.93681 and 0.93686, while the factors for deaths are 0.93844, 0.93670, and 0.93861. For derivation of revised totals see text.

registered to total births in the decade 1901–10.[8] This ratio is higher than for the preceding 30 years when the ratio was very close to unity. He explains the change as due to the better registration of young children in the 1911 census which included additional questions about fertility based on numbers of children ever born and still alive. The greater completeness of census coverage thus brought to light deficiencies in coverage which were concealed in the earlier censuses. If under-registration at a level of 1½ per cent or more continued after 1874 it is almost certain that it was at a higher level before the 1874 Act, suggesting that the higher ratios produced by the new estimates are credible.

It remained to convert the new estimated decadal birth totals into annual totals by selecting inflation factors to apply to the registered totals in each year. This was achieved by using the following inflation ratios for the years listed and obtaining inflation factors for intervening years by linear interpolation: 1841, 1.1200; 1846, 1.0700; 1851, 1.0555; 1861, 1.0425; and 1871, 1.0240. The individual annual totals are shown in table A8.5. It will be recalled that a factor of 1.1200 had already been selected for 1841.[9] The several factors result in decadal totals which are so close to those of table A8.4 as to be taken as identical. Annual totals of deaths are also given. Totals of deaths 1841–5 were increased by the ratio 1.02. Deaths in 1850 and thereafter are the registered totals. Between 1845 (1.02) and 1850 (1.00) inflation ratios were obtained by linear interpolation. Glass assumes a deficiency in death registration of 2 per cent in the period 1841–5.[10] We have made the same assumption, and since any subsequent improvement is likely to have been gradual, we have reduced the inflation ratio to zero by equal steps over the next five years.

8. Teitelbaum. 'Birth under-registration', p. 332.
9. See above table 5.20.
10. Glass, 'A note on under-registration', p. 84.

Appendix 9

A real-wage series 1500–1912 using the Phelps Brown and Hopkins wage and price data

Phelps Brown and Hopkins published two articles in 1955 and 1956 in which they drew together published material on wages and on the price of a basket of consumables over a period of seven centuries.[1] Their series remain the only continuous series from which real wages can be calculated for the whole period covered by our demographic data. Phelps Brown and Hopkins themselves published a real-wage index but it contains many gaps in the sixteenth and seventeenth centuries and a few even in the eighteenth and nineteenth centuries.

The gaps arise because Phelps Brown and Hopkins did not calculate a real wage for any year in which the evidence from their wage data suggested that wages were fluctuating over a range rather than predominantly at one level. Thus, for the years 1655–87 the daily craftsman's wage is given in their wage series as 18d. and a real wage was calculated throughout this 33-year period. But from 1688 to 1700 the prevailing wage is held to lie in the range 18–20 d. and no real-wage figure is quoted. Their adherence to this method of determining a real wage has other disadvantages. When their wage data suggest that one prevailing wage level was replaced by another very quickly without a long intervening period of uncertainty, the PBH method sometimes produces unrealistically sharp apparent changes in the real wage. For example, from 1736 to 1773 the prevailing daily craftsman's wage is given as 24 d., and a new higher plateau of 29 d. is reported for the period 1776–91. Consequently, after a two-year gap in the real-wage series (1774–5) there is a very marked jump in the real-wage index from 47 in 1773 to 61 in 1776 of which only a small part is attributable to a price fall between the two dates. The revised real-wage series which we reproduce below was designed both to produce a continuous real-wage series and to avoid the abrupt changes of level found in the original PBH series. Before describing the method employed, however, it is convenient to review briefly the data that Phelps Brown and Hopkins assembled.

For wages Phelps Brown and Hopkins relied upon material collected by Thorold Rogers down to 1700. It consists in rates paid to building craftsmen and labourers, which come from counties in the south of England and from Oxford and Cambridge. Data for craftsmen are more numerous than for labourers and we have used the former exclusively (the ratio between the rates for craftsmen and labourers was very stable throughout the period 1500–1912 at about 3:2). The PBH series switches to reliance on Maidstone wage data between 1730 and 1800. These were collected by Gilboy, and during a period of overlap with the Oxford material in the early eighteenth century can be shown to run closely in parallel with the Oxford series. In the nineteenth

---

1. Phelps Brown and Hopkins, 'Seven centuries of building wages', and 'Seven centuries of the prices of consumables'.

century Bowley's London wage series was used adjusted down by a fifth to get a good join with the Maidstone series in 1800.

The PBH price series is predominantly a measure of changes in the cost of food and drink, which comprise 80 per cent of the commodity basket. The balance is made up of fuel and clothing. Most of the data refer either to raw materials or partly processed commodities and come either from wholesale markets or from bulk purchase by large local consumers. They were drawn primarily from the published work of Thorold Rogers and Beveridge and suffer from intermittent breaks in the series for some commodities, from the difficulty of taking account of the introduction of important new commodities, such as potatoes or tea, and from the difficulties common to any index of this type that attempts to cover very long periods of time. These defects are very properly stressed by Phelps Brown and Hopkins who relied heavily upon their personal judgement in attempting to overcome the various problems. They point out that their series probably fluctuates more, and more violently, than would a comparable series based on retail prices, and that the relative weights of different commodities should in principle be changed substantially with changes in the real wage.

Since both the wage and price data are open to criticism it is inevitable that any real-wage series produced by combining them must be equally if not more lacking in authority. Some of the defects are sufficiently serious to place in doubt even such questions as the timing of a change in the secular trend of real wages. For example, the fact the wage series is entirely southern and cannot capture the influence of the favourable trend in real wages in parts of the north of England in the later eighteenth century may mean that the downturn in real wages (which began in 1743 if measured by a 25-year moving average) is placed too early in the century and that the subsequent fall is exaggerated. Nevertheless the PBH data are valuable in providing a guide to the approximate timing and magnitude of changes in real wages over a very long period.

To produce an unbroken real-wage series from the material published by Phelps Brown and Hopkins, and to ensure that there were no spurious sharp jumps in the real wage of the type already described, we proceeded as follows. Phelps Brown and Hopkins provide a daily wage series for craftsmen which is reproduced in table A9.1 (the PBH wages reproduced are only a part of their full series which covers seven centuries). In the right-hand panel of the table are listed the dates and rates we have used in our reworking of their material. Each figure is either the first year of a period in which wage rates were stable at one level or represents a year in which there was a movement from a lower to a higher wage band. In the latter case the wage figure common to both bands was used.

The wage figure of 6d. at the beginning of the series in 1500 was expressed as an index figure of 10,000 and other wage levels were similarly converted. Thus 10d. becomes 16,667, and so on. Between any two data points not more than 25 years apart the wage index level for all intervening years was obtained by linear interpolation. For example, the index figure for 1776 is 48,333 (29d.) and for 1796 60,000 (36d.) and

therefore the figure for 1777 is $48,333 + (\dfrac{60,000 - 48,333}{20}) = 48,916$. Where data

points were more than 25 years apart the later figure was reduced linearly over a 25-year period moving backwards in time to the level of the early figure. For example, the index figures for 1580 and 1642 are 20,000 (12d.) and 26,667 (16d.).

Table A9.1: Daily wage rates of building craftsmen in southern England

PBH series		Points in revised series	
Date	Wage in pence	Date	Wage in pence
1412–1532	6	1500	6
1532–48	6–7	1532	6
1548–52	7–8	1548	7
1552–61	8–10	1552	8
1561–73	10	1561	10
1573–80	10–12	1580	12
1580–1629	12	1642	16
1629–42	12–16	1655	18
1642–55	16–18	1701	20
1655–87	18	1710	22
1687–1701	18–20	1736	24
1701–10	20–22	1776	29
1710–30	22	1796	36
1730–36	22–24	1806	43
1736–73	24	1810	48
1773–6	24–29	1847	49
1776–91	29	1853	54
1791–6	29–36	1861	56
1796–1802	36	1866	64
1802–6	36–43	1873	72
1806–9	43	1893	75
1810–46	48	1899	80
1847–52	49	1914	85
1853–60	54		
1861–4	56		
1864–6	56–64		
1866–71	64		
1871–3	64–72		
1873–92	72		
1893–8	75		
1899–1913	80		
1914	85		

Source: Phelps Brown and Hopkins, 'Seven centuries of building wages', pp. 177–8.

The lower figure was therefore maintained from 1580 to 1617 (25 years back from 1642) but thereafter the index is made to rise steadily to the higher figure in 1642.

In this fashion both breaks and jumps in the wage series are avoided, though the device employed is quite arbitrary since the period of time over which pressure was building up for a change in the conventional daily wage is not known. The decision to use wage band overlap years as reference points is equally arbitrary. In a sense, of course, the assumption of a period of development towards a higher wage level which may be as long as 25 years goes directly against the PBH evidence since the PBH data are presented in a way intended to define periods during which pressure for change was detectable. Moreover, sometimes an abrupt change from one level to another in the PBH nominal wage data took place when prices were changing equally quickly, and the abruptness of change was probably genuine. When this was so our method of correction will antedate the beginning of the rise in the real wage and will also exaggerate any short-term fall at the time of the sharp price rise. For example, wages in our series were increased linearly between 1866 and 1873 (see table A9.1) but the PBH series is flat from 1866 to 1871, rising abruptly thereafter to 1873, a brief period in which prices were also moving sharply upwards. There are therefore losses as well as gains from treating the PBH series in the manner described, though for our purposes any inaccuracies introduced in this way are usually of slight importance since the real-wage data have been used primarily to calculate 11-year and 25-year moving averages.

Having produced an unbroken wage series it is possible to take advantage of the fact that there are very few breaks in the PBH price series to calculate a full real-wage series. The PBH price series contains only three missing values in the whole period 1500–1912, those for 1563, 1564, and 1575. Values for these years were estimated by linear interpolation from the values in the years at either side of the gap. The wage index was then divided by the PBH price index to produce a real-wage index. For example, the wage index figure for 1561 is 16,667, the price index figure 283, and the real-wage index figure is therefore 58.9 (16,667/283). It should be noted that the PBH price data were collected for the year running from Michaelmas to Michaelmas, and that the PBH consumables index for, say, 1561 refers to the harvest year *ending* at Michaelmas 1561. Therefore the real-wage figure for 1561 should be regarded as notionally applicable to the last three months of 1560 and the first nine months of 1561. To avoid ambiguity it is shown as 1560–1 in table A9.2 (overleaf). The real-wage figures in the table were multiplied by 10 to simplify presentation and to preserve detail without the inconvenience of a decimal point.

Table A9.2: A real-wage index for England 1500–1912

Date	Real-wage index	Date	Real-wage index	Date	Real-wage index
1499–1500	1 064	1549–50	477	1599–1600	436
1500–1	935	1550–1	453	1600–1	373
1501–2	820	1551–2	483	1601–2	425
1502–3	877	1552–3	529	1602–3	446
1503–4	935	1553–4	510	1603–4	495
1504–5	971	1554–5	535	1604–5	446
1505–6	943	1555–6	400	1605–6	427
1506–7	1 020	1556–7	371	1606–7	445
1507–8	1 000	1557–8	676	1607–8	394
1508–9	1 087	1558–9	624	1608–9	358
1509–10	971	1559–60	615	1609–10	398
1510–1	1 031	1560–1	589	1610–1	432
1511–2	990	1561–2	633	1611–2	382
1512–3	833	1562–3	[621]	1612–3	364
1513–4	848	1563–4	[610]	1613–4	353
1514–5	935	1564–5	599	1614–5	357
1515–6	909	1565–6	611	1615–6	356
1516–7	901	1566–7	628	1616–7	372
1517–8	862	1567–8	637	1617–8	387
1518–9	775	1568–9	655	1618–9	416
1519–20	730	1569–70	608	1619–20	429
1520–1	599	1570–1	695	1620–1	457
1521–2	625	1571–2	689	1621–2	408
1522–3	735	1572–3	685	1622–3	367
1523–4	752	1573–4	506	1623–4	403
1524–5	775	1574–5	[559]	1624–5	415
1525–6	752	1575–6	624	1625–6	406
1526–7	680	1576–7	536	1626–7	457
1527–8	559	1577–8	560	1627–8	492
1528–9	629	1578–9	608	1628–9	455
1529–30	592	1579–80	585	1629–30	394
1530–1	649	1580–1	576	1630–1	348
1531–2	559	1581–2	583	1631–2	414
1532–3	598	1582–3	617	1632–3	430
1533–4	704	1583–4	601	1633–4	402
1534–5	787	1584–5	592	1634–5	416
1535–6	635	1585–6	568	1635–6	423
1536–7	679	1586–7	407	1636–7	408
1537–8	770	1587–8	578	1637–8	362
1538–9	730	1588–9	565	1638–9	426
1539–40	686	1589–90	505	1639–40	479
1540–1	663	1590–1	436	1640–1	451
1541–2	642	1591–2	541	1641–2	479
1542–3	652	1592–3	562	1642–3	487
1543–4	632	1593–4	525	1643–4	512
1544–5	594	1594–5	388	1644–5	478
1545–6	462	1595–6	396	1645–6	487
1546–7	500	1596–7	292	1646–7	419
1547–8	605	1597–8	345	1647–8	366
1548–9	565	1598–9	422	1648–9	347

Table A9.2: *(cont.)*

Date	Real-wage index	Date	Real-wage index	Date	Real-wage index
1649-50	342	*1699-1700*	495	*1749-50*	678
1650-1	412	*1700-1*	569	*1750-1*	697
1651-2	451	*1701-2*	579	*1751-2*	671
1652-3	509	*1702-3*	618	*1752-3*	695
1653-4	548	*1703-4*	587	*1753-4*	667
1654-5	565	*1704-5*	635	*1754-5*	715
1655-6	537	*1705-6*	603	*1755-6*	692
1656-7	490	*1706-7*	670	*1756-7*	573
1657-8	464	*1707-8*	629	*1757-8*	579
1658-9	429	*1708-9*	521	*1758-9*	634
1659-60	439	*1709-10*	459	*1759-60*	669
1660-1	463	*1710-1*	412	*1760-1*	706
1661-2	390	*1711-2*	577	*1761-2*	684
1662-3	444	*1712-3*	622	*1762-3*	672
1663-4	457	*1713-4*	584	*1763-4*	622
1664-5	487	*1714-5*	576	*1764-5*	605
1665-6	452	*1715-6*	579	*1765-6*	602
1666-7	520	*1716-7*	622	*1766-7*	574
1667-8	498	*1717-8*	654	*1767-8*	585
1668-9	524	*1718-9*	620	*1768-9*	641
1669-70	520	*1719-20*	596	*1769-70*	649
1670-1	504	*1720-1*	629	*1770-1*	602
1671-2	539	*1721-2*	688	*1771-2*	548
1672-3	513	*1722-3*	729	*1772-3*	554
1673-4	462	*1723-4*	652	*1773-4*	552
1674-5	434	*1724-5*	632	*1774-5*	589
1675-6	460	*1725-6*	607	*1775-6*	606
1676-7	509	*1726-7*	651	*1776-7*	616
1677-8	478	*1727-8*	600	*1777-8*	599
1678-9	495	*1728-9*	574	*1778-9*	662
1679-80	538	*1729-30*	654	*1779-80*	694
1680-1	541	*1730-1*	711	*1780-1*	674
1681-2	513	*1731-2*	708	*1781-2*	668
1682-3	527	*1732-3*	728	*1782-3*	603
1683-4	545	*1733-4*	767	*1783-4*	606
1684-5	479	*1734-5*	753	*1784-5*	639
1685-6	560	*1735-6*	742	*1785-6*	646
1686-7	542	*1736-7*	688	*1786-7*	656
1687-8	573	*1737-8*	710	*1787-8*	638
1688-9	593	*1738-9*	731	*1788-9*	653
1689-90	621	*1739-40*	621	*1789-90*	649
1690-1	649	*1740-1*	562	*1790-1*	656
1691-2	593	*1741-2*	634	*1791-2*	653
1692-3	495	*1742-3*	691	*1792-3*	641
1693-4	467	*1743-4*	772	*1793-4*	602
1694-5	504	*1744-5*	758	*1794-5*	545
1695-6	469	*1745-6*	673	*1795-6*	517
1696-7	473	*1746-7*	697	*1796-7*	585
1697-8	429	*1747-8*	668	*1797-8*	610
1698-9	428	*1748-9*	657	*1798-9*	553

Table A9.2: (*cont.*)

Date	Real-wage index	Date	Real-wage index	Date	Real-wage index
1799–1800	413	1839–40	631	1879–80	1 037
1800–1	376	1840–1	647	1880–1	1 006
1801–2	497	1841–2	701	1881–2	1 072
1802–3	538	1842–3	790	1882–3	1 036
1803–4	530	1843–4	792	1883–4	1 146
1804–5	464	1844–5	756	1884–5	1 199
1805–6	493	1845–6	727	1885–6	1 324
1806–7	517	1846–7	650	1886–7	1 293
1807–8	514	1847–8	752	1887–8	1 303
1808–9	481	1848–9	816	1888–9	1 308
1809–10	479	1849–50	886	1889–90	1 312
1810–1	493	1850–1	908	1890–1	1 247
1811–2	436	1851–2	906	1891–2	1 253
1812–3	425	1852–3	793	1892–3	1 368
1813–4	487	1853–4	715	1893–4	1 287
1814–5	545	1854–5	713	1894–5	1 320
1815–6	595	1855–6	722	1895–6	1 364
1816–7	524	1856–7	712	1896–7	1 356
1817–8	523	1857–8	774	1897–8	1 344
1818–9	536	1858–9	762	1898–9	1 404
1819–20	591	1859–60	707	1899–1900	1 347
1820–1	672	1860–1	717	1900–1	1 364
1821–2	777	1861–2	744	1901–2	1 402
1822–3	729	1862–3	862	1902–3	1 350
1823–4	672	1863–4	844	1903–4	1 382
1824–5	573	1864–5	840	1904–5	1 382
1825–6	607	1865–6	823	1905–6	1 351
1826–7	649	1866–7	807	1906–7	1 336
1827–8	669	1867–8	856	1907–8	1 326
1828–9	677	1868–9	903	1908–9	1 313
1829–30	703	1869–70	921	1909–10	1 403
1830–1	640	1870–1	880	1910–1	1 423
1831–2	691	1871–2	857	1911–2	1 407
1832–3	737	1872–3	835		
1833–4	799	1873–4	845		
1834–5	787	1874–5	920		
1835–6	709	1875–6	881		
1836–7	693	1876–7	910		
1837–8	689	1877–8	947		
1838–9	642	1878–9	1 004		

Source: See text for derivation of real-wage figures.

Appendix 10

Local mortality crises

The timing and concomitants of mortality crises visible in the national data have been discussed in chapter 8. A sharp rise in the national death rate, however, tells us little about the experiences of individual parishes, since it may result from a uniform but relatively modest increase in mortality throughout the country, or from violent surges in a few populous parishes. Again, a national crisis may reflect a country-wide peppering of local epidemics, or be widely present but only within a limited region. A fuller understanding of the local characteristics of mortality crises therefore adds a greater depth to their study at the national level, besides revealing much else that is independently interesting. This appendix is devoted to such issues; it begins with a description of the technique adopted to identify local crises and then turns to the discussion of the substantive topics that may be studied using data obtained in this way, notably the temporal incidence of local crises, their geographical distribution, and their relationship to the local social, economic, and physical environment.

The data used to plot local mortality crises were the monthly burial totals available for each of the 404 parishes.[1] The conventions used to convert burial to death totals on a national scale cannot be paralleled in each parish, but the use of burial rather than death totals causes no problem in this context because the factors that caused the registration of the former to be an imperfect record of the latter changed only slowly over time and so are of negligible significance for the detection of short-term fluctuations.[2] On the other hand, the variation from parish to parish in the date range for which monthly burial totals are available means that the overall prevalence of crisis mortality has to be measured in relative, rather than absolute terms, i.e. as a proportion of the parishes in observation at a given date. All parishes provide data for the years 1662/3 to 1810/11, but before and after this period coverage is not complete. Only 39 parishes (10 per cent) were in observation in 1540/1, a figure that grew to 16, 33, and 59 per cent by 1550/1, 1560/1, and 1570/1, respectively. By 1600/1 72 per cent of the parishes were contributing data and by 1620/1 the proportion had risen to 87 per cent. After 1810/1 the percentage of parishes in observation falls to 70, a figure maintained until the establishment of civil registration in 1837. By 1838/9, the last year for which parish monthly data are available, only 21 per cent of the parishes were in observation.[3]

Throughout the appendix when data are tabulated on an annual basis, the year beginning on 1 July has been used in preference to the calendar year, partly to

---

1. The south-west is under-represented with no parishes from Cornwall; see tables 2.15–6 and fig. 2.1.
2. The monthly totals include corrections for under-registration as described in chapter 1 and appendices 12 and 13. Care was taken to ensure that no spurious crises were generated in this way.
3. For finer detail see table 2.19 and fig. 2.4, which illustrate the very similar observational profile for baptismal registration.

preserve comparability with the national results reported in chapter 8, but primarily because mid summer was usually a period of seasonally low mortality (table 8.3).

Identifying local crises

In order to investigate the local incidence of crisis mortality it is first necessary to define what constitutes a crisis in terms of the monthly frequencies of events. On the national level the definition could be couched in terms of the death rate, but the general lack of information about local population sizes precludes this possibility in the case of individual parishes. However parish population sizes very seldom changed markedly in the short run so that a large short-term increase in the number of deaths can be taken to indicate a major rise in mortality. In this context there are two issues to be decided: how the 'normal' number of deaths at any point in time is to be determined, and how large a surge above the normal level may be taken to indicate a crisis.

A number of different methods have been employed in other studies to estimate the normal number of deaths, usually based on an average of the frequencies of deaths recorded in non-crisis periods, either in the immediate past, or in a period centred on the year or month in question.[4] The problem with trailing moving averages is that their estimate of the trend level of the current month lags behind the true figure by half the length of the moving average. The centred moving average avoids this difficulty but runs the risk of including future monthly totals which may turn out to be at crisis level.[5] A technique known as double exponential smoothing escapes both drawbacks by deriving an estimate of the current trend in the series from the behaviour of past, and hence already tested, monthly frequencies, exponentially weighted so that the most recent frequencies are given most, and the most distant frequencies least, weight in determining the trend in the series.[6] Once the trend in the series has been identified it can be projected forward in time to forecast the numbers of burials that might be expected to occur in the next month, or at any point in the future. The forecasts can then be compared with the actual numbers of burials recorded.

In distinguishing a crisis from random fluctuations it is obviously important to take account of the variability of the burial series, for while a small upward fluctuation in the number of burials may be quite unremarkable in a highly variable series, it can be very significant in an extremely stable series. We have investigated the variability of monthly series of burials in a large number of parishes of different sizes and at

4. Several methods are presented and discussed by contributors to Charbonneau and Larose, *The great mortalities*. See especially Hollingsworth, 'A preliminary suggestion for the measurement of mortality crises', with comments by Johansen (pp. 153–6) and Marschalck (pp. 171–8); del Panta and Livi-Bacci, 'Chronology, intensity and diffusion of mortality in Italy' (p. 72); Dupâquier, 'L'analyse statistique des crises de mortalité' (pp. 85–93).

5. This risk can be diminished by taking a truncated moving average (e.g. dropping the highest and lowest values from the period covered by the moving average), as suggested by del Panta and Livi-Bacci, *op. cit.*

6. Double smoothing means that the results of the exponential smoothing of the original data are themselves smoothed exponentially, and it is this that enables an estimate to be made of the effects of linear trends in the underlying processes (death rate and population size). After considerable experiment with parishes of widely differing sizes and rates of growth we settled on a smoothing constant of 0.0083, which corresponds to a *double* moving average of a trailing period of 20 years. We also experimented with triple smoothing to capture non-linear (second-degree polynomial) elements in the trend, but with the small populations being examined here we found the estimates less stable than those derived from a simple linear model of the trend. The technique of exponential smoothing is described in most textbooks on time-series analysis, for example Montgomery and Johnson, *Forecasting and time series analysis*, chapter 3.

different times and have found that the standard deviations of the series are reasonably well approximated by the formula $0.1f + \sqrt{f}$, where f is the current trend value of the monthly totals of burials.[7] Since f can be forecast for any month in the future the formula also makes it possible to estimate the standard deviation of the series at any future date. Very small parishes, however, involve a special problem in that the formula may result in an f which is only a fraction of one and in these circumstances the standard deviation is understated. To overcome this difficulty 0.75 was arbitrarily added to f in all cases.

If all parishes had been large and if the fluctuations in the monthly burial totals had been independent of each other, the normal distribution could have been used to find the probability that a recorded value was a random fluctuation by noting how many standard deviations higher than the projected trend value it lay. However, many parishes were small, and fluctuations in individual months were influenced by those that had occurred in previous months.[8] Although in these circumstances the normal distribution does not give an accurate measure of the probability that an individual monthly total is a random fluctuation from trend, it can still be used as a rough yardstick to identify totals that are so far above trend that it is reasonable to conclude that the death rate had risen substantially.

After much experiment, the rule was adopted that any single monthly total that was 3.36 or more standard errors above the forecast trend value for that month was classified as a month of crisis mortality. The probability of so high a monthly total occurring by chance with no change in the underlying trend is very remote (less than 1 in 10,000 under strictly independent random conditions). Furthermore any run of two or more consecutive months, each of which was at least 2.05 standard errors above the forecast trend value, was also held to constitute a crisis (the equivalent probability that each monthly total could have occurred by chance with no change in the underlying trend is less than 1 in 100 under strictly independent random conditions). To allow for random, downward fluctuations within a crisis period, up to two consecutive months were permitted to return frequencies less than 2.05 standard errors above the trend value without terminating the crisis provided that they were followed by at least one month above this level. However, if a third consecutive month failed under this rule, or if any month with *fewer* burials than the forecast trend value interposed, the crisis was terminated with the last month to reach the crisis level.

As a concrete illustration of the operation of these rules, we may consider a parish of 1,000 inhabitants with a crude burial rate of 27 per 1,000. In such a parish 27 burials a year would be registered, or 2.25 per month. If for convenience we assume that there was no trend in the stream of deaths (because the population was stationary and the death rate constant), then the forecast monthly trend value would be 2.25 burials for the next and all future months. According to the formula given above the standard deviation of the trend value (to which 0.75 is added) would be $0.3 + \sqrt{3} = 2.032$. Thus any month with at least 10 deaths would be adjudged a crisis

7. A similar result was found in an investigation of a number of French and Belgian registers. See appendix 12, fn. 1. We experimented with using an updated estimate of the prediction error (i.e. the discrepancy between the observed and forecast monthly totals) as a guide to the variance in the series, but it proved too unstable for the purpose of identifying crises.

8. The internal structure in the series of annual national death rates is discussed on pp. 344–8 above. The most likely reason for the serial correlation in the annual rates was the influence of past fluctuations on the size of the populations at risk to die, and this consideration would also be likely to induce a serial correlation in the parish burial totals.

$(2.25 + (2.032 \times 3.36) = 9.08)$, while the qualifying level for each potential member of a sequence of months, as defined above, would be at least 7 burials $(2.25 + (2.032 \times 2.05) = 6.42)$. In this example, therefore, to qualify as a crisis a single month must score at least 4.04 times the trend value, or alternatively a sequence of months must score at least 2.85 times their trend values.[9]

Because the variability of the series of burials is *proportionately* higher in small than in large parishes, the ratio by which monthly totals of deaths has to exceed the trend value to be accounted a crisis is also higher. For example, in a parish of 500 inhabitants with the same burial rate of 27 per 1,000 the crisis-qualifying ratios corresponding to the figures of 4.04 and 2.85 would be 5.65 and 3.84. In contrast, in a parish of 2,000 inhabitants the comparable ratios would be lower at 3.10 and 2.28. Thus the larger the size of the parish the smaller the rise in the burial rate that can be distinguished from a random fluctuation.

A set of criteria of this kind makes it possible to step a month at a time through the monthly frequencies of burials in each parish. At each step the expected frequency for the current month is calculated on the basis of the information already acquired about the nature of the trend in the series. If the current month is judged not to be a crisis, the current value is accepted and included in the updating of the calculation of the trend ready for the next monthly step. If, however, the current month exceeds the crisis level, the information about the trend is frozen in its current state, and subsequent months are tested sequentially against the expected values forecast on the basis of the current estimate of the trend. Once the first month following the crisis has been identified, the intervening crisis months are skipped and the calculation of the underlying trend is updated by including the first month after the crisis, and the process of stepping through the series month by month is resumed.

Two further points about this method of identifying crises should be noted. First, it is necessary to gain some idea of the trend at the beginning of the series in order to be able to test whether the first month was part of a crisis. To achieve this, the testing process was begun 20 years after the beginning of the monthly series with an initial estimate of the trend value at that point calculated from a simple average of the monthly frequencies over a period of 10 years. The standard testing procedure was then used, but moving backwards in time towards the start of the series, before turning round to begin its main run forwards through the data. A preliminary period of 20 years was chosen to allow ample time for the influence of any crisis months that may have been included in the initial estimate of the trend value to be decayed exponentially to negligible proportions before the main run started.

Second, the seasonal pattern of mortality, as seen in table 8.3, clearly needs to be taken into account in forecasting burial frequency. Otherwise the expected level of burials will be underestimated in the spring, when burials were at their seasonal maximum, with a consequent risk of finding too many crises, and overestimated in the late summer, with an opposite risk. Although a seasonal component could have been built into the forecasting procedure, the simpler expedient was adopted of estimating the seasonal pattern of mortality in each parish and then 'de-seasonalizing' the monthly series of burials before testing for the existence of crises.[10]

9. To avoid the unevenness due to the fact that deaths occur in integer units these ratios have been calculated using the fractional cut-off points (i.e. $4.04 = 9.08/2.25$ and $2.85 = 6.42/2.25$).

10. For each of the 12 months in the year a ratio was calculated between the observed number of burials recorded during the entire period covered by the register and one twelfth of the total number of burials. Each monthly total was then divided by the appropriate ratio for the month. The procedure assumes that the

It scarcely needs to be remarked that the criteria adopted for the identification of crises will to a large extent determine the results: the numbers of crises found, their length, and severity. Crises are usually defined by reference to a fixed ratio between the observed numbers of burials and an estimate of the underlying trend. For example, annual or monthly totals that are more than double the trend level may be classified as crisis periods.[11] Unfortunately, despite an appearance of impartiality, such a procedure will not measure the incidence of crises accurately. In the case of very small parishes where the monthly totals of recorded events were very low, quite small random fluctuations could exceed the fixed ratio and generate spurious crises. In contrast, in large parishes purely random fluctuations were much smaller in proportion to the normal monthly totals of events so the risk of finding spurious crises would be correspondingly less. Furthermore, large parishes were often geographically extensive, so that epidemics might take some time to spread through the parish, or might fail to reach some parts of it at all, resulting in lower proportionate increases in the numbers of burials recorded. Consequently the use of a fixed ratio to identify crises will tend to understate the frequency of crises in larger parishes compared with smaller ones.[12]

The method of identifying crises adopted here, which uses a flexible ratio linked to the variability of the burial series, has been designed to avoid misclassifying random fluctuations in smaller parishes as crises. But the greater variability of the series in smaller parishes means that only large upward movements in burials will be adjudged to constitute crises in them, while more modest movements can qualify as crises in larger parishes.[13] The severity of the local crises identified in this way is therefore correlated negatively with parish size.[14] Moreover, the method may also produce an artificial positive relationship between the frequency and duration of crises and parish size unless its greater sensitivity to relatively small upward movements in the burial rate in larger parishes is offset by the generally lower levels of crisis death rates in these populations. This is a difficult point to evaluate, partly for technical reasons, but also because the greater exposure of larger parishes to infectious disease together with their greater geographical extent furnish plausible grounds for supposing the existence of a genuine positive relationship between the frequency and duration of local crises and parish size. On the other land, other characteristics of local crises, such as their seasonality and their distribution over time, are less dependent on the method of determining the cut-off point between crisis and non-crisis mortality, since crises are but the peaks of more general surges in mortality.

The distribution of local crises through time

A total of 5,470 periods of crisis mortality was found in the 404 parishes in the

---

seasonal pattern of burials was constant over time, an assumption that is reasonable at the national level (see table 8.3). For methods of forecasting a seasonal time series see Montgomery and Johnson, *Forecasting and time series analysis*, chapter 5.

11. See references cited in fn. 4, above.

12. The point is discussed extensively by Hollingsworth, Johansen, and Marschalck. See fn. 4, above.

13. The negative relationship between variability and parish size is contained in the $\sqrt{f}$ term in the expression for the estimate of the standard deviation of the burial series $(0.1f + \sqrt{f})$ discussed in the text (the term $0.1f$ being proportional to population size). The $\sqrt{f}$ term dominates when population size is very small and becomes progressively less important as population size increases.

14. Mean severity rates (observed burials in a crisis period/forecast total) ranged from 12.5 in parishes with under 250 inhabitants (in 1811), through 8.8 in parishes with 250–499 inhabitants, down to 3.3 in parishes with 3,750 or more inhabitants.

aggregative set using the method of identification just described. Table A10.1 summarizes the distribution of the crises over time, by quarter century and decade. To avoid the problems of comparability arising from the different time spans covered by the burial registers of individual parishes, the number of months of crisis mortality occurring in each period has been expressed as a rate per 1,000 parish-months in observation. The first panel of the table shows a steady, but not uninterrupted, fall in

Table A10.1: Crisis months in 404 parishes per 1 000 months observed, by quarter century and decade

Quarter century	Months observed	Crisis months (per 1 000 observed)	Quarter century	Months observed	Crisis months (per 1 000 observed)
1550–74	50 064	14.6	*1700–24*	121 200	10.4
1575–99	86 256	13.4	*1725–49*	121 200	16.2
1600–24	105 960	12.6	*1750–74*	121 200	9.8
1625–49	113 760	12.9	*1775–99*	121 200	9.2
1650–74	119 916	10.8	*1800–24*	100 296	6.0
1675–99	121 200	10.0			
Decade			Decade		
1540–9	6 660	15.0	*1690–9*	48 480	5.5
1550–9	9 660	27.7	*1700–9*	48 480	6.5
1560–9	25 224	5.5	*1710–9*	48 480	13.2
1570–9	31 092	8.1	*1720–9*	48 480	27.0
1580–9	34 116	11.1	*1730–9*	48 480	7.7
1590–9	36 228	17.7	*1740–9*	48 480	11.9
1600–9	40 680	13.2	*1750–9*	48 480	9.4
1610–9	43 188	9.2	*1760–9*	48 480	11.1
1620–9	44 388	15.0	*1770–9*	48 480	9.8
1630–9	45 384	14.2	*1780–9*	48 480	9.4
1640–9	46 080	12.2	*1790–9*	48 480	7.9
1650–9	47 268	11.2	*1800–9*	48 480	7.0
1660–9	48 408	11.2	*1810–9*	35 136	5.0
1670–9	48 480	12.0	*1820–9*	33 336	6.6
1680–9	48 480	12.1	*1830–8*	22 536	10.7

Note: Years run from July to June, and are identified by the calendar year in which they begin.

Source: Original parish monthly burial totals corrected for deficient registration. The equivalent annual totals, summed over the 404 parishes, are given in table A4.1, column 2.

the crisis rate over time. Over the four quarter centuries between 1550 and 1649 the rate fell from 14.6 to 12.9 per 1,000 months observed. On average, therefore, in this period a parish would experience one crisis month about every six or seven years. Such a figure gives a general impression of the intensity of crisis mortality, but is not typical of the actual intervals occurring between crises for, as will become apparent later, crises did not always come in single months nor was the experience of crisis mortality uniform across the parishes.

From 1650 to the end of the eighteenth century the general level of the incidence of crisis mortality continued to fall but only slightly, from 10.8 to 9.2 per 1,000 months observed. After 1800 there was a further sharp fall to a rate of 6 crisis months per 1,000. In outline, therefore, the first panel of the table provides further confirmation of the general stabilization of mortality over time. The decline in the incidence of crisis mortality after 1700 is particularly impressive because it occurred against a background of rising parish population sizes which might be expected to have led to an increase in the number of local crises identified.[15]

However, the figures in the first panel of the table contain some anomalies, notably the very high figure of 16.2 for the period 1725–49, suggesting that there were considerable fluctuations within the three lengthy sub-periods outlined above. The second panel of the table, which aggregates the results on a decadal basis, confirms this. Several decades emerge as having been relatively lightly afflicted by crisis mortality at the parish level. The rates for the periods 1560–89, 1610–9, 1690–1709, and 1730–9 are below those generally obtaining at the time, in some instances with figures as low as those prevailing in the nineteenth century. These were in general decades in which the level of mortality, as measured by the crude death rate or the expectation of life at birth, was low, lending credence to the view that a diminished frequency of crisis mortality helped to secure lower death rates.[16]

The decadal figures suggest the existence of a plateau in the incidence of crisis mortality extending from the 1640s to the 1680s, which contrasted with the more variable and often higher rates that had obtained previously. This stabilization at a somewhat lower level might be taken to imply a fall in mortality between the late sixteenth and late seventeenth centuries. But, as was shown in chapter 7, this was a period when the general level of mortality rose rather than fell. Thus the diminishing incidence of crises at the parish, no less than at the national, level can be an untrustworthy guide to the long-term trends in mortality. On the other hand, the decadal figures in the table also indicate a decline in the incidence of local crisis mortality after the 1770s which did coincide with a period of secular improvement in mortality.

In some decades, such as the 1590s, 1620s, 1630s, and 1740s, the incidence of local crises was higher than usual, and it was very much higher in the 1550s and 1720s. These were all decades in which the national death rate fluctuated violently upwards in one or more years, indicating that the crises in these decades were widespread and that the surges in the national death rates were not simply the product of heavy mortality in a few large parishes.

The generality of the incidence of crisis mortality can be investigated more fully by referring to figure A10.1 which shows the percentage of the parishes in observation that experienced at least one crisis month in each year between 1540/1 and 1838/9. The percentages of parishes experiencing at least one month of crisis mortality were highest in 1557/8 and 1558/9, years that witnessed the most extreme upward fluctuations in the national death rate, but by no means every parish suffered a massive increase in mortality. In 1558/9, when the death rate was at the highest annual figure ever recorded, only 39 per cent of the parishes recorded a rise in mortality severe enough to be adjudged a crisis. In the previous year, when the death rate was at its second highest annual figure, only 33 per cent of the parishes were affected. The only other years which approached these figures were two of the three successive year of exceptionally high mortality in the late 1720s (1727/8 and 1728/9), when 28 per cent of the parishes in each year recorded at least one month of crisis mortality.

Table A10.2 summarizes the information contained in figure A10.1 for each of the

---

15. Whether for substantive, or for artificial reasons connected with the method of identifying crises, as discussed in the text above. For the increase in parish population sizes between 1676 and 1811 see table 2.2.
16. See tables A3.1, A3.3.

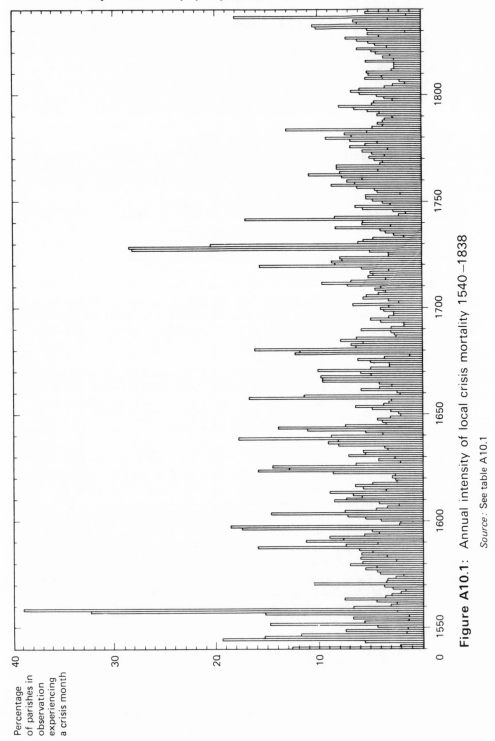

Figure A10.1: Annual intensity of local crisis mortality 1540–1838

Source: See table A10.1

Table A10.2: Percentage of parishes experiencing a crisis in 45 national crisis years (in descending order of severity)

Year	(1) National death rate (per cent above trend)	(2) 404 Parishes (per cent affected)[1]	(3) No. in observation
1558/9	124.2	39.1	92
1557/8	60.5	32.5	83
1625/6	43.0	14.6	370
1657/8	42.9	16.8	399
1728/9	41.2	28.5	404
1727/8	37.2	28.2	404
1680/1	36.5	16.3	404
1741/2	36.3	17.1	404
1729/30	35.4	20.5	404
1638/9	35.1	17.9	380
1665/6	31.7	9.7	404
1592/3	29.8	9.1	298
1587/8	29.5	16.1	292
1643/4	29.3	14.0	385
1624/5	26.6	13.0	369
1545/6	26.6	15.5	58
1597/8	25.6	18.7	305
1658/9	25.1	11.5	400
1762/3	24.2	10.9	404
1544/3	23.3	19.6	56
1603/4	21.0	14.8	338
1596/7	20.9	17.6	301
1623/4	18.3	16.0	369
1559/60	18.1	6.8	132
1590/1	18.1	11.4	297
1783/4	16.7	13.1	404
1684/5	15.7	7.9	404
1639/40	15.2	8.9	380
1670/1	15.2	10.1	404
1846/7[2]	15.1	—	—
1681/2	14.8	6.4	404
1742/3	14.6	8.4	404
1546/7	14.2	11.9	59
1781/2	14.1	7.4	404
1613/4	13.7	9.0	357
1719/20	13.6	15.8	404
1542/3	12.9	0.0	52
1678/9	12.4	12.4	404
1682/3	11.8	6.9	404
1802/3	11.2	5.9	404
1609/10	10.8	8.6	350
1854/5[2]	10.7	—	—
1779/80	10.5	9.2	404
1766/7	10.4	8.2	404
1679/80	10.3	11.9	404

Notes: [1] With at least one month with a crisis-level burial frequency.
[2] 1846/7 and 1854/5 lie outside the period covered by the aggregative tabulations though the national death rate is, of course, known.

Sources: National death rate: table 8.11. Local crises: see table A10.1.

45 years in which the national death rate rose above trend by more than 10 per cent.[17] It shows that in most of the years when the death rate was more than 20 per cent above trend, between 15 and 20 per cent of the parishes experienced at least one month of crisis mortality. In other years in the table the proportion was in general lower, from 5 to 10 per cent, but there were some years in which the percentage of parishes affected was considerably higher. There was therefore a rough, but only a rough, correspondence between the severity of the crisis in terms of the fluctuation in the annual national death rate and the percentage of parishes experiencing a crisis. In some cases the anomalies are readily explicable, for example the appearance of 1665/6 high in the list of major national crises owes much to the very large numbers of deaths from plague in London as only 10 per cent of the 404 parishes recorded a crisis level of mortality in that year. Indeed the same percentage of parishes suffered a crisis in each of the two subsequent years, but without the powerful support of London there was only a modest rise in the national death rates.[18] A similar anomaly can be seen in the table in the case of the year 1592/3, another plague year in London when only 9.1 per cent of the parishes experienced crisis mortality. Although relatively few parishes were affected, an unusual feature of the plague epidemic in this year both in London and elsewhere was its very long duration, beginning in the late autumn of 1592 and lasting until the autumn of 1593.[19] In such circumstances the numbers of deaths will have been very large and it is evident from column 1 of the table A10.2 that they had a considerable impact on the national death rate.

Towards the foot of table A10.2 there are a number of years that are anomalous in the reverse sense, in that comparatively small fluctuations in the national death rate were accompanied by relatively large percentages of parishes experiencing crisis mortality. Such a combination suggests that although mortality rose sharply in a substantial number of places the impact on the national death rate was muffled because the crises were of short duration with few other places affected. Such would be the case with rural plague which might decimate some parishes in a short period of time while neighbouring parishes escaped altogether. The year 1546/7 seems to be an example of this pattern: a study of mortality crises in Devon found the plague epidemic to have been 'the most wide-spread crisis of the whole century between 1540 and 1640' yet the national death rate was not particularly high.[20] Other similar

17. There is a general, but not perfect, agreement between the information in column 2 of the table and an earlier study of the increase of local crisis mortality based on 54 parishes drawn as a systematic (1 in 10) sample from a set of parish returns that included the 404 parishes on which the present study is based. The earlier study employed calendar year divisions and a very crude definition of a crisis year. Schofield, ' "Crisis" mortality', p. 19. There is also a fair correspondence with the list of 'sickly years' compiled by Short in the eighteenth century, despite the limited geographical range of his data (mainly from Yorkshire and Derbyshire) and the discrepancy between his definition of 'sickliness' (depending upon an unstated proportion of parishes registering more burials than baptisms) and the definition of crisis mortality employed here. Short, *New observations*, pp. 86–9, 187–9.
18. For details of local outbreaks of plague in 1666 and 1667 see Shrewsbury, *Bubonic plague*, pp. 488–537.
19. Creighton, *Epidemics in Britain*, 1, pp. 351–7. Shrewsbury, *Bubonic plague*, pp. 245–51. The local nature of plague mortality is attested by the fact that a massive outbreak in Lichfield in the summer of 1593 did not spread to the nearby villages: Palliser, 'Dearth and disease in Staffordshire', pp. 60–1. There were several localized outbreaks of plague in Devon between 1589 and 1593. Slack, 'Mortality crises', pp. 45–7. For the epidemiological and zoological factors influencing the spread of plague see Biraben, 'Current medical views on plague'.
20. Slack, 'Mortality crises', p. 52. For the sporadic incidence of rural plague see Bradley, 'Some medical aspects of plague', pp. 15–6.

years were 1590/1 (another plague period) and 1623/4, 1670/1, 1679/80, 1680/1, 1719/20, and 1783/4.

A further group of years of some interest is that in which a fairly large percentage of parishes experienced crises without the national death rate rising even 10 per cent above trend (and therefore not listed in the table). Two such years, following the London plague of 1665, have already been noted; other conspicuous examples are 1551/2, 1556/7, 1570/1, 1642/3, 1831/2, 1832/3, and 1836/7. Reference to table 8.13 which summarizes fluctuations in the national monthly death rates shows that in four of these seven years the discrepancy between the local parish experience and the movement in the annual national death rate arose from the fact that very few of the months in these years were affected. The extreme examples of 1551/2 and 1836/7, when the 'sweat' and influenza respectively produced very large upward fluctuations in the death rate in one or two months, were noted in chapter 8.[21] In these years 14.9 and 18.1 per cent of the parishes were affected respectively. In 1831/2 and 1832/3, when 10.1 and 10.5 per cent of the parishes experienced a local crisis, not only were the epidemics short but the diseases concerned (late summer diarrhoea in 1831, the first outbreak of asiatic cholera in England in the late summer and autumn of 1832, and influenza in the late spring of 1833) had only a weak effect on the national monthly death rate.[22]

In contrast to these short epidemics the crises in 1556/7, 1570/1, and 1642/3 were spread more evenly through the year, though again without provoking a national crisis. In 1556 a very poor harvest had driven the real wage index 34 per cent below trend, and in the previous year another harvest failure had brought real wages down to a level 28 per cent below trend. In the circumstances it is noteworthy that only 15 per cent of the parishes experienced crisis mortality in 1556/7.[23] Such a figure, nonetheless, was usually accompanied by a substantial rise in the national death rate, but large increases in the monthly national death rate occured only in September and December 1556 and June 1557, and the annual death rate for 1556/7 was only 7 per cent above trend. The unresponsiveness of mortality to harvest failure is thrown into sharp relief by the more marked reactions of the annual birth and marriage rates, which fell 13 and 42 per cent below trend respectively.

In 1570/1 and 1642/3, on the other hand, when 11 per cent of the parishes experienced local crises, real wages were above trend by 14 and 11 per cent respectively.[24] Neither year has been much discussed in the literature as a year of crisis mortality. Outbreaks of plague have been noted for several towns in the summer and autumn of the former year, but the seasonality of parish crises, which fell mainly on the winter months, suggests that other diseases may also have been prevalent.[25] In 1642/3 the parish crises were more frequent in the summer (July to November), and then picked up again in May and June as a prelude to the major national crisis which

21. See table 8.13 and pp. 332–40, above.

22. For a discussion of the incidence of these epidemics see Creighton *Epidemics in Britain*, II, pp. 789 (1831), 820–35 (1832), 380–3 (1833).

23. The parishes affected did not appear to be drawn disproportionately from any particular size group, economic context, or region.

24. For real wages see appendix 9. The annual death rates were 7 and 4 per cent above trend, respectively.

25. The seasonal pattern of local crises is reflected in the national monthly death rates, which were furthest above trend in September–October 1570 and January 1571 (table 8.13). For outbreaks of plague see Slack, 'Mortality crises', table 2, p. 20; Palliser, 'Dearth and disease in Staffordshire', p. 59; and Jones, 'Parish registers: north Shropshire', pp. 205–6. Information on the seasonal pattern in Devon is given in Oswald, 'Epidemics in Devon', p. 80.

reigned in the succeeding year (1643/4) and the reason for the seasonal pattern may well have been local outbreaks of plague.[26]

The occurrence of years in which a relatively high proportion of parishes experienced crisis mortality without there being any violent upswing in the national death rate leads naturally to a more general point, namely that in every year some parishes were affected by crisis mortality even though the national death rate may have been well below average. Figure A10.1 shows that there was always a minimum of 2 to 3 per cent of the parishes experiencing crisis mortality at the level defined in the present study, providing a continuous backdrop against which the more celebrated crisis years stand out in bold relief. At the local level, therefore, crisis mortality was never entirely absent in normal years. Potentially lethal micro-organisms were always present and circumstances might change so as to produce a burst of mortality in epidemic form. For example, very hot summers increased the soil temperature, thereby raising the rate at which flies' eggs hatched, and so increasing the risk of infection from contaminated food especially in the case of the more densely populated communities where excreta were left lying in the street.[27] Moreover micro-organisms could also be carried from community to community either by individuals in the normal course of daily life, or by insect and animal vectors. In this way infections could assume a peripatetic character, striking individual parishes infrequently while remaining continuously present on a regional or national level.[28]

The national crises discussed in chapter 8 were therefore produced by a synchrony of local crises which typically affected somewhere between 10 and 20 per cent of the parishes in the country, though the absolute percentage depends upon the degree of severity of mortality taken to constitute a local crisis. It should not be forgotten in this connexion that other parishes also often experienced a rise in the number of burials in crisis periods which, though insufficient to constitute clear evidence of crisis mortality, may still have reflected a genuine rise in the death rate. Yet there was always a substantial proportion of parishes whose registers betrayed no sign of an increase in the death rate. Thus crisis mortality was continuously present in the country, though never universal in its incidence.

---

26. Shrewsbury notes several outbreaks of plague in 1642 and only one in 1643, *Bubonic Plague*, pp. 400–4.

27. For the influence of temperature on the developmental cycle of flies and their rôle in the transmission of disease, see Snow, *Insects and disease*, pp. 61–2. For sanitary conditions in the pre-industrial era see Clarkson, *Death, disease and famine*, pp. 107–10. The presence of human excreta in crowded areas of early Victorian cities is a commonplace of contemporary descriptions. See, for example, 'Report of the Statistical Society on the dwellings in Church Lane, St Giles's', pp. 2–17. Furthermore, it has been estimated that there were 1.5 million town horses in the late nineteenth century, each producing 22lbs of manure a day. Thompson, 'Nineteenth century horse-sense', p. 77.

28. Many airborne infections, such as measles or smallpox, are endemic at the national or regional level but occur locally in an epidemic form. This is because they can only be continuously present when the pool of susceptible hosts is very large, for example in cities of 200,000 to 300,000 inhabitants. In small communities the infection will die out once everyone has been infected, and only return in an epidemic form when a sufficient new pool of susceptibles has grown up. For example, in the Swedish data from the late eighteenth century, where deaths are tabulated by age and disease, it is very evident that smallpox returns to parishes every six to eight years and very rarely kills anyone over that age, implying a near universal exposure to the infection, Imhof, *Aspekte der Bevölkerungsentwicklung*, 1, pp. 496–8. For the position in England, see Razzell, *The conquest of smallpox*, pp. 115–7. For the internal dynamics of epidemiological processes leading to recurrent epidemic outbreaks of an endemic disease, see Bailey, *Mathematical theory of infectious diseases*, chapters 3, 4, and 7.

The seasonality of local crises

As defined by the criteria outlined earlier in this appendix, local crises were overwhelmingly of a short duration: 37 per cent lasted only one month, 30 per cent two months, 12 per cent three months, 9 per cent four months, 5 per cent five months, and only 7 per cent persisted for six months or more.[29] This pattern showed no tendency to change over time despite the growth in parish population sizes. The short duration of the crises facilitates a discussion of their seasonality, since most of them began and ended quickly.

Table A 10.3 displays the seasonal distribution of the months in which the parish crises were at their maximum, by quarter century. To bring out the seasonal patterns more clearly the monthly frequencies have been re-expressed as index numbers scaled so that 100 represents the number of maxima that would have been recorded in each month if they had been distributed evenly throughout the year, taking into account the number of days in each month. For example, an index number of 110 would indicate that the number of crises reaching a maximum in that month was 10 per cent more than would be expected if there were no seasonality in the distribution. Since the normal seasonal rhythm of burials was controlled for in identifying the crises, the table provides information on the 'pure' seasonality of crisis mortality, though in interpreting the figures for periods before the reform of the calendar in 1751, it must be remembered that by then the Julian calendar was lagging behind the true season by 11 days.[30] Thus, for example, events registered in May 1752 occurred between 12 May and 11 June correctly reckoned; and so on.

A very clear and regular pattern emerges from the table. While crises occurred throughout the year, they were generally much more frequent in the late summer and autumn. For the period as a whole the index numbers for the months from July to November were all above 100, and they were at their maximum in August and September at 143 and 156 respectively. In contrast the index numbers for the months from December through to May were below 100, indicating a relative deficiency of crises in the winter and the spring. The seasonality of crisis mortality was thus very different from the normal seasonality of burials, which peaked in the spring.[31]

It was also much more pronounced. The overall figure for the mean absolute deviation of the monthly index numbers for the period as a whole (in the penultimate column of the table) shows an average deviation of 26 per cent from an even split across the year, while the comparable figure for burials as a whole, given in table 8.3, was about 10 per cent. Figures for the individual quarter-centuries show a similar dispersion but in three periods the seasonal pattern of crisis mortality was much more marked. In 1650–74 and 1725–49 the mean absolute monthly deviation from 100 exceeded 40 per cent, and in both cases this was mainly due to an even greater clustering of crisis mortality in August and September. In the period 1625–49 the mean absolute monthly deviation was 39 per cent, but this time there was a greater excess in July and larger shortfalls in December and January.

The overall domination of August and September as the peak months of crisis mortality is remarkable: only in 1550–74, 1675–99, and 1750–1824 were they displaced as the two months with the highest monthly indices. Crisis mortality at this

---

29. 1.4 per cent lasted for 10 or more months.
30. To correct the discrepancy 2 September 1751 was followed by 14 September. Cheney, *Handbook of dates*, pp. 10–1.
31. See table 8.3.

Table A10.3: Seasonality of parish crises

Period	Jan.	Feb.	Mar.	Apr.	May	Jun.	Jul.	Aug.	Sept.	Oct.	Nov.	Dec.	Mean absolute deviation	No. of crises
1550–74	128	115	76	128	66	79	90	114	88	105	123	90	18.7	248
1575–99	39	100	81	78	68	94	104	149	167	99	119	104	23.7	452
1600–24	63	100	73	90	84	75	98	138	148	131	109	91	21.0	503
1625–49	38	74	49	63	85	92	135	169	177	131	122	66	38.9	557
1650–74	43	62	47	46	76	114	97	189	218	153	79	76	45.7	525
1675–99	60	77	65	78	70	91	113	123	127	113	150	135	26.7	471
1700–24	59	75	52	73	86	117	134	125	171	114	101	91	27.2	519
1725–49	62	67	73	68	68	55	78	182	206	140	127	71	42.8	681
1750–74	82	85	48	60	85	135	162	118	102	87	130	106	25.5	488
1775–99	85	88	56	55	53	135	121	111	133	121	143	102	27.4	487
1800–24	70	76	116	44	46	136	143	128	108	100	128	104	27.3	305
1825–38	104	107	31	50	61	107	116	153	139	147	114	73	31.0	193
All years	64	82	63	69	73	100	114	143	156	120	120	91	25.9	5 470

Note: Years run from July to June and are referenced by the calendar year in which they begin.

Source: See table A10.1.

time of the year is often assumed to have been associated with bubonic plague, but the pattern persists long after plague disappeared from England.[32] Although several diseases can break out in epidemic form in August and September, the late summer and early autumn is the classic season for epidemics of diarrhoeal infections such as dysentery.[33] Dysentry has been little noticed in earlier discussions of crisis mortality in England, possibly because attention has been confined to specific mentions of cause of death such as 'the flux' or 'the bloody flux', ignoring the many descriptions of abdominal pains and frequent motions accompanying 'fevers' which could equally well be signs of dysentery.[34] On the continent dysentery has more readily been acknowledged as a major source of crisis mortality.[35] It was also significant for overall mortality: for example in eighteenth-century Sweden it was the fourth most important specified cause of death accounting for 5 per cent of all deaths, and 10 per cent of the age-group 1–14 years.[36] In England in the mid nineteenth century, when national data on cause of death are first available, intestinal infections accounted for 8 per cent of all deaths.[37] The seasonal pattern of local crisis mortality that emerges from table A10.3 suggests that they may also have been major killers in the pre-industrial period.[38]

In the first of the three periods with an anomalous seasonal pattern of local crisis mortality, 1550–74, high monthly index numbers were scored by several of the winter and spring months, while, in contrast, in the late seventeenth century and in the period from 1750 to 1824 crisis mortality fell more often in mid summer (June, July) and in November. These exceptions to the general pattern reflect the influence of the major crises falling in these periods.

Local crisis characteristics by quinquennium

To help bring out more clearly the differences in the characteristics of local crises over time, information has been tabulated on a quinquennial basis in table A10.4. Almost all of the major crisis periods occurred within the quinquennial divisions used, though occasionally a split is forced, as at July 1625. It should be remembered, however, that at all times there was also a background hum of crisis mortality scattered amongst the parishes unrelated to the major outbursts. In quinquennia dominated by national

32. Shrewsbury takes summer seasonality combined with heavy mortality as an indicator of bubonic plague: 50 per cent of an annual total of burials falling between June and October is 'suggestive', and more than 66 per cent occurring between July and September 'almost certainly indicative' of plague. *Bubonic plague*, pp. 174–5.
33. For a summary of the seasonality of the main epidemic diseases see Schofield, 'An anatomy of an epidemic', p. 121. For the seasonality of dysentery, see Engleson, *Dysenteriestudien*, pp. 101–13, and Imhof, *Aspekte der Bevölkerungsentwicklung*, I, pp. 548–51.
34. Dysentery cases present a wide variety of symptoms: sometimes the stools are bloody in the classic manner, but sometimes they are diarrhoeal suggesting enteritis. On other occasions the symptoms are indistinguishable from those of influenza. Bulmer, 'Dysentery', p. 546.
35. Engleson, *op. cit.*, Imhof, *op. cit.*, I, pp. 578–90; II, pp. 591–613; Goubert, 'La mortalité en France', p. 88.
36. Bronchitis/pneumonia, tuberculosis, and smallpox accounted for 12, 11, and 10 per cent of all deaths respectively. Other causes, including unspecified, accounted for 43 per cent. Widén, 'Mortality and causes of death in Sweden', p. 100.
37. In the period 1848–54 the infections, mainly comprising cholera, diarrhoea, and dysentery, accounted for 8 per cent of all deaths. They also accounted for 10 per cent of the reduction in the (age-standardized) national death rate between 1848–54 and 1971, 33 per cent of the reduction from these diseases occurring before 1901. McKeown, *The modern rise of population*, pp. 54, 58.
38. Probably dysentery since Asiatic cholera only appeared in October 1831, Morris, *Cholera*, p. 11.

Table A10.4: Aspects of local mortality crises by quinquennium

Quinquennium[1]	(1) Total months Observed	(2) Crisis	(3) Per cent crisis	(4) Maximum crisis month Parishes affected (per cent)	(5) (year; month)	(6) Duration[2] 1 mth	(7) Duration[2] ≥ 4 mths	(8) Seasonality[2] maximum[3]	(9) National crises[4]
1540-4	2 916	56	1.9	8.9	(44:9)	40	25	Oct.	42/3, 44/5**
1545-9	3 744	40	1.1	6.9	(45:10)	57	19	Jun.	45/6**, 46/7
1550-4	4 152	36	0.9	10.4	(51:7)	55	5	Jul.	
1555-9	5 508	249	4.5	20.5	(57:11)	25	33	Feb.	57/8***, 58/9****, 59/60
1560-4	11 316	87	0.8	3.8	(63:10)	44	9	Oct.	
1565-9	13 908	53	0.4	1.3	(65:12)	59	6	Dec.	
1570-4	15 180	100	0.7	4.1	(71:1)	54	7	Jan.	
1575-9	15 912	152	1.0	4.1	(79:8)	34	18	Aug.	
1580-4	16 632	110	0.7	2.9	(82:10)	60	10	Oct.	
1585-9	17 484	274	1.6	6.2	(88:2)	39	22	Sep.[11]	87/8**
1590-4	17 880	267	1.5	4.4	(90:8)	42	21	Aug.	90/1, 92/3**
1595-9	18 348	366	2.0	8.9	(97:9)	30	27	Jul.	96/7**, 97/8***
1600-4	19 812	365	1.8	7.1	(03:10)	37	34	Sep.[10]	03/4**
1605-9	20 868	172	0.8	2.9	(10:3)	42	21	Nov.	09/10
1610-4	21 312	230	1.1	3.4	(10:9)	40	15	Sep.	13/4
1615-9	21 876	170	0.8	3.0	(16:8)	43	20	Aug.[9]	
1620-4	22 092	407	1.8	6.8	(23:11)	37	28	Dec.	23/4, 24/5**
1625-9	22 296	258	1.2	8.4	(25:9)	36	22	Sep.	25/6***
1630-4	22 620	178	0.8	2.4	(31:7)	50	16	Jul.	
1635-9	22 764	462	2.0	9.7	(38:9)	40	21	Sep.	38/9***, 39/40
1640-4	22 980	409	1.8	5.5	(43:9)	33	31	Sep.	43/4**
1645-9	23 100	152	0.6	2.3	(46:8)	34	19	Aug.[11]	
1650-4	23 304	190	0.8	2.8	(53:12)	48	23	Sep.	
1655-9	23 964	341	1.4	8.0	(57:8)	34	22	Aug.	57/8***, 58/9**
1660-4	24 168	170	0.7	2.5	(61:8)	41	25	Jul.[8]	
1665-9	24 240	383	1.6	5.0	(65:10)	40	21	Aug.[9]	65/6***
1670-4	24 240	221	0.9	6.7	(70:9)	40	17	Sep.	70/1
1675-9	24 240	358	1.5	4.5	(79:8)	37	25	Nov.	78/9, 79/80
1680-4	24 240	402	1.7	6.4	(80:11)	31	24	Oct.	80/1***, 81/2, 82/3, 84/5
1685-9	24 240	184	0.8	2.5	(89:10)	30	26	Jul.	
1690-4	24 240	123	0.5	2.0	(95:6)	41	17	Jun.	

1695–9	24 240	143	0.6	(95:7)	1.7	25	21	Aug.	
1700–4	24 240	148	0.6	(01:7)	2.7	53	11	Jul.	
1705–9	24 240	163	0.7	(06:7)	2.0	41	16	Aug.	
1710–4	24 240	312	1.3	(12:7)	3.5	36	27	Jul.	19/20
1715–9	24 240	328	1.4	(19:8)	8.2	28	25	Aug.	
1720–4	24 240	302	1.2	(20:9)	3.7	36	19	Sep.	
1725–9	24 240	1 014	4.2	(27:9)	16.3	25	32	Sep.	27/8***, 28/9***, 29/30***
1730–4	24 240	167	0.7	(31:3)	2.0	49	17	Sep.	
1735–9	24 240	207	0.9	(37:11)	4.2	37	20	Nov.	
1740–4	24 240	376	1.6	(41:9)	6.4	30	33	Aug.[9]	41/2***, 42/3
1745–9	24 240	195	0.8	(47:8)	2.5	31	26	Aug.[9]	
1750–4	24 240	172	0.7	(50:11)	2.5	48	24	Nov.	
1755–9	24 240	281	1.2	(57:12)	2.7	26	22	Jun.	
1760–4	24 240	292	1.2	(63:1)	3.5	37	18	Jul.	62/3**
1765–9	24 240	249	1.0	(66:7)	2.7	33	21	Jul.	66/7
1770–4	24 240	198	0.8	(70:7)	2.2	24	25	Jul.[8,12]	
1775–9	24 240	288	1.2	(80:1)	3.0	32	23	Nov.	79/80
1780–4	24 240	295	1.2	(83:9)	6.4	38	15	Oct.	81/2, 83/4
1785–9	24 240	157	0.6	(87:8)	1.7	35	20	Jun.[10,12]	
1790–4	24 240	241	1.0	(93:6)	2.5	36	19	Jun.	
1795–9	24 240	140	0.6	(95:7)	1.5	43	10	Jul.	
1800–4	24 240	211	0.9	(01:6)	2.0	43	18	Nov.	02/3
1805–9	24 240	130	0.5	(10:6)	2.2	53	19	Mar.[8]	
1810–4	18 348	89	0.5	(11:11)	1.8	48	9	Jun.	
1815–9	16 788	96	0.6	(15:11)	1.8	35	8	Dec.	
1820–4	16 680	100	0.6	(24:8)	2.5	48	12	Aug.	
1825–9	16 656	123	0.7	(25:10)	2.9	46	8	Aug.	
1830–4	16 596	208	1.3	(31:9)	4.3	35	13	Oct.	
1835–8	5 940	55	0.9	(37:2)	10.8	32	9	Jan.[2]	
All						37	21	Sep.	

Notes:

1 Years run from July to June and are referenced by the calendar year in which they begin.

2 Crises are allocated to the quinquennium in which they begin.

3 In the case of ties, the earliest month is specified, other months being indicated by superscripts (e.g. May[7,10] represents a tie between May, July, and October).

4 1-star unless otherwise indicated.

Sources: Local crises: see table A10.1; national crises: table 8.12

crises most of the local crises will be related to them but in more tranquil quinquennia (such as 1695–9) the information contained in the table summarizes the characteristics of a scattering of independent local crises.

For each quinquennium the table first provides two measures of the intensity of crisis mortality: the overall percentage of months in which a crisis level of mortality was recorded, and the maximum percentage of parishes affected in any single month in the period. Later columns of the table contain information on the duration of the crises and their seasonality, summarized by the month in which the peaks of the individual crises most often fell. To help to provide a context for the subsequent discussion, the national crisis years occurring in each quinquennium are also listed in the table with an indication of their severity using the 'starring' system described in connexion with table 8.12, whereby 1, 2, and 3 star crises respectively represent fluctuations in the annual crude death rate of 10–9, 20–9, and over 30 per cent above a 25-year centred moving average.

The table both amplifies some of the general characteristics of local crisis mortality outlined above and provides a background against which the anomalous characteristics of the crises in certain periods can be better be appreciated. The third column of the table shows that in quinquennia in which there were no national crises, between about a half and one per cent of the monthly burial totals of the parishes in observation reached a crisis level. In general the more severe the national crises falling within a quinquennium, the higher the percentage of monthly totals classified as local crises. Very roughly it may be said that in quinquennia with 1-star crises between 1.0 and 1.5 per cent, and in quinquennia with 2- and 3-star crises between 1.5 and 2 per cent, of all months were crisis months. Only two quinquennia exceeded the 2 per cent mark, the late 1550s and the late 1720s, which are already familiar as periods of exceptional mortality at the national level. In these periods 4.5 and 4.2 per cent respectively of the monthly parish totals reached crisis level, illustrating a point made earlier: that even major national crises were made up of a scattering of short-lived local crises which were far from universal in their incidence. The point is underlined by the data for the period 1680–4, which contained one 3-star and three 1-star national crisis years, yet only 1.7 per cent of the parish monthly totals were at crisis level. This long period of high annual death rates was therefore produced by a general, and relatively modest, rise in mortality rather than by a large number of local crises.

The overall quinquennial figures of the incidence of crisis mortality reflect the joint influence of two factors: the proportion of parishes affected and the duration of the local crises. The first factor has already been examined for the individual years of national crisis in terms of the percentage of parishes with *any* monthly burial total at a crisis level (table A10.2). The fourth column of table A10.4 extends this analysis by showing the maximum percentage of parishes affected in any single month in a quinquennium, which is identified in the fifth column. The percentages are influenced both by the geographical and the temporal spread of crisis mortality. Once again the quinquennia with the most severe national crises, 1555–9 and 1725–9, head the list. The month that saw the most widespread incidence of local crisis mortality was November 1557 when 20.5 per cent of the parishes in observation were affected and it was followed by September 1727 with 16.3 per cent. It is interesting that the next two months with the most widespread local crisis mortality were July 1551 and February 1837, both of which have already been singled out as the peaks of unusually short national crises affecting communities scattered all over the country but only for a very short time, and so having only a minor impact on the annual death rates.

The duration of crisis mortality is summarized in the next two columns of the table, the first reporting the proportion of crises lasting only one month and the second the proportion of crises of four or more months' duration. The quinquennium with the highest proportion of single month crises was 1580–4, with 60 per cent, and it is noteworthy that five of the eight quinquennia with more than 50 per cent fell in the sixteenth century. Reference to earlier columns in the table shows that they were also periods with a low overall incidence of crisis mortality and with a low percentage of parishes affected in the worst crisis month. The same pattern also obtained in the other three periods with more than 50 per cent of the crises lasting only one month: in 1630–4, 1700–4, and 1805–9. Short crises suggest either a prevalence of airborne infections, as in the case of the 'sweat' of 1551, or plague, whether in its pneumonic (airborne) form or when a bubonic outbreak strikes a community in hot, humid weather.[39]

In contrast, the quinquennia in which a substantial proportion of crises were of four or more months' duration were periods of national crisis mortality in which a relatively high proportion of parishes were affected. About one third of the crises lasted four or more months in 1555–9, 1600–4, 1640–4, 1725–9, and 1740–4. Crisis mortality of several months' duration cannot be sustained by airborne infections in populations of the size of most villages and market towns in pre-industrial England. These local crises were therefore likely either to have been caused by diseases transmitted by insect vectors (e.g. typhus or in certain circumstances bubonic plague)[40] or to have encompassed a series of onslaughts by a number of different micro-organisms, as the resistance of the human hosts was progressively weakened by successive infections.[41] For example, bubonic plague was widely reported in the quinquennium 1600–4, typhus has been suspected in connexion with the military upheavals of the early 1640s, and either typhus or a fly-borne disease such as dysentery may have been responsible for the outbreaks of 1741–3.[42] Composite crises comprising successive infections are more probable in the cases of 1555–9 and 1725–9, for in these periods an unusually large proportion of parishes were affected by separate crises in quick succession.[43] Moreover, in the late 1720s local doctors noted the presence of several diseases.[44]

39. In the case of pneumonic plague the mean interval from infection to death, which is a certain outcome, is from 3 to 6 days (1 to 3 days incubation and 2 to 3 days development). Optimal conditions for the rat flea *Xenopsylla cheopis*, which is the usual vector transmitting bubonic plague, are an air temperature of 15 to 20°C with a relative humidity of 90 to 95 per cent. Cold limits the flea's activity and heat retards its rate of reproduction; the moister the atmosphere the longer it lives. Biraben, 'Current medical views on plague', pp. 28, 30.
40. Typhus is generally transmitted by the body-louse and is often associated with over-crowded conditions such as institutions or armies. Megaw, 'Typhus fevers', pp. 392–3. Plague epidemics could last several months when the weather was cold or dry, or where the susceptible populations of rats and people were large, as in London. For examples of long drawn-out epidemics of bubonic plague see fn. 19 above and the literature cited in Schofield, 'An anatomy of an epidemic', fn. 33.
41. For example, an attack of influenza can be followed by secondary bacterial invasions causing bronchitis or reviving a previously quiescent focus of pulmonary tuberculosis. Baker-Bates 'Influenza', pp. 136–7.
42. Shrewsbury, *Bubonic plague*, pp. 399–403, notes plague epidemics in the early 1640s. For typhus and dysentery see Creighton, *Epidemics in Britain*, I, pp. 547–57 (1640–4): II, pp. 78–83 (1740–4); and Oswald, 'Epidemics in Devon', pp. 103–4. See also p. 669 below.
43. The proportions of crises that were followed by another crisis within six months of their end were 30 and 29 per cent in 1555–9 and 1725–9 respectively. No other quinquennium approached these figures, the next highest being 1625–9 with 19 per cent. The overall figure for the whole period (1540–1839) was 10 per cent.
44. For example Short, a practising doctor in correspondence with colleagues elsewhere, noted several

The seasonality of the months of maximum incidence of the crises is shown in column 8 of table A10.4. Overall the quinquennial results confirm the predominance of August or September established on a quarter-century basis in table A10.3, though there was a tendency for June and July to feature fairly prominently amongst quinquennia in the later eighteenth century. As has already been noted, late summer and early autumn epidemics were typical of both plague and dysentery, while airborne infections such as influenza were more likely to produce mortality crises in the colder months of the year. The quinquennia in which the local crises were most often at their maximum in the winter months (December to February) were 1555–9, 1565–9, 1570–4, 1620–4, 1815–9, and 1835–9, and it is therefore likely that in these crises airborne infections predominated. However each quinquennium covered a wide variety of crises and the month in which crisis peaks occurred most frequently within the quinquennium was not always that in which crisis mortality was most widespread, as may be seem from column 5 of table A10.4. Here, too, August and September predominated amongst the 3- and 2-star national crisis years, not only in plague years (such as 1544/5 and 1625/6) but also in other years both before and after the disappearance of plague in the late seventeenth century. In other plague years (e.g. 1545/6, 1603/4 and 1665/6) the seasonal maximum occurred a little later in October.[45]

Some extended periods of local crisis mortality

In several instances the seasonal pattern in the longer periods of national crisis did not build up smothly to the peak month indicated in column 5 of table A10.4 and then fall back to normal levels in a symmetrical manner. Table A10.5 displays the seasonal incidence of the intensity of local crises for five extended periods of high mortality. The first began with two very deficient harvests (in 1555 and 1556), and it is unfortunate that the figures in the first panel of the table are based on rather too few parishes for it to be possible to draw any firm conclusions about their effect on local crisis mortality.[46] Yet of the 78 parishes in observation in 1556 no more than four experienced a local crisis until the very end of the harvest year 1556/7.[47] The proportion of parishes affected then rose during the autumn to reach an all-time peak of 20.5 per cent in November 1557, two to three months after the next harvest which was unusually plentiful.[48] Thereafter this very high intensity of local crisis mortality fell to a much more modest level in January 1558, but another surge occurred in the following August and on this occasion a high frequency of crisis mortality was maintained throughout the autumn and winter. Normal levels were regained only in

diseases as common in these years. '1729 . . .chincough [whooping cough], Rheumatisms, Inflammations and a general scabbiness. All low grounds sore afflicted with obstinate Quartans and Tertians [probably malaria]. At Plymouth Rheumatisms, Arthritis, suffocating coughs, fatal to the Asthmatic and Consumptive. In May inflammatory fevers and Chicken Pox; in June Erysipelas and Small-Pox; in July a putrid Fever, Itch and Scabbiness, in November a universal catarrh'. *Comparative History*, p. 91. Creighton, *Epidemics in Britain*, II, pp. 71–4, quotes extensively from contemporary accounts by Hillary at Ripon, Wintringham at York, and Huxham at Plymouth, all of whom noted several diseases.

45. The unusually extended seasonal distribution of plague deaths in 1592–3 has already been remarked. The month with the highest incidence of crises in the quinquennium 1590–4 was August 1591, another period of bubonic plague. Shrewsbury, *op. cit.*, p. 242.

46. Real wages were 28 and 34 per cent below trend in 1555/6 and 1556/7 respectively.

47. From January 1557 five further parishes came into observation raising the total to 83.

48. Real wages were 20 per cent above trend.

Table A10.5: Seasonality of local crises in selected periods of high mortality

	Jan.	Feb.	Mar.	Apr.	May	Jun.	Jul.	Aug.	Sept.	Oct.	Nov.	Dec.	No. of parishes
	Percentage of parishes in observation experiencing a crisis												
1556–60													
1556	0.0	1.3	1.3	0.0	0.0	0.0	1.3	5.1	3.8	2.6	2.6	2.6	78
1557	2.4	1.2	1.2	2.4	3.6	7.2	6.0	13.3	13.3	13.3	20.5	9.6	83
1558	3.2	4.3	3.2	2.3	2.2	2.2	2.2	13.0	12.0	15.2	13.0	10.9	92
1559	9.8	11.4	8.4	3.3	3.8	2.3	0.0	3.0	2.3	1.5	1.5	1.5	132
1560	0.7	1.3	1.3	8.4	0.0	0.7	6.0	0.0	0.0	0.0	0.0	0.0	154
1596–8													
1596	0.7	1.0	0.7	0.0	0.3	1.0	2.0	1.3	1.3	2.0	3.7	4.0	301
1597	3.9	5.5	6.9	7.2	6.2	5.2	5.9	6.6	8.9	6.6	7.2	6.6	305
1598	4.2	3.6	2.0	1.0	0.7	2.0	1.0	0.6	0.6	1.0	0.6	0.0	309
1622–5													
1622	0.5	0.5	0.3	0.3	0.0	0.3	0.5	0.3	0.0	0.3	1.4	4.3	368
1623	2.7	2.4	2.2	3.5	3.5	3.0	5.1	5.7	5.7	6.5	6.8	6.0	369
1624	4.3	3.8	0.8	1.4	1.1	1.6	1.6	3.5	3.3	3.0	2.4	2.4	369
1625	2.2	2.2	1.9	2.2	1.4	2.4	3.5	5.7	8.4	7.0	4.9	2.7	370
1678–81													
1678	0.2	0.2	0.0	0.0	0.0	0.2	1.2	2.0	3.5	4.2	3.0	3.5	404
1679	4.2	3.5	3.5	1.7	2.5	2.0	2.5	4.5	3.7	3.5	3.5	4.2	404
1680	1.0	1.0	1.2	1.0	0.5	0.7	0.7	1.0	4.0	5.9	6.4	5.2	404
1681	3.5	3.5	2.5	3.0	3.5	3.0	2.0	2.0	1.2	1.2	1.2	1.2	404
1727–30													
1727	0.7	0.5	0.5	0.5	0.5	0.5	1.7	9.2	16.3	16.1	12.9	8.4	404
1728	4.7	3.5	3.2	2.5	2.0	2.5	2.5	13.1	10.9	6.7	5.4	5.7	404
1729	5.0	5.2	8.7	9.2	7.4	4.5	4.0	7.4	9.7	9.7	7.9	5.9	404
1730	4.5	4.5	3.0	2.7	2.2	1.5	1.0	0.5	1.5	1.5	1.5	0.5	404

Source: See table A10.1.

the summer of 1559, and were not thereafter disturbed except by a sudden outbreak of local crises in April 1560.

There were therefore two extended periods of crisis mortality (in the summer and autumn of 1557 and from the late summer of 1558 to the winter of 1559), and an isolated surge in the spring of 1560. The timing of the first period indicates that if there was any link with the deficient harvest of the previous year it only became operative after a delay of eight or nine months. Alternatively the crisis mortality may have been due to other infections quite independent of the scarcity of food. Epidemic infection is the probable explanation in the case of the second period of crisis mortality which started late in the next summer (1558) when the harvest was abundant. The persistence of crisis mortality right through the following winter coupled with the high proportion of recurrent local crises in this period suggests that a succession of infections may have taken their toll.[49]

The second panel of the table shows the monthly distribution of the percentage of parishes affected by crisis mortality during the 2-star crisis years of 1596/7 and 1597/8 when food prices were very high.[50] The proportion of parishes affected began to rise fairly soon after the disastrous harvest of 1596, remaining at 6 or 7 per cent right through 1597. The peak of 8.9 per cent occurred in September 1597 after another very bad harvest and the intensity of local crisis did not fall to the normal background level until the spring of 1598.[51]

In 1622/3 the harvest was again deficient, although to a much lesser extent than in 1555/6 or 1596/7.[52] However, the food price data used in the present study mainly refer to the south of England, and the harvest failure appears to have been much more severe in the north.[53] The third panel of table A10.5 shows that the incidence of local crises began to rise soon after the deficient harvest and continued at a high level throughout the following year (1623), falling back to a lower level in the spring of 1624. The pattern was similar to that of the years of harvest failure in 1596–8, though, in this case, there was a further temporary increase in the late summer and autumn of 1624, followed by a separate, and much more severe, surge in the intensity of local crises in the same months of 1625. These later crises were geographically distinct from those occurring in the wake of the deficient harvest of 1622, as is shown below, and many of the crises towards the end of 1625 were probably connected with a severe outbreak of bubonic plague from July to September in London.

The years from 1678/9 to 1684/5 comprised an exceptionally long period of high mortality, though the proportions of parishes experiencing a crisis were comparatively low. The fourth panel of the table concentrates on the first four years of this period when local crises were more frequent, and shows that there was one autumn season of local crisis mortality (August to December 1679) and two long winter seasons (September 1678 to March 1679, and September 1680 to May 1681).

49. Contemporary descriptions of cause of death (e.g. 'burning' and 'spotted' fevers, 'the new ague', the 'bloody flux', and 'pining sickness') are discussed in Slack, 'Mortality crises', pp. 31–2.
50. Real wages were 36 and 23 per cent below trend in 1596/7 and 1597/8, respectively.
51. A similar pattern obtained in 1587/8 with between 4.5 and 5.8 per cent of the parishes experiencing local crises between September 1587 and March 1588. Although famine aided by typhus has been suggested as the probable cause of local crises in Cumbria at this time, it should be noted that while it is true that the harvest of 1586 was very deficient (real wages were 21 per cent below trend), the main period of local crises followed immediately after the harvest of 1587 which was plentiful (real wages were 12 per cent above trend). Appleby, 'Disease or famine?', pp. 408–14.
52. Real wages were 9 per cent below trend.
53. See p. 340 above.

The fifth panel of the table also reveals that the four years of generally high mortality in the late 1720s contained distinct periods when local crises were more intense than at other times. Indeed there are strong parallels between the seasonal pattern in these years and that obtaining for the four crisis years in the late 1550s. In 1727, as in 1557, the intensity of local crisis mortality began to increase rapidly in the summer and tailed off in the winter months, though in 1727 the build-up began a little later in the year (in August) to reach maximum intensity in the next month, while in 1557 there had been a slower rise from June to a maximum in November. In both the 1720s and the 1550s, local crisis mortality picked up again in the August of the second year (1558, 1728), but whereas in the former period it remained at a high level through the winter into the spring of 1559 and then declined to normal levels by midsummer, in 1728 the intensity declined somewhat with the onset of winter, but then maintained this level with occasional spurts right through 1729. The decline began in the early months of 1730 and, as in 1559, normal levels were regained by midsummer. In the late 1720s, therefore, as in the late 1550s, the seasonality of local crisis-mortality was unusual in that it was mainly confined to the autumn and winter.

The concentration of crisis mortality in the autumn and winter, together with the length of the period of crisis mortality and the relatively high proportion of repeated crises in individual parishes, accords well with the succession of infections reported by doctors at the time.[54] The feature of crisis mortality in the late 1720s that distinguished it from that of the late 1550s was the persistence of a relatively high intensity of local crises throughout 1729. It will be remembered that an extended period of months with a high incidence of local crises was a feature of the years following the deficient harvests of 1596 and 1622 and it is not surprising to find that the harvest in 1728 was deficient, though more on the modest scale of 1622/3 than the more serious shortfall of 1596/7.[55] However it should be noted that this pattern of mortality was by no means an inevitable consequence of high food prices, for there are many examples of deficient harvests not followed by a whole year of local crises.[56] The late 1720s, therefore, appear to have differed from the late 1550s in that a deficient harvest prolonged the second wave of local crises through the spring and summer to join up with a further round of epidemics in the autumn and winter and so produce very high death rates for a period of two consecutive years (in 1728/9 and 1729/30).[57]

The causes of local crises

While the duration, severity, and seasonal incidence of local crises can provide some clues as to the general nature of mortality at the time, they do not enable a clear identification to be made of the specific diseases responsible. In order to distinguish between the probable causes of crisis mortality it is necessary to consider more detailed aspects of the pattern of deaths, for example the incidence of mortality by age and by household, a task beyond the scope of this volume.[58] Unfortunately, English

54. See fn. 44 above.
55. Real wages were 14 per cent below trend.
56. Examples of years with major downward fluctuations in real wages but no spate of local crises are 1594/5, 1647/8, 1648/9, 1649/50, 1697/8, 1689/90, 1811/2, 1812/3.
57. For a detailed study of the relationship between movements in burials and local food prices see Gooder, 'The population crisis of 1727–30'.
58. See, for example, Schofield, 'An anatomy of an epidemic', and 'Microdemography and epidemic mortality'.

parish registers outside London rarely record the cause of death in a consistent manner. Even in times of crisis an annotation in a register such as 'plague' may be used in a generic rather than a specific sense, and indicate the existence of some 'pestilence' rather than refer to bubonic plague. Medical descriptions of crisis mortality proliferate throughout the period but suffer from two disadvantages: they are often biased in their coverage, reporting urban rather than rural experience, and, with the exception of a few clearly recognizable diseases such as bubonic plague and smallpox, they describe diseases in ways that are difficult to translate into modern terminology, and that sometimes convey little more than that the patient experienced an increased temperature in response to a severe infection.[59]

Although many contemporary references have been gathered together by Short and Creighton, the difficulties of interpretation are severe, especially with regard to the many outbreaks of fevers and the hazy distinctions drawn between typhus and other diseases.[60] Nevertheless it seems clear that plague was an important cause of crisis mortality in the sixteenth and, to a lesser extent in the seventeenth century. It is mentioned frequently in the urban sources, and it is consistent with some of the patterns examined here, notably the predominance of short crises in several of the quinquennia in the later sixteenth century. Furthermore, detailed investigations of some local outbreaks, by Shrewsbury and Slack, have confirmed the continuing importance of plague in the period.[61] Outside London, where some plague deaths were recorded in most years, the disease occurred in sporadic epidemics particularly common in the mid 1540s, 1563, the late 1570s, and the early 1590s. While not entirely absent, it was only a minor element in the periods of heavy crisis mortality in the late 1550s, mid 1580s, and late 1590s, which are more likely to have been caused by airborne infections.[62] In the seventeenth century plague became relatively rare except in large urban centres and, when it occurred, was often an accompaniment to a major epidemic in London, as in 1603, 1625, and 1665.[63]

Smallpox was also endemic in London where in addition it occasionally flared up in an epidemic form.[64] Smallpox epidemics are often referred to in contemporary literature, especially in the late seventeenth and eighteenth centuries, both in towns and in the countryside.[65] The disease was present during the late 1720s, but so were many others and it is impossible to establish its relative importance in this crisis period.[66] A few years earlier, between 1721 and 1725, contemporaries referred

---

59. For example, fevers were classified according to the periodicity of recurrence: e.g. 'tertians', 'quartans', or, more vaguely, as 'remittents'.

60. Short, *New observations* and *Comparative history*. Creighton conflates what are probably several separate diseases under the heading 'Typhus and other continued fevers', *Epidemics in Britain*, II, chapter 1. A further complication is that typhus was not distinguished from typhoid until 1869. McKeown, *The modern rise of population*, p. 59.

61. Shrewsbury, *Bubonic plague*. Slack, 'Mortality crises'.

62. Shrewsbury, however, argues for the presence of plague in some localities in the late 1550s, *op. cit.*, pp. 195–200.

63. Slack, 'Mortality crises', notes a decline in the incidence of plague in rural Devon between the sixteenth and seventeenth centuries but a rise in its incidence in rural Essex. Since in the latter area plague mainly occurred in towns and in villages near the main roads, the contrary development in Essex may reflect the growing involvement of the county in the London market. Slack, 'Mortality crises', pp. 45, 52–3.

64. Marshall, *Mortality in the metropolis*, unpaginated tables headed 'An account of the number of deaths . . . under . . . heads of diseases and casualties'.

65. Creighton, *Epidemics in Britain*, II, chapter 4; Razzell, *The conquest of smallpox*, pp. 128–32.

66. See the sources cited in fn. 44 above and Jones, 'Parish registers: north Shropshire', p. 205.

extensively to outbreaks of smallpox but, as a glance at figure A 10.1 will show, the intensity of local crisis mortality did not rise significantly above the normal background level.[67] Thus smallpox, unlike a disease such as influenza, did not sweep across the country as a national epidemic. Rather it seems to have been endemic at a regional level, returning to individual communities when there was a sufficient number of susceptible young children who had not previously been exposed to it, thereby contributing to the background rumble of crisis mortality.[68]

With other diseases, where the problems of identification are still more severe, it is very difficult to discover their specific contribution to crisis mortality in the period before the establishment of civil registration. For example, typhus has been suspected as a major cause of the heavy mortalities accompanying military activities in the early 1640s, and as the disease behind the 3-star national crisis in 1741/2.[69] Unfortunately many of the contemporary descriptions are couched in terms that might refer to any infection producing fever and a rash on the skin. In the absence of pathological analysis, the age-specific incidence of mortality is probably the best indicator because typhus is unusual in rarely killing very young children.[70] On these grounds typhus has been implicated in the crisis mortality in 1587/8 in the north-west.[71] A proper appreciation of the impact of typhus must await a more detailed investigation, but it would seem likely that the disease played a role in the crisis attending troop movements in the 1640s. On the other hand, the spate of local crises that ran from July 1741 to October 1742 appears to have been unconnected with the apparent introduction of typhus in Plymouth and Bristol in the summer of 1740. There was relatively little crisis mortality in 1740 and the first half of 1741, and it is noteworthy that the surge in the intensity of local crises in July 1741 coincided with an exceptionally hot summer.[72] Huxham in Plymouth noted that in the course of the first half of 1741 the original infection 'seemed to become lost in a fever of the bilious kind', and intestinal complications feature in accounts of other local crises in 1741 and 1742.[73] It is therefore likely that it was dysentery rather than typhus which produced the heavy mortality in these years.

The delay in the main onset of epidemic outbreaks until July 1741 also counts against the view that they were produced by the poor harvest of 1740 or, even more implausibly, by the exceptionally cold winter of 1739–40.[74] It is also uncertain how much the high mortality of 1741/2 was due to the rather poor harvest of 1741, which was deficient, though not on the same scale as that of 1740 (real wages were 9 per cent below trend). As in England, the harvest of 1740 was seriously deficient in Brabant, and there too there was no major outbreak of crisis mortality in the following months. In 1741, however, Brabant, unlike England, enjoyed a plentiful harvest, yet in

67. Creighton, *op. cit.*, II, pp. 517–20. Razzell, *op. cit.*, pp. 130–2.

68. See fn. 28 above.

69. See fn. 42 above.

70. Megaw, 'Typhus fevers', p. 393.

71. Appleby, 'Disease or famine?', pp. 408–14.

72. Lamb, *Climate*, II, p. 573. Short remarked that 'This was the hottest and calmest summer since 1719', *Comparative history*, p. 94. The summer of 1719 was also a period with a high incidence of local crises and the national death rates in August and September were well above average (table 8.13).

73. Quoted in Creighton, *Epidemics in Britain*, II, p. 79. See also p. 83.

74. As suggested, for example, by Chambers, *Population, economy and society*, p. 93, where he refers to crises in 1740–1, even though his earlier work, cited there, makes it clear that the high mortality occurred later, in 1741 and 1742. Real wages were 19 per cent below trend in 1740/1 (see appendix 9). For the cold winter of 1739–40 see Short, *Comparative history*, p. 94 and Lamb, *Climate*, II, p. 573.

September and October a violent epidemic broke out and raged until the early months of 1742.[75]

The geographical spread of local crisis mortality

The point has already been made that local crisis mortality was never universal in its incidence: even in the worst years of national crisis less than 40 per cent of the parishes experienced a local crisis, as defined here, and in most national crisis years the proportion of parishes affected was as low as 7 to 15 per cent. The geographical incidence of local crisis mortality varied considerably over time reflecting differences in the underlying causes in each crisis period. To help abbreviate the discussion the location of the parishes affected will be shown in map form for only a selection of the periods with the most severe crisis mortality. For each period the parishes that experienced the onset of a local crisis are represented by an asterisk, while parishes that were in observation but unaffected are indicated by a cross.[76] In interpreting the maps it must always be remembered that the definition of crisis-level mortality is an arbitrary one, and that parishes shown as having been unaffected may still have experienced some rise in mortality, but insufficiently pronounced to be distinguished from a random fluctuation.

Unfortunately the numbers of parishes in observation are rather too small for any meaningful geographical patterns to be visible for the early plague crises of the 1540s and the 'sweat' of 1551. However, the parishes affected were scattered fairly widely across the country. For the period of exceptionally high mortality in the late 1550s enough parishes are in observation for figure A 10.2 to give a reasonable indication of the spread of local crises. It will be remembered that at all times there was a continuous background rumble of crises. Accordingly, in order to reduce the interference from unconnected local crises the temporal scope of figure A 10.2 has been confined to the core of the crisis period, namely to local outbreaks beginning between May 1557 and June 1559. The figure confirms the widespread incidence of local crisis mortality in this period, but also shows that some areas, such as the north midlands, Essex, and the south-west were affected relatively lightly.

Figure A 10.3 shows the geographical distribution of the incidence of local crises at the time of the harvest failures in 1596 and 1597.[77] Unlike the late 1550s, the geographical pattern is much more clustered with every parish in observation in the far north experiencing crisis level mortality, and almost no parishes in eastern England and the central midlands being affected. In other regions there were some crises; relatively few in the south-east, but rather more in west Yorkshire, much of the midlands, and in the south-west. Not surprisingly, in years of harvest failure caused largely by too much rain, the incidence of crises was relatively heavy in upland parishes (more than 350 feet above sea level) and in parishes situated in open fell

75. Bruneel, *La mortalité dans les campagnes*, I, pp. 276– 82. The author concludes 'Apparemment le lien avec la disette est inexistant' (p. 280). A detailed study of mortality in northern France during the years 1738– 43 finds that increased mortality accompanied the severe winter of 1740–1, but not the deficient harvest of 1740. The authors conclude: 'la mortalité . . . a fréquemment précédé ou suivi de très loin les crises; la simultanéité n'a été souvent que pure coincidence'. Bricourt, Lachiver, and Queruel, 'La crise des années 1740', pp. 304–8, 328, 332–3.
76. To be in observation a parish register must have begun registering burials before the crisis period begins.
77. The period for the onset of local crises was October 1596 to June 1598.

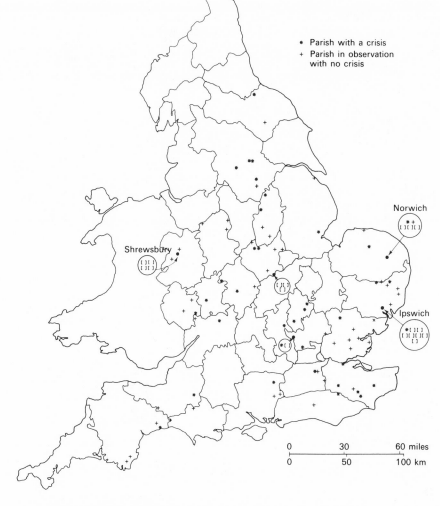

* Parish with a crisis
+ Parish in observation with no crisis

Norwich
Shrewsbury
Ipswich

0   30   60 miles
0   50   100 km

Figure A10.2: Geographical distribution of local crises beginning
May 1557 to June 1559

Source: See table A10.1

pasture country or in the valleys in areas of mixed agriculture.[78] The particularly heavy incidence of crisis mortality in the north-west in these years is well known.[79] Figure A10.3 shows that local crises also occurred over much, but by no means all, of the country, and suggests that their geographical distribution was in general related to

78. Twenty-nine per cent of the parishes experiencing a crisis were situated 350 or more feet above sea level compared to 14 per cent of the parishes not experiencing a crisis. Eleven per cent of the parishes with a local crisis were situated in open fell pasture and 35 per cent in valley parishes in mixed agricultural regions. The equivalent figures for parishes without crises were 5 and 26 per cent respectively.
79. Appleby, 'Disease or famine?', and *Famine in Tudor and Stuart England*, chapter 8.

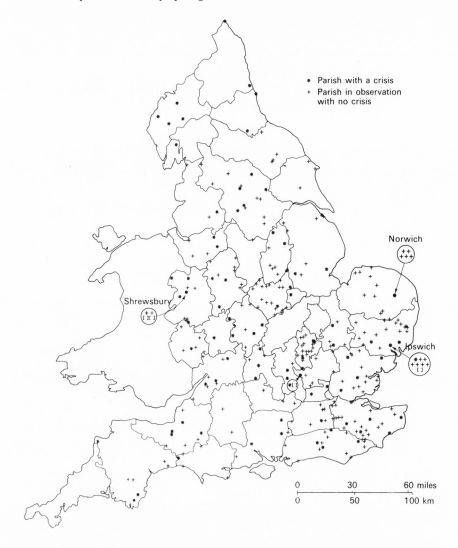

- • Parish with a crisis
- + Parish in observation with no crisis

Norwich
```
+ +
+ + +
```

Shrewsbury
```
+ +
[ ][ ]
```

Ipswich
```
• + + +
[ ]
```

0	30	60 miles
0	50	100 km

Figure A10.3: Geographical distribution of local crises beginning
Oct. 1596 to June 1598

Source: See table A10.1

difficulty of access to grain supplies. Interestingly, figure A10.4 shows that a similar geographical pattern obtained in 1587/8, another year of dearth with crises common in the north, the west midlands, and the south-west, but very infrequent in the central midlands, East Anglia, and the whole of the south and east.[80]

A very different pattern emerges if a period is taken in which plague was predominant. In the seventeenth century most of the national outbreaks of the disease

---

80. The period for the onset of local crises was January 1586 to June 1588. Crises in the north-west in this period are discussed by Appleby, *op. cit.*, chapter 7.

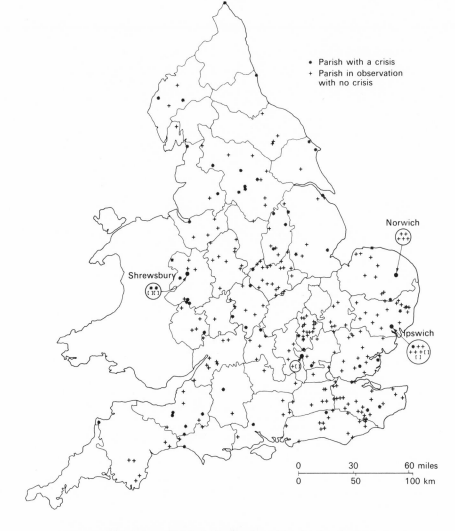

Norwich

Shrewsbury

Ipswich

* Parish with a crisis
+ Parish in observation
  with no crisis

0		30		60 miles
0	50		100 km	

Figure A10.4: Geographical distribution of local crises beginning
Jan. 1586 to June 1588

Source: See table A10.1

were associated with an epidemic in London and the distribution of local crises
reflects proximity to, or connexions with, the capital. Figure A10.5 shows that in the
period May 1603 to December 1604, which includes one of the major outbreaks of
plague in London (July to October 1603), there was a tendency for local crises to
cluster around London, along the Thames estuary, and in parts of East Anglia near
Colchester, Ipswich, and Norwich. In addition there were some outbreaks in
Yorkshire, the south midlands, and the south-west. Apart from the south-west, most
of the areas relatively badly affected in 1596–8 were largely free of local crises in this
period.

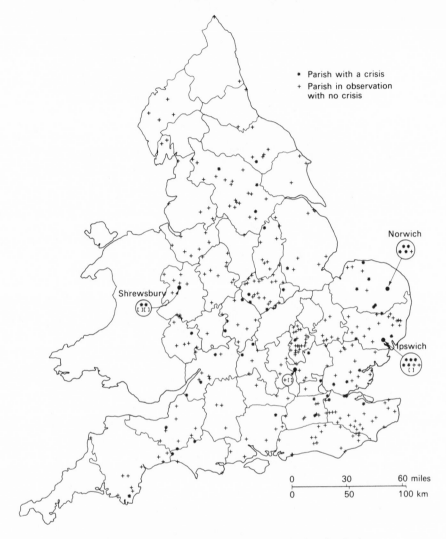

Figure A10.5: Geographical distribution of local crises beginning
May 1603 to Dec. 1604

Source: See table A10.1

Figure A 10.6 shows that a similar pattern obtained at the time of the Great Plague of London, when once again the greatest incidence fell near London and the coast of East Anglia, while much of the interior of the country, the north, and the south-west recorded no local crises.[81] However, when outbreaks of plague were not associated with an epidemic in London, as was sometimes the case in the sixteenth century, the geographical pattern of local crises reflected the distribution of the local centres of infection and the lines of communication radiating from them. For example, in the

81. The period for the onset of local crises was April 1665 to October 1666.

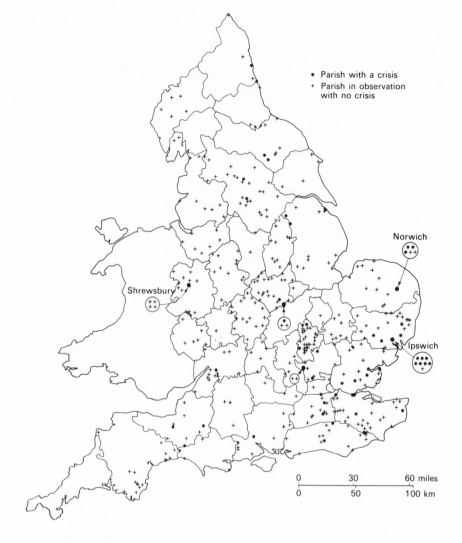

- Parish with a crisis
+ Parish in observation with no crisis

Norwich

Shrewsbury

Ipswich

0		30		60 miles
0		50		100 km

Figure A10.6: Geographical distribution of local crises beginning
April 1665 to Oct. 1666

Source: See table A10.1

plague period 1590–1, local crises were particularly frequent in Yorkshire, the north-west midlands, and the south-west.[82]

The contrast between the patterns of crisis mortality to be found in periods of harvest failure or plague are summarized by figure A10.7 which shows the geographical distribution of local crises during the period from November 1622 to December 1625. In 1622 the harvest was deficient, especially in the north, and the

82. The spread of plague in Devon, from Plymouth through the south and east of the country in the period 1589–93, is described in Slack, 'Mortality crises', pp. 45–6.

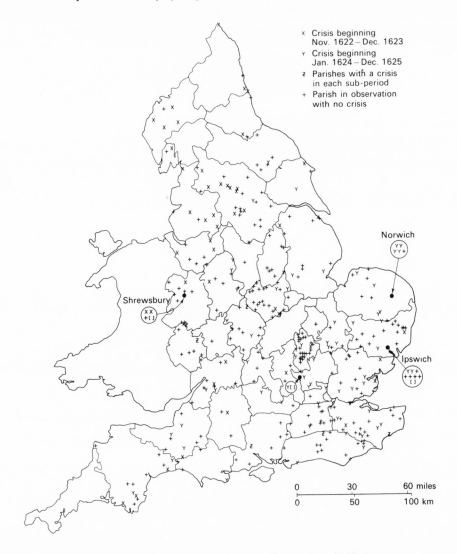

x Crisis beginning
   Nov. 1622 – Dec. 1623
y Crisis beginning
   Jan. 1624 – Dec. 1625
z Parishes with a crisis
   in each sub-period
+ Parish in observation
   with no crisis

Figure A10.7: Geographical distribution of local crises beginning
Nov. 1622 to Dec. 1625

Source: See table A10.1

local crises starting between November 1622 and December 1623 are distinguished
on the map by the letter 'X'. As in 1596–8 the far north and the north-west were fairly
heavily affected, with only a scattering of outbreaks elsewhere. Quite the reverse was
true of the local crises beginning between January 1624 and December 1625, a period
that was afflicted by fevers in the first year and contained a severe outbreak of plague
in London from June to October 1625.[83] Parishes experiencing a crisis beginning in

83. Creighton associates some of these fevers with typhus; *Epidemics in Britain*, I, pp. 504–7. For the
plague in London, see Marshall, *Mortality in the metropolis*, p. 66.

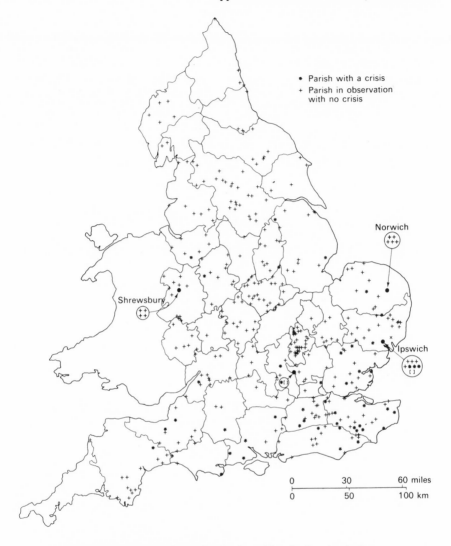

Figure A10.8: Geographical distribution of local crises beginning
March to Sept. 1638

Source: See table A10.1

this period are indicated on the map by the letter 'Y', and they were heavily
concentrated in the south-east midlands, East Anglia, and the south-east, again with a
scattering elsewhere. The areas in the far north and north-west that were affected in
1622–3 were almost entirely free from crises in this period. The relatively few
parishes that experienced a crisis in both periods are indicated by the letter 'Z' on the
map.

Before the mid seventeenth century there would therefore seem to be two Englands:
one pastoral and remote, and the other engaged in arable farming but with a high
degree of occupational specialization reflected in a relatively dense network of small

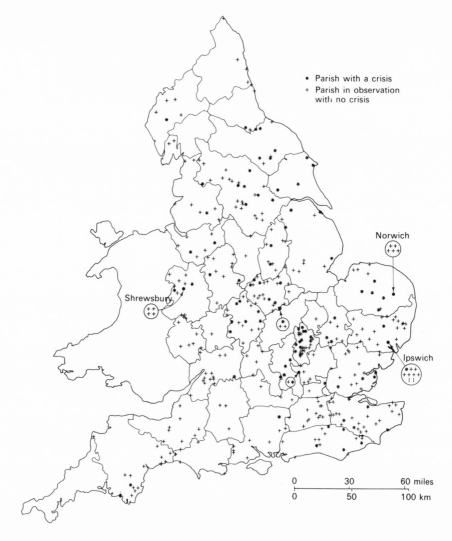

Figure A10.9: Geographical distribution of local crises beginning
July 1657 to March 1659

Source: See table A10.1

towns. While access to grain, together with ease of transport and the well-developed communications in the south-east made the area much less vulnerable to harvest failures, its greater economic integration facilitated the spread of disease. The same contrast can also be seen in microcosm in a county such as Devon where crisis mortality in bad harvest years was largely confined to the remote upland parishes, while it was parishes in the mixed farming lowlands in the south of the county near the coast that were infected in times of bubonic plague.[84]

84. Slack, 'Mortality crises', pp. 34–5, 45.

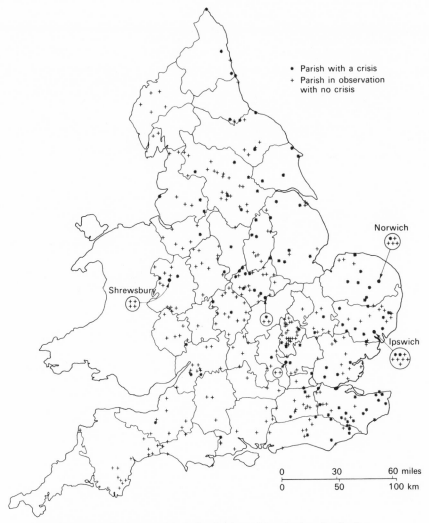

Figure A10.10: Geographical distribution of local crises beginning
July 1678 to June 1681

Source: See table A10.1

The vulnerability of the upland north-west to harvest failure disappeared after
1623[85], but the greater susceptibility of the south-east to the spread of infectious
disease continued throughout the seventeenth century. For example, in the heavy
mortality associated with fever (with some outbreaks of plague) in 1638, figure A10.8
shows that local crises were almost entirely confined to the south-east; very few
occurred north-west of a line running from the New Forest to the Wash.[86] In the

85. Appleby, *Famine in Tudor and Stuart England*, p. 155.
86. The period for the onset of local crises was March to September 1638. There was no plague epidemic in
London and few other places were reported affected. Some of the fevers were described as 'spotted'.
Creighton, *Epidemics in Britain*, 1, pp. 541–3. The lack of crises in the areas traditionally vulnerable to

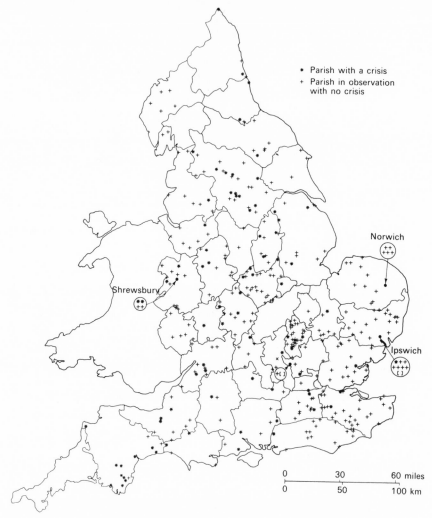

* Parish with a crisis
+ Parish in observation
  with no crisis

Norwich

Shrewsbury

Ipswich

0		30		60 miles
0		50		100 km

Figure A10.11: Geographical distribution of local crises beginning
April 1642 to Oct. 1644

Source: See table A10.1

national 3- and 2-star crisis years 1657/8 and 1658/9 local crises were more widespread, with the south-east midlands and Yorkshire particularly badly affected, but once again the far north and the west of the country escaped almost completely (figure A10.9).[87] A rather similar pattern obtained during the years 1678/9 to 1680/1

---

harvest failure together with the long interval that elapsed between the deficient harvest of 1637 and the onset of high mortality in the late summer of 1638, which then continued for many months after the normal harvest of 1638, make it unlikely that the crises of 1638/9 were due to a failure of subsistence as has been suggested (Appleby, *Famine in Tudor and Stuart England*, p. 191). Real wages in 1637 were 15 per cent below trend, and in 1638 were exactly on trend. The monthly pattern of crisis national death rates is summarized in table 8.13.

87. The period for the onset of local crises was July 1657 to March 1659.

which ushered in a six-year period of very heavy mortality. Figure A10.10 shows that local crisis mortality was fairly widespread, though on this occasion the areas of the greatest intensity were Kent and Sussex, the east midlands, and the far north-east. But once again the west of the country was relatively little affected.[88]

The contrast between the eastern and western sides of the country could be upset by unusual circumstances, such as obtained during the civil war. Figure A10.11 shows that local crises beginning between April 1642 and October 1644 were more likely to occur in the south-west, in parts of the midlands and Yorkshire. These were areas that were particularly subject to invasion by armies from other regions, and several of the crises can be linked with military activities.[89] Nor did the east-west contrast persist into the eighteenth century. In the late 1720s the country experienced several years of very high death rates and a succession of local crises on a scale unparalleled since the late 1550s. As was shown in table A10.5 the intensity of local crisis mortality built up very quickly from August 1727 and did not fall back to normal levels until the spring of 1730. We have also noted that several aspects of the local crises during this period suggested a succession of infections, and that a moderately deficient harvest in 1728 may have helped prevent the usual seasonal decline in crisis mortality during the spring and early summer of 1729.

Figure A10.12 shows the geographical spread of local crisis mortality in this period according to the month in which each parish first experienced a surge in burials up to crisis level. Between August 1727 and February 1730 166 of the 404 parishes (41 per cent) were affected. Of the 166 parishes 19 per cent first suffered crisis level mortality in August 1727, and they are represented by a 'W' on the map. It is clear that at the onset the local crises were mainly to be found in the north–west with the parishes affected lying along a belt running from Lancashire to Warwickshire. In the following month (September 1727) crisis mortality first struck a further 20 per cent of the parishes ever to be affected. The geographical distribution of these parishes, marked by a 'X' in the figure, shows a movement east from the southern end of the area affected in the previous month, as crises spread into Leicestershire, Bedfordshire, and across into central East Anglia. There were also signs of a movement towards the south–west.

The pace of the spread of crisis mortality then slackened with the next 20 per cent of the parishes being first affected over a period of 10 months, from October 1727 to July 1728. Some of these parishes, represented by a 'Y' in the figure, show a continuation of earlier trends towards East Anglia and the south-west, but the chief area of expansion lay in the east midlands, Lincolnshire, and eastern Yorkshire. In the final 19 months of the crisis period (August 1728 to February 1730) there was a small extension of this movement up into the far north-east, but many of the parishes experiencing a crisis for the first time in this prolonged period, represented by a 'Z' in the figure, lay in regions that had already been affected in the first two months: the north-west, the west midlands, the south-west, and East Anglia. The deficient harvest of 1728, inasmuch as it may have influenced crisis mortality, did not make new areas vulnerable but may possibly have undermined resistance still further in areas already badly hit by infectious diseases.

The late return of crisis mortality to the areas originally attacked meant that a high

88. The period for the onset of local crises was July 1678 to June 1681.
89. Information on troop movements was kindly supplied by Dr. J. S. Morrill of Selwyn College, Cambridge. For specific examples see references cited in fn. 42 above.

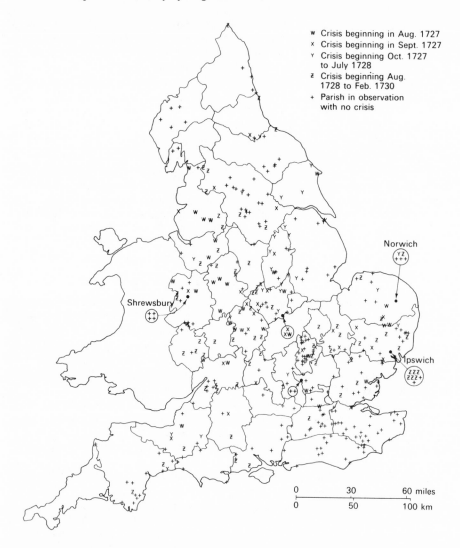

Figure A10.12: Geographical distribution of local crises beginning
Aug. 1727 to Feb. 1730

Source: See table A10.1

proportion of the parishes in observation in the belt running from the midlands to Lancashire were affected at some point in the late 1720s. Since many of the influential studies of local crises used data from this region, the severity and universality of the heavy mortalities of this period have received much emphasis.[90] It should therefore be stressed that figure A10.12 shows that some parts of the country escaped infection almost entirely. Throughout England south of a line running through Gloucester,

90. Two such studies are Chambers, *Vale of Trent*, and Eversley, 'A survey of population in an area of Worcestershire'.

Figure A10.13: Geographical distribution of local crises beginning
June 1741 to Oct. 1742

Source: See table A10.1

Oxford, and Chelmsford, and including London, there were very few instances of
local crises.[91] Other areas producing little or no evidence of crisis mortality were the
far north and the central area of Yorkshire. Consequently the main brunt of the crisis
mortality was borne in the midlands with extensions into Lancashire, east Yorkshire,
and East Anglia. The geographical distribution of local crises in the late 1720s

91. However in the few localities where crisis mortality did occur, a large number of neighbouring
parishes might be affected. For example, a study of 12 Exeter parishes and 28 rural parishes within a radius
of about 10 miles of the city, found that in the period 1727–32 burial totals rose to more than 1.5 times their
normal level in 75 per cent of the city parishes and 57 per cent of the country parishes. Study by Dr.
R. Sellman, reported in Schofield, 'An anatomy of an epidemic', p. 98 and fn. 21.

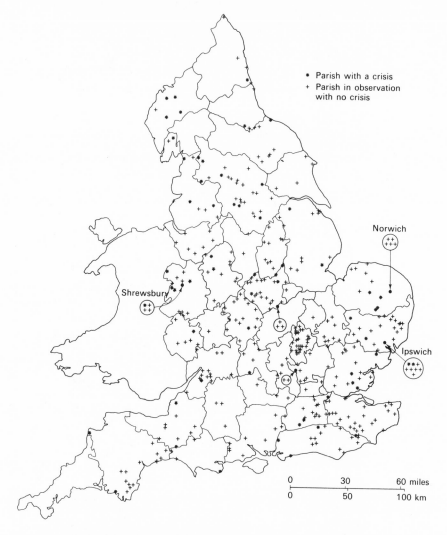

Figure A10.14: Geographical distribution of local crises beginning
June 1762 to Oct. 1763

Source: See table A10.1

therefore no longer conforms to the division between a remote and pastoral north-west
and an arable and more inter-connected south-east that had been so marked a feature
of years of heavy mortality in the seventeenth century.

The same is true of the next period of heavy mortality in the eighteenth century in
1741/2, when local crises were scattered all over the country (figure A10.13)[92]
However the intensity of local crises was somewhat greater in an area extending
diagonally north-east from the far south-west through the south midlands to northern

92. The period for the onset of local crises was June 1741 to October 1742.

East Anglia. Local crises were also to be found in all regions in 1762/3, the last year to achieve a 2-star ranking as a national crisis, though on this occasion the far north and the north-west were particularly badly affected (figure A10.14).[93] Although this pattern is reminiscent of that which obtained in years of harvest deficiency in the period before 1650, in 1761 and 1762 the harvest was plentiful and real wages were above trend.[94] The earlier dichotomy in the geographical distribution of local crises between the north-west and the south-east appears to have been related to major regional differences in economic life. Its disappearance in the eighteenth century, therefore, probably reflected the progressive geographical integration of the two areas as agricultural practices changed, market networks developed, and the geographical centre of gravity of industry and population began to move towards the north.[95]

The structure of local crisis mortality

The geographical patterns of the incidence of local crises may have reflected regional differences in such matters as climate or the local economy. On the other hand the incidence of crisis mortality may have been more directly linked to specific characteristics of individual communities, such as their size or remoteness, and the geographical patterns noted above may simply have reflected different regional mixes of these primary characteristics. To test this latter possibility we have examined the degree to which the variation in the incidence of crisis mortality was related to factors such as parish location and size. The individual parishes were not all in observation for the same length of time, though none was in observation for less than 150 years (1662–1811). Therefore the incidence of crisis mortality in each of them has been expressed as a decadal crisis rate (i.e. the number of months of crisis mortality per 10 years in observation). Since this rate is calculated over the whole period in observation, parishes for which data are available from an early date, such as the 1550s, when the incidence of crisis mortality was high, have a greater chance of acquiring a high decadal crisis rate, and this point will need to be taken into account when evaluating the results.

Amongst the set of 404 parishes the mean experience was 13.4 months of crisis per decade, occurring in 6.0 crisis periods of 2.2 months duration and with 5.5 times as many burials recorded as in normal times.[96] Around these average figures there was considerable variation in the experience of individual parishes. Table A10.6 reveals that at one extreme five of the parishes escaped without a single month of crisis mortality, while at the other 42 (10 per cent) suffered 30 or more months per decade. The existence of this group of parishes particularly prone to crisis mortality,

93. The period for the onset of local crises was June 1762 to October 1763. Creighton reports both influenza and dysentery in 1762, which accords with the monthly fluctuations in the death rate, summarized in table 8.13. *Epidemics in Britain*, II, pp. 356–8, 779.

94. By 8 and 6 per cent, respectively.

95. For the end of the economic isolation of Cumbria see Appleby, *Famine in Tudor and Stuart England*, chapter 11. Agricultural developments and the widening of market networks both in agriculture and industry are discussed in Holderness, *Pre-industrial England*, pp. 68–71, 139–46. For changes in the regional balance of industry and population in the eighteenth century see Deane and Cole, *British economic growth*, pp. 98–106.

96. Mean duration was calculated as the total number of crisis months divided by the total number of crisis periods. The product of the mean numbers of periods and durations may not equal the mean rate because of rounding. The mean severity ratio was calculated as the total number of recorded burials in all crisis periods divided by the total number of burials according to the forecast trend in these periods.

Table A10.6: Frequency distribution of parish
decadal crisis rates

Rate	Frequency	Cumulative percent
0.0	5	1
0.1–	4	2
1.0–	23	8
2.0–	23	14
3.0–	27	20
4.0–	25	26
5.0–	23	32
6.0–	20	37
7.0–	18	42
8.0–	14	45
9.0–	19	50
10.0–	16	54
11.0–	13	57
12.0–	19	62
13.0–	14	65
14.0–	12	68
15.0–	11	71
16.0–	9	73
17.0–	9	75
18.0–	10	78
19.0–	5	79
20.0–	6	80
21.0–	8	82
22.0–	5	84
23.0–	1	84
24.0–	5	85
25.0–	7	87
26.0–	3	88
27.0–	4	89
28.0–	3	89
29.0–	1	90
30.0+	42	100

Source: See table A10.1.

influences the mean figures quoted above, and the *median* parish experience was 9.6 crisis months per decade falling in 5.5 periods of 1.7 months duration, with 4.1 times as many burials as in normal times. Measured against a normal *monthly* death rate of 2.158 per 1,000, the median parish crisis therefore implied the death of 1.5 per cent of the population ($4.1 \times 0.002158 \times 1.7$), only just over half the normal annual death rate and very much less than the massive mortality that is sometimes thought to have been typical of local crises.[97] One quarter of the parishes suffered less than 5 crisis months

---

97. The mean annual death rate for the period 1541–1871 was 25.9 (see p. 311 above). Stone provides particularly melodramatic view of the incidence and severity of crises: 'Barely half the country dwellers and hardly any inhabitants of the towns could hope to live out their lives in a community which did not experience at least one of these psychologically devastating events, during which anything between a third and a half of the population would die in a matter of months'. *Causes of the English revolution*, p. 111. The source cited for this statement turns out to refer to two epidemics in one town (Northampton, in 1605 and 1638) in which only *one sixth* of the population died. Everitt, *Change in the provinces*, p. 30.

The death of as much as a third of the population implies an increase in the normal number of burials by a factor of 12 over a whole year, or by a factor of 48 for three months, a degree of severity that was almost

per decade, while a further quarter had a decadal rate of 18 crisis months or above. The central experience, comprising half of the parishes, therefore lay between 5 and 17 crisis months per decade. There was much less variation in the mean duration of crisis, which was 1 or 2 months in 40 and 44 per cent of the parishes respectively, and in only 6 parishes was the mean duration more than three months.

In examining how far the variation in the incidence of crisis mortality was linked to specific characteristics of the individual communities it is important to remember that the method used to identify crises may have created a positive association between the size of the parish and the number of crises observed. This arose from the need to distinguish genuine short-run increases in the death rate from random fluctuations.[98] Such an association is indeed a marked feature of the data: the mean decadal crisis rate rose from 1.7 in parishes of less than 250 inhabitants enumerated in the 1811 census to 44.2 in parishes with populations of 7,500 or more. While part of this large increase may have been an artificial consequence of the method of identifying crises, there may also have been a genuinely greater propensity for larger settlements to experience crisis mortality, being more densely populated and more exposed to infection because of their more frequent contacts with the outside world.[99] Since parish size confounds these substantive reasons with a methodological artefact, it would be desirable to examine their relationship with the incidence of crisis mortality more directly. Unfortunately the first of the two substantive factors is hard to test because, although the area of the parish and its population size in 1811 are known, the resulting measure of density means little. For example, a relatively small population living in a parish of many acres may nonetheless be densely settled in a single settlement. However, the second factor, remoteness, can be measured approximately in terms of the distance from the nearest market town, and this can be related to the incidence of crisis mortality. Other factors that may have influenced the regional differences in the incidence of crisis mortality are altitude and the nature of the farming carried on in the area.

Preliminary inspection of the data suggested that the incidence of local crises may have been linked systematically and negatively to remoteness. On the other hand the connexion with altitude and farming type appeared to have been partial, being confined to certain categories rather than obtaining generally. Nor did the regional incidence of crisis mortality exhibit any uniform gradation across the map. Most of southern and central England extending up into central Yorkshire experienced relatively low decadal crisis rates, while higher rates characterized the areas north-east and north-west of this central triangle, and the far south-west.

There were therefore several variables that at first sight appeared to have influenced the variation in the decadal crisis rates of the individual parishes. Since several of the variables were inter-related, the importance of each needed to be estimated after controlling for the effects of the others. This was investigated in two ways: by

---

unknown in the parish register period. Even in London in 1665 the plague raised the annual number of burials only to 5.7 times the usual level (97,000 compared to an annual average of 17,000 for the rest of the decade), killing about 20 per cent of the population (Marshall, *Mortality in the metropolis*, pp. 66 and 73; Sutherland, 'Mortality in London', p. 310). Some earlier London plagues, however, may have been more severe; and in plague periods some deaths escaped registration.

98. See pp. 646–9 above.

99. For examples of the positive relationship between density and mortality see Wrigley, *Population and history*, pp. 173–6. In the nineteenth century Farr found that the death rate varied as a function of the 12th root of the density of population; *Vital statistics*, pp. 173–6.

stepwise regression and by multiple classification analysis. In the former approach the variables were successively introduced into a regression equation depending on which accounted for most of the inter-parish variation in the decadal crisis rate not already accounted for by other previously linked variables.[100] Since date of entry into observation, and, to some extent, population size were linked artificially to the decadal crisis rate they were explicitly introduced first so that the remaining variables could be related to the decadal crisis rates net of their effects.[101] Remoteness was measured by the distance in kilometers to the nearest market town and altitude by height above sea-level in 50 ft steps.[102] The 'farming type' of the parishes was dichotomized into 'pasture' and 'other' to investigate whether the lack of a local supply of grain was related to the decadal crisis rate.[103] Finally, 'region' was decomposed into two variables using the national grid co-ordinates of the parishes to test whether there was any tendency for the decadal crisis rate to vary with the location of the parish on each of two axes, one running north–south and the other east–west.

Table A10.7: Stepwise regression of parish decadal crisis rates

Step	Variable added	Zero-order r	Partial r at step 2	At each step R^2	R^2 change
1	Date of entry into observation	0.016	—	0.000	0.000
2	Population size	0.663	—	0.441	0.441
3	Distance from market town	−0.356	−0.318	0.498	0.057
4	Altitude	−0.129	−0.254	0.527	0.029
5	East	−0.148	−0.033	0.538	0.011
6	North	0.176	0.046	0.541	0.003
7	Pasture	0.053	0.043	0.541	0.000

Notes:
1 Steps 1 and 2 were forced in order to control for the effect of variables artificially correlated with the decadal crisis rate.
2 Partial r values are the correlation coefficients of each variable with the decadal crisis rate after the effects of population size and date of entry into observation have been eliminated.
3 R^2 denotes the multiple correlation coefficient.

Sources: Decadal crisis rates and date of entry into observation: see table A10.1; other variables; table 2.3.

The first column of table A10.7 displays the zero order correlation coefficients between the decadal crisis rates and each of the explanatory variables. Of the two variables accorded an arbitrary priority in the regression, the date of entry into observation had almost no effect on the incidence of crisis mortality which, however, was heavily influenced by population size.[104] The second column of the table

100. The analysis used SPSS, version H, release 8.0, with default options. See Nie *et al.*, *SPSS*, pp 345–6.
101. Population size as in the 1811 census. For date of entry into observation see above, pp. 56–62.
102. The location of each parish and market town was measured as the national grid reference of the church, rounded to the nearest 100 meters. Distance was calculated as a straight line, ignoring physiographical realities, and is therefore a minimal measure of true distance.
103. Thirsk, 'Farming regions', p. 4. 'Pasture' included both wood and open pasture types, and 'other' comprised Thirsk's 'mixed' farming types and entirely urban parishes. Similar results were obtained when pasture was restricted to either the 'wood' or the 'open' type.
104. The negligible effect of the date of entry into observation is consonant with the lack of any differences

recalculates the correlation coefficients between the incidence of crisis mortality and the remaining variables after the effects of these variables have been removed. The modest relationships that at first sight appeared to have obtained between the decadal crisis rate and location turn out to have been spurious effects of a higher frequency of large parishes in the north and the west. After controlling for this there was little relationship between incidence of crisis mortality and the location of the parish on either a north–south or an east–west axis. In contrast, the fairly strong negative relationship with distance from market town remained virtually unchanged even though market towns themselves had larger than average populations and the more distant villages were often small. Remoteness therefore seems to have been a genuine factor diminishing the incidence of crisis mortality. So was altitude, a relationship that was orginally somewhat obscured by the greater frequency of larger parishes on higher ground. Finally, controlling for population size and date of entry into observation turned a weak positive association between pastoral parishes and the incidence of crisis mortality into a weak negative one.

Although remoteness and altitude emerge as factors that exercised a general influence over the incidence of crisis mortality, in neither case was it strong. The third column of table A10.7 shows the proportion of the variation in the parish crisis decadal rates accounted for by all the variables included at each stage of the stepwise regression and the fourth column indicates by how much the proportion changed as a result of the addition of a new variable at each step. It is evident that once the effects of the date of entry into observation and population size had been removed, the other variables accounted for very little of the variation in the parish crisis decadal rates. Distance from market town, the most powerful of these factors, accounted for only a further 5.7 per cent, altitude 2.9 per cent, and location on an east–west axis a further 1.1 per cent. Location on a north–south axis and farming type had a negligible effect on the incidence of crisis mortality.

The method of analysis may have done less than justice to the strengths of the links between some of the variables and the decadal crisis rate. This would have been the case if the relationships had not been uniform over the whole range of values attained by the variables, or if combinations of certain values of the variables had produced an unusual effect on the decadal crisis rate. For example, the effects of regional differences are unlikely to have been captured adequately by a reduction to two simple (north–south and east–west) gradients in the incidence of crisis mortality.

A second approach was therefore tried using multiple classification analysis in which the parishes were divided into categories on each of four factors (distance from market town, altitude, farming type, and region). The basic categories were dictated by the form in which the data were collected, but it seemed sensible to group some categories so as to maximize the contrast in their decadal crisis rates. For farming type a division was made into 'mixed', 'wood pasture', and 'open pasture';[105] and seven regions were distinguished (the south–west, the south–east, East- and Mid-Anglia, the south midlands, the north midlands and Yorkshire, the east coast, and the north and north–west), as shown in figure A10.15. Since some of the factors were

---

in the general trends in the numbers of events recorded by parishes entering observation at different dates (as shown in figure 2.3), and lends further justification to the simple inflation procedures adopted in chapter 2 to create a national series of events extending back to 1539. See above, pp. 56–62.

105. Farming types from Thirsk, 'Farming regions', p. 4. The category 'mixed' consists in parishes that were in primarily arable regions and includes 17 urban parishes on the grounds that they probably had good access to grain supplies.

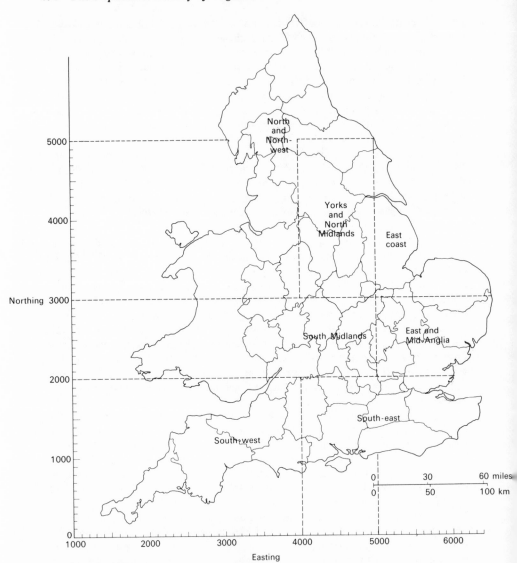

Figure A10.15: Crisis mortality regions (national grid co-ordinates)

intercorrelated (for example region, farming type, and altitude), differences between the mean decadal crisis rates of the categories of any one factor reflect the influence of the other factors. To remove this source of contamination, and so isolate the net effect of each factor on the incidence of crisis mortality, multiple classification analysis calculates the means for each category holding the distributions of the parishes for the other factors constant and controlling for the effects of date of entry into observation and parish population size.[106]

106. Population size and date of entry into observation were treated as covariates. The statistical

Table A10.8: Multiple classification analysis of parish decadal crisis rates

Factor and category	No.	Deviation of category mean from overall mean[1]	Beta
Distance from market town (kilometers)			
0	88	6.20	
1	34	5.51	
2	15	−0.16	
3	26	−3.65	
4–5	79	−2.89	
6–7	77	−3.43	
8–9	56	−1.88	
10+	29	−1.30	0.34
Altitude (feet above sea level)			
0–49	41	4.27	
50–199	159	1.59	
200–99	88	−0.74	
300+	116	−2.85	0.19
Region			
South-west	35	4.41	
South-east	83	−2.09	
East and mid Anglia	78	−1.97	
South midlands	63	0.47	
N. midlands and Yorks.	68	0.05	
East coast	23	1.43	
North and north-west	54	1.99	0.17
Farming type			
Mixed/arable[2]	223	−0.13	
Wood pasture	95	0.33	
Open pasture	86	−0.04	0.02

Overall mean 13.40
No. of cases 404

Notes:
1 Deviations from overall mean are adjusted for effects of other factors, and for parish size and date of entry into observation (treated as covariates).
2 Including 17 urban parishes.

Sources: See table A10.7.

Table A10.8 presents the mean decadal crisis rates for each category expressed as a deviation from the overall mean of 13.40. Distance from market town and altitude are confirmed as factors that influenced the incidence of crisis mortality. In the case of altitude the relationship was a regular one: the higher the parish was situated, the lower the decadal crisis rate. The impact of altitude was more marked in extreme cases, with parishes situated less than 50, or more than 300 feet, above sea-level being

procedures employed assume that the effect of each factor on the incidence of crisis mortality was uniform across the categories of the other factors. This assumption was tested and no significant two-way interactions between the factors were found (the significance of the associated F-statistics ranged from 0.15 to 0.68). Since there were artificial links between the covariates and the incidence of crisis mortality, covariate by factor interaction was considered improbable and not tested. The analysis used SPSS, version H, release 8.0, with variance partitioned following the classic experimental approach, and with options 3 and 8. Factor interactions were tested with option 4. See Nie *et al.*, *SPSS*, chapter 22, especially pp. 408–10, 416–9.

particularly heavily, and lightly, affected respectively. The position with regard to distance from market town was more complicated. Market towns themselves, and parishes lying within a distance of a kilometer, experienced a higher than average incidence of crises, thereafter, up to a distance of about 3 kilometers, there was a negative relationship between the incidence of crisis mortality and distance from market, as might be expected on the grounds that the more remote the parish the less its exposure to infectious diseases. However, from 3 to 7 kilometers this relationship disppeared, and it was reversed for parishes lying 8 or more kilometers from a market town though they still showed a below-average frequency of crises.

The absence of any strong deviations from the overall mean decadal crisis rate for the farming-type categories confirms the results of stepwise regression in which farming type was merely dichotomized into 'pasture' and 'other'. On the other hand, the categorization by region brings out some strong relationships that were obscured when location was represented by position on two independent (north–south and east–west) axes. After the effects of all other factors had been controlled for, the central area of England (the south midlands, and the north midlands with Yorkshire) emerged as having experienced an average incidence of crisis mortality. Local crises were less frequent in the south-east, and in East- and Mid-Anglia, and more frequent in the east-coast region and in the north and north-west. But by far the highest overall incidence of crisis mortality occurred in the south–west, in an area extending from south Gloucestershire and west Wiltshire through Dorset to Devon.

The figures in the final column of table A10.8, labelled 'Beta' indicate the relative importance of the four factors in accounting for the variation in the parish decadal crisis rates after the effects of date of entry into observation and parish population size have been removed.[107] As in the case of stepwise regression, remoteness, as measured by distance from market town, explained twice as much of the variation in the incidence of local crises as altitude, which was the next most closely linked factor. Farming-type is also confirmed as having been of negligible significance, but the ability to specify region more effectively shows that it had an influence only a little weaker than that of altitude.

Unfortunately the beta coefficients cannot be used to find the proportion of the variation in the parish crisis rates accounted for by the four factors combined.[108] For this purpose it is necessary to refer back to the stepwise regression results in the final column of table A10.7. If the figures for 'East' and 'North' are now increased to allow for a greater influence of regionality on the scale suggested by multiple classification analysis, the four factors of remoteness, altitude, region, and farming type still only account for about 11 per cent of the local variation in crisis mortality over and above the 44 per cent attributable to population size.[109] While the latter figure may contain a spurious element arising from the way in which mortality crises were identified, it is also possible that the greater density of settlement and greater exposure to infection typical of larger parishes made population size a genuinely determining factor in the

107. They are standardized partial regression coefficients calculated from the multiple classification analysis scores for the categories of each factor. Nie *et al.*, *SPSS*, p. 410.

108. The beta scores for each factor include the effects of the covariates (population size and date of entry into observation). They do not necessarily sum to R^2 due to unequal cell frequencies.

109. Calculated by summing the figures for R^2-change at steps 3 to 7, substituting a figure of 2.6 per cent to represent regionality for the 1.4 per cent contributed by 'East' and 'North' combined. The regional figure was estimated by multiplying the figure for R^2-change attributable to altitude (0.029) by the ratio obtaining between the beta coefficients for region and altitude in table A10.8 (0.17/0.19). The effect of date of entry into observation was negligible (table A10.7, col. 4).

incidence of crisis mortality. The relatively weak additional explanatory power of the other four factors is perhaps not surprising, because the decadal crisis rate summarizes the incidence of crisis mortality over several centuries when, it has already been argued, the patterns of crisis mortality altered in response to changes in the social and economic life. Since these wider changes will have affected the ways in which each of the factors were associated with the intensity of local mortality crises, the summary picture that has emerged probably reflects only the basic and enduring features of the structure of crisis mortality in the past.

Appendix 11

Sequential sampling to estimate the proportion of monthly totals wrongly recorded

Statistical basis

An efficient way of estimating some characteristic of a population is to draw a random sample of items and calculate the value of the characteristic for the sample. The precision of the sample estimate depends both on the amount of variation in the population and on the size of the sample with which it is hoped to capture a representative picture of this variation. The larger the sample, and the less varied the population, the more precise the sample estimate will be. The greater the precision of the estimate, the greater the confidence with which conclusions may be drawn about the population on the basis of information contained in the sample, though there is always some further uncertainty due to the element of chance introduced by the random selection of the sample items. The usual sampling strategy is to tackle the problem from both ends, that is to make a rough estimate of the amount of variation in the population, and to reach some decision about what degrees of precision and confidence will be required of the final result. The size of the sample can then be calculated, the sample drawn, and the desired estimates made for the population.[1]

An alternative approach is to draw the sample items one at a time and to update the sample estimates for the population after each item. As more sample items enter into the calculation the estimate becomes more precise, and, depending on how much confidence needs to be placed in the result, sooner or later a point is reached at which an acceptable decision can be taken about the population. This approach is very useful in circumstances when an underlying characteristic, such as the proportion of months wrongly recorded, is unknown, and all that is needed is to discover whether it is greater than some critical figure or less than another, at which point a decision can be made and sampling terminated. Often the point of decision can be reached with a smaller sample size than would have been taken using a conventional approach.[2]

In this case there are four quantities that need to be specified in order to calculate the point during the sampling process at which decision can be made.

p_0 the maximum proportion of erroneous monthly totals considered acceptable.

p_1 – the minimum proportion of erroneous monthly totals considered unacceptable.

a – the highest acceptable risk of asserting on the basis of a sample that there is a difference between these proportions when in fact no such difference exists.

1. Sampling procedures for historical research are discussed in Schofield, 'Sampling in historical research', especially pp. 161–5.
2. Sequential sampling is described in many statistical texts. The presentation in this appendix follows Davies, *Design and analysis of industrial experiments*, pp. 79–84.

b — a similar risk of asserting there is no difference when a difference does exist.

The first two quantities can be used to calculate two scores, one for each erroneous monthly total and one for each correct monthly total encountered in the data. The monthly scores can then be cumulated until they become high or low enough to indicate that the proportion of errors in the data is high or low enough to warrant the acceptance or rejection of the tabulation as a whole. If P is $\log(p_1/p_0)$ and Q is $\log((1-p_0)/(1-p_1))$ and R is $Q/(P+Q)$, then the score for an erroneous monthly total is $(1-R)$ and the score for a correct monthly total is $(0-R)$. If, further, A is $\log((1-b)/a)$ and B is $\log((1-a)/b)$ then the critical cumulative score for rejecting the tabulation is $A/(P+Q)$ and the corresponding score for accepting the tabulation is $-B/(P+Q)$.

Practical operation

It was decided to accept a tabulation if not more than 3.5 per cent of the monthly totals were wrongly recorded and to reject it if 4.5 per cent or more of the monthly totals were in error. The degree of confidence in the sample estimate of the true error rate was set at 95 per cent, that is a 5 per cent risk was taken of drawing the wrong conclusion from the sample.

Thus: $p_0 = 0.035$, $p_1 = 0.045$, and $a = b = 0.05$,
from which were calculated
score for a correct month: -0.04
score for an incorrect month: 0.96
acceptance level: -11.25
rejection level: 11.25

Decimal scores are inconvenient to handle, so both scores and critical levels were multiplied by 25. Each correct month scored -1 and each incorrect month scored 24. If the cumulative score reached -281, sampling ceased and the tabulation was accepted, while if it reached $+281$ the tabulation was rejected. Since a single 20-year sample form contains only 240 months, even if it were entirely free of error the cumulative score (-240) would fall short of the -281 needed to be confident that the error rate was not more than 3.5 per cent. On the other hand a very large number of errors on a single 20-year sample form would be sufficient evidence on which to reject the whole tabulation (21 errors would score 504, less 219 correct months = 285).

In the event, it was rare for a decision to be reached on the basis of the first form, which had already failed the 1 per cent overall value discrepancy test,[3] for few of those who totalled up the registers made more than 21 errors on a single form. A second 20-year form, and if necessary a third, were then selected at random and the results checked against a careful independent count of the register. In almost every case a firm decision either to accept or reject the tabulation could be made by the end of the third sample form. In the few cases where the error rate still hovered in the zone of uncertainty between 3.5 per cent and 4.5 per cent the tabulation was accepted if the

3. See pp. 17–8.

cumulative score were nearer to the acceptance line than to the rejection line, otherwise it was rejected.

Both the underlying statistical logic of sequential sampling and the selection of sample months in 20-year blocks, rather than individually, involve the assumption that the errors in recording the monthly totals were randomly distributed throughout the period for which a tabulation was made. In practice this was often not the case: some styles of register entry, and some vicars' scripts were more difficult to read than others, and errors in extracting information from the register tended to cluster in such periods. We therefore decided wherever possible to increase the severity of the test by checking baptism and burial entries, which can occasionally refer to more than one event, rather than marriage entries, and by checking totals from the sixteenth and seventeenth centuries, when the registers were generally less tidily kept than was the case in the eighteenth and nineteenth centuries.

Appendix 12

The detection of periods of defective registration

General strategy

To classify a period of registration as defective is to make a relative judgement: the period appears to be defective because the total number of events recorded in it seems implausibly low in the context of the numbers recorded for neighbouring periods of time. While it is easy to detect periods of gross under-registration by eye, the task becomes much harder when the normal frequency of events is so low that one or more months may occur with no recorded events. It is also difficult to maintain comparable standards of judgement when scanning some 3.689 million monthly frequencies. It therefore seemed sensible to develop a computer program that would parallel the same kind of relative judgement of defectiveness that an historian makes by eye and apply consistent criteria over a wide range of differing conditions.

The relative nature of the notion of defectiveness implies both a standard of reference (a normal frequency of events) and a decision as to how far observed frequencies may legitimately stray from the standard of reference, beyond which point they are to be classified as defective. Both points imply some knowledge of the normal variation to be found in a series of baptisms, burials, and marriages. With a smooth series of events, a short reference period will give a good indication of the current level of events. In these circumstances relatively modest shortfalls will be unlikely occurrences and may be taken as evidence of defective registration. The more variable the series, the longer the reference period needs to be in order to capture a reasonably typical level, and the greater the tolerance of low values in the period under review before they are classified as defective.

After examining a large number of baptism, burial, and marriage series in parishes of all sizes we found, as expected, that the degree of variation in a series was fairly straightforwardly related to the size of the parish. Indeed, theoretically, if the monthly frequencies had been independent random samples of a vital rate (p) applied to a constant parish population (N), the standard deviation of the frequencies (Np) would be given by the binomial formula (Npq). In practice the parish populations were rarely constant and the monthly events were variously auto- and inter-correlated, so the standard deviations of the series of events were usually greater than what would be expected in independent random conditions. Over the range of values assumed by the monthly frequencies in pre-industrial parishes we found that the standard deviation of a series is reasonably well approximated by the formula $0.1 f + \sqrt{f}$, where f (or Np in binomial terms) is the mean expected frequency.[1] Thus the standard deviation of a

1. It should be noted that our formula $0.1f + \sqrt{f}$ slightly understates the standard deviation of a series of burials and exaggerates the standard deviation of samples with a very high mean frequency of events (f > 1000). An independent study has found similar results by applying linear regression analysis to annual series of baptisms and marriages from some French and Belgian parishes in the seventeenth and eighteenth

series of monthly events is approximately one tenth of the prevailing frequency plus the square root of that frequency. Since the last term is equivalent to the standard deviation of Poisson distribution it follows that the variation in the series is greater than that of the Poisson distribution. Furthermore, since the latter is a limiting case of the binomial distribution it follows that the variation in the series is greater than that of the binomial distribution too. This result is not surprising given the inability of the series of events to meet the assumptions of statistical independence on which these two theoretical distributions are based.

If the empirical formula for the standard deviation of the series of events is expressed in terms of the coefficient of variation (i.e. the standard deviation as a proportion of the mean), it would appear that over the range of values normally found in pre-industrial parishes the coefficient of variation assumes a minimum value of 0.1 with a supplement equal to the square root of the mean monthly frequency. Since variations in the level of vital rates (p) were relatively modest in the past, the prevailing mean values of recorded events (f or Np) were largely reflections of the size of the parish (N). Proportionately, therefore, series of events drawn from small parishes were more variable than series from large parishes. However, we also found that if we took successive runs of several months in small parishes sufficient to yield about 20 events, the degree of variation in the total numbers of events these months produced was similar to the variation we found when sampling 20 events from a larger parish taking one month at a time.[2] This is perhaps not surprising because the underlying process is one of a successive application of a vital rate to a population, and the time period (day, month, year) over which the outcomes (baptisms, burials, marriages) are aggregated is an arbitrary choice made after the event. Thus, for example, to consider the total frequency of baptisms recorded for a parish over 10 months rather than 1 month is nearly tantamount to increasing the size of the population under observation by a factor of 10.

This is a useful result because it provides a way to get round the problem of how to distinguish under-registration from genuine variation when the normal monthly frequency of events is very low, as for example in the case of marriages celebrated in tiny parishes where one a year may be par for the course. Since runs of several months with no recorded events are awkward to handle statistically it seemed more sensible to consider a fixed, and reasonably large, number of events rather than a fixed number of months. After considerable trial and error we decided to take a period containing 100 events as our reference period from which to calculate the 'normal' frequency for a series, and a period estimated to contain 20 events as the test period for under-registration.

The reference period

The length of the '100 event' reference period for each series in each parish was calculated by summing the entire series, and then deriving the mean monthly

---

centuries aggregated over a number of different time periods. In that study variability was expressed in terms of a linear regression equation for the percentage coefficient of variation, and in these terms our own expression for the standard deviation of a series becomes $y = 10 + 100\sqrt{f}$. This is similar to several of the expressions obtained for the Belgian and French parishes, especially those involving larger numbers of events. The variability of burial series was not investigated because of heavy disturbance from crisis mortality. Spencer, 'Variability of demographic data', pp. 18–24, 32–5.

2. Again our experience duplicated that reported by Spencer. See above chapter 1, fn. 13.

frequency and hence the number of months required on average to capture 100 events. Experience suggested, however, that the 100 event rule would have led to rather short reference periods being taken for large parishes and very long periods being selected for small parishes. Brief reference periods were sometimes influenced by short-term variations and hence gave a misleading view of the normal frequency of events being recorded, while very long periods sometimes spanned years in which the parish population grew or declined and thus provided a figure not typical of any particular point in time. The reference period was therefore constrained to lie within the bounds of 10 and 40 years. It was treated like a moving average, trailing behind the under-registration test period. As the latter advanced through the series the trailing reference period was updated by dropping off its oldest monthly value and adding in the latest acceptable monthly frequency. Since the whole point of the reference period was to provide an estimate of the normal monthly frequency of events, care had to be taken to ensure that neither under- nor over-registered months (e.g. epidemics or temporary 'marriage-shops') were included. The means by which such months were detected are described below.

Clearly the initial reference period would be made up of untested months, and should they be untypical any judgement of a test period based on them would be faulty. We tried to avoid this difficulty by beginning the scan through the data six reference period lengths after the start of the series (i.e. a minimum of 720 months into the data) and then tracking backwards towards the beginning of the series. By the time the program had reached the start of the series, turned round and begun its main scan forwards along the series, the original reference period had been left far behind and each of the intervening months used to update the reference period would have been checked for typicality. Thus any initial bias in the reference period should have been 'washed out' during the run-in back to the start of the series. However, a seriously deviant initial reference period, such as a prolonged period of defective registration or a 'marriage-shop', might permanently bias the expectations of the normal level of events. We therefore rejected any initial reference period that recorded events at a monthly frequency less than one quarter, or more than three times, the overall average monthly frequency for the series, and took the nearest period that did not fail this test.

Once the main forward scan through the series has begun, the trailing moving average reference period, based on a minimum of 100 events, gives an estimate of the local average monthly frequency. Strictly speaking, the estimate refers to the centre of the reference period, not the leading edge, from which the test period is to be projected. This means that the estimated monthly frequency will be an underestimate when population is growing and an overestimate when it is declining. However, the inaccuracy in the estimation is not large even for the fastest growing parishes, and is of negligible significance compared to the crudity of the rules employed to identify under- or over-registered periods.

The test period

The test period itself is one that is estimated to contain 20 events, and the length of the period can easily be calculated on the basis of the average monthly frequency obtained from the reference period. The length of the test period therefore not only varies between parishes and series but also during the course of a scan of a single series. When the estimated length is not an exact number of months it is rounded up to the nearest whole number, and the observed number of events recorded in the period is adjusted accordingly. For example, if the reference period suggests an average monthly frequency of 15 events, 1.33 months would be needed to obtain 20 events. The test period is therefore two months and the total number of events found to have been recorded in the two-month test period is deflated by the ratio 1.33/2. The test period is rounded up, rather than down, to ensure that it is always at least one month long, though only large parishes with more than about 8,000 inhabitants produce enough events to yield a test period as short as this. Small parishes of around 200 inhabitants, on the other hand, take about a dozen years to produce 20 marriages. With very long test periods there is a danger that short periods of under-registration may be missed, so an arbitrary upper limit of 10 years was imposed on the length of the test period.

Once the test period had been defined and the number of events recorded in it summed, it was then checked for either over- or under-registration. In both cases, once a test period had been judged to be untypical as a whole, steps were taken to find the point within it at which under- or over-registration appeared to begin. The reference period was brought forward until it trailed back from the last acceptable month, and it was then frozen until the end of the peak or trough had been located. To accomplish this, the test period continued to advance one month at a time until the frequencies it contained implied a return to normality. Thereafter a more detailed search was carried out within the test period to find the month at which the peak or trough ended. The individual months comprising the over- or under-registered periods were then tagged so as not to be included in the reference period as the scan resumed its advance, a month at a time along the series.

Testing for 'peaks'

The criteria by which peaks and troughs were identified were rather different. The only reason for identifying peaks was to prevent untypically high monthly frequencies from contaminating the reference period and producing unrealistically high estimates of the normal average monthly frequency of events, so they were identified in a rough and ready way. A test period was classified as a peak if its average monthly frequency was more than 2.75 times the average monthly frequency in the reference period. When the test period frequency fell below this figure the peak was deemed to have ended. In order to prevent a spurious permanent peak being generated, as might happen when the test period was long and the number of events was increasing rapidly to a new plateau, the qualifying level for peak status was raised to six times the normal monthly frequency eight years after the beginning of the peak. These figures were chosen so as not to rule out the genuine peaks in the data produced by 'marriage-shops' and epidemic mortality. Eight years is far longer than any recorded epidemic, and the 'marriage-shops' amongst our parishes produced more than six times the normal number of marriages.

Finding the edges of a 'peak'

In most cases the test period was several months long, so in order to find the month in which the peak began an internal sub-period was defined of one third the length of the original test period. Starting at the beginning of the original test period the sub-period was advanced one month at a time until its average monthly frequency was more than twice the normal monthly frequency given by the reference period. If the sub-period was more than two months long its length was then again divided into three and the same search was carried out, starting at the beginning of the sub-period in which the monthly frequency first became more than twice the normal level. If the new part sub-period was still more than two months long the same process of subdividing by a factor of three and searching internally was pursued until the sub-period containing the start of the peak was reduced to a length of one or two months. Starting with the first month in this final sub-period the edge of the peak was more finely tuned by moving backwards or forwards in time to locate the first monthly frequency that was more than 1.75 times the average monthly frequency.

Once the month in which the peak began had been identified, the trailing reference period was brought up to that point and the standard test period reformed. The scanning of the series then proceeded until the test period yielded a monthly frequency less than 2.75 times the normal monthly frequency derived from the reference period. Then the same procedure of successive subdivision and fine-tuning was employed to locate the month within this test period at which the peak might be said to end.

It should be emphasized that the various critical factors such as 1.75 and 2.75, which were used to define the peaks, have no theoretical justification. They were arrived at after experimenting with a large number of registers, and appeared to be successful in identifying the boundaries of the overwhelming majority of epidemics, mass baptisms, and 'marriage-shops' to be found in the data.

Testing for 'troughs'

The criteria by which periods of under-registration can be identified, however, need rather more careful elaboration. The starting point was the hope that the sampling variation in the series might prove to be 'well behaved' so that some simple rules based on sampling theory could reasonably be applied, even though both the data and the sampling process violated some of the theoretical assumptions of simple random sampling. Having decided that sampling a fixed number of events would prove more tractable than sampling a fixed number of months, we chose a sample size of 20 events as being one that would be small enough to yield fairly short search periods of a year or less for most parishes, while being large enough for the sampling variation to be well behaved. This latter point was crucial so we drew many successive test samples of 20 events in the sense described above. That is, for each series in a number of parishes of different sizes we calculated how many months would yield 20 events at particular points in time, and then tabulated the actual number of frequencies of events yielded by a large number of samples of that number of months. In almost every case, across each of the three kinds of registration (baptisms, burials, marriages) and over parishes of very different sizes, we found that the sample frequencies were approximately normally distributed around a mean of 20 events, which is what one would expect if they had indeed been simple random samples. Furthermore the standard deviations of these sampling distributions were very close to each other, around 6.0 to 6.5, with burials as the most variable series.

This immediately suggested how we might formalize our 'implausibility' approach to identifying under-registration, for the apparent normality of the sampling distribution and the regularity of the dispersion of the sample results around a mean of 20 events enabled us to calculate the probability of random variation producing test periods with very low numbers of recorded events. If the probability turned out to be very low, we discounted random variation as the explanation and labelled the period as one of under-registration. In the event we found it convenient to set two arbitrary decision levels, one for unconditional condemnation to an under-registered status, and a second for a conditional judgement, to be confirmed or revised by reference to what was happening to the other series at the same point in time.

We began by setting our *unconditional* decision level at a frequency that corresponded approximately to the 0.5 per cent level of significance in simple random-sampling terms. In other words we wanted to keep the chance of falsely claiming under-registration, when it was really random variation that was responsible, down to a figure of less than 1 in 200. For our *conditional* judgement of under-registration we took a decision level corresponding approximately to the 1.25 per cent level of significance, that is the chance of falsely claiming under-registration was about 1 in 80. In practical terms, therefore, our unconditional decision was taken when the test period frequency reached a figure lower than 2.58 standard deviations away from the mean test frequency of 20 and a conditional judgement of under-registration was made when the test period frequency was more than 2.25 standard deviations below the mean. For baptisms and marriages this meant that any test period yielding less than 4.5 events was unconditionally declared to be under-registered, periods yielding between 4.5 and 6.5 were conditionally judged to be under-registered, while periods with more than 6.5 recorded events were considered to be subject to normal random fluctuations. In the case of burials, which fluctuated more than the other two series, the limits were set a little lower at 5.5 for conditional, and 3.5 for unconditional under-registration. A problem arose with epidemics, which anticipate much normal mortality and often leave several months following them with few burials recorded. To avoid classifying such periods as under-registered, the unconditional level was lowered even further to 2.5 events for a period of 2 years after an epidemic.[3]

Although we began by choosing the figures for these cut-off points by thinking in probabilistic terms, we followed the conventional 'significance'-level approach only as a very general guide to the level of fluctuation beyond which random variation would have been a highly improbable explanation. Before we settled on the figures cited here, we experimented with a large number of both clear-cut and borderline cases of under-registration in the registers of parishes of different sizes. By definition, the results of any test of this kind are bound to be arbitrary, and wherever the cut-off point happens to be set there will always be marginal cases for which one might have preferred a different result. But our overall impression was that these cut-off points gave reasonable results in the vast majority of cases. They usually confirmed the decision one would make scanning a register oneself, and when applied systematically by computer showed again and again the fallibility of a visual inspection of very long series of numbers by finding clear cases of under-registration that had quite escaped the eye.

This was particularly so in the borderline cases for which special steps had to be taken. If a test period had been conditionally declared to be under-registered, reference was made to the number of events being recorded in one of the other two series. In the case of burials, the conditional judgement was confirmed if the frequency of baptisms recorded during the same time period also lay below the conditional under-registration level (6.5 events), but was reversed if baptisms showed

3. For references to sampling theory see chapter 1, fn. 14.

no signs of being under-registered. Conditional judgements with respect to baptisms and marriages were verified by checking whether the burial frequency was below the conditional level and confirming the provisional judgement only if this were so.

In this way periods that recorded very low frequencies of events were failed outright. But if the shortfall was only just beyond what might reasonably occur by chance, taking account of the overall degree of fluctuation in the series, the period was failed only if it appeared that another series was also defective at the same time.[4] The choice of baptisms as the reference series for burials, and burials as the reference series for baptisms and marriages, helped to ensure that the genuinely low frequencies occurring in each series either during or immediately after periods of crisis mortality were not erroneously considered to be signs of under-registration. For if the numbers of baptisms and marriages fell off sharply during a mortality crisis, as they sometimes did, there would be a good chance that they would only attract a conditional judgement of under-registration which would be reversed by the large numbers of burials being recorded. Similarly a conditional judgement of under-registration attached to a period immediately after a mortality crisis, when low numbers of burials were usually recorded, would be reversed by the large numbers of baptisms typically occurring at such times.

Finding the edges of a 'trough'

Once a test period had been judged to be under-registered, if it was more than one month in length, the next task was to find the month within the period at which the under-registration might be said to begin. The same general procedure was adopted as has been described in the case of peaks, that is a sub-period was defined of one third the length of the test period, and the sub-period was advanced one month at a time, starting at the beginning of the test period. This time the progress of the sub-period was halted when it contained less than 3 events. Since the test period as a whole could only at most contain between 2.5 and 6.5 events, and since there would be a strong probability that these events would be found near the start of the test period next to the period of registration already judged to be sound, there would also be a strong chance that by the time the sub-period was recording less than 3 events it would have passed over any 'shoulder' of sound registration within the test period and would be descending into the under-registered 'trough'. As with the procedure adopted for delimiting peaks, the process of dividing the length of the current sub-period by three and advancing internally until less than three events were recorded was continued until the sub-period was reduced to a length of one or two months. The final result was more finely tuned as follows. If the first month of the final sub-period was found to be preceded by one or more successive months with no recorded events the detection process was considered to have overshot the mark and the start of under-registration was moved back to the first month with no recorded events. On the other hand, if the first month of the final sub-period was found to contain more than one third of the

---

4. Note, however, that if the registration of one series were to fail conditionally *before* the other, the conditional judgement would be overturned and the partly defective months incorporated into the reference period. When the second series in turn became conditionally defective, this judgement would also be overturned because the first series would apparently be running at a genuinely low level. We have found only one example of a failure to detect a staggered onset of defective registration. This occurred in Almondbury, Yorks. W. R., in the spring of 1718 when burials in outlying chapelries were omitted from the main register two months earlier than was the case with baptisms.

normal frequency of events the detection process was considered to have under-shot, and the start of under-registration was moved forward until a month with less than this frequency was found.

The trailing reference period was then advanced up to the month before that in which under-registration had been adjudged to begin and the test period was reformed. Under-registration was deemed to have continued until the test period returned at least 11 events, that is only 1.5 standard deviations below the mean test frequency. This higher figure was chosen, rather than the figures of 6.5 and 5.5 which were the lowest acceptable figures in a period of normal registration, because it was felt that some substantial evidence of a change of state was required before a period of registration deficiency could be considered to have ended. Once a test period containing 11 events had been located, the point within it at which under-registration could be said to have ended was determined by applying the same procedure of sub-division as was used for identifying the month when under-registration began, but this time looking for the point at which the sub-period yielded at least three events.

When the end of under-registration had been identified, the months comprising the defective period were noted, and flagged so as not to be included in the trailing reference period as the scan continued on its way along the series, beginning with the month after the end of under-registration.

It will have been clear from this account that the identification of the months within a test period at which a period of under-registration began and ended was effected by a rather *ad hoc* set of procedures, in contrast to the way in which the test periods as a whole were evaluated by analogy with the more formal rules of sampling theory. This informal approach was forced upon us because we could no longer finesse the problem of sequences of months with no recorded events by adopting the device of considering a number of months together. Indeed the difficulty lay in finding some rule that would not only identify a single month as the beginning or end of a period of under-registration, but that would also work for large and small parishes, for abrupt breaks in the register, and for long, gradual descents into defective registration. The procedures we finally adopted have no theoretical justification; they emerged as the most effective of a large number of approaches which we tried out on a wide variety of different profiles of under-registration selected for test purposes from the data. If they have any virtue, it is a practical one, for they reach a decision as to the month in which under-registration begins or ends quite quickly, an important consideration even if large computers are available when there is a file of some 3:689 million monthly frequencies to be scanned. Accordingly a computer program was written embodying the various tests and procedures described above that produced a list of the periods of under-registration it had detected.

As was stressed at the beginning of this appendix, the reduction of a continuum in the quality of registration to a dichotomy is an arbitrary act; but it was one that we could not escape. It was very evident from the most casual inspection by eye that the data contained periods in which registration was marginally incomplete as well as yawning chasms. Clearly something had to be done to make good the deficiencies, and that entailed making a decision about what constituted a 'deficiency'. We believe that the rules we have formulated to that end give reasonable results. There are undoubtedly marginal cases where special circumstances might lead one to disagree with the formalized decision reached by the program, but in our experience these are rare occurrences.

Appendix 13

The replacement of defective monthly frequencies

Interpolation

We considered estimating the trend lines to be interpolated across the defective periods by a variety of curve fitting procedures, but decided that the gain in precision was of insufficient importance to justify the heavy computational costs involved. We therefore opted for a simple geometric interpolation between local average monthly frequencies calculated for each end of the defective period. These were usually based on the two periods of 60 months immediately adjacent to the defective period, though in the case of a few small parishes which had not recorded 20 events within the five-year period, the period was extended until 20 events had been encountered. If a further period of defective registration intervened while the local average was being calculated, the period on which the average was based was extended by the appropriate number of months. If a period of defective registration was too close to the beginning or end of registration to allow a local average to be calculated on that side of the period, the local average calculated for the other side was substituted, thereby implying a flat trend through the defective period.

Monthly variation

A simple geometric interpolation fails to capture short-run variation. Although a seasonal pattern could have been derived for each parish internally by referring to the well-registered periods, we were anxious to take account of other important short-run and geographically widespread variations, such as those associated with weather and the harvest. There was no way of telling what these might have been during a defectively registered period from the surrounding well-registered months, but the pattern could be recovered by referring to the experience of other, well-registered parishes during the same period. But to construct such a reference template was no simple matter, because the prevalence of under-registration amongst the set of parishes at several points in time meant that the number of other parishes whose registers could be used to construct the reference template varied during the course of the period.

To avoid complications of this kind we decided to construct the reference template for each series from parishes with no periods of defective registration. We found we could use only 35 parishes for baptisms, 50 parishes for burials, and 37 parishes for marriages. However, most of the defective periods fell in the period before January 1662, for which there was the added complication that not all the parishes were in observation all the time. We therefore decided to divide the replacement operation into two phases. In the first phase we considered only the period between January 1662 and December 1811 when all parishes were registering. Many more parishes had no periods of defective registration in this period (174, 161, and 158 parishes for baptisms, burials, and marriages respectively). A reference template was compiled from the monthly variation in these parishes and used in conjunction with the interpolation procedure to find replacement monthly totals for the defective periods occurring between the years 1667 and 1806.[1]

Once the first replacement phase had been completed several parishes, whose periods of defective registration were confined to these years, now had no defective registration and so could boost the number of parishes contributing to the monthly template for the second replacement phase which covered the years before 1667 and after 1806. Although the template for the later sixteenth century could now be based on a more reasonable number of parishes, the fall-off in the number of parishes beginning registration before 1566 was sharp and still left an insufficient basis for the construction of a monthly template for the mid sixteenth century. To overcome this

Table A13.1: Number of parishes with no defective periods, starting registration by selected dates

Date	Baptisms	Series Burials	Marriages
1661	53	76	60
1601	38	51	43
1571	29	36	37
1566	28	32	35
1561	16	23	24
1556	7	5	9
1551	6	4	8
1541	5	2	5

difficulty a special search was made for registers in operation by 1542 and that had no defective periods before 1571. This yielded 15 baptism registers, 17 burial registers, and 28 marriage registers. The monthly pattern of each of these sets of registers was compared to the monthly pattern of the larger sets of registers enumerated in table A13.1 over the period 1566 to 1570 with a view to discovering whether they could legitimately be spliced together. In fact the monthly variation of the two sets was identical for each series, so for the period 1542–66 the monthly template based on the dwindling number of parishes in table A13.1 was replaced by one based on the specially located set of early registering parishes, inflated by the ratio obtaining between the two sets during the test period 1566–70. As there were practically no registers without defects operating during the period before 1542, we abandoned the attempt to calculate a contemporary template of monthly variation, and gave each month a value equal to the average monthly frequency computed over the period 1542–50, but omitting the epidemic years 1544–6.

The final problem to be overcome in the construction of the monthly template was to ensure that the monthly frequencies were all comparable, even though they were

1. The replacement period was indented so that there would always be at least five years adjacent to a defective period which were covered by the reference template and from which a local average frequency could be calculated for the purposes of interpolation. Only very small parishes which could not register 20 events between the outer edge of the defective period and the bounds of the template period would fail to acquire a local average on the outer edge of the defective period and be assigned a flat trend through the period by the interpolation procedure.

based on different numbers of registers as a result of the differences in the dates at which the parishes began and ended registration. We had already established that the date of commencement of registration appeared to be random with respect to subsequent demographic experience, so we raised the earlier and later totals by a process of successive proportional inflation, working outwards from the period 1662–1811, when all registers were in operation.[2]

Replacement

Once a reference template of monthly variation had been compiled, the replacement values for each defective period were calculated by interpolating a smooth geometric trend through the period, as described above, and then subjecting each month to the same proportional deviation from trend as obtained in the template series over the same period of time.

The replacement value for each month was estimated as a real number and then rounded to the nearest integer. If the replacement value for a month happened to be less than the value originally recorded, the original value was retained. The integer replacement values, overridden where necessary by original values, were then totalled and their sum compared to the rounded sum of the real replacement values before rounding or substitution had taken place. If the monthly integer values fell short of the total number apparently required to fill the defective period, the missing events were assigned at random to the months within the period. In order to preserve the influence of short-term variation the probabilities of selection were made proportionate to the monthly frequencies in the template series. If, however, there was a surplus of monthly integer values, the extra events were subtracted from the months at random with a probability inverse to the size of each month in the template series, except that no subtraction was allowed if it would reduce a monthly total below its original recorded value. When the total number of integer events in the defective period had been corrected, the annual totals for every calendar year involved in the period were recomputed. If, however, a new, revised annual total were less than that originally recorded, which might happen in a period of bad registration if events had been ascribed to the year but not to individual months, then the original annual total was allowed to stand.

Although some effort was made to make the monthly replacement values sensitive both to short-term variations and to the general trend in the individual parish series, the differences between individual months on both counts were relatively slight and tended to be obliterated in small parishes when the finely calculated replacement values were rounded to whole numbers. In large parishes, however, both trend and short-term variation were well preserved in the integer numbers of events finally chosen to replace the monthly totals in periods of defective registration.

2. The process is described on pp. 56–62 above.

Appendix 14

The derivation of two families of 'English' life tables

Both the operation of aggregative back projection and the calculation of decadal birth totals in the period 1781–1871 depend upon the creation of a family of life tables spanning a wide range of mortality levels. In the case of back projection a known total of deaths has to be distributed among the several age groups of a population whose age structure is known. Any life table linked to a particular age structure implies a determinate total of deaths, and within a family of life tables two adjacent tables can always be found with implied death totals which bracket the known total for the period in question. The exact mortality level experienced can then be established by interpolation between the two tables.[1] Similarly, the selection of a set of L_xs suitable for the calculation of a decadal birth total depends upon searching among a family of life tables to find the table that best fits the changing totals of individual cohorts between successive censuses.[2]

Faced with the necessity of finding a family of life tables, the simplest solution would have been to adopt an existing set. If that were to have been done the obvious choice would have been model North of the Princeton regional model life tables.[3] Table A14.1 shows how much better is the correspondence between the third English life table and model North than between it and model West.[4] There is, however, sufficient difference between the third life table and model North to make it desirable to derive an independent set of life tables rather than to use model North itself. For example, in model North female rates in early adult life are always lower than male whereas in the third life table female rates are consistently the higher from $_5q_{10}$ to $_5q_{35}$. As a result, whereas there is a good fit between the male rates of the third life table and the North tables almost throughout, the fit is much less good in the case of female rates.

To use the third life table as a base for a new family of life tables implies, of course, the large assumption that the peculiarities in the age structure of English death rates in the mid nineteenth century were also present in earlier periods, albeit at varying absolute mortality levels. This may have been broadly true of the latter part of the parish register period but was probably not true of the first century after registers began to be kept.[5] Nevertheless a family of life tables derived from the third life table appeared to be the most appropriate starting point for aggregative back projection when using English birth and death data.[6]

1. See appendix 15.
2. See pp. 730–2.
3. Coale and Demeny, *Regional model life tables*.
4. This point has not always been appreciated. Both Hollingsworth and Teitelbaum assumed that model West was the appropriate model to use when making inferences from mid-nineteenth-century English census data. Hollingsworth, *Historical demography*, appendix 1; Teitelbaum, 'Birth under-registration'.
5. See Schofield and Wrigley, 'Infant and child mortality'.
6. We hope to investigate the effect of modifying assumptions about the age structure of mortality in the course of back projection in due course but have not incorporated this refinement in the present study.

Table A14.1: Life table death rates $(1\,000q_x)$ of the third English life table and nearest levels in Princeton North and West tables

	Third life table (1838–54)		North levels		West levels	
	M	F	M	F	M	F
0	163.6	134.7	10	11	11	12
1	134.7	132.6	10	9	8	8
5	46.8	46.3	11	11	5	6
10	24.8	26.3	11	11	8	9
15	31.0	32.7	10	11	9	10
20	42.5	44.2	11	7	10	9
25	46.7	49.0	10	8	10	9
30	51.5	53.6	10	9	10	9
35	58.1	58.7	10	9	11	10
40	67.5	64.9	10	9	11	9
45	80.8	72.8	10	8	12	9
50	101.5	84.3	10	9	12	11
55	129.8	113.9	10	9	12	10
60	173.3	155.8	11	10	13	11
65	241.4	219.0	11	10	13	11
70	337.4	309.5	11	11	13	12
75	457.4	425.7	12	11	14	12

Source: Third life table q_xs were calculated from l_xs in *Supplement to 65th Annual Report,* Pt I, pp. xlviii–li, tables H and I. Princeton North and West tables in Coale and Demeny, *Regional model life tables.*

The third life table was not, however, used without modification. It is not difficult to show that there was a marked overstatement of age by the elderly in the censuses of 1841 and 1851 and the accuracy of the third life table suffered as a result in the higher age groups. So much was clear from an initial review of the census age data.[7] A first

7. As an example of the acuteness of the problem of overstatement of age, it is interesting to note that if the 1841 female census totals in the higher age groups are inflated back to 1821 using the L_xs of the unmodified third life table, the following pattern appears (in both censuses those of unknown age were distributed among the age groups proportionately to those of known age; totals refer to England less Monmouth).

	(1) 1841 census		(2) 1821 totals inflated from 1841	(3) 1821 census	(4) Ratio (2)/(3)
50–9	492 959	30–9	662 978	695 285	0.9535
60–9	342 181	40–9	543 005	535 592	1.0138
70–9	170 245	50–9	417 378	375 245	1.1123
80 and over	52 127	60 and over	645 234	434 146	1.4862

Note: The calculation for those aged 80 and over was made using the approximations employed by Coale and Demeny, $T_{80} = e_{80}l_{80}$ and $e_{80} = 3.725 + 0.0000625\,l_{80}$. Coale and Demeny, *Regional model life tables,* p.20.

In constructing the third life table, however, Farr did take into account two other potential causes of inaccuracy – the effect of under-registration of births in the early years of vital registration and the tendency of young women to misrepresent their age. Farr, *English life table,* pp. xxi–xxii.

set of life tables was therefore constructed using as a base the rates of the third life table up to age 55, but for $_5q_{55}$ and above the rates of the 1891–1900 life table. These were used in the calculations described in chapter 5 which yielded estimates of the decennial birth cohorts from 1781 to 1841 and indirectly determined the final inflation ratios for both baptisms and burials. At all ages above 55 the q_xs of the 1891–1900 life table are higher than those of the third life table if rates are calculated for the two series combined (the 1891–1900 rates are higher from age 50 for men and from age 60 for women). Later, in the course of experiment with back projection, it began to appear probable that still higher rates were more plausible in middle and later life. This is not surprising since at ages below 55 the third life table rates are higher than those of the 1891–1900 table for the sexes combined. The latter had been used initially on the general ground that by the end of the century age reporting in the census at higher ages had greatly improved and that the fall in mortality rates was progressively less pronounced with increasing age,[8] so that the rates late in the century were likely to have been similar to those in its middle decades.

The life table death rates of the third life table and those of the 1891–1900 table are shown in table A14.2. Only female rates are given since the operations of chapter 5 were confined to the female population. The rates used as a base to generate a family of life tables are printed in heavier type.

The second modification of the third life table was made by splicing rates derived

Table A14.2: Female life table death rates ($1\,000q_x$) of the third English life table and of the life table of 1891–1900

	Third life table (1838–54)	1891–1900 life table
0	**134.7**	140.7
1	**132.6**	89.8
5	**46.3**	21.6
10	**26.3**	12.8
15	**32.7**	18.2
20	**44.2**	22.1
25	**49.0**	27.0
30	**53.6**	33.5
35	**58.7**	42.7
40	**64.9**	51.8
45	**72.8**	62.8
50	**84.3**	81.4
55	113.9	**112.7**
60	155.8	**158.0**
65	219.0	**223.8**
70	309.5	**318.5**
75	425.7	**439.6**
80	557.6	**577.2**
85	689.3	**713.0**
90	804.1	**826.0**

Source: Rates calculated from l_xs in *Supplement to 65th Annual Report*, Pt I, pp. xlviii–li, tables H and I.

8. See McKeown and Record, 'Reasons for the decline of mortality'.

from model North to those of the third life table above age 50. The details are set out in table A14.3. Rates for the sexes combined are needed in this case because back projection was carried out for the population as a whole. The rates were obtained by combining information from the separate male and female tables.[9]

Table A14.3: Life table death rates ($1\,000q_x$) of the third English life table (sexes combined) extended above age 50 from model North

0	149.5
1	133.7
5	46.6
10	25.5
15	31.9
20	43.3
25	47.8
30	52.6
35	58.4
40	66.2
45	76.8
50	94.3
55	123.3
60	170.7
65	242.8
70	350.7
75	480.9
80	618.9
85	769.8
90	878.8

Sources: Third life table rates calculated from male and female l_xs in *Supplement to 65th Annual Report,* Pt. I, pp. xlviii–li, tables H and I. Model North rates from Coale and Demeny, *Regional model life tables* modified as indicated in text.

In middle life the trend of death rates for the sexes combined in the third life table is closely in accord with those of model North as may be seen in table A14.4. They lie about half way between level 9 and level 10 from $_5q_{35}$ to $_5q_{45}$, continue to fluctuate between these two levels until $_5q_{55}$, but then show a steadily falling trend in model North terms at higher ages. If rates taken from the 1891–1900 life table are substituted for those of the third life table from age 55, they remain in the range between level 9 and level 10 until $_5q_{65}$ but thereafter once again fall below the levels that would be expected on the model North pattern.

In view of the close agreement of the increase of rates with age between the third life table and model North in middle life it seemed reasonable to use model North data to extend the third life table at ages where defects in age reporting in the census began

9. For details of the method used see below, pp. 730–2.

Table A14.4: Life table death rates ($1\,000q_x$) of model North and English life tables compared (sexes combined)

	Third life table	1891–1900 life table	Model North level 9	Model North level 10	Expressed as Model North levels Third life table	Expressed as Model North levels 1891–1900 life table
35	58.4		60.6	55.5	9.43	
40	66.2		69.4	63.7	9.56	
45	76.8		79.3	73.1	9.40	
50	93.0		97.5	90.5	9.64	
55	121.8	125.6	127.3	118.4	9.62	9.19
60	164.4	172.5	175.9	164.5	10.01	9.30
65	229.9	239.7	249.5	234.7	10.35	9.66
70	323.0	336.0	359.4	340.0	10.94	10.22
75	440.6	457.9	490.9	468.7	11.35	10.52

Sources: English life table rates calculated from male and female l_xs in *Supplement to 65th Annual Report,* Pt I, pp. xlviii–li, tables H and I. Model North rates calculated from male and female l_xs given in Coale and Demeny, *Regional model life tables,* pp. 228–9. See text for further details.

to affect its accuracy. Accordingly, rates derived from model North were substituted for third life tables rates for $_5q_{50}$ and above. The pattern of rates from $_5q_{35}$ to $_5q_{45}$ shown in table A14.4 suggests that level 9.45 is appropriate. This represents the average location of the third life table rates between level 9 and level 10 over the age span 35–50. For example, $_5q_{35}$ is 60.6 in level 9, 55.5 in level 10, and in the third life table 58.4. The third life table rate is therefore located at level 9.43 ((60.6–58.4) (60.6–55.5) = 0.43). Rates for level 9.45 were calculated by linear interpolation between level 9 and level 10 for all ages above 50.

Although the third life table and the two variants just described show substantial differences in death rates in the higher age groups, the differences between them in expectation of life at birth are slight because most of the attrition of the population base occurs before the rates diverge. Expectation of life for the sexes combined in the third life table is 40.86 years; in the life table produced by using elements drawn from the 1891–1900 life table 40.78 years; and in the life table modified in accordance with model North rates 40.70 years. All three are very similar to the comparable figure for level 10 North which is 40.99 years. The two revisions of the third life table were therefore each treated as level 10 in the new 'English' life table families, and, taking advantage of the general similarity between the third life table and model North of the Princeton tables, other levels in the 'English' tables were calculated from the model North pattern. The ratios of rates (q_x) between any two levels in the North tables were used to manufacture levels in the 'English' tables. For example, $_5q_{30}$ female in North level 10 is 46.9 per 1,000 and the comparable rate in North level 5 is 73.3 ($e_0 = 30.0$ years). The female rate $_5q_{30}$ in the third life table is 53.6 and therefore the rate in level 5 of the 'English' tables is 53.6 × 73.3/46.9, or 83.3. Since the levels in the Princeton life tables are constructed to ensure that female e_0 increases by 2.5 years with each increase in level (level 1 = 20.0 years, level 2 = 22.5 years, and so on), it follows that adjacent levels in the 'English' sets differ by approximately 2.5 years in expectation of life at birth.

Because the Princeton tables do not specify mortality rates for ages above 80, they could not be used to derive q_xs above age 80 for the 'English' life table sets, and yet the specification of rates up to $_5q_{90}$ is of great importance in aggregative back projection.[10] Mortality at advanced ages has not attracted much study and reliable data are scarce.[11] Our solution was to derive the rates $_5q_{80}$, $_5q_{85}$, and $_5q_{90}$ from $_5q_{75}$ in each life table. Ledermann provides regression equations for deriving $_5q_{85}$ and $_5q_{90}$ from $_5q_{80}$.[12] This leaves only the problem of obtaining $_5q_{80}$ from $_5q_{75}$. The work of Gabriel and Ronen offers an indirect solution.[13] In the course of reviewing the set of model life tables published by the United Nations, which were based on about 150 life tables with a fairly wide geographic and temporal spread,[14] they expressed the relation between $_1q_0$ and mortality at all later ages in a series of regression formulae designed to obviate the distortions present in the United Nations' rates due to 'chaining'. In so doing they provided the opportunity of making an estimate of the death rate at a given age from the known mortality in an adjacent age group. The mortality rate $_5q_{75}$ expressed as a function of $_1q_0$ is 325.27 + 0.8082x where x equals the rate $_1q_0$. The comparable formula for $_5q_{80}$ is 485.57 + 0.6927x.[15] For any given $_5q_{75}$, therefore, the matching $_1q_0$ can be calculated, and from this in turn an estimate of $_5q_{80}$ can be made. We have preferred to use Ledermann's equations for calculating $_5q_{85}$ and $_5q_{90}$ rather than to continue to use those of Gabriel and Ronen, since the former were explicitly intended to cover the issue in question.

By using the method just described the rates found in each level of model North were extended from $_5q_{75}$ to $_5q_{90}$, thus completing the grid of rates necessary to convert rates found in the two new 'English' life tables into two families of life tables. The two modified forms of the third English life tables (tables A 14.2 and A 14.3) were treated as level 10 and every other level derived from them using the ratios found in the model North tables extended to $_5q_{90}$.

Once a set of q_xs has been specified for all age groups, other life table functions can be derived from them. The following methods were used to this end:

$_nq_x$ The probability at age x of dying before attaining age x + ·n. Values for q_x were obtained as described above.

$_nm_x$ The number of deaths between age x and age x + n in the life table population expressed as a rate obtained by relating the deaths to the number of years lived by the population between age x and age x + n. The m_xs of a life table may be derived from the q_xs and vice versa using the formulae of Reed and Merrell. We have used them in the form reproduced by Pressat with the simplified relationships between q_0 and m_0.[16]

l_x The total of survivors to age x from the original birth cohort. The l_xs can be obtained directly from the q_x values. Thus if l_5 is 80,000 (from an original cohort of 100,000) and $_5q_5$ is 50 per 1,000, l_{10} will be 80,000 − (80,000 × .05) = 76,000.

$_nL_x$ The number of years lived between age x and age x + n by the survivors from the original birth cohort. The L_x for any given age group can be derived from the l_xs that enclose it and the m_x for the age group. For $_5L_5$ to

10. See chapter 7 and appendix 15.

11. Much useful data may, however, be found in Vincent, 'La mortalité des vieillards' and, for ages up to 85 years, in *Age and sex patterns of mortality*. See also *Methods for population projections*.

12. Ledermann, *Nouvelles tables-types de mortalité*, pp. 46–7. He gives the following equations: $_5q_{85}$ = 337.80 + 0.69798 × $_5q_{80}$; and $_5q_{90}$ = 637.51 + 0.38990 × $_5q_{80}$

13. Gabriel and Ronen, 'Estimates of mortality'.

14. *Age and sex patterns of mortality*.

15. Gabriel and Ronen, 'Estimates of mortality', p. 166.

16. Pressat, *Demographic analysis*, pp. 138 and 481. It should be noted that the exponent of the final *m* is missing in the formulae reproduced on p. 481.

$_5L_{90}$ the value was obtained by the formula $_5L_x = (l_x - l_{x+5})/_5m_x$.[17] For $_1L_0$ and $_4L_1$ the method described by Coale and Demeny was used.[18] Model North separation factors for the sexes combined were calculated by combining the male and female factors weighted in the ratio 105/100.

P_x The proportion of persons living in one five-year age group who survive for five years or $_5L_{x+5}/_5L_x$.

e_x The average number of years of life remaining at age x. Thus e_0 represents expectation of life at birth.

All aggregative back projection was carried out for the sexes combined. In compiling life table functions for the sexes combined the sex ratio at birth was assumed to be 105. The male and female l_xs were therefore weighted in the ratio 105/100 in constructing a combined sex set of l_xs from which in turn q_xs and all other life table functions were derived.

Table A14.5 shows the q_xs of the family of life tables used in aggregative back projection and produced in the manner described. Only a section of the full set is reproduced covering the range of mortality levels most commonly encountered in early modern England. Levels 3 to 12 are shown; the full set runs from level 1 to level 24, as with the Princeton tables.

Table A14.5: Life table death rates ($1\,000q_x$) of the third English life table extended above age 50 by Princeton model North tables (sexes combined)

Level	3	4	5	6	7	8	9	10	11	12
e_0	23.54	25.98	28.42	30.86	33.31	35.77	38.23	40.70	43.18	45.66
Age										
0	279.2	255.8	234.4	214.7	196.6	179.8	164.1	149.5	135.8	123.0
1	265.7	241.8	220.1	200.1	181.6	164.5	148.6	133.7	119.7	106.6
5	91.9	83.7	76.2	69.4	63.0	57.2	51.7	46.6	41.8	37.3
10	49.3	45.0	41.1	37.5	34.2	31.1	28.2	25.5	23.0	20.7
15	58.3	53.5	49.2	45.2	41.5	38.0	34.8	31.9	29.1	26.5
20	77.6	71.4	65.7	60.6	55.8	51.3	47.2	43.3	39.7	36.3
25	86.3	79.3	73.0	67.2	61.8	56.8	52.2	47.8	43.8	39.9
30	95.4	87.7	80.6	74.1	68.1	62.6	57.4	52.6	48.0	43.8
35	106.5	97.8	89.8	82.6	75.9	69.6	63.8	58.4	53.3	48.6
40	118.4	109.0	100.4	92.5	85.2	78.4	72.1	66.2	60.7	55.5
45	135.0	124.5	114.9	106.1	98.0	90.4	83.4	76.8	70.7	64.9
50	158.2	146.7	136.2	126.5	117.6	109.3	101.6	94.3	87.6	81.2
55	205.8	191.0	177.4	164.9	153.3	142.6	132.6	123.3	114.5	106.0
60	275.2	256.4	239.2	223.4	208.8	195.2	182.6	170.7	159.7	149.0
65	377.8	353.4	331.2	310.7	291.9	274.4	258.1	242.8	228.6	214.9
70	527.2	495.4	466.3	439.6	414.9	392.0	370.7	350.7	332.0	313.8
75	682.4	646.1	613.0	582.5	554.3	528.1	503.7	480.9	459.5	438.4
80	790.1	759.3	731.2	705.3	681.3	659.1	638.3	618.9	600.8	582.8
85	888.4	867.1	847.6	829.6	813.0	797.6	783.2	769.8	757.2	744.8
90	944.8	932.9	922.1	912.1	902.9	894.3	886.3	878.8	871.8	864.9

Note: The methods used for the calculation of the rates for the sexes combined, and for the extension of rates for ages above $_5q_{75}$, are described in the text.

Source: Third life table rates table A14.1; model North rates Coale and Demeny, *Regional model life tables.*

17. This is a rearrangement of the formula given in Keyfitz and Flieger, *Population*, p. 137.
18. Coale and Demeny, *Regional model life tables*, p. 20.

Appendix 15

Aggregative back projection

Jim Oeppen

This appendix is chiefly devoted to a description, by means of a simple illustration, of the technique of back projection, which reconstructs the size and age structure of past populations from a knowledge of the totals of births and deaths stretching back from a reliable census. It also includes, however, a summary specification of the logical structure of the full system, and short sections dealing with the methods used to derive standard measures of fertility and mortality, with the testing of back projection as a technique, and with the construction of hypothetical birth and death series stretching back for 95 years before 1541. The appendix should be read in conjunction with the first section of chapter 7 which describes the general strategy of back projection, and with appendix 14 in which the method used to construct 'English' life tables is set out.

Back projection

The example used below to illustrate back projection was devised to clarify the sequence of operations which comprise it, but the imaginary population used has been simplified to the point of caricature, and the birth and death series have been reduced to the minimum length necessary to specify the operation of the system. Accordingly, the example should be regarded simply as a formal attempt to set out the internal accounting of the system in a way that facilitates comparison with other approaches, such as Lee's method of inverse projection. The equations introduced in the example are then incorporated in a 'flow-chart' specifying the overall logical structure of the full back projection system as set out in figure A15.6. The testing or verification of the full system is a separate issue briefly considered in a later section.

It is convenient to preface the example of back projection by a forward projection in order to introduce the concepts and notation used in a more familiar guise, and to provide the input data for the back-projection example. Figure A15.1 shows the accounting framework that will be used to describe back projection, but which is equally well adapted to detailing a forward projection exercise. The initial age structure of the population at time t = 0 is denoted

$n_{i,0}$ where i = 1, 2 . . . k age groups

and the slight difference between this notation and that of the conventional life table form used in appendix 14, namely

$n_{x,0}$ where x = 0, 1, 5, 10 . . . ω years

is extended where necessary to the life table function P_x which is used to denote the proportion of all individuals in a given age group who survived to the next age group at the next 'census'. In both cases the age-group interval is constrained to be equal to the length of the inter-censal period. This greatly simplifies the description of the

715

model. B_t and D_t are the totals of births and deaths respectively that occur between t and t+1. Where convenient the birth cohort B_t is denoted $n_{0,t}$. Thus $P_{0,t}$ is the proportion of $n_{0,t}$ who survive to become $n_{1,t+1}$. N_t is the population total; M_t is the period total of net migrants who leave during the period t to t+1 (in the case of net immigration M_t is negative); and C_t is the lifetime total of net migrants entering or

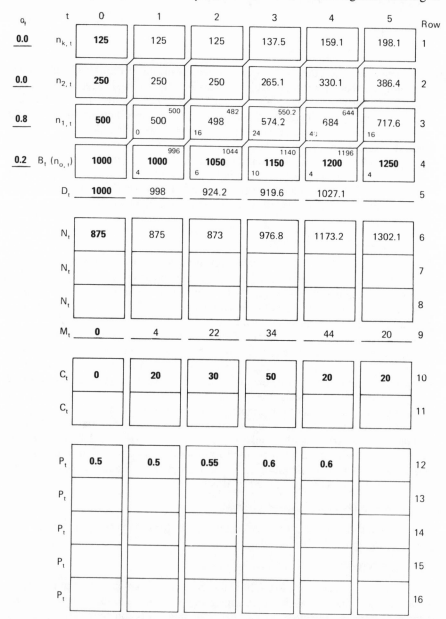

Figure A15.1: A forward-projection simulation

leaving the cohort B_t. It is assumed that C_t is distributed over time according to the age-specific cohort migration schedule

c_i where i = 1, 2 . . . k.

In this and subsequent examples the mortality system is a highly simplified version of that used in full back projection. A family of life tables is used in both cases but whereas those used in the full system involve all the usual complexities of a life table (table A14.5), the family used here has artificially simple P values covering values from 0.1 to 0.9, where level 0.1 refers to a P value of 0.1, level 0.2 to a P value of 0.2, and so on. The level indicates the P value for all age groups, except that there are no survivors from the final age group as may be seen in table A15.1.

Table A15.1: A simple family of life tables

	Level (P_t)		
	0.1	0.2 . . . . .0.9	
P_0	0.1	0.2 . . . . .0.9	
P_1	0.1	0.2 . . . . .0.9	
P_2	0.1	0.2 . . . . .0.9	
P_k	0.0	0.0 . . . . .0.0	

The simulated population history shown in figure A15.1 begins with a census age distribution at time 0 which is the result of a P value of 0.5, constant birth and death totals of 1,000, and zero cohort migration over the period t $= -k$ to 0. Time series for B_t, C_t, and P_t (survivorship level) for t = 0 to 5 have been arbitrarily selected as shown, and these, together with the cohort migration schedule and the family of life tables shown in table A15.1, exactly determine the behaviour of the system (the input values are shown in bold type).

Any cohort passes through k steps of migration and survival while it exists within the system. At each step the cohort loses or gains an appropriate share of migrants and the resulting total is 'survived' to the next 'census' by referring to the appropriate life table. Table A15.2 follows these steps for one such cohort in figure A15.1, namely B_2 or $n_{0,2}$, the successive cohort census totals being shown bold. The 'corner' totals in small type in figure A15.1 and in figures A15.3–5 show the migration totals for each cohort and time period and also the population totals which result after the migration has taken place.

Table A15.2: An example of the forward projection of a cohort

Step
1 t = 2 migration $n'_{0,2} = n_{0,2} - c_0 C_2$ $1044 = 1050 - 0.2(30)$
        survival $n_{1,3} = n'_{0,2} (P_{0,2})$ **574.2** $= 1044(0.55)$

2 t = 3 migration $n'_{1,3} = n_{1,3} - c_1 C_2$ $550.2 = 574.2 - 0.8(30)$
        survival $n_{2,4} = n'_{1,3} (P_{1,3})$ **330.1** $= 550.2(0.6)$

3 t = 4 migration $n'_{2,4} = n_{2,4} - c_2 C_2$ $330.1 = 330.1 - 0.0(30)$
        survival $n_{k,5} = n'_{2,4} (P_{2,4})$ **198.1** $= 330.1(0.6)$

4 t = 5 extinction $n_{k+1,6} = n_{k,5} (P_{3,5}) = 0$ **0** $= 198.1(0.0)$

Filling in the rest of the table in a similar fashion allows the period totals D_t, N_t, and M_t to be accumulated. For example,

$$D_2 = (1{,}044 - 574.2) + (482 - 265.1) + (250 - 137.5) + (125 - 0) = 924.2^1$$

We now have the history of a demographic system that has been constrained by two assumptions: first, that the period mortality is determined by a family of life tables with very simple characteristics; and second, that cohort migration totals are distributed over time in fixed proportions which bear the same sign throughout the cohort's history. Individual cohort migration totals may vary both in sign and magnitude, and therefore successive *period* migration totals may vary in both respects also. The assumptions are artificially simple but they help to make the operation of the system easier to understand.

There have been many attempts to infer the demographic history of a system such as that described in figure A15.1 using very simple methods linked to the assumption that $N_{t-1} = N_t + D_{t-1} - B_{t-1}$.[2] Recently Lee achieved a major advance by developing a technique that he termed inverse projection.[3] His method involves moving forwards in time and therefore requires an initial age structure to be specified. As the projection advances the observed period totals of births are successively introduced into the base of the population pyramid, and the observed period totals of deaths are obtained by depleting all age groups in accordance with the age structure of mortality defined by a reference life table. The life table is rescaled to make it more or less severe as required to match the observed period death totals. The process is repeated for each inter-censal period up to the date of a reliable census. No migration is allowed, and the size of the starting population is therefore obtained from the formula given earlier in the paragraph.

The results of applying inverse projection to the data derived from the forward projection are set out in figure A15.2, but it should be noted that the method of selecting an appropriate life table has been changed to conform to the method used in back projection which is described later in this section. Input data are again indicated in bold type. The size of the initial population at t = 0 is fixed by subtracting births and adding deaths between t = 5 and t = 0, as already noted. The age structure of the initial population was obtained by exploiting the constraints implied by an assumption that $B = D = 1{,}000$ indefinitely before time t = 0 (i.e. the population was stationary). The next step is to select a survivorship level within the family of life tables that satisfies the equation

$$D_t = \sum_{i=0}^{k} n_{i,t}\,(1.0 - P_{i,t}) \tag{A15.1}$$

$P_0 = 0.5$ would result in too few deaths (944) while $P_0 = 0.4$ produces too many (1,109). After making appropriate allowance for the fact that all those in the age group $n_{k,t}$ will die, the survivorship level that satisfies the equation may be obtained by interpolation and proves to be $P_0 = 0.4662$. Each age is then advanced from t = 0 to t = 1 according to

1. All the results shown in the various figures and tables are presented after rounding to one decimal place where necessary.
2. Most of the attempts to uncover the population history of England in the eighteenth century fall into this category (see appendix 5).
3. Lee, 'Estimating vital rates'. See pp. 576–87 above for further comments on Lee's method.

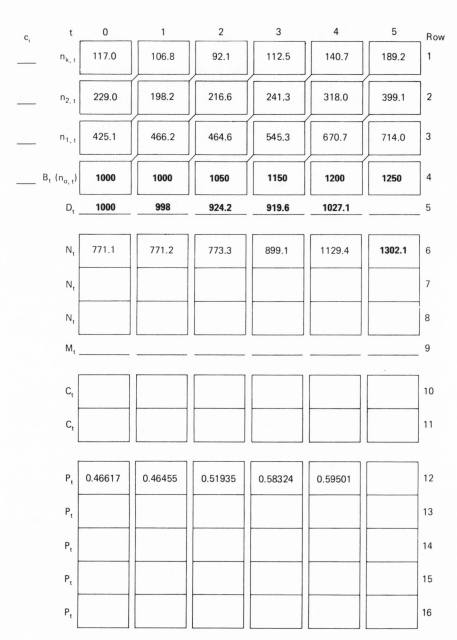

Figure A15.2: An illustration of Lee's inverse projection method

Note: The age groups totals n_t and t = 5 do not sum exactly to the
known population at that date (there is a discrepancy of 0.2).
This arises because of rounding in the intermediate steps
between t = 0 and t = 5.

$$n_{i+1,\,t+1} = n_{i,\,t}P_{i,\,t} \qquad i = 0, 1 \ldots k \tag{A15.2}$$

Inverse projection assumes population closure (zero net migration), so that we can proceed immediately to the second step, repeating the operations just described, and continue until $t = 5$. It will be noted that the failure to take migration into account causes serious inaccuracies at the beginning of the projection, but that the data in figures A15.1 and A15.2 converge thereafter, though significant discrepancies remain even at $t = 5$.

Back projection was designed to overcome, or at least to reduce inaccuracies arising from two weaknesses in inverse projection. First, it was essential to develop a technique capable of estimating net migration flows since few historical populations were uninfluenced by the effects of migration, especially over long periods of time. Second, inverse projection entails specifying an initial population size and age structure. The former can only be estimated where population closure is assumed and the latter involves making assumptions about the prevailing levels of fertility and mortality at a time when any such estimates are likely to be subject to wide margins of uncertainty. We therefore preferred to move backwards in time from a date at which the size and age structure of the population were known tolerably accurately using a reliable census. It will become clear that this reversal of the normal direction of population projections also permits estimates of period and cohort migration to be made, thus solving the first problem also.

We may begin by noting that if initially the effects of migration are ignored the relationship between one age structure and its predecessor can be redefined from equation A15.2 as

$$n_{i-1,\,t-1} = n_{i,\,t}/P_{i-1,\,t-1} \qquad i = 1, 2 \ldots k \tag{A15.3}$$

Equation A15.3 does not, however, define the final age group, $n_{k,t-1}$, as it is assumed that there is a zero probability of survival beyond age group k. As a result the following equation only determines the selection of a unique survivorship level from the family of such levels if a way can be found of estimating $n_{k,t-1}$. Assuming this is possible, we can select a life table that satisfies

$$D_{t-1} = \sum_{i=1}^{k} n_{i,\,t}(1.0 - P_{i-1,\,t-1})/P_{i-1,\,t-1} + n_{k,\,t-1} \tag{A15.4}$$

It will be seen that $(1 - P)/P$ represents the ratio between the mortality and survivorship rates between successive 'censuses' and when an age group at time t is multiplied by this ratio the product will equal the number of deaths occurring between t and $t-1$, the next earliest 'census'. Solving for $P_{i-1,t-1}$ allows equation A15.3 to be used to estimate the age structure at the previous 'census', but this is only achieved on the implicit assumption that natural increase is the sole cause of population change. Since the population cannot be assumed to be closed, we can do no more than to define the size of a combined estimate of two unknowns. Expressed in aggregate terms

$$(N_{t-1} - M_{t-1}) = N_t + D_{t-1} - B_{t-1} \tag{A15.5}$$

The inclusion of a migration term means that the behaviour of the system can no longer be determined in a straightforward way from the series of births and deaths alone. A method must be found to estimate M_{t-1} and its distribution by age if age structural information for a series of 'censuses' stretching back from the starting census is to be obtained.

Although other solutions to this problem are possible, experiment suggested that the best solution could be obtained by exploiting the fact that the system is constrained in a cohort as well as a period sense. Equation A15.4 represents a period constraint; the period total of deaths is given as part of the input data. However, in addition, any given age group $n_{i,t}$ must eventually, moving backward in time, expand to equal the birth cohort B_{t-i} from which it sprang, by gaining its appropriate share of deaths and net migrants at each period. Thus there is also a cohort constraint which permits the combined total of deaths and net migrants to be estimated for each age group.

For illustration, we can return to table A15.2 and rewrite the set of relationships as

$$n_{0,t} = \{[(n_{k,t+3} + c_3 C_t)/P_{2,t+2} + c_2 C_t]/P_{1,t+1} + c_1 C_t\}/P_{0,t} + c_0 C_t$$

or   (A15.6)

$$1{,}050 = \{[(198.1 + 0.0(30))/0.6 + 0.0(30)]/0.6 + 0.8(30)\}/0.55 + 0.2(30)$$

To exploit the possibility of estimating migration in this way in the course of back projection, it is clearly necessary to be able to forecast mortality in order to obtain the P values for an equation comparable to A15.6.

One possible solution to the problem of forecasting mortality is to use the known history of mortality later in time than the initial census point to make a statistical projection of its probable course moving further back in time. Such a solution is open not only to the objection that secular changes in mortality were not always smooth or predictable, but also that the haphazard incidence of severe epidemic mortality in the early modern period invalidates the assumptions on which any statistical projection must be based. Despite these objections, the method has proved capable of producing very accurate results for countries where there is independent evidence of population totals and age structure over long periods of time. Test results for Norway, Sweden, and Finland show that their population histories can be recovered successfully from birth and death totals alone using this method.[4] It appears to be particularly well suited to cases where the level of net migration was high and variable.

Where net migration was a less important component of population change, however, as in England or France, better results can be obtained by using the death series itself as an indicator of mortality change over the period for which mortality levels must be predicted. Since the totals of deaths are not independent of the size and age structure of the population, however, they cannot be used directly.

It is convenient at this point to provide a worked example of back projection in order to show how the forecasting of mortality is carried out, and to draw together the loosely connected points that have been made above by giving them operational definition. The totals shown in bold type in figure A15.3 represent the information drawn from figure A15.1 which we can assume to be known.

In order to convert death totals into estimates of mortality levels over the forecast period, it is first necessary to estimate the population totals and age structures to which they must be related. Initial estimates of population totals are made by subtracting natural increase from the current 'census' total and assuming that the current proportion of net migrants holds constant over $k + 1$ periods backwards in time (an estimate of the population size for the period t-k-1 must also be made for reasons that

4. We hope in due course to publish details of these exercises and an assessment of the alternative methods of forecasting mortality separately.

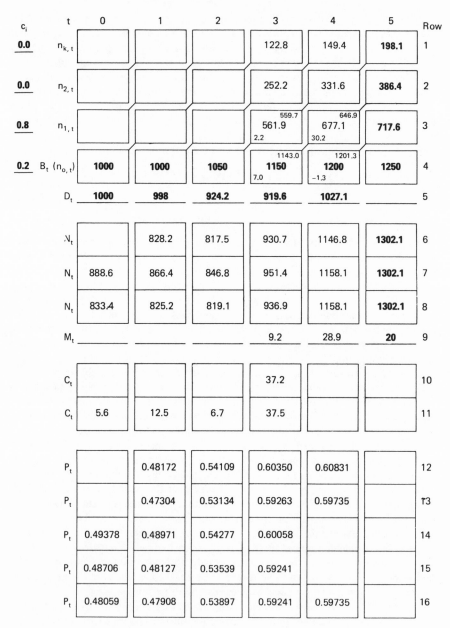

Figure A15.3: Results of the first back-projection pass

will become apparent when the problem of estimating $n_{k,\,t-1}$, the highest age group, is discussed). It is assumed at this stage that the age structure of the population did not change during the forecast period.

We therefore have, for example,

$$\hat{N}_{t-1} = (N_t - B_{t-1} + D_{t-1}) . N_t/(N_t - M_t) \tag{A15.7}$$
$$= (1,302.1 - 1,200 + 1,027.1) . 1,302.1/(1,302.1 - 20)$$
$$= 1,146.8$$

and this is repeated recursively until we obtain

$$828.2 = (817.5 - 1,000 + 998) . 1,302.1/(1,302.1 - 20)$$

These estimates have been entered in row 6 of figure A15.3. To derive estimates of mortality levels at each of the $k + 1$ periods, we use the proportionate age structure that obtained at time t in conjunction with equation A15.4. For example, if $P_4 = 0.6$ then $(1 - P)/P = 0.6666$ and

$$\hat{D}_4 = 717.6(0.6666) + 386.4(0.6666) + 198.1(0.6666) + n_{k, 4} \tag{A15.8}$$

To obtain an estimate of $n_{k,4}$ (the highest age group, all of whom die in the period) we exploit the fact that if any two cohorts have the same mortality experience and are exposed to the same age-specific net migration rates, then their relative sizes at any age will depend only on the ratio of their birth cohort sizes. As a first approximation to the size of the highest age group $(n_{k,t-1})$, therefore, we can write

$$n_{k, t-1} = n_{k, t} . B_{t-k-1}/B_{t-k} \tag{A15.9}$$
$$= 198.1 \times (1,000/1,050)$$
$$= 188.7$$

From equation A15.8 it is evident that $P_4 = 0.6$ would then imply 1,057 deaths, whereas $P_4 = 0.7$ implies 747 deaths. Making due allowance for the fixed number of deaths at $n_{k,t-1}$ it is then possible to estimate P_4 by linear interpolation between $(1.0 - 0.6)/0.6$ and $(1.0 - 0.7)/0.7$ and then solving to obtain P. In this simplified form of back projection since $P = P_{0,t} = P_{1,t} = P_{2,t}$ the same result can, of course, be obtained more easily and directly by solving for P where

$$(1 - P)/P = (D_{t-1} - n_{k,t-1})/N_t = (1,027.1 - 188.7)/1,302.1 = 0.64388.$$

In a full back projection using a family of complex life tables, however, no such simple solution is possible and the interpolation method just described has to be followed. It should be noted, incidentally, that in our illustration $n_{k,t-1}$ is very large in relation to the total of deaths at younger ages. In a back projection relating to a 'real' population deaths in this age group (the age group 90–4) would form only a tiny fraction of all deaths and would therefore have only a very slight influence on the choice of mortality level. In this respect, therefore, the example given in figure A15.3 is highly misleading.

The same procedure used to estimate P_4 can be used for earlier periods, maintaining the assumption that the relative age structure at earlier 'censuses' is the same as that of the current period. Thus, for example, to obtain an estimate of P_3 we may begin by trying $P_3 = 0.6$ and equation A15.8 becomes

$$\hat{D}_3 = 717.6(1,146.8/1,302.1) (0.6666) + 386.4(1,146.8/1,302.1) (0.6666)$$
$$+ 198.1(1,146.8/1,302.1) (0.6666) + 188.7(1,146.8/1,302.1) \tag{A15.10}$$
$$= 930.7$$

By interpolation between $P_3 = 0.6$ and $P_3 = 0.7$, we find that $P_3 = 0.60350$ gives 919.6. The rest of row 12 is completed in the same way to give preliminary estimates of the mortality history of all age groups in the initial census (N_5) and its predecessors.

We are now in a position to re-estimate D_4 in equation A15.8 making allowance for differential mortality in estimating $n_{k,4}$, the highest age group. In the simple version of back projection used here for illustration this can be done directly by using the mortality levels set out out on row 12 of figure A15.3. In the full version a more complex algorithm is needed because where full life tables with widely differing age-specific death rates are used survivorship is modified in a more complex way with any change of level and therefore the selection of any given mortality level for P_4 affects $n_{k,4}$ and modifies the total of deaths to be allocated to N_5, those living at t_5. A mortality level must therefore be found whose joint effect on these two variables is to produce a total of deaths, $\hat{D}_4$, that equals the known total (1,027). The search for the appropriate survivorship level proceeds by interpolation much as before, and at each step in the search the mortality levels for earlier periods can be calculated directly because they stand in the same ratio to earlier estimates as the new estimate of P_4 does to its earlier estimate. This is because the set of levels possesses internal consistency since they are based on the same age structure and period migration rate. Thus when trying alternative values for the $(1 - P)/P$ expression used in equation A15.8, row 12 is rescaled to preserve its internal consistency by

$$\hat{P}_{t-j-1} = \left(\frac{\hat{P}_{t-1}}{P_{t-1}}\right) \cdot P_{t-j-1} \qquad j = 1, 2 \ldots k \tag{A15.11}$$

For example setting $P_4 = 0.6$ would convert the row 9 values to 0.4751, 0.5337, 0.5953, and 0.6000.

Equation A15.9 then becomes

$$n_{k,4} = 198.1 \times \left(\frac{1,000 \times 0.4751 \times 0.5337 \times 0.5953}{1,050 \times 0.5337 \times 0.5953 \times 0.6000}\right) = 149.4 \tag{A15.12}$$

By interpolation the appropriate level of survivorship is found to be 0.59735 and the P_t are rescaled appropriately and entered as row 13 in figure A15.3. In this example $n_{k,4}$ remains 149.4 with the new survivorship level but this is not necessarily the case in the full version of back projection, and it is for this reason that the more complex method of estimation is required.[5]

A start can now be made in the estimation of net migration levels. Using equation A15.3 and $P_4 = 0.59735$ we get estimates at $t = 4$ of the size of each age group before taking migration into account ($n_{k,4}$ has already been found): $n'_{0,4} = 1,201.3$, $n'_{1,4} = 646.9$, $n'_{2,4} = 331.6$. In the simplified back-projection system used here for illustration, migration only affects two age groups. Migration in the youngest age group ($n'_{0,4}$) can be calculated directly as the difference between the estimated size of the birth cohort and the number of births that occurred ($-1.3 = 1,200 - 1,201.3$), but those who migrated between age groups 2 and 1 (entering $n'_{1,4}$) must be calculated

---

5. It will be noted that the size of $n_{k,4}$ could be set by direct calculation by reducing its related birth cohort by the intervening survivorship ratios. To do so, however, would mean placing reliance on the *absolute* survivorship levels, which is likely to be more prone to error than using *relative* levels as in equation A15.12. The latter method also reduces the volatility of the estimates of the size of the final age groups.

It will also be noted that although the population totals and sub-totals are presented after rounding, the survivorship levels are presented in much greater precision to make it easier to appreciate the effects of the re-estimations of the levels after successive passes through the data.

by rearranging an equation similar to equation A15.6. The age-group totals before migration is taken into account, and the migration totals are shown in small type as 'corner' totals in figure A15.3 in the box in which their sum is printed in larger type. The cohort migration for $n'_{1,4}$ is given as

$$C_3 = \left(B_3 - \frac{n'_{1,4}}{P_{0,3}}\right) \bigg/ \left(\frac{c_1/(c_0 + c_1)}{P_{0,3}} + c_0/(c_0 + c_1)\right) \qquad (A15.13)$$

$$= (1{,}150 - 646.9/0.59263) \bigg/ \left(\frac{0.8/(0.2+0.8)}{0.59263} + 0.2/(0.2+0.8)\right)$$

$$= 37.7$$

and the period share is equal to

$$c_1 C_3 = 0.8(37.7) = 30.2$$

The numerator in equation A15.13 represents the discrepancy between the current cohort size and its birth total after accounting for the intervening mortality history. The denominator is a correction term that is always greater than or equal to unity by definition. It is necessary because back projection is recursive, and does not solve all estimation problems simultaneously. As a result, those individuals who enter as migrants in one period form part of the cohort at earlier stages in its history. Thus 1 migrant added to $n'_{1,4}$ will become $1/0.59263$ persons in $n'_{0,3}$ if the survivorship estimate is correct, and an allowance must also be made for migration in the youngest age group, $n'_{0,3}$. This is covered by the final term in the denominator.[6] Put another way, the numerator in equation A15.13 only accounts for those deaths attributable to survivors in the cohort present at time $t=4$. The equation is designed to capture the way in which migrants who return to the system 'expand' as they grow younger in parallel with the expansion of the pool of those who did not migrate.

It should be noted in relation to net migration flows that back projection treats all migration, whether in or out, as occurring on the first day of any inter-censal period (that is, when moving backward in time deaths are allocated over the age groups before net migrants are added or subtracted). In this connexion it is also appropriate to stress that although the P values calculated in back projection are referred to as survivorship ratios, they are not identical with the survivorship ratios which can be calculated from a life table, but they should be regarded rather as transition ratios used in moving between adjacent 'censuses'.

As a result of obtaining the migration estimates produced by equation A15.13 the 'census' total at $t=4$ can be recalculated, and proves to amount to 1,158.1. The period total of net emigrants M_4 is found to be 28.9. The new population and migration totals call for a revision of the population totals in row 6 of figure A15.3 and they are re-estimated from equation A15.7 and placed in row 7. The sequence of operations that comprised the first step from $t=5$ to $t=4$ is now repeated exactly for $t=4$ to $t=3$. The preliminary estimates of survivorship levels based on the age

6. To ensure that all the estimated cohort migration is accounted for in an equation of the A15.13 type the relevant cohort migration proportions are rescaled to sum to 1 at each step. If, for example, the schedule were 0.6, 0.2, 0.2, 0.0, then $c_1/(c_0+c_1)$ would be $0.2/(0.6+0.2)=0.25$ and $c_0/(c_0+c_1)$ would be $0.6(0.6+0.2)=0.75$. In such a case, however, unlike the present example, the pairs of c values bracketed together in the denominator would not equal 1.

structure at t=4 are placed in row 14. After re-estimating the $n_{k,3}$ age group (the highest age group) to reflect the changed mortality estimates a survivorship level of $P_3 = 0.59241$ is obtained to match the recorded total of 919.6 deaths and the levels of row 14 are rescaled as row 15. The period total of net emigrants is calculated after the distribution of the total of inter-censal deaths between the several age groups.

No further steps can be taken in the example shown in figure A15.3 because the birth cohort of $n_{k,2}$ is unknown. However, the estimates of N_t and P_t for periods 0, 1, and 2 have been outmoded and can be re-estimated using the age structure and net migration proportion found at t=3. These estimates are placed in rows 8 and 16, the latter augmented by the levels for the two complete steps.

It will be evident that the estimates made at each step as the back projection progresses are based on assumptions about the history of the population at earlier periods which become outdated as the successive steps are taken. In conventional population projections the future is conditional on the past alone because of a one-way temporal causality, 'the arrow of time', but in back projection each step taken is influenced both by the future and by a changing view, or prediction, of the past. In the example given in figure A15.3 this is evident from the way in which estimates of N_t and P_t have to be updated at each step. Nor is the future fixed except at dates later than the starting point of the back projection (the future in back projection is, of course, analogous to the past in a conventional forward projection). The age group totals in populations between the current 'census' and the initial census from which the back projection departs are all conditional only, since the assumptions on which their calculation was based may not be realized as the back projection progresses. At the end of the first back-projection pass through the data, therefore, there will be many internal inconsistencies in the estimates it has produced.

For example, even though the period constraints and the cohort constraints on the combined effect of mortality and net migration for each age group are satisfied for each period, the results may not satisfy equations of the type shown as A15.6 when they are taken together. This inconsistency is apparent in figure A15.3 in the period distribution of emigrants from cohort B_3, the only cohort with a complete migration history in our brief example. The age-specific ratio is actually 0.19 : 0.81, whereas all the period calculations were based on a schedule ratio of 0.2 : 0.8. This is only a modest discrepancy (it can be much more substantial in other instances). If equation A15.13 is re-estimated from the final observed age group in the cohort we find

$$C_3 = \left(1{,}150 - \frac{386.4}{0.59241 \times 0.59735}\right) \bigg/ \left(\frac{0.8(0.2 + 0.8)}{0.59241} + 0.2(0.2 + 0.8)\right)$$

$$= 37.5$$

compared with a total of 37.2 (30.2 + 7.0) in figure A15.3, which was derived from two steps in the program having different estimates of P_3 (0.59263 and 0.59241).

Such inconsistencies raise the question of how to make best use of the information they contain. Our strategy has been to introduce iteration into the estimation procedure in recognition of the fact that the inconsistencies arise because as the first pass progresses backwards through the data it constantly outdates earlier estimates. The information available is more reliable when the program reaches any given 'census' date than at a distance since estimates of N and P will have improved. Further passes through the data are therefore made, designed both to avoid a simple repetition of the 'mistakes' of the first pass and to achieve a greater degree of internal consistency than could be gained in the first pass.

In the second pass the information about survivorship levels which was the output of the first pass is used as input data, together with the totals of cohort migration which

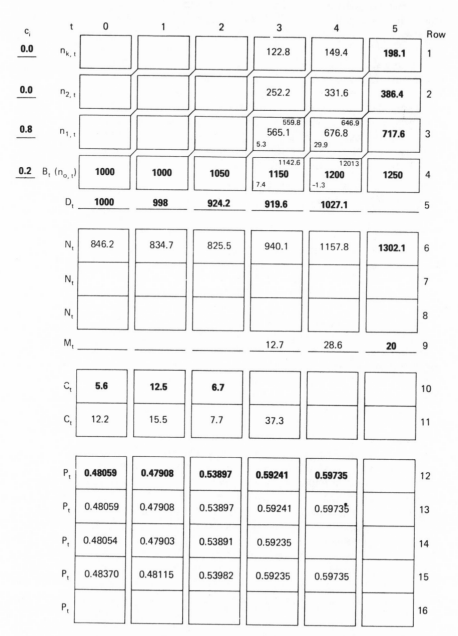

Figure A15.4: Results of the second back-projection pass

are consistent with them (the former are in row 16 of figure A15.3; the latter are in row 11 and were derived from an equation in the form of A15.13 in the same manner as the C_3 total of 37.5 which was described above). That the latter is forced to match the former reflects our view that mortality is the dominant member of the pair and is directly constrained by the data. This implies, of course, that the degree of error in the initial estimates of migration is likely to prove greater than in the parallel mortality estimates.

In figure A15.4 the new input data are again shown in bold type. The P_t in row 12 allow us to dispense with preliminary estimates based on a fixed age structure and a constant migration proportion, and we can turn directly to the estimation of P_4. Since there are now estimates of cohort migration totals, the assumption that $n_{k,t}$ and $n_{k,t-1}$ experienced the same age-specific migration proportions can be dropped. As before the program proceeds by interpolation between survivorship levels in seeking to find the new P_4. For example, as a first step in trying to match the D_4 total of deaths (1,027.1), the mortality levels of row 12 are rescaled in accordance with equation A15.11 and equation A15.12 emerges in a modified form as

$$n_{k,4} = 198.1 \left(\frac{\{[1,000 - 0.2(12.5)] \times 0.48121 - 0.8(12.5)\} \times 0.54136 \times 0.59504}{\{[1,050 - 0.2(6.7)] \times 0.54136 - 0.8(6.7)\} \times 0.59504 \times 0.60000} \right)$$

$$= 149.4$$

The appropriate survivorship level is found to be 0.59735, the same as in the first pass. Indeed in this highly simplified example all the P values in row 13 are the same as the input values of row 12, but all the age-group totals whose size is affected by net migration and therefore partly determined by the forecast levels of P will change because the input estimate of P_3 (0.59241) differs from the estimate used when the calculation was last made in the first pass (0.59263). After two steps we have the direct mortality estimates for P_4 and P_3, 0.59735 and 0.59235, but the estimates for the three preceding 'census' dates, although they have been rescaled as necessary, are still dependent for their relative values on the age structure and migration proportion at $t=3$ on the first pass. To update these estimates of P we return to the indirect method of mortality estimation. Row 6 gives the estimated populations and row 14 the associated survivorship estimates, augmented by the direct estimates from the first two steps of the second pass. Finally, the cohort migration totals are recalculated to match the mortality levels and entered in row 11.

As a result of the changes to estimates of population and migration made in the course of the second pass, the degree of internal consistency in the age-specific cohort migration ratio of C_3 is improved. It now stands at 0.198 : 0.802. When a third pass is made, as shown in figure A15.5 the changes in the N_t, P_t, and C_t compared to the second pass are much smaller than was the case between the first and second passes. The system is rapidly stabilizing and would change little if further passes were made. It has become internally consistent.

There are, of course, substantial differences between the example used here to illustrate the accounting methods used in back projection and the full back projection system. The latter is inevitably far more complex since 19 five-year age groups are employed (0–94 years),[7] and because the family of life tables used reflects the

---

7. The first age group, 0–4, however, is split in the conventional manner into two parts, 0–1 and 1–4, when moving backwards from the 5–9 age group.

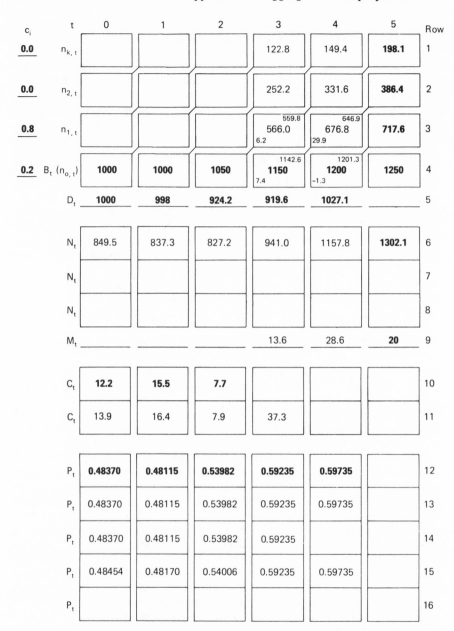

Figure A15.5: Results of the third back-projection pass

empirical patterning of death rates by age, rather than the artificially simple
assumptions of the life tables of table A15.1. Again net migration affects all the age
groups up to age 45 and requires a correspondingly elaborate age-specific schedule.
The example was confined to two full steps in each pass which restricts its ability to
modify the output of the first pass; and so on. Nevertheless the main features of the

detailed *modus operandi* of back projection can be grasped from a consideration of figures A15.3 to A15.5 and the accompanying text.

A more general view of the overall logical structure of back projection is provided by the 'flow chart' in figure A15.6, which illustrates the sequence of steps followed by the full system as it tracked back 330 years from the 1871 census in the manner described in chapter 7. The description of each individual step is necessarily brief, but cross-references have been provided to the equations discussed in the example above where the estimating and calculating procedures have been more fully specified.

The derivation of measures of fertility and mortality

We turn now to a description of the derivation of demographic measures from the data produced by back projection. The methods used are based on standard procedures for estimation in cases where the distribution of births and deaths by age is unknown. They require that the series of births and deaths should first be re-grouped into quinquennial blocks centring on a 'census'; for example, the block centring on the 1871 census runs from 1 July 1868 to 30 June 1873. This is in contrast with their grouping for back projection when the quinquennial blocks run between 'census' dates.

Mortality measurement begins by deriving a series of m_xs for each 'census'.[8] A family of m_x tables can be obtained directly from the sets of q_xs in table A14.5, which form the basis of the 'English' life table system, by using Reed-Merrell conversion factors.[9] Linear interpolation in the m_xs is used to select a mortality level that produces a total of deaths equal to the annual average of deaths during the quinquennial period centring on the 'census' in question. The specification of the appropriate level enables all the other life table measures defined in appendix 14 to be derived by standard methods.[10]

In the same way that totals of deaths are allocated to age groups by a family of life tables, totals of births can be allocated to the age groups 15–9 to 45–9 by the use of an appropriate fertility schedule. Coale and Demeny provide empirically based fertility schedules with mean ages at maternity equal to 27, 29, 31, and 33 years.[11] For reasons discussed elsewhere[12] we have chosen 32 years as an appropriate mean age at maternity to use in the main back projection exercise,[13] and this was obtained by interpolation between the schedules for 31 and 33 years to give the proportional distribution of births by age group shown in table A15.3. The application of such a schedule, which relates to female births only, requires knowledge of the number of women in each age group and the number of female births. Neither was directly available from the output of back projection but both could be estimated. The first was obtained by constructing a family of female life tables using the method described in appendix 14, and basing the set on the third English life table in the same way as with the set for the sexes combined. Using these it is possible to calculate the proportion of survivors in each 'census' age group who were women. In order to do this we have assumed that there was a constant sex ratio at birth of 105 (i.e. 105 males per 100

8. For a definition of m_x, see appendix 14, p. 713.
9. The factors used were those reproduced by Pressat. See appendix 14, fn. 16 for additional details.
10. The methods used are those described by Keyfitz and Flieger, *Population*, pp. 127–39.
11. Coale and Demeny, *Regional model life tables*, p. 30.
12. See above, pp. 233–5.
13. The effect of making other assumptions about the mean age at maternity may be seen in figure 7.7.

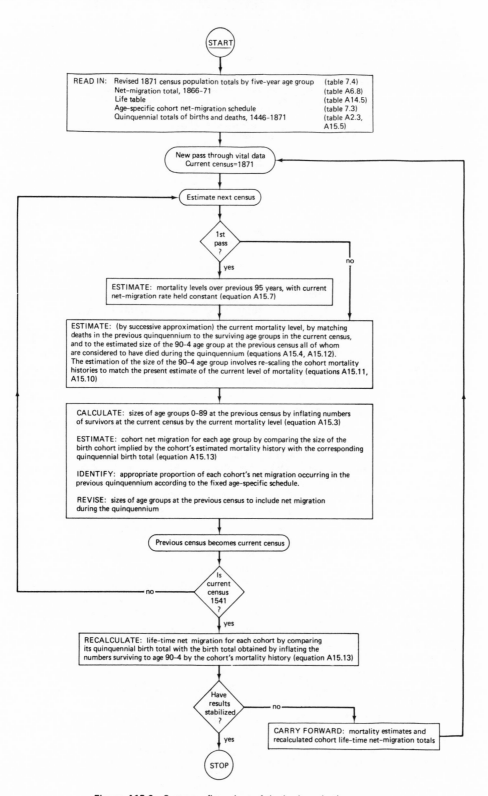

Figure A15.6: Summary flow chart of the back-projection program

Table A15.3: A fertility schedule with a mean age at maternity of 32 years

Age group	Proportionate share of births
15–9	0.0250
20–4	0.1275
25–9	0.2525
30–4	0.2650
35–9	0.2000
40–4	0.1075
45–9	0.0225
	1.0000

Source: Coale and Demeny, *Regional model life tables*, p. 30.

females), and in the absence of any firm data we have further assumed that net emigration rates were the same for both sexes and can therefore be excluded from the calculation, even though this latter assumption is clearly unwarranted.[14] We have also assumed, of course, that the mortality levels estimated for the sexes combined apply equally to the female population, so that if, for example, mortality was at level 7 in a particular cohort as a whole, it was also at level 7 in the female part of the cohort.

Applying the maternity schedule given in table A15.3 to the estimated total of women in each child-bearing age group of a 'census' gives a total of female births that is consistent with a GRR equal to unity. The average annual total of female births that took place in each quinquennial period can be obtained by multiplying the observed total of births by 100/205. The resulting total divided by the total of births which represents a GRR of unity will provide an estimate of the prevailing level of the GRR.

Using the age-specific female fertility rates consonant with a GRR of unity (i.e. the age-specific proportions shown in table A15.3 divided by 5), and a knowledge of the prevailing level of the GRR, the prevailing age-specific female fertility rates may be obtained. These in turn permit the calculation of the NRR using the female life table appropriate to the current level of mortality for the sexes combined. The intrinsic growth rate, r, may then also be calculated, using data from the fertility and mortality schedules that have already been derived as appropriate.[15]

Gross reproduction rates and expectations of life at birth can also be calculated on a cohort rather than a period basis using the data obtained from the operations just described. For each five-year birth cohort a cohort life table can be constructed by following the appropriate diagonal of q_xs through the sets of period rates. Thus a cohort life table for the birth cohort of time t would be derived from the period rates $_5q_{0,t}, _5q_{5,t+5}, _5q_{10,t+10} \cdots _5q_{90,t+90}$, with any derivative measures calculated in the normal way. The last quinquennial birth cohort whose history can be covered completely is that centred on 1781 (i.e. that of 1779–83). Similarly, using female cohort life tables and the appropriate female age-specific fertility rates cohort fertility measures can also be constructed. Since the fertile period is assumed to end at age 49, the last quinquennial cohort GRR that can be obtained from the back projection data is that for the birth cohort centred on 1826 (i.e. that of 1824–8).

14. See above, pp. 118–22, 218–28.
15. The net reproduction and intrinsic growth rates were derived using the methods described in Shryock and Siegel, *Methods and materials of demography*, pp. 315–8.

Testing the technique of back projection

Adequate testing of the set of algorithms which comprise back projection presents great difficulties. Systematic tests of the major assumptions embodied in the model, even if taken singly rather than in combination, would require the commitment of very large human and computing resources. We have undertaken a limited amount of testing under three main heads – simulation tests, sensitivity tests, and empirical tests – using data from countries that have long runs of good demographic data so that the results obtained by back projection can be effectively monitored.

The results of a number of sensitivity tests are reported in chapter 7 in connexion with the presentation of the main empirical findings of back projection. They cover the degree to which the results are affected by alternative assumptions about the totals in the birth and death series, about the mortality and net migration schedules, and about the size of the age group 90–4 in the initial census (which has a special importance because it is the base total from which all other $n_{k,t}$s are derived by 'chaining').[16]

The simulation and empirical tests were too extensive to be reported here in full.[17] The simulation tests took the form of forward projection of the type used in this appendix followed by back-projection runs that attempted to recover the population and migration totals from the birth and death series. The results of the simulation tests were in the main satisfactory. They showed, for example, that back projection can cope successfully with abrupt changes in mortality level or in population trends, though, as might be expected, it is not able to do justice to sudden, sharp peaks in period net migration, even when it may successfully estimate total net migration over lengthier periods.

Empirical testing of back projection is only possible where information about fertility, mortality, and migration, as well as reliable birth and death series, are available over long periods of time. Testing of this type, therefore, has had to be confined largely to Scandinavian examples, and back-projection runs using Norwegian, Swedish, and Finnish data have been made with encouraging results. Once again, a full description of the data sets and results would be out of place here. It may be of interest, however, to present in summary form an example of this third form of testing.

The population history of the city of Stockholm presents a particularly severe test for back projection because Stockholm's population was far less 'closed' than that of any national population. At all times migration has supplied all or most of the city's growth. There are birth and death series for Stockholm from 1721 onwards which makes it possible to run back as far as 1815 in a back projection (birth and death totals stretching back 95 years before each census date in back projection are necessary in order to permit the estimation of the size of the 90–4 age group introduced at the top of the age pyramid in each step taken by the program). Between 1815 and 1940, the period covered in the back projection, the city's population increased by 517,554 from 72,989 to 590,543, but the surplus of births over deaths during the same period was only 58,392.[18]

Figures A15.7 and A15.8 show in summary form the results obtained by back

16. See above, pp. 269–84.
17. We hope to deal with both simulation and empirical tests at greater length in a separate publication.
18. The data on births, deaths, and population totals were taken from *Statistisk Årsbok för Stockholms Stad* 1913, table 20, pp. 81–5.

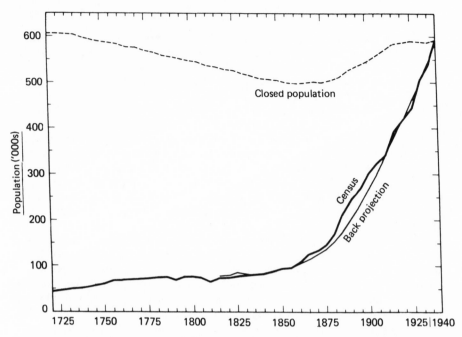

Figure A15.7: A back projection of the population of Stockholm
1815–1940

Source: The census totals and estimates were taken from the
Statistisk Årsbok för Stockholms Stad 1913, table 20
pp. 81–5.

projection compared with the official data. The upper line of figure A15.7 shows the path which would have been traced out moving backwards from 1940 had the population been closed (obtained by adding deaths and subtracting births from the starting population). Its path emphasizes the scale of the problem created by the very high level of net immigration. The two figures show clearly that back projection was generally successful in identifying the path of population growth, but that the use of a fixed age schedule of net cohort migration caused it to fail to pick up the very marked short-term fluctuations in totals of net immigration (the net migration schedule used was based on data for the 1890s for all Swedish towns;[19] the family of life tables employed was the Princeton model North set). Both the fluctuations in migration and the effect of mortality crises had a powerful influence in modifying the age structure of the population of Stockholm from time to time in ways that back projection by its nature is unlikely to mirror effectively. Nevertheless, as may be seen in table A15.4, the broad outlines of age structure are tolerably well reflected in the back projection data, even in 1820, the earliest date at which census and back-projection data on age structure can be compared.

During the period 1815 to 1940 Stockholm's population grew eight-fold and predominantly by migration. The fact that the back-projection population total in

19. *Emigrationsutredningen*, Bilaga V (Stockholm), p. 17*, table 20.

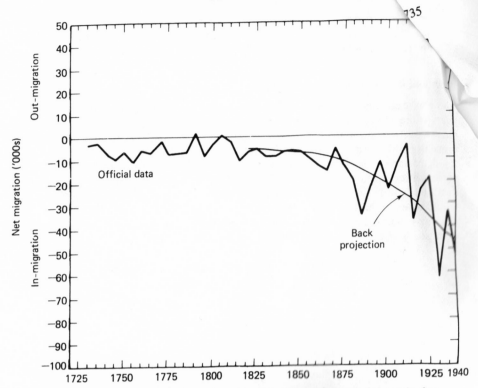

Figure A15.8: Net migration into Stockholm (quinquennial totals for periods ending at the years indicated)

Source: The migration totals labelled 'official data' are inferences drawn from the population totals and totals of births and deaths published in the *Statistisk Årsbok för Stockholms Stad 1913*, table 20, pp.81–5.

Table A15.4: A comparison of age data for Stockholm in 1820 drawn from the census and from back projection (percentages of the total population in each age group)

	Census	Back projection
0–4	8.2	10.1
5–9	7.5	7.9
10–9	13.7	14.2
20–9	22.9	19.3
30–9	18.2	16.7
40–59	21.8	23.6
60 and over	7.8	8.1
Total population	75 569	79 822

Source: Statistisk Årsbok för Stockholm Stad 1913, table 23, p. 91.

is less than 6 per cent different from the census total at that date constitutes
ng evidence of its capacity to deal satisfactorily even with data sets which *prima
cie* appear intractable.

Birth and death totals before 1541

As we have already noted, birth and death totals extending back over a period of 95
years before any given date must be obtained if back projection is to reach that date
since the estimation of the highest age group, 90–4, at each 'census' depends upon
preceding birth and death series of this length. Since we wished to obtain estimates of
the demographic characteristics of the population of England from the beginning of
parochial registration onwards, it was necessary to invent quinquennial birth and
death totals from 1446 onwards so that the first estimates of fertility and mortality
would relate to the five-year period centring on 1541.[20]

There is no available evidence that can much reduce the arbitrariness of any such
exercise. The totals used are shown in table A15.5. They were constructed in

Table A15.5: Annual totals of births and deaths
in the quinquennia before 1541 used in back
projection

	Births ('000s)	Deaths ('000s)
1446–51	72	72
1451–6	72	72
1456–61	72	72
1461–6	72	72
1466–71	72	72
1471–6	72	70
1476–81	73	71
1481–6	75	70
1486–91	75	71
1491–6	76	71
1496–1501	77	72
1501–6	77	73
1506–11	79	71
1511–6	83	75
1516–21	84	72
1521–6	88	67
1526–31	94	75
1531–6	96	82
1536–41	100	87

conformity with three main assumptions. First, the recovery in population totals after
the large falls of the later fourteenth and early fifteenth centuries did not begin until
after 1471.[21] Second, population growth should be modest until early in the sixteenth
century but thereafter should accelerate to a rate broadly similar to that obtaining later

20. Parochial registration began, of course, in 1538, but the earliest 'census' is in 1541, and the next
earliest quinquennial block of data therefore covers the period 1536–41 and must include a substantial
period before parochial registration had begun.
21. See Hatcher, *Plague, population*, p. 63; Gottfried, 'Population, plague', p. 36.

in the sixteenth century, that is about 0.6 per cent per annum. Third, throughout the whole period before 1541 the population was treated as closed with no net migration (the program constrained net migration to be zero before 1541). The birth and death totals shown in table A15.5 imply population growth conforming to these assumptions. They produce a total increase of population of 610,000 between 1471 and 1541. If therefore the back-projection population total for 1541 were precisely accurate (2.774 million), this would imply a population total of 2.164 million before growth began. Some attempt was made to match the level of natural increase in each quinquennium after 1471 to the mortality conditions that may have prevailed, using Creighton's consolidation of available descriptive evidence as a guide.[22] It is for this reason that natural increase totals fluctuate rather than changing smoothly from one quinquennium to the next, but it is very doubtful whether the fluctuations that have been imposed are well founded.

The series of birth and death totals shown in table A15.5 have no greater claim to accuracy than many other such series might have. For example, it would have been possible to secure the same cumulative surplus of births over deaths between 1471 and 1541 by employing higher quinquennial totals of births and deaths and 'freezing' the pre-1471 totals at a higher level also. It will be noted that the series used imply that in the mid fifteenth century birth rates were somewhat below the levels reached in the mid sixteenth century but that death rates were substantially higher. Different assumptions would be equally plausible provided that the resultant birth and death rates were roughly equal.

If the pre-1541 totals of births and deaths were changed, the findings of back projections for the period after 1541 would also change. Estimates of population size and age structure, and consequently of fertility and mortality, are increasingly affected by the pre-1541 series as the back-projection program nears 1541. It would require drastic changes to the pre-1541 series totals to make more than a marginal difference to back projection results, except for the two or three decades immediately after 1541, but it should not be forgotten that all the data produced by back projection are subject to greater uncertainty before about 1580 than at other times because of the arbitrary choice of pre-1541 birth and death totals. Estimates of migration are particularly prone to error because migration is in a sense a residual. Since only the age groups under age 45 are affected by net migration movements, it is only earlier than about 1580 that the influence of any mis-estimation of pre-1541 birth and death totals will directly involve distortion of the path followed by back projection. Indirectly the effects of mis-estimation can involve later periods, however, though to a lesser extent.[23]

Finally, it may be convenient to note that the other empirical inputs to the English back projection are listed elsewhere in this volume. The annual totals of births and deaths may be found in table A2.3. The age structure of the starting population in 1871 is given in table 7.4, except that those aged 95 and over were excluded to suit the back-projection life-table system, and the total of those aged 90–4 was slightly altered.[24] The family of life tables used was the 'English' set whose q_xs are given in table A14.5: from these the other standard functions and special measures such as

22. Creighton, *Epidemics in Britain*, I, chapters 4–6.
23. The extent to which the assumption about the totals of events before 1541 can affect population estimates even after 1636 (the first date at which their size directly affects a computation of the size of the age group 90–4) is discussed above, p. 283.
24. For a discussion of the reasons for changing the total of those aged 90–4 see above, pp. 204–5.

$(1-P)/P$ used in back projection were all derived.[25] The cohort net migration schedule is set out in table 7.3, while the initial net migration data used in the first pass to calculate the ratio $N_t/(N_t-M_t)$ (see equation A15.7) were taken from table A6.8 (the level of net migration prevailing in 1871 was assumed to be that found during the decade 1861–71).

---

25. Some additional information about the life table functions may be found in appendix 14, pp. 713–4.

Appendix 16

Econometric procedures

Ronald Lee

When dealing with monthly data, a 121-point moving average was used to divide into the original series, $Z_{1,t}$, to form a new series, $Z_{2,t}$:

$$Z_{2,t} = 121 \cdot Z_{1,t} \bigg/ \sum_{i=-60}^{60} Z_{1,t+i} \tag{A16.1}$$

Note that series transformed in this way will have an average value very close to unity. The properties of this transform are discussed in Granger and Hughes, and Lee.[1]

If this transformation is performed on series of births ($b_{1,t}$), deaths ($d_{1,t}$), marriages ($m_{1,t}$), and prices ($p_{1,t}$), then new series of short run fluctuations will be obtained, which we may label $b_{2,t}$, $d_{2,t}$, $m_{2,t}$ and $p_{2,t}$. Consider the relation between short-run fluctuations in births and prices. This can be represented as:

$$b_{2,t} = \alpha + \sum_{i=0}^{n} \beta_i p_{t-i} + \varepsilon_t \tag{A16.2}$$

The α is a constant term, and the β_i are distributed lag coefficients.

If $b_{2,t}$ and $p_{2,t}$ are monthly series, then the constant term should actually vary by calendar month, in order to express that portion of the seasonal variance in births not explained by seasonal price variation. Rather than including such seasonal constants, the procedure used here was to difference the data series to form $b_{3,t}$ and $p_{3,t}$ as follows:

$$b_{3,t} = b_{2,t} - b_{2,t-12} \tag{A16.3}$$

Inspection of A16.2 will confirm that when this is done, the new series will be related by:

$$b_{3,t} = \sum_{i=0}^{n} \beta_i p_{3,t-i} + \eta_t \tag{A16.4}$$

where the β_i are unchanged, but the constant (or seasonal constants) has disappeared, and the error term has changed. This procedure will correct quite well for seasonal patterns even if they change over time.[2]

It is very likely that the error term in each of these equations is autoregressive; that is, error values are likely to be systematically related to earlier error values in the series. For example, if fertility is higher in month t than predicted on the basis of prices, it will probably also be higher than predicted in month t+ 1. This renders the

1. Granger and Hughes, 'A new look at some old data' and Lee, 'Comment on "A new look"'
2. Box and Jenkins, *Time series analysis*, pp. 300–6.

ordinary least squares estimate of the β_i inefficient (although they are unbiased and consistent), and it leads to biased estimates of the confidence regions for the estimated coefficients. To correct for second-order autoregressive disturbances, the iterative Cochrane–Orcutt procedure was used.[3] Because of the 12-month differencing to remove seasonality, there will also be 12th-order autoregression in the disturbances, but this should not have an important effect on the results.

With annual data, we will let n in equations A16.2 and A16.4 be four years; this allows the price level of a given year to influence fertility up to five years later. With the length of the data series available, estimating this many β_i is no problem. But with monthly data, to allow for effects delayed by five years would require estimating 60 βs, which is prohibitive. Here, the maximum lag with monthly data has been set at 36 months, at the cost of losing information about the demographic rebound, which annual data show to take place two to five years after the initial stimulus. Even with this shorter maximum lag, the estimated coefficients are extremely erratic; they oscillate wildly, and appear quite random despite attaining statistical significance rather frequently. Two methods were used to 'smooth' the estimated β_i, in order to make the underlying pattern discernible. One procedure, which is frankly *ad hoc*, is to form a moving average of the estimated coefficients. Another procedure, with well-established statistical properties, is to assume that the true β_i change smoothly as a function of i, and can therefore be represented as a polynomial in i:

$$\beta_i = \gamma_0 + \gamma_1 i + \gamma_2 i^2 + \ldots + \gamma_q i^q \qquad (A16.5)$$

where q is the prespecified degree of the polynomial. This is called a 'polynomial distributed lag' or 'Almon lag', and it reduces the number of coefficients to be estimated from n+1 to q+1.[4] Here, q has generally been taken to be five, which is high enough to express the expected oscillating demographic echo effects. In one case, each of two segments of the distributed lag was allowed its own polynomial expression. Generally there was an excellent agreement between the results from the moving-average approach and the Almon-lag approach. When the results of the methods differed substantially, it was usually clear that the averaged coefficients were preferable; for example, at the earliest and latest lags, the Almon-lag estimates tended to take on very high or very low values, which is a well-known difficulty with the method. In chapter 9, therefore, only the coefficients smoothed by moving averages are shown in the diagrams, although the Almon-lag results are occasionally referred to.

Equation A16.2 expressed a distributed lag relation between two variables. Often, another distributed lag variable will also be involved, and this has been treated in a similar manner. Sometimes the true structural relations are recursive. If the disturbances in recursive equations are uncorrelated, consistent and asymptotically efficient estimates can be obtained by single-equation methods.[5] This is the assumption underlying the estimated relation of births to adjusted deaths and prices. However, if the disturbances are correlated, biassed estimates of coefficients will result. This was the case with the equation relating births to marriages (with or without deaths and prices included); the problem was dealt with at the stage of interpreting the estimated equations, rather than at estimation, since no alternative procedure, such as instrumental variables, seemed feasible.

3. Kmenta, *Econometrics*, pp. 287–9.
4. Kmenta, *Econometrics*, pp. 492–5.
5. Kmenta, *Econometrics*, p. 586.

Bibliography

The works listed below are not a full or even a select bibliography of English population history in the early modern period. They consist simply of books, articles, and other sources to which reference was made in footnotes and source notes in the book, where only short titles were given. The bibliography is divided into two sections. The first comprises works that can be classified by author's name. Works that cannot be so classified, official sources, and maps are listed in the second section. Since the short titles used in the main body of the book did not include date of publication, where several books and articles by the same author are listed they are given in alphabetical order represented by the key words of the short title.

The following abbreviations of journal titles have been used:

A. A. G. Bijdragen	*Afdeling Agrarische Geschiedenis Bijdragen*
Ag. Hist. Rev.	*Agricultural History Review*
Amat. Hist.	*Amateur Historian*
Amer. Hist. Rev.	*American Historical Review*
Amer. Soc. Rev.	*American Sociological Review*
Annales dém. hist.	*Annales de démographie historique*
Annales, E.S.C.	*Annales. Economies, sociétés, civilisations*
B.M.J.	*British Medical Journal*
Bull. soc. dém. hist.	*Bulletin de la société de démographie historique*
Econ. Hist. Rev.	*Economic History Review*
Explor. Econ. Hist.	*Explorations in Economic History*
Geneal. Mag.	*Genealogists' Magazine*
J. Amer. Stat. Ass.	*Journal of the American Statistical Association*
J. Biosoc. Sci.	*Journal of Biosocial Science*
J. Br. Stud.	*Journal of British Studies*
J. Econ. Hist.	*Journal of Economic History*
J. Eur. Econ. Hist.	*Journal of European Economic History*
J.I.H.	*Journal of Interdisciplinary History*
J.R.S.S.	*Journal of the Royal Statistical Society*
L.P.S.	*Local Population Studies*
Med. Hist.	*Medical History*
Met. Mag.	*Meteorological Magazine*
Milbank Mem. Fd Qu.	*Milbank Memorial Fund Quarterly*
P.P.	*Parliamentary Papers*
P. & P.	*Past and Present*
Pop.	*Population*
Pop. Index	*Population Index*
Pop. Stud.	*Population Studies*
Proc. Amer. Phil. Soc.	*Proceedings of the American Philosophical Society*
Qu. J. Econ.	*Quarterly Journal of Economics*
Qu. J. Roy. Met. Soc.	*Quarterly Journal of the Royal Meteorological Society*
Rev. Econ. Stat.	*Review of Economic Statistics*

Scand. Econ. Hist. Rev.   *Scandinavian Economic History Review*
Soc. Hist.   *Social History*
Trans. Roy. Hist. Soc.   *Transactions of the Royal Historical Society*
U.N.   *United Nations*

Section 1

Note that where the work listed is a chapter within a collaborative volume, only the short title of the volume is given; full details of the volume will be found elsewhere listed under the editor's name.

Abrams, P. and Wrigley, E. A. (eds.), *Towns in societies. Essays in economic history and historical sociology* (Cambridge, 1978).

Adams, J., *Index villaris* (London, 1700).

Appleby, A. B., 'Disease or famine? Mortality in Cumberland and Westmorland', *Econ. Hist. Rev.*, 2nd ser., xxvi (1973), pp. 403–32.

Appleby, A. B., *Famine in Tudor and Stuart England* (Stanford, 1978).

Appleby, A. B., 'Grain prices and subsistence crises in England and France, 1590–1740', *J. Econ. Hist.*, xxxix (1979), pp. 865–87.

Appleby, A. B., 'Nutrition and disease: the case of London 1550–1750', *J.I.H.*, vi (1975), pp. 1–22.

Bailey, N. T. J., *The mathematical theory of infectious diseases and its applications*, 2nd ed. (London, 1975).

Baker-Bates, E. T., 'Influenza', *British encyclopaedia of medical practice*, vii, pp. 129–44.

Bardet, J.-P., 'La démographie des villes de la modernité (XVI\ᵉ–XVIII\ᵉ siècles): mythes et réalités', *Annales dém. hist.*, 1974, pp. 101–26.

Baugh, D. A., 'The cost of poor relief in south-east England, 1790–1834', *Econ. Hist. Rev.*, 2nd ser., xxviii (1975), pp. 50–68.

Beier, A. L., 'Poor relief in Warwickshire, 1630–60', *P. & P.*, xxxv (1966), pp. 77–100.

Beresford, M. W., 'The poll taxes of 1377, 1379 and 1381', *Amat. Hist.*, iii (1958), pp. 271–8.

Berg, F. T., 'Årstidernas inflytelse på dödligheten', *Statistisk Tidskrift*, vii (1879), pp. 87–121.

Berkner, L. K., 'The stem family and the developmental cycle of the peasant household: an eighteenth century Austrian example', *Amer. Hist. Rev.*, lxxvii (1972), pp. 398–418.

Berry, B. M. and Schofield, R. S., 'Age at baptism in pre-industrial England', *Pop. Stud.*, xxv (1971), pp. 453–63.

Beveridge, W. H. and others, *Prices and wages in England*, i, Price tables: mercantile era (London, 1939).

Bickmore, D. P. and Shaw, M. A., *The atlas of Great Britain and Northern Ireland* (Oxford, 1963).

Biraben, J.-N., *Les hommes et la peste en France et dans les pays européens et méditerranéens*, 2 vols. (Paris and the Hague, 1975–6).

Biraben, J.-N., 'Current medical and epidemiological views on plague' in *The plague reconsidered*, pp. 25–36.

Blayo, Y., 'La mortalité en France de 1740 à 1829', *Pop.*, xxx (1975), pp. 123–42.

Blayo, Y., 'Mouvement naturel de la population française de 1740 à 1829', *Pop.*, xxx (1975), pp. 15–64.

Bongaarts J., 'Does malnutrition affect fecundity? A summary of evidence', *Science*, ccviii (1980), pp. 564–9.

Boserup, E., *The conditions of agricultural growth. The economics of agrarian change under population pressure* (London, 1965).

Bourgeois-Pichat, J., 'The general development of the population of France since the eighteenth century', in Glass and Eversley, *Population in history*, pp. 474–506.

Bourgeois[-Pichat], J., 'Le mariage coutume saisonnière', *Pop.*, ɪ (1946), pp. 623–42.

Bourgeois-Pichat, J., 'La mesure de la mortalité infantile', *Pop.*, vɪ (1951), pp. 233–48, 459–80.

Bowden, P., 'Agricultural prices, farm prices, and rents', in Thirsk, *The agrarian history of England and Wales*, pp. 593–695, 814–70 (statistical appendix).

Box, G. and Jenkins, G., *Time series analysis: forecasting and control* (San Francisco, 1970).

Bradley, L., 'An enquiry into seasonality in baptisms, marriages and burials', pt III, 'Burial seasonality', *L.P.S.*, vɪ (1971), pp. 15–31.

Bradley, L., 'Some medical aspects of plague' in *The plague reconsidered*, pp. 11–23.

Braudel, F., *Capitalism and material life 1400–1800* (New York, 1974).

Brent, C., 'Devastating epidemic in the countryside of eastern Sussex between harvest years 1558 and 1640', *L.P.S.*, xɪv (1975), pp. 42–8.

Bricourt, M., Lachiver, M., and Queruel, J., 'La crise de subsistance des années 1740 dans le resort du parlement de Paris', *Annales dém. hist.*, 1974, pp. 281–333.

Bringéus, N.-A., *Arets festseder* (Stockholm, 1976).

Brown, R. L., *Clandestine marriages in London, especially within the Fleet prison, and their effects on Hardwicke's Act, 1753* (unpub. London M.A. thesis, 1972).

Brownlee, J., 'The history of the birth and death rates in England and Wales taken as a whole, from 1570 to the present time', *Public Health*, xxɪx (1915–6), pp. 211–22, 228–38.

Bruneel, C., *La mortalité dans les campagnes: le duché de Brabant au XVIIe et XVIIIe siècles*, 2 vols. (Louvain, 1977).

Bull, G. M. and Morton, J., 'Relationship of temperature with death rates from all causes and from certain respiratory and arteriosclerotic diseases in different age groups', *Age and Ageing*, ɪv (1975), pp. 232–46.

Bulmer, E., 'Dysentery, bacillary (Shigellosis)', *British encyclopaedia of medical practice*, ɪv, pp. 545–73.

Burn, J. S., *The history of the French, Dutch and other protestant refugees settled in England from the reign of Henry VIII to the revocation of the edict of Nantes* (London, 1846).

Burn, R., *The ecclesiastical law*, 8th ed., 4 vols. (London, 1824).

Cairncross, A. K., *Home and foreign investment 1870–1913* (Cambridge, 1953).

Call, J., 'An abstract of baptisms and burials in four parishes of fifty counties in England', *Communications to the Board of Agriculture on subjects relative to the husbandry, and internal improvement of the country*, ɪɪ (1800) pp. 479–93.

Carlsson, G., 'Nineteenth century fertility oscillations', *Pop. Stud.*, xxɪv (1970), pp. 413–22.

Carrier, N. H. and Jeffrey, J. R., *External migration. A study of the available statistics 1815–1950*. General Register Office studies on medical and population subjects, no. 6 (London, 1953).

Carus-Wilson, E. M. (ed.), *Essays in economic history*, ɪ and ɪɪ (London, 1954 and 1962).

Chalklin, C. W. and Havinden, M. A. (eds.), *Rural change and urban growth 1500–1800; essays in English regional history in honour of W. G. Hoskins* (London, 1974).

Chalmers, G., *An estimate of the comparative strength of Great Britain during the present and four preceding reigns* (London, 1786).

Chamberlayne, E., *Angliae notitia; or the present state of England, together with divers reflections upon the antient state thereof*, 5th ed. (London, 1671).

Chambers, J. D., *Population, economy and society in pre-industrial England* (Oxford, 1972).

Chambers, J. D., *The vale of Trent 1670–1800: a regional study of economic change*, Econ. Hist. Rev. supplement, ɪɪɪ (1957).

Charbonneau, H. and Larose, A. (eds.), *The great mortalities: methodological studies of demographic crises in the past* (Liège, n.d.).

Cheney, C.R. (ed.), *Handbook of dates for students of English history* (London, 1945).

Christ, C. F., *et al.*, *Measurement in economics* (Stanford, 1963).

Cipolla, C. M., *Cristofano and the plague. A study in the history of public health in the age of Galileo* (London, 1973).

Cipolla, C. M., *The economic history of world population* ([London], 1962).

Cipolla, C. M., 'Four centuries of Italian demographic development', in Glass and Eversley, *Population in history*, pp. 570–87.

Clapham, J., *A concise economic history of Britain* (Cambridge, 1951).

Clark, P., *English provincial society from the Reformation to the Revolution: religion, politics and society in Kent 1500–1640* (Hassocks, 1977).

Clark, P., 'Migration in England during the late seventeenth and early eighteenth centuries', *P. & P.*, LXXXIII (1979), pp. 57–90.

Clarkson, L. A., *Death, disease and famine in pre-industrial England* (Dublin, 1975).

Clarkson, L. A., *The pre-industrial economy in England* (London, 1971).

Coale, A. J. (ed.), *Economic factors in population growth* (London and Basingstoke, 1976).

Coale, A. J., 'The effects of changes in mortality and fertility on age composition', *Milbank Mem. Fd Qu.*, XXXIV (1956), pp. 79–114.

Coale, A. J., *The growth and structure of human populations* (Princeton, 1972).

Coale, A. J. and Demeny, P., *Regional model life tables and stable populations* (Princeton, 1966).

Cochran, W. G., *Sampling techniques* (New York, 1963).

Coleman, D. C., *The economy of England 1450–1750* (Oxford, 1977).

Coleman, D. C., 'Labour in the English economy of the seventeenth century', *Econ. Hist. Rev.*, 2nd ser., VIII (1956), pp. 280–95.

Conze, W. (ed.), *Sozialgeschichte der Familie in der Neuzeit Europas* (Stuttgart, 1976).

Cornwall, J., 'English country towns in the 1520s', *Econ. Hist. Rev.*, 2nd ser., XV (1962), pp. 54–69.

Cornwall, J., 'English population in the early sixteenth century', *Econ. Hist. Rev.*, 2nd ser., XXIII (1970), pp. 32–44.

Corsini, C., 'Problemi di utilizzazione dei dati dai registri di sepolture e morti', *Problemi di utilizzazione delle fonti di demografia storica* (Comitato italiano per lo studio della demografia storica: atti del seminario 1972–3), (Roma, n.d.), II, pp. 93–136.

Cox, J. C., *The parish registers of England* (London, 1910).

Crafts, N. F. R., 'Average age at first marriage for women in mid-nineteenth century England and Wales: a cross-section study', *Pop. Stud*, XXXII (1978), pp. 21–5.

Crafts, N. F. R. and Ireland, N. J., 'A simulation of the impact of changes in age at marriage before and during the advent of industrialisation in England', *Pop. Stud.*, XXX (1976), pp. 495–510.

Creighton, C., *A history of epidemics in Britain*, 2 vols., reprinted with additional material (London, 1965).

Dalle, D., *De bevolking van Veurne-Ambacht in de 17de en de 18de eeuw* (Brussels, 1963).

Dalrymple, J., *Memoirs of Great Britain and Ireland from the dissolution of the last parliament of Charles II until the sea battle off La Hogue*, 2 vols. (Edinburgh and London, 1771–3).

Daunton, M. J., 'Towns and economic growth in eighteenth century England', in Abrams and Wrigley, *Towns in societies*, pp. 245–77.

Davenant, C., 'An essay upon the probable methods of making a people gainers in the balance of trade' in *The politic and commercial works of that celebrated writer Charles Davenant. LL. D.*, collected and revised by C. Whitworth, 5 vols. (London, 1771).

Davies, O. L., *The design and analysis of industrial experiments* (London, 1963).

Deane P. and Cole, W. A., *British economic growth 1688–1959* (Cambridge, 1962).

del Panta, L., and Livi-Bacci, M., 'Chronology, intensity and diffusion of mortality in Italy, 1600–1850' in Charbonneau and Larose, *The great mortalities*, pp. 69–81.

Deprez, P., 'The demographic development of Flanders in the eighteenth century' in Glass and Eversley, *Population in history*, pp. 608–30.

de Vries, J., *The Dutch rural economy in the golden age, 1500–1700* (New Haven and London, 1974).

de Vries, J., 'Histoire du climat et économie', *Annales, E. S. C.*, xxxii (1977), pp. 198–226.

de Zeeuw, J. W., 'Peat and the Dutch golden age. The historical meaning of energy availability', *A. A. G. Bijdragen*, xxi (Wageningen, 1978), pp. 3–31.

di Comite, L., 'I matrimoni nel XVII secolo', *Problemi di utilizzazione delle fonti di demografia storica* (Comitato italiano per lo studio della demografia storica: atti del seminario 1972–3), (Roma, n.d.), ii, pp. 7–89.

Drake, M., 'An elementary exercise in parish register demography', *Econ. Hist. Rev.*, 2nd ser., xiv (1962), pp. 427–45.

Drake, M., 'Norway', in Lee, *European demography and economic growth*, pp. 284–318.

Drake, M., *Population and society in Norway 1735–1865* (Cambridge, 1969).

Dupâquier, J., 'L'analyse statistique des crises de mortalité' in Charbonneau and Larose, *The great mortalities*, pp. 83–112.

Durand, J., 'The modern expansion of world population', *Proc. Amer. Phil. Soc.*, cxi (1967), pp. 136–59.

Dyer, A. D., 'Seasonality of baptisms: an urban approach', *L. P. S.* (forthcoming).

Dyer, A. D., *The city of Worcester in the sixteenth century* (Leicester, 1973).

Edwards, W. J., 'National marriage data: a re-aggregation of John Rickman's marriage returns', *L. P. S.*, xvii (1976), pp. 25–41.

Edwards, W. J., 'National parish register data: an evaluation of the comprehensiveness of the areal cover', *L.P.S.*, xvii (1976), pp. 16–24.

Engleson, H., *Dysenteriestudien*, Acta Medica Scandinavica, supplementum, lxxxiii (Lund, 1937).

Everitt, A., *Change in the provinces; the seventeenth century*, Univ. of Leicester, Dept of Local History, Occasional Papers (Leicester, 1969).

Everitt, A., 'Farm labourers', in Thirsk, *The agrarian history of England and Wales*, pp. 396–465.

Everitt, A., 'The marketing of agricultural produce' in Thirsk, *The agrarian history of England and Wales*, pp. 466–592.

Eversley, D. E. C., 'A survey of population in an area of Worcestershire from 1660 to 1850 on the basis of parish registers' in Glass and Eversley (eds.), *Population in history*, pp. 394–419.

Fåhraeus, E., 'Om förhållandet mellan de särskilda månaderna i fråga om befolkningens årliga förändringar', *Statistisk Tidskrift*, ii (1864), pp. 223–34.

Farr, W., *English life table* (London, 1864).

Farr, W., *Vital statistics* (London, 1885).

Finlay, R. A. P., 'Gateways to death? London child mortality experience, 1570–1653', *Annales dém. hist.*, 1978, pp. 105–34.

Finlay, R. A. P., *The population of London, 1580–1650* (unpub. Cambridge Ph.D. thesis, 1976).

Firth, C. H., and Rait, R. S., *Acts and ordinances of the Interregnum, 1642–1660*, 3 vols. (London, 1911).

Fisher, F. J., 'Commercial trends and policy in sixteenth century England', in Carus-Wilson, *Essays in economic history*, i, pp. 152–72.

Fisher, F. J., 'Influenza and inflation', *Econ. Hist. Rev.*, 2nd ser., xviii (1965), pp. 120–9.

Fisher, F. J., *Essays in the economic and social history of Tudor and Stuart England* (Cambridge, 1961).

Fleury, M. and Henry, L., *Nouveau manuel de dépouillement et d'exploitation sommaire de l'état civil ancien* (Paris, 1956).

Flinn, M. W., *British population growth 1700–1850* (London, 1970).

Flinn, M. W. *et al.*, *Scottish population history from the seventeenth century to the 1930s* (Cambridge, 1977).

Flinn, M. W., 'The stabilization of mortality in pre-industrial western Europe', *J. Eur. Econ. Hist.*, iii (1974), pp. 285–318.

Flinn, M. W., 'Trends in real wages, 1750–1850', *Econ. Hist. Rev.*, 2nd ser., xxvii (1974), pp. 395–413.

Floud, R. C., (ed.), *Essays in quantitative economic history* (Oxford, 1974).

Floud, R. C., and McCloskey, D. (eds.), *The economic history of Britain since 1700*, 2 vols. (Cambridge, 1981).

Forster, R. and Ranum, O., (eds.), *Biology of man in history* (Baltimore, 1975).

Frere, W. H., and Douglas, C. E., *Puritan manifestoes*, reprinted with new preface by N. Sykes (London, 1954).

Frere, W. H. and Kennedy, W. M., (eds.), *Visitation articles and injunctions of the period of the Reformation*, Alcuin Club Collections, xiv–xvi (1910).

Frisch, R. E., 'Nutrition, fatness and fertility: the effect of food intake on reproductive ability', in Mosley, *Nutrition and human reproduction*, pp. 91–122.

Gabriel, K. R. and Ronen, I., 'Estimates of mortality from infant mortality rates', *Pop. Stud.*, xii (1958), pp. 164–9.

Galenson, D. W., 'British servants and the colonial indenture system in the eighteenth century', *Journal of Southern History*, xliv (1978), pp. 41–66.

Gaunt, D., 'Early Swedish parish records and their background', in S. Pascu (ed.), *Population et société, iii–iv: sources de démographie historique. Les travaux du colloque international de démographie historique, Cluj-Napoca, Septembre 1977* (Cluj-Napoca, 1980).

Gautier, E. and Henry, L., *La population de Crulai* (Paris, 1958).

Gayer, A. D., Rostow, W. W., and Schwartz, A. J., *The growth and fluctuation of the British economy 1790–1850*, 2 vols. (Oxford, 1953).

Gemery, H. A., 'Emigration from the British Isles to the New World, 1630–1700: inferences from colonial populations', *Research in economic history*, v (1980), pp. 179–231.

George, M. D., *London life in the eighteenth century* (London, 1930).

Gibson, E., *Codex iuris ecclesiastici anglicani* (London, 1713).

Gilboy, E. W., 'The cost of living and real wages in eighteenth century England', *Rev. Econ. Stat.*, xviii (1936), pp. 134–43.

Gilboy, E. W., *Wages in eighteenth century England* (Cambridge, Mass., 1934).

Glass, D. V., 'Changes in fertility in England and Wales, 1851 to 1931' in Hogben, *Political arithmetic*, pp. 161–212.

Glass, D. V., 'Notes on the demography of London at the end of the seventeenth century' in Glass and Revelle, *Population and social change*, pp. 275–85.

Glass, D. V., 'Introduction', in Glass and Eversley, *Population in history*, pp. 1–22.

Glass, D. V., 'Marriage frequency and economic fluctuations in England and Wales, 1851 to 1934' in Hogben, *Political Arithmetic*, pp. 251–82.

Glass, D. V., *Numbering the people. The eighteenth century population controversy and the development of census and vital statistics in Britain* (Farnborough, 1973).

Glass, D. V., 'Population and population movements in England and Wales, 1700 to 1850' in Glass and Eversley, *Population in history*, pp. 221–46.

Glass, D. V., 'Two papers on Gregory King', in Glass and Eversley, *Population in history*, pp. 159–220.

Glass, D. V., 'A note on the under-registration of births in Britain in the nineteenth century', *Pop. Stud.*, v (1951), pp. 70–88.

Glass, D. V. and Eversley, D. E. C., (eds.), *Population in history* (London, 1965).

Glass, D. V. and Revelle, R., (eds.), *Population and social change* (London, 1972).

Glasspoole, J., 'Two centuries of rainfall', *Met. Mag.*, LXIII, no. 745 (1928), pp. 1–7.

Gooder, A., 'The population crisis of 1727–30 in Warwickshire', *Midland History*, I (1972), pp. 1–22.

Goodman, L. A., 'Tests based on the movements in and the comovements between *m*-dependent time series', in Christ, *Measurement in economics*, pp. 253–69.

Gottfried, R. S., *Epidemic disease in fifteenth century England: the medical response and the demographic consequences* (Brunswick, 1978).

Gottfried, R. S., 'Population, plague, and the sweating sickness: demographic movements in late fifteenth century England', *J. Br. Stud.*, XVII (1977), pp. 12–37.

Goubert, P., *Beauvais et le Beauvaisis de 1600 à 1730*, 2 vols. (Paris, 1960).

Goubert, P., 'En Beauvaisis: problèmes démographiques du XVII siècle', *Annales, E.S.C.*, VII (1952), pp. 453–68.

Goubert, P., 'La mortalité en France sous l'ancien régime: problèmes et hypothèses', in Harsin and Hélin, *Actes du colloque international*, pp. 79–82.

Goubert, P., 'Recent theories and research in French population between 1500 and 1700', in Glass and Eversley, *Population in history*, pp. 457–73.

Granger, C. W. J. and Hughes, A. O., 'A new look at some old data: the Beveridge wheat price series', *J.R.S.S.*, ser. A, CXXXIV (1971), pp. 413–28.

Griffith, G. T., *Population problems of the age of Malthus* (Cambridge, 1926).

Guillaume, P. and Poussou, J.-P., *Démographie historique* (Paris, 1970).

Habakkuk, H. J., 'The economic history of modern Britain', *J. Econ. Hist.*, XVIII (1958), pp. 486–501.

Habakkuk, H. J., 'English population in the eighteenth century', in Glass and Eversley, *Population in history*, pp. 269–84.

Hair, P. E. H., 'Bridal pregnancy in rural England in earlier centuries', *Pop. Stud.*, XX (1966), pp. 233–43.

Hair, P. E. H., 'Bridal pregnancy in earlier rural England further examined', *Pop. Stud.*, XXIV (1970), pp. 59–70.

Hajnal, H. J., 'Age at marriage and proportions marrying', *Pop. Stud.*, VII (1953), pp. 111–36.

Hakluyt, R., 'Discourse of western planting', in *The original writings and correspondence of the two Richard Hakluyts*, ed. E. G. R. Taylor (Hakluyt Society; London, 1935), II, pp. 211–326.

Hampson, E. M., *The treatment of poverty in Cambridgeshire, 1597–1834* (Cambridge, 1934).

Hansen, M. H., Hurwitz, W. N., and Pritzker, L., 'The accuracy of census results', *Amer. Soc. Rev.*, XVIII (1953), pp. 416–23.

Harsin, P. and Hélin, E., (eds.), *Actes du colloque international de démographie historique* (Liege, 1965).

Hatcher, J., *Plague, population and the English economy, 1348–1530* (London, 1977).

Helleiner, K. F., 'The vital revolution reconsidered', in Glass and Eversley, *Population in history*, pp. 79–86.

Henry, L., 'Étude de la nuptialité après reconstitution de familles', *Bull. soc. dém. hist.*, XXIV (1978), pp. 2–12.

Henry, L., *On the measurement of human fertility* (New York, 1972).

Henry, L., *Manuel de démographie historique* (Geneva and Paris, 1967).

Henry, L., *Population, analysis and models* (London, 1976).

Henry, L. and Blayo, Y., 'La population de la France de 1740 à 1860', *Pop.*, XXX (1975), pp. 71–122.

Henry, L. and Houdaille, J., 'Célibat et age au mariage aux XVIIIe et XIXe siècles en France. I. Célibat définitif. II. Age au premier mariage', *Pop.*, XXXIII (1978), pp. 43–84; XXXIV (1979), pp. 403–42.

Hill, C., *Reformation to industrial revolution* (London, 1969).

Hocking, F., *Starvation* (Sydney, 1969).

Hofsten, E. and Lundström, H., *Swedish population history. Main trends from 1750 to 1970*, Urval, VIII (Stockholm, 1976).

Hogben, L. (ed.), *Political arithmetic* (London, 1938).

Holderness, B. A., ' "Open" and "close" parishes in England in the eighteenth and nineteenth centuries', *Ag. Hist. Rev.*, xx (1972), pp. 126–39.

Holderness, B. A., *Pre-industrial England: economy and society from 1500 to 1750* (London, 1976).

Hollingsworth, T. H., 'The demography of the British peerage', supplement to *Pop. Stud.*, xVIII, no. 2 (1964).

Hollingsworth, T. H., *Historical demography* (London, 1969).

Hollingsworth, T. H., 'Mortality in the British peerage families since 1600', *Pop.*, xxxII (September, 1977) [special number entitled *La mesure des phénomènes démographiques*], pp. 323–52.

Hollingsworth, T. H., 'A preliminary suggestion for the measurement of mortality crises', in Charbonneau and Larose, *The great mortalities*, pp. 21–8.

Hoskins, W. G., 'Early Tudor towns', *Trans. Roy. Hist. Soc.*, vI (1956), pp. 1–19.

Hotelling, H. and Hotelling, F., 'Causes of birth rate fluctuations', *J. Amer. Stat . Ass.*, xxvI (1931), pp. 135–49.

Hotten, J. C., *The original lists of persons of quality; emigrants; religious exiles; political rebels ... and others who went from Great Britain to the American plantations, 1600–1700* (London, 1874).

Houdaille, J., 'Mouvement saisonnier des conceptions en France de 1740 à 1869', *Pop.*, xxxIV (1979), pp. 452–7.

Houdaille, J., 'La population de Boulay (Moselle) avant 1850', *Pop.*, xxII (1967), pp. 1,055–84.

Imhof, A. E., *Aspekte der Bevölkerungsentwicklung in den nördischen Ländern*, 2 vols. (Bern, 1976).

Imhof, A. E., (ed.), *Historische Demographie als Sozialgeschichte: Giessen und Umgebung vom 17 zum 19 Jahrhundert*, 2 vols. (Darmstadt, 1975).

Imhof, A. E., 'Die nicht-namentliche Auswertung der Kirchenbücher von Giessen und Umgebung. Die Resultate', in Imhof, *Historische Demographie*, I, pp. 85–278.

Isichei, E., *Victorian Quakers* (Oxford, 1970).

Johansen, H.-C., *Bevolkningsudvikling og familiestruktur i de 18 århundrede* (Odense, 1975).

Johnston, J. A. 'The impact of the epidemics of 1727–30 in south-west Worcestershire', *Med. Hist.*, xv (1971), pp. 278–92.

Jones, E. L., and Mingay, G. E. (eds.), *Land, labour and population in the industrial revolution* (London, 1967).

Jones, P. E. and Judges, A. V., 'London population in the late seventeenth century', *Econ. Hist. Rev.*, vI (1935), pp. 45–63.

Jones, R. E., *Parish registers and population history: north Shropshire, 1538–1837* (unpub. London Ph.D. thesis, 1973).

Jutikkala, E., 'Finland's population movement in the eighteenth century' in Glass and Eversley, *Population in history*, pp. 549–69.

Kennedy, R. E., *The Irish. Emigration, marriage and fertility* (Berkeley, Los Angeles, and London, 1973).

Kerridge, E., *The agricultural revolution* (London, 1967).

Keyfitz, N., 'Changes in birth and death rates and their demographic effects' in *Rapid population growth: consequences and policy implications*. National Academy of Sciences (Baltimore, 1971), pp. 639– 80.

Keyfitz, N. and Flieger, W., *Population: facts and methods of demography* (San Francisco, 1971).

Keys, A., *et al., The biology of human starvation*, 2 vols. (Minneapolis, 1950).

Kintz, J.-P., 'Aspekte einer städtetypischen demographischen Verhaltens im 17 und 18 Jahrhundert, Strassburg als Beispiel' in Imhof, *Historische Demographie*, ii, pp. 1,049– 57.

Kmenta, J. *Elements of econometrics* (New York, 1971).

Knappen, M. M., *Tudor puritanism* (Gloucester, Mass., 1963).

Knodel, J., 'Breast feeding and population growth', *Science*, cxcviii, (1977), pp. 1,111–5.

Knodel, J., 'Law, marriage and illegitimacy in nineteenth century Germany', *Pop. Stud.*, xx (1967), pp. 279– 94.

Krantz, F. and Hohenberg, P. M. (eds.), *Failed transitions to modern industrial society: Renaissance Italy and seventeenth century Holland* (Montreal, 1975).

Krause, J. T., 'The changing adequacy of English registration' in Glass and Eversley, *Population in history*, pp. 379–93.

Krause, J. T., 'Changes in English fertility and mortality, 1780–1850', *Econ. Hist. Rev.*, 2nd ser., xi (1958), pp. 52–70.

Krause, J. T., 'Some aspects of population change, 1690–1790', in Jones and Mingay, *Land, labour and population*, pp. 187–205.

Kussmaul, A. S., *Servants in husbandry in early modern England* (unpub. Ph.D. thesis, Toronto, 1978).

Ladurie, E. Le Roy, 'Famine amenorrhoea (seventeenth–twentieth centuries)', in Forster and Ranum, *Biology of man in history*, pp. 163–78.

Ladurie, E. Le Roy, *Histoire du climat depuis l'an mil* (Paris, 1967).

Lamb, H. H., *Climate: present, past and future*, 2 vols. (London, 1972–7).

Laslett, P., *Family life and illicit love in earlier generations* (Cambridge, 1977).

Laslett, P., *The world we have lost* (London, 1965).

Laslett, P., Oosterveen, K., and Smith, R. M., (eds.), *Bastardy and its comparative history* (London, 1980).

Laslett, P., and Wall, R., (eds.), *Household and family in past time* (Cambridge, 1972).

Ledermann, S., *Nouvelles tables-types de mortalité* (Paris, 1969).

Lee, R. D., 'Comment on "A new look at some old data: the Beveridge wheat price series"', *J.R.S.S.*, ser.A, cxxxviii (1975), p. 296.

Lee, R. D., *Econometric studies of topics in demographic history* (New York, 1978).

Lee, R. D., 'Estimating series of vital rates and age structures from baptisms and burials: a new technique, with applications to pre-industrial England', *Pop. Stud.*, xxviii (1974), pp. 495–512.

Lee, R. D., 'Methods and models for analysing historical series of births, deaths and marriages' in Lee, *Population patterns in the past*, pp. 337–70.

Lee, R. D., 'Models of pre-industrial population dynamics, with applications to England', in Tilly, *Historical studies of changing fertility*, pp. 155–207.

Lee, R. D., 'Natural fertility, population cycles, and the spectral analysis of births and marriages', *J. Amer. Stat. Ass.*, lxx (1975), pp. 295–304.

Lee, R. D., 'Population in pre-industrial England: an econometric analysis', *Qu. J. Econ.*, lxxxvii (1973), pp. 581–607.

Lee, R. D., (ed.), *Population patterns in the past* (New York, 1977).

Lee, R. D., and Schofield, R. S., 'British population in the eighteenth century' in Floud and McCloskey, *Economic history of England*, i, pp. 17–35.

Lee, W. R. (ed.), *European demography and economic growth* (London, 1979).

Leonard, E. M., *The early history of English poor relief* (Cambridge, 1900).

Leridon, H., *Human fertility* (Chicago, 1977).

Leridon, H., *Natalité, saisons et conjoncture économique* (Paris, 1973).

Lesthaeghe, R., 'Nuptiality and population growth', *Pop. Stud.*, xxv (1971), pp. 415–32.

Lesthaeghe, R., and van de Walle, E., 'Economic factors and fertility decline in France and Belgium' in Coale, *Economic factors in population growth*, pp. 205–28.

Levine, D., *Family formation in an age of nascent capitalism* (New York and London, 1977).

Levine, D., 'The reliability of parochial registration and the representiveness of family reconstitution', *Pop. Stud.*, xxx (1976), pp. 107–22.

Linde, H. 'Die Bedeutung von Th. Robert Malthus für die Bevölkerungs-soziologie', *Zeitschrift für die gesamte Staatswissenschaft*, cxviii (1962), pp. 705–20.

Linde, H., 'Generative strukturen', *Studium Generale*, xii (1959), pp. 343–50.

Livi Bacci, M., ' Can anything be said about demographic trends when only aggregate vital statistics are available?', in Lee, *Population patterns in the past*, pp. 311–36.

Loschky, D. J. and Krier, D. F., 'Income and family size in three eighteenth century Lancashire parishes: a reconstitution study', *J. Econ. Hist.*, xxix (1969), pp. 429–48.

Lyndwood, W., *Provinciale seu constitutiones Angliae* [first published 1481] (Oxford, 1679).

Macfarlane, A., *Reconstructing historical communities* (Cambridge, 1977).

Machin, R., 'The great rebuilding: a reassessment', *P. & P.*, lxxvii (1977), pp. 33–56.

Mackenroth, G., *Bevölkerungslehre. Theorie, Soziologie und Statistik der Bevölkerung* (Berlin, 1953).

McKeown, T., *The modern rise of population* (London, 1976).

McKeown, T., and Record, R. G., 'Reasons for the decline of mortality in England and Wales during the nineteenth century', *Pop. Stud.*, xvi (1962), pp. 94–122.

McNeill, W. H., *Plagues and peoples* (New York, 1976).

Malthus, T. R., *An essay on the principle of population* (London, 1798). reprinted for the Royal Economic Society (London, 1926).

Manley, G., 'Central England temperatures: monthly means 1659 to 1973', *Qu. J. Roy. Met. Soc.*, C (1974), pp. 389–405.

Marshall, J., *Mortality in the metropolis* (London, 1832).

Marshall, J. D., 'Social structure and wealth in pre-industrial England', *Proceedings of British Association for the Advancement of Science*, Section H, Anthropology, 1977.

Mathias, P., *The first industrial nation. An economic history of Britain 1700–1914* (London, 1969).

Medick, H., 'The proto-industrial family economy: the structural function of the household and family during the transition from peasant society to industrial capitalism', *Soc. Hist.*, no. 3 (1976), pp. 291–315.

Megaw, J. W. D., 'Typhus fevers and other rickettsial fevers', *British encyclopaedia of medical practice*, xii, pp. 390–414.

Menard, R., 'From servants to slaves: the transformation of the Chesapeake labor system', *Southern Studies*, xvi (1977), pp. 355–90.

Mendels, F., 'Proto-industrialisation: the first phase of the industrialisation process', *J. Econ. Hist.*, xxxii (1972), pp. 241–61.

Mendels, F., 'Industry and marriages in Flanders before the industrial revolution', in P. Deprez (ed.), *Population and economics* (Winnipeg, 1970) (Proceedings of the Fourth Congress of the International Economic History Association, 1968, section V), pp. 81–93.

Mirowski, P., 'The plague and the penny-loaf: the disease–dearth nexus in Stuart and Hanoverian London' (unpub. MS, Dept of Economics, Univ. of Michigan, 1976).

Mitchell, B. R. and Deane, P., *Abstract of British historical statistics* (Cambridge, 1962).

Moheau, M., *Recherches et considérations sur la population de la France, 1778*, with an introduction and index by R. Gonnard (Paris, 1912).

Montgomery, D. C. and Johnson, L. A., *Forecasting and time series analysis* (New York, 1976).

Morris, R. J., *Cholera 1832: the social response to an epidemic* (London, 1976).

Mosley, H. W., *Nutrition and human reproduction* (New York, 1978).

Mueller, E. 'The economic value of children in peasant agriculture' in Ridker, *Population and development*, pp. 98–153.

Nef, J. U., *The rise of the British coal industry*, 2 vols. (London, 1932).

Nicholson, C. D. P., 'Some early emigrants to America', *Geneal. Mag.*, xii (1955–8), pp. 11–4, 48–53, 89–92, 122–5, 157–62, 191–6, 228–33, 269–72, 303–9, 340–4, 379–82, 404–6, 440–2, 478–82, 516–20; xiii (1959–61), pp. 10–3, 46–50, 78–80, 105–8, 145–8, 175–9, 209–12, 236.

Nie, N. H. *et al.*, *SPSS: statistical package for the social sciences*, 2nd ed. (New York, 1975).

Ohlin, P. G., 'Mortality, marriage and growth in pre-industrial populations', *Pop. Stud.*, xiv (1961), pp. 190–7.

Ohlin, P. G., 'No safety in numbers: some pitfalls of historical statistics' in Floud, *Quantitative economic history*, pp. 59–78.

Ohlin, P. G., *The positive and the preventive check: a study of the rate of growth of pre-industrial populations* (unpub. Harvard Ph.D. thesis, 1955).

Ormrod, D., 'Dutch commercial and industrial decline and British growth in the late seventeenth and early eighteenth centuries' in Krantz and Hohenberg, *Failed transitions*, pp. 36–43.

Oswald, N., 'Epidemics in Devon, 1538–1837', *Transactions of the Devon Association for the Advancement of Science*, cix (1977), pp. 73–116.

Outhwaite, R. B., 'Food crises in early modern England: patterns of public response' in M. W. Flinn (ed.), *Proceedings of the Seventh International Economic History Conference* (Edinburgh, 1978), pp. 367–74.

Palliser, D. M., 'Dearth and disease in Staffordshire, 1540–1670', in Chalklin and Havinden, *Rural change and urban growth*, pp. 54–75.

Parkes, A. S., 'Environmental influences on human fertility', *J. Biosoc. Sci.*, supplement 3, Biological aspects of human fertility (1971), pp. 13–28.

Patten, J. H., 'The hearth taxes, 1682–1689', *L.P.S.*, vii (1971), pp. 14–27.

Patten, J. H., *English towns 1500–1700* (Folkestone, 1978).

Pentland, H. C., 'Population and labour growth in Britain in the eighteenth century', *Proceedings of the Third International Conference of Economic History*, Munich 1965, section VII, Demography and economy (Paris, 1972), pp. 157–89.

Perrenoud, A., *La population de Genève du seizième au début du dix-neuvième siècle*, 2 vols. (Geneva, 1979–).

Phelps Brown, E. H. and Hopkins, S. V., 'Seven centuries of building wages', in Carus-Wilson, *Essays in economic history*, ii, pp. 168–78.

Phelps Brown, E. H. and Hopkins, S. V., 'Seven centuries of the prices of consumables compared with builders' wage rates', in Carus-Wilson, *Essays in economic history*, ii, pp. 179–96.

Phythian-Adams, C., 'Urban decay in late medieval England', in Abrams and Wrigley, *Towns in societies*, pp. 159–85.

Pollard, A. F., *The history of England from the accession of Edward VI to the death of Elizabeth* (London, 1910).

Poole, R. L., *A history of the Huguenots of the dispersion* (London, 1880).

Potter, J., 'The growth of population in America 1700–1860' in Glass and Eversley, *Population in history*, pp. 631–88.

Pressat, R., *Demographic analysis* (London, 1972).

Razzell, P. E., *The conquest of smallpox: the impact of inoculation on smallpox mortality in eighteenth century Britain* (Firle, 1977).

Razzell, P. E., 'The evaluation of baptism as a form of birth registration through cross-matching census and parish register data', *Pop. Stud.*, xxvi (1972), pp. 121–46.

Rebaudo, D., 'Le mouvement annuel de la population française rurale de 1670 à 1740', *Pop.*, xxxiv (1979), pp. 589–606.

Redford, A., *Labour migration in England, 1800–1850*, 2nd ed., revised and edited by W. H. Chaloner (Manchester, 1964).

Reinhard, M., Armengaud, A., and Dupâquier, J., *Histoire générale de la population mondiale* (Paris, 1968).

Ricardo, D., *On the principles of political economy and taxation* ([London], 1971).

Rich, E. E., 'The population of Elizabethan England', *Econ. Hist. Rev.*, 2nd ser., iii (1950), pp. 247–65.

Ridker, R. G. (ed.), *Population and development* (Baltimore, 1976).

Rogers, C. D., *The Lancashire population crisis of 1623* (Manchester, 1975).

Russell, J. C., *British medieval population* (Albuquerque, 1948).

Ryder, N. B., 'Notes on stationary populations', *Pop. Index*, xli (1975), pp. 3–28.

Rye, W., 'Dutch refugees in Norwich', *Norfolk Antiquarian Miscellany*, iii (Norwich, 1887), pp. 185–248.

Sauvy, A., *Théorie générale de la population*, 2 vols. (Paris, 1956–9).

Schofield, R. S., 'An anatomy of an epidemic: Colyton, November 1645 to November 1646' in *The plague reconsidered*, pp. 95–126.

Schofield, R. S., 'Comment on correspondence on age at baptism in pre-industrial England', *L.P.S.*, xix (1977), p. 52.

Schofield, R. S., ' "Crisis" mortality', *L.P.S.*, ix (1972), pp. 10–22.

Schofield, R. S., 'The relationship between demographic structure and environment in pre-industrial western Europe', in Conze, *Sozialgeschichte*, pp. 147–60.

Schofield, R. S., 'Dimensions of illiteracy, 1750–1850', *Explor. Econ. Hist.*, x (1973), pp. 437–54.

Schofield, R. S., 'Microdemography and epidemic mortality: two case studies' in Sundin and Söderlund (eds.), *Time, space and man*, pp. 53–67.

Schofield, R. S., *Parliamentary lay taxation, 1485–1547* (unpub. Cambridge Ph.D. thesis, 1963).

Schofield, R. S., 'Perinatal mortality in Hawkshead, Lancashire, 1581–1710', *L.P.S.*, iv (1970), pp. 11–6.

Schofield, R. S., 'Representativeness and family reconstitution', *Annales dém. hist.*, (1972), pp. 121–5.

Schofield, R. S., 'Sampling in historical research', in Wrigley, *Nineteenth century society*, pp. 146–90.

Schofield, R. S. and Wrigley, E. A., 'Infant and child mortality in England in the late Tudor and early Stuart period' in Webster, *Health, medicine and mortality*, pp. 61–95.

Schofield, R. S. and Wrigley, E. A., 'Remarriage intervals and the effect of marriage order on fertility', in J. Dupâquier et al. (eds.), *Marriage and remarriage in past populations* (London, 1981), pp. 211–27.

Scott Smith, D., 'A homeostatic demographic regime: patterns in west European family reconstitution studies', in Lee, *Population patterns in the past*, pp. 19–52.

Scrimshaw, N. S., Taylor, C. E., and Gordon, J. E., *Interactions of nutrition and infection* (Geneva, 1968).

Sharlin, A., 'Natural decrease in early modern cities: a reconsideration', *P. & P.*, LXXIX (1978), pp. 126–38.

Sheail, J., *The distribution of regional wealth in England as indicated in the lay subsidy returns of 1524/5*, 2 vols. (unpub. London Ph.D. thesis, 1968).

Short, T., *A comparative history of the increase and decrease of mankind* (London, 1767), reprinted with an introduction by R. Wall (London, 1973).

Short, T., *New observations on city, town and country bills of mortality* (London, 1750), reprinted with an introduction by R. Wall (London, 1973).

Shrewsbury, J. F. D., *A history of bubonic plague in the British Isles* (Cambridge, 1970).

Shryock, H. S., Siegel, J. S., and associates, *The methods and materials of demography*, condensed edition by E. G. Stockwell (London, 1976).

Skipp, V., *Crisis and development. An ecological case study of the Forest of Arden, 1570–1640* (Cambridge, 1978).

Slack, P., 'Mortality crises and epidemic disease in England, 1485–1610', in Webster, *Health, medicine and mortality*, pp. 9–59.

Slicher van bath, B. H., *The agrarian history of western Europe, 500–1850* (London, 1963).

Smith, A. E., *Colonists in bondage* (Gloucester, Mass., 1965).

Smith, T. C., 'Pre-modern economic growth: Japan and the West', *P. & P.*, LX (1973), pp. 127–60.

Snow, K. R., *Insects and disease* (London, 1974).

Sogner, S., 'Aspects of the demographic situation in seventeen parishes in Shropshire, 1711–60', *Pop. Stud.*, XVII (1963), pp. 126–46.

Spencer, B., 'Size of population and variability of demographic data, 17th and 18th centuries', *Genus*, XXXII (1976), pp. 11–42.

Spengler, J. J., 'Demographic factors and early modern economic development', in Glass and Revelle, *Population and social change*, pp. 87–98.

Steel, D. J., *National index of parish registers*, I, Sources of births, marriages and deaths before 1837 (London, 1968); II, Sources for nonconformist genealogy and family history (London, 1973).

Stone, L., *The causes of the English revolution, 1529–1642* (London, 1972).

Strype, J., *Annals of the Reformation*, 4 vols. (Oxford, 1824).

Sundbärg, G., *Bevölkerungsstatistik Schwedens, 1750–1900* (Stockholm, 1907), reprinted with preface and vocabulary in English, Urval, III (Stockholm, 1970).

Sundin, J. and Söderlund E., (eds.), *Time, space and man* (Stockholm, 1979).

Sutherland, I., 'When was the Great Plague? Mortality in London, 1563 to 1665' in Glass and Revelle, *Population and society*, pp. 287–320.

Tate, W. E., *The parish chest* (Cambridge, 1960).

Taylor, A. J., 'The taking of the census, 1801–1951', *B.M.J.*, 7 April 1951, I, pp. 715–20.

Teitelbaum, M. S., *The British fertility decline* (Princeton, forthcoming).

Teitelbaum, M. S., 'Birth under-registration in the constituent counties of England and Wales: 1841–1910', *Pop. Stud.*, XXVIII (1974), pp. 329–43.

Thirsk, J. (ed.), *The agrarian history of England and Wales, 1500–1640*, IV (Cambridge, 1967).

Thirsk, J., *Economic policy and projects. The development of a consumer society in early modern England* (Oxford, 1978).

Thirsk, J., 'The farming regions of England' in Thirsk, *The agrarian history of England and Wales*, pp. 1–112.

Thirsk, J., 'Industries in the countryside' in Fisher, *Tudor and Stuart England*, pp. 70–88.

Thirsk, J., 'Sources of information on population', *Amat. Hist.*, IV (1959), pp. 129–32, 182–4.

Thirsk, J. and Cooper, J. P. (eds.), *Seventeenth century economic documents* (Oxford, 1972).

Thomas, B., *Migration and economic growth* (Cambridge, 1954).

Thomas, D. S., *Social and economic aspects of Swedish population movements, 1750–1933* (New York, 1941).

Thompson, F. M. L., 'Nineteenth century horse-sense', *Econ. Hist. Rev.*, 2nd ser., xxix (1976). pp. 60–79.

Tierney, B., *Medieval poor law; a sketch of canonical theory and its application to England* (Berkeley, 1959).

Tilly, C. (ed.), *Historical studies of changing fertility* (Princeton, 1978).

Tooke, T., *A history of prices and of the state of the circulation*, 6 vols. (London, 1838–57).

Tooke, T., *Thoughts and details on the high and low prices of the last thirty years* (London, 1823).

Tromp, S. W., *Medical biometeorology* (Amsterdam, 1963).

Tucker, G. S. L., 'English pre-industrial population trends', *Econ. Hist. Rev.*, 2nd ser., xvi (1963), pp. 205–18.

Tucker, G. S. L., 'Population in history', *Econ. Hist. Rev.*, 2nd ser., xx (1967), pp. 131–40.

Tukey, J. W., *Exploratory data analysis* (Reading, Mass., 1977).

Turpeinen, O., 'Fertility and mortality in Finland since 1750', *Pop. Stud.*, xxxiii (1979) pp. 101–14.

Utterström, G., 'Climatic fluctuations and population problems in early modern history', *Scand. Econ. Hist. Rev.*, iii (1955), pp. 3–47.

van de Walle, E., 'Alone in Europe: the French fertility decline until 1850', in Tilly, *Historical studies of changing fertility*, pp. 257–88.

van de Walle, E., *The female population of France in the nineteenth century* (Princeton, 1974).

van der Woude, A. M., *Het Noorderkwartier*, 3 vols. (Wageningen, 1972).

Vincent, P., 'La mortalité des vieillards', *Pop.*, vi (1951), pp. 181–204.

von Tunzelmann, G. N., 'Trends in real wages, 1750–1850, revisited', *Econ. Hist. Rev.*, 2nd ser., xxxii (1979), pp. 33–49.

Wall, R., 'Mean household size in England from printed sources', in Laslett and Wall, *Household and family*, pp. 159–204.

Wareing, J., 'Some early emigrants to America, 1683–4. A supplementary list', *Geneal. Mag.*, xviii (1976), pp. 239–46.

Webster, C. (ed.), *Health, medicine and mortality in the sixteenth century* (Cambridge, 1979).

Welch, E., 'Nonconformist registers: a general survey' in Steel, *National index of parish registers*, ii, pp. 507–18.

Whiteman, E. A. O., 'The census that never was: a problem in authorship and dating', in Whiteman (ed.), *Statesmen, scholars and merchants: essays in eighteenth century history presented to Dame Lucy Sutherland* (Oxford, 1973), pp. 1–16.

Whiteman, E. A. O., *The Compton census, 1676: a critical edition* (Cambridge, forthcoming).

Widén, L., 'Mortality and causes of death in Sweden during the 18th century', *Statistisk Tidskrift*, 3rd ser., xiii (1975), pp. 93–104.

Wilson, C., *England's apprenticeship, 1603–1763* (London, 1965).

Wright, A. P., *British calendar customs: England*, 3 vols. (London, 1936–40).

Wrigley, E. A., 'Baptism coverage in early nineteenth century England: the Colyton area', *Pop. Stud.*, xxix (1975), pp. 299–316.

Wrigley, E. A., 'Births and baptisms: the use of Anglican baptism registers as a source of information about the numbers of births in England before the beginning of civil registration', *Pop. Stud.*, xxxi (1977), pp. 281–312.

Wrigley, E. A., 'Checking Rickman', *L.P.S.*, xvii (1976), pp. 9–15.

Wrigley, E. A., 'Clandestine marriage in Tetbury in the late seventeenth century', *L.P.S.*, x (1973), pp. 15–21.

Wrigley, E. A. (ed.), *An introduction to English historical demography* (London, 1966).

Wrigley, E. A., 'Family limitation in pre-industrial England', *Econ. Hist. Rev.*, 2nd ser., xix (1966), pp. 82–109.

Wrigley, E. A., 'Fertility strategy for the individual and the group', in Tilly, *Historical studies of changing fertility*, pp. 135–54.

Wrigley, E. A., 'A simple model of London's importance in changing English society and economy 1650–1750', *P. & P.*, xxxvii (1967), pp. 44–70.

Wrigley, E. A., 'Mortality in pre-industrial England: the example of Colyton, Devon, over three centuries', *Daedalus*, xcvii (1968), pp. 546–80.

Wrigley, E. A. (ed.), *Nineteenth century society: essays in the use of quantitative methods for the study of social data* (Cambridge, 1972).

Wrigley, E. A., *Population and history* (London, 1969).

Wrigley, E. A., 'The process of modernisation and the industrial revolution in England', *J.I.H.*, iii (1972), pp. 225–59.

Wrigley, E. A., 'The supply of raw materials in the industrial revolution', *Econ. Hist. Rev.*, 2nd ser., xv (1962), pp. 1–16.

Wrigley, E. A., 'Some problems of family reconstitution using English parish register material: the example of Colyton', *Proceedings of the Third International Conference of Economic History*, Munich 1965, Section VII, Demography and Economy (Paris, 1972), pp. 199–221.

Wynne-Edwards, V. C., *Animal dispersion in relation to social behaviour* (Edinburgh and London, 1962).

Yasumoto, M., 'Industrialisation and population change in a Yorkshire parish (Methley), 1780–1830', research paper (1979) deposited in Cambridge Group library.

Section 2

Note that the list of county maps used is placed at the end of this section.

Age and sex patterns of mortality. Model life tables for under-developed countries. U.N., Dept of Economic and Social Affairs, Population Studies no. 22 (New York, 1955).

Annual Report of the Registrar General for England and Wales, 1838– (London, 1839–)

Bidrag till Sveriges officiela statistik, 1856– (Stockholm, 1863–).

British encyclopaedia of medical practice, ed. Lord Horder, 12 vols., 2nd ed. (London, 1950–2).

Census [the following is a list of the sections of censuses of England and Wales taken between 1801 and 1911 to which reference is made in this book]

1801 Census. Enumeration, *P.P.* 1802, VII

Observations on the results, *P. P.* 1802, VII

Parish registers, *P. P.* 1802, VI

1811 Census. Enumeration, *P. P.* 1812, XI

Parish registers, *P. P.* 1812, XI

Preliminary observations, *P. P.* 1812, XI

1821 Census. Enumeration abstract, *P. P.* 1822, XV

Parish register abstract, *P. P.* 1822, XV
Preliminary observations, *P. P.* 1822, XV
1831 Census. Enumeration abstract, vols I and II, *P.P.* 1833, XXXVI and XXXVII
Parish register abstract, *P.P.* 1833, XXXVIII
Preface, *P.P.* 1833, XXXVI
1841 Census. Age abstract, *P.P.* 1843, XXIII
Enumeration abstract, *P.P.* 1833, XXXII
1851 Census. Population tables I. Numbers of the inhabitants, vols. I and II, *P.P.* 1852–3, LXXXV and LXXXVI
Population tables II. Ages, civil condition, occupations and birth place of the people, vols. I and II, *P.P.* 1852–3, LXXXVIII, parts I and II.
Religious workshop (England and Wales), *P. P.* 1852–3, LXXXIX
1861 Census. General report, *P.P.* 1863, LIII, part I
Population tables II. Ages, civil condition, occupations and birth places of the people, *P.P.*, 1863, LIII, parts I and II.
1871 Census. General report, *P.P.* 1873, LXXI, part II
Population abstracts. Ages, civil condition, occupations, and birth places of the people, *P.P.* 1873, LXXI, part I.
1881 Census. Ages, condition as to marriage, occupations and birthplaces of people, *P.P.* 1883, LXXX.
1891 Census. Ages, condition as to marriage, occupations, birthplaces, and infirmities, *P.P.* 1893–4, CVI.
1901 Census. General report, *P.P.* 1904, CVIII.
Summary tables. Area, houses and population; also population classified by ages, condition as to marriage, occupations, birthplaces, and infirmities, *P.P.* 1903, LXXXIV
1911 Census. Ages and condition as to marriage, *P.P.*, 1912–3, CXIII.
Comparative account of the population of Great Britain in 1801, 1811, 1821, 1831 with the annual value of real property, 1815; also a statement of progress in the inquiry regarding the occupations of families and persons, and the duration of life, as required by the Population Act, 1830. *P.P.* 1831, XVIII, pp. 1–417.

Demographic Yearbook. U.N., Dept of Social Affairs, 1948– (New York, 1949–)
The determinants and consequences of population trends. U.N., Dept of Economic and Social Affairs, Population Studies, no. 50, revised ed., 2 vols. (New York, 1973–8).
Dissenters' Places of Worship, *P.P.* 1852–3, LXXVIII, pp. 83–170.

Emigrationsutredningen, Bilaga V, Bygdestatistik (Stockholm, 1908–13).

Historisk statistik för Sverige. Del I. Befolkning, Statistiska Centralbyrån, 2nd ed. (Stockholm, 1969).

Lists of non-parochial registers and records in the custody of the Registrar General (London, 1859).
London inhabitants within the walls 1695, with an introduction by D. V. Glass. London Record Society Publications, II (London, 1966).

Methods for population projections by sex and age, U.N., Dept of Economic and Social Affairs, Population Studies, no. 25 (New York, 1956).
Methods of using census statistics for the calculation of life tables and other demographic measures. U.N., Dept. of Social Affairs, Population Studies, no. 7 (New York, 1949).

Parish register abstract 1841, *P.P.* 1845, XXV, pp. 493–718.

The plague reconsidered, a *Local Population Studies* supplement (Matlock, 1977).
Population trends, 1–, Office of Population Censuses and Surveys (London, 1975–).

'Report of the Statistical Society on the dwellings in Church Lane, St Giles's', *Journal of the Statistical Society of London* [later the Royal Statistical Society], xi (1848), pp. 1–18, reprinted in R. Wall (ed.), *Slum conditions in London and Dublin* (London, 1974).
Royal college of Physicians of London, *Report of the Committee on Accidental Hypothermia* (London, 1966).

Statistisk Årsbok för Stockholms Stad 1913 (Stockholm, 1914).

County maps.
  The maps are listed in the alphabetical order of the counties concerned (Southampton being listed in the position of Hampshire).
    C. and J. Greenwood, *Map of the county of Bedford* (London, 1826).
    C. and J. Greenwood *Map of the county of Berkshire* (London, 1824).
    A. Bryant, *Map of the county of Buckinghamshire* (1925).
    R. G. Baker, *Map of the county of Cambridge* (Bluntisham, 1821).
    C. Greenwood, *Map of the county palatine of Chester* (1819).
    C. and J. Greenwood, *Map of the county of Cornwall* (1827).
    C. and J. Greenwood, *Map of the county of Cumberland* (1823).
    C. and J. Greenwood, *Map of the county of Derby* (London, 1825).
    C. and J. Greenwood, *Map of the county of Devon* (London, 1827).
    C. and J. Greenwood, *Map of the county of Dorset* (1826).
    C. Greenwood, *Map of the county palatine of Durham* (1820).
    C. and J. Greenwood, *Map of the county of Essex* (London, 1825).
    C. and J. Greenwood, *Map of the county of Gloucester* (London, 1824).
    C. and J. Greenwood, *Map of the county of Southampton* (1826).
    A. Bryant, *Map of the county of Hereford* (1835).
    A. Dury and J. Andrews, *A topographical map of Hartfordshire* (1766).
    C. and J. Greenwood, *Map of the county of Huntingdon* (1831).
    C. Greenwood, *Map of the county of Kent* (1821).
    C. Greenwood, *Map of the county palatine of Lancaster* (Wakefield, 1818).
    C. and J. Greenwood, *Map of the county of Leicester* (London, 1826).
    C. and J. Greenwood, *Map of the county of Lincoln* (London, 1830).
    C. Greenwood, *Map of the county of Middlesex* (London, 1819).
    A. Bryant, *Map of the county of Norfolk* (1826).
    C. and J. Greenwood, *Map of the county of Northampton* (London, 1826).
    C. and J. Greenwood, *Map of the county of Northumberland* (1828).
    C. and J. Greenwood, *Map of the county of Nottingham* (London, 1826).
    A. Bryant, *Map of the county of Oxford* (1824).
    C. and J. Greenwood, *Map of the county of Rutland* (1826).
    C. and J. Greenwood, *Map of the county of Salop* (1827).
    C. and J. Greenwood, *Map of the county of Somerset* (London, 1822).
    C. Greenwood, *Maps of the county of Stafford* (1820).
    C. and J. Greenwood, *Map of the county of Suffolk* (London, 1825).
    C. and J. Greenwood, *Map of the county of Surrey* (1823).
    C. and J. Greenwood, *Map of the county of Sussex* (London, 1824–5).
    C. and J. Greenwood, *Map of the county of Warwick* (London, 1822).
    C. and J. Greenwood, *Map of the county of Westmorland* (London, 1824).
    C. Greenwood, *Map of the county of Wiltshire* (1820).
    C. and J. Greenwood, *Map of the county of Worcester* (1822).
    C. Greenwood, *Map of the county of York* (Wakefield, 1817–8).

Index

Adams, J., 39, 48

Agbrigg wapentake, Yorkshire, 171n

age, at baptism, 289; at marriage, 233–4, 255–6, 261–3, 265, 422–4, 429, 436–7; age at marriage and illegitimacy, 266; mean age at maternity, 232–4, 256–7, 266–9; misrepresentation by elderly, 109–11, 202–3, 282

age structure, back projection, 195–8, 200–7, 215–9, 282–3, 455; changes in, 443–50; female population, 104–18; life tables, 708–14; migrants, 200–2, 277–8, 633–5; mortality rates, 110–1, 215–6, 249–53; quinquennial totals by back projection, 528–9; sex ratios, 591; size of age groups, 103–4

aggregative tabulations, 5–6; back projection, 7–8; compensating for differences in length of registration, 56–62; correction for delayed baptisms, 97–102; correction of nonconformity, 100–2; final inflation ratios, 136–42; geographical distribution of sample, 38–45; names of local historians providing tabulations, 490–2; national inflation ratios, 66–76, 83–8, 96; parishes contributing data, 485–9; population size bias, 46–56, 61–5; quality control, 16–8; representativeness of data, 33–56; sequential sampling, 694–6; time limits, 18–9; uses of, 7–8

agricultural regions, distribution of mortality crises, 687–92; distribution of sample parishes, 43–6; population size weighting, 55–6

agriculture and balance of population, 458–9, 461; as basis of prosperity, 1, 406; harvest failure and mortality crises, 340–1, 655, 666–7, 669–72, 675–81; harvest fluctuations, 305–7, 312–3, 325, 340–1, 345–7; improvements in productivity, 404, 407, 451, 475; industrialization of, 476; and population growth ratios, 38; and seasonality of births, 292; and seasonality of marriages, 303–5; and vital rates, 319, 345–7; see also famine; food prices; wheat prices

Alcester, Warwickshire, 233n, 248

Aldenham, Hertfordshire, 233n, 248

Almon lags, 359

Almondbury, Yorkshire, 703n

altitude, distribution of sample parishes and incidence of mortality crises, 45, 687–9, 691–2

amenorrhea, 363, 370

Andrews, J., 9

Anglican church, causes of non-registration, 103; communicants, 563–6, 569–70; 574; and growth of nonconformity, 89–92; marriage laws, 29; registration quality, 4, 15, 130–7, 152–3; and seasonality of marriages, 298; see also parish registers

annual crude rates, births, deaths, and marriages, 311–2, 531–5; migration, 531–5

Appleby, A. B., 313n, 329n, 335n, 340n, 341n, 354n, 371n, 416n, 666n, 669n, 671n, 672n, 679n, 680n, 685n

Armengaud, A., 580n

army, effect of warfare on sex ratios of burials, 128; exclusion from censuses, 104, 199–200, 592–3; loss of life, 220

Ashbrittle, Somerset, 126

Asia, 482